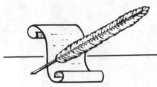

HISTORIC DOCUMENTS OF 1982

Cumulative Index 1978-82

Congressional Quarterly Inc.

Congressional Quarterly Inc.
1414 22nd St. N.W., Washington, D.C. 20037

The following have given permission to reprint copyrighted material: From an interview with Secretary of Defense Caspar W. Weinberger, copyright © 1982 by ABC News. From *U.S. and Soviet Agriculture: The Shifting Balance of Power*, by Lester R. Brown, copyright © 1982 by Worldwatch Institute. From the Pastoral Letter of the National Conference of Catholic Bishops On War And Peace, Second Draft, *The Challenge of Peace: God's Promise and Our Response*, copyright © 1982 United States Catholic Conference, Inc. All rights reserved. From *External Debt of Developing Countries, 1982 Survey*, copyright © by the Organization for Economic Cooperation and Development.

The Library of Congress cataloged the first issue of this title as follows:

Historic documents.   1972—
    Washington. Congressional Quarterly Inc.

    1. United States—Politics and government—1945—   —Yearbooks.
2. World politics—1945— —Yearbooks. I. Congressional Quarterly Inc.

E839.5.H57   917.3'03'9205   72-97888
ISBN 0-87187-257-9

FOREWORD

Publication of *Historic Documents of 1982* carries through an eleventh year the project launched by Congressional Quarterly with *Historic Documents 1972.* The purpose of this continuing series of volumes is to give students, scholars, librarians, journalists and citizens convenient access to documents of basic importance in the broad range of public affairs.

To place the documents in perspective, each entry is preceded by a brief introduction containing background materials, in some cases a short summary of the document itself and, where necessary, relevant subsequent developments. We believe these introductions will prove increasingly useful in future years when the events and questions now covered are less fresh in one's memory and the documents may be difficult to find or unobtainable.

Chronicled in 1982 was the growing concern about the danger of the arms race between the superpowers. The year was marked by increasing tension between the Reagan administration and those in favor of a nuclear freeze. The president, seeking to strengthen the U.S military, asked for huge budget increases for weapons. At the same time, the administration proposed several arms reduction schemes to the Soviets, while assuring the nation that the Soviet way of life was doomed to failure.

In the area of health, one report dealing with cancer found links between nutrition and the disease; another reiterated the connection between smoking and cancer. The health consequences of marijuana use were examined, and the Supreme Court decided that regulation of shops selling drug-related paraphernalia was constitutional.

The year saw at least two wars break out — the conflict between Britain and Argentina for control of the Falkland Islands and the invasion by Israel of Lebanon, resulting in the expulsion of the Palestine Liberation Organization's army from Lebanon. In ongoing struggles, the State Department found new evidence of the use of toxic chemicals in Afghanistan and Southeast Asia. Some martial law restrictions were lifted in Poland, but the Solidarity labor union was banned.

These and other developments added substantially to the usual outpouring of presidential statements, court decisions, committee reports, special studies and speeches of national or international importance. We have selected for inclusion in this book as many as possible of the documents that in our judgment will be of more than transitory interest. Where space limitations prevented reproduction of the full texts, the excerpts used were chosen to set forth the essentials and, at the same time, to preserve the flavor of the materials.

Carolyn Goldinger
Editor

Washington, D.C.
April 1983

Historic Documents of 1982

Editor: Carolyn Goldinger
Contributing Editors: John L. Moore, Martha V. Gottron
Contributors: Carolyn H. Crowley, Suzanne de Lesseps, James R. Ingram,
        Mary L. McNeil, Patricia M. Russotto, Elizabeth H. Sum-
        mers, Margaret C. Thompson, Esther D. Wyss
Cumulative Index: Nancy A. Blanpied

Congressional Quarterly Inc.

Book Department

How to Use This Book

The documents are arranged in chronological order. If you know the approximate date of the report, speech, statement, court decision or other document you are looking for, glance through the titles for that month in the Table of Contents below.

If the Table of Contents does not lead you directly to the document you want, turn to the index at the end of the book. There you may find references not only to the particular document you seek but also to other entries on the same or a related subject. The index in this volume is a **five-year cumulative index** of Historic Documents covering the years 1978-1982.

The introduction to each document is printed in italic type. The document itself, printed in roman type, follows the spelling, capitalization and punctuation of the original or official copy. In some cases, boldface headings in brackets have been added to highlight the organization of the text. Where the full text is not given, omissions of material are indicated by the customary ellipsis points.

TABLE OF CONTENTS

January

February

March

May

June

July

August

September

October

November

December

HISTORIC

DOCUMENTS

OF

1982

JANUARY

FEDERAL DISTRICT COURT ON 'CREATION SCIENCE'

January 5, 1982

A federal district judge in Arkansas struck down that state's law requiring public schools to give balanced treatment to "creation science" and the theory of evolution. Judge William Ray Overton issued a 38-page decision January 5 stating that the intent of Act 590 was "the advancement of religion," which violated the separation of church and state guaranteed by the First Amendment. The same day Overton issued a permanent injunction against implementation of the law.

Act 590 had been signed March 19, 1981, by Arkansas Gov. Frank White. The bill had passed the Arkansas Senate by a vote of 22-2 and the House of Representatives by a vote of 69-18. Reviewing the history of the legislation, Overton said that the bill had been introduced by State Sen. James L. Holsted, "a self-described 'born again' Christian Fundamentalist." Holsted had not consulted any science educators, the state education department or the Arkansas attorney general about the content or the constitutionality of the legislation. The bill had passed the Arkansas Senate without any committee hearings and with only a few minutes' discussion on the Senate floor. The Arkansas House Education Committee had conducted a fifteen minute hearing but had heard no testimony from scientists or educators.

Background

Passage of the law was seen by some observers as another round in the continuing battle to teach creationism in school. Previously the attack

3

had been from the other direction — the prohibition of the teaching of Darwinism in public schools.

Overton traced briefly the history of Fundamentalism and its effects on the teaching of biology in the United States. After World War I many Fundamentalists, who believed in a literal interpretation of the Bible and in the Book of Genesis as the sole source of knowledge about the origin of man, blamed the teaching of evolution for what they saw as a decline in traditional morality. One method of coping with this problem was to seek passage of laws forbidding the teaching of evolution in public schools. In the celebrated 1925 "monkey trial," John Scopes was convicted of violating a Tennessee law that made it illegal to teach anything but a literal Biblical theory of creation. A similar Arkansas law was struck down in a unanimous decision by the U.S. Supreme Court on November 12, 1968, in Epperson v. Arkansas.

Between the 1920s and early 1960s many biology textbooks, especially those used in the South, avoided the subject of evolution and did not mention the name of Charles Darwin. But following the launch of the Soviet Sputnik satellite in 1957, many educators and politicians became alarmed at what was seen as poor science teaching in U.S. schools. Many school districts began to modernize science teaching. Overton stated that the appearance of new biology texts may have stimulated a response from the Fundamentalists.

In the 1960s and early 1970s several Fundamentalist organizations were formed to promote the idea that the biblical story of creation was supported by scientific data. Their goal was to introduce "creation science" into the public schools, and at least one organization published pamphlets outlining methods for convincing school officials to add creationism to their curricula.

The decision stated that Arkansas' Act 590 was drafted by Paul Ellwanger, founder of Citizens For Fairness in Education, based in Anderson, S.C. Ellwanger had collected several proposed legislative acts requiring balanced treatment for "creation science" and evolution, with the idea of preparing a model state act. Overton said the draft legislation passed through several hands but was virtually unchanged when it was introduced by Holsted. Trial evidence showed that Ellwanger believed that neither creationism nor evolution was a science. Overton's decision stated that Ellwanger knew he was embarked on a religious campaign and that he made deliberate efforts to conceal that fact.

Effects of Case

Writing in The New York Times *January 5, 1982, Fred M. Hechinger said that the court case in Arkansas did more than focus on what "most scientists consider a silly issue." Hechinger said the case was an example of the vulnerability of the public schools to political pressure. State legislators may have felt that they could not afford to ignore the wishes of a large vocal group of constituents. But Overton's decision stated, "The application and content of First Amendment principles are not determined by public opinion polls or by a majority vote. Whether the proponents of Act 590 constitute the majority or the minority is quite irrelevant under a constitutional system of government. No group, no matter how large or small, may use the organs of government, of which the public schools are the most conspicuous and influential, to foist its religious beliefs on others."*

Because the issue of "creation science" was current in several other Southern states, textbook publishers were faced with the problem of how to continue to sell books and not offend large groups of people. Frank Press, president of the National Academy of Sciences, wrote, "We simply cannot afford to teach pseudo-science in the guise of science. And creationism, which, arguably, may have a place elsewhere in teaching and comparative religion, is not science."

But the "creation science" battle was far from over. The same day Overton struck down the Arkansas law, a similar bill passed the Mississippi Senate by a vote of 48-4. In Louisiana a suit filed by the American Civil Liberties Union against that state's law was pending. The Louisiana law, also drafted by Ellwanger, was thought to be different enough from Arkansas' to warrant another court test. Louisiana's law was ruled unconstitutional in federal district court November 22, 1982.

Following are excerpts from the U.S. District Court's decision in McLean v. Arkansas Board of Education, *issued January 5, 1982:*

IN THE UNITED STATES DISTRICT COURT
EASTERN DISTRICT OF ARKANSAS
WESTERN DIVISION

Rev. Bill McLean, et al. Plaintiffs *vs.* The Arkansas Board of Education, et al. Defendants	No. LR C 881 322 Memorandum Opinion

[January 5, 1982]

Introduction

On March 19, 1981, the Governor of Arkansas signed into law Act 590 of 1981, entitled the "Balanced Treatment for Creation-Science and Evolution-Science Act." ... Its essential mandate is stated in its first sentence:

5

"Public schools within this State shall give balanced treatment to creation-science and to evolution-science." On May 27, 1981, this suit was filed challenging the constitutional validity of Act 590 on three distinct grounds.

First, it is contended that Act 590 constitutes an establishment of religion prohibited by the First Amendment to the Constitution, which is made applicable to the states by the Fourteenth Amendment. Second, the plaintiffs argue the Act violates a right to academic freedom which they say is guaranteed to students and teachers by the Free Speech Clause of the First Amendment. Third, plaintiffs allege the Act is impermissibly vague and thereby violates the Due Process Clause of the Fourteenth Amendment.

The individual plaintiffs include the resident Arkansas Bishops of the United Methodist, Episcopal, Roman Catholic and African Methodist Episcopal Churches, the principal official of the Presbyterian Churches in Arkansas, other United Methodist, Southern Baptist and Presbyterian clergy, as well as several persons who sue as parents and next friends of minor children attending Arkansas public schools. One plaintiff is a high school biology teacher. All are also Arkansas taxpayers. Among the organizational plaintiffs are the American Jewish Congress, the Union of American Hebrew Congregations, the American Jewish Committee, the Arkansas Education Association, the National Association of Biology Teachers and the National Coalition for Public Education and Religious Liberty, all of which sue on behalf of members living in Arkansas.

The defendants include the Arkansas Board of Education and its members, the Director of the Department of Education, and the State Textbooks and Instructional Materials Selecting Committee....

I

There is no controversy over the legal standards under which the Establishment Clause portion of this case must be judged. The Supreme Court has on a number of occasions expounded on the meaning of the clause, and the pronouncements are clear. Often the issue has arisen in the context of public education, as it has here. In *Everson v. Board of Education* (1947), Justice Black stated:

> "The 'establishment of religion' clause of the First Amendment means at least this: Neither a state nor the Federal Government can set up a church. Neither can pass laws which aid one religion, aid all religions, or prefer one religion over another. Neither can force nor influence a person to go to or to remain away from church against his will or force him to profess a belief or disbelief in any religion. No person can be punished for entertaining or professing religious beliefs or disbeliefs, for church-attendance or non-attendance. No tax, large or small, can be levied to support any religious activities or institutions, whatever they may be called, or whatever form they may adopt to teach or practice religion. Neither a state nor the Federal Government can,

openly or secretly, participate in the affairs of any religious organizations or groups and *vice versa*. In the words of Jefferson, the clause . . . was intended to erect 'a wall of separation between church and State.' "

The Establishment Clause thus enshrines two central values: voluntarism and pluralism. And it is in the area of the public schools that these values must be guarded most vigilantly. . . .

The specific formulation of the establishment prohibition has been refined over the years, but its meaning has not varied from the principles articulated by Justice Black in *Everson*. In *Abbington School District v. Schempp*, (1963), Justice Clark stated that "to withstand the strictures of the Establishment Clause there must be a secular legislative purpose and a primary effect that neither advances nor inhibits religion." The Court found it quite clear that the First Amendment does not permit a state to require the daily reading of the Bible in public schools, for "[s]urely the place of the Bible as an instrument of religion cannot be gainsaid." Similarly, in *Engel v. Vitale* (1962), the Court held that the First Amendment prohibited the New York Board of Regents from requiring the daily recitation of a certain prayer in the schools. With characteristic succinctness, Justice Black wrote, "Under [the First] Amendment's prohibition against governmental establishment of religion, as reinforced by the provisions of the Fourteenth Amendment, government in this country, be it state or federal, is without power to prescribe by law any particular form of prayer which is to be used as an official prayer in carrying on any program of governmentally sponsored religious activity." Black also identified the objective at which the Establishment Clause was aimed: "Its first and most immediate purpose rested on the belief that a union of government and religion tends to destroy government and to degrade religion."

Most recently, the Supreme Court has held that the clause prohibits a state from requiring the posting of the Ten Commandments in public school classrooms for the same reasons that officially imposed daily Bible reading is prohibited. *Stone v. Graham* (1980). The opinion in *Stone* relies on the most recent formulation of the Establishment Clause test, that of *Lemon v. Kurtzman* (1971):

> "First, the statute must have a secular legislative purpose; second, its principal or primary effect must be one that neither advances nor inhibits religion . . .; finally, the statute must not foster 'an excessive government entanglement with religion.' " *Stone v. Graham*

It is under this three part test that the evidence in this case must be judged. Failure on any of these grounds is fatal to the enactment.

II

The religious movement known as Fundamentalism began in nineteenth century America as part of evangelical Protestantism's response to social changes, new religious thought and Darwinism. Fundamentalists viewed these developments as attacks on the Bible and as responsible for a decline in traditional values.

The various manifestations of Fundamentalism have had a number of common characteristics, but a central premise has always been a literal interpretation of the Bible and a belief in the inerrancy of the Scriptures. Following World War I, there was again a perceived decline in traditional morality, and Fundamentalism focused on evolution as responsible for the decline. One aspect of their efforts, particularly in the South, was the promotion of statutes prohibiting the teaching of evolution in public schools. In Arkansas, this resulted in the adoption of Initiated Act 1 of 1929. . . .

The State of Arkansas, like a number of states whose citizens have relatively homogeneous religious beliefs, has a long history of official opposition to evolution which is motivated by adherence to Fundamentalist beliefs in the inerrancy of the Book of Genesis. This history is documented in Justice Fortas' opinion in *Epperson v. Arkansas* (1968), which struck down Initiated Act 1 of 1929, prohibiting the teaching of the theory of evolution. To this same tradition may be attributed Initiated Act 1 of 1930, (Repl. 1980), requiring "the reverent daily reading of a portion of the English Bible" in every public school classroom in the State.

The unusual circumstances surrounding the passage of Act 590, as well as the substantive law of the First Amendment, warrant an inquiry into the stated legislative purposes. The author of the Act had publicly proclaimed the sectarian purpose of the proposal. The Arkansas residents who sought legislative sponsorship of the bill did so for a purely sectarian purpose. These circumstances alone may not be particularly persuasive, but when considered with the publicly announced motives of the legislative sponsor made contemporaneously with the legislative process; the lack of any legislative investigation, debate or consultation with any educators or scientists; the unprecedented intrusion in school curriculum; and official history of the State of Arkansas on the subject, it is obvious that the statement of purposes has little, if any, support in fact. The State failed to produce any evidence which would warrant an inference or conclusion that at any point in the process anyone considered the legitimate educational value of the Act. It is simply and purely an effort to introduce the Biblical version of creation into the public school curricula. The only inference which can be drawn from these circumstances is that the Act was passed with the specific purpose by the General Assembly of advancing religion. The Act therefore fails the first prong of the three-pronged test, that of secular legislative purpose, as articulated in *Lemon v. Kurtzman* and *Stone v. Graham.*

III

If the defendants are correct and the Court is limited to an examination of the language of the Act, the evidence is overwhelming that both the purpose and effect of Act 590 is the advancement of religion in the public schools.

Section 4 of the Act provides:

Definitions. As used in this Act:

(a) "Creation-science" means the scientific evidences for creation and inferences from those scientific evidences. Creation-science includes the scientific evidences and related inferences that indicate: (1) Sudden creation of the universe, energy, and life from nothing; (2) The insufficiency of mutation and natural selection in bringing about development of all living kinds from a single organism; (3) Changes only within fixed limits of originally created kinds of plants and animals; (4) Separate ancestry for man and apes; (5) Explanation of the earth's geology by catastrophism, including the occurrence of a worldwide flood; and (6) A relatively recent inception of the earth and living kinds.

(b) "Evolution-science" means the scientific evidences for evolution and inferences from those scientific evidences. Evolution-science includes the scientific evidences and related inferences that indicate: (1) Emergence by naturalistic processes of the universe from disordered matter and emergence of life from nonlife; (2) The sufficiency of mutation and natural selection in bringing about development of present living kinds from simple earlier kinds; (3) Emergence by mutation and natural selection of present living kinds from simple earlier kinds; (4) Emergence of man from a common ancestor with apes; (5) Explanation of the earth's geology and the evolutionary sequence by uniformitarianism; and (6) An inception several billion years ago of the earth and somewhat later of life. . . .

The evidence establishes that the definition of "creation science" contained in 4 (a) has as its unmentioned reference the first 11 chapters of the Book of Genesis. Among the many creation epics in human history, the account of sudden creation from nothing, or *creatio ex nihilo*, and subsequent destruction of the world by flood is unique to Genesis. The concepts of 4 (a) are the literal Fundamentalists' view of Genesis. Section 4 (a) is unquestionably a statement of religion, with the exception of 4 (a) (2) which is a negative thrust aimed at what the creationists understand to be the theory of evolution.

Both the concepts and wording of Section 4 (a) convey an inescapable religiosity. Section 4 (a) (1) describes "sudden creation of the universe, energy and life from nothing." Every theologian who testified, including defense witnesses, expressed the opinion that the statement referred to a supernatural creation which was performed by God.

Defendants argue that: (1) the fact that 4 (a) conveys ideas similar to the literal interpretation of Genesis does not make it conclusively a statement of religion; (2) that reference to a creation from nothing is not necessarily a religious concept since the Act only suggests a creator who has power, intelligence and a sense of design and not necessarily the attributes of love,

9

compassion and justice; and (3) that simply teaching about the concept of a creator is not a religious exercise unless the student is required to make a commitment to the concept of a creator.

The evidence fully answers these arguments. The ideas of 4 (a) (1) are not merely similar to the literal interpretation of Genesis; they are identical and parallel to no other story of creation.

The argument that creation from nothing in 4 (a) (1) does not involve a supernatural deity has no evidentiary or rational support. To the contrary, "creation out of nothing" is a concept unique to Western religions. In traditional Western religious thought, the conception of a creator of the world is a conception of God. Indeed, creation of the world "out of nothing" is the ultimate religious statement because God is the only actor. As Dr. Langdon Gilkey noted, the Act refers to one who has the power to bring all the universe into existence from nothing. The only "one" who has this power is God.

The leading creationist writers, [Henry M.] Morris and [Duane] Gish, acknowledge that the idea of creation described in 4 (a) (1) is the concept of creation by God and make no pretense to the contrary. The idea of sudden creation from nothing, or *creatio ex nihilo*, is an inherently religious concept. . . .

The argument advanced by defendants' witness, Dr. Norman Geisler, that teaching the existence of God is not religious unless the teaching seeks a commitment, is contrary to common understanding and contradicts settled case law. *Stone v. Graham* (1980); *Abbington School District v. Schempp* (1963). . . .

IV (A)

The approach to teaching "creation science" and "evolution science" found in Act 590 is identical to the two-model approach espoused by the Institute for Creation Research and is taken almost verbatim from ICR writings. It is an extension of Fundamentalists' view that one must either accept the literal interpretation of Genesis or else believe in the godless system of evolution.

The two model approach of the creationists is simply a contrived dualism which has no scientific factual basis or legitimate educational purpose. It assumes only two explanations for the origins of life and existence of man, plants and animals: It was either the work of a creator or it was not. Application of these two models, according to creationists, and the defendants, dictates that all scientific evidence which fails to support the theory of evolution is necessarily scientific evidence in support of creationism and is, therefore, creation science "evidence" in support of Section 4 (a).

IV (B)

The emphasis on origins as an aspect of the theory of evolution is peculiar to creationist literature. Although the subject of origins of life is within the province of biology, the scientific community does not consider origins of life a part of evolutionary theory. The theory of evolution assumes the existence of life and is directed to an explanation of *how* life evolved. Evolution does not presuppose the absence of a creator or God and the plain inference conveyed by Section 4 is erroneous.

As a statement of the theory of evolution, Section 4 (b) is simply a hodgepodge of limited assertions, many of which are factually inaccurate.

For example, although 4 (b) (2) asserts, as a tenet of evolutionary theory, "the sufficiency of mutation and natural selection in bringing about the existence of present living kinds from simple earlier kinds," Drs. [Francisco] Ayala and [Stephen Jay] Gould both stated that biologists know that these two processes do not account for all significant evolutionary change. They testified to such phenomena as recombination, the founder effect, genetic drift and the theory of punctuated equilibrium, which are believed to play important evolutionary roles. Section 4 (b) omits any reference to these. . . . Additionally, the Act presents both evolution and creation science as "package deals." Thus, evidence critical of some aspect of what the creationists define as evolution is taken as support for a theory which includes a worldwide flood and a relatively young earth.

IV (C)

In addition to the fallacious pedagogy of the two model approach, Section 4 (a) lacks legitimate educational value because "creation science" as defined in that section is simply not science. Several witnesses suggested definitions of science. A descriptive definition was said to be that science is what is "accepted by the scientific community" and is "what scientists do." The obvious implication of this description is that, in a free society, knowledge does not require the imprimatur of legislation in order to become science.

More precisely, the essential characteristics of science are:

(1) It is guided by natural law;

(2) It has to be explanatory by reference to natural law;

(3) It is testable against the empirical world;

(4) Its conclusions are tentative, i.e., are not necessarily the final word; and

(5) It is falsifiable. (Ruse and other science witnesses).

Creation science as described in Section 4 (a) fails to meet these essential characteristics. First, the section revolves around 4 (a) (1) which asserts a sudden creation "from nothing." Such a concept is not science because it depends upon a supernatural intervention which is not guided by natural law. It is not explanatory by reference to natural law, is not testable and is not falsifiable.

If the unifying idea of supernatural creation by God is removed from Section 4, the remaining parts of the section explain nothing and are meaningless assertions.

Section 4 (a) (2), relating to the "insufficiency of mutation and natural selection in bringing about development of all living kinds from a single organism," is an incomplete negative generalization directed at the theory of evolution.

Section 4 (a) (3) which describes "changes only within fixed limits of originally created kinds of plants and animals" fails to conform to the essential characteristics of science for several reasons. First, there is no scientific definition of "kinds" and none of the witnesses was able to point to any scientific authority which recognized the term or knew how many "kinds" existed. One defense witness suggested there may be 100 to 10,000 different "kinds." Another believes there were "about 10,000, give or take a few thousand." Second, the assertion appears to be an effort to establish outer limits of changes within species. There is no scientific explanation for these limits which is guided by natural law and the limitations, whatever they are, cannot be explained by natural law.

The statement in 4 (a) (4) of "separate ancestry of man and apes" is a bald assertion. It explains nothing and refers to no scientific fact or theory.

Section 4 (a) (5) refers to "explanation of the earth's geology by catastrophism, including the occurrence of a worldwide flood." This assertion completely fails as science. The Act is referring to the Noachian flood described in the Book of Genesis. The creationist writers concede that *any* kind of Genesis Flood depends upon supernatural intervention. A worldwide flood as an explanation of the world's geology is not the product of natural law, nor can its occurrence be explained by natural law.

Section 4 (a) (6) equally fails to meet the standards of science. "Relatively recent inception" has no scientific meaning. It can only be given meaning by reference to creationist writings which place the age at between 6,000 and 20,000 years because of the genealogy of the Old Testament. Such a reasoning process is not the product of natural law; not explainable by natural law; nor is it tentative.

Creation science, as defined in Section 4 (a), not only fails to follow the canons defining scientific theory, it also fails to fit the more general descriptions of "what scientists think" and "what scientists do." The scientific community consists of individuals and groups, nationally and internationally, who work independently in such varied fields as biology, paleontology, geology and astronomy. Their work is published and subject to review and testing by their peers. The journals for publication are both numerous and varied. There is, however, not one recognized scientific journal which has published an article espousing the creation science theory described in Section 4 (a). Some of the State's witnesses suggested that the scientific community was "close-minded" on the subject of creationism and that explained the lack of acceptance of the creation science arguments. Yet no witness produced a scientific article for which publication had been refused. Perhaps some members of the scientific community are resistant to new ideas. It is, however, inconceivable that such a loose knit group of independent thinkers in all the varied fields of science could, or would, so effectively censor new scientific thought.

The creationists have difficulty maintaining among their ranks consistency in the claim that creationism is science. The author of Act 590, [Paul] Ellwanger, said that neither evolution nor creationism was science. He thinks both are religion. . . .

The methodology employed by creationists is another factor which is indicative that their work is not science. A scientific theory must be tentative and always subject to revision or abandonment in light of facts that are inconsistent with, or falsify, the theory. A theory that is by its own terms dogmatic, absolutist and never subject to revision is not a scientific theory.

The creationists' methods do not take data, weigh it against the opposing scientific data, and thereafter reach the conclusions stated in Section 4 (a). Instead, they take the literal wording of the Book of Genesis and attempt to find scientific support for it. . . . The Creation Research Society employs the same unscientific approach to the issue of creationism. Its applicants for membership must subscribe to the belief that the Book of Genesis is "historically and scientifically true in all of the original autographs." The Court would never criticize or discredit any person's testimony based on his or her religious beliefs. While anybody is free to approach a scientific inquiry in any fashion they choose, they cannot properly describe the methodology used as scientific, if they start with a conclusion and refuse to change it regardless of the evidence developed during the course of the investigation. . . .

IV (D)

In efforts to establish "evidence" in support of creation science, the defendants relied upon the same false premise as the two model approach contained in Section 4, i.e., all evidence which criticized evolutionary theory was proof in support of creation science. For example, the defendants established that the mathematical probability of a chance chemical combination resulting in life from non-life is so remote that such an occurrence is almost beyond imagination. Those mathematical facts, the defendants argue, are scientific evidences that life was the product of a creator. While the statistical figures may be impressive evidence against the theory of chance chemical combinations as an explanation of origins, it requires a leap of faith to interpret those figures so as to support a complex doctrine which includes a sudden creation from nothing, a worldwide flood, separate ancestry of man and apes, and a young earth. . . .

The testimony of Marianne Wilson was persuasive evidence that creation science is not science. Ms. Wilson is in charge of the science curriculum for Pulaski County Special School District, the largest school district in the State of Arkansas. Prior to the passage of Act 590, Larry Fisher, a science teacher in the District, using materials from the ICR, convinced the School Board that it should voluntarily adopt creation science as part of its science curriculum. The District Superintendent assigned Ms. Wilson the job of producing a creation science curriculum guide. Ms. Wilson's testimony about the project was particularly convincing because she obviously approached the assignment with an open mind and no preconceived notions about the subject. She had not heard of creation science until about a year ago and did not know its meaning before she began her research.

Ms. Wilson worked with a committee of science teachers appointed from the District. They reviewed practically all of the creationist literature. Ms. Wilson and the committee members reached the unanimous conclusion that creationism is not science; it is religion. They so reported to the Board. The Board ignored the recommendation and insisted that a curriculum guide be prepared.

In researching the subject, Ms. Wilson sought the assistance of Mr. Fisher who initiated the Board action and asked professors in the science departments of the University of Arkansas at Little Rock and the University of Central Arkansas for reference material and assistance, and attended a workshop conducted at Central Baptist College by Dr. Richard Bliss of the ICR staff. Act 590 became law during the course of her work so she used Section 4 (a) as a format for her curriculum guide.

Ms. Wilson found all available creationists' materials unacceptable because they were permeated with religious references and reliance upon religious beliefs.

It is easy to understand why Ms. Wilson and other educators find the creationists' textbook material and teaching guides unacceptable. The materials misstate the theory of evolution in the same fashion as Section 4 (b) of the Act, with emphasis on the alternative mutually exclusive nature of creationism and evolution. Students are constantly encouraged to compare and make a choice between the two models, and the material is not presented in an accurate manner. . . .

Biology, A Search For Order in Complexity is a high school biology text typical of creationists' materials. The following quotations are illustrative:

> "Flowers and roots do not have a mind to have purpose of their own; therefore, this planning must have been done for them by the Creator." [p. 12]

> "The exquisite beauty of color and shape in flowers exceeds the skill of poet, artist, and king. Jesus said (from Matthew's gospel), 'Consider the lilies of the field, how they grow; they toil not, neither do they spin . . .' " [p. 363]

The "public school edition" texts written by creationists simply omit Biblical references but the content and message remain the same. For example, *Evolution — The Fossils Say No!,* contains the following:

> Creation. By creation we mean the bringing into being by a supernatural Creator of the basic kinds of plants and animals by the process of sudden, or fiat, creation.
>
> We do not know how the Creator created, what processes He used, *for He used processes which are not now operating anywhere in the*

natural universe. This is why we refer to creation as Special Creation. We cannot discover by scientific investigation anything about the creative processes used by the Creator." [p. 40]

Gish's book also portrays the large majority of evolutionists as "materialistic atheists or agnostics."...

Without using creationist literature, Ms. Wilson was unable to locate one genuinely scientific article or work which supported Section 4 (a). In order to comply with the mandate of the Board she used such materials as an article from *Readers Digest* about "atomic clocks" which inferentially suggested that the earth was less than 4 1/2 billion years old. She was unable to locate any substantive teaching material for some parts of Section 4 such as the worldwide flood. The curriculum guide which she prepared cannot be taught and has no educational value as science. The defendants did not produce any text or writing in response to this evidence which they claimed was usable in the public school classroom.

The conclusion that creation science has no scientific merit or educational value as science has legal significance in light of the Court's previous conclusion that creation science has, as one major effect, the advancement of religion. The second part of the three-pronged test for establishment reaches only those statutes having as their *primary* effect the advancement of religion. Secondary effects which advance religion are not constitutionally fatal. Since creation science is not science, the conclusion is inescapable that the *only* real effect of Act 590 is the advancement of religion. The Act therefore fails both the first and second portions of the test in *Lemon v. Kurtzman* (1971).

IV (E)

Act 590 mandates "balanced treatment" for creation science and evolution science. The Act prohibits instruction in any religious doctrine or references to religious writings. The Act is self-contradictory and compliance is impossible unless the public schools elect to forego significant portions of subjects such as biology, world history, geology, zoology, botany, psychology, anthropology, sociology, philosophy, physics and chemistry. Presently, the concepts of evolutionary theory as described in 4 (b) permeate the public school textbooks. There is no way teachers can teach the Genesis account of creation in a secular manner.

The State Department of Education, through its textbook selection committee, school boards and school administrators will be required to constantly monitor materials to avoid using religious references. The school boards, administrators and teachers face an impossible task. How is the teacher to respond to questions about a creation suddenly and out of nothing? How will a teacher explain the occurrence of a worldwide flood? How will a teacher explain the concept of a relatively recent age of the earth? The answer is obvious because the only source of this information is ultimately contained in the Book of Genesis.

References to the pervasive nature of religious concepts in creation science texts amply demonstrate why State entanglement with religion is inevitable under Act 590. Involvement of the State in screening texts for impermissible religious references will require State officials to make delicate religious judgments. The need to monitor classroom discussion in order to uphold the Act's prohibition against religious instruction will necessarily involve administrators in questions concerning religion. These continuing involvements of State officials in questions and issues of religion create an excessive and prohibited entanglement with religion. . . .

V (D)

The defendants presented Dr. Larry Parker, a specialist in devising curricula for public schools. He testified that the public school's curriculum should reflect the subjects the public wants taught in schools. The witness said that polls indicated a significant majority of the American public thought creation science should be taught if evolution was taught. The point of this testimony was never placed in a legal context. No doubt a sizeable majority of Americans believe in the concept of a Creator or, at least, are not opposed to the concept and see nothing wrong with teaching school children about the idea.

The application and content of First Amendment principles are not determined by public opinion polls or by a majority vote. Whether the proponents of Act 590 constitute the majority or the minority is quite irrelevant under a constitutional system of government. No group, no matter how large or small, may use the organs of government, of which the public schools are the most conspicuous and influential, to foist its religious beliefs on others.

The Court closes this opinion with a thought expressed eloquently by the great Justice Frankfurter:

> "We renew our conviction that 'we have staked the very existence of our country on the faith that complete separation between the state and religion is best for the state and best for religion.'" *Everson v. Board of Education.* If nowhere else, in the relation between Church and State, 'good fences make good neighbors.'" *McCollum v. Board of Education* (1948).

An injunction will be entered permanent prohibiting enforcement of Act 590.

It is so ordered this January 5, 1982.

AT&T ANTITRUST SETTLEMENT
January 8, 1982

A new agreement requiring the American Telephone & Telegraph Co. (AT&T) to divest itself of its 22 Bell System operating companies settled the Justice Department's pending antitrust suit against the communications giant. The agreement, announced January 8, 1982, promised far-reaching changes in the structure of the traditional phone company and left AT&T free to concentrate its resources in other rapidly expanding telecommunications fields.

AT&T Background

AT&T's domination of telephone communications began in the early 1900s when the company agreed to offer affordable telephone service to all who wanted it, provided the government protected its monopoly and allowed AT&T to charge profitable rates for service. The government retained the right to regulate AT&T and place ceilings on telephone rates.

As AT&T expanded its communications empire, doubts arose as to whether the arrangement was good public policy and whether AT&T really provided efficient service at the lowest possible cost. A federal antitrust suit, brought against AT&T by the Justice Department in 1949, was settled in 1956 by an agreement confining the company to providing only regulated telephone service.

In 1974 the Justice Department again charged AT&T with monopolizing telephone service by consistently taking steps to keep competitors out of the industry. A non-jury trial of the case began January 15, 1981, in Washington, D.C., with U.S. District Judge Harold H. Greene presiding. Greene immediately recessed the trial until March 2 pending the outcome of talks between Justice and AT&T to reach an out-of-court settlement. The inauguration of President Ronald Reagan and subsequent leadership changes at the Justice Department, however, prevented the parties from meeting the March 2 deadline. After more than six years of research and preparation, Justice called its first witness in the trial on March 4.

Why AT&T Settled

Prompted by an increasing inability to compete effectively in the rapidly changing telecommunications industry and moving to head off unfavorable legislation and possible defeat in the courts, AT&T decided to settle its eight-year-old antitrust case with the Justice Department.

Beginning in the mid-1970s, a series of court rulings and Federal Communications Commission decisions permitted other long distance companies and computer and electronic firms to challenge AT&T. Most of these companies competed for the lucrative long distance routes and big business clients, leaving local phone service, the unprofitable end of the telecommunications business, to AT&T. The 1956 consent decree further restricted AT&T's competitive ability in the rapidly growing telecommunications field because it confined the company to providing only regulated telephone service and prevented its expansion into more technologically advanced areas, such as computer-oriented data processing. In addition, AT&T, bogged down in government regulations, was hampered in developing and marketing new technologies and services.

By 1976 Congress had taken an active interest in revising telecommunications policy, attempting to rewrite the Communications Act of 1934 in each subsequent session. In 1981 the Senate passed a bill deregulating much of the industry, restructuring the phone company and allowing AT&T to enter certain unregulated markets through a separate subsidiary. In the House, however, sentiment was growing for a more restrictive bill that would regulate strictly any entry by AT&T into other telecommunications areas. It became clear that any legislation emerging from Congress would subject AT&T to layer upon layer of new regulations and further hamper its ability to compete.

Finally, as of September 1981, the antitrust case seemed to be going badly for AT&T. Judge Greene denied the company's request that the case be dismissed, saying that Justice had proved AT&T had "violated antitrust laws in a number of ways over a lengthy period of time. On the three principal factual issues the evidence sustains the Government's basic contentions, and the burden is on the defendants to refute the factual showings."

As AT&T executives reviewed the situation, they decided that the least painful and most profitable solution would be to streamline the company by dropping its local operating companies and to concentrate its vast resources in technological research and development, equipment manufacture and long distance service.

The Settlement

The new agreement required AT&T to divest itself of its 22 Bell operating companies, which provided the bulk of the nation's local telephone service and local connections for long distance service. The local operating units accounted for two-thirds or $80 billion of AT&T's total assets and 80 percent of AT&T employees. The settlement permitted AT&T to retain its research arm (Bell Laboratories), manufacturing subsidiary (Western Electric Co.) and long distance service (Long Lines Deparment). The local units divested by AT&T would remain under federal and state regulation and would be required to grant equal access to all long distance companies seeking local connections for their services. The settlement also cleared the way for AT&T to expand into the unregulated telecommunications areas prohibited it by the 1956 consent decree.

Congressional Reaction

Congressional reaction to the announced settlement centered on the possible adverse effects of divestiture on local telephone rates and services. Members were particularly concerned about potential local rate increases because the divested local firms would lose their current subsidies from long distance charges, Yellow Pages and other services remaining at AT&T. In hearings before the Senate Commerce Committee January 25, AT&T Chairman Charles Brown said that local rates would rise regardless of the settlement because of inflation and increasing competition from other long distance companies, but that state and federal regulations would help keep them down. Brown also suggested that local firms could charge long distance companies enough for access to the local telephone network to subsidize local service. Critics of the settlement were quick to point out, however, that no legislative device existed to provide for setting access charges or long distance service subsidies.

Members of Congress from both sides of the aisle also expressed concern that the divested companies might be left in such poor financial condition that telephone service would deteriorate. Local service traditionally had been the high-cost, slow-growth end of the communications business. Industry analysts predicted that as local phone rates increased, big business customers would turn to private telephone systems, thereby

19

forcing residential consumers to pay even higher rates or face further cutbacks in service.

Legal Confusion

The Justice Department and AT&T filed the new agreement with U.S. District Judge Vincent P. Biunno in Newark, N.J., for approval. Biunno, who had presided over the AT&T antitrust case resulting in the 1956 consent decree, approved the settlement and transferred it to Greene in Washington. But Greene maintained that because he had presided over the case since its trial stages and was familiar with all of the evidence, final judicial approval of the accord rested in him. Greene then nullified Biunno's approval and refused to dismiss the suit. Although he was "delighted a settlement [had] been reached," Greene said he could "not permit the case to be dismissed without proper scrutiny" of the agreement. Greene also noted that any settlement of the case was subject to the Antitrust Procedures and Penalties Act (also known as the Tunney Act) that required a 60-day waiting period for public comment and a study of possible effects.

In the months that followed, Greene received comments on the implications of the agreement from AT&T, the Justice Department and concerned citizens groups. On August 11, 1982, Greene issued his opinion on the agreement. While ruling that the proposed settlement was in the public interest, Greene requested some changes before granting his final approval.

First, AT&T would be barred from entering the field of electronic publishing for a minimum of seven years. Newspapers in particular had requested this restriction, fearing that AT&T would use its resources to provide news, advertising and financial reports on home computers using its telephone lines.

Second, Greene ordered that the local Bell companies be permitted to publish their own Yellow Pages advertising directories. Under terms of the original arrangement, publication of the Yellow Pages remained at AT&T.

Third, Greene ordered that the divested Bell companies be permitted to sell, but not manufacture, telephones and switchboards, thus opening the telephone equipment market to competition as well.

Greene ordered these changes to make the newly independent local Bell companies financially viable operations, and threatened to withhold approval of the agreement unless AT&T and Justice agreed. Without income from the Yellow Pages and telephone equipment sales, the local operating companies would lose much of their ability to generate revenue and provide affordable telephone service. AT&T and Justice agreed to the proposed modifications, and Greene gave final approval to the accord

August 24. Greene directed AT&T to present a final divestiture plan to his court and Justice within six months for approval.

Greene's approval of the agreement did not, however, mark the end of the legal dispute. Several state regulatory commissions and public interest groups appealed portions of the settlement, claiming it interfered with states' rights to regulate telephone companies. Greene sent the appeals directly to the U.S. Supreme Court to expedite a ruling. On February 28, 1983, the high court affirmed Greene's opinion, thus denying the appeals.

Following are excerpts from The Modification of Final Judgment between AT&T and the Justice Department, issued January 8, 1982, but not approved by Judge Harold H. Greene; and the text of the conclusion of Judge Greene's August 11 opinion, containing the changes he required:

DISTRICT COURT DECISION

UNITED STATES DISTRICT COURT
FOR THE DISTRICT OF NEW JERSEY

United States of America
Plaintiff
v.
Western Electric Company, Inc.,
and American Telephone and
Telegraph Company,
Defendants

Civil Action
No. 17-49

[January 8, 1982]

Modification of Final Judgment

Plaintiff, United States of America, having filed its complaint herein on January 14, 1949; the defendants having appeared and filed their answer to such complaint denying the substantive allegations thereof; the parties, by their attorneys, having severally consented to a Final Judgment which was entered by the Court on January 24, 1956, and the parties having subsequently agreed that modification of such Final Judgment is required by the technological, economic and regulatory changes which have occurred since the entry of such Final Judgment;

Upon joint motion of the parties and after hearing by the Court, it is hereby

ORDERED, ADJUDGED, AND DECREED that the Final Judgment entered on January 24, 1956, is hereby vacated in its entirety and replaced by the following items and provisions:

I

AT&T Reorganization

A. Not later than six months after the effective date of this Modification of Final Judgment, Defendant AT&T shall submit to the Department of Justice for its approval, and thereafter implement, a plan of reorganization. Such plan shall provide for the completion, within 18 months after the effective date of this Modification of Final Judgment, of the following steps:

1. The transfer from AT&T and its affiliates to the BOCs [Bell Operating Companies], or to a new entity subsequently to be separated from AT&T and to be owned by the BOCs, of sufficient facilities, personnel, systems, and rights to technical information to permit the BOCs to perform, independently of AT&T, exchange telecommunications and exchange access functions, including the procurement for, and engineering, marketing and management of, those functions, and sufficient to enable the BOCs to meet the equal exchange access requirements of Appendix B;

2. The separation within the BOCs of all facilities, personnel and books of account between those relating to the exchange telecommunications or exchange access functions and those relating to other functions (including the provision of interexchange switching and transmission and the provision of customer premises equipment to the public); provided that there shall be no joint ownership of facilities, but appropriate provision may be made for sharing, through leasing or otherwise, of multifunction facilities so long as the separated portion of each BOC is ensured control over the exchange telecommunications and exchange access functions;

3. The termination of the License Contracts between AT&T and the BOCs and other subsidiaries and the Standard Supply Contract between Western Electric and the BOCs and other subsidiaries; and

4. The transfer of ownership of the separated portions of the BOCs providing local exchange and exchange access services from AT&T by means of a spin-off of stock of the separated BOCs to the shareholders of AT&T, or by other disposition; provided that nothing in this Modification of Final Judgment shall require or prohibit the consolidation of the ownership of the BOCs into any particular number of entities.

B. Notwithstanding separation of ownership, the BOCs may support and share the costs of a centralized organization for the provision of engineering, administrative and other services which can most efficiently be provided on a centralized basis. The BOCs shall provide, through a centralized organization, a single point of contact for coordination of BOCs to meet the requirements of national security and emergency preparedness.

C. Until September 1, 1987, AT&T, Western Electric, and the Bell Telephone Laboratories, shall, upon order of any BOC, provide on a priority basis all research, development, manufacturing, and other support services to enable the BOCs to fulfill the requirements of this Modification of Final Judgment. AT&T and its affiliates shall take no action that interferes with the BOCs' requirements of nondiscrimination established by section II.

D. After the reorganization specified in paragraph A (4), AT&T shall not acquire the stock or assets of any BOC.

II

BOC Requirements

A. Subject to Appendix B, each BOC shall provide to all interexchange carriers and information service providers exchange access, information access, and exchange services for such access on an unbundled, tariffed basis, that is equal in type, quality, and price to that provided to AT&T and its affiliates.

B. No BOC shall discriminate between AT&T and its affiliates and their products and services and other persons and their products and services in the:

1. procurement of products and services;

2. establishment and dissemination of technical information and procurement and interconnection standards;

3. interconnection and use of the BOC's telecommunications service and facilities or in the charges for each element of service; and

4. provision of new services and the planning for and implementation of the construction or modification of facilities, used to provide exchange access and information access.

C. Within six months after the reorganization specified in I (A) 4, each BOC shall submit to the Department of Justice procedures for ensuring compliance with the requirements of paragraph B.

D. After completion of the reorganization specified in Section I, no BOC shall, directly or through any affiliated enterprise:

1. provide interexchange telecommunications services or information services;

2. manufacture or provide telecommunications products or customer premises equipment (except for provision of customer premises equipment for emergency services); or

3. provide any other product or service, except exchange telecommunications and exchange access service, that is not a natural monopoly service actually regulated by tariff.

III

Applicability and Effect

The provisions of this Modification of Final Judgment, applicable to each defendant and each BOC, shall be binding upon said defendants and BOCs, their affiliates, successors and assigns, officers, agents, servants, employees, and attorneys, and upon those persons in active concert or participation with each defendant and BOC who receives actual notice of this Modification of Final Judgment by personal service or otherwise. Each defendant and each person bound by the prior sentence shall cooperate in ensuring that the provisions of this Modification of Final Judgment are carried out. Neither this Modification of Final Judgment nor any of its terms or provisions shall constitute any evidence against, an admission by, or an estoppel against any party or BOC. The effective date of this Modification of Final Judgment shall be the date upon which it is entered.

IV

Definitions

For the purposes of this Modification of Final Judgment:

A. "Affiliate" means any organization or entity, including defendant Western Electric Company, Incorporated, and Bell Telephone Laboratories, Incorporated, that is under direct or indirect common ownership with or control by AT&T or is owned or controlled by another affiliate. For the purposes of this paragraph, the terms "ownership" and "owned" mean a direct or indirect equity interest (or the equivalent thereof) of more than fifty (50) percent of an entity. "Subsidiary" means any organization or entity in which AT&T has stock ownership, whether or not controlled by AT&T.

B. "AT&T" shall mean defendant American Telephone and Telegraph Company and its affiliates.

C. "Bell Operating Companies" and "BOCs" mean the corporations listed in Appendix A attached to this Modification of Final Judgment and any entity directly or indirectly owned or controlled by a BOC or affiliated through substantial common ownership.

D. "Carrier" means any person deemed a carrier under the Communications Act of 1934 or amendments thereto, or, with respect to intrastate telecommunications, under the laws of any state.

E. "Customer premises equipment" means equipment employed on the premises of a person (other than a carrier) to originate, route, or terminate telecommunications, but does not include equipment used to multiplex, maintain, or terminate access lines.

F. "Exchange access" means the provision of exchange services for the purpose of originating or terminating interexchange telecommunications. Exchange access services include any activity or function performed by a

BOC in connection with the origination or termination of interexchange telecommunications, including but not limited to, the provision of network control signalling, answer supervision, automatic calling number identification, carrier access codes, directory services, testing and maintenance of facilities and the provision of information necessary to bill customers. Such services shall be provided by facilities in an exchange area for the transmission, switching, or routing, within the exchange area, of interexchange traffic originating or terminating within the exchange area, and shall include switching traffic within the exchange area above the end office and delivery and receipt of such traffic at a point or points within an exchange area designated by an interexchange carrier for the connection of its facilities with those of the BOC. Such connections, at the option of the interexchange carrier, shall deliver traffic with signal quality and characteristics equal to that provided similar traffic of AT&T, including equal probability of blocking, based on reasonable traffic estimates supplied by each interexchange carriers [sic]. Exchange services for exchange access shall not include the performance by any BOC of interexchange traffic routing for any interexchange carrier. In the reorganization specified in section I, trunks used to transmit AT&T's traffic between end offices and class 4 switches shall be exchange access facilities to be owned by the BOCs.

G. "Exchange area," or "exchange" means a geographic area established by a BOC in accordance with the following criteria:

1. any such area shall encompass one or more contiguous local exchange areas serving common social, economic, and other purposes, even where such configuration transcends municipal or other local governmental boundaries;

2. every point served by a BOC within a State shall be included within an exchange area;

3. no such area which includes part or all of one standard metropolitan statistical area (or a consolidated statistical area, in the case of densely populated States) shall include a substantial part of any other standard metropolitan statistical area (or a consolidated statistical area, in the case of densely populated States), unless the Court shall otherwise allow; and

4. except with approval of the Court, no exchange area located in one State shall include any point located within another State.

H. "Information" means knowledge or intelligence represented by any form of writing, signs, signals, pictures, sounds, or other symbols.

I. "Information access" means the provision of specialized exchange telecommunications services by a BOC in an exchange area in connection with the origination, termination, transmission, switching, forwarding or routing of telecommunications traffic to or from the facilities of a provider of information services. Such specialized exchange telecommunications services include, where necessary, the provision of network control signalling, answer supervision, automatic calling number identification, carrier access codes, testing and maintenance of facilities, and the provision of information necessary to bill customers.

J. "Information service" means the offering of a capability for generating, acquiring, storing, transforming, processing, retrieving, utilizing, or making available information which may be conveyed via telecommunications, except that such service does not include any use of any such capability for the management, control, or operation of a telecommunications system or the management of a telecommunications service.

K. "Interexchange telecommunications" means telecommunications between a point or points located in one exchange telecommunications area and a point or points located in one or more other exchange areas or a point outside an exchange area.

L. "Technical information" means intellectual property of all types, including, without limitation, patents, copyrights, and trade secrets, relating to planning documents, designs, specifications, standards, and practices and procedures, including employee training.

N. "Telecommunications equipment" means equipment, other than customer premises equipment, used by a carrier to provide telecommunications services.

O. "Telecommunications" means the transmission, between or among points specified by the user, of information of the user's choosing, without change in the form or content of the information as sent and received, by means of electromagnetic transmission, with or without benefit of any closed transmission medium, including all instrumentalities, facilities, apparatus, and services (including the collection, storage, forwarding, switching, and delivery of such information) essential to such transmission.

P. "Telecommunications service" means the offering for hire of telecommunications facilities, or of telecommunications by means of such facilities.

Q. "Transmission facilities" means equipment (including without limitation wire, cable, microwave, satellite, and fibre-optics) that transmit information by electromagnetic means or which directly support such transmission, but does not include customer-premises equipment.

V

Compliance Provisions

The defendants, each BOC, and affiliated entities are ordered and directed to advise their officers and other management personnel with significant responsibility for matters addressed in this Modification of Final Judgment of their obligations hereunder. Each BOC shall undertake the following with respect to each such officer or management employee:

1. The distribution to them of a written directive setting forth their employer's policy regarding compliance with the Sherman Act and with this Modification of Final Judgment, with such directive to include:

(a) an admonition that non-compliance with such policy and this Modification of Final Judgment will result in appropriate disciplinary action determined by their employer and which may include dismissal; and

(b) advice that the BOCs' legal advisors are available at all reasonable times to confer with such persons regarding any compliance questions or problems.

2. The imposition of a requirement that each of them sign and submit to their employer a certificate in substantially the following form:

> The undersigned hereby (1) acknowledges receipt of a copy of the 1982 *United States* v. *Western Electric*, Modification of Final Judgment and a written directive setting forth Company policy regarding compliance with the anti-trust laws and with such Modification of Final Judgment, (2) represents that the undersigned has read such Modification of Final Judgment and directive and understands those provisions for which the undersigned has responsibility, (3) acknowledges that the undersigned has been advised and understands that non-compliance with such policy and Modification of Final Judgment will result in appropriate disciplinary measures determined by the Company and which may include dismissal, and (4) acknowledges that the undersigned has been advised and understands that non-compliance with the Modification of Final Judgment may also result in conviction for contempt of court and imprisonment and/or fine.

VI

Visitorial Provisions

A. For the purpose of determining or securing compliance with this Modification of Final Judgment, and subject to any legally recognized privilege, from time to time:

1. Upon written request of the Attorney General or of the Assistant Attorney General in charge of the Antitrust Division, and on reasonable notice to a defendant or after the reorganization specified in Section I, a BOC, made to its principal office, duly authorized representatives of the Department of Justice shall be permitted access during office hours of such defendants or BOCs to depose or interview officers, employees, or agents, and inspect and copy all books, ledgers, accounts, correspondence, memoranda and other records and documents in the possession or under the control of such defendant, BOC, or subsidiary companies, who may have counsel present, relating to any matters contained in this Modification of Final Judgment; and

2. Upon the written request of the Attorney General or of the Assistant Attorney General in charge of the Antitrust Division made to a defendant's principal office or, after the reorganization specified in Section I, a BOC, such defendant, or BOC, shall submit such written reports, under oath if requested, with respect to any of the matters contained in this Modification of Final Judgment as may be requested.

B. No information or documents obtained by the means provided in this Section shall be divulged by any representative of the Department of Justice to any person other than a duly authorized representative of the Executive Branch of the United States or the Federal Communications Commission, except in the course of legal proceedings to which the United

States is a party, or for the purpose of securing compliance with this Final Judgment, or as otherwise required by law.

C. If at the time information or documents are furnished by a defendant to a plaintiff, such defendant or a BOC represents and identifies in writing the material in any such information or documents to which a claim of protection may be asserted under Rule 26 (c) (7) of the Federal Rules of Civil Procedure, and said defendant or BOC marks each pertinent page of such material, "Subject to claim of protection under Rule 26 (c) (7) of the Federal Rules of Civil Procedure," then 10 days' notice shall be given by plaintiff to such defendant or BOC prior to divulging such material in any legal proceeding (other than a grand jury proceeding) to which that defendant BOC is not a party.

VII

Retention of Jurisdiction

Jurisdiction is retained by this Court for the purpose of enabling any of the parties to this Modification of Final Judgment, or, after the reorganization specified in Section I, a BOC to apply to this Court at any time for such further orders or directions as may be necessary or appropriate for the construction or carrying out of this Modification of Final Judgment, for the modification of any of the provisions hereof, for the enforcement of compliance herewith, and for the punishment of any violation hereof.

JUDGE GREENE'S OPINION

Conclusion

The proposed reorganization of the Bell System raises issues of vast complexity. Because of their importance, not only to the parties but also to the telecommunications industry and to the public, the Court has discussed the various problems in substantial detail. It is appropriate to summarize briefly the major issues and the Court's decisions which are central to the proceeding.

A. The American telecommunications industry is presently dominated by one company — AT&T. It provides local and long-distance telephone service; it manufactures and markets the equipment used by telephone subscribers as well as that used in the telecommunications network; and it controls one of the leading communications research and development facilities in the world. According to credible evidence, this integrated structure has enabled AT&T for many years to undermine the efforts of competitors seeking to enter the telecommunications market.

The key to the Bell System's power to impede competition has been its control of local telephone service. The local telephone network functions as the gateway to individual telephone subscribers. It must be used by long-distance carriers seeking to connect one caller to another. Customers will only purchase equipment which can readily be connected to the local network through the telephone outlets in their homes and offices. The enormous cost of the wires, cables, switches, and other transmission facilities which comprise that network has completely insulated it from competition. Thus, access to AT&T's local network is crucial if long distance carriers and equipment manufacturers are to be viable competitors.

AT&T has allegedly used its control of this local monopoly to disadvantage these competitors in two principal ways. First, it has attempted to prevent competing long distance carriers and competing equipment manufacturers from gaining access to the local network, or to delay that access, thus placing them in an inferior position vis-a-vis AT&T's own services. Second, it has supposedly used profits earned from the monopoly local telephone operations to subsidize its long distance and equipment businesses in which it was competing with others.

For a great many years, the Federal Communications Commission has struggled, largely without success, to stop practices of this type through the regulatory tools at its command. A lawsuit the Department of Justice brought in 1949 to curb similar practices ended in an ineffectual consent decree. Some other remedy is plainly required; hence the divestiture of the local Operating Companies from the Bell System. This divestiture will sever the relationship between this local monopoly and the other, competitive segments of AT&T, and it will thus ensure — certainly better than could any other type of relief — that the practices which allegedly have lain heavy on the telecommunications industry will not occur.

B. With the loss of control over the local network, AT&T will be unable to disadvantage its competitors, and the restrictions imposed on AT&T after the government's first antitrust suit — which limited AT&T to the provision of telecommunications services — will no longer be necessary. The proposed decree accordingly removes these restrictions.

The decree will thus allow AT&T to become a vigorous competitor in the growing computer, computer-related, and information markets. Other large and experienced firms are presently operating in these markets, and there is therefore no reason to believe that AT&T will be able to achieve monopoly dominance in these industries as it did in telecommunications. At the same time, by use of its formidable scientific, engineering, and management resources, including particularly the capabilities of Bell Laboratories, AT&T should be able to make significant contributions to these fields, which are at the forefront of innovation and technology, to the benefit of American consumers, national defense, and the position of American industry vis-a-vis foreign competition.

All of these developments are plainly in the public interest, and the Court will therefore approve this aspect of the proposed decree, with one exception. Electronic publishing, which is still in its infancy, holds promise to become an important provider of information — such as news, entertainment, and advertising — in competition with the traditional print, television, and radio media; indeed, it has the potential, in time, for actually replacing some of these methods of disseminating information.

Traditionally, the Bell System has simply distributed information provided by others; it has not been involved in the business of generating its own information. The proposed decree would, for the first time, allow AT&T to do both, and it would do so at a time when the electronic publishing industry is still in a fragile state of experimentation and growth and when electronic information can still most efficiently and most economically be distributed over AT&T's long distance network. If, under these circumstances, AT&T were permitted to engage both in the transmission and the generation of information, there would be a substantial risk not only that it would stifle the efforts of other electronic publishers but that it would acquire a substantial monopoly over the generation of news in the more general sense. Such a development would strike at a principle which lies at the heart of the First Amendment: that the American people are entitled to a diversity of sources of information. In order to prevent this from occurring, the Court will require, as a condition of its approval of the proposed decree, that it be modified to preclude AT&T from entering the field of electronic publishing until the risk of its domination of that field has abated.

C. After the divestiture, the Operating Companies will possess a monopoly over local telephone service. According to the Department of Justice, the Operating Companies must be barred from entering all competitive markets to ensure that they will not misuse their monopoly power. The Court will not impose restrictions simply for the sake of theoretical consistency. Restrictions must be based on an assessment of the realistic circumstances of the relevant markets, including the Operating Companies' ability to engage in anticompetitive behavior, their potential contribution to the market as an added competitor for AT&T, as well as upon the effects of the restrictions on the rates for local telephone service.

This standard requires that the Operating Companies be prohibited from providing long distance services and information services, and from manufacturing equipment used in the telecommunications industry. Participation in these fields carries with it a substantial risk that the Operating Companies will use the same anticompetitive techniques used by AT&T in order to thwart the growth of their own competitors. Moreover, contrary to the assumptions made by some, Operating Company involvement in these areas could not legitimately generate subsidies for local rates. Such involvement could produce substantial profits only if the local companies used their monopoly position to dislodge competitors or to provide subsidy for their competitive services or products — the very behavior the decree seeks to prevent.

Different considerations apply, however, to the marketing of customer premises equipment — the telephone and other devices used in subscribers' homes and offices — and the production of the Yellow Pages advertising directories. For a variety of reasons, there is little likelihood that these companies will be able to use their monopoly position to disadvantage competitors in these areas. In addition, their marketing of equipment will provide needed competition for AT&T, and the elimination of the restriction on their production of the Yellow Pages will generate a substantial subsidy for local telephone rates. The Court will therefore require that the proposed decree be modified to remove the restrictions on these two types of activities.

D. With respect to a number of subjects, the proposed decree establishes merely general principles and objectives, leaving the specific implementing details for subsequent action, principally by the plan of reorganization which AT&T is required to file within six months after entry of the judgment. The parties have also made informal promises, either to each other or to the Court, as to how they intend to interpret or implement various provisions. The Court has decided that its public interest responsibilities require that it establish a process for determining whether the plan of reorganization and other, subsequent actions by AT&T actually implement these principles and promises in keeping with the objectives of the judgment. Absent such a process, AT&T would have the opportunity to interpret and implement the broad principles of the decree in such a manner as to disadvantage its competitors, the Operating Companies, or both, or otherwise to act in a manner contrary to the public interest as interpreted by the Court in this opinion.

For that reason, the Court is requiring that the judgment be modified (1) to vest authority in the Court to enforce the provisions and principles of that judgment on its own rather than only at the request of a party; and (2) to provide for a proceeding, accessible to third party intervenors and to the chief executives of the seven new regional Operating Companies, in which the Court will determine whether the plan of reorganization is consistent with the decree's general principles and promises.

E. For the reasons stated in this opinion, the Court will approve the proposed decree as in the public interest provided that the parties agree to the addition of the following new section:

VIII

Modifications

A. Notwithstanding the provisions of section II (D) (2), the separated BOCs shall be permitted to provide, but not manufacture, customer premises equipment.

B. Notwithstanding the provisions of section II (D) (3), the separated BOCs shall be permitted to produce, publish, and distribute printed directories which contain advertisements and which list general product and business categories, the service or product providers under these categories, and their names, telephone numbers, and addresses.

Notwithstanding the provisions of sections I (A) (1), I (A) (2), I (A) (4), all facilities, personnel, systems, and rights to technical information owned by AT&T, its affiliates, or the BOCs which are necessary for the production, publication, and distribution of printed advertising directories shall be transferred to the separated BOCs.

C. The restrictions imposed upon the separated BOCs by virtue of section II (D) shall be removed upon a showing by the petitioning BOC that there is no substantial possibility that it could use its monopoly power to impede competition in the market it seeks to enter.

D. AT&T shall not engage in electronic publishing over its own transmission facilities. "Electronic publishing" means the provision of any information which AT&T or its affiliates has, or has caused to be, originated, authored, compiled, collected, or edited, or in which it has a direct or indirect financial or proprietary interest, and which is disseminated to an unaffiliated person through some electronic means.

Nothing in this provision precludes AT&T from offering electronic directory services that list general product and business categories, the service or product providers under these categories, and their names, telephone numbers, and addresses; or from providing the time, weather, and such other audio services as are being offered as of the date of the entry of the decree to the geographic areas of the country receiving those services as of that date.

Upon application of AT&T, this restriction shall be removed after seven years from the date of entry of the decree, unless the Court finds that competitive conditions clearly require its extension.

E. If a separated BOC provides billing services to AT&T pursuant to Appendix B (C) (2), it shall include upon the portion of the bill devoted to interexchange services the following legend:

This portion of your bill is provided as a service to AT&T. There is no connection between this company and AT&T. You may choose another company for your long distance telephone calls while still receiving your local telephone service from this company.

F. Notwithstanding the provisions of Appendix B (C) (3), whenever, as permitted by the decree, a separated BOC fails to offer exchange access to an interexchange carrier that is equal in type and quality to that provided for the interexchange traffic of AT&T, the tariffs filed for such less-than-equal access shall reflect the lesser cost, if any, of such access as compared to the exchange access provided AT&T.

G. Facilities and other assets which serve both AT&T and one or more BOCs shall be transferred to the separated BOCs if the use made by such BOC or BOCs predominates over that of AT&T. Upon application by a party or a BOC, the Court may grant an exception to this requirement.

H. At the time of the transfer of ownership provided for in section

I (A) (4), the separated BOCs shall have debt ratios of approximately forty-five percent (except for Pacific Telephone and Telegraph Company which shall have a debt ratio of approximately fifty percent), and the quality of the debt shall be representative of the average terms and conditions of the consolidated debt held by AT&T, its affiliates and the BOCs at that time. Upon application by a party or a BOC, the Court may grant an exception to this requirement.

I. The Court may act *sua sponte* to issue orders or directions for the construction or carrying out of this decree, for the enforcement of compliance herewith, and for the punishment of any violation thereof.

J. Notwithstanding the provisions of section I (A), the plan of reorganization shall not be implemented until approved by the Court as being consistent with the provisions and principles of the decree.

F. The United States and AT&T shall within fifteen days hereof submit to the Court their proposed decree, including the modifications listed above, or their statements that they are not prepared to incorporate such modifications. If a modified decree is submitted, the Court will promptly approve it as being in the public interest, and the *AT&T* action will be dismissed. If the parties do not agree to incorporate the modifications, the Court will decline to approve the proposed decree, the 1956 consent decree in the *Western Electric* action will remain in effect, and the *AT&T* trial will resume at a date to be set by the Court.

Harold H. Greene
United States District Judge

Dated: August 11, 1982

COURT ON ANTITRUST
IMMUNITY OF CITIES
January 13, 1982

The Supreme Court ruled 5-3 January 13 that cities, unless acting under specific state laws, are subject to federal antitrust laws when they regulate private business. In Community Communications Company, Inc. v. City of Boulder, Colorado, *the majority decided that Boulder was not exempt from the Sherman Antitrust Act when it prohibited a local cable television firm from temporarily expanding its business.*

Justice William J. Brennan Jr. wrote the majority opinion, in which Justices Thurgood Marshall, Harry A. Blackmun, Lewis F. Powell Jr. and John Paul Stevens joined. Stevens also wrote a concurring opinion. Justice William H. Rehnquist, joined by Chief Justice Warren E. Burger and Justice Sandra Day O'Connor, wrote the dissenting opinion. Justice Byron R. White took no part in the case.

Background

Since 1966 Community Communications Co. had served an area of Boulder that was unable to receive broadcast TV signals for geographic reasons. From 1966 to 1980, this service consisted essentially of retransmitting programs broadcast elsewhere. When dramatic improvements in cable television technology occurred in the late 1970s, the company was able to offer many more services and wanted to extend its business into other areas of the city.

Boulder's city council enacted an "emergency" ordinance prohibiting the company from expanding for three months. During those three months, the council intended to draft a model cable television ordinance and to invite new businesses to compete in the market. The council feared that if the already established Community Communications Co. expanded immediately, new firms would be unable to compete and the city's best interests might not be served.

Community Communications filed suit in federal district court, alleging that the city's action violated Section 1 of the Sherman Act. Passed in 1890, the Sherman Act is the major federal antitrust law, prohibiting any contract, combination or conspiracy in restraint of trade.

Boulder argued that because it was a "home rule" municipality, it was entitled to the same immunity to federal antitrust laws that state governments have. Boulder's argument was based on the 1943 Parker v. Brown decision, in which the Supreme Court held that Congress had not intended the Sherman Act to cover state regulation of private enterprise. In the Community Communications case, a district court had ruled that Boulder was not immune to the antitrust laws, but the court of appeals had reversed the lower court's decision.

Majority Opinion

The Supreme Court reversed the appeals court decision and ruled that Boulder was not exempt from the antitrust law. "Ours is a dual system of government, which has no place for sovereign cities," wrote Brennan. Unless a local government has a "precise, clearly articulated and affirmatively expressed state grant of power to engage in specific anticompetitive actions," he stated, it was subject to antitrust regulation as if it were a private entity.

The case was remanded to the district court to decide whether there was, in fact, any antitrust violation. For, as Stevens pointed out in his concurring opinion, the court had not ruled that antitrust laws had been violated, merely that Boulder was not exempt from them.

Dissent

Rehnquist, writing in dissent, maintained that the decision would "impede, if not paralyze, local governments' efforts to enact ordinances and regulations aimed at protecting public health, safety and welfare, for fear of subjecting the local government to liability under the Sherman Act." Rehnquist said the court's decision "effectively destroys the 'home rule' movement in this country, through which local governments have obtained, not without persistent state opposition, a limited autonomy over matters of local concern."

Reaction

Because the case involved the relationship between local and state governments, it generated great interest among these groups. Several cities joined in the litigation with Boulder, while 23 states (including Colorado) filed a "friend-of-the-court" brief on behalf of Community Communications Co.

Many city officials clearly were upset with the court's decision. Local governments contended that the decision made them vulnerable to long and costly lawsuits that, regardless of outcome, would interfere with their efforts to govern and serve the public. Many cities already were struggling with service cutbacks because of the recession and federal budget cuts.

Testifying before the Senate Judiciary Committee on behalf of the National League of Cities on June 30, Mayor Tom Moody of Columbus, Ohio, deplored the court's decision. He advocated amending the antitrust laws to establish a municipal exemption that would parallel that of the states. "We are not asking for blanket immunity for cities, but rather a limited exemption that will allow cities to govern without being subject to inappropriate antitrust challenges," he said.

Following are excerpts from the January 13, 1982, decision of the Supreme Court in Community Communications Company, Inc. v. City of Boulder, Colorado *and excerpts from the dissenting opinion by Justice Rehnquist:*

No. 80-1350

Community Communications Company, Inc., Petitioner *v.* City of Boulder, Colorado, et al.	On writ of certiorari to the United States Court of Appeals for the Tenth Circuit

[January 13, 1982]

JUSTICE WHITE took no part in the consideration or decision of this case.

JUSTICE BRENNAN delivered the opinion of the Court.

The question presented in this case, in which the District Court for the District of Colorado granted preliminary injunctive relief, is whether a "home rule" municipality, granted by the state constitution extensive powers of self-government in local and municipal matters, enjoys the "state action" exemption from Sherman Act liability announced in *Parker v. Brown* (1943).

I

Respondent City of Boulder is organized as a "home rule" municipality under the Constitution of the State of Colorado. The City is thus entitled to exercise "the full right of self-government in both local and municipal matters," and with respect to such matters the City Charter and ordinances supersede the laws of the State. Under that Charter, all municipal legislative powers are exercised by an elected City Council. In 1964 the City Council enacted an ordinance granting to Colorado Televents, Inc., a 20-year, revocable, non-exclusive permit to conduct a cable television business within the City limits. This permit was assigned to petitioner in 1966, and since that time petitioner has provided cable television service to the University Hill area of Boulder, an area where some 20% of the City's population lives, and where, for geographical reasons, broadcast television signals cannot be received.

From 1966 until February 1980, due to the limited service that could be provided with the technology then available, petitioner's service consisted essentially of retransmissions of programming broadcast from Denver and Cheyenne, Wyo. Petitioner's market was therefore confined to the University Hill area. However, markedly improved technology became available in the late 1970s, enabling petitioner to offer many more channels of entertainment than could be provided by local broadcast television. Thus presented with an opportunity to expand its business into other areas of the City, petitioner in May 1979 informed the City Council that it planned such an expansion. But the new technology offered opportunities to potential competitors, as well, and in July 1979 one of them, the newly formed Boulder Communications Company (BCC), also wrote to the City Council, expressing its interest in obtaining a permit to provide competing cable television service throughout the City.

The City Council's response, after reviewing its cable television policy, was the enactment of an "emergency" ordinance prohibiting petitioner from expanding its business into other areas of the City for a period of three months. The City Council announced that during this moratorium it planned to draft a model cable television ordinance and to invite new businesses to enter the Boulder market under its terms, but that the moratorium was necessary because petitioner's continued expansion during the drafting of the model ordinance would discourage potential competitors from entering the market.

Petitioner filed this suit in the United States District Court for the District of Colorado, and sought, *inter alia,* a preliminary injunction to prevent the City from restricting petitioner's proposed business expansion, alleging that such a restriction would violate § 1 of the Sherman Act. The City responded that its moratorium ordinance could not be violative of the antitrust laws, either because that ordinance constituted an exercise of the City's police powers, or because Boulder enjoyed antitrust immunity under the *Parker* doctrine. The District Court considered the City's status as a home rule municipality, but determined that that status gave autonomy to the City only in matters of local concern, and that the operations of cable television embrace "wider concerns, including interstate commerce ... [and] the First Amendment rights of communicators." (1980). Then, assuming *arguendo* that the ordinance was within the City's authority as a home rule municipality, the District Court considered *City of Lafayette* v. *Louisiana Power & Light Co.* (1978) and concluded that the *Parker* exemption was "wholly inapplicable," and that the City was therefore subject to antitrust liability. Petitioner's motion for a preliminary injunction was accordingly granted.

On appeal, a divided panel of the United States Court of Appeals for the Tenth Circuit reversed. (1980). The majority, after examining Colorado law, rejected the District Court's conclusion that regulation of the cable television business was beyond the home rule authority of the City. The majority then addressed the question of the City's claimed *Parker* exemption. It distinguished the present case from *City of Lafayette* on the ground that, in contrast to the municipally operated revenue-producing utility companies at issue there, "no proprietary interest of the City is here involved." After noting that the City's regulation "was the only control or active supervision exercised by state or local government, and ... represented the only expression of policy as to the subject matter," the majority held that the City's actions therefore satisfied the criteria for a *Parker* exemption. We granted certiorari (1981). We reverse.

II

A

Parker v. *Brown* addressed the question whether the federal antitrust laws prohibited a State, in the exercise of its sovereign powers, from imposing certain anticompetitive restraints. These took the form of a "marketing program" adopted by the State of California for the 1940 raisin crop; that program prevented appellee from freely marketing his crop in interstate commerce. *Parker* noted that California's program "derived its authority ... from the legislative command of the state" and went on to hold that the program was therefore exempt, by virtue of the Sherman Act's own limitations, from antitrust attack:

> "We find nothing in the language of the Sherman Act or in its history which suggests that its purpose was to restrain a state or its officers or agents from activities directed by its legislature. In a dual system of government in which, under the Constitution, the states are sovereign, save only as Congress may constitutionally subtract from their authority, an unexpressed purpose to nullify a state's control over its officers and agents is not lightly to be attributed to Congress."

The availability of this exemption to a State's municipalities was the question presented in *City of Lafayette*. In that case, petitioners were Louisiana cities empowered to own and operate electric utility systems both within and beyond their municipal limits. Respondent brought suit against petitioners under the Sherman Act, alleging that they had committed various antitrust offenses in the conduct of their utility systems, to the injury of respondent. Petitioners invoked the *Parker* doctrine as entitling them to dismissal of the suit. The District Court accepted this argument and dismissed. But the Court of Appeals for the Fifth Circuit reversed, holding that a "subordinate state governmental body is not *ipso facto* exempt from the operation of the antitrust laws" (1976) and directing the District Court on remand to examine "whether the state legislature contemplated a certain type of anticompetitive restraint."

This Court affirmed. In doing so, a majority rejected at the outset petitioners' claim that, quite apart from *Parker*, 'Congress never intended to subject local governments to the antitrust laws." A plurality opinion for four Justices then addressed petitioners' argument that *Parker*, properly construed, extended to "all governmental entities, whether state agencies or subdivisions of a State, . . . simply by reason of their status as such." The plurality opinion rejected this argument, after a discussion of *Parker*, *Goldfinch* v. *Virginia State Bar* (1975), and *Bates* v. *State Bar of Arizona* (1977). These precedents were construed as holding that the *Parker* exemption reflects the federalism principle that we are a nation of *States*, a principle that makes no accommodation for sovereign subdivisions of States. The plurality opinion said that:

> "Cities are not themselves sovereign; they do not receive all the federal deference of the States that create them. *Parker*'s limitation of the exemption to 'official action directed by a state,' is consistent with the fact that the States' subdivisions generally have not been treated as equivalents of the States themselves. In light of the serious economic dislocation which could result if cities were free to place their own parochial interests above the Nation's economic goals reflected in the antitrust laws, we are especially unwilling to presume that Congress intended to exclude anticompetitive municipal action from their reach."

The opinion emphasized, however, that the state as sovereign might sanction anticompetitive municipal activities and thereby immunize municipalities from antitrust liability. Under the plurality's standard, the *Parker* doctrine would shield from antitrust liability municipal conduct engaged in "pursuant to state policy to displace competition with regulation or monopoly public service." This was simply a recognition that a State may frequently choose to effect its policies through the instrumentality of its cities and towns. It was stressed, however, that the "state policy" relied upon would have to be "clearly articulated and affirmatively expressed." This standard has since been adopted by a majority of the Court. *New Motor Vehicle Board of California* v. *Orrin W. Fox Co.* (1978); *California Retail Liquor Dealers Assn.* v. *Midcal Aluminum, Inc.* (1980).

B

Our precedents thus reveal that Boulder's moratorium ordinance cannot be exempt from antitrust scrutiny unless it constitutes the action of the

State of Colorado itself in its sovereign capacity, see *Parker*, or unless it constitutes municipal action in furtherance or implementation of clearly articulated and affirmatively expressed state policy, see *City of Lafayette, Orrin W. Fox. Co.*, and *Midcal*. Boulder argues that these criteria are met by the direct delegation of powers to municipalities through the Home Rule Amendment to the Colorado Constitution. It contends that this delegation satisfies both the *Parker* and the *City of Lafayette* standards. We take up these arguments in turn.

(1)

Respondent's *Parker* argument emphasizes that through the Home Rule Amendment the people of the State of Colorado have vested in the City of Boulder "*every power* theretofore possessed by the legislature ... in local and municipal affairs." The power thus possessed by Boulder's City Council assertedly embraces the regulation of cable television, which is claimed to pose essentially local problems. Thus, it is suggested, the City's cable television moratorium ordinance is an "act of government" performed by the City *acting as the state* in local matters, which meets the "state action" criterion of *Parker*.

We reject this argument: it both misstates the letter of the law and misunderstands its spirit. The *Parker* state action exemption reflects Congress' intention to embody in the Sherman Act the federalism principle that the States possess a significant measure of sovereignty under our Constitution. But this principle contains its own limitation: Ours is a "*dual* system of government," *Parker* (emphasis added), which has no place for sovereign cities. As this Court stated long ago, all sovereign authority "within the geographical limits of the United States" resides either with

> "the Government of the United States, or [with] the States of the Union. *There exist within the broad domain of sovereignty but these two*. There may be cities, counties, and other organized bodies with limited legislative functions, but they are all derived from, or exist in, subordination to one or the other of these." *United States* v. *Kagama* (1886) (emphasis added).

The dissent in the Court of Appeals correctly discerned this limitation upon the federalism principle: "We are a nation not of 'city-states' but of States." *Parker* itself took this view. When *Parker* examined Congress' intentions in enacting the antitrust laws, the opinion noted that "nothing in the language of the Sherman Act or in its history ... suggests that its purpose was to restrain a state or its officers or agents from activities *directed by its legislature*. ... [And] an unexpressed purpose to nullify a *state's control over its officers and agents* is not lightly to be attributed to Congress." ([E]mphasis added.) Thus *Parker* recognized Congress' intention to limit the state action exemption based upon the federalism principle of limited state sovereignty. ... It was expressly recognized by the plurality opinion in *City of Lafayette* that municipalities "are not themselves sovereign and that accordingly they could partake of the

Parker exemption only to the extent that they acted pursuant to a clearly articulated and affirmatively expressed state policy.... We turn then to Boulder's contention that its actions were undertaken pursuant to a clearly articulated and affirmatively expressed state policy.

(2)

Boulder first argues that the requirement of "clear articulation and affirmative expression" is fulfilled by the Colorado Home Rule Amendment's "guarantee of local autonomy." It contends, quoting from *City of Lafayette*, that by this means Colorado has "comprehended within the powers granted" to Boulder the power to enact the challenged ordinance and that Colorado has thereby "contemplated" Boulder's enactment of an anticompetitive regulatory program. Further, Boulder contends that it may be inferred, "from the authority given" to Boulder "to operate in a particular area" — here, the asserted home rule authority to regulate cable television — "that the *legislature* contemplated the kind of action complained of." (Emphasis supplied.) Boulder therefore concludes that the "adequate state mandate" required by *City of Lafayette* is present here.

But plainly the requirement of "clear articulation and affirmative expression" is not satisfied when the State's position is one of mere *neutrality* respecting the municipal actions challenged as anticompetitive. A State that allows its municipalities to do as they please can hardly be said to have "contemplated" the specific anticompetitive actions for which municipal liability is sought.... The relationship of the State of Colorado to Boulder's moratorium ordinance is one of precise neutrality. As the majority in the Court of Appeals below acknowledged, "we are here concerned with City action in the absence of any regulation whatever by the State of Colorado. Under these circumstances there is no interaction of state and local regulation. We have only the action or exercise of authority by the City." Indeed, respondent argues that as to local matters regulated by a home rule city, the Colorado General Assembly is without power to act.... Acceptance of such a proposition — that the general grant of power to enact ordinances necessarily implies state authorization to enact specific anticompetitive ordinances — would wholly eviscerate the concepts of "clear articulation and affirmative expression" that our precedents require.

III

Respondent argues that denial of the *Parker* exemption in the present case will have serious adverse consequences for cities, and will unduly burden the federal courts. But this argument is simply an attack upon the wisdom of the longstanding congressional commitment to the policy of free markets and open competition embodied in the antitrust laws. Those laws, like other federal laws imposing civil or criminal sanctions upon "persons," of course apply to municipalities as well as to other corporate entities. Moreover, judicial enforcement of Congress' will regarding the state action exemption renders a State "no less able to allocate governmental power between itself and its political subdivisions. It means only that when the State itself has not directed or authorized an anticompetitive practice, the State's subdivisions in exercising their delegated power must obey the antitrust laws." *City of Lafayette.* As was observed in that case,

> Today's decision does not threaten the legitimate exercise of governmental power, nor does it preclude municipal government from providing services on a monopoly basis. *Parker* and its progeny make clear that a State properly may ... direct or authorize its instrumentalities to act in a way which, if it did not reflect state policy, would be inconsistent with the antitrust laws. . . . [A]ssuming that the municipality is authorized to provide service on a monopoly basis, these limitations on municipal action will not hobble the execution of legitimate governmental programs.

The judgment of the Court of Appeals is reversed, and the action remanded for further proceedings consistent with this opinion.

It is so ordered.

JUSTICE REHNQUIST, with whom THE CHIEF JUSTICE and JUSTICE O'CONNOR join, dissenting.

The Court's decision in this case is flawed in two serious respects, and will thereby impede, if not paralyze, local governments' efforts to enact ordinances and regulations aimed at protecting public health, safety, and welfare, for fear of subjecting the local government to liability under the Sherman Act, 15 U.S.C. § 1 *et seq.* First, the Court treats the issue in this case as whether a municipality is "exempt" from the Sherman Act under our decision in *Parker* v. *Brown* (1943). The question addressed in *Parker* and in this case is not whether State and local governments are *exempt* from the Sherman Act, but whether statutes, ordinances, and regulations enacted as an act of government are *preempted* by the Sherman Act under the operation of the Supremacy Clause. Second, in holding that a municipality's ordinances can be "exempt" from antitrust scrutiny only if the enactment furthers or implements a "clearly articulated and affirmatively expressed state policy," the Court treats a political subdivision of a State as an entity indistinguishable from any privately owned business. As I read the Court's opinion, a municipality may be said to *violate* the antitrust laws by enacting legislation in conflict with the Sherman Act, unless the legislation is enacted pursuant to an affirmative state policy to supplant competitive market forces in the area of the economy to be regulated.

I

Preemption and exemption are fundamentally distinct concepts. Preemption, because it involves the Supremcy Clause, implicates our basic notions of federalism. Preemption analysis is invoked whenever the Court is called upon to examine "the interplay between the enactments of two *different* sovereigns — one federal and the other state." We are confronted with questions under the Supremacy Clause when we are called upon to resolve a purported conflict between the enactments of the federal government and those of a State or local government, or where it is claimed that the federal government has occupied a particular field exclusively, so as to foreclose any state regulation. Where preemption is found, the state enactment must fall without any effort to accommodate the State's purposes or interests. Because preemption treads on the very sensitive area of Federal-State relations, this Court is "reluctant to infer preemption," *Exxon Corp.* v. *Governor of Maryland* (1978), and the presumption is that preemption is not to be found absent the clear and manifest intention of Congress that the federal act should supersede the police powers of the States. *Ray* v. *Atlantic Richfield Co.* (1978).

In contrast, exemption involves the interplay between the enactments of a single sovereign — whether one enactment was intended by Congress to relieve a party from the necessity of complying with a prior enactment. See, *e.g., National Broiler Marketing Ass'n* v. *United States* (1978) (Sherman Act and Capper-Volstead Act); *United States* v. *Philadelphia National Bank* (1963) (Clayton Act and Bank Merger Act of 1960); *Silver* v. *New York Stock Exchange* (1963) (Sherman Act and Securities Exchange Act). Since the enactments of only one sovereign are involved, no problems of federalism are present. The court interpreting the statute must simply attempt to ascertain congressional intent, whether the exemption is claimed to be express or implied. The presumptions utilized in exemption analysis are quite distinct from those applied in the preemption context. In examining exemption questions, "the proper approach . . . is an analysis which reconciles the operation of both statutory schemes with one another rather than holding one completely ousted." *Silver* v. *New York Stock Exchange.*

With this distinction in mind, I think it quite clear that questions involving the so-called "state action" doctrine are more properly framed as being ones of preemption rather than exemption. Issues under the doctrine inevitably involve state and local regulation which, it is contended, are in conflict with the Sherman Act.

Our decision in *Parker* v. *Brown* was the genesis of the "state action" doctrine. That case involved a challenge to a program established pursuant to the California Agricultural Prorate Act, which sought to restrict competition in the State's raisin industry by limiting the producer's ability to distribute raisins through private channels. The program thus sought to maintain prices at a level higher than those maintained in an unregulated market. This Court assumed that the program would violate the Sherman Act were it "organized and made effective solely by virtue of a contract, combination or conspiracy of private persons, individual or corporate," and that "Congress could, in the exercise of its commerce power, prohibit a state from maintaining a stabilization program like the present because of its effect on interstate commerce." In this regard, we noted that "[o]ccupation of a legislative field by Congress in the exercise of a granted power is a familiar example of its constitutional power to suspend state laws." We then held, however, that "[w]e find nothing in the language of the Sherman Act or its history which suggests that its purpose was to restrain a state or its officers or agents from activities directed by its legislature. In a dual system of government in which, under the Constitution, the states are sovereign, save only as Congress may constitutionally subtract from their authority, an unexpressed purpose to nullify a state's control over its officers and agents is not lightly to be attributed to Congress."

This is clearly the language of federal preemption under the Supremacy Clause. This Court decided in *Parker* that Congress did not intend the Sherman Act to override state legislation designed to regulate the economy. There was no language of "exemption," either express or implied, nor the usual incantation that "repeals by implication are disfavored." Instead, the Court held that state regulation of the economy is not necessarily preempted by the antitrust laws even if the same acts by purely private parties would constitute a violation of the Sherman Act. The Court recognized, however, that some state regulation is preempted by the Sherman Act, explaining that "a state does not give immunity to those who violate the Sherman Act by authorizing them to violate it, or by declaring that their action is lawful. . . ."

Our two most recent *Parker* doctrine cases reveal most clearly that the "state action" doctrine is not an exemption at all, but instead a matter of federal preemption.

In *New Motor Vehicle Bd.* v. *Orrin W. Fox Co.* (1978), we examined the contention that the California Automobile Franchise Act conflicted with the Sherman Act. That Act required a motor vehicle manufacturer to secure the approval of the California New Motor Vehicle Board before it could open a dealership within an existing franchisee's market area, if the competing franchisee objected. By so delaying the opening of a new dealership whenever a competing dealership protested, the Act arguably gave effect to privately initiated restraints of trade, and thus was invalid under *Schwegmann Bros.* v. *Calvert Distillers Corp.* (1951). We held that the Act was outside the purview of the Sherman Act because it contemplated "a system of regulation, clearly articulated and affirmatively expressed, designed to displace unfettered business freedom in the matter of the establishment and relocation of automobile dealerships." We also held that a state statute is not invalid under the Sherman Act merely because the statute will have an anticompetitive effect. Otherwise, if an adverse effect upon competition were enough to render a statute invalid under the Sherman Act, "the States' power to engage in economic regulation would be effectively destroyed." In *New Motor Vehicle Bd.*, we held that a state statute could stand in the face of a purported conflict with the Sherman Act.

In *California Retail Liquor Dealers Ass'n* v. *Midcal Aluminum, Inc.* (1980), we invalidated California's wine-pricing system in the face of a challenge under the Sherman Act. We first held that the price-setting program constituted resale price maintenance, which this Court has consistently held to be a *"per se"* violation of the Sherman Act. We then concluded that the program could not fit within the *Parker* doctrine. Although the restraint was imposed pursuant to a clearly articulated and affirmatively expressed state policy, the program was not actively supervised by the State itself. The State merely authorized and enforced price-fixing established by private parties, instead of establishing the prices itself or reviewing their reasonableness. In the absence of sufficient state supervision, we held that the pricing system was invalid under the Sherman Act.

Unlike the instant case, *Parker, Midcal,* and *New Motor Vehicle Bd.* involved challenges to a state statute. There was no suggestion that a State *violates* the Sherman Act when it enacts legislation not saved by the *Parker* doctrine from invalidation under the Sherman Act. Instead, the statute is simply unenforceable because it has been preempted by the Sherman Act. By contrast, the gist of the Court's opinion is that a municipality may actually violate the antitrust laws when it merely enacts an ordinance invalid under the Sherman Act, unless the ordinance implements an affirmatively expressed state policy. According to the majority, a municipality may be liable under the Sherman Act for enacting anticompetitive legislation, unless it can show that it is acting simply as the "instrumentality" of the State.

Viewing the *Parker* doctrine in this manner will have troubling consequences for this Court and the lower courts who must now adapt antitrust principles to adjudicate Sherman Act challenges to local regulation of the economy. . . . Among the many problems to be encountered will be whether the *"per se"* rules of illegality apply to municipal defendants in the same manner as they are applied to private defendants. Another is the question of remedies. The Court understandably leaves open the question whether municipalities may be liable for treble damages for enacting anticompetitive ordinances which are not protected by the *Parker* doctrine.

Most troubling, however, will be questions regarding the factors which may be examined by the Court pursuant to the Rule of Reason. In *National Society of Professional Engineers* v. *United States* (1978), we held that an anticompetitive restraint could not be defended on the basis of a private party's conclusion that competition posed a potential threat to public safety and the ethics of a particular profession. "[T]he Rule of Reason does not support a defense based on the assumption that competition itself is unreasonable." *Professional Engineers* holds that the decision to replace competition with regulation is not within the competence of private entities. Instead, private entities may defend restraints only on the basis that the restraint is not unreasonable in its effect on competition or because its pro-competitive effects outweigh its anticompetitive effects. See *Continental T.V., Inc.* v. *G.T.E. Sylvania, Inc.* (1977).

Applying *Professional Engineers* to municipalities would mean that an ordinance could not be defended on the basis that its benefits to the community, in terms of traditional health, safety, and public welfare concerns, outweigh its anticompetitive effects. A local government would be disabled from displacing competition with regulation. Thus, a municipality would violate the Sherman Act by enacting restrictive zoning ordinances, by requiring business and occupational licenses, and by granting exclusive franchises to utility services, even if the city determined that it would be in the best interests of its inhabitants to displace competition with regulation. Competition simply does not and cannot further the interests that lie behind most social welfare legislation. . . . Unless the municipality could point to an affirmatively expressed state policy to displace competition in the given area sought to be regulated, the municipality would be held to violate the Sherman Act and the regulatory scheme would be rendered invalid. Surely, the Court does not seek to require a municipality to justify every ordinance it enacts in terms of its pro-competitive effects. If municipalities are permitted only to enact ordinances that are consistent with the pro-competitive policies of the Sherman Act, a municipality's power to regulate the economy would be all but destroyed. . . .

On the other hand, rejecting the rationale of *Professional Engineers* to accommodate the municipal defendant opens up a different sort of Pandora's Box. If the Rule of Reason were "modified" to permit a municipality to defend its regulation on the basis that its benefits to the community outweigh its anticompetitive effects, the courts will be called upon to review social legislation in the manner reminiscent of the *Lochner* era. Once again, the federal courts will be called upon to engage in the same wide-ranging, essentially standardless inquiry into the reasonableness of local regulation that this Court has properly rejected. Instead of "liberty of contract" and "substantive due process," the pro-competitive principles of the Sherman Act will be the governing standard by which the reasonableness of all local regulation will be determined. Neither the Due Process Clause nor the Sherman Act authorizes federal courts to invalidate local regulation of the economy simply upon opining that the municipality has acted unwisely. . . .

Before this Court leaps into the abyss and holds that municipalities may *violate* the Sherman Act by enacting economic and social legislation, it ought to think about the consequences of such a decision in terms of its effect both upon the very antitrust principles the Court desires to apply to local governments and on the role of the federal courts in examining the validity of local regulation of the economy.

Analyzing this problem as one of federal preemption rather than exemption will avoid these problems. We will not be confronted with the anomaly of holding a municipality liable for enacting anticompetitive ordinances. The federal courts will not be required to engage in a standardless review of the reasonableness of local legislation. Rather, the question simply will be whether the ordinance enacted is preempted by the

Sherman Act. I see no reason why a different rule of preemption should be applied to testing the validity of municipal ordinances than the standard we presently apply in assessing state statutes. I see no reason why a municipal ordinance should not be upheld if it satisfies the *Midcal* criteria: the ordinance survives if it is enacted pursuant to an affirmative policy on the part of the city to restrain competition and if the city actively supervises and implements this policy. As with the case of the State, I agree that a city may not simply authorize private parties to engage in activity that would violate the Sherman Act. See *Parker* v. *Brown*. As in the case of a State, a municipality may not become "a participant in a private agreement or combination by others for restraint of trade."

Apart from misconstruing the *Parker* doctrine as a matter of "exemption" rather than preemption, the majority comes to the startling conclusion that our Federalism is in no way implicated when a municipal ordinance is invalidated by the Sherman Act. I see no principled basis to conclude, as does the Court, that municipal ordinances are more susceptible to invalidation under the Sherman Act than are state statutes. The majority concludes that since municipalities are not States, and hence are not "sovereigns," our notions of federalism are not implicated when federal law is applied to invalidate otherwise constitutionally valid municipal legislation. I find this reasoning remarkable indeed. Our notions of federalism are implicated when it is contended that a municipal ordinance is preempted by a federal statute. This Court has made no such distinction between States and their subdivisions with regard to the preemptive effects of federal law. The standards applied by this Court are the same regardless of whether the challenged enactment is that of a State or one of its political subdivisions. . . . I suspect that the Court has not intended to so dramatically alter established principles of Supremacy Clause analysis. Yet, this is precisely what it appears to have done by holding that a municipality may invoke the *Parker* doctrine only to the same extent as can a private litigant. Since the *Parker* doctrine is a matter of federal preemption under the Supremacy Clause, it should apply in challenges to municipal regulation in similar fashion as it applies in a challenge to a state regulatory enactment. The distinction between cities and States created by the majority has no principled basis to support it if the issue is properly framed in terms of preemption rather than exemption.

As with the States, the *Parker* doctrine should be employed to determine whether local legislation has been preempted by the Sherman Act. Like the State, a municipality should not be haled into federal court in order to justify its decision that competiton should be replaced with regulation. The *Parker* doctrine correctly holds that the federal interest in protecting and fostering competition is not infringed so long as the state or local regulation is so structured to ensure that it is truly the government, and not the regulated private entities, which is replacing competition with regulation.

II

By treating the municipal defendant as no different from the private litigant attempting to invoke the *Parker* doctrine, the Court's decision today will radically alter the relationship between the States and their political subdivisions. Municipalities will no longer be able to regulate the local economy without the imprimatur of a clearly expressed state policy to displace competition. The decision today effectively destroys the "home rule" movement in this country, through which local governments have obtained, not without persistent state opposition, a limited autonomy over matters of local concern. The municipalities that stand most to lose by the decision today are those with the most autonomy. Where the State is totally disabled from enacting legislation dealing with matters of local concern, the municipality will be defenseless from challenges to its regulation of the local economy. In such a case, the State is disabled from articulating a policy to displace competition with regulation. Nothing short of altering the relationship between the municipality and the State will enable the local government to legislate on matters important to its inhabitants. In order to defend itself from Sherman Act attacks, the home rule municipality will have to cede its authority back to the State. It is unfortunate enough that the Court today holds that our Federalism is not implicated when municipal legislation is invalidated by a federal statute. It is nothing less than a novel and egregious error when this Court uses the Sherman Act to regulate the relationship between the States and their political subdivisions.

COURT ON DEATH PENALTY
January 19, 1982

The U.S. Supreme Court January 19 voted 5-4 to reverse the death sentence imposed on Monty Lee Eddings, who was 16 years old when he murdered an Oklahoma highway patrolman in 1977. The case represented another attempt by the court to define humane and uniform standards by which states could impose the death penalty. But the court decided the case, Eddings v. Oklahoma, *on a procedural point and skirted the issue of whether a minor could be sentenced to death. In reversing the sentence, the court ruled that the lower courts had not considered all mitigating factors offered by the defendant as a basis for a lesser sentence. The case was sent back to the Oklahoma courts, leaving open the possibility that the death penalty could be reimposed on Eddings.*

Justice Lewis F. Powell Jr. delivered the opinion of the court in which Justices Thurgood Marshall and John Paul Stevens joined. Justices William J. Brennan and Sandra Day O'Connor each wrote brief concurring opinions. Brennan stated his belief that the death penalty was always cruel and unusual punishment. Chief Justice Warren E. Burger and Justices Byron R. White, Harry A. Blackmun and William H. Rehnquist dissented.

Background

In 1972 the court held in Furman v. Georgia *that existing death penalty laws were unconstitutional because they gave judges and juries too little guidance in deciding when to impose a death sentence. Justice Potter*

Stewart wrote that, under the then-existing laws, a sentence of death was imposed in such a random way that it was "cruel and unusual in the same way that being struck by lightning is cruel and unusual." (Historic Documents of 1972, p. 499)

The court addressed the issue again in 1976. In a series of cases involving newly enacted death penalty laws, the court refused to hold that death was always so cruel and unusual a punishment that it violated the Constitution. The court held, however, that the problems pointed out in Furman *were not remedied satisfactorily by laws making death the mandatory penalty for all persons convicted of first-degree murder.*

In the case of Gregg v. Georgia, *the court upheld the type of capital punishment law adopted by Georgia. (Historic Documents of 1976, p. 489) Under Georgia's new law, a person charged with murder was first tried to determine his innocence or guilt. Upon conviction, a sentencing hearing followed at which evidence was presented concerning any aggravating or mitigating circumstances with regard to the crime or the defendant.*

In 1978 the court held in Lockett v. Ohio *that judges and juries charged with sentencing convicted murderers must consider any factors that might argue for a lesser punishment than death. Chief Justice Burger wrote in the majority opinion that the sentencing authority "in all but the rarest kind of capital case, [may] not be precluded from considering, as a mitigating factor, any aspect of a defendant's character or record and any of the circumstances of the offense that the defendant proffers as a basis for a sentence less than death." (Historic Documents of 1978, p. 505)*

The court continued to refine the constitutional limitations on capital punishment in the 1980 case of Godfrey v. Georgia. *In the 1976* Gregg *decision, the court had upheld Georgia's capital punishment statute, which permitted imposition of a death sentence if the offense was "outrageously or wantonly vile, horrible or inhuman in that it involved torture, depravity of mind, or an aggravated battery to the victim."* Godfrey *had been sentenced to death under the provisions of this statute. The court overturned the sentence, ruling that the Georgia courts had interpreted the statutory provision too broadly in this instance. (Historic Documents of 1980, p. 460)*

The Eddings *Opinion*

Oklahoma's death penalty statute, like Georgia's, provides for a separate sentencing procedure to consider mitigating circumstances following a conviction for first-degree murder. Justice Powell wrote that the court, in deciding Eddings, *had based its ruling on the standard set in* Lockett. *At the original sentencing hearing, the trial judge had considered Eddings' youth a mitigating circumstance, but had not considered his disturbed childhood. ". . . [T]he Court cannot be persuaded entirely by the ... fact that the youth was sixteen years old when this heinous crime was committed.* Nor can the Court in following the law, in my opinion, consider the fact of this young man's violent background." *The Oklahoma Court of Criminal Appeals agreed with the trial judge, stating that while "the petitioner's family history is useful in explaining why he behaved the way he did ... it does not excuse his behavior."*

The majority inferred from these remarks that the trial judge and the appeals court had not considered Eddings' background at all in determining his sentence. Powell wrote that the trial judge "did not evaluate the evidence in mitigation and find it wanting as a matter of fact, rather he found that as a matter of law he was unable even to consider the evidence." The court concluded that such refusal to consider evidence introduced in mitigation violated the defendant's Eighth and 14th Amendment rights.

In a brief concurring opinion, Justice O'Connor, noting that the court had always taken care to ensure that the death penalty "was not imposed out of whim, passion, prejudice, or mistake," held that Eddings' sentence should be reversed to prevent the imposition of capital punishment despite ambiguities surrounding remarks made by the lower courts.

Sending the case back, the court directed Oklahoma courts to "consider all relevant mitigating evidence and weigh it against the evidence of the aggravating circumstances" in determining a proper sentence for Eddings.

The Dissent

Chief Justice Burger argued in dissent that the majority had misinterpreted the remarks of the trial judge and the appellate court. Although neither of the Oklahoma courts had termed the evidence of Eddings' unhappy childhood a "mitigating factor," Burger said there was "no reason to read [the courts'] statements as reflecting anything more than a conclusion that Eddings' background was not a sufficiently mitigating factor to tip the scales given the aggravating circumstances..." Burger also chided the court for deciding Eddings *on "a matter of semantics." The court, in taking the case for review, had agreed to examine only whether the Eighth and 14th Amendments prohibit imposition of the death penalty on a person who was 16 when he committed the offense. Instead, the court had gone beyond that issue "to decide the case on a point raised for the first time in [the] petitioner's brief to this Court." Burger said he and the other dissenters would have upheld the sentence and ruled that capital punishment might constitutionally be imposed on juveniles.*

Following are excerpts from the Supreme Court's January 19 ruling in Eddings v. Oklahoma *that all mitigating evi-*

dence must be considered by the courts in capital cases and from the dissenting opinion by Chief Justice Burger:

No. 80-5727

Monty Lee Eddings, Petitioner *v.* Oklahoma	On writ of Certiorari to the Court of Criminal Appeals of Oklahoma

[January 19, 1982]

JUSTICE POWELL delivered the opinion of the Court.

Petitioner Monty Lee Eddings was convicted of first degree murder and sentenced to death. Because this sentence was imposed without "the type of individualized consideration of mitigating factors . . . required by the Eighth and Fourteenth Amendments in capital cases," *Lockett* v. *Ohio* (1978) (opinion of BURGER, C. J.), we reverse.

I

On April 4, 1977, Eddings, a 16 year old youth, and several younger companions ran away from their Missouri homes. They travelled in a car owned by Eddings' brother, and drove without destination or purpose in a southwesterly direction eventually reaching the Oklahoma turnpike. Eddings had in the car a shotgun and several rifles he had taken from his father. After he momentarily lost control of the car, he was signalled to pull over by Officer Crabtree of the Oklahoma Highway Patrol. Eddings did so, and when the Officer approached the car, Eddings stuck a loaded shotgun out of the window and fired, killing the Officer.

Because Eddings was a juvenile, the State moved to have him certified to stand trial as an adult. Finding that there was prosecutive merit to the complaint and that Eddings was not amenable to rehabilitation within the juvenile system, the trial court granted the motion. The ruling was affirmed on appeal. Eddings was then charged with murder in the first degree, and the District Court of Creek County found him guilty upon his plea of nolo contendere.

The Oklahoma death penalty statute provides, in pertinent part:

"Upon conviction . . . of guilt of a defendant of murder in the first degree, the court shall conduct a separate sentencing proceeding to determine whether the defendant should be sentenced to death or life imprisonment. . . . In the sentencing proceeding, evidence may be presented as to *any mitigating circumstances* or as to any of the aggravating circumstances enumerated in this act." ([E]mphasis added.)

Section 701.12 lists seven separate aggravating circumstances; the statute nowhere defines what is meant by "any mitigating circumstances."

At the sentencing hearing, the State alleged three of the aggravating circumstances enumerated in the statute: that the murder was especially heinous, atrocious, or cruel, that the crime was committed for the purpose of avoiding or preventing a lawful arrest, and that there was a probability that the defendant would commit criminal acts of violence that would constitute a continuing threat to society.

In mitigation, Eddings presented substantial evidence at the hearing of his troubled youth. The testimony of his supervising Juvenile Officer indicated that Eddings had been raised without proper guidance. His parents were divorced when he was 5 years old, and until he was 14 Eddings lived with his mother without rules or supervision. There is the suggestion that Eddings' mother was an alcoholic and possibly a prostitute. By the time Eddings was 14 he no longer could be controlled, and his mother sent him to live with his father. But neither could the father control the boy. Attempts to reason and talk gave way to physical punishment. The Juvenile Officer testified that Eddings was frightened and bitter, that his father overreacted and used excessive physical punishment: "Mr. Eddings found the only thing that he thought was effectful with the boy was actual punishment, or physical violence — hitting with a strap or something like this."

Testimony from other witnesses indicated that Eddings was emotionally disturbed in general and at the time of the crime, and that his mental and emotional development were at a level several years below his age. A state psychologist stated that Eddings had a sociopathic or anti-social personality and that approximately 30% of youths suffering from such a disorder grew out of it as they aged. A sociologist specializing in juvenile offenders testified that Eddings was treatable. A psychiatrist testified that Eddings could be rehabilitated by intensive therapy over a 15 to 20 year period. He testified further that Eddings "did pull the trigger, he did kill someone, but I don't even think he knew that he was doing it." The psychiatrist suggested that, if treated, Eddings would no longer pose a serious threat to society.

At the conclusion of all the evidence, the trial judge weighed the evidence of aggravating and mitigating circumstances. He found that the State had proved each of the three alleged aggravating circumstances beyond a reasonable doubt. Turning to the evidence of mitigating circumstances, the judge found that Eddings' youth was a mitigating factor of great weight: "I have given very serious consideration to the youth of the Defendant when this particular crime was committed. Should I fail to do this, I think I would not be carrying out my duty." But he would not consider in mitigation the circumstances of Eddings' unhappy upbringing and emotional disturbance: ". . . the Court cannot be persuaded entirely by the . . . fact that the youth was sixteen years old when this heinous crime was committed. *Nor can the Court in following the law, in my opinion, consider the fact of this young man's violent background.*" ([E]mphasis added). Finding that the only mitigating circumstance could not outweigh the aggravating circumstances present, the judge sentenced Eddings to death.

The Court of Criminal Appeals affirmed the sentence of death. *Eddings* v. *State* (Okla. Crim. App. 1980). It found that each of the aggravating circumstances alleged by the State had been present. It recited the mitigating evidence presented by Eddings in some detail, but in the end it agreed with the trial court that only the fact of Eddings' youth was properly considered as a mitigating circumstance:

> "[Eddings] also argues his mental state at the time of the murder. He stresses his family history in saying he was suffering from severe psychological and emotional disorders, and that the killing was in actuality an inevitable product of the way he was raised. There is no doubt that the petitioner has a personality disorder. But all the evidence tends to show that he knew the difference between right and wrong at the time he pulled the trigger, and that is the test of criminal responsibility in this State. For the same reason, the petitioner's family history is useful in explaining why he behaved the way he did, but it does not excuse his behavior."

II

In *Lockett* v. *Ohio* (1978), CHIEF JUSTICE BURGER, writing for the plurality, stated the rule that we apply today:

> "[W]e conclude that the Eighth and Fourteenth Amendments require that the sentencer ... not be precluded from considering, *as a mitigating factor,* any aspect of a defendant's character or record and any of the circumstances of the offense that the defendant proffers as a basis for a sentence less than death." ([E]mphasis in original).

Recognizing "that the imposition of death by public authority is ... profoundly different from all other penalties," the plurality held that the sentencer must be free to give "independent mitigating weight to aspects of the defendant's character and record and to circumstances of the offense proferred in mitigation. ..." Because the Ohio death penalty statute only permitted consideration of three mitigating circumstances, the Court found the statute to be invalid.

As THE CHIEF JUSTICE explained, the rule in *Lockett* is the product of a considerable history reflecting the law's effort to develop a system of capital punishment at once consistent and principled but also humane and sensible to the uniqueness of the individual. Since the early days of the common law, the legal system has struggled to accommodate these twin objectives. Thus, the common law began by treating all criminal homicides as capital offenses, with a mandatory sentence of death. Later it allowed exceptions, first through an exclusion for those entitled to claim benefit of clergy and then by limiting capital punishment to murders upon "malice prepensed." In this country we attempted to soften the rigor of the system of mandatory death sentences we inherited from England, first by grading murder into different degrees of which only murder of the first degree was a capital offense and then by committing use of the death penalty to the absolute discretion of the jury. By the time of our decision in *Furman* v. *Georgia* (1972), the country had moved so far from a mandatory system that the imposition of capital punishment frequently had become arbitrary and capricious.

Beginning with *Furman*, the Court has attempted to provide standards for a constitutional death penalty that would serve both goals of measured, consistent application and fairness to the accused. Thus, in *Gregg* v. *Georgia* (1976), the plurality held that the danger of an arbitrary and capricious death penalty could be met "by a carefully drafted statute that ensures that the sentencing authority is given adequate information and guidance." By its requirement that the jury find one of the aggravating circumstances listed in the death penalty statute, and by its direction to the jury to consider "any mitigating circumstances," the Georgia statute properly confined and directed the jury's attention to the circumstances of the particular crime and to "the characteristics of the person who committed the crime...."

Similarly, in *Woodson* v. *North Carolina* (1976), the plurality held that mandatory death sentencing was not a permissible response to the problem of arbitrary jury discretion. As the history of capital punishment had shown, such an approach to the problem of discretion could not succeed while the Eighth Amendment required that the individual be given his due: "the fundamental respect for humanity underlying the Eighth Amendment ... requires consideration of the character and record of the individual offender and the circumstances of the particular offense as a constitutionally indispensable part of the process of inflicting the penalty of death." See *Roberts (Harry)* v. *Louisiana; Roberts (Stanislaus)* v. *Louisiana* (1976).

Thus, the rule in *Lockett* followed from the earlier decisions of the Court and from the Court's insistence that capital punishment be imposed fairly, and with reasonable consistency, or not at all. By requiring that the sentencer be permitted to focus "on the characteristics of the person who committed the crime," *Gregg* v. *Georgia,* the rule in *Lockett* recognizes that "justice ... requires ... that there be taken into account the circumstances of the offense together with the character and propensities of the offender." *Pennsylvania* v. *Ashe* (1937). By holding that the sentencer in capital cases must be permitted to consider any relevant mitigating factor, the rule in *Lockett* recognizes that a consistency produced by ignoring individual differences is a false consistency.

III

We now apply the rule in *Lockett* to the circumstances of this case. The trial judge stated that "in following the law," he could not "consider the fact of this young man's violent background." There is no dispute that by "violent background" the trial judge was referring to the mitigating evidence of Eddings' family history. From this statement it is clear that the trial judge did not evaluate the evidence in mitigation and find it wanting as a matter of fact, rather he found that *as a matter of law* he was unable even to consider the evidence.

The Court of Criminal Appeals took the same approach. It found that the evidence in mitigation was not relevant because it did not tend to provide a legal excuse from criminal responsibility. Thus the court conceded that Eddings had a "personality disorder," but cast this evidence aside on the basis that "he knew the difference between right and wrong ... and that is the test of criminal responsibility." *Eddings* v. *State*. Similarly, the evidence of Eddings' family history was "useful in explaining" his behavior, but it did not "excuse" the behavior. From these statements it appears that the Court of Criminal Appeals also considered only that evidence to be mitigating which would tend to support a legal excuse from criminal liability.

We find that the limitations placed by these courts upon the mitigating evidence they would consider violated the rule in *Lockett*. Just as the state may not by statute preclude the sentencer from considering any mitigating factor, neither may the sentencer, refuse to consider, *as a matter of law,* any relevant mitigating evidence. In this instance, it was as if the trial judge had instructed a jury to disregard the mitigating evidence Eddings proferred on his behalf. The sentencer, and the Court of Criminal Appeals on review, may determine the weight to be given relevant mitigating evidence. But they may not give it no weight by excluding such evidence from their consideration.

Nor do we doubt that the evidence Eddings offered was relevant mitigating evidence. Eddings was a youth of 16 years at the time of the murder. Evidence of a difficult family history and of emotional disturbance is typically introduced by defendants in mitigation. See *McGautha* v. *California* (1971). In some cases, such evidence properly may be given little weight. But when the defendant was 16 years old at the time of the offense there can be no doubt that evidence of a turbulent family history, of beatings by a harsh father, and of severe emotional disturbance is particularly relevant.

The trial judge recognized that youth must be considered a relevant mitigating factor. But youth is more than a chronological fact. It is a time and condition of life when a person may be most susceptible to influence and to psychological damage. Our history is replete with laws and judicial recognition that minors, especially in their earlier years, generally are less mature and responsible than adults. Particularly "during the formative years of childhood and adolescence, minors often lack the experience, perspective, and judgment" expected of adults. *Bellotti* v. *Baird* (1979).

Even the normal 16 year old customarily lacks the maturity of an adult. In this case, Eddings was not a normal 16 year old; he had been deprived of the care, concern and paternal attention that children deserve. On the contrary, it is not disputed that he was a juvenile with serious emotional problems, and had been raised in a neglectful, sometimes even violent, family background. In addition, there was testimony that Eddings' mental and emotional development were at a level several years below his chronological age. All of this does not suggest an absence of responsibility for the crime of murder, deliberately committed in this case. Rather, it is to say that just as the chronological age of a minor is itself a relevant mitigating factor of great weight, so must the background and mental and emotional development of a youthful defendant be duly considered in sentencing.

We are not unaware of the extent to which minors engage increasingly in violent crime. Nor do we suggest an absence of legal responsibility where crime is committed by a minor. We are concerned here only with the manner of the imposition of the ultimate penalty: the death sentence imposed for the crime of murder upon an emotionally disturbed youth with a disturbed child's immaturity.

On remand, the state courts must consider all relevant mitigating evidence and weigh it against the evidence of the aggravating circumstances. We do not weigh the evidence for them. Accordingly, the judgment is reversed to the extent that it sustains the imposition of the death penalty, and the case is remanded for further proceedings not inconsistent with this opinion.

So ordered.

JUSTICE O'CONNOR, concurring.

I write separately to address more fully the reasons why this case must be remanded in the light of *Lockett* v. *Ohio* (1978), which requires the trial court to consider and weigh all of the mitigating evidence concerning the petitioner's family background and personal history.

Because sentences of death are "qualitatively different" from prison sentences, *Woodson* v. *North Carolina* (1976) (opinion of Stewart, J.), this Court has gone to extraordinary measures to ensure that the prisoner sentenced to be executed is afforded process that will guarantee, as much as is humanly possible, that the sentence was not imposed out of whim, passion, prejudice, or mistake. Surely, no less can be required when the defendant is a minor. . . . In order to ensure that the death penalty was not erroneously imposed, the *Lockett* plurality concluded that "the Eighth and Fourteenth Amendments require that the sentencer, in all but the rarest kind of capital case, not be precluded from considering, *as a mitigating factor,* any aspect of a defendant's character or record and any of the circumstances of the offense that the defendant proffers as a basis for a sentence less than death." ([E]mphasis in the original.) . . .

THE CHIEF JUSTICE may be correct in concluding that the Court's opinion reflects a decision by some Justices that they would not have imposed the death penalty in this case had they sat as the trial judge. I, however, do not read the Court's opinion either as altering this Court's opinions establishing the constitutionality of the death penalty or as deciding the issue of whether the Constitution permits the imposition of the death penalty on an individual who committed a murder at age 16.

Rather, by listing in detail some of the circumstances surrounding the petitioner's life, the Court has sought to emphasize the variety of mitigating information that may not have been considered by the trial court in deciding whether to impose the death penalty or some lesser sentence.

CHIEF JUSTICE BURGER, with whom JUSTICE WHITE, JUSTICE BLACKMUN, and JUSTICE REHNQUIST join, dissenting.

It is important at the outset to remember — as the Court does not — the narrow question on which we granted certiorari. We took care to limit our consideration to whether the Eighth and Fourteenth Amendments prohibit the imposition of a death sentence on an offender because he was 16 years old in 1977 at the time he committed the offense; review of all other questions raised in the petition for certiorari was denied. Yet the Court today goes beyond the issue on which review was sought — and granted — to decide the case on a point raised for the first time in petitioner's brief to this Court. This claim was neither presented to the Oklahoma courts nor presented to this Court in the petition for certiorari. Relying on this "eleventh-hour" claim, the Court strains to construct a plausible legal theory to support its mandate for the relief granted.

I

In *Lockett* v. *Ohio* (1978), we considered whether Ohio violated the Eighth and Fourteenth Amendments by sentencing Lockett to death under a statute that "narrowly limit[ed] the sentencer's discretion to consider the circumstances of the crime and the record and character of the offense as mitigating factors." The statute at issue ... required the trial court to impose the death penalty upon Lockett's conviction for "aggravated murder with specifications," unless it found "that (1) the victim had induced or facilitated the offense, (2) it was unlikely that Lockett would have committed the offense but for the fact that she 'was under duress, coercion, or strong provocation,' or (3) the offense was 'primarily the product of [Lockett's] psychosis or mental deficiency.' " It was plain that although guilty of felony homicide under Ohio law, Lockett had played a relatively minor role in a robbery which resulted in a homicide actually perpetrated by the hand of another. Lockett had previously committed no major offenses; in addition, a psychological report described her "prognosis for rehabilitation" as "favorable." However, since she was not found to have acted under duress, did not suffer from "psychosis," and was not "mentally deficient," the sentencing judge concluded that he had " 'no alternative, whether [he] like[d] the law or not' but to impose the death penalty."

We held in *Lockett* that the "Eighth and Fourteenth Amendments require that the sentencer ... not be precluded from considering, *as a mitigating factor,* any aspect of a defendant's character or record and any of the circumstances of the offense that the defendant proffers as a basis for a sentence less than death." ([E]mphasis in original). We therefore found the Ohio statute flawed, because it did not permit individualized consideration of mitigating circumstances — such as the defendant's comparatively minor role in the offense, lack of intent to kill the victim, or age. We did not, however, undertake to dictate the *weight* that a sentencing court must ascribe to the various factors that might be categorized as "mitigating," nor did we in any way suggest that this Court may substitute its sentencing judgment for that of state courts in capital cases.

In contrast to the Ohio statute at issue in *Lockett,* the Oklahoma death penalty statute provides:

"In the sentencing proceeding, evidence may be presented as to *any* mitigating circumstances or as to any of the aggravating circumstances enumerated in this act." ([E]mphasis added).

The statute further provides that

"[u]nless at least one of the statutory aggravating circumstances enumerated in this act is [found to exist beyond a reasonable doubt] or if it is found that any such aggravating circumstance is outweighed by the finding of one or more mitigating circumstances, the death penalty shall not be imposed."

This provision, of course, instructs the sentencer to weigh the mitigating evidence introduced by a defendant against the aggravating circumstances proven by the state.

The Oklahoma statute thus contains provisions virtually identical to those cited with approval in *Lockett,* as examples of proper legislation which highlighted the Ohio statute's "constitutional infirmities." Indeed, the Court does not contend that the Oklahoma sentencing provisions are inconsistent with *Lockett.* Moreover, the Court recognizes that, as mandated by the Oklahoma statute, Eddings was permitted to present "substantial evidence at the [sentencing] hearing of his troubled youth."

In its attempt to make out a violation of *Lockett,* the Court relies entirely on a single sentence of the trial court's opinion delivered from the bench at the close of the sentencing hearing. After discussing the aggravated nature of petitioner's offense, and noting that he had "given very serious consideration to the youth of the Defendant when this particular crime was committed," the trial judge said that he could not

"be persuaded entirely by the ... fact that the youth was sixteen years old when this heinous crime was committed. Nor can the Court in following the law, in my opinion, consider the fact of this young man's violent background."

From this statement, the Court concludes "it is clear that the trial judge did not evaluate the evidence in mitigation and find it wanting as a matter of fact, rather he found that *as a matter of law* he was unable even to consider the evidence." This is simply not a correct characterization of the sentencing judge's action.

In its parsing of the trial court's oral statement, the Court ignores the fact that the judge was delivering his opinion extemporaneously from the bench, and could not be expected to frame each utterance with the specificity and precision that might be expected of a written opinion or statute. Extemporaneous courtroom statements are not often models of clarity. Nor does the Court give any weight to the fact that the trial court had spent considerable time listening to the testimony of a probation officer and various mental health professionals who described Eddings' personality and family history — an obviously meaningless exercise if, as the Court asserts, the judge believed he was barred "as a matter of law" from "considering" their testimony. Yet even examined in isolation, the trial court's statement is at best ambiguous; it can just as easily be read to say that, while the court had taken account of Eddings' unfortunate childhood, it did not consider that either his youth or his family background was sufficient to offset the aggravating circumstances that the evidence revealed. Certainly nothing in *Lockett* would preclude the court from making such a determination.

The Oklahoma Court of Criminal Appeals independently examined the evidence of "aggravating" and "mitigating" factors presented at Eddings' sentencing hearing. After reviewing the testimony concerning Eddings' personality and family background, and after referring to the trial court's discussion of mitigating circumstances, it stated that while Eddings' "family history is useful in explaining why he behaved the way he did, ... *it does not excuse his behavior.*" ([E]mphasis added). From this the Court concludes that "the Court of Criminal Appeals also considered only that evidence to be mitigating which would tend to support a legal excuse from criminal liability." However, there is no reason to read that court's statements as reflecting anything more than a conclusion that Eddings' background was not a sufficiently mitigating factor to tip the scales, given the aggravating circumstances, including Eddings' statements immediately before the killing. The Court of Criminal Appeals most assuredly did *not*, as the Court's opinion suggests, hold that this "evidence in mitigation was not relevant;" indeed, had the Court of Criminal Appeals thought the evidence irrelevant, it is unlikely that it would have spent several paragraphs summarizing it. The Court's opinion offers no reasonable explanation for its assumption that the Court of Criminal Appeals considered itself bound by some unstated legal principle not to "consider" Eddings' background.

To be sure, neither the Court of Criminal Appeals nor the trial court labelled Eddings' family background and personality disturbance as "mitigating factors." It is plain to me, however, that this was purely a matter of semantics associated with the rational belief that "evidence in mitigation" must rise to a certain level of persuasiveness before it can be said to consitute a "mitigating circumstance." In contrast, the court seems to require that any potentially mitigating evidence be described as a "mitigating factor" — regardless of its weight; the insubstantiality of the evidence is simply to be a factor in the process of weighing the evidence against aggravating circumstances. Yet if this is all the Court's opinion stands for, it provides scant support for the result reached. For it is clearly the choice of the Oklahoma courts — a choice not inconsistent with

Lockett or any other decision of this Court — to accord relatively little weight to Eddings' family background and emotional problems as balanced against the circumstances of his crime and his potential for future dangerousness.

II

It can never be less than the most painful of our duties to pass on capital cases, and the more so in a case such as this one. However, there comes a time in every case when a court must "bite the bullet."

Whether the Court's remand will serve any useful purpose remains to be seen, for petitioner has already been given an opportunity to introduce whatever evidence he considered relevant to the sentencing determination. Two Oklahoma courts have weighed that evidence and found it insufficient to offset the aggravating circumstances shown by the state. The Court's opinion makes clear that some Justices who join it would not have imposed the death penalty had they sat as the sentencing authority. Indeed, I am not sure I would have done so. But the Constitution does not authorize us to determine whether sentences imposed by state courts are sentences we consider "appropriate"; our only authority is to decide whether they are constitutional under the Eighth Amendment. The Court stops far short of suggesting that there is any constitutional proscription against imposition of the death penalty on a person who was under age 18 when the murder was committed. In the last analysis, the Court is forced to conclude that it is "the state courts [which] must consider [petitioner's mitigating evidence] and weigh it against the evidence of the aggravating circumstances. We do not weigh the evidence for them."

Because the sentencing proceedings in this case were in no sense inconsistent with *Lockett* v. *Ohio* (1978), I would decide the sole issue on which we granted certiorari, and affirm the judgment.

COURT ON LAWYER ADS
January 25, 1982

The Supreme Court in a unanimous decision January 25 struck down Missouri's rules governing advertising by attorneys, saying that the law was so restrictive that it violated the appellant's right of free speech. The decision said that states could regulate such advertising only to prevent deceptive or misleading ads.

The opinion by Justice Lewis F. Powell extended the 1977 ruling of the high court in Bates *v.* State Bar of Arizona. *Until 1977 most states forbade lawyers to advertise at all, holding such practice unethical. In* Bates *the court ruled 5-4 that such flat bans violated the First Amendment's guarantee of free speech, but the ruling made clear the states' right to regulate the advertising.*

After Bates, *Missouri and most other states revised their rules concerning advertising by attorneys. Missouri's law restricted the kinds of information in the ads to certain categories and set forth the exact phrases to be used to describe the areas of legal practice by the lawyer.*

The case, In re R. M. J., *concerned a young lawyer who opened his practice in 1977 in St. Louis. He placed ads in the local newspapers and in the Yellow Pages of the telephone directory and had announcement cards printed with language that differed from that prescribed by the rules of the Missouri bar. He was charged with unprofessional conduct and reprimanded by the Missouri Supreme Court. He appealed to the U.S. Supreme Court on the grounds that the state's restriction unduly curtailed his freedom of speech. The justices agreed, pointing out that in*

some areas the lawyer's phrases were clearer and conveyed more informa-
tion than those prescribed by the rules.

Following are excerpts from the January 25, 1982, decision
by the Supreme Court finding that Missouri's rules govern-
ing advertising by attorneys to be unconstitutionally
restrictive:

No. 80-1431

In the Matter of	
R ——— M. J ———, Appellant	} On appeal from the Supreme Court of Missouri

[January 25, 1982]

JUSTICE POWELL delivered the opinion of the Court.

The Court's decision in *Bates* v. *State Bar of Arizona* (1977) required a re-examination of long held perceptions as to "advertising" by lawyers. This appeal presents the question whether certain aspects of the revised ethical rules of the Supreme Court of Missouri regulating lawyer advertising conform to the requirements of *Bates*.

I

As with many of the states, until the decision in *Bates,* Missouri placed an absolute prohibition on advertising by lawyers. After the Court's invalidation of just such a prohibition in *Bates,* the Committee on Professional Ethics and Responsibility of the Supreme Court of Missouri revised that court's Rule 4 regulating lawyer advertising. The Committee sought to "strike a midpoint between prohibition and unlimited advertising," and the revised regulation of advertising, adopted with slight modification by the State Supreme Court, represents a compromise. Lawyer advertising is permitted, but it is restricted to certain categories of information, and in some instances, to certain specified language.

Thus, part B of DR 2-101 of the Rule states that a lawyer may "publish ... in newspapers, periodicals and the yellow pages of telephone directories" ten categories of information: name, address and telephone number; areas of practice; date and place of birth; schools attended; foreign language ability; office hours; fee for an initial consultation; availability of a schedule of fees; credit arrangements; and the fixed fee to be charged for certain specified "routine" legal services. Although the Rule does not state explicitly that these ten categories of information or the three indicated forms of printed advertisement are the only information and the only means of advertising that will be permitted, that is the interpretation given the Rule by the State Supreme Court and the Advisory Committee charged with its enforcement.

In addition to these guidelines, and under authority of the Rule, the Advisory Committee has issued an addendum to the Rule providing that if the lawyer chooses to list areas of practice in his advertisement, he must do so in one of two prescribed ways. He may list one of three general descriptive terms specified in the Rule — "General Civil Practice," "General Criminal Practice," or "General Civil and Criminal Practice." Alternatively, he may use one or more of a list of twenty-three areas of practice, including, for example, "Tort Law," "Family Law," and "Probate and Trust Law." He may not list both a general term and specific subheadings, nor may he deviate from the precise wording stated in the rule. He may not indicate that his practice is "limited" to the listed areas and he must include a particular disclaimer of certification of expertise following any listing of specific areas of practice.

Finally, one further aspect of the Rule is relevant in this case. DR 2-102 of Rule 4 regulates the use of professional announcement cards. It permits a lawyer or firm to mail a dignified "brief professional announcement card stating new or changed associates or addresses, change of firm name, or similar matters." The rule, however, does not permit a general mailing; the announcement cards may be sent only to "lawyers, clients, former clients, personal friends, and relatives."

II

Appellant graduated from law school in 1973 and was admitted to the Missouri and Illinois bars in the same year. After a short stint with the Securities and Exchange Commission in Washington, D.C., appellant moved to St. Louis, Missouri in April, 1977, and began practice as a solo practitioner. As a means of announcing the opening of his office, he mailed professional announcement cards to a selected list of addresses. In order to reach a wider audience, he placed several advertisements in local newspapers and in the yellow pages of the local telephone directory.

The advertisements at issue in this litigation appeared in January, February, and August of 1978, and included information that was not expressly permitted by Rule 4. They included the information that appellant was licensed in Missouri and Illinois. They contained, in large capital letters, a statement that appellant was "Admitted to Practice Before the United States Supreme Court." And they included a listing of areas of practice that deviated from the language prescribed the Advisory Committee — e.g., "personal injury" and "real estate" instead of "tort law" and "property law" — and that included several areas of law without analogue in the list of areas prepared by the Advisory Committee — e.g., "contract," "zoning & land use," "communication," "pension & profit sharing plans." In addition, and with the exception of the advertisement appearing in August, 1978, appellant failed to include the required disclaimer of certification of expertise after the listing of areas of practice.

On November 19, 1979, the Advisory Committee filed an information in the Supreme Court of Missouri charging appellant with unprofessional conduct. The information charged appellant with publishing three advertisements that listed areas of law not approved by the Advisory Committee, that listed the courts in which appellant was admitted to practice, and, in the case of two of the advertisements, that failed to include the required disclaimer of certification. The information also charged appellant with sending announcement cards to "persons other than lawyers, clients, former clients, personal friends, and relatives" in violation of DR 2-102 (A) (2). In response, appellant argued that, with the exception of the disclaimer requirement, each of these restrictions upon advertising was unconstitutional under the First and Fourteenth Amendments.

In a disbarment proceeding, the Supreme Court of Missouri upheld the constitutionality of DR 2-101 of Rule 4 and issued a private reprimand. *In the Matter of R. M. J.* (Mo. 1981). But the court did not explain the reasons for its decision, nor did it state whether it found appellant to have violated each of the charges lodged against him or only some of them. Indeed, the court only purported to uphold the constitutionality of DR 2-101; it did not mention the propriety of DR 2-102, which governs the use of announcement cards.

Writing in separate dissenting opinions, Chief Justice Bardgett and Judge Seiler argued that the information should be dismissed. The dissenters suggested that the State did not have a significant interest either in requiring the use of certain, specified words to describe areas of practice or in prohibiting a lawyer from informing the public as to the States and courts in which he was licensed to practice. Nor would the dissenters have found the mailing of this sort of information to be unethical.

III

In *Bates* v. *State Bar of Arizona* (1977), the Court considered whether the extension of First Amendment protection to commercial speech announced in *Virginia Pharmacy Board* v. *Virginia Citizens Consumer Council* (1976) applied to the regulation of advertising by lawyers. The *Bates* Court held that indeed lawyer advertising was a form of commercial speech, protected by the First Amendment, and that "advertising by attorneys may not be subjected to blanket suppression."

More specifically, the *Bates* Court held that lawyers must be permitted to advertise the fees they charge for certain "routine" legal services. The Court concluded that this sort of price advertising was not "inherently" misleading, and therefore could not be prohibited on that basis. The Court also rejected a number of other justifications for broad restrictions upon advertising including the potential adverse effect of advertising on professionalism, on the administration of justice, and on the cost and quality of legal services, as well as the difficulties of enforcing standards short of an outright prohibition. None of these interests was found to be sufficiently strong or sufficiently affected by lawyer advertising to justify a prohibition.

But the decision in *Bates* nevertheless was a narrow one. The Court emphasized that advertising by lawyers still could be regulated. False, deceptive, or misleading advertising remains subject to restraint, and the Court recognized that advertising by the professions poses special risks of deception — "[B]ecause the public lacks sophistication concerning legal services, misstatements that might be overlooked or deemed unimportant in other advertising may be found quite inappropriate in legal advertising." The Court suggested that claims as to quality or in-person solicitation might be so likely to mislead as to warrant restriction. And the Court noted that a warning or disclaimer might be appropriately required, even in the context of advertising as to price, in order to dissipate the possibility of consumer confusion or deception. "[T]he bar retains the power to correct omissions that have the effect of presenting an inaccurate picture, [although] the preferred remedy is more disclosure, rather than less."

In short, although the Court in *Bates* was not persuaded that price advertising for "routine" services was necessarily or inherently misleading, and although the Court was not receptive to other justifications for restricting such advertising, it did not by any means foreclose restrictions on potentially or demonstrably misleading advertising. Indeed, the Court recognized the special possibilities for deception presented by advertising for professional services. The public's comparative lack of knowledge, the limited ability of the professions to police themselves, and the absence of any standardization in the "product" renders advertising for professional services especially susceptible to abuses that the States have a legitimate interest in controlling.

Thus, the Court has made clear in *Bates* and subsequent cases that regulation — and imposition of discipline — are permissible where the particular advertising is inherently likely to deceive or where the record indicates that a particular form or method of advertising has in fact been deceptive. . . .

Commercial speech doctrine, in the context of advertising for professional services, may be summarized generally as follows: Truthful advertising related to lawful activities is entitled to the protections of the First Amendment. But when the particular content or method of the advertising suggests that it is inherently misleading or when experience has proven that in fact such advertising is subject to abuse, the states may impose appropriate restrictions. Misleading advertising may be prohibited entirely. But the states may not place an absolute prohibition on certain types of potentially misleading information, *e.g.*, a listing of areas of practice, if the information also may be presented in a way that is not deceptive. Thus, the Court in *Bates* suggested that the remedy in the first instance is not necessarily a prohibition but preferably a requirement of disclaimers or explanation. Although the potential for deception and confusion is particularly strong in the context of advertising professional services, restrictions upon such advertising may be no broader than reasonably necessary to prevent the deception. . . .

IV

We now turn to apply these generalizations to the circumstances of this case.

The information lodged against appellant charged him with four separate kinds of violation of Rule 4: listing the areas of his practice in language or in terms other than that provided by the rule, failing to include a disclaimer, listing the courts and States in which he had been admitted to practice, and mailing announcement cards to persons other than "lawyers, clients, former clients, personal friends, and relatives." Appellant makes no challenge to the constitutionality of the disclaimer requirement, and we pass on to the remaining three infractions.

Appellant was reprimanded for deviating from the precise listing of areas of practice included in the Advisory Committee addendum to Rule 4. The Advisory Committee does not argue that appellant's listing was misleading. The use of the words "real estate" instead of "property" could scarcely mislead the public. Similarly, the listing of areas such as "contracts" or "securities," that are not found on the Advisory Committee's list in any form, presents no apparent danger of deception. Indeed, as Chief Justice Bardgett explained in dissent, in certain respects appellant's listing is more informative than that provided in the addendum. Because the listing published by the appellant has not been shown to be misleading, and because the Advisory Committee suggests no substantial interest promoted by the restriction, we conclude that this portion of Rule 4 is an invalid restriction upon speech as applied to appellant's advertisements.

Nor has the Advisory Committee identified any substantial interest in a rule that prohibits a lawyer from identifying the jurisdictions in which he is licensed to practice. Such information is not misleading on its face. Appellant was licensed to practice in both Illinois and Missouri. This is factual and highly relevant information particularly in light of the geography of the region in which appellant practiced.

Somewhat more troubling is appellant's listing, in large boldface type, that he was a member of the bar of the Supreme Court of the United States. The emphasis of this relatively uninformative fact is at least bad taste. Indeed, such a statement could be misleading to the general public unfamiliar with the requirements of admission to the bar of this Court. Yet there is no finding to this effect by the Missouri Supreme Court. There is nothing in the record to indicate that the inclusion of this information was misleading. Nor does the Rule specifically identify this information as potentially misleading or, for example, place a limitation on type size or require a statement explaining the nature of the Supreme Court bar.

Finally, appellant was charged with mailing cards announcing the opening of his office to persons other than "lawyers, clients, former clients, personal friends and relatives." Mailings and handbills may be more difficult to supervise than newspapers. But again we deal with a silent record. There is no indication that an inability to supervise is the reason the State restricts the potential audience of announcement cards. Nor is it clear that an absolute prohibition is the only solution. . . .

In sum, none of the three restrictions in the Rule upon appellant's First Amendment rights can be sustained in the circumstances of this case. There is no finding that appellant's speech was misleading. Nor can we say that it was inherently misleading, or that restrictions short of an absolute prohibition would not have sufficed to cure any possible deception. We emphasize, as we have throughout the opinion, that the States retain the authority to regulate advertising that is inherently misleading or that has proven to be misleading in practice. There may be other substantial state interests as well that will support carefully drawn restrictions. But although the states may regulate commercial speech, the First and Fourteenth Amendments require that they do so with care and in a manner no more extensive than reasonably necessary to further substantial interests. The absolute prohibition on appellant's speech, in the absence of a finding that his speech was misleading, does not meet these requirements.

Accordingly, the judgment of the Supreme Court of Missouri is

Reversed.

STATE OF THE UNION ADDRESS
January 26, 1982

In his first State of the Union address, President Ronald Reagan January 26 unveiled a sweeping proposal to transfer many existing federal functions to the states. His plan became known as the "new federalism" in the news media.

The plan involved a phased swap of about $47 billion in programs and revenues between the federal government and the states beginning in 1984. In his nationally televised address before a joint session of Congress, Reagan said that, according to an intergovernmental commission, the growth in federal programs had made the government "more pervasive, more intrusive, more ineffective and costly, and above all, more [un]accountable." The president added, "Let's solve this problem with a single, bold stroke...."

While proposing the far-reaching restructuring of the government, Reagan offered no major initiative to deal with mounting fiscal and economic problems, nor did he propose any major foreign policy move. He did, however, promise to "act with firmness" toward "those who would export terrorism ... especially Cuba and Libya."

'New Federalism'

Although substantial support for Reagan's "new federalism" was evident, many observers believed that it would result in such a broad governmental restructuring and in such a diminution of congressional power that chances that Congress would approve the plan seemed slim.

The proposal called for a shift of about 40 social, transportation and community development programs to the states. In the early phase, there would be a shift of revenues from the federal government to help pay for the programs.

The proposal also included a "swap" of the three principal welfare programs for the poor. Under the plan, the federal government would assume the full costs of the Medicaid health programs while the states would take over the food stamps and Aid to Families with Dependent Children (AFDC) programs. The New York Times *pointed out that under the president's proposal the federal government and states would trade responsibility for the poor and the sick.*

Costs of Program

Administration officials said that because health care outlays were among the fastest rising costs in the entire economy, they expected the states, under the proposal, to do better financially in the long run than the federal government.

They estimated that Medicaid costs would rise from the current level of about $19 billion to $25.4 billion by 1987 and that in the same period welfare and food stamp costs would rise from $16.5 billion to about $17.6 billion.

Reaction

Congressional reaction to the "new federalism" proposal was mixed. Senate Majority Leader Howard H. Baker Jr., R-Tenn., hailed the plan as "a brave, courageous statement that will impact not only on the budget but the basic structure of government." Sen. Mark O. Hatfield, R-Ore., chairman of the Appropriations Committee, told reporters that the plan was "brilliant, fantastically creative."

But Sen. Alan Cranston, D-Calif., criticized the program as "a prescription for abdicating our national commitment to meeting the most basic human needs of our poor, disabled and elderly citizens and the children of tomorrow." Sen. Daniel Patrick Moynihan, D-N.Y., said, "To turn these programs back to the states is to turn us back to the 1920s."

Several governors met at the White House with Reagan on February 1 to discuss the complex proposal. Gov. George Busbee of Georgia, a Democrat, said that while the governors had a number of concerns they were hopeful that they could be met. Shifting an array of education, transportation and social programs to the states together with the money to run them had long been advocated by many of the governors.

Following is the text of President Reagan's nationally televised State of the Union address to Congress January 26,

1982. (Boldface headings in brackets have been added by Congressional Quarterly to highlight the organization of the text.):

Mr. Speaker, Mr. President, distinguished Members of the Congress, honored guests, and fellow citizens:

Today marks my first State of the Union address to you, a constitutional duty as old as our Republic itself.

President Washington began this tradition in 1790 after reminding the Nation that the destiny of self-government and the "preservation of the sacred fire of liberty" is "finally staked on the experiment entrusted to the hands of the American people." For our friends in the press, who place a high premium on accuracy, let me say: I did not actually hear George Washington say that. But it is a matter of historic record.

But from this podium, Winston Churchill asked the free world to stand together against the onslaught of aggression. Franklin Delano Roosevelt spoke of a day of infamy and summoned a nation to arms. Douglas MacArthur made an unforgettable farewell to a country he loved and served so well. Dwight Eisenhower reminded us that peace was purchased only at the price of strength. And John F. Kennedy spoke of the burden and glory that is freedom.

When I visited this chamber last year as a newcomer to Washington, critical of past policies which I believed had failed, I proposed a new spirit of partnership between this Congress and this administration and between Washington and our State and local governments. In forging this new partnership for America, we could achieve the oldest hopes of our Republic — prosperity for our nation, peace for the world, and the blessings of individual liberty for our children and, somebody [*sic*], for all of humanity.

It's my duty to report to you tonight on the progress that we have made in our relations with other nations, on the foundation we've carefully laid for our economic recovery and, finally, on a bold and spirited initiative that I believe can change the face of American government and make it again the servant of the people.

[The Economy]

Seldom have the stakes been higher for America. What we do and say here will make all the difference to autoworkers in Detroit, lumberjacks in the Northwest, steelworkers in Steubenville who are in the unemployment lines; to black teenagers in Newark and Chicago; to hard-pressed farmers and small businessmen; and to millions of everyday Americans who harbor the simple wish of a safe and financially secure future for their children. To understand the state of the Union, we must look not only at where we are and where we're going but where we've been. The situation at this time last year was truly ominous.

The last decade has seen a series of recessions. There was a recession in 1970, in 1974, and again in the spring of 1980. Each time, unemployment increased and inflation soon turned up again. We coined the word "stagflation" to describe this.

Government's response to these recessions was to pump up the money supply and increase spending. In the last 6 months of 1980, as an example, the money supply increased at the fastest rate in postwar history — 13 percent. Inflation remained in double digits, and government spending increased at an annual rate of 17 percent. Interest rates reached a staggering 21-1/2 percent. There were 8 million unemployed.

Late in 1981 we sank into the present recession, largely because continued high interest rates hurt the auto industry and construction. And there was a drop in productivity, and the already high unemployment increased.

This time, however, things are different. We have an economic program in place, completely different from the artificial quick-fixes of the past. It calls for a reduction of the rate of increase in government spending, and already that rate has been cut nearly in half. But reduced spending alone isn't enough. We've just implemented the first and smallest phase of a 3-year tax-rate reduction designed to stimulate the economy and create jobs. Already interest rates are down to 15-3/4 percent, but they must still go lower. Inflation is down from 12.4 percent to 8.9, and for the month of December it was running at an annualized rate of 5.2 percent. If we had not acted as we did, things would be far worse for all Americans than they are today. Inflation, taxes, and interest rates would all be higher.

['An Era of American Renewal']

A year ago, Americans' faith in their governmental process was steadily declining. Six out of 10 Americans were saying they were pessimistic about their future. A new kind of defeatism was heard. Some said our domestic problems were uncontrollable, that we had to learn to live with this seemingly endless cycle of high inflation and high unemployment.

There were also pessimistic predictions about the relationship between our administration and this Congress. It was said we could never work together. Well, those predictions were wrong. The record is clear, and I believe that history will remember this as an era of American renewal, remember this administration as an administration of change, and remember this Congress as a Congress of destiny.

Together, we not only cut the increase in government spending nearly in half, we brought about the largest tax reductions and the most sweeping changes in our tax structure since the beginning of this century. And because we indexed future taxes to the rate of inflation, we took away government's built-in profit on inflation and its hidden incentive to grow larger at the expense of American workers.

Together, after 50 years of taking power away from the hands of the people in their States and local communities, we have started returning power and resources to them.

Together, we have cut the growth of new Federal regulations nearly in half. In 1981 there were 23,000 fewer pages in the *Federal Register* which lists new regulations, than there were in 1980. By deregulating oil we've come closer to achieving energy independence and helped bring down the costs of gasoline and heating fuel.

Together, we have created an effective Federal strike force to combat waste and fraud in Government. In just 6 months it has saved the taxpayers more than $2 billion, and it's only getting started.

Together we've begun to mobilize the private sector, not to duplicate wasteful and discredited government programs, but to bring thousands of Americans into a volunteer effort to help solve many of America's social problems.

Together we have begun to restore that margin of military safety that ensures peace. Our country's uniform is being worn once again with pride.

Together we have made a New Beginning, but we have only begun.

[Continued Recovery]

No one pretends that the way ahead will be easy. In my Inaugural Address last year, I warned that the "ills we suffer have come upon us over several decades. They will not go away in days, weeks or months, but they will go away . . . because we as Americans have the capacity now, as we've had it in the past, to do whatever needs to be done to preserve this last and greatest bastion of freedom."

The economy will face difficult moments in the months ahead. But the program for economic recovery that is in place will pull the economy out of its slump and put us on the road to prosperity and stable growth by the latter half of this year. And that is why I can report to you tonight that in the near future the state of the Union and the economy will be better — much better — if we summon the strength to continue on the course that we've charted.

And so, the question: If the fundamentals are in place, what now? Well, two things. First, we must understand what's happening at the moment to the economy. Our current problems are not the product of the recovery program that's only just now getting underway, as some would have you believe; they are the inheritance of decades of tax and tax and spend and spend.

Second, because our economic problems are deeply rooted and will not respond to quick political fixes, we must stick to our carefully integrated plan for recovery. That plan is based on four commonsense fundamentals: continued reduction of the growth in Federal spending; preserving the individual and business tax reductions that will stimulate saving and investment; removing unnecessary Federal regulations to spark productivity; and maintaining a healthy dollar and a stable monetary policy, the latter a responsibility of the Federal Reserve System.

The only alternative being offered to this economic program is a return to the policies that gave us a trillion-dollar debt, runaway inflation, runaway interest rates and unemployment. The doubters would have us turn back the clock with tax increases that would offset the personal tax-rate reductions already passed by this Congress. Raise present taxes to cut future deficits, they tell us. Well, I don't believe we should buy that argument.

There are too many imponderables for anyone to predict deficits or surpluses several years ahead with any degree of accuracy. The budget in place, when I took office, had been projected as balanced. It turned out to have one of the biggest deficits in history. Another example of the imponderables that can make deficit projections highly questionable — a change of only one percentage point in unemployment can alter a deficit up or down by some $25 billion.

As it now stands, our forecast, which we're required by law to make, will show major deficits starting at less than a hundred billion dollars and declining, but still too high. More important, we're making progress with the three keys to reducing deficits: economic growth, lower interest rates, and spending control. The policies we have in place will reduce the deficit steadily, surely and, in time, completely.

[Taxes]

Higher taxes would not mean lower deficits. If they did, how would we explain that tax revenues more than doubled just since 1976; yet in that same 6-year period we ran the largest series of deficits in our history. In 1980 tax revenues increased by $54 billion and in 1980 we had one of our alltime biggest deficits. Raising taxes won't balance the budget; it will encourage more government spending and less private investment. Raising taxes will slow economic growth, reduce production, and destroy future jobs, making it more difficult for those without jobs to find them and more likely that those who now have jobs could lose them. So, I will not ask you to try to balance the budget on the backs of the American taxpayers.

I will seek no tax increases this year, and I have no intention of retreating from our basic program of tax relief. I promise to bring the American people — to bring their tax rates down and to keep them down, to provide them incentives to rebuild our economy, to save, to invest in America's future. I will stand by my word. Tonight I'm urging the American people: Seize these new opportunities to produce, to save, to invest, and together we'll make this economy a mighty engine of freedom, hope, and prosperity again.

[Federal Budget]

Now, the budget deficit this year will exceed our earlier expectations. The recession did that. It lowered revenues and increased costs. To some extent, we're also victims of our own success. We've brought inflation down faster than we thought we could, and in doing this, we've deprived government of those hidden revenues that occur when inflation pushes people into higher income tax brackets. And the continued high interest rates last year cost the government about $5 billion more than anticipated.

We must cut out more nonessential Government spending and root out more waste, and we will continue our efforts to reduce the number of employees in the Federal work force by 75,000.

The budget plan I submit to you on February 8th will realize major savings by dismantling the Departments of Energy and Education and by eliminating ineffective subsidies for business. We'll continue to redirect our resources to our two highest budget priorities — a strong national defense to keep America free and at peace and a reliable safety net of social programs for those who have contributed and those who are in need.

[Entitlement Programs]

Contrary to some of the wild charges you may have heard, this administration has not and will not turn its back on America's elderly or America's poor. Under the new budget, funding for social insurance programs will be more than double the amount spent only 6 years ago. But it would be foolish to pretend that these or any programs cannot be made more efficient and economical.

The entitlement programs that make up our safety net for the truly needy have worthy goals and many deserving recipients. We will protect them. But there's only one way to see to it that these programs really help those whom they were designed to help. And that is to bring their spiraling costs under control.

Today we face the absurd situation of a Federal budget with three-quarters of its expenditures routinely referred to as "uncontrollable." And a large part of this goes to entitlement programs.

Committee after committee of this Congress has heard witness after witness describe many of these programs as poorly administered and rife with waste and fraud. Virtually every American who shops in a local supermarket is aware of the daily abuses that take place in the food stamp program, which has grown by 16,000 percent in the last 15 years. Another example is Medicare and Medicaid — programs with worthy goals but whose costs have increased from 11.2 billion to almost 60 billion, more than 5 times as much, in just 10 years.

Waste and fraud are serious problems. Back in 1980, Federal investigators testified before one of your committees that "corruption has permeated virtually every area of the Medicare and Medicaid health care industry." One official said many of the people who are cheating the system were "very confident that nothing was going to happen to them." Well, something is going to happen. Not only the taxpayers are defrauded; the people with real dependency on these programs are deprived of what they need, because available resources are going not to the needy but to the greedy.

The time has come to control the uncontrollable. In August we made a start. I signed a bill to reduce the growth of these programs by $44 billion over the next 3 years while at the same time preserving essential services for the truly needy. Shortly you will receive from me a message on further reforms we intend to install — some new, but others long recommended by your own congressional committees. I ask you to help make these savings for the American taxpayer.

The savings we propose in entitlement programs will total some $63 billion over 4 years and will, without affecting social security, go a long way toward bringing Federal spending under control.

But don't be fooled by those who proclaim that spending cuts will deprive the elderly, the needy and the helpless. The Federal Government will still subsidize 95 million meals every day. That's one out of seven of all the meals served in America. Head Start, senior nutrition programs, and child welfare programs will not be cut from the levels we proposed last year. More than one-half billion dollars has been proposed for minority business assistance. And research at the National Institute of Health will be increased by over $100 million. While meeting all these needs, we intend to plug unwarranted tax loopholes and strengthen the law which requires all large corporations to pay a minimum tax.

I am confident the economic program we've put into operation will protect the needy while it triggers a recovery that will benefit all Americans. It will stimulate the economy, result in increased savings and provide capital for expansion, mortgages for homebuilding, and jobs for the unemployed.

[The New Federalism]

Now that the essentials of that program are in place, our next major undertaking must be a program — just as bold, just as innovative — to make government again accountable to the people, to make our system of federalism work again.

Our citizens feel they've lost control of even the most basic decisions made about the essential services of government, such as schools, welfare, roads, and even garbage collection. And they're right. A maze of interlocking jurisdictions and levels of government confronts average citizens in trying to solve even the simplest of problems. They don't know where to turn for answers, who to hold accountable, who to praise, who to blame, who to vote for or against. The main reason for this is the overpowering growth of Federal grants-in-aid programs during the past few decades.

In 1960 the Federal Government had 132 categorical grant programs, costing $7 billion. When I took office, there were approximately 500, costing nearly a hundred billion dollars — 13 programs for energy, 36 for pollution control, 66 for social services, 90 for education. And here in the Congress, it takes at least 166 committees just to try to keep track of them.

You know and I know that neither the President nor the Congress can properly oversee this jungle of grants-in-aid; indeed, the growth of these grants has led to a distortion in the vital functions of government. As one

Democratic Governor put it recently: The national government should be worrying about "arms controls, not potholes."

The growth in these Federal programs has — in the words of one intergovernmental commission — made the Federal Government "more pervasive, more intrusive, more unmanageable, more ineffective, more costly, and above all, more [un]accountable." Let's solve this problem with a single bold stroke: the return of some $47 billion in Federal programs to State and local government, together with the means to finance them and a transition period of nearly 10 years to avoid unnecessary disruption.

I will shortly send this Congress a message describing this program. I want to emphasize, however, that its full details will have been worked out only after close consultation with congressional, State, and local officials.

Starting in fiscal 1984, the Federal Government will assume full responsibility for the cost of the rapidly growing Medicaid program to go along with its existing responsibility for Medicare. As part of a financially equal swap, the States will simultaneously take full responsibility for Aid to Families with Dependent Children and food stamps. This will make welfare less costly and more responsive to genuine need, because it'll be designed and administered closer to the grassroots and the people it serves.

In 1984 the Federal Government will apply the full proceeds from certain excise taxes to a grassroots trust fund that will belong in fair shares to the 50 States. The total amount flowing into this fund will be $28 billion a year. Over the next 4 years the States can use this money in either of two ways. If they want to continue receiving Federal grants in such areas as transportation, education, and social services, they can use their trust fund money to pay for the grants. Or to the extent they choose to forgo the Federal grant programs, they can use their trust fund money on their own for those or other purposes. There will be a mandatory pass-through of part of these funds to local governments.

By 1988 the States will be in complete control of over 40 Federal grant programs. The trust fund will start to phase out, eventually to disappear, and the excise taxes will be turned over to the States. They can then preserve, lower, or raise taxes on their own and fund and manage these programs as they see fit.

In a single stroke we will be accomplishing a realignment that will end cumbersome administration and spiraling costs at the Federal level while we ensure these programs will be more responsive to both the people they are meant to help and the people who pay for them.

[Urban Enterprise Zones]

Hand in hand with this program to strengthen the discretion and flexibility of State and local governments, we're proposing legislation for an experimental effort to improve and develop our depressed urban areas in the 1980's and 90's. This legislation will permit States and localities to apply to the Federal Government for designation as urban enterprise zones. A broad range of special economic incentives in the zones will help attract new business, new jobs, new opportunity to America's inner cities and rural towns. Some will say our mission is to save free enterprise. Well, I say we must save free enterprise so that together we can save America.

Some will also say our States and local communities are not up to the challenge of a new and creative partnership. Well, that might have been true 20 years ago before reforms like reapportionment and the Voting Rights Act, the 10-year extension of which I strongly support. It's no longer true today. This administration has faith in State and local governments and the constitutional balance envisioned by the Founding Fathers. We also believe in the integrity, decency, and sound, good sense of grassroots Americans.

[Private Sector Initiatives Task Force]

Our faith in the American people is reflected in another major endeavor. Our Private Sector Initiatives Task Force is seeking out successful community models of school, church, business, union, foundation, and civic programs that help community needs. Such groups are almost invariably far more efficient than government in running social programs.

We're not asking them to replace discarded and often discredited government programs dollar for dollar, service for service. We just want to help them perform the good works they choose and help others to profit by their example. Three hundred and eighty-five thousand corporations and private organizations are already working on social programs ranging from drug rehabilitation to job training, and thousands more Americans have written us asking how they can help. The volunteer spirit is still alive and well in America.

[Other Concerns]

Our nation's long journey toward civil rights for all our citizens — once a source of discord, now a source of pride — must continue with no backsliding or slowing down. We must and shall see that those basic laws that guarantee equal rights are preserved and, when necessary, strengthened.

Our concern for equal rights for women is firm and unshakable. We launched a new Task Force on Legal Equity for Women and a Fifty-States Project that will examine State laws for discriminatory language. And for the first time in our history a woman sits on the highest court in the land.

So, too, the problem of crime — one as real and deadly serious as any in America today. It demands that we seek transformation of our legal system, which overly protects the rights of criminals while it leaves society and the innocent victims of crime without justice.

We look forward to the enactment of a responsible Clean Air Act to increase jobs while continuing to improve the quality of our air. We're encouraged by the bipartisan initiative of the House and are hopeful of further progress as the Senate continues its deliberations.

[Foreign Policy]

So far, I've concentrated largely, now, on domestic matters. To view the state of the Union in perspective, we must not ignore the rest of the world. There isn't time tonight for a lengthy treatment of social — or foreign policy, I should say, a subject I intend to address in detail in the near future. A few words, however, are in order on the progress we've made over the past year, reestablishing respect for our nation around the globe and some of the challenges and goals we will approach in the year ahead.

At Ottawa and Cancún, I met with leaders of the major industrial powers and developing nations. Now, some of those I met were a little surprised that I didn't apologize for America's wealth. Instead, I spoke of the strength of the free marketplace system and how that system could help them realize their aspirations for economic development and political freedom. I believe lasting friendships were made, and the foundation was laid for future cooperation.

In the vital region of the Caribbean Basin, we're developing a program of aid, trade, and investment incentives to promote self-sustaining growth and a better, more secure life for our neighbors to the south. Toward those who would export terrorism and subversion in the Caribbean and elsewhere, especially Cuba and Libya, we will act with firmness.

Our foreign policy is a policy of strength, fairness, and balance. By restoring America's military credibility, by pursuing peace at the negotiating table wherever both sides are willing to sit down in good faith, and by regaining the respect of America's allies and adversaries alike, we have strengthened our country's position as a force for peace and progress in the world.

[Poland]

When action is called for, we're taking it. Our sanctions against the military dictatorship that has attempted to crush human rights in Poland — and against the Soviet regime behind that military dictatorship — clearly demonstrated to the world that America will not conduct "business as usual" with the forces of oppression. If the events in Poland continue to deteriorate, further measures will follow.

Now, let me also note that private American groups have taken the lead in making January 30th a day of solidarity with the people of Poland. So, too, the European Parliament has called for March 21st to be an international day of support for Afghanistan. Well, I urge all peace-loving peoples to join together on those days, to raise their voices, to speak and pray for freedom.

[National Security]

Meanwhile, we're working for reduction of arms and military activities, as I announced in my address to the nation last November 18th. We have proposed to the Soviet Union a far-reaching agenda for mutual reduction of military forces and have already initiated negotiations with them in Geneva on intermediate range nuclear forces. In those talks it is essential that we negotiate from a position of strength. There must be a real incentive for the Soviets to take these talks seriously. This requires that we rebuild our defenses.

In the last decade, while we sought the moderation of Soviet power through a process of restraint and accommodation, the Soviets engaged in an unrelenting buildup of their military forces. The protection of our national security has required that we undertake a substantial program to enhance our military forces.

We have not neglected to strengthen our traditional alliances in Europe and Asia, or to develop key relationships with our partners in the Middle East and other countries. Building a more peaceful world requires a sound strategy and the national resolve to back it up. When radical forces threaten our friends, when economic misfortune creates conditions of instability, when strategically vital parts of the world fall under the shadow of Soviet power, our response can make the difference between peaceful change or disorder and violence. That's why we've laid such stress not only on our own defense but on our vital foreign assistance program. Your recent passage of the Foreign Assistance Act sent a signal to the world that America will not shrink from making the investments necessary for both peace and security. Our foreign policy must be rooted in realism, not naivete or self-delusion.

A recognition of what the Soviet empire is about is the starting point. Winston Churchill, in negotiating with the Soviets, observed that they respect only strength and resolve in their dealings with other nations. That's why we've moved to reconstruct our national defenses. We intend to keep the peace. We will also keep our freedom.

We have made pledges of a new frankness in our public statements and worldwide broadcasts. In the face of a climate of falsehood and misinformation, we've promised the world a season of truth — the truth of our great civilized ideas: individual liberty, representative government, the rule of law under God. We've never needed walls or minefields or barbed wire to keep our people in. Nor do we declare martial law to keep our people from voting for the kind of government they want.

[Everyday Heroes in America]

Yes, we have our problems; yes, we're in a time of recession. And it's true, there's no quick fix, as I said, to instantly end the tragic pain of unemployment. But we will end it. The process has already begun, and we'll see its effect as the year goes on.

We speak with pride and admiration of that little band of Americans who overcame insuperable odds to set this Nation on course 200 years ago. But our glory didn't end with them. Americans ever since have emulated their deeds.

We don't have to turn to our history books for heroes. They're all around us. One who sits among you here tonight epitomized that heroism at the end of the longest imprisonment ever inflicted on men of our Armed Forces. Who will ever forget that night when we waited for television to bring us the scene of that first plane landing at Clark Field in the Philippines, bringing our POW's home? The plane door opened and Jeremiah Denton came slowly down the ramp. He caught sight of our flag, saluted it, and said, "God bless America," and then thanked us for bringing him home.

Just 2 weeks ago, in the midst of a terrible tragedy on the Potomac, we saw again the spirit of American heroism at its finest — the heroism of dedicated rescue workers saving crash victims from icy waters. We saw the heroism of one of our young government employees, Lenny Skutnik, who, when he saw a woman lose her grip on the helicopter line, dived into the water and dragged her to safety.

And then there are countless, quiet, everyday heroes of American life — parents who sacrifice long and hard so their children will know a better life than they've known; church and civic volunteers who help to feed, clothe, nurse and teach the needy; millions who've made our nation and our nation's destiny so very special — unsung heroes who may not have realized their own dreams themselves but then who reinvest those dreams in their children.

Don't let anyone tell you that America's best days are behind her, that the American spirit has been vanquished. We've seen it triumph too often in our lives to stop believing in it now.

One hundred and twenty years ago, the greatest of all our Presidents delivered his second State of the Union message in this Chamber. "We cannot escape history," Abraham Lincoln warned. "We of this Congress and this administration will be remembered in spite of ourselves." The "trial through which we pass will light us down, in honor or dishonor, to the latest generation."

Well, that President and that Congress did not fail the American people. Together they weathered the storm and preserved the Union. Let it be said of us that we, too, did not fail; that we, too, worked together to bring America through difficult times. Let us so conduct ourselves that two centuries from now, another Congress and another President, meeting in this Chamber as we are meeting, will speak of us with pride, saying that we met the test and preserved for them in their day the sacred flame of liberty — this last, best hope of man on Earth.

God bless you, and thank you.

RICKOVER'S PARTING SHOT
January 28, 1982

In his "farewell address" to Congress before the Joint Economic Committee, Admiral Hyman G. Rickover blasted big business, particularly defense contractors, for neglecting traditional business values in favor of the "so-called bottom line of profit and loss." Responding to questions from committee members, Rickover criticized the Defense Department bureaucracy and questioned the need for dramatic increases in U.S. defense spending.

Rickover Background

Born January 27, 1900, in Makow, Russia, Rickover was known as the "father" of the nuclear navy. He graduated from the U.S. Naval Academy in Annapolis, Md., in 1922 and served in a number of naval posts, including submarine duty. Following World War II, Rickover was assigned to the Atomic Energy Commission's Manhattan Project, where he first conceived the idea of using a reactor to propel a ship. Despite Navy objections, Rickover convinced Congress to appropriate funds for a nuclear-powered submarine. Construction of the Nautilus *began in June 1952 and was completed in January 1954.*

Rickover's abrasive personality and criticism of Defense Department policy made him unpopular with his naval and civilian superiors, and he was passed over twice for promotion from captain to rear admiral. A congressional investigation resulted in his promotion in 1953, and the same year he became director of the Naval Nuclear Propulsion Division, a post he held until his retirement. He became a full admiral in 1973. Always a strong advocate of the nuclear navy, Rickover constantly clashed with administration and Navy officials over the practicality and cost of additional ships.

During his tenure as director of the Nuclear Propulsion Division, Rickover repeatedly deplored the poor workmanship on Navy ships and launched extensive investigations of defense contractors who delivered inferior products or tried to charge the Navy for huge cost overruns. In his January 28 testimony Rickover blamed large corporations for the existing state of defense procurement, charging that they had created a business environment "where responsibility is increasingly disassociated from the exercise of power; where skill in financial manipulation is valued more than actual knowledge and experience in the business; where attention and effort is directed mostly to short-term considerations, regardless of long-range consequences."

Rickover was scheduled to retire from the Navy in 1964 at the mandatory retirement age of 64, but was retained by presidential order. In January 1982 the secretary of the Navy decided not to permit Rickover to remain on active duty. Rickover retired January 31.

Testimony

In remarks to Sen. William Proxmire, D-Wis., Rep. Henry S. Reuss, D-Wis., and Rep. Fred Richmond, D-N.Y. of the Joint Economic Committee, Rickover reiterated his charges of attempted fraud by defense contractors, spoke out against dramatic increases in defense spending, criticized the Defense Department civilian bureaucracy, defended the feasiblility of safe nuclear power and called for an end to nuclear proliferation.

Rickover charged that because of mismanagement and preoccupation with large profits, defense contractors often were either unable or unwilling to honor their contract obligations. To cover their own inefficiency and ensure the desired profit levels, the companies delivered inferior products or billed the Navy for cost overruns. "It used to be that a businessman's honor depended on his living up to his contract — a deal was a deal. Now, honoring contracts is becoming more a matter of convenience."

Although a career Navy man, Rickover questioned the need for dramatic increases in defense spending and the Reagan administration's buildup of U.S. military strength. "At a certain point," said Rickover, "there is sufficiency.... We can sink everything on the oceans several times over with the number we have, and so can they." Rickover believed that the United States should be more selective in defense spending, concentrating financial resources in specific areas where any future danger might arise.

Rickover also had harsh words for the Defense Department, an institution whose creation he had opposed in the 1940s because he believed it was a "behemoth" that would become "mired in its own internal problems." Responding to questions on how to improve Defense Department efficiency, Rickover replied: "To increase the efficiency of the Defense Department, you must first abolish it." The secretaries of defense and of the individual services, Rickover pointed out, were civilians with little or no military expertise. The duties and obligations inherent in their political appointments rendered this civilian military bureaucracy unfamiliar with the departments they tried to manage.

Safety of Nuclear Reactors

Rickover cited the record of the Naval Nuclear Propulsion Program, which had logged 2,300 reactor years without an accident, as an example of the safe use of nuclear power. He said he believed civilian reactors could be operated safely with tighter supervision and more responsible operating procedures.

Although he acknowledged the feasibility of nuclear power as an energy source, Rickover pointed out the dangers of radioactive waste. In essence, said Rickover, man was creating something (radioactivity) that nature had been working for millions of years to eliminate. "In this broad philosophical sense, I do not believe that nuclear power is worth the present benefits since it creates radiation. You may ask why do I design nuclear-powered ships? That is because it is a necessary evil. I would sink them all."

Rickover said he was proud of his role in developing naval nuclear power because it was necessary for national security. Attempts to outlaw war had always failed, Rickover noted, and one had to assume that should a serious war break out, nations would use all weapons at their disposal, including nuclear weapons, to win. Rickover said he feared that humanity would ultimately destroy itself in a nuclear war and urged an international meeting to outlaw all nuclear weapons.

Following are excerpts from the testimony of Adm. Hyman G. Rickover before the Joint Economic Committee January 28, 1982. (Boldface headings in brackets have been added by Congressional Quarterly to highlight the organization of the text.):

... Over the years the Joint Economic Committee has done an outstanding job educating the Congress, the executive branch, and the public regarding the important economic issues confronting the Nation. ...

One of these issues is how to promote greater efficiency and economy in the Defense Department. As you know, I have testified often before congressional committees, including yours, on various aspects of this problem. In some cases, Congress implemented my recommendations for reforms. Eventually, however, defense contractor lobbyists have generally learned how to get around them or have them rescinded. . . .

Cost Accounting Standards

In the late 1960s, Senator William Proxmire, Congressman Henry Gonzalez, and former Congressman Wright Patman were instrumental in enacting legislation requiring the establishment of cost accounting standards for defense contracts and a Cost Accounting Standards Board to set these standards. In 1980, Congress eliminated the Cost Accounting Standards Board by cutting off its funding. And today, defense contractor lobbyists are promoting legislation that would give the Office of Management and Budget authority to waive or amend the standards. I predict that within a few years the standards established by the Cost Accounting Standards Board will have been watered down to the point that they will be worthless. . . .

. . . Today the defense contractors have carte blanche. They can do anything they wish. All the safeguards so painfully and meticulously passed through Congress were all thrown away. Perhaps it is not possible to make significant improvements in defense procurement. It is an arcane subject in which defense contractors, who have a strong financial interest in such matters, tend to be most influential. . . .

Influence of Large Corporations

I also recommend that the Joint Economic Committee assign high priority to addressing the problems growing out of the increasing power and influence of large corporations in our society. If our free enterprise, capitalistic system is to survive, it is incumbent upon corporate executives to exercise greater self-restraint and to accept moral responsibility for their actions, many of which appear to be having a negative influence on our economy and our society.

A preoccupation with the so-called bottom line of profit and loss statements, coupled with a lust for expansion, is creating an environment in which fewer businessmen honor traditional values; where responsibility is increasingly disassociated from the exercise of power; where skill in financial manipulation is valued more than actual knowledge and experience in the business; where attention and effort is directed mostly to short-term considerations, regardless of long-range consequences.

Political and economic power is increasingly being concentrated among a few large corporations and their officers — power they can apply against society, government, and individuals. Through their control of vast resources, these large corporations have become, in effect, another branch of government. They often exercise the power of government, but without the checks and balances inherent in our democratic system.

With their ability to dispense money, officials of large corporations may often exercise greater power to influence society than elected or appointed Government officials — but without assuming any of the responsibilities and without being subject to public scrutiny. . . .

Many large corporations, because of their economic power and influence, have ready access to high level Government officials who, although not always familiar with the subtleties of the issues presented to them all too often act without consulting their subordinates. This undermines the subordinates and does not always protect the interests of the taxpayer. Some large defense contractors know this and exploit it.

In the business world itself, many corporate executives, aided by shrewd, high-priced lawyers, seek to evade moral and legal responsibility for the companies they own and control by insulating themselves from the details, and they can always say they did not know what was going on — in many cases they probably don't.

Executives at corporate headquarters often can control their subsidiaries and draw out profits without assuming responsibility for contract obligations. This is the so-called corporate veil through which profits and cash can flow upwards to corporate headquarters, but which cuts off financial or legal responsibility.

[Need for Corporate Responsibility]

Where responsibility is increasingly divorced from authority, traditional business values tend to be lost. Contracts often become meaningless. It used to be that a businessman's honor depended on his living up to his contract — a deal was a deal. Now, honoring contracts is becoming more a matter of convenience. Corporations are increasingly turning to high-priced law firms which, by legal maneuvering, obfuscation, and delay, can effectively void almost any contract — probably even the Ten Commandments. Probably, even Moses was not shrewd enough to deal with present-day claims lawyers. Under these circumstances, Government contracts with some large companies are binding only to the extent the company wishes to be bound.

Ever since the famous *Santa Clara County* v. *Southern Pacific Railroad* case in 1886, the Supreme Court has accorded corporations — which are considered as "persons" in law — the rights of individuals under the 14th amendment.

I submit that if a corporation is to be accorded protection as a natural person under the 14th amendment, then all the obligations incumbent on "natural persons" ought also to be binding on corporations. And, since a corporation acts through its officials, they should be held personally liable for illegal corporate acts.

Mr. Chairman, if you start along that line and you get one of those characters, take him on and throw him into jail, this would have an exemplary effect. A number of years ago some General Electric officials were thrown into jail for a week. That had a tremendous effect not only on the General Electric Co. but on other large corporations. But that lesson must be learned again every few years. . . .

Certainly the profit motive is and should be the driving force in the capitalist system — the free enterprise system is based on it. However, in today's large corporations, managerial performance too often is measured solely in financial terms. In their world of financial statements, statistical reports, stock certificates, tender offers, press releases, and so on, managers of large corporations often lose sight of the men, materials, machines, and customers of the companies they control. Preoccupied with reports and numbers rather than people and things, there is a tendency to oversimplify operating problems and their solutions. Further, by focusing too strongly on so-called bottom line results, corporate officials can generate pressures that cause subordinates to act in ways they would not consider proper in their personal affairs.

Under pressure to meet assigned corporate profit objectives, subordinates sometimes overstep the bounds of propriety — even the law. The corporate officials who generate these pressures, however, are hidden behind the remote corporate screen, and are rarely, if ever, held accountable for the results.

Shipbuilding Claims

In recent years, several major Navy shipbuilders, when faced with large projected cost overruns, resorted to making large claims against the Navy. These large claims were greatly inflated and based on how much extra money the contractor wanted rather than how much he actually was owed by the Government. By ignoring their own responsibility for poor contract performance, they generated claims which attributed all the problems to Government actions and demanded hundreds of millions of dollars in extra payments — enough to recover all their costs overruns and yield the desired profit — the profit originally desired.

I could tell you many stories about that. For example, the very large shipbuilder who claimed he was not making enough profit on Navy contracts. So I had my people search through financial reports and they found that he was making less on commercial contracts than he wanted on Government contracts. Apparently he felt we were too stupid to look at the records.

Sen. Proxmire: What was the name of that shipbuilder?

Adm. Rickover: Newport News Shipbuilding and Dry Dock Co. Look, don't just pick on those poor people. This is endemic throughout the system. I would appreciate it if you not make an issue of that. I answered you because you asked me and I knew the answer.

Sometimes the claims were many times the desired objective so that the company could appear to be accommodating the Navy by settling for a fraction of the claimed amount.

It was also quite possible for those companies to get well-known lawyers — I believe all members here are members of the legal profession — you're a lawyer, aren't you, Senator?

Proxmire: I am not a lawyer.

Rickover: You're not? How the hell did you ever get into Congress?

Proxmire: That's one of the reasons, Admiral....

Rep. Reuss: We hate lawyers in Wisconsin. That's why Senator Proxmire is so successful.

Rickover: Are you a lawyer?

Rep. Richmond: No, sir.

Rickover: You mean you have a committee of three and you have no lawyer?

Proxmire: It's very rare. There's nothing better than to tell an audience of farmers, for example, that one of the qualifications I have is I'm not a lawyer.

Rickover: Are you a farmer?

Proxmire: I am not a farmer. That's why I tell lawyers I'm not a farmer.

Rickover: I know farming is an essential profession. I do not think lawyers are.

You know, there's a story that when Peter the Great first visited England he went to observe their customs. He attended a law court. When he came back to Russia he asked: "Who were those people who were arguing?" They said, "Those were lawyers." He asked: "How many are there in Russia?" They said: "Four." And he said: "Go and hang the four of them." Now that is a true story by the way.

I am not really blaming lawyers. I don't think lawyers are worse than many other people.

[Fraud Referred to Justice]

In evaluating these claims, I found numerous instances of apparent fraud. I documented these instances in great detail and, in accordance with Navy directives, sent these reports of fraud to my superiors, recommending that they be referred to the Justice Department for investigation. Other Navy officials made similar reports....

In the 1970s, the Navy referred the claims of four large shipbuilders to the Justice Department for investigation. The Justice Department, however, seems incapable of dealing with sophisticated procurement fraud — or perhaps undesirous of doing so. After nearly a decade of work, the status of the Justice Department's record in these cases is as follows:

Litton was indicted 4 years ago for fraud, but the Justice Department has taken no action to try the case.

The Justice Department conducted a lengthy investigation of Lockheed claims but did not issue an indictment. By now, the statute of limitations has expired.

After investigating General Dynamics, our biggest defense contractor, for 4 years, the Department of Justice recently announced they could find no evidence of criminal intent, although the claims were almost five times what the Navy actually owed.

The Newport News investigation was recently dealt a serious blow when the Justice Department split up the investigating team and assigned the leading investigators other work. This happened shortly after they had reported their findings in the Newport News case and had asked the department for more help to track down other promising leads.

Responsibilities of Congress

Being responsible Government officials, what reaction do Members of Congress have? You are responsible for the laws. What reaction do you expect from Government officials when they see this? How do you expect any Government official to stick his neck out and try to do his job when he's faced with this bunch of superiors who make speeches asking their employees to be honest and save money. When some clerk figures out a way to save 10 cents a week on stamps they make a big deal out of it, have a ceremony, and present him with a medal. But when large contractors submit multimillion-dollar inflated claims, nothing is done. That is the way it goes. It's all a lot of nonsense.

So what I am saying is that until the people at the top of Government mean what they say when they utter their vacuous speeches about Federal employees doing a good job and saving money; it will never be done.

The only place I see where it is possible to get anything done is Congress — I know you're not the executive branch, but you do make the laws. You can do something. There are things that you can do that I believe you have not done. I would like to get an answer from you on that, Senator Proxmire.

Proxmire: Well, you see, the last part of your observation is correct. We cannot act directly. We can only act through the laws, call attention to it, try to make our laws more effective. In your opening statement you pointed out that the provisions that we have been able to incorporate into law to provide a discipline and control of defense contractors have gone. We have lost them. They have been overridden. So we just have to try again.

Rickover: Do you think it's possible in this day to really get a law passed that would protect the public?

Proxmire: Sure, it's possible, but it's very difficult — I think testimony like yours today will help — for a whole series of reasons. You know better than I do, Admiral. As you said so well in your prepared statement, these defense contractors and others lobby very hard. They contribute to campaigns for candidates for the House and Senate and the Presidency of the United States. They contribute very heavily. Members of Congress feel obligated to them. They are impressive people. When they come down here it's very hard to stand up [to] them.

Rickover: Make it legally impossible for them to directly or indirectly contribute to campaign funds — that no defense contractor or subcontractor shall be allowed to contribute to campaigns.

Proxmire: I don't think you could possibly sustain that if you passed a law. The Supreme Court would say that would infringe on —

Rickover: Or limit it to the State and local representatives.

Proxmire: I don't think you can even do that. You have to treat them like everybody else. As you know, if a very wealthy person wants to run for office, the Supreme Court has said he could spend as much as he wants to be elected to the House or Senate.

Rickover: And that cannot be limited?

Proxmire: Not so far, unless we can change the mind of the Supreme Court.

Rickover: You mean the Supreme Court has declared candidates for public office can do that?

Proxmire: That's right.

Rickover: Maybe we need a new Supreme Court. They are supposed to protect the people, too, you know. They are not above the law.

Proxmire: Well, we could pass a constitutional amendment, but that would be — you know how difficult that is and how long it takes. . . .

Complaints About Overregulation

Rickover: . . . Businessmen regularly complain that overregulation by Government inhibits their freedom and accomplishments, yet it is the very acts of some of them that have made government regulation necessary. Adolf Berle perceptively observed that when business threatens to engulf the state, it forces the state to engulf business. That should be a dire warning to business. I believe that ultimately there will be enough aroused citizens that there will again be a serious move against business.

The notion that we have a self-regulating, free market economy that will itself encourage a high standard of ethical business conduct is not realistic in today's complex society. Those who advocate exclusive reliance on the market do disservice to capitalism, since the result is often increased government intervention — the very antithesis of their expressed goal. On the other hand, the destruction of capitalism and the establishment of complete state control are inimical to economic and political freedom, and I deeply detest that just as much as I know all of you detest it and yet we are approaching that state.

The survival of our capitalist system therefore depends on finding a proper middle ground between these two extremes.

I believe that businessmen must treat Government regulation realistically, rather than with instinctive opposition. Much of Government regulation is essential to protect the public against the recurrence of past abuses, and because it is unrealistic to expect any group to truly police itself. . . .

Often the largest businesses — those least subject to the restraints of free enterprise — are the most outspoken advocates of the capitalist, free enterprise system as an effective safeguard against these excesses. They want the public to believe that they behave in accordance with the free enterprise system, when in fact they escape many restraints of that system. And they all have public relations people who know little about the business but do know how to do public relations. Consistently they lobby against new Government regulations. They herald the virtues of competition and the marketplace as if they were small businessmen subject to these forces. Yet at the same time they lobby for Government — that is, taxpayer, assistance, in the form of tax loopholes, protected markets, subsidies, guaranteed loans, contract bailouts, and so on.

Businessmen should vigorously advocate respect for law because law is the foundation of our entire society including business. Few areas of society are as dependent on law as is business. The law protects such essential rights of business as integrity of contracts. When businessmen break the law, ignore or destroy its spirit, or use its absence to justify unethical conduct, they undermine business itself as well as their own welfare.

They should be concerned with the poor record of law enforcement as it relates to them. They should be concerned about the double standard where an ordinary citizen is punished more severely for a petty crime than corporate officials convicted of white collar crimes involving millions of dollars. . . .

Capitalism

Although I have been critical of some current trends in business, I am not hostile to business. Despite its present moral obtuseness, I believe in free enterprise and the capitalist system. No other system offers as much opportunity for individual freedom and accomplishment.

Capitalism, based as it is on freedom of choice, helps preserve all other freedoms. Despite its man-designed imperfections, it is still the best system yet devised by man to foster a high level of economic well-being together with individual freedom. Should our capitalist system be destroyed, its destruction will be accompanied by the loss of most of our other liberties as well. . . .

Defense Spending

Proxmire: A big issue in this country today is how much we're spending for defense. It is an issue that relates to our economic health. It is an issue that relates, of course, also to our military security.

In your opinion . . . are we spending more than we need to spend on national defense? Is it possible to spend such amounts well or is the pace of the buildup too fast?

Rickover: I think we are spending too much. I think we should be more selective in our spending. There are certain areas from where it is obvious danger is going to come if it does come. I believe we should concentrate on those areas. When anyone has a large business establishment, it is self-limiting because, if it expands too far, too fast, you stop making a profit. In Government there is no such limitation and there is little strict scrutiny, sir. . . .

Nuclear Submarines

For example, take the number of nuclear submarines. I will hit right close to home. I see no reason why we must have just as many as the Russians. At a certain point there is sufficiency. What is the difference whether we have 100 nuclear submarines or 200? . . . We can sink everything on the oceans several times over with the number we have, and so can they. That is the point I am making.

There has to be some judgment used. Submarines are very expensive items. They take a lot of time and money to build — taxpayers' money. . . .

Proxmire: Let me get specific on the nuclear submarines. We now have 91 submarines.

Rickover: We have more than that. We now have 121.

Proxmire: I was talking about attack submarines.

Rickover: I will give you the total. We have 33 ballistic missile submarines including one Trident; 88 nuclear attack submarines which includes 7 converted ballistic missile submarines. We have 21 additional attack submarines and 8 additional Tridents authorized. If you add the operational and authorized attack submarines, that is enough. . . . We need to continue to build submarines to maintain an adequate level and to replace those that wear out or become obsolete. However, the way we design them and build submarines now, they should last for 30 years. . . . In my opinion, a future naval war may well be decided under the polar ice. That probably will be the only place were submarines can operate unfettered in the future. . . .

Aircraft Carriers

Proxmire: Now the Defense Department's fiscal year 1983 budget requests funding for two nuclear-powered aircraft carriers at a construction cost of about $6 billion. It doesn't include the cost of the planes which is considerably more than $6 billion. In fact, it's more than twice that. Considering the capability of the Soviet submarines, how long do you think one of these aircraft carriers would last in the case of an all-out war?

Rickover: About 2 days.

Proxmire: About 2 days?

Rickover: Is that a direct answer?

Proxmire: Yes, sir. How about the whole fleet of carriers?

Rickover: If they are in port they will last a little longer.

Proxmire: How much longer?

Rickover: I don't know. If you use ballistic missiles, it does not make any difference whether or not you have carriers.

Proxmire: Wouldn't they be more vulnerable in port than at sea?

Rickover: If the enemy decided to use ballistic missiles, they probably would be.

Proxmire: I'm talking about a confrontation with the Soviet Union in which nuclear weapons are used.

Rickover: Well, if there is a confrontation with nuclear weapons, there is no point to discussing it. . . .

Civilian Defense Officials

Nobody ever asks the question: What is the expertise of the Secretary of Defense, for example, for his job? Or what is the expertise of the Secretary of the Navy for his job? Nobody ever asks those questions.

Proxmire: You asked the question. You answer it. What is the expertise of our Secretary of Defense and Secretary of the Navy?

Rickover: The Secretary of Defense is a businessman. He has experience in business and that is what we generally get to run the military. I am not criticizing the individual, you understand, I am criticizing the system. He has experience in business. The reason he is in his defense job is because of the Founding Fathers' fear, based on their experience with the English Government, that if the military gets too powerful they could take over the Government. That is the only basic reason for having civilians run the military. There is no other reason.

However, when these civilians get appointed to the job, they feel they must make something out of it.

They have a short time to prove their worth. They can do all manner of things they could never have done in civilian life. There is no profit and loss sheet, and no board of directors to monitor them. . . . Most of the work in the Defense Department is writing reports. I once made a recommendation about this situation to Congress. . . .

How would I fix the problem? I would split up the Defense Department officials into three distinct groups. One-third would do the work. The other two-thirds would sit in offices with no secretaries or aides and would write letters in longhand to each other and get replies in longhand but never do anything more.

If we did that — it sounds funny — we would do more to promote military efficiency than anything I know. Try it sometime. . . .

[Government Shipyards]

I believe you have got to act unequivocally to nationalize them [the arms industry]. I will tell you what this means. Take shipbuilding, with which I am quite familiar. I believe you will find it ultimately much cheaper overall to have a lot of shipbuilding work done in Government yards. I am not a proponent of doing things in Government facilities, but the issue has come to this point. Now it costs more to do work in Government shipyards. But why does it cost more? Because the shipyards — I am sticking to that one because I know a lot about it — the salaries Government shipyards pay is mandated by law. There are many other regulations to which Government shipyards must conform. These regulations are not binding on private industry. So the cost comparison is an unfair and an unrealistic one. In my opinion, based on what I see industry doing, it will be just as efficient overall for the U.S. Government to build a ship in Government yards. . . .

Every time I recommend building ships in Navy shipyards the Defense Department refuses to go along. They will not. They protect private industry because that is where the civilian superiors come from and that is where they are going back when they leave Government. . . .

Secretary of Defense

. . . [The Secretary of Defense] has problems that I do not have. I think if I were made Secretary of Defense I could reduce the money spent. But he has other problems. He has the administration to deal with. He is their appointee. They want certain things done and they have programs. I will not say whether they are right or wrong. I am not in the position to judge. Furthermore, the Secretary of Defense really has so many duties, obligations, meetings, trips abroad, and so on, that I doubt he actually knows much about what is going on. No man could. . . .

. . . I said in the 1940's and I still believe it was wrong to set up the Defense Department. I was involved in this to some extent, toward the end of the war. I was against the concept because I saw that this behemoth would be mired in its own internal problems. I do not know why we have a Defense Department. I really do not know. I do not know what it does. Nobody knows.

Recommendations Made to OMB

Richmond: Admiral, you made a lot of recommendations to David Stockman on various economies in the Defense Department I believe.

Rickover: Yes, sir.

Richmond: Have any of those been put into work at all?

Rickover: No, sir.

Richmond: Can you give us an idea of some of the recommendations you made?

Rickover: Yes. I have an appendix to my prepared statement which explains the gist of it. You have before you this thick document on my recommendations for improvement of the Defense Department. First I talk about the organization of the Department. Then I mention excess organizational layering. I mention the large number of people staffing the offices at each level. I am just reading the titles. Here are some more examples: Stop the undue reliance of the military on management information systems and system analysis; reduce the number of flag officers. In other words, there are too many such as me in the damned place. . . . We have too many officers and we don't know what to do with them. So we assign them to shore duty, and they must do things to demonstrate they are activists — and so become known to their superiors. This helps for their promotion and assignment to the next duty. . . .

Shipbuilding and Steel Industries

Richmond: The shipbuilding capacity of the United States . . . is down to the barest minimum, to a point where my understanding is that even in commercial ships we're building fewer or no ships at all in the commercial shipyards in the United States as against Japan and Korea where they are building hundreds of ships. Don't you think as a matter of defense readiness two industries in the United States should be modernized, namely our shipbuilding facilities and steelmaking facilities? How can you fight a war if you can't make modern steel and ships?

Rickover: The basic reason is that it is too expensive to build ships in this country. . . . A man who has to build a ship for commercial purposes — and he has to pay out money he borrowed at high interest rates — has to go abroad to get his ships. That is why the Japanese are building so many ships. . . .

Mismanagement

. . . You have to face the fact that we are paying people in industry much more than they get in other countries, with equivalent intellectual capability and standard of living. Therefore, we ought to find out why this is. One of the reasons is mismanagement.

I will be specific with the shipbuilding industry because I know something about that. The people in charge of it do not know much about shipbuilding. That is not why they are there. They are simply put in their jobs for their financial acumen on how to make a profit. I once testified and offended the shipbuilding industry very much. I said they would just as soon sell horse turds as ships. They didn't like it. That's the best I can say. What they want is to make money. . . .

Circumstances Surrounding Retirement

Proxmire: Admiral, questions have been raised in the press about the circumstances surrounding your retirement. Will you give us the facts?

Rickover: I will sir. On November 13, 1981, I met with the Secretary of Defense at his invitation; the Secretary of the Navy was there. He said nothing during this meeting. The Secretary of Defense told me that I would be replaced when my current tour expired. He offered me a position as Adviser to the President on Civilian Nuclear Matters.

I declined that offer but told him that if the President ever wanted my advice, I would be honored to give it, and that had applied throughout my entire career. In fact, some Presidents have asked — President Truman, President Carter, and President Eisenhower. But this President has never asked me.

I later informed the Secretary of the Navy that I would like to continue on active duty as a special Navy adviser, but still be available as needed to offer advice to other government officials. The Chief of Naval Operations proceeded to make arrangements for me to have an office and small staff at the Washington Navy Yard.

On January 25, 1982, the Secretary of the Navy informed me that he had decided not to recall me to active duty, but that I would have use of an office and certain administrative support for 3 to 6 months. In other words, he wanted me completely terminated in the Navy within 3 to 6 months. . . .

Naval Nuclear Propulsion

The safety record of the naval nuclear propulsion program remains excellent — 2,300 reactor years of operation without a reactor accident involving a nuclear propulsion plant.

Our nuclear-powered ships continue to be the most reliable yet hardest worked ships in the fleet.

Our latest nuclear-powered ships are superior in key propulsion attributes, such as ship silencing and endurance, to any ships in the world.

We know how to increase the speed of our submarines substantially if the Navy and Congress are willing to spend the money for a new class of submarines.

Despite an expanding nuclear fleet, the amount of radioactive waste and the total occupational radiation exposure is declining. Radiation exposure to people in the program has always been kept well below allowable Federal standards. It is lower than any other nuclear power program in the United States or, I believe, in the world.

Listen to this one: We have under development nuclear cores that will last the entire life of the ship. This will eliminate the expense, radioactive waste, occupational radiation exposure, and ship time out of service involved in refueling nuclear-powered ships. . . .

Excessive Rotation in Jobs

Proxmire: Admiral, is it possible in today's military structure for another Admiral Rickover to come up through the ranks?

Rickover: Well, what if Jesus Christ were to come back?

Proxmire: I didn't hear that?

Rickover: I think you're asking rather the wrong question. Certainly there are people who can do that.

Proxmire: I think there are people. I am just wondering if the system would permit a man who is —

Rickover: The system would prevent it. You cannot do that because the most sacred thing about the Navy is the officer must change duties every 2 to 4 years. That is absolutely sacred and you know there's a reason for that. When an officer gets up for promotion, the more duties he has had, the more likely he is to be promoted. For example, in interviewing senior officers, captains, I find that in the 20-year time some of them had 20 different duties. Now what can one learn about a job in a year? So, in my opinion, the whole system of rotation in the Defense Department is giving each officer an equal chance to fill every billet so he can be considered for promotion. The system does [not] pick out the best officers. It can't. . . .

Department of Defense

Proxmire: Admiral, the Office of Management and Budget has received great publicity for its efforts to balance the budget and they have tried hard and they have cut programs very sharply. What's that organization doing, if anything, about increasing the efficiency of the Defense Department, and what is the Defense Department and the Navy doing?

Rickover: To increase the efficiency of the Defense Department, you first must abolish it. I am not joking about this at all. It is too large, as I mentioned earlier in my testimony. You should get back to having an Army, a Navy, and an Air Force. You should get back to that. The Defense Department is far too large for any human being to handle. . . .

Nuclear Reactor Safety

Proxmire: In view of the experience in Three Mile Island and the other accidents and mishaps, do you believe that civilian nuclear reactors can be operated safely?

Rickover: Absolutely, sir.

Proxmire: What's wrong with the way the civilian nuclear industry is managed now? Why are there accidents?

Rickover: Supervision, and I can give you a perfect example of that. Most of the civilian industry is manned by people who were trained in the naval program and yet they run into these problems. . . .

We have trained about 54,000 people. Many of them have gotten jobs in the civilian nuclear industry. The senior watchstander at Three Mile Island had been in a nuclear ship. But the difference is that in the Navy we truly supervise. We require proper watchstanding. We check on everything. I get reports all the time, every week, from every one of our ships.

In the civilian nuclear industry, there are no similar reports to one central authority. There is no equivalent supervision. One of the serious things wrong at Three Mile Island was the lack of supervision and carelessness in operation. . . .

I do not believe the Government should spend money fostering nuclear power. Government should have people checking on their operation. I do not believe the Government should subsidize the development of commercial nuclear power. They have done enough now. . . .

I think that ultimately we will need nuclear power because we are exhausting our nonrenewable energy resources; that is, coal and oil. I think this exhaustion will go far more rapidly than we believe. The cost is already going up. I believe that nuclear power for commercial purposes may show itself to be more economic, but that is not the only line of reasoning to consider. We must also take into account the potential damage a major release of radioactivity could cause. . . .

I will be philosophical. Until about 2 billion years ago it was impossible for there to be any life on Earth. That is, there was so much heat and radiation on Earth that there could be no life — fish or any other form of life. Gradually, about 2 billion years ago, the amount of heat and radiation on this planet, and probably in the entire system, became reduced. This made it possible for some form of life to begin. It started in the seas, I understand. The amount of radiation has gradually decreased, because all radiation has a half-life; which means ultimately there could be no radiation.

Now when we use nuclear weapons or nuclear power we are creating something which nature has been eliminating. That is the philosophical aspect, and it pertains whether it is radiation from nuclear weapons, nuclear power, use of radiation for medical or industrial purposes. Of course, some radiation is not bad because it doesn't last long, or has little effect on the surroundings. We live with a certain amount of natural radiation all the time. But every time you produce radiation, you produce something that has a certain half-life, which in some cases is billions of years.

There are, of course, many other things mankind is doing which, in the broadest sense, are having an adverse impact, such as using up scarce resources. I think the human race is ultimately going to wreck itself. It is important that we control these forces and try to eliminate them.

In this broad philosophical sense, I do not believe that nuclear power is worth the present benefits since it creates radiation. You might ask why do I design nuclear-powered ships? That is because it is a necessary evil. I would sink them all. . . .

I am proud of the part I have played in it. I did it because it was necessary for the safety of our country. That is why I am such a great exponent of stopping this whole nonsense of war. Unfortunately, attempts to outlaw war have always failed. One lesson of history is when a war erupts every nation will ultimately use whatever weapon is available. That is a lesson learned time and again. Therefore, we must expect, if another war — a serious war — were to break out, we will use nuclear energy in some form. That is due to the imperfection of human beings.

Prospect of Nuclear War

Proxmire: What do you think is the prospect, then, of nuclear war?

Rickover: I think we will probably destroy ourselves. So what difference will it make? Some new species will arise eventually; it might be wiser than we are....

From a long-range standpoint — I am talking about humanity — the most important thing we could do at present is to have an international meeting where first we outlaw nuclear weapons. Eventually we could outlaw nuclear reactors too....

... I do not believe in divine intercession. I think we are making our own bed and we have to lie on it. We can go to church every Sunday and pray, but the Lord has many demands made on him from many other worlds and in the eyes of the Lord we are not the most important thing in the universe....

FEBRUARY

STATE DEPARTMENT REPORT ON HUMAN RIGHTS

February 2, 1982

In its annual human rights report dated February 2 and submitted to the House Foreign Affairs and the Senate Foreign Relations committees February 4, the State Department strongly criticized the Soviet Union and its activities in Afghanistan and Poland during 1981. The report also noted deterioration in the protection of human rights in several Central American, Asian and African nations.

The introduction to Country Reports on Human Rights Practices for 1981 *defined human rights as first "the right to be free from governmental violations of the integrity of the person — violations such as torture, cruel, inhuman or degrading treatment or punishment; arbitrary arrest or imprisonment; denial of fair public trial; and invasion of the home." Second, according to the report, human rights also meant the "right to enjoy civil and political liberties, including freedom of speech, press, religion and assembly; the right to participate in government; the right to travel freely within and outside one's own country; the right to be free from discrimination based on race or sex."*

The 158 countries reviewed in the 1,142-page report were analyzed on the basis of these human rights definitions. The report also contained an assessment of the economic and social circumstances inside each country "because of the moral imperative of conquering poverty and since an understanding of these circumstances is useful" in assessing a nation's human rights situation. Each country report concluded with a chart indicating the amount of aid the nation received from the United States and from international agencies through direct economic and relief aid, technical expertise or military assistance.

Opposing 'Selective Indignation'

Since the mid-1970s the State Department had been required to produce an annual report on human rights worldwide for the House and Senate committees on foreign affairs. These requirements first applied only to those countries receiving aid from the United States, but they were extended in 1979 to include all members of the United Nations. The 1981 report was the first issued during the Reagan administration under Assistant Secretary of State for Human Rights Elliott Abrams, who had stepped into this post after the controversial nomination of Ernest Lefever was withdrawn. (Historic Documents of 1981, p. 449)

The report's introduction reasserted the importance of human rights as an essential element in the formulation of a coherent U.S. foreign policy. It said the international community had accused the Carter administration of maintaining "a double standard which focuses solely on certain countries, almost ignoring the violations of human rights in Communist lands. ..." In what the Reagan administration described as "an evenhanded approach," the report said that U.S. human rights policy would no longer be one of "selective indignation." An instance of human rights abuse, no matter where and under what kind of government it took place, was to be regarded with equal repugnance by the United States. (Historic Documents of 1981, p. 779)

Abuses by the Soviet Union

The report assailed the Soviet Union's abuse of human rights, which it said "intensified" in 1981. About 10,000 dissidents were imprisoned, exiled or sentenced to forced labor, the report said. In all, some four million Soviet citizens were undergoing forced labor. The State Department strongly criticized Soviet involvement in Poland, declaring that "the Polish authorities acted under strong pressure from the Soviet Union" in imposing martial law. This action led to at least 2,000 arrests and to the "harassment and intimidation of major segments of the Polish population." The report also assailed Soviet activities in Afghanistan, especially "the reported use of chemical weapons and the indiscriminate bombing and shelling of the Afghan people." (Historic Documents of 1981, pp. 881, 681)

The report stated that the most effective course of action to promote human rights was to counter Soviet policy with American diplomacy. ". .. [I]t is a significant service to the cause of human rights to limit the influence the U.S.S.R. (together with its clients and proxies) can exert. A consistent and serious policy for human rights in the world must counter the U.S.S.R. politically and bring Soviet bloc human rights violations to the attention of the world over and over again."

Abuses in Other Countries

The report found no marked general improvement or deterioration in human rights during 1981, and abuses were noted in all corners of the world, in "developed" as well as "developing" nations. The report cited abuses in Kampuchea, where, three years after the overthrow of the Pol Pot regime, 180,000 Vietnamese troops occupied the Khmer country. In Kampuchea, as in Afghanistan, evidence indicated the use of chemical/biological agent warfare by the communist powers. Both situations had resulted in the flight of hundreds of thousands of refugees into Thailand and Pakistan.

Political instability in many Central American nations posed a threat to human rights, according to the report. In El Salvador, for example, 400 violent deaths were reported monthly by the U.S. Embassy, with no way of determining whether the government or insurgent political groups could be held responsible. In South America the continued mysterious disappearance of several hundred political prisoners marred the human rights record of the Argentine government.

Pakistan and Chile were both scheduled to resume receiving U.S. aid in 1982. According to the report, government response to human rights problems in these countries remained questionable. Although Pakistan provided a sanctuary and relief aid for two million Afghan refugees in the Northern part of its territory, allegations of electric shock torture, brutal treatment of prisoners and widespread censorship tainted the country's human rights record. Similarly, in Chile a significant number of unexplained political arrests undermined the country's human rights record.

Following are excerpts from the State Department Country Reports on Human Rights Practices for 1981, *released February 2, 1982.* (Boldface headings in brackets have been added by Congressional Quarterly to highlight the organization of the text.):

Afghanistan

Human rights in Afghanistan must be seen in the context of the bitter war in which a highly independent people is pitted against a powerful and determined invader. The Soviet Union seeks not only to dominate Afghanistan strategically with its 90,000-man expeditionary force, but also to reshape this traditional Muslim society into the Soviet mold. To achieve this purpose the Soviets are using not only military force and control of a pervasive secret police network, but also a comprehensive program aimed at indoctrinating the younger generation through large-scale and long-term educational programs in the Soviet Union. These efforts are accepted in Afghanistan by a small minority of hard-core communist sympathizers.

They are rejected, however, by the vast majority of Afghans, whose resistance, both active and passive, has fueled the continuing, devastating conflict. The Afghan war has caused enormous physical damage to the country and inflicted great hardship on the general populace.

Wanton brutality and summary executions continue under the present regime, although probably at a lower level than during the two preceeding Marxist regimes of [Nur Mohammad] Taraki and [Hafizullah] Amin. At the same time, the scope and efficiency of Babrak's [Karmal] secret police operations are increasing in areas of the country under government control (chiefly the cities). The regime has developed more technical and human means with which to restrict freedom of expression and assembly and is using these tools to create a pervasive atmosphere of suspicion and fear in the cities and towns which it controls. The sanctity of the home is being systematically violated as the army and secret police search for arms caches, new recruits, and political opponents. . . .

Refugees frequently refer to torture by the Afghan security services in recounting their own experiences, and those of relatives and friends, in Afghan prisons. For example, an Afghan who was detained at Kabul's Pol-e-Charkhi prison in mid-1981 has reported being hung upside down for an extended period of time, and seeing and hearing other detainees undergoing torture as well. In August 1981, a second Kabul resident reported seeing his brother in a semi-conscious state at secret police headquarters with his face distorted by swelling and his hands and legs trussed behind him. There also are reports that Soviet security officers have used electric shock torture in interrogating Afghan detainees in whom they have taken an interest. . . .

There are reports that summary execution of prisoners taken by the government continues at a high rate, although probably less frequently under the Babrak regime than under either of the two preceeding Marxist governments. On several occasions in the past year, the official press has reported the execution of persons found guilty of attacks on government officials or installations very shortly after such attacks took place. It seems unlikely that those deemed guilty of these offenses were given an adequate opportunity to defend themselves. There are also occasional reports of assassinations, presumably government-inspired, of persons suspected of harboring anti-regime sentiments. In mid-1981, one of the few members of the religious Mojaddedi family left alive in the country was shot while sitting in the garden of his home in the town of Charikar north of Kabul. Mojaddedi's young son was also shot when he tried to go for help. . . .

In the fall of 1981, Afghan and Soviet forces conducting an offensive against the resistance made extensive use of scorched-earth tactics. In Parwan province, north of Kabul, tanks were used to destroy grape arbors and piles of freshly threshed wheat. Private houses and other buildings were bombarded both from the air and the ground, and other buildings were booby-trapped so that returning residents would be injured or killed. . . .

Non-lethal chemicals, such as riot-control agents and incapacitants, have been used rather regularly by the Soviets in Afghanistan. In addition, there is growing evidence that Soviet forces have used lethal chemical agents against resistance forces. Evidence includes first-hand accounts of victims and bystanders, as well as testimony of Afghan Army defectors. Information from regime sources confirms that equipment has been issued to Afghan soldiers and officials to protect them against chemical agents presumably being used by security forces against the resistance....

Argentina

... The number of reported violations of all kinds fell dramatically compared to previous years. At the same time, the total number of prisoners held on other than common criminal charges was reduced to a reported 1,050. This figure includes approximately 640 people who are being held under the president's special state of siege powers (the P.E.N. prisoners). In comparison, a total of 8,200 people were detained for various periods under PEN powers between 1974 and 1980. However, a substantial number of these PEN prisoners still in detention are being held without trial or charge. In 1981 there were no new PEN arrests.

Against the overall record, several points should be noted. In December, Argentine human rights organizations asserted that two cases of disappearances had taken place in 1981 (the person involved in the second case subsequently reappeared . . .). These were the only such incidents reported as having occurred in 1981. In March there were two other cases in which individuals were apparently detained by security forces, but their detention was not acknowledged before they were released. They, like a woman who was arrested in December, were reportedly mistreated during their detention. In addition, in April a man was found dead of multiple bullet wounds several days after allegedly being arrested by security forces.

During the year, human rights organizations joined by political groups continued to seek an accounting for those who disappeared in the past, but there was no positive response from the government. In general, human rights organizations remained active throughout the year. On several occasions their leaders complained of harassment and intimidation. In February 1981, the leaders of one human rights group were arrested by court order, held several days and then freed....

The constitution prohibits the use of torture. There were reports that two of the men detained in March were subjected to electric shocks. A member of the Communist Party who was arrested as part of a court-ordered investigation reportedly stated in court that while detained she was mistreated, including being dangled from a window by her heels....

El Salvador

Throughout 1981 the human rights situation in El Salvador remained troubled. The civil strife and endemic violence which has convulsed the country for years continued. Human rights violations were frequent, but there was a downward trend in political violence. Extreme leftist terrorists and guerrillas, right-wing death squads and some members of the government's internal security forces all had a hand in the violence. At the same time, significant strides were made by El Salvador's government in moving toward a democratic process for resolving conflicts and in implementing socio-economic reforms aimed at reducing the social causes of the present division and strife....

Statistics on numbers of people killed as a result of El Salvador's current political violence are difficult to obtain and are unreliable. Available figures are useful principally to set trend lines. Two Salvaderan institutions, the Legal Aid Office which identifies itself with the Archbishopric, and the staff of the Central American Unversity (UCA), maintain statistics on the number of persons murdered. Both institutions are sympathetic to anti-government forces. Their statistics often have a monthly variance numbering in the hundreds. The United States Embassy in San Salvador maintains its own count of deaths attributable to political violence, gleaned primarily from press reports. According to the embassy's count, there were 6,116 violent deaths during the twelve-month period ending January 1, 1982. The embassy's figures also show a decline in average monthly totals from around 800 per month in late 1980 and in the beginning of 1981 to 200-400 per month at the end of the year. Some Church sources claim that perhaps twice as many non-combatants have been killed.

In only a small percentage of political murders is it possible to determine who or which group bears responsibility. In most cases, no organization has sufficient information about the sources of violence to support specific allocations of responsibility. Some killings clearly are the result of combat activity between the military and the guerrillas. Other killings or terrorist acts are the work of extreme leftists who claim responsibility for them. Other murders and bombings are committed by rightist elements who acknowledge responsibility. Sometimes members of the official and local security forces, acting against standing regulations, are associated with these acts. In the vast majority of cases, however, no one claims responsibility, and it is virtually impossible to determine exactly who is responsible for such crimes. Moreover, many apparent acts of political violence are probably common crimes or crimes of vengeance. (El Salvador has long had a very high homicide rate.)...

The 1952 constitution prohibits "all forms of torture." There have been numerous reports that terrorists of both the left and the right have used torture to gain information and to intimidate their opponents. Bodies bearing clear signs of torture have been discovered. Despite constitutional bans and government policy against using torture, individual members of the security forces may have been involved in unsolved crimes of murder with torture. There have been credible accounts of torture and abuse at interrogation centers operated by the security forces, especially the treasury police, during investigations of people suspected of subversion. Some persons who have been captured by government forces have alleged that they were tortured during interrogation. Psychological torture by leftist and rightist terrorists in the form of threats against or murders of family members of prisoners has also been claimed....

Ethiopia

After the 1974 revolution, the level of human rights abuses in Ethiopia, high under the previous regime, increased sharply. The human rights situation was at its worst in 1977 and 1978, when the military leadership and its civilian opponents fought for control of the government. Perhaps 10,000 men, women and children were killed, while tens of thousands of others were imprisoned or exiled during this "red terror" campaign. Because the government has since consolidated its control over most of the country, the level of human rights abuses is now significantly lower. However, there is no legal protection against abuses.

The legitimacy of the Provisional Military Government of Socialist Ethiopia (PMGSE) is not accepted by many of the country's constituent ethnic groups. Most notably, the Eritreans, Tigreans, Oromos and ethnic Somalis are in varying degrees of revolt. The government's 1976 promise of greater regional autonomy to these groups has not been fulfilled. Its efforts to suppress the insurgencies have given rise to many human rights violations. In Eritrea, there is a continuing pattern of arbitrary arrests, reported torture and summary execution of those suspected of independence sympathies. About one-third of a million Eritreans have become refugees in the Sudan and elsewhere. The Ogaden war and drought in eastern Ethiopia produced an initially-reported million refugees in Somalia; the number living in camps is now estimated to be substantially less than a million....

There are no enforceable legal protections for the civil and political rights of the individual. Although the PMGSE claims that religious freedom is respected, 1981 saw increased repression and harassment directed against churches associated with foreign missionaries....

Use of torture is not prohibited by law, although it has declined since the worst excesses of the 1977-78 red terror. Reports indicate that torture is still used occasionally on military and political prisoners, including those accused of secessionist tendencies. In its 1981 report, Amnesty International reports that torture is still widespread....

Conditions in many Ethiopian prisons are poor, in particular in the PMGSE Headquarters basement cells (the GIBI) and in the prison at the 3rd Police Precinct in Addis Ababa. At the latter, prisoners are kept in semi-darkness in vastly overcrowded conditions. They sleep on the floor in crowded cells and corridors. Sanitary conditions are inadequate. Families, who are expected to provide for the prisoners' daily food and personal needs, are allowed to bring changes of clothing and linen only twice a month....

The United Kingdom based Anti-Slavery Society submitted a report to the United Nations Human Rights Subcommission's Working Group on Slavery asserting that in 1980 thousands of people, many inexperienced in agriculture, were forcibly transported to the State sesame farm in Humera in northeastern Ethiopia. Conditions in the workers' camps were described as extremely crowded and unsanitary. According to the report, a total of 1,626 people died at the farm that year. Some were reportedly shot while trying to escape. In addition, the report states that women workers were raped by the army personnel in charge of guarding them.

In 1981, workers were again transported to the Humera farm. While some may have gone voluntarily, many were forced to go. Workers who have escaped back to Addis Ababa report that conditions this year are still poor. . . .

Haiti

Haiti has had a long and troubled history of autocratic rule characterized by many periods of political instability and human rights abuses. The country is constitutionally a republic. Executive authority is vested in a president for life. The legislature is a unicameral chamber, with members elected for six-year terms. In practice, virtually all effective government powers are concentrated in the presidency. During the eight months that the legislative assembly is in recess, major sections of the constitution concerning protection of individual liberties are suspended, and the president has full powers to rule by decree. Considerable open political opposition to the government was permitted in Haiti during the period 1976-80. In November 1980, however, dozens of persons were arrested on various charges of conspiracy and subversion. . . .

In September 1981 the governments of the United States and Haiti signed an agreement to stop the illegal migration of Haitians to the United States. An estimated 800,000 Haitians have left the country over the past 20 years, primarily in search of better economic opportunities and in some cases, for political reasons. More than 5,000 Haitians per year are issued immigrant visas and travel legally to the United States. In addition, during January-September 1981 more than 1,000 Haitians per month illegally entered the United States. The Haitian government has made an effort to stem the illegal immigrant tide by seizing vessels on occasion, and fining or imprisoning boat captains and crews. . . .

The government does not impede domestic movement. Foreign travel requires a passport and exit visa, which together can cost up to a maximum of $97, but there is no indication the Haitian government attempts to control travel for political or other arbitrary reasons. Those who leave illegally are subject to fine or imprisonment, but the government has given assurances it will not prosecute or punish such migrants who have left Haiti without fulfilling these requirements. Checks on a sample of returnees from the United States indicates [sic] that these assurance have been kept to date. . . .

Kampuchea

The central features of human rights in Kampuchea are the continuing violation by Vietnam (SRV) of the Khmer nation's and people's right to national integrity and sovereignty, the repressive policies of both the Heng Samrin and Pol Pot contenders for power, and the thin margin of survival for most Khmer. 180,000 Vietnamese troops continue to occupy and administer Kampuchea three years after the invasion and overthrow of the brutally oppressive Pol Pot Democratic Kampuchea (DK) regime. Although the People's Republic of Kampuchea (PRK) regime in June promulgated a constitution which claims to "recognize and respect" human rights and purports to set up a judicial system, Vietnamese forces and administrators stand above the law with respect to any and all human rights for the Khmer people. The Hanoi-controlled Heng Samrin administration has facilitated some resuscitation of normal Kampuchean life. Basic food and medical needs go first to Khmer who work directly within or around the administration Heng Samrin and his Vietnamese sponsors are attempting to construct.

In 1981, ordinary Khmer slowly began to benefit from large-scale international relief donated to Kampuchea. The Khmer people are still caught between their fears of a restoration to power by the Pol Pot regime, the dangers of associating or not associating with the fledgling Heng Samrin administration, and their resentment over subjugation by their traditional enemy, the Vietnamese. In the regions controlled by the People's Republic of Kampuchea, there have been improvements, if circumscribed, in education, cultural, and religious activities. The Khmer people, largely on their own initiative, have begun reconstruction of a rudimentary economy, based on subsistance agriculture and on trading of commodities from the Thai-Kampuchean border and from international relief. There has been no real institutional progress which promises any meaningful relief from Vietnamese violation of basic Khmer human rights. Government repression, restrictions, and surveillance are increasing as resistance to the regime grows. Convincing evidence now exists that the regime may be employing lethal chemical/biological agents against groups along the Thai-Kampuchean border who continue to resist its authority. The continuing failure of the regime to provide for basic human rights has led to a small, but steady flow of refugees to the Thai border....

Knowledgeable Khmer citizens and Khmer refugees, based on their contacts with inmates or from personal experience, now report only rare instances of torture in areas of Kampuchea controlled by either the DK or the PRK....

Summary executions were widespread by the DK regime from 1975 to 1978. Very limited information available in 1981 suggests that such executions still occur for serious offenses, but that they no longer seem the rule. DK soldiers reportedly massacred a number of civilian Vietnamese refugees near the Thai border in June. There are no recent reports of summary executions by PRK authorities.

According to first-hand reports, in the central prison in Phnom Penh there is no provision of medical care or medicines, clothing or soap, and there are cases of malnutrition and malnutrition-related deaths among the prisoners. Some prisoners are reportedly kept in tiny cells in total isolation and darkness, and lose the ability to walk after several months. Some inmates allegedly have been beaten to death. . . .

Pakistan

Throughout its three decades of independence, Pakistan has been preoccupied with a search for its national identity. The social, political, economic and regional differences which characterize Pakistan's diverse society have led frequently to instability and deterioration in the human rights environment. As a result, Pakistan has been governed by martial law or other undemocratic regimes for most of its thirty-four years. Presently it is under military rule. . . .

Pakistani society is Islamic and traditional, largely rural and poor. Development is often slow paced and sometimes related only indirectly to basic human needs. The government is seeking to make Pakistani law and custom consistent with Islamic precepts. Some innovations, such as the distribution of revenues from compulsory "zakat" (a tax levied on savings accounts), have been directly beneficial to the poor.

Pakistan is providing generous humanitarian assistance to over two million Afghan refugees. The presence of this large and growing number of displaced persons, largely concentrated in Pakistan's Northwest Frontier province and in Baluchistan, creates a serious economic burden. It also contributes to social tensions stemming from competition with the local population for scarce resources. . . .

The 1973 Constitution bans torture. During 1981 there were at least four cases in which prisoners allegedly died while in police custody. In all four cases, allegations of police brutality were reported in the local press. . . . All four cases were investigated, and in two cases murder charges were filed against the policemen involved. . . .

. . . A former prisoner in Lahore claimed that he received electrical shocks and was repeatedly slapped in the face by police interrogators; also in Lahore, a political leader convicted for holding a political meeting in his residence was reported to have been denied medical treatment on orders of military authorities; in Sialkot, a police assistant sub-inspector was formally charged with having beaten a prisoner who received serious injuries; and a student in Faisalabad alleged that he was stripped and beaten, then tied to a charpoy (a portable bed) and hung upside down. . . .

[Poland]

Poland's progress towards a freer and more open society ceased on December 13 when the regime initiated martial law throughout the country. There is reason to believe that Polish authorities acted under strong pressure from the Soviet Union. The regime acknowledged a severe curtailment of individual freedom in the proclamation issued on December 13: "The introduction of the state of martial law causes, among other things, a temporary suspension or limitation of the basic rights of citizens, defined in the constitution of the Polish People's Republic and other laws as well as international agreements to which Poland is a signatory, and, in particular, personal immunity, the inviolability of residences and the secrecy of correspondence, the right of association, freedom of speech, publications, meetings, rallies, public marches and demonstrations."

Since December 13, the state security organs have undertaken a far-reaching and concerted campaign of harassment and intimidation against major segments of Polish society. Security forces are carrying out a harsh punitive effort against members and sympathizers of Solidarity. The government has admitted to the forcible detention of over 6,000 persons suspected of hostility towards the regime, including most of the national leadership of Solidarity. At least 2,000 people have been arrested as a result of martial law. Unofficial estimates of detentions are much higher. Formal charges have been pressed against only a few detainees. They are being held for an indefinite period, possibly as long as martial law remains in effect. Many of these prisoners have not been permitted personal contact or correspondence with their families. Representatives of the church and other non-official agencies have been granted access to some of the 49 detention centers reported to be in operation throughout Poland. These independent observers have reported generally humane conditions in the facilities they were able to visit, but there are also reports of far worse conditions in those to which observers were denied access.

A process called "verification" has been taking place at work places through the country at all levels of the economy. Government officials are demanding that workers sign oaths of loyalty to the regime and renounce all allegience to Solidarity. Failure to comply normally results in the dismissal from work. . . .

The regime used force to crush peaceful or passive resistance. The authorities have employed tanks, small arms, clubs, tear gas, rubber bullets, and water cannon to break up non-violent strikes and demonstrations. Official statements so far have acknowledged nine deaths as a result of government suppression of protest actions, but unofficial and unconfirmed reports indicate a higher number of fatalities. No firm estimates have been made of the number of persons injured and wounded in the course of government "pacification" actions. The statements of the regime's leaders have been filled with abhorrence of inflicting death or injury on fellow Poles. The decision to implement martial law in the first place, they insist, resulted from their revulsion at the thought of Polish blood being shed in fratricidal strife. It is difficult to reconcile such a statement with the employment of special heavily armed riot police and elite international security troops of the Interior Ministry to quell the actions of unarmed workers and students. . . .

[U.S.S.R.]

The Soviet Union is a one-party, centralized state in which a small group within the Communist Party attempts to direct all political, economic, social, cultural and other developments. Although the Soviet constitution formally provides for all internationally recognized human rights, in fact there is little tolerance for actions and practices incompatible with Communist Party control. Suppression of constitutional rights is accomplished under the auspices of a number of broadly-worded provisions stating that constitutional rights may not be exercised in a manner contrary to the interests of society as defined by the party.

The primary instrument for the suppression of dissent within the Soviet Union remains the Committee for State Security — the KGB. This organization is one of the largest employers in the country. Its divisions devoted to domestic operations number several hundred thousand men and include the Border Guards, a corps devoted to surveillance of economic crimes, an armed forces directorate which infiltrates and controls the military, and numerous other directorates which infiltrate almost every social organization so these will not serve as fronts for organized opposition.

The KGB concentrates on protecting party rule by attempting to suppress all dissent, seal all information flowing to the Soviet people from outside influences (controlling borders, jamming broadcasts, infiltrating writers' unions, operating systems of local informers, etc.), stifle nationalism and religion, and assure complete conformity with the party line. There are organic links between this police system and the party and the other organs of state control, such as the ministry of internal affairs, which run the network of prisons, forced labor camps, and "psychiatric" hospitals.

The Soviet government's intolerance for activity deemed incompatible with Communist Party control continued to be particularly evident in 1981. The precise number of persons who are presently imprisoned, exiled, or undergoing forced labor for engaging in dissident activities is not known, but the number is believed to be about 10,000. . . .

Another area in which the Soviet authorities engage in extensive domestic violations of human rights is in the area of emigration. Restrictions on Jewish, Armenian and Volga German emigration have increased greatly in the last year. Jewish emigration is now at a ten-year low.

A detailed examination of the Soviet Union's external conduct is beyond the scope of this report, but several developments nevertheless require brief mention. Soviet armed forces continue to occupy Afghanistan, and their number there has recently been increased to 90,000 men. Soviet practices in Afghanistan have continued to include the reported use of chemical weapons, "trick" explosives, and the indiscriminate bombing, shelling, and terrorizing of the Afghan population. In Poland, there is little doubt that Soviet authorities have played a major behind-the-scenes role in the effort to crush Solidarity. Thus, Soviet authorities have a major responsibility for the situation in which the Polish people now find themselves, and for the efforts of the present Polish government to turn back the clock and halt social progress. . . .

. . . Approximately 4 million Soviet citizens are undergoing forced labor, half of them confined to prisons and camps. Working inmates comprise nearly 4 percent of the Soviet work force, engaging in a wide variety of economic activity. Although article 20 of the Russian Republic criminal code states that "punishment does not have the goal of causing physical suffering or the destruction of human dignity," a number of reliable sources have described the stark conditions in Soviet labor camps. These conditions include isolation, inadequate protection against extremely cold weather, a poor diet causing hunger and, eventually, medical problems associated with malnutrition; compulsory, hard labor in difficult conditions; inadequate medical care; and frequent, arbitrary deprivation of the prisoners' limited rights to receive correspondence and family visits. Prisoners are denied the right to practice their religion and may be punished for attempts to do so.

. . . The Soviet government continues to use pseudo-scientific procedures to confine perfectly sane political and religious activists to special psychiatric hospitals (SPHs) run by the ministry of internal affairs. In these SPHs, the "patients" are kept under control by "therapy" which amounts to little more than torture through the administration of unbalanced doses of powerful and painful drugs such as sulphazin, insulin, sanapax, seduxin, and motiden-depo. Some sources estimate that up to 1,000 sane persons are confined in Soviet psychiatric hospitals for political reasons. Another 3,000-4,000 persons are confined to SPHs simply for complaining about deficiencies in the Soviet bureaucratic apparatus. . . . In 1977, the World Psychiatric Association adopted a resolution condemning political abuse of psychiatry and naming the Soviet Union as an offender in this regard. . . .

PRESIDENT'S ECONOMIC REPORT, ECONOMIC ADVISERS' REPORT
February 6, 10, 1982

In his first Economic Report to Congress, President Reagan on February 10 pointed to the "first decisive steps" he said his administration had taken toward a "fundamental reorientation" of the federal government's role in the economy. The president's message stressed that the economic programs of his administration represented a sharp break with the policies of the past.

The changes he had initiated, Reagan said, were in the spending, taxing and regulatory policies of the federal government. Moreover, he continued, his administration in its first year had supported the Federal Reserve Board in a monetary policy "that will steadily bring down inflation."

The "historic" Economic Recovery Tax Act of 1981, President Reagan said, had "restructured" the tax system to encourage people to work, save and invest. Then, too, he said, regulatory actions of the federal government had fallen off in number in 1981 "after increasing steadily for a decade." (Reagan budget and tax package, Historic Documents of 1981, p. 639)

Economic Advisers

The Annual Report of the Council of Economic Advisers, which accompanied the president's message, also stressed the new course in economic policy on which the Reagan administration had embarked. The president's economists referred to the "dramatic changes" in economic policy that the administration had initiated.

The council's report, presented to the president on February 6, hewed closely to the broad outlines of the economic philosophy espoused by Reagan, frequently described in the news media as "Reaganomics." For example, the report pointed to the policy of the Reagan administration to "reduce a large number of [special interest] programs simultaneously" rather than one at a time. In that way, the report said, most people would see that "while they lose from cuts in a specific program, they gain enough from cuts in other programs and in lower taxes to compensate for their losses."

The report said that the economy was currently experiencing a "cyclical decline" in inflation. But a major objective of the Reagan program, the economists said, was to "achieve the elimination of inflation in the long run."

There currently was more agreement "than a decade ago," the advisers said, that "inflation is essentially a monetary phenomenon." Consequently, the appropriate policy for reducing the rate of inflation was a "decrease in the rate of money growth." The president's advisers did write that there was a "short-lived tradeoff" between unemployment and the rate of inflation.

Forecasts

The economists forecast that they expected the recession to end early in 1982. They said that the "moderating pattern" of price increases would become "more generalized and significant."

They predicted that the unemployment rate would reach "the vicinity of 9 percent" in the spring of 1982. From that time, the "rapid pace of expansion" should pull the jobless rate down between one-quarter and one-half of a percentage point a quarter, they wrote.

Following are excerpts from the February 10, 1982, Economic Report of the President and the Annual Report of the Council of Economic Advisers, issued February 6, 1982. (Boldface headings in brackets have been added by Congressional Quarterly to highlight the organization of the texts.):

ECONOMIC REPORT OF THE PRESIDENT

To the Congress of the United States:

In the year just ended, the first decisive steps were taken toward a fundamental reorientation of the role of the Federal Government in our economy — a reorientation that will mean more jobs, more opportunity, and more freedom for all Americans. This long overdue redirection is designed to foster the energy, creativity, and ambition of the American people so that they can create better lives for themselves, their families, and the communities in which they live. Equally important, this redirection puts the economy on the path of less inflationary but more rapid economic growth.

My economic program is based on the fundamental precept that government must respect, protect, and enhance the freedom and integrity of the individual. Economic policy must seek to create a climate that encourages the development of private institutions conducive to individual responsibility and initiative. People should be encouraged to go about their daily lives with the right and the responsibility for determining their own activities, status, and achievements. . . .

The Legacy of the Past

For several decades, an ever-larger role for the Federal Government and, more recently, inflation have sapped the economic vitality of the Nation.

In the 1960s Federal spending averaged 19.5 percent of the Nation's output. In the 1970s it rose to 20.9 percent, and in 1980 it reached 22.5 percent. The burden of tax revenues showed a similar pattern, with increasingly high tax rates stifling individual initiative and distorting the flow of saving and investment.

The substantially expanded role of the Federal Government has been far deeper and broader than even the growing burden of spending and taxing would suggest. Over the past decade the government has spun a vast web of regulations that intrude into almost every aspect of every American's working day. This regulatory web adversely affects the productivity of our Nation's businesses, farms, educational institutions, State and local governments, and the operations of the Federal Government itself. That lessened productivity growth, in turn, increases the costs of the goods and services we buy from each other. And those regulations raise the cost of government at all levels and the taxes we pay to support it.

Consider also the tragic record of inflation — that unlegislated tax on everyone's income — which causes high interest rates and discourages saving and investment. During the 1960s, the average yearly increase in the consumer price index was 2.3 percent. In the 1970s the rate more than doubled to 7.1 percent; and in the first year of the 1980s it soared to 13.5 percent. We simply cannot blame crop failures and oil price increases for our basic inflation problem. The continuous, underlying cause was poor government policy.

The combination of these two factors — ever higher rates of inflation and ever greater intrusion by the Federal Government into the Nation's economic life — have played a major part in a fundamental deterioration in the performance of our economy. In the 1960s productivity in the American economy grew at an annual rate of 2.9 percent; in the 1970s productivity growth slowed by nearly one-half, to 1.5 percent. Real gross national product per capita grew at an annual rate of 2.8 percent in the 1960s compared to 2.1 percent in the 1970s. This deterioration in our economic performance has been accompanied by inadequate growth in employment opportunities for our Nation's growing work force.

Reversing the trends of the past is not an easy task. I never thought or stated it would be. The damage that has been inflicted on our economy was done by imprudent and inappropriate policies over a period of many years; we cannot realistically expect to undo it all in a few short months. But during the past year we have made a substantial beginning.

Policies for the 1980s

Upon coming into office, my Administration set out to design and carry out a long-run economic program that would decisively reverse the trends of the past, and make growth and prosperity the norm, rather than the exception for the American economy. To that end, my first and foremost objective has been to improve the performance of the economy by reducing the role of the Federal Government in all its many dimensions. This involves a commitment to reduce Federal spending and taxing as a share of gross national product. It means a commitment to reduce progressively the size of the Federal deficit. It involves a substantial reform of Federal regulation, eliminating it where possible and simplifying it where appropriate. It means eschewing the stop-and-go economic policies of the past which, with their short-term focus, only added to our long-run economic ills.

A reduced role for the Federal Government means an enhanced role for State and local governments. A wide range of Federal activities can be more appropriately and efficiently carried out by the States. I am proposing in my *Budget Message* a major shift in this direction. This shift will eliminate the "freight charge" imposed by the Federal Government on the taxpayers' money when it is sent to Washington and then doled out again. It will permit a substantial reduction in Federal employment involved in administering these programs. Transfers of programs will permit public sector activities to be more closely tailored to the needs and desires of the electorate, bringing taxing and spending decisions closer to the people. Furthermore, as a result of last year's Economic Recovery Tax Act, Federal taxation as a share of national income will be substantially reduced, providing States and localities with an expanded tax base so that they can finance those transferred programs they wish to continue. That tax base will be further increased later in this decade, as Federal excise taxes are phased out.

These initiatives follow some common sense approaches to making government more efficient and responsive:

● We should leave to private initiative all the functions that individuals can perform privately.

● We should use the level of government closest to the community involved for all the public functions it can handle. This principle includes encouraging intergovernmental arrangements among the State and local communities.

● Federal Government action should be reserved for those needed functions that only the national government can undertake.

The accompanying report from my Council of Economic Advisers develops the basis for these guidelines more fully.

To carry out these policies for the 1980s, my Administration has put into place a series of fundamental and far-reaching changes in Federal Government spending, taxing, and regulatory policy, and we have made clear our support for a monetary policy that will steadily bring down inflation.

[Slowing Government Spending]

Last February I promised to bring a halt to the rapid growth of Federal spending. To that end, I made budget control the cutting edge of my program for economic recovery. Thanks to the cooperation of the Congress and the American people, we have taken a major step forward in accomplishing this objective, although much more remains to be done.

The Congress approved rescissions in the fiscal 1981 budget of $12.1 billion, by far the largest amount ever cut from the budget through this procedure. Spending for fiscal 1982 was subsequently reduced by another $35 billion. The Omnibus Budget Reconciliation Act of 1981 also cut $95 billion from the next 2 fiscal years, measured against previous spending trends. Many of these cuts in so-called "uncontrollable" programs were carried out by substantive changes in authorizing legislation, demonstrating that we can bring government spending under control — if only we have the will. These spending cuts have been made without damaging the programs that many of our truly needy Americans depend upon. Indeed, my program will continue to increase the funds, before and after allowing for inflation, that such programs receive in the future.

In this undertaking to bring spending under control, I have made a conscious effort to ensure that the Federal Government fully discharges its duty to provide all Americans with the needed services and protections that only a national government can provide. Chief among these is a strong national defense, a vital function which had been allowed to deteriorate dangerously in previous years.

As a result of my program, Federal Government spending growth has been cut drastically — from nearly 14 percent annually in the 3 fiscal years ending last September to an estimated 7 percent over the next 3 years — at the same time that we are rebuilding our national defense capabilities.

We must redouble our efforts to control the growth in spending. We face high, continuing, and troublesome deficits. Although these deficits are undesirably high, they will not jeopardize the economic recovery. We must understand the reasons behind the deficits now facing us: recession, lower inflation, and higher interest rates than anticipated. Although my original timetable for a balanced budget is no longer achievable, the factors which have postponed it do not mean we are abandoning the goal of living within our means. The appropriate ways to reducing the deficit will be working in our favor in 1982 and beyond. . . .

Reducing Tax Burdens

We often hear it said that we work the first few months of the year for the government and then we start to work for ourselves. But that is backwards. In fact, the first part of the year we work for ourselves. We begin working for the government only when our income reaches taxable levels. After that, the more we earn, the more we work for the government, until rising tax rates on each dollar of extra income discourage many people from further work effort or from further saving and investment.

As a result of passage of the historic Economic Recovery Tax Act of 1981, we have set in place a fundamental reorientation of our tax laws. Rather than using the tax system to redistribute existing income, we have significantly restructured it to encourage people to work, save, and invest more. Across-the-board cuts in individual income tax rates phased-in over 3 years and the indexing of tax brackets in subsequent years will help put an end to making inflation profitable for the Federal Government. The reduction in marginal rates for all taxpayers, making Individual Retirement Accounts available to all workers, cutting the top tax bracket from 70 percent to 50 percent, and reduction of the "marriage penalty" will have a powerful impact on the incentives for all Americans to work, save, and invest.

These changes are moving us away from a tax system which has encouraged individuals to borrow and spend to one in which saving and investment will be more fully rewarded.

To spur further business investment and productivity growth, the new tax law provides faster write-offs for capital investment and a restructured investment tax credit. Research and development expenditures are encouraged with a new tax credit. Small business tax rates have been reduced.

Regulatory Reform

My commitment to regulatory reform was made clear in one of my very first acts in office, when I accelerated the decontrol of crude oil prices and eliminated the cumbersome crude oil entitlements system. Only skeptics of the free market system are surprised by the results. For the first time in 10 years, crude oil production in the continental United States has begun to rise. Prices and availability are now determined by the forces of the market, not dictated by Washington. And, helped by world supply and demand developments, oil and gasoline prices have been falling, rather than rising.

I have established, by Executive order, a process whereby all executive agency regulatory activity is subject to close and sensitive monitoring by the Executive Office of the President. During the first year of my Administration, 2,893 regulations have been subjected to Executive Office review. The number of pages in the *Federal Register,* the daily publication that contains a record of the Federal Government's official regulatory actions, has fallen by over one-quarter after increasing steadily for a decade. . . .

Controlling Money Growth

Monetary policy is carried out by the independent Federal Reserve System. I have made clear my support for a policy of gradual and less volatile reduction in the growth of the money supply. Such a policy will ensure that inflationary pressures will continue to decline without impairing the operation of our financial markets as they mobilize savings and direct them to their most productive uses. It will also ensure that high interest rates, with their large inflation premiums, will no longer pose a threat to the well-being of our housing and motor vehicle industries, to small business and farmers, and to all who rely upon the use of credit in their daily activities. In addition, reduced monetary volatility will strengthen confidence in monetary policy and help lower interest rates.

[Program's International Aspects]

The poor performance of the American economy over the past decade and more has had its impact on our position in the world economy. Concern about the dollar was evidenced by a prolonged period of decline in its value on foreign exchange markets. A decline in our competitiveness in many world markets reflected, in part, problems of productivity at home.

A strengthened domestic economy will mean a faster growing market for our trading partners and greater competitiveness for American exports abroad. At the same time it will mean that the dollar should increase in its attractiveness as the primary international trading currency, and thus provide more stability to world trade and finance. . . .

1981: Building for the Future

In 1981 not only were the far-reaching policies needed for the remainder of the 1980s developed and put into place, their first positive results also began to be felt.

The most significant result was the contribution these policies made to a substantial reduction in inflation, bringing badly needed relief from inflationary pressures to every American. For example, in 1980 the consumer price index rose 13.5 percent for the year as a whole; in 1981 that rate of increase was reduced substantially, to 10.4 percent. This moderation in the rate of price increases meant that inflation, "the cruelest tax," was taking less away from individual savings and taking less out of every working American's paycheck.

There are other, more indirect but equally important benefits that flow from a reduction in inflation. The historically high level of interest rates of recent years was a direct reflection of high rates of actual and expected in-

127

flation. As the events of this past year suggested, only a reduction in inflationary pressures will lead to substantial, lasting reductions in interest rates.

In the 6 months preceding this Administration's taking office, interest rates had risen rapidly, reflecting excessively fast monetary growth. Since late last summer, however, short- and long-term interest rates have, on average, moved down somewhat in response to anti-inflationary economic policies.

Unfortunately, the high and volatile money growth of the past, and the high inflation and high interest rates which accompanied it, were instrumental in bringing about the poor and highly uneven economic performance of 1980 and 1981, culminating in a sharp fall in output and a rise in unemployment in the latter months of 1981.

This Administration views the current recession with concern. I am convinced that our policies, now that they are in place, are the appropriate response to our current difficulties and will provide the basis for a vigorous economic recovery this year. It is of the greatest importance that we avoid a return to the stop-and-go policies of the past. The private sector works best when the Federal Government intervenes least. The Federal Government's task is to construct a sound, stable, long-term framework in which the private sector is the key engine to growth, employment, and rising living standards.

The policies of the past have failed. They failed because they did not provide the environment in which American energy, entrepreneurship, and talent can best be put to work. Instead of being a successful promoter of economic growth and individual freedom, government became the enemy of growth and an intruder on individual initiative and freedom. My program — a careful combination of reducing incentive-stifling taxes, slowing the growth of Federal spending and regulations, and a gradually slowing expansion of the money supply — seeks to create a new environment in which the strengths of America can be put to work for the benefit of us all. That environment will be an America in which honest work is no longer discouraged by ever-rising prices and tax rates, a country that looks forward to the future not with uncertainty but with the confidence that infused our forefathers.

THE ANNUAL REPORT OF THE
COUNCIL OF ECONOMIC ADVISERS

Economic Policy for the 1980s

The year just ended was an especially significant one for the economy and for economic policymaking. When future *Reports* are written, we hope that 1981 will be described as the watershed year in which the more than decade-old rising trend of inflation was finally arrested. This development should contribute to more rapidly rising standards of living, more productive patterns of investment and saving, and a strengthened U.S. position in the world economy.

At the same time that inflation was moderating, a far-reaching set of economic policies was being developed to provide a framework for growth and stability in the years ahead, reversing more than a decade of declining productivity growth and wide swings in economic activity.

The speed with which the economy adjusts to the Administration's policies will be largely determined by the extent to which individuals, at home and at work, believe the Administration will maintain, unchanged, its basic approach to personal and business taxation, Federal spending and regulation, and monetary policy. When public expectations fully adjust to this commitment, a necessary condition for both reduced inflation and higher growth will be fully established. In short, as this *Report* attempts to demonstrate, what some people have referred to as "monetarism" and "supply-side economics" should be seen as two sides of the same coin — compatible and necessary measures to both reduce inflation and increase economic growth.

THE LEGACY OF 'STAGFLATION'

Over the last 15 years the U.S. economy has experienced progressively higher rates of inflation and unemployment, a combination of conditions commonly called "stagflation." This development was associated with a substantial increase in the Federal Government's role in the economy. Federal spending and tax revenues absorbed an increasing share of national output, Federal regulations were extended to a much broader scope of economic activity, and the rate of money growth increased substantially. . . .

A full explanation of stagflation in the United States and other countries has yet to be developed. An important lesson of this period, however, is that there is no long-term tradeoff between unemployment and inflation. The increasing role of the Federal Government in the economy — whether that role was to aid the poor and aged, to protect consumers and the environment, or to stabilize the economy — contributed to our declining economic performance. Most of the increase in Federal spending over the past 15 years has been in the form of transfer payments, which tend to reduce employment of the poor and of older workers. A combination of increases in some tax rates and inflation raised marginal tax rates on real wages and capital income. The rapid growth in regulatory activity — however measured — has significantly increased production costs. The Federal Government bears the most direct responsibility for the increases in inflation and interest rates, which were due to excessive expansion of the money supply. In short, Federal economic policies bear the major responsibility for the legacy of stagflation.

[PRESIDENT'S PROGRAM]

For the economy, the most important event of 1981 was the dramatic change in Federal policy. On February 18 the President announced a long-term program designed to increase economic growth and to reduce inflation. The key elements of the proposed program were:

- cutting the rate of growth in Federal spending;
- reducing personal income tax rates and creating jobs by accelerating depreciation for business investment in plant and equipment;
- instituting a far-reaching program of regulatory relief; and
- in cooperation with the Federal Reserve, making a new commitment to a monetary policy that will restore a stable currency and healthy financial markets.

Over the year, with the support of the Congress and the Federal Reserve System, most of this program was approved and implemented. The Federal Government's budget underwent its most significant reorientation since the mid-1960s. The rate of increase in total Federal outlays declined from 17.5 percent in fiscal 1980 to 14.0 percent in fiscal 1981 and to an anticipated 10.4 percent in fiscal 1982. The composition of Federal spending was also substantially changed. Real defense spending was accelerated, real spending for the major transfer programs for the poor and aged was maintained, and most of the spending reductions were made in other domestic programs....

A SUMMARY OF ECONOMIC CONDITIONS

General economic conditions during 1981 reflected the transitory effects of the necessary changes in Federal economic policies. The major elements of the Administration's economic policy are designed to increase long-term economic growth and to reduce inflation. Uniformly favorable near-term effects were not expected.

The primary redirection of economic policy that affected economic conditions during the year was the reduction in the growth of the money supply relative to the record high rate of growth in late 1980. This monetary restraint reduced inflation and short-term interest rates but also influenced the decline in economic activity in late 1981.

Beginning in late 1979, substantial variability in money growth rates was associated with unusually large swings in interest rates. By the end of 1980, as a result of an unprecedented degree of monetary stimulus, interest rates had risen to new peaks. In December 1980 the Federal funds rate reached more than 20 percent, the prime rate was 21½ percent, and 3-month Treasury bills had doubled in yield from their midyear lows. Long-term interest rates had risen by as much as 3 full percentage points from their midyear lows.

The rise in interest rates that began in late 1979 gradually produced an ever-widening circle of weakness centering on the most interest-sensitive industries, notably homebuilding and motor vehicles. Falling demand for housing and autos gradually affected an increasing number of other sectors, ranging from forest products to steel and rubber to appliances and home furnishings. The high interest rates also contributed to a squeeze on farm incomes — already under pressure from weaker farm prices — and weakness in industries and services closely tied to the farm sector.

Excessive monetary expansion in the latter half of 1980 helped to drive interest rates to record highs. Rates were kept at those levels for the next 6 months or so by a variety of factors, including the transitory impact of the shift to monetary restraint. Rates then fell because of the monetary restraint that characterized Federal Reserve policy during most of 1981. The high interest rates were an important factor in precipitating the downturn in the final quarter of 1981, when real output fell at an annual rate of 5.2 percent.

In short, the conflict between continued expectations of rising inflation, based on the history of the last 15 years, and the more recent monetary restraint explains many recent problems. Continued monetary restraint and a reduction of the within-year variability of money growth, however, are necessary both to reduce inflation and provide the basis for sustained economic growth.

PROSPECTS FOR RECOVERY

The series of tax cuts enacted in 1981 provides the foundation for increased employment, spending, saving, and business investment. Inflation and short-term interest rates are now substantially lower than they were at the beginning of 1981. At the time this *Report* was prepared, it appeared that the recession which started in August — as determined by the National Bureau of Economic Research — will be over by the second quarter of 1982. This would make it about average in length for a post-World War II downturn. Output and employment are expected to increase slightly in the second quarter and at a brisk pace through the rest of the year, when growth in output is expected to be in excess of a 5 percent annual rate. Inflation is likely to continue to decline and to average about 7 percent for the year, with further reductions in 1983 and beyond.

The outlook for 1983 and subsequent years is based on continuation of the Administration's spending, tax, and regulatory policies, continued monetary restraint, and broader public recognition that the Administration is committed to each of these key elements of its program. Prospective budget deficits are a consequence of the difference in the timing of the spending and tax policy actions, and of the impact on nominal gross national product growth of continued monetary restraint. Although the prospective deficits are undesirably high, they are not expected to jeopardize the economic recovery program.

Concerns have been expressed that the Federal Reserve's targets for money growth are not compatible with the vigorous upturn in economic activity envisioned later in 1982. Any such upturn, it is feared, will lead to a renewed upswing in interest rates and thus choke off recovery. We believe that such fears, while understandable on the basis of recent history and policies, are unjustified in light of current policies and the Administration's determination to carry them through.

Interest rates, after more than a decade of rising inflation, contain sizable premiums to compensate lenders for the anticipated loss in value of future repayments of principal. It is our estimate, however, that such premiums will decline over the course of 1982 and beyond. Such a decline would occur while "real" (inflation-adjusted) interest rates remain high as a result of private and public sector credit demands even as private saving flows increase. In other words, the market rate of interest is likely to continue on a downward trend, even though short-run fluctuations around the trend can be expected.

A critical element in this outlook is the assumption that inflationary expectations will, in fact, continue to recede. If they recede at a relatively fast rate, market rates of interest will decline significantly, wage demands will continue to moderate, and the pro-inflationary biases that have developed throughout the economy over the past decade will quickly disappear. Thus, the greater the degree of cooperation between the Administration, the Congress, and the Federal Reserve in continuing to support a consistent, credible anti-inflation policy, as embodied in the Administration's program, the more rapidly will real growth and employment increase. . . .

Government and the Economy

Political freedom and economic freedom are closely related. Any comparison among contemporary nations or examination of the historical record demonstrates two important relationships between the nature of the political system and the nature of the economic system:

• All nations which have broad-based representative government and civil liberties have most of their economic activity organized by the market.

• Economic conditions in market economies are generally superior to those in nations (with a comparable culture and a comparable resource base) in which the government has the dominant economic role.

The evidence is striking. No nation in which the government has the dominant economic role (as measured by the proportion of gross national product originating in the government sector) has maintained broad political freedom; economic conditions in such countries are generally inferior to those in comparable nations with a predominantly market economy. Voluntary migration, sometimes at high personal cost, is uniformly to nations with both more political freedom and more economic freedom.

The reasons for these two relationships between political and economic systems are simple but not widely understood. Everyone would prefer higher prices for goods sold and lower prices for goods bought. Since the farmer's wheat is the consumer's bread, however, both parties cannot achieve all they want. The most fundamental difference among economic systems is how these conflicting preferences are resolved.

A market system resolves these conflicts by allowing the seller to get the highest price at which others will buy and the buyer to get the lowest price at which others will sell, by consensual exchanges that are expected to benefit both parties. Any attempt by one party to improve his outcome relative to the market outcome requires a coercive activity at the expense of some other party. The politicization of price decisions — whether of wages, commodities, or interest rates — tends to reduce both the breadth of popular support for the government and the efficiency of the economy. A rich nation can tolerate a good bit of such mischief, but not an unlimited amount. One should not be surprised that all nations in which the government has dominant control of the economy are run by a narrow oligarchy and in most economic conditions are relatively poor. In the absence of limits on the economic role of government, the erosion of economic freedom destroys both political freedom and economic performance.

Only a few dozen nations now guarantee their citizens both political and economic freedom. The economic role of government in these nations differs widely, without serious jeopardy to political freedom. Within the range of experience of the United States and other free nations, the relation between the political system and the government's economic role is more subtle. Expansion of the economic role of the government tends to reduce both the level of agreement on government policies and the inclination to engage in political dissent. The link between political and economic freedom is important. Increasing economic freedom will also provide greater assurance of our political freedom.

A major objective of this Administration's economic program is to reduce the Federal Government's role in economic decisionmaking while strengthening the economic role of individuals, private organizations, and State and local governments. This shift will entail substantial reductions in the size and number of Federal spending programs, significant reductions in both personal and business Federal tax rates, major reforms of Federal regulatory activities, and a reduced rate of money growth. While an important element in this redefinition of the Federal Government's economic role is a political judgment and the appropriate relationship among individuals, the States, and the Federal Government, this redefinition also is supported by an extensive body of economic analysis. . . .

Monetary Policy, Inflation, and Employment

The economic story of the late 1960s and the 1970s was a story of rising inflation, slackening growth, and rising unemployment. The challenge of the 1980s is to eliminate inflation, restore growth, and reduce unemployment. Despite differences over the precise combination of policies that will do the job, there is widespread agreement that inflation can and must be reduced if the economy is to operate successfully. The obstacles to successful implementation of an anti-inflation policy have been largely political, although public understanding of this has been complicated by the economic consequences of the oil price shocks of 1974-75 and 1979-80. The proper policy would be one based on a careful weighing of the long-term benefits of ending inflation against the costs which are essentially short run. It is the nature of the political process, however, to focus primarily on the short-run costs of dealing with inflation, as these appear to be more easily quantifiable, and to ignore the more distant but equally important benefits of price stability.

As the acute costs of rising inflation have become more widely recognized, the public has demanded action. That has made possible the implementation of the current set of fiscal and monetary policies aimed at reducing inflation. The decision to end inflation over a period of several years will be sustained by this Administration, even though short-run costs will be suffered before long-term benefits begin to accrue. A broad public understanding of the nature of the immediate but transitory costs and the longer run benefits of reducing inflation can contribute to the overall success of the current policies. On the other hand, any perception that the policies may soon be reversed would cause transitional costs to rise, since upward adjustments in inflation expectations — and, subsequently, prices and wages — would then be realized. In short, any lack of credibility would greatly extend the period of adjustment, thereby increasing the size and duration of short-term costs. . . .

. . . [G]ood economic policy also means resisting the previous tendency in our system to change the course of policies prematurely.

[PHENOMENON OF STAGFLATION]

The irony of the 1970s was that the attempt to trade inflation for employment resulted in more inflation and rising unemployment. This period was characterized by relatively high unemployment rates and high rates of inflation, a phenomenon often called "stagflation." The growth of real output in the United States was slower than during the preceding two decades, even though the growth rate of the labor force increased. The rate of increase in the productivity of labor declined, in part because of the effects of externally imposed oil price shocks. The combination of inflation with progressive income tax rates led to steady increases in actual and prospective taxes on real income in the latter part of the 1970s. Government appeared unable to reduce inflation without increasing unemployment or to reduce unemployment without, sooner or later, increasing inflation. The actual result was that rates of inflation and unemployment rose with each succeeding round of expansion and recession, and measured productivity growth was disappointing at best. . . .

THE NATURE OF THE INFLATION PROCESS

Inflation is essentially a monetary phenomenon. This is not to deny the importance of other factors, such as changes in the price of petroleum, in causing increases in the general price level. What the statement does deny, however, is that persistent inflation can be explained by nonmonetary factors.

Monetary policy actions affect primarily nominal quantities — exchange rates, the price level, national income, and the quantity of money — as well as the rate of change in nominal quantities. But central bank actions do not have significant long-run effects in achieving *specific* values of real magnitudes — the real rate of interest, the rate of unemployment, the level of real national income, the real quantity of money — or rates of growth of real magnitudes.

Economists recognized long ago that output and employment may be no higher when prices are high than when they are low. A main point of Adam Smith's *Wealth of Nations* is that a country's wealth and income depend on the country's real resources and the way in which production is organized, and not on the level of prices. It was realized that changes in the price level had some short-term effects on output, but these effects were recognized as the result of transitory changes in demand.

The classical gold-standard mechanism embodied these principles. Unanticipated increases in the flow of gold from abroad stimulated domestic production but gradually raised domestic prices relative to foreign prices. The rise in domestic prices then reduced exports and raised imports, thereby lowering domestic production and employment and eventually lowering prices. The continuous ebb and flow of gold was expected, but the timing of the movements could not be predicted accurately. Inability to predict the movements was recognized as a cause of changes in prices and output.

Once people anticipate that prices will rise, they seek higher wages for their labor and higher prices for their products. The increase in employment produced by stimulative policies vanishes, but the inflation remains. Attempts to reduce unemployment by increasing inflation will work only if people are fooled by the changes in policy. Once people learn to expect inflation, the short-run gains in employment disappear.

It is often stated that inflation is an intractable problem, caused by forces beyond our control. But the monetary nature of inflation suggests that this is not so. More importantly, it suggests that a decrease in money growth is the necessary strategy to end inflation. Frequent use of monetary policy to reduce unemployment at certain times and inflation at others would raise the prospect of generating the same kind of cyclical behavior in economic activity that we have experienced in the past....

Stop-and-go policies cause uncertainty, hamper the ability of monetary authorities to achieve noninflationary conditions, and ultimately raise the transitional costs of eliminating inflation. The next section discusses in detail the nature of these costs.

THE COSTS OF INFLATION

Over the last decade, as inflation worsened, the attention of the general public focused on the detrimental effects that rapidly rising prices have on economic performance. These effects were felt in many ways, but the mechanisms by which inflation generated them were not well understood.

The effects of inflation fall into two general categories: (1) those that occur because no one is able to predict the precise rate of inflation; and (2) those that occur even when the rate of inflation is fully anticipated.

The concept of a "fully anticipated inflation" implies a rate of inflation that people can predict and hence take action to minimize its effects. But it is doubtful that a high rate of inflation that was also predictable could ever exist because the same lack of monetary discipline which leads to unacceptably high inflation is also likely to lead to more variable inflation. Indeed, periods of high inflation rates generally have been associated with periods of higher variability of inflation rates. It would take at least as much monetary discipline to maintain a constant high inflation rate as it takes to maintain price-level stability. Once a positive rate of inflation is accepted it becomes difficult to argue against a slightly higher rate.

One of the most important costs of unanticipated inflation is its arbitrary redistribution of wealth and income. Economic transactions are often formalized in contracts that require one party to pay a fixed dollar amount to the other party at some point in the future. When both parties anticipate inflation during the life of the contract, these future dollar payments will be adjusted upward to compensate for their expected lower real value. This upward adjustment is the so-called inflation premium. If, however, the actual rate of inflation turns out to be different from the anticipated rate, the real terms of the contract will have been altered arbitrarily. If the actual rate is higher than anticipated, the fixed payments in dollars will have a lower than expected real value, and the debtor will gain at the expense of the creditor. The same kind of arbitrary transfer occurs when workers and firms agree to wage contracts that implicitly or explicitly assume rates of inflation which later turn out to be incorrect.

In a market economy, changes in the price of one good relative to another signal changes in demand and supply conditions among various markets. An uncertain rate of inflation obscures these signals and thereby reduces economic efficiency. Since prices are rising more or less together during a general inflationary period, the fact that a price has risen is no guarantee that it has risen relative to other prices. The difficulty of distinguishing between relative and absolute price changes increases as inflation and its variability increase. This leads people to use more time and resources to attempt to decipher relative price changes, as opposed to engaging in more productive activities. Differently stated, inflation tends to make the economic information that people accumulate through experience more rapidly obsolescent than when prices are stable.

Perhaps more importantly, inability to correctly anticipate inflation creates confusion about relative prices over time and compounds the problem of efficient resource allocation. Economic decisionmaking, especially in the private sector, is inherently forward-looking. Decisions made today determine tomorrow's levels of capital stock, production, and consumption. Decisions based on correct anticipation of future relative prices lead to a more efficient allocation of resources over time. High and variable inflation, on the other hand, leads to divergent inflation expectations, and therefore to a larger proportion of incorrect decisions....

THE COSTS OF REDUCING INFLATION

There is, as noted above, a short-lived tradeoff between unemployment and the rate of inflation. This means that policies designed to reduce inflation significantly will temporarily increase unemployment and reduce output growth. The temporary decline in output growth induced by anti-inflation policies forms a rough benchmark against which the subsequent benefits of reduced inflation can be compared. The extent of these costs of reducing inflation depends on four factors: (1) the institutional process of setting wages and prices; (2) the role of expectations in this process; (3) the policy instruments employed to reduce inflation; and (4) the initial rate of inflation.

Flexibility in wages and prices reduces the transitional costs of ending inflation. A policy-induced decline in the growth rate of monetary aggregates will be associated with a decline in the growth of real output, but the more rapidly this decline in output is followed by a moderating of inflation, the more rapidly will output growth return to a rising trend. One important factor affecting the flexibility of wages and prices is the institutional environment in which they are determined. The costs of continuously negotiating and resetting prices and wages, for example, has given rise to the common practice of changing wage and price agreements relatively infrequently. While this practice makes economic sense for individuals and firms, it builds a degree of inertia into the system....

The primary policy tool for ending inflation is a decrease in the rate of growth of money. The question of how rapidly the monetary deceleration should proceed must be answered in the context of public expectations. In view of past experience, when efforts to reduce inflation were abandoned as the short-run costs began to accrue, the public has come to expect that such policies will continue to be short-lived and that inflation will persist. Frequent swings from restrictive to stimulative policy and back have led to a "wait and see" attitude on the part of the public. The mere announcement of new policies is not sufficient to convince people that they will be carried out. Rather, public expectations regarding the future course of policy are adjusted only gradually as policy actions turn out to be consistent with policy pronouncements. The credibility of policy authorities, like the credibility of anyone else, is enhanced when they do what they say they are going to do. For the Federal Reserve, this means setting money growth targets consistent with a sustained decrease in the rate of inflation and then adhering to those targets. The more success the Federal

Reserve has in meeting those targets, the less time it will take before the public is convinced of the policy's credibility.

In the current environment, even if a successful effort is made to reduce money growth, past experience with high and variable inflation will affect the speed at which financial markets reflect progress toward a long-run noninflationary policy. Having repeatedly suffered sizable capital losses on their holdings of long-term bonds, investors will be unwilling to commit new funds to these markets unless they are compensated for the risk that the current commitment to overcome inflation might be abandoned. Without adequate compensation for this risk, individuals will continue to prefer to invest in short-lived rather than long-lived financial assets. While this preference may prevent investors from maximizing the expected return on their assets, it allows them to minimize the adverse effects of future increases in inflation and interest rates.

Present concern about future monetary growth, inflation, and interest rates is related to the knowledge that the Federal budget will continue to show large deficits for the next several years. Financial investors fear that these deficits will cause either a sharp increase in interest rates — which would slow the recovery from recession — or an increase in monetary growth if the Federal Reserve attempts to hold interest rates down by adding reserves to the banking system through open market purchases of government securities.

Interest rates that are considerably higher than the current rate of inflation can have an adverse effect on investment and real economic growth. The level of long-term interest rates at the end of 1981 did not reflect investor willingness to believe that inflation will decline over the next several years. The presumably large but unmeasurable premiums being demanded by investors constitute a major obstacle to achieving rising output and employment with falling inflation. . . .

Review and Outlook

Economic developments in 1981 reflected the inflationary economic policies of more than a decade and the transitory effects of reversing those policies. Past policies alternated periodically between short-run efforts to reduce unemployment and short-lived attempts to fight inflation. Economic forecasting, however, was not sufficiently accurate to produce finely tuned countercyclical policies that made proper allowance for the lag between policy actions and their effects. Stimulative policies had relatively immediate effects on employment, followed by delayed effects in the form of higher inflation. Restrictive policies for fighting the inflation were not seen by the public as part of a credible long-term commitment and therefore were not expected to be sustained. Consequently, they tended to have a more severe impact on output and employment than on inflation. The result has been a ratcheting-up in the trend rate of inflation from one cycle to the next.

This legacy of stop-and-go policies prevented a direct move to lower inflation and higher real growth in 1981. During the first half of 1980, restrictive policies — in the form of credit controls and a sharp reduction in monetary growth — had produced a brief, sharp recession. The subsequent removal of these controls and a postwar record high rate of monetary growth then led to an unsustainable rate of economic expansion through early 1981. . . .

PROSPECTS FOR 1982 and 1983

The current recession is expected to end early in 1982, followed by a resumption of growth by mid-year. The moderating pattern of price increases which began last year should become more generalized and significant this year. With money growth expected to be moderate, the extent of the deceleration of inflation will become the critical factor in sustaining economic recovery beyond 1982. Apart from the very high rate of expected inflation reflected in current interest rates, the economy is generally free of impediments to expansion.

The proportion of employed working-age adults will turn upward by this summer, reversing the general decline that began in 1979. Even at the expected low point of the employment ratio this spring, the proportion of people with jobs will be significantly higher than at the trough of all past recessions, except the very short 1980 contraction. The strong economic recovery this year and next is expected to expand civilian employment to over 103.5 million for 1983, well above the 98.8 million employed in 1979 before output declined. . . .

The decline in inflation, which has so far been most evident in the consumer price index and in producer prices, will influence trends in wages as 1982 progresses. But the expected 1 to 1½ percentage point slowdown of inflation in product prices will be only slightly less than the slowdown of labor costs. Therefore, the currently narrow margin of corporate profits is likely to recover only modestly during the year.

The unemployment rate is expected to reach the vicinity of 9 percent this spring until growth strengthens in the summer. Thereafter, the rapid pace of expansion should pull the unemployment rate down between one-quarter and one-half of a percentage point a quarter.

The growth in household consumption was restrained last year by high interest rates as well as by modest income growth. By the last quarter of 1981, consumption was approximately 1 percent higher in real terms than a year earlier, and new auto sales had fallen to an annual rate of 7.4 million. The decline in interest rates that began last fall, and improvements in household financial positions due to the reduced consumer debt burden and the first step of the personal tax cut, should lead to increased consumption early this year. The second step of the tax cut and the scheduled step-up in social security benefits will raise household disposable income roughly 2 percent this summer. It is difficult to predict how much of this increase will be allocated to saving or consumption. If between one-quarter and one-half of it is saved and the remainder is spent, the addition to the growth rate of consumption in the second half of this year would be about 3 percent at an annual rate. A large share of this would be expected to be used for the purchase of durables, whose annual growth rate in the second half is projected to approach 10 percent.

The recent improvement in early indicators of housing activity presages a rapid recovery that should be apparent by spring and proceed through the year. In 1980 the decline in housing early in the year was quickly reversed, and the ensuing recovery was quite rapid. Though the second reversal in the housing industry in as many years has forced some builders out of business, a rapid expansion this year is still possible. The necessary capital equipment remains, and additions to the stock of construction equipment and tools can be made rapidly. Though the supply of unsold homes relative to monthly sales is large, the absolute number of available new homes is not. Hence, rising sales will quickly generate faster building activity. While housing starts for 1982 as a whole may only exceed last year's by 10 percent, the increase during the year could exceed 50 percent. This would raise the pace of new housing starts from about 900,000 at an annual rate for the last quarter of 1981 to the vicinity of 1.5 million by the end of this year....

PROSPECTS BEYOND 1983

Continuing deceleration in money growth, fairly rapid adaptation of expectations to lower inflation, and growth aided by tax policies that are weighted toward investment are expected to be characteristic of the mid-1980s. The combination of growth-oriented fiscal policy and anti-inflationary monetary policy should mean substantial progress toward the economic goals embodied in the Full Employment and Balanced Growth Act of 1978.

The general objectives of this act — and those of the Administration — are to achieve full employment, growth in productivity, price stability, and a reduced share of governmental spending in the Nation's output. The act states clearly that ultimate price stability means eliminating inflation altogether. Although it does not define full employment as any specific unemployment rate, the act establishes as a national goal "the fulfillment of the right to full opportunities for useful paid employment at fair rates of compensation of all individuals able, willing, and seeking to work." It places emphasis on encouraging capital formation and relying on the private sector to meet the act's objectives of full employment, growth in productivity, and price stability. It requires an annual Investment Policy Report.... In addition, the act responds to the widespread desire for reduced governmental intervention by calling for steady reductions in the share of the Nation's output accounted for by governmental spending, and for the ultimate reduction of Federal outlays to 20 percent of GNP....

The Council emphasizes two points about the setting of a timetable for reaching these goals and about targeting economic performance in general. First, as has been emphasized elsewhere in this *Report,* the speedy adaptation of inflationary expectations to the anti-inflationary monetary regime set for the 1980s is of central importance in turning away from the rising inflation and unemployment of the last decade to an extended period of declining inflation with prosperous growth. However, as this *Report* points out . . . government efforts to intervene directly in wage and price setting in the private sector are essentially destabilizing and do not alter the longer term path of the economy. Second, the Federal Government cannot fully anticipate the course of the economy; neither can it direct economic outcomes precisely. In view of these limits the annual goals should best be viewed as benchmarks of economic progress. . . .

PRESIDENT'S BUDGET MESSAGE
February 8, 1982

President Reagan sent his budget requests for fiscal 1983 to Congress on February 8, proposing $757.6 billion in expenditures. The president's budget projected huge deficits — $91.5 billion in fiscal 1983 and $82.9 billion in fiscal 1984 — despite major new cuts in domestic programs. Moreover, forecasts in the budget appeared to quash any hope that the budget could be balanced before 1988 at the earliest.

Although political opposition was sure to coalesce around the issue of the deficit, Reagan proposed no major new tax increases. Nor did he cut back on an increase in fiscal 1983 Defense Department expenditures to $221.1 billion — a sharp boost from $187.5 billion in fiscal 1982. Later in the year, Reagan urged Congress to pass legislation to raise $98.3 billion in taxes and to reduce spending by $17.5 billion over three years. The tax bill passed the House August 19, with more Democrats than Republicans voting in favor of it. Reagan signed it into law September 3.

Deficit

In the message to Congress accompanying the budget, the president said, "...[O]ur incentive-minded tax policy and our security-based defense programs are right and necessary for long-run peace and prosperity, and must not be tampered with in a vain attempt to cure deficits in the short run."

Reagan blamed the large deficit on a number of problems. He said that "the most important setback to our budgetary timetable is the recession *now underway." Another cause, he said, was the rising cost of interest payments on the nation's trillion-dollar debt. The lowering of the rate of inflation was itself a cause of the deficit, as seen by the president, because the lower rate resulted in lower tax receipts. Finally, the president held Congress responsible for failing in its previous session to make all the spending cuts he had requested earlier.*

Political supporters and opponents of the president alike, however, generally saw the projected deficits as largely a reflection of Reagan's deep philosophical commitment both to a program of "supply-side" tax cuts and to a strengthening of the nation's defense posture. Few doubted the president's conviction that cuts in personal and corporate taxes would spur investment, creating jobs and raising productivity in the bargain. Moreover, to beef up the nation's defense was to fulfill a promise Reagan had made in dozens of speeches. But the means required to achieve the two goals were not easily reconcilable.

Clearly sensitive about the size of the deficit, the administration stressed that as a percentage of the gross national product (GNP) the fiscal 1983 deficit was not so large as the one in fiscal 1968. And the president told an audience in Bloomington, Minn., on the day the budget was released, that it had not been "easy for a conservative like myself to recommend a $91.5 billion deficit."

Economic Assumptions

Despite the significance attached to any president's budget, it was always, in a sense, a structure built on sand. That is, underlying all the figures was a collection of economic assumptions on which predictions of revenues and spending were based.

Reagan's fiscal 1983 budget assumed that the recession would come to a quick end, that it would be followed by sustained prosperity and that inflation, interest rates and unemployment would all come down. Specifically, it assumed a 6 percent inflation rate and a jobless rate of only 7.9 percent. But in recent years the U.S. economy could almost be said to have defied current economic theory, and, in looking to the future, the president's budget planners faced many imponderables.

Defense Budget

The budget proposed a $43.4 billion increase — to $257.5 billion — in the Defense Department's budget authority. Of that jump, officials estimated, $29.8 billion would be above the inflation rate — a real increase in defense spending of 13.2 percent.

Much of the hike reflected an administration decision to try to estimate fully the likely cost of weapons and to buy them in a way most *likely to reduce the total cost in the long run. Under the most dramatic of such "spend now, save later" plans, two nuclear-powered aircraft carriers would be funded at a cost of $6.8 billion in fiscal 1983 budgetary authority.*

Social Programs

The president's budget proposed cutting the core income support programs for the poor — Aid to Families with Dependent Children (AFDC), food stamps and Supplemental Security Income (SSI) — by a total of $3.7 billion in fiscal 1983. Under the plan, states would be required to set up AFDC "workfare" programs. The programs would require adult recipients to perform community service work in exchange for their benefits.

Budget reductions also were recommended in such related programs for the poor and elderly as Medicare, Medicaid, federal retirement benefits, unemployment compensation and housing assistance. The administration defended the cuts as restoring the "original safety net character of welfare programs."

Congressional Reaction

By and large, the reaction of members of Congress to the fiscal 1983 budget was sharply negative, and it focused on the deficit. Moreover, criticism came from both sides of the aisle in the House and Senate. Republicans were described as groping for a way to distance themselves from the budget without renouncing the president himself.

House Speaker Thomas P. O'Neill Jr., D-Mass., called the president's plan a "Beverly Hills budget." House Minority Leader Robert H. Michel, R-Ill., a key player in Reagan's budget victories a year earlier, said, "That deficit is just mind-boggling to most of our people." Rep. James R. Jones, D-Okla., chairman of the House Budget Committee, called some of the economic assumptions in the budget "Alice in Wonderland views."

Following is the text of President Reagan's February 8, 1982, budget message to Congress. (Boldface headings in brackets have been added by Congressional Quarterly to highlight the organization of the text.):

To the Congress of the United States:
One year ago, in my first address to the country, I went before the American people to report on the condition of our economy. It was not a happy occasion.

Inflation, interest, and unemployment rates were at painfully high levels, while real growth, job creation, new investment, personal savings, and productivity gains had virtually ceased. Our economy was staggering under the burden of excessive tax rates, double-digit inflation, runaway Government spending, counter-productive regulations, and uneven money supply growth. The economy, I declared, was in the "worst mess" in half a century.

To our great good fortune, there were many in the Congress who understood the nature of our difficulties and who rose with us to meet the challenge. Fundamental and long-overdue remedies were proposed and put in place. Together, we enacted the biggest spending and tax reductions in history. Counter-productive regulations have been swept away, and the Federal Reserve has taken action to bring excessive monetary growth under control.

The first year of the 97th Congress will be remembered for its decisive action to hold down spending and cut tax rates. Today, the question before us is whether the second year of this Congress will bring forward equal determination, courage, and wisdom. Clearly, there is a great deal more to be done.

Some seek instant relief from the economic problems we face. There is no such panacea. Our program began October 1, and it cannot solve in 4 months problems that have been building for more than 4 decades. All the quick fixes tried in the past not only failed to solve but actually aggravated our economic difficulties. They simply ensured a new cycle of boom and bust, of exaggerated hopes and eventual disappointment.

We did not promise the American people a miracle. We did promise them progress, and progress they will get.

Our goal was and remains economic recovery — the return of noninflationary and sustained prosperity. We seek a larger economic pie to provide all Americans more jobs, more after-tax income, and a better life. Quick fixes won't get us there.

What will get us there is firm resolve and unwavering adherence to the four fundamentals of our economic recovery program that I outlined to the Congress 1 year ago:

• Reducing personal and business taxes to stimulate saving, investment, work effort, and productivity.

• Reducing the growth of overall Federal spending by eliminating Federal activities that overstep the proper sphere of Federal Government responsibilities.

• Reducing the Federal regulatory burden in areas where the Federal Government intrudes unnecessarily into our private lives or interferes unnecessarily with the efficient conduct of private business or of State or local government.

• Supporting a moderate and steady monetary policy, to bring inflation under control.

At the same time, I have proposed strengthening the Nation's defenses, to restore our margin of safety and counter the Soviet military buildup.

Congressional response to these proposals has been positive and gratifying. While much remains to be done, we have made a good beginning.

The Nation's fiscal policy is now firmly embarked on a new, sound, and sustainable course. For the first time in 2 decades, the destructive pattern of runaway spending, rising tax rates, and expanding budgetary commitments has been slowed, and with the cooperation of the Congress this year, will finally be broken.

● Where the growth rate of spending had soared to 17.4% in 1980, it is now declining dramatically — to 10.4% this year, and, under the budget I am submitting, to 4.5% next year.

● Where budget growth totaled $166 billion from 1979 to 1981, spending will rise by only 60% of that amount from 1981 to 1983, despite cost-of-living adjustments and the needed defense buildup.

● After having reached 23% of GNP in 1981, the Federal Government's claim on our economy will steadily recede — to 22% in 1983 and to below 20% by 1987.

● After a decade of tax-flation in which fiscal and monetary excess fueled the unrelenting rise of prices and the automatic increase of taxes, significant tax rate reductions have been enacted. A permanent safeguard against bracket creep and Government profiteering on inflation — income tax indexing — has also been created.

● Where Government had passively tolerated the swift, continuous growth of automatic entitlements and had actively shortchanged the national security, a long-overdue reordering of priorities has begun, entitlement growth is being checked, and the restoration of our defenses is underway.

The Budget Totals

[In billions of dollars]

	1981 actual	1982 estimate	1983 estimate	1984 estimate	1985 estimate
Budget receipts	599.3	626.8	666.1	723.0	796.6
Budget outlays	657.2	725.3	757.6	805.9	868.5
Surplus or deficit (−)	− 57.9	− 98.6	− 91.5	− 82.9	− 71.9
Budget authority	718.4	765.5	801.9	858.0	943.5

This dramatic progress in reordering fiscal policy has been paralleled by a similar redirection of monetary policy. The excessive, unsustainable, and eventually ruinous growth of money and credit of the past decade has been curbed. The inflation spiral has been broken. The growth of prices is slowing down. Peoples' savings are beginning to flow out of unproductive speculation, tangible assets, and other inflation hedges back into the Nation's financial arteries where they will be available to power economic recovery, more jobs, and growing incomes and opportunities.

In short, we are putting the false prosperity of overspending, easy credit, depreciating money, and financial excess behind us. A solid foundation has been laid for a sound dollar, sustained real economic growth, lasting financial stability, and noninflationary prosperity for all Americans.

We are also moving to shackle the regulatory juggernaut that burdened production, consumed jobs, and diminished productivity growth. During the past year no significant new regulatory statutes were enacted and few major new regulations were imposed. Additions to the Federal Register declined by 23,000 pages. Benefit-cost analysis was made mandatory for regulations. Dozens of existing regulations were reviewed, modified, or eliminated. Without taking into account billions of dollars of savings from regulations never formally proposed because of the changed climate our program has created, quantifiable one-time cost savings of over $3 billion and recurring annual savings of nearly $2 billion have been realized. And the effort has just begun.

A Year of Historic Achievement

These remarkable achievements are the cornerstones of our national economic recovery program. They far exceed anything that the skeptics and critics ever dreamed possible just 1 year ago. They occurred because the executive and legislative branches of our Government joined together to respond to the mandate of the American people and overcome the impediments that had paralyzed Washington for a decade. Together, we have launched a process of reform and change that can transform the course of events.

The Economic Recovery Tax Act of 1981 is the largest, most comprehensive, and most constructive tax bill ever adopted. With the cooperation of the Congress and support of the public, it was enacted in just 5 months. It addressed and substantially remedied most of the tax system's shortcomings and disincentives that had accumulated over decades — distortions that were imposing an increasingly heavy toll on investment, economic growth, and job creation.

● The penalty tax rate on investment income has been eliminated. By dropping the top rate from 70 to 50%, the attractiveness of tax shelters will be reduced and the incentives for productive investment in stocks, bonds, new business ventures, and other financial assets will be increased. Our Nation's capital will again flow to the growth of business and jobs rather than to the vendors of protection from punitive taxation.

● Marginal tax rates have been significantly lowered for the first time in two decades. The 23% across-the-board rate reduction will mean $183 billion in lower taxes for individuals over the first 3 years. The financial reward for savings, work effort, and new production will stop diminishing and start rising once again.

● Powerful new incentives for savings have been established. Beginning this year, 50 million workers will be eligible for the first time to set aside tax-free up to $2,000 per year for Individual Retirement Accounts. The annual limit for existing Keogh and IRA investors will also be raised. By sharply altering the incentives for saving as opposed to consumption, a huge new flow of current income will be channeled toward restoring our productivity and lifting our national savings rate from last place in the industrial world.

• The taxation of phantom corporate profits has also been significantly curtailed. The new accelerated cost recovery system will shorten depreciation periods to 5 years for machinery and 15 years for structures. This will permit fuller recovery of asset costs, a more valid accounting of taxable profits, and a reasonable after-tax return on investments for the first time in years. By eliminating the drastic under-depreciation provided in previous tax law, after-tax business cash flow will be increased by $10 1/2 billion this year and $211 billion over the next 6 years. This growing stream of funds for modernization, new machinery, new technology, new products, and new plants will revive our lagging productivity, restore our competitiveness in world markets, and spur the steady growth of jobs, production, and real incomes.

• The confiscatory taxing of estates and inheritances has been halted as well. By raising the exemption to $600,000, by lowering the rate to 50%, and by removing the limits on the marital deduction, 99.7% of all estates will eventually be exempt from estate taxation. Hard-working American farmers, small businessmen, investors, and workers can once again be confident that the sweat, sacrifices, and accumulations of a lifetime will belong to their heirs rather than their Government.

• Government profiteering on inflation has been abolished. Beginning in 1985, the individual income tax brackets, the zero-bracket amount, and the personal exemption will be corrected annually for inflation. Bracket creep will never again systematically plunder the rewards for production and effort. Government will never again use inflation to take a rising share of the peoples' income without a vote of their representatives.

The past year's achievements on spending control and the reestablishment of budgetary discipline are no less impressive than the sweeping tax changes. For the first time ever, the Congress activated its central budgetary machinery and overcame the spending impulses of its fragmented parts. The Omnibus Budget Reconciliation Act of 1981 was a watershed in fiscal history — a giant step toward the restoration of fiscal discipline. By the accounting of its own Congressional Budget Office, spending will be $35 billion lower this year and about $130 billion lower over the next 3 years due to just one bill passed in only 5 months after having been considered by 30 different committees, a bill that reduced, reformed or eliminated hundreds of programs. The growth of budgetary outlays is at last being brought in line with the growth of the tax base and the national income. Excess spending commitments, unnecessary programs and overlapping activities were meaningfully addressed in the Reconciliation Act for the first time in decades.

• As a result of congressional action in 1981, the growth of entitlements will be reduced by $41 billion during the next 3 years. For the first time, eligibility standards for food stamps and student loans have been tightened. Unemployment benefits have been targeted to States where they are needed. Subsidies for non-needy students have been reduced in the school lunch program. Abuses of the medicaid, nutrition, and AFDC programs have been curtailed, saving $14.4 billion over the next 3 years. Overly generous and unaffordable twice-a-year cost-of-living adjustments for Federal retirees have been eliminated. The "uncontrollables" are being brought under control, and benefits have been retargeted where they are most needed.

• Dozens of ineffective or counter-productive programs have been eliminated or reduced. The $4 billion make-work CETA public sector jobs program was abolished. Extravagant dairy subsidies have been cut substantially. The ineffective $700 million Economic Development Administration is being phased out. The Community Services Administration has been eliminated. An unnecessary $2 billion in Government subsidies for new energy supplies and technologies has been cut. The excessively-funded impact aid program was substantially scaled back. In short, a long-overdue housecleaning of excess budgetary commitments was accomplished.

• Inappropriate Federal subsidies have been withdrawn. Legislation to return Conrail to the private sector has been enacted. The National Consumer Cooperative Bank has been privatized. Subsidies to the auto industry for new technology demonstrations have been eliminated. Operating subsidies to local mass transit systems are being phased out. Subsidies to exporters have been sharply curtailed. Subsidized disaster loans to financially viable businesses have been eliminated.

• A major stride toward rationalizing the structure, reducing the cost, and increasing State and local flexibility in the Nation's $91 billion grant-in-aid system has been enacted. Fifty-seven narrow, redtape-ridden categorical grants programs have been replaced with 9 block grants. The pages of regulation imposed on State and local governments have been reduced from over 300 to 6, while the cost to the Federal budget has been reduced.

• Total funding for nondefense discretionary programs has been reduced. After continuous growth for two decades, the budget cost of these programs will actually decline from $137 billion in 1981 to $130 billion in 1982.

• An impressive start at reducing fraud, waste, abuse, and unnecessary Government overhead was made. The President's Council on Integrity and Efficiency, established to coordinate a Government-wide attack on fraud and waste, saved $2 billion in the last 6 months of 1981 alone. A comprehensive effort to collect $33 billion in delinquent debts has been launched and will recover $1.5 billion in 1982 and $4.0 billion in 1983. These estimates include recoveries of delinquent taxes due to the Internal Revenue Service. Federal nondefense employment has been reduced by 35,000 since January 1981. The cost of Government travel, publications, and consultants has been reduced substantially.

At the same time that the Congress joined in these long-overdue efforts to pare back the size of the Federal budget and slow its momentum of growth, it has fully supported our ambitious but essential plan to rebuild our national defense. A year ago every component of military strength was flashing warning lights of neglect, under-investment, and deteriorating capability. Today, health is being restored.

● Pervasive deficiencies in readiness — including too many units not ready for combat, too many weapons systems out of commission, too few people with critical combat skills, and too few planes and ships fully capable of their missions — are being corrected. Funds for operations and maintenance, including training and aircraft flying hours, have been boosted. Backlogs of combat equipment needing repair are being eliminated. Adequate supplies of spare parts necessary to support high operating rates for training, as well as to provide war reserves, are being purchased.

● The serious inadequacy in pay and benefits that threatened the all-volunteer force, caused an exodus of skilled personnel, and sapped morale throughout the armed services has been corrected. Last year's 14.3% pay increase has improved recruit quality, boosted reenlistment rates, stopped the drain of critical skills, and contributed to the dramatic revival of morale in our military services. End-strength goals are now being exceeded. In addition, the percentage of recruits with higher test scores has risen in the past year.

● Critical investments in conventional and strategic force modernization are now moving rapidly forward. A new bomber for early deployment and an advanced (Stealth) bomber for the 1990's have been approved to retain our capability to penetrate Soviet air defenses. Development of a new, larger, and more accurate MX missile to preserve our land-based deterrent is proceeding. A 5-year shipbuilding program including 133 new ships and a total investment of $96 billion — double the 5-year program of the previous administration — has been launched. Rapid production of new combat systems including the M-1 Abrams tank, the AV-8B Marine Corps attack aircraft and the F/A-18 Navy tactical fighter have been approved. Improvements in our airlift and sealift forces to transport equipment and soldiers rapidly to counter military aggression anywhere in the world, are moving forward.

No Time to Retreat

These achievements of the first year truly constitute a new beginning. In every major dimension of national strength and well-being we have launched the redirection of policy that was so desperately needed and so long overdue. We are ending the destructive inflation and the financial disorder built up over a decade. We have removed the yoke of over-taxation from our workers and our business enterprises. We have begun to dismantle the regulatory straitjacket that impeded our commerce and sapped our prosperity. And we have reversed the dangerous erosion of our military capabilities.

The task before us now is a different one, but no less crucial. Our task is to persevere; to stay the course; to shun retreat; to weather the temporary dislocations and pressures that must inevitably accompany the restoration of national economic, fiscal, and military health.

The correction of previous fiscal and monetary excesses has come too late to avert an unwelcome, painful, albeit temporary business slump. In the months ahead there will be temptation to resort to pump-priming and spending stimulus programs. Such efforts have failed in the past, are not needed now, and must be resisted at every turn. Our program for permanent economic recovery is already in place. Artificial stimulants will undermine that program, not reinforce it.

Likewise, previous excesses in money and credit growth have resulted in financial strain in many regions and sectors of our national economy. The adjustment to lower inflation and a more moderate money and credit policy did not come soon enough to avoid interest rates and unemployment far higher than we would like, and that we are working to reduce. But these effects are temporary. They cannot be remedied by a return to rapid, unsustainable expansion of Federal spending and money growth, which would drive inflation and interest rates to new highs. Our hard-won gains in reducing inflation must be preserved and extended — because permanent reduction of interest rates and unemployment is impossible if the fight against inflation is abandoned, just when it is being won.

Similarly, our budget deficits will be large because of the current recession, and because it is impossible in a short period of time to correct the mistakes of decades. But our incentive-minded tax policy and our security-based defense programs are right and necessary for long-run peace and prosperity, and must not be tampered with in a vain attempt to cure deficits in the short-run. The answer to deficits is economic growth and indefatigable efforts to control spending and borrowing. These principles we dare not abandon.

The Deficit Problem: Its Origins

Despite the new course we have charted and the gains we have achieved, the voices of doubt, retreat and rejection are beginning to rise. They conveniently forget that the present business slump was not caused by our program but is the result of the accumulated burdens of past policy errors, which we have taken action to redress. They fail to comprehend that our spending cuts and tax reductions were not designed to redistribute the output of a stagnant economy, but to revive the economy's growth and to increase its size — for the jobless as well as the affluent, for those who aspire to get ahead as well as those who have already arrived.

Increasingly, the larger budget deficits that we unavoidably face are offered as evidence that our entire course should be recharted. The matter of budget deficits, therefore, must be addressed squarely. We must fully comprehend why they have grown from our original projections, why they may remain with us for some time to come, what dangers they pose if not vigorously combatted and what steps we can and must take to steadily reduce their size and drain on our available savings.

Our original plan called for a balanced budget in 1984. Balance is no longer achievable in 1984, but the factors that have postponed its realization are neither permanent nor cause for abandoning the goal of eventually living within our means.

In the near term, the most important setback to our budgetary timetable is the recession now underway. During 1982, receipts will decline by $31 billion and outlays rise by $8 billion due to the falloff of business activity and the increase of unemployment-related payments. This factor alone accounts for nearly all of the difference between the $45 billion 1982 deficit we projected last year and our current estimate of $98.6 billion.

While the recession will end before this fiscal year is over, its budgetary impact will spill over for many years into the future. It will take time for the unemployment rate to come down and safety net payments to diminish. The growth of receipts will recover, but not at the levels previously projected. This will add billions to deficits for 1983 and 1984.

The second major factor widening the deficit projection is interest payments on our trillion dollar debt. Here we are being penalized doubly for the misguided policies of the past.

The discredited philosophy of spend and spend, borrow and borrow, saddled us with a permanent debt burden of staggering dimensions. This year's interest payment of $83 billion exceeds the size of the entire Federal budget as recently as 1958.

In addition, past fiscal, monetary, and credit excesses have resulted in temporarily high interest rates — rates that will come down, but only as inflation abates, private and public financing practices adjust, and long-term confidence rebuilds. Since market confidence has been so badly shaken by runaway inflation and interest rates in the past 3 years, it is apparent that interest rates over the next several years will fall less rapidly than we had originally anticipated. Between the huge inherited base of national debt, the high interest rates, and the large prospective additions to the national debt in the next several years, our total debt service costs will rise substantially.

Interest payments on the debt will exceed our original projections by $18 billion in 1982, $32 billion in 1983, and $182 billion over 1982-86 taken as a whole. The interest rate/debt service factor, then, constitutes a major source of the setback to our budget timetable. But let us be clear about its origins: it arises primarily from a legacy of past excesses, not from a shortfall in our current budget control effects, nor from a flaw in our overall program.

The third and most important factor contributing to the growth in deficit projections is quite simply the ironic by-product of our rapid and decisive success in bringing down the rate of inflation. Our economic forecast last February projected a 9.5% inflation rate in calendar year 1981 and a further decline to 7.7% in 1982. This projection was scorned by many as too rosy just 1 year ago. Yet the actual inflation rate in 1981 turned out to be lower than our projection, and the inflation decline this year and next year almost certainly will exceed our earlier projections.

This is welcome news to every American and we have adjusted our inflation forecast accordingly. But lower rates of price increase also mean lower inflation components in wages and incomes and a reduced flow of inflation-swollen tax receipts to the Treasury.

This point is not merely academic. Over the next 5 years, our forecast projects a 9.9% average rate of growth in nominal GNP reflecting a steady fall of inflation to about 4 1/2% by 1987. If nominal GNP growth were just 2% higher each year, reflecting a continuation of higher inflation, Federal receipts would be enlarged by the staggering sum of $353 billion over the 5 years. On paper, at least, the budget would be nearly balanced in 1987 rather than more than $50 billion in deficit.

But if the last decade offers any lesson, it is that we cannot inflate our way to budget balance. Indeed, every budget from 1975 forward projected a balanced budget 2 years into the future and growing surpluses in the out-years. Not one of these surpluses materialized for a very compelling reason: the monetary excesses needed to finance inflationary growth of wages and incomes are the enemy of savings, investment, real economic growth, and fundamental business confidence and financial stability. They lead to the kind of pervasive economic breakdown that we experienced during 1979-81 — a breakdown that swells Government spending, interrupts the flow of receipts, and causes prospective budgetary surpluses to vanish in a flow of red ink.

Thus, we cannot and will not pursue the will-o'-the-wisp of reflation nor the phantom of future budget surpluses premised on a continuance of high inflation.

Instead, we must recognize that for a period of time, success in our unyielding battle against inflation will appear to work against our goal of a balanced budget. Thus, while our current revenues will reflect the decline of inflation today, part of our current outlays will reflect the higher rates of inflation in years past. This is especially true in the case of some $249 billion in indexed programs. Generally, the inflation rate used to adjust indexed benefits lags a year or more behind the current payment period. During 1983, for example, an inflation rate of 6.5% is projected, but cost-of-living adjustments to social security and other program benefits will be 8.1% based largely on the actual inflation experience of 1981. Much the same is true of the $96.4 billion in debt service for 1983. Some part of that will reflect the higher cost of debt securities issued in 1980-82 when inflation and interest rates will have been higher than is now projected for 1983.

Thus, the conquest of inflation will contribute to budgetary imbalance for some years to come. But these deficits will prove manageable if we understand why we have them and redouble our efforts to reduce them.

The final factor contributing to the worsening of the deficit outlook is that all of the budget savings we had planned for last year were not actually achieved. Most importantly, our plan to ensure the short- and long-run solvency of social security was discarded by the Congress. In an effort to eliminate partisanship and facilitate movement toward a constructive solution, our reform proposal has been withdrawn in favor of a bipartisan commission charged with developing a plan to rescue the social security system by next fall. I am confident that the commission will do just that, but in the meanwhile our outlay projections must be increased by $6 billion in 1983 and $18 billion for 1987.

Likewise, the Congress failed to adopt all of the reforms we proposed for medicaid, guaranteed student loans, food stamps and other entitlements. Without further action, about $4 billion would be added to the 1983 deficit in these areas alone. While major and unprecedented action was taken to curb the growth of entitlements last year, the shortfall is still substantial. Entitlement reforms not acted upon by the Congress last year will add nearly $20 billion to the deficit over the next 3 years. When this is combined with substantial added outlays for farm subsidies and for discretionary programs that were not reformed, it is clear that the task of budget control is far from complete.

The Budget Deficit in Perspective

Taken together, the effects of recession, higher interest rates, declining inflation, and incomplete congressional action will mean high, continuing, and troublesome Federal budget deficits. Constant vigilance and relentless efforts to pare back future spending and borrowing will be imperative to ensure that they are not permitted to worsen and add further pressure to financial markets and interest rates.

Nevertheless, three features of these high deficit numbers must not be lost sight of even as we seek eventually to eliminate them.

First, even the 1982 deficit of $98.6 billion is not unprecedented in the context of a recession and recovery cycle. Relative to the present size of the U.S. economy, the budget deficit would have been $94 billion for 1975, followed by deficits of $139 billion, $91 billion and $97 billion in the next 3 years, respectively.

Second, these deficits reflect the excess spending commitments of past rather than new spending programs with potential to grow in the future. That means that by remaining firm in our efforts to reduce waste and excess, reform entitlements, reduce low priority spending, and gradually return domestic programs back to State and local governments, the gap between spending subject to firm fiscal discipline and revenues being lifted by steady economic expansion will gradually diminish.

Finally, the share of GNP taken in taxes will be substantially lower and the incentives for savings markedly stronger. This expansion of the total savings supply will increase our capacity to absorb deficits and give us additional time to work toward their elimination.

$239 Billion Deficit Reduction Plan

The prospect of high deficits during the transition to strong economic growth and low inflation contains a profound warning: any relaxation of our budget control efforts, any backsliding to spending politics as usual, any retreat to time-worn excuses about "uncontrollables" — that results in spending growth significantly above our projections, will mean a serious threat to the progress of our entire economic recovery program. There is precious little margin for shirking or diluting the task the American people have charged us with. That task is nothing less than a constant, comprehensive, ceaseless search for ways to reduce the size of Government and the future growth of its spending.

The 1983 budget I am presenting to the Congress faithfully adheres to that mandate. If all proposed measures are adopted, the prospective deficit will be reduced by $56 billion next year, $84 billion in 1984, and $99 billion in 1985. In short, the budget this year represents much more than simply a tabulation of accounts or a compilation of spending decisions, large and small. Instead, it represents a far-reaching, resourceful, and integrated blueprint for reducing the prospective deficit by $239 billion over the next 3 years. It is a bold action plan that, if faithfully implemented, can cut the prospective deficits over that period by nearly 50%.

Our plan for deficit reduction consists of five parts. It addresses each area of the budget where actions to reduce the gap between spending and revenues are possible and desirable.

The first area concerns nonsocial security entitlements. Despite the heartening progress we made toward reform last year, the cost of these automatic spending programs will rise to $201 billion in 1983 without further action. This figure compares to only $119 billion in 1979.

Thus, our 1983 budget proposals continue the objective set out previously: to reduce the swift growth of automatic entitlements while preserving benefits for the truly needy. If acted upon fully by the Congress, these new reform measures will save $12 billion next year and $52 billion over the next 3 years. They include new steps to tighten eligibility, reduce errors and abuse and curtail unwarranted benefits in the welfare, medical, and nutrition programs. The explosive growth of medical programs — 16.7% per year since 1978 — will be contained with tighter reimbursement standards for providers, modest copayment requirements for medicaid beneficiaries, and, later in the year, a comprehensive plan to reform the health care reimbursement system and provide new cost control incentives for all participants. We have also proposed measures to target guaranteed student loans better to those with financial need and to limit the cost growth of Federal military and civilian retirement programs.

Nevertheless, let me be clear on this point. Our administration has not and will not turn its back on our elderly or needy citizens. Under our new budget, funding for social insurance programs will be more than double the amount spent only 6 years ago. For example, the Federal Government will subsidize 95 million meals every day. That is one of every seven of all meals served in America. Headstart, senior nutrition programs, and child welfare programs will not be cut from the levels we proposed last year.

The second component of our deficit reduction plan covers domestic discretionary and other programs for purposes ranging from agricultural research to housing subsidies and manpower training. Our proposed savings here total $14 billion next year and $76 billion over the next 3 years.

These savings measures involve two essential principles. First, where programs are unnecessary, can be better targeted or can be significantly streamlined, we have proposed substantial reductions. Our proposals to convert the fragmented and wasteful CETA training program to a block grant, to target low-income energy assistance to the colder States where it is needed, to combine the WIC program with the child and maternal health block grant, and to further reduce subsidies to business for energy technology development and commercialization are all examples of this principle.

The other principle governing discretionary programs is that we have generally not provided inflation allowances for them. This will provide a powerful incentive to reduce overhead, waste, and low-priority activities and ensure that the money we spend for many worthwhile purposes in the areas of education, transportation, community development, and research is utilized in the most efficient and productive manner possible. Our deficit problem is simply too severe to permit business as usual to continue any longer.

The third component of the deficit reduction program involves user fees, or more appropriately, the recovery of costs borne by the taxpayers generally, but that predominantly benefit a limited group of businesses, communities or individuals. Total savings would amount to $2.5 billion in 1983 and $10 billion over the next 3 years.

While the Congress made great strides on most of our proposed budget cuts last year, the user fees proposals were a noticeable and disappointing departure from this pattern. The case for action now is even stronger than it was last year. With sacrifices required of almost every beneficiary of Federal programs, it is simply inexcusable and intolerable that yacht owners escape without paying even a small part of the Coast Guard services; or that commercial and general aviation are not paying the cost of the air traffic control system that ensures their safety; or that ship and barge operators do not pay a fair share of the costs of waterways maintained by the Federal Government. Our user fee package corrects these and similar shortcomings in current budget policy and will contribute signifcantly toward reducing the deficit.

The fourth part of the plan is aimed at the executive branch and the most inexcusable of all forms of spending: lax management, the toleration of fraud and abuse, the failure to recover debts owed the Government or to dispose of properties it does not need, and outdated, inefficient, procurement practices.

Our fiscal plan has always assumed that our new management would take hold, and that savings would be possible in areas we have simply never looked at before. After 1 year, our new management team has indeed taken hold, the results to date have been impressive, and our plans for future savings are bold and far-reaching. All told, these efforts will reduce the budget deficit by $20 billion next year and $68 billion over the next 3 years.

We will collect the debts we are owed and the taxes we are due. New legislation will be needed in some cases, but much of these savings will flow from tighter, more aggressive management throughout executive branch agencies.

Likewise, we will move systematically to reduce the vast Federal holdings of surplus land and real property. It is estimated that the Federal Government owns approximately 775 million acres, and 405,000 buildings, covering about 2.6 billion square feet. Some of this real property is not in use and would be of greater value to society if transferred to the private sector. During the next 3 years we will save $9 billion by shedding these unnecessary properties while fully protecting and preserving our national parks, forests, wildernesses and scenic areas.

Our management efforts will also be directed toward the more cost-effective procurement of the goods and services required by the Federal Government. The changes we seek will increase competition for the Government's business, reduce and simplify paperwork and regulations, and develop better standards for our procurement processes and personnel. Over time these efforts will yield large outyear savings not included in the budget totals.

Finally, our emphasis thus far has been on reducing excessive tax rates and shrinking the Government's take from the paychecks of workers and the profits of business. On that principle we will not waver. But that does not mean unintended loopholes should go uncorrected, that obsolete tax incentives should be continued, or that profitable business should not contribute at least some minimum fair share to the cost of financing Government. Thus, our deficit reduction plan includes $34 billion over the next 3 years in additional receipts from new initiatives in these areas.

About one-third of this total is attributable to our proposal to strengthen the minimum corporate tax, and a substantial share of the other tax revisions will also affect business. In every case, these measures involve the collection of a tax that is owed now or that was intended by the Congress, or elimination of incentives that are no longer needed due to the sweeping reform of business taxation contained in the Economic Recovery Act of 1981.

These new proposals will have no adverse impact on our economic recovery program, are fair and equitable, and will contribute significantly to the reduction of future deficits.

[Restoration of National Defense]

Our 1983 budget plan continues the effort begun last year to strengthen our military posture in four primary areas: strategic forces, combat readiness, force mobility, and general purpose forces.

A thorough 8-month review of U.S. strategic forces and objectives preceded my decision this past October to strengthen our strategic forces.

The review found that the relative imbalance with the Soviet Union will be at its worst in the mid-1980's and hence needs to be addressed quickly. It also concluded that the multiple protective structure basing proposal for MX did not provide long-term survivability since the Soviets could counter it (at about the same cost) by simply deploying more warheads.

In addition, our review pointed to serious deficiencies in force survivability, endurance, and the capability to exercise command and control during nuclear war. Current communications and warning systems were found to be vulnerable to severe disruption from an attack of very modest scale.

The 1983 budget funds programs to correct these deficiencies. The 1983 strategic program of $23.1 billion, an increase of $6.9 billion over 1982, provides for both near-term improvements and longer-term programs. These initiatives include:

● Early deployment of cruise missiles on existing bombers and attack submarines.

● Acquisition of a new bomber (the B-1B) and development of advanced technology (Stealth) bomber for deployment in the 1990's to provide a continued capability to penetrate Soviet defenses.

● Development and procurement of a new, larger, and more accurate land-based missile, the MX.

● Continued deployment of Trident ballistic missile submarines to strengthen the sea-based leg of our strategic deterrent.

Longer-term programs include: development of a survivable deployment plan for the MX missile, development of a new submarine-launched ballistic missile, continued improvements in the survivability of warning and communications systems, and improvements in strategic defenses against both bomber and missile attacks.

The 1983 budget provides $114.3 billion in operations and military personnel costs, an increase of over $13 billion from the 1982 level to improve the combat readiness of our forces.

Today a major conflict involving the United States could occur without adequate time to upgrade U.S. force readiness. Our concerns with military readiness reflect both the long lead time required to procure sophisticated equipment (both parts and finished equipment) and past failures to provide adequate peacetime support for combat units. We cannot wait for a period of rising tensions before bringing forces up to combat readiness.

My program will continue to bolster combat readiness by increasing training, operating rates, and equipment support. There will be increased aircraft flying hours and supply inventories. In addition, backlogs of combat equipment and real property awaiting maintenance will be reduced. Also, the 1983 budget will provide levels of military compensation that will improve the readiness and capability of the All Volunteer Force.

Current U.S. mobility forces cannot move the required combat or combat support units fast enough to counter effectively military aggression in Europe, Korea or in the Southwest Asia/Persian Gulf region. For example, at present only a small light combat force could be moved rapidly to the Southwest Asia region. Major mobility shortages include wide-body military cargo aircraft; fast logistics ships; and prepositioned ships and associated support equipment. Elimination of these shortages is an essential first step toward improving U.S. military capability during the first 30 days after the beginning of a crisis.

The 1983 budget provides $4.4 billion for:

• Initial procurement of a fleet of improved C-5 cargo aircraft, and additional KC-10A tanker/cargo aircraft that will double our wide-bodied military airlift capability by the 1990's.

• Continued upgrading of existing C-5A aircraft to extend their effectiveness beyond the year 2000.

• Conversion of four additional fast logistic ships that will provide the capability to move heavy combat forces rapidly.

• Chartering a fleet of supply ships that can be stationed with equipment and supplies in Southwest Asia to reduce the time required for deployment of heavy forces.

In the last decade, the Soviet Union introduced large quantities of highly capable, new-generation tactical equipment including combat ships, tanks and aircraft, which must be countered by modernized U.S. forces. Also, the traditional U.S. superiority in system quality has been considerably narrowed, making Soviet quantitative advantages more serious. The Soviet military force buildup has increased the risk that they may rely on military power to support their foreign policy goals. For the U.S. to maintain, in concert with our allies, sufficient conventional forces to deter potential aggression, our forces must be provided with adequate numbers of new, modern tactical equipment.

My 1983 budget includes $106.2 billion for general purpose forces (including both operations and investment), and $18 billion increase over 1982. A key initiative is an expanded shipbuilding program. The United States, dependent on open seas for commerce and military resupply, must have the naval capability to maintain control of vital sea lanes. While our naval forces have declined from the mid-1960's, the Soviets have in existence or under construction eight new classes of submarines and eight new classes of major surface warships, including nuclear-powered cruisers and new aircraft carriers.

The budget provides an $18.6 billion shipbuilding program including full funding for two nuclear-powered aircraft carriers, to be constructed during 1983-87. Other ships included in my 1983 program are three large cruisers equipped with an advanced air defense system; two nuclear-powered attack submarines; two frigates for convoy protection and four mine countermeasure ships to improve fleet capability to operate in mined waters. My longer term objective is to increase the deployable battle force from 513 ships in 1982 to over 600 by the end of the decade.

In addition, the budget provides for increased production of ground and tactical air force weapons. Production rates will be increased for a variety of new systems such as the M-1 Abrams tank, light armored vehicles, and the AV-8B Marine corps attack aircraft.

All of this will be done with a major reform of the acquisition process and vastly improved management of defense operations, which will save $51 billion by 1987. In a continuing fight against fraud, waste, and inefficiency, the Secretary of Defense has appointed an Assistant for Review and Oversight and a Council on Integrity and Management Improvement.

[American Federalism]

The Constitution provides clear distinctions between the roles of the Federal Government and of the States and localities. In their wisdom, our founding fathers provided for considerable flexibility so that in following centuries these responsibilities could be adapted to new conditions. But in recent years we have not adapted well to new conditions. We have created confusion as to who is responsible for what. During the past 20 years, what had been a classic division of functions between the Federal Government and the States and localities has become a confused mess. Traditional understandings about the roles of each level of government have been violated.

Governments at all levels have had and will continue to face various problems. But, as Governor of California, I learned that a problem in one part of the country does not automatically mean that we need a new Federal program in all 50 States. Yet that is what has happened.

In 1964, total Federal grants to State and local governments were $10 billion. By 1980, total Federal grants to States and localities exceeded $90 billion, meaning that 18% of Federal tax receipts were being passed through to States and localities for one reason or another. However, these funds were not passed through entirely benignly. Attached to them were Federal rules, mandates, and requirements. This massive Federal grantmaking system has distorted State and local decisions and usurped State and local functions.

I propose that over the coming years we clean up this mess. I am proposing a major effort to restore American federalism. This transition over nearly 10 years will give States and localities the time they need to plan for themselves when and how to meet State and local needs that are now being met with Federal Government funds. My proposal will also make available to the States and localities the tax resources that would otherwise fund these programs by the Federal Government.

In coming weeks, we will have intensive discussions with local and State officials, the Congress, and many others to hammer out a proposal I will soon send to the Congress. Essentially, I believe the Federal Government should assume full responsibility for the medicaid program which assures adequate health care for the poor. In contrast, financial assistance to the poor is a legitimate responsibility of States and localities. I am proposing, therefore, that the aid to families with dependent children (AFDC) and food stamp programs be turned over to the States. This swap will clarify responsibilities substantially because these programs will become the clear responsibility of one level of government or another. That responsibility is now mixed.

In addition, I propose that more than 40 current grant-in-aid programs costing the Federal Government about $30 billion a year be turned back to the States and localities, along with the funds to pay for them. During the period 1984-87, these programs will be funded by a specially designated set of taxes to be used exclusively for financing this transition program. These taxes will be deposited in a fund that will belong to the States. Each State will be able to make its own decision on how rapidly to phase out the turnback programs. This is because each State will have two options: it may use its share of the federalism trust fund to reimburse Federal agencies for continuing to carry out turnback programs, or it may ask that the programs be terminated and then use the funds directly for whatever purposes it desires.

Beginning in 1987, the federalism trust fund will gradually be dissolved and the tax sources themselves will be made available to the States.

The key to this program is that the States and localities make the critical choices. They have the time to make them in an orderly way. A major sorting out of Federal, State and local responsibilities will occur, and the Federal presence and intervention in State and local affairs will gradually diminish.

Conclusion

While some administration proposals have been turned down, turned aside, or compromised by the Congress, the overall assessment of the past year's action on the budget is heartening. Cooperation, support, goodwill, and a genuine sense of national purpose have enabled us to make significant progress in setting the Federal Government's affairs in order and America on the road to economic recovery.

I urge the Congress to approach the new, or renewed, proposals in this budget in the same spirit and with the same goodwill as it did my proposals of a year ago. Much has been accomplished. This budget proposes that more be done.

The proposals set forth in this budget will not be accepted readily. They are a second challenging installment of a politically difficult, yet necessary, program. In their specifics, these proposals will undoubtedly be altered by the Congress. The general direction we must travel, however, is clear. I urge the Congress to weigh these budget proposals thoughtfully, and to join me, and my administration, in a constructive effort to curb the growth of Federal spending and to provide for the Nation's security. We must, in the end, roll up our sleeves, face our responsibilities squarely, and persevere at the unending task of setting, and keeping, the Nation's affairs in order.

SURGEON GENERAL'S REPORT ON SMOKING AND CANCER

February 22, 1982

The surgeon general's annual report on smoking and health, released February 22, focused solely on smoking and the development of cancer in one of the strongest indictments of cigarettes since the landmark report by the Surgeon General's Advisory Committee on Smoking and Health in 1962. The link between smoking and cancer had been the subject of extensive scientific research ever since.

The 1982 report, The Health Consequences of Smoking: Cancer, *said that cigarette smoking was the "major single cause of cancer mortality in the United States" and "the chief preventable cause of illness and premature death in the nation," resulting in 340,000 "potentially avoidable" cancer deaths annually.*

The list of cancers caused directly by smoking included not only cancer of the lung, but also of the mouth, larynx and esophagus. Smoking was determined a "contributory factor" in cancer of the bladder, kidney and pancreas. The report also noted an association between smoking and stomach and cervical cancer and it called for further research in these areas. In many cases, the use of alcohol in conjunction with smoking was said to increase the risk of these cancers.

According to the report, "30 percent of all deaths are attributable to smoking and lung cancer caused by smoking constituted 25 percent of all cancer deaths. A male smoker was two times more likely to die of cancer than a non-smoking male; a similar statistic was said to exist for females. In the coming five years, lung cancer was expected to overtake breast cancer as the leading fatal cancer among women. The report stated that smoking filtered or lower tar cigarettes decreased only slightly the risk of cancer. (Historic Documents of 1981, p. 3)

The report shed little light on the effects of "passive" smoking — the inhalation of tobacco smoke by a non-smoker — or on non-smokers' rights. There was thus far no conclusive evidence that this type of smoke inhalation led to the development of cancer. However, according to Assistant Secretary for Health Edward N. Brandt Jr., "prudence dictates that nonsmokers avoid exposure to second-hand tobacco smoke." The report recommended more research on this aspect of smoking.

Reducing the Cancer Risk

The report noted that the single most effective way to reduce the risk of cancer is not to smoke. "It is estimated that 85 percent of lung cancer mortality could have been avoided if individuals never took up smoking," said Surgeon General C. Everett Koop. Furthermore, his report contended that after "fifteen years ... [of] quitting cigarette smoking, the former smoker's lung cancer risk ... is reduced close to that [of] nonsmokers." Studies of smoking habits demonstrated that the "cold turkey" approach to quitting was more effective than were lengthy smoking-cessation programs. According to the report, warning words from the family doctor also provided an incentive for the individual to quit.

The report stressed the importance of informing adolescents on the health consequences of smoking before they start. According to the director of the National Institute on Drug Abuse, Dr. William Pollin, "[C]igarette smoking has greater addictive power than heroin." Social pressures to start smoking among adolescents also were cited as an issue to be studied.

Because it had undergone cutbacks in staff and funding during 1981, the Office of Smoking and Health within the Department of Health and Human Services said it had to count on the cooperation of other groups to help with the task of educating the public on the dangers of smoking. Koop cited the voluntary efforts of non-governmental health groups as an important force in the drive to convince people to join smoking-prevention programs.

Smoking-Prevention Legislation in Congress

The Office of Smoking and Health supported a bill in Congress that would require stronger, more specific warning labels on cigarette packages. The proposed Comprehensive Smoking Prevention Act closely followed recommendations by the Federal Trade Commission in 1981 to replace the general warning on cigarette packages and advertising with specific warnings about the risks of lung cancer, emphysema, birth defects and heart disease.

Despite Reagan administration endorsement of the bill, opposition to it was considerable. Sen. John P. East, R-N.C., termed it "a prohibitional move." Interest groups, such as the Tobacco Institute, contended that the question of smoking as a direct cause of cancer was "still open." Walker Merriman, spokesman for the institute, dismissed as "asinine" the premise that stronger warning labels prevented more people from smoking in a country where 60 million American adults continued to smoke an annual total of 3,850 cigarettes each.

Following is the text of the foreword of The Health Consequences of Smoking: Cancer, *released February 22, 1982, by the Department of Health and Human Services. (Boldface headings in brackets have been added by Congressional Quarterly to highlight the organization of the text.):*

Foreword

The 1982 report on *The Health Consequences of Smoking* presents a comprehensive evaluation of the relationship between cigarette smoking and cancer.

Since 1937, cancer has been the second most important cause of death in the United States and will account for an estimated 430,000 deaths this year. Surveys have shown that Americans fear dying of cancer more than any other disease. We have yet to observe, however, a decline in the cancer mortality rate as is currently occurring for other chronic diseases, such as the 30 percent decline in the cardiovascular disease mortality rate and the 50 percent decline in the cerebrovascular disease mortality rate observed over the last three decades. The mortality rate for cancer has changed little over two decades, and that change has been a small, but measurable, increase. This increase in mortality has occurred in the face of remarkable improvements in survival rates for some cancer sites through earlier or better diagnosis and treatment. Unfortunately, however, these advances have failed to counter the remarkable increases in mortality from smoking-related cancers, many of which have a poor prognosis for long-term survival or cures.

[PUBLIC HEALTH SIGNIFICANCE]

Cigarette smoking is the major single cause of cancer mortality in the United States. Tobacco's contribution to *all* cancer deaths is estimated to be 30 percent. This means we can expect that 129,000 Americans will die of cancer this year because of the higher overall cancer death rates that exist among smokers as compared with nonsmokers. Cigarette smokers have total cancer death rates two times greater than do nonsmokers. Heavy smokers have a three to four times greater excess risk of cancer mortality. If large numbers of our population did not smoke, the cancer death rate in this country could be reduced, and instead of the small but continued increase in the total cancer death rate, there could be a substantial decline. There is no single action an individual can take to reduce the risk of cancer more effectively than quitting smoking, particularly cigarettes.

Cigarette smoking is a major cause of cancers of the lung, larynx, oral cavity, and esophagus, and is a contributory factor for the development of cancers of the bladder, pancreas, and kidney. The term contributory factor by no means excludes the possibility of a causal role for smoking in cancer of these sites.

LUNG CANCER

Lung cancer, first correlated with smoking over 50 years ago, is the single largest contributor to the total cancer death rate. Lung cancer alone accounts for fully 25 percent of all cancer deaths in this country; it is estimated that 85 percent of lung cancer cases are due to cigarette smoking. Overall, smokers are 10 times more likely to die from lung cancer than are nonsmokers. Heavy smokers are 15 to 25 times more at risk than nonsmokers. The total number of lung cancer deaths in the United States increased from 18,313 in 1950 to 90,828 in 1977. The lung cancer death rate for women is currently rising faster than the lung cancer death rate for men, a fact that reflects the later adoption of smoking by large numbers of women. The lung cancer death rate for women will soon surpass that of breast cancer (perhaps as early as next year), currently the leading cause of cancer mortality in women. This remarkable increase in lung cancer mortality for women mimics that observed among men some 30 years ago. However, since the early 1960s, large numbers of men have given up cigarette smoking or have not begun to smoke, whereas only recently has the prevalence of cigarette smoking by women started to decline. These differences in patterns of smoking have a decided effect on lung cancer mortality trends in this country, with a decline in lung cancer mortality already apparent for younger men. These differences will clearly affect lung cancer mortality experience by sex in the United States. The American Cancer Society estimates there will be 111,000 lung cancer-related deaths in 1982, of which 80,000 will be in men and 31,000 in women.

The 5-year survival rate for cancer of the lung is less than 10 percent. This rate has not changed in 20 years. Early diagnosis and treatment do not appreciably alter this dismal survival rate — the best preventive measure a smoker can take to reduce the risk of lung cancer is to quit smoking, and for a nonsmoker, to not take up the habit.

LARYNX AND ORAL CAVITY CANCER

Laryngeal and oral cancers will strike an estimated 40,000 individuals and will be responsible for approximately 13.000 deaths this year in the

United States. These sites have 5-year survival rates of 60 and 40 percent, respectively. An estimated 50 to 70 percent of oral and laryngeal cancer deaths are associated with smoking. These cancers are strongly associated with the use of cigars and pipes in addition to cigarettes. All carry approximately the same excess relative risk of at least fivefold. The use of alcohol in conjunction with smoking acts synergistically to greatly increase the risk of these cancers.

ESOPHAGEAL CANCER

This year, 8,300 deaths due to cancer of the esophagus are expected. Cancer of the esophagus has one of the poorest survival rates of all cancers — only about 4 percent of esophageal cancer patients live 5 years after diagnosis and most die within 6 months. Cigarette smoking is estimated to be a factor in over half of esophageal cancer deaths. Smokers have mortality ratios approximately 4 to 5 times higher than nonsmokers. The use of alcohol has a synergistic interaction with smoking that greatly increases this risk.

BLADDER AND KIDNEY CANCERS

Over 50,000 Americans are expected to develop bladder and kidney cancer this year. Bladder and kidney cancers will be responsible for a total of 20,000 deaths this year. The 5-year survival rates are approximately 50 to 60 percent. Various investigators have estimated that between 30 and 40 percent of bladder cancers are smoking related, with slightly higher estimates for males than for females.

PANCREATIC CANCER

Approximately 24,000 people will develop cancer of the pancreas this year, and there will be an estimated 22,000 deaths. Like cancers of the lung and esophagus, cancer of the pancreas is often fatal, with a 5-year survival of less than 10 percent. While few estimates are available as to the proportion of these deaths attributable to smoking, it would appear to be about 30 percent. Pancreatic cancer appears to be increasing at a more rapid rate than most other cancer sites.

STOMACH AND UTERINE CERVIX CANCER

A link between smoking and stomach cancer and cancer of the uterine cervix is noted. However, no judgment can be reached on the significance of any association, because of insufficient data.

INVOLUNTARY SMOKING AND LUNG CANCER

In recent months, the popular press has generated interest in the controversy of whether passive or involuntary smoking causes lung cancer in nonsmokers. Three epidemiological studies examined this issue in the past year. Evidence from two of the studies demonstrated a statistically significant correlation between involuntary smoking and lung cancer risk in nonsmoking wives of husbands who smoked. A third noted a positive association, but it was not statistically significant. While the nature of this association is unresolved, it does raise the concern that involuntary smoking may pose a carcinogenic risk to the nonsmoker. Any health risk resulting from involuntary smoke exposure is a serious public health concern because of the large numbers of nonsmokers in the population who are potentially exposed. Therefore, for the purpose of preventive medicine, prudence dictates that nonsmokers avoid exposure to second-hand tobacco smoke to the extent possible.

LOWER TAR CIGARETTES

This report also notes that smokers who use filtered or lower tar cigarettes have statistically lower death rates from lung cancer than do cigarette smokers who use nonfiltered or higher tar brands. This reduced risk was also noted for laryngeal cancer. However, cancer death rates for smokers of lower tar cigarettes were still significantly higher than those noted for nonsmokers.

CESSATION OF SMOKING

Since cigarette smoking is a cause of many cancers, encouraging data about cessation are presented in this Report. Quitting smoking reduces one's cancer risk substantially, compared with the continuing smoker, even after many years of cigarette smoking. The more years one is off cigarettes, the greater the reduction in excess cancer risk. Fifteen years after quitting cigarette smoking, the former smoker's lung cancer risk, for example, is reduced close to that observed in nonsmokers. This same reduction in cancer risk is observed for the other cancer sites associated with smoking.

Part V of this Report contains a review of cessation research among adults and adolescents. In summary, many promising techniques are available to smokers who have been unable to quit on their own. It is nonetheless interesting to note that the vast majority of former smokers, probably close to 95 percent, quit on their own, without the aid of formal smoking cessation programs.

As a physician, I encourage all health care providers, particularly other physicians, to counsel cigarette smokers to quit and to give them as much support as possible. As this Report notes, a few minutes' discussion with patients about their smoking behavior can have a decisive impact on whether they quit smoking or continue the habit.

TRENDS IN SMOKING PREVALENCE

I am encouraged by the recent decline in cigarette smoking rates in this country. Today, only one-third of adults smoke, a decline from 42 percent in 1965. Teenage smoking, particularly among adolescent girls, also appears to be declining.

While these figures are encouraging, there are still 53 million cigarette smokers in this country — about the same number of smokers as 20 years ago.

Furthermore, while per capita use of cigarettes has declined to its lowest level since 1957, there has been a substantial increase in the consumption of chewing tobacco and snuff, particularly among the young. What impact the use of these products will have on future cancer mortality is unclear; knowledge of the type and extent of the health effects of these tobacco products is limited. Current evidence indicates, however, that their use is not without risk. Studies conducted in this country and others have demonstrated an increased risk for oral cancer and other noncancerous oral diseases.

EDUCATIONAL EFFORTS

This Department is committed to continuing the programs of education and information for all our citizenry regarding the adverse health consequences of smoking. There is no more important aspect of this than the health education of our young, to convince them not to start smoking, or to quit the habit before it becomes difficult to break.

This problem cannot be left solely to government to solve. I call upon the rest of the health care community, the voluntary health agencies, and our schools to increase their efforts to control one of this country's most pressing health problems. Reducing smoking will reduce the devastating toll that cancer, as well as other smoking-related diseases, exacts on this Nation's health.

Edward N. Brandt, Jr., M.D.
Assistant Secretary for Health

COURT ON CONFIDENTIALITY
OF CENSUS DATA
February 24, 1982

Citing Congress' intent that raw census data be kept private and confidential, the Supreme Court ruled unanimously February 24 that the Census Bureau not be required to turn over its master address lists to state and local officials challenging the accuracy of the 1980 census.

Officials from Denver, Colo., (McNichols v. Baldrige) had sought the address lists under the "discovery" provisions of federal court rules, whereby litigants claimed the right to gather information pertinent. to their cases. Officials from Essex County, N.J., (Baldrige v. Shapiro) had tried to obtain the data under the Freedom of Information Act.

Both localities claimed the census had undercounted their populations by treating certain dwellings as vacant when they were, in fact, occupied. Both were seeking the master address lists to substantiate their challenges.

Writing for the court, Chief Justice Warren E. Burger agreed with the government's contention that census information must be kept confidential to ensure citizen cooperation in the counting process. "Congress concluded . . . that only a bar on disclosure of all raw data reported by or on behalf of individuals would serve the function of assuring public confidence," Burger wrote. "The wisdom of its classifications is not for us to decide in light of Congress' 180 years experience with the census process."

"Congress, of course, can authorize disclosure in executing its constitutional obligation to conduct a decennial census," he said. "But until

Congress alters its clear provisions under ... the Census Act, its mandate is to be followed by the courts."

Census counts had a direct effect on state and local governments because many federal program funds were allocated, at least in part, according to population. Congressional redistricting, which took place every 10 years, also was based on census figures.

At the time of the Supreme Court ruling, a number of suits challenging the 1980 census were in progress. But the February 24 decision, plus the court's refusal to hear a challenge two days earlier from the city of Detroit, portended little optimism for the suits remaining.

> *Following are excerpts from the opinions of the Supreme Court in* Baldrige v. Shapiro *and* McNichols v. Baldrige, *both decided February 24, 1982:*

Nos. 80-1436 and 80-1781

Malcolm Baldrige, Secretary of Commerce, et al., Petitioners
v.
Peter Shapiro,
Essex County Executive

On Writ of Certiorari to the United States Court of Appeals for the Third Circuit

William H. McNichols, Jr., etc., et al., Petitioners
v.
Malcolm Baldrige, Secretary of the United States Department of Commerce, et al.

On Writ of Certiorari to the United States Court of Appeals for the Tenth Circuit

[February 24, 1982]

CHIEF JUSTICE BURGER delivered the opinion of the Court.

We granted certiorari to determine whether lists of addresses collected and utilized by the Bureau of the Census are exempt from disclosure, either by way of civil discovery or the Freedom of Information Act, under the confidentiality provisions of the Census Act, 13 U.S.C. §§ 8 and 9 (1976).

I

Under Art. 1, § 2, cl. 3 of the United States Constitution, responsibility for conducting the decennial census rests with Congress. Congress has delegated to the Secretary of Commerce the duty to conduct the decennial census; the Secretary in turn has delegated this function to the Bureau of the Census.

The 1980 enumeration conducted by the Bureau of the Census indicated that Essex County, New Jersey, which includes the city of Newark, and Denver, Colorado, among other areas, had lost population during the 1970s. This information was conveyed to the appropriate officials in both Essex County and Denver. Under Bureau procedures a City has ten working days from receipt of the preliminary counts to challenge the accuracy of the census data. Both Essex County and Denver challenged the census count under the local review procedures. Both proceeded on the theory that the Bureau had erroneously classified occupied dwellings as vacant, and both sought to compel disclosure of a portion of the address lists used by the Bureau in conducting its count in their respective jurisdictions.

A

Baldrige v. Shapiro (No. 80-1436)

The Essex County Executive filed suit in the United States District Court for the District of New Jersey to compel the Bureau to release the "master address" register under the Freedom of Information Act (FOIA). The master address register is a listing of such information as addresses, householder's names, number of housing units, type of census inquiry and, where applicable, the vacancy status of the unit. The list was compiled initially from commercial mailing address lists and census postal checks, and was updated further through direct responses to census question-naires, pre- and post-enumeration canvassing by census personnel, and in some instances by a cross-check with the 1970 census data. The Bureau resisted disclosure of the master address list, arguing that 13 U.S.C. §§ 8 (b) and 9 (a) of the Census Act prohibit disclosure of all raw census data pertaining to particular individuals, including addresses. The Bureau argued that it therefore could lawfully withhold the information under the FOIA pursuant to Exemption 3, which provides that the FOIA does not apply where information is specifically exempt from disclosure by statute.

The District Court concluded that the FOIA required disclosure of the requested information. The court began its analysis by noting that public policy favors disclosure under the FOIA unless the information falls within the statutory exemptions. The District Court concluded that the Census Act did not provide a "blanket of confidentiality" for all census materials. Rather, the confidentiality limitation is "solely to require that census material be used in furtherance of the Bureau's statistical mission and to ensure against disclosure of any particular individual's response." The court noted that Essex County did not seek access to individual census reports or information relative to particular individuals, but sought access to the address list exclusively for statistical purposes in conjunction with the Bureau's own program of local review. In addition, the Secretary is authorized by the Census Act to utilize County employees if they are sworn to observe the limitations of the statute. The District Court concluded that the Bureau's claim of confidentiality impeded the goal of accurate and complete enumeration. Finally, the District Court found that the information sought was not derived from the questionnaires received, but rather from data available prior to the census. The District Court ordered the Bureau to make available the address register of all property in the county, with the proviso that all persons using the records be sworn to secrecy. The United States Court of Appeals for the Third Circuit affirmed for the reasons stated by the District Court.

B

McNichols v. Baldrige (No. 80-1781)

The City of Denver, through its officials, filed suits in the United States District Court for the District of Colorado seeking a preliminary injunction to require the Bureau to cooperate with the City in verifying its vacancy data. The District Court did not rule on the preliminary injunction, but instead focused on whether the City of Denver was entitled to the vacancy information contained in the updated master address registers maintained by the Bureau. The District Court granted the City of Denver's discovery request for this information. The court concluded that the city should have access to the information because without the address list the City was denied any meaningful ability to challenge the Bureau's data. In light of what it deemed the important constitutional and statutory rights involved, the District Court concluded that the purposes of § 9 of the Census Act should be maintained without denying the City the right of discovery. The District Court entered a detailed order to protect the confidentiality of the information.

The United States Court of Appeals for the Tenth Circuit reversed. (1981). The Court of Appeals relied on the "express language" of the statute and on the "emphatically expressed intent of Congress to protect census information." [Q]uoting Seymour v. Barabba (CADC 1977). The court reasoned that Congress has the power to make census information immune from direct discovery or disclosure. The court concluded that Congress has neither made nor implied an exception covering this case. The Court of Appeals also found no indication that Congress is constitutionally required to provide the City with information to challenge the census data. The court concluded that the City of Denver's remedy must lie with Congress.

Thus, the United States Court of Appeals for the Third Circuit ordered disclosure of the master address list under the FOIA. The United States Court of Appeals for the Tenth Circuit denied discovery of similar information, concluding that the data was privileged from disclosure. (1981). We granted certiorari in these cases to determine whether such information is to be disclosed under either of the requested procedures.

II

A

The broad mandate of the FOIA is to provide for open disclosure of public information. The act expressly recognizes, however, that public disclosure is not always in the public interest and consequently provides that agency records may be withheld from disclosure under any one of the nine exemptions defined in 5 U.S.C. § 522 (b). Under Exemption 3 disclosure need not be made as to information "specifically exempted from disclosure by statute" if the statute affords the agency no discretion on disclosure, or establishes particular criteria for withholding the data, or refers to the particular type of material to be withheld. The question in Baldrige v. Shapiro, No. 80-1436, is twofold: first, do §§ 8 (b) and 9 (a) of the Census Act constitute a statutory exception to disclosure within the meaning of Exemption 3; and second, is the requested data included within the protection of §§ 8 (b) and 9 (a).

B

Although the national census mandated by Art. I, § 2 of the Constitution fulfills many important and valuable functions for the benefit of the country as a whole, its initial constitutional purpose was to provide a basis for apportioning representatives among the States in the Congress. The census today serves an important function in the allocation of federal grants to States based on population. In addition, the census also provides important data for Congress and ultimately for the private sector.

Although Congress has broad power to require individuals to submit responses, an accurate census depends in large part on public cooperation. To stimulate that cooperation Congress has provided assurances that information furnished to the Secretary by individuals is to be treated as confidential. Section 8 (b) of the Census Act provides that subject to specified limitations, "the Secretary [of Commerce] may furnish copies of tabulations and other statistical materials which do not disclose the information reported by, or on behalf of, any particular respondent...". Section 9 (a) provides further assurances of confidentiality:

> Neither the Secretary, nor any other officer or employee of the Department of Commerce or bureau or agency thereof, may, except as provided in section 8 of this title—
> (1) use the information furnished under the provisions of this title for any purpose other than the statistical purposes for which it is supplied; or
> (2) make any publication whereby the data furnished by any particular establishment or individual under this title can be identified; or
> (3) permit anyone other than the sworn officers and employees of the Department or bureau or agency thereof to examine the individual reports.

Sections 8 (b) and 9 (a) explicitly provide for the nondisclosure of certain census data. No discretion is provided to the Census Bureau on whether or not to disclose the information referred to in §§ 8 (b) and 9 (a).

Sections 8 (b) and 9 (a) of the Census Act therefore qualify as withholding statutes under an Exemption 3. Raw census data is protected under the §§ 8 (b) and 9 (a) exemptions, however, only to the extent that the data is within the confidentiality provisions of the Act.

C

Essex County and various amici vigorously argue that §§ 8 (b) and 9 (a) of the Census Act are designed to prohibit disclosure of the identities of individuals who provide raw census data; for this reason, they argue, the confidentiality provisions protect raw data only if the individual respondent can be identified. The unambiguous language of the confidentiality provisions, as well as the legislative history of the Act, however, indicate that Congress plainly contemplated that raw data reported by or on behalf of individuals was to be held confidential and not available for disclosure. . . .

The legislative history also makes clear that Congress was concerned not solely with protecting the identity of individuals. Since 1879 Congress has expressed its concern that confidentiality of data reported by individuals also be preserved. . . .

The . . . history of the Census Act reveals a congressional intent to protect the confidentiality of census information by prohibiting disclosure of raw census data reported by or on behalf of individuals. Subsequent congressional action is consistent with this interpretation. In response to claimed undercounts in the census of 1960 and of 1970, Congress considered, but ultimately rejected proposals to allow local officials limited access to census data in order to challenge the census count.

A list of vacant addresses is part of the raw census data — the information — intended by Congress to be protected. The list of addresses requested by the County of Essex constitutes "information reported by, or on behalf of," individuals responding to the census. The initial list of addresses is taken from prior censuses and mailing lists. This information then is verified both by direct mailings and census enumerators who go to areas not responding. See, e.g., 1980 Census Question[n]aire, Question No. H4 ("How many living quarters, occupied and vacant, are at this address?") As with all the census material, the information on vacancies was updated from data obtained from neighbors and others who speak with the follow-up census enumerators. The final master address list therefore includes data reported by or on behalf of individuals.

Under the clear language of the Census Act it is not relevant that the municipalities seeking the data will use it only for statistical purposes. Section 9 (a) (1) permits use of the data only for "the statistical purposes for which it is supplied." There is no indication in the Census Act that the hundreds of municipal governments in the 50 states were intended by Congress to be the "monitors" of the Census Bureau. In addition, limiting use of data only for "statistical" purposes in no way indicates that raw data may be revealed outside the strict requirements of the Census Act that data be handled by Census employees sworn to secrecy.

Because §§ 8 (b) and 9 (a) of the Census Act constitute withholding statutes under Exemption 3 of the FOIA and because the raw census data in this case was intended to be protected from disclosure within those provisions of the Census Act, the requested information is not subject to disclosure under the FOIA.

III

The discovery provisions of the Federal Rules of Civil Procedure, similar to the FOIA, are designed to encourage open exchange of information by litigants in federal courts. Unlike the FOIA, however, the discovery provisions under the federal rules focus upon the need for the information rather than a broad statutory grant of disclosure. Federal Rule of Civil Procedure 26 (b) (1) provides for access to all information "relevant to the subject matter involved in the pending action" unless the information is privileged. If a privilege exists, information may be withheld, even if relevant to the lawsuit and essential to the establishment of plaintiff's claim.

It is well recognized that a privilege may be created by statute. A statute granting a privilege is to be strictly construed so as "to avoid a construction that would suppress otherwise competent evidence." *St. Regis Paper Co.* v. *United States* (1961). In the case of the City of Denver, the central inquiry is whether §§ 8 (b) and 9 (a) create a privilege so as to protect against disclosure of the raw census data requested.

As noted above, §§ 8 (b) and 9 (a) of the Census Act embody explicit congressional intent to preclude *all* disclosure of raw census data reported by or on behalf of individuals. This strong policy of nondisclosure indicates that Congress intended the confidentiality provisions to constitute a "privilege" within the meaning of the Federal Rules. Disclosure by way of civil discovery would undermine the very purpose of confidentiality contemplated by Congress. One such purpose was to encourage public participation and maintain public confidence that information given to the Census Bureau would not be disclosed. The general public, whose cooperation is essential for an accurate census, would not be concerned with the underlying rationale for disclosure of data that had been accumulated under assurances of confidentiality. Congress concluded in §§ 8 (b) and 9 (a) that only a bar on disclosure of all raw data reported by or on behalf of individuals would serve the function of assuring public confidence. This was within congressional discretion, for Congress is vested by the Constitution with authority to conduct the census "as they shall by Law direct." The wisdom of its classifications is not for us to decide in light of Congress' 180 years experience with the census process.

This is not to say that the City of Denver does not also have important reasons for requesting the raw census data for purposes of its civil suit. A finding of "privilege," however, shields the requested information from disclosure despite the need demonstrated by the litigant.

IV

We hold that whether sought by way of requests under the FOIA or by way of discovery rules, raw data reported by or on behalf of individuals need not be disclosed. Congress, of course, can authorize disclosure in executing its constitutional obligation to conduct a decennial census. But until Congress alters its clear provisions under §§ 8 (b) and 9 (a) of the Census Act, its mandate is to be followed by the courts.

Accordingly the judgment of the United States Court of Appeals for the Third Circuit in No. 80-1436 is reversed, and the judgment of the United States Court of Appeals for the Tenth circuit in No. 80-1781 is affirmed.

It is so ordered.

REAGAN CARIBBEAN PLAN

February 24, 1982

In an address to Latin American leaders at the Organization of American States February 24, President Reagan outlined an economic and military aid package designed to ensure Caribbean security and bring prosperity to the region. Labeled the Caribbean Basin Initiative, the president's proposal included duty-free access to the United States for Caribbean exports and investment incentives for U.S. businesses, as well as supplementary military and economic aid totaling $410 million.

The centerpiece of Reagan's economic aid package was a free trade provision that would permit exports from participating Caribbean nations to enter the United States duty free for 12 years. Eighty-seven percent of Caribbean exports already enjoyed this special trade status under the Generalized System of Preferences. Duty-free access to the United States would provide expanded market opportunities for current Caribbean exports, as well as a market incentive for Caribbean private sector investment in new products and services, since the 12-year free trade provision would be in place long enough for firms at least to pay off their initial investment. Textile, apparel and sugar exports, governed by other international agreements, would be exempted.

Reagan noted that fuel costs had skyrocketed since 1977, resulting in economic crisis for many Caribbean nations. In 1977 one barrel of oil was roughly equivalent to five pounds of coffee or 155 pounds of sugar, but by 1982 it took 26 pounds of coffee or 283 pounds of sugar to equal one barrel of oil. To help those nations particularly hard hit economically, the president said he would ask Congress to provide supplemental appropri-

ations of $350 million in economic aid during the 1982 fiscal year.

The president directed other portions of his Caribbean Basin Initiative to the U.S. private sector, saying he would ask Congress for tax incentives to encourage investment by U.S. firms in Caribbean nations. In an April 28 address to U.S. corporate officers, Reagan requested that the private sector make available to government and international aid programs "highly qualified mid-career people" to provide Basin countries with technical assistance and training. The president also reassured corporate officers of the administration's commitment to protecting U.S. industry, agriculture and labor against "disruptive imports."

Reagan promised to work closely with other American nations, specifically Canada, Mexico, Venezuela and Colombia, to coordinate economic assistance in the Caribbean and said he would encourage additional international aid for the area from Europe and Japan. The president also indicated that, while eager to extend the free trade provision to Basin countries, the United States would maintain the special trade status of Puerto Rico and the U.S. Virgin Islands.

New Colonialism

Addressing the question of political unrest in the Caribbean, Reagan noted that U.S. economic and security interests were inextricably tied to the stability and well-being of the Basin countries and spoke of the threat posed by forces outside the region trying to expand their "colonialist ambitions." The president denounced continuing armed conflicts in El Salvador and Guatemala as "Soviet-backed, Cuban-managed" bids to establish "Cuban-style Marxist-Leninist dictatorships" in Latin America. He warned that unless the United States acted quickly, "new Cubas [would] arise from the ruins of today's conflicts." Reagan was particularly concerned that the continuing violence would impede the chances for success of his economic program for the Caribbean.

Reagan criticized Nicaragua for its role in smuggling Cuban arms to leftist guerrillas in El Salvador and Guatemala, but left open the possibility that it too could enjoy the economic benefits of the Caribbean Basin Initiative if it changed its policies. "We seek to exclude no one," stated the president.

Attempting to ease concerns about U.S. involvement in El Salvador, Reagan declared that the United States would not "follow Cuba's lead in attempting to resolve human problems by brute force." The president promised, however, to do "whatever is prudent and necessary to ensure the peace and security of the Carribean." He announced that he would ask Congress for an additional $60 million in supplementary military aid for the region.

Congressional Reaction

The president's proposal received a mixed reaction on Capitol Hill. Most members welcomed the plan as a positive step toward improving economic and political conditions in the Caribbean, but expressed fears that it would face a tough fight. The cool atmosphere in Congress toward foreign aid and the natural urge to protect domestic interests, particularly in an election year, indicated that passage of legislation to implement the plan would be difficult at best.

"It's too little too late but it's the best we're going to get, and I intend to support it," said Michael D. Barnes, D-Md., chairman of the House Inter-American Affairs Subcommittee. "It obviously will be very difficult to get through Congress." Paul Findley, R-Ill., a member of the House Foreign Affairs and Agriculture committees, said he was "strongly in favor of a Caribbean policy that is less militaristic than the one we seem to have now, but I think this is going to have tough sledding." Findley noted that the proposal for tax incentives for U.S. firms to invest in Caribbean nations would stir some controversy. "We need incentives for U.S. firms to invest here and create jobs," he said. Clement J. Zablocki, D-Wis., chairman of the House Foreign Affairs Committee, regretted that Reagan had "cloaked [the plan] in the mantle of Soviet-Cuban subversion," and said it would be "necessary and in the best interest of the United States with or without outside subversion. Even without Soviet intervention there would exist poverty and social inequality."

Many members of Congress expressed concern over provisions for additional military aid for El Salvador and promised that any such proposals would be subject to intense congressional scrutiny. "Most people don't even know where El Salvador is," noted Bill Alexander, D-Ark., "but the ghost of Vietnam hangs over every instance of military support or action in a foreign country."

Caribbean Reaction

Caribbean leaders also welcomed Reagan's plan, though many believed the U.S. Congress would balk at providing legislation to implement it. Some leaders also expressed concern that the president's proposal relied too heavily on free enterprise to cure Caribbean economic ills in a region of mixed economies and severe development problems. Jamaican Prime Minister Edward P. G. Seaga, in a February 25 New York Times article, praised Reagan's initiative, calling it "bold, historic and far-reaching in concept." But Barbadian Ambassador Charles A. T. Skeete was skeptical of the free market emphasis. "We cannot accept the thesis that any one approach can solve all our problems. Development is a little more complex than that. We would love it if it were that simple."

The U.S. president's obvious concern over the situation in El Salvador and Guatemala left some leaders wondering how much of the proposed aid would remain for the Caribbean area after the United States had fulfilled its commitments in Central America. "On the positive side, [the plan] is certainly an innovation, a new approach," noted Haitian Ambassador Georges N. Leger. "If it is implemented as described it will give each country the chance to have a custom-made assistance package. But we are not going to expect a miracle overnight."

Following is the text of President Reagan's speech February 24 in Washington, D.C., to the Permanent Council of the Organization of American States. (Boldface headings in brackets have been added by Congressional Quarterly to highlight the organization of the text.):

Mr. Chairman, distinguished permanent representatives, Mr. Secretary General, distinguished members of the diplomatic corps, ladies and gentlemen:

It's a great honor for me to stand before you today. The principles which the Organization of American States embodies — democracy, self-determination, economic development, and collective security — are at the heart of U.S. foreign policy. The United States of America is a proud member of this organization. What happens anywhere in the Americas affects us in this country. In that very real sense, we share a common destiny.

We, the peoples of the Americas, have much more in common than geographical proximity. For over 400 years our peoples have shared the dangers and dreams of building a new world. From colonialism to nationhood our common quest has been for freedom.

Most of our forebears came to this hemisphere seeking a better life for themselves. They came in search of opportunity and, yes, in search of God. Virtually all descendants of the land and immigrants alike have had to fight for independence. Having gained it, they've had to fight to retain it. There were times when we even fought each other.

Gradually, however, the nations of this hemisphere developed a set of common principles and institutions that provided the basis for mutual protection. Some 20 years ago, John F. Kennedy caught the essence of our unique mission when he said it was up to the New World "to demonstrate that man's unsatisfied aspiration for economic progress and social justice can best be achieved by free men working within a framework of democratic institutions."

In the commitment to freedom and independence, the peoples of this hemisphere are one. In this profound sense, we are all Americans. Our principles are rooted in self-government and nonintervention. We believe in the rule of law. We know that a nation cannot be liberated by depriving its people of liberty. We know that a state cannot be free when its independence is subordinated to a foreign power. And we know that a government cannot be democratic if it refuses to submit to the test of a free election.

We have not always lived up to these ideals. All of us at one time or another in our history have been politically weak, economically backward, socially unjust, or unable to solve our problems through peaceful means. My own country, too, has suffered internal strife including a tragic civil war. We have known economic misery, and once tolerated racial and social injustices. And, yes, at times we have behaved arrogantly and impatiently toward our neighbors. These experiences have left their scars, but they also help us today to identify with the struggle for political and economic development in the other countries of this hemisphere.

Out of the crucible of our common past, the Americas have emerged as more equal and more understanding partners. Our hemisphere has an unlimited potential for economic development and human fulfillment. We have a combined population of more than 600 million people; our continents and our islands boast vast reservoirs of food and raw materials; and the markets of the Americas have already produced the highest standard of living among the advanced as well as the developing countries of the world. The example we could offer to the world would not only discourage foes; it would project like a beacon of hope to all of the oppressed and impoverished nations of the world. We are the New World, a world of sovereign and independent states that today stand shoulder to shoulder with a common respect for one another and a greater tolerance of one another's shortcomings.

[North American Accord]

Some 2 years ago when I announced as a candidate for the Presidency, I spoke of an ambition I had to bring about an accord with our two neighbors here on the North American continent. Now, I was not suggesting a common market or any kind of formal arrangement. "Accord" was the only word that seemed to fit what I had in mind.

I was aware that the U.S. has long enjoyed friendly relations with Mexico and Canada, that our borders have no fortifications. Yet it seemed to me that there was a potential for a closer relationship than had yet been achieved. Three great nations share the North American continent with all its human and natural resources. Have we done all we can to create a relationship in which each country can realize its potential to the fullest?

Now, I know in the past the United States has proposed policies that we declared would be mutually beneficial not only for North America but also for the nations of the Caribbean and Central and South America. But there was often a problem. No matter how good our intentions were, our very size may have made it seem that we were exercising a kind of paternalism. At the time I suggested a new North American accord, I said I wanted to approach our neighbors not as someone with yet another plan, but as a friend seeking their ideas, their suggestions as to how we could become better neighbors.

I met with President López Portillo in Mexico before my inauguration and with Prime Minister Trudeau in Canada shortly after I had taken office. We have all met several times since — in the U.S., Mexico, and Canada — and I believe we have established a relationship better than any our three countries have ever known before.

Today I would like to talk about our other neighbors — neighbors by the sea — some two dozen countries of the Caribbean and Central America. These countries are not unfamiliar names from some isolated corner of the world far from home. They're very close to home. The country of El Salvador, for example, is nearer to Texas than Texas is to Massachusetts. The Caribbean region is a vital strategic and commercial artery for the United States. Nearly half our trade, two-thirds of our imported oil, and over half of our imported strategic minerals pass through the Panama Canal or the Gulf of Mexico. Make no mistake: The well-being and security of our neighbors in this region are in our own vital interest.

Economic health is one of the keys to a secure future for our Caribbean Basin neighbors. I am happy to say that Mexico, Canada, and Venezuela have joined in the search for ways to help these countries realize their economic potential.

Each of our four nations has its own unique position and approach. Mexico and Venezuela are helping to offset energy costs to Caribbean Basin countries by means of an oil facility that is already in operation. Canada is doubling its already significant economic assistance. We all seek to ensure that the people of this area have the right to preserve their own national identities; to improve their economic lot and to develop their political institutions to suit their own unique social and historical needs. The Central American and Caribbean countries differ widely in culture, personality, and needs. Like America itself, the Caribbean Basin is an extraordinary mosaic of Hispanics, Africans, Asians, and Europeans, as well as native Americans.

[Economic Siege]

At the moment, however, these countries are under economic siege. In 1977, 1 barrel of oil was worth 5 pounds of coffee or 155 pounds of sugar. Well, to buy that same barrel of oil today, these small countries must provide 5 times as much coffee — nearly 26 pounds — or almost twice as much sugar — 283 pounds. This economic disaster is consuming our neighbors' money, reserves, and credit, forcing thousands of people to leave for the United States, often illegally, and shaking even the most established democracies. And economic disaster has provided a fresh opening to the enemies of freedom, national independence, and peaceful development.

We've taken the time to consult closely with other governments in the region, both sponsors and beneficiaries, to ask them what they need and what they think will work. And we've labored long to develop an economic program that integrates trade, aid, and investment — a program that represents a long-term commitment to the countries of the Caribbean and Central America to make use of the magic of the marketplace, the market of the Americas, to earn their own way toward self-sustaining growth.

At the Cancún Summit last October, I presented a fresh view of a development which stressed more than aid and government intervention. As I pointed out then, nearly all of the countries that have succeeded in their development over the past 30 years have done so on the strength of market-oriented policies and vigorous participation in the international economy. Aid must be complemented by trade and investment.

The program I'm proposing today puts these principles into practice. It is an integrated program that helps our neighbors help themselves, a program that will create conditions under which creativity and private entrepreneurship and self-help can flourish. Aid is an important part of this program because many of our neighbors need it to put themselves in a starting position from which they can begin to earn their own way. But this aid will encourage private sector activities, not displace them.

[Free Trade for Caribbean Exports]

The centerpiece of the program that I am sending to the Congress is free trade for Caribbean Basin products exported to the United States. Currently some 87 percent of Caribbean exports already enter U.S. markets duty free under the Generalized System of Preferences. These exports, however, cover only the limited range of existing products — not the wide variety of potential products these talented and industrious peoples are capable of producing under the free trade arrangement that I am proposing.

Exports from the area will receive duty free treatment for 12 years. Thus, new investors will be able to enter the market knowing that their products will receive duty-free treatment for at least the pay-off lifetime of their investments. Before granting duty-free treatment, we will discuss with each country its own self-help measures.

The only exception to the free trade concept will be textile and apparel products because these products are covered now by other international agreements. However, we will make sure that our immediate neighbors have more liberal quota arrangements.

This economic proposal is as unprecedented as today's crisis in the Caribbean. Never before has the United States offered a preferential trading arrangement to any region. This commitment makes unmistakably clear our determination to help our neighbors grow strong.

The impact of this free trade approach will develop slowly. The economies we seek to help are small. Even as they grow, all the protections now available to U.S. industry, agriculture and labor against disruptive imports will remain. And growth in the Caribbean will benefit everyone, with American exports finding new markets.

[Tax Incentives]

Secondly, to further attract investment, I will ask the Congress to provide significant tax incentives for investment in the Caribbean Basin. We also stand ready to negotiate bilateral investment treaties with interested Basin countries.

Third, I'm asking for a supplemental fiscal year 1982 appropriation of $350 million to assist those countries which are particularly hard hit economically. Much of this aid will be concentrated on the private sector. These steps will help foster the spirit of enterprise necessary to take advantage of the trade and investment portions of the program.

Fourth, we will offer technical assistance and training to assist the private sector in the Basin countries to benefit from the opportunities of this program. This will include investment promotion, export marketing, and technology transfer efforts, as well as programs to facilitate adjustments to greater competition and production in agriculture and industry. I intend to seek the active participation of the business community in this joint undertaking. The Peace Corps already has 861 volunteers in Caribbean Basin countries, and will give special emphasis to recruiting volunteers with skills in developing local enterprise.

[Other International Efforts]

Fifth, we will work closely with Mexico, Canada, and Venezuela, all of whom have already begun substantial and innovative programs of their own, to encourage stronger international efforts to coordinate our own development measures with their vital contributions, and with those of other potential donors like Colombia. We will also encourage our European, Japanese, and other Asian allies, as well as multilateral development institutions, to increase their assistance in the region.

Sixth, given our special valued relationship with Puerto Rico and the U.S. Virgin Islands, we will propose special measures to ensure that they also will benefit and prosper from this program. With their strong traditions of democracy and free enterprise, they can play leading roles in the development of the area.

This program has been carefully prepared. It represents a farsighted act by our own people at a time of considerable economic difficulty at home. I wouldn't propose it if I were not convinced that it is vital to the security interests of this Nation and of this hemisphere. The energy, the time, and the treasure we dedicate to assisting the development of our neighbors now can help to prevent the much larger expenditures of treasure as well as human lives which would flow from their collapse.

One early sign is positive. After a decade of falling income and exceptionally high unemployment, Jamaica's new leadership is reducing bureaucracy, dismantling unworkable controls, and attracting new investment. Continued outside assistance will be needed to tide Jamaica over until market forces generate large increases in output and employment — but Jamaica is making freedom work.

[New Colonialism]

I've spoken up to now mainly of the economic and social challenges to development. But there are also other dangers. A new kind of colonialism stalks the world today and threatens our independence. It is brutal and totalitarian. It is not of our hemisphere, but it threatens our hemisphere and has established footholds on American soil for the expansion of its colonialist ambitions.

The events of the last several years dramatize two different futures which are possible for the Caribbean area: either the establishment or restoration of moderate, constitutional governments with economic growth and improved living standards, or further expansion of political violence from the extreme left and the extreme right, resulting in the imposition of dictatorships and, inevitably, more economic decline and human suffering.

The positive opportunity is illustrated by the two-thirds of the nations in the area which have democratic governments. The dark future is foreshadowed by the poverty and repression of Castro's Cuba, the tightening grip of the totalitarian left in Grenada and Nicaragua, and the expansion of Soviet-backed, Cuban-managed support for violent revolution in Central America.

The record is clear. Nowhere in its whole sordid history have the promises of Communism been redeemed. Everywhere it has exploited and aggravated temporary economic suffering to seize power and then to institutionalize economic deprivation and suppress human rights. Right now, 6 million people worldwide are refugees from Communist systems. Already, more than a million Cubans alone have fled Communist tyranny.

[Economic Progress Impeded]

Our economic and social program cannot work if our neighbors cannot pursue their own economic and political future in peace, but must divert their resources, instead, to fight imported terrorism and armed attack. Economic progress cannot be made while guerrillas systematically burn, bomb, and destroy bridges, farms and power and transportation systems — all with the deliberate intention of worsening economic and social problems in hopes of radicalizing already suffering people.

Our Caribbean neighbors' peaceful attempts to develop are feared by the foes of freedom, because their success will make the radical message a hollow one. Cuba and its Soviet backers know this. Since 1978 Havana has trained, armed and directed extremists in guerrilla warfare and economic sabotage as part of a campaign to exploit troubles in Central America and the Caribbean. Their goal is to establish Cuban-style, Marxist-Leninist dictatorships.

Last year, Cuba received 66,000 tons of war supplies from the Soviet Union — more than in any year since the 1962 missile crisis. Last month, the arrival of additional high performance MIG-23 Floggers gave Cuba an arsenal of more than 200 Soviet warplanes — far more than the military aircraft inventories of all other Caribbean Basin countries combined.

For almost 2 years, Nicaragua has served as a platform for covert military action. Through Nicaragua, arms are being smuggled to guerrillas in El Salvador and Guatemala. The Nicaraguan Government even admits the forced relocation of about 8,500 Miskito Indians. And we have clear evidence that since late 1981, many Indian communities have been burned to the ground and men, women, and children killed.

The Nicaraguan junta cabled written assurances to the OAS in 1979 that it intended to respect human rights and hold free elections. Two years later, these commitments can be measured by the postponement of elections until 1985, by repression against free trade unions, against the media, minorities, and in defiance of all international civility, by the continued export of arms and subversion to neighboring countries.

Two years ago, in contrast, the Government of El Salvador began an unprecedented land reform. It has repeatedly urged the guerrillas to renounce violence, to join in the democratic process, an election in which the people of El Salvador could determine the government they prefer. Our own country and other American nations through the OAS have urged such a course. The guerrillas have refused. More than that, they now threaten violence and death to those who participate in such an election.

Can anything make more clear the nature of those who pretend to be supporters of so-called wars of liberation?

A determined propaganda campaign has sought to mislead many in Europe and certainly many in the U.S. as to the true nature of the conflict in El Salvador. Very simply, guerrillas, armed and supported by and through Cuba, are attempting to impose a Marxist-Leninist dictatorship on the people of El Salvador as part of a larger imperialistic plan. If we do not act promptly and decisively in defense of freedom, new Cubas will arise from the ruins of today's conflicts. We will face more totalitarian regimes, more regimes tied militarily to the Soviet Union — more regimes exporting subversion, more regimes so incompetent yet so totalitarian that their citizens' only hope becomes that of one day migrating to other American nations, as in recent years they have come to the United States.

[Increased Security Aid]

I believe free and peaceful development of our hemisphere requires us to help governments confronted with aggression from outside their borders to defend themselves. For this reason, I will ask the Congress to provide increased security assistance to help friendly countries hold off those who would destroy their chances for economic and social progress and political democracy. Since 1947, the Rio Treaty has established reciprocal defense responsibilities linked to our common democratic ideals. Meeting these responsibilities is all the more important when an outside power supports terrorism and insurgency to destroy any possibility of freedom and democracy. Let our friends and our adversaries understand that we will do whatever is prudent and necessary to ensure the peace and security of the Caribbean area.

In the face of outside threats, security for the countries of the Caribbean and Central American area is not an end in itself, but a means to an end. It is a means toward building representative and responsive institutions, toward strengthening pluralism and free private institutions — churches, free trade unions, and an independent press. It is a means to nurturing the basic human rights freedom's foes would stamp out. In the Caribbean we above all seek to protect those values and principles that shape the proud heritage of this hemisphere.

I have already expressed our support for the coming election in El Salvador. We also strongly support the Central American Democratic Community formed this January by Costa Rica, Honduras and El Salvador. The United States will work closely with other concerned democracies inside and outside the area to preserve and enhance our common democratic values.

We will not, however, follow Cuba's lead in attempting to resolve human problems by brute force. Our economic assistance, including the additions that are part of the program I've just outlined, is more than five times the amount of our security assistance. The thrust of our aid is to help our neighbors realize freedom, justice, and economic progress.

We seek to exclude no one. Some, however, have turned from their American neighbors and their heritage. Let them return to the traditions and common values of this hemisphere and we will all welcome them. The choice is theirs.

As I have talked these problems over with friends and fellow citizens here in the United States, I'm often asked "Well, why bother?" Why should the problems of Central America or the Caribbean concern us? Why should we try to help?" Well, I tell them we must help, because the people of the Caribbean and Central America are in a fundamental sense fellow Americans. Freedom is our common destiny. And freedom cannot survive if our neighbors live in misery and oppression. In short, we must do it because we're doing it for each other.

Our neighbors' call for help is addressed to us all here in this country — to the administration, to the Congress, to millions of Americans from Miami to Chicago, from New York to Los Angeles. This is not Washington's problem; it is the problem of all the people of this great land and of all the other Americas — the great and sovereign republics of North America, the Caribbean Basin, and South America. The Western Hemisphere does not belong to any one of us; we belong to the Western Hemisphere. We are brothers historically as well as geographically.

Now, I'm aware that the United States has pursued good neighbor policies in the past. These policies did some good, but they're inadequate for today. I believe that my country is now ready to go beyond being a good neighbor to being a true friend and brother in a community that belongs as much to others as to us. That, not guns, is the ultimate key to peace and security for us all.

We have to ask ourselves why has it taken so long for us to realize the God-given opportunity that is ours? These two great land masses north and south, so rich in virtually everything we need — together our more than 600 million people can develop what is undeveloped, can eliminate want and poverty, can show the world that our many nations can live in peace, each with its own customs, language and culture, but sharing a love for freedom and a determination to resist outside ideologies that would take us back to colonialism.

We return to a common vision. Nearly a century ago, a great citizen of the Caribbean and the Americas, José Martí, warned that "Mankind is composed of two sorts of men, those who love and create and those who hate and destroy." Today more than ever the compassionate, creative peoples of the Americas have an opportunity to stand together, to overcome injustice, hatred, and oppression, and to build a better life for all the Americas.

I have always believed that this hemisphere was a special place with a special destiny. I believe we are destined to be the beacon of hope for all mankind. With God's help, we can make it so. We can create a peaceful, free, and prospering hemisphere based on our shared ideas and reaching from pole to pole of what we proudly call the New World.

Thank you.

CBO ANALYSIS
OF FY 1983 REAGAN BUDGET
February 25, 1982

The Congressional Budget Office (CBO), in an analysis of President Ronald Reagan's proposed 1983 budget, calculated that the president's proposed deficit of $91.5 billion for fiscal 1983 was underestimated by $29 billion. The report released February 25 stated that even if the administration's complete deficit reduction plan were enacted, the deficit in fiscal 1985 would be $140 billion — almost double the White House estimate of $71.9 billion. (Reagan budget, p. 143)

CBO is a non-partisan arm of Congress that annually re-estimates the administration's budget proposal, using its own economic assumptions and technical analysis.

Revenue and Spending

The chief difference between the Reagan and CBO analyses centered on revenue and spending projections. The CBO study estimated that revenues would be lower in 1983-85 than the administration projected and that budget outlays would be higher.

Specifically, the CBO report predicted that the Reagan budget had overestimated revenues by about $5 billion in 1983, $13 billion in 1984 and $16 billion in 1985. In terms of outlays, the differences were larger, "averaging more than $20 billion during 1983-1985."

According to the CBO study, most of the deviation in revenue predictions resulted from varying estimates on the effect of the 1981 tax cut. On

191

the outlay side, differences involved the cost of farm price supports, the rate of spending for defense procurement, likely receipts from the administration's accelerated leasing of the Outer Continental Shelf and net interest costs.

Economic Assumptions

In the area of economic assumptions, the administration and CBO were in general agreement for fiscal 1982. However, the CBO was more pessimistic than the president in terms of forecasts for inflation and real growth in fiscal 1983.

The White House projected a real economic growth rate of 5.2 percent in 1983, while CBO estimated 3.7 percent. "The slower growth expected by CBO is largely the consequence of higher interest rates in its forecast, which would dampen the recovery in economic activity," the report said.

Risks in Reagan Budget

The CBO study cautioned that "several risks are inherent in the administration's budget proposals." First, it stated that the White House may have underpriced its projected defense spending requests by not considering a higher inflation rate and an increase in the real cost of defense purchases.

Second, the report noted that it would be very difficult to reduce budget deficits over the next few years by concentrating primarily on lowering spending. "The sharp increases proposed for national defense programs, the rising outlays for Social Security and other benefit payments indexed for inflation, and the growing net interest costs place enormous pressure on the remaining portion of the budget," the report stated. It continued: "The difficulty of finding still further significant reductions in this area of the budget is very great."

Finally, the study warned that the economic growth rate could be weaker than that projected by either the White House or CBO. Using more pessimistic economic assumptions, the CBO estimated the budget deficit would reach $184 billion in fiscal 1985.

> *Following are excerpts from the summary of "An Analysis of the President's Budgetary Proposals for Fiscal Year 1983,"* prepared by the Congressional Budget Office and released February 25, 1982. (Boldface headings in brackets have been added by Congressional Quarterly to highlight the organization of the text.):

Summary

The budget deficit for fiscal year 1982 is now expected to exceed $100 billion. The sharp rise from previously estimated levels can be attributed largely to the current economic recession, which was not anticipated in last year's budget estimates by either the Administration or the Congress. The economy is expected to recover during 1982 and to move upward thereafter. But budget deficits are projected to increase steadily for the foreseeable future, even after economic recovery, unless existing tax and spending policies change.

The President's 1983 budget contains proposals — mostly affecting spending policies — to reduce projected deficits during the next three years by $239 billion. According to Administration estimates, adoption of these proposals would result in only marginal reductions in the budget deficit from the record high level of 1982. The Administration anticipates deficits of $92 billion in 1983, $83 billion in 1984, and $72 billion in 1985, all substantially above the 1981 level of $58 billion.

The Congressional Budget Office (CBO) has analyzed the President's budgetary proposals and finds that revenues are likely to be slightly lower than projected by the Administration and outlays significantly higher. Hence, even if the President's proposals are adopted, CBO estimates that the budget deficit will climb steadily from an estimated $111 billion in 1982 to $121 billion in 1983, $129 billion in 1984, and $140 billion in 1985. Furthermore, there is the possibility that the budget deficits could be even larger, if tight credit conditions produce a weaker economy than assumed by either the Administration or CBO.

THE BUDGET OUTLOOK UNDER CURRENT POLICIES

Under existing law, the future growth in federal revenues will be sharply reduced from rates experienced over the past decade as a result of the tax cuts contained in the Economic Recovery Tax Act of 1981. Without further cuts in spending, budget outlays will grow at a faster rate than revenues. Consequently, without steps to raise revenues or to lower the growth in spending, the budget deficit will continue to grow.

This budget outlook is portrayed clearly by both the CBO baseline budget projections and the Administration's projection of current services (which includes the Administration's defense spending proposals). These projections are shown in Summary Table 1.

The budget deficit under baseline assumptions is projected by CBO as almost doubling between 1982 and 1985, from $109 billion to $208 billion. The Administration's projections also show a sharp rise in the budget deficit during this period, although not quite so much as CBO's, largely because of different economic assumptions. In the absence of tax increases or spending reductions, the CBO projections show the deficit rising to 5.0 percent of GNP in both 1984 and 1985; the Administration's show it rising to 4.3 percent of GNP in 1984 and 4.0 percent in 1985. The last time the budget deficit was this large relative to GNP was in 1976 when it was 4.0 percent as a result of the 1974 recession.

SUMMARY TABLE 1

THE BUDGET OUTLOOK UNDER CURRENT POLICIES

[By fiscal year, in billions of dollars]

	1981 Actual	1982 Estimate	1983	Projections 1984	1985
CBO Baseline Projections					
Revenues	602	631	652	701	763
Outlays	660	740	809	889	971
Deficit	58	109	157	188	208
Administration Current Services Baseline with Proposed Defense Spending Growth[a]					
Revenues	599	626	653	704	778
Outlays	657	728	799	869	946
Deficit	58	101	146	165	168

[a] The President's 1983 budget has reclassified certain social insurance contributions as offsetting collections to spending, thereby reducing both revenues and outlays but leaving unchanged the deficit.

THE ADMINISTRATION'S BUDGETARY PROPOSALS

President Reagan's budget for fiscal year 1983 recommends outlays of $757.6 billion, revenues of $666.1 billion, and a unified budget deficit of $91.5 billion. The main features of the President's 1983 budget include:

● No change in the scheduled individual income tax cuts enacted in 1981, but some significant increases in corporate taxes;

● Rapid real growth in defense spending;

● Further reforms in entitlement programs, but no reductions in Social Security benefits;

● Additional cuts in discretionary nondefense spending programs; and

● Substantial savings from various management initiatives.

Total revenues under the Administration's proposals would increase by 27 percent from an estimated $627 billion in 1982 to $797 billion in 1985. Outlays would grow by only 20 percent, from an estimated $725 billion in 1982 to $869 billion in 1985. Net spending by off-budget entities — primarily the Federal Financing Bank and oil purchases for the strategic petroleum reserve — is projected to decline from an estimated $20 billion in 1982 to $11 billion by 1985. . . . [T]he total budget deficit — including off-budget entities — would decline by 30 percent from $118 billion in

1982 to $83 billion in 1985. Relative to GNP, however, the reduction in the total deficit would be larger — falling from 3.8 percent in 1982 to 2.0 percent in 1985. The federal debt subject to statutory limit is projected to grow from $1.0 trillion at the end of fiscal year 1981 to $1.5 trillion by the end of 1985.

[Administration Deficit Reduction Program]

The Administration's proposals to reduce the size of the federal deficit from the levels indicated by current policies are concentrated largely on the spending side of the budget. ... [A]lmost 80 percent of the deficit reduction proposals over the next three years are calculated as reductions in outlays from the Administration's projected current services baseline. The biggest share of the outlay reductions — 40 percent — would be accomplished largely through the appropriation process by holding back increases or cutting nondefense discretionary programs. Another 29 percent of these outlay reductions are to be achieved through legislative proposals to reform entitlement programs, primarily Medicare, Medicaid, food stamps, and Aid to Families with Dependent Children (AFDC). No entitlement reforms for Social Security are proposed in the President's budget. ...

An estimated 28 percent of outlay savings would be achieved through various management initiatives, such as accelerated leasing of Outer Continental Shelf (OCS) lands, the sale of surplus or underused federal property, improved debt collection procedures, and further restraint on increases in federal pay. Fully two-thirds of these management initiatives would reduce net outlays by increasing receipts that are recorded on the spending side of the budget. Finally, proposed increases in user fees that would be counted as offsetting receipts make up the remaining 3 percent of the proposed outlay savings.

Only a little more than 20 percent of the Administration's deficit reduction proposals involve revenue increases. About 75 percent of the increases during 1983-1985 would come in corporate income taxes, and would substantially offset the corporate tax reduction enacted in the Economic Recovery Tax Act (ERTA) for that period. No proposals are made in the February budget to delay or eliminate any of the scheduled rate reductions in individual income taxes that also were enacted in ERTA. ...

Defense Spending Proposals

The President's February budget includes a 1982 program supplemental appropriation request of $2.6 billion for the Defense Department, and proposes a further increase of $44 billion in national defense appropriations for 1983. The Administration's 1983 budget for national defense programs totals $263 billion in new budget authority. Further large increases in defense appropriations are projected for 1984 and 1985. Measured in constant (fiscal year 1983) dollars, these projected increases for national defense appropriations for 1983-1985 would mean an average real growth of 9.2 percent per year using the Administration's economic assumptions.

Overall, the President's 1983 budget reflects relatively small funding increases for forces and manpower, and large increases to acquire new weapons for future force expansion and modernization. The most significant new policy proposal is the Administration's plan to increase the size of the naval fleet from 514 ships to over 600.

Restructuring of the Federal Budget

The President's budget proposals would dramatically affect the relative composition of federal spending. Outlays for national defense would increase by 56 percent in the next three years — from $187.5 billion in 1982 to $292 billion in 1985. The share of the budget allocated to national defense would rise sharply from 26 percent in 1982 to 34 percent in 1985. Direct federal payments to individuals, which include Social Security, Medicare, and federal employee retirement benefits, would increase by $57 billion between 1982 and 1985 — maintaining their relative share of the budget at about 42 percent. Net interest costs are also projected to rise during the next three years and would claim another 11 percent of total outlays in 1985, the same share as estimated for 1982.

All other federal spending would be reduced by 25 percent — about $37 billion — between 1982 and 1985. ... [P]ayments for individuals made through state and local governments — which include Medicaid and AFDC — would be cut back in 1983 from 1982 levels and then allowed to grow slightly in 1984 and 1985. Outlays for other grants to states and localities would be reduced steadily from about $50 billion in 1982 to $41 billion in 1985. Net outlays for "all other federal programs" would have the sharpest cutback, falling by more than one-half, from an estimated $54 billion in 1982 to $25 billion in 1985. This decline, however, masks a projected 60 percent increase in offsetting receipts from the sale of OCS leases, surplus federal property, and other sources. Gross outlays for this sector would be cut back in 1983 by about 15 percent but then held approximately level in current dollars during 1984 and 1985.

CBO ANALYSIS OF THE PRESIDENT'S BUDGET

The Congressional Budget Office's analysis of the President's February budget finds that revenues would be slightly lower than estimated by the Administration for 1983-1985 and budget outlays would be higher. This finding results from CBO's technical analysis of the Administration's budget estimates and a substitution of CBO's economic assumptions for the Administration's. The CBO budget reestimates are shown in Summary Table 5.

SUMMARY TABLE 5

CBO BUDGET REESTIMATES

[By fiscal year, in billions of dollars]

	1982	1983	1984	1985
CBO Technical Reestimates				
Revenues	4.3	−5.2	−13.0	−15.6
Outlays				
Unified budget	12.2	19.9	22.1	23.0
Off-budget entities	0.6	0.8	0.9	1.1
CBO Baseline Economic Assumptions				
Revenues	−3.4	−0.8	5.6	−4.9
Outlays	1.2	3.2	16.4	24.2
Total Reestimates				
Revenues	0.9	− 6.0	− 7.4	−20.5
Outlays				
Unified budget	13.5	23.1	38.5	47.2
Off-budget entities	0.6	0.8	0.9	1.1

These reestimates produce a dramatic increase in the budget deficit. . . . Under CBO's technical and economic reestimates, the unified budget deficit rises from $111 billion in 1982 to $140 billion by 1985, almost twice the level projected by the Administration. Over the three-year period, 1983 to 1985, CBO estimates that the President's budgetary proposals would result in budget deficits that exceed the Administration's estimates by more than $140 billion. Almost $100 billion, or about 70 percent, of these higher deficits results from technical estimating differences. Another $44 billion results from using CBO's baseline economic assumptions instead of the Administration's. . . .

CBO Technical Reestimates

CBO's technical analysis of the Administration's budget estimates suggests that revenues may be overestimated in the February budget by about $5 billion in 1983, $13 billion in 1984, and $16 billion in 1985. The technical reestimates for revenues result mainly from different estimates of the revenue effects of the Economic Recovery Tax Act. On the outlay side, CBO's technical reestimates suggest larger differences, averaging more than $20 billion during 1983-1985. The major differences involve the cost of farm price supports, the rate of spending for defense procurement activities, likely receipts to be derived from the proposed accelerated leasing of OCS lands, and net interest costs. These four areas account for three-fourths of all the differences in CBO's technical reestimates for 1983-1985 outlays.

CBO Economic Reestimates

The economic forecasts of both the Administration and CBO are in close agreement for 1982. Real gross national product (GNP) is projected to rise by about 3 percent over the four quarters of the year, and the unemployment rate is expected to be in the neighborhood of 8 1/2 percent at year's end. The forecasts of inflation and short-term interest rates are also similar in 1982.

In 1983, however, the Administration forecast for inflation and real growth is more optimistic than CBO's. While both forecasts imply virtually the same expansion of nominal GNP, the Administration looks for real GNP to grow by 5.2 percent over the four quarters of 1983, and for inflation (as measured by the GNP deflator) to fall to a rate of 5.5 percent. CBO expects real GNP to grow by about 1 1/2 percentage points less than the Administration does in 1983, and the GNP deflator to rise by about 1 1/2 percentage points more. The slower growth expected by CBO is largely the consequence of higher interest rates in its forecast, which would dampen the recovery in economic activity. . . .

The Administration's economic assumptions for 1984 and beyond are also more optimistic than CBO's. Compared with CBO's baseline assumptions, the Administration projects higher real growth and sharper declines in inflation, unemployment, and interest rates.

The Administration's real growth assumptions for 1984-1987 are near the upper end of historical experience. In comparable four-year periods following previous postwar recoveries, real growth averaged 3.4 percent a year and ranged between 2.0 and 5.2 percent a year. The Administration assumes an average rate of growth of 4.6 percent a year between 1984 and 1987. CBO, in its baseline projections, assumes an average annual growth rate of 3.5 percent.

As shown in Summary Table 5, the effect of the somewhat less optimistic CBO baseline assumptions with respect to real growth, inflation, unemployment, and interest rates would be to raise unified budget outlays by $1 billion in 1982, $3 billion in 1983, over $16 billion in 1984, and $24 billion in 1985. Over the entire four-year period, budget outlays would be $45 billion higher than projected by the Administration. Revenues, on the other hand, would be very close to the Administration's estimates because of the similar assumption about nominal GNP.

The Administration's Budget Reestimated

The CBO economic and technical reestimates assume that all of the President's legislative proposals for taxes and spending are approved by the Congress, and also that the Administration is successful in meeting most of its targets for revenue increases and outlay savings from various management initiatives. CBO has not been able to develop its own independent estimates for outlay savings from several of the management initiatives, particularly those that are clearly targets and not allocated to agency accounts. Based on past history, the unallocated targets for reduction of waste, fraud, and abuse; for improved debt collection; and for the sale of surplus or underused federal property appear to be very optimistic.

Summary Table 7 shows the effect on the Administration's budget of CBO's technical reestimates and of substituting CBO's baseline economic assumptions for the Administration's economic assumptions. Under CBO's pricing of the Administration's budgetary proposals, revenues would grow by less than 25 percent between 1982 and 1985, rising from an estimated $628 billion to $776 billion. Unified budget outlays would grow at approximately the same rate as revenues during this period, rising by 24 percent from $739 billion in 1982 to $916 billion in 1985.

The unified budget deficit rises from $111 billion in 1982 to $140 billion in 1985. When net outlays of off-budget federal entities are included, the total deficit rises from $131 billion in 1982 to more than [$1.51 billion in 1985. The debt subject to limit increases from] $1.0 trillion at the end of 1981 to more than $1.6 trillion at the end of 1985, or by more than 60 percent.

SUMMARY TABLE 7
THE ADMINISTRATION'S BUDGET REESTIMATED
[By fiscal year, in billions of dollars]

	Actual 1981	CBO Estimates			
		1982	1983	1984	1985
Revenues	599.3	627.7	660.1	715.6	776.1
Outlays					
Unified budget	657.2	738.8	780.7	844.5	915.7
Off-budget entities	21.0	20.2	16.5	15.2	12.0
Total Outlays	678.2	759.0	797.2	859.7	927.7
Deficit (−)					
Unified budget	−57.9	−111.1	−120.6	−128.9	−139.6
Off-budget entities	−21.0	−20.2	−16.5	−15.2	−12.0
Total Deficit	−78.9	−131.3	−137.1	−144.1	−151.6
Debt Subject to Limit	998.8	1,143.0	1,297.1	1,458.4	1,640.5

MAJOR RISKS

Several risks are inherent in the Administration's budget proposals. One is that the Administration may have underpriced its projected defense appropriation requests. CBO has identified two major elements of concern in this regard. First, inflation may not decline as rapidly as assumed in the

Administration's budget estimates. This would require additional funds to complete the Administration's plans for defense purchases. Otherwise, higher than anticipated inflation could cause a scaling back of purchases to stay within available funds. CBO's reestimates of the President's budget did not adjust the Administration's proposed budget authority for defense programs for the higher inflation contained in CBO's baseline economic assumptions. If this were done, $61 billion in additional appropriations would be needed during the next five years to achieve the same real growth in defense spending as proposed by the Administration.

Second, the real cost of defense purchases has grown in recent years — averaging about 3 1/2 percent per year since 1975. This has occurred for a variety of reasons, including program changes (such as new specifications for weapons or revised production schedules) and underestimates of real resources (such as manufacturing hours and materials costs). If the Administration is unable to curb this cost growth, further funds would be needed to meet its defense procurement objectives. If the 3 1/2 percent average annual cost growth continues, for example, CBO estimates that an additional $48 billion in new budget authority will be required to fund major weapons procurement during 1983-1987.

A second risk is that it will be very difficult to achieve lower deficits in the next few years if the major effort is focused primarily on the spending side of the budget. The sharp increases proposed for national defense programs, the rising outlays for Social Security and other benefit payments indexed for inflation, and the growing net interest costs place enormous pressure on the remaining portion of the budget. ... [T]hese other federal outlays are projected to shrink steadily. The difficulty of finding still further significant reductions in this area of the budget is very great.

A more fundamental risk is the uncertainty in the economic outlook. The Administration's program implies a strong fiscal stimulus in 1982 and 1983. The large budget deficits projected in this report would result in a marked increase in Treasury borrowing that would put further upward pressure on interest rates. At the same time, the Federal Reserve's targets for monetary growth may act as a brake on economic growth during the next few years. Given the combination of monetary and fiscal policies and the projected economic recovery, high interest rates next year seem likely — although the level is hard to predict because this policy combination of a tight monetary policy and a stimulative fiscal policy is virtually without precedent. Nevertheless, there is a significant risk that the outcome could be even weaker growth than projected by either the Administration or CBO.

Since budget estimates are very sensitive to economic assumptions, policymakers must be prepared for the possibility of developments markedly different from those assumed by both the Administration and CBO. To illustrate the sensitivity of the budget to economic assumptions, CBO also has reestimated the President's February budget using a more pessimistic set of economic assumptions. In the CBO pessimistic alternative assumptions ... real growth averages only 2.0 percent in 1984-1987, unemployment remains at about 8 1/2 percent throughout the period, the rate of inflation remains above 7 percent until the end of the period, and short-term interest rates fall very slowly. ...

Under this more pessimistic set of assumptions, growth in nominal incomes would be somewhat less and federal revenues would be lower by about $25 billion during 1982-1985 than projected by the Administration. The effect on outlays, however, would be much greater. By 1985, outlays would be over $50 billion higher than projected by the Administration, and over $100 billion higher for the entire four-year period. The effect of using the CBO pessimistic economic assumptions would be to raise the estimated level of the budget deficit under the Administration's proposals to $132 billion in 1983, $155 billion in 1984, and $184 billion in 1985.

▼▼▼

MARIJUANA AND HEALTH REPORT
February 26, 1982

A report entitled Marijuana and Health *concluded that marijuana represented a potential health hazard that "justifies serious national concern." The study was conducted by the Institute of Medicine, an organization chartered in 1970 by the National Academy of Sciences to enlist experts to examine public health policy matters. Released February 26, the study was funded by a $454,000 federal grant from the National Institutes of Health.*

Begun at the request of Joseph A. Califano Jr. when he was secretary of the Department of Health, Education and Welfare during the Carter administration, the report constituted the first thorough impartial report on the issues raised by the use of marijuana, particularly among adolescents and young adults.

Surveys suggested that by the time of this study, about a quarter of the American population had tried marijuana and that half of all high school seniors used it with varying regularity. Its widespread use was of concern not only to members of the medical profession but also to local and federal authorities who increasingly had attempted to contain the drug culture surrounding marijuana by curbing paraphernalia traffic. (Court on "head shops," p. 215)

The Report

The report represented 15 months of research conducted by a panel of 22 scientists, chaired by Dr. Arnold S. Relman, editor of The New

England Journal of Medicine. *The panel consulted experts in each area of concern and reviewed all the existing literature on marijuana published since 1975 and relevant studies from before that time. The panel also accepted public comments, although Relman stated that little credence was given to personal testimonials and unverified claims.*

The report was unlikely to satisfy either strong supporters or opponents of the use of marijuana. "Our committee found the present truth of the matter to lie somewhere between the two extremes," said Relman, "so we give no comfort to those with strong positions on either side of the argument." While the panel found "disturbing" the mental phenomena associated with the drug and the possibility that prolonged smoking would lead to lung cancer, it dismissed as "inconclusive" some highly publicized reports linking marijuana to possible chromosome breakage resulting in genetic damage, or a decrease in human fertility.

The panel deplored the lack of available information and insufficient research on almost every topic explored. What made the study especially difficult, members said, was that marijuana use had become widespread only in the last 10 to 20 years and long-term effects, such as lung cancer and psychiatric disorders, often take decades to develop and to detect. Difficulties in designing and executing good experiments, because marijuana was illegal and its smoke had a complex chemical make-up, provided another impeding factor in reaching conclusions.

Findings

The report studied marijuana's effect on functioning of the brain, heart, lungs, reproductive system and chromosome segregation during cell division, concluding that the drug had "possible adverse effects," but that further medical research was still necessary in each of these areas.

Although the findings showed no evidence that the drug caused addiction similar to narcotics, or that physical dependence had much to do with its persistent use, a member of the panel, Dr. Charles P. O'Brien, psychiatrist at the University of Pennsylvania School of Medicine, noted that chemicals found in marijuana, unlike those in alcohol, tended to persist in the brain for many hours after ingestion, a fact that he found "disturbing."

The panel was cautious about attributing to marijuana the "amotivational syndrome," marked by apathy and lack of ambition among some users, and said it was impossible to know if the condition was the cause or the result of drug use. For similar reasons, the report was reluctant to say marijuana was a "stepping stone" to harder drugs.

The report noted a suspected link between marijuana and cancer. Relman said, "We concluded that prolonged, heavy smoking of marijuana would probably lead to cancer of the lungs and to serious impairment of

*the pulmonary function." But he added that "so far there is no direct
confirmation of this." The effects of marijuana on the lungs were
compared with those of cigarettes. The connection between cigarette
smoking and cancer was the subject of the U.S. surgeon general's 1982
report on smoking.* (Surgeon general's report, p. 163)

*The National Institute of Medicine study also examined marijuana's
alleged curative effects in the treatment of glaucoma, the control of the
severe nausea and vomiting caused by cancer chemotherapy, asthma,
epileptic seizures, spastic disorders and other diseases of the nervous
system. It determined that certain components of marijuana could be
"helpful," though again more research for clearer medical evidence was
deemed necessary.*

University of Michigan Report

*Released two days prior to this report were the results of another study,
based on a nationwide survey conducted by the University of Michigan's
Institute for Social Research under a contract with the National Institute on Drug Abuse. This report concluded that students used less
marijuana in 1981 than in previous years. Overall use of drugs among
students was very high; two-thirds of 17,000 high school seniors from the
130 private and public schools surveyed admitted to some use of an illicit
drug. According to the study, marijuana still ranked as the most widely
used of these drugs, with one out of 14 seniors smoking marijuana daily
in 1981, as compared with one out of 11 in 1980 and one out of nine in
1979.*

Following is the text of the summary of Marijuana and
Health, *prepared by the Institute of Medicine and released
February, 26, 1982.* (Boldface headings in brackets have been
added by Congressional Quarterly to highlight the organization of the text.):

Summary

The Institute of Medicine (IOM) of the National Academy of Sciences
has conducted a 15-month study of the health-related effects of marijuana,
at the request of the Secretary of Health and Human Services and the
Director of the National Institutes of Health. The IOM appointed a 22-
member committee to:

 • analyze existing scientific evidence bearing on the possible hazards to
the health and safety of users of marijuana;
 • analyze data concerning the possible therapeutic value and health
benefits of marijuana;
 • assess federal research programs in marijuana;

● identify promising new research directions, and make suggestions to improve the quality and usefulness of future research; and

● draw conclusions from this review that would accurately assess the limits of present knowledge and thereby provide a factual, scientific basis for the development of future government policy.

This assessment of knowledge of the health-related effects of marijuana is important and timely because marijuana is now the most widely used of all the illicit drugs available in the United States. In 1979, more than 50 million persons had tried it at least once. There has been a steep rise in its use during the past decade, particularly among adolescents and young adults, although there has been a leveling-off in its overall use among high school seniors in the past 2 or 3 years and a small decline in the percentage of seniors who use it frequently. Although substantially more high school students have used alcohol than have ever used marijuana, more high school seniors use marijuana on a daily or near-daily basis (9 percent) than alcohol (6 percent). Much of the heavy use of marijuana, unlike alcohol, takes place in school, where effects on behavior, cognition, and psychomotor performance can be particularly disturbing. Unlike alcohol, which is rapidly metabolized and eliminated from the body, the psychoactive components of marijuana persist in the body for a long time. Similar to alcohol, continued use of marijuana may cause tolerance and dependence. For all these reasons, it is imperative that we have reliable and detailed information about the effects of marijuana use on health, both in the long and short term.

What, then, did we learn from our review of the published scientific literature? Numerous acute effects have been described in animals, in isolated cells and tissues, and in studies of human volunteers; clinical and epidemiological observations also have been reported. This information is briefly summarized in the following paragraphs.

[EFFECTS ON NERVOUS SYSTEM AND BEHAVIOR]

We can say with confidence that marijuana produces acute effects on the brain, including chemical and electrophysiological changes. Its most clearly established acute effects are on mental functions and behavior. With a severity directly related to dose, marijuana impairs motor coordination and affects tracking ability and sensory and perceptual functions important for safe driving and the operation of other machines; it also impairs short-term memory and slows learning. Other acute effects include feelings of euphoria and other mood changes, but there also are disturbing mental phenomena, such as brief periods of anxiety, confusion, or psychosis.

There is not yet any conclusive evidence as to whether prolonged use of marijuana causes permanent changes in the nervous system or sustained impairment of brain function and behavior in human beings. In a few unconfirmed studies in experimental animals, impairment of learning and changes in electrical brain-wave recordings have been observed several months after the cessation of chronic administration of marijuana. In the judgment of the committee, widely cited studies purporting to demonstrate that marijuana affects the gross and microscopic structure of the human or monkey brain are not convincing; much more work is needed to settle this important point.

Chronic relatively heavy use of marijuana is associated with behavioral dysfunction and mental disorders in human beings, but available evidence does not establish if marijuana use under these circumstances is a cause or a result of the mental condition. There are similar problems in interpreting the evidence linking the use of marijuana to subsequent use of other illicit drugs, such as heroin or cocaine. Association does not prove a causal relation, and the use of marijuana may merely be symptomatic of an underlying disposition to use psychoactive drugs rather than a "stepping stone" to involvement with more dangerous substances. It is also difficult to sort out the relationship between use of marijuana and the complex symptoms known as the amotivational syndrome. Self-selection and effects of the drug are probably both contributing to the motivational problems seen in some chronic users of marijuana.

Thus, the long-term effects of marijuana on the human brain and on human behavior remain to be defined. Although we have no convincing evidence thus far of any effects persisting in human beings after cessation of drug use, there may well be subtle but important physical and psychological consequences that have not been recognized.

[EFFECTS ON THE HEART AND LUNGS]

There is good evidence that the smoking of marijuana usually causes acute changes in the heart and circulation that are characteristic of stress, but there is no evidence to indicate that a permanently deleterious effect on the normal cardiovascular system occurs. There is good evidence to show that marijuana increases the work of the heart, usually by raising heart rate and, in some persons, by raising blood pressure. This rise in workload poses a threat to patients with hypertension, cerebrovascular disease, and coronary atherosclerosis.

Acute exposure to marijuana smoke generally elicits bronchodilation; chronic heavy smoking of marijuana causes inflammation and pre-neoplastic changes in the airways, similar to those produced by smoking of tobacco. Marijuana smoke is a complex mixture that not only has many chemical components (including carbon monoxide and "tar") and biological effects similar to those of tobacco smoke, but also some unique ingredients. This suggests the strong possibility that prolonged heavy smoking of marijuana, like tobacco, will lead to cancer of the respiratory tract and to serious impairment of lung function. Although there is evidence of impaired lung function in chronic smokers, no direct confirmation of the likelihood of cancer has yet been provided, possibly because marijuana has been widely smoked in this country for only about 20 years, and data have not been collected systematically in other countries with a much longer history of heavy marijuana use.

[EFFECTS ON REPRODUCTION]

Although studies in animals have shown that Δ-9-THC (the major psychoactive constituent of marijuana) lowers the concentration in blood serum of pituitary hormones (gonadotropins) that control reproductive functions, it is not known if there is a direct effect on reproductive tissues. Delta-9-THC appears to have a modest reversible suppressive effect on sperm production in men, but there is no proof that it has a deleterious effect on male fertility. Effects on human female hormonal function have been reported, but the evidence is not convincing. However, there is convincing evidence that marijuana interferes with ovulation in female monkeys. No satisfactory studies of the relation between use of marijuana and female fertility and child-bearing have been carried out. Although Δ-9-THC is known to cross the placenta readily and to cause birth defects when administered in large doses to experimental animals, no adequate clinical studies have been carried out to determine if marijuana use can harm the human fetus. There is no conclusive evidence of teratogenicity in human offspring, but a slowly developing or low-level effect might be undetected by the studies done so far. The effects of marijuana on reproductive function and on the fetus are unclear; they may prove to be negligible, but further research to establish or rule out such effects would be of great importance.

Extracts from marijuana smoke particulates ("tar") have been found to produce dose-related mutations in bacteria; however, Δ-9-THC, by itself, is not mutagenic. Marijuana and Δ-9-THC do not appear to break chromosomes, but marijuana may affect chromosome segregation during cell division, resulting in an abnormal number of chromosomes in daughter cells. Although these results are of concern, their clinical significance is unknown.

[THE IMMUNE SYSTEM]

Similar limitations exist in our understanding of the effects of marijuana on other body systems. For example, some studies of the immune system demonstrate a mild, immunosuppressant effect on human beings, but other studies show no effect.

[THERAPEUTIC POTENTIAL]

The committee also has examined the evidence on the therapeutic effects of marijuana in a variety of medical disorders. Preliminary studies suggest that marijuana and its derivatives or analogues might be useful in the treatment of the raised intraocular pressure of glaucoma, in the control of the severe nausea and vomiting caused by cancer chemotherapy, and in the treatment of asthma. There also is some preliminary evidence that a marijuana constituent (cannabidiol) might be helpful in the treatment of certain types of epileptic seizures, as well as for spastic disorders and other nervous system diseases. But, in these and all other conditions, much more work is needed. Because marijuana and Δ-9-THC often produce troublesome psychotropic or cardiovascular side-effects that limit their therapeutic usefulness, particularly in older patients, the greatest therapeutic potential probably lies in the use of synthetic analogues of marijuana derivatives with higher ratios of therapeutic to undesirable effects.

[MORE RESEARCH NEEDED]

The explanation for all of these unanswered questions is insufficient research. We need to know much more about the metabolism of the various marijuana chemical compounds and their biologic effects. This will require many more studies in animals, with particular emphasis on subhuman primates. Basic pharmacologic information obtained in animal experiments will ultimately have to be tested in clinical studies on human beings.

Until 10 or 15 years ago, there was virtually no systematic, rigorously controlled research on the human health-related effects of marijuana and its major constituents. Even now, when standardized marijuana and pure synthetic cannabinoids are available for experimental studies, and good qualitative methods exist for the measurement of Δ-9-THC and its metabolites in body fluids, well-designed studies on human beings are relatively few. There are difficulties in studying the clinical effects of marijuana in human beings, particularly the effects of long-term use. And yet, without such studies the debate about the safety or hazard of marijuana will remain unresolved. Prospective cohort studies, as well as retrospective case-control studies, would be useful in identifying long-term behavioral and biological consequences of marijuana use.

The federal investment in research on the health-related effects of marijuana has been small, both in relation to the expenditure on other illicit drugs and in absolute terms. The committee considers the research particularly inadequate when viewed in light of the extent of marijuana use in this country, especially by young people. We believe there should be a greater investment in research on marijuana, and that investigator-initiated research grants should be the primary vehicle of support.

The committee considers all of the areas of research on marijuana that are supported by the National Institute on Drug Abuse to be important, but we did not judge the appropriateness of the allocation of resources among those areas, other than to conclude that there should be increased emphasis on studies in human beings and other primates. . . .

CONCLUSIONS

The scientific evidence published to date indicates that marijuana has a broad range of psychological and biological effects, some of which, at least under certain conditions, are harmful to human health. Unfortunately, the available information does not tell us how serious this risk may be.

Our major conclusion is that what little we know for certain about the effects of marijuana on human health — and all that we have reason to suspect — justifies serious national concern. Of no less concern is the extent of our ignorance about many of the most basic and important questions about the drug. Our major recommendation is that there be a greatly intensified and more comprehensive program of research into the effects of marijuana on the health of the American people. . . .

[Use of Marijuana in the U. S.]

. . . There has been a steep rise in the use of marijuana and other illicit drugs in the past decade. So far it is primarily a youth phenomenon. Since 1971 there has been at least a doubling of lifetime experience with marijuana in every cohort in the 12- to 24-year age group. Of all psychoactive drugs investigated (including inhalants, hallucinogens, cocaine, heroin, stimulants, sedatives, and tranquilizers), marijuana is by far the most commonly used illicit drug. Legal drugs for adults, such as alcohol and tobacco, are the most widely used of all drugs among adolescents. Although substantially more students have ever used alcohol in their lifetime than have ever used marijuana, more high school seniors use marijuana on a "daily" basis (9 percent) than use alcohol that frequently (6 percent). "Daily" users report the use of marijuana in school, whereas daily use of alcohol tends to occur after school and on weekends.

Some trends in use of marijuana are apparent. The continuing dramatic rise in the use of marijuana has recently slowed. It is too early to tell whether this decrease will continue or is merely a pause in the rise. The overall prevalence of use of marijuana has remained at approximately 60 percent of high school seniors for the years 1978, 1979, and 1980. Between 1975 and 1978 there was an almost twofold increase in "daily" use of marijuana from 6 percent in 1975 to a peak rate of 11 percent in 1978. In 1980 the "daily" use rate of high school seniors dropped by 1.2 percentage points, or more than 10 percent. This may signal a reversal of the upward trend in "daily" use unless higher absenteeism and school drop-out of daily users are significant factors in the decline. Multiple sources suggest that out-of-school age mates are heavier users than those in school. Other trends have not slowed. There was a continuing rise in 1980 of the proportion of high school seniors who during the year had used some illicit drug other than marijuana, from 28 percent in 1979 to 30 percent in 1980.

Throughout the 1970s, as a correlate of continuing rise in prevalence rates, there was a trend toward younger ages of first use of all of these drugs. For marijuana this age trend continues but has slowed somewhat. In 1979, 23 percent of seniors who had used marijuana started their use in the eighth grade or below as compared to 25 percent in 1980.

"Daily" use of marijuana in high school and in early adult life is very high and merits special attention. Drawing on data from *Monitoring the*

Future, characteristics of "daily" users were described. For high school seniors the rate of "daily" marijuana use in 1980 was 9.1 percent. Such users have very high involvement with other drugs and begin their use of drugs at very early ages. "Daily" users are predominantly urban although rates do not vary by geographical regions of the country, whereas use among white students is double that for blacks. "Daily" use is only slightly higher in disrupted or single parent homes than in nuclear families, and use is associated with poor school achievement, absenteeism, and dropout. Non-college-bound students are twice as likely to be "daily" users as were students planning to attend college. Religious commitment and self-rating of strong belief in law-abiding behavior are associated with lower "daily" use rates. "Daily" users are involved in more automobile accidents and delinquency.

Post-high school "daily" user rates are lowest among full-time college students and those living in a college dormitory. "Daily" use among non-college students was not related to joblessness, employment, or military service. Single persons are twice as likely as married persons to be "daily" users. Among the married, those with children had very low rates of "daily" use. The "daily" use habit has a remarkable stability. By 4 years after high school, 85 percent of "daily" using seniors in the class of 1975 were still using marijuana, with 51 percent of them continuing to be "daily" users.

In these studies, students report reasons for using marijuana: to have a good time with friends, to get "high," to relieve boredom, to enhance the effects of other drugs, and to cope with stress. "Daily" users are deeply immersed in a drug-using circle of friends.

Some "daily" users have discontinued their habit. Reasons given for stopping use of marijuana are loss of interest in getting "high," concern about harmful physical or psychological effects, and concern about their loss of energy or ambition.

More is known about the antecedents of using marijuana than is known about the consequences of using marijuana. . . . Longitudinal studies have established that use of marijuana is preceded by acceptance of a cluster of beliefs and values that are favorable to use of marijuana and also by the adoption of deviant behaviors. The deviant psycho-social attributes of marijuana users that were described almost a decade ago, when use of marijuana was a rare event, are just as characteristic of marijuana users today, when 60 percent of all high school seniors report some experience with the use of marijuana. Daily users show the extremes of these deviant behaviors but less deeply involved users also exhibit some deviancy. Friendship patterns and peer influence play a uniquely powerful role in determining youthful marijuana use. Negative parental relationships do not appear to be associated as an antecedent to use of marijuana. . . .

MARCH

COURT ON 'HEAD SHOPS'

March 3, 1982

An 8-0 vote by the Supreme Court March 3 upheld the power of an Illinois village to curb the sale of drug paraphernalia, reversing a decision by the 7th Circuit Court of Appeals. Although the case of Hoffman Estates v. Flipside *did not address the legality of "head shops" per se, it did officially relegate power over paraphernalia sales to state and local governments. Justice Thurgood Marshall wrote the court's opinion, in which Justice John Paul Stevens did not participate.*

The ordinance at issue was enacted by Hoffman Estates, a village of approximately 38,000 people 25 miles northwest of Chicago. The ordinance required head shops to apply for a $150.00 license and to register, by name and address, any individual purchasing a paraphernalia item. This list would be open to police inspection. The regulation was designed to restrict minors' access to potentially hazardous drugs, the most common of which was marijuana. (Marijuana and health, p. 203)

Flipside sued to have the ordinance declared unconstitutional. Though officially a record store, Flipside, in one of the Hoffman Estates shopping malls, also carried drug-oriented accessories, including roach clips, bongs, pipes, rolling papers and drug publications. Flipside lost the case in federal district court, but the 7th Circuit upheld its appeal, agreeing that the regulation was unconstitutionally vague in defining paraphernalia, a paraphernalia store and "intent to sell material for use with illegal substances." The ordinance's targets included "any item, effect, paraphernalia, accessory or thing which is designed or marketed for use with illegal cannabis or drugs." The 7th Circuit decided that the village's

215

order, besides being vague, was "an infringement on the constitutional guarantee of free speech."

The Supreme Court, however, decided that the ordinance "simply regulates business behavior," and that it was constitutional. According to Marshall, the head-shop operators must have known the meaning of words like "roach clip." If not, he wrote, they could find out "without undue burden" by consulting one American Heritage dictionary definition of roach: "the butt of a marijuana cigarette." The court emphasized that local laws should contain precise definitions of regulated materials and of the retailer's intent in selling these items.

The ruling was expected to aid other jurisdictions in efforts to curtail the use of marijuana and other illegal substances and to restrict the paraphernalia industry, estimated to gross $3 billion annually. The states of New York, New Jersey and Connecticut already had adopted the prohibition approach. The United States Court of Appeals for the 2nd Circuit in 1981 upheld a Westchester County ordinance that banned the sale of material "used, intended for use, or designed for use" with illegal substances. This case had been appealed to the Supreme Court. Thus, a final decision on the legality of head shops was still pending, even after Hoffman Estates v. Flipside.

Following are excerpts from the March 3 decision by the Supreme Court upholding, by a vote of 8-0, a local ordinance regulating the sale of drug paraphernalia:

No. 80-1681

Village of Hoffman Estates, et al., Appellants, *v.* Flipside, Hoffman Estates, Inc.	Appeal from the United States Court of Appeals for the Seventh Circuit

[March 3, 1982]

JUSTICE MARSHALL delivered the opinion of the Court.

JUSTICE STEVENS took no part in the consideration or decision of this case.

This case presents a pre-enforcement facial challenge to a drug paraphernalia ordinance on the ground that it is unconstitutionally vague and overbroad. The ordinance in question requires a business to obtain a license if it sells any items that are "designed or marketed for use with illegal cannabis or drugs." The United States Court of Appeals for the Seventh Circuit held that the ordinance is vague on its face. (1980). We noted probable jurisdiction and now reverse.

COURT ON HEAD SHOPS

I

For more than three years prior to May 1, 1978, appellee The Flipside, Hoffman Estates, Inc. (Flipside) sold a variety of merchandise, including phonographic records, smoking accessories, novelty devices and jewelry, in its store located in the village of Hoffman Estates, Illinois (the village). On February 20, 1978, the village enacted an ordinance regulating drug paraphernalia, to be effective May 1, 1978. The ordinance makes it unlawful for any person "to sell any items, effect, paraphernalia, accessory or thing which is designed or marketed for use with illegal cannabis or drugs, as defined by Illinois Revised Statutes, without obtaining a license therefor." The license fee is $150.00. A business must also file affidavits that the licensee and its employees have not been convicted of a drug-related offense. Moreover, the business must keep a record of each sale of a regulated item, including the name and address of the purchaser, to be open to police inspection. No regulated item may be sold to a minor. A violation is subject to a fine of not less than $10.00 and not more than $500.00, and each day that a violation continues gives rise to a separate offense. A series of licensing guidelines prepared by the village attorney define "Paper," "Roach Clips," "Pipes" and "Paraphernalia," the sale of which is required to be licensed.

After an administrative inquiry, the village determined that Flipside and one other store appeared to be in violation of the ordinance. The village attorney notified Flipside of the existence of the ordinance, and made a copy of the ordinance and guidelines available to Flipside. Flipside's owner asked for guidance concerning which items were covered by the ordinance; the village attorney advised him to remove items in a certain section of the store "for his protection," and he did so. The items included, according to Flipside's description, a clamp, chain ornaments, an "alligator" clip, key chains, necklaces, earrings, cigarette holders, glove stretchers, scales, strainers, a pulverizer, squeeze bottles, pipes, water pipes, pins, an herb sifter, mirrors, vials, cigarette rolling papers, and tobacco snuff. On May 30, 1978, instead of applying for a license or seeking clarification via the administrative procedures that the village had established for its licensing ordinances. Flipside filed this lawsuit in the United States District Court for the Northern District of Illinois.

The complaint alleged, inter alia, that the ordinance is unconstitutionally vague and overbroad, and requested injunctive and declaratory relief and damages. The District Court, after hearing testimony, declined to grant a preliminary injunction. The case was tried without a jury on additional evidence and stipulated testimony. The court issued an opinion upholding the constitutionality of the ordinance, and awarded judgment to the village defendants.

The Court of Appeals reversed, on the ground that the ordinance is unconstitutionally vague on its face. The court reviewed the language of the ordinance and guidelines and found it vague with respect to certain conceivable applications, such as ordinary pipes or "paper clips sold next to *Rolling Stone* magazine." It also suggested that the "subjective" nature of the "marketing" test creates a danger of arbitrary and discriminatory enforcement against those with alternative lifestyles. Finally, the court determined that the availability of administrative review or guidelines cannot cure the defect. Thus, it concluded that the ordinance is impermissibly vague on its face.

II

In a facial challenge to the overbreadth and vagueness of a law, a court's first task is to determine whether the enactment reaches a substantial amount of constitutionally protected conduct. If it does not, then the overbreadth challenge must fail. The court should then examine the facial vagueness challenge and, assuming the enactment implicates no constitutionally protected conduct, should uphold the challenge only if the enactment is impermissibly vague in all of its applications. A plaintiff who engages in some conduct that is clearly proscribed cannot complain of the vagueness of the law as applied to the conduct of others. A court should therefore examine the complainant's conduct before analyzing other hypothetical applications of the law.

The Court of Appeals in this case did not explicitly consider whether the ordinance reaches constitutionally protected conduct and is overbroad, nor whether the ordinance is vague in all of its applications. Instead, the court determined that the ordinance is void for vagueness because it is unclear in *some* of its applications to the conduct of Flipside and of other hypothetical parties. Under a proper analysis, however, the ordinance is not facially invalid.

III

We first examine whether the ordinance infringes Flipside's First Amendment rights or is overbroad because it inhibits the First Amendment rights of other parties. Flipside makes the exorbitant claim that the village has imposed a "prior restraint" on speech because the guidelines treat the proximity of drug-related literature as an indicium that paraphernalia are "marketed for use with illegal cannabis or drugs." Flipside also argues that because the presence of drug-related designs, logos, or slogans on paraphernalia may trigger enforcement, the ordinance infringes "protected symbolic speech."

These arguments do not long detain us. First, the village has not directly infringed the noncommercial speech of Flipside or other parties. The ordinance licenses and regulates the sale of items displayed "with" or "within proximity of" "literature encouraging illegal use of cannabis or illegal drugs," but does not prohibit or otherwise regulate the sale of literature itself. Although drug-related designs or names on cigarette papers may subject those items to regulation, the village does not restrict speech as such, but simply regulates the commercial marketing of items that the labels reveal may be used for an illicit purpose. The scope of the ordinance therefore does not embrace noncommercial speech.

Second, insofar as any *commercial* speech interest is implicated here, it is only the attenuated interest in displaying and marketing merchandise in the manner that the retailer desires. We doubt that the village's restriction on the manner of marketing appreciably limits Flipside's communication of information — with one obvious and telling exception. The ordinance is expressly directed at commercial activity promoting or encouraging illegal drug use. If that activity is deemed "speech," then it is speech proposing an illegal transaction, which a government may regulate or ban entirely. *Central Hudson Gas & Electric Co.* v. *Public Service Comm'n* (1980); *Pittsburgh Press Co.* v. *Human Relations Comm'n* (1973). Finally, it is irrelevant whether the ordinance has an overbroad scope encompassing protected commercial speech of other persons, because the overbreadth doctrine does not apply to commercial speech. . . .

IV

A

A law that does not reach constitutionally protected conduct and therefore satisfies the overbreadth test may nevertheless be challenged on its face as unduly vague, in violation of due process. To succeed, however, the complainant must demonstrate that the law is impermissibly vague in all of its applications. Flipside makes no such showing.

The standards for evaluating vagueness were enunciated in *Grayned* v. *City of Rockford* (1972):

> "Vague laws offend several important values. First, because we assume that man is free to steer between lawful and unlawful conduct, we insist that laws give the person of ordinary intelligence a reasonable opportunity to know what is prohibited, so that he may act accordingly. Vague laws may trap the innocent by not providing fair warning. Second, if arbitrary and discriminatory enforcement is to be prevented, laws must provide explicit standards for those who apply them. A vague law impermissibly delegates basic policy matters to policemen, judges, and juries for resolution on an *ad hoc* and subjective basis, with the attendant dangers of arbitrary and discriminatory applications."

These standards should not, of course, be mechanically applied. The degree of vagueness that the Constitution tolerates — as well as the relative importance of fair notice and fair enforcement — depend in part on the nature of the enactment. Thus, economic regulation is subject to a less strict vagueness test because its subject-matter is often more narrow, and because businesses, which face economic demands to plan behavior carefully, can be expected to consult relevant legislation in advance of action. Indeed, the regulated enterprise may have the ability to clarify the meaning of the regulation by its own inquiry, or by resort to an administrative process. The Court has also expressed greater tolerance of enactments with civil rather than criminal penalties because the consequences of imprecision are qualitatively less severe. And the Court has recognized that a scienter [knowledge of the wrong] requirement may mitigate a law's vagueness, especially with respect to the adequacy of notice to the complainant that his conduct is proscribed.

Finally, perhaps the most important factor affecting the clarity that the Constitution demands of a law is whether it threatens to inhibit the exercise of constitutionally protected rights. If, for example, the law interferes with the right of free speech or of association, a more stringent vagueness test should apply.

B

This ordinance simply regulates business behavior and contains a scienter requirement with respect to the alternative "marketed for use" standard. The ordinance nominally imposes only civil penalties. However, the village concedes that the ordinance is "quasi-criminal," and its prohibitory and stigmatizing effect may warrant a relatively strict test. Flipside's facial challenge fails because, under the test appropriate to either a quasi-criminal or a criminal law, the ordinance is sufficiently clear as applied to Flipside.

The ordinance requires Flipside to obtain a license if it sells "any items, effect, paraphernalia, accessory or thing which is designed or marketed for use with illegal cannabis or drugs, as defined by the Illinois Revised Statutes." Flipside expresses no uncertainty about which drugs this description encompasses; as the District Court noted, Illinois law clearly defines cannabis and numerous other controlled drugs, including cocaine. On the other hand, the words "items, effect, paraphernalia, accessory or thing" do not identify the type of merchandise that the village desires to regulate. Flipside's challenge thus appropriately focuses on the language "designed or marketed for use." Under either the "designed for use" or "marketed for use" standard, we conclude that at least some of the items sold by Flipside are covered. Thus, Flipside's facial challenge is unavailing.

1. "Designed for use"

The Court of Appeals objected that "designed . . . for use" is ambiguous with respect to whether items must be inherently suited only for drug use; whether the retailer's intent or manner of display is relevant; and whether the intent of a third party, the manufacturer, is critical, since the manufacturer is the "designer." For the reasons that follow, we conclude that this language is not unconstitutionally vague on its face.

The Court of Appeals' speculation about the meaning "design" is largely unfounded. The guidelines refer to "paper of colorful design" and to other specific items as conclusively "designed" or not "designed" for illegal use. A principal meaning of "design" is "To fashion according to a plan." Webster's New International Dictionary of the English Language 707 (2d ed. 1957). Cf. *Lanzetta* v. *New Jersey* (1939). It is therefore plain that the standard encompasses at least an item that is principally used with illegal drugs by virtue of its objective features, i.e., features designed by the manufacturer. A business person of ordinary intelligence would understand that this term refers to the design of the manufacturer, not the intent of the retailer or customer. It is also sufficiently clear that items which are principally used for nondrug purposes, such as ordinary pipes, are not "designed for use" with illegal drugs. Moreover, no issue of fair warning is present in this case, since Flipside concedes that the phrase refers to structural characteristics of an item.

The ordinance and guidelines do contain ambiguities. Nevertheless, the "designed for use" standard is sufficiently clear to cover at least some of the items that Flipside sold. The ordinance, through the guidelines, explicitly regulates "roach clips." Flipside's co-operator admitted that the store sold such items, and the village Chief of Police testified that he had never seen a "roach clip" used for any purpose other than to smoke cannabis. The chief also testified that a specially-designed pipe that Flipside marketed is typically used to smoke marijuana. Whether further guidelines, administrative rules, or enforcement policy will clarify the more ambiguous scope of the standard in other respects is of no concern in this facial challenge.

2. "Marketed for use"

Whatever ambiguities the "designed . . . for use" standard may engender, the alternative "marketed for use" standard is transparently clear: it describes a retailer's intentional display and marketing of merchandise. The guidelines refer to the display of paraphernalia, and to the proximity of covered items to otherwise uncovered items. A retail store therefore must obtain a license if it deliberately displays its wares in a manner that appeals to or encourages illegal drug use. The standard requires scienter, since a retailer could scarcely "market" items "for" a particular use without intending that use.

Under this test, Flipside had ample warning that its marketing activities required a license. Flipside displayed the magazine "High Times" and books entitled "Marijuana Grower's Guide," "Children's Garden of Grass," and "The Pleasures of Cocaine," physically close to pipes and colored rolling papers, in clear violation of the guidelines. As noted above, Flipside's co-operator admitted that his store sold "roach clips," which are principally used for illegal purposes. Finally, in the same section of the store, Flipside had posted the sign, "You must be 18 or older to purchase any head supplies."

V

The Court of Appeals also held that the ordinance provides insufficient standards for enforcement. Specifically, the court feared that the ordinance might be used to harass individuals with alternative lifestyles and views. In reviewing a business regulation for facial vagueness, however, the principal inquiry is whether the law affords fair warning of what is proscribed. Moreover, this emphasis is almost inescapable in reviewing a pre-enforcement challenge to a law. Here, no evidence has been, or could be, introduced to indicate whether the ordinance has been enforced in a discriminatory manner or with the aim of inhibiting unpopular speech. The language of the ordinance is sufficiently clear that the speculative danger of arbitrary enforcement does not render the ordinance void for vagueness. Cf. *Papachristou* v. *City of Jacksonville* (1972); *Coates* v. *City of Cincinnati* (1971).

We do not suggest that the risk of discriminatory enforcement is insignificant here. Testimony of the village attorney who drafted the ordinance, the village president, and the police chief revealed confusion over whether the ordinance applies to certain items, as well as extensive reliance on the "judgment" of police officers to give meaning to the ordinance and to enforce it fairly. At this stage, however, we are not prepared to hold that this risk jeopardizes the entire ordinance.

Nor do we assume that the village will take no further steps to minimize the dangers of arbitrary enforcement. The village may adopt administrative regulations that will sufficiently narrow potentially vague or arbitrary interpretations of the ordinance. In economic regulation especially such administrative regulation will often suffice to clarify a standard with an otherwise uncertain scope. We also find it significant that the village ... primarily relied on the "marketing" aspect of the standard, which does not require the more ambiguous item-by-item analysis of whether paraphernalia are "designed for" illegal drug use, and which therefore presents a lesser risk of discriminatory enforcement. "Although it is possible that specific future applications ... may engender concrete problems of constitutional dimension, it will be time enough to consider any such problems when they arise." *Seagram & Sons* v. *Hostetter* (1966).

VI

Many American communities have recently enacted laws regulating or prohibiting the sale of drug paraphernalia. Whether these laws are wise or effective is not, of course, the province of this Court. See *Ferguson* v. *Skrupa* (1963). We hold only that such legislation is not facially overbroad or vague if it does not reach constitutionally protected conduct and is reasonably clear in its application to the complainant.

Accordingly, the judgment of the Court of Appeals is reversed, and the case is remanded for further proceedings consistent with this opinion.

It is so ordered.

[Appendix omitted]

JUSTICE WHITE, concurring in the judgment.

I agree that the judgment of the Court of Appeals must be reversed. I do not, however, believe it necessary to discuss the overbreadth problem in order to reach this result. The Court of Appeals held the ordinance to be void for vagueness; it did not discuss any problem of overbreadth. That opinion should be reversed simply because it erred in its analysis of the vagueness problem presented by the ordinance.

I agree with the majority that a facial vagueness challenge to an economic regulation must demonstrate that "the enactment is impermissibly vague in all of its applications." I also agree with the majority's statement that the "marketed for use" standard in the ordinance is "sufficiently clear." There is, in my view, no need to go any further: If it is "transparently clear" that some particular conduct is restricted by the ordinance, the ordinance survives a facial challenge on vagueness grounds.

Technically, overbreadth is a standing doctrine that permits parties in cases involving First Amendment challenges to government restrictions on noncommercial speech to argue that the regulation is invalid because of its effect on the First Amendment rights of others, not presently before the Court. *Broadrick* v. *Oklahoma* (1973). Whether the appellees may make use of the overbreadth doctrine depends, in the first instance, on whether or not they have a colorable claim that the ordinance infringes on constitutionally protected, noncommercial speech of others. Although appellees claim that the ordinance does have such an effect, that argument is tenuous at best and should be left to the lower courts for an initial determination.

Accordingly, I concur in the judgment reversing the decision below.

BREZHNEV AND REAGAN ON SOVIET NUCLEAR FREEZE
March 16, 1982

At an international trade union convention in Moscow March 16, Soviet President Leonid Brezhnev announced a moratorium, effective immediately, on the deployment of new nuclear medium-range missiles in Western Europe. American officials quickly dismissed Brezhnev's proposal as a propaganda ploy, and President Ronald Reagan, speaking in Oklahoma the same day, said that the Soviet proposal "doesn't go far enough."

In his address the Soviet leader announced that the freeze on the introduction of any new SS-20 medium-range nuclear missiles and on the replacement of old SS-4 and SS-5 missiles west of the Ural Mountains would continue until an arms control agreement was reached with the United States or until the North Atlantic Treaty Organization (NATO) started "practical preparations" for the deployment of 572 new Pershing II and cruise missiles. To counter the Soviets' increased arms buildup and their deployment of new SS-20s, NATO had agreed in December 1979 to deploy the American missiles in late 1983.

Although Brezhnev warned that NATO's deployment of a new generation of missiles would force Moscow to take "retaliatory steps," he did not elaborate on what the steps would be. The Soviet leader also said that Moscow would dismantle some of its medium-range missiles already in place. While Brezhnev did not specify what missiles he meant, U.S. analysts assumed he was referring to long-standing plans to dismantle some older generation missiles.

Response in the United States

Brezhnev spoke a day after the Reagan administration had announced that the Soviet Union recently had deployed 300 new SS-20 medium-range missiles, each capable of delivering three nuclear warheads, and apparently had begun construction of five new bases, each housing up to 50 more missiles.

In response to Brezhnev, Reagan said that, like other nuclear-freeze proposals by the Soviets, this one retained Soviet missile superiority in Europe. He added that a Soviet freeze west of the Urals was meaningless because the SS-20 was powerful enough to hit European targets from east of the Urals.

U. S. State Department officials described Brezhnev's proposal as "an attempt to convey the impression of restraining while diverting attention from the enormous growth in Soviet capability." They claimed that Brezhnev's comments also were intended to fuel the growing antinuclear movement in Western Europe and the United States. (Nuclear freeze movement, p. 885)

Soviet-American Arms Talks

Brezhnev's speech and Reagan's quick response were one of a series of public exchanges between the White House and the Kremlin since talks on reducing medium-range weapons in Europe began in Geneva on November 30, 1981. Although the talks officially were scheduled to continue until an agreement was reached between the two nations, the Geneva conference recessed on March 16 for about two months without any indications of whether progress had been made. Both nations had agreed to a news blackout when the talks first opened.

One fundamental dispute between the two powers promised to remain a barrier in reaching an agreement. Moscow asserted that the East and West were of roughly equal strength in Europe, but Washington contended that the Soviet Union had an advantage because it had been replacing its old SS-4 and SS-5 missiles with the new SS-20s. While the Soviet Union proposed a nuclear freeze, the United States advocated the "zero-option" plan advanced by Reagan on November 18, 1981, and presented at the talks on February 4, 1982. According to this "ground zero" proposal, the Soviet Union would dismantle all its medium-range missiles capable of hitting Western Europe in return for the cancellation of NATO plans to deploy the new generation of 572 modern medium-range missiles. (Reagan on nuclear arms in Europe, Historic Documents of 1981, p. 823)

Following are excerpts from an address by Leonid Brezhnev at the 17th Congress of the Trade Unions of the U. S. S. R., *excerpts from President Reagan's response, delivered before a joint session of the Oklahoma state legislature, in Oklahoma City, and the text of a White House statement, delivered by Larry Speakes, principal deputy press secretary, all March 16, 1982. (Boldface headings in brackets have been added by Congressional Quarterly to highlight the organization of the texts.):*

BREZHNEV STATEMENT

... Now a few words about the international situation as a whole. To say it is complicated and tense would perhaps be saying too little. The situation arouses alarm over the entire further development of international relations.

Take, for instance, what has happened at the Madrid follow-up conference on security and cooperation in Europe.

SECURITY AND COOPERATION — that was the mandate the conference had from the peoples. Instead, however, high-ranking representatives of the governments of the United States and (under obvious Washington pressure) of some other NATO countries have come to Madrid with an entirely different intention, that of poisoning to the maximum the international atmosphere. As a pretext, they chose the internal events in Poland. NATO bloc spokesmen began telling the Sejm [Polish parliament] and the Government of the Polish People's Republic and the leadership of the Polish United Workers' Party what they should do to settle their country's internal problems. Nor did they omit slandering the Soviet Union and other countries of the socialist community. Representatives of governments that patronise in every way the bloodiest and most inhuman regimes now to be found in the world, that persecute people active in trade unions and other democratic organisations in their own countries, held forth unblushingly on the subject of "championing human rights".

[U.S. Plans for Western Europe]

Let me repeat: Polish affairs were no more than a pretext. No one will succeed in overturning socialism in Poland. That is also evidently understood by the foreign inspirers of the Polish counter-revolutionaries. Their true aim in Madrid was to add still more heat to the general tense atmosphere and thereby facilitate implementation of the sinister plans of the United States with regard to Western Europe. They want to make it a launching pad for new American missiles, a lightning rod that would take the retaliatory strike in the event of a conflict. Furthermore, they want to place additional obstacles in the way of development of normal economic ties between Western Europe and the socialist countries. These ties obviously do not suit Washington, because Western Europe is one of its chief economic rivals.

Actions of that sort give food for serious thought about the future of detente and peaceful cooperation in Europe, and not in Europe alone.

Madrid, after all, is only a recent example. One could probably say that international relations as a whole have now come to a distinctly visible crossroads.

[Two Paths]

On the one hand lies the path of strengthening peace and extending peaceful cooperation among all states, cooperation based on strict respect for the independence, rights and interests of each country, on non-interference in internal affairs, and on joint efforts to strengthen world security and mutual confidence. That path is clearly marked out in the provisions of the Helsinki Conference, and in many other inter-state documents of the past decade. And it has been confirmed by the practical experience of nations, especially the European nations, during those ten years.

On the other hand lies the path onto which the world is being intensively pushed by the newly fledged devotees of cold war and dangerous balancing on the brink of a real war.

They would like nothing better than casting aside the legal and ethical norms of relations between states that have taken shape over the centuries and destroying their independence and sovereignty. They are trying to recarve the political map of the world, and have declared large regions on all continents to be zones of their "vital interests". They have arrogated to themselves the "right" to command some countries and to judge and "punish" others. Unashamedly, they publicly announce and try to carry out plans for economic and political "destablisation" of governments and states that are not to their liking. With unexampled cynicism, they gloat over difficulties experienced by this or that nation. They are trying to substitute "sanctions" and blockades for normal communications and international trade, and endless threats of the use of armed force, not short of threats to use nuclear weapons, for contacts and negotiations.

It is simply astonishing to see it all. And you cannot help asking yourself: what is there more of in this policy — thoughtlessness and lack of experience in international affairs, or irresponsibility and, to put it bluntly, an adventurist approach to problems crucial for the destiny of mankind? It is not in our country, but in the columns of respectable organs of the US bourgeois press that this policy has been described as "a course to political disaster". It is hard to deny the validity of this description.

[Effect of U.S. Sanctions]

And now about blockades and "sanctions": the Soviet Union is a large country with a powerful economy and abundant resources. And the socialist community as a whole is even more than that. So we could somehow manage, and let no one have any doubts about that. Among countries which Washington calls its allies many are far more dependent on foreign trade in all their development. It is hard to say, therefore, whose interests are more painfully hit by the policy of cowboy sallies on international trade and normal economic relations.

Objectively speaking, the course of further aggravating the international atmosphere, escalating the arms race, and destroying normal ties between states augurs ill for any nation. And that, of course, includes the Americans. But the troubles it will bring all mankind may be numerous indeed. That is why we are firmly convinced that this course cannot win the support of the peoples, and has no future. The sooner this is understood by its initiators, the better it will be for all concerned.

As for the Soviet Union, we are firmly and unswervingly pursuing a course of lasting peace and peaceful, mutually beneficial cooperation among all states, irrespective of their social and political system. And, certainly, we want all participants in the Madrid meeting, when it resumes its work, to finally get down to the business for which it was convened — security and cooperation in Europe. Also, we want the way cleared for a conference on military detente and disarmament in Europe, so badly needed by the peoples of our continent.

['Reasonable Accords']

Comrades, the militarist line and aggressive policy of the NATO bloc, headed by the United States, are forcing us to maintain our country's defence capability at the due level. That is a grim necessity of the present-day world, and, of course, it requires diverting considerable resources to the detriment of our plans of peaceful construction. But as I have already said more than once, we have not spent, nor will we spend, a single rouble more for these purposes than is absolutely necessary for the security of our people, and that of our friends and allies. And we see the future not in terms of any unrestricted stockpiling of mountains of weapons, but in terms of reaching reasonable accords with the other side on a mutual lowering of the level of military confrontation.

In this connection, of course, the problem of reducing nuclear armaments in Europe merits special attention. One can say that at present this is the key to averting the growing danger of a worldwide nuclear-missile war.

You are aware, comrades, of the concrete and far-reaching proposals put forward by the Soviet Union on this score: from the proposal for reducing by two-thirds the nuclear arsenals of the two sides in Europe and designed for use in Europe, to the proposal for completely ridding the continent of medium-range and tactical nuclear weapons. It is also common knowledge that the US side has so far been evading a serious discussion, let alone solution, of these questions, taking cover behind the absurd demand that the Soviet Union unilaterally disarm, which Washington has, as though in mockery, called the "zero option".

[Soviet Moratorium]

However, we do not lose hope of reaching a reasonable accord on the basis of parity and equal security of the sides. Furthermore, we are doing everything we can to this end, both in words and in actions. I can now inform you, dear comrades, that, in an attempt to facilitate a just agreement on a major reduction of nuclear weapons by both sides in Europe, and desirous of setting a good example, *the Soviet leadership has taken a decision to introduce, unilaterally, a moratorium on the deployment of medium-range nuclear armaments in the European part of the USSR. We are freezing, in both the quantitative and qualitative respects, the armaments of this kind already stationed here, and are suspending the replacement of old missiles, known as the SS-4 and SS-5, by newer SS-20 missiles.*

This moratorium will be in force either until an agreement is reached with the United States on reducing, on the basis of parity and equal security, the medium-range nuclear missile designed for use in Europe, or until such a time when the US leaders, disregarding the security of the nations, should nevertheless go over to practical preparations for the deploying of Pershing II missiles and cruise missiles in Europe.

More, we had said earlier that if the two sides reached agreement on a moratorium we would be prepared, as a sign of good will, to carry out a unilateral reduction of the number of our nuclear missiles in Europe as part of an agreed future reduction. Now we have decided to take a new step thereby demonstrating our will for peace and our faith in the possibility of a mutually acceptable agreement. *The Soviet Union intends already this year, unless there is a new aggravation of the international situation, to reduce a certain number of its medium-range missiles on its own initiative.*

In announcing these decisions we are confident that the peoples of the world will appreciate the peaceable intentions and good will displayed by the Soviet Union. We also hope that our Western counterparts in the talks will be able to respond to this by taking constructive steps in a spirit of good will.

[Soviet Retaliation]

At the same time we regard it as our duty to make the following perfectly clear. If the governments of the United States and its NATO allies, in defiance of the will of the nations for peace, were actually to carry out their plan to deploy in Europe hundreds of new US missiles capable of striking targets on the territory of the Soviet Union, a different strategic situation would arise in the world. There would arise a real additional threat to our country and its allies from the United States. *This would compel us to take retaliatory steps that would put the other side, including the United States itself, its own territory, in an analogous position. This should not be forgotten.*

This circumstance is yet another reminder of how significant the *question of a Soviet-US strategic nuclear arms limitation and reduction agreement* is for the destinies of peace, for lessening the threat of a world-wide nuclear conflagration. As is known, the United States has refused to ratify the treaty on this score that was signed in 1979. Nor has Washington as yet shown any wish to hold further talks on this problem. But the issue is becoming increasingly acute and urgent.

In the first place, implementation of the US plans to station new missiles in Europe could upset — with consequences for the future that are difficult to foresee — the strategic arms balance the sides have reached at present.

Secondly, the development by the sides of new types of mass destruction weapons (unless this is stopped on the basis of a treaty) could undermine the ground on which limitation, reduction and control agreements can still be reached today.

[Halt to Arms Buildup]

Therefore, we call on the Government of the United States not to raise artificial barriers to SALT talks and to get the talks started in the nearest future. *Pending their resumption we would propose that the two sides undertake a mutual commitment not to open a new channel of the arms build-up, not to deploy sea-based or ground-based long-range cruise missiles.*

In general, we believe that the situation in the world calls for maximum restraint in the military activity of the two opposing alliances of countries. We would be prepared, for example, to agree to *a mutual restriction of naval operations. In particular, we would consider it possible to agree that missile submarines of the two sides should be removed from their present extensive combat patrol areas, that their cruises should be restricted by limits mutually agreed upon. We would also be prepared to discuss the question of extending confidence-building measures to the seas and oceans, especially to areas through which the busiest shipping routes pass.* In short, we are for making the largest possible part of the World Ocean a zone of peace in the very nearest future.

Those are our new proposals on the questions of curbing the arms build-up and averting the threat of another world war. As you see, comrades, our Party and the Soviet Government are conscientiously carrying out the people's mandate, are doing everything to justify the hopes of the people of our country, and of all mankind, for a lasting peace, for clear skies above a peaceful Earth. . . .

REAGAN'S REMARKS

... Before I begin my planned remarks this morning, I would like to speak again to the question of controlling nuclear arms, a subject of deep concern to all Americans, to our allies, and to the people of the world. The hope of all men everywhere is peace — peace not only for this generation but for generations to come. To preserve peace, to ensure it for the future, we must not just freeze the production of nuclear arms, we must reduce the exorbitant level that already exists.

Those who are serious about peace, those who truly abhor the potential for nuclear destruction must begin an undertaking for real arms reduction. President Brezhnev has proposed a unilateral moratorium on further deployment of SS-20 missiles in Western Europe. Well, I say today, as I said yesterday, and as I made clear on November 18 [1981], a freeze simply isn't good enough, because it doesn't go far enough. We must go beyond a freeze.

Let's consider some facts about the military balance in Europe. The Soviet Union now has 300 brand new SS-20 missiles with 900 warheads deployed. All can hit targets anywhere in Western Europe. NATO has zero land-based missiles which can hit the U. S. S. R.

When President Brezhnev offers to stop deployments in Western Europe, he fails to mention that these are mobile missiles. It doesn't matter where you put them, since you can move them anywhere you want, including back to Western Europe. And even if east of the Urals, they could still target most of Western Europe.

Our proposal, now on the table in Geneva, is that we not deploy any of the intermediate missiles in Europe, in exchange for Soviet agreement to dismantle what they now have there. And that's fair. That is zero on both sides. And if President Brezhnev is serious about real arms control — and I hope he is — he will join in real arms reduction. ...

WHITE HOUSE STATEMENT

Upon examination, the "unilateral moratorium" offered by President Brezhnev is neither unilateral, nor a moratorium.

The offer, President Brezhnev makes clear, is limited to the European Soviet Union, thus leaving the U. S. S. R. free to continue its SS-20 buildup east of the Urals, well within range of Western Europe. As we have noted on many occasions, given its range and mobility, an SS-20 is a threat to NATO wherever located.

President Brezhnev clearly links his "unilateral" offer to the condition that Western preparations for the deployment of ground launch cruise missiles (GLCM) and Pershing II's, agreed upon in December 1979, do not proceed. This condition, plus the fact that the Soviets have already prepared sites for new SS-20's west as well as east of the Urals, demonstrate that this is a propaganda gesture and that the Soviets do not really intend to stop their SS-20 buildup.

[Soviet Missile Strength]

The Soviet SS-20 force already exceeds the dimensions of the expected threat when NATO took its decision of December 1979 to deploy U.S. GLCM and Pershing II missiles in Europe and to seek, through arms control, to reduce planned levels of long-range intermediate nuclear force (INF) missiles on both sides. The Soviets now have 300 SS-20 missiles deployed, with 900 warheads. Brezhnev's freeze proposal is designed, like previous Soviet statements over the past 3 years, to direct attention away from the enormous growth of Soviet capabilities that has already taken place and the enormous preponderance that the Soviet Union has thereby acquired.

It is unfortunate that the Soviets did not choose to exercise real restraint before their SS-20 buildup began. NATO, for its part, has been observing restraint on INF missiles for well over a decade, which the Soviets simply exploited.

In sum, President Brezhnev's offer is neither evidence of Soviet restraint, nor is it designed to foster an arms control agreement. Like previous such Soviet freeze proposals, this one seeks to legitimize Soviet superiority, to leave the Soviet Union free to continue its buildup, to divide the NATO Alliance, to stop U.S. deployments, and thus to secure for the Soviet Union unchallenged hegemony over Europe.

The United States has put forward concrete proposals in Geneva for the complete elimination of missiles on both sides, cited by Brezhnev in his remarks of today. We regret the Soviet Union apparently prefers propaganda gestures to concentrating on serious negotiations in Geneva. For its part, the United States, with the full support of its Allies, will continue to implement both tracks of the December 1979 decision on the deployment of new systems to Europe and the pursuit of genuine arms control, which we hope will make those deployments unnecessary.

President Brezhnev's proposal to place limits on the operations of missiles submarines is also not a serious proposal. U.S. submarines, by deploying to extensive ocean areas, are able to remain invulnerable to Soviet attack, and thus constitute a stable deterrent force. Reducing their area of operations in the world's oceans would increase their vulnerability and erode our confidence in their deterrent capability. The Soviet proposal, therefore, is entirely self-serving. Having made a large fraction of our land-based ICBM force vulnerable through their large ICBM buildup, the Soviets in this proposal are attempting to reduce the confidence we have in the sea-based leg of our deterrent.

The proposal for a ban on the deployment of ground-based, long-range cruise missiles is yet another transparent effort to disrupt NATO's 1979 two-track decision. Moreover, in focusing on sea-based as well as land-based, long-range cruise missiles, the proposal ignores the hundreds of shorter range cruise missiles that the Soviet Union currently deploys aboard its warships.

[U.S. Approach to Arms Control]

Finally, we want to reiterate the four principles underlying the Reagan administration's approach to arms control. These are to seek agreements that:

1. produce significant reductions in the arsenals of both sides;

2. are equal, since an unequal agreement, like an unequal balance of forces, can encourage coercion or aggression;

3. are verifiable, because when our national security is at stake, agreements cannot be based simply upon trust; and

4. enhance U.S. and Allied security, because arms control is not an end in itself, but an important means toward securing peace and international stability.

These four principles were highlighted by the President in his speech of November 18, 1981. They underlie our position in the current Geneva negotiations on the elimination of U.S. and Soviet intermediate-range nuclear missile forces. They also form the basis for our approach to negotiations with the Soviet Union on the reduction of strategic arms — the START talks.

STATE DEPARTMENT
ON CHEMICAL WARFARE
March 22 and November 29, 1982

On March 22 Secretary of State Alexander M. Haig Jr. issued a report to Congress and the United Nations on the use of chemical and toxic weapons by the Soviets and their allies in Laos, Kampuchea (Cambodia) and Afghanistan.

The 32-page report was a compilation of material gathered since 1975, when the first accounts of chemical warfare began to emerge from Laos. In 1978 and 1979 similar reports of chemical and toxic gas attacks came from Kampuchea and Afghanistan, respectively. The United States began to investigate and in 1979 and 1980 confronted the Soviet Union and the governments of the three countries involved with the reports of chemical warfare. All parties involved denied the validity of U.S. concerns.

In 1980, however, the United States raised the issue publicly in Congress and the United Nations. Reports of toxic and chemical weapons use continued, and in 1981 Haig and Undersecretary of State for Political Affairs Walter J. Stoessel cited analysis of a Kampuchean leaf and stem sample as physical evidence that lethal chemicals were being used in Southeast Asia. (Historic Documents of 1981, p. 681)

The evidence mounted that chemical warfare continued in the three countries and that the Soviet Union was involved in all three cases. Haig's March report was another attempt to publicize the issue. "If the efforts of the United States Government to call attention to chemical warfare in Afghanistan and Southeast Asia stimulate others to discover for themselves, and join in efforts to expose the truth," Haig stated, "this report will have served its purpose."

March Report

The March report claimed that more than 10,000 people had been killed in almost 400 chemical warfare attacks in the three countries. Lao and Vietnamese forces "under direct Soviet control," the report stated, had used nerve gases and other chemical agents, including trichothecene toxins (poisonous chemical substances extracted from biological material) against the H'Mong villagers in Laos and resistance fighters in Kampuchea. In Afghanistan, the report stated, the Soviets had used "a variety of lethal and nonlethal chemical agents on mujahidin resistance forces and Afghan villages since the Soviet invasion in December 1979."

In all three countries, the report said, chemical warfare was a "militarily effective way of breaking the will and resistance of stubborn antigovernment forces operating from relatively inaccessible, protected sanctuaries." The report also suggested that the Soviets likely considered these remote areas as unique opportunities to test and evaluate various chemical weapons.

Contributing to the conclusions contained in the report were scientific analyses of physical samples, medical evidence and interviews with various persons, including survivors of attacks, doctors who treated victims, defectors who took part in chemical attacks and journalists. Included were descriptions of the effects of the chemicals on victims.

November Report

On November 29 the State Department issued an update to the March report, in yet another attempt to call attention to the problem. Secretary of State George P. Shultz, who became head of the department after Haig's resignation in June, stated, "The world cannot be silent in the face of such human suffering and such cynical disregard for international law and agreements." The 12-page update contained further evidence of chemical warfare in the three countries, including the first convincing physical evidence of toxins from Afghanistan. Two captured Soviet gas masks from Afghanistan were found to be contaminated by the toxin T2.

Reactions to the U.S. Reports

Reactions to the U.S. reports were mixed. The Soviet Union called the charges "dirty lies" and noted through its official news agency, Tass, "The world has not forgotten that tens of thousands of chemical agents were dropped over Vietnam, Laos and Cambodia in the years of U.S. aggression in Indochina."

The report persuaded a number of scientists and military specialists, who previously had been skeptical, that chemical warfare was indeed going on. Harvard biologist Matthew Meselson, who had disputed the charges in 1981, said in March he was impressed by the sheer volume of human testimony the United States had collected. Debate continued in the scientific and military areas, however, over the exact nature of the chemicals and the degree of Soviet involvement. A Canadian team, for example, conducted a study of chemical weapons use in Southeast Asia in the spring of 1982. The team agreed with the United States that chemicals were being used but differed with U.S. findings on the nature and effects of the toxins.

A December 6 report submitted by a group of experts from the United Nations offered only lukewarm support to the U.S. charges. The U.N. group had been unable to visit sites of alleged chemical attacks but had interviewed refugees in Thailand and Pakistan. The group concluded that there was "circumstantial evidence suggestive of the possible use of some sort of toxic chemical substance in some instances."

> *Following are excerpts from "Chemical Warfare in Southeast Asia and Afghanistan," issued by the State Department March 22, 1982; and excerpts from the update to the report, issued November 29:*

MARCH 22 REPORT

Introduction

Nearly 7 years ago, reports of the use of lethal chemical weapons began to emerge from Laos. In 1978, similar reports started to come from Kampuchea, and in 1979 from Afghanistan. Early reports were infrequent and fragmentary, reflecting the remoteness of the scene of conflict and the isolation of those subjected to such attacks. In the summer of 1979, however, the State Department prepared a detailed compilation of interviews with refugees from Laos on this subject. That fall, a U.S. Army medical team visited Thailand to conduct further interviews. By the winter of 1979, the United States felt that it had sufficiently firm evidence of chemical warfare to raise the matter with the governments of Laos, Vietnam, and the Soviet Union. All three governments denied that a basis for concern over the use of chemical warfare agents existed.

Dissatisfied with these responses, and possessing further reports that lethal chemical agents were in use in Southeast Asia and Afghanistan, the U.S. Government in 1980 began to raise the issue publicly in the United Nations, with the Congress, and in other forums. In August of that year, the State Department provided extensive documentation containing evidence of chemical weapons attacks to the United Nations and also made this material publicly available. In December, as a result of efforts by the United States and other concerned nations, the U.N. General Assembly voted to initiate an international investigation into the use of chemical weapons. This investigation is still underway. To date, the U.N. investigating team has been denied admission to any of the three countries where these weapons are in use.

Despite the volume of information on chemical warfare in Southeast Asia which had become available by 1980, there remained one major unresolved issue — the exact nature of the chemical agents in use. Collection of physical samples was hindered by the remoteness of the then principal areas of conflict — as many as 6 weeks by foot to the nearest international border. Tests for known chemical warfare agents on those samples that were obtained proved consistently negative.

In order to identify the chemical agents in use, U.S. experts in late 1980 began to go back over all the reporting — as far back as 1975 — looking for new clues. In particular, they sought to match the reported symptomatology of victims — which commonly included skin irritation, dizziness, nausea, bloody vomiting and diarrhea, and internal hemorrhaging — with possible causes. As a result of this review, the U.S. Government in mid-1981 began to test physical samples from Southeast Asia for the presence of toxins. These substances are essentially biologically produced chemical poisons. Although they have never before been used in war, this was a technical possibility, and it was noted that certain toxins could produce the sorts of symptoms observed in Southeast Asian victims of chemical warfare.

In August 1981, unnatural levels and combinations of lethal trichothecene toxins were detected in the first sample to be tested by the United States for such agents. This consisted of vegetation taken from a village in Kampuchea where an attack occurred in which people had died after exhibiting the symptoms described above. In succeeding months, further samples, taken from the sites of attacks in both Kampuchea and Laos, yielded similar results. So did samples of blood taken from victims of a chemical attack in Kampuchea.

Despite a continued flow of reports, dating back over 7 years, of chemical warfare in Southeast Asia and more recently Afghanistan, and despite the still mounting physical evidence of the use of trichothecene toxins as warfare agents, doubts as to the conclusive nature of the available evidence have persisted. These doubts have arisen for several reasons. For one, the evidence of the use of lethal chemical weapons has become available over a period of several years and from a variety of sources. Few governments, journalists, or interested members of the public have been exposed to all of this evidence, nor has it been available in any one place. A second difficulty has been the inevitable need for the U.S. Government to protect some of the relevant information, often gathered at personal risk to individuals who secured it, or obtained through the use of highly sensitive methods. . . .

This report represents an effort of the U.S. Government to correct the first deficiency and to ameliorate the second to the extent possible. In preparation of this report, all of the information available to the U.S. Government on chemical weapons use in Laos, Kampuchea, and Afghanistan was assembled in one place. This information was again reviewed, analyzed, cross-indexed, and organized in a coherent fashion. Based upon this comprehensive analysis, a set of conclusions were drawn, conclusions which have since been reviewed and agreed on without qualification by every relevant agency of the U.S. Government.

The evidence upon which this report is based is of several kinds, including:

- Testimony of those who saw, experienced, and suffered from chemical weapons attacks;

- Testimony of doctors, refugee workers, journalists, and others who had the opportunity to question large numbers of those with firsthand experience of chemical warfare;

- Testimony of those who engaged in chemical warfare or were in a position to observe those who did;

- Scientific evidence, based upon the analysis of physical samples taken from sites where attacks had been conducted;

- Documentary evidence from open sources; and

- Intelligence derived from "national technical means."

These sources provide compelling evidence that tens of thousands of unsophisticated and defenseless peoples have for a period of years been subjected to a campaign of chemical attacks. *Taken together, this evidence has led the U.S. Government to conclude that Lao and Vietnamese forces, operating under Soviet supervision, have, since 1975, employed lethal chemical and toxin weapons in Laos; that Vietnamese forces have, since 1978, used lethal chemical and toxin agents in Kampuchea; and that Soviet forces have used a variety of lethal chemical warfare agents, including nerve gases, in Afghanistan since the Soviet invasion of that country in 1979.*

The implications of chemical warfare in Afghanistan and Southeast Asia are painful to contemplate but dangerous to ignore. This activity threatens not only the peoples of those isolated regions but the international order upon which the security of all depends. Those who today suffer chemical warfare against their homelands are powerless to stop it. The prohibitions of international law and solemn agreement are not self-enforcing. Only an alert and outspoken world community, intent to maintain those standards of international behavior it has so painfully achieved and so tenuously established, can bring sufficient pressure to bear to halt these violations of law and treaty. It is hoped that publication of this report will be one step in this process, the end result of which will be the cessation of chemical warfare and the strengthening of the rule of law in the affairs of nations.

Key Judgments

Laos. The U.S. Government has concluded from all the evidence that selected Lao and Vietnamese forces, under direct Soviet supervision, have employed lethal trichothecene toxins and other combinations of chemical agents against H'Mong resisting government control and their villages since at least 1976. Trichothecene toxins have been positively identified, but medical symptoms indicate that irritants, incapacitants, and nerve agents also have been employed. Thousands have been killed or severely injured. Thousands also have been driven from their homeland by the use of these agents.

Kampuchea. Vietnamese forces have used lethal trichothecene toxins on Democratic Kampuchean (DK) troops and Khmer villages since at least 1978. Medical evidence indicates that irritants, incapacitants, and nerve agents also have been used.

Afghanistan. Soviet forces in Afghanistan have used a variety of lethal and nonlethal chemical agents on *mujahidin* resistance forces and Afghan villages since the Soviet invasion in December 1979. In addition, there is some evidence that Afghan Government forces may have used Soviet-supplied chemical weapons against the *mujahidin* even before the Soviet invasion. Although it has not been possible to verify through sample analysis the specific agents used by the Soviets, a number of Afghan military defectors have named the agents brought into the country by the Soviets and have described where and when they were employed. This information has been correlated with other evidence, including the reported symptoms, leading to the conclusion that nerve agents, phosgene oxime, and various incapacitants and irritants have been used. Other agents and toxic smokes also are in the country. Some reported symptoms are consistent with those produced by lethal or sublethal doses of trichothecene toxins, but this evidence is not conclusive.

The Soviet Connection. The conclusion is inescapable that the toxins and other chemical warfare agents were developed in the Soviet Union, provided to the Lao and Vietnamese either directly or through the transfer of know-how, and weaponized with Soviet assistance in Laos, Vietnam, and Kampuchea. Soviet military forces are known to store agents in bulk and move them to the field for munitions fill as needed. This practice also is followed in Southeast Asia and Afghanistan, as evidenced by many reports which specify that Soviet technicians supervise the shipment, storage, filling, and loading onto aircraft of the chemical munitions. The dissemination techniques reported and observed evidently have been drawn from years of Soviet chemical warfare testing and experimentation. *There is no evidence to support any alternative explanation, such as the hypothesis that the Vietnamese produce and employ toxin weapons completely on their own....*

Discussion of Findings

In September 1981, the U.S. Government declared publicly that toxins — poisonous chemical substances extracted from biological material — probably were the mysterious lethal agents used for many years in Laos and Kampuchea. The statement was prompted by the discovery of high levels of trichothecene toxins in a vegetation sample collected shortly after a March 1981 Vietnamese chemical attack in Kampuchea. This conclusion, however, rested on a much broader base of evidence than analysis of one sample.

By April 1980, the U.S. Government had already concluded that lethal agents almost certainly had been used against H'Mong tribespeople in Laos. There was less certainty then about the use of lethal agents in Kampuchea, mainly because of the already mentioned suspicions about the propaganda campaign of Pol Pot's Democratic Kampuchean forces, although their claims subsequently were shown to be valid. It was also concluded that chances were about even that lethal agents had been used in Afghanistan. There was little doubt by April 1980 that riot-control agents and some form of incapacitants had been used in all three countries. Since that April 1980 assessment, additional evidence has allowed a much firmer conclusion. There is now no doubt that casualties and deaths have resulted from chemical attacks in all three countries.

WHAT CHEMICAL AGENTS ARE BEING USED?

As soon as it was determined that chemical agents had been used, an effort was made to identify the specific agents. To do this it was necessary to collect and analyze at least one of the following: environmental samples contaminated with agents, the munitions used to deliver agents, or biological specimens from victims of an attack. A study by medical-toxicological experts of symptoms exhibited by individuals exposed to toxic agents provides a good indication of the general class of chemical agent used. Thus, the range of clinical manifestations from chemical agents, as reported by a U.S. Army investigative team in Thailand, resulted in the determination that nerve agents, irritants such as CS, and highly toxic hemorrhagic chemicals or mixture of chemicals were used in Laos.

Other medical-toxicological personnel who reviewed the evidence and conducted their own investigation reached the same conclusion. They further indicated that toxins such as the trichothecenes were a probable cause of the lethal hemorrhaging effect seen in Kampuchea and Laos. In many cases, symptoms reported by the Democratic Kampuchean forces in Kampuchea and the *mujahidin* in Afghanistan were similar to those reported by the H'Mong in Laos. Moreover, symptoms reported from Afghanistan and Kampuchea indicated that a highly potent, raid-acting, incapacitant "knockout" chemical also was being used. *Mujahidin* victims and witnesses to chemical attacks reported other unusual symptoms, including a blackening of the skin, severe skin irritation along with multiple small blisters and severe itching, severe eye irritation, and difficulty in breathing — all of which suggests that phosgene oxime or a similar substance was used.

Collecting samples possibly contaminated with a toxic agent during or after a chemical assault is difficult under any circumstances but particularly when the assault is against ill-prepared people without masks or other protective equipment. Obtaining contaminated samples that will yield positive traces of specific chemical agents depends on many factors. These include the persistency of the chemical, the ambient temperature, rainfall, wind conditions, the medium on which the chemical was deposited, and the time, care, and packaging of the sample from collection to laboratory analysis.

Many traditional or known chemical warfare agents are nonpersistent and disappear from the environment within a few minutes to several hours after being dispersed. Such agents include the nerve agents sarin and tabun; the blood agents hydrogen cyanide and cyanogen chloride; the choking agents phosgene and diphosgene; and the irritant phosgene oxime. Other standard chemical warfare agents — such as the nerve agents VX and thickened soman and the blistering agents sulfur mustard, nitrogen mustard, and lewisite — may persist for several days to weeks depending on weather conditions.

The trichothecene toxins have good persistency but may be diluted by adverse weather conditions to below detectable concentrations. To maximize the chances of detection, sample collections need to be made as rapidly as possible after a chemical assault; as with many agents, this means minutes to hours. Under the circumstances of Southeast Asia and Afghanistan, such rapid collection has simply not been possible. Although many samples were collected, few held any realistic prospect of yielding positive results. It is fortunate that trichothecenes are sufficiently persistent and in some cases were not diluted by adverse weather conditions. Thus we were able to detect them several months after the attack.

Samples have been collected from Southeast Asia since mid-1979 and from Afghanistan since May 1980. To date, about 50 individual samples — of greatly varying types and usefulness for analytical purposes — have been collected and analyzed for the presence of known chemical warfare agents, none of which has been detected. Based on recommendations by medical and toxicological experts and findings of investigators from the U.S. Army's Chemical Systems Laboratory, several of the samples have been analyzed for the trichothecene group of mycotoxins. Four samples, two from Kampuchea and two from Laos, were found to contain high levels of trichothecene toxins. In addition, preliminary results of the analysis of blood samples drawn from victims of an attack indicate the presence of a trichothecene metabolite of T-2, namely HT-2.

A review of all reports indicates the use of many different chemical agents, means of delivery, and types of chemical attacks. The use of trichothecene toxins has been identified through symptoms and sample analysis. In some cases, however, the symptoms suggest other agents, such as nerve gas, which have not been identified through sample analysis. Significant differences as well as similarities have surfaced in the reports from the three countries. The evidence from each country, therefore, is described separately, with attention drawn to similarities where appropriate.

LAOS

Reports of chemical attacks against H'Mong villages and guerrilla strongholds in Laos date from the summer of 1975 to the present. Most of the reports were provided by H'Mong refugees who were interviewed in Thailand and the United States. More than 200 interviews were carried out variously by U.S. Embassy officials in Thailand, a Department of Defense team of medical-toxicological experts, U.S. physicians, Thai officials, journalists, and representatives of international aid and relief organizations. According to the interviews, Soviet AN-2 and captured U.S. L-19 and T-28/41 aircraft usually were employed to disseminate toxic chemical agents by sprays, rockets, and bombs. In some cases, Soviet helicopters and jet aircraft were said to have been used.

The reports describe 261 separate attacks in which at least 6,504 deaths were cited as having resulted directly from exposure to chemical agents. The actual number of deaths is almost certainly much higher, since the above figure does not take account of deaths in attacks for which no specific casualty figures were reported. The greatest concentration of reported chemical agent use occurred in the area where the three provinces of Vientiane, Xiangkhoang, and Louangphrabang adjoin. . . .

The medical symptoms reportedly produced by the chemical agents are varied. According to knowledgeable physicians, the symptoms clearly point to at least three types of chemical agents — incapacitant/riot-control agents, a nerve agent, and an agent causing massive hemorrhaging. The last-named was positively identified as trichothecene toxins. This was announced publicly by Secretary Haig in September 1981.

In a number of the refugee reports, eyewitnesses described attacks as consisting of "red gas" or a "yellow cloud." Red gas was considered the more lethal. A former Lao Army captain stated that the "red gas" caused the H'Mong to die within 12 hours. An employee of an international organization interviewed victims of a September 15, 1979 attack in which nonlethal rounds preceded an attack by five or six "red gas" bombs that covered a 500-meter area. Persons within 30-100 meters of the circle died in 10 minutes after severe convulsions. Others had headaches, chest pains, and vomiting but did not die.

Every qualified interrogator who systematically interviewed the H'Mong refugees concluded that they had been subjected to chemical attacks. A U.S. Government medical team returned from Thailand in 1979 convinced that several unidentified chemical warfare agents had produced the symptoms described by the refugees. This evidence was expanded by testimony from a variety of sources, including that of a Lao pilot who flew chemical warfare missions before defecting in 1979. His detailed description of the Lao, Vietnamese, and Soviet program to use chemical agents to defeat the H'Mong resistance helped dispel any lingering suspicions that the refugees had fabricated or embellished the stories. . . .

Obtaining additional data for Laos has been difficult because of the nature of the fighting there. There have been few major operations. The reports reflect numerous minor engagements between the opposing forces. In nearly all cases, the chemical use reported has been directed against villages, in the absence of obvious combat operations. This lends support to the Lao pilot's claim that the Vietnamese and Lao military commands were engaged in a "H'Mong extermination" campaign.

Of particular interest are the circumstances surrounding the collection of two physical samples found to contain lethal toxins. The first was collected after a March 13, 1981 attack on a village between the villages of Muong Chai and Phakhao in the Phou Bia region. In this case, a large two-engine plane reportedly sprayed a mist of a moist, yellow, sticky substance; two villagers and all village animals died. The second sample is from Ban Thonghak, another village in the Phou Bia region, collected following an April 2, 1981 attack in which a jet aircraft reportedly sprayed a yellow substance; 24 of the 450 villagers died. In the spring of 1981, seven separate chemical attacks, resulting in 218 deaths, were reported to have occurred in this region.

It is significant that these attacks took place folowing a period of escalation in overall resistance activities in the Phou Bia area in the winter of 1980-81. During that period, joint suppression operations by Lao People's Liberation Army and Vietnamese Army forces had achieved only limited success, perhaps spurring both forces on to greater effort. The more intense use of chemical weapons may have been part of this effort.

In a December 15, 1981 press conference in Beijing, former Lao Health Ministry Bureau Director Khamsengkeo Sengsathit — who had defected to China — confirmed that chemical weapons were being used "in the air and on the ground" in Laos, killing "thousands." He asserted that the Vietnamese alone were using such weapons, keeping the matter secret from the Lao. He also stated that 3,000 Soviet advisers were in Laos and "have taken control" of the Lao Air Force, while 40,000-50,000 Vietnamese troops had "reduced Laos to the status of a colony."

KAMPUCHEA

Since October 1978, radio broadcasts, press releases, and official protests to the United Nations by the Democratic Kampuchea leadership have accused the Vietnamese and the Hanoi-backed People's Republic of Kampuchea regime of using Soviet-made lethal chemical agents and weapons against DK guerrilla forces and civilians. DK allegations for a time were the only source of information concerning chemical warfare attacks in Kampuchea. In November 1979, however, the guerrilla forces of the Khmer People's National Liberation Front reported that the Vietnamese had attacked them with a tear gas which, from their description, resembled the riot-control agent CS. Subsequently, Thai officials, Democratic Kampuchea informants and refugees, Vietnamese Army defectors, U.S. and Thai medical personnel, officials of international aid and relief organizations, and Canadian and West European officials also have implicated the Vietnamese in the offensive use of lethal and incapacitating chemical agents in Kampuchea.

There are reports of 124 separate attacks in Kampuchea from 1978 to the fall of 1981 in which lethal chemicals caused the deaths of 981 persons. The mortality figure represents a minimum because some reports state only that there were deaths and do not provide a number. The earliest reports cite attacks in Ratanakiri Province, in the northeastern corner of the country. Reports from 1979 to the present show the use of lethal chemicals primarily in the provinces bordering Thailand. The greatest use of chemical agents apparently has been in Battambang Province, with 51 reported incidents; Pursat Province has experienced the next highest frequency, with 25 reported incidents. These numbers are consistent with the overall high level of military activity reported in the border provinces.

A review of information from all sources provides direct and specific support for 28 of 124 reported attacks. There is, in addition, some evidence that in all reported instances some form of attack took place. This evidence includes reports of troop movements, supply transfers, operational plans, postoperation reporting, and air activity. It indicates that military activity took place at the time and place of every incident reported to involve lethal chemical agents. In some cases, it provides strong circumstantial evidence that the action involved chemical substances — for example, the movement of chemicals and personal protection equipment into the area.

There is no doubt that in late 1978 and 1979 the Vietnamese, and what later became the People's Republic of Kampuchea forces, made at least limited use of riot-control chemicals and possible incapacitating agents against both Communist and non-Communist guerrilla forces in Kampuchea. The chemicals used probably included toxic smokes, riot-control agents such as CS, and an unidentified incapacitating agent that caused vertigo and nausea and ultimately rendered victims unconscious with no other signs or symptoms. . . .

Starting in February 1980, reports revealed that the Vietnamese were using 60 mm mortars, 120 mm shells, 107 mm rockets, M-79 grenade launchers filled with chemical agents, as well as munitions delivered by T-28 aircraft. According to the DK, the chemicals used were green and yellow and powderlike in appearance. In some instances the gas was described as yellow or white. The symptoms described were tightening of the chest, disorientation, vomiting, bleeding from the nose and gums, discoloration of the body, and "stiffening" of the teeth. In July 1980, the DK described artillery attacks that produced a black smoke causing itchy skin, weakness, skin lesions, and in some cases decaying skin and blisters. In December

1980, the Vietnamese were once again firing chemical artillery shells, and it was believed that poison chemicals were being brought into Thailand's border region. By March 1981, the Democratic Kampuchea forces had reported numerous attacks directed against them with lethal chemical agents and the poisoning of food and water.

U.S. analysis of contaminated vegetation samples collected within hours of a March 1981 attack showed high levels of three trichothecene toxins in a combination that would not be expected to be found in a natural outbreak in this environment. At the levels found on the vegetation, the three trichothecenes would produce vomiting, skin irritations and itching, and bleeding symptoms. Water samples taken from the area of the same attack also contained trichothecene toxins. Control samples from nearby areas confirmed that these toxins were not indigenous to the locale. . . .

In Kampuchea, as in Laos, the period of late 1980 through spring 1981 was one of intensified Vietnamese operations to suppress the resistance and break the will of the opposing forces. In July 1981, trucks loaded with blue sacks filled with white powder were being moved by the Vietnamese into the Pailin, Battambang, and Siem Reap areas. Vietnamese soldiers told villagers that the chemicals caused blindness, hemorrhaging, and vomiting. . . .

Thailand also has been concerned about chemical attacks against its own forces and civilian population. In March 1981, one Thai died from poisons placed by Vietnamese troops, and others became ill after suffering bleeding from the nose and mouth. In May 1981, Thai forces captured two Vietnamese as they were attempting to poison the water supply in a Kampuchean relocation camp in Thailand. The poison was analyzed by the Thai and found to contain lethal quantities of cyanide. Many reports indicate that it is common practice for Vietnamese units to poison water and food used by the DK forces.

THE SOVIET CONNECTION IN SOUTHEAST ASIA

Much of the Soviet interest in Southeast Asia is dictated by their rivalry with China and their close alliance with the Vietnamese. Regional Communist forces have been strengthened to contain Chinese influence and deter military incursions. The area of northern Laos between Vientiane and the Chinese border — where the H'Mong hill tribes have stubbornly resisted and harassed Vietnamese forces — is strategically significant to the Vietnamese because it adjoins a hostile China. In the last few years the Vietnamese have expanded their military construction and strengthened their forces in Laos which now number 50,000.

Initially there was a tendency to interpret the Soviet role as strictly advisory. Now, however, there is considerable evidence to suggest that the Soviets are far more involved in the Lao and Vietnamese chemical warfare program than was assumed earlier. An estimated 500 Soviet military advisers provide maintenance assistance and technical support, actually running the Lao Air Force, and give advanced training to Lao personnel in conventional as well as chemical warfare.

The Soviets have had advisers and technicians working in Vietnam and Laos for many years and in Kampuchea since 1979. However, it was not until early 1979 that evidence surfaced on the Soviets' direct involvement in chemical warfare activities. For example, the Lao Army chemical section in Xiangkhoang prepared Soviet-manufactured chemical items for inspection by a Soviet military team on February 7, 1979. A seven-man team of Soviet chemical artillery experts, accompanied by Lao chemical officers, inspected chemical supplies and artillery rounds at the Xeno storage facility in Savannakhet on June 1, 1979. One report stated that the Soviets would be inspecting the same chemical explosives used to suppress the H'Mong in the Phou Bia area.

In addition to this information, H'Mong accounts have described Soviet advisers and technicians participating in the preparation of the chemical weapons for the attacks on the H'Mong villages. H'Mong eyewitnesses claim to have seen "Caucasian pilots" in aircraft, and one H'Mong report states that a downed Soviet aircraft was discovered in the jungle along with a dead Soviet pilot. In November 1981, a H'Mong resistance leader described how Soviet soldiers fighting with the Lao Army fired hand-held weapons that dispersed a lethal agent over a 300-meter area. Several Lao defectors have reported seeing Soviet advisers present when aircraft were loaded with chemical-agent rockets.

In July 1981, a Soviet shipment of wooden crates filled with canisters described by the Vietnamese as "deadly toxic chemicals" was unloaded at the port of Ho Chi Minh City. This incident further corroborates the judgment that the Soviets have been shipping chemical warfare materiel to Vietnam for some time. During the unloading, Vietnamese soldiers were caught pilfering the wooden crates containing the canisters. The soldiers dropped one of the wooden cases and intentionally broke it open; they wanted to determine if its contents were edible or valuable for pilferage. When a soldier broke the nylon seal and attempted to pry open a canister, special security personnel isolated the area and told the soldiers that the canisters contained deadly toxic substances from the U.S.S.R. . . .

This incident is only one in a series involving Soviet chemical warfare materiel dating back several years. In 1979, for example, a Soviet captain of a diving support craft engaged in salvaging a sunken ship in the Black Sea, which had been transporting Soviet military supplies to Vietnam, said that his divers came in contact with toxic chemicals, and a special Soviet salvage unit took over the operation after the divers became very ill. The salvage operations, conducted by the ASPTR-12 Salvage, Rescue, and Underwater Technical Services Group based in Odessa, were monitored by high-ranking Soviet naval officers.

The operation began with the removal of tractors and helicopters which cluttered the deck of the ship and prevented access to hold hatches. Once the surface clutter was removed the divers attempted to enter the holds. At this point, however, operations had to be suspended temporarily because of a violent outbreak of chemical poisoning among the divers. . . .

AFGHANISTAN

Attacks with chemical weapons against the *mujahidin* guerrillas in Afghanistan were reported as early as 6 months before the Soviet invasion on December 27, 1979. The information specifies that Soviet-made aircraft were used to drop chemical bombs, with no clear identification of Soviet or Afghan pilots or of the specific agents used. On November 16, 1979, chemical bombs reportedly were dropped along with conventional air munitions on targets in Farah, Herat, and Badghisat Provinces by Soviet-supplied Afghan IL-28 bombers based at Shindand. A number of Afghan military defectors have stated that the Soviets provided the Afghan military with chemical warfare training as well as supplies of lethal and incapacitating agents.

For the period from the summer of 1979 to the summer of 1981, the U.S. Government received reports of 47 separate chemical attacks with a claimed death toll of more than 3,000. Of the 47 reports, 36 came from Afghan Army deserters, *mujahidin* resistance fighters, journalists, U.S. physicians, and others. For 24 of the reported attacks, there is additional independent evidence supporting allegations of chemical attacks. In seven instances, further individual reporting exists. Evidence for 20 of the reported incidents comes from information on Soviet or Afghan Army combat operations in progress in areas and at times approximating those of a reported chemical attack.

The reports indicated that fixed-wing aircraft and helicopters usually were employed to disseminate chemical warfare agents by rockets, bombs, and sprays. Chemical-filled landmines were also reportedly used by the Soviets. The chemical clouds were usually gray or blue-black, yellow, or a combination of the colors.

Symptoms reported by victims and witnesses of attacks indicate that non-lethal incapacitating chemicals and lethal chemicals — including nerve agents, phosgene or phosgene oxime, possibly trichothecene toxins, and mustard — were used. Medical examinations of some of the victims include reports of paralysis, other neurological effects, blisters, bleeding, and sometimes death. While none of the agents being used in Afghanistan has been positively identified through sample analysis, there is no doubt that the agents being used are far more toxic than riot-control agents such as CN and CS or even adamsite.

Several descriptions of the physiological action of a chemical agent or of the condition of the corpses of victims were particularly unusual. In one, victims were rapidly rendered unconscious for 2-6 hours and had few aftereffects. In another, the bodies were characterized by abnormal bloating and blackened skin with a dark-reddish tinge, and the flesh appeared decayed very soon after death. In a third incident, three dead *mujahidin* guerrillas were found with hands on rifles and lying in a firing position, indicating that the attacker had used an extremely rapid-acting lethal chemical that is not detectable by normal senses and that causes no outward physiological responses before death.

Shortly after the Soviet invasion, many reports were received that both Soviet and Afghan forces were using various types of chemical agents. Ten separate chemical attacks, resulting in many deaths, were reported in the first 3 months of 1980. These reports came from northeastern Afghanistan and provide the highest percentage of reported deaths. During the mid-January to February 1980 period, helicopter attacks were reported in northeastern Afghanistan in which a grayish-blue smoke resulted in symptoms similar to those described by the H'Mong refugees from Laos (e.g., heavy tearing or watering of eyes; extensive blistering and discoloration of the skin, later resulting in large sheetlike peeling; swelling in the areas affected by the blister; and finally numbness, paralysis, and death). Medical reports from examinations in Pakistan of refugees from a large attack in the upper Konar Valley in February 1980 described red skin and blisters containing fluid described as "dirty water." Refugees estimated that about 2,000 people were affected after contact with a dirty yellow cloud.

By spring and summer of 1980, chemical attacks were reported in all areas of concentrated resistance activity. Many reports from different sources strongly support the case that irritants were used to drive the insurgents into the open to expose them to attack with conventional weapons and incapacitants to render them tractable for disarming and capture. On several occasions in April 1980, for example, Soviet helicopter pilots dropped "gas bombs" on insurgents, evidently to drive them from caves.

A Dutch journalist, Bernd de Bruin, published an eyewitness account of two chemical attacks occurring in the Jalalabad area on June 15 and June 21, 1980 (*Niewsnet*, August 2, 1980). He filmed an MI-24 helicopter dropping canisters that produced a dirty yellow cloud. A victim with blackened skin, discolored by extensive subcutaneous hemorrhaging, was photographed in the village 5 hours after the attack. The journalist evidently was exposed because he developed blisters on his hands and a swollen and itchy face. He also was exposed in the second attack, and it took about 10 days for him to recover from skin lesions, nausea, diarrhea, and stomach cramps. . . .

Reports of chemical weapons use in 1981 essentially parallel 1980 reporting with respect to frequency and location of attack. Soviet helicopter units participated in chemical attacks from April 20 to April 29, 1981, in areas east and west of Kabul and in the Konar Valley, according to eyewitness accounts. These attacks were intended to drive personnel from sanctuaries, such as caves, in order to engage them with conventional fire. The munitions were described as Soviet 250-kilogram RBK cluster bombs. The Soviets have such a munition, which can be filled with chemical agents. Other reports described similar operations by helicopters north of Qandahar on April 24 and April 26, 1981. . . .

In February 1982, a member of the resistance, with considerable knowledge of Soviet weapons, told a U.S. official that the Soviets were using irritants, a hallucinogenic gas, and what he said was an apparent nerve gas. He described the "nerve agent" as an off-white powdery substance dispersed from helicopters generally during artillery or bombing attacks. Victims realize they have been exposed to chemical attack only when they become faint and dizzy. Subsequently, they begin to vomit and bleed from the eyes, nose, and mouth. Death occurs within a short time. The corpses are extremely relaxed, with no evidence of rigor mortis. Flesh and skin frequently peel off if an effort is made to move the bodies.

According to this account, survivors suffer aftereffects for about 6 months, including chest congestion and pain, dizziness, and mental agitation. The powder-like substance is more effective at lower altitudes where there is less wind to dilute the poison, and *mujahidin* groups have experienced fatality rates as high as 70%. Many survivors of chemical attacks in Laos and Afghanistan have exhibited the same long-term health problems described in this account. . . .

A Soviet military chemical specialist, captured by the *mujahidin*, gave his name as Yuriy Povarnitsyn from Sverdlovsk. During an interview, he said that his mission was to examine villages after a chemical attack to determine whether they were safe to enter or required decontamination. An Afghan pathologist who later defected described accompanying Soviet chemical warfare personnel into contaminated areas to collect soil, vegetation, and water samples after Soviet chemical attacks. According to firsthand experience of former Soviet chemical personnel, the Soviets do not require decontamination equipment in an area where chemical bombs are stored or loaded onto aircraft. Thus, deployment of this equipment in Afghanistan must be assumed to be associated with the active employment of casualty-producing chemical agents.

Afghan military defectors have provided information on ammunition and grenades containing phosgene, diphosgene, sarin, and soman and have described where and when some of them have been used. They also have revealed locations where these agents were stockpiled. The agents used, plus the time and location of the attacks, correspond with the refugee reporters and recorded military operations.

The Soviet Union has stocked a variety of toxic chemical agents and munitions to meet wartime contingencies. Weapons systems capable of delivering chemical munitions available to Soviet forces in Afghanistan include artillery, multiple rocket launchers, and tactical aircraft.

MOTIVATION FOR USING CHEMICAL WEAPONS

In the course of this analysis, the question has been posed: Is there a military-strategic or tactical rationale for the systematic use of chemical weapons by conventional forces in Laos, Kampuchea, and Afghanistan? The military problems faced in these countries — viewed from the perspective of the Soviets and their allies — make the use of chemical weapons a militarily effective way of breaking the will and resistance of stubborn anti-government forces operating from relatively inaccessible, protected sanctuaries.

The Soviets have made a large investment in insuring that Vietnam and its clients succeed in extending their control over Indochina. For Vietnam, the H'Mong resistance in Laos is a major irritant to be removed as quickly and cheaply as possible. The use of chemical agents has played a major role in driving the H'Mong from their mountain strongholds, relieving Vietnamese and Lao ground forces of the need for costly combat in difficult terrain. Much of the H'Mong population that lived in the Phou Bia mountain region has been driven into Thailand, killed, or resettled.

In the mountainous areas of Afghanistan, where rebels are holed up in caves or other inaccessible areas, conventional artillery, high-explosive bombs, and napalm are not particularly effective. Many reports indicate that unidentified chemical agents have been used on such targets. Caves and rugged terrain in Laos and thick jungles in Kampuchea also have frustrated attempts to locate and destroy the resistance forces. Chemical clouds can penetrate the heavy forests and jungle canopy and seep into the mountain caves. Persistent agents linger in the area and cause casualties days and sometimes weeks after the attack. Unprotected forces and civilians have little or no defense against lethal agents like toxins, nerve gas, or blister agents.

Trichothecene toxins, which are known to have been used in Southeast Asia, have the added advantage of being an effective terror weapon that causes bizarre and horrifying symptoms. Severe bleeding, in addition to blisters and vomiting, has instilled fear in the resistance villages. Not only have the villagers and their animals been killed in a gruesome manner, but the vegetation and water also have been contaminated. Survivors are reluctant to return to their inhospitable homes and instead make the long and dangerous trek to camps in Thailand.

There is no clearcut explanation of why trichothecene toxins have been used in addition to irritants, incapacitants, and other traditional chemical warfare agents. Speculation suggests that they are probably cheaper to make and are readily available from Soviet stocks; they are probably safer and more stable to store, transport, and handle in a Southeast Asian environment, and they may require less protective equipment when being prepared for munitions. They are difficult to trace as the causative agent after an attack — as demonstrated by the length of time it took for the United States to detect them. Few laboratories in the world have the analytical capability to identify precisely the type and amount of trichothecene toxin in a sample of vegetation, soil, or water.

The Soviets may well have calculated that they and their allies could successfully deny or counter charges that chemical weapons had been used, recognizing that it would be especially difficult to compile incontrovertible evidence from inaccessible areas of Southeast Asia and Afghanistan. With respect to Kampuchea, they may also have calculated that, in view of the lack of international support for Pol Pot's resistance, chemical weapons could be used on his troops without significant international outcry.

In addition, the Soviet military very likely considers these remote areas as providing unique opportunities for the operational testing and evaluation of chemical weapons under various tactical conditions. Years of aerial and artillery chemical dispersion have undoubtedly provided the Soviets with valuable testing data. Southeast Asia has offered the Soviets an opportunity to test old agents that had been stockpiled for many years as well as more recently developed agents or combinations of agents. This conclusion is supported by information from foreign military officers who have attended the Soviet Military Academy of Chemical Defense in Moscow. . . . The foreign officers' accounts, including detailed descriptions of the Soviet chemical warfare program, support the conclusion that the Soviets consider chemical weapons an effective and acceptable means of warfare in local conflicts. . . .

Evidence accumulated since World War II clearly shows that the Soviets have been extensively involved in preparations for large-scale offensive and defensive chemical warfare. Chemical warfare agents and delivery systems developed by the Soviets have been identified, along with production and storage areas within the U.S.S.R. and continuing research, development, and testing activities at the major Soviet chemical proving grounds. Soviet military forces are extensively equipped and trained for operations in a chemically contaminated environment. None of the evidence indicates any abatement in this program. The Soviets have shown a strong interest in improving or enhancing their standard agents for greater reliability and effect. Their large chemical and biological research and development effort has led them to investigate other kinds of chemical warfare agents, particularly the toxins.

None of the four countries considered in this report — Vietnam, Laos, Kampuchea, and Afghanistan — has any known large-scale facility or organization for the manufacture of chemical and biological materials. Nor are they known to have produced even small quantities of chemical warfare agents or munitions. The technical problems of producing large quantities of weapons-grade toxins, however, are not so great as to preclude any of the four countries from learning to manufacture, purify, and weaponize these materials. It is highly unlikely, however, that they could master these functions without acquiring outside technical know-how. . . .

NOVEMBER 29 REPORT

This report presents conclusions based on further evidence about chemical and toxin warfare activities in Laos, Kampuchea, and Afghanistan that has become available to the U.S. Government since publication of the special report on this subject on March 22, 1982. The evidence includes new information on events occuring since the first of this year as well as additional information from a variety of sources on activities described in that report. . . .

Updated Findings

Based on a thorough analysis of this new information, we are able to conclude the following:

• Reports of chemical attacks from February through October 1982 indicate that Soviet forces continue their selective use of chemicals and toxins against the resistance in Afghanistan. Moreover, new evidence collected in 1982 on Soviet and Afghan Government forces' use of chemical weapons from 1979 through 1981 reinforces the previous judgment that lethal chemical agents were used on the Afghan resistance. Physical samples from Afghanistan also provide new evidence of mycotoxin use.

• Vietnamese and Lao troops, under direct Soviet supervision, have continued to use lethal and incapacitating chemical agents and toxins against the H'Mong resistance in Laos through at least June 1982.

• Vietnamese forces have continued to use lethal and incapacitating chemical agents and toxins against resistance forces in Kampuchea through at least June 1982.

• Trichothecene toxins were found in the urine, blood, and tissue of victims of "yellow rain" attacks in Laos and Kampuchea and in samples of residue collected after attacks.

• We continue to find that a common factor in the evidence is Soviet involvement in the use of these weapons in all three countries. Continued analysis of prior data and newly acquired information about Soviet mycotoxin research and development, chemical warfare training in Vietnam, the presence of Soviet chemical warfare advisers in Laos and Vietnam, and the presence of the same unusual trichothecene toxins in samples collected from all three countries reinforce our earlier conclusion about the complicity of the Soviet Union and about its extent.

Introduction

Our March study showed that casualties and deaths resulted from chemical attacks in Southeast Asia and Afghanistan and that trichothecene toxins were used in both Laos and Kampuchea. The new evidence shows that these attacks are continuing in all three countries and that trichothecene toxins have been used in Afghanistan as well.

The same rigorous analytical processes employed in our March study, and outlined in detail there, were followed to arrive at the judgments contained in this update. In light of the widespread publicity given the March report, special efforts were made by U.S. Government analysts to preclude being led astray by any possible false reports that might be generated for propaganda or other purposes and to eliminate the possibility of making erroneous judgments about the chemical or toxin agents involved because of tampering or improper handling. Every report has been carefully checked.

The evidence in the March study was based on a broad range of data, including testimony by physicians, refugee workers, journalists, and others. Although some of the new reports are anecdotal, we have been able to corroborate most of them by other sources and sample analysis. Moreover, personal testimony tends to add credence to other accounts which, taken together, form a coherent picture. The material presented in this report represents only a relatively small amount of the total accumulated evidence.... Improved sample collection procedures, a better quality of medical histories and physical examinations, documentation including photographs of lesions and hospital charts from Southeast Asia, and interviews by trained personnel have reinforced our earlier conclusions and led to new discoveries.

As international concern about this subject has increased, based on the development of evidence from many countries, independent analyses have been initiated by foreign chemical warfare experts, physicians, journalists, and independent nongovernmental scientists and laboratories. Analysts in the United States have found this research very helpful both in supporting their own conclusions and, more importantly, in expanding on them.

Summary of Evidence

AFGHANISTAN

Evidence indicates that the Soviets have continued the selective use of toxic agents in Afghanistan as late as October 1982. For the first time we have obtained convincing evidence of the use of mycotoxins by Soviet forces through analyses of two contaminated Soviet gas masks acquired from Afghanistan. Analysis and quantification of material taken from the outside surface of one mask have shown the presence of trichothecene mycotoxin. Analysis of a hose from a second Soviet mask showed the presence of several mycotoxins. In addition, a vegetation sample from Afghanistan shows preliminary evidence of the presence of mycotoxins.

Our suspicions that mycotoxins have been used in Afghanistan have now been confirmed.... Because of limited access to survivors who still exhibited symptoms, as well as great difficulties in collecting environmental and other physical samples from attack sites, we were unable to conclude with certainty in the March 22 report that mycotoxins were being used in Afghanistan. We have now concluded that trichothecene mycotoxins have been used by Soviet forces in Afghanistan since at least 1980.

A number of reports indicate that chemical attacks are continuing in 1982. While we cannot substantiate every detail, the pieces of evidence in these reports add up to a consistent picture. For example, a physician in a facility treating casualties among the *mujahidin* (resistance fighters) has reported that he treated 15 *mujahidin* for red skin lesions that he said were caused by Soviet chemical attacks in Qandahar Province in May-June 1982. Three *mujahidin* died within 12 hours of one attack in the general area of Maharijat south of Qandahar. The *mujahidin* claimed that Soviet helicopters fired rockets that emitted black, yellow, and white gases on impact. The physician said that the surviving victims failed to respond to conventional medical treatment.

We have received reports that on September 20, 1982, Soviet soldiers poisoned underground waterways in Lowgar Province south of Kabul where the *mujahidin* were hiding. According to a *mujahidin* commander in Pakistan, a similar event occurred in the same province on September 13, 1982, resulting in the deaths of 60 adults and 13 children. These two independent accounts described a Soviet armored vehicle pumping a yellow gas through a hose into the waterways.

According to the accounts of the September 1982 attacks, the victims' bodies decomposed rapidly, and the flesh peeled away when attempts were made to move the bodies. Since 1979, *mujahidin* resistance leaders, refugees, journalists, and Afghan defectors have described chemical attacks causing almost identical symptoms. Most reports have described the skin as being blue-black after death. Although such symptoms seem bizarre, the large number of reports from a variety of sources since 1979 suggest that they cannot be dismissed. . . .

In 1982, a Soviet soldier who defected to the *mujahidin* said in an interview with a British journalist that a Soviet toxic agent, termed "100 percent lethal," causes the flesh to become very soft. The Soviet defector stated that the Soviets maintained stores of "picric acid" (probably chloropicrin, a potentially lethal tear gas), the "100 percent lethal" agent, and an incapacitating agent near the cities of Qonduz and Kabul. . . .

The defector stated that the Soviets have been preoccupied with protecting the roads and that chemicals were sprayed by planes along the areas adjacent to highways. Chemical grenades reportedly have been used, but the data are inadequate to allow us to hypothesize about the contents, although some symptoms are indicative of mycotoxins.

The reports of rapid skin decomposition as quickly as 1-3 hours after death continue to concern us. There is no recognized class of chemical or biological toxin agents we know of that could affect bodies in such a way. If we assume occasional inaccuracies in reporting by journalists and survivors of attacks, it is possible that phosgene or phosgene oxime could cause such effects after 3-6 hours but with much less softening of tissues than is consistent with stories of "fingers being punched through the skin and limbs falling off." The reported medical effects of other toxic agent attacks are consistent with use of the nerve agent tabun. We have information that both phosgene oxime and tabun are stored by the Soviets in Afghanistan. . . .

LAOS

H'Mong refugees, recounting details of toxic agent attacks and exhibiting severe medical symptoms from exposure to the agents, fled to Thailand every month from January through June 1982. They brought out more samples contaminated by a yellow sticky substance described as a "yellow rain" dropped by aircraft and helicopters on their villages and crops. We have preliminary reports on attacks as recent as October 1982. We now know that the yellow rain contains trichothecene toxins and other substances that cause victims to experience vomiting, bleeding, blistering, severe skin lesions, and other lingering signs and symptoms observed by qualified physicians. Experts agree that these people were exposed to a toxic agent and that no indigenous natural disease, plant, or chemical caused these unique physical effects.

Laboratory analyses of blood samples from these victims and studies on experimental animals have shown that trichothecene toxins are retained in the body for much longer periods of time than previously thought. Scientific research has shown that the multiple-phase distribution pattern in animals includes a secondary half-life of up to 30 days. We believe that the severe skin lesions observed on victims by doctors are also relevant. Victims whose blood proved on analysis to have high levels of trichothecene mycotoxins exhibit such skin lesions. . . .

Medical personnel in Lao refugee camps in Thailand were much better organized in 1982 to screen victims than in past years. Doctors now routinely use extensive questionnaires and conduct comprehensive medical examinations, including some onsite, preliminary blood analysis. Skilled paramedical personnel oversee preparation of blood and serum samples for proper transport and shipment to the United States or other countries for chemical analysis. Some patients with active symptoms are now being monitored extensively over time.

A number of blood samples have been collected from Laos for analysis in the United States. All biological specimens were drawn by qualified medical personnel, and samples were refrigerated until analyzed in the United States. Analysis of these samples show that trichothecene mycotoxins continue to be used against H'Mong villages. . . .

KAMPUCHEA

Most reports of toxic attacks in Kampuchea for the period 1978-June 1982 come from Democratic Kampuchean (DK) sources, including interviews with DK military personnel. Evidence from other sources confirmed most of these reports. In 1982, most reported attacks occurred near the Thai border, making it easier to obtain samples and other direct evidence of toxic agent use.

In the first 6 months of 1982, the number of reported toxic agent attacks in Kampuchea was about half the number reported during the same periods in 1980 and 1981. The number of reported deaths per attack also decreased, but data were insufficient to determine if this decrease was statistically significant. We also have preliminary reports on attacks through early November 1982.

In February and March 1982, several attacks occurred just across the Kampuchean border in Thailand. Analysis of samples collected from the attacks was performed in Canada, Thailand, and the United States.

Although differing sampling techniques give rise to significant sampling error and lead to slightly different analytical results, both the U.S. and Thai analysts, using different analytical techniques, found trichothecene mycotoxins in their samples. The Canadian team investigating these attacks has published a detailed medical assessment of the victims' symptoms; it concluded that illness had in fact occurred and was caused by a toxic agent, although preliminary tests for trichothecenes proved inconclusive in the Canadian sample.

Blood and urine samples from Kampuchean victims of a toxic agent artillery attack on February 13, 1982, contained trichothecene toxins. In addition, post-mortem tissue from a victim of this same attack confirmed the presence of trichothecene toxins. . . .

The Vietnamese conducted toxic agent attacks this year against another resistance group, the Kampuchean People's National Liberation Forces. On several occasions in March-May 1982, the resistance camp at Sokh Sann was hit with toxic artillery shells and bombs. Samples of contaminated vegetation and yellow residue from these attacks are now being analyzed. Attacks occurred in Kampuchea through June 1982, providing new samples; qualitative tests indicate that the presence of trichothecenes is probable. The results of confirmatory analyses are pending.

Several Vietnamese military defectors from Kampuchea have provided valuable information in 1981 and 1982 on chemical weapons use and on the Vietnamese chemical warfare program and have reported that some types of agents are supplied by the Soviet Union. Information from other sources also confirms our earlier view that the Vietnamese possess toxic agent munitions and are equipping their own troops with additional protective equipment. . . .

COURT ON PARENTAL RIGHTS
March 24, 1982

In a 5-4 decision March 24, the Supreme Court struck down a New York law concerning child custody cases. The court ruled that the statute used too lenient a standard of evidence to decide such cases, thereby depriving the parents of due process of law. The ruling concerned the judicial finding of "permanent neglect" by parents, a term that also encompassed physical abuse of children. Thirty-three states already had adopted the more stringent level of evidence in child custody proceedings.

According to the dissent, the majority opinion in the case, Santosky v. Kramer, constituted national court interference in family law, a sphere traditionally assigned to the state legal system.

Santosky Case

The case began in 1973 when social work authorities in Ulster County, New York, temporarily removed the three children, aged 3 days to 3 years, of Annie and John Santosky II to foster homes following reports of bruises, abrasions, cuts, pinpricks, blisters and other wounds on the two older children. One child also was suffering from malnutrition. Officials removed the newborn baby as a precautionary measure.

After four years and $15,000 worth of state expenditures on attempts to "rehabilitate" the parents, officials reported no improvement in their attitudes toward their children. The officials moved to revoke parental rights and put the children up for adoption. The New York law provided that a judge may terminate parental rights if, after a year of foster care, *the agency's "diligent efforts" failed to improve the parents' willingness or ability to care for their child.*

Lawyers for the Santoskys challenged the New York law on how much proof of abuse authorities needed to take the children permanently from the parents. The Appellate Division of State Supreme Court upheld the law, and the New York Court of Appeals declined to hear the case.

The Supreme Court ruling struck down the provision of the New York State Family Court Act that allowed the removal of children on a "fair preponderance of evidence" of permanent neglect, the same level of evidence required when two parties were quarreling in court over money.

Levels of Proof

The U.S. legal system generally recognized three levels of proof, depending on the seriousness of the allegation and the consequences of the finding. "Fair preponderance of the evidence," the least strict standard of proof employed in American judicial proceedings, meant that the evidence presented was "more probable than not." The strictest standard of proof, used in criminal trials, was "beyond a reasonable doubt." Between the two was "clear and convincing evidence," the standard the Supreme Court ruled was necessary to remove children from their parents. The decision left the state free to attempt to end the Santoskys' parental rights by meeting the higher standard.

Opinion and Dissent

Justice Harry A. Blackmun, writing for the majority, held that by demanding only a low level of evidence to revoke parental rights, the New York provision treated child-custody rights as mere property rights. According to Blackmun, who was joined by Justices William J. Brennan Jr., Thurgood Marshall, Lewis F. Powell Jr. and John Paul Stevens, due process in parental rights proceedings required the support of evidence that was "at least" clear and convincing.

The majority believed that the "social cost of even an occasional error is sizable." In the termination of parental rights, parents lose their children forever and are, according to Blackmun, officially "unfit," a label they carry for the rest of their lives. The higher standard of "clear and convincing evidence" was no more stringent than that required to suspend a driver's license and could help avoid possible errors of judgment, Blackmun added.

Justice William H. Rehnquist, joined in the dissent by Chief Justice Warren E. Burger and Justices Sandra Day O'Connor and Byron R. White, wrote that, by focusing on parents' rights, the majority overlooked the essential purpose of parental rights termination laws — the protection of abused and neglected children. In terminating parental rights, they said, the state frees a child from the "unstable world of foster care" to be eligible for adoption and the possibility of a "normal homelife."

Although New York used the lowest standard of proof, Rehnquist wrote that the state protected the parents with a broad variety of hearings and other procedural safeguards, including provision of a lawyer, and with services aimed at rehabilitating problem parents before termination.

Furthermore, Rehnquist assailed the majority for "federal court intervention" in state matters and for supporting the "federalization of family law." According to the minority, family law — divorce, custody, parental rights — had, since "time immemorial and not without good reason," been reserved for the state legal system.

Supreme Court activity in family law was evident in two other recent decisions. Lehman v. Lycoming County Children's Services Agency *(1982) held that parents generally may not turn to federal courts to try to regain custody of children permanently taken from them by state officials.* Lassiter v. *Department of Social Services (1981), often referred to in the majority opinion in the Santosky case, held that the Constitution's due process clause does not entitle indigent parents to be represented by counsel at every termination-of-rights hearing.*

The court ruling in Santosky *affected a long-standing conflict between civil liberties groups and social workers. The ruling had been sought by civil liberties and legal aid groups who argued that many of the parents who had the children taken from them were poor and no match for the local government. State officials and social workers opposed a heightened standard of proof, saying it would rob them of the flexibility to deal with situations where the physical and mental well-being, even the survival of children, was at stake.*

Following are excerpts from the Supreme Court's March 24, 1982, decision in Santosky v. Kramer *that the New York state law governing child custody deprives parents of due process and from the dissenting opinion of Justice Rehnquist:*

No. 80-5889

John Santosky II and Annie Santosky, Petitioners *v.* Bernhardt S. Kramer, Commissioner, Ulster County Department of Social Services, et al.	On writ of certiorari to the Appellate Division, Supreme Court of New York, Third Jud. Dept.

[March 24, 1982]

JUSTICE BLACKMUN delivered the opinion of the Court.

Under New York law, the State may terminate, over parental objection, the rights of parents in their natural child upon a finding that the child is "permanently neglected." The New York Family Court Act § 622 requires that only a "fair preponderance of the evidence" support that finding. Thus, in New York, the factual certainty required to extinguish the parent-child relationship is no greater than that necessary to award money damages in an ordinary civil action.

Today we hold that the Due Process Clause of the Fourteenth Amendment demands more than this. Before a State may sever completely and irrevocably the rights of parents in their natural child, due process requires that the state support its allegations by at least clear and convincing evidence.

I

A

New York authorizes its officials to remove a child temporarily from his or her home if the child appears "neglected," within the meaning of Art. 10 of the Family Court Act. Once removed, a child under the age of 18 customarily is placed "in the care of an authorized agency," usually a state institution or a foster home. At that point, "the state's first obligation is to help the family with services to ... reunite it...." But if convinced that "positive, nurturing parent-child relationships no longer exist," the State may initiate "permanent neglect" proceedings to free the child for adoption.

The State bifurcates its permanent neglect proceeding into "factfinding" and "dispositional" hearings. At the factfinding stage, the State must prove that the child has been "permanently neglected," as defined by Fam. Ct. Act §§ 614.1.(a)-(d) and Soc. Serv. Law § 384-b.7.(a). The Family Court judge then determines at a subsequent dispositional hearing what placement would serve the child's best interests.

At the factfinding hearing, the State must establish, among other things, that for more than a year after the child entered state custody, the agency "made diligent efforts to encourage and strengthen the parental relationship." The State must further prove that during that same period, the child's natural parents failed "substantially and continuously or repeatedly to maintain contact with or plan for the future of the child although physically and financially able to do so." Should the State support its allegations by "a fair preponderance of the evidence," the child may be declared permanently neglected. That declaration empowers the Family Court judge to terminate permanently the natural parents' rights in the child. Termination denies the natural parents physical custody, as well as the rights ever to visit, communicate with, or regain custody of the child.

New York's permanent neglect statute provides natural parents with certain procedural protections. But New York permits its officials to establish "permanent neglect" with less proof than most States require. Thirty-three States, the District of Columbia, and the Virgin Islands currently specify a higher standard of proof, in parental rights termination proceedings, than a "fair preponderance of the evidence." The only analogous federal statute of which we are aware permits termination of parental rights solely upon "evidence beyond a reasonable doubt." The question here is whether New York's "fair preponderance of the evidence" standard is constitutionally sufficient.

B

Petitioners John Santosky II and Annie Santosky are the natural parents of Tina and John III. In November 1973, after incidents reflecting parental neglect, respondent Kramer, Commissioner of the Ulster County Department of Social Services, initiated a neglect proceeding under Fam. Ct. Act § 1022 and removed Tina from her natural home. About 10 months later, he removed John III and placed him with foster parents. On the day John was taken, Annie Santosky gave birth to a third child, Jed. When Jed was only three days old, respondent transferred him to a foster home on the ground that immediate removal was necessary to avoid imminent danger to his life or health.

In October 1978, respondent petitioned the Ulster County Family Court to terminate petitioners' parental rights in the three children. Petitioners challenged the constitutionality of the "fair preponderance of the evidence" standard specified in Fam. Ct. Act § 622. The Family Court judge rejected this constitutional challenge and weighed the evidence under the statutory standard. While acknowledging that the Santoskys had maintained contact with their children, the judge found those visits "at best superficial and devoid of any real emotional content." After deciding that the agency had made " 'diligent efforts' to encourage and strengthen the parental relationship," he concluded that the Santoskys were incapable, even with public assistance, of planning for the future of their children. The judge later held a dispositional hearing and ruled that the best interests of the three children required permanent termination of the Santoskys' custody.

Petitioners appealed, again contesting the constitutionality of § 622's standard of proof. The New York Supreme Court, Appellate Division, affirmed, holding application of the preponderance of the evidence standard "proper and constitutional." *In re John AA* (1980). That standard, the court reasoned, "recognizes and seeks to balance rights possessed by the child ... with those of the natural parents...."

The New York Court of Appeals then dismissed petitioners' appeal to that court "upon the ground that no substantial constitutional question is directly involved." We granted certiorari to consider petitioners' constitutional claim.

II

Last Term, in *Lassiter* v. *Department of Social Services* (1981), this Court, by a 5-4 vote, held that the Fourteenth Amendment's Due Process Clause does not require the appointment of counsel for indigent parents in every parental status termination proceeding. The case casts light, however, on the two central questions here — whether process is constitutionally due a natural parent at a State's parental rights termination proceeding, and, if so, what process is due.

In *Lassiter,* it was "not disputed that state intervention to terminate the relationship between [a parent] and [the] child must be accomplished by procedures meeting the requisites of the Due Process Clause." . . . The absence of dispute reflected this Court's historical recognition that freedom of personal choice in matters of family life is a fundamental liberty interest protected by the Fourteenth Amendment. *Quilloin* v. *Walcott* (1978); *Smith* v. *Organization of Foster Families* (1977) . . . *Pierce* v. *Society of Sisters* (1925); *Meyer* v. *Nebraska* (1923).

The fundamental liberty interest of natural parents in the care, custody, and management of their child does not evaporate simply because they have not been model parents or have lost temporary custody of their child to the State. Even when blood relationships are strained, parents retain a vital interest in preventing the irretrievable destruction of their family life. If anything, persons faced with forced dissolution of their parental rights have a more critical need for procedural protections than do those resisting state intervention into ongoing family affairs. When the State moves to destroy weakened familial bonds, it must provide the parents with fundamentally fair procedures.

In *Lassiter,* the Court and three dissenters agreed that the nature of the process due in parental rights termination proceedings turns on a balancing of the "three distinct factors" specified in *Mathews* v. *Eldridge* (1976): the private interests affected by the proceeding; the risk of error created by the State's chosen procedure; and the countervailing governmental interest supporting use of the challenged procedure. . . . Unlike the Court's right-to-counsel rulings, its decisions concerning constitutional burdens of proof have not turned on any presumption favoring any particular standard. To the contrary, the Court has engaged in a straightforward consideration of the factors identified in *Eldridge* to determine whether a particular standard of proof in a particular proceeding satisfies due process.

In *Addington* v. *Texas* (1979), the Court, by a unanimous vote of the participating Justices, declared: "The function of a standard of proof, as that concept is embodied in the Due Process Clause and in the realm of factfinding, is to 'instruct the factfinder concerning the degree of confidence our society thinks he should have in the correctness of factual conclusions for a particular type of adjudication.'" [Q]uoting *In re Winship* (1970) (Harlan, J., concurring). *Addington* teaches that, in any given proceeding, the minimum standard of proof tolerated by the due process requirement reflects not only the weight of the private and public interests affected, but also a societal judgment about how the risk of error should be distributed between the litigants.

Thus, while private parties may be interested intensely in a civil dispute over money damages, application of a "preponderance of the evidence" standard indicates both society's "minimal concern with the outcome," and a conclusion that the litigants should "share the risk of error in roughly equal fashion." When the State brings a criminal action to deny a defendant liberty or life, however, "the interests of the defendant are of such magnitude that historically and without any explicit constitutional requirement they have been protected by standards of proof designed to exclude as nearly as possible the likelihood of an erroneous judgment." The stringency of the "beyond a reasonable doubt" standard bespeaks the "weight and gravity" of the private interest affected, society's interest in avoiding erroneous convictions, and a judgment that those interests together require that "society impos[e] almost the entire risk of error upon itself.". . .

The "minimum requirements [of procedural due process] being a matter of federal law, they are not diminished by the fact that the State may have specified its own procedures that it may deem adequate for determining the preconditions to adverse official action." *Vitek* v. *Jones* (1980). . . . Moreover, the degree of proof required in a particular type of proceeding "is the kind of question which has traditionally been left to the judiciary to resolve." *Woodby* v. *INS* (1966). "In cases involving individual rights, whether criminal or civil, '[t]he standard of proof [at a minimum] reflects the value society places on individual liberty.'" *Addington* v. *Texas*. . . .

This Court has mandated an intermediate standard of proof — "clear and convincing evidence" — when the individual interests at stake in a state proceeding are both "particularly important" and "more substantial than mere loss of money." *Addington* v. *Texas*. Notwithstanding "the state's 'civil labels and good intentions,'" the Court has deemed this level of certainty necessary to preserve fundamental fairness in a variety of government-initiated proceedings that threaten the individual involved with "a significant deprivation of liberty" or "stigma." See, *e.g.*, *Addington* v. *Texas* (civil commitment); *Woodby* v. *INS* (deportation); *Chaunt* v. *United States* (1960) (denaturalization); *Schneiderman* v. *United States* (1943) (denaturalization).

In *Lassiter*, to be sure, the Court held that fundamental fairness may be maintained in parental rights termination proceedings even when some procedures are mandated only on a case-by-case basis, rather than through rules of general application. But this Court never has approved case-by-case determination of the proper *standard of proof* for a given proceeding. Standards of proof, like other "procedural due process rules[,] are shaped by the risk of error inherent in the truth-finding process as applied to the *generality of cases*, not the rare exception." *Mathews* v. *Eldridge* (emphasis added). Since the litigants and the factfinding must know at the outset of a given proceeding how the risk of error will be allocated, the standard of proof necessarily must be calibrated in advance. Retrospective case-by-case review cannot preserve fundamental fairness when a class of proceedings is governed by a constitutionally defective evidentiary standard.

III

In parental rights termination proceedings, the private interest affected is commanding; the risk of error from using a preponderance standard is substantial; and the countervailing governmental interest favoring that standard is comparatively slight. Evaluation of the three *Eldridge* factors compels the conclusion that use of a "fair preponderance of the evidence" standard in such proceedings is inconsistent with due process.

A

"The extent to which procedural due process must be afforded the recipient is influenced by the extent to which he may be 'condemned to suffer grievous loss.'" *Goldberg* v. *Kelly* (1970), quoting *Joint Anti-Fascist Refugee Committee* v. *McGrath* (1951) (Frankfurter, J., concurring). Whether the loss threatened by a particular type of proceeding is sufficiently grave to warrant more than average certainty on the part of the factfinder turns on both the nature of the private interest threatened and the permanency of the threatened loss.

Lassiter declared it "plain beyond the need for multiple citation" that a natural parent's "desire for and right to 'the companionship, care, custody, and management of his or her children'" is an interest far more precious than any property right. When the State initiates a parental rights termination proceeding, it seeks not merely to infringe that fundamental liberty interest, but to end it. "If the State prevails, it will have worked a unique kind of deprivation.... A parent's interest in the accuracy and justice of the decision to terminate his or her parental status is, therefore, a commanding one."

... Once affirmed on appeal, a New York decision terminating parental rights is *final* and irrevocable. Few forms of state action are both so severe and so irreversible.

Thus, the first *Eldridge* factor — the private interest affected — weighs heavily against use of the preponderance standard at a State-initiated permanent neglect proceeding. We do not deny that the child and his foster parents are also deeply interested in the outcome of that contest. But at the factfinding stage of the New York proceeding, the focus emphatically is not on them.

The factfinding does not purport — and is not intended — to balance the child's interest in a normal family home against the parents' interest in raising the child. Nor does it purport to determine whether the natural parents or the foster parents would provide the better home. Rather, the factfinding hearing pits the State directly against the parents. The State alleges that the natural parents are at fault. The questions disputed and decided are what the State did — "made diligent efforts," and what the natural parents did not do — "maintain contact with or plan for the future of the child." The State marshals an array of public resources to prove its case and disprove the parents' case. Victory by the State not only makes termination of parental rights possible; it entails a judicial determination that the parents are unfit to raise their own children.

At the factfinding, the State cannot presume that a child and his parents are adversaries. After the State has established parental unfitness at the initial proceeding, the court may assume at the *dispositional* stage that the interests of the child and the natural parents do diverge. See Fam. Ct. Act. § 631 (judge shall make his order "solely on the basis of the best interests of the child," and thus has no obligation to consider the natural parents' rights in selecting dispositional alternatives). But until the State proves parental unfitness, the child and his parents share a vital interest in preventing erroneous termination of their natural relationship. . . .

. . . For the foster parents, the State's failure to prove permanent neglect may prolong the delay and uncertainty until their foster child is freed for adoption. But for the natural parents, a finding of permanent neglect can cut off forever their rights in their child. Given this disparity of consequence, we have no difficulty finding that the balance of private interests strongly favors heightened procedural protections.

B

Under *Mathews* v. *Eldridge*, we next must consider both the risk of erroneous deprivation of private interests resulting from use of a "fair preponderance" standard and the likelihood that a higher evidentiary standard would reduce that risk. Since the factfinding phase of a permanent neglect proceeding is an adversary contest between the State and the natural parents, the relevant question is whether a preponderance standard fairly allocates the risk of an erroneous factfinding between these two parties.

In New York, the factfinding stage of a State-initiated permanent neglect proceeding bears many of the indicia of a criminal trial. . . . The Commissioner of Social Services charges the parents with permanent neglect. They are served by summons. The factfinding hearing is conducted pursuant to formal rules of evidence. The State, the parents, and the child are all represented by counsel. The State seeks to establish a series of historical facts about the intensity of its agency's efforts to reunite the family, the infrequency and insubstantiality of the parents' contacts with their child, and the parents' inability or unwillingness to formulate a plan for the child's future. The attorneys submit documentary evidence, and call witnesses who are subject to cross-examination. Based on all the evidence, the judge then determines whether the State has proved the statutory elements of permanent neglect by a fair preponderance of the evidence.

At such a proceeding, numerous factors combine to magnify the risk of erroneous factfinding. Permanent neglect proceedings employ imprecise substantive standards that leave determinations unusually open to the subjective values of the judge. See *Smith* v. *Organization of Foster Families*. In appraising the nature and quality of a complex series of encounters among the agency, the parents, and the child, the court possesses unusual discretion to underweigh probative facts that might favor the parent. Because parents subject to termination proceedings are often poor, uneducated, or members of minority groups, such proceedings are often vulnerable to judgments based on cultural or class bias.

The State's ability to assemble its case almost inevitably dwarfs the parents' ability to mount a defense. No predetermined limits restrict the sums an agency may spend in prosecuting a given termination proceeding. The State's attorney usually will be expert on the issues contested and the procedures employed at the factfinding hearing, and enjoys full access to all public records concerning the family. The State may call on experts in family relations, psychology, and medicine to bolster its case. Furthermore, the primary witnesses at the hearing will be the agency's own professional caseworkers whom the State has empowered both to investigate the family situation and to testify against the parents. Indeed, because the child is already in agency custody, the State even has the power to shape the historical events that form the basis for termination.

The disparity between the adversaries' litigation resources is matched by a striking asymmetry in their litigation options. Unlike criminal defendants, natural parents have no "double jeopardy" defense against repeated state termination efforts. If the State initially fails to win termination, as New York did here, it always can try once again to cut off the parents' rights after gathering more or better evidence. Yet even when the parents have attained the level of fitness required by the State, they have no similar means by which they can forestall future termination efforts.

Coupled with a "preponderance of the evidence" standard, these factors create a significant prospect of erroneous termination.... Given the weight of the private interests at stake, the social cost of even occasional error is sizable.

Raising the standard of proof would have both practical and symbolic consequences. The Court has long considered the heightened standard of proof used in criminal prosecutions to be "a prime instrument for reducing the risk of convictions resting on factual error." *In re Winship*. An elevated standard of proof in a parental rights termination proceeding would alleviate "the possible risk that a factfinder might decide to [deprive] an individual based solely on a few isolated instances of unusual conduct [or] ... idiosyncratic behavior." *Addington* v. *Texas*. "Increasing the burden of proof is one way to impress the factfinder with the importance of the decision and thereby perhaps to reduce the chances that inappropriate" terminations will be ordered.

The Appellate Division approved New York's preponderance standard on the ground that it properly "balanced rights possessed by the child ... with those of the natural parents...." By so saying, the court suggested that a preponderance standard properly allocates the risk of error *between* the parents and the child. That view is fundamentally mistaken.

The court's theory assumes that termination of the natural parents' rights invariably will benefit the child. Yet we have noted above that the parents and the child share an interest in avoiding erroneous termination. Even accepting the court's assumption, we cannot agree with its conclusion that a preponderance standard fairly distributes the risk of error between parent and child. Use of that standard reflects the judgment that society is nearly neutral between erroneous termination of parental rights and erroneous failure to terminate those rights. For the child, the likely consequence of an erroneous failure to terminate is preservation of an uneasy status quo. For the natural parents, however, the consequence of an erroneous termination is the unnecessary destruction of their natural family. A standard that allocates the risk of error nearly equally between those two outcomes does not reflect properly their relative severity.

C

Two state interests are at stake in parental rights termination proceedings — a *parens patriae* interest in preserving and promoting the welfare of the child and a fiscal and administrative interest in reducing the cost and burden of such proceedings. A standard of proof more strict than preponderance of the evidence is consistent with both interests.

"Since the State has an urgent interest in the welfare of the child, it shares the parent's interest in an accurate and just decision" at the *factfinding* proceeding. *Lassiter* v. *Department of Social Services.* As *parens patriae,* the State's goal is to provide the child with a permanent home. Yet while there is still reason to believe that positive, nurturing parent-child relationships exist, the *parens patriae* interest favors preservation, not severance, of natural family bonds. "[T]he State registers no gain towards its declared goals when it separates children from the custody of fit parents." *Stanley* v. *Illinois* [1972].

The State's interest in finding the child an alternative permanent home arises only "when it is *clear* that the natural parent cannot or will not provide a normal family home for the child." At the factfinding, that goal is served by procedures that promote an accurate determination of whether the natural parents can and will provide a normal home.

Unlike a constitutional requirement of hearings, see, *e.g., Mathews* v. *Eldridge,* or court-appointed counsel, a stricter standard of proof would reduce factual error without imposing substantial fiscal burdens upon the State. As we have observed, 33 States already have adopted a higher standard by statute or court decision without apparent effect on the speed, form, or cost of their factfinding proceedings.

Nor would an elevated standard of proof create any real administrative burdens for the State's factfinders. New York Family Court judges already are familiar with a higher evidentiary standard in other parental rights termination proceedings not involving permanent neglect. New York also demands at least clear and convincing evidence in proceedings of far less moment than parental rights termination proceedings.... We cannot believe that it would burden the State unduly to require that its factfinders have the same factual certainty when terminating the parent-child relationship as they must have to suspend a driver's license.

IV

The logical conclusion of this balancing process is that the "fair prepondernace of the evidence" standard prescribed the Fam. Ct. Act § 622 violates the Due Process Clause of the Fourteenth Amendment. The Court noted in *Addington:* "The individual should not be asked to share equally with society the risk of error when the possible injury to the individual is significantly greater than any possible harm to the state." Thus, at a parental rights termination proceeding, a near-equal allocation of risk between the parents and the State is constitutionally intolerable. The next question, then, is whether a "beyond a reasonable doubt" or a "clear and convincing" standard is constitutionally mandated.

In *Addington,* the Court concluded that application of a reasonable-doubt standard is inappropriate in civil commitment proceedings for two reasons — because of our hesitation to apply that unique standard "too broadly or casually in noncriminal cases," and because the psychiatric evidence ordinarily adduced at commitment proceedings is rarely suscepti-ble to proof beyond a reasonable doubt. To be sure, in the Indian Child Welfare Act of 1978 Congress requires "evidence beyond a reasonable doubt" for termination of Indian parental rights, reasoning that "the removal of a child from the parents is a penalty as great, if not greater, than a criminal penalty...." Congress did not consider, however, the evidentiary problems that would arise if proof beyond a reasonable doubt were required in all State-initiated parental rights termination hearings.

Like civil commitment hearings, termination proceedings often require the factfinder to evaluate medical and psychiatric testimony, and to decide issues difficult to prove to a level of absolute certainty, such as lack of pa-rental motive, absence of affection between parent and child, and failure of parental foresight and progress. The substantive standards applied vary from State to State. Although Congress found a "beyond a reasonable doubt" standard proper in one type of parental rights termination case, another legislative body might well conclude that a reasonable-doubt standard would erect an unreasonable barrier to state efforts to free permanently neglected children for adoption.

A majority of the States have concluded that a "clear and convincing evidence" standard of proof strikes a fair balance between the rights of the natural parents and the State's legitimate concerns. We hold that such a standard adequately conveys to the factfinder the level of subjective certainty about his factual conclusions necessary to satisfy due process. We further hold that determination of the precise burden equal to or greater than that standard is a matter of state law properly left to state legislatures and state courts.

We, of course, express no view on the merits of petitioners' claims. At a hearing conducted under a constitutionally proper standard, they may or may not prevail. Without deciding the outcome under any of the standards we have approved, we vacate the judgment of the Appellate Division and remand the case for further proceedings not inconsistent with the opinion.

It is so ordered.

JUSTICE REHNQUIST, with whom the CHIEF JUSTICE, JUSTICE WHITE, and JUSTICE O'CONNOR join, dissenting.

I believe that few of us would care to live in a society where every aspect of life was regulated by a single source of law, whether that source be this Court or some other organ of our complex body politic. But today's decision certainly moves us in that direction. By parsing the New York scheme and holding one narrow provision unconstitutional, the majority invites further federal court intrusion into every facet of state family law. If ever there were an area in which federal courts should heed the admonition of Justice Holmes that "a page of history is worth a volume of logic," it is in the area of domestic relations. This area has been left to the States from time immemorial, and not without good reason.

Equally as troubling is the majority's due process analysis. The Fourteenth Amendment guarantees that a State will treat individuals with "fundamental fairness" whenever its actions infringe their protected liberty or property interests. By adoption of the procedures relevant to this case, New York has created an exhaustive program to assist parents in regaining the custody of their children and to protect parents from the unfair deprivation of their parental rights. And yet the majority's myopic scrutiny of the standard of proof blinds it to the very considerations and procedures which make the New York scheme "fundamentally fair."

I

State intervention in domestic relations has always been an unhappy but necessary feature of life in our organized society. For all of our experience in this area, we have found no fully satisfactory solutions to the painful problem of child abuse and neglect. We have found, however, that leaving the States free to experiment with various remedies has produced novel approaches and promising progress.

Throughout this experience the Court has scrupulously refrained from interfering with state answers to domestic relations questions. "Both theory and the precedents of this Court teach us solicitude for state interests, particularly in the field of family and family-property arrangements." *United States* v. *Yazell* (1966). This is not to say that the Court should blink at clear constitutional violations in state statutes, but rather that in this area, of all areas, "substantial weight must be given to the good faith judgments of the individuals [administering a program] ... that the procedures they have adopted assure fair consideration of the ... claims of individuals." *Mathews* v. *Eldridge* (1976).

This case presents a classic occasion for such solicitude. As will be seen more fully in the next part, New York has enacted a comprehensive plan to *aid* marginal parents in regaining the custody of their child. The central purpose of the New York plan is to reunite divided families. Adoption of the preponderance of the evidence standard represents New York's good faith effort to balance the interest of parents against the legitimate interests of the child and the State. These earnest efforts by state officials should be given weight in the Court's application of due process principles. "Great constitutional provisions must be administered with caution. Some play must be allowed for the joints of the machine, and it must be remembered that legislatures are ultimate guardians of the liberties and welfare of the people in quite as great a degree as the courts." *Missouri, Kansas and Texas Railway Co.* v. *May* (1904).

The majority may believe that it is adopting a relatively unobtrusive means of ensuring that termination proceedings provide "due process of law." In fact, however, fixing the standard of proof as a matter of federal constitutional law will only lead to further federal-court intervention in state schemes. By holding that due process requires proof by clear and convincing evidence the majority surely cannot mean that any state scheme passes constitutional muster so long as it applies that standard of proof. A state law permitting termination of parental rights upon a showing of neglect by clear and convincing evidence certainly would not be acceptable to the majority if it provided no procedures other than one thirty-minute hearing. Similarly, the majority probably would balk at a state scheme that permitted termination of parental rights on a clear and convincing showing merely that such action would be in the best interests of the child. . . .

After fixing the standard of proof, therefore, the majority will be forced to evaluate other aspects of termination proceedings with reference to that point. Having in this case abandoned evaluation of the overall effect of a scheme, and with it the possibility of finding that strict substantive standards or special procedures compensate for a lower burden of proof, the majority's approach will inevitably lead to the federalization of family law. Such a trend will only thwart state searches for better solutions in an area where this Court should encourage state experimentation. "It is one of the happy incidents of the federal system that a single courageous State may, if its citizens choose, serve as a laboratory; and try novel social and economic experiments without risk to the rest of the country. This Court has the power to prevent an experiment." *New State Ice Co.* v. *Liebmann* (1932) (Brandeis, J., dissenting). It should not do so in the absence of a clear constitutional violation. As will be seen in the next part, no clear constitutional violation has occurred in this case.

II

As the majority opinion notes, petitioners are the parents of five children, three of whom were removed from petitioners' care on or before August 22, 1974. During the next four and one-half years, those three children were in the custody of the State and in the care of foster homes or institutions, and the State was diligently engaged in efforts to prepare petitioners for the childrens' return. Those efforts were unsuccessful, however, and on April 10, 1979 the New York Family Court for Ulster County terminated petitioners' parental rights as to the three children removed in 1974 or earlier. This termination was preceded by a judicial finding that petitioners had failed to plan for the return and future of their children, a statutory category of permanent neglect. Petitioners now contend, and the Court today holds, that they were denied due process of law, not because of a general inadequacy of procedural protections, but simply because the finding of permanent neglect was made on the basis of a preponderance of the evidence adduced at the termination hearing.

It is well settled that "[t]he requirements of procedural due process apply only to the deprivation of interests encompassed by the Fourteenth Amendment's protection of liberty and property." *Board of Regents* v. *Roth* (1972). In determining whether such liberty or property interests are implicated by a particular government action, "we must look not to the 'weight' but to the *nature* of the interest at stake." I do not disagree with the majority's conclusion that the interest of parents in their relationship with their children is sufficiently fundamental to come within the finite class of liberty interests protected by the Fourteenth Amendment. See *Smith* v. *Organization of Foster Families* [1977] (Stewart, J., concurring). "Once it is determined that due process applies, [however,] the question remains what process is due." *Morrissey* v. *Brewer* (1972). It is the majority's answer to this question with which I disagree.

A

Due process of law is a flexible constitutional principle. The requirements which it imposes upon governmental actions vary with the situations to which it applies. As the Court previously has recognized, "not all situations calling for procedural safeguards call for the same kind of procedure." *Morrissey* v. *Brewer.* . . . The adequacy of a scheme of procedural protections cannot, therefore, be determined merely by the application of general principles unrelated to the peculiarities of the case at hand.

Given this flexibility, it is obvious that a proper due process inquiry cannot be made by focusing upon one narrow provision of the challenged statutory scheme. Such a focus threatens to overlook factors which may introduce constitutionally adequate protections into a particular government action. Courts must examine *all* procedural protections offered by the State, and must assess the *cumulative* effect of such safeguards. As we have stated before, courts must consider "the fairness and reliability of the existing ... procedures" before holding that the Constitution requires more. *Mathews* v. *Eldridge.* Only through such a broad inquiry may courts determine whether a challenged governmental action satisfies the due process requirement of "fundamental fairness." In some instances, the Court has even looked to non-procedural restraints on official action in determining whether the deprivation of a protected interest was effected without due process of law. *E.g., Ingraham* v. *Wright* (1977). In this case, it is just such a broad look at the New York scheme which reveals its fundamental fairness.

The termination of parental rights on the basis of permanent neglect can occur under New York law only by order of the Family Court. Before a petition for permanent termination can be filed in that court, however, several other events must first occur.

The Family Court has jurisdiction only over those children who are in the care of an authorized agency. Therefore, the children who are the subject of a termination petition must previously have been removed from their parents' home on a temporary basis. Temporary removal of a child can occur in one of two ways. The parents may consent to the removal or, as occurred in this case, the Family Court can order the removal pursuant to a finding that the child is abused or neglected.

Court proceedings to order the temporary removal of a child are initiated by a petition alleging abuse or neglect, filed by a state-authorized child protection agency or by a person designated by the court. Unless the court finds that exigent circumstances require removal of the child before a petition may be filed and a hearing held, the order of temporary removal results from a "dispositional hearing" conducted to determine the appropriate form of alternative care. This "dispositional hearing" can be held only after the court, at a separate "fact-finding hearing," has found the child to be abused or neglected within the specific statutory definition of those terms.

Parents subjected to temporary removal proceedings are provided extensive procedural protections. A summons and copy of the temporary removal petition must be served upon the parents within two days of issuance by the court, and the parents may, at their own request, delay the commencement of the fact-finding hearing for three days after service of the summons. The fact-finding hearing may not commence without a determination by the court that the parents are present at the hearing and have been served with the petition. At the hearing itself, "only competent, material and relevant evidence may be admitted," with some enumerated exceptions for particularly probative evidence. In addition, indigent parents are provided with an attorney to represent them at both the fact-finding and dispositional hearings, as well as at all other proceedings related to temporary removal of their child.

An order of temporary removal must be reviewed every 18 months by the Family Court. Such review is conducted by hearing before the same judge who ordered the temporary removal, and a notice of the hearing, including a statement of the dispositional alternatives, must be given to the parents at least 20 days before the hearing is held. As in the initial removal action, the parents must be parties to the proceedings and are entitled to court appointed counsel if indigent.

One or more years after a child has been removed temporarily from the parents' home, permanent termination proceedings may be commenced by the filing of a petition in the court which ordered the temporary removal. The petition must be filed by a state agency or by a foster parent authorized by the court and must allege that the child has been permanently neglected by the parents. Notice of the petition and the dispositional proceedings must be served upon the parents at least 20 days before the commencement of the hearing, must inform them of the potential consequences of the hearing, and must inform them "of their right to the assistance of counsel, including [their] right ... to have counsel assigned by the court [if] they are financially unable to obtain counsel."

As in the initial removal proceedings, two hearings are held in consideration of the permanent termination petition. At the fact-finding hearing, the court must determine, by a fair preponderance of the evidence, whether the child has been permanently neglected. "Only competent, material and relevant evidence may be admitted in a fact-finding hearing." The court may find permanent neglect if the child is in the care of an authorized agency or foster home and the parents have "failed for a period of more than one year ... substantially and continuously or repeatedly to maintain contact with or plan for the future of the child, although physically and financially able to do so." In addition, because the State considers its "first obligation" to be the reuniting of the child with its natural parents, the court must also find that the supervising state agency has, without success, made "*diligent* efforts to encourage and strengthen the parental relationship." ([E]mphasis added).

Following the fact-finding hearing, a separate, dispositional hearing is held to determine what course of action would be in "the best interests of the child." A finding of permanent neglect at the fact-finding hearing, although necessary to a termination of parental rights, does not control the court's order at the dispositional hearing. The court may dismiss the petition, suspend judgment on the petition and retain jurisdiction for a period of one year in order to provide further opportunity for a reuniting of the family, or terminate the parents' right to the custody and care of the child. The court must base its decision solely upon the record of "material and relevant evidence" introduced at the dispositional hearing ... and may not entertain any presumption that the best interests of the child "will be promoted by any particular disposition."

As petitioners did in this case, parents may appeal any unfavorable decision to the Appellate Division of the New York Supreme Court. Thereafter, review may be sought in the New York Court of Appeals and, ultimately, in this Court if a federal question is properly presented.

As this description of New York's termination procedures demonstrates, the State seeks not only to protect the interests of parents in rearing their own children, but also to assist and encourage parents who have lost custody of their children to reassume their rightful role. Fully understood, the New York system is a comprehensive program to *aid* parents such as petitioners. Only as a last resort, when "diligent efforts" to reunite the family have failed, does New York authorize the termination of parental rights. The procedures for termination of those relationships which cannot be aided and which threaten permanent injury to the child, administered by a judge who has supervised the case from the first temporary removal through the final termination, cannot be viewed as fundamentally unfair. The facts of this case demonstrate the fairness of the system.

The three children to which this case relates were removed from petitioners' custody in 1973 and 1974, before petitioners' other two children were born. The removals were made pursuant to the procedures detailed above and in response to what can only be described as shockingly abusive treatment. At the temporary removal hearing held before the Family Court on September 30, 1974, petitioners were represented by counsel, and allowed the Ulster County Department of Social Services ("Department") to take custody of the three children.

Temporary removal of the children was continued at an evidentiary hearing held before the Family Court in December 1975, after which the court issued a written opinion concluding that petitioners were unable to resume their parental responsibilities due to personality disorders. Unsatisfied with the progress petitioners were making, the court also directed the Department to reduce to writing the plan which it had designed to solve the problems at petitioners' home and reunite the family.

A plan for providing petitioners with extensive counseling and training services was submitted to the court and approved in February 1976. Under the plan, petitioners received training by a mother's aide, a nutritional aide, and a public health nurse, and counseling at a family planning clinic. In addition, the plan provided psychiatric treatment and vocational training for the father, and counseling at a family service center for the mother. Between early 1976 and the final termination decision in April 1979, the State spent more than $15,000 in these efforts to rehabilitate petitioners as parents.

Petitioners' response to the State's effort was marginal at best. They wholly disregarded some of the available services and participated only sporadically in the others. As a result, and out of growing concern over the length of the childrens' stay in foster care, the Department petitioned in September 1976 for permanent termination of petitioners' parental rights so that the children could be adopted by other families. Although the Family Court recognized that petitioners' reaction to the State's efforts was generally "non-responsive even resentful," the fact that they were "at least superficially cooperative" led it to conclude that there was yet hope of further improvement and an eventual reuniting of the family. Accordingly, the petition for permanent termination was dismissed.

Whatever progress petitioners were making prior to the 1976 termination hearing, they made little or no progress thereafter. In October 1978, the Department again filed a termination petition alleging that petitioners had completely failed to plan for the childrens' future despite the considerable efforts rendered in their behalf. This time, the Family Court agreed. The court found that petitioners had "failed in any meaningful way to take advantage of the many social and rehabilitative services that have not only been made available to them but have been diligently urged upon them." In addition, the court found that the "infrequent" visits "between the parents and their children were at best superficial and devoid of any real emotional content." The court thus found "nothing in the situation which holds out any hope that [petitioners] may ever become financially self sufficient or emotionally mature enough to be independent of the services of social agencies. More than a reasonable amount of time has passed and still, in the words of the case workers, there has been no discernible forward movement. At some point in time, it must be said, 'enough is enough.' "

In accordance with the statutory requirements set forth above, the court found that petitioners' failure to plan for the future of their children, who were then seven, five, and four years old and had been out of petitioners' custody for at least four years, rose to the level of permanent neglect. At a subsequent dispositional hearing, the court terminated petitioners' parental rights, thereby freeing the three children for adoption.

As this account demonstrates, the State's extraordinary four-year effort to reunite petitioners' family was not just unsuccessful, it was altogether rebuffed by parents unwilling to improve their circumstances sufficiently to permit a return of their children. At every step of this protracted process petitioners were accorded those procedures and protections which traditionally have been required by due process of law. Moreover, from the beginning to the end of this sad story all judicial determinations were made by one family court judge. After four and one-half years of involvement with petitioners, more than seven complete hearings, and additional periodic supervision of the State's rehabilitative efforts, the judge no doubt was intimately familiar with this case and the prospects for petitioners' rehabilitation.

It is inconceivable to me that these procedures were "fundamentally unfair" to petitioners. Only by its obsessive focus on the standard of proof and its almost complete disregard of the facts of this case does the majority find otherwise. As the discussion above indicates, however, such a focus does not comport, with the flexible standard of fundamental fairness embodied in the Due Process Clause of the Fourteenth Amendment.

B

In addition to the basic fairness of the process afforded petitioners, the standard of proof chosen by New York clearly reflects a constitutionally permissible balance of the interests at stake in this case. The standard of proof "represents an attempt to instruct the factfinder concerning the degree of confidence our society thinks he should have in the correctness of factual conclusions for a particular type of adjudication." *In re Winship* (1970) (Harlan, J. concurring); *Addington* v. *Texas* (1979). In this respect, the standard of proof is a crucial component of legal process, the primary function of which is "to minimize the risk of erroneous decisions." *Greenholtz* v. *Nebraska Penal Inmates* [1979]. See also *Addington* v. *Texas; Mathews* v. *Eldridge.*

In determining the propriety of a particular standard of proof in a given case, however, it is not enough simply to say that we are trying to minimize the risk of error. Because errors in factfinding affect more than one interest, we try to minimize error as to those interests which we consider to be most important. As Justice Harlan explained in his well-known concurrence to *In re Winship:*

> "In a lawsuit between two parties, a factual error can make a difference in one of two ways. First, it can result in a judgment in favor of the plaintiff when the true facts warrant a judgment for the defendant. The analogue in a criminal case would be the conviction of an innocent man. On the other hand, an erroneous factual determination can result in a judgment for the defendant when the true facts justify a judgment in plaintiff's favor. The criminal analogue would be the acquittal of a guilty man.
> The standard of proof influences the relative frequency of these two types of erroneous outcomes. If, for example, the standard of proof for a criminal trial were a preponderance of the evidence rather than proof beyond a reasonable doubt, there would be a smaller risk of factual errors that result in freeing guilty persons, but a far greater risk of factual errors that result in convicting the innocent." ...

When the standard of proof is understood as reflecting such an assessment, an examination of the interests at stake in a particular case becomes essential to determining the propriety of the specified standard of proof. Because proof by a preponderance of the evidence requires that "[t]he litigants ... share the risk of error in a roughly equal fashion," *Addington* v. *Texas,* it rationally should be applied only when the interests at stake are of roughly equal societal importance. The interests at stake in this case demonstrate that New York has selected a constitutionally permissible standard of proof.

On one side is the interest of parents in a continuation of the family unit and the raising of their own children. The importance of this interest cannot easily be overstated. Few consequences of judicial action are so grave as the severance of natural family ties. ... In creating the scheme at issue in this case, the New York legislature was expressly aware of this right of parents "to bring up their own children."

On the other side of the termination proceeding are the often countervailing interests of the child. A stable, loving homelife is essential to a child's physical, emotional, and spiritual well-being. It requires no citation of authority to assert that children who are abused in their youth generally face extraordinary problems developing into responsible, productive citizens. The same can be said of children who, though not physically or emotionally abused, are passed from one foster home to another with no constancy of love, trust, or discipline. If the Family Court makes an incorrect factual determination resulting in a failure to terminate a parent-child relationship which rightfully should be ended, the child involved must return either to an abusive home or to the often unstable world of foster care. The reality of these risks is magnified by the fact that the only families faced with termination actions are those which have voluntarily surrendered custody of their child to the State, or, as in this case, those from which the child has been removed by judicial action because of threatened irreparable injury through abuse or neglect. Permanent neglect findings also occur only in families where the child has been in foster care for at least one year.

In addition to the child's interest in a normal homelife, "the State has an urgent interest in the welfare of the child." *Lassiter* v. *Department of Social Services*. Few could doubt that the most valuable resource of a self-governing society is its population of children who will one day become adults and themselves assume the responsibility of self-governance.... Thus, "the whole community" has an interest "that children be both safeguarded from abuses and given opportunities for growth into free and independent well-developed ... citizens."...

When, in the context of a permanent neglect termination proceeding, the interests of the child and the State in a stable, nurturing homelife are balanced against the interests of the parents in the rearing of their child, it cannot be said that either set of interests is so clearly paramount as to require that the risk of error be allocated to one side or the other. Accordingly, a State constitutionally may conclude that the risk of error should be borne in roughly equal fashion by use of the preponderance of the evidence standard of proof.... This is precisely the balance which has been struck by the New York legislature: "It is the intent of the legislature in enacting this section to provide procedures not only assuring that the rights of the natural parent are protected, but also, where positive, nurturing parent-child relationships no longer exist, furthering the best interests, needs, and rights of the child by terminating the parental rights and freeing the child for adoption."

III

For the reasons heretofore stated, I believe that the Court today errs in concluding that the New York standard of proof in parental-rights termination proceedings violates due process of law. The decision disregards New York's earnest efforts to *aid* parents in regaining the custody of their children and a host of procedural protections placed around parental rights and interests. The Court finds a constitutional violation only by a tunnel-vision application of due process principles that altogether loses sight of the unmistakable fairness of the New York procedure.

Even more worrisome, today's decision cavalierly rejects the considered judgment of the New York legislature in an area traditionally entrusted to state care. The Court thereby begins, I fear, a trend of federal intervention in state family law matters which surely will stifle creative responses to vexing problems. Accordingly, I dissent.

APRIL

FALKLAND ISLANDS WAR

April 2 - June 16, 1982

On April 2 approximately 4,000 Argentine troops seized control of the British-held Falkland Islands in the South Atlantic, beginning a 10-week struggle for control of the islands. The war ended June 16 with the signing of a surrender by Argentina.

The Falklands, located about 250 miles off the southeast coast of Argentina and roughly 8,000 miles southwest of Britain, comprise two main islands, East and West Falkland, and 200 smaller ones, South Georgia and the South Sandwich Islands, about 800 miles farther east. Sheep farming is the primary economic activity on the Falklands. The terrain is rugged and hilly; rain or snow falls two-thirds of the year, and the mean temperature is 42 degrees. Most of the land, home to 700,000 sheep, penguins, albatross and various other sea birds, is owned by absentee British landlords. Approximately 1,800 islanders, almost all of British descent, live in the Falklands, more than half of them in Stanley, the capital on East Falkland. On the island of South Georgia, Britain maintains an antarctic research station. The waters around the Falklands are considered a likely source of oil, and this possibility may have increased Argentina's motivation to invade the islands.

History

Argentina's sudden invasion of the Falklands stunned most of the world, but Britain and Argentina had disputed the sovereignty of the islands for almost 150 years. In the 1700s England, France and Spain *maintained thriving whaling and sealing settlements there. France eventually sold its interest to Spain and, narrowly avoiding war, Spain and Britain agreed to share the islands. In 1774 Britain withdrew its colony but maintained its claim. Spain abandoned its settlement in 1806.*

Argentina gained independence from Spain in 1816 and established its own settlement on the Falklands in 1828. In 1832-33 the British reasserted their claim, forced the Argentines out and established a lasting colony. From that time on Britain and Argentina have argued over whose claim is legitimate. Argentina believed that Britain usurped and maintained control of the islands by force for 149 years. Britain, on the other hand, held that Argentina had no right to have established a colony on the Falklands in the first place.

In 1964 the United Nations urged the two countries to resolve their longstanding dispute through peaceful negotiations. Throughout the 1970s the two held a series of talks and agreed on a variety of trade, communications and social service issues involving the Falklands and their inhabitants. The sovereignty issue, however, remained unresolved.

In 1981 Britain considered ceding the islands to Argentina and then leasing them back. But Argentina insisted on full control, and the islanders were equally determined to remain British. On March 1, 1982, after another round of talks, Argentina warned Britain that unless the sovereignty issue was resolved soon, Argentina would cease negotiating and "seek other means" to end the dispute.

The Conflict

On April 2 Argentina carried out its threat. Four thousand Argentine troops quickly overcame 84 British Royal Marines on the Falklands, and British Gov. Rex Hunt ordered his troops to abandon fighting. The next day Argentine troops took over South Georgia Island where a handful of Royal Marines were stationed at Port Grytviken. The ousted British governor returned to England, and Argentina installed Brig. Gen. Mario Benjamin Menéndez as governor of the Malvinas, as Argentina called the Falklands.

Reacting immediately to the invasion, Britain broke diplomatic ties with Argentina April 2 and imposed a freeze on all Argentine assets in Britain. A few days later the European Common Market approved a total ban on Argentine imports, the harshest punitive action in its 25-year history.

British Prime Minister Margaret Thatcher ordered 36 ships, almost two-thirds of Britain's navy, to the Falklands, a trip of about two weeks. The British fleet included aircraft carriers, nuclear submarines, cruisers, destroyers, frigates, supply ships and oilers. Prince Andrew, Queen

Elizabeth II's second son, served aboard the aircraft carrier Invincible *as a helicopter pilot.*

The Thatcher government received intense criticism, even from members of its own Conservative Party, for not having anticipated or prepared for the Argentine invasion. Foreign Secretary Lord Carrington was forced to resign April 5, admitting that Britain had suffered a "humiliating affront."

In Argentina, meanwhile, the invasion enjoyed great popular support, diverting attention from the country's economic and political troubles and creating a strong wave of national unity and pride. Lt. Gen. Leopóldo Galtieri, president of Argentina, member of its three-man military junta and head of the army, described the invasion in a nationwide broadcast April 2: "We have regained the southern islands that legitimately form part of our national patrimony — safeguarding the national honor — without rancor, but with the firmness demanded by the circumstances."

Peace Attempts

Attempts to resolve the crisis peacefully were made from the start. The United Nations Security Council passed a resolution April 3 calling for Argentina's withdrawal and a cessation of hostilities. On April 7 U.S. Secretary of State Alexander M. Haig Jr. began an intensive peace effort. Throughout the month of April, Haig conducted a series of meetings with both Thatcher and Galtieri, attempting to achieve a diplomatic solution to the crisis. Haig's proposals included simultaneous withdrawal of Argentine and British forces, termination of sanctions and temporary administration of the islands by Britain, Argentina and the United States or other third party.

Haig continued his cross-Atlantic shuttles, but on April 12, with the arrival of at least one nuclear submarine in the Falklands area, Britain put into effect a 200-mile war zone around the islands. This blockade was intended to prevent Argentina from sending supplies and reinforcements to its troops. Any Argentine ship caught crossing the zone would be sunk, Britain warned.

The Falkland crisis simmered for two weeks as attempts to resolve it diplomatically continued and the British fleet approached the islands. On April 25, in their first military maneuver, British troops invaded and regained control of South Georgia Island. Five days later Britain imposed a total air and sea blockade around the Falklands, and the first British troops landed on the islands.

On April 30 the United States gave up its attempts to resolve the dispute through negotiations and officially backed Britain. After the Haig effort collapsed, the United Nations again pressed for peace, with both Peru and U.N. Secretary General Javier Pérez de Cuéllar presenting *plans. All the peace efforts failed, however, because Argentina refused to withdraw until Britain recognized Argentina's sovereignty, and Britain refused to discuss the sovereignty issue until Argentina withdrew.*

Increase in Hostilities

On May 2 a British submarine torpedoed and sank Argentina's only cruiser, the General Belgrano. *More than 320 Argentine troops were reported dead or missing. Two days later, Argentina scored a similar blow against Britain. An Exocet missile fired by an Argentine fighter plane traveled 20 miles and sank the British destroyer* Sheffield. *Twenty British troops were killed. After the loss of the* Sheffield, *Britain extended its military blockade, warning Argentine forces to stay within 12 miles of their mainland coast.*

A week later British warships and helicopters attacked Argentine positions on the Falklands. Additional British troops were on their way to the islands, including 3,000 infantrymen aboard the converted luxury-liner Queen Elizabeth II. *Argentina, meanwhile, had mounted a frantic worldwide search for additional weapons to match Britain's.*

On May 14 British troops destroyed an Argentine aircraft and military installation on Pebble Island, just north of West Falkland, and bombed the Stanley airport on East Falkland. Over the next four weeks the fighting continued. British reinforcements arrived, and by June 1 Britain had seized key hills outside of Stanley, exposing Argentine forces. For the first time since the war began, the Argentine press hinted that the cause might be lost.

Despite the heavy fighting and the failure of various peace efforts, Pope John Paul II repeatedly called for peace. The pontiff carried on with a long-planned trip to Britain in early June despite the Falklands war. To balance the British visit, however, he hastily scheduled a brief trip to Argentina June 11-13. On both trips the pope prayed for an end to the hostilities. (Pope's trip to Britain, p. 409)

The fighting continued nonetheless, and on June 12 the major battle for control of Stanley began. Both sides suffered heavy casualties. By June 14 Britain had forced a large Argentine retreat, and Thatcher announced to the House of Commons that white flags were flying over Stanley. Argentine troops surrendered June 15. Although the military junta in Buenos Aires gave no answer to British demands for a formal pledge to end all hostilities, Argentina clearly had given up. On June 20 Britain reclaimed the last of its South Atlantic possessions; Thule, the southernmost of the South Sandwich Islands, was taken without a fight.

Aftermath

The Falklands victory buoyed Britain in a time of high unemployment and economic woes. In elections held in early May, Thatcher's Conservative Party did better than expected, indicating popular support for her tough stand on the Falklands.

Argentina, in contrast, was devastated by the defeat. Having believed the Argentine press reports and government statements that assured victory right up to the end, the Argentine public was at first disbelieving and then angered by the actual outcome. Long a land of turbulent politics, Argentina again found itself in political upheaval. Galtieri was forced to resign as president June 17 and eventually was replaced by Maj. Gen. Reynaldo Bignone. Hardliner Lt. Gen. Cristino Nicolaider succeeded Galtieri as commander of Argentina's army. The war effort had left Argentina's military forces and economy in trouble and its people desolate and confused.

The war had effects on other countries as well. Relations between the United States and Argentina and other Latin America countries suffered. In late April the Organization of American States (OAS), to which the United States belongs, supported Argentina's claim to the islands. A month later the OAS urged its members to give any support they could to Argentina. These developments left the United States in an awkward position. When the United States finally sided with Britain, it was perceived by many Latin American countries as no longer a fully reliable ally, and they decided to build up their own defenses.

Cuba, meanwhile, had supported Argentina throughout the crisis, and relations between Cuba and South American countries warmed as a result. The Soviet Union, initially maintaining a neutral position, eventually sided with Argentina and provided intelligence aid. Argentina, however, remained wary of Soviet motives and Soviet-Argentine relations did not change significantly as a result of the Falklands struggle.

The war also provided an opportunity to evaluate military equipment and weapons. The conflict demonstrated clearly the vulnerability of older surface ships such as the Sheffield and General Belgrano to advanced, precision-guided missiles and nuclear submarines. Military experts praised the performance of Exocet missiles, Harrier jump jets and Tigerfish torpedoes. The Mirage fighter jets and diesel submarines used by Argentina were found disappointing.

> Following are the texts of U.N. Resolution 502 on the Argentine action in the Falkland Islands, passed by the Security Council April 3, 1982; excerpts from the statement to the Security Council by Argentine Ambassador Nicanor Costa Mendez, April 3; excerpts from statements to the House of Commons by British Prime Minister Margaret Thatcher, April 3, 14, 29, May 20 and June 15; and the text of the surrender document, signed June 16. (Boldface

headings have been added by Congressional Quarterly to highlight the organization of the texts.):

SECURITY COUNCIL RESOLUTION

THE SECURITY COUNCIL,

RECALLING the statement made by the President of the Security Council on 2 April 1982 calling on the Governments of Argentina and the United Kingdom to refrain from the use of threat or force in the region of the Falkland Islands (Islas Malvinas),

DEEPLY disturbed at reports of an invasion on 2 April 1982 by armed forces of Argentina,

DETERMINING that there exists a breach of peace in the region of the Falkland Islands (Islas Malvinas),

1. DEMANDS an immediate cessation of hostilities;

2. DEMANDS an immediate withdrawal of all Argentine forces from the Falkland Islands (Islas Malvinas);

3. CALLS on the Government of Argentina and the United Kingdom to seek a diplomatic solution to their differences and to respect fully the purposes and principles of the Charter of the United Nations.

COSTA MENDEZ SPEECH

Perhaps the beginning of my statement may be considered repetitive, but I consider it none the less useful to state that the reason for the calling of these meetings lies in the Malvinas Islands, which is part of Argentine territory and which was illegally occupied by the United Kingdom in 1833 by an act of force which deprived our country of that archipelago.

The British fleet in 1833 displaced by force the Argentine population and the authorities which were exercising the legitimate rights that belonged to the Republic at that time as the heir to Spain.

Legally speaking, that act of force cannot give rise to any right at all, and politically the events of 1833 were one more reflection of the imperialist policy which the European States carried out in the nineteenth century at the expense of America, Africa and Asia. Hence, we can say today that this is a colonial problem in the most traditional sense of that political and economic phenomenon.

Since 1833, the Republic of Argentina has been claiming reparation from the United Kingdom for the great wrong done. The Republic of Argentina has never consented to that act of usurpation of its national territory, usurpation carried out by unacceptable and illegal means. All the successive Governments of Argentina, regardless of party or faction, have remained united and steadfast in their position during those 149 years of strongly protesting against that arbitrary occupation.

No one can have the slightest doubt as to the historic role of the United Nations in the decolonization process. This is perhaps the area in which the United Nations has proved most fruitful, a task that it has carried out most effectively, one that has changed the course of international relations. Proof of this is that the original membership of 54 has increased to 157. Many of the young nations represented here in the Council have been freed from the colonial yoke, and their contribution to the organized international community is of such magnitude that I do not need to mention it — far less to emphasize it. . . .

One of the last vestiges of colonialism on Latin American territory ended yesterday. The claims that my country has been making repeatedly since 1833 have enjoyed the support of the decisions of the world Organization, and of the individual assistance of these new nations just emerging from the colonial era.

Despite the Organization's efforts and my country's arduous and careful work, time passed and brought with it only continued frustration, resulting from the evasive tactics and time-wasting manoeuvres of Great Britain — and all that despite the many alternatives put forward by Argentina and despite the imagination and flexibility with which we approached negotiations.

Two days ago the Permanent Representative of my country made reference here to the willingness and readiness on our part demonstrated by the facilities offered in 1971 in terms of communications and other concessions to the inhabitants of the islands. Those 1,800 inhabitants, as the United Kingdom representative said yesterday, would fit without difficulty into this chamber. They have been and are the subject of constant concern in Argentina, which has given them attention that I venture to say, with all due respect, they have not received from their "homeland". The Government of Argentina is always careful to respect individual rights and physical integrity.

Yesterday Argentina stated that its position did not represent any kind of aggression against the present inhabitants of the islands, whose rights and way of life — and I stress this — will be respected in the same way as those of the countries freed by our liberators. Troops will be used only when absolutely necessary and they will not in any way disturb the inhabitants of the islands; quite the contrary, they will protect the institutions and inhabitants, since they are part of us. This is a most solemn commitment by the Government of Argentina to the international community.

The United Kingdom has invoked the presence of the inhabitants of the Malvinas Islands as an excuse for its colonial presence in those islands. But I ask members: What, then, is the pretext for that presence in the South Sandwich or South Georgia Islands? I here, as the *Times* of London said in an editorial of 29 March last, the only natives, according to the Commonwealth and Foreign Offices, were seals — and in the present state of international law seals do not enjoy the right to self-determination?

In view of the fact that my country opened up communications, the

British Government did not seem too concerned over the physical and historical isolation in which the inhabitants of the islands lived.

I shall not go into details about the change in the standard of living brought about by the facilities offered by Argentina. As the President of my country has said, we are ready to guarantee all the individual rights of the inhabitants. But we cannot allow anyone to use those 1,800 persons as something enshrined in international law as a "population".

In previous statements the characteristics of that group of persons have been dealt with, but I must say again here that, to a large extent, those persons are officials of the British Government and a large number of them are employees of the Falkland Islands Company, a typical colonial firm — a complete anachronism: a colonial corporation of those who had letters patent from the eighteenth century, the trade branch of colonialism and imperialism. . . .

Some delegations here have stated that my Government acted hastily. I leave it to the Council to judge, but I must point out that it seems difficult to describe my country as acting hastily when, with the greatest respect for peaceful solutions, it has borne with a situation of continued usurpation of its territory by a colonial Power for 150 years. Argentina has wisely, patiently and imaginatively negotiated on its long-standing claim but the United Kingdom has not given the slightest indication of being flexible nor made a single just proposal. Furthermore, we have been accused in this chamber of violating Article 2 (3) and (4) of the United Nations Charter. No provision of the Charter can be taken to mean the legitimization of situations which have their origin in wrongful acts, in acts carried out before the Charter was adopted and which subsisted during its prevailing force. Today, in 1982, the purpose of the Organization cannot be invoked to justify acts carried out in the last century in flagrant violation of principles that are today embodied in international law.

Throughout the years we have celebrated the excellent results of the irreversible march of history typified by decolonization and at the same time, while we were celebrating and taking part in that process, our frustration was growing because of the conviction that the United Kingdom was not ready to give up the territory it had usurped from Argentina. The accession of emerging peoples to international politics and the change in international society are a result of the historic process I mentioned at the beginning of my statement. This is a real force, and this real force in the world order was reflected in the establishment of the Non-Aligned Movement, which my country joined in 1973 and in which it takes part as an active member. That Movement promotes the eradicating of historical injustices, whether they be political or economic. Members of the Non-Aligned Movement, as our Permanent Representative has already said, have repeatedly recognized and acknowledged the justice of the Argentine claim and our country's sovereignty over the Malvinas Islands, the South Georgia and Sandwich Islands, they have already stated that the principle of self-determination does not apply in this case for special historical reasons I have already explained.

The representative of the United Kingdom said that he had doubts about being able to arrive at an agreement with the representative of my country as to the historical vicissitudes. That is possible, but it would seem difficult for us not to agree on the facts of history which are absolutely indisputable.

The Government of Argentina has not invaded any foreign territory, as the United Kingdom claims. As was stated very simply by the President of my country,

> "Safeguarding our national honour and without rancour or bitterness, but with all the strength that comes from being in the right, we have recovered a part of our national heritage".

The same cannot be said of the United Kingdom Government vis-à-vis our country. Apart from the case which concerns us today, in 1806 and 1807 British expeditionary forces attacked and temporarily occupied the city of Buenos Aires and its suburbs, a historical fact that may not be well known to everbody. On both occasions the British troops were repelled by the Argentine people. . . .

We have a clear conscience about our rights; and we shall maintain them with firmness and prudence until we arrive at a proper and peaceful settlement. It is useless to whip up emotions when there is clear justice, as in our case. Our policy, the policy of Argentina has, at all time been lofty, conciliatory and prudent — and there is no evidence to the contrary. I am sure that it will lose none of those attributes here. . . .

[After passage of Resoulution 502]

Argentina deeply regrets the vote just taken by the Security Council. We regret it because after many years during which the Security Council has maintained a constant position in favour of the liquidation of colonialism and all its vestiges the Council has now taken this decision which, in a sense, lends support to an obsolete colonial situation born in a period when America, Africa and Asia were a field in which imperialist Powers, without any respect, infringed upon the sovereignty and freedom of other peoples.

The Argentine Republic is firmly convinced of its rights to the Malvinas Islands. We shall not stop affirming our rights and seeking an appropriate solution on the bases that I have already had occasion to set forth in my previous statement, bases which are just, honourable and acceptable to all the parties.

The Argentine delegation wishes to express its thanks to those members of the Council which supported us; or abstained, for the understanding they have shown. . . .

We call upon all who are acting here in good faith and free of any prejudices, prejudices which today have become archaic, to lend us their co-operation so that we may find a just solution reflecting the lofty principles of sovereignty, non-intervention, territorial integrity — principles that are today at stake.

THATCHER STATEMENTS

April 3

... By late afternoon yesterday it became clear that an Argentine invasion had taken place and that the lawful British Government of the islands had been usurped.

I am sure that the whole House will join me in condemning totally this unprovoked aggression by the Government of Argentina against British territory. It has not a shred of justification and not a scrap of legality.

It was not until 8:30 this morning, our time, when I was able to speak to the Governor, who had arrived in Uruguay, that I learnt precisely what had happened. He told me that the Argentines had landed at approximately 6 a.m. Falklands time, 10 our time. One party attacked the capital from the landward side and another from the seaward side. The Governor then sent a signal to us which we did not receive. Communications had ceased at 8:45 a.m. our time. It is common for atmospheric conditions to make communications with Port Stanley difficult. Indeed, we had been out of contact for a period the previous night.

The Governor reported that the Marines, in the defense of Government House, were superb. He said that they acted in the best tradition of the Royal Marines. They inflicted casualties, but those defending Government House suffered none. He had kept the local people informed of what was happening through a small local transmitter which he had in Government House. He is relieved that the islanders heeded his advice to stay indoors. Fortunately, as far as he is aware, there were no civilian casualties. When he left the Falklands, he said that the people were in tears. They do not want to be Argentine. He said that the islanders are still tremendously loyal. I must say that I have every confidence in the Governor and the action that he took.

[THE ISLANDS MUST BE FREED]

I must tell the House that the Falkland Islands and their dependencies remain British territory, no aggression and no invasion can alter that simple fact; it is the Government's objective to see that the islands are freed from occupation and are returned to British Administration at the earliest possible moment.

Argentina has, of course, long disputed British sovereignty over the islands. We have absolutely no doubt about our sovereignty which has been continuous since 1833 nor have we any doubt about the unequivocal wishes of the Falkland Islanders, who are British in stock and tradition, and they wish to remain British in allegiance. We cannot allow the democratic rights of the islanders to be denied by the territorial ambitions of Argentina. Over the past 15 years, successive British Governments have held a series of meetings with the Argentine Government to discuss the dispute. In many of these meetings elected representatives of the islanders have taken part. We have always made it clear that their wishes were paramount and that there would be no change in sovereignty without their consent and without the approval of the House. . . .

There had, of course, been previous incidents affecting sovereignty before the one in South Georgia to which I shall refer in a moment. In December 1976 the Argentines illegally set up a scientific station on one of the dependencies within the Falklands group — Southern Thule. The last Government attempted to solve the matter through diplomatic exchanges, but without success. The Argentines remained there and are still there.

Two weeks ago — on March 19 — the latest in this series of incidents affecting sovereignty occurred; and the deterioration in relations between the British and Argentine Governments which culminated in yesterday's Argentinian invasion began. The incident appeared at the start to be relatively minor. But we now know it was the beginning of much more.

THE INCIDENT ON SOUTH GEORGIA

The Commander of the British Antarctic Survey base at Grytviken on South Georgia — a dependency of the Falkland Islands over which the United Kingdom has exercised sovereignty since 1775 when the island was discovered by Captain Cook — reported to us that an Argentine Navy cargo ship had landed about 60 Argentines at nearby Leith Harbour. They had set up camp and hoisted the Argentine flag. They were there to carry out a valid commercial contract to remove scrap metal from a former whaling station.

The leader of the commercial expedition, Davidoff, had told our Embassy in Buenos Aires that he would be going to South Georgia in March. He was reminded of the need to obtain permission from the immigration authorities on the island. He did not do so. The base Commander told the Argentines that they had no right to land on South Georgia without the permission of the British authorities. They should go either to Grytviken to get the necessary clearances or leave. The ship and some 50 of them left on March 22. Although about 10 Argentines remained behind, this appeared to reduce the tension.

In the meantime, we had been in touch with the Argentine Government about the incident. They claimed to have had no prior knowledge of the landing and assured us that there were no Argentine military personnel in the party. For our part we made it clear that while we had no wish to interfere in the operation of a normal commercial contract, we could not accept the illegal presence of these people on British territory.

We asked the Argentine Government either to arrange for the departure of the remaining men or to ensure that they obtained the necessary permission to be there. Because we recognized the potentially serious nature of the situation, HMS Endurance was ordered to the area. We told the Argentine Government that if they failed to regularize the position of the party on South Georgia or to arrange for their departure, HMS

Endurance would take them off, without using force, and return them to Argentina.

This was, however, to be a last resort. We were determined that this apparently minor problem of 10 people on South Georgia in pursuit of a commercial contract should not be allowed to escalate and we made it plain to the Argentine Government that we wanted to achieve a peaceful resolution of the problem by diplomatic means. To help in this, HMS Endurance was ordered not to approach the Argentine party at Leith but to go to Grytviken.

But it soon became clear that the Argentine Government had little interest in trying to solve the problem. On March 25 another Argentine Navy ship arrived at Leith to deliver supplies to the 10 men ashore. Our Ambassador in Buenos Aires sought an early response from the Argentine Government to our previous requests that they should arrange for the men's departure. This request was refused. Last Sunday March 28, the Argentine Foreign Minister sent a message to the Foreign Secretary refusing outright to regularize the men's position. Instead it restated Argentine's claim to sovereignty over the Falkland Islands....

The Foreign and Commonwealth Secretary then sent a message to the United States Secretary of State asking him to intervene and to urge restraint. By the beginning of this week it was clear that our efforts to solve the South Georgia dispute through the usual diplomatic channels were getting nowhere. Therefore, on Wednesday March 31 the Foreign Secretary proposed to the Argentine Foreign Minister that we should dispatch a special emissary to Buenos Aires.

PRESIDENT REAGAN'S INTERVENTION

Later that day we received information — on Wednesday — which led us to believe that a large number of Argentine ships, including an aircraft carrier, destroyers, landing craft, troop carriers and submarines were heading for Port Stanley. I contacted President Reagan that evening and asked him to intervene with the Argentine President directly. We promised, in the meantime, to take no action to escalate the dispute for fear of precipitating — the very event that our efforts were directed to avoid....

... On Thursday, the Argentine Foreign Minister rejected the idea of an emissary and told our Ambassador that the diplomatic channel, as a means of solving this dispute, was closed. President Reagan had a very long telephone conversation — of some 50 minutes — with the Argentine President, but his strong representations fell on deaf ears. I am grateful to him and to Secretary Haig for their strenuous and persistent efforts on our behalf....

On Thursday, the United Nations Secretary General Mr. Perez De Cuellar summoned both British and Argentine Permanent Representatives to urge both countries to refrain from the use or threat of force in the South Atlantic. Later that evening we sought an emergency meeting of the Security Council. We accepted the appeal of its President for restraint.

The Argentines said nothing. On Friday, as the House knows, the Argentines invaded the Falklands and I have given a precise account of everything we knew, or did not know about that situation. . . .

THE GOVERNMENT'S ACTIONS

Before indicating some of the measures that the Government have taken in response to the Argentinian invasion, I should like to make three points. First, even if ships had been instructed to sail the day that the Argentines landed on South Georgia to clear the whaling station, the ships could not possibly have got to Port Stanley before the invasion.

Secondly, there have been several occasions in the past when an invasion has been threatened. The only way of being certain to prevent an invasion would have been to keep a very large fleet close to the Falklands, when we are some 8,000 miles away from base. No Government have ever been able to do that and the cost would be enormous. . . .

Thirdly, aircraft unable to land on the Falklands, because of the frequently changing weather, would have had little fuel left and, ironically, their only hope of landing safely would have been to divert to Argentina. Indeed, all of the air and most sea supplies for the Falklands come from Argentina, which is but 400 miles away compared with our 8,000 miles.

This is the background against which we have to make decisions and to consider what action we can best take. I cannot tell the House precisely what dispositions have been made — some ships are already at sea, others were put on immediate alert on Thursday evening.

"A LARGE TASK FORCE WILL SAIL"

The Government have now decided that a large task force will sail as soon as all preparations are complete. HMS Invincible will be in the lead and will leave port on Monday.

I stress that I cannot foretell what orders the task force will receive as it proceeds. That will depend on the situation at the time; meanwhile we hope that our continuing diplomatic efforts, helped by our many friends, will meet with success.

The Foreign Ministers of the European Community member states yesterday condemned the intervention and urged withdrawal. The NATO Council called on both sides to refrain from force and continue diplomacy.

The United Nations Security Council met again yesterday and will continue its discussions today. Opposition members laugh. They would have been the first to urge a meeting of the Security Council if we had not called one. They would have been the first to urge restraint and to urge a solution to the problem by diplomatic means. They would have been the first to accuse us of sabre-rattling and warmongering. . . .

ARGENTINIAN ASSETS FROZEN

We are now reviewing all aspects of the relationship between Argentina and the United Kingdom. The Argentine Charge d'Affaires and his staff were yesterday instructed to leave within four days.

As an appropriate precautionary and, I hope, temporary measure, the Government have taken action to freeze Argentine financial assets held in this country. An order will be laid before Parliament today under the Emergency Laws (Re-Enactments and Repeals) Act 1964 blocking the movement of gold, securities or funds held in the United Kingdom by the Argentine Government or Argentine residents.

As a further precautionary measure, the ECGD (Export Credit Guarantee Department) has suspended new export credit cover for the Argentine. It is the Government's earnest wish that a return to good sense and the normal rules of international behavior on the part of the Argentine Government will obviate the necessity for action across the full range of economic relations....

The people of the Falkland Islands, like the people of the United Kingdom, are an island race. Their way of life is British, their allegiance is to the Crown. They are few in number, but they have the right to live in peace, to choose their own way of life and to determine their own allegiance. Their way of life is British; their allegiance is to the Crown. It is the wish of the British people and the duty of Her Majesty's Government to do everything that we can to uphold that right. That will be our hope and our endeavor and, I believe, the resolve of every Member of this House.

April 14

... First of all, we seek a peaceful solution by diplomatic effort. This, too, is in accordance with the Security Council Resolution. In this approach we have been helped by the widespread disapproval of the use of force which the Argentine aggression has aroused across the world, and also by the tireless efforts of Secretary of State Haig who has now paid two visits to this country and one to Buenos Aires.

On his first visit last Thursday we impressed upon him the great depth of feeling on this issue, not only of Parliament but of the British people as a whole. We may not express our views in the same way as the masses gathered in Buenos Aires, but we feel them every bit as strongly — indeed, even more profoundly, because Britons are involved. We made clear to Mr. Haig that withdrawal of the invaders' troops must come first; that the sovereignty of the islands is not affected by the act of invasion; and that when it comes to future negotiations what matters most is what the Falkland Islanders themselves wish.

On his second visit on Easter Monday and yesterday, Mr. Haig put forward certain ideas as a basis for discussion — ideas concerning the withdrawal of troops and its supervision, and an interim period during which negotiations on the future of the islands would be conducted....

These discussions are complex, changing and difficult, the more so because they are taking place between a military junta and a democratic Government of a free people — one which is not prepared to compromise that democracy and that liberty which the British Falkland Islanders regard as their birthright.

We seek, and shall continue to seek, a diplomatic solution, and the House will realize that it would jeopardize that aim were I to give further details at this stage. Indeed, Secretary Haig has been scrupulous in his adherence to confidentiality in pursuit of the larger objective. We shall continue genuinely to negotiate through the good offices of Mr. Haig, to whose skill and perseverance I pay warm tribute.

MILITARY PRESSURE

Diplomatic efforts are more likely to succeed if they are backed by military strength. At 5 a.m. London time on Monday April 12, the maritime exclusion zone of 200 miles around the Falkland Islands came into effect. From that time any Argentine warships and Argentine naval auxiliaries found within this zone are treated as hostile and are liable to be attacked by British forces....

The naval task force is proceeding with all speed towards the South Atlantic. It is a formidable force, comprising two aircraft carriers, five guided missile destroyers, seven frigates, an assault ship with five landing ships, together with supporting vessels. The composition of the force and the speed with which it was assembled and put to sea clearly demonstrate our determination....

A number of civilian ships have now been chartered or requisitioned. These include the Canberra for use as a troop ship, and the Uganda, which will be available as a hospital ship. Recourse to the merchant marine is traditional in time of naval emergency and its response has been wholehearted on this occasion as in the past.

Men and equipment continue to be flown out to Ascension Island to meet up with the task force. These additional elements will enhance the fighting capability of the force and the range of operations which can be undertaken. Nimrod maritime patrol aircraft are now patrolling the South Atlantic in support of our fleet.

Sustaining a substantial force 8,000 miles from the United Kingdom is a considerable undertaking. As the Ministry of Defence announced this morning, additional measures are now in hand to provide extra capability for the force over an extended period. In particular, the second assault ship, HMS Intrepid, is being recommissioned for operation service. She will significantly add to the amphibious capability of the task force now entering the South Atlantic, which already contains her sister ship HMS Fearless.

Arrangements are in hand to adopt a large cargo ship for the sea lift of additional Harriers. This will nearly double the size of the Harrier force in the South Atlantic. All these aircraft have a formidable air combat and ground attack capability....

ECONOMIC PRESSURE

The third aspect of our pressure against Argentina has been economic. We have been urging our friends and allies to take action parallel to our own, and we have achieved a heartening degree of success. The most significant measure has been the decision of our nine partners in the European Community to join us not just in an arms embargo but also in stopping all imports from Argentina.

This is a very important step, unprecedented in its scope and the rapidity of the decision. Last year about a quarter of all Argentina's exports went to the European Community. The effect on Argentina's economy of this measure will therefore be considerable, and cannot be without influence on her leaders in the present crisis. I should like warmly to thank our European partners for rallying to our support. It was an effective demonstration of Community solidarity....

What have the Argentines been able to produce to balance this solidarity in support of our cause? Some Latin American countries have, of course, repeated their support for the Argentine claim to sovereignty. We always knew they would. But only one of them has supported the Argentine invasion, and nearly all have made clear their distaste and disapproval that Argentina should have resorted to aggression.

Almost the only country whose position has been shifting towards Argentina is the Soviet Union. We can only guess at the cynical calculations which lie behind this move. But Soviet support for Argentina is hardly likely to shake the world's confidence in the justice of our cause and it will not alter our determination to achieve our objectives....

April 29

... As the House knows, the Government have also taken military measures to strengthen our diplomatic efforts. Mr. Haig's initiative would never have got under way if the British Government had not sent the naval task force to the South Atlantic within four days of Argentina's aggression against the Falkland Islands.

What incentive would there have been for the Argentine junta to give Mr. Haig's ideas more than the most cursory glance if Britain had not underpinned its search for a diplomatic settlement with the dispatch of the task force? Gentle persuasion will not make the Argentine Government give up what they have seized by force....

On April 25, as I reported to the House on Monday, British forces recaptured South Georgia. The operation was conducted in exercise of our right of self-defense under Article 51 of the United Nations Charter. The minimum of force was used, consistent with achieving our objective, and no lives — Argentine or British — were lost in the operation, although as was announced yesterday, we deeply regret that an Argentine prisoner lost his life in an incident on April 26. That incident is now being urgently investigated by a Board of Inquiry in accordance with the terms of the relevant Geneva Convention.

THE TOTAL EXCLUSION ZONE

The latest of our military measures is the imposition of the total exclusion zone around the Falkland Islands of which we gave 48 hours notice yesterday. The new zone has the same geographical boundaries as the Maritime Exclusion Zone which took effect on April 12. It will apply from noon London time tomorrow (April 30) to all ships and aircraft, whether military or civil, operating in support of the illegal occupation of the Falkland Islands. A complete blockade will be placed on all traffic supporting the occupation forces of Argentina. Maritime and aviation authorities have been informed of the imposition of the zone, in accordance with our international obligations.

We shall enforce the total exclusion Zone as completely as we have done the Maritime Exclusion Zone. The Argentine occupying forces will then be totally isolated — cut off by sea and air. . . .

THE AMERICAN PROPOSALS

On the diplomatic side, Mr. Haig has put formal American proposals to the Argentine Government and requested an early response. I stress the status of those proposals. They are official American proposals. Mr. Haig judged it right to ask Argentina to give its decision first, as the country to which Security Council Resolution 502 is principally addressed. He saw Mr. Costa Mendez last night, but no conclusion was reached. Mr. Haig has also communicated to us the text of his proposals. . . .

THE DISPATCH OF THE TASK FORCE

With regard to the first argument, when the House debated the Falkland Islands on April 14 the Leader of the Opposition (Mr. Michael Foot) supported the dispatch of the task force. He said: "I support the dispatch of the task force; I support it because I believe that it can have strong diplomatic results." We agreed on that.

But it would be totally inconsistent to support the dispatch of the task force and yet to be opposed to its use. What is more, it would be highly dangerous to bluff in that way. British servicemen and ships would be exposed to hostile action. Argentina would doubt our determination and sense of purpose. The diplomatic pressure would be undermined. Is it really suggested that the use of force in self-defense for the recapture of British territory is not a proper use of force?

As long as the Argentines refuse to comply with the Security Council resolution, we must continue to intensify the pressure on them. And we must not abandon our efforts to re-establish our authority over our own territory and to free our own people from the invader.

U.N. INVOLVEMENT

Let me turn now to the question of greater United Nations involvement. All our action has been on a resolution of the United Nations. The Argentine invasion was carried out in defiance of an appeal issued by the President of the Security Council as our urgent request on April 1.

That solemn appeal was endorsed by the whole of the Security Council, but it was ignored. Immediately after the invasion we asked for another meeting of the Security Council. The meeting passed Resolution 502....

It is quite wrong to suggest that because the invader is not prepared to implement the resolution the principles of the United Nations require that we, the aggrieved party, should forfeit the right of self-defense. Such an argument has no validity in international law. It would be to condone and encourage aggression and to abandon our people.

The question that we must answer is, what could further recourse to the United Nations achieve at the present stage? We certainly need mediation, but we already have the most powerful and the most suitable mediator available, Mr. Haig, backed by all the authority and all the influence of the United States, working to implement a mandatory resolution of the Security Council. If anyone can succeed in mediation, it is Mr. Haig. Of course, we support the United Nations and we believe that respect for the United Nations should form the basis of international conduct. But, alas, the United Nations does not have the power to enforce compliance with its resolutions, as a number of aggressors well know.

Those simple facts are perfectly well understood in the international community. Let me quote the Swedish Foreign Minister, because Sweden is a country second to none in its opposition to the use of force and its respect for the United Nations. The Swedish Foreign Minister said of the South Georgia operation: 'We have no objection to Britain retaking British territory. Time and again one is forced to observe that the United Nations is weak and lacks the authority required to mediate.' — That may not be desirable, but it is a fact of life and we must make our dispositions and judgments accordingly....

May 20

... We have now been negotiating for six weeks. The House will recall the strenuous efforts made over an extended period by Secretary of State Haig. During that period my ministerial colleagues and I considered no less than four sets of proposals. Although these presented substantial difficulties, we did our best to help Mr. Haig continue his mission until Argentine rejection of his last proposals left him no alternative but to abandon his efforts. . . .

Since May 6, when it became clear that the United States/Peruvian proposals were not acceptable to Argentina the United Nations Secretary-General, Sr Perez de Cuellar, has been conducting negotiations with Britain and Argentina. Following several rounds of discussions the United Kingdom representative at the United Nations was summoned to London for consultation last Sunday. On Monday Sir Anthony Parsons returned to New York and presented to the Secretary-General a draft interim agreement between Britain and Argentina which set out the British position in full. He made clear that the text represented the furthest that Britain could go in the negotiations. He requested that the draft should be transmitted to the Argentine representative and that he should be asked to convey his Government's response within two days.

Yesterday we received the Argentine Government's reply. As I have said, it amounted to a rejection of our own proposals, and we have so informed the Secretary-General. . . .

ARGENTINE RESPONSE

I turn now to the Argentinian response; this revived once again all the points which had been obstacles in earlier negotiations.

Their draft interim agreement applied not only to the Falklands but included South Georgia and the South Sandwich Islands as well. They demanded that all forces should withdraw, including our forces on South Georgia, and return to their normal bases and areas of operation. This was plainly calculated to put us at an enormous disadvantage.

They required that the interim administration should be the exclusive responsibility of the United Nations which should take over all executive, legislative, judicial and security functions in the islands. They rejected any role for the island's democratic institutions.

They envisaged that the interim administration would appoint as advisers equal numbers of British and Argentine residents of the islands, despite their huge disparity.

They required freedom of movement and equality of access with regard to residence, work and property for Argentine nationals on an equal basis with the Falkland Islanders. The junta's clear aim was to flood the islands with their own nationals during the interim period, and thereby change the nature of Falklands society and so prejudge the future of the islands.

With regard to negotiations for a long-term settlement, while pretending not to prejudice the outcome, they stipulated that the object was to comply not only with the Charter of the United Nations but with various resolutions of the General Assembly, from some of which the United Kingdom dissented on the grounds that they favored Argentine sovereignty.

And if the period provided for the completion of the negotiation expired, they demanded that the General Assembly should determine the lines to which the final agreement should conform. It was manifestly impossible for Britain to accept such demands.

Argentina began this crisis. Argentina has rejected proposal after proposal. One is bound to ask whether the junta have ever intended to seek a peaceful settlement or whether they have sought merely to confuse and prolong the negotiations while remaining in illegal possession of the islands.

I believe that if we had a dozen more negotiations the tactics and results would be the same. From the course of these negotiations and Argentina's persistent refusal to accept Resolution 502 we are bound to conclude that her objective is procrastination and continuing occupation leading eventually to sovereignty. . . .

June 15

Early this morning, in Port Stanley, 74 days after the Falkland Islands were invaded, General Moore accepted from General Menendez the surrender of all the Argentine forces in East and West Falkland together with their arms and equipment. In a message to the Commander-in-Chief Fleet, General Moore reported: "The Falklands are once more under the Government desired by their inhabitants. God Save the Queen."

General Menendez has surrendered some 11,000 men in Port Stanley and some 2,000 in West Falkland.

In addition we had already captured and were holding elsewhere on the islands 1,800 prisoners, making in all some 15,000 prisoners of war now in our hands.

The advance of our forces in the last few days is the culmination of a determined military effort to compel the Argentine Government to withdraw its forces from the Falkland Islands. On the night of Friday June 11, men of 42 and 45 Commandos and the Third Battalion the Parachute Regiment, supported by elements of the Royal Artillery and Royal Engineers, mounted an attack on Argentine positions on Mount Harriet, Two Sisters and Mount Longdon. They secured all their objectives, and during the next day consolidated their positions in the face of continuing resistance.

I regret to inform the House that 5 Royal Marines, 18 Paratroopers and two Royal Engineers lost their lives in these engagements. Their families are being informed. 72 Marines and Paratroopers were wounded. We have no details of Argentine casualties. Hundreds of prisoners and large quantities of equipment were taken in these operations. The land operations were supported by Harrier attacks and naval gunfire from ships of the task force which made a major contribution to the success of our troops. In the course of the bombardment, however, HMS Glamorgan was hit by enemy fire. We now know that 13 of the crew died in this attack or are missing. . . .

During the night of Sunday, June 13 the second phase of the operations commenced. The Second Battalion the Parachute Regiment secured Wireless Ridge and the Second Battalion the Scots Guards took Tumbledown Mountain by first light on Monday, June 14. The First/Seventh Ghurkas advanced on Mount William. At two o'clock London time large numbers of Argentine troops were reported to be retreating from Mount Williams, Sapper Hill and Moody Brook in the direction of Port Stanley. British forces pressed forward to the outskirts of Port Stanley. Large numbers of Argentines threw down their weapons and surrendered.

At 4 o'clock the Argentine garrison indicated its willingness to talk. Orders were given to our forces to fire only in self defense. Shortly before 5 o'clock a white flag appeared over Port Stanley.

Initial contact was made with the enemy by radio. By midnight General Moore and General Menendez were talking. The surrender of all the Argentine forces on East and West Falkland was agreed at 1 a.m. today London time. Some of our forces are proceeding to West Falkland to organize the surrender of the Argentine forces there.

We are now tackling urgently the immense practical problems of dealing with the Argentine prisoners on the islands. The weather conditions are severe, permanent accommodation is very limited, and much of the temporary accommodation which we had hoped to use was lost when the Atlantic Conveyor was sunk on May 25. We have already repatriated to Argentina almost 1,400 prisoners, and the further 15,000 now in our custody are substantially more than we had expected. With the help of the International Red Cross, we are taking urgent steps to safeguard these prisoners and hope to evacuate them as soon as possible from the islands, in accordance with our responsibilities under the Geneva Convention. This is a formidable task. . . .

After all that has been suffered it is too early to look much beyond the beginning of the return to normal life. In due course the islanders will be able to consider and express their views about the future. When the time is right we can discuss with them ways of giving their elected representatives an expanded role in the Government of the islands.

We shall uphold our commitment to the security of the islands. If necessary we shall do this alone. But I do not exclude the possibility of associating other countries with their security. Our purpose is that the Falkland Islands should never again be a victim of unprovoked aggression. . . .

The battle of the Falklands was a remarkable military operation, boldly planned, bravely executed, and brilliantly accomplished. We owe an enormous debt to the British forces and to the Merchant Marine. We honor them all. They have been supported by a people united in defense of our way of life and of our sovereign territory.

SURRENDER DOCUMENT

I, the undersigned, commander of all the Argentine land, sea and air forces in the Falkland Islands, surrender to Major General J. J. Moore C.B., O.B.E., M.C., as representative of Her Britannic Majesty's Government. Under the terms of this surrender, all Argentine personnel in the Falklands Islands are to muster at assembly points which will be nominated by General Moore, and hand over their arms, ammunition, and all other weapons and warlike equipment as directed by General Moore, or appropriate British officers acting on his behalf.

Following the surrender, all personnel of the Argentinian forces will be treated with honor in accordance with the conditions set out by the Geneva Convention of 1949.

They will obey any directions concerning movement and in connection with accommodation.

This surrender is to be effective from 2359 hours (Greenwich Mean Time) on 14 June (2059 hours local) and includes those Argentine forces presently deployed in and around Port Stanley, those others on East Falkland, West Falkland, and all the outlying islands.

Brig. Gen. Mario Benjamin Menéndez

HAIG ON FIRST STRIKE POLICY
April 6, 1982

In an address April 6 at the Center for Strategic and International Studies of Georgetown University, U.S. Secretary of State Alexander M. Haig Jr. reaffirmed the U.S. "first strike" defense policy as the only one that would permit the "highest possibility" of world peace.

Haig spoke two days prior to the publication of a controversial magazine article by four former U.S. officials. Written by McGeorge Bundy, Robert S. McNamara, George F. Kennan and Gerard Smith, the article called for a reversal of the "first strike" or "flexible response" defense policy in favor of what they called a "no-first-use" plan. In their opinion, the new concept would decrease the possibility of conventional warfare escalating into a nuclear holocaust.

All four of the co-authors had been high-level U.S. defense policy makers during prior administrations: Bundy as national security adviser to Presidents John F. Kennedy and Lyndon Johnson; McNamara as secretary of defense during the same administrations; Kennan as ambassador to the Soviet Union; and Smith as leader of the Nixon administration's Soviet arms talks team.

Proposals by Former Officials

A "no-first-use" policy would guarantee Western European nations that the United States would not be the first to employ its nuclear arsenal in the event of an attack. According to agreements with West European countries, specifically Article 5 of the NATO doctrine, the

United States had pledged to resort to nuclear arms when use of such weapons would quickly end a conflict. As previous proponents of the NATO doctrine, the four men had helped formulate the basis of the Reagan defense policy. The four authors agreed that the NATO pact was generally regarded as a "nuclear guarantee," formulated "at a time when only a conventional Soviet threat existed, so a readiness for first use was plainly implied from the beginning."

According to the four former senior officials, relying on these agreements with Western Europe as the basis for U.S. defense policy was not only inappropriate but also potentially devastating. In a joint statement released at a press conference, they said that "continuation of the present policy will add to the risk of nuclear war."

The Reagan administration's emphasis on developing a strong nuclear arsenal in Western Europe, underscored by the December 1979 agreement to deploy 572 new American intermediate range missiles in Europe, was criticized by the four co-authors. They considered the expenditures to be "enormously excessive." According to them, "the evolution of ... [these] essentially equivalent ... nuclear weapons systems both in the Soviet Union and in the Atlantic Alliance has aroused new concern about the dangers of all forms of nuclear war, [making] it more difficult than ever to construct rational plans for any first use of these weapons by anyone." (Reagan's "zero option" proposal, Historic Documents of 1981, p. 823)

The writers called for a new approach to the nuclear arms problem and stressed the importance of maintaining any confrontation at a conventional level. Together with the NATO alliance, they said, U.S. conventional forces would be sufficiently strong to deter a Warsaw Pact aggression.

Haig's Response

In his personal "first strike," rebutting the proposal appearing in Foreign Affairs *before its release to the public, Haig stood firm behind the Reagan administration's nuclear arms policy. A renewed emphasis on conventional arms, according to him, would not be realistic. The Soviets would have a greater advantage in conventional warfare than in a nuclear confrontation. A "no-first-strike" policy would mean maintaining military forces at a wartime level for the United States and its NATO allies. The United States would have to "reintroduce the draft, triple the size of its armed forces and put its economy on a wartime footing."*

Haig emphasized the strategy behind deterrence as the underlying basis for all U.S. nuclear arms policy formulation. By adopting a "no-first-use" policy and thereby "failing to maintain deterrence, we would risk our freedoms, while actually increasing the likelihood of also suffer-

ing nuclear devastation," he added.

The release of the Foreign Affairs *article and Haig's vehement response indicated a growing rift between the former defense officials and current policy makers. The article also stood out as one of many challenges to U.S. defense policy. Grass-roots efforts and small coalitions had mushroomed all over Europe and the United States to increase public awareness of nuclear warfare.* (Nuclear freeze movement, p. 885)

Haig resigned his post June 25, 1982, and President Reagan appointed George P. Shultz to be the new secretary of state. (Haig resignation, p. 561)

Following is the text of Secretary of State Alexander M. Haig Jr.'s speech, delivered April 6, 1982, at Georgetown University in Washington, D.C. (Boldface headings in brackets have been added by Congressional Quarterly to highlight the organization of the text.):

It is a melancholy fact of the modern age that man has conceived a means capable of his own destruction. For 37 years mankind has had to live with the terrible burden of nuclear weapons. From the dawn of the nuclear age, these weapons have been the source of grave concern to our peoples and the focus of continuous public debate. Every successive president of the United States has shared these concerns. Every Administration has had to engage itself in this debate.

It is right that each succeeding generation should question anew the manner in which its leaders exercise such awesome responsibilities. It is right that each new Administration should have to confront the awful dilemmas posed by the possession of nuclear weapons. It is right that our nuclear strategy should be exposed to continuous examination.

Strategy of Nuclear Deterrence

In debating these issues, we should not allow the complexity of the problems and the gravity of the stakes to blind us to the common ground upon which we all stand. No one has ever advocated nuclear war. No responsible voice has ever sought to minimize its horrors.

On the contrary, from the earliest days of the postwar era, America's leaders have recognized the only nuclear strategy consistent with our values and our survival — our physical existence, and what makes life worth living — is the strategy of deterrence. The massive destructive power of these weapons precludes their serving any lesser purpose. The catastrophic consequences of another world war — with or without nuclear weapons — make deterrence of conflict our highest objective and our only rational military strategy in the modern age.

Thus, since the close of World War II, American and Western strategy has assigned a single function to nuclear weapons: the prevention of war and the preservation of peace. At the heart of this deterrence strategy is the requirement that the risk of engaging in war must be made to outweigh any possible benefits of aggression. The cost of aggression must not be confined to the victims of aggression.

This strategy of deterrence has won the consistent approval of the Western peoples. It has enjoyed the bipartisan support of the American Congress. It has secured the unanimous endorsement of every successive allied government.

Deterrence has been supported because deterrence works. Nuclear deterrence and collective defense have preserved peace in Europe, the crucible of two global wars in this century. Clearly, neither improvement in the nature of man nor strengthening of the international order have made war less frequent or less brutal. Millions have died since 1945 in over 130 international and civil wars. Yet nuclear deterrence has prevented a conflict between the two superpowers, a conflict which even without nuclear weapons would be the most destructive in mankind's history.

Requirements for Western Strategy

The simple possession of nuclear weapons does not guarantee deterrence. Throughout history societies have risked their total destruction if the prize of victory was sufficiently great or the consequences of submission sufficiently grave. War and, in particular, nuclear war can be deterred, but only if we are able to deny an aggressor military advantage from his action and thus insure his awareness that he cannot prevail in any conflict with us. Deterrence, in short, requires the maintenance of a secure military balance, one which cannot be overturned through surprise attack or sudden technological breakthrough. The quality and credibility of deterrence must be measured against these criteria. Successive administrations have understood this fact and stressed the importance of the overall balance. This Administration can do no less.

The strategy of deterrence, in its essentials, has endured. But the requirements for maintaining a secure capability to deter in all circumstances have evolved. In the early days of unquestioned American nuclear superiority the task of posing an unacceptable risk to an aggressor was not difficult. The threat of massive retaliation was fully credible as long as the Soviet Union could not respond in kind. As the Soviet Union's nuclear arsenal grew, however, this threat began to lose credibility.

To sustain the credibility of Western deterrence, the concept of flexible response was elaborated and formally adopted by the United States and its NATO partners in 1967. Henceforth, it was agreed that NATO would meet aggression initially at whatever level it was launched, while preserving the flexibility to escalate the conflict, if necessary, to secure the cessation of aggression and the withdrawal of the aggressor. The purpose of this strategy is not just to conduct conflict successfully if it is forced upon us but, more importantly, to prevent the outbreak of conflict in the first place.

Flexible response is not premised upon the view that nuclear war can be controlled. Every successive allied and American government has been convinced that a nuclear war, once initiated, could escape such control. They have, therefore, agreed upon a strategy which retains the deterrent effect of a possible nuclear response, without making such a step in any sense automatic.

The alliance based its implementation of flexible response upon a spectrum of forces, each of which plays an indispensable role in assuring the credibility of a Western strategy of deterrence. At one end of the spectrum are America's strategic forces, our heavy bombers, intercontinental missiles, and ballistic missile submarines. Since NATO's inception, these forces have been the ultimate guarantee of Western security, a role which they will retain in the future.

At the other end of the spectrum are the alliance's conventional forces, including U.S. forces in Europe. These forces must be strong enough to defeat all but the most massive and persistent conventional aggression. They must be resistant and durable enough to give political leaders time to measure the gravity of the threat, to confront the inherently daunting prospects of nuclear escalation, and to seek through diplomacy the cessation of conflict and restoration of any lost Western territory. The vital role which conventional forces play in deterrence is too often neglected, particularly by those most vocal in their concern over reliance upon nuclear weapons. A strengthened conventional posture both strengthens the deterrent effect of nuclear forces and reduces the prospect of their ever being used.

Linking together strategic and conventional forces are theater nuclear forces, that is, NATO's nuclear systems based in Europe. These systems are concrete evidence of the nature of the American commitment. They are a concrete manifestation of NATO's willingness to resort to nuclear weapons if necessary to preserve the freedom and independence of its members. Further, the presence of nuclear weapons in Europe insures that the Soviet Union will never believe that it can divide the United States from its allies or wage a limited war with limited risks against any NATO member.

The strategy of flexible response and the forces that sustain its credibility reflect more than simply the prevailing military balance. Western strategy also reflects the political and geographical reality of an alliance of 15 independent nations, the most powerful of which is separated from all but one by 4,000 miles of ocean.

Deterrence is consequently more than a military strategy. It is the essential political bargain which binds together the Western coalition. Twice in this century, America has been unable to remain aloof from European conflict but unable to intervene in time to prevent the devastation of Western Europe. In a nuclear age neither we nor our allies can afford to see this pattern repeated a third time. We have, therefore, chosen a strategy which engages American power in the defense of Europe, and gives substance to the principle that the security of the alliance is indivisible.

The Task Ahead

During the past decade the Soviet Union has mounted a sustained buildup across the range of its nuclear forces designed to undermine the credibility of the Western strategy. Soviet modernization efforts have far outstripped those of the West. The development and deployment of Soviet intercontinental ballistic missiles now pose a serious and increasing threat to a large part of our land-based ICBM [intercontinental ballistice missile] force. A new generation of Soviet intermediate range missiles is targeted upon our European allies.

In the last 10 years, the Soviets introduced an unprecedented array of new strategic and intermediate-range systems into their arsenals, including the SS-17, SS-18, and SS-19 ICBMs, the Backfire bomber, the Typhoon submarine and several new types of submarine-launched missiles, and the SS-20 intermediate-range missile. In contrast, during this same period, the United States exercised restraint, introducing only the Trident missile and submarine and the slower air-breathing cruise missile.

In order to deal with the resulting imbalances, President Reagan has adopted a defense posture and recommended programs to the U.S. Congress designed to maintain deterrence, rectify the imbalances, and thereby support the Western strategy I have just outlined. His bold strategic modernization program, announced last October, is designed to insure the maintenance of a secure and reliable capability to deny an adversary advantage from any form of aggression, even a surprise attack.

The President's decision, in his first weeks in office, to go ahead with the production and deployment of the Pershing II and ground-launched cruise missiles, in accordance with NATO's decision of December 1979, represents an effort to reinforce the linkage between our strategic forces in the United States and NATO's conventional and nuclear forces in Europe. A response to the massive buildup of Soviet SS-20s targeted on Western Europe, this NATO decision was taken to insure that the Soviet Union will never launch aggression in the belief that its own territory can remain immune from attack or that European security can ever be decoupled from that of the United States.

The improvements we are making in our conventional forces — in their readiness, mobility, training, and equipment — are designed to insure the kind of tough and resilient conventional capability required by the strategy of flexible response. It is important to recognize the interrelationship of these three types of forces. The requirements in each category are dependent upon the scale of the others. Their functions are similarly linked. The Soviet Union understands this. That is why they have consistently proposed a pledge against the first use of nuclear weapons, an idea which has achieved some resonance here in the West.

NATO has consistently rejected such Soviet proposals, which are tantamount to making Europe safe for conventional aggression. If the

West were to allow Moscow the freedom to choose the level of conflict which most suited it and to leave entirely to Soviet discretion the nature and timing of any escalation, we would be forced to maintain conventional forces at least at the level of those of the Soviet Union and its Warsaw Pact allies.

'No First Use' Policy

Those in the West who advocate the adoption of a "no first use" policy seldom go on to propose that the United States reintroduce the draft, triple the size of its armed forces, and put its economy on wartime footing. Yet in the absence of such steps, a pledge of "no first use" effectively leaves the West nothing with which to counterbalance the Soviet conventional advantages and geopolitical position in Europe.

Neither do Western proponents of a "no first use" policy acknowledge the consequences for the alliance of an American decision not to pose and accept the risk of nuclear war in the defense of Europe. A "no first use" policy would be the end of flexible response and thus of the very credibility of the Western strategy of deterrence. In adopting such a stance, the United States would be limiting its commitment to Europe. But the alliance cannot function as a limited liability corporation. It can only survive as a partnership to which all are equally and fully committed — shared benefits, shared burdens, shared risks.

Another concept which has recently attracted interest is that of a freeze on nuclear weapons. While being sensitive to the concerns underlying this proposal, we have had to underscore the flaws in such an approach. A freeze at current levels would perpetuate an unstable and unequal military balance. It would reward a decade of unilateral Soviet buildup and penalize the United States for a decade of unilateral restraint. As President Reagan stressed last week, such a freeze would remove all Soviet incentive to engage in meaningful arms control designed to cut armaments and reduce the risk of war.

Much of the argumentation for a nuclear freeze revolves around the question of how much is enough. Each side possesses thousands of deliverable nuclear weapons. Does it then really make any difference who is ahead? The question itself is misleading, as it assumes that deterrence is simply a matter of numbers of weapons, or numbers of casualties which could be inflicted. It is not.

● Let us remember, first and foremost, that we are trying to deter the Soviet Union, not ourselves. The dynamic nature of the Soviet nuclear buildup demonstrates that the Soviet leaders do not believe in the concept of "sufficiency." They are not likely to be deterred by a strategy or a force based upon it.

● Let us also recall that nuclear deterrence must work not just in times of peace and moments of calm. Deterrence faces its true test at the time of maximum tension, even in the midst of actual conflict. In such extreme circumstances, when the stakes on the table may already be immense, when Soviet leaders may feel the very existence of their regime is threatened, who can say whether or not they would run massive risks if they believed that in the end the Soviet state would prevail?

● Deterrence thus does not rest on a static comparison of the number or size of nuclear weapons. Rather, deterrence depends upon our capability, even after suffering a massive nuclear blow, to prevent an aggressor from securing a military advantage, and prevailing in a conflict. Only if we maintain such a capability can we deter such a blow. Deterrence, in consequence, rests upon a military balance measured not in warhead numbers but in a complex interaction of capabilities and vulnerabilities.

[Diplomacy and Military Balance]

The state of the military balance and its impact upon the deterrent value of American forces cast a shadow over every significant geopolitical decision. It affects on a day-to-day basis the conduct of American diplomacy. It influences the management of international crises and the terms upon which they are resolved.

The search for national interest and national security is a principal preoccupation of the leaders of every nation on the globe. Their decisions and their foreign policies are profoundly affected by their perception of the military balance between the United States and the Soviet Union and the consequent capacity of either to help provide for their security or to threaten that security.

More important still, perceptions of the military balance also affect the psychological attitude of both American and Soviet leaders, as they respond to events around the globe. For the foreseeable future the relationship between the United States and the Soviet Union will be one in which our differences outnumber points of convergence. Our objective must be to restrain this competition, to keep it below the level of force, while protecting our interests and those of our allies. Our ability to secure these objectives will be crucially influenced by the state of the strategic balance. Every judgment we make and every judgment the Soviet leadership makes will be shaded by it.

Thus the Soviet leadership, in calculating the risks of subversion or aggression, of acquiring new clients or propping up faltering proxies, must carefully evaluate the possibilities and prospects for an effective American response. Soviet calculations must encompass not only American capabilities to influence regional developments, but American willingness to face the prospect of U.S.-Soviet confrontation and consequent escalation. American leaders, for their part, must go through comparable calculations in reacting to regional conflicts, responding to Soviet adventurism, and seeking to resolve international crises in a manner consistent with U.S. interests.

Put simply, our own vulnerability to nuclear blackmail, as well as the susceptibility of our friends to political intimidation, depends upon our ability and willingness to cope credibly with any Soviet threat. A strong and credible strategic posture enhances stability by reducing for the Soviets the temptations toward adventurism, at the same time that it strengthens our hand in responding to Soviet political-military threats.

Arms Control and Nuclear Deterrence

In no area of diplomacy does the military balance have greater effect than in arms control. Arms control can reinforce deterrence and stabilize a military balance at lower levels of risk and effort. Arms control cannot, however, either provide or restore a balance we are unwilling to maintain through our defense efforts.

Just as the only justifiable nuclear strategy is one of deterrence, so the overriding objective for arms control is reducing the risk of war. The essential purpose of arms control is not to save money, although it may do so. Its purpose is not to generate good feelings or improve international relationships, although it may have that effect as well. Arms control's central purpose must be to reinforce the military balance, upon which deterrence depends, at reduced levels of weapons and risk.

On November 18, [1981] President Reagan laid out the framework for a comprehensive program of arms control designed to serve these objectives. He committed the United States to seek major reductions in nuclear and conventional forces, leading to equal agreed limits on both sides. Last week he reviewed the steps we have taken:

• In Geneva we have put forth detailed proposals designed to limit intermediate-range nuclear forces and to eliminate entirely the missiles of greatest concern to each side. This proposal has won the strong and unified support of our allies.

• In Vienna we are negotiating, alongside our allies, on reductions in conventional force levels in Europe. These negotiations have gone on without real progress for over 8 years. Because we are now facing diplomatic atrophy, we must urgently consider how to revitalize East-West discussions of conventional force reductions and stimulate progress in these talks.

• Our highest priority, in the past several months, has been completing preparations for negotiations with the Soviet Union on strategic arms. Here too we will be proposing major reductions to verifiable, equal agreed levels. Here too we will be presenting detailed proposals when negotiations open.

The prospects for progress in each of these areas of arms control depend upon support of the President's defense programs. This imperative has been caricatured as a policy of building up arms in order to reduce them. This is simply not true. As President Reagan's proposals for intermediate-range missiles make clear, we hope that we never have to deploy those systems. But we must demonstrate a willingness to maintain the balance through force deployments if we are to have any prospect of reducing and stabilizing it through arms control.

Negotiations in the early 1970s on a treaty limiting antiballistic missile (ABM) systems provide an historic example. At the time, the Soviets had already built a system of ballistic missile defenses around Moscow. The United States had deployed no such system. Arms control offered the only means of closing off an otherwise attractive and expensive new avenue for arms competition. Yet it was not until the American Administration sought and secured congressional support for an American ABM program that the Soviets began to negotiate seriously. The result was the 1972 treaty limiting anti-ballistic missile systems, which remains in force today.

This same pattern was repeated more recently with intermediate-range missiles. For years the Soviets had sought limits on U.S. nuclear forces in Europe but refused to consider any limits upon their nuclear forces targeted upon Western Europe. Only after NATO took its decision of December 1979 to deploy U.S. Pershing II and ground-launched cruise missiles did the Soviet Union agree to put its SS-20 missiles on the negotiating table.

In the area of strategic arms, as well, there is little prospect the Soviet Union will ever agree to equal limits at lower levels unless first persuaded that the United States is otherwise determined to maintain equality at higher levels. It is, for instance, unrealistic to believe that the Soviet Union will agree to reduce the most threatening element of its force structure, its heavy, multiwarheaded intercontinental missiles unless it is persuaded that otherwise the United States will respond by deploying comparable systems itself.

For many opposed to reliance on nuclear weapons — even for defense or deterrence — the issue is a moral one. For those who first elaborated the strategy of deterrence, and for those who seek to maintain its effect, this issue is also preeminently moral. A familiar argument is that, in a nuclear age, we must choose between our values and our existence. If nuclear weapons offer the only deterrent to nuclear blackmail, some would argue we should submit rather than pose the risk of nuclear conflict. This choice, however, is a false one. By maintaining the military balance and sustaining deterrence, we protect the essential values of Western civilization — democratic government, personal liberty, and religious freedom — and preserve the peace. In failing to maintain deterrence, we would risk our freedoms, while actually increasing the likelihood of also suffering nuclear devastation.

As human beings and free men and women, we must reject this false alternative and avoid the extremes of nuclear catastrophe and nuclear blackmail. In the nuclear age, the only choice consistent with survival and civilization is deterrence.

An eminent theologian once described our age as one in which "the highest possibilities are inextricably intermingled with the most dire perils." The scientific and technological advances so vital to our civilization also make possible its destruction. This reality cannot be wished away.

Americans have always been conscious of the dilemmas posed by the nuclear weapon. From the moment that science unleashed the atom, our instinct and policy have been to control it. Those who direct America's defense policies today share completely the desire of people everywhere to end the nuclear arms race and to begin to achieve substantial reductions in nuclear armament.

Confronted by the dire perils of such weapons, America has responded in a manner that best preserves both security and peace, that protects our society and our values, and that offers hope without illusion. The strategy of deterrence has kept the peace for over 30 years. It has provided the basis for arms control efforts. And it offers the best chance to control and to reduce the dangers that we face.

Deterrence is not automatic. It cannot be had on the cheap. Our ability to sustain it depends upon our ability to maintain the military balance now being threatened by the Soviet buildup. If we are to reinforce deterrence through arms control and arms reduction, we must convince the Soviets that their efforts to undermine the deterrent effect of our forces will not succeed.

The control and reduction of nuclear weapons, based on deterrence, is the only effective intellectual, political, and moral response to nuclear weapons. The stakes are too great and the consequences of error too catastrophic to exchange deterrence for a leap into the unknown. The incentives for real arms control exist, and we have both the means and the duty to apply them.

Let us be clear about our objectives in the nuclear era. We seek to reduce the risk of war and to establish a stable military balance at lower levels of risk and effort. By doing so today, we may be able to build a sense of mutual confidence and cooperation, offering the basis for even more ambitious steps tomorrow. But above all, we shall be pursuing the "highest possibility" for peace.

CANADIAN CONSTITUTION BROUGHT HOME
April 17, 1982

In a proclamation ceremony in Ottawa on April 17, Queen Elizabeth II formally transferred full authority over the Canadian constitution from Britain to Canada. The event culminated years of attempts at constitutional reform and broke the last statutory link between the two countries after more than two centuries of colonial ties.

Canada gained formal independence from Britain in 1931, but the power to amend its constitution remained with the British Parliament because the Canadian provinces and federal government could not agree on an amending procedure.

Pierre Elliott Trudeau, Canada's prime minister since 1968, was determined to resolve the constitutional debate. In addition to a satisfactory amending formula, Trudeau wanted a U.S.-style bill of rights to guarantee basic freedoms across the land. He negotiated repeatedly with the premiers of the provinces, and in November 1981 a compromise finally was reached between the federal government and nine of the 10 provinces.

Under the agreement, the British North America Act of 1867, which founded the Canadian federation, would be modified to become a strictly Canadian constitution, with the addition of a charter of rights and an amending procedure. In early December 1981, the new constitution was approved by the Canadian Parliament, and the British Parliament on March 25, 1982, passed the Canada Act that provided for the patriation and amendment of the Canadian constitution. (Historic Documents of 1981, p. 813)

317

Quebec was the only province to oppose the compromise. Premier René Lévesque feared that the new constitution would limit his province's powers to protect its distinctive culture, particularly in the areas of language and education rights. Quebec challenged the constitution, but on April 7, 1982, the Quebec Court of Appeal unanimously upheld the legality of the November accord. Lévesque maintained that his government would appeal the case to the Canadian Supreme Court.

While the premiers of the nine English-speaking provinces attended the proclamation ceremony and lunched with the queen in Ottawa, Lévesque led a protest rally of thousands in Montreal. Terming the new constitution a "horror" made against Quebec and behind its back, Lévesque called for separation from Canada, although Quebec voters had rejected this idea in a May 1980 referendum. (Historic Documents of 1980, p. 401)

Both Queen Elizabeth and Prime Minister Trudeau, however, refused to separate Quebec from the other provinces at the Ottawa ceremony. Trudeau, speaking first, cited the 1980 referendum results as evidence of Quebec's support for Canadian unity. The queen declared, "Although we regret the absence of the premier of Quebec, it is right to associate the people of Quebec with this celebration...."

With the queen's formal proclamation, the new constitution became the basic instrument of government. Canada remains a constitutional monarchy, with Elizabeth II its queen.

Following are excerpts from remarks by Prime Minister Pierre Elliott Trudeau, the text of Queen Elizabeth II's proclamation, and excerpts from the queen's speech, all in Ottawa, April 17, 1982:

TRUDEAU'S SPEECH

Today, at long last, Canada is acquiring full and complete national sovereignty. The Constitution of Canada has come home. The most fundamental law of the land will now be capable of being amended in Canada, without any further recourse to the Parliament of the United Kingdom....

We became an independent country for all practical purposes in 1931, with the passage of the Statute of Westminster. But by our own choice, because of our inability to agree upon an amending formula at that time, we told the British Parliament that we were not ready to break this last colonial link.

After fifty years of discussion we have finally decided to retrieve what is properly ours. It is with happy hearts, and with gratitude for the patience displayed by Great Britain, that we are preparing to acquire today our complete national sovereignty. It is my deepest hope that Canada will match its new legal maturity with that degree of political maturity which will allow us all to make a total commitment to the Canadian ideal.

I speak of a Canada where men and women of aboriginal ancestry, of French and British heritage, of the diverse cultures of the world, demonstrate the will to share this land in peace, in justice, and with mutual respect. I speak of a Canada which is proud of, and strengthened by its essential bilingual destiny, a Canada whose people believe in sharing and in mutual support, and not in building regional barriers.

I speak of a country where every person is free to fulfill himself or herself to the utmost, unhindered by the arbitrary actions of governments.

The Canadian ideal which we have tried to live, with varying degrees of success and failure for hundreds of years, is really an act of defiance against the history of mankind. Had this country been founded upon a less noble vision, or had our forefathers surrendered to the difficulties of building this nation, Canada would have been torn apart long ago. It should not surprise us, therefore, that even now we sometimes feel the pull of those old reflexes of mutual fear and distrust.

—Fear of becoming vulnerable by opening one's arms to other Canadians who speak a different language or live in a different culture.

—Fear of becoming poorer by agreeing to share one's resources and wealth with fellow citizens living in regions less favoured by nature.

The Canada we are building lies beyond the horizon of such fears. Yet it is not, for all that, an unreal country, forgetful of the hearts of men and women. We know that justice and generosity can flourish only in an atmosphere of trust.

For if individuals and minorities do not feel protected against the possibility of the tyranny of the majority, if French-speaking Canadians or native peoples or new Canadians do not feel they will be treated with justice, it is useless to ask them to open their hearts and minds to their fellow Canadians.

Similarly, if provinces feel that their sovereign rights are not secure in those fields in which they have full constitutional jurisdiction, it is useless to preach to them about cooperation and sharing.

The Constitution which is to be proclaimed today goes a long way toward removing the reasons for the fears of which I have spoken.

We now have a Charter which defines the kind of country in which we wish to live, and guarantees the basic rights and freedoms which each of us shall enjoy as a citizen of Canada.

It reinforces the protection offered to French-speaking Canadians outside Quebec, and to English-speaking Canadians in Quebec. It recognizes our multicultural character. It upholds the equality of women, and the rights of disabled persons.

The Constitution confirms the longstanding division of powers among governments in Canada, and even strengthens provincial jurisdiction over natural resources and property rights. It entrenches the principle of equalization, thus helping less healthy provinces to discharge their obligations without excessive taxation. It offers a way to meet the legitimate demands of our native peoples. And, of course, by its amending formula, it now permits us to complete the task of constitutional renewal in Canada.

The government of Quebec decided that it wasn't enough. It decided not to participate in this ceremony, celebrating Canada's full independence. I know that many Quebecers feel themselves pulled in two directions by that decision. But one need look only at the results of the referendum in May 1980, to realize how strong is the attachment to Canada among the people of Quebec. By definition, the silent majority does not make a lot of noise; it is content to make history.

History will show, however, that in the guarantees written into the Charter of Rights and Freedoms, and in the amending formula — which allows Quebec to opt out of any constitutional arrangement which touches upon language and culture, with full financial compensation — nothing essential to the originality of Quebec has been sacrificed.

Moreover, the process of constitutional reform has not come to an end. The two orders of government have made a solemn pledge to define more precisely the rights of native peoples. At the same time, they must work together to strengthen the Charter of Rights, including language rights in the various provinces. Finally, they must try to work out a better division of powers among governments. . . .

It is true that our will to live together has sometimes appeared to be in deep hibernation, but it is there nevertheless, living and tenacious, in the hearts of Canadians of every province and territory. I simply wish that the bringing home of our Constitution marks the end of a long winter, the breaking up of the ice-jams and the beginning of a new spring.

What we are celebrating today is not so much the completion of our task, but the renewal of our hope — not so much an ending, but a fresh beginning.

Let us celebrate the renewal and patriation of our Constitution; but let us put our faith, first and foremost, in the people of Canada who will give it life. . . .

QUEEN'S PROCLAMATION

WHEREAS in the past certain amendments to the Constitution of Canada have been made by the Parliament of the United Kingdom at the request and with the consent of Canada;

AND WHEREAS it is in accord with the status of Canada as an independent state that Canadians be able to amend their Constitution in Canada in all respects;

AND WHEREAS it is desirable to provide in the Constitution of Canada for the recognition of certain fundamental rights and freedoms and to make other amendments to the Constitution;

AND WHEREAS the Parliament of the United Kingdom has therefore, at the request and with the consent of Canada, enacted the Canada Act, which provides for the patriation and amendment of the Constitution of Canada;

AND WHEREAS Section 58 of the Constitution Act, 1982, set out in Schedule B to the Canada Act, provides that the Constitution Act, 1982, shall, subject to Section 59 thereof, come into force on a day to be fixed by proclamation issued under the Great Seal of Canada:

NOW KNOW You that We, by and with the advice of Our Privy Council for Canada, do by this Our Proclamation, declare that the Constitution Act, 1982, shall, subject to Section 59 thereof, come into force on the Seventeenth day of April, in the year of Our Lord One Thousand Nine Hundred and Eighty-Two.

OF ALL WHICH Our Loving Subjects and all others whom these Presents may concern and hereby required to take notice and to govern themselves accordingly.

IN TESTIMONY WHEREOF we have caused these Our Letters to be made Patent and the Great Seal of Canada to be hereunto affixed.

At Our City of Ottawa, this Seventeenth day of April in the Year of Our Lord One Thousand Nine Hundred and Eighty-Two and in the Thirty-first Year of Our Reign.

QUEEN ELIZABETH'S SPEECH

It was on the 29th March, 1867, that the assent of my great-great grandmother, Queen Victoria, was signified in Parliament in Westminster to the British North America Act, which created the Canadian federation. Precisely one hundred and fifteen years later, on 29th of March of this year, my assent was signified at Westminster to the Canada Act, embodying the Constitution Act which, as Queen of Canada, I have just had the great pleasure of bringing into force by proclamation here on Parliament Hill in Ottawa.

I want to offer my personal congratulations to the Prime Minister of Canada and my Canadian Government and the Premiers and Governments of the Provinces on the wisdom and statesmanship they have shown in reaching agreement on this new Canadian Constitution. It has been a long and difficult process of negotiation which I have followed closely for many years. Concessions had to be made on all sides and the people of Canada can be grateful to their leaders for the good sense and tolerance which they have displayed in bringing about a successful conclusion. . . .

It is one of the quirks of history that over a century should have passed before Canada obtained her own Constitution formulated by Canadians and approved by her own Parliament. But the years have not been wasted and a great nation has grown up in this magnificent land. . . .

Your confident spirit has produced splendid achievements in every field of human endeavour. You have carried forward the daring and pioneering spirit of your forefathers into mammoth engineering projects and into agricultural development on a vast scale. Your reputation is high in science and medicine, in education and the arts.

At the same time, your social policies have stressed the value and importance of the individual, protecting the weak, the sick, the elderly and the unemployed. One of Canada's most notable achievements in the twentieth century has been the creation of a caring and sharing society, a society fair to all — and this has been reflected in the generous and far sighted help Canada has given to less fortunate countries all over the world. . . .

If the ideal of the country which Canadians wish to continue building together may seem a defiant challenge to history, there is nevertheless reason to believe it can be realized. I have seen Canadians working together, for the good of all the people. I have seen the vision of this country take shape in the lives of Canadians. There is now a greater confidence among Canadians that people of the two official language communities can live fuller and richer lives together than in mutual isolation. Among French-speaking Canadians I sense a stronger realization that there are growing opportunities for them to play their rightful role in the development of Canada in every field and indeed at every level.

Perhaps the most significant step in Canada's history was the decision of the communities to take pride in their several languages and cultures, rather than to deplore the differences. Quebec was both the inspiration and the principal agent of the profound transformation which has resulted from that decision. Although we regret the absence of the Premier of Quebec, it is right to associate the people of Quebec with this celebration because, without them, Canada would not be what it is today.

You spoke, Prime Minister, of the Charter of Rights and Freedoms, which guarantees to every person in this country the right to equal opportunity. The Charter also embodies notable progress in other areas. I am glad, glad to see that the equality of women is accorded full respect, that disabled persons are protected against discrimination, and that the rights of the aboriginal people are recognized, with full opportunity for further definition.

We must realize, however, that no law by itself can create or maintain a free society, or a united society, or a fair society. It is the commitment of the people that alone can transform a printed constitution or charter into a living and dynamic reality. The strength of Canada's new constitution lies not in the words it contains, but in the foundation upon which it rests, the desire of the people of Canada that their country remain strong and united.

That spirit, however assailed it may have been through the years by differences and rivalries, has endured, making this nation a model of freedom, good sense and democracy.

Differences persist. In this vast and vigorous land, they always will. The genius of Canadian federalism, however, lies in your consistent ability to overcome differences through reason and compromise. That ability is reflected in the willingness of the ordinary people of French-speaking and English-speaking Canada, and of the various regions, to respect each other's rights, and to create together the conditions under which all may prosper in freedom.

There is a historic relationship between the Crown and Canada's aboriginal peoples and I am therefore particularly pleased that this innate respect for fellow Canadians is also reflected in the willingness of the national and provincial governments to consult with the representatives of native peoples and to work out solutions to longstanding problems of rights and opportunities.

Constitutional revision is really a matter of adapting to changing needs and circumstances, while safeguarding stability, and providing protection for guaranteed rights. Change and movement are essential signs of life. The Constitution which so splendidly met the needs of the very young Canada of the late nineteenth century could not have anticipated the conditions of national life in 1982 and beyond. It is fitting, therefore, that the main features of Canada's new Constitution should be that it strengthens the rights of its people, while establishing a process of amendment which will make needed changes easier to accomplish than they were in the past.

Today I have proclaimed this new Constitution — one that is truly Canadian at last. There could be no better moment for me, as Queen of Canada, to declare again my unbounded confidence in the future of this wonderful country.

May God bless and keep you all.

JONES ON REORGANIZATION OF JOINT CHIEFS OF STAFF

April 21, 1982

In a series of articles and interviews in the spring of 1982, Gen. David C. Jones, chairman of the Joint Chiefs of Staff, critiqued the current organization of the Joint Chiefs and recommended changes. Problems with the Joint Chiefs system had been pointed out many times over the years, but Jones' proposals renewed interest in the issue. Congress held hearings, and other top military officials offered a variety of criticisms and suggested reforms. All agreed, however, that the existing Joint Chiefs system must be changed.

President Franklin D. Roosevelt informally set up the Joint Chiefs of Staff in 1942, and the National Security Act of 1947 made the organization official. The Joint Chiefs of Staff is a five-member committee consisting of a chairman and the heads of the four military services: the chiefs of staff of the Army and Air Force, the chief of naval operations, and the Marine Corps commandant. All five are appointed by the president and confirmed by the Senate. The four service chiefs serve four-year terms; the chairman serves a two-year term and can be reappointed to a second term.

By law, the Joint Chiefs as a body is the principal military adviser to the president, secretary of defense and National Security Council. The chiefs meet with foreign military leaders and represent the U.S. military at arms control talks. They supervise, but do not command, U.S. forces in the field.

The chiefs meet several times a week to work on a variety of military matters. They are supported both by staffs from the individual services and by a joint staff. Traditionally, they have relied more heavily on their service staffs for advice and assistance than on the joint staff.

The chairman is the only member of the Joint Chiefs who devotes all of his time to joint matters. The other four chiefs have service duties, and in joint work they tend to guard the interests and traditions of their respective services.

Problems

Jones, chairman of the Joint Chiefs from 1978 until June 1982, spent most of his last months in office urging reform of the Joint Chiefs system.

The primary personnel problem Jones described was inadequate cross-service and joint experience throughout the military system. "[W]e cannot escape the fact that our national security today requires the integration of Service efforts more than at any time in our history," he wrote in an article published in Directors and Boards in February.

The committee structure of the Joint Chiefs created a number of problems, according to Jones. Because so much time was spent trying to reach compromises among the four services, he said, advice offered by the Joint Chiefs too often was "not crisp, timely, very useful or very influential." And frequently, Jones warned, individual service interests dominated the chiefs' actions at the expense of broader interests. In addition, the dual roles of the four service chiefs were overly time-consuming and created scheduling difficulties.

Proposed Reforms

Jones proposed several major changes in the existing Joint Chiefs system. In part, he suggested:

● The position of chairman shoud be strengthened. The chairman, not the Joint Chiefs as a body, should be designated the principal adviser to the president, secretary of defense and National Security Council. The president and secretary, however, could request corporate advice from the Joint Chiefs, and the chiefs could give their individual views directly to the president and secretary.

● A deputy chairman should be appointed to assist the chairman.

● The training, experience and rewards for joint duty should be expanded.

● The joint staff should respond directly to the chairman rather than to the Joint Chiefs as a group.

● The involvement of the individual service staffs should be severely limited, and the joint staff used to provide truly interservice advice.

Jones' criticisms and proposals sparked debate and led several other military leaders to offer their views. Gen. Edward C. Meyer, the Army chief of staff, for example, proposed creation of an independent panel of four-star generals and admirals "not charged with any service responsibilities" who would "never return" to their respective military services.

The House Armed Services Committee held hearings in the spring regarding the reorganization of the Joint Chiefs. Scores of military officials and experts testified. On August 16 the House passed the Joint Chiefs of Staff Reorganization Act of 1982 (HR 6954) that included elements of both Jones' and Meyer's proposals. The bill was sent to the Senate Armed Services Committee but received no action in 1982.

> *Following are excerpts from a statement by Gen. David C. Jones to the Investigations Subcommittee of the House Armed Services Committee, April 21, 1982. (Boldface headings in brackets have been added by Congressional Quarterly to highlight the organization of the text.):*

Mr. Chairman and Members of the committee, I welcome these hearings and commend you for addressing what I consider one of the most important and difficult defense issues of the day. . . .

As one of the first witnesses, I have been called upon to help kick off the discussion of JCS [Joint Chiefs of Staff] organizational improvements, but this should not be thought of as a David Jones crusade. You will be hearing many witnesses with experience in the JCS arena, the unified command structure and civilian leadership positions of the Department of Defense. I trust that you will listen carefully to their views and proposals as well as to mine. I have studied the problems intently, but I would not presume to have found the only acceptable solutions to the difficult problems that have plagued the JCS system for so long. I have pored over the many studies which have examined the system over the years. Many have recommended solutions similar to those I will outline to you today. Others have proposed different approaches. I commend all of those studies to you so that you can critically examine all of the alternatives before deciding where we should go from here. Regardless of differences of opinion on how to solve our organizational problems, a large number of military and civilian leaders, past and present, have strongly supported the *need* for structural change.

[Organizational Problems]

Historically, our military organization has tended to lag behind the changing demands of the defense environment. Organizational change has come more often in the aftermath of wartime failures than as a result of foreward [sic] planning. War and Navy Department organizational problems created both operational and logistics difficulties in the Spanish-

American War. Some reorganization took place, but even with plenty of time to prepare for World War I, our logistics system almost broke down because of inadequate war planning and disjointed organizational responsibilities.

Again some adjustments were made but we were still inadequately prepared for World War II. Pearl Harbor not only awakened us to the realities of modern warfare but served as a clear example of how diffused responsibilities and bureaucratic approaches to problems can contribute to a disaster. One of the first things done after the attack was to reorganize — an ad hoc JCS arrangement was developed, multi-Service and multi-national commands were formed, and the Army Staff was streamlined — but interservice difficulties persisted. In his December 1945 Message to Congress, President Truman said that, while unity of command for operations allowed us to win the war,

> "...we never had comparable unified direction in Washington. And even in the field our unity of operations was greatly impaired by the differences in training, in doctrine, in communication systems, and in supply and distribution systems that stemmed from the division of leadership in Washington ... [I]t is now time to take stock, to discard obsolete organizational forms...."

President Truman strongly urged the formation of an integrated Department of National Defense, but many within the War and Navy Departments and the respective Congressional Committees feared that integration would undermine the esprit and confuse the functions of the established Services. Thus the National Security Act of 1947 was a compromise that led to but limited integration of effort among our separate land, sea and air arms. We have been trying ever since — with very limited success — to overcome this handicap.

Vietnam was perhaps our worst example of confused objectives and unclear responsibilities. The organizational arrangements were a nightmare; for example, each Service fought its own air war. Since that time we have been concerned with how to react more effectively to contingencies, but have not as yet devised a way to integrate our efforts to achieve maximum joint effectiveness without undue regard to Service doctrines, missions and command prerogatives.

Clearly our record has not been what it could and should have been. We got by in the past because of our industrial base and the factors of time and space which allowed us to mobilize that base. In the World Wars we had the buffers of geography and of allies who could carry the fight until we mobilized and deployed. After World War II we depended largely on our nuclear superiority to cover a growing imbalance in conventional capabilities and deter direct clashes with the Soviets.

[Problems Faced in Modern Warfare]

However, today we no longer have the luxury of the buffers which in the past had allowed us to mobilize, organize and deploy after a conflict began. In fact, today the factors of time, geography and the strategic balance work largely to our disadvantage; they compound rather than mitigate our deficiencies in conventional force size, readiness and deployability. We must reaffirm our commitment to redress the balance through sustained investment in our defense capabilities. But we must do more to see us through the dangerous period ahead and ensure that our defense resources, both current and planned, are applied most effectively. To do so, we must free ourselves of the institutional and conceptual constraints of the past so that we can develop better strategy and tactics and imaginative solutions to the defense problems of today and tomorrow.

Quite frankly, we in this country have never applied those principles very well, particularly in developing strategy and tactics for truly joint operations. Because of our past successes with superior resources in wars of attrition, our military institutions have not been forced to reexamine established doctrine or to break down the institutional barriers in the interests of achieving greater force effectiveness through imaginative combinations of the resources and doctrines of the separate Services. We have bureaucratized our military institutions — and the great strength of a bureaucracy is its ability to protect and preserve institutional interests and self-image against the demands of a changing environment. We are comfortable with the past because it is the future, not the past, that challenges outmoded concepts, doctrines and organizational arrangements.

I have outlined the basic organizational deficiencies of the joint system in writing. Rather than repeat myself here, I would like to enter my article into the record. What I want to emphasize today is that the problems I have outlined are not new, nor am I the first to discover them. Their long-time existence and their persistence in the face of occasional attempts to overcome them have been attested to by a long series of studies dating from World War II to the present. The latest study was commissioned by me. It was conducted by a distinguished group of retired senior officers who have lived with the problems in the past, but who are now freed from the institutional pressures and constraints that tend to preclude detailed and objective evaluations of the system. This latest study found very serious deficiencies in the joint system, but what is most striking is that, for the most part, those very deficiencies have been articulated by virtually every study conducted over the past twenty-four years, and in some cases much longer. Let me demonstrate the point by outlining just four major problems.

[Diffuse Responsibility and Authority]

First, responsibility and authority are diffused, both in Washington and in the field. Because of this, we are neither able to achieve the maximum effective capability of the combined resources of the four Services nor to hold our military leadership accountable for this failure. As

I have already pointed out, the problem was highlighted by President Truman in 1945. Since that time:

- President Truman in 1949 recommended amendments to the National Security Act to fix responsibility, but less modest changes were enacted. Secretary of Defense Lovett in his November 1952 letter to President Truman wrote:

    "I do not consider the present organization adequate, not only because it leaves certain responsibilities obscure but also because in its purest form it does not provide the type of military guidance needed if the full benefits of unification are to be attained."

- Some additional changes were made in 1953, but in 1958 President Eisenhower still found that:

    "The unified commander's authority over [his] component commands is short of the full command required for maximum efficiency. . . . When military responsibility is unclear, civilian control is uncertain."

- Again some minimal changes were made, yet in 1970, the Blue Ribbon Defense Panel found that in Washington:

    ". . . the diffusion of responsibility and accountability, the freedom to 'pass the buck' to the top on hard decisions, and the opportunity to use the extensive coordination process to advance parochial objectives, are circumstances to which many in the Department have adapted comfortably." . . .

- Finally, the 1982 Special Study Group concluded that:

    "The military organizations given the responsibility for the planning and execution of Joint activities — notably the JCS, the Joint Staff and its subordinate agencies such as the Joint Deployment Agency, and the various Unified Command headquarters — simply do not have the authority, stature, trained personnel, or support needed to carry out their jobs effectively."

[Quality of Advice]

Second, the corporate advice provided by the Joint Chiefs of Staff is not crisp, timely, very useful or very influential. And that advice is often watered down and issues are papered over in the interest of achieving unanimity, even though many have contended that the resulting lack of credibility has caused the national leadership to look elsewhere for recommendations that properly should come from the JCS. Dissatisfaction with the corporate advice of the JCS was evident from the very beginning:

- The 1949 Eberstadt Committee found that,

    ". . . it has proven difficult to expedite decision on the part of the

Joint Chiefs, or to secure from them soundly unified and integrated plans and programs and clear, prompt advice."

- In 1960, the Symington Report stated:

  "Action by the Joint Chiefs of Staff takes place, if at all, only after prolonged debate, coordination and negotiation...."

- And finally, the Special Study Group recently concluded that the JCS staffing process:

  "...tends to water down or 'waffle' both the exposition of the issue and the recommended position as the constraints imposed by the protection of Service interests are applied at each echelon. The process is viewed as unproductive by most action officers, one of the reasons many fine officers do not seek Joint Staff assignments. It is also perceived as unproductive by its civilian consumers, one of the reasons that JCS formal advice is frequently not requested or heeded."

[Individual Service Interests]

Third, individual Service interests too often dominate JCS recommendations and actions at the expense of broader defense interests. This occurs not only within the JCS itself but in the Unified Commands and throughout the multi-layered JCS committee structure where joint issues are addressed. It occurs within the JCS because four of the five members are charged with the responsibility to maintain the traditions, esprit, morale and capabilities of their Services. It occurs in the field and within the Pentagon staff structure because officers assigned to joint billets come from and return to their Services who have complete control over their future promotions and assignments. It has never been considered very beneficial for an officer's career to champion causes that lead to greater joint effectiveness at the expense of the institutional interests of his own Service. Once again, this problem has been recognized from the beginning but has persisted to this very day.

- In 1945, with the war not yet ended, a JCS Special Committee observed that:

  "...even in areas where unity of command has been established, complete integration of effort has not yet been achieved because we are still struggling with inconsistencies, lack of understanding, jealousies and duplications which exist in all theaters of operations."

- President Eisenhower found that the problem persisted in 1958:

  "I know well, from years of military life, the constant concern of service leaders for the adequacy of their respective programs, each of which is intended to strengthen the Nation's defense...."

But service responsibilities and activities must always be only the branches, not the central trunk of the national security tree. The present organization fails to apply this truth.

While at times human failure and misdirected zeal have been responsible for duplications, inefficiencies, and publicized disputes, the truth is that most of the service rivalries that have troubled us in recent years have been made inevitable by the laws that govern our defense organization.". . .

● The 1978 Steadman Report found that:

"The nature of the [JCS] organization virtually precludes effective addressal of those issues involving allocation of resources among the Services, such as budget levels, force structures, and procurement of new weapons systems — except to agree that they should be increased without consideration of resource constraints."

● And finally, the 1982 Special Study Group concluded:

"A certain amount of Service independence is healthy and desirable, but the balance now favors the parochial interests of the Services too much and the larger needs of the nation's defenses too little."

[Dual Role of Service Chief]

And fourth, a Service Chief does not have enough time to perform his two roles as a member of the Joint Chiefs and as the head of a Service — and these two roles have a built-in conflict of interest. The involvement of the Service Chiefs and their staffs in every facet of joint actions contributes greatly to these problems. The time demands on a Service Chief not only contribute to the difficulty of managing Service programs and resolving such problems as procurement cost and time overruns, personnel discipline, training, morale and force readiness, they also prevent him from being fully conversant with the joint and cross-Service issues he must address in the JCS forum. His Service staff generally briefs him on these issues from a Service perspective and thus reinforces the conflict of interest he faces when attempting to trade off his own Service's programs and needs from the broader perspective demanded by his JCS responsibilities. This problem too has been with us from the beginning.

● The 1949 Eberstadt Report stated that:

"A further source of the deficiencies of the Joint Chiefs lies in the fact that they are, as individuals, too busy with their service duties to give to Joint Chiefs of Staff matters the attention their great importance demands. Three of the four members of the Joint Chiefs of Staff are also the military commanders of their respective services."

● Secretary of Defense Lovett concluded in 1952:

"It is extremely difficult for a group composed of the Chiefs of the three Military Departments and charged, with the exception of the Chairman, with heavy responsibilities placed upon them by law with respect to each individual Service to decide matters involving the splitting of manpower, supplies, equipment, facilities, dollars, and similar matters."

● President Eisenhower emphasized in his 1958 Message to Congress that:

". . . the Joint Chiefs' burdens are so heavy that they find it very difficult to spend adequate time on their duties as members of the Joint Chiefs of Staff. This situation is produced by their having the dual responsibilities of chiefs of the military services and members of the Joint Chiefs of staff. The problem is not new but has not yielded to past efforts to solve it."

● The 1958 reorganization directed that the Service Chiefs delegate Service responsibilities to their Vice Chiefs, yet the Symington Report in 1960 declared:

"No different results can be expected as long as the members of the Joint Chiefs of Staff retain their two-hatted character, with their positions preconditioned by the Service environment to which they must return after each session of the Joint Chiefs of Staff."

● And the problem persisted, as found by the Blue Ribbon Defense Panel in 1970:

"The numerous functions now assigned to members of the Joint Chiefs of Staff impose an excessive workload and a difficult mix of functions and loyalties. . . . The difficulty is caused by the system, not the people."

● The Steadman Report in 1978:

"A Chief's responsibility to manage and lead his Service conflicts directly with his agreement in the joint forum to recommendations which are inconsistent with programs desired by his own Service. . . ."

● And the [1982] Study Group also confirmed that the conflict of interest problem still exists:

"What the current system demands of the Chiefs is often unrealistic. They have one job that requires them to be effective advocates for their own Service; they have another that requires them to subordinate Service interests to broader considerations; and they are faced with issues where the two positions may well be antithetical. . . ."

Clearly, these problems have been with us far too long. Clearly, these problems are inherent in organizational arrangements which violate established principles of good management. They are not the fault of individuals, for they have persisted through a long line of extremely dedicated and talented men who have filled the various positions on the Joint Chiefs of Staff....

[Recommendations for Reform]

Most studies have recommended one of two general courses of action to resolve these problems. The first alternative is to strengthen the authority and capability of the Chairman and hold him, rather than the Joint Chiefs as a body, responsible for JCS functions. The second alternative — most recently espoused by General Meyer, the Army Chief of Staff — is to resolve the dual-hat problem by replacing the Joint Chiefs with a group of senior military advisers who have no further Service responsibilities. My preference is for the first alternative, although I agree with General Meyer that the second has clear advantages over the current system.

I have recently provided my specific recommendations. My proposals are designed to strengthen the role of the Chairman by incorporating the following features into basic statutes, executive orders and departmental directives:

1. *The Chairman, rather than the Joint Chiefs of Staff as a body, should be designated the principal military adviser to the President, the Secretary of Defense, and the National Security Council.* In developing his advice, the Chairman would receive the counsel of the Service Chiefs and the Unified and Specified Commanders; however, he should give his advice based on his own responsibility for broader defense interests. In this clarified role, the Chairman should have oversight of the combatant commands; and the current chain of command to the CINCs [Commanders of the Unified and Specified Commands], established by DOD [Department of Defense] directive, should be changed to run from the President and the Secretary of Defense through the Chairman instead of through the JCS. The statutes should be amended to reflect this change. These actions would resolve the problem of diffused responsibilities while retaining Service involvement in the joint process, allow the Service Chiefs to spend more time on their Service responsibilities, provide better access for the views of the combatant commanders to be incorporated in planning and programming issues, and free the Joint Staff to interact more frequently with the Unified Command staffs.

2. *The Secretary of Defense or the President would continue to seek the corporate advice of the Joint Chiefs of Staff on subjects they deem appropriate.* There are subjects such as national security strategy, industrial mobilization, arms control and major military personnel matters which would be particularly appropriate for the

Joint Chiefs to address as a body.

3. *Each Service Chief would have the right to submit his individual views and recommendations directly to the Secretary of Defense, and to the President as appropriate, on any joint issue on which that Chief had particularly strong feelings.* This would assure that a Chairman would carefully consider the views of the Service Chiefs. It would also provide the Chiefs the opportunity to present alternative views more clearly drawn in terms of national security objectives and Service contributions to joint defense capabilities.

4. *A Deputy Chairman of four-star rank should be authorized to assist in carrying out the Chairman's responsibilities,* to allow more time to interact with the CINCs, to provide continuity in crisis management and in interagency and defense forums, and to assure a balance of expertise and viewpoints.

5. *The Joint Staff should be made responsible directly to the Chairman rather than to the Joint Chiefs of Staff as a body.* In addition, we must improve the experience and military education levels of officers serving in joint assignments and provide greater incentives and rewards for distinguished joint duty. This will require removing the legislative restrictions on the Joint Staff and establishing joint procedures for selecting, schooling, insuring enhanced promotion and assignment opportunities, and managing the careers of those officers best qualified for joint duty. Actions are already being addressed by the Joint Chiefs to properly manage well qualified joint officers as a valuable national asset; repealing the legislative constraints on Joint Staff duty will allow sufficient flexibility to do this job properly.

We have also recently agreed to make organizational changes in the Joint Staff as a first step to overcoming some of the problems that have been created by our internal procedures. These changes, which are currently in progress, will improve our contingency and mobilization planning and execution processes, allow us to deal better with important cross-cutting budget and program management issues such as C^3 [command, control, and communications], strategic mobility and force readiness, and to focus more attention on joint staffing and personnel matters. These initiatives can serve as first steps to even greater progress if, with the cooperation of Congress and the Administration, the broader reforms I have outlined are enacted.

I believe the proposed reorganization of the joint system would strengthen civilian control, provide the opportunity for the civilian leadership to make decisions based on more incisive military advice, and at the same time assure that Service viewpoints are available to Executive and Congressional decisionmakers. My proposals would also bring the Unified Commanders ... who will be charged with the joint operations of the future — more clearly and continuously into the OSD-JCS [Office of the

Secretary of Defense-Joint Chiefs of Staff] dialog on questions of strategy, priorities and force development. There would still be competition among the Services, but that competition could be turned to the goal of making the most effective and efficient contributions to our total — our joint — deterrence and war fighting capabilities, and away from divisive debates centering on Service roles, missions and budgets.

[What Proposals Will Not Do]

Let me dwell for a moment on what my proposals will *not* do. This is equally important if we are to avoid the pitfalls of the past and not be diverted once again by side issues. First, my proposals will *not* create an all-powerful single Chief of Staff who could monopolize military advice. The right of the Service Chiefs to present their views and arguments directly to the civilian leadership charged with decision responsibility would be protected by law, and the civilian leadership would continue to exercise fully the power of decision and control. Second, my proposals will *not* weaken civilian control. The Military Departments would still report directly to the Secretary of Defense. Responsibility for oversight of the combatant commands would be clearly fixed on the Chairman rather than on a committee, and the Chairman would just as clearly remain subordinate and accountable to the Secretary of Defense and the President. Third, my proposals will *not* create an independent, elite or pervasive General Staff. I do not propose the establishment of a group of planners who sit in an ivory tower, oblivious to what is going on in the field. Officers who prove best qualified for joint assignments would alternate between joint and Service assignments — and they would be rewarded rather than discriminated against for serving the broader interests of national security. . . .

I am convinced that we will reorganize our joint system. The only question is whether we will do so with foresight and measured purpose, or once again wait until forced to do so by our failure to deter aggression. In this age, I fear we would not be able to recover from our unpreparedness as we have in the past.

RETURN OF SINAI
TO EGYPT
April 25, 1982

Israel withdrew the last of its troops from the Sinai Peninsula April 25, returning the territory to Egypt. Israel had seized the Sinai during the 1967 Six-Day War and subsequently established settlements there. Under the terms of the Camp David accords, however, Israel agreed to relinquish the Sinai and on May 25, 1979, turned over the first of six sections of the territory. (Historic Documents of 1978, p. 605.) The final portion returned to Egypt on April 25 was the largest, totaling 7,500 square miles. This section bordered Israel and stretched from the Mediterranean south to the Gulf of Aqaba.

The Sinai covers more than 23,000 square miles — almost twice the size of Israel. Much of the land is desert wilderness, but there are lush oases and miles of beaches along the northern and southern coasts.

Relinquishing the land was a costly step for Israel. The Israeli military gave up vast areas used for air and ground maneuvers, as well as military warning stations high in the Sinai mountains. In addition, Israel lost several oil fields, 16 civilian settlements and an estimated $17 billion worth of roads, pipelines, electric lines and other investments.

Egypt's plans for developing the Sinai included 175 projects, ranging from tourist facilities and new towns to agricultural and fishing ventures.

Pullout Problems

The period just prior to the final turnover was marked with difficulties.

Egypt and Israel disputed the exact boundaries of the remaining territory at 15 different points. In addition, Israel accused Egypt of overstaffing its military units in the Sinai sections already returned, of making public statements circumventing the Camp David accords and of permitting Palestinians to smuggle arms into the Gaza Strip.

Fearing that the last phase of Israel's pullout was in jeopardy, the United States sent a special envoy, Deputy Secretary of State Walter J. Stoessel Jr., to smooth things out. Stoessel shuttled between Egypt and Israel, and the turnover was completed on schedule.

The most dramatic impediment to withdrawal was the resistance of some Israeli Sinai settlers to the move, primarily in the town of Yamit. The Israeli government instructed all Sinai settlers to leave the territory by midnight March 31. Approximately 2,000 protesters, however, refused to vacate their homes. On April 19 the Israeli military moved in to evict the remaining settlers. Some resisters had to be pried from their homes and dragged to waiting buses. Bulldozers then leveled the town of Yamit, returning it to the desert sands.

The resistance both symbolized and exacerbated Israel's national anguish over the withdrawal. Defense Minister Ariel Sharon vowed that the Sinai return would be Israel's last territorial concession to peace, and he promised new settlement expansion in the Golan Heights, West Bank and Gaza Strip.

Muted Ceremonies

The last of Israel's soldiers left the Sinai April 25. Shortly after dawn they lowered Israeli flags at the southern outpost of Sharm el Sheik. Several hours later Egypt raised its flags at Sharm el Sheik and at the Mediterranean coast town of Rafah, newly divided by the Sinai border. There were no joint Israeli-Egyptian ceremonies to mark the occasion, and Egypt's celebrations were notably low-key.

The pullout marked one step in the fragile Mideast peace process. In a speech to the Egyptian Parliament April 26, Egyptian President Hosni Mubarak praised Israel's "enthusiasm for the peace process and readiness to shoulder its consequences and requirements," and he stated Egypt's determination to work for a lasting and comprehensive peace. Nonetheless, the Middle East remained an area of tension and uncertainty. The Sinai withdrawal left Israel grim and embittered; many Arab states remained hostile to the Camp David agreements; and strife in Lebanon threatened peace throughout the region. (War in Lebanon, p. 741)

Following are the text of a White House statement, issued April 25, 1982, on the return of the Sinai to Egypt and excerpts from a speech by President Hosni Mubarak to Egypt's Parliament, April 26. (Boldface headings in brackets have been added by Congressional Quarterly to highlight the organization of the texts.):

WHITE HOUSE STATEMENT

We note today the successful completion by Israel of the withdrawal of its forces from the Sinai Peninsula and the reestablishment there of full Egyptian sovereignty. The President believes that withdrawal represents a truly major sacrifice by Israel, and he admires its courage in taking the great risks which true peace requires. He admires as well the courageous Egyptian initiative without which peace with Israel would not have been achieved.

Israeli withdrawal from Sinai marks the beginning of a new era in the peaceful relations between Israel and Egypt, peaceful relations which should be taken by us all as the model for the future in that troubled region. The President is determined that the United States, together with Egypt and Israel, will continue to pursue the course of peace, under Camp David, with renewed vigor and dedication. It will not be an easy task but, with the example of Egypt and Israel before us, it can be achieved.

MUBARAK'S ADDRESS TO PARLIAMENT

... The liberation of the Egyptian land, which is an Arab and African land, is a tremendous accomplishment, compared to which great events pale. It is an accomplishment which the Egyptian people have achieved through their constant struggle and continuous work, hope, sacrifices, offerings, suffering, sweat, blood and tears. . . .

In these blessed moments we turn to those heroes who worked silently to prepare for the battle of liberation. They worked long hours so that Egypt would be secure; and they suffered so that Egypt might prosper. . . .

It is a gigantic historic achievement that has been realized by one of Egypt's faithful sons: Muhammad Anwar as-Sadat . . . the leader in war and the hero of peace . . . who was born on the soil of immortal Egypt, drank from its great Nile, drew from its deep-rooted civilization, upheld its spiritual ideals and tolerant principles and shared his people's joys and sadnesses, their pains and dreams. . . .

It is with a feeling of grief that we celebrate liberation day in his absence, while the credit for this day goes to him, and that he is not among us to share in raising Egypt's flags over every inch of its sacred land. He waited all his life for that moment. . . .

Dear brothers, the liberation of the land and the prevalence of Egyptian sovereignty on the land of immortal Egypt are a great accomplishment by any standard; this was achieved by the interaction of the Egyptian will with the dreams of the masses in all parts of the great Arab homeland. We will never forget the noble, principled stand adopted by our brothers who remained loyal to the pledge, adhered to what is right and rejected the logic of defeat and inability and remained confident in the Arab ability to make peace and preserve its value and principles. . . .

It pleases me to convey heartfelt and sincere greetings from here to all the glorious African peoples . . . who stood alongside us and supported with all their power our just struggle in its various stages. They have rejected any harm to the Egyptian people's struggle and have expressed by this great stand the true essence of the principle of solidarity between nations and peoples. Solidarity is not a mere slogan, but it is a full partnership in austerity and prosperity, a true support in secret and in public, a priority given to joint questions and cooperation within the one group.

The peoples of our glorious continent have realized through their cultural heritage and experience in their long struggle that the struggle waged by the Egyptian people was the battle of all the African peoples, and that the noble principles for which they are fighting are the goals of all free men everywhere — justice, peace and freedom.

Blessed greetings to the Islamic peoples who supported our march along the road to justice and who embraced the true religion that calls for peace and for forebearance and coexistence among all races, religions and peoples; and rejects fanaticism, rancor and hatred. These peoples and their conscious leadership have shown that Islamic fraternity constitutes an inseparable sacred tie from which there is no return, because what God ties, man cannot untie. . . .

Warm greetings to the friendly American people . . . and to President Reagan . . . who has undertaken to complete and add to the great work which former President Jimmy Carter started. . . . The efforts which the U.S. President and his aides have made since he took office have been of utmost importance to completing the peace march and to consolidating its pillars. The United States has been with us in every step we have taken calling for moderation, for constructive positive action, and working to bring the viewpoints closer.

I would like to mention specifically the intensive efforts which the U.S. administration has exerted in the past few days to remove obstacles, clear the atmosphere in the relations between Egypt and Israel and iron out the differences which had arisen over some technical aspects — differences which could have cast their dark shadow on the situation at this critical phase.

Greetings to the friendly states in Europe, Asia and Latin America. These states have never denied us their support and backing ever since they believed in our just cause, legitimate struggle and sound course. . . .

[Relations Between Egypt and Israel]

Brothers and sisters, members of the People's Assembly and of the Consultative Council, brother citizens: The Israeli withdrawal from Sinai is an event which bolsters the peace process. It also opens new avenues for communication and exchange between the two peoples. This is because the liberation of the national soil removes an obstacle from the road of good neighborliness and friendship. We view peace in its capacity as a strategic and fundamental goal to which we unswervingly adhere. The reason is that peace is the way leading to the future and it is the safeguard of security and stability in the area. It is also the obligation to which the two peoples have committed themselves in the Camp David documents, in the Egyptian-Israeli treaty and its appendices and in subsequent agreements.

It is in keeping with justice that we determine that the Israeli people have shown clear enthusiasm for the peace process and readiness to shoulder its consequences and requirements. The people advocating moderation and coexistence are becoming stronger and more capable of action. This is a positive development; we must put it on record and seek to strengthen it and widen its scope. The reason is that the future depends on an increase in the number of those who believe in peace on both sides, on dissipating deep-seated doubts from hearts, demolishing barriers and surmounting obstacles by finding new ways of dealing, of deepening mutual understanding, of planting hope and confidence in lieu of suspicion and despair.

We hope the future will witness new momentum generated for the construction of bridges for liaison and cooperation based on respect for rights and legal conditions and the honoring of obligations.

Egypt has always been and will remain in the forefront of the states that adhere to legality, respect international treaties and agreements and fulfill legal commitments and obligations. This is because a civilized society can only be founded on the rule of the law, respect for rights and duties and prevention and deterrence of aggression.

Therefore, we intend to fulfill our obligations with goodwill and great integrity and without retreat or vacillation. We also hope Israel will keep all its commitments so that the peace march will be upheld and gain new ground every day and so that its concepts will become entrenched in the conscience of the peoples.

We are earnestly striving to reach a quick and just end to the dispute which Israel has raised over the location of the demarcation line in the Tabah area. We demand only right and justice. We have no interest in any regional expansion. However, at the same time we will not and cannot relinquish ... one inch of the holy land. We do not accept any bargaining in this matter because safeguarding the land is a responsibility shouldered by the successive generations, and the October generation will not be the generation that will relinquish land or right ... but will remain the guardian of the national soil and watchful over the safety of its country, which God has mentioned in his holy book.

Therefore, we insist on restoring our control and exercising our sovereignty over that piece of land that lies within the territory of our country and to which the provisions of Clause Two of the peace treaty applies.

Brothers: Since it began its gigantic steps on the road to peace, Egypt has declared that it is striving to achieve a comprehensive peace which all the parties to the conflict will participate in establishing and enjoying its fruits. This stand is not due to a committment [sic] to promises which we have accepted, rather, it is a decision that stems from our vision of reality, our understanding of the lessons of history and our faith that the desired peace is a comprehensive peace that deals with the roots of the problem and not just with some of its aspects.

The bloody incidents that occurred recently in the West Bank, the Gaza Strip and in Lebanon are another indication that it is necessary to move quickly to enlarge the scope of peace and to spread the umbrella of security and stability over all parts of our region, which has been bled by wounds, so that ultimately peace treaties will be concluded between Israel and all its neighbors. The Egyptian-Israeli treaty can be an example to be emulated in these treaties, given the precedent principles and provisions it has established and the tangible aspects it contains, which are represented by specific arrangements to guarantee the security of the two sides — arrangements that are totally removed from the concept of territorial expansion and annexation of territories.

[Palestinian Problem]

From this premise, in all the talks that have been held with Israel we have insisted that the Palestinian problem is the key to a solution and that reaching a just settlement of this problem within the framework of international legality is the sure guarantee for establishing stability and security in the region.

This is the principle on which the philosophy of the peace framework, was agreed upon in September 1978, and the letter exchanged among the parties on 26 March 1979 regarding the establishment of autonomy in the West Bank and Gaza Strip as an interim transitional arrangement paving the way for the final solution of the problem, were based.

We look forward to the resumption of autonomy negotiations in the coming days in a way leading to a declaration of principles that would permit the fraternal Palestinian people to come forward and participate in the making of peace. It is absolutely certain that the continuation of the present situation does not serve anyone's interests. This situation leads to the escalation of tension and an increase in the acts of violence, the victims of which are often innocent children and women, and to the establishment of unacceptable and unsafe neighborhood patterns between the Palestinians and the Israelis because the planning of Israeli settlements in Palestinian territory will only led to more tension, the widening of the gulf separating the two sides, reviving fears and doubts in hearts, and weakening hope in the future.

While asserting the fact that we do not represent the Palestinian people, nor do we speak in their name or claim for ourselves the right to make commitments on their behalf and negotiate their rights and demands, none of us can accept that the state of occupation should continue, or that Israeli control should firmly consolidate itself. Therefore, it was necessary that we make the first step permitting the fraternal Palestinian people, if they want, to reach the beginning of the road by cancelling the Israeli military government and its civil administration and by electing an autonomous authority enjoying wide powers drawing this people, with whom we are linked by ties of kinship and joint interests, closer to the achievement of their legitimate rights in the stage of final settlement.

I would like to reiterate at this place that nothing will be imposed on the Palestinian people. They have the first and last word in their cause. Our aim is to provide them with more options so that [they] don't feel surrounded in a narrow area, choosing between a continuation of the occupation, with all the suffering and pain it means, and desperate acts of violence, which achieve no benefits and avert no harm, but create an appropriate atmosphere for more suppression and repression. . . .

We are seeking good relations with all states and peoples. We harbor no evil intentions toward anyone. We deal with various states without complexes or sensitivity within limits that achieve our joint interests. This is conditional upon their respect for the independence of our will, our right to freedom of option, to safeguard our national security and to defend our strategic interests. Egypt will always remain in the vanguard of the forces defending the interests of peoples and human rights, calling for adherence to international legitimacy and the rule of law and seeking the establishment of a new international system that will allow all states to achieve further justice, equality and stability.

[Plans for the Future]

Dear brothers and sisters, sons of immortal Egypt. The stage that begins today with the liberation of the national soil is no less ferocious and delicate than the past stages. The liberation imposes on us new obligations and additional burdens that must be confronted with strong will and the same spirit that enabled us to achieve this glorious national aim — a spirit of responsibility, vigilance, wisdom and placing public interests above individual interests and selfish whims. . . .

The appraisal of our economic situation, which we carried out in the past few months, has disclosed a dire need to increase investments in fields related to development, step up production and productivity, change many of the consumption patterns that have increased in the past years and create new job opportunities that would not constitute a numerical addition to the marked unemployment but would actually lead to an increase in the general national production and to the absorption of the latest technology. This is so Egypt will not lag behind the procession, because its natural place is one of prominence and leadership and of setting examples. . . .

We must reconstruct the Sinai and spread civilization throughout its area while preserving its unique natural environment. . . .

LAW OF THE SEA TREATY
April 30, 1982

Chiefly because of the document's seabed mining provisions, the United States and several other major industrial countries refused to support a Law of the Sea Treaty approved April 30 by the United Nations. The vote was 130 to 4 in favor of the treaty; joining the United States in voting against it were Venezuela, Turkey and Israel. Seventeen nations abstained, including Britain, West Germany and other countries from the European Economic Community, and several Soviet bloc nations. On December 10 in Jamaica 117 countries formally signed the treaty, which had undergone minor revisions in June and October.

The treaty's 320 articles and nine annexes governed the use of the ocean and its resources. The Third United Nations Conference on the Law of the Sea had negotiated the terms since 1974. Scheduled to take effect one year after 60 nations have ratified it, the treaty then would bind only the ratifiers.

Objections to the Treaty

The United States rejected the treaty primarily because of the feature Third World countries sought most — a global authority to determine who can mine the metals in the deep seas and how much they can extract. The treaty demanded that private companies or their governments sell technical know-how to a global mining enterprise. Analysts believed the cost of this venture was the reason for the abstention by the Soviet Union and its allies.

If the treaty becomes effective, it will give each nation sovereign control of waters 12 miles from its shores, but countries must grant passage to all vessels that do not harm their security. The treaty would give each nation control of the fish and other marine resources over a 200-mile "economic zone" and the oil and gas in the continental shelves for 350 miles. In addition, planes and ships could pass through straits inside the 12-mile limit. This provision was considered crucial for military powers because it opened up 100 straits or choke points that otherwise would fall within the 12-mile limit.

Although previous U.S. administrations had accepted most of the treaty's provisions, President Ronald Reagan delayed concluding negotiations for more than a year and then unsuccessfully sought major changes to satisfy U.S. mining interests. Believers in the free-market system persuaded Reagan that it was unnecessary to share the profits of seabed mining with Third World countries that had not mastered the technology. They disagreed with the treaty's statement that "the sea-bed and ocean floor ... as well as their resources, are the common heritage of mankind, the exploration and exploitation of which shall be carried out for the benefit of mankind."

Parts of the ocean floor contain rich deposits of minerals such as cobalt, manganese, nickel and copper. Experts refer to these minerals as strategic or critical because they are essential to alloys needed for advanced aircraft and weapons. The United States imports 91 percent of the cobalt it uses, 98 percent of its manganese and 72 percent of its nickel.

The overwhelming vote in favor of the treaty indicated that the United States might have to curtail its oceanic mining ventures. There was a strong legal case for allowing only treaty signers, following treaty rules, to mine the ocean's wealth. It was expected that few banks would lend the $1.5 billion to $2 billion currently estimated as the cost to develop a mine site, because with an international treaty in place ownership of the metals would be uncertain.

Question of Legality

The United States also had a constitutional objection to the treaty. The treaty allowed "amendments to come into force for a state without its consent," said U.S. conference delegate James L. Malone. In 20 years the code's provisions would enable three-fourths of the treaty signers to impose amendments. The United States insisted it could not be bound to any such procedures and that any amendments would amount to a new treaty that would have to be submitted to the Senate for approval.

Following are excerpts from provisions of the Law of the Sea Treaty, adopted by the United Nations, April 30, 1982; and the text of a July 9 statement by President Reagan, outlining U.S. objections to the treaty:

LAW OF THE SEA TREATY

The States Parties to this Convention,

Prompted by the desire to settle, in a spirit of mutual understanding and co-operation, all issues relating to the law of the sea and aware of the historic significance of this Convention as an important contribution to the maintenance of peace, justice and progress for all the peoples of the world,

Noting that the developments that have occurred since the United Nations Conferences on the Law of the Sea held at Geneva in 1958 and 1960 have accentuated the need for a new and generally acceptable Convention on the law of the sea,

Conscious that the problems of ocean space are closely interrelated and need to be considered as a whole,

Recognizing the desirability of establishing, through this Convention, and with due regard for the sovereignty of all States, a legal order for the seas and oceans which would facilitate international communication and promote their peaceful uses, the equitable and efficient utilization of their resources, the study, protection and preservation of the marine environment and the conservation of the living resources thereof,

Bearing in mind that the achievement of such goals will contribute to the realization of a just and equitable international economic order which would take into account the interests and needs of mankind as a whole and, in particular, the special interests and needs of developing countries, whether coastal or land-locked,

Desiring by this Convention to develop the principles embodied in resolution 2749 (XXV) of 17 December 1970 in which the General Assembly solemnly declared *inter alia* that the area of the sea-bed and ocean floor and the subsoil thereof, beyond the limits of national jurisdiction, as well as its resources, is the common heritage of mankind, the exploration and exploitation of which shall be carried out for the benefit of mankind as a whole, irrespective of the geographical location of States,

Believing that the codification and progressive development of the law of the sea achieved in this Convention will contribute to the strengthening of peace, security, co-operation and friendly relations among all nations in conformity with the principles of justice and equal rights and promote the economic and social advancement of all peoples of the world, in accordance with the Purposes and Principles of the United Nations as set forth in its Charter,

Affirming that matters not regulated by this Convention continue to be governed by the rules and principles of general international law,

Have agreed as follows:

Part I

USE OF TERMS

Article 1
Use of terms

For the purposes of this Convention:

1. "Area" means the sea-bed and ocean floor and subsoil thereof beyond the limits of national jurisdiction;

2. "Authority" means the International Sea-Bed Authority;

3. "activities in the Area" means all activities of exploration for, and exploitation of, the resources of the Area....

Part II

Territorial Sea and Contiguous Zone

Section 1. General Provisions

Article 2
Legal status of the territorial sea, of the air space over the territorial sea and of its bed and subsoil

1. The sovereignty of a coastal State extends, beyond its land territory and internal waters and, in the case of an archipelagic State, its archipelagic waters, to an adjacent belt of sea, described as the territorial sea.

2. This sovereignty extends to the air space over the territorial sea as well as to its bed and subsoil.

3. The sovereignty over the territorial sea is exercised subject to this Convention and to other rules of international law.

Section 2. Limits of the Territorial Sea

Article 3
Breadth of the territorial sea

Every State has the right to establish the breadth of its territorial sea up to a limit not exceeding 12 nautical miles, measured from baselines determined in accordance with this Convention....

Section 3. Innocent Passage in the Territorial Sea

Subsection A. Rules Applicable to All Ships

Article 17
Right of innocent passage

Subject to this Convention, ships of all States, whether coastal or landlocked, enjoy the right of innocent passage through the territorial sea.

Article 18
Meaning of passage

1. Passage means navigation through the territorial sea for the purpose of:

(a) traversing that sea without entering internal waters or calling at a roadstead or port facility outside internal waters; or

(b) proceeding to or from internal waters or a call at such roadstead or port facility.

2. Passage shall be continuous and expeditious. However, passage includes stopping and anchoring, but only in so far as the same are incidental to ordinary navigation or are rendered necessary by *force majeure* or distress or for the purpose of rendering assistance to persons, ships or aircraft in danger or distress.

Article 19
Meaning of innocent passage

1. Passage is innocent so long as it is not prejudicial to the peace, good order or security of the coastal State. Such passage shall take place in conformity with this Convention and with other rules of international law.

2. Passage of a foreign ship shall be considered to be prejudicial to the peace, good order or security of the coastal State if in the territorial sea it engages in any of the following activities:

(a) any threat or use of force against the sovereignty, territorial integrity or political independence of the coastal State, or in any other manner in violation of the principles of international law embodied in the Charter of the United Nations;

(b) any exercise or practice with weapons of any kind;

(c) any act aimed at collecting information to the prejudice of the defence or security of the coastal State;

(d) any act of propaganda aimed at affecting the defence or security of the coastal State;

(e) the launching, landing or taking on board of any aircraft;

(f) the launching, landing or taking on board of any military device;

(g) the loading or unloading of any commodity, currency or person contrary to the customs, fiscal, immigration or sanitary laws and regulations of the coastal State;

(h) any act of wilful and serious pollution, contrary to this Convention;

(i) any fishing activities;

(j) the carrying out of research or survey activities;

(k) any act aimed at interfering with any systems of communication or any other facilities or installations of the coastal State;

(l) any other activity not having a direct bearing on passage. . . .

Article 22
Sea lanes and traffic separation schemes
in the territorial sea

1. The coastal State may, where necessary having regard to the safety of navigation, require foreign ships exercising the right of innocent passage through its territorial sea to use such sea lanes and traffic separation schemes as it may designate or prescribe for the regulation of the passage of ships.

2. In particular, tankers, nuclear-powered ships and ships carrying nuclear or other inherently dangerous or noxious substances or materials may be required to confine their passage to such sea lanes.

Article 23
Foreign nuclear-powered ships and ships carrying nuclear
or other inherently dangerous or noxious substances

Foreign nuclear-powered ships and ships carrying nuclear or other inherently dangerous or noxious substances shall, when exercising the rights of innocent passage through the territorial sea, carry documents and observe special precautionary measures established for such ships by international agreements. . . .

Article 25
Rights of protection of the coastal State

1. The coastal State may take the necessary steps in its territorial sea to prevent passage which is not innocent.

2. In the case of ships proceeding to internal waters or a call at a port facility outside internal waters, the coastal State also has the right to take the necessary steps to prevent any breach of the conditions to which admission of those ships to internal waters or such a call is subject.

3. The coastal State may, without discrimination in form or in fact among foreign ships, suspend temporarily in specified areas of its territorial sea the innocent passage of foreign ships if such suspension is essential for the protection of its security, including weapons exercises. Such suspension shall take effect only after having been duly published. . . .

Part V

EXCLUSIVE ECONOMIC ZONE

Article 55
Specific legal régime of the exclusive economic zone

The exclusive economic zone is an area beyond and adjacent to the territorial sea, subject to the specific legal régime established in this Part, under which the rights and jurisdictions of the coastal State and the rights and freedoms of other States are governed by the relevant provisions of this Convention.

Article 56
Rights, jurisdiction and duties of the coastal State
in the exclusive economic zone

1. In the exclusive economic zone, the coastal State has:
   (a) sovereign rights for the purpose of exploring and exploiting, conserving and managing the natural resources, whether living or non-living, of the sea-bed and subsoil and the superjacent waters, and with regard to other activities for the economic exploitation and exploration of the zone, such as the production of energy from the water, currents and winds. . . .

Article 57
Breadth of the exclusive economic zone

The exclusive economic zone shall not extend beyond 200 nautical miles from the baselines from which the breadth of the territorial sea is measured.

Article 58
Rights and duties of other States
in the exclusive economic zone

1. In the exclusive economic zone, all States, whether coastal or land-locked, enjoy, subject to the relevant provisions of this Convention, the freedoms referred to in article 87 of navigation and overflight and of the laying of submarine cables and pipelines, and other internationally lawful uses of the sea related to these freedoms, such as those associated with the operation of ships, aircraft and submarine cables and pipelines, and compatible with the other provisions of this Convention. . . .

Article 60
Artificial islands, installations and structures
in the exclusive economic zone

1. In the exclusive economic zone, the coastal State shall have the exclusive right to construct and to authorize and regulate the construction, operation and use of:
   (a) Artificial islands;
   (b) installations and structures for the purposes provided for in article 56 and other economic purposes;
   (c) installations and structures which may interfere with the exercise of the rights of the coastal State in the zone.
2. The coastal State shall have exclusive jurisdiction over such artificial

islands, installations and structures, including jurisdiction with regard to customs, fiscal, health, safety and immigration laws and regulations.

3. Due notice must be given of the construction of such artificial islands, installations or structures, and permanent means for giving warning of their presence must be maintained. Any installations or structures which are abandoned or disused shall be removed to ensure safety of navigation, taking into account any generally accepted international standards established in this regard by the competent international organization. Such removal shall also have due regard to fishing, the protection of the marine environment and the rights and duties of other States. Appropriate publicity shall be given to the depth, position and dimensions of any installations or structures not entirely removed.

4. The coastal State may, where necessary, establish reasonable safety zones around such artificial islands, installations and structures in which it may take appropriate measures to ensure the safety both of navigation and of the artificial islands, installations and structures.

5. The breadth of the safety zones shall be determined by the coastal State, taking into account applicable international standards....

6. All ships must respect these safety zones and shall comply with generally accepted international standards regarding navigation in the vicinity of artificial islands, installations, structures and safety zones.

7. Artificial islands, installations and structures and the safety zones around them may not be established where interference may be caused to the use of recognized sea lanes essential to international navigation....

Article 61
Conservation of the living resources

1. The coastal State shall determine the allowable catch of the living resources in its exclusive economic zone.

2. The coastal State, taking into account the best scientific evidence available to it, shall ensure through proper conservation and management measures that the maintenance of the living resources in the exclusive economic zone is not endangered by over-exploitation. As appropriate, the coastal State and competent international organizations, whether subregional, regional or global, shall co-operate to this end.

3. Such measures shall also be designed to maintain or restore populations of harvested species at levels which can produce the maximum sustainable yield, as qualified by relevant environmental and economic factors, including the economic needs of coastal fishing communities and the special requirements of developing States, and taking into account fishing patterns, the interdependence of stocks and any generally recommended international minimum standards, whether subregional, regional or global.

4. In taking such measures the coastal State shall take into consideration the effects on species associated with or dependent upon harvested species with a view to maintaining or restoring populations of such

associated or dependent species above levels at which their reproduction may become seriously threatened.

5. Available scientific information, catch and fishing effort statistics, and other data relevant to the conservation of fish stocks shall be contributed and exchanged on a regular basis through competent international organizations, whether subregional, regional or global, where appropriate and with participation by all States concerned, including States whose nationals are allowed to fish in the exclusive economic zone.

Article 62
Utilization of the living resources

1. The coastal State shall promote the objective of optimum utilization of the living resources in the exclusive economic zone without prejudice to article 61.

2. The coastal state shall determine its capacity to harvest the living resources of the exclusive economic zone. Where the coastal State does not have the capacity to harvest the entire allowable catch, it shall ... give other States access to the surplus of the allowable catch. . . .

4. Nationals of other States fishing in the exclusive economic zone shall comply with the conservation measures and with the other terms and conditions established in the laws and regulations of the coastal State. . . .

Article 65
Marine mammals

Nothing in this Part restricts the right of a coastal State or the competence of an international organization, as appropriate, to prohibit, limit or regulate the exploitation of marine mammals more strictly than provided for in this Part. States shall co-operate with a view to the conservation of marine mammals and in the case of cetaceans shall in particular work through the appropriate international organizations for their conservation, management and study. . . .

Article 69
Right of land-locked States

1. Land-locked States shall have the right to participate, on an equitable basis, in the exploitation of an appropriate part of the surplus of the living resources of the exclusive economic zones of coastal States of the same subregion or region, taking into account the relevant economic and geographical circumstances of all the States concerned and in conformity with the provisions of this article and of articles 61 and 62. . . .

Part VI

CONTINENTAL SHELF

Article 76
Definition of the continental shelf

1. The continental shelf of a coastal State comprises the sea-bed and subsoil of the submarine areas that extend beyond its territorial sea throughout the natural prolongation of its land territory to the outer edge of the continental margin, or to a distance of 200 nautical miles from the baselines from which the breadth of the territorial sea is measured where the outer edge of the continental margin does not extend up to that distance. . . .

3. The continental margin comprises the submerged prolongation of the land mass of the coastal State, and consists of the sea-bed and subsoil of the shelf, the slope and the rise. It does not include the deep ocean floor with its oceanic ridges or the subsoil thereof. . . .

Article 81
Drilling on the continental shelf

The coastal State shall have the exclusive right to authorize and regulate drilling on the continental shelf for all purposes. . . .

Part XI

THE AREA

Section 1. General Provisions

Article 133
Use of terms

For the purposes of this Part:

(a) "resources" means all solid, liquid or gaseous mineral resources *in situ* in the Area at or beneath the sea-bed, including polymetallic nodules;

(b) resources, when recovered from the Area, are referred to as "minerals". . . .

Section 2. Principles Governing the Area

Article 136
Common heritage of mankind

The Area and its resources are the common heritage of mankind.

Article 137
Legal status of the Area and its resources

1. No State shall claim or exercise sovereignty or sovereign rights over any part of the Area or its resources, nor shall any State or natural or juridicial person appropriate any part thereof. No such claim or exercise of sovereignty or sovereign rights, nor such appropriation shall be recognized.

2. All rights in the resources of the Area are vested in mankind as a whole, on whose behalf the Authority shall act. These resources are not subject to alienation. The minerals recovered from the Area, however, may only be alienated in accordance with this Part and the rules, regulations and procedures of the Authority.

3. No State or natural or juridicial person shall claim, acquire or exercise rights with respect to the minerals recovered from the Area except in accordance with this Part. Otherwise, no such claim, acquisition or exercise of such rights shall be recognized. . . .

Article 140
Benefit of mankind

1. Activities in the Area shall, as specifically provided for in this Part, be carried out for the benefit of mankind as a whole, irrespective of the geographical location of States, whether coastal or land-locked, and taking into particular consideration the interests and needs of developing States and of peoples who have not attained full independence or other self-governing status recognized by the United Nations in accordance with General Assembly resolution 1514 (XV) and other relevant General Assembly resolutions. . . .

Article 141
Use of the Area exclusively for peaceful purposes

The Area shall be open to use exclusively for peaceful purposes by all States, whether coastal or land-locked, without discrimination and without prejudice to the other provisions of this Part. . . .

Article 145
Protection of the marine environment

Necessary measures shall be taken in accordance with this Convention with respect to activities in the Area to ensure effective protection for the marine environment from harmful effects which may arise from such activities. To this end the Authority shall adopt appropriate rules, regulations and procedures for *inter alia:*

    (a) the prevention, reduction and control of pollution and other hazards to the marine environment, including the coastline, and of interference with the ecological balance of the marine environment, particular attention being paid to the need for protection from harmful effects of such activities as drilling, dredging, excavation, disposal of waste, construction and operation or maintenance of installations, pipelines and other devices related to such activities;

(b) the protection and conservation of the natural resources of the Area and the prevention of damage to the flora and fauna of the marine environment.

Article 146
Protection of human life

With respect to activities in the Area, necessary measures shall be taken to ensure effective protection of human life. To this end the Authority shall adopt appropriate rules, regulations and procedures to supplement existing international law as embodied in relevant treaties....

Article 148
Participation of developing States
in activities in the Area

The effective participation of developing States in activities in the Area shall be promoted as specifically provided for in this Part, having due regard to their special interests and needs, and in particular to the special need of the land-locked and geographically disadvantaged among them to overcome obstacles arising from their disadvantaged location, including remoteness from the Area and difficulty of access to and from it.

Article 149
Archaeological and historical objects

All objects of an archaeological and historical nature found in the Area shall be preserved or disposed of for the benefit of mankind as a whole, particular regard being paid to the preferential rights of the State or country of origin, or the State of cultural origin, or the State of historical and archaeological origin.

Section 3.   Development of Resources of the Area

Article 150
Policies relating to activities in the Area

Activities in the Area shall, as specifically provided for in this Part, be carried out in such a manner as to foster healthy development of the world economy and balanced growth of international trade, and to promote international co-operation for the over-all development of all countries, especially developing States, and with a view to ensuring:

(a) the development of the resources of the Area;

(b) orderly, safe and rational management of the resources of the Area, including the efficient conduct of activities in the Area and, in accordance with sound principles of conservation, the avoidance of unnecessary waste;

(c) the expansion of opportunities for participation in such activities consistent in particular with articles 144 and 148;

(d) participation in revenues by the Authority and the transfer of technology to the Enterprise and developing States as provided for in this Convention;

(e) increased availability of the minerals derived from the Area as needed in conjunction with minerals derived from other sources, to ensure supplies to consumers of such minerals;

(f) the promotion of just and stable prices remunerative to producers and fair to consumers for minerals derived both from the Area and from other sources, and the promotion of long-term equilibrium between supply and demand;

(g) the enhancement of opportunities for all States Parties, irrespective of their social and economic systems or geographical location, to participate in the development of the resources of the Area and the prevention of monopolization of activities in the Area;

(h) the protection of developing countries from adverse effects on their economies or on their export earnings resulting from a reduction in the price of an affected mineral, or in the volume of exports of that mineral, to the extent that such reduction is caused by activities in the Area, as provided in article 151;

(i) the development of the common heritage for the benefit of mankind as a whole; and

(j) conditions of access to markets for the imports of minerals produced from the resources of the Area and for imports of commodities produced from such minerals shall not be more favourable than the most favourable applied to imports from other sources.

Article 151
Production policies

1. (a) Without prejudice to the objectives set forth in article 150 and for the purpose of implementing subparagraph (h) of that article, the Authority, acting through existing forums or such new arrangements or agreements as may be appropriate, in which all interested parties, including both producers and consumers, participate, shall take measures necessary to promote the growth, efficiency and stability of markets for those commodities produced from the minerals derived from the Area, at prices remunerative to producers and fair to consumers. All States Parties shall co-operate to this end.

(b) The Authority shall have the right to participate in any commodity conference dealing with those commodities and in which all interested parties including both producers and consumers participate. The Authority shall have the right to become a party to any arrangement or agreement resulting from such conferences. Participation of the Authority in any organs established under those arrangements or agreements shall be in respect of production in the Area and in accordance with the relevant rules of those organs. . . .

2. (a) During the interim period specified in paragraph 3, commercial production shall not be undertaken pursuant to an approved plan of work until the operator has applied for and has been issued a production authorization by the Authority. Such production authorizations may not be applied for or issued more than five years prior to the planned commencement of commercial production under the plan of work unless, having regard to the nature and timing of project development, the rules, regulations and procedures of the Authority prescribe another period.

(b) In the application for the production authorization, the operator shall specify the annual quantity of nickel expected to be recovered under the approved plan of work. The application shall include a schedule of expenditures to be made by the operator after he has received the authorization which are reasonably calculated to allow him to begin commercial production on the date planned. . . .

(d) The Authority shall issue a production authorization for the level of production applied for unless the sum of that level and the levels already authorized exceeds the nickel production ceiling, as calculated pursuant to paragraph 4 in the year of issuance of the authorization, during any year of planned production falling within the interim period. . . .

4. (a) The production ceiling for any year of the interim period shall be the sum of:

(i) the difference between the trend line values for nickel consumption, as calculated pursuant to subparagraph (b), for the year immediately prior to the year of the earliest commercial production and the year immediately prior to the commencement of the interim period; and

(ii) sixty per cent of the difference between the trend line values for nickel consumption, as calculated pursuant to subparagraph (b), for the year for which the production authorization is being applied for and the year immediately prior to the year of the earliest commercial production.

(b) For the purposes of subparagraph (a):

(i) trend line values used for computing the nickel production ceiling shall be those annual nickel consumption values on a trend line computed during the year in which a production authorization is issued. The trend line shall be derived from a linear regression of the logarithms of actual nickel consumption for the most recent 15-year period for which such data are available, time being the independent variable. This trend line shall be referred to as the original trend line;

(ii) if the annual rate of increase of the original trend line is less than 3 per cent, then the trend line used to determine the quantities referred to in subparagraph (a) shall instead be one passing through the original trend line at the value for the first year of the relevant 15-year period, and increasing at 3 per cent annually; provided however that the production ceiling established for any year of the interim period may not in any case exceed the difference between the original trend line value for that year and the original trend line value for the year immediately prior to the commencement of the interim period. . . .

6. (a) An operator may in any year produce less than or up to 8 per cent more than the level of annual production of minerals from polymetallic nodules specified in his production authorization, provided that the over-all amount of production shall not exceed that specified in the authorization. Any excess over 8 per cent and up to 20 per cent in any year, or any excess in the first and subsequent years following two consecutive years in which excesses occur, shall be negotiated with the Authority, which may require the operator to obtain a supplementary production authorization to cover additional production.

(b) Applications for such supplementary production authorizations shall be considered by the Authority only after all pending applications by operators who have not yet received production authorizations have been acted upon and due account has been taken of other likely applicants. The Authority shall be guided by the principle of not exceeding the total production allowed under the production ceiling in any year of the interim period. It shall not authorize the production under any plan of work of a quantity in excess of 46,500 metric tonnes of nickel per year.

7. The levels of production of other metals such as copper, cobalt and manganese extracted from the polymetallic nodules that are recovered pursuant to a production authorization should not be higher than those which would have been produced had the operator produced the maximum level of nickel from those nodules pursuant to this article. The Authority shall establish rules, regulations and procedures pursuant to Annex III, article 17, to implement this paragraph.

8. Rights and obligations relating to unfair economic practices under relevant multilateral trade agreements shall apply to the exploration and exploitation of minerals from the Area. In the settlement of disputes arising under this provision, States Parties which are Parties to such multilateral trade agreements shall have recourse to the dispute settlement procedures of such agreements.

9. The Authority shall have the power to limit the level of production of minerals from the Area, other than minerals from nodules, under such conditions and applying such methods as may be appropriate by adopting

regulations in accordance with article 161, paragraph 8.

10. Upon the recommendation of the Council on the basis of advice from the Economic Planning Commission, the Assembly shall establish a system of compensation or take other measures of economic adjustment assistance including co-operation with specialized agencies and other international organizations to assist developing countries which suffer serious adverse effects on their export earnings or economies resulting from a reduction in the price of an affected mineral or in the volume of exports of that mineral, to the extent that such reduction is caused by activities in the Area. The Authority on request shall initiate studies on the problems of those States which are likely to be most seriously affected with a view to minimizing their difficulties and assisting them in their economic adjustment.

Article 152
Exercise of powers and functions by the Authority

1. The Authority shall avoid discrimination in the exercise of its powers and functions, including the granting of opportunities for activities in the Area.

2. Nevertheless, special consideration for developing States, including particular consideration for the land-locked and geographically disadvantaged among them, specifically provided for in this Part shall be permitted....

REAGAN STATEMENT

The United States has long recognized how critical the world's oceans are to mankind and how important international agreements are to the use of those oceans. For over a decade, the United States has been working with more than 150 countries at the Third United Nations Conference on Law of the Sea to develop a comprehensive treaty.

On January 29 of this year, I reaffirmed the United States commitment to the multilateral process for reaching such a treaty and announced that we would return to the negotiations to seek to correct unacceptable elements in the deep seabed mining part of the draft convention. I also announced that my administration would support ratification of a convention meeting six basic objectives.

On April 30 the conference adopted a convention that does not satisfy the objectives sought by the United States. It was adopted by a vote of 130 in favor, with 4 against (including the United States) and 17 abstentions. Those voting "no" or abstaining appear small in number but represent countries which produce more than 60 percent of the world's gross national product and provide more than 60 percent of the contributions to the United Nations.

We have now completed a review of that convention and recognize that it contains many positive and very significant accomplishments. Those extensive parts dealing with navigation and overflight and most other provisions of the convention are consistent with United States interests and, in our view, serve well the interests of all nations. That is an important achievement and signifies the benefits of working together and effectively balancing numerous interests. The United States also appreciates the efforts of the many countries that have worked with us toward an acceptable agreement, including efforts by friends and allies at the session that concluded on April 30.

Our review recognizes, however, that the deep seabed mining part of the convention does not meet United States objectives. For this reason, I am announcing today that the United States will not sign the convention as adopted by the conference, and our participation in the remaining conference process will be at the technical level and will involve only those provisions that serve United States interests.

These decisions reflect the deep conviction that the United States cannot support a deep seabed mining regime with such major problems. In our view, those problems include:

—Provisions that would actually deter future development of deep seabed mineral resources, when such development should serve the interest of all countries.

—A decisionmaking process that would not give the United States or others a role that fairly reflects and protects their interests.

—Provisions that would allow amendments to enter into force for the United States without its approval. This is clearly incompatible with the United States approach to such treaties.

—Stipulations relating to mandatory transfer of private technology and the possibility of national liberation movements sharing in benefits.

—The absence of assured access for future qualified deep seabed miners to promote the development of these resources.

We recognize that world demand and markets currently do not justify commercial development of deep seabed mineral resources, and it is not clear when such development will be justified. When such factors become favorable, however, the deep seabed represents a potentially important source of strategic and other minerals. The aim of the United States in this regard has been to establish with other nations an order that would allow exploration and development under reasonable terms and conditions.

MAY

REPORT ON TV AND VIOLENCE
May 5, 1982

A major study by the National Institute of Mental Health (NIMH), released May 5, concluded that violence on television can lead directly to aggressive and violent behavior among children and teen-agers. The report, Television and Behavior: Ten Years of Scientific Progress and Implications for the Eighties, *was undertaken to update the 1972* Report of the Surgeon General's Advisory Committee on Television and Behavior, *which tentatively affirmed a connection between television viewing and aggressive behavior among children. The earlier report saw a short-run link, but it was uncertain about any connection in the long run.*

After reviewing research studies done since the 1972 report, NIMH concluded that the evidence was now "overwhelming" that a definite link existed between watching televised violence and aggressive behavior in children.

"Not all children become aggressive, of course, but the correlations between violence and aggression are positive," it stated. "In magnitude, television violence is as strongly correlated with aggressive behavior as any other behavioral variable that has been measured."

Theories Explored

Addressing the question of what explains the viewing-behavior connection, the report discussed several theories. According to the "observational learning" theory, for example, children learned aggressive behavior from watching television in much the same way they learned social skills from watching their parents, teachers and others. Other theorists said watching television makes children more accepting of aggressive behavior and can change their attitudes toward such values as discipline and obedience.

On the plus side, the report noted that television also had the potential to teach children "constructive social behavior," such as helpfulness, cooperation and friendliness. But it noted that it was not clear whether these benefits were actually being achieved and said that additional research was needed in this area.

Other Findings

In addition to violence, the NIMH report focused on other behavioral areas of television watching. Some general findings included:

- *Television, especially commercials, seemed to encourage poor nutrition. Children who watched a lot of television had poorer eating habits than those who did not watch as much.*
- *Television commercials taught children to be avid consumers. Teenagers, however, seemed to be more skeptical about commercials.*
- *People who watched television a great deal were more likely to view the world as a violent, "mean and scary" place. They also had less trust in other people.*
- *Findings were mixed as to television's effects on educational achievement. Some studies showed more television viewing produced higher achievement, some found lower achievement and some found no relation at all.*
- *Almost everyone watched television, although not necessarily every day. Women and minority groups tended to watch more than others. Those who watched the most tended to be less educated, although college students also watched a great deal.*

Following are excerpts from Chapters I, IV and X of Television and Behavior, *released May 5, 1982, by the National Institute of Mental Health:*

HIGHLIGHTS OF TEN YEARS OF RESEARCH

Television's Health-Promoting Possibilities

In its programs, television contains many messages about health, messages that may be important to promotion of health and prevention of illness. Television seems to be doing a rather poor job of helping its audiences to attain better health or better understanding of health practices. That is, of course, not a goal of commercial television; nevertheless, incidental learning from television stories and portrayals may be contributing to lifestyles and habits that are not conducive to good health. Portrayal of mental illness on television is not frequent, but when it does appear, it is related to both violence and victimization; compared with "normal" characters, twice as many mentally ill characters on television are violent or are the victims of others' violence. Even though very few characters on television are ill, many more doctors are evident than are in real life. Much of television's content seems to foster poor nutrition, especially in commercials for sweets and snack foods. Children who watch a lot of television have poorer nutritional habits than children who do not watch as much. Alcohol consumption is common; it is condoned and is presented as a part of the social milieu. When people drive cars, which occurs often on television, they almost never wear seat belts. Correlational studies suggest that people's attitudes are influenced by these portrayals. One study, for example, indicated that television ranked second to physicians and dentists as a source of health information.

There has been almost no research on people in institutions, even though it is known that they often watch television. One study in a psychiatric setting found that staff believed television had a beneficial effect on patients, especially the chronic and elderly. Increased use of television for therapeutic purpose should be considered; for example, films and videotape have been used successfully to help people learn to cope with fears and phobias. An experimental study of emotionally disturbed children reported that, for some of the children, prosocial programs increased their altruistic behavior and decreased their aggressive behavior. More research is needed to explore the therapeutic potential of television.

With the pervasiveness of television viewing, it can be assumed that campaigns to promote better health would be effective. There have been campaigns on community mental health, against drug abuse and smoking, for seat-belt wearing, for dental health, and against cancer, venereal disease, and alcoholism. An example of a successful campaign to reduce risk of cardiovascular disease in California had programs in both English and Spanish and face-to-face instruction, in addition to the television messages, for some of the groups. After 2 years, communities exposed to the campaign, even without the personal instruction, had significantly reduced the likelihood of heart attack and stroke, while in a "control" community where there was no campaign risk levels remained high. Carefully planned and evaluated campaigns built on an understanding of the ways in which messages are conveyed and incorporated into people's lives hold great promise.

Cognitive and Emotional Functioning

Research on cognitive processes has asked such questions as: What are the factors involved in paying attention to television? What is remembered? How much is understood? The research shows that duration of paying attention is directly related to age. Infants watch sporadically; little children gradually pay more attention visually until, at about age 4, they look at television about 55 percent of the time, even when there are many other distractions in the room. Auditory cues are very important in attracting and holding attention. Up to the second and third grades, children cannot report much of what they see and hear on television, but they probably remember more than they can report, and memory improves with growing up. Young children remember specific scenes better than relationships, and they often do not understand plot or narrative. Making inferences and differentiating between central and peripheral content are difficult for young children, but these skills also improve with age. The changes may be partly developmental and partly the result of experience with television.

The "medium as the message" came to be studied again in the 1970s. Much of what children, and others, see on television is not only the content. They learn the meaning of television's forms and codes — its camera techniques, sound effects, and organization of programs. Some of the effects of television can be traced to its forms, such as fast or slow action, loud or soft music, camera angles, and so on. Some researchers suggest that fast action, loud music, and stimulating camera tricks may account for changes in behavior following televised violence.

Although television producers and viewers alike agree that television can arouse the emotions, there has been very little research on television's effects on emotional development and functioning. It is known that some people have strong emotional attachments to television characters and personalities and that children usually prefer characters most like themselves. Research on television and the emotions should be given a top priority.

Violence and Aggression

The report of the Surgeon General's committee states that there was a high level of violence on television in the 1960s. Although in the 1970s there was considerable controversy over definitions and measurement of violence, the amount of violence has not decreased. Violence on television seems to be cyclical, up a little one year, down a little the next, but the percentage of programs containing violence has remained essentially the same over the past decade.

. . . What is the effect of all this violence? After 10 more years of research, the consensus among most of the research community is that violence on television does lead to aggressive behavior by children and teenagers who watch the programs. This conclusion is based on laboratory experiments and on field studies. Not all children become aggressive, of course, but the correlations between violence and aggression are positive. In magnitude, television violence is as strongly correlated with aggressive behavior as any other behavioral variable that has been measured. The research question has moved from asking whether or not there is an effect to seeking explanations for the effect.

According to observational learning theory, when children observe television characters who behave violently, they learn to be violent or aggressive themselves. Observational learning from television has been demonstrated many times under strict laboratory conditions, and there is now research on when and how it occurs in real life. Television is also said to mold children's attitudes which later may be translated into behavior. Children who watch a lot of violence on television may come to accept violence as normal behavior.

Although a causal link between televised violence and aggressive behavior now seems obvious, a recent panel study by researchers at the National Broadcasting Company found no evidence for a long-term enduring relation between viewing violent television programs and aggressive behavior. Others doing television research wil no doubt examine this new study to try to learn why it does not agree with many other findings.

Imaginative Play and Prosocial Behavior

Since children spend many hours watching the fantasy world of television it can be asked whether television enriches their imaginative capacities and whether it leads to a distortion of reality. Evidence thus far is that television does not provide material for imaginative play and that watching violent programs and cartoons is tied to aggressive behavior and to less imaginative play. Most young children do not know the difference between reality and fantasy on television, and of course, they do not understand how television works or how the characters appear on the screen. Television, however, can be used to enhance children's imaginative play if an adult watches with the child and interprets what is happening.

During the past 10 years research on television's influence on prosocial behavior has burgeoned. As a result evidence is persuasive — children can learn to be altruistic, friendly and self-controlled by looking at television programs depicting such behavior patterns. It appears that they also learn to be less aggressive.

Socialization and Conceptions of Social Reality

Most studies on socialization have been in the form of content analyses concerned with sex, race, occupation, age and consumer roles. There are more men than women on entertainment television, and the men on the average are older. The men are mostly strong and manly, the women usually passive and feminine. Both, according to some analysts are stereotyped but the women are even more stereotyped than the men. Lately there has been more sexual reference, more innuendo, and more seductive actions and dress. Both parents and behavioral scientists consider television to be an important sex educator not only in depictions specifically related to sex but in the relationships between men and women throughout all programs.

For a while, after organized protest removed degrading stereotyped portrayals from the air, there were almost no blacks to be seen on television. About 12 years ago, they emerged again, and now about 10 percent of television characters are black. There are not many Hispanics, Native Americans or Asian Americans.

Television characters usually have higher status jobs than average people in real life. A large proportion of them are professionals or managers, and relatively few are blue-collar workers.

The elderly are underrepresented on television, and, as with the younger adults, there are more old men than old women.

Research shows that consumer roles are learned from television. Children are taught to be avid consumers; they watch the commercials, they ask their parents to buy the products, and they use or consume the products. Not much research has been done with teenagers, but they seem to be more skeptical about advertisements.

In general, researchers seem to concur that television has become a major socializing agent of American children.

In addition to socialization, television influences how people think about the world around them or what is sometimes called their conceptions of "social reality." Studies have been carried out on the amount of fear and mistrust of other people, and on the prevalence of violence, sexism, family values, racial attitudes, illness in the population, criminal justice, and affluence. On the whole, it seems that television leads its viewers to have television-influenced attitudes. The studies on prevalence of violence and mistrust have consistent results: People who are heavy viewers of television are more apt to think the world is violent than are light viewers. They also trust other people less and believe that the world is a "mean and scary" place.

The Family and Interpersonal Relations

There are many television families — about 50 families can be seen weekly — and most of them resemble what people like to think of as the typical American family. The husbands tend to be companions to their wives and friends to their children; many of the wives stay home and take care of the house and children. Recently, however, on entertainment television there have been more divorces, more single-parent families, and more unmarried couples living together. In black families, there are more single parents and more conflict than in white families. The actual effects of these portrayals on family life have been the subject of practically no research.

Television, of course, takes place in the context of social relations, mainly in the family. Parents do not seem to restrict the amount of time their children spend in front of the television set, nor do they usually prevent them from looking at certain programs. They seldom discuss programs with their children except perhaps to make a few favorable comments now and then. Many families look at television together, which brings up the question of who decides what to look at. Usually the most powerful member of the family decides — father first, then mother, then older children. But, surprisingly often, parents defer to the wishes of their young children.

Television in American Society

Television seems to have brought about changes in society and its institutions. Television's effects on laws and norms have been the subject of discussion, but no firm conclusions have been reached. Television, according to some observers, reinforces the status quo and contributes to a homogenization of society and a promotion of middle-class values. Television's ubiquity in bringing events — especially violent and spectacular events — throughout the world to millions of people may mean that television itself is a significant factor in determining the events. Television broadcasts of religious services bring religion to those who cannot get out, but they also may reduce attendance at churches and thus, opportunities for social interactions. Television has certainly changed leisure time activities. For many people, leisure time means just about the same as television time; their off-duty hours are spent mainly in front of the television set. Many of these effects of television, however, are still speculative and need further research to provide more accurate and reliable information.

Education and Learning About Television

Parents, teachers, and others blame television for low grades and low scores on scholastic aptitude tests, but causal relationships are complex, as in television and violence, and they need careful analysis. Among adults, television viewing and education are inversely related: the less schooling, the more television viewing. Although children with low IQs watch television more than others, it is not known if heavy viewing lowers IQ scores or if those with low IQ choose to watch more television. There have been no experimental studies on these questions. Research on television and educational achievement has mixed findings. Some studies found higher achievement with more television viewing, while others found lower, and still others found no relation. There seems to be a difference at different ages. At the lower grades, children who watch a moderate amount of television get higher reading scores than those who watch either a great deal or very little. But at the high school level (a time when heavy viewing tends to be less common), reading scores are inversely related to amount of viewing, with the better readers watching less television.

In terms of educational aspiration, it appears that heavy viewers want high status job but do not intend to spend many years in school. For girls, there is even more potential for conflict between aspirations and plans; the girls who are heavy viewers usually want to get married, have children, and stay at home to take care of them, but at the same time they plan to remain in school and to have exciting careers.

Finally, one of the most significant developments of the decade is the rise of interest in television literacy, critical viewing skills, and intervention procedures. "Television literacy" is a way to counteract the possible deleterious effects of television and also to enhance its many benefits. Several curricula and television teaching guides have been prepared, containing lessons on all facets of television technology and programing — camera techniques, format, narratives, commercials, differences between reality and fantasy, television's effect on one's life, and so on. Use of these educational and intervention procedures has demonstrated that parents, children, and teachers can achieve much greater understanding of television and its effects, but whether this understanding changes their social behavior is not yet known. . . .

Violence and Aggression

Public interest and concern have long focused on the issue of violence on television. Attention to that issue began in the 1950s and has remained there ever since. Although the field of television and human behavior has gone far beyond the study of violence, many researchers are still committed to finding an answer to the question about the effects of televised violence on the viewer.

One reason for this continued commitment is that, despite all the research that has been done both for the report of the Surgeon General's advisory committee and since then, the conclusions are not completely unequivocal. While much of the research shows a causal relationship between televised violence and aggressive behavior, proponents of the "no effects" position, while in diminished number, continue to argue their case. . . .

EFFECTS OF TELEVISED VIOLENCE

The discussion about the effects of televised violence needs to be evaluated not only in the light of existing evidence but also in terms of how that evidence is to be assessed. Most of the researchers look at the totality of evidence and conclude, as did the Surgeon General's advisory committee, that the convergence of findings supports the conclusion of a causal relationship between televised violence and later aggressive behavior. The evidence now is drawn from a large body of literature. Adherents to this convergence approach agree that the conclusions reached in the Surgeon General's program have been significantly strengthened by more recent research. Not only has the evidence been augmented, but the processes by which the aggressive behavior is produced have been further examined.

In the past 10 years, several important field studies have found that televised violence results in aggressive behavior. Here are some examples:

A study funded by the Columbia Broadcasting System reported that teenage boys in London, according to their own accounts of their activities, were more likely to engage in "serious violence" after [being] exposed to television violence.

Two independent studies by the same investigators followed 3- and 4-year-old children over a year's time and correlated their television viewing at home with the various types of behavior they showed during free-play periods at daycare centers. In each study there were consistent associations between heavy television viewing of violent programs and unwarranted aggressive behavior in their free play. It was concluded that, for these preschool children, watching violence on television was a cause of heightened aggressiveness.

In a 5-year study of 732 children, several kinds of aggression — conflict with parents, fighting, and delinquency — were all positively correlated with the total amount of television viewing, not just viewing of violent programs.

Two additional studies were able to compare aggressiveness in children before and after their communities had television. In one study there was a significant increase in both verbal and physical aggression following the introduction of television. In the other study, after the introduction of television, aggressiveness increased in those children who looked at it a great deal.

Another long-term study currently has been collecting extensive data on children in several countries. Results are available for grade-school children in the United States, Finland, and Poland. In all three countries, a positive relationship was found between television violence and aggression in both boys and girls. In previous studies by these investigators, the relationship was found only for boys. The sheer amount of television viewing, regardless of the kind of program, was the best predictor of aggression.

Two other field studies reported similar results with different groups of children. One on teenagers found that those who perceived a program as violent or who thought that violence is an acceptable way to achieve a goal were more violent than the others. The other study reported that the positive correlations between violence and aggression in English school children were just about the same as in American school children.

In contrast, in a large scale study sponsored by the National Broadcasting Company a group of researchers reached a different conclusion. In this technically sophisticated panel study, data were collected on several hundred elementary school boys and girls and teenage high school boys. For the elementary school children, measurements of aggression were taken six times during a 3-year period, and for the high school boys the measurements were taken five times. The elementary school children gave "peer nominations" of aggression, and the teenagers gave "self reports." Both the elementary school children and the teenagers reported on which television programs they watched, and, for purposes of the analyses, the investigators picked those programs that could be classified as violent. The results showed that for the measures of violence on television and aggressive behavior taken at the same time, there were small but positive correlations. This is consistent with other cross-sectional survey results. But, when the measurements taken at different times were compared, no relationship was found. These investigators wanted to learn whether the short-term effects of television would accumulate over time and produce stable patterns of aggressive behavior in the real world. They found: the study did not provide evidence that television violence was causally implicated in the development of aggressive behavior patterns in children and adolescents over the time periods studied.

But according to many researchers, the evidence accumulated in the 1970s seems overwhelming that televised violence and aggression are positively correlated in children. The issue now is what processes produce the relation. Four such processes have been suggested; observational learning, attitude changes, physiological arousal, and justification processes.

Observational Learning

Proponents of the observational learning theory hold that children learn to behave aggressively from the violence they see on television in the same way they learn cognitive and social skills from watching their parents, siblings, peers, teachers, and others. Laboratory studies have demonstrated many times that children imitate aggressive behavior immediately after they have seen it on film or television, but there are still questions about the role of observational learning in field studies. What do the data show? A longitudinal study published in 1977 gave the first substantial evidence that observational learning is the most plausible explanation for the positive relation between televised violence and aggressive behaviors. Several other observational and field studies agree with these results. Although these studies can be criticized on methodological grounds — and, indeed, the "clean" outcomes of laboratory experiments are rarely found in field studies — they nevertheless are important supports for the learning of behaviors from the observations of models.

Researchers have also analyzed specific issues related to observational learning. In the first place, if children see someone rewarded for doing certain things, more likely they also will perform these acts. Thus, if children see a television character rewarded for aggressive behavior, they will probably imitate that behavior. If the actor is punished, the children are less apt to imitate the aggressive behavior. These vicarious reinforcements — either reward or punishment — can influence the behavior's occurrence. The persistence of the behavior, however, seems to be related to the children's own reinforcement, in other words, if the children themselves are rewarded or punished.

Observational learning may be related to age. Some investigators say that, by the time children reach their teens, behavior may no longer be affected significantly by observational learning. Young children, however, who do not see the relation between the aggression and the motives for it, may be more prone to imitate the aggressive behavior. Children start to imitate what they see on television when they are very young, some as early as 2-years-old.

Identification with the actor or actress whose behavior is being imitated is also thought to be important, but the evidence is not clear-cut. For example, it has been shown that both boys and girls are more likely to imitate male than female characters, and the males are the more aggresive. Girls who are aggressive may, it is true, identify more with the men characters. When children were asked to try to think in the same way as an aggressive character, they become more aggressive. It appears that there are no simple relations between observational learning and identification.

Another approach had been to tie the observational learning to specific cues on the programs, even apparently irrelevant cues. A tragic case from real life is the incident of a gang who burned a woman to death after a similar event occurred on a television show. In both the show and the real incident, the person was carrying a red gasoline can.

If these ideas about observational learning are analyzed in cognitive-processing terms, it can be hypothesized that children encode what they see and hear and then store it in their memories. To be encoded, the behavior must be salient or noticeable, and, to be retrieved in future behavior, it must be rehearsed with the same cues as those in the first observation present. If a child rehearses aggressive acts by daydreaming about them or uses them in make-believe play, the probability is increased that these acts will occur. There is some evidence that aggressive fantasies are related to aggressive acts.

These hypotheses are relevant to another theory, namely, disinhibition. In disinhibition theory, it is assumed that children and others are inhibited by training and experience from being aggressive. But if they see a lot of violence on television, they lose their inhibitions — they are disinhibited. This is an interesting idea, but some theorists say that cognitive-processing theory does not need to call upon disinhibition functions to explain observational learning, even though disinhibition probably occurs. Rather, if children see a great deal of aggressive behavior on television, they will store and retrieve that behavior for future action.

Attitude Change

Watching television influences people's attitudes. The more television children watch, the more accepting they are of aggressive behavior. It has been shown that persons who often watch television tend to be more suspicious and distrustful of others, and they also think there is more violence in the world than do those who do not watch much television.

Attitudes in psychological theory are "attributions, rules, and explanations" that people gradually learn from observations of behavior. Therefore, it can be assumed that, if someone watches a lot of television, attitudes will be built up on the basis of what is seen, and the attitudes will, in turn, have an effect on behavior. A clever experiment showed how the television movie *Roots* changed attitudes and subsequent behavior. Unruly behavior of white and black high school students was recorded

375

before, during, and after the show was broadcast. During the week that *Roots* was shown, the black students were more unruly, as measured by after-school detentions. This change was interpreted to mean that the black students had a change in attitudes toward obedience after watching *Roots*.

Looking at violent scenes for even a very brief time makes young children more willing to accept aggressive behavior of other children. This acceptance of aggression makes it likely that the children will themselves be more aggressive.

Other studies have shown that children's attitudes are changed if adults discuss the program. In an experimental study, one group of children who regularly watched violent programs were shown excerpts from violent shows and then took part in sessions about the unreality of television violence and wrote essays about it. The other group who also watched many violent programs were shown nonviolent excerpts, followed by a discussion of the content. The group who saw the violent television and then took part in the sessions on unreality were much less aggressive than the other group.

Arousal Processes

Processes involving physiological arousal are thought to have three possible consequences. One is desensitization. For example boys who regularly looked at violent programs showed less physiological arousal when they looked at new violent programs. Another possibility is that merely the increase of general arousal level will boost aggressiveness. A third alternative suggests that people seek an optimal level of arousal; aggressive behavior is arousing, and the persons who are desensitized may act aggressively to raise their levels of arousal. Then, once the desired level is reached, aggression will continue, because the behavior most likely to be continued is the behavior readily retrievable from memory. All these theories need more empirical verification.

Justification Processes

In the justification theory, it is assumed that people who are already aggressive like to look at violent television programs because they can then justify their own behavior, even if only to themselves. They can believe that they are acting like a favorite television hero. In this theory, watching televised violence is a result, rather than a cause, of aggressive behavior. So little research has been done on this theory that it cannot be evaluated.

Catharsis Theory

Contrary to these four theories is the catharsis theory, which predicts that aggression will be reduced after watching violence on television. Supposedly through catharsis, the need or desire to be aggressive is dissipated by looking at violence on television. Since practically all the evidence points to an increase in aggressive behavior, rather than a decrease, the theory is contradicted by the data.

In general, it appears that observational learning and attitude changes are the most likely explanations of television's effects on aggressive behavior. . . .

In conclusion, the interesting characteristics of violence on television are its overall stability and regularity, despite fluctuations by networks, genre, and time. The percentage of programs containing violence has remained about the same since 1967, although the number of violent acts per program has increased. Children's shows are violent in a cyclical way, up one year and down the next.

The amount of violence on television, according to some researchers, will almost certainly remain about the same as it has been, and they do not call for its total elimination. The concern is more with the kinds of violence, who commits violence, and who is victimized, because these portrayals may be critical mechanisms of social control.

The cultivation analysis aspects of the Cultural Indicators Project has a basic thesis that the more time viewers spend watching television, the more they will conceive the world to be similar to television portrayals. Thus, as stated in the discussion of attitude change, people who view a great deal of television — and who consequently see a great deal of violence — are more likely to view the world as a mean and scary place. These heavy viewers also exhibit more fear, mistrust, and apprehension than do light viewers. Because there are more victims than there are aggressors, this finding may ultimately be of more significance than the direct relationship between televised violence and aggression. . . .

Implications for the Eighties

It is now time to look at the total array of research on television and behavior in the 1970s and to discern the import and implications for the coming decade.

First, an impressive body of scientific knowledge has been accumulated since 1972, when the report of the Surgeon General's Advisory Committee was published. Some 3,000 reports, papers, and books have been published. The number of scientists engaged in research on television began to proliferate as a result of the report of the Surgeon General's committee, and the number has continued to grow. Yet, in relation to the magnitude of the research field and the many questions to which answers are urgently needed, the number of scientists involved in the study of television is still miniscule [sic] compared with other research specialists. If the momentum of research productivity achieved in the 1970s is to continue into the 1980s, the number will have to be increased. . . .

The research findings of the past decade have reaffirmed the powerful influence of television on the viewers. Almost all the evidence testifies to television's role as a formidable educator whose effects are both pervasive and cumulative. Television can no longer be considered as a casual part of daily life, as an electronic toy. Research findings have long since destroyed the illusion that television is merely innocuous entertainment. While the learning it provides is mainly incidental rather than direct and formal, it is a significant part of the total acculturation process. Furthermore, indications are that future technological developments in programming, distribution, and television usage will probably increase television's potential influence on the viewer.

Extending over all other findings is the fact that television is so large a part of daily life. Within American society, television is now a universal phenomenon. About half the present population never knew a world without it. Television is, in short, an American institution. It has changed or influenced most other institutions, from the family to the functioning of the government. . . .

In contrast to previous research, the bulk of the current findings no longer focuses on specific cause-effect or input-output results. Television viewing is so entrenched in American daily life that it can only be regarded as a major socializing influence almost comparable to the family, the schools, the church, and other socializing institutions. Socialization can be thought of as the accumulation of the many specific learning experiences throughout one's life. It is not limited to the developing child, although children have an especially strong need to acquire knowledge and skills as they grow up. But at any age, a person represents the product of cumulative learning, and thinking and behavior are affected by a mixture of recent learning and of learning earlier in life. As people go through life-cycle transitions, the importance of television changes for them. Old people, for example, are more like very young people in their use of television than they are like middle-age adults. Further studies of socialization and general learning from television need be continued with children and expanded to include the entire lifespan.

HEALTH

With television a central feature of daily life, it is somewhat surprising that little attention has been given to its influences on physical and mental health. Television's portrayals [sic] of mentally ill persons as often being either violent or victimized is particularly unfortunate, because it may be contributing to the well-known stigma borne by those suffering from mental illness. The widespread consumption of alcoholic beverages on television, together with the fact that such consumption is presented as a pleasant aspect of social life with no deleterious consequences, may also be fostering attitudes and subsequent behavior that reinforce the use of alcohol by viewers. Similarly, the portrayals of snacks and other nonnutritious foods may be affecting eating habits, especially those of children. Health portrayals on television thus are distorted frequently and have the possibility of unwittingly encouraging poor health. But the fact that very little smoking appears on television is noteworthy and perhaps an indication that television has been responsive to an important health problem. Other efforts to eliminate depictions detrimental to good health would not inhibit the dramatic impact of the programs and could have positive social consequences.

Another area, perhaps more difficult to implement, would be the possibility of programming for special populations, such as institutionalized individuals in psychiatric settings, in homes for the elderly, and in hospitals. This kind of programming offers an excellent opportunity for constructive change.

In the 1980s, it can be predicted that there will be increased use of television for health campaigns. Such campaigns should be very carefully planned and the more recent theories and practices of evaluation research applied to them. Campaigns can be a valuable resource to improve the Nation's health, but they require at least the talent and financial backing that go into making a good commercial.

There have been no attempts to assess in systematic studies the direct effect of television viewing on health. For example, the passivity of television viewing has not been studied in connection with physical fitness of children and adults. The relationship, if any, of the amount of physical exercise to the amount of viewing is not known, nor is there any clue concerning whether early and continued heavy viewing establishes enduring patterns of passive, rather than active, participation in daily life. Eating behavior during television viewing could be significant. For example, eating junk foods while watching television is common, and it is possible that some adults link television viewing with drinking wine and beer. The cumulative effects of these conditioned eating and drinking patterns might have serious long-term effects.

Television as a stressor needs to be studied. At times, it can be stress reducing and at other times stress enhancing. The noise levels of television may operate as a chronic stressor for some persons. It is not known whether stress can be induced by the synergistic effect of television arousal and other psychosocial variables that may be operating.

There is a dearth of studies on the psychophysiological implications of television watching. Possible areas for research, to name only a few, include sleep and sleep disturbances, autonomic nervous system functioning, rigorous studies on brain lateralization, biological rhythms, and perhaps even on neurotransmitters, all as related to television....

COGNITIVE PROCESSES

Several issues have emerged from the innovative research on cognitive processes in the 1970s, all with implications for continued research into the 1980s.

Children growing up with television must learn cognitive strategies for dealing with the medium. At very early ages, children already demonstrate active and selective viewing strategies, for example, watching animation, turning away from dialog they do not understand, turning back when music or sound effects suggest lively action or "pixillation" (animated activity). Age factors as well as properties of the medium interact to determine how children develop useful viewing strategies.

Television differs from real life by using structural symbols or codes that may be difficult to understand. A character who is remembering things from the past may fade out of view, and actual past scenes then show the character's memories. Children at young ages may not recognize these "flashback" conventions and be confused. Conventions, such as split screens (screen divided into two parts with a different picture on each part), may not be understood, and magical effects, for example, superheroes leaping over buildings, may be taken literally. While children eventually learn television conventions and viewing strategies and incorporate some of them into more general thinking, there are suggestions that some forms of presentation are more effective than others in helping children to learn the television codes and also in enhancing general cognitive effectiveness.

Age differences are highly significant in television viewing. These differences, which themselves reflect differences in conceptual capacities (for example, the inability of preschoolers to engage in conversation), lead to sizable differences in how much sense children can make of stories on television. Structural factors, such as rapid shifts of scene, may lead young children to misunderstand the intended plots, to overemphasize the more obvious features of a story (for example, violence), and to be confused about causality. The fact that young children do not easily relate consequences to earlier actions makes the adult interpretation of the story quite different from that of the child. The contention is often made that children's programs, or adult programs watched by children, really are prosocial programs because the "bad guy" gets punished at the end. What is not recognized in this argument is the critical fact that young children simply do not see the relation between the punishment and the earlier antisocial behavior. This finding can be generalized to include a large number of other age-specific responses to, and attributes of, television viewing. The dilemma — and the challenge — raised by these research findings is that it is difficult to produce programs that simultaneously satisfy the needs and capabilities of a widely diverse audience.

Although there is some evidence that young children's imaginativeness and the stories they use in spontaneous play are enhanced by television materials, the predominant evidence suggests that heavy viewing is associated with lower imagination and less creativity. Under special circumstances with carefully designated programing and with adult mediation, children can increase their spontaneous playfulness, imagination, and enjoyment after television viewing. There is reason to believe, however, that under conditions of unsupervised viewing children may not learn necessary distinctions between "realism" and "fantasy" in stories.

More research is needed to explore ways of presenting material that will maximize not only attention but also comprehension and reflective thought. . . .

EMOTIONAL DEVELOPMENT AND FUNCTIONING

Children show a wide range of emotional reactions to television. The evidence suggests that moderately rapid pacing leads to arousal and enjoyment in children. For adolescents and young adults, a good balance of lively pace and some (but not too much) humor may enhance attention and comprehension. There is not yet adequate evidence to support some current beliefs that children have been led by lively television programing to be inattentive to verbal presentations and detailed material presented in the classroom. While children can learn to be more emphatic and to express or understand emotions from television presentations with guidance from adults, the data on heavy viewing suggest that they tend to be less empathic or to show negative reactions, such as unhappy or fearful emotions. . . .

VIOLENCE AND AGGRESSION

Recent research confirms the earlier findings of a causal relationship between viewing televised violence and later aggressive behavior. A distinction must be made, however, between groups and individuals. All the studies that support the causal relationships demonstrate group differences. None supports the case for particular individuals. As with most statistical analyses of complex phenomena, group trends do not predict individual or isolated events. This distinction does not, of course, minimize the significance of the findings, even though it delimits their applicability. Moreover, no single study unequivocally confirms the conclusion that televised violence leads to aggressive behavior. Similarly, no single study unequivocally refutes that conclusion. The scientific support for the causal relationship derives from the convergence of findings from many studies, the great majority of which demonstrate a positive relationship between televised violence and later aggressive behavior.

During the 1970s, research on violence and aggression yielded interesting new information. Recent studies have extended the age range in which the relationship between televised violence and aggressive behavior can be demonstrated. Earlier research had been primarily with children from 8 to 13 years old. The evidence has now been extended to include preschoolers at one end of the age spectrum and older adolescents at the other. In addition, most of the earlier studies had indicated that boys, but not girls, were influenced by watching televised violence, while recent research in both the United States and other countries shows similar relationships in samples of girls as well as boys.

Despite some argument about how to measure the amount of television violence, the level of violence on commercial television has not markedly decreased since the Surgeon General's committee published its report. What this means for the 1980s is difficult to discern. If one extrapolates from the past 20 years, it can be predicted that violence on television will continue to be about the same. Yet there may be various social forces and groups that will work to bring about a diminution.

Research evidence accumulated during the past decade suggests that the viewer learns more than aggressive behavior from televised violence. The viewer learns to be a victim and to identify with victims. As a result, many heavy viewers may exhibit fear and apprehension, while other heavy viewers may be influenced toward aggressive behavior. Thus, the effects of televised violence may be even more extensive than suggested by earlier studies, and they may be exhibited in more subtle forms of behavior than aggression. . . .

PROSOCIAL BEHAVIOR AND SOCIALIZATION

Potentially, as research suggests, children (and to some degree adults) can learn constructive social behavior, for example, helpfulness, cooperation, friendliness, and imaginative play, from television viewing, especially if adults help them grasp the material or reinforce the program content. It is less certain whether these positive benefits are actually being achieved, since analyses of television content and form suggest that such potentially useful material is embedded in a complicated format and is viewed at home by children under circumstances not conducive to effective generalization. Additional research is required to determine the conditions under which prosocial behavior is most likely to be learned.

If almost everybody is learning from television, the question of television's influence needs to be rephrased in terms not only of what specific content is acquired but of what constraints or qualifications television imposes on people's learning capacities. Thus, television content reflecting certain stereotypes may limit or distort how people view women, ethnic groups, or the elderly, for example, and how people interpret the extent to which there are dangers that confront them in daily life. . . .

EDUCATIONAL ACHIEVEMENT AND ASPIRATION

The evidence now supports the opinion that heavy television viewing tends to displace time required to practice reading, writing, and other school-learning skills. These effects are particularly noticeable for children from middle socioeconomic levels who might in the past have spent more time in practicing reading. Television on the whole also seems to interfere with educational aspirations. The cultivation effects leading to increased cognitive skills and educational aspirations in heavy-viewing girls from lower socioeconomic levels are evident, suggesting that amount of viewing may influence social class or IQ groups differently. Unfortunately, studies examining the value of specific types of programing for reading interest and skill development have not been carried out.

The sheer attractiveness of television may preempt other activities which were part of daily life, such as sports or hobbies, social activities like playing cards, and, for children, studying and homework activity. Thus the medium's pervasive attraction may also be interfering with certain social and cognitive skill developments formerly acquired through direct exchanges between people or through reading. In this sense, television viewing may be influencing how people learn generally, not only from watching television.

CRITICAL VIEWING SKILLS

Recognition of the pervasiveness of television has led during the past decade to the beginnings of a new effort to teach children and others to understand the medium. Several school curricula have been constructed. Programs for elementary school children that include teacher-taught lessons, sometimes with videotape segments to enhance effectiveness, have been tested increasingly in the schools. Accumulating evidence suggests that such educational programs are welcomed by teachers and pupils and that the programs do produce changes in awareness of television production, special effects, the nature of commercials, the excesses of violence, and so on. Longer term effects of genuine critical viewing at home or of reduced viewing or more selective viewing have yet to be demonstrated. Teaching about television is considered by many television researchers to be one of the most significant practical developments of the 1970s, one that needs to be continued, expanded, and evaluated in the 1980s.

NEW TECHNOLOGIES

The report of the Surgeon General's committee predicted that new technologies would result in many changes in television programing and viewing. These changes were slow in coming, but it appears that they will be made in the 1980s. Cable television and videodiscs may gradually alter the content of entertainment television. They also may make it feasible to have different programing for various special populations. Interactive television is considered by many people to be a desirable advance because it will require greater effort and thus result in more effective learning.

Ten years ago, the report of the Surgeon General's committee led to significant increases in the research on television and behavior. This research also expanded in many directions from the original focus on the effects of televised violence. Now, 10 years after the appearance of that report, it is clear that research on television is still growing and expanding and that the research in the 1970s has opened new vistas and posed new questions. Compared with the 1970s, the decade of the 1980s should witness an even greater intensity of necessary research effort on television and behavior.

REAGAN PROPOSAL
FOR ARMS REDUCTION
May 9, 1982

In a commencement speech at his alma mater, Eureka College in Eureka, Ill., President Reagan shifted markedly his previous confrontational stance against the Soviet Union by proposing the opening of Strategic Arms Reduction Talks (START) between the United States and Moscow.

After leveling a series of criticisms against the Soviet Union, including the charge that it was increasing the threat of nuclear war, Reagan softened the tone of his speech to offer the START proposal. "The focus of our efforts," he said, "will be to reduce significantly the most destabilizing systems, the ballistic missiles, the number of warheads they carry, and their overall destructive potential." He added he hoped the arms talks could begin by the end of June, and it was announced later that they were scheduled to begin June 29.

The Eureka College speech marked the president's second major initiative in nuclear arms reduction. In November 1981 Reagan had proposed his "zero-option" plan, offering to cancel U.S. plans to deploy intermediate-range nuclear missiles in Europe if the Soviets would dismantle similar weapons aimed at Western European targets. (Zero-option speech, Historic Documents of 1981, p. 823)

The first phase of the START talks, according to Reagan, would involve a one-third reduction by both countries in the number of warheads on long-range land-based missiles (ICBMs) and submarine-launched missiles. "To enhance stability, I would ask that no more than half of those warheads be land-based," he said.

According to administration officials, the United States and the Soviet Union each maintained about 7,500 missile warheads. However, because ICBMs made up a larger percentage of the Soviet arsenal as compared with that of the United States, the Soviets would be required to make greater reductions in this area.

During the second stage of the START process, the president said, both countries would seek to lower and equalize the "throw weight" (a measure of the total weight of nuclear warheads that missiles can carry) of their respective arsenals. Because the average size of the Soviet ICBMs was much larger, the Russians surpassed the United States by a ratio of almost 3-1 in the "throw weight" category.

Differences existed within the Reagan administration as to whether arms reductions should be negotiated on the basis of number of missiles or on the basis of "throw weight." Reportedly, Secretary of Defense Caspar W. Weinberger favored the "throw weight" approach, while Secretary of State Alexander M. Haig Jr. favored limiting the number of missiles first.

Following the president's speech, speculation centered on whether Reagan was responding to pressures from the nuclear freeze movement in Europe and the United States, in preparation for his visit to several European capitals in June. European leaders had complained that the United States was being too tough-minded in its dealings with the Soviet Union, and the Reagan speech seemed geared toward calming fears that he might be leading the Western alliance in the direction of war.

On Capitol Hill, two sponsors of a nuclear freeze resolution — Sen. Edward M. Kennedy, D-Mass., and Sen. Mark O. Hatfield, R-Ore., — argued that the START proposal would not stop the drive within the administration to modernize U.S. nuclear weapons, including building the MX missile and B-1 bomber.

>*Following are excerpts from President Reagan's speech proposing Strategic Arms Reduction Talks, delivered May 9, 1982, at Eureka College. (Boldface headings in brackets have been added by Congressional Quarterly to highlight the organization of the text.):*

... In about a month I will meet in Europe with the leaders of nations who are our closest friends and allies. At Versailles, leaders of the industrial powers of the world will seek better ways to meet today's economic challenges. In Bonn, I will join my colleagues from the Atlantic Alliance nations to renew those ties which have been the foundation of Western, free-world defense for 37 years. There will also be meetings in Rome and London.

Now, these meetings are significant for a simple but very important reason. Our own Nation's fate is directly linked to that of our sister democracies in Western Europe. The values for which America and all democratic nations stand represent the culmination of Western culture. Andrei Sakharov, the distinguished Nobel Laureate and courageous Soviet human rights advocate, has written in a message smuggled to freedom, "I believe in Western man. I have faith in his mind which is practical and efficient and, at the same time, aspires to great goals. I have faith in his good intentions and in his decisiveness."

This glorious tradition requires a partnership to preserve and protect it. Only as partners can we hope to achieve the goal of a peaceful community of nations. Only as partners can we defend the values of democracy and human dignity that we hold so dear.

There's a single, major issue in our partnership which will underlie the discussions that I will have with the European leaders: the future of Western relations with the Soviet Union. How should we deal with the Soviet Union in the years ahead? What framework should guide our conduct and our policies toward it? And what can we realistically expect from a world power of such deep fears, hostilities, and external ambitions?

I believe the unity of the West is the foundation for any successful relationship with the East. Without Western unity, we'll squander our energies in bickering while the Soviets continue as they please. With unity, we have the strength to moderate Soviet behavior. We've done so in the past and we can do so again.

Our challenge is to establish a framework in which sound East-West relations will endure. I'm optimistic that we can build a more constructive relationship with the Soviet Union. To do so, however, we must understand the nature of the Soviet system and the lessons of the past.

[Soviet Empire]

The Soviet Union is a huge empire ruled by an elite that holds all power and all privilege, and they hold it tightly because, as we've seen in Poland, they fear what might happen if even the smallest amount of control slips from their grasp. They fear the infectiousness of even a little freedom and because of this in many ways their system has failed. The Soviet empire is faltering because it is rigid — centralized control has destroyed incentives for innovation, efficiency, and individual achievement. Spiritually, there is a sense of malaise and resentment.

But in the midst of social and economic problems, the Soviet dictatorship has forged the largest armed force in the world. It has done so by pre-empting the human needs of its people, and, in the end, this course will undermine the foundations of the Soviet system. Harry Truman was right when he said of the Soviets that, "When you try to conquer other people or extend yourself over vast areas you cannot win in the long run."

Yet Soviet aggressiveness has grown as Soviet military power has increased. To compensate, we must learn from the lessons of the past. When the West has stood unified and firm, the Soviet Union has taken heed. For 35 years Western Europe has lived free despite the shadow of

Soviet military might. Through unity . . . the West secured the withdrawal of occupation forces from Austria and the recognition of its rights in Berlin.

Other Western policies have not been successful. East-West trade was expanded in the hope of providing incentives for Soviet restraint, but the Soviets exploited the benefits of trade without moderating their behavior. Despite a decade of ambitious arms control efforts, the Soviet buildup continues. And despite its signature of the Helsinki agreements on human rights, the Soviet Union has not relaxed its hold on its own people or those of Western [Eastern] Europe.

During the 1970's, some of us forgot the warning of President Kennedy who said that the Soviets "have offered to trade us an apple for an orchard. We don't do that in this country." But we came perilously close to doing just that.

If East-West relations in the détente era in Europe have yielded disappointment, détente outside of Europe has yielded a severe disillusionment for those who expected a moderation of Soviet behavior. The Soviet Union continues to support Vietnam in its occupation of Kampuchea and its massive military presence in Laos. It is engaged in a war of aggression against Afghanistan. Soviet proxy forces have brought instability and conflict to Africa and Central America.

We are now approaching an extremely important phase in East-West relations as the current Soviet leadership is succeeded by a new generation. Both the current and the new Soviet leadership should realize aggressive policies will meet a firm Western response. On the other hand, a Soviet leadership devoted to improving its people's lives, rather than expanding its armed conquests, will find a sympathetic partner in the West. The West will respond with expanded trade and other forms of cooperation. But all of this depends on Soviet actions. Standing in the Athenian marketplace 2,000 years ago, Demosthenes said: "What sane man would let another man's words rather than his deeds proclaim who is at peace and who is at war with him?"

Peace is not the absence of conflict, but the ability to cope with conflict by peaceful means. I believe we can cope. I believe that the West can fashion a realistic, durable policy that will protect our interests and keep the peace, not just for this generation, but for your children and your grandchildren.

I believe such a policy consists of five points: military balance, economic security, regional stability, arms reductions, and dialog. Now, these are the means by which we can seek peace with the Soviet Union in the years ahead. Today, I want to set this five-point program to guide the future of our East-West relations, set it out for all to hear and see.

[Military Balance and Economic Security]

First, a sound East-West military balance is absolutely essential. Last week NATO published a comprehensive comparison of its forces with those of the Warsaw Pact. Its message is clear. During the past decade, the Soviet Union has built up its forces across the board. During that same period, the defense expenditures of the United States declined in real terms. The United States has already undertaken steps to recover from that decade of neglect. And I should add that the expenditures of our European allies have increased slowly but steadily, something we often fail to recognize here at home.

The second point on which we must reach consensus with our allies deals with economic security. Consultations are under way among Western nations on the transfer of militarily significant technology and the extension of financial credits to the East, as well as on the question of energy dependence on the East, that energy dependence of Europe. We recognize that some of our allies' economic requirements are distinct from our own. But the Soviets must not have access to Western technology with military applications, and we must not subsidize the Soviet economy. The Soviet Union must make the difficult choices brought on by its military budgets and economic shortcomings.

[Regional Stability]

The third element is regional stability with peaceful change. Last year in a speech in Philadelphia and in the Summit meetings at Cancún, I outlined the basic American plan to assist the developing world. These principles for economic development remain the foundation of our approach. They represent no threat to the Soviet Union. Yet in many areas of the developing world we find that Soviet arms and Soviet-supported troops are attempting to destabilize societies and extend Moscow's influence.

High on our agenda must be progress toward peace in Afghanistan. The United States is prepared to engage in a serious effort to negotiate an end to the conflict caused by the Soviet invasion of that country. We are ready to cooperate in an international effort to resolve this problem, to secure a full Soviet withdrawal from Afghanistan, and to ensure self-determination for the Afghan people.

In southern Africa, working closely with our Western allies and the African States, we've made real progress toward independence for Namibia. These negotiations, if successful, will result in peaceful and secure conditions throughout southern Africa. The simultaneous withdrawal of Cuban forces from Angola is essential to achieving Namibian independence, as well as creating long-range prospects for peace in the region.

Central America also has become a dangerous point of tension in East-West relations. The Soviet Union cannot escape responsibility for the violence and suffering in the region caused by its support for Cuban activities in Central America and its accelerated transfer of advanced military equipment to Cuba.

However, it was in Western Europe — or Eastern Europe, I should say — that the hopes of the 1970's were greatest, and it's there that they have

been the most bitterly disappointed. There was hope that the people of
Poland could develop a freer society. But the Soviet Union has refused to
allow the people of Poland to decide their own fate, just as it refused to allow the people of Hungary to decide theirs in 1956, or the people of
Czechoslovakia in 1968.

If martial law in Poland is lifted, if all the political prisoners are
released, and if a dialog is restored with the Solidarity Union, the United
States is prepared to join in a program of economic support. Water
cannons and clubs against the Polish people are hardly the kind of dialog
that gives us hope. It is up to the Soviets and their client regimes to show
good faith by concrete actions.

[Arms Reduction]

The fourth point is arms reduction. I know that this weighs heavily on
many of your minds. In our 1931 *Prism*, we quoted Carl Sandburg, who in
his own beautiful way quoted the Mother Prairie, saying, "Have you seen a
red sunset drip over one of my cornfields, the shore of night stars, the wave
lines of dawn up a wheat valley?" What an idyllic scene that paints in our
minds — and what a nightmarish prospect that a huge mushroom cloud
might someday destroy such beauty. My duty as President is to ensure
that the ultimate nightmare never occurs, that the prairies and the cities
and the people who inhabit them remain free and untouched by nuclear
conflict.

I wish more than anything there were a simple policy that would
eliminate that nuclear danger. But there are only difficult policy choices
through which we can achieve a stable nuclear balance at the lowest
possible level.

I do not doubt that the Soviet people, and, yes, the Soviet leaders have
an overriding interest in preventing the use of nuclear weapons. The Soviet
Union within the memory of its leaders has known the devastation of total
conventional war and knows that nuclear war would be even more
calamitous. Yet, so far, the Soviet Union has used arms control negotiations primarily as an instrument to restrict U.S. defense programs and, in
conjunction with their own arms buildup, a means to enhance Soviet power
and prestige.

Unfortunately, for some time suspicions have grown that the Soviet
Union has not been living up to its obligations under existing arms control
treaties. There is conclusive evidence the Soviet Union has provided toxins
to the Laotians and Vietnamese for use against defenseless villagers in
Southeast Asia. And the Soviets themselves are employing chemical
weapons on the freedom fighters in Afghanistan.

We must establish firm criteria for arms control in the 1980's if we're to
secure genuine and lasting restraint on Soviet military programs throughout arms control. We must seek agreements which are verifiable, equitable,
and militarily significant. Agreements that provide only the appearance of
arms control breed dangerous illusions.

Last November, I committed the United States to seek significant reductions on nuclear and conventional forces. In Geneva, we have since proposed limits on U.S. and Soviet intermediate-range missiles, including the complete elimination of the most threatening systems on both sides. In Vienna, we're negotiating, together with our allies, for reductions of conventional forces in Europe. In the 40-nation Committee on Disarmament, the United Nations [United States] seeks a total ban on all chemical weapons.

Since the first days of my administration, we've been working on our approach to the crucial issue of strategic arms and the control and negotiations for control of those arms with the Soviet Union. The study and analysis required has been complex and difficult. It had to be undertaken deliberately, thoroughly, and correctly. We've laid a solid basis for these negotiations. We're consulting with Congressional leaders and with our allies, and we are now ready to proceed.

The main threat to peace posed by nuclear weapons today is the growing instability of the nuclear balance. This is due to the increasingly destructive potential of the massive Soviet buildup in its ballistic missile force.

Therefore, our goal is to enhance deterrence and achieve stability through significant reductions in the most destabilizing nuclear systems, ballistic missiles, and especially the giant intercontinental ballistic missiles, while maintaining a nuclear capability sufficient to deter conflict, to underwrite our national security and to meet our commitment to allies and friends.

[Strategic Arms Reduction Talks]

For the immediate future, I'm asking my START — and START really means — we've given up on SALT — START means "Strategic Arms Reduction Talks," and that negotiating team to propose to their Soviet counterparts a practical, phased reduction plan. The focus of our efforts will be to reduce significantly the most destabilizing systems, the ballistic missiles, the number of warheads they carry and their overall destructive potential.

At the first phase, or the end of the first phase of START, I expect ballistic missile warheads, the most serious threat we face, to be reduced to equal levels, equal ceilings, at least a third below the current levels. To enhance stability, I would ask that no more than half of those warheads be land-based. I hope that these warhead reductions, as well as significant reductions in missiles themselves, could be achieved as rapidly as possible.

In a second phase, we'll seek to achieve an equal ceiling on other elements of our strategic nuclear forces, including limits on the ballistic missile throw-weight at less than current American levels. In both phases, we shall insist on verification procedures to insure compliance with the agreement.

This, I might say, will be the twentieth time that we have sought such negotiations with the Soviet Union since World War II. The monumental task of reducing and reshaping our strategic forces to enhance stability will take many years of concentrated effort. But I believe that it will be possible to reduce the risks of war by removing the instabilities that now exist and by dismantling the nuclear menace.

I have written to President Brezhnev and directed Secretary Haig to approach the Soviet government concerning the initiation of formal negotiations on the reduction of strategic nuclear arms, START, at the earliest opportunity. We hope negotiations will begin by the end of June.

We will negotiate seriously, in good faith, and carefully consider all proposals made by the Soviet Union. If they approach these negotiations in the same spirit, I'm confident that together we can achieve an agreement of enduring value that reduces the number of nuclear weapons, halts the growth in strategic forces and opens the way to even more far-reaching steps in the future.

I hope the Commencement today will also mark the commencement of a new era, in both senses of the word a new start toward a more peaceful and secure world.

[East-West Talks]

The fifth and final point I propose for East-West relations is dialog. I've always believed that people's problems can be solved when people talk to each other instead of about each other. And I've already expressed my own desire to meet with President Brezhnev in New York next month. If this can't be done, I'd hope we could arrange a future meeting where positive results can be anticipated. And when we sit down, I'll tell President Brezhnev that the United States is ready to build a new understanding based upon the principles I've outlined today.

I'll tell him that his government and his people have nothing to fear from the United States. The free nations living at peace in the world community can vouch for the fact that we seek only harmony. And I'll ask President Brezhnev why our two nations can't practice mutual restraint. Why can't our peoples enjoy the benefits that would flow from real cooperation? Why can't we reduce the number of horrendous weapons?

Perhaps I should also speak to him of this school and these graduates who are leaving it today — of your hopes for the future, of your deep desire for peace, and yet your strong commitment to defend your values if threatened. Perhaps if he someday could attend such a ceremony as this, he'd better understand America. In the only system he knows, you would be here by the decision of government and on this day the government representatives would be here telling most, if not all, of you where you were going to report to work tomorrow.

But as we go to Europe for the talks and as we proceed in the important challenges facing this country, I want you to know that I will be thinking of you and of Eureka and what you represent. In one of my yearbooks, I remember reading that, "The work of the prairie is to be the soil for the growth of a strong Western culture." I believe Eureka is fulfilling that work. You, the members of the 1982 graduating class, are this year's harvest.

I spoke of the difference between our two countries. I try to follow the humor of the Russian people. We don't hear much about the Russian people. We hear about the Russian leaders. But you can learn a lot, because they do have a sense of humor, and you can learn from the jokes they're telling. And one of the most recent jokes I found kind of, well, personally interesting. Maybe you might — tell you something about your country.

The joke they tell is that an American and a Russian were arguing about the differences between our two countries. And the American said, "Look, in my country I can walk into the Oval Office; I can hit the desk with my fist and say, 'President Reagan, I don't like the way you're governing the United States.' " And the Russian said, "I can do that." The American said, "What?" He says, "I can walk into the Kremlin, into Brezhnev's office. I can pound Brezhnev's desk, and I can say, 'Mr. President, I don't like the way Ronald Reagan is governing the United States.' " (Laughter.)

Eureka as an institution and you as individuals are sustaining the best of Western man's ideals. As a fellow graduate and in the office I hold, I'll do my best to uphold these same ideals.

To the Class of '82, congratulations and God bless you.

▼▼▼

REAGAN ADMINISTRATION ON SECURITY STRATEGY

May 21, June 20, and August 23, 1982

Controversy over the Reagan administration's national security planning arose in late spring when a sensitive "guidance paper" was leaked to the press. Media and public attention focused on whether the administration's strategy included plans for a "protracted" nuclear war.

Before the existence of the paper became public knowledge, William P. Clark, in his first speech since becoming President Ronald Reagan's assistant for national security affairs, revealed the president's approval of a new military strategy. Clark, speaking May 21 at Georgetown University's Center for Strategic and International Studies, said U.S. forces need not engage those of the Soviet Union on all fronts at the same time in the event of war.

Drawing from a secret, eight-page National Security Decision Memorandum, Clark said that "any conflict with the Soviet Union could expand to global dimensions." The United States, he said, would "procure balanced forces and establish priorities for sequential operations to insure that military power would be applied in the most effective way on a priority basis."

Clark stressed that the main goal of the administration's global strategy was peace. He reiterated the administration's intention to keep any war limited in scope but warned that the decision to expand a conflict may not lie with the United States. "Therefore," he said, "U.S. forces must be capable of responding to a major attack with unmistakable global implications early on in any conflict."

Five-Year Defense Plan

Clark's speech was overshadowed on May 29 when The New York Times *published a detailed account of a classified five-year defense plan that had been leaked to the newspaper. The plan had been used as the basic source of the strategy outlined by Clark, according to the* Times. *The plan, "Fiscal Year 1984-1988 Defense Guidance," allegedly confirmed U.S. preparations for a protracted nuclear war. As reported in the* Times, *the document said that "United States forces might be required simultaneously in geographically separated theatres" and that "it is essential that the Soviet Union be confronted with the prospect of a major conflict should it seek to reach the oil resources of the Persian Gulf."*

The guidance paper formed the basis for the Defense Department's budget requests for fiscal years 1984-1988 and provided the overall strategy for proposed programs in the military budget. Emphasis was on the development and upgrading of a variety of new communications and intelligence systems and on preparation for conducting simultaneous war in different parts of the world.

The plan would give first priority to defense of the American homeland, second priority to Western Europe and the oil resources of the Persian Gulf and third priority to Asia and countries of the Western Pacific. Military assistance would be given to China to keep Soviet forces along the Chinese border tied down in case of war. Peacetime efforts would include implementing trade policies to put as much pressure as possible on the militarily burdened Soviet economy.

The document also described the U.S. plan to "decapitate" the Soviet Union by striking first at political and military leadership and communication lines in case of attack. Special operations (guerrilla warfare, sabotage, psychological warfare) would be upgraded and existing U.S. forces would be maintained for combat readiness.

The leaked document surfaced amidst congressional and popular debate over nuclear arms limitations. On May 26, 113 Roman Catholic bishops endorsed a resolution urging Reagan to begin nuclear arms freeze negotiations. On June 12 approximately three quarters of a million people gathered in New York City to protest the U.S. nuclear arms buildup. The demonstration was the largest disarmament rally in U.S. history. (Nuclear freeze movement, p. 885)

The leaked document added to the uproar over the administration's defense program, with opponents arguing that the plan would cause an escalation in the nuclear arms race. On July 21, 50 members of Congress wrote to Reagan protesting the administration's policy as outlined in the five-year plan. The letter said, "We are extremely alarmed with those sections of the guidance calling for planning to wage a protracted nuclear war. In our minds, such a strategy will result in a futile renewal of the nu-clear arms race in which neither side will relent."

Weinberger's Clarifications

On June 20 Weinberger was interviewed on the ABC news program, This Week. Questioned about U.S. plans to fight a protracted nuclear war, he said, "[T]he story was so wrong and it's caused so much trouble that I'm glad to have an opportunity to clear it up." The United States was not planning to launch a nuclear war, he said, but was trying to demonstrate to the Soviet Union the futility of such a plan. "[W]e are trying to acquire the capacity that will demonstrate that it cannot be won, and therefore deter it."

On August 23 Weinberger defended the administration's position further in a letter to newspaper editors around the world. The letter claimed that the leaked accounts of the five-year plan had been "completely inaccurate" and that "It is the first and foremost goal of this administration to take every step to ensure that nuclear weapons are never used again, for we do not believe there could be any winners in a nuclear war."

> *Following are excerpts from a speech by National Security Adviser William P. Clark, delivered at the Center for Strategic and International Studies, May 21, 1982; excerpts from an interview with Secretary of Defense Caspar W. Weinberger on ABC's This Week, June 20; and the text of Weinberger's letter to newspaper editors, dated August 23. (Boldface headings in brackets have been added by Congressional Quarterly to highlight the organization of the texts.):*

CLARK'S SPEECH

... [I]n early February of this year — February 5, to be exact — the President directed a review of our national security strategy. At that time our strategy was a collection of departmental policies which had been developed during the Administration's first year in office. The President wanted to review the results of that first year with decisions often being made at the departmental level, to see where we were, to make sure our various policies were consistent and to set the course for the future.

In particular, he wanted to make sure that any discussions we had with the leadership of Congress on reductions in our defense budget, any discussions with the leadership of the Soviet Union regarding arms reductions, were based both on a well thought-through and integrated strategy for preserving our national security. ...

Now that the work is done or at least the first major portion and we're at a plateau here today. We have come to several conclusions, I believe, seven.

First, the purpose of our strategy should be to preserve our institutions of freedom and democracy — to protect our citizens, to promote their economic well-being and to foster an international orderliness supportive of these institutions and these principles.

Second, we're confident that the policies of our first year have been internally consistent and that they do lay the groundwork for a strategy that will protect the security of the United States.

Third conclusion, a successful strategy must have diplomatic, political, economic, informational components built on a foundation of military strength.

Fourthly, our strategy must be forward looking and active. We must offer hope. As the President said last year at Notre Dame, collectivism and the subordination of the individual to the state is now perceived around the world as a bizarre and evil episode of history whose last pages are even now being written. We have something better to offer — namely freedom. To secure the America we all want and the global stability and prosperity we all seek, we cannot sit back and hope that somehow it all will happen. We must believe in what we're doing and that requires initiative, patience, persistence. We find we must be prepared to respond vigorously to opportunities as they arise and to create opportunities where they have not existed before. We must be steadfast in those efforts.

[Strategy Must Include Allies]

The fifth conclusion, ours must be a coalition strategy. We, together with our friends, our allies, must pull together. And that effort will certainly be evidenced as . . . the President proceeds on the third of June to Versailles, Rome, London, Bonn, Berlin, New York.

There's no other way, we must achieve an even closer linkage with regional allies and friends. Next month's NATO [North Atlantic Treaty Organization] summit is a case in point, of course. There may be a vocal minority questioning the basic assumptions of the Atlantic Alliance. It's not the first time, nor will it be the last. But when President Reagan and other NATO leaders meet in Bonn, there should be a strong reaffirmation of Alliance unity, vitality, and resolve. A strong, unified NATO remains indispensible for the protection of all of our Western interests.

The differences among NATO members involve shaping NATO, not whether there should be an Alliance. At Bonn, we will witness fundamental agreement on the need to strengthen our deterrent posture. We will see a balanced approach to arms control and NATO remains dedicated to the common task of preserving democracy.

Sixth, the economic component of our strategy is particularly important. We must promote a well-functioning international economic system with minimal distortion to trade and broadly agreed rules for resolving differences. . . .

The seventh and final conclusion, the maintenance of peace requires a strong, flexible, and responsive military. The rebuilding of our nation's defenses is now our urgent task.

[Defense Policy]

For obvious reasons, I cannot discuss the defense portion of our review in the detail that I did to select members of Congress this morning or perhaps in the detail that you might desire. I will try, however, to provide the highlights where I can, some degree of specificity.

Our interests are global and they conflict with those of the Soviet Union, a state which pursues worldwide policies, most unfriendly to our own. The Soviet Union maintains the most heavily armed military establishment in history and possesses the capability to project its military forces far beyond its own borders. It's a given that, of course, we have vital interests around the world, including maritime sea lanes of communication. The hard fact is that the military power of the Soviet Union is now able to threaten these vital interests as never before. The Soviet Union also complements its direct military capabilities with proxy forces and surrogates with extensive arms sales and grants by manipulation of terrorist and subversive organizations, and through support to a number of insurgencies and separatist movements — providing arms, advice, military training, political backing.

Our military force and those of our allies must protect our common interests in our increasingly turbulent environment. We must be prepared to deter attack and to defeat such attack when deterrence fail.

In this regard, the modernization of our strategic nuclear forces will receive first priority in our efforts to rebuild the military capabilities of the United States. Nuclear deterrence can only be achieved if our strategic nuclear posture makes Soviet assessment of the risks of war, under any contingency, so great as to remove any incentive for initiating attack.

The decisions reached on strategic nuclear forces, which the President announced last fall, remain the foundation of our policy. The highest priority was to be accorded to survivable strategic communications systems.

In addition we plan to modernize the manned bomber force, increase the accuracy and payload of our submarine launched ballistic missiles, add sea launched cruise missiles, improve strategic defenses, and deploy a new larger, more accurate land based ballistic missile.

The latter decision was reaffirmed by the President last Monday. He views the production of a modern ICBM, with the earliest possible introduction into the operational force, as absolutely essential.

[MX Missile]

The President provided some guidance to the Department of Defense on priorities he wished accorded to various basing and defense schemes, but he essentially asked Defense for their recommendation on a permanent basing mode by early fall so that he could comply with congressional desires for an administration position, well before the end of this year.

At the same time, the President made it clear that until a more survivable basing mode has been selected, funded, cleared for construction, he wishes to retain the option of deploying a limited number of MX and Minuteman silos as an integral part of the overall MX program.

The silo basing option provides a hedge against unforeseen technical developments, program changes. It is a clear incentive to the Soviets to negotiate arms reductions, and even in silos, MX gains in survivability as all three legs of the strategic triad are modernized.

The MX program, the President has said, is too important to allow the risk of technical environmental or arms control debates to delay introduction of the missile into force.

[Conventional Deterrence]

While the failure to strengthen our nuclear deterrent could be disastrous, recent history makes clear that conventional deterrence is now more important than ever. Current overseas deployments will be maintained to provide a capability for timely and flexible response to contingencies and to demonstrate resolve to honor our commitments. Ground, naval and air forces will remain deployed in Europe, in the western Pacific, in Southwest Asia and elsewhere as appropriate. In this hemisphere, naval forces will maintain a presence in the North Atlantic, the Caribbean Basin, the Mediterranean, the western Pacific and in the Indian Ocean. Forward-deployed forces will be postured to facilitate rapid response. Intermittent overseas developments from the United States will be made as necessary.

Now, our strategic reserve of U.S.-based forces, both active and reserve components, will be maintained at a high state of readiness and will be periodically exercised. Last year's Bright Star exercise in the Middle East, last month's Ocean Venture 82 in the Caribbean provided a valuable experience for those forces. They also demonstrated a multi-national, multi-force capability to defend our interests and those of our friends worldwide. Our need to swiftly reinforce worldwide means that improvements in our strategic mobility and in our reserve structure are terribly important.

Although the most prominent threat to our vital interests worldwide is the Soviet Union, our interests can also be put in jeopardy by actions of other states, other groups. In contingencies not involving the Soviet Union, we hope to rely on friendly regional states to provide military force.

Should the threat exceed our capabilities within regional states, we must be prepared within the framework of our constitutional processes to commit U.S. forces to assist our allies. This, of course, does not mean that we must push ourselves into areas where we are neither wanted nor desired or needed. What is does mean is that we cannot reject in advance any options we might need to protect those same vital interests. To do so is to invite aggression, undermine our credibility and place at risk all global objectives.

[Security Assistance]

Now, this highlights the importance of security assistance. By this term we mean military sales, grant assistance, international military education and training, economic support funds and peacekeeping operations. If we do not assist our allies and friends in meeting their legitimate defense requirements, then their ability to cope with conflict goes down and the pressure for eventual U.S. involvement goes up. Yet today security assistance is not doing the job it should, as discovered by these same studies.

Resources are inadequate, often of the wrong kind. During the 1950s, the security assistance budget ranged from 5 to 10 percent of the defense budget. But today, it's about 1.5 percent. While it is not necessary to return to the post war levels that rearmed and secured Western Europe, some steady growth in security assistance can be our most cost-effective investment. Again, found by our studies.

The annual budget cycle constrains long-range planning. Countries participating in our security assistance program and procurement officers at the Defense Department both need to plan ahead. Procurement lead times limit the responsiveness of the overall program. And, finally, legislative restrictions reduce the ability of our government to react appropriately to emergency conditions.

An effective security assistance program, again, is a critical element in meeting our security objectives abroad. At times recently, [we] have had difficulty explaining that on the Hill. Thus, it is a real compliment to our own force structure. Security assistance can help deter conflict, can increase the ability of our friends and allies to defend themselves without the commitment of our own combat forces. Effective programs can establish a degree of compatibility between U.S. forces and the forces of recipient countries so we can work together in combat if necessary. Not only does security assistance offer a cost-effective way of enhancing our security worldwide but it also strengthens our economy in general and our defense production base in particular. In short, a little assistance buys a lot of security.

For these reasons, we are planning a priority effort to improve the effectiveness, the responsiveness of this vital component of our national security strategy. We will be looking at ways of reducing lead times. We will take a hard look at existing legislation future resources. Programs require predictability. This points toward more extensive use of multiyear commitments and a larger capitalization of the special defense acquisition fund.

In sum, security assistance needs fixing and we have a plan to fix it.

[Goal Is Peace]

No one should mistake the main goal of American global strategy. The goal, of course, as the President has said over and again, is peace.

We have devoted too large a portion of our national resources and emotion over the past 40 years to the alleviation of want, hunger, suffering and distress throughout the world, to want anything but peace in every corner of the planet. And those who slander the United States with charges of warmongering can barely paper over their own guilty consciences in this very regard.

In particular, the record of the Soviet Union in armed suppression of popular movements since 1945 is unparalleled among modern nations. To maintain peace with freedom, therefore, we are forced, reluctantly, to plan carefully for the possibility that our adversaries may prove unwilling to keep that peace. And when we turn to a strategy for our military forces, we enter the world of assumptions, scenarios, and hypothetical projections. It would be our strategy to employ military force to achieve specific political objectives quickly on terms favorable to the United States and our Allies.

We need a better, more detailed strategy in order to buy the right equipment, develop forces, and lay detailed plans. This strategy must provide flexibility and yet allow preplanning. In trying to solve this problem we have looked at such strategy as a planning continuum over the last four months. At the lower end of the spectrum our guidance emphasizes the integration of economic aid and security assistance, foreign military training, and supplementary support capability.

At the higher end our strategy guidance takes into account the global military capabilities of the Soviet Union and the interrelationship of strategic theaters. We recognize that in spite of our efforts [to] preserve peace, any conflict with the Soviet Union could expand to global dimension.

[Military Priorities]

Thus, global planning is a necessity. This does not mean that we must have the capability to successfully engage Soviet forces simultaneously on all fronts. We can't, simply can't. What it does mean is that we must procure balanced forces and establish priorities for sequential operations to insure that military power would be applied in the most effective way on a priority basis.

It is in the interest of the United States to limit the scope of any conflict. The capability for counteroffensives on other fronts is an essential element of our strategy, but it is not a substitute for adequate military capability to defend our vital interests in the area in which they are threatened.

On the other hand, the decision to expand a conflict may well not be ours to make. Therefore, U.S. forces must be capable of responding to a major attack with unmistakable global implications early on in any conflict.

The President has established priorities in the way our forces would be used in combat, in terms of geography, in terms of force development. We must ask, what do we fix first?

We have tried to analyze the risks we face. We cannot fix them all at once, in part because things take time, and in part because the Soviet military advantage results from a whole decade of investment and top priority. There is not enough money available to eliminate the risks we face overnight.

What we have tried to do is analyze those risks, put first things first, and develop for how we will conduct ourslves if the worst comes to worst.

On the other hand, we want to hope for the best, and we want to offer that hope to others, our Allies, our friends, the Third World, and especially to the citizens of the Soviet Union.

It is our fondest hope that with an active yet prudent national security policy, we might one day convince the leadership of the Soviet Union to turn their attention inward, to seek the legitimacy that only comes from the consent of the governed, and thus to address the hopes and the dreams of their own people. . . .

WEINBERGER INTERVIEW

Mr. [George] Will: Mr. Secretary, the sequence that Secretary Haig [Alexander M. Haig Jr.] described was a five-step one. It began with an anti-satellite move, which would be the first step, perhaps, in a nuclear war — to blind the United States, and went through the launching of ground-based and sea-based missiles, intermediate missiles, and wound up with the firing of an ABM to block a retaliatory strike coming in. In other words, this looked to some people like a scenario for fighting a nuclear war. Is that the construction you put on it?

Sec. [Caspar W.] Weinberger: Well, I've said for a long time — first, yes, I agree with you. And I've said for a long time that the Soviets are now, by a number of pieces of evidence, and this is just another in that long chain, giving — displaying the fact that they believe a nuclear war can be fought, can be won. And that's one of the things that we think is so dangerous. We don't think a nuclear war can be won, and our policy is based entirely on trying to acquire the necessary strength to keep our deterrent credible.

Mr. Will: Some people thought they heard in the Gromyko speech — leaving aside the no-first-use pledge in Europe by Brezhnev — they thought they heard the outlines of a strategic nuclear deal. Did you detect that in that speech?

Sec. Weinberger: No, I didn't, and I don't know that he had checked with the Ministry of Defense over there because it didn't sound — the sequence of events that you've correctly described didn't sound as if there'd been anything remotely resembling that. It sounded, in the whole way it took place, it looked as if it was to be a clear demonstration to the world that they were bringing their forces of all kinds, through command and control communications and this kind of unprecedented exercise, to the point where they could show the world they plan to use some of this immense arsenal they've been accumulating at rapidly increasing rates for 21 years.

Mr. [Sam] Donaldson: Well, if we don't think a nuclear war can be won, why are you studying plans to fight a protracted nuclear war?

Sec. Weinberger: Well, I'm glad you asked that question —

Mr. Donaldson: Well, I'm glad I did too.

Sec. Weinberger: — because we're not studying plans to fight —

Mr. [David] Brinkley: Because you've got an answer all ready.

Sec. Weinberger: We're not studying — well, the story was so wrong and it's caused so much trouble that I'm glad to have an opportunity to clear it up. We're not studying plans to fight a protracted nuclear war. What we're trying to do is to make sure, through modernization and improvement of our weapons, that we have an enduring survivability of our weapons so that we can indeed meet and deal with, and have the capability to deal with, a protracted nuclear war fought by the Soviets against us. And that's one of the dangers —

Mr. Donaldson: Wait a moment.

Sec. Weinberger: — that's one of the dangers of wrenching a few sentences out of context —

Mr. Donaldson: But it takes two to fight.

Sec. Weinberger: Well, what —

Mr. Donaldson: We're not going to fight a protracted nuclear war, but the Soviets might against us?

Sec. Weinberger: No. No. No, no. We're not going to launch a protracted nuclear war. We don't believe a nuclear war can be won. But we are certainly not going to sit by quietly and do nothing while they develop the capability to fight, and — as they believe, apparently — to win what they call a protracted nuclear war. And the whole word "protracted" here was wrenched out of the context of the statement, and the statement was never published in full; it was a sensitive statement. It was leaked or somebody stole it or something, but one way or another, the impression had been given that we are sitting down saying we will now plan to fight a protracted nuclear war. What we're trying to do is develop an enduring sustainability of our forces, which we don't have sufficiently now, so that it will be very apparent to the Soviets that their plan for fighting a protracted nuclear war will be useless and should be discarded. And that is a very great difference. If you only have the capability to fight a very short time — if you can only use your weapons once and they are then wiped out, then you have a hair-trigger situation in which every intendment is that you have to use yours immediately, and you put a hair trigger on the most dangerous kind of all wars. So what we're trying our best to do is to acquire the capability that will demonstrate to them and deter them from making any kind of attack on us.

Mr. Donaldson: I'm belaboring the point, but let me try one more time. Why not say to the Soviets, "Don't even think about fighting protracted nuclear war because it can't happen. We will destroy you in a massive series of exchanges"? Instead you seem to be saying, "Don't try to think about fighting a protracted nuclear war, because we have plans to be able to fight one also."

Sec. Weinberger: "To counter anything that you might do." And there is a most peculiar syndrome around in which we are criticized for this use of the term "prevail." And —

Mr. Donaldson: I didn't criticize you for the use of —

Sec. Weinberger: Well, others have, and they say that you shouldn't think about a protracted nuclear war because that's part of this philosophy of trying to prevail in any sort of contest. And I would say to you —

Mr. Donaldson: But you said you can't win.

Sec. Weinberger: I'd say to you that we are planning to prevail if we are attacked. We are not planning to sit by meekly and say it can't be won so we aren't going to plan to do it. You show me a secretary of defense who is not planning to prevail, and I'll show you a secretary —

Mr. Donaldson: In other worlds, you're saying —

Sec. Weinberger: I'll show you a secretary of defense who ought to be impeached.

Mr. Donaldson: Wait a minute. You can't win a nuclear war —

Sec. Weinberger: You can't do that.

Mr. Donaldson: — but we can prevail?

Sec. Weinberger: We don't think a nuclear war is winnable, and that's why we think —

Mr. Donaldson: But we can prevail?

Sec. Weinberger: That's — we are trying to acquire the capacity that will demonstrate that it cannot be won, and therefore deter it. And that's exactly what we've been doing from the very beginning....

WEINBERGER LETTER TO EDITORS

I am increasingly concerned with news accounts that portray this Administration as planning to wage protracted nuclear war, or seeking to acquire a nuclear "warfighting" capability. This is completely inaccurate, and these stories misrepresent the Administration's policies to the American public and to our allies and adversaries abroad.

It is the first and foremost goal of this Administration to take every step to ensure that nuclear weapons are never used again, for we do not believe there could be any "winners" in a nuclear war. Our entire strategy aims to deter war of all kinds, but most particularly to deter nuclear war. To accomplish this objective, our forces must be able to respond in a measured and prudent manner to the threat posed by the Soviet Union. That will require the improvements in our strategic forces that the President has proposed. But it does *not* mean that we endorse the concept of protracted nuclear war, or nuclear "warfighting." It is the Soviet Union that appears to be building forces for a "protracted" conflict (the doctrine of ZATYAZHNAYA VOYNA).

[Paradox of Deterrence]

The policy of deterrence is difficult for some to grasp because it is based on a paradox. But this is quite simple: to make the cost of nuclear war much higher than any possible "benefit" to the country starting it. If the Soviets know in advance that a nuclear attack on the United States could and would bring swift nuclear retaliation, they would never attack in the first place. They would be "deterred" from ever beginning a nuclear war.

There is nothing new about our policy. Since the awful age of nuclear weapons began, the United States has sought to prevent nuclear war through a policy of deterrence. This policy has been approved, through the political processes of the democratic nations it protects, since at least 1950. More important, it works. It has worked in the face of major international tensions involving the great powers and it has worked in the face of war itself.

But for detererence to continue to be successful in the future we must take steps to offset the Soviet military buildup. If we do not modernize our arsenal now, as the Soviets have been doing for more than 20 years, we will, within a few years, no longer have the ability to retaliate. The Soviet Union would then be in a position to threaten or actually to attack us with the knowledge that we would be incapable of responding. We have seen in Poland, in Afghanistan, in Eastern Europe and elsewhere that the Soviet Union does not hesitate to take advantage of a weaker adversary. We cannot allow the Soviet Union to think it could begin a nuclear war with us and win.

[Soviet Military Buildup]

This is not just idle speculation. The Soviet Union has engaged in a frenzied military buildup, in spite of their economic difficulties. They have continued to build greater numbers of nuclear weapons far beyond those necessary for deterrence. They now have over 5,000 nuclear warheads on ICBMs compared to about 2,000 only five years ago. They have modified the design of these weapons and their launchers so that many of their land based missiles are now more accurate, more survivable, and more powerful than our own. They have also developed a refiring capability that will allow them to reload their delivery systems several times. They have elaborate plans for civil defense and air defense against any retaliation we might attempt. And finally, their writings and military doctrine emphasize a nuclear war-fighting scenario. Whatever they claim their intentions to be, the fact remains that they are designing their weapons in such a way and in sufficient numbers to indicate to us that they think they could begin, and win, a nuclear war.

In the face of all this, it is my responsibility and duty as Secretary of Defense to make every effort to modernize our nuclear forces in such a way that the United States retains the capability to deter the Soviet Union from ever beginning a nuclear war. We must take the steps necessary to match the Soviet Union's greatly improved nuclear capability.

That is exactly why we must have a *capability* for a survivable and enduring response — to demonstrate that our strategic forces *could* survive Soviet strikes over an extended period. Thus we believe we could deter any attack. Otherwise we would be tempting them to employ nuclear weapons or try to blackmail us. In short, we cannot afford to place ourselves in the position where the survivability of our deterrent would force the President to choose between using our strategic forces before they were destroyed or surrendering.

[Danger of Weakness]

Those who object to a policy that would strengthen our deterrent, then, would force us into a more dangerous, hairtriggered posture. Forces that must be used in the very first instant of any enemy attack are not the tools of a prudent strategy. A posture that encourages Soviet nuclear adventurism is not the basis of an effective deterrent. Our entire strategic program, including the development of a response capability that has been so maligned in the press recently, has been developed with the express intention of assuring that nuclear war will never be fought.

I know this doctrine of deterrence is a difficult paradox to understand. It is an uncomfortable way to keep the peace. We understand deterrence and accept the fact that we must do much more in order to continue to keep the peace. It is my fervent hope that all can understand and accept this so that we can avoid the sort of sensationalist treatment of every mention of the word "nuclear" that only serves to distort our policy and to frighten people all over the world. Our policy is peace, and we deeply believe that the best and surest road to peace is to secure and maintain an effective and credible deterrent.

The purpose of U.S. policy remains to prevent aggression through an effective policy of deterrence, the very goal which prompted the formation of the North Atlantic Alliance, an alliance which is as vital today as it was the day it was formed.

POPE'S TRIP TO BRITAIN
May 28 - June 2, 1982

Pope John Paul II, leader of the Roman Catholic Church, became the first pope to visit Britain when he arrived in London May 28. Hoping to mend a break between England and the Vatican that was more than four centuries old, the pope spent six days touring England, Scotland and Wales. His itinerary called for more than 50 events and included stops in London, Canterbury, Coventry, Liverpool, Manchester and York in England; Edinburgh and Glasgow in Scotland and Cardiff in Wales.

For almost 450 years, the Church of Rome and the Church of England have been divided. Catholicism came to Britain in Anglo-Saxon times. In 597 Pope Gregory I sent Augustine to England as a missionary, and he became the first archbishop of Canterbury. During medieval times, Catholicism reigned supreme in Britain as it did elsewhere in Western Europe. But when Pope Clement VII refused to allow King Henry VIII to divorce Catharine of Aragon and marry Anne Boleyn, the king broke with the Vatican. In 1534 Henry had himself proclaimed head of the Church of England.

From that time on, the Anglican Church grew in power and number, and Catholics became a persecuted minority. As late as the 19th century, they were barred from the English army and navy, from Oxford and Cambridge universities and from Parliament. Today less than 10 percent of England's 55 million people are Catholics.

Unity and Reconciliation

Queen Elizabeth II, head of the Anglican Church, welcomed Pope John Paul II at Buckingham Palace May 28 in a meeting of symbolic and historic significance. This greeting was the first of several scenes of unity and reconciliation, the major themes of the pontiff's trip. At a service in Westminster Cathedral May 28, the pope explained, "I come among you as the visible sign and source of unity for the whole church."

Perhaps the spiritual highlight of the visit was an ecumenical service led by the pope and the archbishop of Canterbury, Dr. Robert Runcie, in Canterbury Cathedral May 29. In an emotional moment the two church leaders embraced as the congregation applauded enthusiastically. Both men spoke and later issued a joint statement declaring the establishment of an international commission to work toward unifying the Anglican and Roman Catholic churches.

On March 29 an earlier commission issued its final report after 12 years of study. The group concluded that progress toward reconciliation had been made. Not everyone in Britain approved of reconciliation between the two churches, however. Militant Protestants, some with links to extremists in Northern Ireland, protested the pope's visit.

Prayers for Peace

Peace was another of the pontiff's themes, and in Coventry May 29 he made his strongest appeal: "Today, the scale and horror of modern warfare, whether nuclear or not, makes it totally unacceptable as a means of settling differences between nations. War should belong to the tragic past, to history; it should find no place on humanity's agenda for the future."

The pope was addressing a nation at war and, at almost every stop on his British tour, he called for an end to the Falkland Islands hostilities. In fact, the crisis in the South Atlantic between Argentina and Britain had threatened the pope's trip. But after two years of planning, rescheduling the visit seemed virtually impossible, and the pope decided to go through with his plans. In a letter to Argentine Catholics, however, the pontiff stressed that the British visit was of a purely pastoral and ecumenical nature — not political. And the Vatican hurriedly scheduled a papal visit to Argentina later in June. (Falkland Islands war, p. 283)

The pope's pastoral and ecumenical activities in Britain included celebration of several outdoor masses, participation in prayer services in Protestant churches and meetings with leaders of Britain's other faiths.

> *Following are excerpts from Pope John Paul II's homily at Westminster Cathedral May 28; from his speech in Canterbury Cathedral May 29; from remarks made by Dr. Robert Runcie, archbishop of Canterbury, May 29; from the text of a joint statement made May 29 by Pope John Paul II and Dr. Runcie; and from the pope's remarks at an outdoor mass near Coventry May 30:*

ADDRESS AT WESTMINSTER CATHEDRAL

... Today, for the first time in history, a bishop of Rome sets foot on English soil. I am deeply moved at this thought. This fair land, once a distant outpost of the pagan world, has become through the preaching of the Gospel a beloved and gifted portion of Christ's vineyard.

Yours is a tradition embedded in the history of Christian civilization. The roll of your saints and of your great men and women, your treasures of literature and music, your cathedrals and colleges, your rich heritage of parish life speak of a tradition of faith. And it is to the faith of your fathers — living still — that I wish to pay tribute by my visit. . . .

2. Let us reflect on the spiritual significance of this moment.

Christ, "the chief shepherd" (1 Pt. 5:4), gave to Peter — as we have heard proclaimed in the passage from St. John's Gospel — the task of confirming his brothers in their faith and in their pastoral duty: "Feed my lambs. . . . Look after my sheep" (Jn. 21:15-16).

I come among you in response to this command of the Lord. I come to confirm the faith of my brother bishops. I come to remind all believers who today inherit the faith of their fathers that in each diocese the bishop is the visible sign and source of the church's unity. I come among you as the visible sign and source of unity for the whole church. I come at the service of unity in love: in the humble and realistic love of the repentant fisherman: "Lord, you know everything; you know that I love you."

Christians down the ages often traveled to that city where the apostles Peter and Paul had died in witness to their faith and were buried. But during 400 years the steady flow of English pilgrims to the tombs of the apostles shrank to a trickle. Rome and your country were estranged. Now the bishop of Rome comes to you. I truly come at the service of unity in love, but I come as a friend too and I am deeply grateful for your welcome.

I have always admired your love of freedom, your generous hospitality to other peoples in their adversity; as a son of Poland I have the strongest, most personal reason for this admiration and the thanks that go with it. . . .

... This fine church where we meet is a symbol of the faith and energy of the English Catholic community in modern times. Its architecture is unusual for this country: It evokes memories of other parts of the Christian world, reminding us of our universality. Tomorrow I shall be welcomed in the much older cathedral of Canterbury, where St. Augustine, sent by my predecessor St. Gregory, first built a little church whose foundations remain. There indeed everything speaks of ancient common traditions, which in this modern age we are ready to stress together. I too want to speak in this way — to mourn the long estrangement between Christians, to hear gladly our blessed Lord's prayer and command that we should be completely one, to thank him for that inspiration of the Holy Spirit which has filled us with a longing to leave behind our divisions and aspire to a common witness to our Lord and Savior. My deep desire, my ardent hope and prayer, is that my visit may serve the cause of Christian unity.

7. . . . In baptism we are given a name — we call it our Christian name. In the tradition of the church it is a saint's name, a name of one of the heroes among Christ's followers — an apostle, a martyr, a religious founder, like St. Benedict, whose monks founded Westminster Abbey nearby, where your sovereigns are crowned. Taking such names reminds us again that we are being drawn into the communion of saints, and at the same time that great models of Christian living are set before us. London is particularly proud of two outstanding saints, great men also by the world's standards, contributors to your national heritage, John Fisher and Thomas More.

John Fisher, the Cambridge scholar of Renaissance learning, bishop of Rochester. He is an example to all bishops in his loyalty to the faith and in his devoted attention to the people of his diocese, especially the poor and the sick.

Thomas More was a model layman living the Gospel to the full. He was a fine scholar and an ornament to his profession, a loving husband and father, humble in prosperity, courageous in adversity, humorous and godly. Together they served God and their country — bishop and layman. Together they died, victims of an unhappy age. Today we have the grace, all of us, to proclaim their greatness and to thank God for giving such men to England.

In this England of fair and generous minds no one will begrudge the Catholic community pride in its own history. So I speak last of another Christian name, less famous but no less deserving honor. Bishop Richard Challoner guided the Catholics of this London district in the 18th century, at what seemed the lowest point of their fortunes. They were few. It seemed they might well not survive. Yet Bishop Challoner bravely raised his voice to prophesy a better future for his people. And now, two centuries later, I am privileged to stand here and to speak to you, in no triumphal spirit, but as a friend, grateful for your kind welcome and full of love for all of you.

Bishop Challoner's courage may remind all of us where the seeds of courage lie, where the confidence of renewal comes from. It is through water and the Holy Spirit that a new people is born, whatever the darkness of the time.

8. As the reading from the prophet Ezekiel reminds us, it is the Lord himself who is the true shepherd of this new people. He himself pastures his sheep. . . .

My dear brothers and sisters, as we proceed to celebrate the mysteries of our faith we cannot forget that an armed conflict is taking place. Brothers in Christ are fighting in a war that imperils peace in the world.

In our prayers let us remember the victims of both sides. We pray for the dead — that they may rest in Christ — and for the wounded, and for all the afflicted families. I ask you to join me at each step of my pastoral visit, praying for peaceful solution of the conflict, praying that the God of peace will move men's hearts to put aside the weapons of death and to pursue the path of fraternal dialogue. With all our hearts we turn to Jesus, the Prince of Peace.

ADDRESS AT CANTERBURY

... Today's gospel passages have called attention in particular to two aspects of the gift of the Holy Spirit which Jesus invoked upon his disciples: He is the spirit of truth and the spirit of unity. On the first Pentecost day the Holy Spirit descended on that small band of disciples to confirm them in the truth of God's salvation of the world through the death and resurrection of his Son, and to unite them into the one body of Christ, which is the church. Thus we know that when we pray "that all may be one" as Jesus and his Father are one, it is precisely in order that "the world may believe" and by this faith be saved (cf. Jn. 17:21). For our faith can be none other than the faith of Pentecost, the faith in which the apostles were confirmed by the spirit of truth. We believe that the risen Lord has authority to save us from sin and the powers of darkness. We believe too that we are called to "become one body, one spirit in Christ" (Eucharistic Prayer III).

3. In a few moments we shall renew our baptismal vows together. We intend to perform this ritual, which we share in common as Anglicans and Catholics, as a clear testimony to the one sacrament of baptism by which we have been joined to Christ. At the same time we are humbly mindful that the faith of the church to which we appeal is not without the marks of our separation. Together we shall renew our renunciation of sin in order to make it clear that we believe that Jesus Christ has overcome the powerful hold of Satan upon "the world" (Jn. 14:17). We shall profess anew our intention to turn away from all that is evil and to turn toward God who is the author of all that is good and the source of all that is holy. As we again make our profession of faith in the triune God — Father, Son and Holy Spirit — we find great hope in the promise of Jesus: "The counselor, the Holy Spirit, whom the Father will send in my name, he will teach you all things, and bring to your remembrance all that I have said to you" (Jn. 14:26). Christ's promise gives us confidence in the power of this same Holy Spirit to heal the divisions introduced into the church in the course of the centuries since that first Pentecost day. In this way the renewal of our baptismal vows will become a pledge to do all in our power to cooperate with the grace of the Holy Spirit, who alone can lead us to the day when we will profess the fullness of our faith together....

5. My dear brothers and sisters of the Anglican Communion, "whom I love and long for" (Phil. 4:1), how happy I am to be able to speak directly to you today in this great cathedral! The building itself is an eloquent witness both to our long years of common inheritance and to the sad years of division that followed. Beneath this roof St. Thomas Becket suffered martyrdom. Here too we recall Augustine and Dunstan and Anselm and all those monks who gave such diligent service in this church. The great events of salvation history are retold in the ancient stained glass windows above us. And we have venerated here the manuscript of the Gospels sent from Rome to Canterbury 1,300 years ago. Encouraged by the witness of so

many who have professed their faith in Jesus Christ through the centuries — often at the cost of their own lives — a sacrifice which even today is asked of not a few, as the new chapel we shall visit reminds us — I appeal to you in this holy place, all my fellow Christians, and especially the members of the Church of England and the members of the Anglican Communion throughout the world, to accept the commitment to which Archbishop Runcie and I pledge ourselves anew before you today. This commitment is that of praying and working for reconciliation and ecclesial unity according to the mind and heart of our savior Jesus Christ.

6. On this first visit of a pope to Canterbury, I come to you in love — the love of Peter to whom the Lord said, "I have prayed for you that your faith may never fail. You in turn must strengthen your brothers" (Lk. 22:32). I come to you also in the love of Gregory, who sent St. Augustine to this place to give the Lord's flock a shepherd's care (cf. 1 Pt. 5:2). Just as every minister of the Gospel must do, so today I echo the words of the Master: "I am among you as one who serves" (Lk. 22:27). With me I bring you, beloved brothers and sisters of the Anglican Communion, the hopes and the desires, the prayers and good will of all who are united with the church of Rome, which from earliest times was said to "preside in love" (Ignatious, *Ad Rom; Proem.*).

7. In a few moments Archbishop Runcie will join me in reading a common declaration in which we give recognition to the steps we have already taken along the path of unity and state the plans we propose and the hopes we entertain for the next stage of our common pilgrimage. And yet these hopes and plans will come to nothing if our striving for unity is not rooted in our union with God; for Jesus said, "In that day you will know that I am in my Father, and you in me, and I in you. He who has my commandments and keeps them, he it is who loves me; and he who loves me will be loved by my Father, and I will love him and manifest myself to him" (Jn. 14:20-21). This love of God is poured out upon us in the person of the Holy Spirit, the spirit of truth and of unity. Let us open ourselves to his powerful love, as we pray that, speaking the truth in love, we may all grow up in every way into him who is the head, into our Lord Jesus Christ (cf. Eph. 4:15). May the dialogue we have begun lead us to the day of full restoration of unity in faith and love. . . .

ARCHBISHOP'S ADDRESS

We welcome you, Your Holiness, with words of friendship for this is a service of celebration. But the present moment is full of pain for so many in the world. Millions are hungry and the secret gift of life is counted cheap, while the nations of the world use some of their best resources and much of their store of human ingenuity in refining weapons of death. With so much to celebrate in life and so much to be done to combat life's enemies, disease and ignorance, energy is being wasted in conflict. Our minds inevitably turn to the conflict and tragic loss of life in the South Atlantic and we also remember the suffering of Your Holiness' own fellow countrymen in Poland.

But Christians do not accept hunger, disease and war as inevitable. The present moment is not empty of hope, but waits to be transformed by the power which comes from remembering our beginnings and by a power which comes from a lively vision of the future; remembering our beginnings, celebrating our hope for the future, freeing ourselves from cynicism and despair in order to act in the present....

At this season of the year we particularly remember the gift of the Holy Spirit at the first Pentecost, and the sending out of the apostles to carry the faith of Jesus Christ to the furthest ends of the world. We recall one of the first missionary endeavors of the Roman church and its efforts to recapture for Christ a Europe overwhelmed by the barbarians. In the year 597, in the words of the English historian, the Venerable Bede, Your Holiness' great predecessor Gregory, prompted by divine inspiration, sent a servant of God named Augustine and several more God-fearing monks with him to preach the word of God to the English race. Augustine became the first archbishop of Canterbury and I rejoice that the successors of Gregory and Augustine stand here today in the church which is built on their partnership in the Gospel.

We shall trace and celebrate our beginnings in this service, by reaffirming our baptismal vows, made at the font at the beginning of the Christian life, and by saying together the Creed, an expression of the heart of our common Christian faith, composed in the era before our unhappy division. The emphasis then will be on the richness of what we share and upon the existing unity of the Christian church, which transcends all political divisions and frontiers imposed on the human family.

One of the gifts which Christians have to make to the peace of the world is to live out the unity that has already been given to them in their common love of Christ. But our unity is not in the past only, but also in the future. We have a common vision which also breaks up the lazy prejudices and easy assumptions of the present. Our chapel here of the martyrs of the 20th century will be the focus for the celebration of a common vision. We believe, even in a world like ours which exalts and applauds self-interest and derides self-sacrifice, that the blood of the martyrs shall create the holy places of the earth.

Our own century has seen the creation of ruthless tyranny by the use of violence and cynical disregard of truth. We believe that such energies, founded on force and lies, destroy themselves. The kingdom spoken of by our Lord Jesus Christ is built by self-sacrificing love, which can even turn places of sorrow and suffering into signs of hope.

... We remember all the martyrs of our century of martyrs who have confirmed Christ's church in the conviction that even in the places of horror, the concentration camps, and prisons and slums of the world, nothing in all creation can separate us from the active and creative love of God in Christ Jesus our Lord....

JOINT STATEMENT

1. In the cathedral church of Christ at Canterbury the pope and the archbishop of Canterbury have met on the eve of Pentecost to offer thanks to God for the progress that has been made in the work of reconciliation between our communions. Together with leaders of other Christian churches and communities we have listened to the word of God; together we have recalled our one baptism and renewed the promises then made; together we have acknowledged the witness given by those whose faith has led them to surrender the precious gift of life itself in the service of others, both in the past and in modern times.

2. The bond of our common baptism into Christ led our predecessors to inaugurate a serious dialogue between our churches, a dialogue founded on the Gospels and the ancient common traditions, a dialogue which has as its goal the unity for which Christ prayed to his Father "so that the world may know that Thou has sent me and hast loved them even as Thou has loved me" (Jn. 17:23). In 1966, our predecessors Pope Paul VI and Archbishop Michael Ramsey made a common declaration announcing their intention to inaugurate a serious dialogue between the Roman Catholic Church and the Anglican Communion which would "include not only theological matters such as scripture, tradition and liturgy, but also matters of practical difficulty felt on either side" (Common Declaration, 6). After this dialogue had already produced three statements on eucharist, ministry and ordination, and authority in the church, Pope Paul VI and Archbishop Donald Coggan, in their common declaration in 1977, took the occasion to encourage the completion of the dialogue on these three important questions so that the commission's conclusions might be evaluated by the respective authorities through procedures appropriate to each communion. The Anglican-Roman Catholic International Commission has now completed the task assigned to it with the publication of its final report, and as our two communions proceed with the necessary evaluation, we join in thanking the members of the commission for their dedication, scholarship and integrity in a long and demanding task undertaken for love of Christ and for the unity of his church.

3. . . . We are agreed that it is now time to set up a new international commission. Its task will be to continue the work already begun: to examine, especially in the light of our respective judgments on the final report, the outstanding doctrinal differences which still separate us, with a view toward their eventual resolution; to study all that hinders the mutual recognition of the ministries of our communions; and to recommend what practical steps will be necessary when, on the basis of our unity in faith, we are able to proceed to the restoration of full communion. . . .

4. While this necessary work of theological clarification continues, it must be accompanied by the zealous work and fervent prayer of Roman Catholics and Anglicans throughout the world as they seek to grow in mutual understanding, fraternal love and common witness to the Gospel. Once more then, we call on the bishops, clergy and faithful people of both

our communions in every country, diocese and parish in which our faithful live side by side. We urge them all to pray for this work and to adopt every possible means of furthering it through their collaboration in deepening their allegiance to Christ and in witnessing to him before the world....

5. Our aim is not limited to the union of our two communions alone, to the exclusion of other Christians, but rather extends to the fulfillment of God's will for the visible unity of all his people. Both in our present dialogue and in those engaged in by other Christians among themselves and with us, we recognize in the agreements we are able to reach, as well as in the difficulties which we encounter, a renewed challenge to abandon ourselves completely to the truth of the Gospel. Hence we are happy to make this declaration today in the welcome presence of so many fellow Christians whose churches and communities are already partners with us in prayer and work for the unity of all.

6. With them we wish to serve the cause of peace, of human freedom and human dignity, so that God may indeed be glorified in all his creatures. With them we greet in the name of God all men of good will, both those who believe in him and those who are still searching for him.

7. This holy place reminds us of the vision of Pope Gregory in sending St. Augustine as an apostle to England, full of zeal for the preaching of the Gospel and the shepherding of the flock. On this eve of Pentecost, we turn again in prayer to Jesus, the Good Shepherd, who promised to ask the Father to give us another advocate to be with us forever, the spirit of truth (cf. Jn. 14:16), to lead us to the full unity to which he calls us. Confident in the power of this same Holy Spirit, we commit ourselves anew to the task of working for unity with firm faith, renewed hope and ever deeper love.

ADDRESS AT COVENTRY

... We are close to the city of Coventry, a city devastated by war but rebuilt in hope. The ruins of the old cathedral and the building of the new are recognized throughout the world as a symbol of Christian reconciliation and peace. We pray at this Mass: "Send forth your spirit, O Lord, and renew the face of the earth." In this prayer we call upon God to enable us to bring about that reconciliation and peace not simply in symbol, but in reality too.

2. Our world is disfigured by war and violence. The ruins of the old cathedral constantly remind our society of its capacity to destroy. And today that capacity is greater than ever. People are having to live under the shadow of a nuclear nightmare. Yet people everywhere long for peace. Men and women of good will desire to make common cause in their search for a worldwide community of brotherhood and understanding.

What is this peace for which we long? What is this peace symbolized by the new cathedral of Coventry? Peace is not just the absence of war. It involves mutual respect and confidence between peoples and nations. It involves collaboration and binding agreements. Like a cathedral, peace has to be constructed patiently and with unshakable faith.

Wherever the strong exploit the weak; wherever the rich take advantage of the poor; wherever great powers seek to dominate and to impose ideologies, there the work of making peace is undone; there the cathedral of peace is again destroyed. Today, the scale and the horror of modern warfare — whether nuclear or not — makes it totally unacceptable as a means of settling differences between nations. War should belong to the tragic past, to history; it should find no place on humanity's agenda for the future.

And so, this morning I invite you to pray with me for the cause of peace. Let us pray earnestly for the special session of the United Nations on disarmament which begins soon. The voices of Christians join with others in urging the leaders of the world to abandon confrontation and to turn their backs on policies which require the nations to spend vast sums of money for weapons of mass destruction. We pray this Pentecost that the Holy Spirit may inspire the leaders of the world to engage in fruitful dialogue. May the Holy Spirit lead them to adopt peaceful ways of safeguarding liberty which do not involve the threat of nuclear disaster.

Yet the cathedral of peace is built of many small stones. Each person has to become a stone in that beautiful edifice. All people must deliberately and resolutely commit themselves to the pursuit of peace. Mistrust and division between nations begin in the heart of individuals. Work for peace starts when we listen to the urgent call of Christ: "Repent and believe in the Gospel" (Mk. 1:15). We must turn from domination to service; we must turn from violence to peace; we must turn from ourselves to Christ, who alone can give us a new heart, a new understanding. Each individual, at some moment in his or her life, is destined to hear this call from Christ. Each person's response leads to death or to life. Faith in Christ, the incarnate word of God, will bring us into the way of peace....

▼▼▼

SPAIN'S ENTRY INTO NATO

May 30, 1982

Spain became the 16th member of the North Atlantic Treaty Organization (NATO) by depositing an "instrument of adhesion" with the U.S. State Department in Washington, D.C., May 30. NATO's treaty procedures required the document, signed May 29 in Madrid, to be brought to Washington as the final step in the membership process.

Both houses of the Spanish parliament had approved the plan to join NATO by November 26, 1981, and NATO issued its formal invitation to Spain December 10, 1981. At that time NATO Secretary General Joseph Luns termed the move one of the most significant events in NATO's history. By May 24, 1982, all other NATO countries had ratified Spain's entry.

Background

NATO was established as a defense alliance in 1949 by the United States, Canada, Great Britain, France, the Netherlands, Belgium, Luxembourg, Italy, Norway, Denmark, Iceland and Portugal. Greece and Turkey joined in 1951, and the Federal Republic of Germany (West Germany) in 1955. France withdrew from all military aspects of NATO in 1968, remaining an active but informal member.

The organization, headquartered in Brussels, has both a civilian policy-making body, called the North Atlantic Council, and a military structure that oversees three commands: the Channel, Atlantic Ocean and European. NATO military forces operate under integrated command, but retain their national identities.

Spain's membership increased NATO's conventional forces, considered the alliance's weakest elements, according to Spanish Defense Minister Albert Oliart. To NATO's current forces, Spain added 340,000 troops, more than 190 war planes, 29 warships and eight submarines. These additions were particularly welcome at a time when Greece refused to participate in the joint NATO command that covered defense of Greece and Turkey. (Greece left NATO's military command in 1974 after fellow-member Turkey invaded Cyprus. The Greeks returned in late 1980, but they complained bitterly of insufficient NATO guarantees against potential Turkish attacks.)

Although increasing NATO's conventional forces, Spain, like members Denmark and Norway, stipulated it would not permit nuclear weapons to be stored in or used from its territory. Spain's foreign affairs minister also made clear that Spain would veto any use of its bases by NATO or U.S. forces for actions against nations friendly to Spain.

Political Issue

NATO membership became a political issue in Spain. The decision to join the alliance, made by Spain's ruling party, the Democratic Center Union, came after several years of deliberation. Shortly after the government made public its decision in August 1981, opponents rallied against the move.

The Spanish Socialist and Communist parties led the opposition and called for a national referendum on the NATO issue. They argued that Spain had never been a member of a military bloc and that NATO membership would not increase the security of Spain or her North African enclaves — Ceuta and Melilla. The government rejected the referendum suggestion and held that NATO membership would improve Spain's defense system and would supersede the bilateral treaty between Spain and the United States.

In September 1981 the Soviet Embassy in Madrid warned that Spain's entry would increase world tension. The Spanish government rebuffed the message as unacceptable interference in Spain's affairs. During his visit to the United States in October 1981, King Juan Carlos sought American support for Spain's attempt to join the alliance. President Reagan assured the monarch of U.S. backing.

Following is the text of the instrument of adhesion, marking Spain's May 30, 1982, entry into the North Atlantic Treaty Organizaton, as translated by the State Department:

Juan Carlos I
King of Spain

Bestowed by the Cortes Generales the authorization foreseen in Article 94.1 of the Constitution and, pursuantly, fulfilled the requirements demanded by Spanish legislation, I hereby extend this Instrument of Adhesion of the Kingdom of Spain to the North Atlantic Treaty, such that with its deposit and in conformity with the provision of its Article, the Kingdom of Spain becomes party to said Treaty.

In faith of which, I hereby sign this Instrument, duly sealed and authenticated by the undersigned Minister of Foreign Affairs.

Done in Madrid on the twenty-ninth day of May, 1982.

[Juan Carlos Rey]

The Minister of Foreign Affairs,
[Jose Pedro Perez Llorca]

JUNE

COURT ON AUTOMOBILE SEARCH AND SEIZURE

June 1, 1982

In a landmark search and seizure case, United States v. Ross, *the Supreme Court ruled June 1 that law enforcement officers with probable cause to search an automobile for contraband could examine any containers found within the car. The ruling reversed the court's 1981 decision in* Robbins v. California *and extended the "automobile exception" to the Fourth Amendment requirement for a search warrant.*

Justice John Paul Stevens wrote the court's opinion in which Chief Justice Warren E. Burger and Justices Harry A. Blackmun, Lewis F. Powell Jr., William H. Rehnquist and Sandra Day O'Connor joined. Justice Thurgood Marshall filed a dissenting opinion joined by Justice William J. Brennan Jr. Justice Byron R. White wrote a brief dissenting opinion.

The Carroll Decision

Since the 1925 decision in Carroll v. United States, *the court had distinguished between automobile and fixed-location searches. That case involved two known bootleggers who were stopped and searched by federal agents without a warrant. When the officers removed a seat cushion from the car, they discovered contraband liquor hidden inside. The bootleggers were found guilty of transporting liquor in violation of the National Prohibition Act.*

In upholding the conviction, the Supreme Court said that the police must have probable cause to believe a vehicle carried contraband before they could conduct a warrantless search and not violate the owner's Fourth Amendment rights. The probable cause determination had to be based on objective facts that would justify issuance of a warrant by a magistrate, not simply on the subjective good faith of the officers. The court recognized that contraband goods located in a car or other vehicle easily could be moved beyond the reach of a warrant and, with this case, established the automobile exception to the warrant requirement.

The court also noted that while it was necessary and practical for officers to obtain a warrant to search for contraband thought to be in a fixed location (such as a house or an office), securing such a warrant might be impractical "in cases involving the transportation of contraband goods."

Other Search and Seizure Decisions

Since Carroll *the court has handed down a number of decisions involving the automobile exception that may have caused confusion among law enforcement officials about what parts and containers in a car may be constitutionally searched.*

In both U.S. v. Chadwick *(1977) and* Arkansas v. Sanders *(1979), police officers had probable cause to believe that pieces of personal luggage were being used to transport marijuana. Although police were interested only in the contents of the luggage, in both cases they waited until the objects had been placed in a car before they seized and examined the bags. The court in these cases held the warrantless searches unconstitutional because "a person's expectations of privacy in personal luggage are substantially greater than in an automobile." Because the luggage, not the cars themselves, was the object of suspicion, the court ruled that the automobile exception did not apply in these cases.*

Robbins, *decided without a written opinion, concerned the search of plastic-wrapped packages that were found in the recessed luggage compartment of a station wagon. The car was stopped by officers because Robbins was driving erratically and searched when the officers smelled marijuana smoke in the car. Robbins was convicted, and the California Court of Appeal upheld the legality of the search. The Supreme Court reversed, saying that* Chadwick *and* Sanders *had established that a closed piece of luggage is constitutionally protected from search and that there was no difference between luggage and "less worthy containers."*

The Ross Case

The Ross *decision reflected the court's desire to end the confusion surrounding the search and seizure question and, thereby, to provide guidelines for the police.*

In November 1978 police in Washington, D.C., acting on a tip from a reliable source, stopped and arrested a man believed to be selling narcotics from his car. In a search of the vehicle, the officers discovered a paper bag and leather pouch in the trunk. The officers, without a warrant, opened both containers and found heroin in the paper bag and $3,200 in the leather pouch. On the basis of this evidence, Ross was convicted of possession of heroin with intent to distribute.

The Court of Appeals reversed Ross' conviction. The case first was reviewed by a three-judge panel of the appellate court, which tried to distinguish between the opening of a paper bag and a leather pouch. In applying the Sanders test to the Ross case, the panel held that the warrantless search of the paper bag was valid, but the search of the leather pouch was not because the owner's expectation of privacy in the contents of the pouch was far greater.

The full Court of Appeals then heard the Ross case and rejected the panel's attempt to distinguish between "worthy" and "unworthy" containers, that is, the leather pouch and the paper bag. The Fourth Amendment, held the appellate court, protected from warrantless search all closed containers in a stopped automobile, regardless of the degree of sophistication.

The Majority Opinion

The Supreme Court reversed the appellate court ruling. At issue in Ross, said Stevens, was whether the scope of a warrantless search authorized by Carroll permitted the opening of containers found within the automobile. Contraband goods by their very nature must be hidden from public view, noted Stevens. To permit the search of an automobile, without also authorizing a search of any containers within the vehicle, would rob the Carroll decision of any practical purpose. In effect, Carroll "...'merely relaxed the requirements for a warrant on the grounds of impracticability.' It neither broadened nor limited the scope of a lawful search based on probable cause.... Only the prior approval of the magistrate is waived; the search otherwise is as the magistrate could authorize."

Stevens concluded that "[t]he scope of a warrantless search of an automobile thus is not defined by the nature of the container in which the contraband is secreted. Rather, it is defined by the object of the search and the places in which there is probable cause to believe that it may be found."

The Dissent

Marshall argued that the decision disregarded "the value of a neutral and detatched magistrate" and showed contempt for the protections of *the Fourth Amendment. He wrote that the court long had insisted that only a magistrate could authorize search and seizure by issuing a warrant. In addition, said Marshall, this magistrate had to meet two criteria: "He must be neutral and detached, and he must be capable of determining whether probable cause exists for the requested arrest or search." Police officers, "engaged in the often competitive enterprise of ferreting out crime," could be not be expected to satisfy those standards, he said.*

Marshall also criticized the majority's argument concerning the mobility of the containers in question. Marshall argued that while the mobility of the car itself might justify an immediate search, the same did not apply to containers within a car that legally may be removed and held while a warrant is obtained.

Following are excerpts from the Supreme Court's June 1, 1982, decision in United States v. Ross *that police search of containers within automobiles does not violate the Fourth Amendment; and excerpts from the dissenting opinion by Justice Marshall:*

No. 80-2209

United States, petitioner ⎫   On writ of certiorari to the United
      v. ⎬   States Court of Appeals for the
Albert Ross, Jr. ⎭   District of Columbia Circuit

[June 1, 1982]

JUSTICE STEVENS delivered the opinion of the Court.

In *Carroll* v. *United States* [1925] the Court held that a warrantless search of an automobile stopped by police officers who had probable cause to believe the vehicle contained contraband was not unreasonable within the meaning of the Fourth Amendment. The Court in *Carroll* did not explicitly address the scope of the search that is permissible. In this case, we consider the extent to which police officers — who have legitimately stopped an automobile and who have probable cause to believe that contraband is concealed somewhere within it — may conduct a probing search of compartments and containers within the vehicle whose contents are not in plain view. We hold that they may conduct a search of the vehicle that is as thorough as a magistrate could authorize in a warrant "particularly describing the place to be searched."

I

In the evening of November 28, 1978, an informant who had previously proved to be reliable telephoned Detective Marcum of the District of Columbia Police Department and told him that an individual known as "Bandit" was selling narcotics kept in the trunk of a car parked at 439 Ridge Street. The informant stated that he had just observed "Bandit" complete a sale and that "Bandit" had told him that additional narcotics were in the trunk. The informant gave Marcum a detailed description of "Bandit" and stated that the car was a "purplish maroon" Chevrolet Malibu with District of Columbia license plates.

Accompanied by Detective Cassidy and Sergeant Gonzales, Marcum immediately drove to the area and found a maroon Malibu parked in front of 439 Ridge Street. A license check disclosed that the car was registered to Albert Ross; a computer check on Ross revealed that he fit the informant's description and used the alias "Bandit." In two passes through the neighborhood the officers did not observe anyone matching the informant's description. To avoid alerting persons on the street, they left the area.

The officers returned five minutes later and observed the maroon Malibu turning off Ridge Street onto Fourth Street. They pulled alongside the Malibu, noticed that the driver matched the informant's description, and stopped the car. Marcum and Cassidy told the driver — later identified as Albert Ross, the respondent in this action — to get out of the vehicle. While they searched Ross, Sergeant Gonzales discovered a bullet on the car's front seat. He searched the interior of the car and found a pistol in the glove compartment. Ross then was arrested and handcuffed. Detective Cassidy took Ross' keys and opened the trunk, where he found a closed brown paper bag. He opened the bag and discovered a number of glassine bags containing a white powder. Cassidy replaced the bag, closed the trunk, and drove the car to Headquarters.

At the police station Cassidy thoroughly searched the car. In addition to the "lunch-type" brown paper bag, Cassidy found in the trunk a zippered red leather pouch. He unzipped the pouch and discovered $3,200 in cash. The police laboratory later determined that the powder in the paper bag was heroin. No warrant was obtained.

Ross was charged with possession of heroin with intent to distribute, in violation of 21 U.S.C. § 841(a). Prior to trial, he moved to suppress the heroin found in the paper bag and the currency found in the leather pouch. After an evidentiary hearing, the District Court denied the motion to suppress. The heroin and currency were introduced in evidence at trial and Ross was convicted.

A three-judge panel of the Court of Appeals reversed the conviction. It held that the police had probable cause to stop and search Ross' car and that, under *Carroll* v. *United States* and *Chambers* v. *Maroney* [1970], the officers lawfully could search the automobile — including its trunk —

without a warrant. The court considered separately, however, the warrantless search of the two containers found in the trunk. On the basis of *Arkansas* v. *Sanders* [1979], the court concluded that the constitutionality of a warrantless search of a container found in an automobile depends on whether the owner possesses a reasonable expectation of privacy in its contents. Applying that test, the court held that the warrantless search of the paper bag was valid but the search of the leather pouch was not. The court remanded for a new trial at which the items taken from the paper bag, but not those from the leather pouch, could be admitted.

The entire Court of Appeals then voted to rehear the case en banc. A majority of the court rejected the panel's conclusion that a distinction of constitutional significance existed between the two containers found in respondent's trunk; it held that the police should not have opened either container without first obtaining a warrant. The court reasoned:

> "No specific, well-delineated exception called to our attention permits the police to dispense with a warrant to open and search 'unworthy' containers. Moreover, we believe that a rule under which the validity of a warrantless search would turn on judgments about the durability of a container would impose an unreasonable and unmanageable burden on police and courts. For these reasons, and because the Fourth Amendment protects all persons, not just those with the resources or fastidiousness to place their effects in containers that decisionmakers would rank in the luggage line, we hold that the Fourth Amendment warrant requirement forbids the warrantless opening of a closed, opaque paper bag to the same extent that it forbids the warrantless opening of a small unlocked suitcase or a zippered leather pouch."

The en banc Court of Appeals considered, and rejected, the argument that it was reasonable for the police to open both the paper bag and the leather pouch because they were entitled to conduct a warrantless search of the entire vehicle in which the two containers were found. The majority concluded that this argument was foreclosed by *Sanders.*

Three dissenting judges interpreted *Sanders* differently. Other courts also have read the *Sanders* opinion in different ways. Moreover, disagreement concerning the proper interpretation of *Sanders* was at least partially responsible for the fact that *Robbins* v. *California* [1981], was decided last Term without a Court opinion.

There is, however, no dispute among judges about the importance of striving for clarification in this area of the law. For countless vehicles are stopped on highways and public streets every day and our cases demonstrate that it is not uncommon for police officers to have probable cause to believe that contraband may be found in a stopped vehicle. In every such case a conflict is presented between the individual's constitutionally protected interest in privacy and the public interest in effective law enforcement. No single rule of law can resolve every conflict, but our conviction that clarification is feasible led us to grant the Government's petition for certiorari in this case and to invite the parties to address the question whether the decision in *Robbins* should be reconsidered.

II

We begin with a review of the decision in *Carroll* itself. In the fall of 1921, federal prohibition agents obtained evidence that George Carroll and John Kiro were "bootleggers" who frequently traveled between Grand Rapids and Detroit in an Oldsmobile Roadster. On December 15, 1921, the agents unexpectedly encountered Carroll and Kiro driving west on that route in that car. The officers gave pursuit, stopped the roadster on the highway, and directed Carroll and Kiro to get out of the car.

No contraband was visible in the front seat of the Oldsmobile and the rear portion of the roadster was closed. One of the agents raised the rumble seat but found no liquor. He raised the seat cushion and again found nothing. The officer then struck at the "lazyback" of the seat and noticed that it was "harder than upholstery ordinarily is in those backs." He tore open the seat cushion and discovered 68 bottles of gin and whiskey concealed inside. No warrant had been obtained for the search.

Carroll and Kiro were convicted of transporting intoxicating liquor in violation of the National Prohibition Act. On review of those convictions, this Court ruled that the warrantless search of the roadster was reasonable within the meaning of the Fourth Amendment. In an extensive opinion written by Chief Justice Taft, the Court held:

> "On reason and authority the true rule is that if the search and seizure without a warrant are made upon probable cause, that is, upon a belief, reasonably arising out of circumstances known to the seizing officer, that an automobile or other vehicle contains that which by law is subject to seizure and destruction, the search and seizure are valid. The Fourth Amendment is to be construed in the light of what was deemed an unreasonable search and seizure when it was adopted, and in a manner which will conserve public interests as well as the interests and right of individual citizens."

The Court explained at length the basis for this rule. The Court noted that historically warrantless searches of vessels, wagons, and carriages — as opposed to fixed premises such as a home or other building — had been considered reasonable by Congress. . . .

. . . [S]ince its earliest days Congress had recognized the impracticability of securing a warrant in cases involving the transportation of contraband goods. It is this impracticability, viewed in historical perspective, that provided the basis for the *Carroll* decision. Given the nature of an automobile in transit, the Court recognized that an immediate intrusion is necessary if police officers are to secure the illicit substance. In this class of cases, the Court held that a warrantless search of an automobile is not unreasonable.

In defining the nature of this "exception" to the general rule that "[i]n cases where the securing of a warrant is reasonably practicable, it must be used," the Court in *Carroll* emphasized the importance of the requirement that officers have probable cause to believe that the vehicle contains contraband.

"Having thus established that contraband goods concealed and illegally transported in an automobile or other vehicle may be searched for without a warrant, we come now to consider under what circumstances such search may be made. It would be intolerable and unreasonable if a prohibition agent were authorized to stop every automobile on the chance of finding liquor and thus subject all persons lawfully using the highways to the inconvenience and indignity of such a search. Travellers may be so stopped in crossing an international boundary because of national self protection reasonably requiring one entering the country to identify himself as entitled to come in, and his belongings as effects which may be lawfully brought in. But those lawfully within the country, entitled to use the public highways, have a right to free passage without interruption or search unless there is known to a competent official authorized to search, probable cause for believing that their vehicles are carrying contraband or illegal merchandise."

Moreover, the probable cause determination must be based on objective facts that could justify the issuance of a warrant by a magistrate and not merely on the subjective good faith of the police officers. " '[A]s we have seen, good faith is not enough to constitute probable cause. That faith must be grounded on facts within knowledge of the [officer], which in the judgment of the court would make his faith reasonable.' "

In short, the exception to the warrant requirement established in *Carroll* — the scope of which we consider in this case — applies only to searches of vehicles that are supported by probable cause. In this class of cases, a search is not unreasonable if based on facts that would justify the issuance of a warrant, even though a warrant has not actually been obtained.

III

The rationale justifying a warrantless search of an automobile that is believed to be transporting contraband arguably applies with equal force to any movable container that is believed to be carrying an illicit substance. That argument, however, was squarely rejected in *United States* v. *Chadwick* [1977].

Chadwick involved the warrantless search of a 200-pound footlocker secured with two padlocks. Federal railroad officials in San Diego became suspicious when they noticed that a brown footlocker loaded onto a train bound for Boston was unusually heavy and leaking talcum power, a substance often used to mask the odor of marijuana. Narcotics agents met the train in Boston and a trained police dog signaled the presence of a controlled substance inside the footlocker. The agents did not seize the footlocker, however, at this time: they waited until respondent Chadwick arrived and the footlocker was placed in the trunk of Chadwick's automobile. Before the engine was started, the officers arrested Chadwick and his two companions. The agents then removed the footlocker to a secured place, opened it without a warrant, and discovered a large quantity of marijuana.

In a subsequent criminal proceeding, Chadwick claimed that the warrantless search of the footlocker violated the Fourth Amendment. In the District Court, the Government argued that as soon as the footlocker was placed in the automobile a warrantless search was permissible under *Carroll*. The District Court rejected that argument, and the Government did not pursue it on appeal. Rather, the Government contended in this Court that the warrant requirement of the Fourth Amendment applied only to searches of homes and other "core" areas of privacy. The Court unanimously rejected that contention. Writing for the Court, THE CHIEF JUSTICE stated:

> "[I]f there is little evidence that the Framers intended the Warrant Clause to operate outside the home, there is no evidence at all that they intended to exclude from protection of the Clause all searches occurring outside the home.... What we do know is that the Framers were men who focused on the wrongs of that day but who intended the Fourth Amendment to safeguard fundamental values which would far outlast the specific abuses which gave it birth."

The Court in *Chadwick* specifically rejected the argument that the warrantless search was "reasonable" because a footlocker has some of the mobile characteristics that support warrantless searches of automobiles. The Court recognized that "a person's expectations of privacy in personal luggage are substantially greater than in an automobile" and noted that the practical problems associated with the temporary detention of a piece of luggage during the period of time necessary to obtain a warrant are significantly less than those associated with the detention of an auto-mobile. In ruling that the warrantless search of the footlocker was unjustified, the Court reaffirmed the general principle that closed pack-ages and containers may not be searched without a warrant.... In sum, the Court in *Chadwick* declined to extend the rationale of the "automobile exception" to permit a warrantless search of any movable container found in a public place.

The facts in *Arkansas* v. *Sanders* were similar to those in *Chadwick*. In *Sanders*, a Little Rock police officer received information from a reliable informant that Sanders would arrive at the local airport on a specified flight that afternoon carrying a green suitcase containing marijuana. The officer went to the airport. Sanders arrived on schedule and retrieved a green suitcase from the airline baggage service. Sanders gave the suitcase to a waiting companion who placed it in the trunk of a taxi. Sanders and his companion drove off in the cab; police officers followed and stopped the taxi several blocks from the airport. The officers opened the trunk, seized the suitcase, and searched it on the scene without a warrant. As predicted, the suitcase contained marijuana.

The Arkansas Supreme Court ruled that the warrantless search of the suitcase was impermissible under the Fourth Amendment, and this Court affirmed. As in *Chadwick*, the mere fact that the suitcase had been placed in the trunk of the vehicle did not render the automobile exception of *Carroll* applicable; the police had probable cause to seize the suitcase before it was placed in the trunk of the cab and did not have probable cause to search the taxi itself. Since the suitcase had been placed in the trunk, no danger existed that its contents could have been secreted elsewhere in the vehicle. As THE CHIEF JUSTICE noted in his opinion concurring in the judgment:

> "Because the police officers had probable cause to believe that respondent's green suitcase contained marijuana before it was placed in the trunk of the taxicab, their duty to obtain a search warrant before opening it is clear under *United States* v. *Chadwick* (1977).
>
> Here, as in *Chadwick*, it was the *luggage* being transported by respondent at the time of the arrest, not the automobile in which it was being carried, that was the suspected locus of the contraband. The relationship between the automobile and the contraband was purely coincidental, as in *Chadwick*. The fact that the suitcase was resting in the trunk of the automobile at the time of respondent's arrest does not turn this into an 'automobile' exception case. The Court need say no more."

The Court in *Sanders* did not, however, rest its decision solely on the authority of *Chadwick*. In rejecting the State's argument that the warrantless search of the suitcase was justified on the ground that it had been taken from an automobile lawfully stopped on the street, the Court broadly suggested that a warrantless search of a container found in an automobile could never be sustained as part of a warrantless search of the automobile itself. The Court did not suggest that it mattered whether probable cause existed to search the entire vehicle. It is clear, however, that in neither *Chadwick* nor *Sanders* did the police have probable cause to search the vehicle or anything within it except the footlocker in the former case and the green suitcase in the latter.

Robbins v. *California*, however, was a case in which suspicion was not directed at a specific container. In that case the Court for the first time was forced to consider whether police officers who are entitled to conduct a warrantless search of an automobile stopped on a public roadway may open a container found within the vehicle. In the early morning of January 5, 1975, police officers stopped Robbins' station wagon because he was driving erratically. Robbins got out of the car, but later returned to obtain the vehicle's registration papers. When he opened the car door, the officers smelled marijuana smoke. One of the officers searched Robbins and discovered a vial of liquid; in a search of the interior of the car the officer found marijuana. The police officers then opened the tailgate of the station wagon and raised the cover of a recessed luggage compartment. In the compartment they found two packages wrapped in green opaque plastic. The police unwrapped the packages and discovered a large amount of marijuana in each.

Robbins was charged with various drug offenses and moved to suppress the contents of the plastic packages. The California Court of Appeal held that "[s]earch of the automobile was proper when the officers learned that appellant was smoking marijuana when they stopped him" and that the warrantless search of the packages was justified because "the contents of the packages could have been inferred from their outward appearance, so that appellant could not have held a reasonable expectation of privacy with respect to the contents." (1980).

This Court reversed. Writing for a plurality, Justice Stewart rejected the argument that the outward appearance of the packages precluded Robbins from having a reasonable expectation of privacy in their contents. He also squarely rejected the argument that there is a constitutional distinction between searches of luggage and searches of "less worthy" containers. Justice Stewart reasoned that all containers are equally protected by the Fourth Amendment unless their contents are in plain view. The plurality concluded that the warrantless search was impermissible because *Chadwick* and *Sanders* had established that "a closed piece of luggage found in a lawfully searched car is constitutionally protected to the same extent as are closed pieces of luggage found anywhere else."

In a concurring opinion, JUSTICE POWELL, the author of the Court's opinion in *Sanders*, stated that "[t]he plurality's approach strains the rationales of our prior cases and imposes substantial burdens on law enforcement without vindicating any significant values of privacy." He noted that possibly "the controlling question should be the scope of the automobile exception to the warrant requirement" and explained that under that view:

> "when the police have probable cause to search an automobile, rather than only to search a particular container that fortuitously is located in it, the exigencies that allow the police to search the entire automobile without a warrant support the warrantless search of every container found therein. This analysis is entirely consistent with the holdings in *Chadwick* and *Sanders*, neither of which is an 'automobile case,' because the police there had probable cause to search the double-locked footlocker and the suitcase respectively before either came near an automobile."

The parties in *Robbins* had not pressed that argument, however, and JUSTICE POWELL concluded that institutional constraints made it inappropriate to re-examine basic doctrine without full adversary presentation. He concurred in the judgment, since it was supported — although not compelled — by the Court's opinion in *Sanders*, and stated that a future case might present a better opportunity for thorough consideration of the basic principles in this troubled area.

That case has arrived. Unlike *Chadwick* and *Sanders*, in this case police officers had probable cause to search respondent's entire vehicle. Unlike *Robbins*, in this case the parties have squarely addressed the question whether, in the course of a legitimate warrantless search of an automobile, police are entitled to open containers found within the vehicle. We now address that question. Its answer is determined by the scope of the search that is authorized by the exception to the warrant requirement set forth in *Carroll*.

IV

In *Carroll* itself, the whiskey that the prohibition agents seized was not in plain view. It was discovered only after an officer opened the rumble seat and tore open the upholstery of the lazyback. The Court did not find the scope of the search unreasonable.... The scope of the search was no greater than a magistrate could have authorized by issuing a warrant based on the probable cause that justified the search. Since such a warrant could have authorized the agents to open the rear portion of the roadster and to rip the upholstery in their search for concealed whiskey, the search was constitutionally permissible.

In *Chambers* v. *Maroney* the police found weapons and stolen property "concealed in a compartment under the dashboard." No suggestion was made that the scope of the search was impermissible. It would be illogical to assume that the outcome of *Chambers* — or the outcome of *Carroll* itself — would have been different if the police had found the secreted contraband enclosed within a secondary container and had opened that container without a warrant. If it was reasonable for prohibition agents to rip open the upholstery in *Carroll*, it certainly would have been reasonable for them to look into a burlap sack stashed inside; if it was reasonable to open the concealed compartment in *Chambers*, it would have been equally reasonable to open a paper bag crumpled within it. A contrary rule could produce absurd results inconsistent with the decision in *Carroll* itself.

In its application of *Carroll*, this Court in fact has sustained warrantless searches of containers found during a lawful search of an automobile In *Husty* v. *United States* [1931], the Court upheld a warrantless seizure of whiskey found during a search of an automobile, some of which was discovered in "whiskey bags" that could have contained other goods. In *Scher* v. *United States* [1938], federal officers seized and searched packages of unstamped liquor found in the trunk of an automobile searched without a warrant.... In these cases it was not contended that police officers needed a warrant to open the whiskey bags or to unwrap the brown paper packages. These decisions nevertheless "have much weight, as they show that this point neither occurred to the bar or the bench." *Bank of the United States* v. *Deveaux* [1809]. The fact that no such argument was even made illuminates the profession's understanding of the scope of the search permitted under *Carroll*. Indeed, prior to the decisions in *Chadwick* and *Sanders*, courts routinely had held that containers and packages found during a legitimate warrantless search of an automobile also could be searched without a warrant.

As we have stated, the decision in *Carroll* was based on the Court's appraisal of practical considerations viewed in the perspective of history. It is therefore significant that the practical consequences of the *Carroll* decision would be largely nullified if the permissible scope of a warrantless search of an automobile did not include containers and packages found inside the vehicle. Contraband goods rarely are strewn across the trunk or floor of a car; since by their very nature such goods must be withheld from public view, they rarely can be placed in an automobile unless they are enclosed within some form of container. The Court in *Carroll* held that "contraband goods *concealed* and illegally transported in an automobile or other vehicle may be searched for without an warrant."([E]mphasis added). As we noted in *Henry* v. *United States* [1959], the decision in *Carroll* "merely relaxed the requirement for a warrant on grounds of impracticability." It neither broadened nor limited the scope of a lawful search based on probable cause.

A lawful search of fixed premises generally extends to the entire area in which the object of the search may be found and is not limited by the possibility that separate acts of entry or opening may be required to complete the search. Thus, a warrant that authorizes an officer to search a home for illegal weapons also provides authority to open closets, chests, drawers, and containers in which the weapon might be found. A warrant to open a footlocker to search for marijuana would also authorize the opening of packages found inside. A warrant to search a vehicle would support a search of every part of the vehicle that might contain the object of the search. When a legitimate search is underway, and when its purpose and its limits have been precisely defined, nice distinctions between closets, drawers, and containers, in the case of a home, or between glove compartments, upholstered seats, trunks, and wrapped packages, in the case of a vehicle, must give way to the interest in the prompt and efficient completion of the task at hand.

This rule applies equally to all containers, as indeed we believe it must. One point on which the Court was in virtually unanimous agreement in *Robbins* was that a constitutional distinction between "worthy" and "unworthy" containers would be improper. Even though such a distinction perhaps could evolve in a series of cases in which paper bags, locked trunks, lunch buckets, and orange crates were placed on one side of the line or the other, the central purpose of the Fourth Amendment forecloses such a distinction. For just as the most frail cottage in the kingdom is absolutely entitled to the same guarantees of privacy as the most majestic mansion, so also may a traveler who carries a toothbrush and a few articles of clothing in a paper bag or knotted scarf claim an equal right to conceal his possessions from official inspection as the sophisticated executive with the locked attaché case.

As Justice Stewart stated in *Robbins*, the Fourth Amendment provides protection to the owner of every container that conceals its contents from plain view. But the protection afforded by the Amendment varies in different settings. The luggage carried by a traveler entering the country may be searched at random by a customs officer; the luggage may be searched no matter how great the traveler's desire to conceal the contents may be. A container carried at the time of arrest often may be searched without a warrant and even without any specific suspicion concerning its contents. A container that may conceal the object of a search authorized by a warrant may be opened immediately; the individual's interest in privacy must give way to the magistrate's official determination of probable cause.

In the same manner, an individual's expectation of privacy in a vehicle and its contents may not survive if probable cause is given to believe that the vehicle is transporting contraband. Certainly the privacy interests in a car's trunk or glove compartment may be no less than those in a movable container. An individual undoubtedly has a significant interest that the upholstery of his automobile will not be ripped or a hidden compartment within it opened. These interests must yield to the authority of a search, however, which — in light of *Carroll* — does not itself require the prior approval of a magistrate. The scope of a warrantless search based on probable cause is no narrower — and no broader — than the scope of a search authorized by a warrant supported by probable cause. Only the prior approval of the magistrate is waived; the search otherwise is as the magistrate could authorize.

The scope of a warrantless search of an automobile thus is not defined by the nature of the container in which the contraband is secreted. Rather, it is defined by the object of the search and the places in which there is probable cause to believe that it may be found. Just as probable cause to believe that a stolen lawnmower may be found in a garage will not support a warrant to search an upstairs bedroom, probable cause to believe that undocumented aliens are being transported in a van will not justify a warrantless search of a suitcase. Probable cause to believe that a container placed in the trunk of a taxi contains contraband or evidence does not justify a search of the entire cab.

V

Our decision today is inconsistent with the disposition in *Robbins* v. *California* and with the portion of the opinion in *Arkansas* v. *Sanders* on which the plurality in *Robbins* relied. Nevertheless, the doctrine of *stare decisis* does not preclude this action. Although we have rejected some of the reasoning in *Sanders*, we adhere to our holding in that case; although we reject the precise holding in *Robbins*, there was no Court opinion supporting a single rationale for its judgment and the reasoning we adopt today was not presented by the parties in that case. Moreover, it is clear that no legitimate reliance interest can be frustrated by our decision today. Of greatest importance, we are convinced that the rule we apply in this case is faithful to the interpretation of the Fourth Amendment that the Court has followed with substantial consistency throughout our history.

We reaffirm the basic rule of Fourth Amendment jurisprudence stated by Justice Stewart for a unanimous Court in *Mincey* v. *Arizona* [1978]:

> "The Fourth Amendment proscribes all unreasonable searches and seizures, and it is a cardinal principle that 'searches conducted outside the judicial process, without prior approval by judge or magistrate, are *per se* unreasonable under the Fourth Amendment — subject only to a few specifically established and well-delineated exceptions.' *Katz* v. *United States* [1967]."

The exception recognized in *Carroll* is unquestionably one that is "specifically established and well-delineated." We hold that the scope of the warrantless search authorized by that exception is no broader and no narrower than a magistrate could legitimately authorize by warrant. If probable cause justified the search of a lawfully stopped vehicle, it justifies the search of every part of the vehicle and its contents that may conceal the object of the search.

The judgment of the Court of Appeals is reversed. The case is remanded for further proceedings consistent with this opinion.

It is so ordered.

JUSTICE MARSHALL, with whom JUSTICE BRENNAN joins, dissenting.

The majority today not only repeals all realistic limits on warrantless automobile searches, it repeals the Fourth Amendment warrant requirement itself. By equating a police officer's estimation of probable cause with a magistrate's, the Court utterly disregards the value of a neutral and detached magistrate. For as we recently, and unanimously, reaffirmed:

> "The warrant traditionally has represented an independent assurance that a search and arrest will not proceed without probable cause to believe that a crime has been committed and that the person or place named in the warrant is involved in the crime. Thus, an issuing magistrate must meet two tests. He must be neutral and detached, and he must be capable of determining whether probable cause exists for the requested arrest or search. This Court long has insisted that inferences of probable cause be drawn by 'a neutral and detached magistrate instead of being judged by the officer engaged in the often competitive enterprise of ferreting out crime.' " *Shadwick* v. *City of Tampa* (1972), citing *Johnson* v. *United States* (1984).

A police officer on the beat hardly satisfies these standards. In adopting today's new rule, the majority opinion shows contempt for these Fourth Amendment values, ignores this Court's precedents, is internally inconsistent, and produces anomalous and unjust consequences. I therefore dissent.

I

According to the majority, whenever police have probable cause to believe that contraband may be found within an automobile that they have stopped on the highway, they may search not only the automobile but also any container found inside it, without obtaining a warrant. The scope of the search, we are told, is as broad as a magistrate could authorize in a warrant to search the automobile. The majority makes little attempt to justify this rule in terms of recognized Fourth Amendment values. The Court simply ignores the critical function that a magistrate serves. And although the Court purports to rely on the mobility of an automobile and the impracticability of obtaining a warrant, it never explains why these concerns permit the warrantless search of a *container*, which can easily be seized and immobilized while police are obtaining a warrant.

The new rule adopted by the Court today is completely incompatible with established Fourth Amendment principles, and takes a first step toward an unprecedented "probable cause" exception to the warrant requirement. In my view, under accepted standards, the warrantless search of the container in this case clearly violates the Fourth Amendment.

A

"[I]t is a cardinal principle that 'searches conducted outside the judicial process, without prior approval by judge or magistrate, are *per se* unreasonable under the Fourth Amendment — subject only to a few specifically established and well-delineated exceptions.'" *Mincey* v. *Arizona* (1978), citing *Katz* v. *United States* (1967). The warrant requirement is crucial to protecting Fourth Amendment rights because of the importance of having the probable cause determination made in the first instance by a neutral and detached magistrate. Time and again, we have emphasized that the warrant requirement provides a number of protections that a post-hoc judicial evaluation of a policeman's probable cause does not.

The requirement of prior review by a detached and neutral magistrate limits the concentration of power held by executive officers over the individual, and prevents some overbroad or unjustified searches from occurring at all. See *United States* v. *United States District Court* (1972); *Abel* v. *United States* (1959) (JUSTICE BRENNAN, with whom Chief Justice Warren, Justice Black, and Justice Douglas join, dissenting). Prior review may also "prevent hindsight from coloring the evaluation of the reasonableness of a search or seizure." *United States* v. *Martinez-Fuerte* (1976); see also *Beck* v. *Ohio* (1964). Furthermore, even if a magistrate would have authorized the search that the police conducted, the interposition of a magistrate's neutral judgment reassures the public that the orderly process of law has been respected.... The safeguards embodied in the warrant requirement apply as forcefully to automobile searches as to any others.

Our cases do recognize a narrow exception to the warrant requirement for certain automobile searches. Throughout our decisions, two major considerations have been advanced to justify the automobile exception to the warrant requirement. We have upheld only those searches that are actually justified by those considerations.

First, these searches have been justified on the basis of the exigency of the mobility of the automobile. See, *e.g.*, *Chambers* v. *Maroney* (1970); *Carroll* v. *United States* (1925). This "mobility" rationale is something of a misnomer ... since the police ordinarily can remove the car's occupants and secure the vehicle on the spot. However, the inherent mobility of the vehicle often creates situations in which the police's only alternative to an immediate search may be to release the automobile from their possession. This alternative creates an unacceptably high risk of losing the contents of the vehicle, and is a principal basis for the Court's automobile exception to the warrant requirement.

In many cases, however, the police will, prior to searching the car, have cause to arrest the occupants and bring them to the station for booking. In this situation, the police can ordinarily seize the automobile and bring it to the station. Because the vehicle is now in the exclusive control of the authorities, any subsequent search cannot be justified by the mobility of the car. Rather, an immediate warrantless search of the vehicle is permitted because of the second major justification for the automobile exception: the diminished expectation of privacy in an automobile.

Because an automobile presents much of its contents in open view to police officers who legitimately stop it on a public way, is used for travel, and is subject to significant government regulation, this Court has determined that the intrusion of a warrantless search of an automobile is constitutionally less significant that a warrantless search of more private areas. See *Arkansas* v. *Sanders* (1979) (collecting cases). This justification has been invoked for warrantless automobile searches in circumstances where the exigency of mobility was clearly not present.... By focusing on the defendant's reasonable expectation of privacy, this Court has refused to require a warrant in situations where the process of obtaining such a warrant would be more intrusive than the actual search itself. Cf. *Katz* v. *United States* (1967). A defendant may consider the seizure of the car a greater intrusion than an immediate search.... Therefore, even where police *can* bring both the defendants and the automobile to the station safely and can house the car while they seek a warrant, the police are permitted to decide whether instead to conduct an immediate search of the car. In effect, the warrantless search is permissible because a warrant requirement would not provide significant protection of the defendant's Fourth Amendment interests.

B

The majority's rule is flatly inconsistent with these established Fourth Amendment principles concerning the scope of the automobile exception and the importance of the warrant requirement. Historically, the automobile exception has been limited to those situations where its application is compelled by the justifications described above. Today, the majority makes no attempt to base its decision on these justifications. This failure is not surprising, since the traditional rationales for the automobile exception plainly do not support extending it to the search of a container found inside a vehicle.

The practical mobility problem — deciding what to do with both the car and the occupants if an immediate search is not conducted — is simply not present in the case of movable containers, which can easily be seized and brought to the magistrate.... The lesser expectation of privacy rationale also has little force. A container, as opposed to the car itself, does not reflect diminished privacy interests....

Ultimately, the majority, unable to rely on the justifications underlying the automobile exception, simply creates a new "probable cause" exception to the warrant requirement for automobiles. We have soundly rejected attempts to create such an exception in the past, see *Coolidge* v. *New Hampshire* (1971), and we should do so again today.

. . .[I]n blithely suggesting that *Carroll* "neither broadened nor limited the scope of a lawful search based on probable cause," the majority assumes what has never been the law: that the scope of the automobile-mobility exception to the warrant requirement is as broad as the scope of a "lawful" probable cause search of an automobile, *i.e.*, one authorized by a magistrate.

The majority's sleight-of-hand ignores the obvious differences between the function served by a magistrate in making a determination of probable cause and the function of the automobile exception. It is irrelevant to a magistrate's function whether the items subject to search are mobile, may be in danger of destruction, or are impractical to store, or whether an immediate search would be less intrusive than a seizure without a warrant. A magistrate's only concern is whether there is probable cause to search them. Where suspicion has focused not on a particular item but only on a vehicle, home, or office, the magistrate might reasonably authorize a search of closed containers at the location as well. But an officer on the beat who searches an automobile without a warrant is not entitled to conduct a broader search than the exigency obviating the warrant justifies. After all, what justifies the warrantless search is not probable cause alone, but *probable cause coupled with the mobility of the automobile*. Because the scope of a *warrantless* search should depend on the scope of the justification for dispensing with a warrant, the entire premise of the majority's opinion fails to support its conclusion.

The majority's rule masks the startling assumption that a policeman's determination of probable cause is the functional equivalent of the determination of a neutral and detached magistrate. This assumption ignores a major premise of the warrant requirement — the importance of having a neutral and detached magistrate determine whether probable cause exists. The majority's explanation that the scope of the warrantless automobile search will be "limited" to what a magistrate could authorize is thus inconsistent with our cases, which firmly establish that an on-the-spot determination of probable cause is *never* the same as a decision by a neutral and detached magistrate.

C

Our recent decisions in *United States* v. *Chadwick* (1977), *Arkansas* v. *Sanders*, and *Robbins* v. *California* clearly affirm that movable containers are different from automobiles for Fourth Amendment purposes. In *Chadwick*, the Court drew a constitutional distinction between luggage and automobiles in terms of substantial differences in expectations of privacy. Moreover, the Court held that the mobility of such containers does not justify dispensing with a warrant, since federal agents had seized the luggage and safely transferred it to their custody under their exclusive control. *Sanders* explicitly held that "the warrant requirement applies to personal luggage taken from an automobile to the same degree it applies to such luggage in other locations." And *Robbins* reaffirmed the *Sanders* rationale as applied to wrapped packages found in the unlocked luggage compartment of a vehicle.

In light of these considerations, I conclude that any movable container found within an automobile deserves precisely the same degree of Fourth Amendment warrant protection that it would deserve if found at a location outside the automobile. . . . *Chadwick*, as the majority notes, "reaffirmed the general principle that closed packages and containers may not be searched without a warrant." Although there is no need to describe the exact contours of that protection in this dissenting opinion, it is clear enough that closed, opaque containers — regardless of whether they are "worthy" or are always used to store personal items — are ordinarily fully protected.

Here, because appellant Ross had placed the evidence in question in a closed paper bag, the container could be seized, but not searched, without a warrant. No practical exigencies required the warrantless searches on the street or at the station: Ross had been arrested and was in custody when both searches occurred, and the police succeeded in transporting the bag to the station without inadvertently spilling its contents.

II

In announcing its new rule, the Court purports to rely on earlier automobile search cases, especially *Carroll* v. *United States*. The Court's approach, however, far from being "faithful to the interpretation of the Fourth Amendment that the Court has followed with substantial consistency throughout our history" is plainly contrary to the letter and the spirit of our prior automobile search cases. Moreover, the new rule produces anomalous and unacceptable consequences.

A

The majority's argument that its decision is supported by our decisions in *Carroll* and *Chambers* is misplaced. The Court in *Carroll* upheld a warrantless search of an automobile for contraband on the basis of the impracticability of securing a warrant in cases involving the transportation of contraband goods. The Court did not, however, suggest that obtaining a warrant for the search of an automobile is always impracticable. "In cases where the securing of a warrant is reasonably practicable, *it must be used*. . . . In cases where seizure is impossible except without warrant, the seizing officer acts unlawfully and at his peril unless he can show the court probable cause." ([E]mphasis added). As this Court reaffirmed in *Chambers* "[n]either *Carroll* nor other cases in this Court require or suggest that in every conceivable circumstance the search of an auto even with probable cause may be made without the extra protection for privacy that a warrant affords."

Notwithstanding the reasoning of these cases, the majority argues that *Carroll* and *Chambers* support its decisions because integral compartments of a car are functionally equivalent to containers found within a car, and because the practical advantages to the police of the *Carroll* doctrine "would be largely nullified if the permissible scope of a warrantless search of an automobile did not include containers and packages found inside the vehicle." Neither of these arguments is persuasive. First, the Court's argument that allowing warrantless searches of certain integral compartments of the car in *Carroll* and *Chambers*, while protecting movable containers within the car, would be "illogical" and "absurd" ignores the reason why this Court has allowed warrantless searches of automobile compartments. Surely an integral compartment within a car is just as mobile, and presents the same practical problems of safekeeping, as the car itself. This cannot be said of movable containers located within the car. The fact that there may be a high expectation of privacy in both containers and compartments is irrelevant, since the privacy rationale is not, and cannot be, the justification for the warrantless search of compartments.

The Court's second argument, which focuses on the practical advantages to police of the *Carroll* doctrine, fares no better. The practical considerations which concerned the *Carroll* Court involved the difficulty of immobilizing a vehicle while a warrant must be obtained. The Court had no occasion to address whether *containers* present the same practical difficulties as the car itself or integral compartments of the car. They do not. *Carroll* hardly suggested, as the Court implies, that a warrantless search is justified simply because it assists police in obtaining more evidence.

Although it can find no support for its rule in this Court's precedents or in the traditional justifications for the automobile exception, the majority offers another justification. In a footnote, the majority suggests that "practical considerations" militate against securing containers found during an automobile search and taking them to the magistrate. The Court confidently remarks: "Certainly no privacy interest is served ... by prohibiting police from opening immediately a container in which the object of the search may most likely be found and instead forcing them first to comb the entire vehicle. Moreover, until the container itself was opened the police could never be certain that the contraband was not secreted in a yet undiscovered portion of the vehicle." The vehicle would have to be seized while a warrant was obtained, a requirement inconsistent with *Carroll* and *Chambers*.

This explanation is unpersuasive. As this Court explained in *Sanders* and as the majority today implicitly concedes, the burden to police departments of seizing a package or personal luggage simply does not compare to the burden of seizing and safeguarding automobiles. Other aspects of the Court's explanation are also implausible. The search will not always require a "combing" of the entire vehicle, since police may be looking for a particular item and may discover it promptly. If, instead, they are looking more generally for evidence of a crime, the immediate opening of the container will not protect the defendant's privacy; whether or not it contains contraband, the police will continue to search for new evidence. Finally, the defendant, not the police, should be afforded the choice whether he prefers the immediate opening of his suitcase or other container to the delay incident to seeking a warrant. The more reasonable presumption, if a presumption is to replace the defendant's consent, is surely that the immediate search of a closed container will be a greater invasion of the defendant's privacy interests than a mere temporary seizure of the container.

B

Finally, the majority's new rule is theoretically unsound and will create anomalous and unwarranted results. These consequences are readily apparent from the Court's attempt to reconcile its new rule with the holdings of *Chadwick* and *Sanders*. The Court suggests that probable cause to search only a container does not justify a warrantless search of an automobile in which it is placed, absent reason to believe that the contents could be secreted elsewhere in the vehicle. This, the majority asserts, is an indication that the new rule is carefully limited to its justification, and is not inconsistent with *Chadwick* and *Sanders*. But why is such a container more private, less difficult for police to seize and store, or in any other relevant respect more properly subject to the warrant requirement, than a container that police discover in a probable cause search of an entire automobile? This rule plainly has peculiar and unworkable consequences: the Government "must show that the investigating officer knew enough but not too much, that he had sufficient knowledge to establish probable cause but insufficient knowledge to know exactly where the contraband was located." *United States* v. *Ross* (CADC 1981) (en banc) (Wilkey, J., dissenting).

Alternatively, the majority may be suggesting that *Chadwick* and *Sanders* may be explained because the connection of the container to the vehicle was incidental in these two cases. That is, because police had preexisting probable cause to seize and search the containers, they were not entitled to wait until the item was placed in a vehicle to take advantage of the automobile exception.... I wholeheartedly agree that police cannot employ a pretext to escape Fourth Amendment prohibitions and cannot rely on an exigency that they could easily have avoided. This interpretation, however, might well be an exception that swallows up the majority's rule. In neither *Chadwick* nor *Sanders* did the Court suggest that the delay of the police was a pretext for taking advantage of the automobile exception. For all that appears, the Government may have had legitimate reasons for not searching as soon as they had probable cause. In any event, asking police to rely on such an uncertain line in distinguishing between legitimate and illegitimate searches for containers in automobiles hardly indicates that the majority's approach has brought clarification to this area of the law.

III

The Court today ignores the clear distinction that *Chadwick* established between movable containers and automobiles. It also rejects all of the relevant reasoning of *Sanders* and offers a substitute rationale that appears inconsistent with the results. *Sanders* is therefore effectively overruled. And the Court unambiguously overrules "the disposition" of *Robbins*, though it gingerly avoids stating that it is overruling the case itself.

The only convincing explanation I discern for the majority's broad rule is expediency: it assists police in conducting automobile searches, ensuring that the private containers into which criminal suspects often place goods will no longer be a Fourth Amendment shield. "When a legitimate search is under way," the Court instructs us, "nice distinctions between . . . glove compartments, upholstered seats, trunks, and wrapped packages . . . must give way to the interest in the prompt and efficient completion of the task at hand." No "nice distinctions" are necessary, however, to comprehend the well-recognized differences between movable containers (which, even after today's decision, would be subject to the warrant requirement if located outside an automobile), and the automobile itself, together with its integral parts. Nor can I pass by the majority's glib assertion that the "prompt and efficient completion of the task at hand" is paramount to the Fourth Amendment interests of our citizens. I had thought it well established that "the mere fact that law enforcement may be made more efficient can never by itself justify disregard of the Fourth Amendment." *Mincey* v. *Arizona* (1978).

This case will have profound implications for the privacy of citizens traveling in automobiles, as the Court well understands. "For countless vehicles are stopped on highways and public streets every day and our cases demonstrate that it is not uncommon for police officers to have probable cause to believe that contraband may be found in a stopped vehicle." A closed paper bag, a tool box, a knapsack, a suitcase, and an attache case can alike be searched without the protection of the judgment of a neutral magistrate, based only on the rarely disturbed decision of a police officer that he has probable cause to search for contraband in the vehicle. The Court derives satisfaction from the fact that its rule does not exalt the rights of the wealthy over the rights of the poor. A rule so broad that all citizens lose vital Fourth Amendment protection is no cause for celebration.

I dissent.

COURT ON FEDERAL POWER
TO REGULATE UTILITIES
June 1, 1982

Dividing over the issue of state versus federal power, the Supreme Court June 1 upheld by one vote a 1978 federal energy law designed to encourage conservation by state utility commissions. The law required state regulatory commissions to consider adopting certain rate-design schemes such as charging more for electricity consumed during peak load hours or charging less for a service that could be interrupted during peak demand periods. It also exempted from certain state and federal regulations small power plants and cogeneration facilities, which produced both electricity and heat.

The state of Mississippi had challenged the law — Public Utility Regulatory Policies Act of 1978 (PURPA) — on grounds that it exceeded Congress' power to regulate interstate commerce and infringed upon the sovereignty reserved to the states under the 10th Amendment. A federal district judge had held the law invalid in February 1981. But the federal government appealed the case — Federal Energy Regulatory Commission v. Mississippi — to the Supreme Court.

Commerce Clause Not Exceeded

Ruling on the case, all nine justices agreed that Congress had not exceeded its power under the Commerce Clause in passing the 1978 law. They split 5-4, however, on the issue of whether utility regulation was a matter properly left to the states under the 10th Amendment.

According to that amendment, powers not given to the federal govern-

447

ment or denied to the states by the Constitution are reserved to the states and the people. Frequently used by the court during the 1930s to strike down parts of President Franklin D. Roosevelt's economic recovery program, the amendment had prompted little discussion since. In the early 1980s, however, it was revived by supporters of states' rights.

Majority Opinion

The majority opinion, written by Justice Harry A. Blackmun and joined by Justices William J. Brennan Jr., Byron R. White, Thurgood Marshall and John Paul Stevens, rejected the argument that the 10th Amendment barred PURPA.

Congress has the power to pre-empt the states in the field of public utility regulation, taking it over as a federal responsibility, Blackmun said. Therefore, he wrote, PURPA should not be struck down "simply because, out of deference to state authority, Congress adopted a less intrusive scheme and allowed the states to continue regulating in the area on the condition that they consider the suggested federal standards."

The law does not require states to adopt the suggested utility rate schemes. They must, however, hold public hearings on the policies and provide written explanations if they refuse to adopt them.

States' Rights Dissent

Taking sharp issue with the majority conclusion regarding the 10th Amendment, Justice Sandra Day O'Connor wrote that "the Constitution permits Congress to govern only through certain channels" and prohibits laws such as PURPA that serve to "conscript utility commissions into the national bureaucratic army."

She concluded further that the court had allowed Congress to "kidnap state utility commissions into the national regulatory family," in direct opposition to the 10th Amendment.

O'Connor was joined in her dissent by Chief Justice Warren E. Burger and Justice William H. Rehnquist. A separate dissent was filed by Justice Lewis F. Powell Jr., who wrote that PURPA imposed "unprecedented burdens on the states."

Following are excerpts from the Supreme Court's June 1, 1982, decision in Federal Energy Regulatory Commission v. Mississippi, in which the court upheld the constitutionality of the Public Utility Regulatory Policies Act of 1978; and excerpts from the dissent by Justice O'Connor:

No. 80-1749

| Federal Energy Regulatory Commission, et al., Appellants, *v.* Mississippi et al. | On appeal from the United States District Court for the Southern District of Mississippi |

[June 1, 1982]

JUSTICE BLACKMUN delivered the opinion of the Court.

In this case, appellees successfully challenged the constitutionality of Titles I and III, and of § 210 of Title II, of the Public Utility Regulatory Policies Act of 1978, Pub. L. No. 95-617, 92 Stat. 3117 (PURPA or Act). We conclude that appellees' challenge lacks merit and we reverse the judgment below.

I

On November 9, 1978, President Carter signed PURPA into law. The Act was part of a package of legislation, approved the same day, designed to combat the nationwide energy crisis.

At the time, it was said that the generation of electricity consumed more than 25% of all energy resources used in the United States. Approximately one-third of the electricity in this country was generated through use of oil and natural gas, and electricity generation was one of the fastest growing segments of the Nation's economy. In part because of their reliance on oil and gas, electricity utilities were plagued with increasing costs and decreasing efficiency in the use of the generating capacities; each of these factors had an adverse effect on rates to consumers and on the economy as a whole. Congress accordingly determined that conservation by electricity utilities of oil and natural gas was essential to the success of any effort to lessen the country's dependence on foreign oil, to avoid a repetition of the shortage of natural gas that had been experienced in 1977, and to control consumer costs.

A

Titles I and III

PURPA's Titles I and III, which relate to regulatory policies for electricity and gas utilities, respectively, are administered (with minor exceptions) by the Secretary of Energy. These provisions are designed to encourage the adoption of certain retail regulatory practices. The Titles share three goals: (1) to encourage "conservation of energy supplied by ... utilities"; (2) to encourage "the optimization of the efficiency of use of facilities and resources" by utilities; and (3) to encourage "equitable rates

449

... to consumers." To achieve these goals, Titles I and III direct state utility regulatory commissions and nonregulated utilities to "consider" the adoption and implementation of specific "rate design" and regulatory standards.

Section 111 (d) of the Act, 16 U.S.C. § 2621 (d), requires each state regulatory authority and nonregulated utility to consider the use of six different approaches to structuring rates: (1) promulgation, for each class of electricity consumers, of rates that, "to the maximum extent practicable," would "reflect the costs of . . . service to such class"; (2) elimination of declining block rates; (3) adoption of time-of-day rates; (4) promulgation of seasonal rates; (5) adoption of interruptible rates; and (6) use of load management techniques. The Act directed each state authority and nonregulated utility to consider these factors not later than two years after PURPA's enactment, that is, by November 8, 1980, and provided that the authority or utility by November 8, 1981, was to have made a decision whether to adopt the standards. The statute does not provide penalties for failure to meet these deadlines; the state authority or nonregulated utility is merely directed to consider the standards at the first rate proceeding initiated by the authority after November 9, 1980.

Section 113 of PURPA requires each state regulatory authority and nonregulated utility to consider the adoption of a second set of standards relating to the terms and conditions of electricity service: (1) prohibition of master-metering in new buildings; (2) restrictions on the use of automatic adjustment clauses; (3) disclosure to consumers of information regarding rate schedules; (4) promulgation of procedural requirements relating to termination of service; and (5) prohibition of the recovery of advertising costs from consumers. Similarly, § 303, 15 U.S.C. § 3203, requires consideration of the last two standards — procedures for termination of service and the nonrecovery of advertising costs — for natural gas utilities. A decision as to the standards contained in §§ 113 and 303 was to have been made by November 1980, although, again, no penalty was provided by the statute for failure to meet the deadline.

Finally, § 114 of the Act, 16 U.S.C. § 2624, directs each state authority and nonregulated utility to consider promulgation of "lifeline rates" — that is, lower rates for service that meets the essential needs of residential consumers — if such rates have not been adopted by November 1980.

Titles I and III also prescribe certain procedures to be followed by the state regulatory authority and the nonregulated utility when considering the proposed standards. Each standard is to be examined at a public hearing after notice, and a written statement of reasons must be made available to the public if the standards are not adopted. "Any person" may bring an action in state court to enforce the obligation to hold a hearing and make determinations on the PURPA standards.

The Secretary of Energy, any affected utility, and any consumer served by an affected utility is given the right to intervene and participate in any rate-related proceeding considering the Title I standards. Under Title III, the Secretary alone has the right to intervene. Any person (including the Secretary) who intervenes or otherwise participates in the proceeding may obtain review in state court of any administrative determination concerning the Title I standards, and the Secretary has the right to participate as an *amicus* in any Title III judicial review proceeding initiated by another. The right to intervene is enforceable against the state regulatory authority by an action in federal court.

Titles I and III also set forth certain reporting requirements. Within one year of PURPA's enactment, and annually thereafter for 10 years, each state regulatory authority and nonregulated utility is to report to the Secretary "respecting its consideration of the standards established." The Secretary, in turn, is to submit a summary and analysis of these reports to Congress. Electricity utilities also are required to collect information concerning their service costs. This information is to be filed periodically with appellant Federal Energy Regulatory Commission (FERC) and with appropriate state regulatory agencies, and is to be made available to the public. Title III requires the Secretary, in consultation with FERC, state regulatory authorities, gas utilities, and gas consumers, to submit a report to Congress on gas utility rate design.

Despite the extent and detail of the federal proposals, however, no state authority or nonregulated utility is required to adopt or implement the specified rate design or regulatory standards. Thus, 16 U.S.C. §§ 2621 (a) and 2623 (a) and 15 U.S.C. § 3203 (a) all provide: "Nothing in this subsection prohibits any State regulatory authority or nonregulated ... utility from making any determination that it is not appropriate to [implement or adopt] any such standard, pursuant to its authority under otherwise applicable State law." Similarly, 16 U.S.C. § 2627 (b) and 15 U.S.C. § 3208 make it clear that any state regulatory authority or nonregulated utility may adopt regulations or rates that are "different from any standard established by this [subchapter or chapter]."

B

Section 210

Section 210 of PURPA's Title II seeks to encourage the development of cogeneration and small power production facilities. Congress believed that increased use of these sources of energy would reduce the demand for traditional fossil fuels. But it also felt that two problems impeded the development of nontraditional generating facilities: (1) traditional electricity utilities were reluctant to purchase power from, and to sell power to, the nontraditional facilities, and (2) the regulation of these alternative energy sources by state and federal utility authorities imposed financial burdens upon the nontraditional facilities and thus discouraged their development.

In order to overcome the first of these perceived problems, § 210 (a) directs FERC, in consultation with state regulatory authorities, to promulgate "such rules as it determines necessary to encourage cogeneration and small power production," including rules requiring utilities to offer to sell electricity to, and purchase electricity from, qualifying cogeneration and small power production facilities. Section 210 (f) requires each state regulatory authority and nonregulated utility to implement FERC's rules. And § 210 (h) authorizes FERC to enforce this requirement in federal court against any state authority or nonregulated utility; if FERC fails to act after request, any qualifying utility may bring suit.

To solve the second problem perceived by Congress, § 210 (e) directs FERC to prescribe rules exempting the favored cogeneration and small power facilities from certain state and federal laws governing electricity utilities.

Pursuant to this statutory authorization, FERC has adopted regulations relating to purchases and sales of electricity to and from cogeneration and small power facilities. These afford state regulatory authorities and nonregulated utilities latitude in determining the manner in which the regulations are to be implemented. Thus, a state commission may comply with the statutory requirements by issuing regulations, by resolving disputes on a case-by-case basis, or by taking any other action reasonably designed to give effect to FERC's rules.

II

In April 1979, the State of Mississippi and the Mississippi Public Service Commission, appellees here, filed this action in the United States District Court for the Southern District of Mississippi against FERC and the Secretary of Energy, seeking a declaratory judgment that PURPA's Titles I and III and § 210 are unconstitutional. Appellees maintained that PURPA was beyond the scope of congressional power under the Commerce Clause and that it constituted an invasion of state sovereignty in violation of the Tenth Amendment.

Following cross-motions for summary judgment, the District Court, in an unreported opinion, held that in enacting PURPA Congress had exceeded its powers under the Commerce Clause. The court observed that the Mississippi Public Service Commission by state statute possessed the "power and authority to regulate and control intrastate activities and policies of all utilities operating within the sovereign state of Mississippi." Relying on *Carter* v. *Carter Coal Co.* (1936), the court stated: "There is literally nothing in the Commerce Clause of the Constitution which authorizes or justifies the federal government in taking over the regulation and control of public utilities. These public utilities were actually unknown at the writing of the Constitution." Indeed, in the court's view, the legislation "does not even attempt to regulate commerce among the several states but it is a clear usurpation of power and authority which the United States simply does not have under the Commerce Clause of the Constitution." Relying on *National League of Cities* v. *Usery* (1976), the court also concluded that PURPA trenches on state sovereignty. It therefore pronounced the statutory provisions void because "they constitute a direct intrusion on integral and traditional functions of the State of Mississippi." For reasons it did not explain, the court also relied on the guarantee of a republican form of government and on the Supremacy Clause.

FERC and the Secretary of Energy appealed directly to this Court pursuant to 28 U.S.C. § 1252. See *Hodel* v. *Virginia Surface Min. & Recl. Assn.* (1981). We noted probable jurisdiction. (1981).

III

The Commerce Clause

We readily conclude that the District Court's analysis and the appellees' arguments are without merit so far as they concern the Commerce Clause. To say that nothing in the Commerce Clause justifies federal regulation of even the intrastate operations of public utilities misapprehends the proper role of the courts in assessing the validity of federal legislation promulgated under one of Congress' plenary powers. The applicable standard was reiterated just last Term in *Hodel* v. *Indiana* (1981):

> "It is established beyond peradventure that 'legislative Acts adjusting the burdens and benefits of economic life come to the Court with a presumption of constitutionality....' *Usery* v. *Turner Elkhorn Mining Co.*, (1978).... A court may invalidate legislation enacted under the Commerce Clause only if it is clear that there is no rational basis for a congressional finding that the regulated activity affects interstate commerce, or that there is no reasonable connection between the regulatory means selected and the asserted ends."

Despite these expansive observations by this Court, appellees assert that PURPA is facially unconstitutional because it does not regulate "commerce"; instead, it is said, the Act directs the nonconsenting State to regulate in accordance with federal procedures. This, appellees continue, is beyond Congress' power: "In exercising the authority conferred by this clause of the Constitution, Congress is powerless to regulate anything which is not commerce, as it is powerless to do anything about commerce which is not regulation." *Carter* v. *Carter Coal Co.* The "governance of commerce" by the State is to be distinguished from commerce itself, for regulation of the former is said to be outside the plenary power of Congress.

It is further argued that the proper test is not whether the regulated activity merely "affects" interstate commerce but, instead, whether it has "a substantial effect" on such commerce, citing JUSTICE REHNQUIST's opinion concurring in the judgment in the *Hodel* cases. PURPA, appellees maintain, does not meet this standard.

The difficulty with these arguments is that they disregard entirely the specific congressional finding, in § 2 of the Act that the regulated activities have an immediate effect on interstate commerce. Congress there determined that "the protection of the public health, safety, and welfare, the preservation of national security, and the proper exercise of congressional authority under the Constitution to regulate interstate commerce require," among other things, a program for increased conservation of electric energy, increased efficiency in the use of facilities and resources by electricity utilities, and equitable retail rates for electricity consumers, as well as a program to improve the wholesale distribution of electric energy, and a program for the conservation of natural gas while ensuring that rates to gas consumers are equitable. The findings, thus, are clear and specific.

The Court heretofore has indicated that federal regulation of intrastate power transmission may be proper because of the interstate nature of the generation and supply of electric power. *FPC* v. *Florida Power & Light Co.* (1972). Our inquiry, then, is whether the congressional findings have a rational basis. *Hodel* v. *Virginia Surface Min. & Recl. Assn.*; *Hodel* v. *Indiana.*

The legislative history provides a simple answer: there is ample support for Congress' conclusions. The hearings were extensive. Committees in both Houses of Congress noted the magnitude of the Nation's energy problems and the need to alleviate those problems by promoting energy conservation and more efficient use of energy resources. Congress was aware that domestic oil production had lagged behind demand and that the Nation had become increasingly dependent on foreign oil. The House Committee observed: "Reliance upon imported oil to meet the bulk of U.S. oil demands could seriously jeopardize the stability of the Nation's economy and could undermine the independence of the United States." Indeed, the Nation had recently experienced severe shortages in its supplies of natural gas. The House and Senate committees both noted that the electricity industry consumed more than 25% of the total energy resources used in this country while supplying only 12% of the user demand for energy. In recent years, the electricity utility industry had been beset by numerous problems, which resulted in higher bills for the consuming public, a result exacerbated by the rate structures employed by most utilities. Congress naturally concluded that the energy problem was nationwide in scope, and that these developments demonstrated the need to establish federal standards regarding retail sales of electricity, as well as federal attempts to encourage conservation and more efficient use of scarce energy resources.

Congress also determined that the development of cogeneration and small power production facilities would conserve energy. The evidence before Congress showed the potential contribution of these sources of energy: it was estimated that if proper incentives were provided, industrial cogeneration alone could account for 7%-10% of the Nation's electrical generating capacity by 1987.

We agree with appellants that it is difficult to conceive of a more basic element of interstate commerce than electric energy, a product used in virtually every home and every commercial or manufacturing facility. No State relies solely on its own resources in this respect. See *FPC* v. *Florida*

Power & Light Co. Indeed, the utilities involved in this very case, Mississippi Power & Light Company and Mississippi Power Company, sell their retail customers power that is generated in part beyond Mississippi's borders, and offer reciprocal services to utilities in other States. The intrastate activities of these utilities, although regulated by the Mississippi Public Service Commission, bring them within the reach of Congress' power over interstate commerce. See *FPC* v. *Florida Power & Light Co.*; *New England Power Co.* v. *New Hampshire* (1982).

Even if appellees were correct in suggesting that PURPA will not significantly improve the Nation's energy situation, the congressional findings compel the conclusion that " 'the means chosen by [Congress are] reasonably adapted to the end permitted by the Constitution' " *Hodel* v. *Virginia Surface Min. & Recl. Assn.*, quoting *Heart of Atlanta Motel, Inc.* v. *United States* (1964). It is not for us to say whether the means chosen by Congress represent the wisest choice. It is sufficient that Congress was not irrational in concluding that limited federal regulation of retail sales of electricity and natural gas, and of relationships between cogenerators and electric utilities, was essential to protect interstate commerce. That is enough to place the challenged portions of PURPA within Congress' power under the Commerce Clause. Because PURPA's provisions concern private nonregulated utilities as well as state commissions, the statute necessarily is valid at least insofar as it regulates private parties. See *Hodel* v. *Virginia Surface Min. & Recl. Assn.*

IV

The Tenth Amendment

Unlike the Commerce Clause question, the Tenth Amendment issue presented here is somewhat novel. This case obviously is related to *National League of Cities* v. *Usery* (1976l), insofar as both concern principles of state sovereignty. But there is a significant difference as well. *National League of Cities*, like *Fry* v. *United States* (1975), presented a problem the Court often confronts: the extent to which state sovereignty shields the States from generally applicable federal regulations. In PURPA, in contrast, the Federal Government attempts to use state regulatory machinery to advance federal goals. To an extent, this presents an issue of first impression.

PURPA, for all its complexity, contains essentially three requirements: (1) § 210 has the States enforce standards promulgated by FERC; (2) Titles I and III direct the States to consider specified rate-making standards; and (3) those Titles impose certain procedures on state commissions. We consider these three requirements in turn:

A. Section 210. On its face, this appears to be the most intrusive of PURPA's provisions. The question of its constitutionality, however, is the easiest to resolve. Insofar as § 210 authorizes FERC to exempt qualified power facilities from "State laws and regulations," it does nothing more than pre-empt conflicting state enactments in the traditional way. Clearly, Congress can pre-empt the States completely in the regulation of retail sales by electricity and gas utilities and in the regulation of transactions between such utilities and congenerators. Cf. *Southern Pacific Co.* v. *Arizona* (1945). The propriety of this type of regulation — so long as it is a valid exercise of the commerce power — was made clear in *National League of Cities*, and was reaffirmed in *Hodel* v. *Virginia Surface Min. & Recl. Assn.*: the Federal Government may displace state regulation even though this serves to "curtail or prohibit the States' prerogatives to make legislative choices respecting subjects the States may consider important."

Section 210's requirement that "each State regulatory authority shall, after notice and opportunity for public hearing, *implement* such rule (or revised rule) for each electric utility for which it has ratemaking authority," (emphasis added), is more troublesome. The statute's substantive provisions require electricity utilities to purchase electricity from, and to sell it to, qualifying cogenerator and small power production facilities. Yet FERC has declared that state commissions may implement this by, among other things, "an undertaking to resolve disputes between qualifying facilities and electric utilities arising under [PURPA]." In essence, then, the statute and the implementing regulations simply require the Mississippi authorities to adjudicate disputes arising under the statute. Dispute resolution of this kind is the very type of activity customarily engaged in by the Mississippi Public Service Commission.

Testa v. *Katt* (1947) is instructive and controlling on this point. There, the Emergency Price Control Act created a treble damages remedy, and gave jurisdiction over claims under the Act to state as well as federal courts. The courts of Rhode Island refused to entertain such claims, although they heard analogous state causes of action. This Court upheld the federal program. It observed that state courts have a unique role in enforcing the body of federal law, and that the Rhode Island courts had "jurisdiction adequate and appropriate under established local law to adjudicate this action." Thus the state courts were directed to heed the constitutional command that "the policy of the federal Act is the prevailing policy in every state," " 'and should be respected accordingly in the courts of the State.' " [Q]uoting *Mondau* v. *New York, N.H. & H.R. Co.* (1912).

So it is here. The Mississippi Commission has jurisdiction to entertain claims analogous to those granted by PURPA, and it can satisfy § 210's requirements simply by opening its doors to claimants. That the Commission has administrative as well as judicial duties is of no significance. Any other conclusion would allow the States to disregard both the pre-eminent position held by federal law throughout the Nation, cf. *Martin* v. *Hunter's Lessee* (1816), and the congressional determination that the federal rights granted by PURPA can appropriately be enforced through state adjudicatory machinery. Such an approach, *Testa* emphasized, "flies in the face of the fact that the States of the Union constitute a nation," and "disregards the purpose and effect of Article VI of the Constitution."

B. Mandatory Consideration of Standards. We acknowledge that "the authority to make ... fundamental ... decisions" is perhaps the quintessential attribute of sovereignty. See *National League of Cities* v. *Usery*. Indeed, having the power to make decisions and to set policy is what gives the State its sovereign nature. See *Bates* v. *State Bar of Arizona* (1977) (State Supreme Court speaks as sovereign because it is the "ultimate body wielding the State's power over the practice of law"). It would follow that the ability of a state legislative (or, as here, administrative) body — which makes decisions and sets policy for the State as a whole — to consider and promulgate regulations of its choosing must be central to a State's role in the federal system. Indeed, the nineteenth century view, expressed in a well known slavery case, was that Congress "has no power to impose upon a State officer, as such, any duty whatever, and compel him to perform it." *Kentucky* v. *Dennison* (1861).

Recent cases, however, demonstrate that this rigid and isolated statement from *Kentucky* v. *Dennison* — which suggests that the States and the Federal Government in all circumstances must be viewed as co-equal sovereigns — is not representative of the law today. While this Court never has sanctioned explicitly a federal command to the States to promulgate and enforce laws and regulations, cf. *EPA* v. *Brown* (1977), there are instances where the Court has upheld federal statutory structures that in effect directed state decision-makers to take or to refrain from taking certain actions. In *Fry* v. *United States* (1975), for example, state executives were held restricted, with respect to state employees, to the wage and salary limitations established by the Economic Stabilization Act of 1970. *Washington* v. *Fishing Vessel Assn.* (1979), acknowledged a federal court's power to enforce a treaty by compelling a state agency to "prepare" certain rules "even if state law withholds from [it] the power to do so." And certainly *Testa* v. *Katt*, by declaring that "the policy of the federal Act is the prevailing policy in every state" reveals that the Federal Government has some power to enlist a branch of state government — there the judiciary — to further federal ends. In doing so, *Testa* clearly cut back on both the quoted language and the analysis of the *Dennison* case of the preceding century.

Whatever all this may forebode for the future, or for the scope of federal authority in the event of a crisis of national proportions, it plainly is not necessary for the Court in this case to make a definitive choice between competing views of federal power to compel state regulatory activity. Titles I and III of PURPA require only *consideration* of federal standards. And if a State has no utilities commission, or simply stops regulating in the field, it need not even entertain the federal proposals. As we have noted, the commerce power permits Congress to pre-empt the States entirely in the regulation of private utilities. . . .

Similarly here, Congress could have pre-empted the field, at least insofar as private rather than state activity is concerned; PURPA should not be invalid simply because, out of deference to state authority, Congress adopted a less intrusive scheme and allowed the States to continue regulating in the area on the condition that they *consider* the suggested federal standards. While the condition here is affirmative in nature — that is, it directs the States to entertain proposals — nothing in this Court's cases suggests that the nature of the condition makes it a constitutionally improper one. There is nothing in PURPA "directly compelling" the States to enact a legislative program. . . .

We recognize, of course, that the choice put to the States — that of either abandoning regulation of the field altogether or considering the federal standards — may be a difficult one. And that is particularly true when Congress, as is the case here, has failed to provide an alternative regulatory mechanism to police the area in the event of state default. Yet in other contexts the Court has recognized that valid federal enactments may have an effect on state policy — and may, indeed, be designed to induce state action in areas that otherwise would be beyond Congress' regulatory authority. Thus in *Oklahoma* v. *Civil Service Comm'n.* (1947), the Court upheld Congress' power to attach conditions to grants-in-aid received by the States, although the condition under attack involved an activity that "the United States is not concerned with, and has no power to regulate." The Tenth Amendment, the Court declared, "has been consistently construed 'as not depriving the national government of authority to resort to all means for the exercise of a granted power which are appropriate and plainly adapted to the permitted end,' " quoting *United States* v. *Darby* (1941) — the end there being the disbursement of federal funds. Thus it cannot be constitutionally determinative that the federal regulation is likely to move the States to act in a given way, or even to "coerc[e] the States" into assuming a regulatory role by affecting their "freedom to make decisions in areas of 'integral governmental functions.' " *Hodel* v. *Virginia Surface Min. & Recl. Assn.*

Equally as important, it has always been the law that state legislative and judicial decisionmakers must give preclusive effect to federal enactments concerning nongovernmental activity, no matter what the strength of the competing local interests. See *Martin* v. *Hunter's Lessee.* This requirement follows from the nature of governmental regulation of private activity. "[I]ndividual businesses necessarily [are] subject to the dual sovereignty of the government of the Nation and the State in which they reside," *National League of Cities* v. *Usery*; when regulations promulgated by the sovereigns conflict, federal law necessarily controls. This is true though Congress exercises its authority "in a manner that displaces the States' exercise of their police powers," *Hodel* v. *Virginia Surface Min. & Recl. Assn.*, or in such a way as to "curtail or prohibit the States' prerogatives to make legislative choices respecting subjects the States may consider important," or, to put it still more plainly, in a manner that is "extraordinarily intrusive." (POWELL, J., concurring). Thus it may be unlikely that the States will or easily can abandon regulation of public utilities to avoid PURPA's requirements. But this does not change the constitutional analysis: as in *Hodel* v. *Virginia Surface Min. & Recl. Assn.*, "[t]he most that can be said is that the . . . Act establishes a program of cooperative federalism that allows the States, within limits established by federal minimum standards, to enact and administer their own regulatory programs, structured to meet their own particular needs." . . .

It is hardly clear on the statute's face, then, that PURPA's standing and appeal provisions grant any rights beyond those presently accorded by Mississippi law, and appellees point to no specific provision of the Act expanding on the State's existing, liberal approach to public participation in ratemaking. In this light, we again find the principle of *Testa* v. *Katt* controlling: the State is asked only to make its administrative tribunals available for the vindication of federal as well as state-created rights. PURPA, of course, establishes as federal policy the requirement that state commissions consider various ratemaking standards, and it gives individuals a right to enforce that policy; once it is established that the requirement is constitutionally supportable, "the obligation of states to enforce these federal laws is not lessened by reason of the form in which they are cast or the remedy which they provide." *Testa* v. *Katt*. See *Second Employers' Liability Cases* (1912).

In short, Titles I and III do not involve the compelled exercise of Mississippi's sovereign powers. And, equally important, they do not set a mandatory agenda to be considered in all events by state legislative or administrative decisionmakers. As we read them, Titles I and III simply establish requirements for continued state activity in an otherwise preemptible field. Whatever the constitutional problems associated with more intrusive federal programs, the "mandatory consideration" provisions of Titles I and III must be validated under the principle of *Hodel* v. *Virginia Surface Min. & Recl. Assn.*

C. The Procedural Requirements. Titles I and III also require state commissions to follow certain notice and comment procedures when acting on the proposed federal standards. In a way, these appear more intrusive than the "consideration" provisions; while the latter are essentially hortatory, the procedural provisions obviously are prescriptive. Appellants and *amici* Maryland, *et al.*, argue that the procedural requirements simply establish minimum due process standards, something Mississippi appears already to provide, and therefore may be upheld as an exercise of Congress' Fourteenth Amendment powers. We need not go that far, however, for we uphold the procedural requirements under the same analysis employed above in connection with the "consideration" provisions. If Congress can require a state administrative body to consider proposed regulations as a condition to its continued involvement in a pre-emptible field — and we hold today that it can — there is nothing unconstitutional about Congress' requiring certain procedural minima as that body goes about undertaking its tasks. The procedural requirements obviously do not compel the exercise of the State's sovereign powers, and do not purport to set standards to be followed in all areas of the state commission's endeavors.

The judgment of the District Court is reversed.

It is so ordered.

JUSTICE O'CONNOR, with whom THE CHIEF JUSTICE and JUS-
TICE REHNQUIST join, concurring in part in the judgment and dissenting in part.

I agree with the Court that the Commerce Clause supported Congress'
enactment of the Public Utility Regulatory Policies Act of 1978 (PURPA).
I disagree, however, with much of the Court's Tenth Amendment analysis.
Titles I and III of PURPA conscript state utility commissions into the
national bureaucratic army. This result is contrary to the principles of
National League of Cities v. *Usery* (1976), antithetical to the values of
federalism, and inconsistent with our constitutional history. Accordingly, I
dissent from subsections IVB and C of the Court's opinion.

I

Titles I and III of PURPA require state regulatory agencies to decide
whether to adopt a dozen federal standards governing gas and electric
utilities. The statute describes, in some detail, the procedures state
authorities must follow when evaluating these standards, but does not
compel the States to adopt the suggested federal standards. The latter,
deceptively generous feature of PURPA persuades the Court that the
statute does not intrude impermissibly into state sovereign functions. The
Court's conclusion, however, rests upon a fundamental misunderstanding
of the role that state governments play in our federalist system.

State legislative and administrative bodies are not field offices of the
national bureaucracy. Nor are they think tanks to which Congress may
assign problems for extended study. Instead, each State is sovereign within
its own domain, governing its citizens and providing for their general
welfare. While the Constitution and federal statutes define the boundaries
of that domain, they do not harness state power for national purposes. The
Constitution contemplates "an indestructible Union, composed of indestructible States," a system in which both the state and national governments retain a "separate and independent existence." *Texas* v. *White*
(1869); *Lane County* v. *Oregon* (1869).

Adhering to these principles, the Court has recognized that the Tenth
Amendment restrains congressional action that would impair "a State's
ability to function as a State." *United Transportation Union* v. *Long
Island R. Co.* (1982); *National League of Cities* v. *Usery* (1976); *Fry* v.
United States (1975). See also *City of Lafayette* v. *Louisiana Power &
Light Co.* (1978) (THE CHIEF JUSTICE, concurring in the judgment).
For example, in *National League of Cities* v. *Usery*, the Court held that
Congress could not prescribe the minimum wages and maximum hours of
state employees engaged in "traditional governmental functions" because
the power to set those wages and hours is an "attribute of state sover-

eignty" that is "essential to [a] separate and independent existence."([Q]uoting *Lane County* v. *Oregon.*)

Just last Term this Court identified three separate inquiries underlying the result in *National League of Cities*. A congressional enactment violates the Tenth Amendment, we observed, if it regulates the " 'States as States,' " addresses "matters that are indisputably 'attribute[s] of state sovereignty,' " and "directly impair[s] [the States'] ability to 'structure integral operations in areas of traditional governmental functions.' " *Hodel* v. *Virginia Surface Mining & Reclamation Association* (1981) (quoting *National League of Cities*. See also *United Transportation Union*.

Application of these principles to the present case reveals the Tenth Amendment defects in Titles I and III. Plainly those titles regulate the "States as States." While the statute's ultimate aim may be the regulation of private utility companies, PURPA addresses its commands solely to the States. Instead of requesting private utility companies to adopt lifeline rates, declining block rates, or the other PURPA standards, Congress directed state agencies to appraise the appropriateness of those standards. It is difficult to argue that a statute structuring the regulatory agenda of a state agency is not a regulation of the "State."

I find it equally clear that Titles I and III address "attribute[s] of state sovereignty." Even the Court recognizes that "the power to make decisions and to set policy is what gives the State its sovereign nature." The power to make decisions and set policy, however, embraces more than the ultimate authority to enact laws; it also includes the power to decide which proposals are most worthy of consideration, the order in which they should be taken up, and the precise form in which they should be debated. PURPA intrudes upon all of these functions. It chooses twelve proposals, forcing their consideration even if the state agency deems other ideas more worthy of immediate attention. In addition, PURPA hinders the agency's ability to schedule consideration of the federal standards. Finally, PURPA specifies, with exacting detail, the content of the standards that will absorb the agency's time.

If Congress routinely required the state legislatures to debate bills drafted by congressional committees, it could hardly be questioned that the practice would affect an attribute of state sovereignty. PURPA, which sets the agendas of agencies exercising delegated legislative power in a specific field, has a similarly intrusive effect.

Finally, PURPA directly impairs the States' ability to "structure integral operations in areas of traditional governmental functions." Utility regulation is a traditional function of state government, and the regulatory commission is the most integral part of that function. By taxing the limited resources of these commissions, and decreasing their ability to address local regulatory ills, PURPA directly impairs the power of state utility commissions to discharge their traditional functions efficiently and effectively.

The Court sidesteps this analysis, suggesting that the States may escape

PURPA simply by ceasing regulation of public utilities. Even the Court recognizes that this choice "may be a difficult one" and that "it may be unlikely that the States will or easily can abandon regulation of public utilities to avoid PURPA's requirements." In fact, the Court's "choice" is an absurdity, for if its analysis is sound, the Constitution no longer limits federal regulation of state governments. Under the Court's analysis, for example, *National League of Cities* v. *Usery* (1976) would have been wrongly decided, because the States could have avoided the Fair Labor Standards Act by "choosing" to fire all employees subject to that Act and to close those branches of state government. Similarly, Congress could dictate the agendas and meeting places of state legislatures, because unwilling States would remain free to abolish their legislative bodies. I do not agree that this dismemberment of state government is the correct solution to a Tenth Amendment challenge.

The choice put to the States by the Surface Mining Control and Reclamation Act of 1977, the federal statute upheld in *Hodel* v. *Virginia Surface Mining & Reclamation Association* (1981), and discussed by the Court, is quite different from the decision PURPA mandates. The Surface Mining Act invites the States to submit proposed surface mining regulations to the Secretary of the Interior. If the Secretary approves a state regulatory program, then the State enforces that program. If a State chooses not to submit a program, the Secretary develops and implements a program for that State. Even States in the latter category, however, may supplement the Secretary's program with consistent state laws. The Surface Mining Act does not force States to choose between performing tasks set by Congress and abandoning all mining or land use regulation. That statute is "a program of cooperative federalism," *Hodel*, because it allows the States to choose either to work with Congress in pursuit of federal surface mining goals or to devote their legislative resources to other mining and land use problems. By contrast, there is nothing "cooperative" about a federal program that compels state agencies either to function as bureaucratic puppets of the Federal Government or to abandon regulation of an entire field traditionally reserved to state authority. Yet this is the "choice" the Court today forces upon the States.

The Court defends its novel decision to permit federal conscription of state legislative power by citing three cases upholding statutes that "in effect directed state decision-makers to take or to refrain from taking certain actions." *Testa* v. *Katt* (1947) is the most suggestive of these decisions. In *Testa*, the Court held that state trial courts may not refuse to hear a federal claim if "th[e] same type of claim arising under [state] law would be enforced by that State's courts." A facile reading of *Testa* might suggest that state legislatures must also entertain congressionally sponsored business, as long as the federal duties are similar to existing state obligations. Application of *Testa* to legislative power, however, vastly expands the scope of that decision. Because trial courts of general jurisdiction do not choose the cases that they hear, the requirement that they evenhandedly adjudicate state and federal claims falling within their jurisdiction does not infringe any sovereign authority to set an agenda. As explained above, however, the power to choose subjects for legislation is a fundamental attribute of legislative power, and interference with this power unavoidably undermines state sovereignty. Accordingly, the existence of a congressional authority to "enlist ... the [state] judiciary ... to further federal ends" does not imply an equivalent power to impress state legislative bodies into federal service.

The court, finally, reasons that because Congress could have preempted the entire field of intrastate utility regulation, the Constitution should not forbid PURPA's "less intrusive scheme." The Court's evaluation of intrusiveness, however, is simply irrelevant to the constitutional inquiry. The Constitution permits Congress to govern only through certain channels. If the Tenth Amendment principles articulated in *National League of Cities* v. *Usery* (1976) and *Hodel* v. *Virginia Surface Mining & Reclamation Association* (1981) foreclose PURPA's approach, it is no answer to argue that Congress could have reached the same destination by a different route. This Court's task is to enforce constitutional limits on congressional power, not to decide whether alternative courses would better serve state and federal interests.

I do not believe, moreover, that Titles I and III of PURPA are less intrusive than preemption. When Congress preempts a field, it precludes only state legislation that conflicts with the national approach. The States usually retain the power to complement congressional legislation, either by regulating details unsupervised by Congress or by imposing requirements that go beyond the national threshold. Most importantly, after Congress preempts a field, the States may simply devote their resources elsewhere. This country does not lack for problems demanding legislative attention. PURPA, however, drains the inventive energy of state governmental bodies by requiring them to weigh its detailed standards, enter written findings, and defend their determinations in state court. While engaged in these congressionally mandated tasks, state utility commissions are less able to pursue local proposals for conserving gas and electric power. The States might well prefer that Congress simply impose the standards described in PURPA; this, at least, would leave them free to exercise their power in other areas.

Federal preemption is less intrusive than PURPA's approach for a second reason. Local citizens hold their utility commissions accountable for the choices they make. Citizens, moreover, understand that legislative authority usually includes the power to decide which ideas to debate, as well as which policies to adopt. Congressional compulsion of state agencies, unlike preemption, blurs the lines of political accountability and leaves citizens feeling that their representatives are no longer responsive to local needs.

The foregoing remarks suggest that, far from approving a minimally intrusive form of federal regulation, the Court's decision undermines the most valuable aspects of our federalism. Courts and commentators frequently have recognized that the fifty States serve as laboratories for the development of new social, economic, and political ideas. This state innovation is no judicial myth. When Wyoming became a State in 1890, it was the only State permitting women to vote. That novel idea did not bear national fruit for another thirty years. Wisconsin pioneered unemployment insurance, while Massachusetts initiated minimum wage laws for women and minors. After decades of academic debate, state experimentation finally provided an opportunity to observe no-fault automobile insurance in operation. Even in the field of environmental protection, an area subject to heavy federal regulation, the States have supplemented national standards with innovative and far-reaching statutes. Utility regulation itself is a field marked by valuable state invention. PURPA, which commands state agencies to spend their time evaluating federally proposed standards and defending their decisions to adopt or reject those standards, will retard this creative experimentation.

In addition to promoting experimentation, federalism enhances the opportunity of all citizens to participate in representative government. Alexis de Tocqueville understood well that participation in local government is a cornerstone of American democracy:

> "It is incontestably true that the love and the habits of republican government in the United States were engendered in the townships and in the provincial assemblies. . . . [I]t is this same republican spirit, it is these manners and customs of a free people, which are engendered and nurtured in the different States, to be afterwards applied to the country at large." Democracy in America.

Citizens, however, cannot learn the lessons of self-government if their local efforts are devoted to reviewing proposals formulated by a far-away national legislature. If we want to preserve the ability of citizens to learn democratic processes through participation in local government, citizens must retain the power to govern, not merely administer, their local problems.

Finally, our federal system provides a salutary check on governmental power. As Justice Harlan once explained, our ancestors "were suspicious of every form of all-powerful central authority." To curb this evil, they both allocated governmental power between state and national authorities, and divided the national power among three branches of government. Unless we zealously protect these distinctions, we risk upsetting the balance of power that buttresses our basic liberties. In analyzing this brake on governmental power, Justice Harlan noted that "[t]he diffusion of power between federal and state authority . . . takes on added significance as the size of the federal bureaucracy continues to grow." Today, the Court disregards this warning and permits Congress to kidnap state utility commissions into the national regulatory family. Whatever the merits of our national energy legislation, I am not ready to surrender this state legislative power to the Federal Energy Regulatory Commission.

II

As explained above, the Court's decision to uphold Titles I and III violates the principles of *National League of Cities* v. *Usery* (1976) and threatens the values promoted by our federal system. The Court's result, moreover, is at odds with our constitutional history, which demonstrates that the Framers consciously rejected a system in which the national legislature would employ state legislative power to achieve national ends.

The principal defect of the Articles of Confederation, eighteenth century writers agreed, was that the new National Government lacked the power to compel individual action. Instead, the central government had to rely upon the cooperation of state legislatures to achieve national goals. Thus, Alexander Hamilton explained that: "The great and radical vice in the construction of the existing Confederation is in the principle of legislation for states or governments, in their corporate or collective capacities and as contradistinguished from the individuals of whom they consist." He pointed out, for example, that the National Government had "an indefinite discretion to make requisitions for men and money," but "no authority to raise either by regulations extending to the individual citizens of America."

The Constitution cured this defect by permitting direct contact between the National Government and the individual citizen, a change repeatedly acknowledged by the delegates assembled in Philadelphia. George Mason, for example, declared that:

> "Under the existing Confederacy, Congress represent[s] the *States* not the *people* of the States: their acts operate on the *States* not on the individuals. The case will be changed in the new plan of government."

Hamilton subsequently explained to the people of New York that the Constitution marked the "difference between a league and a government," because it "extend[ed] the authority of the union to the persons of the citizens, — the only proper objects of government." ...

The speeches and writings of the Framers suggest why they adopted this means of strengthening the National Government. Mason, for example, told the Convention that because "punishment could not [in the nature of things be executed on] the States collectively," he advocated a National Government that would "directly operate on individuals." Hamilton predicted that a National Government forced to work through the States would "degenerate into a military despotism" because it would have to maintain a "large army, continually on foot" to enforce its will against the States.

Thus, the Framers concluded that government by one sovereign through the agency of a second cannot be satisfactory. At one extreme, as under the Articles of Confederation, such a system is simply ineffective. At the other, it requires a degree of military force incompatible with stable government and civil liberty. For this reason, the Framers concluded that "the execution of the laws of the national government ... should not require the intervention of the State Legislatures" and abandoned the Articles of Confederation in favor of direct national legislation.

At the same time that the members of the Constitutional Convention fashioned this principle, they rejected two proposals that would have given the national legislature power to supervise directly state governments. The first proposal would have authorized Congress "to call forth the force of the Union against any member of the Union failing to fulfill its duty under the articles thereof." The delegates never even voted on this suggestion. James Madison moved to postpone it, stating that "the more he reflected on the use of force, the more he doubted the practicability, the justice and the efficacy of it when applied to people collectively and not individually." Several other delegates echoed his concerns, and Madison ultimately reported that "[t]he practicability of making laws, with coercive sanctions, for the States as political bodies [has] been exploded on all hands."

The second proposal received more favorable consideration. Virginia's Governor Randolph suggested that Congress should have the power "to negative all laws passed by the several States, contravening in the opinion of the National Legislature the articles of Union." On May 31, 1787, the Committee of the Whole approved this proposal without debate. A week later, [Charles] Pinckney moved to extend the congressional negative to all state laws "which [Congress] should judge to be improper." Numerous delegates criticized this attempt to give Congress unbounded control over state lawmaking. Hugh Williamson, for example, thought "the State Legislatures ought to possess independent powers in cases purely local," while Elbridge Gerry thought Pinckney's idea might "enslave the States." After much debate, the Convention rejected Pinckney's suggestion.

Late in July, the delegates reversed their approval of even Randolph's more moderate congressional veto. Several delegates now concluded that the negative would be "terrible to the States," "unnecessary," and "improper." Omission of the negative, however, left the new system without an effective means of adjusting conflicting state and national laws. To remedy this defect, the delegates adopted the Supremacy Clause, providing that the federal Constitution, laws, and treaties are "the supreme Law of the Land" and that "the Judges in every State shall be bound thereby." Thus, the Framers substituted judicial review of state laws for congressional control of state legislatures.

While this history demonstrates the Framers' commitment to a strong central government, the means that they adopted to achieve that end are as instructive as the end itself. Under the Articles of Confederation, the national legislature operated through the States. The Framers could have fortified the central government, while still maintaining the same system, if they had increased Congress' power to demand obedience from state legislatures. In time, this scheme might have relegated the States to mere departments of the National Government, a status the Court appears to endorse today. The Framers, however, eschewed this course, choosing instead to allow Congress to pass laws directly affecting individuals, and rejecting proposals that would have given Congress military or legislative power over state governments. In this way, the Framers established independent state and national sovereigns. The National Government received the power to enact its own laws and to enforce those laws over conflicting state legislation. The States retained the power to govern as sovereigns in fields that Congress cannot or will not preempt. This product of the Constitutional Convention, I believe, is fundamentally inconsistent with a system in which either Congress or a state legislature harnesses the legislative powers of the other sovereign.

III

During his last Term of service on this Court, Justice Black eloquently explained that our notions of federalism subordinate neither national nor state interests:

> "The concept does not mean blind deference to 'States' Rights' any more than it means centralization of control over every important issue in our National Government and its courts. The Framers rejected both these courses. What the concept does represent is a system in which there is sensitivity to the legitimate interest of both State and National Governments, and in which the National Government, anxious though it may be to vindicate and protect federal rights and federal interests, always endeavors to do so in ways that will not unduly interfere with the legitimate activities of the States." *Younger* v. *Harris* (1971).

In this case, I firmly believe that a proper "sensitivity to the legitimate interests of both State and National Governments" requires invalidation of Titles I and III of PURPA insofar as they apply to state regulatory authorities. Accordingly, I respectfully dissent from the Court's decision to uphold those portions of the statute.

ECONOMIC SUMMIT
IN VERSAILLES
June 4-6, 1982

The leaders of seven industrialized democracies conferred June 4-6 on reaching a more closely aligned approach to common economic problems. Similarly, they sought a more cautious trade policy with Soviet bloc countries. Attending the summit were officials from Britain, Canada, France, Italy, Japan, the United States and West Germany. The meeting, one of a series held annually since 1975, took place at the royal palace of Versailles, France.

Joining President Ronald Reagan in representing the United States were Secretary of State Alexander M. Haig Jr. and Secretary of the Treasury Donald T. Regan. Both Cabinet officers attended separate conferences on foreign policy and finance matters. The Versailles summit and a subsequent five-day whirlwind trip through Europe marked the president's first diplomatic venture overseas. (Reagan's speech to British Parliament, p. 477)

Trade with Soviet Bloc

Of primary importance to the American delegation was achieving European support for withholding credit to Soviet-allied nations, which, according to the United States, stimulated the massive military spending of those countries. European nations in turn believed that the economic credits helped their own slackening economies and were therefore more reluctant to bend to the wishes of the United States.

After several days of conferences and personal encouragement by

Reagan to take a common stand against the Soviet-allied nations, the summit participants resolved to "pursue a prudent ... economic approach" toward these countries. Although Treasury Secretary Regan termed the decision a "victory," it did not include the sharp trade restrictions on the Soviet Union the United States wanted.

France's President François Mitterand, demonstrating his country's reluctance to join the Soviet trade decision, added a cautionary note to the resolution, as it left each country "sovereignly responsible for deciding what is prudent."

Policy Toward the Third World

The European leaders urged convening a global conference with Third World nations on future aid from industrialized to developing nations. They also sought initiatives to encourage capital flow from North to South and to replenish the funds of the World Bank's soft-loan institution, the International Development Association. These funds were meant to increase assistance to poorer countries in food and energy production and population growth control programs.

The United States, indicating less enthusiasm for the global conference, decided to go along with the Europeans after the Soviet trade resolution had been passed. They insisted, however, that "the independence of the specialized agencies," especially the International Monetary Fund, where industrialized nations held decisive power, not be threatened. Thus, the issue of Third World economic development strategy essentially became a bargaining chip in the decision on Soviet policy.

Other Summit Resolutions

The United States showed its willingness to "use intervention in the exchange markets to counter disorderly conditions," after its allies had complained of dollar fluctuations and the effects of growing American interest rates on international currency markets. This apparent consent to government intervention would have amounted to a significant change in U.S. fiscal policy, which previously had stressed the importance of the free-floating dollar. Regan, however, denied such a shift and asserted that the Europeans had not "read the fine print" of the agreement.

The summit participants agreed to strengthen the General Agreement on Tariffs and Trade (GATT) to resist protectionist measures in international trade and take further steps to reduce trade barriers.

At Mitterand's urging, the summit also recommended a report on technological progress with an eye for job creation. The participating governments promised to pay more attention to the effects of technologi-

cal advances in areas such as labor-saving robots and computerized machines on increasing unemployment and social welfare.

Past Economic Summits

In the past, the economic summit meetings had led to only limited policy change. Underlying tension and disagreements among the industrialized democracies tended to be covered up by overly general and artful language about the importance of international cooperation and breaking down domestic barriers in the statement submitted at the end of the conference.

The summit in Ottawa in 1981 had concluded with similar agreements to "fight to bring down inflation and reduce unemployment," to pursue "undiminished security at lower levels of armament and expenditure," to operate "an open multilateral trading system as embodied in the GATT," and to "accelerate food production in the developing world." Following the conference, however, each country felt free to continue implementing its own domestic economic program, drifting in what appeared to be divergent directions. (Ottawa conference, Historic Documents of 1981, p. 591)

The pattern seemed to be holding true in Versailles as well. Two months after the conference agreement on limiting credit to the Soviet Union, the French and Italian governments promised to assist the Soviet government in financing a 3,700-mile natural gas pipeline that would lead from east of the Soviet Ural Mountains to Western Europe.

On August 2, Britain challenged a U.S. ban on the use of American technology in the Soviet project by ordering British companies to honor contracts relating to the pipeline's construction. According to Lord Cockfield, British trade secretary, "the [U.S] embargo ... is an attempt to interfere with existing contracts and is an unacceptable extension of American extraterritorial jurisdiction in a way which is repugnant in international law." (Soviet pipeline sanctions, p. 879)

Following are the texts of a statement and of a joint communiqué, both issued June 6, 1982, at the conclusion of the Versailles economic summit conference:

CONCLUDING STATEMENT

Since World War II our peoples in Europe, Canada, Japan, and the United States have worked together to lay the foundation for global prosperity. Together, we built the international institutions which have seen us through the greatest economic expansion in the history of the world. This weekend at Versailles, that spirit of partnership was very much alive.

471

In the formal sessions and informal exchanges, the leaders of the major industrial democracies worked on strengthening and solidifying Western cooperation.

We did not ignore the serious difficulties facing our economies. These problems will not go away overnight, but they will be overcome. Beating inflation, convincingly and enduringly, is the key to a strong recovery of growth and employment. This was agreed. And I was pleased to report to my colleagues that in the U.S. we are conquering inflation and are convincing our people that we will not return to the inflationary policies of the past.

In times of economic stress, it is always tempting to seek simple solutions at the expense of others. At Versailles, we resisted this temptation. Instead, we concentrated on ways and means to strengthen our economic performance individually and collectively. We have agreed to reinforce the international institutions which assure cooperation and coordination. In doing so, we are looking to a future with low inflation, greater employment opportunities, rising standards of living through advancing technology, and smoothly functioning international economic relations.

Just to name a few specific areas:

— We will work in association with the IMF [International Monetary Fund] to achieve meaningful coordination of medium-term economic policies, aimed at fiscal and monetary discipline and greater reliance on market forces.

— We have dedicated our efforts to a productive ministerial meeting of the GATT [General Agreements on Tariffs and Trade], which will address the trade problems of the 1980's.

— We have reaffirmed our commitment, made last year at Ottawa, to ensure that our economic relations with the Soviet Union are fully consistent with our political and security objectives. Specifically, we have agreed to exercise prudence in financial relations with the Soviet Union, including limiting export credits.

— We also agreed to work together to develop the considerable energy potential in the West, as another step in assuring a strong, sustained economic recovery, less vulnerable to energy disruptions.

In our informal political discussions, we addressed the major critical issues before the West. We know that the economic growth we seek would be hollow without the collective capacity to defend our democratic principles and our freedom.

We addressed our shared concerns in East-West relations. The continuing buildup of Soviet military power is a major challenge, heightened by Soviet actions in Poland, Afghanistan, and Southeast Asia — issues I look forward to discussing in greater depth at the Bonn summit. At the same time, we agreed that the serious economic problems and impending succession in the Soviet Union provide us with major opportunities to work out a more constructive East-West dialog.

We must maintain dialog with the Soviet Union, based on reciprocity and restraint. In that spirit, my colleagues have endorsed U.S. initiatives for arms control, particularly the negotiations on reducing strategic arms which will begin on June 29.

The tragedy in the Falkland Islands has been a serious concern to us all. Throughout the crisis, we have all been impressed by the British resolve, and in various ways, we have demonstrated our support for the United Kingdom. The United States continues to believe that we must end the fighting in the South Atlantic and achieve a political settlement.

On other matters, we urged restraint on all parties in Lebanon. Increasing bloodshed in that region is something we all abhor. We have also called for a political settlement in the Iran-Iraq conflict which would preserve the territorial integrity of both nations. And we agreed to improve our coordinated fight against international terrorism.

Finally, I believe that we should reach out to new generations. The summit nations can invest in the future with expanded exchanges among young people from North America, Japan, and Europe.

A year ago in Ottawa, we ended the first series of economics summits that began in France. With this summit at Versailles, we have begun a new cycle. We thus reaffirm our strong commitment to economic and political cooperation. In the spirit of partnership with our fellow democracies, I want to say that I very much look forward to welcoming these nations to the United States next year.

JOINT COMMUNIQUE

1. In the course of our meeting at Versailles we have deepened our mutual understanding of the gravity of the world economic situation, and we have agreed on a number of objectives for urgent action with a view to improving it.

2. We affirm that the improvement of the present situation, by a further reduction of inflation and by a return to steady growth and higher levels of employment, will strengthen our joint capacity to safeguard our security, to maintain confidence in the democratic values that we share, and to preserve the cultural heritage of our peoples in all their diversity. Full employment, price stability and sustained and balanced growth are ambitious objectives. They are attainable in the coming years only if we pursue policies which encourage productive investment and technological progress; if, in addition to our own individual efforts, we are willing to join forces, if each country is sensitive to the effects of its policies on others and if we collaborate in promoting world development.

3. In this spirit, we have decided to implement the following lines of action:

— Growth and employment must be increased. This will be attained on a durable basis only if we are successful in our continuing fight against inflation. That will also help to bring down interest rates, which are now unacceptably high, and to bring about more stable exchange rates. In order to achieve this essential reduction of real interest rates, we will as a matter of urgency pursue prudent monetary policies and achieve greater control of budgetary deficits. It is essential to intensify our economic and monetary cooperation. In this regard, we will work towards a constructive and orderly evolution of the international monetary system by a closer cooperation among the authorities representing the currencies of North America, of Japan and of the European Community in pursuing medium-term economic and monetary objectives. In this respect, we have committed ourselves to the undertakings contained in the attached statement.

— The growth of world trade in all its facets is both a necessary element for the growth of each country and a consequence of that growth. We reaffirm our commitment to strengthening the open multilateral trading system as embodied in the GATT and to maintaining its effective operation. In order to promote stability and employment through trade and growth, we will resist protectionist pressures and trade-distorting practices. We are resolved to complete the work of the Tokyo Round and to improve the capacity of the GATT to solve current and future trade problems. We will also work towards the further opening of our markets. We will cooperate with the developing countries to strengthen and improve the multilateral system, and to expand trading opportunities in particular with the newly industrialized countries. We shall participate fully in the forthcoming GATT Ministerial Conference in order to take concrete steps toward these ends. We shall work for early agreement on the renewal of the OECD [Organization for Economic Cooperation and Development] export credit consensus.

— We agree to pursue a prudent and diversified economic approach to the U.S.S.R. and Eastern Europe, consistent with our political and security interests. This includes actions in three key areas. First, following international discussions in January, our representatives will work together to improve the international system for controlling exports of strategic goods to these countries and national arrangements for the enforcement of security controls. Second, we will exchange information in the OECD on all aspects of our economic, commercial and financial relations with the Soviet Union and Eastern Europe. Third, taking into account existing economic and financial considerations, we have agreed to handle cautiously financial relations with the U.S.S.R. and other Eastern European countries, in such a way as to ensure that they are conducted on a sound economic basis, including also the need for commercial prudence in limiting export credits. The development of economic and financial relations will be subject to periodic ex-post review.

— The progress we have already made does not diminish the need for continuing efforts to economise on energy, particularly through the price mechanism, and to promote alternative sources, including nuclear energy and coal, in a long-term perspective. These efforts will enable us further to reduce our vulnerability to interruptions in the supply of energy and instability of prices. Cooperation to develop new energy technologies, and to strengthen our capacity to deal with disruptions, can contribute to our common energy security. We shall also work to strengthen our cooperation with both oil-exporting and oil-importing developing countries.

— The growth of the developing countries and the deepening of a constructive relationship with them are vital for the political and economic well-being of the whole world. It is therefore important that a high level of financial flows and official assistance should be maintained and that their amount and their effectiveness should be increased as far as possible, with responsibilities shared broadly among all countries capable of making a contribution. The launching of global negotiations is a major political objective approved by all participants in the summit. The latest draft resolution circulated by the Group of the 77 is helpful, and the discussion at Versailles showed general acceptance of the view that it would serve as a basis for consultations with the countries concerned. We believe that there is now a good prospect for the early launching and success of the global negotiations, provided that the independence of the specialised agencies is guaranteed. At the same time, we are prepared to continue and develop practical cooperation with the developing countries through innovations within the World Bank, through our support of the work of the Regional Development Banks, through progress in countering instability of commodity export earnings, through the encouragement of private capital flows, including international arrangements to improve the conditions for private investment, and through a further concentration of official assistance on the poorer countries. This is why we see a need for special temporary arrangements to overcome funding problems for IDA [International Development Association] VI, and for an early start to consideration of IDA VII. We will give special encouragement to programmes or arrangements designed to increase food and energy production in developing countries which have to import these essentials, and to programmes to address the implications of population growth.

— In the field of balance of payments support, we look forward to progress at the September IMF annual meeting towards settling the increase in the size of the fund appropriate to the coming Eighth Quota Review.

— Revitalization and growth of the world economy will depend not only on our own effort but also to a large extent upon cooperation among our countries and with other countries in the exploitation of scientific and technological development. We have to exploit the immense opportunities presented by the new technologies, particularly for creating new employment. We need to remove barriers to, and to promote, the development of the trade in new technologies both in the public sector and in the private sector. Our countries will need to train men and women in the new technologies and to create the economic, social and cultural conditions which allow these technologies to develop and flourish. We have considered the report presented to us on these issues by the President of the French Republic. In this context we have decided to set up promptly a working group of representatives of our governments and of the European Community to develop, in close consultation with the appropriate international institutions, especially the OECD, proposals to give help to attain these objectives. This group will be asked to submit its report to us by 31 December 1982. The conclusion of the report and the resulting action will be considered at the next economic summit to be held in 1983 in the United States of America.

Statement of International Monetary Undertakings

1. We accept a joint responsibility to work for greater stability of the world monetary system. We recognize that this rests primarily on convergence of policies designed to achieve lower inflation, higher employment and renewed economic growth; and thus to maintain the internal and external values of our currencies. We are determined to discharge this obligation in close collaboration with all interested countries and monetary institutions.

2. We attach major importance to the role of the IMF as a monetary authority and we will give it our full support in its efforts to foster stability.

3. We are ready to strengthen our cooperation with the IMF in its work of surveillance; and to develop this on a multilateral basis taking into account particularly the currencies constituting the SDR [Special Drawing Rights].

4. We rule out the use of our exchange rate to gain unfair competitive advantages.

5. We are ready, if necessary, to use intervention in exchange markets to counter disorderly conditions, as provided for under Article IV of the IMF Articles of Agreement.

6. Those of us who are members of the EMS [European Monetary System] consider that these undertakings are complementary to the obligations of stability which that [sic] have already undertaken in that framework.

7. We are all convinced that greater monetary stability will assist freer flows of goods, services and capital. We are determined to see that greater monetary stability and freer flows of trade and capital reinforce one another in the interest of economic growth and employment.

REAGAN SPEECH TO PARLIAMENT
June 8, 1982

Following ceremonies ending the economic summit conference in Versailles, President Ronald Reagan embarked June 7 on his first diplomatic venture through Italy, Britain and West Germany. The trip included a meeting with the pope at the Vatican and an address, the first of any U.S. president, to both houses of the British Parliament.

Reagan's first stop was Rome, where he met briefly with President Alessandro Pertini and Premier Giovanni Spadolini before he was received by Pope John Paul II at the Vatican. After a 45-minute private meeting, the pope and Reagan read public statements reflecting their mutual concern with maintaining world peace and reducing tension in certain areas of the world.

The pope warned against the proliferation of "evermore sophisticated and deadly weapons." Reagan stated that he viewed his trip as a "pilgrimage for peace, a journey aimed at strengthening the forces for peace in the free West by offering new opportunities for realistic negotiations with those who may not share the values and the spirit we cherish."

Reagan's Vatican statement set forth his trip's recurring themes of strong anti-Soviet rhetoric and the need to soften the United States' threatening and rather militaristic image in Europe. Because of increasing emphasis on U.S. defense policy, including the North Atlantic Treaty Organization's (NATO) projected deployment of 372 Pershing missiles in Western Europe, Reagan had been subjected to mounting criticism by the European peace movement. (Nuclear freeze movement, p. 885)

477

British Parliament Address

Following their arrival in London on July 7, the president and Mrs. Reagan were escorted to Windsor Castle, where they stayed as guests of Queen Elizabeth II and Prince Philip. The social highlights of their sojourn included a highly publicized royal horseback ride.

Reagan addressed a joint session of Parliament on June 8 and further developed the idea of a "crusade for freedom" that would promote "democratic development" thoughout the world and "leave Marxism-Leninism on the ash heap of history, as it has left other tyrannies which stifle the freedom and muzzle the self-expression of the people."

In his speech, Reagan repeatedly condemned the evils of totalitarianism, communism and the Soviet Union. "It was not the democracies that invaded Afghanistan, or suppressed Polish Solidarity, or used chemical and toxin warfare," Reagan stated.

Reagan expressed the concern with weapons buildup as he had at the Vatican. By increasing U.S. military strength both domestically and abroad, he stressed, the United States wished to "maintain . . . strength in the hope it will never be used."

The speech was often characterized by echoes of the Cold War, reminiscent in tone of Dwight D. Eisenhower's presidential campaigns in the 1950s. Reagan made several references to the famed British leader Sir Winston Churchill, who had coined the phrase "iron curtain" on the occasion of his famous 1946 Fulton, Mo., speech.

Reagan's support for Britain's defense of the Falkland Islands drew enthusiastic applause from the audience. The president stated that the British had to remain tough against military aggression by a government lacking the support of its people. (Falkland Islands war, p. 283)

In a protest against Reagan's politics, most of the 225 British Labor Party members of Parliament did not show up for the address, although party leader Michael Foot and his deputy, Denis Healey, did appear. In a statement released following the address the party declared: "We utterly reject an ideological crusade against the Soviet Union and its identification as the sole or even prime cause of conflict in the world." The Labor Party leadership added that "We can inform you that the peace movement is not Communist-inspired nor pacifist nor necessarily neutralist."

NATO Meeting in Bonn

The NATO meeting in Bonn on June 10 marked the last leg of Reagan's European trip. Reagan emphasized alliance solidarity and limiting conventional forces in both NATO and Warsaw Pact countries to de-

crease the possibility of nuclear warfare. He called for a ceiling of 700,000 ground troops in both East and West as "a major step toward a safer Europe." Upon the urging of the European powers, the idea of "détente," generally regarded as "out" by Americans after its apparent failure in the 1970s, was nonetheless espoused in the communiqué issued at the end of the meeting.

The formal meetings and state receptions for Reagan contrasted dramatically with the mass demonstrations against U.S. defense policy by the European peace activists. Reagan's trip ended on June 11 with a visit to the Berlin Wall, while more than 100,000 anti-American demonstrators marched in another part of the city.

Tight security controls, implemented since the assassination attempt on the president, prevented any public appearances by Reagan to win the hearts of the European population as had President John F. Kennedy in June 1963.

> *Following is the text of President Reagan's speech to both houses of the British Parliament, delivered June 8, 1982. (Boldface headings in brackets have been added by Congressional Quarterly to highlight the organization of the text.):*

My Lord Chancellor, Mr. Speaker:

The journey of which this visit forms a part is a long one. Already it has taken me to two great cities of the West, Rome and Paris, and to the economic summit at Versailles. And there, once again, our sister democracies have proved that even in a time of severe economic strain, free peoples can work together freely and voluntarily to address problems as serious as inflation, unemployment, trade, and economic development in a spirit of cooperation and solidarity.

Other milestones lie ahead. Later this week, in Germany, we and our NATO allies will discuss measures for our joint defense and America's latest initiatives for a more peaceful, secure world through arms reductions.

Each stop of this trip is important, but among them all, this moment occupies a special place in my heart and in the hearts of my countrymen — a moment of kinship and homecoming in these hallowed halls.

Speaking for all Americans, I want to say how very much at home we feel in your house. Every American would, because this is, as we have been so eloquently told, one of democracy's shrines. Here the rights of free people and the processes of representation have been debated and refined.

It has been said that an institution is the lengthening shadow of a man. This institution is the lengthening shadow of all the men and women who have sat here and all those who have voted to send representatives here.

This is my second visit to Great Britain as President of the United States. My first opportunity to stand on British soil occurred almost a year and a half ago when your Prime Minister graciously hosted a diplomatic dinner at the British Embassy in Washington. Mrs. Thatcher said then that she hoped I was not distressed to find staring down at me from the grand staircase a portrait of His Royal Majesty King George III. She suggested it was best to let bygones be bygones, and in view of our two countries' remarkable friendship in succeeding years, she added that most Englishmen today would agree with Thomas Jefferson that "a little rebellion now and then is a very good thing." [*Laughter*]

Well, from here I will go to Bonn and then Berlin, where there stands a grim symbol of power untamed. The Berlin Wall, that dreadful gray gash across the city, is in its third decade. It is the fitting signature of the regime that built it.

And a few hundred kilometers behind the Berlin Wall, there is another symbol. In the center of Warsaw, there is a sign that notes the distances to two capitals. In one direction it points toward Moscow. In the other it points toward Brussels, headquarters of Western Europe's tangible unity. The marker says that the distances from Warsaw to Moscow and Warsaw to Brussels are equal. The sign makes this point: Poland is not East or West. Poland is at the center of European civilization. It has contributed mightily to that civilization. It is doing so today by being magnificently unreconciled to oppression.

Poland's struggle to be Poland and to secure the basic rights we often take for granted demonstrates why we dare not take those rights for granted. Gladstone, defending the Reform Bill of 1866, declared, "You cannot fight against the future. Time is on our side." It was easier to believe in the march of democracy in Gladstone's day — in that high noon of Victorian optimism.

[Strength of Democracy]

We're approaching the end of a bloody century plagued by a terrible political invention — totalitarianism. Optimism comes less easily today, not because democracy is less vigorous, but because democracy's enemies have refined their instruments of repression. Yet optimism is in order, because day by day democracy is proving itself to be a not-at-all-fragile flower. From Stettin on the Baltic to Varna on the Black Sea, the regimes planted by totalitarianism have had more than 30 years to establish their legitimacy. But none — not one regime — has yet been able to risk free elections. Regimes planted by bayonets do not take root.

The strength of the Solidarity movement in Poland demonstrates the truth told in an underground joke in the Soviet Union. It is that the Soviet Union would remain a one-party nation even if an opposition party were permitted, because everyone would join the opposition party. [*Laughter*]

America's time as a player on the stage of world history has been brief. I think understanding this fact has always made you patient with your younger cousins — well, not always patient. I do recall that on one occasion, Sir Winston Churchill said in exasperation about one of our most distinguished diplomats: "He is the only case I know of a bull who carries his china shop with him." [*Laughter*]

But witty as Sir Winston was, he also had that special attribute of great statesmen — the gift of vision, the willingness to see the future based on the experience of the past. It is this sense of history, this understanding of the past that I want to talk with you about today, for it is in remembering what we share of the past that our two nations can make common cause for the future.

[Threats to Freedom]

We have not inherited an easy world. If developments like the Industrial Revolution, which began here in England, and the gifts of science and technology have made life much easier for us, they have also made it more dangerous. There are threats now to our freedom, indeed to our very existence, that other generations could never even have imagined.

There is first the threat of global war. No President, no Congress, no Prime Minister, no Parliament can spend a day entirely free of this threat. And I don't have to tell you that in today's world the existence of nuclear weapons could mean, if not the extinction of mankind, then surely the end of civilization as we know it. That's why negotiations on intermediate-range nuclear forces now underway in Europe and the START talks — Strategic Arms Reduction Talks — which will begin later this month, are not just critical to American or Western policy; they are critical to mankind. Our commitment to early success in these negotiations is firm and unshakable, and our purpose is clear: reducing the risk of war by reducing the means of waging war on both sides.

At the same time there is a threat posed to human freedom by the enormous power of the modern state. History teaches the dangers of government that overreaches — political control taking precedence over free economic growth, secret police, mindless bureaucracy, all combining to stifle individual excellence and personal freedom.

Now, I'm aware that among us here and throughout Europe there is legitimate disagreement over the extent to which the public sector should play a role in a nation's economy and life. But on one point all of us are united — our abhorrence of dictatorship in all its forms, but most particularly totalitarianism and the terrible inhumanities it has caused in our time — the great purge, Auschwitz and Dachau, the Gulag, and Cambodia.

Historians looking back at our time will note the consistent restraint and peaceful intentions of the West. They will note that it was the democracies who refused to use the threat of their nuclear monopoly in the forties and early fifties for territorial or imperial gain. Had that nuclear monopoly been in the hands of the Communist world, the map of Europe — indeed, the world — would look very different today. And certainly they will note it was not the democracies that invaded Afghanistan or suppressed Polish

Solidarity or used chemical and toxin warfare in Afghanistan and Southeast Asia.

[Response from the West]

If history teaches anything it teaches self-delusion in the face of unpleasant facts is folly. We see around us today the marks of our terrible dilemma — predictions of doomsday, antinuclear demonstrations, an arms race in which the West must, for its own protection, be an unwilling participant. At the same time we see totalitarian forces in the world who seek subversion and conflict around the globe to further their barbarous assault on the human spirit. What, then, is our course? Must civilization perish in a hail of fiery atoms? Must freedom wither in a quiet, deadening accommodation with totalitarian evil?

Sir Winston Churchill refused to accept the inevitability of war or even that it was imminent. He said, "I do not believe that Soviet Russia desires war. What they desire is the fruits of war and the indefinite expansion of their power and doctrines. But what we have to consider here today while time remains is the permanent prevention of war and the establishment of conditions of freedom and democracy as rapidly as possible in all countries."

Well, this is precisely our mission today: to preserve freedom as well as peace. It may not be easy to see; but I believe we live now at a turning point.

In an ironic sense Karl Marx was right. We are witnessing today a great revolutionary crisis, a crisis where the demands of the economic order are conflicting directly with those of the political order. But the crisis is happening not in the free, non-Marxist West, but in the home of Marxist-Leninism, the Soviet Union. It is the Soviet Union that runs against the tide of history by denying human freedom and human dignity to its citizens. It also is in deep economic difficulty. The rate of growth in the national product has been steadily declining since the fifties and is less than half of what it was then.

[Failure of Soviet Experiment]

The dimensions of this failure are astounding: A country which employs one-fifth of its population in agriculture is unable to feed its own people. Were it not for the private sector, the tiny private sector tolerated in Soviet agriculture, the country might be on the brink of famine. These private plots occupy a bare 3 percent of the arable land but account for nearly one-quarter of Soviet farm output and nearly one-third of meat products and vegetables. Overcentralized, with little or no incentives, year after year the Soviet system pours its best resource into the making of instruments of destruction. The constant shrinking of economic growth combined with the growth of military production is putting a heavy strain on the Soviet people. What we see here is a political structure that no longer corresponds to its economic base, a society where productive forces are hampered by political ones.

The decay of the Soviet experiment should come as no surprise to us. Wherever the comparisons have been made between free and closed societies — West Germany and East Germany, Austria and Czechoslovakia, Malaysia and Vietnam — it is the democratic countries what [sic] are prosperous and responsive to the needs of their people. And one of the simple but overwhelming facts of our time is this: Of all the millions of refugees we've seen in the modern world, their flight is always away from, not toward the Communist world. Today on the NATO line, our military forces face east to prevent a possible invasion. On the other side of the line, the Soviet forces also face east to prevent their people from leaving.

The hard evidence of totalitarian rule has caused in mankind an uprising of the intellect and will. Whether it is the growth of the new schools of economics in America or England or the appearance of the so-called new philosophers in France, there is one unifying thread running through the intellectual work of these groups — rejection of the arbitrary power of the state, the refusal to subordinate the rights of the individual to the superstate, the realization that collectivism stifles all the best human impulses.

[Struggle for Freedom]

Since the exodus from Egypt, historians have written of those who sacrificed and struggled for freedom — the stand at Thermopylae, the revolt of Spartacus, the storming of the Bastille, the Warsaw uprising in World War II. More recently we've seen evidence of this same human impulse in one of the developing nations in Central America. For months and months the world news media covered the fighting in El Salvador. Day after day we were treated to stories and film slanted toward the brave freedom-fighters battling oppressive government forces in behalf of the silent, suffering people of that tortured country.

And then one day those silent, suffering people were offered a chance to vote, to choose the kind of government they wanted. Suddenly the freedom-fighters in the hills were exposed for what they really are — Cuban-backed guerrillas who want power for themselves, and their backers, not democracy for the people. They threatened death to any who voted, and destroyed hundreds of buses and trucks to keep the people from getting to the polling places. But on election day, the people of El Salvador, an unprecedented 1.4 million of them, braved ambush and gunfire, and trudged for miles to vote for freedom.

They stood for hours in the hot sun waiting for their turn to vote. Members of our Congress who went there as observers told me of a woman who was wounded by rifle fire on the way to the polls, who refused to leave the line to have her wound treated until after she had voted. A grandmother, who had been told by the guerrillas she would be killed when she returned from the polls, and she told the guerrillas, "You can kill me, you can kill my family, kill my neighbors, but you can't kill us all." The real freedom-fighters of El Salvador turned out to be the people of that country — the young, the old, the in-between.

Strange, but in my own country there's been little if any news coverage of that war since the election. Now, perhaps they'll say it's — well, because there are newer struggles now.

On distant islands in the South Atlantic young men are fighting for Britain. And, yes, voices have been raised protesting their sacrifice for lumps of rock and earth so far away. But those young men aren't fighting for mere real estate. They fight for a cause — for the belief that armed aggression must not be allowed to succeed, and the people must participate in the decisions of government — [applause] — the decisions of government under the rule of law. If there had been firmer support for that principle some 45 years ago, perhaps our generation wouldn't have suffered the bloodletting of World War II.

In the Middle East now the guns sound once more, this time in Lebanon, a country that for too long has had to endure the tragedy of civil war, terrorism, and foreign intervention and occupation. The fighting in Lebanon on the part of all parties must stop, and Israel should bring its forces home. But this is not enough. We must all work to stamp out the scourge of terrorism that in the Middle East makes war an ever-present threat.

[Democratic Revolution]

But beyond the troublespots lies a deeper, more positive pattern. Around the world today, the democratic revolution is gathering new strength. In India a critical test has been passed with the peaceful change of governing political parties. In Africa, Nigeria is moving into remarkable and unmistakable ways to build and strengthen its democratic institutions. In the Caribbean and Central America, 16 of 24 countries have freely elected governments. And in the United Nations, 8 of the 10 developing nations which have joined that body in the past 5 years are democracies.

In the Communist world as well, man's instinctive desire for freedom and self-determination surfaces again and again. To be sure, there are grim reminders of how brutally the police state attempts to snuff out this quest for self-rule — 1953 in East Germany, 1956 in Hungary, 1968 in Czechoslovakia, 1981 in Poland. But the struggle continues in Poland. And we know that there are even those who strive and suffer for freedom within the confines of the Soviet Union itself. How we conduct ourselves here in the Western democracies will determine whether this trend continues.

No, democracy is not a fragile flower. Still it needs cultivating. If the rest of this century is to witness the gradual growth of freedom and democratic ideals, we must take actions to assist the campaign for democracy.

Some argue that we should encourage democratic change in right-wing dictatorships, but not in Communist regimes. Well, to accept this preposterous notion — as some well-meaning people have — is to invite the argument that once countries achieve a nuclear capability, they should be allowed an undisturbed reign of terror over their own citizens. We reject this course.

As for the Soviet view, Chairman Brezhnev repeatedly has stressed that the competition of ideas and systems must continue and that this is entirely consistent with relaxation of tensions and peace.

Well, we ask only that these systems begin by living up to their own constitutions, abiding by their own laws, and complying with the international obligations they have undertaken. We ask only for a process, a direction, a basic code of decency, not for an instant transformation.

We cannot ignore the fact that even without our encouragement there has been and will continue to be repeated explosions against repression and dictatorships. The Soviet Union itself is not immune to this reality. Any system is inherently unstable that has no peaceful means to legitimize its leaders. In such cases, the very repressiveness of the state ultimately drives people to resist it, if necessary, by force.

While we must be cautious about forcing the pace of change, we must not hesitate to declare our ultimate objectives and to take concrete actions to move toward them. We must be staunch in our conviction that freedom is not the sole prerogative of a lucky few, but the inalienable and universal right of all human beings. So states the United Nations Universal Declaration of Human Rights, which, among other things, guarantees free elections.

[Reagan's Objective]

The objective I propose is quite simple to state: to foster the infrastructure of democracy, the system of a free press, unions, political parties, universities, which allows a people to choose their own way to develop their own culture, to reconcile their own differences through peaceful means.

This is not cultural imperialism; it is providing the means for genuine self-determination and protection for diversity. Democracy already flourishes in countries with very different cultures and historical experiences. It would be cultural condescension, or worse, to say that any people prefer dictatorship to democracy. Who would voluntarily choose not to have the right to vote, decide to purchase government propaganda handouts instead of independent newspapers, prefer government to worker-controlled unions, opt for land to be owned by the state instead of those who till it, want government repression of religious liberty, a single political party instead of a free choice, a rigid cultural orthodoxy instead of democratic tolerance and diversity?

Since 1917 the Soviet Union has given covert political training and assistance to Marxist-Leninists in many countries. Of course, it also has promoted the use of violence and subversion by these same forces. Over the past several decades, West European and other Social Democrats, Christian Democrats, and leaders have offered open assistance to fraternal, political, and social institutions to bring about peaceful and democratic progress. Appropriately, for a vigorous new democracy, the Federal Republic of Germany's political foundations have become a major force in this effort.

We in America now intend to take additional steps, as many of our allies have already done, toward realizing this same goal. The chairmen and other leaders of the national Republican and Democratic Party organizations are initiating a study with the bipartisan American political foundation to determine how the United States can best contribute as a nation to the global campaign for democracy now gathering force. They will have the cooperation of congressional leaders of both parties, along with representatives of business, labor, and other major institutions in our society. I look forward to receiving their recommendations and to working with these institutions and the Congress in the common task of strengthening democracy throughout the world.

It is time that we committed ourselves as a nation — in both the public and private sectors — to assisting democratic development.

We plan to consult with leaders of other nations as well. There is a proposal before the Council of Europe to invite parliamentarians from democratic countries to a meeting next year in Strasbourg. That prestigious gathering could consider ways to help democratic political movements.

This November in Washington there will take place an international meeting on free elections. And next spring there will be a conference of world authorities on constitutionalism and self-government hosted by the Chief Justice of the United States. Authorities from a number of developing and developed countries — judges, philosophers, and politicians with practical experience — have agreed to explore how to turn principle into practice and further the rule of law.

At the same time, we invite the Soviet Union to consider with us how the competition of ideas and values — which it is committed to support — can be conducted on a peaceful and reciprocal basis. For example, I am prepared to offer President Brezhnev an opportunity to speak to the American people on our television if he will allow me the same opportunity with the Soviet people. We also suggest that panels of our newsmen periodically appear on each other's television to discuss major events.

Now, I don't wish to sound overly optimistic, yet the Soviet Union is not immune from the reality of what is going on in the world. It has happened in the past — a small ruling elite either mistakenly attempts to ease domestic unrest through greater repression and foreign adventure, or it chooses a wiser course. It begins to allow its people to have a voice in their own destiny. Even if this latter process is not realized soon, I believe the renewed strength of the democratic movement, complemented by a global campaign for freedom, will strengthen the prospects for arms control and a world at peace.

[Military Strength]

I have discussed on other occasions, including my address on May 9th, the elements of Western policies toward the Soviet Union to safeguard our interests and protect the peace. What I am describing now is a plan and a hope for the long term — the march of freedom and democracy which will leave Marxism-Leninism on the ash heap of history as it has left other tyrannies which stifle the freedom and muzzle the self-expression of the people. And that's why we must continue our efforts to strengthen NATO even as we move forward with our Zero-Option initiative in the negotiations on intermediate-range forces and our proposal for a one-third reduction in strategic ballistic missile warheads.

Our military strength is a prerequisite to peace, but let it be clear we maintain this strength in the hope it will never be used, for the ultimate determinant in the struggle that's now going on in the world will not be bombs and rockets, but a test of wills and ideas, a trial of spiritual resolve, the values we hold, the beliefs we cherish, the ideals to which we are dedicated.

The British people know that, given strong leadership, time and a little bit of hope, the forces of good ultimately rally and triumph over evil. Here among you is the cradle of self-government, the Mother of Parliaments. Here is the enduring greatness of the British contribution to mankind, the great civilized ideas: individual liberty, representative government, and the rule of law under God.

I've often wondered about the shyness of some of us in the West about standing for these ideals that have done so much to ease the plight of man and the hardships of our imperfect world. This reluctance to use those vast resources at our command reminds me of the elderly lady whose home was bombed in the Blitz. As the rescuers moved about, they found a bottle of brandy she'd stored behind the staircase, which was all that was left standing. And since she was barely conscious, one of the workers pulled the cork to give her a taste of it. She came around immediately and said, "Here now — there now, put it back. That's for emergencies." [*Laughter*]

Well, the emergency is upon us. Let us be shy no longer. Let us go to our strength. Let us offer hope. Let us tell the world that a new age is not only possible but probable.

During the dark days of the Second World War, when this island was incandescent with courage, Winston Churchill exclaimed about Britain's adversaries, "What kind of a people do they think we are?" Well, Britain's adversaries found out what extraordinary people the British are. But all the democracies paid a terrible price for allowing the dictators to underestimate us. We dare not make that mistake again. So, let us ask ourselves, "What kind of people do we think we are?" And let us answer, "Free people, worthy of freedom and determined not only to remain so but to help others gain their freedom as well."

Sir Winston led his people to great victory in war and then lost an election just as the fruits of victory were about to be enjoyed. But he left office honorably, and, as it turned out, temporarily, knowing that the liberty of his people was more important than the fate of any single leader. History recalls his greatness in ways no dictator will ever know. And he left us a message of hope for the future, as timely now as when he first uttered it, as opposition leader in the Commons nearly 27 years ago, when he said, "When we look back on all the perils through which we have passed and at the mighty foes that we have laid low and all the dark and deadly designs that we have frustrated, why should we fear for our future? We have," he said, "come safely through the worst."

Well, the task I've set forth will long outlive our own generation. But together, we too have come through the worst. Let us now begin a major effort to secure the best — a crusade for freedom that will engage the faith and fortitude of the next generation. For the sake of peace and justice, let us move toward a world in which all people are at last free to determine their own destiny.

Thank you.

COURT ON FREE EDUCATION
FOR ALIEN CHILDREN
June 15, 1982

Applying for the first time the Constitution's guarantee of equal protection to illegal aliens, the Supreme Court decided June 15 that states cannot deny free public education to children of such aliens. Specifically, in the case of Plyler v. Doe, *the court declared unconstitutional a Texas law requiring that illegal alien children pay tuition to attend the state's public schools.*

Texas had argued that illegal immigrants were not "persons within the jurisdiction" of the state and thus had no right to equal protection of the laws guaranteed by the 14th Amendment. But this argument was rejected by Justice William J. Brennan Jr., writing for the 5-4 majority.

"Whatever his status under the immigration laws," Brennan wrote, "an alien is surely a 'person' in any ordinary sense of that term." He added, "By denying these children a basic education, we deny them the ability to live within the structure of our civic institutions, and foreclose any realistic possibility that they will contribute in even the smallest way to the progress of our Nation."

Brennan said that Texas had failed to show that denying illegal alien children free public education furthered "some substantial state interest." The state had argued that denial was justified to discourage more illegal aliens from immigrating to the state and to prevent a reduction in the amount of education money available for lawful residents.

"It is difficult to understand precisely what the state hopes to achieve," Brennan concluded, "by promoting the creation and perpetua-

tion of a subclass of illiterates within our boundaries, surely adding to the problems and costs of unemployment, welfare and crime."

Echoing a 1973 decision involving another Texas school case, Brennan emphasized that public education was not a right the Constitution granted to individuals. "But neither is it merely some governmental 'benefit' indistinguishable from other forms of social welfare legislation," he wrote. "Both the importance of education in maintaining our basic institutions, and the lasting impact of its deprivation on the life of the child, mark the distinction."

Joining Brennan in the majority were Justices Thurgood Marshall, Harry A. Blackmun, Lewis F. Powell Jr. and John Paul Stevens. All but Stevens wrote separate concurring opinions. Chief Justice Warren E. Burger was joined in a dissenting opinion by Justices Byron R. White, William H. Rehnquist and Sandra Day O'Connor.

Burger criticized the majority opinion, saying that it was not within the court's jurisdiction to "set the nation's social policy." He wrote, "We trespass on the assigned function of the political branches under our structure of limited and separated powers when we assume a policymakng role as the Court does today."

Burger and the other dissenters also argued that it was reasonable for a state not to provide illegal residents with government services "at the expense of those who are lawfully in the state."

> *Following are excerpts from* Plyler v. Doe, *in which the Supreme Court decided June 15, 1982, that Texas could not deny free public education to the children of illegal aliens, and from the dissenting opinion of Chief Justice Warren E. Burger:*

No. 80-1538

James Plyler, Superintendent of the Tyler Independent School District and its Board of Trustees et al., Appellants *v.* J. and R. Doe et al.	On appeal from the United States Court of Appeals for the Fifth Circuit

[June 15, 1982*]

---

* Together with No. 80-1934, *Texas et al.* v. *Certain Named and Unnamed Undocumented Alien Children et al.*, also on appeal from the same court.

JUSTICE BRENNAN delivered the opinion of the Court.

The question presented by these cases is whether, consistent with the Equal Protection Clause of the Fourteenth Amendment, Texas may deny to undocumented school-age children the free public education that it provides to children who are citizens of the United States or legally admitted aliens.

I

Since the late nineteenth century, the United States has restricted immigration into this country. Unsanctioned entry into the United States is a crime, 8 U.S.C. § 1325, and those who have entered unlawfully are subject to deportation, 8 U.S.C. §§ 1251-1252. But despite the existence of these legal restrictions, a substantial number of persons have succeeded in unlawfully entering the United States, and now live within various States, including the State of Texas.

In May 1975, the Texas legislature revised its education laws to withhold from local school districts any state funds for the education of children who were not "legally admitted" into the United States. The 1975 revision also authorized local school districts to deny enrollment in their public schools to children not "legally admitted" to the country. These cases involve constitutional challenges to those provisions.

No. 80-1538
Plyler v. *Doe*

This is a class action, filed in the United States District Court for the Eastern District of Texas in September 1977, on behalf of certain school-age children of Mexican origin residing in Smith County, Texas, who could not establish that they had been legally admitted into the United States. The action complained of the exclusion of plaintiff children from the public schools of the Tyler Independent School District. The Superintendent and members of the Board of Trustees of the School District were named as defendants; the State of Texas intervened as a party-defendant. After certifying a class consisting of all undocumented school-age children of Mexican origin residing within the School District, the District Court preliminarily enjoined defendants from denying a free education to members of the plaintiff class. In December 1977, the Court conducted an extensive hearing on plaintiffs' motion for permanent injunctive relief.

In considering this motion, the District Court made extensive findings of fact. The court found that neither § 21.031 [of Texas' education code] nor the School District policy implementing it had "either the purpose or effect of keeping illegal aliens out of the State of Texas." Respecting defendants' further claim that § 21.031 was simply a financial measure designed to avoid a drain on the State's fisc, the court recognized that the increases in population resulting from the immigration of Mexican nationals into the United States had created problems for the public schools of

the State, and that these problems were exacerbated by the special educational needs of immigrant Mexican children. The court noted, however,
that the increase in school enrollment was primarily attributable to the
admission of children who were legal residents. It also found that while the
"exclusion of all undocumented children from the public schools in Texas
would eventually result in economies at some level," funding from both the
state and federal governments was based primarily on the number of
children enrolled. In net effect then, barring undocumented children from
the schools would save money, but it would "not necessarily" improve "the
quality of education." The court further observed that the impact of
§ 21.031 was borne primarily by a very small sub-class of illegal aliens,
"entire families who have migrated illegally and — for all practical
purposes — permanently to the United States." Finally, the court noted
that under current laws and practices "the illegal alien of today may well
be the legal alien of tomorrow," and that without an education, these
undocumented children, "[a]lready disadvantaged as a result of poverty,
lack of English-speaking ability, and undeniable racial prejudices, . . . will
become permanently locked into the lowest socio-economic class."

The District Court held that illegal aliens were entitled to the protection
of the Equal Protection Clause of the Fourteenth Amendment, and that
§ 21.031 violated that Clause. Suggesting that "the state's exclusion of
undocumented children from its public schools . . . may well be the type of
invidiously motivated state action for which the suspect classification
doctrine was designed," the court held that it was unnecessary to decide
whether the statute would survive a "strict scrutiny" analysis because, in
any event, the discrimination embodied in the statute was not supported
by a rational basis. The District Court also concluded that the Texas
statute violated the Supremacy Clause.

The Court of Appeals for the Fifth Circuit upheld the District Court's
injunction. (1980). The Court of Appeals held that the District Court had
erred in finding the Texas statute preempted by federal law. With respect
to equal protection, however, the Court of Appeals affirmed in all essential
respects the analysis of the District Court, concluding that § 21.031 was
"constitutionally infirm regardless of whether it was tested using the mere
rational basis standard or some more stringent test." We noted probable
jurisdiction. (1981).

No. 80-1934
In Re: Alien Children Litigation

During 1978 and 1979, suits challenging the constitutionality of § 21.031
and various local practices undertaken on the authority of that provision
were filed in the United States District Courts for the Southern, Western,
and Northern Districts of Texas. Each suit named the State of Texas and
the Texas Education Agency as defendant, along with local officials. In
November 1979, the Judicial Panel on Multidistrict Litigation, on motion
of the State, consolidated the claims against the State officials into a single

action to be heard in the District Court for the Southern District of Texas. A hearing was conducted in February and March 1980. In July 1980, the court entered an opinion and order holding that § 21.031 violated the Equal Protection Clause of the Fourteenth Amendment. The court held that "the absolute deprivation of education should trigger strict judicial scrutiny, particularly when the absolute deprivation is the result of complete inability to pay for the desired benefit." The court determined that the State's concern for fiscal integrity was not a compelling state interest, that exclusion of these children had not been shown to be necessary to improve education within the State, and that the educational needs of the children statutorily excluded was not different from the needs of children not excluded. The court therefore concluded that § 21.031 was not carefully tailored to advance the asserted state interest in an acceptable manner. While appeal of the District Court's decision was pending, the Court of Appeals rendered its decision in No. 81-1538. Apparently on the strength of that opinion, the Court of Appeals, on February 23, 1981, summarily affirmed the decision of the Southern District. We noted probable jurisdiction (1981) and consolidated this case with No. 81-1538 for briefing and argument.

II

The Fourteenth Amendment provides that "No State shall ... deprive any person of life, liberty, or property, without due process of law; nor deny to *any person within its jurisdiction* the equal protection of the laws." Appellants argue at the outset that undocumented aliens, because of their immigration status, are not "persons within the jurisdiction" of the State of Texas, and that they therefore have no right to the equal protection of Texas law. We reject this argument. Whatever his status under the immigration laws, an alien is surely a "person" in any ordinary sense of that term. Aliens, even aliens whose presence in this country is unlawful, have long been recognized as "persons" guaranteed due process of law by the Fifth and Fourteenth Amendments. *Shaughnessy* v. *Mezei* (1953); *Wong Wing* v. *United States* (1896); *Yick Wo* v. *Hopkins* (1886). Indeed, we have clearly held that the Fifth Amendment protects aliens whose presence in this country is unlawful from invidious discrimination by the Federal Government. *Mathews* v. *Diaz* (1976).

Appellants seek to distinguish our prior cases, emphasizing that the Equal Protection Clause directs a State to afford its protection to persons *within its jurisdiction* while the Due Process Clauses of the Fifth and Fourteenth Amendments contain no such assertedly limiting phrase. In appellants' view, persons who have entered the United States illegally are not "within the jurisdiction" of a State even if they are present within a State's boundaries and subject to its laws. Neither our cases nor the logic of the Fourteenth Amendment supports that constricting construction of the phrase "within its jurisdiction." We have never suggested that the class of persons who might avail themselves of the equal protection guarantee is less than coextensive with that entitled to due process. To the contrary, we have recognized that both provisions were fashioned to protect an identical class of persons, and to reach every exercise of State authority.

> "The Fourteenth Amendment to the Constitution is not confined to the protection of citizens. It says: 'Nor shall any state deprive any persons of life, liberty or property without due process of law; nor deny to any persons within its jurisdiction the equal protection of the laws.' *These provisions are universal in their application, to all persons within the territorial jurisdiction,* without regard to any differences of race color, or of nationality; and the protection of the laws is a pledge of the protection of equal laws." *Yick Wo,* (emphasis added).

In concluding that "all persons within the territory of the United States," including aliens unlawfully present, may invoke the Fifth and Sixth Amendment to challenge actions of the Federal Government, we reasoned from the understanding that the Fourteenth Amendment was designed to afford its protection to all within the boundaries of a State. *Wong Wing.* Our cases applying the Equal Protection Clause reflect the same territorial theme:

> "Manifestly, the obligation of the State to give the protection of equal laws can be performed only where its laws operate, that is, within its own jurisdiction. It is there that the equality of legal right must be maintained. That obligation is imposed by the Constitution upon the States severally as governmental entities, — each responsible for its own laws establishing the rights and duties of persons within its borders." *Missouri ex rel. Gaines* v. *Canada* (1938).

There is simply no support for appellants' suggestion that "due process" is somehow of greater stature than "equal protection" and therefore available to a larger class of persons. To the contrary, each aspect of the Fourteenth Amendment reflects an elementary limitation on state power. To permit a State to employ the phrase "within its jurisdiction" in order to identify subclasses of persons whom it would define as beyond its jurisdiction, thereby relieving itself of the obligation to assure that its laws are designed and applied equally to those persons, would undermine the principal purpose for which the Equal Protection Clause was incorporated in the Fourteenth Amendment. The Equal Protection Clause was intended to work nothing less than the abolition of all caste- and invidious class-based legislation. That objective is fundamentally at odds with the power the State asserts here to classify persons subject to its laws as nonetheless excepted from its protection. . . .

Use of the phrase "within its jurisdiction" . . . does not detract from, but rather confirms, the understanding that the protection of the Fourteenth Amendment extends to anyone, citizen or stranger, who *is* subject to the laws of a State, and reaches into every corner of a State's territory. That a person's initial entry into a State, or into the United States, was unlawful, and that he may for that reason be expelled, cannot negate the simple fact of his presence within the State's territorial perimeter. Given such presence, he is subject to the full range of obligations imposed by the

State's civil and criminal laws. And until he leaves the jurisdiction — either voluntarily, or involuntarily in accordance with the Constitution and laws of the United States — he is entitled to the equal protection of the laws that a State may choose to establish.

Our conclusion that the illegal aliens who are plaintiffs in these cases may claim the benefit of the Fourteenth Amendment's guarantee of equal protection only begins the inquiry. The more difficult question is whether the Equal Protection Clause has been violated by the refusal of the State of Texas to reimburse local school boards for the education of children who cannot demonstrate that their presence within the United States is lawful, or by the imposition by those school boards of the burden of tuition on those children. It is to this question that we now turn.

III

The Equal Protection Clause directs that "all persons similarly circumstanced shall be treated alike." *F. S. Royster Guano Co.* v. *Virginia* (1920). But so too, "The Constitution does not require things which are different in fact or opinion to be treated in law as though they were the same." *Tigner* v. *Texas* (1940). The initial discretion to determine what is "different" and what is "the same" resides in the legislatures of the States. A legislature must have substantial latitude to establish classifications that roughly approximate the nature of the problem perceived, that accommodate competing concerns both public and private, and that account for limitations on the practical ability of the State to remedy every ill. In applying the Equal Protection Clause to most forms of state action, we thus seek only the assurance that the classification at issue bears some fair relationship to a legitimate public purpose.

But we would not be faithful to our obligations under the Fourteenth Amendment if we applied so deferential a standard to every classification. The Equal Protection Clause was intended as a restriction on state legislative action inconsistent with elemental constitutional premises. Thus we have treated as presumptively invidious those classifications that disadvantage a "suspect class," or that impinge upon the exercise of a "fundamental right." With respect to such classifications, it is appropriate to enforce the mandate of equal protection by requiring the State to demonstrate that its classification has been precisely tailored to serve a compelling governmental interest. In addition, we have recognized that certain forms of legislative classification, while not facially invidious, nonetheless give rise to recurring constitutional difficulties; in these limited circumstances we have sought the assurance that the classification reflects a reasoned judgment consistent with the ideal of equal protection by inquiring whether it may fairly be viewed as furthering a substantial interest of the State. We turn to a consideration of the standard appropriate for the evaluation of § 21.031.

A

Sheer incapability or lax enforcement of the laws barring entry into this country, coupled with the failure to establish an effective bar to the employment of undocumented aliens, has resulted in the creation of a substantial "shadow population" of illegal migrants — numbering in the millions — within our borders. This situation raises the specter of a permanent caste of undocumented resident aliens, encouraged by some to remain here as a source of cheap labor, but nevertheless denied the benefits that our society makes available to citizens and lawful residents. The existence of such an underclass presents most difficult problems for a Nation that prides itself on adherence to principles of equality under law.

The children who are plaintiffs in these cases are special members of this underclass. Persuasive arguments support the view that a State may withhold its beneficence from those whose very presence within the United States is the product of their own unlawful conduct. These arguments do not apply with the same force to classifications imposing disabilities on the minor *children* of such illegal entrants. At the least, those who elect to enter our territory by stealth and in violation of our law should be prepared to bear the consequences, including, but not limited to, deportation. But the children of those illegal entrants are not comparably situated. Their "parents have the ability to conform their conduct to societal norms," and presumably the ability to remove themselves from the State's jurisdiction; but the children who are plaintiffs in these cases "can affect neither their parents' conduct nor their own status." *Trimble* v. *Gordon* (1977). Even if the State found it expedient to control the conduct of adults by acting against their children, legislation directing the onus of a parent's misconduct against his children does not comport with fundamental conceptions of justice.

> "[V]isiting . . . condemnation on the head of an infant is illogical and unjust. Moreover, imposing disabilities on the . . . child is contrary to the basic concept of our system that legal burdens should bear some relationship to individual responsibility or wrongdoing. Obviously, no child is responsible for his birth and penalizing the . . . child is an ineffectual — as well as unjust — way of deterring the parents." *Weber* v. *Aetna Casualty & Surety Co.* (1972).

Of course, undocumented status is not irrelevant to any proper legislative goal. Nor is undocumented status an absolutely immutable characteristic since it is the product of conscious, indeed unlawful, action. But § 21.031 is directed against children, and imposes its discriminatory burden on the basis of a legal characteristic over which children can have little control. It is thus difficult to conceive of a rational justification for penalizing these children for their presence within the United States. Yet that appears to be precisely the effect of § 21.031.

Public education is not a "right" granted to individuals by the Constitution. *San Antonio School District.* But neither is it merely some governmental "benefit" indistinguishable from other forms of social welfare legislation. Both the importance of education in maintaining our basic institutions, and the lasting impact of its deprivation on the life of the child, mark the distinction. The "American people have always regarded education and the acquisition of knowlege as matters of supreme importance." *Meyer* v. *Nebraska* (1923). We have recognized "the public school as a most vital civic institution for the preservation of a democratic system of government." *Abington School District* v. *Schempp* (1963) (BRENNAN, J., concurring) and as the primary vehicle for transmitting "the values on which our society rests." *Ambach* v. *Norwick* (1979). As noted early in our history, "some degree of education is necessary to prepare citizens to participate effectively and intelligently in our open political system if we are to preserve freedom and independence." *Wisconsin* v. *Yoder* (1972). And these historic "perceptions of the public schools as inculcating fundamental values necessary to the maintenance of a democratic political system have been confirmed by the observations of social scientists." *Ambach* v. *Norwick*. In addition, education provides the basic tools by which individuals might lead economically productive lives to the benefit of us all. In sum, education has a fundamental role in maintaining the fabric of our society. We cannot ignore the significant social costs borne by our Nation when select groups are denied the means to absorb the values and skills upon which our social order rests.

In addition to the pivotal role of education in sustaining our political and cultural heritage, denial of education to some isolated group of children poses an affront to one of the goals of the Equal Protection Clause: the abolition of governmental barriers presenting unreasonable obstacles to advancement on the basis of individual merit. Paradoxically, by depriving the children of any disfavored group of an education, we foreclose the means by which that group might raise the level of esteem in which it is held by the majority. But more directly, "education prepares individuals to be self-reliant and self-sufficient participants in society." *Wisconsin* v. *Yoder*. Illiteracy is an enduring disability. The inability to read and write will handicap the individual deprived of a basic education each and every day of his life. The inestimable toll of that deprivation on the social, economic, intellectual and psychological well-being of the individual, and the obstacle it poses to individual achievement, makes it most difficult to reconcile the cost or the principle of a status-based denial of basic education with the framework of equality embodied in the Equal Protection Clause. What we said 28 years ago in *Brown* v. *Board of Education* (1954), still holds true:

> "Today, education is perhaps the most important function of state and local governments. Compulsory school attendance laws and the great expenditures for education both demonstrate our recognition of the importance of education to our democratic society. It is required in the performance of our most basic public responsibilities, even service in the armed forces. It is the very foundation of good citizenship. Today it is a principal instrument in awakening the child to cultural values, in preparing him for later professional training, and in helping him to adjust normally to his environment. In these days, it is

doubtful that any child may reasonably be expected to succeed in life if he is denied the opportunity of an education. Such an opportunity, where the state has undertaken to provide it, is a right which must be made available to all on equal terms."

B

These well-settled principles allow us to determine the proper level of deference to be afforded § 21.031. Undocumented aliens cannot be treated as a suspect class because their presence in this country in violation of federal law is not a "constitutional irrelevancy." Nor is education a fundamental right; a State need not justify by compelling necessity every variation in the manner in which education is provided to its population. See *San Antonio School Dist.* v. *Rodriguez* (1973). But more is involved in this case than the abstract question whether § 21.031 discriminates against a suspect class, or whether education is a fundamental right. Section 21.031 imposes a lifetime hardship on a discrete class of children not accountable for their disabling status. The stigma of illiteracy will mark them for the rest of their lives. By denying these children a basic education, we deny them the ability to live within the structure of our civic institutions, and foreclose any realistic possibility that they will contribute in even the smallest way to the progress of our Nation. In determining the rationality of § 21.031, we may appropriately take into account its costs to the Nation and to the innocent children who are its victims. In light of these countervailing costs, the discrimination contained in § 21.031 can hardly be considered rational unless it furthers some substantial goal of the State.

IV

It is the State's principal argument, and apparently the view of the dissenting Justices, that the undocumented status of these children *vel non* establishes a sufficient rational basis for denying them benefits that a State might choose to afford other residents. The State notes that while other aliens are admitted "on an equality of legal privileges with all citizens under non-discriminatory laws," *Takahashi* v. *Fish & Game Comm'n* (1948), the asserted right of these children to an education can claim no implicit congressional imprimatur. Indeed, on the State's view, Congress' apparent disapproval of the presence of these children within the United States, and the evasion of the federal regulatory program that is the mark of undocumented status, provides authority for its decision to impose upon them special disabilities. Faced with an equal protection challenge respecting the treatment of aliens, we agree that the courts must be attentive to congressional policy; the exercise of congressional power might well affect the State's prerogatives to afford differential treatment to a particular class of aliens. But we are unable to find in the congressional immigration scheme any statement of policy that might weigh significantly in arriving at an equal protection balance concerning the State's authority to deprive these children of an education.

The Constitution grants Congress the power to "establish a uniform Rule of Naturalization." Art. I., § 8. Drawing upon this power, upon its plenary authority with respect to foreign relations and international commerce, and upon the inherent power of a sovereign to close its borders, Congress has developed a complex scheme governing admission to and status within our borders. See *Mathews* v. *Diaz* (1976); *Harrisades* v. *Shaughnessy* (1952). The obvious need for delicate policy judgments has counselled the Judicial Branch to avoid intrusion into this field. *Mathews*. But this traditional caution does not persuade us that unusual deference must be shown the classification embodied in § 21.031. The States enjoy no power with respect to the classification of aliens. See *Hines* v. *Davidowitz* (1941). This power is "committed to the political branches of the Federal Government." *Mathews*. Although it is "a routine and normally legitimate part" of the business of the Federal Government to classify on the basis of alien status and to "take into account the character of the relationship between the alien and this country," only rarely are such matters relevant to legislation by a State. *Nyquist* v. *Mauclet* (1977)....

To be sure, like all persons who have entered the United States unlawfully, these children are subject to deportation. But there is no assurance that a child subject to deportation will ever be deported. An illegal entrant might be granted federal permission to continue to reside in this country, or even to become a citizen. In light of the discretionary federal power to grant relief from deportation, a State cannot realistically determine that any particular undocumented child will in fact be deported until after deportation proceedings have been completed. It would of course be most difficult for the State to justify a denial of education to a child enjoying an inchoate federal permission to remain.

We are reluctant to impute to Congress the intention to withhold from these children, for so long as they are present in this country through no fault of their own, access to a basic education. In other contexts, undocumented status, coupled with some articulable federal policy, might enhance State authority with respect to the treatment of undocumented aliens. But in the area of special constitutional sensitivity presented by this case, and in the absence of any contrary indication fairly discernible in the present legislative record, we perceive no national policy that supports the State in denying these children an elementary education. The State may borrow the federal classification. But to justify its use as a criterion for its own discriminatory policy, the State must demonstrate that the classification is reasonably adapted to *"the purposes for which the state desires to use it."* *Oyama* v. *California* (1948) (Murphy, J., concurring) (emphasis added). We therefore turn to the state objectives that are said to support § 21.031.

V

Appellants argue that the classification at issue furthers an interest in the "preservation of the state's limited resources for the education of its lawful residents." Of course, a concern for the preservation of resources standing alone can hardly justify the classification used in allocating those resources. *Graham* v. *Richardson.* The State must do more than justify its classification with a concise expression of an intention to discriminate. *Examining Board* v. *Flores de Otero* (1976). Apart from the asserted state prerogative to act against undocumented children solely on the basis of their undocumented status — an asserted prerogative that carries only minimal force in the circumstances of this case — we discern three colorable state interests that might support § 21.031.

First, appellants appear to suggest that the State may seek to protect the State from an influx of illegal immigrants. While a State might have an interest in mitigating the potentially harsh economic effects of sudden shifts in population, § 21.031 hardly offers an effective method of dealing with an urgent demographic or economic problem. There is no evidence in the record suggesting that illegal entrants impose any significant burden on the State's economy. To the contrary, the available evidence suggests that illegal aliens underutilize public services, while contributing their labor to the local economy and tax money to the State fisc. The dominant incentive for illegal entry into the State of Texas is the availability of employment; few if any illegal immigrants come to this country, or presumably to the State of Texas, in order to avail themselves of a free education. Thus, even making the doubtful assumption that the net impact of illegal aliens on the economy of the State is negative, we think it clear that "[c]harging tuition to undocumented children constitutes a ludicrously ineffectual attempt to stem the tide of illegal immigration," at least when compared with the alternative of prohibiting the employment of illegal aliens.

Second, while it is apparent that a state may "not . . . reduce expenditures for education by barring [some arbitrarily chosen class of] children from its schools," *Shapiro* v. *Thompson* (1969), appellants suggest that undocumented children are appropriately singled out for exclusion because of the special burdens they impose on the State's ability to provide high quality public education. But the record in no way supports the claim that exclusion of undocumented children is likely to improve the overall quality of education in the State. As the District Court in No. 80-1934 noted, the State failed to offer any "credible supporting evidence that a proportionately small diminution of the funds spent on each child [which might result from devoting some State funds to the education of the excluded group] will have a grave impact on the quality of education." And, after reviewing the State's school financing mechanism, the District Court in No. 80-1538 concluded that barring undocumented children from local schools would not necessarily improve the quality of education provided in those schools. Of course, even if improvement in the quality of education were a likely result of barring some *number* of children from the schools of the State, the State must support its selection of *this* group as the appropriate target for exclusion. In terms of educational cost and need, however, undocumented children are "basically indistinguishable" from legally resident alien children.

Finally, appellants suggest that undocumented children are appropriately singled out because their unlawful presence within the United States renders them less likely than other children to remain within the boundaries of the State, and to put their education to productive social or political use within the State. Even assuming that such an interest is legitimate, it is an interest that is most difficult to quantify. The State has no assurance that any child, citizen or not, will employ the education provided by the State within the confines of the State's borders. In any event, the record is clear that many of the undocumented children disabled by this classification will remain in this country indefinitely, and that some will become lawful residents or citizens of the United States. It is difficult to understand precisely what the State hopes to achieve by promoting the creation and perpetuation of a sub-class of illiterates within our boundaries, surely adding to the problems and costs of unemployment, welfare, and crime. It is thus clear that whatever savings might be achieved by denying these children an education, they are wholly insubstantial in light of the costs involved to these children, the State, and the Nation.

VI

If the State is to deny a discrete group of innocent children the free public education that it offers to other children residing within its borders, that denial must be justified by a showing that it furthers some substantial state interest. No such showing was made here. Accordingly, the judgment of the Court of Appeals in each of these cases is

Affirmed.

CHIEF JUSTICE BURGER, with whom JUSTICE WHITE, JUSTICE REHNQUIST, and JUSTICE O'CONNOR join, dissenting.

Were it our business to set the Nation's social policy, I would agree without hesitation that it is senseless for an enlightened society to deprive any children — including illegal aliens — of an elementary education. I fully agree that it would be folly — and wrong — to tolerate creation of a segment of society made up of illiterate persons, many having a limited or no command of our language. However, the Constitution does not constitute us as "Platonic Guardians" nor does it vest in this Court the authority to strike down laws because they do not meet our standards of desirable social policy, "wisdom," or "common sense." See *Tennessee Valley Authority* v. *Hill* (1978). We trespass on the assigned function of the political branches under our structure of limited and separated powers when we assume a policymaking role as the Court does today.

The Court makes no attempt to disguise that it is acting to make up for Congress' lack of "effective leadership" in dealing with the serious national problems caused by the influx of uncountable millions of illegal aliens across our borders. The failure of enforcement of the immigration laws over more than a decade and the inherent difficulty and expense of sealing our vast borders have combined to create a grave socio-economic dilemma. It is a dilemma that has not yet even been fully assessed, let alone addressed. However, it is not the function of the judiciary to provide "effective leadership" simply because the political branches of government fail to do so.

The Court's holding today manifests the justly criticized judicial tendency to attempt speedy and wholesale formulation of "remedies" for the failures — or simply the laggard pace — of the political processes of our system of government. The Court employs, and in my view abuses, the Fourteenth Amendment in an effort to become an omnipotent and omniscient problem solver. That the motives for doing so are noble and compassionate does not alter the fact that the Court distorts our constitutional function to make amends for the defaults of others.

I

In a sense, the Court's opinion rests on such a unique confluence of theories and rationales that it will likely stand for little beyond the results in these particular cases. Yet the extent to which the Court departs from principled constitutional adjudication is nonetheless disturbing.

I have no quarrel with the conclusion that the Equal Protection Clause of the Fourteenth Amendment *applies* to aliens who, after the illegal entry into this country, are indeed physically "within the jurisdiction" of a State. However, as the Court concedes, this "only begins the inquiry." The Equal Protection Clause does not mandate identical treatment of different categories of persons. *Jefferson* v. *Hackney* (1972); *Reed* v. *Reed* (1971); *Tigner* v. *Texas* (1940).

The dispositive issue in these cases, simply put, is whether, for purposes of allocating its finite resources, a State has a legitimate reason to differentiate between persons who are lawfully within the State and those who are unlawfully there. The distinction the State of Texas has drawn — based not only upon its own legitimate interests but on classifications established by the federal government in its immigration laws and policies — is not unconstitutional.

A

The Court acknowledges that, except in those cases when state classifications disadvantage a "suspect class" or impinge upon a "fundamental right," the Equal Protection Clause permits a State "substantial latitude" in distinguishing between different groups of persons. Moreover, the Court expressly — and correctly — rejects any suggestion that illegal aliens are a suspect class, or that education is a fundamental right. Yet by patching together bits and pieces of what might be termed quasi-suspect-class and quasi-fundamental-rights analysis, the Court spins out a theory custom-tailored to the facts of these cases.

In the end, we are told little more than that the level of scrutiny employed to strike down the Texas law applies only when illegal alien children are deprived of a public education. If ever a court was guilty of an unabashedly result-oriented approach, this case is a prime example.

(1)

The Court first suggests that these illegal alien children, although not a suspect class, are entitled to special solicitude under the Equal Protection Clause because they lack "control" over or "responsibility" for their unlawful entry into this country. Similarly, the Court appears to take the position that § 21.031 is presumptively "irrational" because it has the effect of imposing "penalties" on "innocent" children. However, the Equal Protection Clause does not preclude legislators from classifying among persons on the basis of factors and characteristics over which individuals may be said to lack "control." Indeed, in some circumstances persons generally, and children in particular, may have little control over or responsibility for such things as their ill-health, need for public assistance, or place of residence. Yet a state legislature is not barred from considering, for example, relevant differences between the mentally-healthy and the mentally-ill, or between the residents of different counties, simply because these may be factors unrelated to individual choice or to any "wrongdoing." The Equal Protection Clause protects against arbitrary and irrational classifications, and against invidious discrimination stemming from prejudice and hostility; it is not an all-encompassing "equalizer" designed to eradicate every distinction for which persons are not "responsible." . . .

. . . This Court has recognized that in allocating governmental benefits to a given class of aliens, one "may take into account the character of the relationship between the alien and this country." *Mathews* v. *Diaz* (1976). When that "relationship" is a federally-prohibited one, there can, of course, be no presumption that a State has a constitutional duty to include illegal aliens among the recipients of its governmental benefits.

(2)

The second strand of the Court's analysis rests on the premise that, although public education is not a constitutionally-guaranteed right, "neither is it merely some governmental 'benefit' indistinguishable from other forms of social welfare legislation." Whatever meaning or relevance this opaque observation might have in some other context, it simply has no bearing on the issues at hand. Indeed, it is never made clear what the Court's opinion means on this score.

The importance of education is beyond dispute. Yet we have held repeatedly that the importance of a governmental service does not elevate it to the status of a "fundamental right" for purposes of equal protection analysis. *San Antonio School District* v. *Rodgriguez* (1973); *Lindsey* v. *Normet* (1972). In *San Antonio School District*, JUSTICE POWELL, speaking for the Court, expressly rejected the proposition that state laws dealing with public education are subject to special scrutiny under the Equal Protection Clause. Moreover, the Court points to no meaningful way to distinguish between education and other governmental benefits in this context. Is the Court suggesting that education is more "fundamental" than food, shelter, or medical care?

The Equal Protection Clause guarantees similar treatment of similarly situated persons, but it does not mandate a constitutional hierarchy of governmental services. JUSTICE POWELL, speaking for the Court in *San Antonio School District,* put it well in stating that to the extent this Court raises or lowers the degree of "judicial scrutiny" in equal protection cases according to a transient Court majority's view of the societal importance of the interest affected, we "assum[e] a legislative role and one for which the Court lacks both authority and competence." Yet that is precisely what the Court does today. . . .

The central question in these cases, as in every equal protection case not involving truly fundamental rights "explicitly or implicitly guaranteed by the Constitution," *San Antonio School District*, is whether there is some legitimate basis for a legislative distinction between different classes of persons. The fact that the distinction is drawn in legislation affecting access to public education — as opposed to legislation allocating other important governmental benefits, such as public assistance, health care, or housing — cannot make a difference in the level of scrutiny applied.

B

Once it is conceded — as the Court does — that illegal aliens are not a suspect class, and that education is not a fundamental right, our inquiry should focus on and be limited to whether the legislative classification at issue bears a rational relationship to a legitimate state purpose. *Vance* v. *Bradley* (1979); *Dandridge* v. *Williams* (1970).

The State contends primarily that § 21.031 serves to prevent undue depletion of its limited revenues available for education, and to preserve the fiscal integrity of the State's school financing system against an ever-increasing flood of illegal aliens — aliens over whose entry or continued presence it has no control. Of course such fiscal concerns alone could not justify discrimination against a suspect class or an arbitrary and irrational denial of benefits to a particular group of persons. Yet I assume no member of this Court would argue that prudent conservation of finite state revenues is *per se* an illegitimate goal. . . .

Without laboring what will undoubtedly seem obvious to many, it simply is not "irrational" for a State to conclude that it does not have the same responsibility to provide benefits for persons whose very presence in the State and this country is illegal as it does to provide for persons lawfully present. By definition, illegal aliens have no right whatever to be here, and the State may reasonably, and constitutionally, elect not to provide them with governmental services at the expense of those who are lawfully in the State. In *DeCamas* v. *Bica* (1976), we held that a State may protect its "fiscal interests and lawfully resident labor force from the deleterious effects on its economy resulting from the employment of illegal aliens." . . .

It is significant that the federal government has seen fit to exclude illegal aliens from numerous social welfare programs, such as the food stamp program, the old age assistance, aid to families with dependent children, aid to the blind, aid to the permanently and totally disabled, and supplemental security income programs, the medicare hospital insurance benefits program, and the medicaid hospital insurance benefits for the aged and disabled program. Although these exclusions do not conclusively demonstrate the constitutionality of the State's use of the same classification for comparable purposes, at the very least they tend to support the rationality of excluding illegal alien residents of a State from such programs so as to preserve the State's finite revenues for the benefit of lawful residents. See *Mathews* v. *Diaz* (1976).

The Court maintains — as if this were the issue — that "barring undocumented children from local schools would not necessarily improve the quality of education provided in those schools." . . . However, the legitimacy of barring illegal aliens from programs such as medicare or medicaid does not depend on a showing that the barrier would "improve the quality" of medical care given to persons lawfully entitled to participate in such programs. Modern education, like medical care, is enormously expensive, and there can be no doubt that very large added costs will fall on the State or its local school districts as a result of the inclusion of illegal aliens in the tuition-free public schools. . . .

Denying a free education to illegal alien children is not a choice I would make were I a legislator. Apart from compassionate considerations, the long-range costs of excluding any children from the public schools may well outweigh the costs of educating them. But that is not the issue; the fact that there are sound *policy* arguments against the Texas legislature's choice does not render that choice an unconstitutional one.

II

The Constitution does not provide a cure for every social ill, nor does it vest judges with a mandate to try to remedy every social problem. . . .

Moreover, when this Court rushes in to remedy what it perceives to be the failings of the political processes, it deprives those processes of an opportunity to function. When the political institutions are not forced to exercise constitutionally allocated powers and responsibilities, those powers, like muscles not used, tend to atrophy. Today's cases, I regret to say, present yet another example of unwarranted judicial action which in the long run tends to contribute to the weakening of our political processes. . . .

DIET AND CANCER REPORT
June 16, 1982

Following a review of approximately 10,000 nutritional studies, a special committee of the National Academy of Sciences recommended June 16 "interim dietary guidelines" for those Americans wishing to reduce their risk of developing cancer. The guidelines, issued as part of a 600-page report titled "Diet, Nutrition, and Cancer," were to be changed or updated as more information became available.

Specifically, the panel recommended less consumption of fat and more consumption of fruits, vegetables and whole grains. Such recommendations had been made previously by other nutrition experts.

The report appeared to contradict a 1980 report issued by the academy's Food and Nutrition Board, which stated that a reduction of fat intake was not necessary except to control weight. That report, however, concentrated mainly on heart disease.

Following issuance of the 1982 guidelines, the American Meat Institute called upon the academy to explain the differences between the two reports. The institute, which represents the meat packing and processing industry, also labeled the 1982 recommendations "misleading advice which does no service to the public."

Among the dietary recommendations by the academy panel were:

● Reduce intake of fatty meats, whole milk products, cooking oils and fats to 30 percent of total calories in the diet.

● Restrict intake of salt-cured, pickled or smoked foods, such as ham, *bacon, hot dogs, smoked sausages and bologna. Such foods, aside from being high in fat, can increase exposure to cancer-causing compounds.*

● *Consume alcoholic beverages in "moderation." According to the report, excessive consumption of alcohol, especially when combined with smoking, has been linked to an increased risk of stomach and lung cancer.*

The panel did not offer advice on increasing consumption of Vitamin E or the mineral selenium, both of which have been purported to inhibit cancer-causing agents.

Following are excerpts from Chapter 1, the executive summary, of Diet, Nutrition, and Cancer, released by ˙the National Academy of Sciences June 16, 1982. (Boldface headings in brackets have been added by Congressional Quarterly to highlight the organization of the text.):

SUMMARY AND CONCLUSIONS

Dietary Patterns and Components of Food

Since the turn of the century, new methods of processing and storage have resulted in a proliferation of the kinds and numbers of food items available to the U.S. population. Unfortunately, little is known about the ways in which such innovations have altered the specific composition of the diet. The only components of food that have been monitored regularly are the nutrients. The dietary levels of most nutrients have changed relatively little over the past 80 years.

Attempting to determine which constituents of food might be associated with cancer, epidemiologists have studied population subgroups, including migrants to the United States, to examine the relationship between specific dietary patterns or the consumption of certain foods and the risk of developing particular cancers. In general, the evidence suggests that some types of diets and some dietary components (e.g., high fat diets or the frequent consumption of salt-cured, salt-pickled, and smoked foods) tend to increase the risk of cancer, whereas others (e.g., low fat diets or the frequent consumption of certain fruits and vegetables) tend to decrease it. The mechanisms responsible for these effects are not fully understood, partly because nutritive and nonnutritive components of foods may interact to exert effects on cancer incidence.

In the laboratory, investigators have attempted to shed light on the mechanisms by which diet may influence carcinogenesis. They have examined the ability of individual nutrients, food extracts, or nonnutritive components of food to enhance or inhibit carcinogenesis and mutagenesis, thereby providing epidemiologists with testable hypotheses regarding specific components of the diet. Because the data from both types of studies are generally grouped according to dietary constituents, the committee found it advantageous to organize its report in a similar fashion.

Total Caloric Intake

The committee reviewed many studies in which the variable examined was the total amount of food consumed by humans or animals, rather than the precise composition of the diet.... [T]he studies did not indicate whether the observed effects resulted from the changes in the proportion of specific nutrients in the diet or from the modification of total caloric intake.

Since very few epidemiologists have been able to examine the effect of caloric intake *per se* on the risk of cancer, their reports have provided largely indirect evidence for such a relationship, and much of it is based on associations between body weight or obesity and cancer.

In laboratory experiments, the incidence of tumors is lower and the lifespan much longer for animals on restricted food intake than for animals fed ad libitum. However, because the intake of all nutrients was simultaneously depressed in these studies, the observed reduction in tumor incidence might have been due to the reduction of some specific nutrient, such as fat. It is also difficult to interpret experiments in which caloric intake has been modified by varying dietary fat or fiber, both of which may by themselves exert effects on tumorigenesis.

Thus, the committee concluded that neither the epidemiological studies nor the experiments in animals permit a clear interpretation of the specific effect of total caloric intake on the risk of cancer. Nonetheless, the studies conducted in animals show that a reduction in total food intake decreases the age-specific incidence of cancer. The evidence is less clear for human beings.

Lipids (Fats and Cholesterol)

Many epidemiological and laboratory studies have been conducted to examine the association between cancer and intake of lipids, i.e., total dietary fat, saturated fat, polyunsaturated fat, and cholesterol.

Fats. Epidemiological studies have repeatedly shown an association between dietary fat and the occurrence of cancer at several sites, especially the breast, prostate, and large bowel. In various populations, both the high incidence of and mortality from breast cancer have been shown to correlate strongly with higher per capita fat consumption; the few case-control studies conducted have also shown this association with dietary fat. Like breast cancer, increased risk of large bowel cancer has been associated with higher fat intake in both correlation and case-control studies. The data on prostate cancer are more limited, but they too suggest that an increased risk is related to high levels of dietary fat. In general, it is not possible to identify specific components of fat as being clearly responsible for the observed effects, although total fat and saturated fat have been associated most frequently.

The epidemiological data are not entirely consistent. For example, the magnitude of the association of fat with breast cancer appears greater in the correlation data than in the case-control data, and several reports on large bowel cancer fail to show an association with fat. Possible reasons for these discrepancies are apparent....

Like epidemiological studies, numerous experiments in animals have shown that dietary lipids influence tumorigenesis, especially in the breast and the colon. An increase in fat intake from 5% to 20% of the weight of the diet (i.e., approximately 10% to 40% of total calories) increases tumor incidence in various tissues; conversely, animals consuming low fat diets have a lower tumor incidence. When the intake of total fat is low, polyunsaturated fats appear to be more effective than saturated fats in enhancing tumorigenesis. However, this distinction becomes less prominent as total fat intake is increased.

Dietary fat appears to have a promoting effect on tumorigenesis. For example, some studies suggest that the development of colon cancer is enhanced by the increased secretion of certain bile steroids and bile acids that accompanies high levels of fat intake. Nonetheless, there is little or no knowledge concerning the specific mechanisms involved in tumor promotion. This lack of understanding contributes to our overall uncertainty about the mechanisms that underlie the effect of diet on carcinogenesis. Although most of the data suggest that dietary fat has promoting activity, there is not enough evidence to warrant the complete exclusion of an effect on initiation.

The committee concluded that of all the dietary components it studied, the combined epidemiological and experimental evidence is most suggestive for a causal relationship between fat intake and the occurrence of cancer. Both epidemiological studies and experiments in animals provide convincing evidence that increasing the intake of total fat increases the incidence of cancer at certain sites, particularly the breast and colon, and, conversely, that the risk is lower with lower intakes of fat. Data from studies in animals suggest that when fat intake is low, polyunsaturated fats are more effective than saturated fats in enhancing tumorigenesis, whereas the data on humans do not permit a clear distinction to be made between the effects of different components of fat. In general, however, the evidence from epidemiological and laboratory studies is consistent.

Cholesterol. The relationship between dietary cholesterol and cancer is not clear. Many studies of serum cholesterol levels and cancer mortality in human populations have demonstrated an inverse correlation with colon cancer among men, but the evidence is not conclusive. Data on cholesterol and cancer risk from studies in animals are too limited to permit any inferences to be drawn....

Protein

The relationship between protein intake and carcinogenesis has been studied in human populations as well as in the laboratory....

Results of epidemiological studies have suggested possible associations between high intake of dietary protein and increased risk for cancers at a number of different sites, although the literature on protein is much more limited than the literature concerning fats and cancer. In addition, because of the very high correlation between fat and protein in the diets of most Western countries, and the more consistent and often stronger association of these cancers with fat intake, it seems likely that dietary fat is the more active component. Nevertheless, the evidence does not completely preclude the existence of an independent effect of protein.

In most laboratory experiments, carcinogenesis is suppressed by diets containing levels of protein at or below the minimum required for optimal growth. Chemically induced carcinogenesis appears to be enhanced as protein intake is increased up to 2 or 3 times the normal requirement; however, higher levels of protein begin to inhibit carcinogenesis. There is some evidence to suggest that protein may affect the initiation phase of carcinogenesis and the subsequent growth and development of the tumor.

Thus, in the judgment of the committee, evidence from both epidemiological and laboratory studies suggests that high protein intake *may* be associated with an increased risk of cancers at certain sites. Because of the relative paucity of data on protein compared to fat, and the strong correlation between the intakes of fat and protein in the U.S. diet, the committee is unable to arrive at a firm conclusion about an independent effect of protein.

Carbohydrates

...[I]nformation concerning the role of carbohydrates in the development of cancer in humans is extremely limited. Although some studies suggest that a high intake of refined sugar or starch increases the risk of cancer at certain sites, the results are insufficient to permit any firm conclusions to be drawn.

The data obtained from studies in animals are equally limited, providing too little evidence to suggest that carbohydrates (possibly excluding fiber) play a direct role in experimentally induced carcinogenesis. However, excessive carbohydrate consumption contributes to caloric excess, and this in turn has been implicated as a modifier of carcinogenesis.

Dietary Fiber

Considerable effort has been devoted to studying the effects of dietary fiber and fiber-containing foods (such as certain vegetables, fruits, and whole grain cereals) on the occurrence of cancer....

Most epidemiological studies on fiber have examined the hypothesis that high fiber diets protect against colorectal cancer. Results of correlation and case-control studies of dietary fiber have sometimes supported and sometimes contradicted this hypothesis. In both types of studies, correlations have been based primarily on estimates of fiber intake obtained by grouping foods according to their fiber content. In the only case-control study and the only correlation study in which total fiber

511

consumption was quantified rather than estimated from the consumption of high fiber foods, no association was found between high fiber intake and a lower risk of colon cancer. However, the correlation study indicated that the incidence of colon cancer was inversely related to the intake of one fiber component — the pentosan fraction, which is found in whole wheat products and other food items.

Laboratory experiments also have indicated that the consumption of some high fiber ingredients (e.g., cellulose and bran) inhibits the induction of colon cancer by certain chemical carcinogens. However, the results are inconsistent. Moreover, they are difficult to equate with the results of epidemiological studies because most laboratory investigations have focused on specific fibers or their individual components, whereas most epidemiological studies have been concerned with fiber-containing foods whose exact composition has not been determined.

Thus, the committee found no conclusive evidence to indicate that dietary fiber (such as that present in certain fruits, vegetables, grains, and cereals) exerts a protective effect against colorectal cancer in humans. Both epidemiological and laboratory reports suggest that if there is such an effect, specific components of fiber, rather than total fiber, are more likely to be responsible.

Vitamins

In recent years, there has been considerable interest in the role of vitamins A, C, and E in the genesis and prevention of cancer. In contrast, less attention has been paid to the B vitamins and others such as vitamin K. . . .

Vitamin A. A growing accumulation of epidemiological evidence indicates that there is an inverse relationship between the risk of cancer and the consumption of foods that contain vitamin A (e.g., liver) or its precursors (e.g., the carotenoids in green and yellow vegetables). Most of the data do not show whether the effects are due to carotenoids, to vitamin A itself, or to some other constituent of these foods. In these studies, investigators found an inverse association between estimates of "vitamin A" intake and carcinoma at several sites, e.g., the lung, the urinary bladder, and the larynx.

Studies in laboratory animals indicate that vitamin A deficiency generally increases susceptibility to chemically induced neoplasia and that an increased intake of the vitamin appears to protect against carcinogenesis in most, but not all cases. Because high doses of vitamin A are toxic, many of these studies have been conducted with its synthetic analogues (retinoids), which lack some of the toxic effects of the vitamin. Retinoids have been shown to inhibit chemically induced neoplasia of the breast, urinary bladder, skin, and lung in animals.

The committee concluded that the laboratory evidence shows that vitamin A itself and many of the retinoids are able to suppress chemically induced tumors. The epidemiological evidence is sufficient to suggest that foods rich in carotenes or vitamin A are associated with a reduced risk of cancer. The toxicity of vitamin A in doses exceeding those required for optimum nutrition, and the difficulty of epidemiological studies to distinguish the effects of carotenes from those of vitamin A, argue against increasing vitamin A intake by the use of supplements.

Vitamin C (Ascorbic Acid). The epidemiological data pertaining to the effect of vitamin C on the occurrence of cancer are not extensive. Furthermore, they provide mostly indirect evidence since they are based on the consumption of foods, especially fresh fruits and vegetables, known to contain high concentrations of the vitamin, rather than on actual measurements of vitamin C intake. The results of several case-control studies and a few correlation studies suggest that the consumption of vitamin-C-containing foods is associated with a lower risk of certain cancers, particularly gastric and esophageal cancer.

In the laboratory, ascorbic acid can inhibit the formation of carcinogenic *N*-nitroso compounds, both *in vitro* and *in vivo*. On the other hand, studies of its inhibitory effect on preformed carcinogens have not provided conclusive results. In recent studies, the addition of ascorbic acid to cells grown in culture prevented the chemically induced transformation of these cells and, in some cases, caused reversion of transformed cells.

Thus, the limited evidence suggests that vitamin C can inhibit the formation of some carcinogens and that the consumption of vitamin-C-containing foods is associated with a lower risk of cancers of the stomach and esophagus.

Vitamin E (α-Tocopherol). Because vitamin E is present in a variety of commonly consumed foods (particularly vegetable oils, whole grain cereal products, and eggs), it is difficult to identify population groups with substantially different levels of intake. Consequently, it is not surprising that there are no epidemiological reports concerning vitamin E intake and the risk of cancer.

Vitamin E, like ascorbic acid, inhibits the formation of nitrosamines *in vivo* and *in vitro*. However, there are no reports about the effect of this vitamin on nitrosamine-induced neoplasia. Limited evidence from studies in animals suggests that vitamin E may also inhibit the induction of tumorigenesis by other chemicals.

The data are not sufficient to permit any firm conclusion to be drawn about the effect of vitamin E on cancer in humans.

The B Vitamins. No specific information has been produced by epidemiological studies, and there have been only a few inadequate laboratory investigations to determine whether there is a relationship between various B vitamins and the occurrence of cancer. Therefore, no conclusion can be drawn.

Minerals

Of the many minerals present in the diet of humans, the committee reviewed the evidence for nine that have been suspected of playing a role in carcinogenesis. The assessment was severely limited by a paucity of relevant studies on all but two minerals — selenium and iron. Where data on dietary exposure and carcinogenesis were insufficient, the committee used information from studies of occupational exposure or laboratory experiments in which the animals were exposed through routes other than diet. . . .

Selenium. Selenium has been studied to determine its role in both the causation and the prevention of cancer. The epidemiological evidence is derived from a few geographical correlation studies, which have shown that the risk of cancer is inversely related to estimates of per capita selenium intake, selenium levels in blood specimens, or selenium concentrations in water supplies. It is not clear whether this relationship applies to all types of cancer or only to cancer at specific sites such as the gastrointestinal tract. There have been no case control or cohort studies.

Experiments in animals have also demonstrated an antitumorigenic effect of selenium. But the relevance of these results to cancer in humans is not apparent since the selenium levels used in most of the studies far exceeded dietary requirements and often bordered on levels that are toxic. Earlier reports suggesting that selenium was carcinogenic in laboratory animals have not been confirmed.

Therefore, both the epidemiological and laboratory studies suggest that selenium may offer some protection against the risk of cancer. However, firm conclusions cannot be drawn from the limited evidence. Increasing the selenium intake to more than 200 μg/day by the use of supplements has not been shown to confer health benefits exceeding those derived from the consumption of a balanced diet. Such supplementation should be considered an experimental procedure requiring strict medical supervision and is not recommended for use by the public.

Iron. Iron deficiency has been related to an increase in the risk of Plummer-Vinson syndrome, which is associated with cancer of the upper alimentary tract. Some evidence suggests that iron deficiency may be related to gastric cancer, also through an indirect mechanism. Although epidemiological reports have suggested that inhalation exposures to high concentrations of iron increase the risk of cancer, there is no evidence pertaining to the effect of high levels of dietary iron on the risk of cancer in humans. The limited evidence from animal experiments suggests that a deficiency of dietary iron may increase susceptibility to some chemically induced tumors.

The data are not sufficient for a firm conclusion to be drawn about the role of iron in carcinogenesis.

Copper, Zinc, Molybdenum, and Iodine. Some epidemiological studies suggest that dietary zinc is associated with an increase in the incidence of cancer at certain sites; others suggest that blood and tissue levels of zinc in cancer patients are lower, and those of copper are higher, than in the controls. Results of experiments in animals are also inconclusive. Different levels of dietary zinc either enhance or retard tumor growth, depending on the specific test design. High levels of copper have been observed to protect against chemical induction of tumors.

There is some epidemiological evidence that a deficiency of molybdenum and other trace elements is associated with an increased risk of esophageal cancer. Limited experiments in animals suggest that dietary molybdenum supplementation may reduce the incidence of nitrosamine-induced tumors of the esophagus and forestomach.

Studies conducted in Colombia, Iceland, and Scotland indicated that iodine deficiency, and also excessive iodine intake, may increase the risk of thyroid carcinoma. These observations have not been confirmed in other countries or in other studies. In general, the results of studies in animals support the association between iodine deficiency and thyroid cancer.

The committee concluded that the data concerning dietary exposure to zinc, copper, molybdenum, and iodine are insufficient and provide no basis for conclusions about the association of these elements with cancer risk.

Arsenic, Cadmium, and Lead. Occupational exposure to these elements is associated with an increased risk of cancer at several sites. Exposure to high concentrations of arsenic in drinking water has been linked with skin cancer. However, the evidence for cancer risk resulting from exposure to the normally low levels of these elements in the diet is not conclusive. No carcinogenic effects of dietary cadmium and arsenic have been observed in laboratory experiments, whereas high intakes of certain lead compounds appear to increase the incidence of cancer in mice and rats.

On this basis, the committee believes that no firm conclusions can be drawn about the risk of cancer due to normal dietary exposure to arsenic, cadmium, and lead.

Inhibitors of Carcinogenesis

Foods and numerous nutritive and nonnutritive components of the diet have been examined for their potential to protect against carcinogenesis. In epidemiological studies, investigators have attempted to correlate the intake of specific foods (and by inference, certain vitamins and trace elements) and the incidence of cancer. In laboratory experiments, vitamins, trace elements, nonnutritive food additives, and other organic constituents of foods (e.g., indoles, phenols, flavones, and isothiocyanates) have been tested for their ability to inhibit neoplasia....

The committee believes that there is sufficient epidemiological evidence to suggest that consumption of certain vegetables, especially carotene-rich (i.e., dark green and deep yellow) vegetables and cruciferous vegetables (e.g., cabbage, broccoli, cauliflower, and brussels sprouts), is associated with a reduction in the incidence of cancer at several sites in humans. A number of nonnutritive and nutritive compounds that are present in these vegetables also inhibit carcinogenesis in laboratory animals. Investigators have not yet established which, if any, of these compounds may be responsible for the protective effect observed in epidemiological studies.

Alcohol

The effects of alcohol consumption on cancer incidence have been studied in human populations. In some countries, including the United States, excessive beer drinking has been associated with an increased risk of colorectal cancer, especially rectal cancer. This observation has not been confirmed in other studies. There is limited evidence that excessive alcohol consumption causes hepatic injury and cirrhosis, which in turn may lead to the formation of hepatomas (liver cancer). When consumed in large quantities, alcoholic beverages appear to act synergistically with inhaled cigarette smoke to increase the risk for cancers of the mouth, larynx, esophagus, and the respiratory tract. . . .

Naturally Occurring Carcinogens

In addition to nutrients, a variety of nonnutritive substances (e.g., hydrazines) are natural constituents of foods. Furthermore, metabolites of molds (e.g., mycotoxins such as the potent carcinogen aflatoxin) and of bacteria (e.g., carcinogenic nitrosamines) may contaminate foods. Many of these are occasional contaminants, whereas others are normal components of relatively common foods. . . .

The committee concluded that certain naturally occurring contaminants in food are carcinogenic in animals and pose a potential risk of cancer to humans. Noteworthy among these are mycotoxins (especially aflatoxin) and N-nitroso compounds, for which there is some epidemiological evidence. Studies in animals indicate that a few nonnutritive constituents of some foods, such as hydrazines in mushrooms, are also carcinogenic.

The compounds thus far shown to be carcinogenic in animals have been reported to occur in the average U.S. diet in small amounts; however, there is no evidence that any of these substances individually makes a major contribution to the total risk of cancer in the United States. This lack of sufficient data should not be interpreted as an indication that these or other compounds subsequently found to be carcinogenic do not present a hazard.

Mutagens in Foods

Mutagens are substances that causes heritable changes in the genetic material of cells. If a chemical is mutagenic to bacteria or other organisms, it is generally regarded as a suspect carcinogen, although carcinogenicity must be confirmed in long-term tests in whole animals.

. . .[C]onsiderable attention has recently been directed toward mutagenic activity in foods. Many vegetables contain mutagenic flavonoids such as quercetin, kaempferol, and their glycosides. Furthermore, some substances found in foods can enhance or inhibit the mutagenic activity of other compounds. Mutagens in charred meat and fish are produced during the pyrolysis of proteins that occurs when foods are cooked at very high temperatures. Mutagens can also be produced during normal cooking of meat at lower temperatures. Smoking of foods as well as charcoal broiling results in the deposition of mutagenic and carcinogenic polynuclear organic compounds such as benzo[a]pyrene on the surface of the food.

Most mutagens detected in foods have not been adequately tested for their carcinogenic activity. Thus, the committee believes that it is not yet possible to assess whether such mutagens are likely to contribute significantly to the incidence of cancer in the United States.

Food Additives

In the United States, nearly 3,000 substances are intentionally added to foods during processing. Another estimated 12,000 chemicals (e.g., vinyl chloride and acrylonitrile, which are used in food-packaging materials) are classified as indirect (or unintentional) additives, and are occasionally detected in some foods. Large amounts of some additives, such as sugar, are consumed by the general population, but the annual per capita exposure to most indirect additives represents only a minute portion of the diet. Although the Food Safety Provisions and, in many cases, the "Delaney Clause" of the Federal Food, Drug, and Cosmetic Act prohibit the addition of known carcinogens to foods, only a small proportion of the substances added to foods have been tested for carcinogenicity according to protocols that are considered acceptable by current standards. Moreover, except for the studies on nonnutritive sweeteners, only a few epidemiological studies have been conducted to assess the effect of food additives on cancer incidence. . . .

Of the few direct food additives that have been tested and found to be carcinogenic in animals, all except saccharin have been banned from use in the food supply. Only minute residues of a few indirect additives that are known either to produce cancer in animals (e.g., acrylonitrile) or to be carcinogenic in humans (e.g., vinyl chloride and diethylstilbestrol) are occasionally detected in foods.

The evidence reviewed by the committee does not suggest that the increasing use of food additives has contributed significantly to the overall risk of cancer for humans. However, this lack of detectable effect may be due to their lack of carcinogenicity, to the relatively recent use of many of these substances, or to the inability of epidemiological techniques to detect the effects of additives against the background of common cancers from other causes.

Environmental Contaminants

Very low levels of a large and chemically diverse group of environmental contaminants may be present in a variety of foods. The dietary levels of some of these substances are monitored by the Market Basket Surveys conducted by the Food and Drug Administration. Many of them have been extensively tested for carcinogenicity. . . .

The results of standard chronic toxicity tests indicate that a number of environmental contaminants (e.g., some organochlorine pesticides, polychlorinated biphenyls, and polycyclic aromatic hydrocarbons) cause cancer in laboratory animals. The committee found no epidemiological evidence to suggest that these compounds individually make a major contribution to the risk of cancer in humans. However, the possibility that they may act synergistically and may thereby create a greater carcinogenic risk cannot be excluded.

[Diet and the Overall Risk of Cancer]

By some estimates, as much as 90% of all cancer in humans has been attributed to various environmental factors, including diet. . . . Other investigators have estimated that diet is responsible for 30% to 40% of cancers in men and 60% of cancers in women. Recently, two epidemiologists suggested that a significant proportion of the deaths from cancer could be prevented by dietary means and that dietary modifications would have the greatest effect on the incidence of cancers of the stomach and large bowel and, to a lesser extent on cancers of the breast, the endometrium, and the lung.

The evidence reviewed by the committee suggests that cancers of most major sites are influenced by dietary patterns. However, the committee concluded that the data are not sufficient to quantitate the contribution of diet to the overall cancer risk or to determine the percent reduction in risk that might be achieved by dietary modifications.

INTERIM DIETARY GUIDELINES

It is not now possible, and may never be possible, to specify a diet that would protect everyone against all forms of cancer. Nevertheless, the committee believes that it is possible on the basis of current evidence to formulate interim dietary guidelines that are both consistent with good nutritional practices and likely to reduce the risk of cancer. These guidelines are meant to be applied in their entirety to obtain maximal benefit.

1. There is sufficient evidence that high fat consumption is linked to increased incidence of certain common cancers (notably breast and colon cancer) and that low fat intake is associated with a lower incidence of these cancers. The committee recommends that the consumption of both saturated and unsaturated fats be reduced in the average U.S. diet. An appropriate and practical target is to reduce the intake of fat from its present level (approximately 40%) to 30% of total calories in the diet. The scientific data do not provide a strong basis for establishing fat intake at precisely 30% of total calories. Indeed, the data could be used to justify an even greater reduction. However, in the judgment of the committee, the suggested reduction (i.e., one-quarter of the fat intake) is a moderate and practical target, and is likely to be beneficial.

2. The committee emphasizes the importance of including fruits, vegetables, and whole grain cereal products in the daily diet. In epidemiological studies, frequent consumption of these foods has been inversely correlated with the incidence of various cancers. Results of laboratory experiments have supported these findings in tests of individual nutritive and nonnutritive constituents of fruits (especially citrus fruits) and vegetables (especially carotene-rich and cruciferous vegetables).

These recommendations apply only to foods as sources of nutrients — not to dietary supplements of individual nutrients. The vast literature examined in this report focuses on the relationship between the consumption of foods and the incidence of cancer in human populations. In contrast, there is very little information on the effects of various levels of individual nutrients on the risk of cancer in humans. Therefore, the committee is unable to predict the health effects of high and potentially toxic doses of isolated nutrients consumed in the form of supplements.

3. In some parts of the world, especially China, Japan, and Iceland, populations that frequently consume salt-cured (including salt-pickled) or smoked foods have a greater incidence of cancers at some sites, especially the esophagus and the stomach. In addition, some methods of smoking and pickling foods seem to produce higher levels of polycyclic aromatic hydrocarbons and N-nitroso compounds. These compounds cause mutations in bacteria and cancer in animals, and are suspected of being carcinogenic in humans. Therefore, the committee recommends that the consumption of food preserved by salt-curing (including salt-pickling) or smoking be minimized.

4. Certain nonnutritive constituents of foods, whether naturally occurring or introduced inadvertently (as contaminants) during production, processing, and storage, pose a potential risk of cancer to humans. The committee recommends that efforts continue to be made to minimize contamination of foods with carcinogens from any source. Where such contaminants are unavoidable, permissible levels should continue to be established and the food supply monitored to assure that such levels are not exceeded. Furthermore, intentional additives (direct and indirect) should continue to be evaluated for carcinogenic activity before they are approved for use in the food supply.

5. The committee suggests that further efforts be made to identify mutagens in food and to expedite testing for their carcinogenicity. Where feasible and prudent, mutagens should be removed or their concentration minimized when this can be accomplished without jeopardizing the nutritive value of foods or introducing other potentially hazardous substances into the diet.

6. Excessive consumption of alcoholic beverages, particularly combined with cigarette smoking, has been associated with an increased risk of cancer of the upper gastrointestinal and respiratory tracts. Consumption of alcohol is also associated with other adverse health effects. Thus, the committee recommends that if alcoholic beverages are consumed, it be done in moderation.

The committee suggests that agencies involved in education and public information should be encouraged to disseminate information on the relationship between dietary and nutritional factors and the incidence of cancer, and to publicize the conclusions and interim dietary guidelines in this report. It should be made clear that the weight of evidence suggests that what we eat during our lifetime strongly influences the probability of developing certain kinds of cancer but that it is not now possible, and may never be possible, to specify a diet that protects all people against all forms of cancer. The cooperation of the food industry should be sought to help implement the dietary guidelines described above.

Since the current data base is incomplete, future epidemiological and experimental research is likely to provide new insights into the relationship between diet and cancer. Therefore, the committee suggests that the National Cancer Institute establish mechanisms to review these dietary guidelines at least every 5 years.

COURT ON RIGHTS
OF MENTALLY RETARDED
June 18, 1982

In its first ruling on the constitutional rights of the mentally retarded, the Supreme Court held June 18 that such persons in state institutions are entitled to safe living conditions, freedom from unreasonable physical restraints and sufficient training in self-care.

The unanimous decision, written by Justice Lewis F. Powell Jr., was based on the due process clause of the 14th Amendment. Powell noted that the rights of the mentally retarded are not "absolute," pointing out that "there are occasions in which it is necessary for the state to restrain the movement of residents — for example, to protect them as well as others from violence." To determine what restrictions and risks are reasonable for mentally retarded persons living in institutions, he wrote, "courts must show deference to the judgment exercised by a qualified professional."

The case began in 1976 after Nicholas Romeo, a resident of the Pennsylvania Pennhurst State School for the retarded, injured himself numerous times through his own violent behavior and the reactions of other residents to him. A suit for damages, based on the violation of Romeo's rights under the Eighth and 14th Amendments, was brought and won by Romeo's mother, acting on his behalf. The lower court's decision was based on the right to protection from cruel and unusual punishment, guaranteed by the Eighth Amendment. In 1980 the Court of Appeals reversed that decision, saying that the 14th Amendment was the proper constitutional basis for the rights demanded by Romeo. The appeals court found that those involuntarily committed retained their "funda-

mental liberties" to freedom of movement and personal security and that "minimally adequate or reasonable training" was necessary to secure these liberties. The Supreme Court upheld that decision.

Among other things, lawyers for the profoundly retarded 33-year-old respondent had argued that he be given enough training in controlling his behavior so as not to injure himself or others. The high court agreed that he was entitled to such "minimally adequate" training.

Chief Justice Warren E. Burger, who concurred with the judgment of the court, refused to sign the Powell opinion, however, arguing that Romeo had "no constitutional right to training, or 'habilitation,' per se."

Following are excerpts from the Supreme Court's June 18, 1982, decision in Youngberg v. Romeo *that mentally re-tarded residents of institutions are entitled to due process protection under the 14th Amendment:*

<u>No. 80-1429</u>

Duane Youngberg, etc., et al.,
        Petitioners,

        v.

Nicholas Romeo, an incompetent,
    by his mother and next friend,
        Paula Romeo

On writ of certiorari to the United States Court of Appeals for the Third Circuit.

[June 18, 1982]

JUSTICE POWELL delivered the opinion of the Court.

The question presented is whether respondent, involuntarily committed to a state institution for the mentally retarded, has substantive rights under the Due Process Clause of the Fourteenth Amendment to (i) safe conditions of confinement; (ii) freedom from bodily restraints; and (iii) training or "habilitation." Respondent sued under U.S.C. § 1983 three administrators of the institution, claiming damages for the alleged breach of his constitutional rights.

I

Respondent Nicholas Romeo is profoundly retarded. Although 33 years old, he has the mental capacity of an eighteen-month old child, with an I.Q. between 8 and 10. He cannot talk and lacks the most basic self-care skills. Until he was 26, respondent lived with his parents in Philadelphia. But after the death of his father in May 1974, his mother was unable to care for him. Within two weeks of the father's death, respondent's mother sought his temporary admission to a nearby Pennsylvania hospital.

Shortly thereafter, she asked the Philadelphia County Court of Common Pleas to admit Romeo to a state facility on a permanent basis. Her petition to the court explained that she was unable to care for Romeo or control his violence. As part of the commitment process, Romeo was examined by a physician and a psychologist. They both certified that respondent was severely retarded and unable to care for himself. On June 11, 1974, the Court of Common Pleas committed respondent to the Pennhurst State School and Hospital, pursuant to the applicable involuntary commitment provision of the Pennsylvania Mental Health and Mental Retardation Act.

At Pennhurst, Romeo was injured on numerous occasions, both by his own violence and by the reactions of other residents to him. Respondent's mother became concerned about these injuries. After objecting to respondent's treatment several times, she filed this complaint on November 4, 1976, in the United States District Court for the Eastern District of Pennsylvania as his next friend. The complaint alleged that "[d]uring the period July, 1974 to the present, plaintiff has suffered injuries on at least sixty-three occasions." The complaint originally sought damages and injunctive relief from Pennhurst's director and two supervisors; it alleged that these officials knew, or should have known, that Romeo was suffering injuries and that they failed to institute appropriate preventive procedures, thus violating his rights under the Eighth and Fourteenth Amendments.

Thereafter, in late 1976, Romeo was transferred from his ward to the hospital for treatment of a broken arm. While in the infirmary, and by the order of a doctor, he was physically restrained during portions of each day. These restraints were ordered by Dr. Gabroy, not a defendant here, to protect Romeo and others in the hospital, some of whom were in traction or were being treated intravenously. Although respondent normally would have returned to his ward when his arm healed, the parties to this litigation agreed that he should remain in the hospital due to the pending law suit. Nevertheless, in December 1977, a second amended complaint was filed alleging that the defendants were restraining respondent for prolonged periods on a routine basis. The second amended complaint also added a claim for damages to compensate Romeo for the defendants' failure to provide him with appropriate "treatment or programs for his mental retardation." All claims for injunctive relief were dropped prior to trial because respondent is a member of the class seeking such relief in another action.

An eight-day jury trial was held in April 1978. Petitioners introduced evidence that respondent participated in several programs teaching basic self-care skills. A comprehensive behavior-modification program was designed by staff members to reduce Romeo's aggressive behavior, but that program was never implemented because of his mother's objections. Respondent introduced evidence of his injuries and of conditions in his unit.

At the close of the trial, the court instructed the jury that "if any or all of the defendants were aware of and failed to take all reasonable steps to prevent repeated attacks upon Nicholas Romeo," such failure deprived him of constitutional rights. The jury also was instructed that if the defendants shackled Romeo or denied him treatment "as a punishment for filing this lawsuit," his constitutional rights were violated under the Eighth Amendment. Finally, the jury was instructed that only if they found the defendants "deliberately indifferent to the serious medical [and psychological] needs" of Romeo could they find that his Eighth and Fourteenth Amendment rights had been violated. The jury returned a verdict for the defendants, on which judgment was entered.

The Court of Appeals for the Third Circuit, sitting en banc, reversed and remanded for a new trial. (1980). The court held that the Eighth Amendment, prohibiting cruel and unusual punishment of those convicted of crimes, was not an appropriate source for determining the rights of the involuntarily committed. Rather, the Fourteenth Amendment and the liberty interest protected by that amendment provided the proper constitutional basis for these rights. In applying the Fourteenth Amendment, the court found that the involuntarily committed retain liberty interests in freedom of movement and personal security. These were "fundamental liberties" that can be limited only by an "overriding, non-punitive" state interest. It further found that the involuntarily committed have a liberty interest in habilitation designed to "treat" their mental retardation.

The en banc court did not, however, agree on the relevant standard to be used in determining whether Romeo's rights had been violated. Because physical restraint "raises a presumption of a punitive sanction," the majority of the Court of Appeals concluded that it can be justified only by "compelling necessity." A somewhat different standard was appropriate for the failure to provide for a resident's safety. The majority considered that such a failure must be justified by a showing of "substantial necessity." Finally, the majority held that when treatment has been administered, those responsible are liable only if the treatment is not "acceptable in the light of present medical or other scientific knowledge."

Chief Judge Seitz, concurring in the judgment, considered the standards articulated by the majority as indistinguishable from those applicable to medical malpractice claims. In Chief Judge Seitz's view, the Constitution "only requires that the courts make certain that professional judgment in fact was exercised." He concluded that the appropriate standard was whether the defendants' conduct was "such a substantial departure from accepted professional judgment, practice or standards in the care and treatment of the plaintiff as to demonstrate that the defendants did not base their conduct on a professional judgment."

We granted the petition for certiorari because of the importance of the question presented to the administration of state institutions for the mentally retarded. (1981).

II

We consider here for the first time the substantive rights of involuntarily-committed mentally retarded persons under the Fourteenth Amendment to the Constitution. In this case, respondent has been committed under the laws of Pennsylvania, and he does not challenge the commitment. Rather, he argues that he has a constitutionally protected liberty interest in safety, freedom of movement, and training within the institution; and that petitioners infringed these rights by failing to provide constitutionally required conditions of confinement.

The mere fact that Romeo has been committed under proper procedures does not deprive him of all substantive liberty interests under the Fourteenth Amendment. See, *e.g., Vitek* v. *Jones* (1980). Indeed, the state concedes that respondent has a right to adequate food, shelter, clothing, and medical care. We must decide whether liberty interests also exist in safety, freedom of movement, and training. If such interests do exist, we must further decide whether they have been infringed in this case.

A

Respondent's first two claims involve liberty interests recognized by prior decisions of this Court, interests that involuntary commitment proceedings do not extinguish. The first is a claim to safe conditions. In the past, this Court has noted that the right to personal security constitutes an "historic liberty interest" protected substantively by the Due Process Clause. *Ingraham* v. *Wright* (1977). And that right is not extinguished by lawful confinement, even for penal purposes. See *Hutto* v. *Finney* (1978). If it is cruel and unusual punishment to hold convicted criminals in unsafe conditions, it must be unconstitutional to confine the involuntarily committed — who may not be punished at all — in unsafe conditions.

Next, respondent claims a right to freedom from bodily restraint. In other contexts, the existence of such an interest is clear in the prior decisions of this Court. Indeed, "[l]iberty from bodily restraint always has been recognized as the core of the liberty protected by the Due Process Clause from arbitrary governmental action." *Greenholtz* v. *Nebraska Penal Inmates* (1979) (POWELL, J., concurring). This interest survives criminal conviction and incarceration. Similarly, it must also survive involuntary commitment.

B

Respondent's remaining claim is more troubling. In his words, he asserts a "constitutional right to minimally adequate habilitation." This is a substantive due process claim that is said to be grounded in the liberty component of the Due Process Clause of the Fourteenth Amendment. The term "habilitation," used in psychiatry, is not defined precisely or consistently in the opinions below or in the briefs of the parties or the amici. As noted previously, the term refers to "training and development of needed skills." Respondent emphasizes that the right he asserts is for "minimal" training, and he would leave the type and extent of training to be determined on a case-by-case basis "in light of present medical or other scientific knowledge."

In addressing the asserted right to training, we start from established principles. As a general matter, a State is under no constitutional duty to provide substantive services for those within its border. See *Harris* v. *McRae* (1980) (publicly funded abortions); *Maher* v. *Roe* (1977) (medical treatment). When a person is institutionalized — and wholly dependent on the State — it is conceded by petitioner that a duty to provide certain services and care does exist, although even then a State necessarily has considerable discretion in determining the nature and scope of its responsibilities. See *Richardson* v. *Belcher* (1971); *Dandridge* v. *Williams* (1970). Nor must a State "choose between attacking every aspect of a problem or not attacking the problem at all."

Respondent, in light of the severe character of his retardation, concedes that no amount of training will make possible his release. And he does not argue that if he were still at home, the State would have an obligation to provide training at its expense. The record reveals that respondent's primary needs are bodily safety and a minimum of physical restraint, and respondent clearly claims training related to these needs. As we have recognized that there is a constitutionally protected liberty interest in safety and freedom from restraint, training may be necessary to avoid unconstitutional infringement of those rights. On the basis of the record before us, it is quite uncertain whether respondent seeks any "habilitation" or training unrelated to safety and freedom from bodily restraints. In his brief to this Court, Romeo indicates that even the self-care programs he seeks are needed to reduce his aggressive behavior. And in his offer of proof to the trial court, respondent repeatedly indicated that, if allowed to testify, his experts would show that additional training programs, including self-care programs, were needed to reduce Romeo's aggressive behavior. If, as seems the case, respondent seeks only training related to safety and freedom from restraints, this case does not present the difficult question whether a mentally retarded person, involuntarily committed to a state institution, has some general constitutional right to training *per se*, even when no type or amount of training would lead to freedom.

Chief Judge Seitz, in language apparently adopted by respondent, observed:

> "I believe that the plaintiff has a constitutional right to minimally adequate care and treatment. The existence of a constitutional right to care and treatment is no longer a novel legal proposition."

Chief Judge Seitz did not identify or otherwise define — beyond the right to reasonable safety and freedom from physical restraint — the "minimally adequate care and treatment" that appropriately may be required for this respondent. In the circumstances presented by this case, and on the basis of the record developed to date, we agree with his view and conclude that respondent's liberty interests require the State to provide minimally adequate or reasonable training to ensure safety and freedom from undue restraint. In view of the kinds of treatment sought by respondent and the evidence of record, we need go no further in this case.

III

A

We have established that Romeo retains liberty interests in safety and freedom from bodily restraint. Yet these interests are not absolute; indeed to some extent they are in conflict. In operating an institution such as Pennhurst, there are occasions in which it is necessary for the State to restrain the movement of residents — for example, to protect them as well as others from violence. Similar restraints may also be appropriate in a training program. And an institution cannot protect its residents from all danger of violence if it is to permit them to have any freedom of movement. The question then is not simply whether a liberty interest has been infringed but whether the extent or nature of the restraint or lack of absolute safety is such as to violate due process.

In determining whether a substantive right protected by the Due Process Clause has been violated, it is necessary to balance "the liberty of the individual" and "the demands of an organized society." *Poe* v. *Ullman* (1961) (Harlan, J., dissenting). In seeking this balance in other cases, the Court has weighed the individual's interest in liberty against the State's asserted reasons for restraining individual liberty. In *Bell* v. *Wolfish* (1979), for example, we considered a challenge to pre-trial detainees' confinement conditions. We agreed that the detainees, not yet convicted of the crime charged, could not be punished. But we upheld those restrictions on liberty that were reasonably related to legitimate government objectives and not tantamount to punishment. We have taken a similar approach in deciding procedural due-process challenges to civil commitment proceedings. In *Parham* v. *J.R.* (1979), for example, we considered a challenge to state procedures for commitment of a minor with parental consent. In determining that *procedural* due process did not mandate an adversarial hearing, we weighed the liberty interest of the individual against the legitimate interests of the State, including the fiscal and administrative burdens additional procedures would entail.

Accordingly, whether respondent's constitutional rights have been violated must be determined by balancing his liberty interests against the relevant state interests. If there is to be any uniformity in protecting these interests, this balancing cannot be left to the unguided discretion of a judge or jury. We therefore turn to consider the proper standard for determining whether a State adequately has protected the rights of the involuntarily-committed mentally retarded.

B

We think the standard articulated by Chief Judge Seitz affords the necessary guidance and reflects the proper balance between the legitimate interests of the State and the rights of the involuntarily committed to reasonable conditions of safety and freedom from unreasonable restraints. He would have held that "the Constitution only requires that the courts make certain that professional judgment in fact was exercised. It is not appropriate for the courts to specify which of several professionally acceptable choices should have been made." Persons who have been involuntarily committed are entitled to more considerate treatment and conditions of confinement than criminals whose conditions of confinement are designed to punish. Cf. *Estelle* v. *Gamble* (1976). At the same time, this standard is lower than the "compelling" or "substantial" necessary tests the Court of Appeals would require a state to meet to justify use of restraints or conditions of less than absolute safety. We think this requirement would place an undue burden on the administration of institutions such as Pennhurst and also would restrict unnecessarily the exercise of professional judgment as to the needs of residents.

Moreover, we agree that respondent is entitled to minimally adequate training. In this case, the minimally adequate training required by the Constitution is such training as may be reasonable in light of respondent's liberty interests in safety and freedom from unreasonable restraints. In determining what is "reasonable" — in this and in any case presenting a claim for training by a state — we emphasize that courts must show deference to the judgment exercised by a qualified professional. By so limiting judicial review of challenges to conditions in state institutions, interference by the federal judiciary with the internal operations of these institutions should be minimized. Moreover, there certainly is no reason to think judges or juries are better qualified than appropriate professionals in making such decisions. See *Parham* v. *J.R.* (1979); *Bell* v. *Wolfish* (Courts should not " 'second-guess the expert administrators on matters on which they are better informed.' "). For these reasons, the decision, if made by a professional, is presumptively valid; liability may be imposed only when the decision by the professional is such a substantial departure from accepted professional judgment, practice or standards as to demonstrate that the person responsible actually did not base the decision on such a judgment. In an action for damages against a professional in his individual capacity, however, the professional will not be liable if he was unable to satisfy his normal professional standards because of budgetary constraints; in such a situation, good-faith immunity would bar liability.

IV

In deciding this case, we have weighed those post-commitment interests cognizable as liberty interests under the Due Process Clause of the

Fourteenth Amendment against legitimate state interests and in light of the constraints under which most state institutions necessarily operate. We repeat that the state concedes a duty to provide adequate food, shelter, clothing and medical care. These are the essentials of the care that the state must provide. The state also has the unquestioned duty to provide reasonable safety for all residents and personnel within the institution. And it may not restrain residents except when and to the extent professional judgment deems this necessary to assure such safety or to provide needed training. In this case, therefore, the state is under a duty to provide respondent with such training as an appropriate professional would consider reasonable to ensure his safety and to facilitate his ability to function free from bodily restraints. It may well be unreasonable not to provide training when training could significantly reduce the need for restraints or the likelihood of violence.

Respondent thus enjoys constitutionally protected interests in conditions of reasonable care and safety, reasonably non-restrictive confinement conditions, and such training as may be required by these interests. Such conditions of confinement would comport fully with the purpose of respondent's commitment. Cf. *Jackson* v. *Indiana* (1972). In determining whether the state has met its obligations in these respects, decisions made by the appropriate professional are entitled to a presumption of correctness. Such a presumption is necessary to enable institutions of this type — often, unfortunately, overcrowded and understaffed — to continue to function. A single professional may have to make decisions with respect to a number of residents with widely varying needs and problems in the course of a normal day. The administrators, and particularly professional personnel, should not be required to make each decision in the shadow of an action for damages.

In this case, we conclude that the jury was erroneously instructed on the assumption that the proper standard of liability was that of the Eighth Amendment. Accordingly, we vacate the decision of the Court of Appeals and remand for further proceedings consistent with this decision.

So ordered.

CHIEF JUSTICE BURGER, concurring in the judgment.

I agree with much of the Court's opinion. However, I would hold flatly that respondent has no constitutional right to training, or "habilitation," *per se*. The parties, and the Court, acknowledge that respondent cannot function outside the state institution, even with the assistance of relatives. Indeed, even now neither respondent nor his family seeks his discharge from state care. Under these circumstances, the State's provision of food, shelter, medical care, and living conditions as safe as the inherent nature of the institutional environment reasonably allows, serve to justify the State's custody of respondent. The State did not seek custody of respondent; his family understandably sought the State's aid to meet a serious need.

I agree with the Court that some amount of self-care instruction may be necessary to avoid unreasonable infringement of a mentally-retarded person's interests in safety and freedom from restraint; but it seems clear to me that the Constitution does not otherwise place an affirmative duty on the State to provide any particular kind of training or habilitation — even such as might be encompassed under the essentially standardless rubric "minimally adequate training," to which the Court refers. Since respondent asserts a right to "minimally adequate" habilitation "[q]uite apart from its relationship to decent care," unlike the Court I see no way to avoid the issue.

I also point out that, under the Court's own standards, it is largely irrelevant whether respondent's experts were of the opinion that "additional training programs, including self-care programs, were needed to reduce [respondent's] aggressive behavior," a prescription far easier for "spectators" to give than for an institution to implement. The training program devised for respondent by petitioners and other professionals at Pennhurst was, according to the Court's opinion, "presumptively valid"; and "liability may be imposed only when the decision by the professional is such a substantial departure from accepted professional judgment, practice or standards as to demonstrate that the person responsible actually did not base the decision on such a judgment." Thus, even if respondent could demonstrate that the training programs at Pennhurst were inconsistent with generally accepted or prevailing professional practice — if indeed there be such — this would not avail him so long as his training regimen was actually prescribed by the institution's professional staff.

Finally, it is worth noting that the District Court's instructions in this case were on the whole consistent with the Court's opinion today; indeed, some instructions may have been overly generous to respondent. Although the District Court erred in giving an instruction incorporating an Eighth Amendment "deliberate indifference" standard, the court also instructed, for example, that petitioners could be held liable if they "were aware of and failed to take all reasonable steps to prevent repeated attacks upon" respondent. Certainly if petitioners took "*all* reasonable steps" to prevent attacks on respondent, they cannot be said to have deprived him either of reasonably safe conditions or of training necessary to achieve reasonable safety.

HINCKLEY VERDICT
June 21, 1982

The jury at the Washington, D.C., trial of John W. Hinckley Jr. decided June 21 that he was not guilty by reason of insanity of 13 charges stemming from his attempt to assassinate President Ronald Reagan. During the March 30, 1981, shooting near the Washington Hilton Hotel, Hinckley had wounded the president, White House press secretary James S. Brady, police patrolman Thomas K. Delahanty and Secret Service agent Timothy J. McCarthy. Although no one was killed in the incident, a bullet entered Reagan's chest near his heart. After surgery and several weeks in the hospital, Reagan made a complete recovery. A head wound, however, left Brady permanently disabled. (Reagan shooting, Historic Documents of 1981, p. 351)

Following the verdict, Hinckley was admitted to St. Elizabeth's, the federal mental hospital in Washington, D.C. He was to remain there for tests for 60 days, after which he would be eligible for release if his mental condition had improved and stabilized.

The jury's decision brought the problems of the insanity plea in the U.S. judicial system into the limelight. The decision also sparked an onslaught of criticism against the system by notable public servants, legal experts and psychiatrists.

Hinckley's Background

Hinckley, the 27-year-old son of an affluent, self-made Colorado oil and gas entrepreneur, had been characterized as a loner who aspired to

531

instant success without having to work. Unable to finish college, he had suffered from anxiety attacks and was prone to delusions.

Several weeks prior to the shootings, Hinckley had been barred from his Colorado home by his parents on the advice of a psychiatrist. They had hoped that casting him out would force him to find a job. According to his mother JoAnn Hinckley, his parents had been watching him go "downhill, downhill, downhill" for years.

After leaving his parents' home, Hinckley remained friendless, wrote morbid poetry and traveled aimlessly by bus all over the country. He identified strongly with Mark David Chapman, who shot the well-known singer John Lennon to death in December 1980. Hinckley previously had sought fame as a player in a rock and roll band.

Hinckley's strongest fantasies involved teen-aged actress Jodie Foster, whom he said he loved. She had appeared in the movie Taxi Driver, *which he had seen at least 15 times. In the movie, the main character goes on a murderous rampage to rescue a young woman (Foster) from prostitution. Hinckley's fantasies further led him to believe that he was to kidnap Foster, hijack a plane and move to the White House with her. He had written to and unsuccessfully attempted to visit Foster in her dormitory at Yale University.*

The Trial: Prosecution and Defense

The trial began April 27 after selection of the jury of seven women and five men, ranging in age from 22 to 64. Their occupations were primarily blue-collar and included a banquet worker, a food service technician, a garage attendant, a shop mechanic, an industrial specialist, two secretaries, one person listed as retired and a research assistant who had studied problems of socially maladjusted persons.

After his arrest, Hinckley was placed under medical observation in the federal correctional institute at Butner, N. C., and in a jail of the Army stockade at Fort Meade, Md., where he was said to have been a generally quiet inmate. During the lengthy trial Hinckley remained mostly motionless and silent. Once, while the actress Foster was testifying by video tape that she had had no relationship with him, Hinckley attempted to walk out of the courtroom without permission. When a prison psychiatrist said that the assassination attempt was not an effort to win Foster's love, he blurted out, "You're wrong."

The trial costs were high both for the public and for Hinckley's parents. The Justice Department, charged with the prosecution, estimated a cost of at least $311,855 in fees and expenses for the government's team of four private experts. Hinckley's defense was headed by Vincent J. Fuller of the Washington, D.C., firm of Williams & Connolly, hired by

Hinckley's parents. They spent several hundred thousand dollars in lawyers' and psychiatrists' fees to prove that their son was not responsible for his actions on the cold and drizzly day of March 30, 1981.

Controversy throughout the trial centered on Hinckley's mental condition on the day of the shooting. The defense psychiatrists portrayed a schizophrenic, psychotic prisoner of an "inner world" who should be pitied, while the prosecution psychiatrists depicted a selfish, manipulative, lazy parasite, with a few minor personality disorders that boiled down to sadness, friendlessness and an exaggerated sense of self-importance. According to District of Columbia law, under which Hinckley was tried, the prosecution had to prove "beyond a reasonable doubt" that Hinckley was sane when he commited the act.

Dr. Park E. Dietz, prosecution psychiatrist and spokesman for the 628-page report that the government compiled as testimony, said that Hinckley had only a "narcissistic personality disorder," and that the prosecution believed he was capable of logical thought. The prosecution demonstrated that Hinckley had prepared for the assassination by studying publicized crimes and practicing with guns. Hinckley was therefore sane and legally responsible for his actions.

According to the defense, Hinckley was schizophrenic and unable to separate his delusions from reality, "a totally irrational individual, driven and motivated by his own world, locked in his own mind." Fuller said Hinckley lacked remorse for shooting the president because he was unaware the deed was wrong and had no ability to conform with law; therefore, he could not be held responsible for it.

During the eight-week trial, 41 witnesses, including 18 psychiatrists and other doctors, produced a mountain of testimony, scientific reports and television footage of the shootings. The jury was also given a special screening of Taxi Driver. *On the last day of presentation of expert testimony, Judge Barrington D. Parker remarked that "there is either enough to guide the jury or confuse the jury."*

After presentation of the evidence, Parker gave instructions on which the jury was to base its decision. He stated that they should find Hinckley "not guilty" unless the government had proved "beyond a reasonable doubt either that the defendant was not suffering from a mental disease or defect, or else that he nevertheless had substantial capacity on that date both to conform his conduct to the requirements of the law and to appreciate the wrongfulness of his conduct." Some commentators believed that these instructions suggested a leaning toward the not guilty by reason of insanity option.

The jury reached its verdict after four days of deliberation. Although the verdict was unanimous, some dissension among the jury members later became apparent. Two jurors claimed they had been coerced into making the decision unanimous and felt that Hinckley should carry more responsibility for his crime. They testified during congressional hearings on the Hinckley decision and on proposed changes for the insanity plea.

Response to the Verdict

The White House, which had maintained consistent silence on the assassination attempt and the trial, refused to comment even after the verdict had been submitted.

Public response, however, was heated, and several prominent citizens responded with outrage. Attorney General William French Smith said, "[T]he verdict demonstrates again the need for responsible reforms [in the American legal system]." Media commentators expressed the need for reassessing the use of the insanity plea. An ABC News poll, conducted shortly after the verdict had been reached, concluded that 76 percent of those questioned believed justice had not been done in the Hinckley case and 75 percent disapproved of laws that allow people to be found not guilty by reason of insanity.

Insanity Defense

Following the trial, the American Psychiatric Association (APA) conducted a study of the issue and in January 1983 issued a report entitled, "Statement on the Insanity Defense." The report traced the judicial history of the insanity plea, examined the previous standards by which an individual was held responsible for his crime and suggested possible reforms.

Proposals for changing the insanity defense included legislation to abolish the insanity defense, the adoption of tougher standards of proof and requirements that the defense, and not the prosecution, carry the burden of proof for the criminals state of mind. At least 18 states had introduced legislation for creating a new verdict of "guilty but insane," which would permit the jury to commit the offender to a mental hospital until he is ruled sane enough to serve his sentence.

Another problem publicized by the Hinckley trial was the need to reassess the role of psychiatric testimony in court. Experts agreed that the testimony could easily confuse juries with multisyllabic, scientific-sounding answers to the ultimate question of criminal responsibility.

Hinckley in St. Elizabeth's

After Hinckley made another court appearance, his stay at St. Elizabeth's Hospital was extended on August 9 for an indefinite period. Hospital testimony described Hinckley as "presently a danger to himself, to Jodie Foster and to any other third party whom he would consider as incidental in his ultimate aims."

Since his arrest, Hinckley attempted suicide three times: the first was an overdose of valium; the next was an attempt to hang himself with a noose made from a jacket; the third try was an overdose of medication.

Following is the text of the verdict form in the case of United States of America *v.* John W. Hinckley Jr., *completed by the jury June 21, 1982:*

United States District Court
for the District of Columbia

United States of America
v.
John W. Hinckley, Jr. } Criminal No. 81-306

JURY VERDICT FORM

GRAND JURY CHARGE   **VERDICT**

(OFFENSES AGAINST PRESIDENT RONALD REAGAN)

First Count

Attempt to Kill Ronald Reagan, President   Guilty _____
of the United States   Not Guilty _____
(Title 18 U.S. Code, Sec. 1751 (c))   Not Guilty by
                                             Reason of Insanity ✔

Second Count

Assault on Ronald Reagan with Intent to   Guilty _____
Kill Him, While Armed   Not Guilty _____
(Title 22 D.C. Code, Secs. 501, 3202)   Not Guilty by
                                             Reason of Insanity ✔

Do not consider Third Count if you find defendant Guilty of Count Two.

Consider Third Count *only* if you find defendant Not Guilty or Not Guilty by Reason of Insanity on Count Two.

Third Count

Assault on Ronald Reagan With A Dan-   Guilty _____
gerous Weapon   Not Guilty _____
(Title 22 D.C. Code, Sec. 502)   Not Guilty by
                                             Reason of Insanity ✔

(OFFENSES AGAINST SECRET SERVICE
AGENT TIMOTHY McCARTHY)

Fourth Count

Assault on Agent McCarthy, a Federal   Guilty _____
Officer, While Performing His Official   Not Guilty _____
Duties   Not Guilty by
(Title 18 U.S. Code, Sec. 111)   Reason of Insanity ✔

Fifth Count

Assault on McCarthy with Intent to Kill   Guilty _____
Him, While Armed   Not Guilty _____
(Title 22 D.C. Code, Secs. 501 & 3202)   Not Guilty by
                                         Reason of Insanity ✔

Do not consider Sixth Count if you find defendant Guilty of Fifth Count.

Consider Sixth Count *only* if you find defendant Not Guilty or Not Guilty by Reason of Insanity on Count Five.

Sixth Count

Assault on McCarthy With A Dangerous   Guilty _____
Weapon   Not Guilty _____
(Title 22 D.C. Code, Sec. 502)   Not Guilty by
                                         Reason of Insanity ✔

(OFFENSES AGAINST JAMES BRADY)

Seventh Count

Assault on Brady With Intent to Kill Him,   Guilty _____
While Armed   Not Guilty _____
(Title 22 D.C. Code, Secs. 501 & 3202)   Not Guilty by
                                         Reason of Insanity ✔

Do not consider Eighth Count if you find defendant Guilty of Seventh Count.

Consider Eighth Count *only* if you find defendant Not Guilty or Not Guilty by Reason of Insanity on Count Seven.

Eighth Count

Assault on Brady with A Dangerous   Guilty _____
Weapon   Not Guilty _____
(Title 22 D.C. Code, Sec. 502)   Not Guilty by
                                         Reason of Insanity ✔

(OFFENSES AGAINST POLICE OFFICER THOMAS DELAHANTY)

Ninth Count

Assault on Police Officer Delahanty With
A Dangerous Weapon
(Title 22 D.C. Code, Sec. 505 (b))

Guilty ____
Not Guilty ____
Not Guilty by
Reason of Insanity ✔

Tenth Count

Assault on Delahanty With Intent to Kill
Him, While Armed
(Title 22 D.C. Code, Secs. 501 & 3202)

Guilty ____
Not Guilty ____
Not Guilty by
Reason of Insanity ✔

Do not consider Eleventh Count if you find defendant Guilty of Tenth Count.

Consider Eleventh Count *only* if you find defendant Not Guilty or Not Guilty by Reason of Insanity of Count Ten.

Eleventh Count

Assault on Delahanty With A Dangerous
Weapon
(Title 22 D.C. Code, Sec. 502)

Guilty ____
Not Guilty ____
Not Guilty by
Reason of Insanity ✔

(WEAPONS OFFENSES)

Twelfth Count

Carrying a Pistol Without a License
(Title 22, D.C. Code, Sec. 3204)

Guilty ____
Not Guilty ____
Not Guilty by
Reason of Insanity ✔

Thirteenth Count

Use of Firearm During Commission of
Federal Offense
(Title 18 U.S. Code, Sec. 924 (c))

Guilty ____
Not Guilty ____
Not Guilty by
Reason of Insanity ✔

Date: June 21, 1982

▼▼▼

COURT ON
PRESIDENTIAL IMMUNITY
June 24, 1982

In a deeply divided 5-4 ruling, the Supreme Court held June 24 that a U.S. president cannot be sued for civil damages for any official actions taken while in office. He may, however, be prosecuted under criminal laws.

"We consider this immunity a functionally mandated incident of the president's unique office, rooted in the constitutional tradition of the separation of powers and supported by our history," wrote Justice Lewis F. Powell Jr. for the majority. Judges, prosecutors and Supreme Court justices themselves are the only other public officials granted absolute immunity from civil suits by earlier decisons of the Supreme Court. The concept of qualified immunity of state officials, based on "good faith," was decided in Scheuer v. Rhodes *(1974), and in* Butz v. Economou *(1978) the court extended the same degree of immunity to federal government officials.*

Powell's opinion was joined by Chief Justice Warren E. Burger, who wrote a brief concurring opinion, and Justices John Paul Stevens, William H. Rehnquist and Sandra Day O'Connor. But three other justices — William J. Brennan Jr., Thurgood Marshall and Harry A. Blackmun — joined Justice Byron R. White in a vigorous dissent. Calling the decision both "tragic" and "bizarre," White wrote: "Attaching absolute immunity to the office of the president, rather than to particular activities that the president might perform, places the president above the law. It is a reversion to the old notion that the king can do no wrong."

Background

Specifically, the case of Nixon v. Fitzgerald arose out of a dispute between former President Richard Nixon and A. Ernest Fitzgerald over Fitzgerald's dismissal from his Air Force job in 1970. The former civilian cost analyst had alleged in a civil suit that Nixon, along with former White House aides Bryce N. Harlow and Alexander P. Butterfield, had conspired to punish him for exposing large cost overruns in the C-5A transport plane project.

The Supreme Court had agreed to hear the case even though Nixon and Fitzgerald had settled out of court in 1980, with Nixon paying Fitzgerald $142,000. The former president had agreed to pay another $28,000 if he lost his appeal on the immunity question to the high court.

Companion Ruling

While granting absolute immunity to U.S. presidents, the court held in a companian case, Harlow v. Fitzgerald, that presidential aides were entitled only to "qualified immunity." This meant that aides would not be subject to civil damage suits if they could show "their conduct does not violate clearly established statutory or constitutional rights of which a reasonable person would have known."

Under this new definition of "qualified immunity," which eliminated a previous requirement that sued officials prove they had not acted with malicious intent, it was expected to be more difficult for frivolous suits to be brought against government officials.

Following are excerpts from the Supreme Court's June 24, 1982, opinion in Nixon v. Fitzgerald, in which the court ruled that a president is immune from civil damages arising from an official act; excerpts from Chief Justice Burger's concurring opinion and excerpts from the dissent by Justice White:

No. 79-1738

Richard Nixon, petitioner v. A. Ernest Fitzgerald	On writ of certiorari to the United States Court of Appeals for the District of Columbia Circuit

[June, 24, 1982]

JUSTICE POWELL delivered the opinion of the Court.

The plaintiff in this lawsuit seeks relief in civil damages from a former President of the United States. The claim rests on actions allegedly taken in the former President's official capacity during his tenure in office. The issue before us is the scope of the immunity possessed by the President of the United States.

I

In January 1970 the respondent A. Ernest Fitzgerald lost his job as a management analyst with the Department of the Air Force. Fitzgerald's dismissal occurred in the context of a departmental reorganization and reduction in force, in which his job was eliminated. In announcing the reorganization, the Air Force characterized the action as taken to promote economy and efficiency in the armed forces.

Respondent's discharge attracted unusual attention in Congress and in the press. Fitzgerald had attained national prominence approximately one year earlier, during the waning months of the presidency of Lyndon B. Johnson. On November 13, 1968, Fitzgerald appeared before the Subcommittee on Economy in Government of the Joint Economic Committee of the United States Congress. To the evident embarrassment of his superiors in the Department of Defense, Fitzgerald testified that cost-overruns on the C-5A transport plane could approximate $2 billion. He also revealed that unexpected technical difficulties had arisen during the development of the aircraft.

Concerned that Fitzgerald might have suffered retaliation for his congressional testimony, the Subcommittee on Economy in Government convened public hearings on Fitzgerald's dismissal. The press reported those hearings prominently, as it had the earlier announcement that his job was being eliminated by the Department of Defense. At a news conference on December 8, 1969, President Richard Nixon was queried about Fitzgerald's impending separation from government service. The President responded by promising to look into the matter. Shortly after the news conference the petitioner asked White House Chief of Staff H. R. Haldeman to arrange for Fitzgerald's assignment to another job within the Administration. It also appears that the President suggested to Budget Director Robert Mayo that Fitzgerald might be offered a position in the Bureau of the Budget.

Fitzgerald's proposed reassignment encountered resistance within the Administration. In an internal memorandum of January 20, 1970, White House aide Alexander Butterfield reported to Haldeman that "Fitzgerald is no doubt a top-notch cost expert, but he must be given very low marks in loyalty; and after all, loyalty is the name of the game." Butterfield therefore recommended that "We should let him bleed, for a while at least." There is no evidence of White House efforts to reemploy Fitzgerald subsequent to the Butterfield memorandum.

Absent any offer of alternative federal employment, Fitzgerald complained to the Civil Service Commission. In a letter of January 20, 1970, he alleged that his separation represented unlawful retaliation for his truthful testimony before a congressional committee. The Commission convened a closed hearing on Fitzgerald's allegations on May 4, 1971. Fitzgerald, however, preferred to present his grievances in public. After he had brought suit and won an injunction, *Fitzgerald* v. *Hampton* (CADC 1972), public hearings commenced on January 26, 1973. The hearings again generated publicity, much of it devoted to the testimony of Air Force Secretary Robert Seamans. Although he denied that Fitzgerald had lost his position in retaliation for congressional testimony, Seamans testified that he had received "some advice" from the White House before Fitzgerald's job was abolished. But the Secretary declined to be more specific. He responded to several questions by invoking "executive privilege."

At a news conference on January 31, 1973, the President was asked about Mr. Seamans' testimony. Mr. Nixon took the opportunity to assume personal responsibility for Fitzgerald's dismissal:

> "I was totally aware that Mr. Fitzgerald would be fired or discharged or asked to resign. I approved it and Mr. Seamans must have been talking to someone who had discussed the matter with me. No, this was not a case of some person down the line deciding he should go. It was a decision that was submitted to me. I made it and I stick to it."

A day later, however, the White House press office issued a retraction of the President's statement. According to a press spokesman, the President had confused Fitzgerald with another former executive employee. On behalf of the President, the spokesman asserted that Mr. Nixon had not had "put before him the decision regarding Mr. Fitzgerald."

After hearing over 4,000 pages of testimony, the Chief Examiner for the Civil Service Commission issued his decision in the Fitzgerald case on September 18, 1973. The Examiner held that Fitzgerald's dismissal had offended applicable civil service regulations. The Examiner based this conclusion on a finding that the departmental reorganization in which Fitzgerald lost his job, though purportedly implemented as an economy measure, was in fact motivated by "reasons purely personal to" respondent. As this was an impermissible basis for a reduction in force, the Examiner recommended Fitzgerald's reappointment to his old position or to a job of comparable authority. The Examiner, however, explicitly distinguished this narrow conclusion from a suggested finding that Fitzgerald had suffered retaliation for his testimony to Congress. As found by the Commission, "the evidence in the record does not support [Fitzgerald's] allegation that his position was abolished and that he was separated . . . in retaliation for his having revealed the C-5A cost overrun in testimony before the Proxmire Committee on November 13, 1968."

Following the Commission's decision, Fitzgerald filed a suit for damages in the United States District Court. In it he raised essentially the same claims presented to the Civil Service Commission. As defendants he named eight officials of the Defense Department, White House aide Alexander Butterfield, and "one or More" unnamed "White House Aides" styled only as "John Does."

The District Court dismissed the action under the District of Columbia's three-year statute of limitations, *Fitzgerald* v. *Seamans* (D.D.C. 1974), and the Court of Appeals affirmed as to all but one defendant, White House aide Alexander Butterfield, *Fitzgerald* v. *Seamans* (CADC 1977). The Court of Appeals reasoned that Fitzgerald had no reason to suspect White House involvement in his dismissal at least until 1973. In that year, reasonable grounds for suspicion had arisen, most notably through publication of the internal White House memorandum in which Butterfield had recommended that Fitzgerald at least should be made to "bleed for a while" before being offered another job in the Administration. Holding that concealment of illegal activity would toll the statute of limitations, the Court of Appeals remanded the action against Butterfield for further proceedings in the District Court.

Following the remand and extensive discovery thereafter, Fitzgerald filed a Second Amended Complaint in the District Court on July 5, 1978. It was in this amended complaint — more than eight years after he had complained of his discharge to the Civil Service Commission — that Fitzgerald first named the petitioner Nixon as a party defendant. Also included as defendants were White House aide Bryce Harlow and other officials of the Nixon administration. Additional discovery ensued. By March 1980, only three defendants remained: the petitioner Richard Nixon and White House aides Harlow and Butterfield. Denying a motion for summary judgment, the District Court ruled that the action must proceed to trial. Its order of March 26 held that Fitzgerald had stated triable causes of action under two federal statutes and the First Amendment to the Constitution. The Court also ruled that petitioner was not entitled to claim absolute presidential immunity.

Petitioner took a collateral appeal of the immunity decision to the Court of Appeals for the District of Columbia Circuit. The Court of Appeals dismissed summarily. It apparently did so on the ground that its recent decision in *Halperin* v. *Kissinger* (CADC 1979), aff'd by an equally divided vote (1981), had rejected this claimed immunity defense.

As this Court has not ruled on the scope of immunity available to a President of the United States, we granted certiorari to decide this important issue. (1981).

II

Before addressing the merits of this case, we must consider two challenges to our jurisdiction. In his opposition to the petition for certiorari, respondent argued that this Court is without jurisdiction to review the non-final order in which the District Court rejected petitioner's claim to absolute immunity. We also must consider an argument that an agreement between the parties had mooted the controversy.

A

Petitioner invokes the jurisdiction of this Court under 28 U.S.C. § 1254, a statute that invests us with authority to review "[c]ases in" the courts of appeals. When the petitioner in this case sought review of an interlocutory order denying his claim to absolute immunity, the Court of Appeals dismissed the appeal for lack of jurisdiction. Emphasizing the "jurisdictional" basis for the Court of Appeals' decision, respondent argued that the District Court's order was not an appealable "case" properly "in" the Court of Appeals within the meaning of § 1254. We do not agree.

Under the "collateral order" doctrine of *Cohen* v. *Beneficial Industrial Loan Corp.* (1949), a small class of interlocutory orders are immediately appealable to the courts of appeals. As defined by *Cohen*, this class embraces orders that "conclusively determine the disputed question, resolve an important issue completely separate from the merits of the action, and [are] effectively unreviewable on appeal from a final judgment." *Coopers & Lybrand* v. *Livesay* (1978). . . . As an additional requirement, *Cohen* established that a collateral appeal of an interlocutory order must "presen[t] . . . a serious and unsettled question." At least twice before this Court has held that orders denying claims of absolute immunity are appealable under the *Cohen* criteria. See *Helstoski* v. *Meanor* (1979) (claim of immunity under the Speech and Debate Clause); *Abney* v. *United States* (1977) (claim of immunity under Double Jeopardy Clause). In previous cases the Court of Appeals for the District of Columbia Circuit also has treated orders denying absolute immunity as appealable under *Cohen*. See *Briggs* v. *Goodwin* (CADC 1977) (Wilkey, J., writing for the Court on the appealability issue); *McSurely* v. *McClellan* (1975), aff'd in pertinent part en banc (1976), cert dismissed *sub nom. McAdams* v. *McSurely* (1978).

In "dismissing" the appeal in this case, the Court of Appeals appears to have reasoned that petitioner's appeal lay outside the *Cohen* doctrine because it raised no "serious and unsettled question" of law. This argument was pressed by the respondent, who asked the Court of Appeals to dismiss on the basis of that court's "controlling" decision in *Halperin* v. *Kissinger.*

Under the circumstances of this case, we cannot agree that petitioner's interlocutory appeal failed to raise a "serious and unsettled" question. Although the Court of Appeals had ruled in *Halperin* v. *Kissinger* that the President was not entitled to absolute immunity, this Court never had so held. And a petition for certiorari in *Halperin* was pending in this Court at the time petitioner's appeal was dismissed. In light of the special solicitude due to claims alleging a threatened breach of essential Presidential prerogatives under the separation of powers, see *United States* v. *Nixon* (1974), we conclude that petitioner did present a "serious and unsettled" and therefore appealable question to the Court of Appeals. It follows that the case was "in" the Court of Appeals under § 1254 and properly within our certiorari jurisdiction.

B

Shortly after petitioner had filed his petition for certiorari in this Court and respondent had entered his opposition, the parties reached an agreement to liquidate damages. Under its terms the petitioner Nixon paid the respondent Fitzgerald a sum of $142,000. In consideration Fitzgerald agreed to accept liquidated damages of $28,000 in the event of a ruling by this Court that petitioner was not entitled to absolute immunity. In case of a decision upholding petitioner's immunity claim, no further payments would be made.

The limited agreement between the parties left both petitioner and respondent with a considerable financial stake in the resolution of the question presented in this Court. As we recently concluded in a case involving a similar contract, "Given respondents' continued active pursuit of monetary relief, this case remains 'definite and concrete, touching the legal relations of parties having adverse legal interests.'" *Havens Realty Co.* v. *Coleman* (1982), quoting *Aetna Life Ins. Co.* v. *Haworth* (1937).

III

A

This Court consistently has recognized that government officials are entitled to some form of immunity from suits for civil damages. In *Spalding* v. *Vilas* (1896), the Court considered the immunity available to the Postmaster General in a suit for damages based upon his official acts. Drawing upon principles of immunity developed in English cases at common law, the Court concluded that "[t]he interests of the people" required a grant of absolute immunity to public officers. In the absence of immunity, the Court reasoned, executive officials would hesitate to exercise their discretion in a way "injuriously affect[ing] the claims of particular individuals," even when the public interest required bold and unhesitating action. Considerations of "public policy and convenience" therefore compelled a judicial recognition of immunity from suits arising from official acts.

> "In exercising the functions of his office, the head of an Executive Department, keeping within the limits of his authority, should not be under an apprehension that the motives that control his official conduct may, at any time, become the subject of inquiry in a civil suit for damages. It would seriously cripple the proper and effective administration of public affairs as entrusted to the executive branch of the government, if he were subjected to any such restraint."

Decisions subsequent to *Spalding* have extended the defense of immunity to actions besides those at common law. In *Tenney* v. *Brandhove* (1951), the Court considered whether the passage of 42 U.S.C. § 1983, which made no express provision for immunity for any official, had abrogated the privilege accorded to state legislators at common law.

Tenney held that it had not.... Similarly, the decision in *Pierson* v. *Ray* (1967), involving a § 1983 suit against a state judge, recognized the continued validity of the absolute immunity of judges for acts within the judicial role. This was a doctrine " 'not for the protection or benefit of a malicious or corrupt judge, but for the benefit of the public, whose interest it is that the judges should be at liberty to exercise their functions with independence and without fear of consequences.' " ... The Court in *Pierson* also held that police officers are entitled to a qualified immunity protecting them from suit when their official acts are performed in "good faith."

In *Scheuer* v. *Rhodes* (1974), the Court considered the immunity available to state executive officials in a § 1983 suit alleging the violation of constitutional rights. In that case we rejected the officials' claim to absolute immunity under the doctrine of *Spalding* v. *Vilas*, finding instead that state executive officials possessed a "good faith" immunity from § 1983 suits alleging constitutional violations. Balancing the purposes of § 1983 against the imperatives of public policy, the Court held that "in varying scope, a qualified immunity is available to officers of the executive branch of government, the variation being dependent upon the scope of discretion and responsibilities of the office and all the circumstances as they reasonably appeared at the time of the action on which liability is sought to be based."

As construed by subsequent cases, *Scheuer* established a two-tiered division of immunity defenses in § 1983 suits. To most executive officers *Scheuer* accorded qualified immunity. For them the scope of the defense varied in proportion to the nature of their official functions and the range of decisions that conceivably might be taken in "good faith." This "functional" approach also defined a second tier, however, at which the especially sensitive duties of certain officials — notably judges and prosecutors — required the continued recognition of absolute immunity. See, *e.g., Imbler* v. *Pachtman* (1976) (state prosecutors possess absolute immunity with respect to the initiation and pursuit of prosecutions); *Stump* v. *Sparkman* (1978) (state judge posseses absolute immunity for all judicial acts).

This approach was reviewed in detail in *Butz* v. *Economou* (1978), when we considered for the first time the kind of immunity possessed by *federal* executive officials who are sued for constitutional violations. In *Butz* the Court rejected an argument, based on decisions involving federal officials charged with common law torts, that all high federal officials have a right to absolute immunity from constitutional damage actions. Concluding that a blanket recognition of absolute immunity would be anomalous in light of the qualified immunity standard applied to state executive officials, we held that federal officials generally have the same qualified immunity possessed by state officials in cases under § 1983. In so doing we reaffirmed our holdings that some officials, notably judges and prosecutors, "because of the special nature of their responsibilities," "require a full exemption from liability." In *Butz* itself we upheld a claim of absolute immunity for administrative officials engaged in functions analogous to those of judges and prosecutors. We also left open the question whether other federal officials could show that "public policy requires an exemption of that scope."

B

Our decisions concerning the immunity of government officials from civil damages liability have been guided by the Constitution, federal statutes, and history. Additionally, at least in the absence of explicit constitutional or congressional guidance, our immunity decisions have been informed by the common law. See *Butz* v. *Economou*; *Imbler* v. *Pachtman* (1976). This Court necessarily also has weighed concerns of public policy, especially as illuminated by our history and the structure of our government. . . .

This case now presents the claims that the President of the United States is shielded by absolute immunity from civil damages liability. In the case of the President the inquiries into history and policy, though mandated independently by our cases, tend to converge. Because the Presidency did not exist through most of the development of common law, any historical analysis must draw its evidence primarily from our constitutional heritage and structure. Historical inquiry thus merges almost at its inception with the kind of "public policy" analysis appropriately undertaken by a federal court. This inquiry involves policies and principles that may be considered implicit in the nature of the President's office in a system structured to achieve effective government under a constitutionally mandated separation of powers.

IV

Here a former President asserts his immunity from civil damages claims of two kinds. He stands named as a defendant in a direct action under the Constitution and in two statutory actions under federal laws of general applicability. In neither case has Congress taken express legislative action to subject the President to civil liability for his official acts.

Applying the principles of our cases to claims of this kind, we hold that petitioner, as a former President of the United States, is entitled to absolute immunity from damages liability predicated on his official acts. We consider this immunity a functionally mandated incident of the President's unique office, rooted in the constitutional tradition of the separation of powers and supported by our history. Justice Story's analysis remains persuasive:

> "There are . . . incidental powers, belonging to the executive department, which are necessarily implied from the nature of the functions, which are confided to it. Among these, must necessarily be included the power to perform them. . . . The President cannot, therefore, be liable to arrest, impris-

onment, or detention, while he is in the discharge of the duties of his office; and for this purpose his person must be deemed, in civil cases at least, to possess an official inviolability." J. Story, Commentaries on the Constitution of the United States, (1833 ed.).

A

The President occupies a unique position in the constitutional scheme. Article II of the Constitution provides that "[t]he executive Power shall be vested in a President of the United States. . . ." This grant of authority establishes the President as the chief constitutional officer of the Executive Branch, entrusted with supervisory and policy responsibilities of utmost discretion and sensitivity. These include the enforcement of federal law — it is the President who is charged constitutionally to "take care that the laws be faithfully executed"; the conduct of foreign affairs — a realm in which the Court has recognized that "[i]t would be intolerable that courts, without the relevant information, should review and perhaps nullify actions of the Executive taken on information properly held secret"; and management of the Executive Branch — a task for which "imperative reasons requir[e] an unrestricted power [in the President] to remove the most important of his subordinates in their most important duties."

In arguing that the President is entitled only to qualified immunity, the respondent relies on cases in which we have recognized immunity of this scope for governors and cabinet officers. *E.g., Butz* v. *Economou; Scheuer* v. *Rhodes*. We find these cases to be inapposite. The President's unique status under the Constitution distinguishes him from other executive officials.

Because of the singular importance of the President's duties, diversion of his energies by concern with private lawsuits would raise unique risks to the effective functioning of government. As is the case with prosecutors and judges — for whom absolute immunity now is established — a President must concern himself with matters likely to "arouse the most intense feelings." *Pierson* v. *Ray*. Yet, as our decisions have recognized, it is in precisely such cases that there exists the greatest public interest in providing an official "the maximum ability to deal fearlessly and impartially with" the duties of his office. *Ferri* v. *Ackerman* (1979). This concern is compelling where the officeholder must make the most sensitive and far-reaching decisions entrusted to any official under our constitutional system. Nor can the sheer prominence of the President's office be ignored. In view of the visibility of his office and the effect of his actions on countless people, the President would be an easily identifiable target for suits for civil damages. Cognizance of this personal vulnerability frequently could distract a President from his public duties, to the detriment not only of the President and his office but also the Nation that the Presidency was designed to serve.

B

Courts traditionally have recognized the President's constitutional responsibilities and status as factors counselling judicial deference and restraint. For example, while courts generally have looked to the common law to determine the scope of an official's evidentiary privilege, we have recognized that the Presidential privilege is "rooted in the separation of powers under the Constitution." *United States* v. *Nixon* (1974). It is settled law that the separation of powers doctrine does not bar every exercise of jurisdiction over the President of the United States. . . . But our cases also have established that a court, before exercising jurisdiction, must balance the constitutional weight of the interest to be served against the dangers of intrusion on the authority and functions of the Executive Branch. . . . When judicial action is needed to serve broad public interests — as when the Court acts, not in derogation of the separation of powers, but to maintain their proper balance . . . or to vindicate the public interest in an ongoing criminal prosecution . . . the exercise of jurisdiction has been held warranted. In the case of this merely private suit for damages based on a President's official acts, we hold it is not.

C

In defining the scope of an official's absolute privilege, this Court has recognized that the sphere of protected action must be related closely to the immunity's justifying purposes. Frequently our decisions have held that an official's absolute immunity should extend only to acts in performance of particular functions of his office. . . . But the Court also has refused to draw functional lines finer than history and reason would support. See, *e.g., Spalding* v. *Vilas* (privilege extends to all matters "committed by law to [an official's] control or supervision"); *Barr* v. *Matteo* (fact "that the action here taken was within the outer perimeter of petitioner's line of duty is enough to render the privilege applicable. . . ."); *Stump* v. *Sparkman* (judicial privilege applies even to acts occuring outside "the normal attributes of a judicial proceeding"). In view of the special nature of the President's constitutional office and functions, we think it appropriate to recognize absolute Presidential immunity from damages liability for acts within the "outer perimeter" of his official responsibility.

Under the Constitution and laws of the United States the President has discretionary responsibilities in a broad variety of areas, many of them highly sensitive. In many cases it would be difficult to determine which of the President's innumerable "functions" encompassed a particular action. In this case, for example, respondent argues that he was dismissed in retaliation for his testimony to Congress — a violation of 5 U.S.C. § 7211 and 18 U.S.C. § 1505. The Air Force, however, has claimed that the underlying reorganization was undertaken to promote efficiency. Assuming that the petitioner Nixon ordered the reorganization in which respondent lost his job, an inquiry into the President's motives could not be avoided under the kind of "functional" theory asserted both by respondent and the dissent. Inquiries of this kind could be highly intrusive.

Here respondent argues that petitioner Nixon would have acted outside the outer perimeter of his duties by ordering the discharge of an employee who was lawfully entitled to retain his job in the absence of "such cause as will promote the efficiency of the service." Because Congress has granted this legislative protection, respondent argues, no federal official could, within the outer perimeter of his duties of office, cause Fitzgerald to be dismissed without satisfying this standard in prescribed statutory proceedings.

This construction would subject the President to trial on virtually every allegation that an action was unlawful, or was taken for a forbidden purpose. Adoption of this construction thus would deprive absolute immunity of its intended effect. It clearly is within the President's constitutional and statutory authority to prescribe the manner in which the Secretary will conduct the business of the Air Force. Because this mandate of office must include the authority to prescribe reorganizations and reductions in force, we conclude that petitioner's alleged wrongful acts lay well within the outer perimeter of his authority.

V

A rule of absolute immunity for the President will not leave the Nation without sufficient protection against misconduct on the part of the chief executive. There remains the constitutional remedy of impeachment. In addition, there are formal and informal checks on Presidential action that do not apply with equal force to other executive officials. The President is subjected to constant scrutiny by the press. Vigilant oversight by Congress also may serve to deter Presidential abuses of office, as well as to make credible the threat of impeachment. Other incentives to avoid misconduct may include a desire to earn re-election, the need to maintain prestige as an element of Presidential influence, and a President's traditional concern for his historical stature.

The existence of alternative remedies and deterrents establishes that absolute immunity will not place the President "above the law." For the President, as for judges and prosecutors, absolute immunity merely precludes a particular private remedy for alleged misconduct in order to advance compelling public ends.

VI

For the reasons stated in this opinion, the decision of the Court of Appeals is reversed and the case remanded for action consistent with this opinion.

So ordered.

CHIEF JUSTICE BURGER, concurring.

I join the Court's opinion, but I write separately to underscore that the presidential immunity derives from and is mandated by the constitutional doctrine of separation of powers. Indeed, it has been taken for granted for nearly two centuries. In reaching this conclusion we do well to bear in mind that the focus must not be simply on the matter of judging individual conduct in a fact-bound setting; rather, in those familiar terms of John Marshall, it is a *Constitution* we are expounding. Constitutional adjudication often bears unpalatable fruit. But the needs of a system of government sometimes must outweigh the right of individuals to collect damages.

It strains the meaning of the words used to say this places a President "above the law." *Nixon* v. *United States* (1974). The dissents are wide of the mark to the extent that they imply that the Court today recognized sweeping immunity for a President for all acts. The Court does no such thing. The immunity is limited to civil damage claims. Moreover, a President, like Members of Congress, judges, prosecutors, or congressional aides — all having absolute immunity — are not immune for acts outside official duties. Even the broad immunity of the Speech and Debate Clause has its limits.

At note 2 of his dissenting opinion, JUSTICE WHITE confuses "judicial process" in the subpoena sense with a civil damage suit. He quotes language from *United States* v. *Nixon* (1974), as though that language has some relevance to the matter of immunity from civil damages:

> "[N]either the doctrine of separation of powers, not the need for confidentiality ... without more, can sustain an absolute, unqualified Presidential privilege of immunity from *judicial process* under all circumstances." (Emphasis added.)

First, it is important to remember that the context of that language is a *criminal* prosecution. Second, the "judicial process" referred to was, as in *Aaron Burr* ... a *subpoena* to the President to produce relevant evidence in a criminal prosecution. No issue of damage immunity was involved either in *Burr* or *United States* v. *Nixon*. In short, the quoted language has no bearing whatever on a *civil* action for damages. It is one thing to say that a President must produce evidence relevant to a criminal case, as in *Burr* and *United States* v. *Nixon,* and quite another to say a President can be held for civil damages for dismissing a federal employee. If the dismissal is wrongful the employee can be reinstated with back pay, as was done here.

The immunity of a President from civil suits is not simply a doctrine derived from this Court's interpretation of common law or public policy. Absolute immunity for a President for acts within the official duties of the Chief Executive is either to be found in the constitutional separation of powers or it does not exist. The Court today holds that the Constitution mandates such immunity and I agree. . . .

Exposing a President to civil damage actions for official acts within the scope of the Executive authority would inevitably subject Presidential actions to undue judicial scrutiny as well as subject the President to harassment. The enormous range and impact of Presidential decisions — far beyond that of any one Member of Congress — inescapably means that many persons will consider themselves aggrieved by such acts. Absent absolute immunity, every person who feels aggrieved would be free to bring a suit for damages, and each suit — especially those that proceed on the merits — would involve some judicial questioning of Presidential acts, including the reasons for the decision, how it was arrived at, the information on which it was based, and who supplied the information. . . .

Judicial intervention would also inevitably inhibit the processes of Executive Branch decision-making and impede the functioning of the Office of the President. The need to defend damage suits would have the serious effect of diverting the attention of a President from his executive duties since defending a lawsuit today — even a lawsuit ultimately found to be frivolous — often requires significant expenditures of time and money, as many former public officials have learned to their sorrow. This very case graphically illustrates the point. . . .

I fully agree that the constitutional concept of separation of independent co-equal powers dictates that a President be immune from civil damage actions based on acts within the scope of Executive authority while in office. Far from placing a President above the law, the Court's holding places a President on essentially the same footing with judges and other officials whose absolute immunity we have recognized.

JUSTICE WHITE, with whom JUSTICE BRENNAN, JUSTICE MARSHALL, and JUSTICE BLACKMUN join, dissenting.

The four dissenting members of the Court in *Butz* v. *Economou* (1978) argued that all federal officials are entitled to absolute immunity from suit for any action they take in connection with their official duties. That immunity would extend even to actions taken with express knowledge that the conduct was clearly contrary to the controlling statute or clearly violative of the Constitution. Fortunately, the majority of the Court rejected that approach: We held that although public officials perform certain functions that entitle them to absolute immunity, the immunity attaches to particular functions — not to particular offices. Officials performing functions for which immunity is not absolute enjoy qualified immunity; they are liable in damages only if their conduct violated well-established law and if they should have realized that their conduct was illegal.

The Court now applies the dissenting view in *Butz* to the office of the President: A President acting within the outer boundaries of what Presidents normally do may, without liability, deliberately cause serious injury to any number of citizens even though he knows his conduct violates a statute or tramples on the constitutional rights of those who are injured. Even if the President in this case ordered Fitzgerald fired by means of a trumped-up reduction in force, knowing that such a discharge was contrary to the civil service laws, he would be absolutely immune from suit. By the same token, if a President, without following the statutory procedures which he knows apply to himself as well as to other federal officials, orders his subordinates to wiretap or break into a home for the purpose of installing a listening device, and the officers comply with his request, the President would be absolutely immune from suit. He would be immune regardless of the damage he inflicts, regardless of how violative of the statute and of the Constitution he knew his conduct to be, and regardless of his purpose.

The Court intimates that its decision is grounded in the Constitution. If that is the case, Congress can not provide a remedy against presidential misconduct and the criminal laws of the United States are wholly inapplicable to the President. I find this approach completely unacceptable. I do not agree that if the office of President is to operate effectively, the holder of that office must be permitted, without fear of liability and regardless of the function he is performing, deliberately to inflict injury on others by conduct that he knows violates the law. . . .

In *Marbury* v. *Madison* [1803], the Court, speaking through the Chief Justice, observed that while there were "important political powers" committed to the President for the performance of which neither he nor his appointees were accountable in court, "the question, whether the legality of the act of the head of a department be examinable in a court of justice or not, must always depend on the nature of that act." The Court nevertheless refuses to follow this course with respect to the President. It makes no effort to distinguish categories of presidential conduct that should be absolutely immune from other categories of conduct that should not qualify for that level of immunity. The Court instead concludes that whatever the President does and however contrary to law he knows his conduct to be, he may, without fear of liability, injure federal employees or any other person within or without the government.

Attaching absolute immunity to the office of the President, rather than to particular activities that the President might perform, places the President above the law. It is a reversion to the old notion that the King can do no wrong. Until now, this concept had survived in this country only in the form of sovereign immunity. That doctrine forecloses suit against the government itself and against government officials, but only when the suit against the latter actually seeks relief against the sovereign. *Larson* v. *Domestic and Foreign Corp.* (1949). Suit against an officer, however, may be maintained where it seeks specific relief against him for conduct contrary to his statutory authority or to the Constitution. Now, however, the Court clothes the office of the President with sovereign immunity, placing it beyond the law.

In *Marbury* v. *Madison*, the Chief Justice, speaking for the Court, observed that the "Government of the United States has been emphatically termed a government of laws, and not of men. It will certainly cease to deserve this high appellation, if the laws furnish no remedy for the violation of a vested legal right." Until now, the Court has consistently adhered to this proposition. In *Scheuer* v. *Rhodes* (1974), a unanimous Court held that the governor of a state was entitled only to a qualified immunity. . . .

Unfortunately, the Court now abandons basic principles that have been powerful guides to decision. It is particularly unfortunate since the judgment in this case has few, if any, indicia of a judicial decision; it is almost wholly a policy choice, a choice that is without substantial support and that in all events is ambiguous in its reach and import.

We have previously stated that "the law of privilege as a defense to damage actions against officers of Government has 'in large part been of judicial making.' " *Butz* v. *Economou* (1978), quoting *Barr* v. *Mateo* (1959). But this does not means that the Court has simply "enacted" its own view of the best public policy. No doubt judicial convictions about public policy — whether and what kind of immunity is necessary or wise — have played a part, but the courts have been guided and constrained by common-law tradition, the relevant statutory background and our constitutional structure and history. Our cases dealing with the immunity of members of Congress are constructions of the Speech or Debate Clause and are guided by the history of such privileges at common law. The decisions dealing with the immunity of state officers involve the question of whether and to what extent Congress intended to abolish the common-law privileges by providing a remedy in the predecessor of 42 U.S.C. § 1983 for constitutional violations by state officials. Our decisions respecting immunity for federal officials — including absolute immunity for judges, prosecutors and those officials doing similar work — also in large part reflect common law views, as well as judicial conclusions as to what privileges are necessary if particular functions are to be performed in the public interest.

Unfortunately, there is little of this approach in the Court's decision today. The Court casually, but candidly, abandons the functional approach to immunity that has run through all of our decisions. Indeed, the majority turns this rule on its head by declaring that because the functions of the President's office are so varied and diverse and some of them so profoundly important, the office is unique and must be clothed with office-wide, absolute immunity. This is policy, not law, and in my view, very poor policy. . . .

[Section I Omitted]

II

The functional approach to the separation of powers doctrine and the Court's more recent immunity decisions converge on the following principle: The scope of immunity is determined by function, not office. The wholesale claim that the President is entitled to absolute immunity in all of his actions stands on no firmer ground than did the claim that all presidential communications are entitled to an absolute privilege, which was rejected in favor of a functional analysis, by a unanimous Court in *United States* v. *Nixon* [1974]. Therefore, whatever may be true of the necessity of such a broad immunity in certain areas of executive responsibility, the only question that must be answered here is whether the dismissal of employees falls within a constitutionally assigned executive function, the performance of which would be substantially impaired by the possibility of a private action for damages. I believe it does not.

Respondent has so far proceeded in this action on the basis of three separate causes of action: two federal statutes — 5 U.S.C. § 7211 and 18 U.S.C. § 1505 — and the First Amendment. At this point in the litigation, the availability of these causes of action is not before us. Assuming the correctness of the lower court's determination that the two federal statutes create a private right of action, I find the suggestion that the President is immune from those causes of action to be unconvincing. The attempt to found such immunity upon a separation of powers argument is particularly unconvincing.

The first of these statutes, 5 U.S.C. § 7211, states that "[t]he right of employees . . . to . . . furnish information to either House of Congress, or to a committee or a Member thereof, may not be interfered with or denied." The second, 18 U.S.C. § 1505, makes it a crime to obstruct congressional testimony. It does not take much insight to see that at least one purpose of these statutes is to assure congressional access to information in the possession of the Executive Branch, which Congress believes it requires in order to carry out its responsibilities. Insofar as these statutes implicate a separation of powers argument, I would think it to be just the opposite of that suggested by petitioner and accepted by the majority. In enacting these statutes, Congress sought to preserve its own constitutionally mandated functions in the face of a recalcitrant Executive. Thus, the separation of powers problem addressed by these statutes was first of all presidential behavior that intruded upon, or burdened, Congress' performance of its own constitutional responsibilities. It is no response to this to say that such a cause of action would disrupt the President in the furtherance of his responsibilities. That approach ignores the separation of powers problem that lies behind the congressional action; it assumes that presidential functions are to be valued over congressional functions. . . .

. . . Personnel decisions of the sort involved in this case are emphatically not a constitutionally assigned presidential function that will tolerate no interference by either of the other two branches of government. More important than . . . "quantitative" analysis of the degree of intrusion in presidential decisionmaking permitted in this area, however, is the "qualitative" analysis. . . .

Absolute immunity is appropriate when the threat of liability may bias the decisionmaker in ways that are adverse to the public interest. But as the various regulations and statutes protecting civil servants from arbitrary executive action illustrate, this is an area in which the public interest is demonstrably on the side of encouraging less "vigor" and more "caution" on the part of decisionmakers. That is, the very steps that Congress has taken to assure that executive employees will be able freely to testify in Congress and to assure that they will not be subject to arbitrary adverse actions indicate that those policy arguments that have elsewhere justified absolute immunity are not applicable here. Absolute immunity would be nothing more than a judicial declaration of policy that directly contradicts the policy of protecting civil servants reflected in the statutes and regulations. . . .

III

Because of the importance of this case, it is appropriate to examine the reasoning of the majority opinion.

The opinion suffers from serious ambiguity even with respect to the most fundamental point: How broad is the immunity granted the President? The opinion suggests that its scope is limited by the fact that under none of the asserted causes of action "has Congress taken express legislative action to subject the President to civil liability for his official acts." We are never told, however, how or why Congressional action could make a difference. It is not apparent that any of the propositions relied upon by the majority to immunize the President would not apply equally to such a statutory cause of action; nor does the majority indicate what new principles would operate to undercut those propositions.

In the end, the majority seems to overcome its initial hesitation, for it announces that, "[w]e consider [absolute] immunity a functionally mandated incident of the President's unique office, rooted in the constitutional tradition of the separation of powers and supported by our history." . . . While the majority opinion recognizes that "[i]t is settled law that the separation of powers doctrine does not bar every exercise of jurisdiction over the President of the United States," it bases its conclusion, at least in part, on a suggestion that there is a special jurisprudence of the presidency.

But in *United States* v. *Nixon* (1974), we upheld the power of a federal district court to issue a subpoena *duces tecum* against the President. In other cases we have enjoined executive officials from carrying out presidential directives. See *e.g., Youngstown Sheet & Tube Co.* v. *Sawyer* (1952). Not until this case has there ever been a suggestion that the mere formalism of the name appearing on the complaint was more important in resolving separation of powers problems than the substantive character of the judicial intrusion upon executive functions.

The majority suggests that the separation of powers doctrine permits exercising jurisdiction over the President only in those instances where "judicial action is needed to serve broad public interests — as when the Court acts, not in derogration of the separation of powers, but to maintain their proper balance." Without explanation, the majority contends that a "merely private suit for damages" does not serve this function.

The suggestion that enforcement of the rule of law — *i.e.*, subjecting the President to rules of general applicability — does not further the separation of powers, but rather is in derogation of this purpose, is bizarre. At stake in a suit of this sort, to the extent that it is based upon a statutorily created cause of action, is the ability of Congress to assert legal restraints upon the Executive and of the courts to perform their function of providing redress for legal harm. Regardless of what the Court might think of the merits of Mr. Fitzgerald's claim, the idea that pursuit of legal redress offends the doctrine of separation of powers is a frivolous contention passing as legal argument.

Similarly, the majority implies that the assertion of a constitutional cause of action — the whole point of which is to assure that an officer does not transgress the constitutional limits on his authority — may offend separation of powers concerns. This is surely a perverse approach to the Constitution: Whatever the arguments in favor of absolute immunity may be, it is untenable to argue that subjecting the President to constitutional restrictions will undercut his "unique" role in our system of government. It cannot be seriously argued that the President must be placed beyond the law and beyond judicial enforcement of constitutional restraints upon executive officers in order to implement the principle of separation of powers.

Focusing on the actual arguments the majority offers for its holding of absolute immunity for the President, one finds surprisingly little. As I read the relevant section of the Court's opinion, I find just three contentions from which the majority draws this conclusion. Each of them is little more than a makeweight; together they hardly suffice to justify the wholesale disregard of our traditional approach to immunity questions.

First, the majority informs us that the President occupies a "unique position in the constitutional scheme," including responsibilities for the administration of justice, foreign affairs, and management of the Executive Branch. True as this may be, it says nothing about why a "unique" rule of immunity should apply to the President. The President's unique role may indeed encompass functions for which he is entitled to a claim of absolute immunity. It does not follow from that, however, that he is entitled to absolute immunity either in general or in this case in particular.

For some reason, the majority believes that this uniqueness of the President shifts the burden to respondent to prove that a rule of absolute immunity does not apply. The respondent has failed in this effort, the Court suggests, because the President's uniqueness makes "inapposite" any analogy to our cases dealing with other executive officers. Even if this were true, it would not follow that the President is entitled to absolute immunity; it would only mean that a particular argument is out of place. But the fact is that it is not true. There is nothing in the President's unique role that makes the arguments used in those other cases inappropriate.

Second, the majority contends that because the President's "visibility" makes him particularly vulnerable to suits for civil damages, a rule of absolute immunity is required. The force of this argument is surely undercut by the majority's admission that "there is no historical record of numerous suits against the President." Even granting that a *Bivens* cause of action did not become available until 1971, in the eleven years since then there have been only a handful of suits. Many of these are frivolous and dealt with in a routine manner by the courts and the Justice Department. There is no reason to think that, in the future, the protection afforded by summary judgment procedures would not be adequate to protect the President, as they currently protect other executive officers from unfounded litigation. Indeed, given the decision today in *Harlow & Butterfield* v. *Fitzgerald*, No. 80-945, there is even more reason to believe that frivolous claims will not intrude upon the President's time. Even if judicial procedures were found not to be sufficient, Congress remains free to address this problem if and when it develops.

Finally, the Court suggests that potential liability "frequently could distract a President from his public duties." Unless one assumes that the President himself makes the countless high level executive decisions required in the administration of government, this rule will not do much to insulate such decisions from the threat of liability. The logic of the proposition cannot be limited to the President; its extension, however, has been uniformly rejected by this Court. See *Butz*; *Harlow & Butterfield*. Furthermore, in no instance have we previously held legal accountability in itself to be an unjustifiable cost. The availability of the courts to vindicate constitutional and statutory wrongs has been perceived and protected as one of the virtues of our system of delegated and limited powers. ... [O]ur concern in fashioning absolute immunity rules has been that liability may pervert the decisionmaking process in a particular function by undercutting the values we expect to guide those decisions. Except for the empty generality that the President should have " 'the maximum ability to deal fearlessly and impartially with' the duties of his office," the majority nowhere suggests a particular, disadvantageous effect on a specific presidential function. The caution that comes from requiring reasonable choices in areas that may intrude on individuals' legally protected rights has never before been counted as a cost.

IV

The majority may be correct in its conclusion that "a rule of absolute immunity will not leave the Nation without sufficient remedies for misconduct on the part of the chief executive." Such a rule will, however, leave Mr. Fitzgerald without an adequate remedy for the harms that he may have suffered. More importantly, it will leave future plaintiffs without a remedy, regardless of the substantiality of their claims. The remedies in which the Court finds comfort were never designed to afford relief for individual harms. Rather, they were designed as political safety-valves.

Politics and history, however, are not the domain of the courts; the courts exist to assure each individual that he, as an individual, has enforceable rights that he may pursue to achieve a peaceful redress of his legitimate grievances.

I find it ironic, as well as tragic, that the Court would so casually discard its own role of assuring "the right of every individual to claim the protection of the laws," *Marbury* v. *Madison*, in the name of protecting the principle of separation of powers. Accordingly, I dissent.

HAIG RESIGNATION
June 25, 1982

In a surprise announcement June 25, President Reagan made public the resignation of Secretary of State Alexander M. Haig Jr. Reagan offered no explanation for Haig's departure. Haig himself gave no specific reasons for his decision when he appeared on television a short time after the president, although he indicated some dissatisfaction with the direction of U.S. foreign policy. The nomination of former Treasury Secretary George P. Shultz as Haig's successor was confirmed by the Senate on July 15, and Shultz was sworn in July 16.

Haig was the first ranking Cabinet member to resign. He was known as a man with a strong temperament and as a supporter of a hard-line U.S. foreign policy. In the resignation letter, Haig, a retired four-star general and former commander of NATO forces, stated that the current trend in U.S. foreign policy was drifting from the "careful course" laid out at the onset of the administration.

Public Surprise and Speculation

According to the media, the public and congressional leadership were "stunned" at news of the resignation. Speculation was widespread about Haig's reasons and whether he had acted on his own or had been asked to resign. When questioned September 30, 1982, by interviewer Barbara Walters, Haig stated that he had been planning to leave his office for "many months." As to the actual timing of his resignation, Haig stated, "I was pushed."

Major factors contributing to the resignation were thought to be Haig's foreign policy disputes with Secretary of Defense Caspar W. Weinberger, with former National Security Adviser Richard V. Allen and with Allen's successor, William P. Clark. Just prior to his announcement, Haig's relations with the White House had been strained; officials there complained of his "grandstanding," his reputation of frequently threatening to quit over presumed slights to his rank and his alleged attempts to undercut the power of other Cabinet members.

The thinly disguised and highly publicized clashes between Haig and U.S. Ambassador to the United Nations Jeane J. Kirkpatrick added to the friction between the State Department and the White House. Kirkpatrick had openly accused Haig of pro-European bias and of being "totally insensitive to [Latin] cultures" when he supported Britain during the Falkland crisis.

The U.S. decision to ban the sale of American-designed equipment for the Soviet Union's natural gas pipeline to Western Europe, overriding Haig's opposition, was thought to be another source of conflict between Haig and Reagan's major policy officials. (Pipeline controversy, p. 879)

Haig's undaunted support of Israel, even after its invasion of Lebanon, had caused similar friction with some Cabinet members demanding a public rebuke of Israel. (War in Lebanon, p. 741)

President Reagan frequently had been criticized for his lack of international experience and for allowing Haig to run the foreign policy scene. Some commentators anticipated the resignation because of Reagan's need to assert Oval Office jurisdiction over foreign policy decision making.

Shultz's Background

A Californian like Reagan, Shultz had both government experience and an international background. A former dean at the University of Chicago Graduate School of Business, he had joined the Nixon administration in 1969 as secretary of labor, then as director of the Office of Management and Budget and as Treasury secretary. He later became Nixon's chief economic policy adviser.

The main obstacle to Shultz' nomination was his previous position as president of Bechtel Group Inc., an international construction and engineering company with substantial interests in Saudi Arabia. Some commentators believed this background would lead to an American bias against Israel in the Middle East, but Shultz assured the Senate that this would not be the case.

During the confirmation hearings Shultz, in contrast to Haig, emphasized the "Palestinian problem" and the need for a solution to the "legitimate needs and problems" of the Palestinians. He also indicated his support of the administration's firm approach to the Soviet Union and the economic sanctions against the U.S.S.R. after the establishment of martial law in Poland in December 1981. He regarded his job as secretary of state as an adviser to the president because "he's the boss."

Other 1982 Cabinet Changes

Haig's resignation was the first of three from Reagan's Cabinet in 1982. Secretary of Energy James B. Edwards resigned in early November and was replaced by Donald P. Hodel, formerly under secretary of the Department of the Interior. In late December Secretary of Transportation Drew Lewis was replaced by Elizabeth Hanford Dole, who had served in the White House as the president's assistant for public liaison.

Following are the texts of President Reagan's June 25, 1982, announcement of the resignation of Secretary of State Alexander M. Haig Jr. and Haig's statement, as they appeared in The New York Times, *June 26; the text of the president's letter to Haig, June 25; and the texts of remarks by Reagan and Secretary of State George P. Shultz at Shultz's swearing in, July 16:*

REAGAN ANNOUNCEMENT

Ladies and gentlemen, let me say first of all, I'm going to make an announcement, very brief. I will take no questions on it. I understand that a press conference is scheduled next week.

It's an announcement that I make with great regret regarding a member of our Administration who has served this country for 40 years above and beyond the call of duty, who has served me so well and faithfully with his wisdom and counsel I have respected and admired for all the time that our Administration has been here, but who now is resigning and leaving Government service after all this great time.

And with great regret, I have accepted the resignation of Secretary of State Al Haig. I am nominating as his successor, and he has accepted, George Schultz to replace him. And that's the extent of the announcement.

Again, as I say, I do this with great regret. I said no questions, I said no questions.

HAIG STATEMENT

Thank you very much. Ladies and gentlemen, I'd like to read a copy of the text of the letter which I presented to President Reagan today.

Dear Mr. President: Your accession to office on Jan. 20, 1981, brought an opportunity for a new and forward-looking foreign policy resting on the cornerstones of strength and compassion. I believe that we shared a view of America's role in the world as the leader of free men and an inspiration for all. We agreed that consistency, clarity and steadiness of purpose were essential to success. It was in this spirit that I undertook to serve you as Secretary of State.

In recent months it has become clear to me that the foreign policy on which we embarked together was shifting from that careful course which we laid out. Under these circumstances I feel it necessary to request that you accept my resignation. I shall always treasure the confidence which you reposed in me. It has been a great honor to serve in your Administration, and I wish you every success in the future. Sincerely.

Now I am extremely pleased, ladies and gentlemen, that Mr. George Shultz, an old friend of many years, has accepted the President's request that he assume my post. My own knowledge of George and his experience, professionalism and integrity gives me the utmost confidence that our country, the American people and our President will be well served by his incumbency.

Over the past 18 months, I have come to develop the most profound respect and admiration for the talents and dedication of the people of the Foreign Service and of the employees of the State Department. They've been and continue to be absolutely superb.

I've asked my associates here at the Department to serve the President and my successor as ably and as loyally as they have served me, and more than that, the American people cannot ask. I have assured the President, furthermore, that I will stay on in my post for as long as is necessary to insure an orderly transition for my successor.

And now, finally, ladies and gentlemen of the press, I would like to thank and compliment each of you for the professionalism and the objectivity that you have shown to me and the business of this department as you carry out your critical role in the service of the American people.

REAGAN LETTER TO HAIG

Dear Al:

It is with the most profound regret that I accept your letter of resignation. Almost forty years ago you committed yourself to the service of your country. Since that time your career has been marked by a succession of assignments demanding the highest level of personal sacrifice, courage and leadership. As a soldier and statesman facing challenges of enormous complexity and danger, you have established a standard of excellence and achievement seldom equalled in our history. On each occasion you have reflected a quality of wisdom which has been critical to the resolution of the most anguishing problems we have faced during the past generation — the conclusion of the Vietnam war, the transfer of executive authority at a time of national trauma and most recently, advancing the cause of peace among nations.

The nation is deeply in your debt. As you leave I want you to know of my deep personal appreciation, and in behalf of the American people I express my gratitude and respect. You have been kind enough to offer your continued counsel and you may be confident that I will call upon you in the years ahead. Nancy joins me in extending our warmest personal wishes to you and Pat.

REMARKS AT SHULTZ SWEARING IN

The President. Ladies and gentlemen, please. Today, I'm reminded of the old saying, "Let George do it." [*Laughter*] And, George, from now on, I think I'll have a few things for you to do.

On behalf of the American people, I want to compliment the Senate for its wisdom in approving so rapidly and decisively the nomination of George Shultz as our next Secretary of State. The Senate's swift action augurs well for continued cooperation between the Congress and the executive branch and for strong leadership at the State Department.

I also want to compliment George Shultz on his impressive performance before the Senate Foreign Relations Committee. His articulate and convincing presentation sent a strong signal to friend and foe alike. Our country is fortunate to have a man of exceptional character and qualifications for this vital position.

America's always been blessed in times such as these with citizens of stature who come forward to make certain the job gets done and done right. George Shultz follows in that tradition. He has served three previous Presidents. He has been immensely successful in his endeavors in the private sector, and he's highly respected for his academic achievements. Those who know him testify that he's a man with character and common sense, affable, yet decisive. He's a man who inspires confidence and leaves no doubt that he's capable of the vital task that we're giving him.

Of all the responsibilities of the Presidency, shaping American foreign policy is the most awesome. It's in this arena that we come to grips with the decisions which most directly affect the delicate balance of peace and which secure both the immediate and long-term well-being of the United States.

When looking for the best, sometimes one finds that the paths of talented men cross. Recently, George, there's been some criticism of your similar background to another member of my Cabinet. Now, I admit we may be dipping from the same well to find quality people. I just want everyone to know that I'm fully aware that George and Don Regan, as well as many other high-ranking members of my administration, are all former Marines. [*Laughter*] And I don't find that a handicap in any way. [*Laughter*]

Seriously, George's background gives him a unique opportunity to be of service to his country. Over the last few years in the private sector leading one of the giants of American enterprise, he has first-hand knowledge of the dynamics of economic progress. He brings with him perhaps a deeper understanding of world economics than any previous Secretary of State, having dealt internationally with leaders of commerce as well as heads of state. This experience will, I have no doubt, add depth and meaning to the decisions that he'll be making. I look forward to his counsel.

And with all of that said, George, welcome to the team.

[*At this point, Attorney General William French Smith administered the oath of office to Mr. Shultz.*]

Secretary Shultz. Thank you very much.

Mr. President, I thank you. You have done me a great honor, and I recognize fully the responsibilities placed upon me.

I said in my statement to the Committee on Foreign Relations that I would muster every ounce of energy and intelligence and dedication I could and pour all of it into performance on this job, and I restate that and remake that pledge to you on this occasion, Mr. President.

In the period of time that I've been preparing for this job and preparing for my examination by the Committee on Foreign Relations, of course I've been impressed with the importance and depth and difficulty of the problems that we face. But also, Mr. President, as you so characteristically do, I think it's essential that we take that coin that has "problems" as its label on one side and turn it over and see that on the other side is the word "opportunities." And I certainly want to approach this task fully conscious and realistic about the problems, but even more, conscious of the opportunities which with creative and constructive effort we may be able to do something wonderful with. I say that with some confidence here, because I am with friends. And I feel the warmth of this gathering and that it's a family affair, and it gives me a certain sense of both humility but also a sense of support.

And in that regard I would like to thank especially the Members of Congress, the Members of the Senate who gave me such a thorough working-over and examination — and, I think, in a very constructive way and thorough way — and in the end voted promptly and decisively to confirm me as Secretary of State. And I appreciate that, and I recognize it as a kind of marker that we should approach these things together and in the spirit of bipartisanship and in trying to find the broad consensus that sustains our policies abroad and has done so for so many decades.

Mr. President, in your Inaugural Address you said that no arsenal, no weapon in the world "is so formidable as the will and moral courage of free men and women." I think, as you often do, you put succinctly the essence of the matter, and I say to you that I will take these words of yours as my touchstone and foundation as I approach the conduct of this great office.

I thank you very much, Mr. President, and my friends.

SUPREME COURT ON
SCHOOL BOOK BANNING
June 25, 1982

In a 5-4 decision issued June 25, the Supreme Court held that the First Amendment limits the authority of public school boards to remove books from school libraries. The case, Board of Education, Island Trees Union Free School District *v.* Pico, *was returned to lower court for trial to determine whether the board had acted under "constitutionally valid concerns" in removing the books. Rather than go to trial, the school board for the Long Island, N.Y., community decided August 12, 1982, to restore the books to the shelves, with orders to the librarians to notify the parents of students checking them out.*

The books that the board had barred from the high school library were Eldridge Cleaver's *Soul on Ice;* Kurt Vonnegut Jr.'s *Slaughterhouse Five;* Desmond Morris' *The Naked Ape;* Piri Thomas' *Down These Mean Streets;* Richard Wright's *Black Boy;* Oliver LaFarge's *Laughing Boy;* Alice Childress' *A Hero Ain't Nothin' but a Sandwich;* Go Ask Alice, *by an anonymous author and* Best Short Stories by Negro Writers, *edited by Langston Hughes. From the junior high school library, the board removed* A Reader for Writers, *edited by Jerome Archer. Bernard Malamud's* The Fixer *was taken out of the curriculum of a 12th grade literature class.*

Background

The case began in 1976 when the Island Trees board banished the books, calling them "anti-American, anti-Christian, anti-Semitic and just plain filthy." Two years later several students filed suit, saying the ban violated their rights under the freedom of speech and press guarantees of the First Amendment.

In 1979 a federal district court ruled summarily without a trial in the board's favor. A summary judgment was allowed under federal court procedure when the facts were not disputed and the issue turned merely on a point of law. In 1980 the 2nd Circuit Court of Appeals reversed the lower federal court's decision, arguing that a trial should be held to determine, as a question of fact, what the board's motives were in banning the books and whether the motives were permissible under the First Amendment.

Majority Opinion

In its ruling the Supreme Court upheld the appeals court's decision that a trial should be held. In the majority opinion, joined by Justices Thurgood Marshall and John Paul Stevens, Justice William J. Brennan Jr. wrote that if the board was motivated to remove the books because it felt they were vulgar or otherwise unsuitable, then the banning was permissible. But if the board acted to remove unpopular ideas, he argued, then it acted in violation of the First Amendment.

School boards "rightly possess significant discretion to determine the content of their school libraries," Brennan wrote. "But that discretion may not be exercised in a narrowly partisan or political manner."

Justice Byron R. White, who cast the deciding vote to order the trial, did not join in the Brennan plurality but wrote a short opinion merely affirming the students' right to bring their case to trial. Justice Harry A. Blackmun filed a separate opinion, agreeing with the decision but not with the entire majority opinion.

The Dissent

In the dissent Chief Justice Warren E. Burger labeled the Brennan opinion "a lavish expansion going beyond any holding under the First Amendment." He added: "Were this to become the law, this court would come perilously close to becoming a 'super censor' of school board library decisions."

The Burger dissent was endorsed by Justices Lewis F. Powell Jr., William H. Rehnquist and Sandra Day O'Connor, with Powell expressing "genuine dismay" over the Brennan opinion. "For me," he wrote, "today's decision symbolizes a debilitating encroachment upon the institutions of a free people."

The court's opinion in Board of Education v. Pico *came at a time of increasing attempts at schoolbook censorship, many of them organized by conservative groups. In a few cases, even some educators questioned the use of classics such as* Huckleberry Finn *and* The Diary of Anne Frank *as classroom material.*

> *Following are excerpts from the Supreme Court's decision in* Board of Education *v.* Pico, *issued June 25, 1982, stating that a school board's authority to remove books from a school library was subject to First Amendment consider-ations, and excerpts from dissents by the chief justice and Justice Powell:*

No. 80-2043

Board of Education, Island Trees Union Free School District No. 26 et al., Petitioners, *v.* Steven A. Pico, by his next friend, Frances Pico et al.	On writ of Certiorari to the United States Court of Appeals for the Second Circuit

[June 25, 1982]

JUSTICE BRENNAN announced the judgment of the Court, and delivered an opinion in which JUSTICE MARSHALL and JUSTICE STEVENS joined, and in which JUSTICE BLACKMUN joined except for Part II-A-(1).

[JUSTICE WHITE wrote a separate concurring opinion.]

The principal question presented is whether the First Amendment imposes limitations upon the exercise by a local school board of its discretion to remove library books from high school and junior high school libraries.

I

Petitioners are the Board of Education of the Island Trees Union Free School District No. 26, in New York, and Richard Ahrens, Frank Martin, Christina Fasulo, Patrick Hughes, Richard Melchers, Richard Michaels, and Louis Nessim. When this suit was brought, Ahrens was the President of the Board, Martin was the Vice-President, and the remaining petition-ers were Board members. The Board is a state agency charged with responsibility for the operation and administration of the public schools within the Island Trees School District, including the Island Trees High School and Island Trees Memorial Junior High School. Respondents are Steven Pico, Jacqueline Gold, Glenn Yarris, Russell Rieger, and Paul Sochinski. When this suit was brought, Pico, Gold, Yarris, and Rieger were students at the High School, and Sochinski was a student at the Junior High School.

In September 1975, petitioners Ahrens, Martin, and Hughes attended a conference sponsored by Parents of New York United (PONYU), a politically conservative organization of parents concerned about education legislation in the State of New York. At the conference these petitioners obtained lists of books described by Ahrens as "objectionable," and by Martin as "improper fare for school students." It was later determined that the High School library contained nine of the listed books, and that another listed book was in the Junior High School library. In February 1976, at a meeting with the superintendent of schools and the principals of the High School and Junior High School, the Board gave an "unofficial direction" that the listed books be removed from the library shelves and delivered to the Board's offices, so that Board members could read them. When this directive was carried out, it became publicized, and the Board issued a press release justifying its action. It characterized the removed books as "anti-American, anti-Christian, anti-Semitic, and just plain filthy," and concluded that "It is our duty, our moral obligation, to protect the children in our schools from this moral danger as surely as from physical and medical dangers."

A short time later, the Board appointed a "Book Review Committee," consisting of four Island Trees parents and four members of the Island Trees schools staff, to read the listed books and to recommend to the Board whether the books should be retained, taking into account the books' "educational suitability," "good taste," "relevance," and "appropriateness to age and grade level." In July, the Committee made its final report to the Board, recommending that five of the listed books [*The Fixer, Laughing Boy, Black Boy, Go Ask Alice* and *The Best Short Stories by Negro Writers*] be retained and that two others [*The Naked Ape* and *Down These Mean Streets*] be removed from the school libraries. As for the remaining four books, the Committee could not agree on two [*Soul on Ice* and *A Hero Ain't Nothin' But a Sandwich*], took no position on one [*A Reader for Writers*], and recommended that the last book [*Slaughterhouse Five*] be made available to students only with parental approval. The Board substantially rejected the Committee's report later that month, deciding that only one book [*Laughing Boy*] should be returned to the High School library without restriction, that another [*Black Boy*] should be made available subject to parental approval, but that the remaining nine books should "be removed from elementary and secondary libraries and [from] use in the curriculum." The Board gave no reasons for rejecting the recommendations of the committee that it had appointed.

Respondents reacted to the Board's decision by bringing the present action under 42 U.S.C. § 1983 in the United States District Court for the Eastern District of New York. They alleged that petitioners had

"ordered the removal of the books from school libraries and proscribed their use in the curriculum because particular passages in the books offended their social, political and moral tastes and not because the books, taken as a whole, were lacking in educational value."

Respondents claimed that the Board's actions denied them their rights under the First Amendment. They asked the court for a declaration that the Board's actions were unconstitutional, and for preliminary and permanent injunctive relief ordering the Board to return the nine books to the school libraries and to refrain from interfering with the use of those books in the schools' curricula.

The District Court granted summary judgment in favor of petitioners. (1979). In the court's view, "the parties substantially agree[d] about the motivation behind the board's actions," namely, that

> "the board acted not on religious principles but on its conservative educational philosophy, and on its belief that the nine books removed from the school library and curriculum were irrelevant, vulgar, immoral, and in bad taste, making them educationally unsuitable for the district's junior and senior high school students."

With this factual premise as its background, the court rejected respondents' contention that their First Amendment rights had been infringed by the Board's actions. Noting that statute, history, and precedent had vested local school boards with a broad discretion to formulate educational policy, the court concluded that it should not intervene in " 'the daily operations of school systems' " unless " 'basic constitutional values' " were " 'sharply implicate[d],' " and determined that the conditions for such intervention did not exist in the present case. Acknowledging that the "removal [of the books] ... clearly was content-based," the court nevertheless found no constitutional violation of the requisite magnitude....

A three judge panel of the United States Court of Appeals for the Second Circuit reversed the judgment of the District Court, and remanded the action for a trial on respondents' allegations. (1980).... We granted certiorari (1981).

II

We emphasize at the outset the limited nature of the substantive question presented by the case before us. Our precedents have long recognized certain constitutional limits upon the power of the State to control even the curriculum and classroom. For example, *Meyer* v. *Nebraska* (1923) struck down a state law that forbade the teaching of modern foreign languages in public and private schools, and *Epperson* v. *Arkansas* (1968), declared unconstitutional a state law that prohibited the teaching of the Darwinian theory of evolution in any state-supported school. But the current action does not require us to re-enter this difficult terrain, which *Meyer* and *Epperson* traversed without apparent misgiving. For as this case is presented to us, it does not involve textbooks, or indeed any books that Island Trees students would be required to read. Respondents do not seek in this Court to impose limitations upon their school board's discretion to prescribe the curricula of the Island Trees schools. On the contrary, the only books at issue in this case are *library* books, books that by their nature are optional rather than required reading. Our adjudication of the present case thus does not intrude into the classroom, or into the compulsory courses taught there. Furthermore, even as to library books, the action before us does not involve the *acquisition* of books. Respondents have not sought to compel their school board to add to the school library shelves any books that students desire to read. Rather, the only action challenged in this case is the *removal* from school libraries of books originally placed there by the school authorities, or without objection from them.

The substantive question before us is still further constrained by the procedural posture of this case. Petitioners were granted summary judgment by the District Court. The Court of Appeals reversed that judgment, and remanded the action for a trial on the merits of respondents' claims. We can reverse the judgment of the Court of Appeals, and grant petitioners' request for reinstatement of the summary judgment in their favor, only if we determine that "there is no genuine issue as to any material fact," and that petitioners are "entitled to a judgment as a matter of law." In making our determination, any doubt as to the existence of a genuine issue of material fact must be resolved against petitioners as the moving party. *Adickes* v. *Kress & Co.* (1970). Furthermore, "On summary judgment the inferences to be drawn from the underlying facts contained . . . in the affadavits, attached exhibits, and depositions submitted below . . . must be viewed in the light most favorable to the party opposing the motion." *United States* v. *Diebold, Inc.* (1962).

In sum, the issue before us in this case is a narrow one, both substantively and procedurally. It may best be restated as two distinct questions. First, Does the First Amendment impose *any* limitations upon the discretion of petitioners to remove library books from the Island Trees High School and Junior High School? Second, If so, do the affidavits and other evidentiary materials before the District Court, construed most favorably to respondents, raise a genuine issue of fact whether petitioners might have exceeded those limitations? If we answer either of these questions in the negative, then we must reverse the judgment of the Court of Appeals and reinstate the District Court's summary judgment for petitioners. If we answer both questions in the affirmative, then we must affirm the judgment below. We examine these questions in turn.

A

(1)

The Court has long recognized that local school boards have broad discretion in the management of school affairs. See, *e.g.*, *Meyer* v. *Nebraska* (1923); *Pierce* v. *Society of Sisters* (1925). *Epperson* v. *Arkan-*

sas reaffirmed that, by and large, "public education in our Nation is committed to the control of state and local authorities," and that federal courts should not ordinarily "intervene in the resolution of conflicts which arise in the daily operation of school systems." *Tinker* v. *Des Moines School Dist.* (1969) noted that we have "repeatedly emphasized ... the comprehensive authority of the States and of school officials ... to prescribe and control conduct in the schools." We have also acknowledged that public schools are vitally important "in the preparation of individuals for participation as citizens," and as vehicles for "inculcating fundamental values necessary to the maintenance of a democratic political system." *Ambach* v. *Norwick* (1979). We are therefore in full agreement with petitioners that local school boards must be permitted "to establish and apply their curriculum in such a way as to transmit community values," and that "there is a legitimate and substantial community interest in promoting respect for authority and traditional values be they social, moral, or political."

At the same time, however, we have necessarily recognized that the discretion of the States and local school boards in matters of education must be exercised in a manner that comports with the transcendent imperatives of the First Amendment. In *West Virginia* v. *Barnette* (1943) we held that under the First Amendment a student in a public school could not be compelled to salute the flag. We reasoned that

> "Boards of Education ... have, of course, important, delicate, and highly discretionary functions, but none that they may not perform within the limits of the Bill of Rights. That they are educating the young for citizenship is reason for scrupulous protection of Constitutional freedoms of the individual, if we are not to strangle the free mind at its source and teach youth to discount important principles of our government as mere platitudes."

Later cases have consistently followed this rationale. Thus *Epperson* v. *Arkansas* invalidated a State's anti-evolution statute as violative of the Establishment Clause, and reaffirmed the duty of federal courts "to apply the First Amendment's mandate in our education system where essential to safeguard the fundamental values of freedom of speech and inquiry." And *Tinker* v. *Des Moines School Dist.* held that a local school board had infringed the free speech rights of high school and junior high school students by suspending them from school for wearing black armbands in class as a protest against the Government's policy in Vietnam; we stated there that the "comprehensive authority ... of school officials" must be exercised "consistent with fundamental constitutional safeguards." In sum, students do not "shed their rights to freedom of speech or expression at the schoolhouse gate," and therefore local school boards must discharge their "important, delicate, and highly discretionary functions" within the limits and constraints of the First Amendment.

The nature of students' First Amendment rights in the context of this case requires further examination. *West Virginia* v. *Barnette* is instructive. There the Court held that students' liberty of conscience could not be infringed in the name of "national unity" or "patriotism." We explained that

> "the action of the local authorities in compelling the flag salute and pledge transcends constitutional limitations on their power and invades the sphere of intellect and spirit which it is the purpose of the First Amendment to our Constitution to reserve from all official control."

Similarly, *Tinker* v. *Des Moines School Dist.* held that students' rights to freedom of expression of their political views could not be abridged by reliance upon an "undifferentiated fear or apprehension of disturbance" arising from such expression:

> "Any departure from absolute regimentation may cause trouble. Any variation from the majority's opinion may inspire fear. Any word spoken, in class, in the lunchroom, or on the campus, that deviates from the views of another person may start an argument or cause a disturbance. But our Constitution says we must take this risk, *Terminiello* v. *Chicago* (1949); and our history says that it is this sort of hazardous freedom — this kind of openness — that is the basis of our national strength and of the independence and vigor of Americans who grow up and live in this ... often disputatious society."

In short, "First Amendment rights, applied in light of the special characteristics of the school environment, are available to ... students."

Of course, courts should not "intervene in the resolution of conflicts which arise in the daily operations of school systems" unless "basic constitutional values" are "directly and sharply implicate[d]" in those conflicts. *Epperson* v. *Arkansas*. But we think that the First Amendment rights of students may be directly and sharply implicated by the removal of books from the shelves of a school library. Our precedents have focused "not only on the role of the First Amendment in fostering individual self-expression but also on its role in affording the public access to discussion, debate, and the dissemination of information and ideas." *First National Bank of Boston* v. *Bellotti* (1978). And we have recognized that "the State may not, consistently with the spirit of the First Amendment, contract the spectrum of available knowledge." *Griswold* v. *Connecticut* (1965). In keeping with this principle, we have held that in a variety of contexts "the Constitution protects the right to receive information and ideas." *Stanley* v. *Georgia* (1969).... This right is an inherent corollary of the rights of free speech and press that are explicitly guaranteed by the Constitution, in two senses. First, the right to receive ideas follows ineluctably from the *sender's* First Amendment right to send them: "The right of freedom of speech and press ... embraces the right to distribute literature, ... and necessarily protects the right to receive it." *Martin* v. *Struthers* (1943). "The dissemination of ideas can accomplish nothing if otherwise willing addressees are not free to receive and consider them. It would be a barren marketplace of ideas that had only seller and no buyers." *Lamont* v. *Postmaster General* (1965) (BRENNAN, J., concurring).

More importantly, the right to receive ideas is a necessary predicate to the *recipient's* meaningful exercise of his own rights of speech, press, and political freedom. Madison admonished us that

"A popular Government, without popular information, or the means of acquiring it, is but a Prologue to a Farce or a Tragedy; or, perhaps both. Knowledge will forever govern ignorance: And a people who mean to be their own Governors, must arm themselves with the power which knowledge gives."

As we recognized in *Tinker,* students too are beneficiaries of this principle:

"In our system, students may not be regarded as closed-circuit recipients of only that which the State chooses to communicate. . . . [S]chool officials cannot suppress 'expressions of feeling with which they do not wish to contend.' "

In sum, just as access to ideas makes it possible for citizens generally to exercise their rights of free speech and press in a meaningful manner, such access prepares students for active and effective participation in the pluralistic, often contentious society in which they will soon be adult members. Of course all First Amendment rights accorded to students must be construed "in light of the special characteristics of the school environment." *Tinker* v. *Des Moines School Dist*. But the special characteristics of the school *library* make that environment especially appropriate for the recognition of the First Amendment rights of students.

A school library, no less than any other public library, is "a place dedicated to quiet, to knowledge, and to beauty." *Brown* v. *Louisiana* (1966) (Opinion of Fortas, J.). *Keyishian* v. *Board of Regents* (1967) observed that "students must always remain free to inquire, to study and to evaluate, to gain new maturity and understanding." The school library is the principal locus of such freedom. . . . Petitioners emphasize the inculcative function of secondary education, and argue that they must be allowed *unfettered* discretion to "transmit community values" through the Island Trees schools. But that sweeping claim overlooks the unique role of the school library. It appears from the record that use of the Island Trees school libraries is completely voluntary on the part of students. Their selection of books from these libraries is entirely a matter of free choice; the libraries afford them an opportunity at self-education and individual enrichment that is wholly optional. Petitioners might well defend their claim of absolute discretion in matters of *curriculum* by reliance upon their duty to inculcate community values. But we think that petitioners' reliance upon that duty is misplaced where, as here, they attempt to extend their claim of absolute discretion beyond the compulsory environment of the classroom, into the school library and the regime of voluntary inquiry that there holds sway.

(2)

In rejecting petitioners' claim of absolute discretion to remove books from their school libraries, we do not deny that local school boards have a substantial legitimate role to play in the determination of school library content. We thus must turn to the question of the extent to which the First Amendment places limitations upon the discretion of petitioners to remove books from their libraries. In this inquiry we enjoy the guidance of several precedents. *West Virginia* v. *Barnette* stated that

> "If there be any fixed star in our constitutional constellation, it is that no official, high or petty, can prescribe what shall be orthodox in politics, nationalism, religion, or other matters of opinion.... If there are any circumstances which permit an exception, they do not now occur to us."

This doctrine has been reaffirmed in later cases involving education. For example, *Keyishian* v. *Board of Regents* noted that "the First Amendment ... does not tolerate laws which cast a pall of orthodoxy over the classroom;" see also *Epperson* v. *Arkansas*....

With respect to the present case, the message of these precedents is clear. Petitioners rightly possess significant discretion to determine the content of their school libraries. But that discretion may not be exercised in a narrowly partisan or political manner. If a Democratic school board, motivated by party affiliation, ordered the removal of all books written by or in favor of Republicans, few would doubt that the order violated the constitutional rights of the students denied access to those books. The same conclusion would surely apply if an all-white school board, motivated by racial animus, decided to remove all books authored by blacks or advocating racial equality and integration. Our Constitution does not permit the official suppression of *ideas*. Thus whether petitioners' removal of books from their school libraries denied respondents their First Amendment rights depends upon the motivation behind petitioners' actions. If petitioners *intended* by their removal decision to deny respondents access to ideas with which petitioners disagreed, and if this intent was the decisive factor in petitioners' decision, then petitioners have exercised their discretion in violation of the Constitution. To permit such intentions to control official actions would be to encourage the precise sort of officially prescribed orthodoxy unequivocally condemned in *Barnette*. On the other hand, respondents implicitly concede that if it were demonstrated that the removal decision was based solely upon the "educational suitability" of the books in question, then their removal would be "perfectly permissible." In other words, in respondents' view such motivations, if decisive of petitioners' actions, would not carry the danger of an official suppression of ideas, and thus would not violate respondents' First Amendment rights.

As noted earlier, nothing in our decision today affects in any way the discretion of a local school board to choose books to *add* to the libraries of their schools. Because we are concerned in this case with the suppression of ideas, our holding today affects only the discretion to *remove* books. In brief, we hold that local school boards may not remove books from school library shelves simply because they dislike the ideas contained in those books and seek by their removal to "prescribe what shall be orthodox in politics, nationalism, religion, or other matters of opinion." *West Virginia* v. *Barnette*. Such purposes stand inescapably condemned by our precedents.

B

We now turn to the remaining question presented by this case: Do the evidentiary materials that were before the District Court, when construed most favorably to respondents, raise a genuine issue of material fact whether petitioners exceeded constitutional limitations in exercising their discretion to remove the books from the school libraries? We conclude that the materials do raise such a question, which forecloses summary judgment in favor of petitioners.

Before the District Court, respondents claimed that petitioners' decision to remove the books "was based upon [their] personal values, morals and tastes." Respondents also claimed that petitioners objected to the books in part because excerpts from them were "anti-American." The accuracy of these claims was partially conceded by petitioners, and petitioners' own affidavits lent further support to respondents' claims. In addition, the record developed in the District Court shows that when petitioners offered their first public explanation for the removal of the books, they relied in part on the assertion that the removed books were "anti-American," and "offensive to ... Americans in general." Furthermore, while the Book Review Committee appointed by petitioners was instructed to make its recommendation based upon criteria that appear on their face to be permissible — the books' "educational suitability," "good taste," "relevance," and "appropriateness to age and grade level" — the Committee's recommendations that five of the books be retained and that only two be removed were essentially rejected by petitioners, without any statement of reasons for doing so. Finally, while petitioners originally defended their removal decision with the explanation that "these books contain obscenities, blasphemies, and perversion beyond description," one of the books, *A Reader for Writers*, was removed even though it contained no such language.

Standing alone, this evidence respecting the substantive motivations behind petitioners' removal decision would not be decisive. This would be a very different case if the record demonstrated that petitioners had employed established, regular, and facially unbiased procedures for the review of controversial materials. But the actual record in the case before us suggests the exact opposite. Petitioners' removal procedures were vigorously challenged below by respondents, and the evidence on this issue sheds further light on the issue of petitioners' motivations. Respondents alleged that in making their removal decision petitioners ignored "the advice of literary experts," the views of "librarians and teachers within the Island Trees School system," the advice of the superintendent of schools, and the guidance of "publications that rate books for junior and senior high school students." Respondents also claimed that petitioners' decision was based solely on the fact that the books were named on the PONYU list received by petitioners Ahrens, Martin, and Hughes, and that petitioners "did not undertake an independent review of other books in the [school] libraries." Evidence before the District Court lends support to these claims.

The record shows that immediately after petitioners first ordered the books removed from the library shelves, the superintendent of schools reminded them that "we already have a policy . . . designed expressly to handle such problems," and recommended that the removal decision be approached through this established channel. But the Board disregarded the superintendent's advice, and instead resorted to the extraordinary procedure of appointing a Book Review Committee — the advice of which was later rejected without explanation. In sum, respondents' allegations and some of the evidentiary materials . . . do not rule out the possibility that petitioners' removal procedures were highly irregular and ad hoc — the antithesis of those procedures that might tend to allay suspicions regarding petitioners' motivations.

Construing these claims, affidavit statements, and other evidentiary materials in a manner favorable to respondents, we cannot conclude that petitioners were "entitled to a judgment as a matter of law." The evidence plainly does not foreclose the possibility that petitioners' decision to remove the books rested decisively upon disagreement with constitutionally protected ideas in those books, or upon a desire on petitioners' part to impose upon the students of the Island Trees High School and Junior High School a political orthodoxy to which petitioners and their constituents adhered. Of course, some of the evidence before the District Court might lead a finder of fact to accept petitioners' claim that their removal decision was based upon constitutionally valid concerns. But that evidence at most creates a genuine issue of material fact on the critical question of the credibility of petitioners' justifications for their decision: On that issue, it simply cannot be said that there is no genuine issue as to any material fact.

The mandate shall issue forthwith.

Affirmed.

JUSTICE BLACKMUN, concurring in part and concurring in the judgment. . . .

In my view, we strike a proper balance here by holding that school officials may not remove books for the *purpose* of restricting access to the political ideas or social perspectives discussed in them, when that action is motivated simply by the officials' disapproval of the ideas involved. It does not seem radical to suggest that state action calculated to suppress novel ideas or concepts is fundamentally antithetical to the values of the First Amendment. At a minimum, allowing a school board to engage in such conduct hardly teaches children to respect the diversity of ideas that is fundamental to the American system. In this context, then, the school board must "be able to show that its action was caused by something more than a mere desire to avoid the discomfort and unpleasantness that always accompanies an unpopular viewpoint," *Tinker* v. *Des Moines School Dist.* [1969], and that the board had something in mind in addition to the suppression of partisan or political views it did not share.

As I view it, this is a narrow principle. School officials must be able to choose one book over another, without outside interference, when the first book is deemed more relevant to the curriculum, or better written, or when one of a host of other politically neutral reasons is present. These decisions obviously will not implicate First Amendment values. And even absent space or financial limitations, First Amendment principles would allow a school board to refuse to make a book available to students because it contains offensive language, cf. *FCC* v. *Pacifica Foundation* (1978) (POWELL, J., concurring), or because it is psychologically or intellectually inappropriate for the age group, or even, perhaps, because the ideas it advances are "manifestly inimical to the public welfare." *Pierce* v. *Society of Sisters* (1925). And, of course, school officials may choose one book over another because they believe that one subject is more important, or is more deserving of emphasis.

As is evident from this discussion, I do not share JUSTICE REHNQUIST's view that the notion of "suppression of ideas" is not a useful analytical concept. Indeed, JUSTICE REHNQUIST's discussion itself demonstrates that "access to ideas" has been given meaningful application in a variety of contexts. . . . And I believe that tying the First Amendment right to the *purposeful* suppression of ideas makes the concept more manageable than JUSTICE REHNQUIST acknowledges. Most people would recognize that refusing to allow discussion of current events in Latin class is a policy designed to "inculcate" Latin, not to suppress ideas. Similarly, removing a learned treatise criticizing American foreign policy from an elementary school library because the students would not understand it is an action unrelated to the *purpose* of suppressing ideas. In my view, however, removing the same treatise because it is "anti-American" raises a far more difficult issue. . . .

Concededly, a tension exists between the properly inculcative purposes of public education and any limitation on the school board's absolute discretion to choose academic materials. But that tension demonstrates only that the problem here is a difficult one, not that the problem should be resolved by choosing one principle over another. As the Court has recognized, school officials must have the authority to make educationally appropriate choices in designing a curriculum: "the State may 'require teaching by instruction and study of all in our history and in the structure and organization of our government, including the guaranties of civil liberty, which tend to inspire patriotism and love of country.' " *Barnette*, quoting *Minersville School District* v. *Gobitis* (1940) (Stone, J., dissenting). Thus school officials may seek to instill certain values "by persuasion and example," or by choice of emphasis. That sort of positive educational action, however, is the converse of an intentional attempt to shield students from certain ideas that officials find politically distasteful. Arguing that the majority in the community rejects the ideas involved does not refute this principle: "The very purpose of a Bill of Rights was to withdraw certain subjects from the vicissitudes of political controversy, to place them beyond the reach of majorities and officials. . . ." *Barnette.*

As THE CHIEF JUSTICE notes, the principle involved here may be difficult to apply in an individual case. But on a record as sparse as the one before us, the plurality can hardly be faulted for failing to explore every possible ramification of its decision. And while the absence of a record "underscore[s] the views of those of us who originally felt that the [case] should not be taken," *Ferguson* v. *Moore-McCormack Lines* (1957) (Harlan, J., concurring and dissenting), the case is here, and must be decided.

Because I believe that the plurality has derived a standard similar to the one compelled by my analysis, I join all but Part IIA(1) of the plurality opinion.

CHIEF JUSTICE BURGER, with whom JUSTICE POWELL, JUSTICE REHNQUIST, and JUSTICE O'CONNOR join, dissenting.

The First Amendment, as with other parts of the Constitution, must deal with new problems in a changing world. In an attempt to deal with a problem in an area traditionally left to the states, a plurality of the Court, in a lavish expansion going beyond any prior holding under the First Amendment, expresses its view that a school board's decision concerning what books are to be in the school library is subject to federal court review. Were this to become the law, this Court would come perilously close to becoming a "super censor" of school board library decisions. Stripped to its essentials, the issue comes down to two important propositions: *first*, whether local schools are to be administered by elected school boards, or by federal judges and teenage pupils; and *second*, whether the values of morality, good taste, and relevance to education are valid reasons for school board decisions concerning the contents of a school library. In an attempt to place this case within the protection of the First Amendment, the plurality suggests a new "right" that, when shorn of the plurality's rhetoric, allows this Court to impose its own views about what books must be made available to students.

I

A

I agree with the fundamental proposition that "students do not 'shed their rights to freedom of speech or expression at the schoolhouse gate.'" ... Here, however, no restraints of any kind are placed on the students. They are free to read the books in question, which are available at public libraries and bookstores; they are free to discuss them in the classroom or elsewhere. Despite this absence of any direct external control on the students' ability to express themselves, the plurality suggest that there is a new First Amendment "entitlement" to have access to particular books in a school library.

The plurality cites *Meyer* v. *Nebraska* (1923), which struck down a state law that restricted the teaching of modern foreign languages in public and private schools, and *Epperson* v. *Arkansas* (1968), which declared unconstitutional under the Establishment Clause a law banning the teaching of

Darwinian evolution, to establish the validity of federal court interference with the functioning of schools. The plurality finds it unnecessary "to re-enter this difficult terrain," yet in the next breath relies on these very cases and others to establish the previously unheard of "right" of access to particular books in the public school library. The apparent underlying basis of the plurality's view seems to be that students have an enforceable "right" to receive the information and ideas that are contained in junior and senior high school library books. This "right" purportedly follows "ineluctably" from the sender's First Amendment right to freedom of speech and as a "necessary predicate" to the recipient's meaningful exercise of his own rights of speech, press, and political freedom. No such right, however, has previously been recognized.

It is true that where there is a willing distributor of materials, the government may not impose unreasonable obstacles to disseminate by the third party. *Virginia State Board of Pharmacy* v. *Virginia Citizens Consumer Council, Inc.* (1976). And where the speaker desires to express certain ideas, the government may not impose unreasonable restraints. *Tinker* v. *Des Moines School Dist.* It does not follow, however, that a school board must affirmatively aid the speaker in its communication with the recipient. In short the plurality suggests today that if a writer has something to say, the government through its schools must be the courier. None of the cases cited by the plurality establish this broad-based proposition.

First, the plurality argues that the right to receive ideas is derived in part from the sender's first amendment rights to send them. Yet we have previously held that a sender's rights are not absolute. *Rowan* v. *Post Office Dept.* (1970). Never before today has the Court indicated that the government has an *obligation* to aid a speaker or author in reaching an audience.

Second, the plurality concludes that "the right to receive ideas is a necessary predicate to the *recipient's* meaningful exercise of his own rights of speech, press, and political freedom." However, the "right to receive information and ideas," *Stanley* v. *Georgia* (1969), does not carry with it the concomitant right to have those ideas affirmatively provided at a particular place by the government. The plurality cites James Madison to emphasize the importance of having an informed citizenry. We all agree with Madison, of course, that knowledge is necessary for effective government. Madison's view, however, does not establish a *right* to have particular books retained on the school library shelves if the school board decides that they are inappropriate or irrelevant to the school's mission. . . .

The plurality also cites *Tinker* to establish that the recipient's right to free speech encompasses a right to have particular books retained in the school library shelf. But the cited passage of *Tinker* notes only that school officials may not *prohibit* a student from expressing his or her view on a subject unless that expression interferes with the legitimate operations of the school. The government does not "contract the spectrum of available knowledge," *Griswold* v. *Connecticut* (1965) by choosing not to retain certain books on the school library shelf; it simply chooses not to be the conduit for that particular information. In short, even assuming the desirability of the policy expressed by the plurality, there is not a hint in the First Amendment, or in any holding of this Court, of a "right" to have the government provide continuing access to certain books.

B

Whatever role the government might play as a conduit of information, schools in particular ought not be made a slavish courier of the material of third parties. The plurality pays homage to the ancient verity that in the administration of the public schools "there is a legitimate and substantial community interest in promoting respect for authority and traditional values be they social, moral, or political." If, as we have held, schools may legitimately be used as vehicles for "inculcating fundamental values necessary to the maintenance of a democratic political system," *Ambach* v. *Norwick* (1979), school authorities must have broad discretion to fufill that obligation. Presumably all activity within a primary or secondary school involves the conveyance of information and at least an implied approval of the worth of that information. How are "fundamental values" to be inculcated except by having school boards make content-based decisions about the appropriateness of retaining materials in the school library and curriculum. In order to fulfill its function, an elected school board *must* express its views on the subjects which are taught to its students. In doing so those elected officials express the views of their community; they may err, of course, and the voters may remove them. It is a startling erosion of the very idea of democratic government to have this Court arrogate to itself the power the plurality asserts today.

The plurality concludes that under the Constitution school boards cannot choose to retain or dispense with books if their discretion is exercised in a "narrowly partisan or political manner." The plurality concedes that permissible factors are whether the books are "pervasively vulgar" or educationally unsuitable. "Educational suitability," however, is a standardless phrase. This conclusion will undoubtedly be drawn in many — if not most — instances because of the decisionmaker's content-based judgment that the ideas contained in the book or the idea expressed from the author's method of communication are inappropriate for teenage pupils.

The plurality also tells us that a book may be removed from a school library if it is "pervasively vulgar." But why must the vulgarity be "pervasive" to be offensive? Vulgarity might be concentrated in a single poem or a single chapter or a single page, yet still be inappropriate. Or a school board might reasonably conclude that even "random" vulgarity is inappropriate for teenage school students. A school board might also reasonably conclude that the school board's retention of such books gives those volumes an implicit endorsement. Cf. *FCC* v. *Pacifica Foundation* (1978).

Further, there is no guidance whatsoever as to what constitutes "political" factors. This Court has previously recognized that public education involves an area of broad public policy and "go[es] to the heart of representative government." *Ambach* v. *Norwick* (1979). As such, virtually all educational decisions necessarily involve "political" determinations.

What the plurality views as valid reasons for removing a book at their core involve partisan judgments. Ultimately the federal courts will be the judge of whether the motivation for book removal was "valid" or "reasonable." Undoubtedly the validity of many book removals will ultimately turn on a judge's evaluation of the books. Discretion must be used, and the appropriate body to exercise that discretion is the local elected school board, not judges.

We can all agree that as a matter of *educational policy* students should have wide access to information and ideas. But the people elect school boards, who in turn elect administrators, who select the teachers, and these are the individuals best able to determine the substance of that policy. The plurality fails to recognize the fact that local control of education involves democracy in a microcosm. In most public schools in the United States the *parents* have a large voice in running the school. Through participation in the election of school board members, the parents influence, if not control, the direction of their children's education. A school board is not a giant bureaucracy far removed from accountability for its actions; it is truly "of the people and by the people." A school board reflects its constituency in a very real sense and thus could not long exercise unchecked discretion in its choice to acquire or remove books. If the parents disagree with the educational decisions of the school board, they can take steps to remove the board members from office. Finally, even if parents and students cannot convince the school board that book removal is inappropriate, they have alternative sources to the same end. Books may be acquired from books stores, public libraries, or other alternative sources unconnected with the unique environment of the local public schools.

II

No amount of "limiting" language could rein in the sweeping "right" the plurality would create. The plurality distinguishes library books from textbooks because library books "by their nature are optional rather than required reading." It is not clear, however, why this distinction requires *greater* scrutiny before "optional" reading materials may be removed. It would appear that required reading and textbooks have a greater likelihood of imposing a " 'pall of orthodoxy' " over the educational process than do optional reading. In essence, the plurality's view transforms the availability of this "optional" reading into a "right" to have this "optional" reading maintained at the demand of teenagers.

The plurality also limits the new right by finding it applicable only to the *removal* of books once acquired. Yet if the First Amendment commands that certain books cannot be *removed*, does it not equally require that the same books be *acquired?* Why does the coincidence of timing become the basis of a constitutional holding? According to the plurality, the evil to be avoided is the "official suppression of ideas." It does not follow that the decision to *remove* a book is less "official suppression" than the decision not to acquire a book desired by someone. Similarly, a decision to eliminate certain material from the curriculum, history for example, would carry an equal — probably greater — prospect of "official suppression." Would the decision be subject to our review?

III

Through use of bits and pieces of prior opinions unrelated to the issue of this case, the plurality demeans our function of constitutional adjudication. Today the plurality suggests that the *Constitution* distinguishes between school libraries and school classrooms, between *removing* unwanted books and *acquiring* books. Even more extreme, the plurality concludes that the Constitution *requires* school boards to justify to its teenage pupils the decision to remove a particular book from a school library. I categorically reject this notion that the Constitution dictates that judges, rather than parents, teachers, and local school boards, must determine how the standards of morality and vulgarity are to be treated in the classroom.

JUSTICE POWELL, dissenting.

The plurality opinion today rejects a basic concept of public school education in our country: that the States and locally elected school boards should have the responsibility for determining the educational policy of the public schools. After today's decision any junior high school student, by instituting a suit against a school board or teacher, may invite a judge to overrule an educational decision by the official body designated by the people to operate the schools.

I

School boards are uniquely local and democratic institutions. Unlike the governing bodies of cities and counties, school boards have only one responsibility: the education of the youth of our country during their most formative and impressionable years. Apart from health, no subject is closer to the hearts of parents than their children's education during those years. For these reasons, the governance of elementary and secondary education traditionally has been placed in the hands of a local board, responsible locally to the parents and citizens of school districts. Through parent-teacher associations (PTAs), and even less formal arrangements that vary with schools, parents are informed and often may influence decisions of the board. Frequently, parents know the teachers and visit classes. It is fair to say that no single agency of government at any level is closer to the people whom it serves than the typical school board.

I therefore view today's decision with genuine dismay. Whatever the final outcome of this suit and suits like it, the resolution of educational policy decisions through litigation, and the exposure of school board members to liability for such decisions, can be expected to corrode the school board's authority and effectiveness. As is evident from the generality of the plurality's "standard" for judicial review, the decision as to the educational worth of a book is a highly subjective one. Judges rarely are as competent as school authorities to make this decision; nor are judges responsive to the parents and people of the school district. . . .

DONOVAN REPORTS
June 25, September 10, 1982

Twice during 1982 Secretary of Labor Raymond J. Donovan was cleared of allegations that before his appointment he engaged in illegal labor practices and was linked to organized crime. The first investigation took six months and resulted in a 1,025-page report, dated June 25. Making his findings public June 28, Special Prosecutor Leon Silverman said that there was "no evidence" to charge Donovan with any crimes while he was an executive of a New Jersey corporation, Schiavone Construction Co. While Silverman was winding up his activities as prosecutor, he was told of additional allegations concerning Donovan. The second investigation ended with a much shorter report issued September 10, also clearing Donovan.

The probes were conducted under the Federal Ethics in Government Act that required the appointment of a special investigator to look into charges and, if necessary, to prosecute allegations of wrongdoing by high government officials. Silverman, a New York lawyer with Fried, Frank, Harris, Shriver & Jacobson since 1949, was named special prosecutor December 29, 1981. Known for his participation in public affairs, he formerly headed the Legal Aid Society and is the president of the American College of Trial Lawyers.

The first investigation was sparked by an allegation made by former union leader Mario Montuoro that Donovan had witnessed an illegal labor payoff in 1977 while lunching at Prudenti's Restaurant in Long Island City, N.Y. Montuoro said that Joseph A. DiCarolis, senior vice-president of Schiavone Construction, gave an envelope containing $2,000 to Louis C. Sanzo, a union official. Montuoro said that the money was *given to Sanzo in plain view of all in attendance, including Donovan, and that DiCarolis said it was given by the construction company as a token of appreciation. The grand jury refused to bring charges based on this allegation, and Silverman concluded that the alleged luncheon never took place.*

At the conclusion of the first investigation, three matters not cleared up were forwarded to the appropriate federal agencies. The first was the gangland-style murder of a witness, Frederick S. Furino; the second was alleged evidence that Donovan's company paid employees who were not actually working on a construction site. The third was the possibility that Donovan's firm may have violated campaign fund-raising laws.

A new set of allegations, not disclosed to the public, led Silverman to reopen his inquiry. This investigation attracted media attention when Nathan Masselli, son of scheduled witness William Masselli, was murdered August 25, 48 hours before his father was to testify before the grand jury. Silverman did not disclose why William Masselli was going to be questioned. The older Masselli said he did not know why his son had been killed, but he did not connect it to the Donovan probe. In the September 10 report Silverman denied that Nathan Masselli was an undercover informant working for Silverman. The report stated that no prosecutable evidence had been found of organized crime links to Donovan and that some allegations had been fabricated.

Reports of Donovan's alleged connections with organized crime first surfaced in late 1980 when President-elect Ronald Reagan chose him as his labor secretary. Donovan's confirmation was delayed two weeks while the FBI and the Senate Labor and Human Resources Committee investigated his background. Routine FBI "name checks" run on Donovan and Schiavone Construction in December 1980 uncovered no evidence of criminality or organized crime ties. The September 10 report contained memorandums written by FBI Director William H. Webster on the Donovan check.

Donovan was confirmed by the Senate February 3, 1981, by a vote of 80-17, the largest number of votes against any Reagan Cabinet nominee. All the votes against came from Democrats.

Donovan was born August 31, 1930, in Bayonne, N.J. He graduated from Notre Dame Seminary in New Orleans in 1952 and worked for the American Insurance Co. until 1958 when he went to work for Schiavone Construction. In 1971 he became its executive vice president. Schiavone, located in Secaucus, N.J., was one of the largest U.S. construction companies, building mostly bridges and tunnels.

At the close of the September investigation Donovan said, "I am not pleased and I am not gratified. I am angry. Angry that I have had to endure months and months of relentless press coverage of groundless charges made by nameless accusers; angry that my wife and children have suffered as only a family can suffer; angry that my former business associates have been unfairly maligned. I have always known that the charges against me were lies, and I have told you so."

Silverman estimated the cost of the inquiry to be nearly $1 million; $300,000 borne by the federal government and about $600,000 absorbed by Silverman's legal firm.

Following are excerpts from two reports on the investigation into alleged criminal activities of Secretary of Labor Raymond J. Donovan, issued by Special Prosecutor Leon Silverman June 25, 1982, and September 10:

JUNE 25 REPORT
Part Two: Results of Investigation
GENERAL SUMMARY

In accordance with the December 29 [1981] Order, the Special Prosecutor's investigation (the "investigation") initially focused on the Prudenti's [Restaurant] allegation. Exhaustive efforts were undertaken in the search for any corroboration, testimonial or documentary, for the assertion of the source of the allegation, Mario Montuoro. As Section IV of this Report reflects, no such corroboration was forthcoming from any source. It is the conclusion of the Special Prosecutor that there is insufficient credible evidence upon which to base a prosecution of Secretary Donovan with respect to the Prudenti's allegation. The grand jury so concluded on June 8, 1982, when it unanimously returned a no true bill with respect to that allegation.

In addition to the Prudenti's allegation, other allegations were presented by Montuoro and others. Pursuant to decretal paragraph 3 of the December 29 Order, the Special Prosecutor investigated all such allegations. Each of the additional allegations made by Montuoro, however, related to alleged wrongdoing which, Montuoro acknowledged, did not necessarily involve Secretary Donovan. Montuoro presented no facts implicating the Secretary. The Special Prosecutor's investigation of those additional Montuoro allegations led to the conclusion that there was no evidence linking Secretary Donovan to any of the alleged wrongdoing. The grand jury declined on June 18, 1982, to indict the Secretary for any offense with respect to his testimony before the grand jury concerning the additional Montuoro allegations.

However, the investigation revealed evidence corroborating one of the Montuoro allegations — that there were so-called "no-show" employees on one of Schiavone Construction Company's New York City construction projects. Moreover, in the view of the Special Prosecutor, there is evidence that perjury was committed before the Special Prosecutor's grand jury with respect to the no-show allegation. However, because that perjury was not committed by Secretary Donovan, and because it did not involve or implicate the Secretary or any other person covered by the Ethics in Government Act, the Special Prosecutor determined to refer that matter to the Department of Justice for further action.

Aside from Montuoro, a number of other sources, many of them anonymous, alleged that Secretary Donovan was in one fashion or another connected to reputed organized crime figures. More than two dozen organized crime ties were alleged, many of them by more than one source. Extensive investigation produced insufficient credible evidence upon which to base any prosecution that the Secretary was untruthful in his denials, either before the Senate Labor Committee or the grand jury, of any and all such associations. The Special Prosecutor concluded that, despite the disturbing number of such allegations, a prosecution would not be warranted. On June 18 and 22, 1982, the grand jury unanimously returned a no true bill with respect to all organized crime allegations put before it.

Shortly after the Special Prosecutor's appointment, there surfaced in the media an allegation that Secretary Donovan had in 1978 made an illegal payoff to a union leader in connection with *The Trib*, a short-lived New York City newspaper. Some months later, an anonymous source made a similar allegation. The Special Prosecutor's investigation disclosed that the anonymous source's charge was unsupported. The investigation also produced no evidence that any illegal payoff had in fact been made. In the absence of sufficient credible evidence that Secretary Donovan testified falsely before the grand jury concerning *The Trib*, the Special Prosecutor concluded that no prosecution was warranted. The grand jury unanimously voted not to indict the Secretary with respect to that allegation on June 18, 1982.

As a result of information that came to the Special Prosecutor during the investigation, the Special Prosecutor also investigated to determine whether Secretary Donovan had committed any violations of the Federal Elections Campaign Act of 1971 in connection with the Secretary's campaign efforts on behalf of Ronald Reagan during the Presidential campaign of 1979-1980. A detailed investigation into the Secretary's, and Schiavone Construction Company's, campaign activities produced no evidence of violations sufficient under the established guidelines of the Department of Justice to warrant the recommendation of a criminal prosecution. In conformance with DOJ [Department of Justice] policy, the matter is being referred to the Federal Election Commission to determine whether any action within its jurisdiction is appropriate.

Three other allegations of Taft-Hartley Act violations were also investigated by the Special Prosecutor. In two of the three cases, there was no evidence that any such violation had occurred. The third case did not involve the payment of money to any union officials but, rather, the entertainment of union officials at Fiddler's Elbow Country Club, a Schiavone Construction Company subsidiary. Although an arguable, technical violation may have been committed, the Special Prosecutor determined that no prosecution was appropriate under settled Department of Justice prosecutive guidelines.

The Special Prosecutor also investigated an allegation that the Secretary was involved in certain improprieties on New Jersey Turnpike Authority projects. The allegation included a charge that Mr. Donovan received inside information from the Turnpike Authority's Executive Director. The investigation revealed no evidence of any bid-rigging, provision or receipt of inside information or any other wrongdoing on the part of Secretary Donovan, and the Special Prosecutor determined that no prosecution was warranted. On June 18, 1982, the grand jury voted unanimously not to indict Secretary Donovan on that charge.

In sum, there was insufficient credible evidence to warrant a prosecution of Secretary Donovan on any charge. The grand jury declined to indict the Secretary with respect to every allegation it considered. The Special Prosecutor concludes that no prosecution of the Secretary, on any of the allegations investigated, is warranted or could successfully be maintained.

IV. The Prudenti's Allegation

The December 29 Order appoints the Special Prosecutor to investigate, *inter alia*, "the allegation that in May or June 1977, at Long Island City, New York, Secretary of Labor Raymond J. Donovan, who at that time was Executive Vice President of Schiavone Construction Company, was present when an official of the company made an illegal cash payment to a union official in violation of 29 U.S.C. § 186...."

Summary

1. *Allegation.* The Prudenti's allegation is the charge of Mario Nicholas Montuoro that, in 1977, Mr. Donovan attended a luncheon at Prudenti's Vicin O Mare Ristorante ("Prudenti's" or the "restaurant") in Long Island City, Queens, together with Schiavone Construction Company ("SCC") Chairman and President Ronald A. Schiavone, Senior Vice President Joseph A. DiCarolis, and Project Manager Gennaro (Jerry) Liguori, and two New York City union officials, Louis C. Sanzo and Montuoro himself. During the luncheon, Montuoro maintains, DiCarolis handed an envelope containing $2,000 to Sanzo in plain view of all in attendance, with words to the effect that the envelope contained a token of appreciation from SCC. Mr. Donovan was allegedly sitting beside DiCarolis, who, in the SCC corporate hierarchy, was Mr. Donovan's subordinate.

2. *Results of Investigation.* Each of the other persons identified by Montuoro as having attended the alleged luncheon categorically denied Montuoro's allegations. Both of the individuals whom Montuoro also

claimed to have seen at the restaurant specifically denied Montuoro's assertions as related to them. None of Prudenti's waitresses employed in 1977, nor the bartender nor any of the three family members who owned the establishment, corroborated Montuoro's charges.

In an exhaustive search, no documentary evidence of the alleged luncheon was found to exist. Moreover, none of Montuoro's efforts to fix the date of the luncheon proved availing; quite the contrary, they conflicted irreconcilably with one another. Furthermore, substantial physical evidence contradicted elements of Montuoro's story — a story which varied in significant detail each time it was repeated.

The grand jury unanimously returned a no true bill on June 8, 1982.

The Special Prosecutor concludes that no credible evidence exists that a luncheon as alleged by Montuoro ever occurred. . . .

SEPTEMBER 10 REPORT

IX. SUBSEQUENT DOCUMENTS

A. The Documents

Subsequent to the Special Prosecutor's submission of his report on June 26, 1982, he was provided with the following three documents relating to communications between Director William H. Webster of the FBI and Edwin Meese, then Chief of [the] President-Elect Reagan Transition effort and currently Counsellor to the President.

1. **December 5, 1980, Memorandum.** On December 5, 1980, Director Webster prepared a handwritten notation following a conference with Edwin Meese. The director's personal note stated, in pertinent part:

> 12-5-8 [0]
> Cf. Ed Meese - 3 p.m.
> 1) P. [or R.] Donovan inq. OK to do full field if any OC - but I will call Ed first
> 2) Wants to direct contact with *James Baker* for W.H. appointments - C. Monroe

2. **December 15, 1980, Memorandum.** Following the December 5, 1980, conference with Edwin Meese, Director Webster had further communications with Transition personnel, including Counsellor Meese, on the subject of the proposed nomination of Mr. Donovan. The following memorandum to then FBI Executive Assistant Director (and currently DEA [Drug Enforcement Administration] acting head) Mullen [Francis M. Mullen Jr.], the Director wrote as follows concerning these communications:

> RE: TRANSITION —
> Mr. Edwin Meese called during my absence at 10:15 a.m. 12/12/80, and said that he would return the call upon my return. He was tied up

with President-elect Reagan and asked Mr. Pen [E. Pendleton] James to return the call. Mr. James asked whether we had reached any conclusion as a result of our inquiry into Pat [sic] Donovan. I checked with Mr. [Oliver B.] Revell and based on information which he supplied, as well as my recollection of conversation with Mr. Mullen while I was in New York on December 10th, that we had reviewed all our indices and had checked with all field offices and nothing negative had been disclosed. I advised that a company, Chivone (PH), in which he apparently had a very substantial interest, had appeared a number of times in reports in our HOFEX [sic: Hoffex] [Hoffa investigation] case, but that none of these suggested any criminality or organized crime associations.

I further advised that it did not appear necessary, in our view, to conduct a full field investigation based on the results of the name check. Mr. James said that he might need our assistance in the course of the confirmation proceedings and, I, of course, stated that we would do whatever we could to help.

I advised that the report had been sent to Miss Jane Danower (PH), Mr. Fielding's secretary. Mr. Fielding was present with Mr. James at the time of our conversation, and was not aware that the report had been delivered.

3. **Addendum to December 15, 1980, Memorandum.** The Director also dictated an addendum to the December 15, 1980, memorandum, which recited:

ADDENEDUM:
Mr. Meese called at 4:40 p.m., 12/12/80, and wanted to be certain that there were no on-going investigations involving Donovan. I confirmed to him, based on what I had been previously advised, that this was the case. We will certainly be asked for a full field following the nomination, but I told him that I know of nothing to hold up the nomination at this time.

B. The Investigation

1. **Edwin Meese.** In the course of his interview with the Special Prosecutor on August 12, 1982, Edwin Meese stated that he had not recalled the December 5, 1980, meeting between himself and Director Webster until he saw the Director's notation and had discussed the matter with another former member of the Transition Effort. Mr. Meese described the December 5, 1980, meeting with Webster as "kind of a get acquainted meeting," his first conference with the Director. Mr. Meese stated that he mentioned the possibility of organized crime ties involving Mr. Donovan because a newspaper columnist had suggested to a Transition official that some such ties might exist. Mr. Meese stated that he advised Director Webster purely as a precaution. There was no specific

allegation, to the best of Mr. Meese's knowledge.

2. **William H. Webster.** The Special Prosecutor spoke with Director Webster of the FBI on August 13, 1982. With respect to the December 5, 1980, memorandum, the Director stated that, to the best of his recollection, neither he nor Edwin Meese had any specific information concerning possible organized crime connections involving Secretary Donovan. Mr. Meese conveyed none to him, the Director said. It was agreed that, if, in the ordinary name check performed by the FBI, the Bureau came upon any organized crime links to Mr. Donovan, it might be advisable to do a full field check prior to the time that the President finally decided to nominate Mr. Donovan. Mr. Meese stated that he would prefer to be called in advance of any full field investigation.

With respect to the December 15, 1980, memorandum, Director Webster stated that the Hoffex reference is incorrect — that, at the time of the December 12, 1980, communications, the Hoffex files had not been checked. Moreover, the Director stated that files had recently been checked and it was determined that there were no references to SCC [Schiavone Construction Co.] therein.

The Director attributed that erroneous Hoffex reference to information which he received from certain subordinates. He was uncertain as to which of the subordinates provided it. He stated that he did not know where he would independently come up with the Hoffex reference since he was not particularly familiar with the details of that file.

The Director concluded by noting that, at the December 5, 1980, meeting, he had advised Meese what the FBI would do if it were to learn any facts associating Mr. Donovan with organized crime in any fashion. The December 15, 1980, communications were to confirm that the Bureau had in fact found nothing in that regard.

3. **Oliver B. Revell.** Oliver B. Revell, Assistant Director in Charge of the FBI Criminial Investigative Division, was interviewed by a member of the Special Prosecutor's staff on September 3, 1982. Among other things, Revell confirmed that on or before December 12, 1980, he had informed Director Webster that the "name check" of Secretary Donovan — consisting of a review of headquarters' central indices and the Identification Division records — had been completed and was negative. Revell informed the Director that the Bureau's Organized Crime Information System, which was then relatively new and which included information from 22 offices, had been accessed and was negative.

Revell did not direct a review of the Hoffex file in December 1980; he had no reason to do so, he said. During the summer of 1982, after the Director's December 15 memorandum became a topic of public discussion, a review was conducted. No references to Raymond (or Pat) Donovan or Schiavone (or Chiavone) Construction Company were found. Moreoever, no one associated with the Hoffa investigation had any recollection that the name of either Mr. Donovan or SCC ever arose in the course of that investigation. Revell did not know the source of the reference to the Hoffex investigation contained in the December 15 memorandum. . . .

C. Conclusion of the Special Prosecutor

The December 5 and 15, 1980, documents became the subject of investigation because they reflected the first mention of possible organized crime ties of Mr. Donovan. The Special Prosecutor sought to determine if this mention arose out of specific information which had not previously come to light and which might provide additional investigative leads. Further, the reference in the December 15 memorandum to the Hoffex file conflicted with the Special Prosecutor's understanding that neither Mr. Donovan nor SCC were mentioned therein. The Special Prosecutor is satisfied that no specific information has been overlooked and that no further investigation is warranted.

X. FURTHER MATTERS

A. On September 8, 1982, the FBI showed the Special Prosecutor the transcript of a conversation recorded in the course of a major organized crime investigation in which there was a reference to Secretary Donovan. The Special Prosecutor's review of the transcript revealed the reference to be casual and non-incriminating in nature.

In a meeting with the Special Prosecutor on September 8, 1982, FBI officials expressed concern to the Special Prosecutor that an investigation into the reference to Mr. Donovan would lead to identifying, and thereby jeopardizing, the source of the conversation and the on-going FBI investigation. By letter dated September 8, 1982, the officials reiterated those concerns and urged the Special Prosecutor not to pursue this lead.

In view of the lack of any criminal aspects to the reference to Secretary Donovan and the risk both to the source and to the major organized crime investigation if the reference were pursued, the Special Prosecutor determined not to pursue the information further.

B. On August 25, 1982, at approximately 8:30 p.m., Nat Masselli, the son of William Masselli, was murdered. Nat Masselli had been interviewed by the Special Prosecutor in early May 1982, in the first phase of the investigation.[14] He had no role in the reopened investigation and was not interviewed or scheduled either to be interviewed or summoned as a witness.

Because Nat Masselli's murder occurred less than 48 hours before his father's scheduled grand jury testimony, the possibility that there existed some link between the murder and this investigation could not be ignored. Therefore, on the very night of the murder, the Special Prosecutor requested a fullscale FBI investigation into any possible federal criminal offense arising out of the murder, including but not limited to obstruction of justice. The FBI commenced its investigation at once.

---

[14] Contrary to innumerable media reports following his death, Nat Masselli was never a federal informant nor did he ever wear any electronic surveillance or eavesdropping devices ("body wires") on behalf of the Special Prosecutor. . . .

On the basis of the investigation to date, there appears to be no evidence of a relationship between the Masselli murder and Secretary Donovan. Nor is there any reason to believe that any such relationship will or might later be established. Accordingly, the FBI has been directed to report the results of its investigation to the Attorney General for any action which might be required by reason thereof.

COURT ON BANKRUPTCY LAW
June 28, 1982

Ruling on a key portion of the Bankruptcy Reform Act of 1978, the Supreme Court held June 28 that the law's bankruptcy court system was unconstitutional because it gave those courts more power than Article III of the Constitution allows for judges with less than complete independence from the other branches of government. The court gave Congress three months to rewrite the law, a deadline that was not met even though it was later extended to December 24.

Justice William J. Brennan Jr. wrote the majority opinion, which was joined by Justices Thurgood Marshall, Harry A. Blackmun and John Paul Stevens. Justice William H. Rehnquist wrote a separate opinion concurring in the decision, joined by Justice Sandra Day O'Connor. Justice Byron R. White wrote the dissenting opinion, joined by Chief Justice Warren E. Burger and Justice Lewis F. Powell Jr. Burger also filed a brief dissenting opinion.

Background

In the cases under consideration, Northern Pipeline Construction Co. v. Marathon Pipe Line Co. and the United States and United States v. Marathon Pipe Line Co., Northern had filed for reorganization in a bankruptcy court and had also filed for damages against Marathon for alleged breach of contract, misrepresentation, coercion and duress. Marathon sought dismissal on the ground that the bankruptcy law unconstitutionally conferred Article III judicial powers upon judges who lacked life tenure and protection against cuts in salary. The bankruptcy court

597

denied the motion to dismiss, but the district court granted the motion on appeal.

Before passage of the 1978 law, bankruptcy cases had been handled by specially appointed officials called "referees." Because these "referees" did not have the power to rule on certain matters considered peripheral to bankruptcy cases, such matters often had to be referred to federal district court judges.

The 1978 act was passed in an attempt to simplify this inefficient procedure and to avoid disputes over what bankruptcy questions fell under the jurisdiction of federal courts. Under the law, new bankruptcy courts were created and new bankruptcy judges were given broad jurisdiction in resolving any kind of civil case relating to a bankrupt individual or organization, such as a contract, antitrust or labor relations case.

The new judges were to be appointed by the president for 14-year terms. Their salaries were to be fixed by law, but subject to adjustment. In these respects, the position of the judges differed from federal district judges, whose independence is protected by life tenure and salaries that cannot be reduced.

In its 6-3 decision, the court held that Congress had conferred too much power on the new judges without giving them the complete independence required by Article III. To accept the new bankruptcy courts would be to endorse "a rule of broad legislative discretion that could effectively eviscerate the constitutional gurarantee of an independent judicial branch of the federal government," wrote Brennan in the majority opinion.

By the end of 1982, Congress had failed to make any changes in the bankruptcy reform law and bankruptcy cases were once again being referred to federal district judges.

White's Dissent

In the dissent White argued that the bankruptcy law was constitutional because its judgments could be appealed to Article III courts, the U.S. courts of appeal or the Supreme Court. He stated that he would have deferred to the judgment of Congress in creating the bankruptcy law and that the "majority's position on adjudication of state law claims is based on an abstract theory that has little to do with the reality of bankruptcy proceedings."

Following are excerpts from the Supreme Court's June 28 opinion in Northern Pipeline Construction Co. v. Marathon Pipe Line Co. *that the bankruptcy court system was unconstitutional:*

No. 81-150

Northern Pipeline Construction Co., Appellant *v.* Marathon Pipe Line Company and United States	On appeals from the United States District Court for the District of Minnesota

[June 28, 1982*]

JUSTICE BRENNAN announced the judgment of the Court and delivered an opinion in which JUSTICE MARSHALL, JUSTICE BLACKMUN and JUSTICE STEVENS joined.

The question presented is whether the assignment by Congress to bankruptcy judges of the jurisdiction granted in § 241 (a) of the Bankruptcy Act of 1978, 28 U.S.C. § 1471, violates Art. III of the Constitution.

I

A

In 1978, after almost ten years of study and investigation, Congress enacted a comprehensive version of the bankruptcy laws. The Bankruptcy Act of 1978 (Act) made significant changes in both the substantive and procedural law of bankruptcy. It is the changes in the latter that are at issue in this case.

Before the Act, federal district courts served as bankruptcy courts and employed a "referee" system. Bankruptcy proceedings were generally conducted before referees, except in those instances in which the district court elected to withdraw a case from a referee. The referee's final order was appealable to the district court. The bankruptcy courts were vested with "summary jurisdiction" — that is, with jurisdiction over controversies involving property in the actual or constructive possession of the court. And, with consent, the bankruptcy court also had jurisdiction over some "plenary" matters — such as disputes involving property in the possession of a third person.

The Act eliminates the referee system and establishes "in each judicial district, as an adjunct to the district court for such district, a bankruptcy court which shall be a court of record known as the United States Bankruptcy Court for the district." The judges of these courts are appointed to office for 14-year terms by the President, with the advice and consent of the Senate. They are subject to removal by the "judicial council

---

*Together with No. 81-546, *United States* v. *Marathon Pipe Line Co. et al.*, also on appeal from the same court.

of the circuit" on account of "incompetence, misconduct, neglect of duty or physical or mental disability." In addition, the salaries of the bankruptcy judges are set by statute and are subject to adjustment under the Federal Salary Act.

The jurisdiction of the bankruptcy courts created by the Act is much broader than that exercised under the former referee system. Eliminating the distinction between "summary" and "plenary" jurisdiction, the Act grants the new courts jurisdiction over all "civil proceedings arising under title 11 [the Bankruptcy title] or arising in or *related to* cases under title 11." ([E]mphasis added). This jurisdictional grant empowers bankruptcy courts to entertain a wide variety of cases involving claims that may affect the property of the estate once a petition has been filed under title 11 of the Act. Included within the bankruptcy courts' jurisdiction are suits to recover accounts, controversies involving exempt property, actions to avoid transfers and payments as preferences or fraudulent conveyances, and causes of action owned by the debtor at the time of the petition for bankruptcy. The bankruptcy courts can hear claims based on state law as well as those based on federal law.

The judges of the bankruptcy courts are vested with all of the "powers of a court of equity, law and admiralty," except that they "may not enjoin another court or punish a criminal contempt not committed in the presence of the judge of the court or warranting a punishment of imprisonment." In addition to this broad grant of power, Congress has allowed bankruptcy judges the power to hold jury trials, to issue declaratory judgments, to issue writs of habeas corpus under certain circumstances, to issue all writs necessary in aid of the bankruptcy court's expanded jurisdiction and to issue any order, process or judgment that is necesary or appropriate to carry out the provisions of title 11, 11 U.S.C. § 105 (a).

The Act also establishes a special procedure for appeals from orders of bankruptcy courts. The circuit council is empowered to direct the Chief Judge of the circuit to designate panels of three bankruptcy judges to hear appeals. These panels have jurisdiction of all appeals from final judgments, orders, and decrees of bankruptcy courts, and, with leave of the panel, of interlocutory appeals. If no such appeals panel is designated, the district court is empowered to exercise appellate jurisdiction. The court of appeals is given jurisdiction over appeals from the appellate panels or from the district court. If the parties agree, a direct appeal to the court of appeals may be taken from a final judgment of a bankruptcy court.

The Act provides for a transition period before the new provisions take full effect in April 1984. During the transition period, previously existing bankruptcy courts continue in existence. Incumbent bankruptcy referees, who served six-year terms for compensation subject to adjustment by Congress, are to serve as bankruptcy judges until March 31, 1984, or until their successors take office. During this period they are empowered to exercise essentially all of the jurisdiction and powers discussed above. The procedure for taking appeals is similar to that provided after the transition period.

B

This case arises out of proceedings initiated in the United States Bankruptcy Court for the District of Minnesota after appellant Northern Pipeline Construction Co. (Northern) filed a petition for reorganization in January 1980. In March 1980 Northern, pursuant to the Act, filed in that court a suit against appellee Marathon Pipeline Co. (Marathon). Appellant sought damages for alleged breaches of contract and warranty, as well as for alleged misrepresentation, coercion, and duress. Marathon sought dismissal of the suit, on the ground that the Act unconstitutionally conferred Art. III judicial power upon judges who lacked life tenure and protection against salary diminution. The United States intervened to defend the validity of the statute.

The bankruptcy judge denied the motion to dismiss. But on appeal the District Court entered an order granting the motion, on the ground that "the delegation of authority in 28 U.S.C. § 1471 to the Bankruptcy Judges to try cases otherwise relegated under the Constitution to Article III judges" was unconstitutional. Both the United States and Northern filed notices of appeal in this Court. We noted probable jurisdiction. (1981).

II

A

Basic to the constitutional structure established by the Framers was their recognition that "The accumulation of all powers, legislative, executive, and judiciary, in the same hands, whether of one, a few, or many, and whether hereditary, self-appointed, or elective, may justly be pronounced the very definition of tyranny." To ensure against such tyranny, the Framers provided that the Federal Government would consist of three distinct Branches, each to exercise one of the governmental powers recognized by the Framers as inherently distinct. "The Framers regarded the checks and balances that they had built into the tripartite Federal Government as a self-executing safeguard against the encroachment or aggrandizement of one branch at the expense of the other." *Buckley* v. *Valeo* (1976).

The Federal Judiciary was therefore designed by the Framers to stand independent of the Executive and Legislature — to maintain the checks and balances of the constitutional structure, and also to guarantee that the process of adjudication itself remained impartial. . . . The Court has only recently reaffirmed the significance of this feature of the Framers' design: "A Judiciary free from control by the Executive and Legislature is essential if there is a right to have claims decided by judges who are free from potential domination by other branches of government." *United States* v. *Will* (1980).

As an inseparable element of the constitutional system of checks and balances, and as a guarantee of judicial impartiality, Art. III both defines the power and protects the independence of the Judicial Branch. It provides that "The judicial Power of the United States, shall be vested in one supreme Court, and in such inferior Courts as the Congress may from time to time ordain and establish." The inexorable command of this provision is clear and definite: The judicial power of the United States must be exercised by courts having the attributes prescribed in Art. III. Those attributes are also clearly set forth:

> "The Judges, both of the supreme and inferior Courts, shall hold their Offices during good Behaviour, and shall, at stated Times, receive for their Services, a Compensation, which shall not be diminished during their Continuance in Office."

The "good Behaviour" Clause guarantees that Art. III judges shall enjoy life tenure, subject only to removal by impeachment. *Toth* v. *Quarles* (1955). The Compensation Clause guarantees Art. III judges a fixed and irreducible compensation for their services. *United States* v. *Will.* Both of these provisions were incorporated into the Constitution to ensure the independence of the judiciary from the control of the executive and legislative branches of government. As we have only recently emphasized, "The Compensation Clause has its roots in the longstanding Anglo-American tradition of an independent Judiciary," while the principle of life tenure can be traced back at least as far as the Act of Settlement in 1701. To be sure, both principles were eroded during the late colonial period, but that departure did not escape notice and indignant rejection by the Revolutionary generation. Indeed, the guarantees eventually included in Art. III were clearly foreshadowed in the Declaration of Independence, "which, among the injuries and usurpations recited against the King of Great Britain, declared that he had 'made judges dependent on his will alone, for the tenure of their offices, and the amount and payment of their salaries.'" *O'Donoghue* v. *United States* (1933). The Framers thus recognized that

> "Next to permanency in office, nothing can contribute more to the independence of the judges than a fixed provision for their support. . . . In the general course of human nature, *a power over a man's subsistence amounts to a power over his will."* The Federalist No. 79 (A Hamilton).

In sum, our Constitution unambiguously enunciates a fundamental principle — that the "judicial Power of the United States" must be reposed in an independent Judiciary. It commands that the independence of the Judiciary be jealously guarded, and it provides clear institutional protections for that independence.

B

It is undisputed that the bankruptcy judges whose offices were created by the Bankruptcy Act of 1978 do not enjoy the protections constitutionally afforded to Art. III judges. The bankruptcy judges do not serve for life subject to their continued "good Behaviour." Rather, they are appointed for 14-year terms, and can be removed by the judicial council of the circuit in which they serve on grounds of "incompetence, misconduct, neglect of duty or physical or mental disability." Second, the salaries of the bankruptcy judges are not immune from diminution by Congress. In short, there is no doubt that the bankruptcy judges created by the Act are not Art. III judges.

That Congress chose to vest such broad jurisdiction in non-Art. III bankruptcy courts, after giving substantial consideration to the constitutionality of the Act, is of course reason to respect the congressional conclusion. See *Fullilove* v. *Klutznick* (1980) (opinion of BURGER, C.J.); *Palmore* v. *United States* (1973). See also *National Ins. Co.* v. *Tidewater Co.* (1949) (Frankfurter, J., dissenting). But at the same time,

> "Deciding whether a matter has in any measure been committed by the Constitution to another branch of government, or whether the action of that branch exceeds whatever authority has been committed, is itself a delicate exercise in constitutional interpretation, and is a responsibility of this Court as ultimate interpreter of the Constitution." *Baker* v. *Carr* (1962).

With these principles in mind, we turn to the question presented for decision: whether the Bankruptcy Act of 1978 violates the command of Art. III, that the judicial power of the United States must be vested in courts whose judges enjoy the protections and safeguards specified in that Article.

Appellants suggest two grounds for upholding the Act's conferral of broad adjudicative powers upon judges unprotected by Art. III. First, it is argued that "pursuant to its enumerated Article I powers, Congress may establish legislative courts that have jurisdiction to decide cases to which the Article III judicial power of the United States extends." Referring to our precedents upholding the validity of "legislative courts," appellants suggest that "the plenary grants of power in Article I permit Congress to establish non-Article III tribunals in 'specialized areas having particularized needs and warranting distinctive treatment,'" such as the area of bankruptcy law. . . . Second, appellants contend that even if the Constitution does require that this bankruptcy-related action be adjudicated in an Art. III court, the Act in fact satisfies that requirement. "Bankruptcy jurisdiction was vested in the district court" of the judicial district in which the bankruptcy court is located, "and the exercise of that jurisdiction by the adjunct bankruptcy court was made subject to appeal as of right to an Art. III court." Analogizing the role of the bankruptcy court to that of a special master, appellants urge us to conclude that this "adjunct" system established by Congress satisfies the requirements of Art. III. We consider these arguments in turn.

III

Congress did not constitute the bankruptcy courts as legislative courts. Appellants contend, however, that the bankruptcy courts could have been

so constituted, and that as a result the "adjunct" system in fact chosen by
Congress does not impermissibly encroach upon the judicial power. In
advancing this argument, appellants rely upon cases in which we have
identified certain matters that "congress may or may not bring within the
cognizance of [Art. III] courts, as it may deem proper." *Murray's Lessee* v.
Hoboken Land and Improvement Co. (1855). But when properly understood, these precedents represent no broad departure from the constitutional command that the judicial power of the United States must be
vested in Art. III courts. Rather, they reduce to three narrow situations not
subject to that command, each recognizing a circumstance in which the
grant of power to the Legislative and Executive Branches was historically
and constitutionally so exceptional that the congressional assertion of a
power to create legislative courts was consistent with, rather than threatening to, the constitutional mandate of separation of powers. These
precedents simply acknowledge that the literal command of Art. III,
assigning the judicial power of the United States to courts insulated from
Legislative or Executive interference, must be interpreted in light of the
historical context in which the Constitution was written, and of the
structural imperatives of the Constitution as a whole.

Appellants first rely upon a series of cases in which this Court has
upheld the creation by Congress of non-Art. III "territorial courts." This
exception from the general prescription of Art. III dates from the earliest
days of the Republic, when it was perceived that the Framers intended
that as to certain geographical areas, in which no State operated as
sovereign, Congress was to exercise the general powers of government. . . .
The Court followed the same reasoning when it reviewed Congress'
creation of non-Art. III courts in the District of Columbia. . . .

Appellants next advert to a second class of cases — those in which this
Court has sustained the exercise by Congress and the Executive of the
power to establish and administer courts martial. The situation in these
cases strongly resembles the situation with respect to territorial courts: It
too involves a constitutional grant of power that has been historically
understood as giving the political branches of Government extraordinary
control over the precise matter at issue. . . .

Finally, appellants rely on a third group of cases, in which this Court has
upheld the constitutionality of legislative courts and administrative agencies created by Congress to adjudicate cases involving "public rights.". . .

This doctrine may be explained in part by reference to the traditional
principle of sovereign immunity, which recognizes that the Government
may attach conditions to its consent to be sued. . . . [S]ee also *Ex parte Bakelite Corp.* (1929). But the public-rights doctrine also draws upon the
principle of separation of powers, and a historical understanding that
certain prerogatives were reserved to the political branches of government.
The doctrine extends only to matters arising "between the Government
and persons subject to its authority in connection with the performance of
the constitutional functions of the executive or legislative departments,"

Crowell v. *Benson* (1932), and only to matters that historically could have been determined exclusively by those departments. . . . The understanding of these cases is that the Framers expected that Congress would be free to commit such matters completely to non-judicial executive determination, and that as a result there can be no constitutional objection to Congress' employing the less drastic expedient of committing their determination to a legislative court or an administrative agency. *Crowell* v. *Benson.*

The public-rights doctrine is grounded in a historically recognized distinction between matters that could be conclusively determined by the Executive and Legislative Branches and matters that are "inherently . . . judicial." *Ex parte Bakelite Corp.* See *Murray's Lessee* v. *Hoboken Land & Improvement Co.* For example, the Court in *Murray's Lessee* looked to the law of England and the States at the time the Constitution was adopted, in order to determine whether the issue presented was customarily cognizable in the courts. Concluding that the matter had not traditionally been one for judicial determination, the Court perceived no bar to Congress' establishment of summary procedures, outside of Art. III courts, to collect a debt due to the Government from one of its customs agents. On the same premise, the Court in *Ex parte Bakelite Corp.* held that the Court of Customs Appeals had been properly constituted by Congress as a legislative court:

> "The *full* province of the court under the act creating it is that of determining matters arising between the Government and others in the executive administration and application of the customs laws. . . . The appeals include nothing which inherently or necessarily requires judicial determination, but only matters the determination of *which may be, and at times has been, committed exclusively to executive officers."* ([E]mphasis added).

The distinction between public rights and private rights has not been definitively explained in our precedents. Nor is it necessary to do so in the present case, for it suffices to observe that a matter of public rights must at a minimum arise "between the government and others." *Ex Parte Bakelite Corp.* In contrast, "the libility of one individual to another under the law as defined," *Crowell* v. *Benson,* is a matter of private rights. Our precedents clearly establish that *only* controversies in the former category may be removed from Art. III courts and delegated to legislative courts or administrative agencies for their determination. . . . Private-rights disputes, on the other hand, lie at the core of the historically recognized judicial power.

In sum, this Court has identified three situations in which Art. III does not bar the creation of legislative courts. In each of these situations, the Court has recognized certain exceptional powers bestowed upon Congress by the Constitution or by historical consensus. Only in the face of such an exceptional grant of power has the Court declined to hold the authority of Congress subject to the general prescriptions of Art. III.

We discern no such exceptional grant of power applicable in the case before us. The courts created by the Bankruptcy Act of 1978 do not lie exclusively outside the States of the Federal Union, like those in the District of Columbia and the territories. Nor do the bankruptcy courts bear any resemblance to courts martial, which are founded upon the Constitution's grant of plenary authority over the Nation's military forces to the Legislative and Executive Branches. Finally, the substantive legal rights at issue in the present action cannot be deemed "public rights." Appellants argue that a discharge in bankruptcy is indeed a "public right," similar to such congressionally created benefits as "radio station license, pilot licenses, and certificates for common carriers" granted by administrative agencies. But the restructuring of debtor-creditor relations, which is at the core of the federal bankruptcy power, must be distinguished from the adjudication of state-created private rights, such as the right to recover contract damages that is at issue in this case. The former may well be a "public right," but the latter obviously is not. Appellant Northern's right to recover contract damages to augment its estate is "one of private right, that is, of the liability of one individual to another under the law as defined." *Crowell* v. *Benson.*

Recognizing that the present case may not fall within the scope of any of our prior cases permitting the establishment of legislative courts, appellants argue that we should recognize an additional situation beyond the command of Art. III, sufficiently broad to sustain the Act. Appellants contend that Congress' constitutional authority to establish "uniform Laws on the subject of Bankruptcies throughout the United States," Art. I, § 8, cl. 4, carries with it an inherent power to establish legislative courts capable of adjudicating "bankruptcy related controversies." In support of this argument, appellants rely primarily upon a quotation from the opinion in *Palmore* v. *United States* (1973), in which we stated that

> "both Congress and this Court have recognized that ... the requirements of Art III, which are applicable where laws of national applicability and affairs of national concern are at stake, must in proper circumstances give way to accommodate plenary grants of power to Congress to legislate with respect to specialized areas having particularized needs and warranting distinctive treatment."

Appellants cite this language to support their proposition that a bankruptcy court created by Congress under its Art. I powers is constitutional, because the law of bankruptcy is a "specialized area," and Congress has found a "particularized need" that warrants "distinctive treatment."

Appellants' contention, in essence, is that pursuant to any of its Art. I powers, Congress may create courts free of Art. III's requirements whenever it finds that course expedient. This contention has been rejected in previous cases. See, *e.g., Atlas Roofing* v. *Occupational Safety Comm'n* [1977], *Toth* v. *Quarles* (1955). Although the cases relied upon by appellants demonstrate that independent courts are not required for *all* federal adjudications, those cases also make it clear that where Art. III does apply, all of the legislative powers specified in Art. I and elsewhere are subject to it....

The flaw in appellants' analysis is that it provides no limiting principle. It thus threatens to supplant completely our system of adjudication in independent Art. III tribunals and replace it with a system of "specialized" legislative courts. True, appellants argue that under their analysis Congress could create legislative courts pursuant only to some "specific" Art. I power, and "only when there is a particularized need for distinctive treatment." They therefore assert that their analysis would not permit Congress to replace the independent Art. III judiciary through a "wholesale assignment of federal judicial business to legislative courts." But these "limitations" are wholly illusory. For example, Art. I, § 8, empowers Congress to enact laws, *inter alia*, regulating interstate commerce and punishing certain crimes. On appellants' reasoning Congress could provide for the adjudication of these and "related" matters by judges and courts within Congress' exclusive control. The potential for encroachment upon powers reserved to the Judicial Branch through the device of "specialized" legislative courts is dramatically evidenced in the jurisdiction granted to the courts created by the Act before us. The broad range of questions that can be brought into a bankruptcy court because they are "related to cases under title 11" is the clearest proof that even when Congress acts through a "specialized" court, and pursuant to only one of its many Art. I powers, appellants' analysis fails to provide any real protection against the erosion of Art. III jurisdiction by the unilateral action of the political branches. In short, to accept appellants' reasoning would require that we replace the principles delineated in our precedents, rooted in history and the Constitution, with a rule of broad legislative discretion that could effectively eviscerate the constitutional guarantee of an independent Judicial Branch of the Federal Government. . . .

In sum, Art. III bars Congress from establishing legislative courts to exercise jurisdiction over all matters related to those arising under the bankruptcy laws. The establishment of such courts does not fall within any of the historically recognized situations in which the general principle of independent adjudication commanded by Art. III does not apply. Nor can we discern any persuasive reason, in logic, history, or the Constitution, why the bankruptcy courts here established lie beyond the reach of Art. III.

IV

Appellants advance a second argument for upholding the constitutionality of the Act: that "viewed within the entire judicial framework set up by Congress," the bankruptcy court is merely an "adjunct" to the district court, and that the delegation of certain adjudicative functions to the bankruptcy court is accordingly consistent with the principle that the judicial power of the United States must be vested in Art. III courts. As support for their argument, appellants rely principally upon *Crowell* v. *Benson* and *United States* v. *Raddatz* (1980), cases in which we approved the use of administrative agencies and magistrates as adjuncts to Art. III courts. . . .

Together these cases establish two principles that aid us in determining the extent to which Congress may constitutionally vest traditionally judicial functions in non-Art. III officers. First, it is clear that when Congress creates a substantive federal right, it possesses substantial discretion to prescribe the manner in which that right may be adjudicated — including the assignment to an adjunct of some functions historically performed by judges. Thus *Crowell* recognized that Art. III does not require "all determinations of fact [to] be made by judges"; with respect to congressionally created rights, some factual determinations may be made by a specialized factfinding tribunal designed by Congress, without constitutional bar. Second, the functions of the adjunct must be limited in such a way that "the essential attributes" of judicial power are retained in the Art. III court. Thus in upholding the adjunct scheme challenged in *Crowell*, the Court emphasized that "the reservation of full authority to the court to deal with matters of law provides for the appropriate exercise of the judicial function in this class of cases." And in refusing to invalidate the Magistrates Act at issue in *Raddatz*, the Court stressed that under the congressional scheme " '[t]he authority — and the responsibility — to make an informed, final determination . . . remains with the judge,' " quoting *Mathews* v. *Weber* (1976); the statute's delegation of power was therefore permissible, since "the ultimate decision is made by the district court."

These two principles assist us in evaluating the "adjunct" scheme presented in this case. Appellants assume that Congress' power to create "adjuncts" to consider all cases related to those arising under title 11 is as great as it was in the circumstances of *Crowell*. But while *Crowell* certainly endorsed the proposition that Congress possesses broad discretion to assign factfinding functions to an adjunct created to aid in the adjudication of congressionally created statutory rights, *Crowell* does not support the further proposition necessary to appellants' argument — that Congress possesses the same degree of discretion in assigning traditionally judicial power to adjuncts engaged in the adjudication of rights *not* created by Congress. Indeed, the validity of this proposition was expressly denied in *Crowell*, when the Court rejected "the untenable assumption that the constitutional courts may be deprived in all cases of the determination of facts upon evidence even though a *constitutional* right may be involved" (emphasis added) and stated that

> "the essential independence of the exercise of judicial power of the United States in the enforcement of *constitutional* rights requires that the Federal court should determine . . . an issue [of agency jurisdiction] upon its own record and the facts elicited before it." ([E]mphasis added).

Appellants' proposition was also implicitly rejected in *Raddatz*. Congress' assignment of adjunct functions under the Federal Magistrates Act was substantially narrower than under the statute challenged in *Crowell*. Yet the Court's scrutiny of the adjunct scheme in *Raddatz* — which played a role in the adjudication of *constitutional* rights — was far stricter than it had been in *Crowell*. Critical to the Court's decision to uphold the Magistrates Act was the fact that the ultimate decision was made by the district court.

Although *Crowell* and *Raddatz* do not explicitly distinguish between rights created by Congress and other rights, such a distinction underlies in part *Crowell's* and *Raddatz's* recognition of a critical difference between rights created by federal statute and rights recognized by the Constitution. Moreover, such a distinction seems to us to be necessary in light of the delicate accommodations required by the principle of separation of powers reflected in Art. III. The constitutional system of checks and balances is designed to guard against "encroachment or aggrandizement" by Congress at the expense of the other branches of government. *Buckley* v. *Valeo*. But when Congress creates a statutory right, it clearly has the discretion, in defining that right, to create presumptions, or assign burdens of proof, or prescribe remedies; it may also provide that persons seeking to vindicate that right must do so before particularized tribunals created to perform the specialized adjudicative tasks related to that right. Such provisions do, in a sense, affect the exercise of judicial power, but they are also incidental to Congress' power to define the right that it has created. No comparable justification exists, however, when the right being adjudicated is not of congressional creation. In such a situation, substantial inroads into functions that have traditionally been performed by the judiciary cannot be characterized merely as incidental extensions of Congress' power to define rights that it has created. Rather, such inroads suggest unwarranted encroachments upon the judicial power of the United States, which our Constitution reserves for Art. III courts.

We hold that the Bankruptcy Act of 1978 carries the possibility of such an unwarranted encroachment. Many of the rights subject to adjudication by the Act's bankruptcy courts, like the rights implicated in *Raddatz*, are not of Congress' creation. Indeed, the case before us, which centers upon appellant Northern's claim for damages for breach of contract and misrepresentation, involves a right created by *state* law, a right independent of and antecedent to the reorganization petition that conferred jurisdiction upon the bankruptcy court. Accordingly, Congress' authority to control the manner in which that right is adjudicated, through assignment of historically judicial functions to a non-Art. III "adjunct," plainly must be deemed at a minimum. Yet it is equally plain that Congress has vested the "adjunct" bankruptcy judges with powers over appellant's state-created right that far exceed the powers that it has vested in administrative agencies that adjudicate only rights of Congress' own creation.

Unlike the administrative scheme that we reviewed in *Crowell*, the Act vests all "essential attributes" of the judicial power of the United States in the "adjunct" bankruptcy court. First, the agency in *Crowell* made only specialized, narrowly confined factual determinations regarding a particularized area of law. In contrast, the subject matter jurisdiction of the bankruptcy courts encompasses not only traditional matters of bankruptcy, but also "all civil proceedings arising under title 11 or arising in or *related to* cases arising under title 11." ([E]mphasis added). Second, while the agency in *Crowell* engaged in statutorily channeled factfinding functions, the bankruptcy courts exercise "*all* of the jurisdiction" conferred by the Act on the district courts, § 1471 (b) (emphasis added). Third, the agency in *Crowell* possessed only a limited power to issue compensation orders pursuant to specialized procedures, and its orders could be enforced only by order of the district court. By contrast, the bankruptcy courts exercise all ordinary powers of district courts, including the power to preside over jury trials, the power to issue declaratory judgments, the power to issue writs of habeas corpus, and the power to issue any order, process or judgment appropriate for the enforcement of the provisions of title 11. Fourth, while orders issued by the agency in *Crowell* were to be set aside if "not supported by the evidence," the judgments of the bankruptcy courts are apparently subject to review only under the more deferential "clearly erroneous" standard. Finally, the agency in *Crowell* was required by law to seek enforcement of its compensation orders in the district court. In contrast, the bankruptcy courts issue final judgments, which are binding and enforceable even in the absence of an appeal. In short, the "adjunct" bankruptcy courts created by the Act exercise jurisdiction behind the facade of a grant to the district courts, and are exercising powers far greater than those lodged in the adjuncts approved in either *Crowell* or *Raddatz.*

We conclude that § 241 (a) of the Bankruptcy Act of 1978 has impermissibly removed most, if not all, of "the essential attributes of the judicial power" from the Art. III district court, and has vested those attributes in a non-Art. III adjunct. Such a grant of jurisdiction cannot be sustained as an exercise of Congress' power to create adjuncts to Art. III courts.

V

... The judgment of the District Court is affirmed. However, we stay our judgment until October 4, 1982. This limited stay will afford Congress an opportunity to reconstitute the bankruptcy courts or to adopt other valid means of adjudication, without impairing the interim administration of the bankruptcy laws. . . .

It is so ordered.

EXPIRATION OF ERA
June 30, 1982

The Equal Rights Amendment (ERA) forbidding discrimination on the basis of sex expired June 30 when it fell three states short of the three-fourths necessary to become the 27th amendment to the U.S. Constitution. Only 35 of the required 38 states approved the brief amendment during the 10-year ratification period. The original deadline for ratification was March 22, 1979. A bill granting 39 additional months was passed by Congress October 6, 1978, and signed by President Jimmy Carter October 20. The extension of the ratification period was the first given since Congress began setting time limits in 1917.

Only two weeks after ERA's demise, 51 cosponsors in the Senate and 201 in the House of Representatives re-introduced the amendment with exactly the same wording: "Equality of rights under the law shall not be denied or abridged by the United States or by any state on account of sex." Approval of a two-thirds majority of both houses of Congress was needed to send the proposed amendment back to the states for another attempt at ratification.

Political and Legal Opposition

Soon after Congress passed ERA in 1972, opponents mounted a strong campaign, arguing the amendment would result in forced military service for women, a dilution of existing laws protecting women in the workplace, homosexual marriages and unisex public toilets. They argued further

611

that existing laws provided equality for women. Proponents rebutted or minimized allegations of such consequences.

The Republican Party platform for 1980 did not include backing for ERA — the first such omission since 1940. Candidate Ronald Reagan opposed passage of the amendment and continued to oppose it as president. The Democratic platform gave full support to passage and opposed the efforts of several states to rescind earlier passage. (Party platforms, Historic Documents of 1980, p. 567; p. 711)

Two states, Idaho and Arizona, sued in federal district court to force Congress to reverse the deadline extension and to remove Idaho from official records indicating its earlier approval of ERA, thus making its rescission legal. Judge Marion J. Callister ruled against the ERA. Early in 1982 the U.S. Supreme Court agreed to hear an appeal of the Idaho decision and stayed enforcement of Callister's ruling. The court had not acted by the time the second deadline passed. (Federal judge on ERA ratification, Historic Documents of 1981, p. 923)

Grass-roots Support and Opposition

Eleanor Smeal, then president of the National Organization for Women (NOW), attributed ERA's defeat to lackluster support from the Democrats and to the Republican Party. She said the GOP "actually led the attack" against the amendment. While critical of state legislators who voted against ERA, Smeal said, "The real opposition, behind the visible political opposition ... has been the special corporate interests that profit from sex discrimination." Major corporate interests, she said, gave financial backing to ERA opponents.

Phyllis Schlafly, a leader of the ERA opposition, said its triumph was "the most remarkable political victory of the 20th century." She said ERA failed because its supporters "could never show any benefit, any advantage to women in ERA."

The effort to achieve such an amendment dated from 1923, when it was first introduced in Congress. Public opinion polls showed more than 60 percent of the American public supported ERA before its June expiration.

> *Following are excerpts from a statement by Eleanor Smeal announcing the end of the campaign to pass the Equal Rights Amendment, released June 24, 1982; excerpts from President Reagan's press conference, June 30; and excerpts from a speech by Phyllis Schlafly, June 30.* (Boldface headings in brackets have been added by Congressional Quarterly to highlight the organization of the texts.):

SMEAL STATEMENT

We are announcing today that the Equal Rights Amendment [ERA] Countdown Campaign, coordinated by the National Organization for Women [NOW], has ended. However, the fight for equality for women will go on, stronger than ever, until justice is ours.

In this long and intensive fight for the ERA, a number of political realities have emerged which must be changed before ratification can be achieved.

1. The Republican Party has not only deserted women's rights, it has actually led the attack against them. In both Oklahoma and North Carolina, Republicans bloc-voted against the Amendment, and overall, 83% of Republicans in unratified states opposed it.

2. While the Democrats provided words of encouragement, and undeniably supported the ERA in greater numbers than Republicans, that support was not strong enough, and lacked the political cohesiveness to achieve victory. In short, women's rights were not high on their agenda and there was significant defection in their ranks. In fact, several Democrats, among them Florida's Senator Dempsey Barron and North Carolina's Lt. Governor Jimmy Green, led the opposition in their states.

3. The real opposition, behind the visible political opposition and behind the women in red, has been the special corporate interests that profit from sex discrimination.

On the list of organizations that support the ERA, which includes hundreds of organizations from nearly every walk of life, major business interests are notable by their absence. There are no Chambers of Commerce, no Associations of Manufacturers, no Insurance Councils. On the other hand, many major corporate interests do appear on the list of contributors to the Mountain States Legal Foundation, the group that spearheaded opposition to the extension of the deadline to ratify the ERA, and led the court fight against it.

After June 30, we expect to see these special interests out in the open again, fighting us as we work to ban sex discrimination in insurance or to win better wages for women. Their tendency is to fight the limited battles in the open, while maintaining that they support equal rights for women in principle. We will no longer allow them to perpetuate that hypocrisy.

4. Another major source of ERA opposition has been, simply, sex bias in the legislatures. In those legislative bodies, women have had token representation at best. They are only 12.9% of the state legislators in North Carolina, 13.6% in Illinois, 8.3% in Oklahoma, 10% in Florida. Men are 94% of all state senators and 86% of all state representatives.

The preponderance of men in the legislatures has created a "stag club" atmosphere which keeps those bodies from being representative of women or responsive to women's concerns. Nowhere is this more clear than on ERA votes, where 75% of the women legislators in the four key unratified states support the Amendment, as opposed to 46% of the men.

[Future Political Strategy]

What we need to do on the political front is twofold: one, we need to increase the numbers of women in legislatures so that an effective female
presence will ensure full and fair consideration of women's issues; and two,
we need to increase the number of women and men in the legislatures who
are committed to equality.

Unquestionably, the most significant and historic outcome of this
campaign is that it will usher in a new era of direct political participation
for women. Untold thousands of women have lobbied legislators in the
course of this campaign, and what many of them discovered, time and time
again, was that they were better qualified to hold office than the men they
were lobbying. As a direct result, there is a dramatic increase in the
number of women who want to run for political office — indeed, who are
now committed to doing so.

In Florida, for example, we have already identified 11 candidates, 7 of
them women, to run against 11 of the 22 state senators who voted against
the ERA last Monday. And we still have a month to search for more
candidates in that state.

We are determined to seek direct and just representation for women in
government; we are determined to build an independent political force,
with the freedom and flexibility to support candidates or not support
candidates based upon their proven commitment to women's rights. NOW
fully intends to work toward removing from office as many of those
opponents of equality as possible and to support those who have supported
women's rights. But more importantly, NOW seeks to recruit and elect a
new breed of candidate.

[Economic Action]

On the economic front, we are going to use industry-wide approaches for
exposing and attacking sex discrimination, and we will take direct economic action to combat it. We have proved in Florida, Missouri, Illinois,
and other unratified states the effectiveness of the economic boycott. This
time we will use the boycott as a tool to make sex discrimination costly to
those who practice it, instead of a source of profit. We will also reach the
public through media education campaigns, one of which we have already
begun in the area of sex discrimination in insurance, and we will fight the
bias they promote in every type of insurance: in life, health, disability,
auto, annuities, and pensions. While our opposition will certainly be able
to outspend us, ultimately their arguments will not hold up to public
scrutiny. Their case for sex discrimination will not sell.

You have undoubtedly also heard that the Equal Rights Amendment
will be reintroduced. We agree with its numerous co-sponsors that it
should remain an item of prime consideration on the nation's agenda.
However, we will not again seriously pursue the ERA until we've made a

major dent in changing the composition of Congress as well as the state legislatures to include a significantly larger proportion of women and of men who are genuinely feminists. . . .

We close this campaign buoyant and stronger than when we began.

We have developed a network of 750 phone banks which have worked and will continue to work for women's rights, a funding base which is bringing in more money monthly than the Democratic Party, an experienced nationwide volunteer and professional corps which numbers in the thousands, and an award-winning media advertising program. The campaign also generated such widespread, enthusiastic support that it has been able to continually produce mass public events, ranging from such single-site events as the ERA Extension March in 1978 that brought 100,000 people to Washington, DC, to the simultaneous rallies of more than 10,000 each in four unratified state capitols on June 6.

As the campaign intensified activist support, it developed a parallel phenomenon in the general public. Most respected public opinion polls show that nationwide the ERA enjoys a strong 2-1 margin of support. As Louis Harris has stated, such support in any election would be considered a landslide.

REAGAN NEWS CONFERENCE

. . . **Q.** Mr. President, Since Maureen Reagan today mentioned what she termed, "the myopic views of the political establishment, a Bohemian Grove society that comes from rubbing elbows with the mighty" — that's what she said, it's not mine — [*laughter*]

The President. Mm-hm.

Q. . . . and she told us to ask you why you changed your mind on ERA. I have a two-part question. The first is, why? And the second, did you ever at any time consider the possibility of selecting a female runningmate like, say, Barbara Bush? [*Laughter*]

P. Well, I came as close to Barbara as I could. [*Laughter*]

My daughter's very eloquent. [*Laughter*] But since you've opened that subject, let me just make a comment of my own on that subject.

I know that this was the day and the decision day, the day of reckoning. I don't think however, that the effort over the last 10 years — while there's been a difference in how to handle the problem of discrimination against women, I don't think that the effort was wasted because they didn't get the constitutional amendment. The only debate has been over the method of eliminating or erasing discrimination.

But in these 10 years, I think that their effort has brought to the attention of the people this problem. I know it did for me when I was Governor to the extent that in California we found 14 statutes that did discriminate. And we eliminated those 14 statutes or altered them; we removed the provisions in them that were discriminatory.

Now, I believe in equal rights. And when I came here I asked the 50 Governors individually if each one of them would appoint someone in their own State to start looking, searching for statutes and regulations to do what we had done there in California — and this included in California to see if there are more that we didn't find. I promised to appoint and have appointed a person in our government here and our administration also to bring this together into a concerted movement and to keep helping move it along. And I found that there was a task force in the Justice Department — and I think that maybe we've made it more active since we've been here — to do the same thing with regard to Federal laws and regulations and to eliminate those that are discriminatory.

And now I know that many say that they will continue to try for an amendment. And I just wonder if any of them have ever thought how much of that effort and the resources that are employed in that, if used in behalf of this program that I've just mentioned, if they could not achieve what it is they want to achieve and much faster, just as we did in California, and eliminate. And we're going to continue to try and do that. . . .

SCHLAFLY SPEECH

. . . The most encouraging thing we learned from our ten-year battle to defeat the Equal Rights Amendment is that, out across America, there are hundreds of public officials who literally cannot be bought at any price. . . .

In the last analysis, the pitched battle came down to Oklahoma, Florida, North Carolina and Illinois. The legislators in those states were put to an incredible test. Efforts were made to buy them with outright bribes. Efforts were made to bribe them with public funds, with all the power and perks that the executive branch of the government can offer. Some Governors were determined to pass ERA at any price. The legislators received repeated calls from the White House when Jimmy Carter was President, and from many other prominent officials. The legislators received invitations to the White House where they were offered whatever they wanted — write your own ticket, write your own check; we'll give you any job you want, any appointment or favor. . . .

Then there was the ugliness when they didn't fall in line: the obscene telephone calls, the harassment of their families, the bags of chicken manure that were sent to the legislators in North Carolina who voted No, the attempts to ruin the businesses of their financial contributors, the picketing at their homes on Sundays, the harassment of their wives and children, the threats on their wives and family.

In the last weeks in Illinois, the shock troops brought in gallons of blood, and they wrote in blood all over the marble floors of our Capitol. They wrote in blood the names of the ones they hated the most. They defaced our Flags, the Illinois Flag and the American Flag. . . .

In Illinois we also had the "Chain Gang" that came in and chained themselves to the House and Senate Chamber doors, and closed down our House of Representatives. In the Capitol Rotunda were the Hunger Strikers, including their leader who said in her book, "If I could have got hold of God, I would have killed Him." That's the kind of people who agitated for ERA. . . .

In the moment of truth, we had enough courageous legislators who knew what was right and wrong; and there were enough who stood firm. In Oklahoma there were a wonderful 27, in North Carolina there were a wonderful 27, in Florida there were a great 23, in Illinois there were 27 in the Senate and 72 in the House. This is the great hope for America. . . .

So my cheerful word is that America does have public officials with strength of character all across this country. I think they are the same type of people who had that strength of character 206 years ago, who were willing to pledge their lives, their fortunes and their sacred honor to make sure that our country is free and independent.

. . . They have stood the test. We can build this victory into a mighty movement that can set America on the right path. . . .

COURT ON BUSING
June 30, 1982

In two related cases the Supreme Court June 30 defined ways in which states may restrict the use of busing to achieve school desegregation. Specifically the court held that voters may limit busing by changing a state's laws or passing a state constitutional amendment only when constitutional rights are not restricted and a special burden is not imposed on minorities.

One case, Crawford v. Los Angeles Board of Education, *centered on the legality of a voter-initiated amendment to California's constitution. The amendment barred state courts from going further than federal courts in ordering busing. As a result the California courts had been forced to cancel a mandatory busing program in Los Angeles, which had been ordered to correct de facto segregation.*

The California Decision

In upholding the constitutionality of the California initiative, called Proposition I, the court ruled 8-1 that it would be "destructive of a state's democratic processes" to hold that "once a State chooses to do 'more' than the Fourteenth Amendment requires, it may never recede."

Writing for the majority, Justice Lewis F. Powell Jr. said that states should be allowed to rescind legislation "that has proven unworkable or harmful when the state was under no obligation to adopt the legislation in the first place." The amendment, he noted, "does not inhibit enforcement of any federal law or constitutional requirement." On the contrary, he said, it linked state law directly to federal standards.

Justice Thurgood Marshall, the sole dissenter, said that in passing Proposition I the voters had deprived minorities of "the only method of redress that has proved effective — the full remedial powers of the state judiciary." He said he could not understand how the court could find the limitation of the powers of a state's courts to be constitutional while similar limits on school boards are unconstitutional with respect to the same racial issue.

The Washington Case

While the court found the California initiative non-discriminatory, it struck down as discriminatory in intent a Washington state voter initiative involving busing. The 1978 Washington measure had prohibited local school boards from requiring busing to correct racial imbalances but made exceptions for other reasons.

Justice Harry A. Blackmun wrote the opinion in the 5-4 decision, in which Justices William J. Brennan Jr., Byron R. White, John Paul Stevens and Marshall joined. Blackmun noted that while the 1978 law appeared to be racially neutral, "there is little doubt that the initiative was effectively drawn for racial purposes ... [and] carefully tailored to interfere only with desegregative busing." He noted further that the initiative placed "substantial and unique burdens on racial minorities."

Justice Powell wrote the dissent, calling the decision an "unprecedented intrusion into the structure of a state government." Powell was joined by Chief Justice Warren E. Burger and Justices William H. Rehnquist and Sandra Day O'Connor.

Concurring in the California case, Blackmun wrote that although the state's voters "may have made it more difficult to achieve desegregation when it enacted Proposition I, to my mind it did so not by working a structural change in the political process so much as by simply repealing the right to invoke a judicial busing remedy." In the Washington case, however, the court held that the state had restructured its educational decision making process, making it difficult for racial minorities to win favorable legislation and thus violating the equal protection clause of the 14th Amendment.

> *Following are excerpts from the Supreme Court's opinion in* Washington v. Seattle, *striking down Proposition 350 that prohibited school boards from ordering busing for racial balance, and excerpts from the dissent by Justice Powell; and excerpts from* Crawford v. Los Angeles Board of Education, *upholding California's Proposition I that prohibited court-ordered busing for racial balance, and from the dissent by Justice Marshall; both June 30:*

No. 81-9

Washington, et al.,
Appellants
v.
Seattle School District
No. 1, et al.

On writ of certiorari to the United
States Court of Appeals for the
Ninth Circuit

[June 30, 1982]

JUSTICE BLACKMUN delivered the opinion of the Court.

We are presented here with an extraordinary question: whether an elected local school board may use the Fourteenth Amendment to *defend* its program of busing for integration from attack by the State.

I

A

Seattle School District No. 1 (District), which is largely coterminous with the city of Seattle, Wash., is charged by state law with administering 112 schools and educating approximately 54,000 public school students. About 37% of these children are of Negro, Asian, American Indian, or Hispanic ancestry. Because segregated housing patterns in Seattle have created racially imbalanced schools, the District historically has taken steps to alleviate the isolation of minority students; since 1963, it has permitted students to transfer from their neighborhood schools to help cure the District's racial imbalance.

Despite these efforts, the District in 1977 came under increasing pressure to accelerate its program of desegation. In response, the District's Board of Directors (School Board) enacted a resolution defining "racial imbalance" as "the situation that exists when the combined minority student enrollment in a school exceeds the districtwide combined average by 20 percentage points, provided that the single minority enrollment ... of no school will exceed 50 percent of the student body." The District resolved to eliminate all such imbalance from the Seattle public schools by the beginning of the 1979-1980 academic year.

In September 1977, the District implemented a "magnet" program, designed to alleviate racial isolation by enhancing educational offerings at certain schools, thereby encouraging voluntary student transfers. A "disproportionate amount of the overall movement" inspired by the program was undertaken by Negro students, however, and racial imbalance in the Seattle schools was found to have actually increased between the 1970-1971 and 1977-1978 academic years. The District therefore concluded that mandatory reassignment of students was necessary if racial isolation in its schools was to be eliminated. Accordingly, in March 1978, the School Board enacted the so-called "Seattle Plan" for desegregation. The plan, which makes extensive use of busing and mandatory reassignments, desegregates elementary schools by "pairing" and "triading" predominantly minority with predominantly white attendance areas, and by basing student assignments on attendance zones rather than on race. The racial makeup of secondary schools is moderated by "feeding" them from the desegregated elementary schools. The District represents that the plan results in the reassignment of roughly equal numbers of white and minority students, and allows most students to spend roughly half of their academic careers attending a school near their homes.

The desegregation program, implemented in the 1978-1979 academic year, apparently was effective: the District Court found that the Seattle Plan "has substantially reduced the number of racially imbalanced schools in the district and has substantially reduced the percentage of minority students in those schools which remain racially imbalanced."

B

In late 1977, shortly before the Seattle Plan was formally adopted by the District, a number of Seattle residents who opposed the desegregation strategies being discussed by the School Board formed an organization called the Citizens for Voluntary Integration Committee (CiVIC). This organization, which the District Court found "was formed because of its founders' opposition to The Seattle Plan," attempted to enjoin implementation of the Board's mandatory desegregation program th[r]ough litigation in state court; when these efforts failed, CiVIC drafted a statewide initiative designed to terminate the use of mandatory busing for purposes of racial integration. This proposal, known as Initiative 350, provided that "no school board . . . shall directly or indirectly require any student to attend a school other than the school which is geographically nearest or next nearest the student's place of residence . . . and which offers the course of study pursued by such student. . . ." (1981). The initiative then set out, however, a number of broad exceptions to this requirement: a student may be assigned beyond his neighborhood school if he "requires special education, care or guidance," or if "there are health or safety hazards, either natural or man made, or physical barriers or obstacles . . . between the student's place of residence and the nearest or next nearest school," or if "the school nearest or next nearest to his place of residence is unfit or inadequate because of overcrowding, unsafe conditions or lack of physical facilities." Initiative 350 also specifically proscribed use of seven enumerated methods of "indirec[t]" student assignment — among them the redefinition of attendance zones, the pairing of schools, and the use of "feeder" schools — that are a part of the Seattle Plan. The initiative envisioned busing for racial purposes in only one circumstance: it did not purport to "prevent any court of competent jurisdiction from adjudicating constitutional issues relating to the public schools."

Its proponents placed Initiative 350 on the Washington ballot for the November 1978 general election. During the ensuing campaign, the District Court concluded, the leadership of CiVIC "acted legally and responsibly," and did not address "its appeals to the racial biases of the voters." At the same time, however, the court's findings demonstrate that the initiative was directed solely at desegregative busing in general, and at the Seattle Plan in particular. Thus, "[e]xcept for the assignment of students to effect racial balancing, the drafters of Initiative 350 attempted to preserve to school districts the maximum flexibility in the assignment of students" and "[e]xcept for racially-balancing purposes" the initiative "permits local school districts to assign students other than to their nearest or next nearest schools for most, if not all, of the major reasons for which students are at present assigned to schools other than their nearest or next nearest schools." In campaigning for the measure, CiVIC officials accurately represented that its passage would result in "no loss of school district flexibility other than in busing for desegregation purposes," and it is evident that the campaign focused almost exclusively on the wisdom of "forced busing" for integration.

On November 8, 1978, two months after the Seattle Plan went into effect, Initiative 350 passed by a substantial margin, drawing almost 66% of the vote statewide. The initiative failed to attract majority support in two state legislative districts, both in Seattle. In the city as a whole, however, the initiative passed with some 61% of the vote. Within the month, the District, together with the Tacoma and Pasco school districts, initiated this suit against the State in United States District Court for the Western District of Washington, challenging the constitutionality of Initiative 350 under the Equal Protection Clause of the Fourteenth Amendment. The United States and several community organizations intervened in support of the District; CiVIC intervened on behalf of the defendants.

After a nine-day trial, the District Court made extensive and detailed findings of fact. The court determined that "[t]hose Seattle schools which are most crowded are located in those areas of the city where the preponderance of minority families live." Yet the court found that Initiative 350, if implemented, "will prevent the racial balancing of a significant number of Seattle schools and will cause the school system to become more racially imbalanced than it presently is," "will make it impossible for Tacoma schools to maintain their present racial balance," and will make "doubtful" the prospects for integration of the Pasco schools. Except for desegregative busing, however, the court found that "almost all of the busing of students currently taking place in [Washington] is permitted by Initiative 350." And while the court found that "racial bias . . . is a factor in the opposition to the 'busing' of students to obtain racial balance," it also found that voters were moved to support Initiative 350 for "a number of reasons," so that "[i]t is impossible to ascertain all of those reasons [o]r to determine the relative impact of those reasons upon the electorate."

The District Court then held Initiative 350 unconstitutional, for three independent reasons. The court first concluded that the initiative established an impermissible racial classification, in violation of *Hunter* v.

Erickson (1969) and *Lee* v. *Nyquist* (1971) "because it permits busing for non-racial reasons but forbids it for racial reasons." The court next held Initiative 350 invalid because "a racially discriminatory purpose was one of the factors which motivated the conception and adoption of the initiative." Finally, the District Court reasoned that Initiative 350 was unconstitutionally overbroad, because in the absence of a court order it barred even school boards that had engaged in *de jure* segregation from taking steps to foster integration. The court permanently enjoined implementation of the initiative's restrictions.

On the merits, a divided panel of the United States Court of Appeals for the Ninth Circuit affirmed, relying entirely on the District Court's first rationale. By subjecting desegregative student assignments to unique treatment, the Court of Appeals concluded, Initiative 350 "both creates a constitutionally-suspect racial classification and radically restructures the political process of Washington by allowing a state-wide majority to usurp traditional local authority over local school board educational policies." In doing so, the court continued, the initiative *"remove[s]* from local school boards their existing authority, and in large part their capability, to enact programs designed to desegregate the schools." ([E]mphasis in original). The court found such a result contrary to the principles of *Hunter* v. *Erickson* and *Lee* v. *Nyquist.* The court acknowledged that the issue would be a different one had a successor school board attempted to rescind the Seattle Plan. Here, however, "a different governmental body — the state-wide electorate — rescinded a policy voluntarily enacted by locally elected school boards already subject to local political control."

The State appealed to this Court. We noted probable jurisdiction to address an issue of significance to our Nation's system of education. (1981).

II

The Equal Protection Clause of the Fourteenth Amendment guarantees racial minorities the right to full participation in the political life of the community. It is beyond dispute, of course, that given racial or ethnic groups may not be denied the franchise, or precluded from entering into the political process in a reliable and meaningful manner. See *White* v. *Regester* (1973); *Nixon* v. *Herndon* (1927). But the Fourteenth Amendment also reaches "a political structure that treats all individuals as equals," *Mobile* v. *Bolden* (1980) (STEVENS, J., concurring in the judgment), yet more subtly distorts governmental processes in such a way as to place special burdens on the ability of minority groups to achieve beneficial legislation.

This principle received its clearest expression in *Hunter* v. *Erickson,* a case that involved attempts to overturn antidiscrimination legislation in Akron, Ohio. The Akron city council, pursuant to its ordinary legislative processes, had enacted a fair housing ordinance. In response, the local citizenry, using an established referendum procedure, amended the city charter to provide that ordinances regulating real estate transactions "on the basis of race, color, religion, national origin or ancestry must first be approved by a majority of the electors voting on the question at a regular or general election before said ordinance shall be effective." This action "not only suspended the operation of the existing ordinance forbidding housing discrimination, but also required the approval of the electors before any future [fair housing] ordinance could take effect." In essence, the amendment changed the requirements for the adoption of one type of local legislation: to enact an ordinance barring housing discrimination on the basis of race or religion, proponents had to obtain the approval of the city council *and* of a majority of the voters city-wide. To enact an ordinance preventing housing discrimination on other grounds, or to enact any other type of housing ordinance, proponents needed the support of only the city council.

In striking down the charter amendment, the *Hunter* Court recognized that, on its face, the provision "draws no distinctions among racial and religious groups." But it did differentiate "between those groups who sought the law's protection against racial ... discriminations in the sale and rental of real estate and those who sought to regulate real property transactions in the pursuit of other ends," thus "disadvantag[ing] those who would benefit from laws barring racial ... discriminations as against those who would bar other discriminations or who would otherwise regulate the real estate market in their favor." In "reality," the burden imposed by such an arrangement necessarily "falls on the minority. The majority needs no protection against discrimination and if it did, a referendum might be bothersome but no more than that." In effect, then, the charter amendment served as an "explicitly racial classification treating racial housing matters differently from other racial and housing matters." This made the amendment constitutionally suspect: "the State may no more disadvantage any *particular* group by making it more difficult to enact legislation in its behalf than it may dilute any person's vote or give any group a smaller representation than another of comparable size." ([E]mphasis added).

Lee v. *Nyquist* offers an application of the *Hunter* doctrine in a setting strikingly similar to the one now before us. That case involved the New York education system, which made use of both elected and appointed school boards and which conferred extensive authority on state education officials. In an effort to eliminate *de facto* segregation in New York's schools, those officials had directed the city of Buffalo — a municipality with an appointed school board — to implement an integration plan. While these developments were proceeding, however, the New York Legislature enacted a statute barring state education officials and appointed — though not elected — school boards from "assign[ing] or compell[ing] [students] to attend any school on account of race ... or for the purpose of achieving [racial] equality in attendance ... at any school."

Applying *Hunter*, the three-judge District Court invalidated the statute, noting that under the provision "[t]he Commissioner [of Education] and local appointed officials are prohibited from acting in [student assignment] matters only where racial criteria are involved." In the court's view, the statute therefore "place[d] *burdens* on the implementation of educational policies designed to deal with race on the local level" by "treating educational matters involving racial criteria differently from other educational matters and making it more difficult to deal with racial imbalance in the public schools." This drew an impermissible distinction "between the treatment of problems involving racial matters and that afforded other problems in the same area." This Court affirmed the District Court's judgment without opinion. (1971).

These cases yield a simple but central principle. As Justice Harlan noted while concurring in the Court's opinion in *Hunter*, laws structuring political institutions or allocating political power according to "neutral principles" — such as the executive veto, or the typically burdensome requirements for amending state constitutions — are not subject to equal protection attack, though they may "make it more difficult for minorities to achieve favorable legislation." Because such laws make it more difficult for *every* group in the community to enact comparable laws, they "provid[e] a just framework within which the diverse political groups in our society may fairly compete." Thus, the political majority may generally restructure the political process to place obstacles in the path of everyone seeking to secure the benefits of governmental action. But a different analysis is required when the State allocates governmental power nonneutrally, by explicitly using the *racial* nature of a decision to determine the decisionmaking process. State action of this kind, the Court said, "places *special* burdens on racial minorities within the governmental process," (emphasis added), thereby "making it *more* difficult for certain racial and religious minorities [than for other members of the community] to achieve legislation that is in their interest." Such a structuring of the political process, the Court said, was "no more permissible than [is] denying [members of a racial minority] the vote, on an equal basis with others."

III

We believe that the Court of Appeals properly focused on *Hunter* and *Lee,* for we find the principle of those cases dispositive of the issue here. In our view, Initiative 350 must fall because it does "not attemp[t] to allocate governmental power on the basis of any general principle." *Hunter* v. *Erickson.* Instead, it uses the racial nature of an issue to define the governmental decisionmaking structure, and thus imposes substantial and unique burdens on racial minorities.

A

Noting that Initiative 350 nowhere mentions "race" or "integration," appellants suggest that the legislation has no racial overtones; they maintain that *Hunter* is inapposite because the initiative simply permits busing for certain enumerated purposes while neutrally forbidding it for all other reasons. We find it difficult to believe that appellants' analysis is seriously advanced, however, for despite its facial neutrality there is little doubt that the initiative was effectively drawn for racial purposes. Neither the initiative's sponsors, nor the District Court, nor the Court of Appeals had any difficulty perceiving the racial nature of the issue settled by Initiative 350. Thus, the District Court found that the text of the referendum was carefully tailored to interfere only with desegregative busing. Proponents of the initiative candidly "represented that there would be no loss of school district flexibility other than in busing for desegregation purposes." And, as we have noted, Initiative 350 in fact allows school districts to bus their students "for most, if not all," of the non-integrative purposes required by their educational policies. The Washington electorate surely was aware of this, for it was "assured" by CiVIC officials that " '99% of the school districts in the state' " — those that lacked mandatory integration programs — "would not be affected by the passage of 350." It is beyond reasonable dispute, then, that the initiative was enacted " 'because of,' not merely 'in spite of,' its adverse effects upon" busing for integration. *Personnel Administrator of Massachusetts* v. *Feeney* (1979).

Even accepting the view that Initiative 350 was enacted for such a purpose, the United States — which has changed its position during the course of this litigation, and now supports the State — maintains that busing for integration, unlike the fair housing ordinance involved in *Hunter*, is not a peculiarly "racial" issue at all. Again, we are not persuaded. It undoubtedly is true, as the United States suggests, that the proponents of mandatory integration cannot be classified by race: Negroes and whites may be counted among both the supporters and the opponents of Initiative 350. And it should be equally clear that white as well as Negro children benefit from exposure to "ethnic and racial diversity in the classroom." *Columbus Board of Education* v. *Penick* (1979) (POWELL, J., dissenting). . . .

In any event, our cases suggest that desegregation of the public schools, like the Akron open housing ordinance, at bottom inures primarily to the benefit of the minority, and is designed for that purpose. Education has come to be "a principal instrument in awakening the child to cultural values, in preparing him for later professional training, and in helping him to adjust normally to his environment." *Brown* v. *Board of Education* (1954). When that environment is largely shaped by members of different racial and cultural groups, minority children can achieve their full measure of success only if they learn to function in — and are fully accepted by — the larger community. Attending an ethnically diverse school may help accomplish this goal by preparing minority children "for citizenship in our pluralistic society," *Estes* v. *Metropolitan Branches of the Dallas NAACP* (1980) (POWELL, J., dissenting), while, we may hope, teaching members of the racial majority "to live in harmony and mutual respect" with children of minority heritage. *Columbus Board of Education* v. *Penick*, (POWELL, J., dissenting). *Lee* v. *Nyquist* settles this point, for the Court there accepted the proposition that mandatory desegregation strategies present the type of racial issue implicated by the *Hunter* doctrine.

It is undeniable that busing for integration — particularly when ordered by a federal court — now engenders considerably more controversy than does the sort of fair housing ordinance debated in *Hunter*. . . . But in the absence of a constitutional violation, the desirability and efficacy of school desegregation are matters to be resolved through the political process. For present purposes, it is enough that minorities may consider busing for integration to be "legislation that is in their interest." *Hunter* v. *Erickson*, (Harlan, J., concurring). Given the racial focus of Initiative 350, this suffices to trigger application of the *Hunter* doctrine.

B

We are also satisfied that the practical effect of Initiative 350 is to work a reallocation of power of the kind condemned in *Hunter*. The initiative removes the authority to address a racial problem — and only a racial problem — from the existing decisionmaking body, in such a way as to burden minority interests. Those favoring the elimination of *de facto* school segregation now must seek relief from the state legislature, or from the statewide electorate. Yet authority over all other student assignment decisions, as well as over most other areas of educational policy, remains vested in the local school board. Indeed, by specifically exempting from Initiative 350's proscriptions most non-racial reasons for assigning students away from their neighborhood schools, the initiative expressly requires those championing school integration to surmount a considerably higher hurdle than persons seeking comparable legislative action. As in *Hunter*, then, the community's political mechanisms are modified to place effective decisionmaking authority over a racial issue at a different level of government. In a very obvious sense, the initiative thus "disadvantages those who would benefit from laws barring" *de facto* desegregation "as against those who . . . would otherwise regulate" student assignment decisions; "the reality is that the law's impact falls on the minority." *Hunter* v. *Erickson*.

The state appellants and the United States, in response to this line of analysis, argue that Initiative 350 has not worked *any* reallocation of power. They note that the State necessarily retains plenary authority over Washington's system of education, and therefore they suggest that the initiative amounts to nothing more than an unexceptional example of a State's intervention in its own school system. In effect, they maintain that the State functions as a "super school board," which typically involves itself in all areas of educational policy. And, the argument continues, if the State is the body that usually makes decisions in this area, Initiative 350 worked a simple change in policy rather than a forbidden reallocation of power. Cf. *Crawford* v. *Los Angeles Board of Education* [1982].

This at first glance would seem to be a potent argument, for States traditionally have been accorded the widest latitude in ordering their internal governmental processes, see *Holt Civic Club* v. *Tuscaloosa* (1978), and school boards, as creatures of the State, obviously must give effect to policies announced by the state legislature. But "insisting that a State may distribute legislative power as it desires . . . furnish[es] no justification for a legislative structure which otherwise would violate the Fourteenth Amendment. Nor does the implementation of this change through popular referendum immunize it." *Hunter* v. *Erickson*. The issue here after all, is not whether Washington has the authority to intervene in the affairs of local school boards; it is, rather, whether the State has exercised that authority in a manner consistent with the Equal Protection Clause. As the Court noted in *Hunter*, "though Akron might have proceeded by majority vote . . . on all its municipal legislation, it has instead chosen a more complex system. Having done so, the State may no more disadvantage any particular group by making it more difficult to enact legislation in its behalf than it may dilute any person's vote." Washington also has chosen to make use of a more complex governmental structure, and a close examination both of the Washington statutes and of the Court's decisions in related areas convinces us that *Hunter* is fully applicable here.

At the outset, it is irrelevant that the State might have vested all decisionmaking authority in itself, so long as the political structure it in fact erected imposes comparative burdens on minority interests; that much is settled by *Hunter* and by *Lee*. And until the passage of Initiative 350, Washington law in fact had established the local school board, rather than the State, as the entity charged with making decisions of the type at issue here. Like all 50 States, Washington of course is ultimately responsible for providing education within its borders . . . and it therefore has set certain procedural requirements and minimum educational standards to be met by each school. . . . But Washington has chosen to meet its educational responsibilities primarily through "state and local officials, boards, and committees," and the responsibility to devise and tailor educational programs to suit local needs has emphatically been vested in the local school boards.

Thus "each common school district board of directors" is made "accountable for the proper operation of [its] district to the local community and its electorate." To this end, each school board is "vested with the *final* responsibility for the setting of policies ensuring quality in the content and extent of its educational program" (emphasis added). . . . School boards, of course, are given broad corporate powers. Significantly for present purposes, school boards are directed to determine which students should be bused to school and to provide those students with transportation.

Indeed, the notion of school board responsibility for local educational programs is so firmly rooted that local boards are subject to disclosure and reporting provisions specifically designed to ensure the board's "accountability" to the people of the community for "the educational programs in the school distric[t]." And, perhaps most relevantly here, before the adoption of Initiative 350 the Washington Supreme Court had found it within the general discretion of local school authorities to settle problems related to the denial of "equal educational opportunity." *Citizens Against Mandatory Bussing* v. *Palmason* (1972). It therefore had squarely held that a program of desegregative busing was a proper means of furthering the school board's responsibility to "administe[r] the schools in such a way as to provide a sound education for all children."...

Given this statutory structure, we have little difficulty concluding that Initiative 350 worked a major reordering of the State's educational decisionmaking process. Before adoption of the initiative, the power to determine what programs would most appropriately fill a school district's educational needs — including programs involving student assignment and desegregation — was firmly committed to the local board's discretion. The question whether to provide an integrated learning environment rather than a system of neighborhood schools surely involved a decision of that sort. See *Citizens Against Mandatory Bussing* v. *Palmason*. After passage of Initiative 350, authority over all but one of those areas remained in the hands of the local board. By placing power over desegregative busing at the state level, then, Initiative 350 plainly "differentiates between the treatment of problems involving racial matters and that afforded other problems in the same area." *Lee* v. *Nyquist*. The District Court and the Court of Appeals similarly concluded that the initiative restructured the Washington political process, and we see no reason to challenge the determinations of courts familiar with local law....

In any event, we believe that the question here is again settled by *Lee*. There, state control of the educational system was fully as complete as it now is in Washington.... The state statute under attack reallocated power over mandatory desegregation in two ways: it transferred authority from the State Commissioner of Education to local elected school boards, and it shifted authority from local appointed school boards to the state legislature. When presented with this restructuring of the political process, the District Court declared that it could "conceive of no more compelling case for the application of the *Hunter* principle." This Court of course affirmed the District Court's judgment. We see no relevant distinction between this case and *Lee*; indeed, it is difficult to imagine a more precise parallel.

C

To be sure, "the simple repeal or modification of desegregation or anti-discrimination laws, without more, never has been viewed as embodying a presumptively invalid racial classification." *Crawford* v. *Los Angeles Board of Education*. See *Dayton Board of Education* v. *Brinkman* (1979); *Hunter* v. *Erickson*. As Justice Harlan noted in *Hunter*, the voters of the polity may express their displeasure through an established legislative or referendum procedure when particular legislation "arouses passionate opposition." Had Akron's fair housing ordinance been defeated at a referendum, for example, "Negroes would undoubtedly [have lost] an important political battle, but they would not thereby [have been] denied equal protection."

Initiative 350, however, works something more than the "mere repeal" of a desegregation law by the political entity that created it. It burdens all future attempts to integrate Washington schools in districts throughout the State, by lodging decisionmaking authority over the question at a new and remote level of government. Indeed, the initiative, like the charter amendment at issue in *Hunter*, has its most pernicious effect on integration programs that do "*not* arouse extraordinary controversy." In such situations the initiative makes the enactment of racially beneficial legislation difficult, though the particular program involved might not have inspired opposition had it been promulgated through the usual legislative processes used for comparable legislation. This imposes direct and undeniable burdens on minority interests. "If a governmental institution is to be fair, one group cannot always be expected to win"; by the same token, one group cannot be subjected to a debilitating and often insurmountable disadvantage.

IV

In the end, appellants are reduced to suggesting that *Hunter* has been effectively overruled by more recent decisions of this Court. As they read it, *Hunter* applied a simple "disparate impact" analysis: it invalidated a facially neutral ordinance because of the law's adverse effects upon racial minorities. Appellants therefore contend that *Hunter* was swept away, along with the disparate impact approach to equal protection, in *Washington* v. *Davis* (1976), and *Arlington Heights* v. *Metropolitan Housing Dev. Corp.* (1977). Cf. *James* v. *Valtierra* (1971).

Appellants unquestionably are correct when they suggest that "purposeful discrimination is 'the condition that offends the Constitution,'" *Personnel Administrator of Massachusetts* v. *Feeney*, quoting *Swann* v. *Charlotte-Mecklenberg Board of Education* (1971), for the "central purpose of the Equal Protection Clause ... is the prevention of official conduct discriminating on the basis of race." *Washington* v. *Davis*. Thus, when facially neutral legislation is subjected to equal protection attack, an inquiry into intent is necessary, to determine whether the legislation in some sense was designed to accord disparate treatment on the basis of racial considerations. Appellants' suggestion that this analysis somehow conflicts with *Hunter*, however, misapprehends the basis of the *Hunter* doctrine. We have not insisted on a particularized inquiry into motivation in all equal protection cases: "A racial classification, regardless of purported motivation, is presumptively invalid and can be upheld only upon an extraordinary justification." *Personnel Administrator of Massachusetts* v. *Feeney*. And legislation of the kind challenged in *Hunter* similarly falls into an inherently suspect category.

There is one immediate and crucial difference between *Hunter* and the cases cited by appellants. While decisions such as *Washington* v. *Davis* and *Arlington Heights* considered classifications facially unrelated to race, the charter amendment at issue in *Hunter* dealt in explicitly racial terms with legislation designed to benefit minorities "as minorities," not legislation intended to benefit some larger group of underprivileged citizens among whom minorities were disproportionately represented. This does not mean, of course, that every attempt to address a racial issue gives rise to an impermissible racial classification. See *Crawford* v. *Los Angeles Board of Education*. But when the political process or the decisionmaking mechanism used to *address* racially conscious legislation — and only such legislation — is singled out for peculiar and disadvantageous treatment, the governmental action plainly "rests on 'distinctions based on race.' " *James* v. *Valtierra* quoting *Hunter* v. *Erickson*. And when the State's allocation of power places unusual burdens on the ability of racial groups to enact legislation specifically designed to overcome the "special condition" of prejudice, the governmental action seriously "curtail[s] the operation of those political processes ordinarily to be relied upon to protect minorities." *United States* v. *Carolene Products Co.* (1938). In a most direct sense, this implicates the judiciary's special role in safeguarding the interests of those groups that are "relegated to such a position of political powerlessness as to command extraordinary protection from the majoritarian political process." *San Antonio School Dist.* v. *Rodriguez* (1973).

Hunter recognized the considerations addressed above, and it therefore rested on a principle that has been vital for over a century — that "the core of the Fourteenth Amendment is the prevention of meaningful and unjustified official distinctions based on race." Just such distinctions infected the reallocation of decisionmaking authority considered in *Hunter*, for minorities are no less powerless with the vote than without it when a racial criterion is used to assign governmental power in such a way as to exclude particular racial groups "from effective participation in the political proces[s]." *Mobile* v. *Bolden* (WHITE, J., dissenting). Certainly, a state requirement that "desegregation or anti-discrimination laws," *Crawford* v. *Los Angeles Board of Education*, and only such laws, be passed by unanimous vote of the legislature would be constitutionally suspect. It would be equally questionable for a community to require that laws or ordinances "designed to ameliorate race relations or to protect racial minorities," be confirmed by popular vote of the electorate as a whole, while comparable legislation is exempted from a similar procedure. The amendment addressed in *Hunter* — and, as we have explained, the legislation at issue here — was less obviously pernicious than are these examples, but was no different in principle.

V

In reaching this conclusion, we do not undervalue the magnitude of the State's interest in its system of education. Washington could have reserved to state officials the right to make all decisions in the areas of education and student assignment. It has chosen, however, to use a more elaborate system; having done so, the State is obligated to operate that system within the confines of the Fourteenth Amendment. That, we believe, it has failed to do.

Accordingly, the judgment of the Court of Appeals is

Affirmed.

JUSTICE POWELL, with whom THE CHIEF JUSTICE, JUSTICE REHNQUIST, and JUSTICE O'CONNOR join, dissenting.

The people of the State of Washington, by a two to one vote, have adopted a neighborhood school policy. The policy is binding on local school districts but in no way affects the authority of state or federal courts to order school transportation to remedy violations of the Fourteenth Amendment. Nor does the policy affect the power of local school districts to establish voluntary transfer programs for racial integration or for any other purpose.

In the absence of a constitutional violation, no decision of this Court compels a school district to adopt or maintain a mandatory busing program for racial integration. Accordingly, the Court does not hold that the adoption of a neighborhood school policy by *local* school districts would be unconstitutional. Rather, it holds that the adoption of such a policy at the *State* level — rather than at the local level — violates the Equal Protection Clause of the Fourteenth Amendment.

I dissent from the Court's unprecedented intrusion into the structure of a state government. The School Districts in this case were under no Federal Constitutional obligation to adopt mandatory busing programs. The State of Washington, the governmental body ultimately responsible for the provision of public education, has determined that certain mandatory busing programs are detrimental to the education of its children. "[T]he Fourteenth Amendment leaves the States free to distribute the powers of government as they will between their legislative and judicial branches." *Hughes* v. *Superior Court* (1950). In my view, that Amendment leaves the States equally free to decide matters of concern to the State at the State, rather than local, level of government.

I

At the November, 1978, general election, the voters of the State adopted Initiative 350 by a two to one majority. . . .

The Initiative includes two significant limitations upon the scope of its neighborhood school policy. It expressly provides that nothing in the Initiative shall "preclude the establishment of schools offering specialized or enriched educational programs which students may voluntarily choose to attend, or of any other voluntary option offered to students." Moreover, and critical to this case, the authority of state and federal courts to order mandatory school assignments to remedy constitutional violations is left untouched by the Initiative: "This chapter shall not prevent any court of competent jurisdiction from adjudicating constitutional issues relating to the public schools."

This suit was filed in United States District Court shortly after the Initiative was enacted. The Seattle School District, joined by the Tacoma and Pasco School Districts and certain individual plaintiffs, argued that the Initiative violated the Equal Protection Clause of the Fourteenth Amendment. The District Court agreed, and, in a split decision the Court of Appeals affirmed. Relying on *Hunter* v. *Erickson* (1969), the Court of Appeals concluded that Initiative 350 "both creates a constitutionally-suspect racial classification and radically restructures the political process of Washington by allowing a state-wide majority to usurp traditional local authority over local school board educational policies."

II

The principles that should guide us in reviewing the constitutionality of Initiative 350 are well established. To begin with, we have never held, or even intimated, that absent a federal constitutional violation, a State *must* choose to treat persons differently on the basis of race. In the absence of a federal constitutional violation requiring race-specific remedies, a policy of strict racial neutrality by a State would violate no federal constitutional principle. Cf. *University of California Regents* v. *Bakke* (1978).

In particular, a neighborhood school policy and a decision *not* to assign students on the basis of their race, does not offend the Fourteenth Amendment. The Court has never held that there is an affirmative duty to integrate the schools in the absence of a finding of unconstitutional segregation. See *Swann* v. *Charlotte-Mecklenburg Board of Education* (1971); *Dayton Board of Education* v. *Brinkman* (1977). Certainly there is no constitutional duty to adopt mandatory busing in the absence of such a violation. Indeed, even where desegregation is ordered because of a constitutional violation, the Court has never held that racial balance itself is a constitutional requirement. And even where there have been segregated schools, once desegregation has been accomplished no further constitutional duty exists upon school boards or States to maintain integration. See *Pasadena City Board of Education* v. *Spangler* (1976).

Moreover, it is a well established principle that the States have "extraordinarily wide latitude ... in creating various types of political subdivisions and conferring authority upon them." *Holt Civic Club* v. *Tuscaloosa* (1978). The Constitution does not dictate to the States a particular division of authority between legislature and judiciary or between state and local governing bodies. It does not define institutions of local government.

Thus, a State may choose to run its schools from the state legislature or through local school boards just as it may choose to address the matter of race relations at the State or local level. There is no constitutional requirement that the State establish or maintain local institutions of government or that it delegate particular powers to these bodies. The only relevant constitutional limitation on a State's freedom to order its political institutions is that it may not do so in a fashion designed to "[place] *special* burdens on racial minorities within the government process." *Hunter* v. *Erickson* (emphasis added).

In sum, in the absence of a prior constitutional violation, the States are under no constitutional duty to adopt integration programs in their schools, and certainly they are under no duty to establish a regime of mandatory busing. Nor does the Federal Constitution require that particular decisions concerning the schools or any other matter be made on the local as opposed to the State level. It does not require the States to establish local governmental bodies or to delegate unreviewable authority to them.

III

Application of these settled principles demonstrates the serious error of today's decision — an error that cuts deeply into the heretofore unquestioned right of a State to structure the decisionmaking authority of its government. In this case, by Initiative 350, the State has adopted a policy of racial neutrality in student assignments. The policy in no way interferes with the power of State or Federal Courts to remedy constitutional violations. And if such a policy had been adopted by any of the school districts in this litigation there could have been no question that the policy was constitutional.

The issue here arises only because the Seattle School District — in the absence of a then established State policy — chose to adopt race specific school assignments with extensive busing. It is not questioned that the District itself, at any time thereafter, could have changed its mind and cancelled its integration program without violating the Federal Constitution. Yet this Court holds that neither the legislature or the people of the State of Washington could alter what the District had decided.

The Court argues that the people of Washington by Initiative 350 created a racial classification, and yet must agree that identical action by the Seattle School District itself would have created no such classification. This is not an easy argument to answer because it seems to make no sense. School boards are the creation of supreme State authority, whether in a State Constitution or by legislative enactment. Until today's decision no one would have questioned the authority of a State to abolish school boards altogether, or to require that they conform to any lawful State policy. And in the State of Washington, a neighborhood school policy would have been lawful.

Under today's decision this heretofore undoubted supreme authority of a State's electorate is to be curtailed whenever a school board — or indeed any other state board or local instrumentality — adopts a race specific program that arguably benefits racial minorities. Once such a program is adopted, *only* the local or subordinate entity that approved it will have authority to change it. The Court offers no authority or relevant explanation for this extraordinary subordination of the ultimate sovereign power of a State to act with respect to racial matters by subordinate bodies. It is a strange notion — alien to our system — that local governmental bodies can forever preempt the ability of a State — the sovereign power — to address a matter of compelling concern to the State. The Constitution of the United States does not require such a bizarre result.

This is certainly not a case where a State — in moving to change a locally adopted policy — has established a racially discriminatory requirement. Initiative 350 does not impede enforcement of the Fourteenth Amendment. If a Washington school district should be found to have established a segregated school system, Initiative 350 will place no barrier in the way of a remedial busing order. Nor does Initiative 350 authorize or approve segregation in any form or degree. It is neutral on its face, and racially neutral as public policy. Children of all races benefit from neighborhood schooling, just as children of all races benefit from exposure to "ethnic and racial diversity in the classroom." [Q]uoting *Columbus Board of Education* v. *Penick* (1979) (POWELL, J., dissenting).

Finally, Initiative 350 places no "special burdens on racial minorities within the governmental process," *Hunter* v. *Erickson*, such that interference with the State's distribution of authority is justified. Initiative 350 is simply a reflection of the State's political process at work. It does not alter that process in any respect. It does not require, for example, that all matters dealing with race — or with integration in the schools — must henceforth be submitted to a referendum of the people. Cf. *Hunter* v. *Erickson*. The State has done no more than precisely what the Court has said that it should do: It has "resolved through the political process" the "desirability and efficacy of [mandatory] school desegregation" where there has been no unlawful segregation.

The political process in Washington, as in other States, permits persons who are dissatisfied at a local level to appeal to the State legislature or the people of the State for redress. It permits the people of a State to preempt local policies, and to formulate new programs and regulations. Such a process is inherent in the continued sovereignty of the States. This is our system. Any time a State chooses to address a major issue some persons or groups may be disadvantaged. In a democratic system there are winners and losers. But there is no inherent unfairness in this and certainly no Constitutional violation.

IV

. . . Nothing in *Hunter* supports the Court's extraordinary invasion into the State's distribution of authority. Even could it be assumed that Initiative 350 imposed a burden on racial minorities, it simply does not place unique political obstacles in the way of racial minorities. In this case, unlike in *Hunter*, the political system has *not* been redrawn or altered. The authority of the State over the public school system, acting through Initiative or the legislature, is plenary. Thus, the State's political system is not altered when it adopts for the first time a policy, concededly within the area of its authority, for the regulation of local school districts. And certainly racial minorities are not uniquely or comparatively burdened by the State's adoption of a policy that would be lawful if adopted by any School District in the State.

Hunter, therefore, is simply irrelevant. It is the *Court* that by its decision today disrupts the normal course of State government. Under its unprecedented theory of a vested constitutional right to local decisionmaking, the State apparently is now forever barred from addressing the perplexing problems of show best to educate fairly *all* children in a multi-racial society where, as in this case, the local school board has acted first.

V

We are not asked to decide the wisdom of a State policy that limits the ability of local school districts to adopt — on their own volition — mandatory reassignments for racial balance. We must decide only whether the Federal Constitution permits the State to adopt such a policy. The School Districts in this case were under no federal constitutional obligation to adopt mandatory busing. Absent such an obligation, the State — exercising its sovereign authority over all subordinate agencies — should be free to reject this debatable restriction on liberty. But today's decision denies this right to a State. In this case, it deprives the State of Washington of all opportunity to address the unresolved questions resulting from extensive mandatory busing. The Constitution does not dictate to the States at what level of government decisions affecting the public schools must be taken. It certainly does not strip the States of their sovereignty. It therefore does not authorize today's intrusion into the State's internal structure.

No. 81-38

Mary Ellen Crawford, a minor, etc., *et al.*, Petitioners, *v.* Board of Education of the City of Los Angeles *et al.*	On writ of certiorari to the Court of Appeal of California, Second Appellate District

[June 30, 1982]

JUSTICE POWELL delivered the opinion of the Court.

An amendment to the California Constitution provides that state courts shall not order mandatory pupil assignment or transportation unless a federal court would do so to remedy a violation of the Equal Protection Clause of the Fourteenth Amendment of the United States Constitution. The question for our decision is whether this provision is itself in violation of the Fourteenth Amendment.

I

This litigation began almost twenty years ago in 1963, when minority students attending school in the Los Angeles Unified School District (District) filed a class action in state court seeking desegregation of the District's schools. The case went to trial some five years later, and in 1970 the trial court issued an opinion finding that the District was substantially segregated in violation of the State and Federal Constitutions. The court ordered the District to prepare a desegregation plan for immediate use.

On the District's appeal, the California Supreme Court affirmed, but on a different basis. *Crawford* v. *Board of Education* (1976). While the trial court had found *de jure* segregation in violation of the Fourteenth Amendment of the United States Constitution, the California Supreme Court based its affirmance solely upon the Equal Protection Clause of the State Constitution. The court explained that under the California Constitution "state school boards . . . bear a constitutional obligation to take reasonable steps to alleviate segregation in the public schools, whether the segregation be de facto or de jure in origin." The court remanded to the trial court for preparation of a "reasonably feasible" plan for school desegregation.

On remand, the trial court rejected the District's mostly voluntary desegregation plan but ultimately approved a second plan that included substantial mandatory school reassignment and transportation — "busing" — on a racial and ethnic basis. The plan was put into effect in the fall of 1978, but after one year's experience, all parties to the litigation were dissatisfied. See *Crawford* v. *Board of Education* (1980). Although the plan continued in operation, the trial court began considering alternatives in October 1979.

In November 1979 the voters of the State of California ratified Proposition I, an amendment to the Due Process and Equal Protection Clauses of the State Constitution. Proposition I conforms the power of state courts to order busing to that exercised by the federal courts under the Fourteenth Amendment:

> "[N]o court of this state may impose upon the State of California or any public entity, board, or official any obligation or responsibility with respect to the use of pupil school assignment or pupil transportation, (1) except to remedy a specific violation by such party that would also constitute a violation of the Equal Protection Clause of the 14th Amendment to the United States Constitution, and (2) unless a federal court would be permitted under federal decisional law to impose that obligation or responsibility upon such party to remedy the specific violation of the Equal Protection Clause. . . ."

Following approval of Proposition I, the District asked the Superior Court to halt all mandatory reassignment and busing of pupils. On May 19, 1980, the court denied the District's application. The court reasoned that Proposition I was of no effect in this case in light of the court's 1970 finding of de jure segregation by the District in violation of the Fourteenth Amendment. Shortly thereafter, the court ordered implementation of a revised desegregation plan, one that again substantially relied upon mandatory pupil reassignment and transportation.

The California Court of Appeal reversed. (1980). The court found that the trial court's 1970 findings of fact would not support the conclusion that the District had violated the Federal Constitution through intentional segregation. Thus, Proposition I was applicable to the trial court's desegregation plan and would bar that part of the plan requiring mandatory student reassignment and transportation. Moreover, the court concluded that Proposition I was constitutional under the Fourteenth Amendment. The court found no obligation on the part of the State to retain a greater remedy at state law against racial segregation than was provided by the Federal Constitution. The court rejected the claim that Proposition I was adopted with a discriminatory purpose.

Determining Proposition I to be applicable and constitutional, the Court of Appeal vacated the orders entered by the Superior Court. The California Supreme Court denied hearing. We granted certiorari. (1981).

II

We agree with the California Court of Appeal in rejecting the contention that once a State chooses to do "more" than the Fourteenth Amendment requires, it may never recede. We reject an interpretation of the Fourteenth Amendment so destructive of a state's democratic processes and of its ability to experiment. This interpretation has no support in the decisions of this Court.

Proposition I does not inhibit enforcement of any federal law or constitutional requirement. Quite the contrary, by its plain language the Proposition seeks only to embrace the requirements of the Federal Constitution with respect to mandatory school assignments and transportation. It would be paradoxical to conclude that by adopting the Equal Protection Clause of the Fourteenth Amendment, the voters of the State thereby had violated it. Moreover, even after Proposition I, the California Constitution still imposes a greater duty of desegregation than does the Federal Constitution. The state courts of California continue to have an obligation under state law to order segregated school districts to use voluntary desegregation techniques, whether or not there has been a finding of intentional segregation. The school districts themselves retain a state law obligation to take reasonably feasible steps to desegregate, and they remain free to adopt reassignment and busing plans to effectuate desegregation.

Nonetheless, petitioners contend that Proposition I is unconstitutional on its face. They argue that Proposition I employs an "explicit racial classification" and imposes a "race-specific" burden on minorities seeking to vindicate state created rights. By limiting the power of state courts to enforce the state created right to desegregated schools, petitioners contend, Proposition I creates a "dual court system" that discriminates on the basis of race. They emphasize that other state created rights may be vindicated by the state courts without limitation on remedies. Petitioners argue that the "dual court system" created by Proposition I is unconstitutional unless supported by a compelling state interest.

We would agree that if Proposition I employed a racial classification it would be unconstitutional unless necessary to further a compelling state interest. "A racial classification, regardless of purported motivation is presumptively invalid and can be upheld only upon an extraordinary justification." *Personnel Administrator of Massachusetts* v. *Feeney* (1979). ... But Proposition I does not embody a racial classification. It neither says nor implies that persons are to be treated differently on account of their race. It simply forbids state courts from ordering pupil school assignment or transportation in the absence of a Fourteenth Amendment violation. The benefit it seeks to confer — neighborhood schooling — is made available regardless of race in the discretion of school boards. Indeed, even if Proposition I had a racially discriminatory effect, in view of the demographic mix of the District it is not clear which race or races would be affected the most or in what way. In addition, this Court previously has held that even when a neutral law has a disproportionately adverse effect on a racial minority, the Fourteenth Amendment is violated only if a discriminatory purpose can be shown.

Similarly, the Court has recognized that a distinction may exist between state action that discriminates on the basis of race and state action that addresses, in neutral fashion, race related matters. This distinction is implicit in the Court's repeated statement that the Equal Protection Clause is not violated by the mere repeal of race related legislation or policies that were not required by the Federal Constitution in the first place. ... [T]he simple repeal or modification of desegregation or anti-discrimination laws ... never has been viewed as embodying a presumptively invalid racial classification.

Were we to hold that the mere repeal of race related legislation is unconstitutional, we would limit seriously the authority of States to deal with the problems of our heterogeneous population. States would be committed irrevocably to legislation that has proven unsuccessful or even harmful in practice. And certainly the purposes of the Fourteenth Amendment would not be advanced by an interpretation that discouraged the States from providing greater protection to racial minorities. Nor would the purposes of the Amendment be furthered by requiring the States to maintain legislation designed to ameliorate race relations or to protect racial minorities but which has produced just the opposite effects. Yet these would be the results of requiring a State to maintain legislation that has proven unworkable or harmful when the State was under no obligation to adopt the legislation in the first place. Moreover, and relevant to this case, we would not interpret the Fourteenth Amendment to require the people of a State to adhere to a judicial construction of their State Constitution when that Constitution itself vests final authority in the people.

III

Petitioners seek to avoid the force of the foregoing considerations by arguing that Proposition I is not a "mere repeal." Relying primarily on the decision in *Hunter* v. *Erickson* [1969], they contend that Proposition I does not simply repeal a state created right but fundamentally alters the judicial system so that "those seeking redress from racial isolation in violation of state law must be satisfied with less than full relief from a state court." We do not view *Hunter* as controlling here, nor are we persuaded by petitioners' characterization of Proposition I as something more than a mere repeal.

In *Hunter* the Akron city charter had been amended by the voters to provide that no ordinance regulating real estate on the basis of race, color, religion, or national origin could take effect until approved by a referendum. As a result of the charter amendment, a fair housing ordinance, adopted by the City Council at an earlier date, was no longer effective. In holding the charter amendment invalid under the Fourteenth Amendment, the Court held that the charter amendment was not a simple repeal of the fair housing ordinance. The amendment "not only suspended the operation of the existing ordinance forbidding housing discrimination, but also required the approval of the electors before any future [anti-discrimination] ordinance could take effect." Thus, whereas most ordinances regulating real property would take effect once enacted by the City Council, ordinances prohibiting racial discrimination in housing would be forced to clear an additional hurdle. As such, the charter amendment placed an impermissible, "special burde[n] on racial minorities within the governmental process."

Hunter involved more than a "mere repeal" of the fair housing ordinance; persons seeking anti-discrimination housing laws — presumptively racial minorities — were "singled out for mandatory referendums while no other group ... face[d] that obstacle." *James* v. *Valtierra* [1971]. By contrast, even on the assumption that racial minorities benefitted [*sic*] from the busing required by state law, Proposition I is less than a "repeal" of the California Equal Protection Clause. As noted above, after Proposition I, the State Constitution still places upon school boards a greater duty to desegregate than does the Fourteenth Amendment.

Nor can it be said that Proposition I distorts the political process for racial reasons or that it allocates governmental or judicial power on the basis of a discriminatory principle. "The Constitution does not require things which are different in fact or opinion to be treated in law as though they were the same." *Tigner* v. *Texas* (1940). Remedies appropriate in one area of legislation may not be desirable in another.... Yet a "dual court system" — one for the racial majority and one for the racial minority — is not established simply because civil rights remedies are different from those available in other areas. Surely it was constitutional for the California Supreme Court to caution that although "in some circumstances busing will be an appropriate and useful element in a desegregation plan," in other circumstances "its 'costs,' both in financial and educational terms, will render its use inadvisable." It was equally constitutional for the people of the State to determine that the standard of the Fourteenth Amendment was more appropriate for California courts to apply in desegregation cases than the standard repealed by Proposition I.

In short, having gone beyond the requirements of the Federal Constitution, the State was free to return in part to the standard prevailing generally throughout the United States. It could have conformed its law to the Federal Constitution in every respect. That it chose to pull back only in part, and by preserving a greater right to desegregation than exists under the Federal Constitution, most assuredly does not render the Proposition unconstitutional on its face.

IV

The California Court of Appeal also rejected petitioners' claim that Proposition I, if facially valid, was nonetheless unconstitutional because enacted with a discriminatory purpose. The court reasoned that the purposes of the Proposition were well stated in the Proposition itself. Voters may have been motivated by any of these purposes, chief among them the educational benefits of neighborhood schooling. The Court found that voters also may have considered that the extent of mandatory busing, authorized by state law, actually was aggravating rather than ameliorating the desegregation problem. It characterized petitioners' claim of discriminatory intent on the part of millions of voters as but "pure speculation."

In *Reitman* v. *Mulkey* (1967), the Court considered the constitutionality of another California Proposition. In that case, the California Supreme Court had concluded that the Proposition was unconstitutional because it gave the State's approval to private racial discrimination. This Court agreed, deferring to the findings made by the California court. The Court noted that the California court was "armed ... with the knowledge of the facts and circumstances concerning the passage and potential impact" of the Proposition and "familiar with the milieu in which that provision would operate." Similarly, in this case, again involving the circumstances of passage and the potential impact of a Proposition adopted at a state-wide election, we see no reason to differ with the conclusions of the state appellate court.

Under decisions of this Court, a law neutral on its face still may be unconstitutional if motivated by a discriminatory purpose. In determining whether such a purpose was the motivating factor, the racially disproportionate effect of official action provides "an important starting point."

Personnel Administrator of Massachusetts v. *Feeney* (1979), quoting *Arlington Heights* v. *Metropolitan Housing Dev. Corp.* [1977].

Proposition I in no way purports to limit the power of state courts to remedy the effects of intentional segregation with its accompanying stigma. The benefits of neighborhood schooling are racially neutral. This manifestly is true in Los Angeles where over 75% of the public school body is composed of groups viewed as racial minorities. Moreover, the Proposition simply removes one means of achieving the state created right to desegregated education. School districts retain the obligation to alleviate segregation regardless of cause. And the state courts still may order desegregation measures other than pupil school assignment or pupil transportation.

Even if we could assume that Proposition I had a disproportionate adverse effect on racial minorities, we see no reason to challenge the Court of Appeal's conclusion that the voters of the State were not motivated by a discriminatory purpose. In this case the Proposition was approved by an overwhelming majority of the electorate. It received support from members of all races. The purposes of the Proposition are stated in its text and are legitimate, nondiscriminatory objectives. In these circumstances, we will not dispute the judgment of the Court of Appeal or impugn the motives of the State's electorate.

Accordingly the judgment of the California Court of Appeal is

Affirmed.

JUSTICE BLACKMUN, with whom JUSTICE BRENNAN joins, concurring.

While I join the opinion of the Court, I write separately to address what I believe are the critical distinctions between this case and *Washington* v. *Seattle School District No. 1.*

The Court always has recognized that distortions of the political process have special implications for attempts to achieve equal protection of the laws. Thus the Court has found particularly pernicious those classifications that threaten the ability of minorities to involve themselves in the process of self-government, for if laws are not drawn within a "just framework," *Hunter* v. *Erickson* (1969) (Harlan, J., concurring), it is unlikely that they will be drawn on just principles.

The Court's conclusion in *Seattle* followed inexorably from these considerations. In that case the statewide electorate reallocated decisionmaking authority to " 'mak[e] it *more* difficult for certain racial and religious minorities [than for other members of the community] to achieve legislation that is in their interest.' " *Washington* v. *Seattle School District No. 1*, quoting *Hunter* v. *Erickson* (Harlan, J., concurring). The Court found such a political structure impermissible, recognizing that if a class cannot participate effectively in the process by which those rights and remedies that order society are created, that class necessarily will be "relegated, by state fiat, in a most basic way to second-class status." *Plyler* v. *Doe* (1982) (BLACKMUN, J., concurring).

In my view, something significantly different is involved in this case. State courts do not create the rights they enforce; those rights originate elsewhere — in the state legislature, in the State's political subdivisions, or in the state constitution itself. When one of those rights is repealed, and therefore is rendered unenforceable in the courts, that action hardly can be said to restructure the State's decisionmaking mechanism. While the California electorate may have made it more difficult to achieve desegregation when it enacted Proposition I, to my mind it did so not by working a structural change in the political *process* so much as by simply repealing the right to invoke a judicial busing remedy. Indeed, ruling for petitioner on a *Hunter* theory seemingly would mean that statutory affirmative action or antidiscrimination programs never could be repealed, for a repeal of the enactment would mean that enforcement authority previously lodged in the state courts was being removed by another political entity.

In short, the people of California — the same "entity" that put in place the state constitution, and created the enforceable obligation to desegregate — have made the desegregation obligation judicially unenforceable. The "political process or the decisionmaking mechanism used to *address* racially conscious legislation" has not been "singled out for peculiar and disadvantageous treatment," *Washington* v. *Seattle School District No. 1* (emphasis in original) for those political mechanisms that create and repeal the rights ultimately enforced by the courts were left entirely unaffected by Proposition I. And I cannot conclude that the repeal of a state-created right — or, analogously, the removal of the judiciary's ability to enforce that right — "curtail[s] the operation of those political processes ordinarily to be relied upon to protect minorities." [Q]uoting *United States* v. *Carolene Products Co.* [1938].

Because I find *Seattle* distinguishable from this case, I join the opinion and judgment of the Court.

JUSTICE MARSHALL, dissenting.

The Court today addresses two state constitutional amendments, each of which is admittedly designed to substantially curtail, if not eliminate, the use of mandatory student assignment or transportation as a remedy for *de facto* segregation. In *Washington* v. *Seattle School District No. 1*, the Court concludes that Washington's Initiative 350, which effectively prevents school boards from ordering mandatory school assignment in the absence of a finding of *de jure* segregation within the meaning of the Fourteenth Amendment, is unconstitutional because "it uses the racial nature of an issue to define the governmental decisionmaking structure, and thus imposes substantial and unique burdens on racial minorities." Inexplicably, the Court simultaneously concludes that California's Proposition I, which effectively prevents a state court from ordering the same mandatory remedies in the absence of a finding of *de jure* segregation, *is* constitutional because "having gone beyond the requirements of the

Federal Constitution, the State was free to return in part to the standard prevailing generally throughout the United States." Because I fail to see how a fundamental redefinition of the governmental decisionmaking structure with respect to the same racial issue can be unconstitutional when the state seeks to remove the authority from local school boards, yet constitutional when the state attempts to achieve the same result by limiting the power of its courts, I must dissent from the Court's decision to uphold Proposition I.

I

In order to understand fully the implications of the Court's action today, it is necessary to place the facts concerning the adoption of Proposition I in their proper context. Nearly two decades ago, a unanimous California Supreme Court declared that "[t]he segregation of school children into separate schools because of their race, even though the physical facilities and the methods and quality of instruction in the several schools may be equal, deprives the children of the minority group of equal opportunities for education and denies them equal protection and due process of the law." *Jackson* v. *Pasadena City School District* (1963). Recognizing that the "right to an equal opportunity for education and the harmful consequences of segregation" do not differ according to the *cause* of racial isolation, the California Supreme Court declined to adopt the distinction between *de facto* and *de jure* segregation engrafted by this Court on the Fourteenth Amendment. Instead, the court clearly held that "school boards [must] take steps, insofar as reasonably feasible, to alleviate racial imbalance in schools regardless of its cause."

As the California Supreme Court subsequently explained, the duty established in *Jackson* does not require that "each school in a district . . . reflect the racial composition of the district as a whole." *Crawford* v. *Board of Education* (1976) (*Crawford I*). Rather, it is sufficient that school authorities "take reasonable and feasible steps to eliminate *segregated* schools, i.e., schools in which the minority student enrollment is so disproportionate as realistically to isolate minority students from other students and thus deprive minority students of an integrated educational experience." Moreover, the California courts have made clear that the primary responsibility for implementing this state constitutional duty lies with local school boards. "[S]o long as a local school board initiates and implements reasonably feasible steps to alleviate school segregation in its district, and so long as such steps produce meaningful progress in the alleviation of such segregation, and its harmful consequences, . . . the judiciary should [not] intervene in the desegregation process." If, however, a school board neglects or refuses to implement meaningful programs designed to bring about an end to racial isolation in the public schools, "the court is left with no alternative but to intervene to protect the constitutional rights of minority children." When judicial intervention is necessary, the court "may exercise broad equitable powers in formulating and supervising a plan which the court finds will insure meaningful progress to alleviate the harmful consequences of school segregation in the district." Moreover, "once a school board defaults in its constitutional task, the court, in devising a remedial order, is not precluded from requiring the busing of children as part of a reasonably feasible desegregation plan."

Like so many other decisions protecting the rights of minorities, California's decision to eradicate the evils of segregation regardless of cause has not been a popular one. In the nearly two decades since the state Supreme Court's decision in *Jackson*, there have been repeated attempts to restrain school boards and courts from enforcing this constitutional guarantee by means of mandatory student transfers or assignments. In 1970, shortly after the San Francisco Unified School District voluntarily adopted a desegregation plan involving mandatory student assignment, the California legislature enacted Education Code § 1009.5, currently codified at Cal. Educ. Code Ann. § 35350 (West), which provides that "no governing board of a school district shall require any student or pupil to be transported for any purpose or for any reason without the written permission of the parent or guardian." In *San Francisco Unified School District* v. *Johnson* (1971), the California Supreme Court interpreted this provision only to bar a school district from compelling students, without parental consent, to use means of transportation furnished by the district. Construing the statute to prohibit nonconsensual assignment of students for the purpose of eradicating *de jure* or *de facto* segregation, the court concluded, would clearly violate both the state and the federal constitution by "exorcising a method that in many circumstances is the sole and exclusive means of eliminating racial segregation in the schools."

The very next year, opponents of mandatory student assignment for the purpose of achieving racial balance again attempted to eviscerate the state constitutional guarantee recognized in *Jackson*. Proposition 21, which was enacted by referendum in November 1972, stated that "no public school student shall, because of his race, creed, or color, be assigned to or be required to attend a particular school." Predictably, the California Supreme Court struck down Proposition 21 "for the same reasons set forth by us in *Johnson*." *Santa Barbara School District* v. *Superior Court* (1975).

Finally, in 1979, the people of California enacted Proposition I. That Proposition, like all of the previous initiatives, effectively deprived California courts of the ability to enforce the state constitutional guarantee that minority children will not attend racially isolated schools by use of what may be "the sole and exclusive means of eliminating racial segregation from the schools," *San Francisco Unified School District* v. *Johnson*, mandatory student assignment and transfer. Unlike the earlier attempts to accomplish this objective, however, Proposition I does not purport to prevent mandatory assignments and transfers when such measures are predicated on a violation of the Federal constitution. Therefore, the only question presented by this case is whether the fact that mandatory transfers may still be made to vindicate federal constitutional rights saves this initiative from the constitutional infirmity presented in the previous attempts to accomplish this same objective. In my view, the recitation of the obvious — that a state constitutional amendment does not override federal constitutional guarantees — cannot work to deprive minority children in California of their federally protected right to the equal protection of the laws.

II

A

In *Seattle*, the Court exhaustively set out the relevant principles that control the present inquiry. We there found that a series of precedents, exemplified by *Hunter* v. *Erickson* (1969) and *Lee* v. *Nyquist* (1971), establish that the Fourteenth Amendment prohibits a State from allocating "governmental power non-neutrally, by explicitly using the *racial* nature of a decision to determine the decisionmaking process." *Seattle* (emphasis in original). We concluded that "State action of this kind . . . 'places *special* burdens on racial minorities within the governmental process' . . . thereby 'making it *more* difficult for certain racial and religious minorities [than for other members of the community] to achieve legislation that is in their interest.'" ([E]mphasis in original), quoting *Hunter* v. *Erickson* (Harlan, J., concurring). *Seattle*.

It is therefore necessary to determine whether Proposition I works a "non-neutral" reallocation of governmental power on the basis of the racial nature of the decision. This determination is also informed by our decision in *Seattle*. In that case we were presented with a state-wide initiative which effectively precluded local school boards from ordering mandatory student assignment or transfer except where required to remedy a constitutional violation. We concluded that the initiative violated the Fourteenth Amendment because it reallocated decisionmaking authority over racial issues from the local school board to a "new and remote level of government." *Seattle*. In reaching this conclusion, we specifically affirmed three principles that are particularly relevant to the present inquiry.

First, we rejected the State's argument that a state-wide initiative prohibiting mandatory student assignment has no "racial overtones" simply because it does not mention the words "race" or "integration." *Seattle*. We noted that "[n]either the initiative's sponsors, nor the District Court, nor the Court of Appeals had any difficulty perceiving the racial nature of the issue settled by Initiative 350." In light of its language and the history surrounding its adoption, we found it "beyond reasonable dispute . . . that the initiative was enacted " 'because of,'" not merely "in spite of," its adverse effects upon' busing for integration." *Seattle*, quoting *Personnel Administrator of Massachusetts* v. *Feeney* (1979). Moreover, we rejected the Solicitor General's remarkable contention, a contention also pressed here, that "busing for integration . . . is not a peculiarly 'racial' issue at all." *Seattle*. While not discounting the value of an integrated education to non-minority students, we conclude that *Lee* v. *Nyquist* definitively established that "desegregation of the public schools ... at bottom inures primarily to the benefit of the minority, and is designed for that purpose," thereby bringing it within the *Hunter* doctrine. *Seattle.*

Second, the *Seattle* Court determined that Initiative 350 unconstitutionally reallocated power from local school boards to the state legislature or the state-wide electorate. After the enactment of Initiative 350, local school boards continued to exercise considerable discretion over virtually all educational matters, including student assignment. Those seeking to eradicate *de facto* segregation, however, were forced to "surmount a considerably higher hurdle than persons seeking comparable legislative action," *Seattle,* for instead of seeking relief from the local school board, those pursuing this racial issue were forced to appeal to a different and more remote level of government. Just as in *Hunter* v. *Erickson,* where those interested in enacting fair housing ordinances were compelled to gain the support of a majority of the electorate, we held that this reallocation of governmental power along racial lines offends the Equal Protection Clause.... We found it sufficient that Initiative 350 had deprived those seeking to redress a racial harm of the right to seek a particularly effective form of redress from the level of government ordinarily empowered to grant the remedy.

Finally, the Court's decision in *Seattle* implicitly rejected the argument that state action that reallocates governmental power along racial lines can be immunized by the fact that it specifically leaves intact rights guaranteed by the Fourteenth Amendment. The fact that mandatory pupil reassignment was still available as a remedy for *de jure* segregation did not alter the conclusion that an unconstitutional reallocation of power had occurred with respect to those seeking to combat *de facto* racial isolation in the public schools.

B

In my view, these principles inexorably lead to the conclusion that California's Proposition I works an unconstitutional reallocation of state power by depriving California courts of the ability to grant meaningful relief to those seeking to vindicate the state's guarantee against *de facto* segregation in the public schools. Despite Proposition I's apparent neutrality, it is "beyond reasonable dispute," *Seattle,* and the majority today concedes, that "court ordered busing in *excess* of that required by the Fourteenth Amendment ... prompted the initiation and probably the adoption of Proposition I." Because "minorities may consider busing for integration to be 'legislation that is in their interest,' " *Seattle,* quoting *Hunter* v. *Erickson* (Harlan, J., concurring.) Proposition I is sufficiently "racial" to invoke the *Hunter* doctrine.

Nor can there be any doubt that Proposition I works a substantial reallocation of state power. Prior to the enactment of Proposition I, those seeking to vindicate the rights enumerated by the California Supreme Court in *Jackson* v. *Pasadena City School District* (1963), just as those interested in attaining any other educational objective, followed a two-stage procedure. First, California's minority community could attempt to convince the local school board voluntarily to comply with its constitutional obligation to take reasonably feasible steps to eliminate racial isolation in the public schools. If the board was either unwilling or unable to carry out its constitutional duty, those seeking redress could petition the California state courts to require school officials to live up to their obligations. Busing could be required as part of a judicial remedial order. *Crawford I* (1976).

Whereas Initiative 350 attempted to deny minority children the first step of this procedure, Proposition I eliminates by fiat the second stage: the ability of California courts to order meaningful compliance with the requirements of the state constitution. After the adoption of Proposition I, the only method of enforcing against a recalcitrant school board the state constitutional duty to eliminate racial isolation is to petition either the state legislature or the electorate as a whole. Clearly, the rules of the game have been significantly changed for those attempting to vindicate this state constitutional right.

The majority seeks to conceal the unmistakable effects of Proposition I by calling it a "mere repeal" of the State's earlier commitment to do " 'more' than the Fourteenth Amendment requires." Although it is true that we have never held that the "mere repeal of an existing [anti-discrimination] ordinance violates the Fourteenth Amendment," *Hunter* v. *Erickson*, it is equally clear that the reallocation of governmental power created by Proposition I is not a "mere repeal" within the meaning of any of our prior decisions. . . .

. . . [I]n *Seattle*, *Hunter*, and *Reitman* v. *Mulkey* (1967), the three times that this Court has explicitly rejected the argument that a proposed change constituted a "mere repeal" of an existing policy, the alleged rescission was accomplished by a governmental entity other than the entity that had taken the initial action, and resulted in a drastic alteration of the substantive effect of existing policy. This case falls squarely within this latter category. To be sure, the *right* to be free from racial isolation in the public schools remains unaffected by Proposition I. . . . But Proposition I does repeal the power of the state court to *enforce* this existing constitutional guarantee through the use of mandatory pupil assignment and transfer.

The majority asserts that the Fourteenth Amendment does not "require the people of a state to adhere to a judicial construction of their state constitution when that constitution itself vests final authority in the people." A state court's authority to order appropriate remedies for state constitutional violations, however, is no more based on the "final authority" of the people than the power of the local Seattle school board to make decisions regarding pupil assignment is premised on the State's ultimate control of the educational process. Rather, the authority of California courts to order mandatory student assignments in this context springs from the same source as the authority underlying other remedial measures adopted by state and federal courts in the absence of statutory authorization: the "courts power to provide equitable relief" to remedy a constitutional violation. *Swann* v. *Charlotte-Mecklenburg Board of Education* (1970); *Crawford I* (1976) ("a trial court may exercise broad equitable powers in formulating and supervising a plan which the court finds will insure meaningful progress to alleviate ... school segregation"). Even assuming that the source of a court's power to remedy a constitutional violation can be traced back to "the people," the majority's conclusion that "the people" can therefore confer that remedial power on a discriminatory basis is plainly inconsistent with our prior decisions.... [I]n *Seattle* we concluded that the reallocation of power away from local school boards offended the Equal Protection clause even though the State of Washington "is ultimately responsible for providing education within its borders." The fact that this change was enacted through popular referendum, therefore, cannot immunize it from constitutional review. See *Lucas* v. *Colorado General Assembly* (1964).

As in *Seattle*, *Hunter*, and *Reitman*, Proposition I's repeal of the state court's enforcement powers was the work of an independent governmental entity, and not of the state courts themselves. That this repeal drastically alters the substantive rights granted by existing policy is patently obvious from the facts of this litigation. By prohibiting California courts from ordering mandatory student assignment when necessary to eliminate racially isolated schools, Proposition I has placed an enormous barrier between minority children and the effective enjoyment of their constitutional rights, a barrier that is not placed in the path of those who seek to vindicate other rights granted by state law. This Court's precedents demonstrate that, absent a compelling state interest, which respondents have hardly demonstrated, such a discriminatory barrier cannot stand.

The fact that California attempts to cloak its discrimination in the mantle of the Fourteenth Amendment does not alter this result. Although it might seem "paradoxical" to some members of this Court that a referendum that adopts the wording of the Fourteenth Amendment might violate it, the paradox is specious. Because of the Supremacy Clause, Proposition I would have precisely the same legal effect if it contained no reference to the Fourteenth Amendment. The lesson of *Seattle* is that a state, in prohibiting conduct that is not required by the Fourteenth Amendment, may nonetheless create a discriminatory reallocation of governmental power that does violate equal protection. The fact that some less effective avenues remain open to those interested in mandatory student assignment to eliminate racial isolation ... does not justify the discriminatory reallocation of governmental decisionmaking.

... As we have long recognized, courts too often have been "the sole practicable avenue open to a minority to petition for redress of grievances." *NAACP* v. *Button* (1963).... It is no wonder, as the present case amply illustrates, that whatever progress that has been made towards the elimination of *de facto* segregation has come from the California courts. Indeed, Proposition I, by denying full access to the only branch of government that has been willing to vindicate the plainly unpopular cause of racial integration in the public schools than a simple reallocation of an often unavailable and unresponsive legislative process. . . .

III

Even if the effects of Proposition I somehow can be distinguished from the enactments at issue in *Hunter* and *Seattle*, the result reached by the majority today is still plainly inconsistent with our precedents. Because it found that the segregation of the California public schools violated the Fourteenth Amendment, the state trial court never considered whether Proposition I was itself unconstitutional because it was the product of discriminatory intent. Despite the absence of *any* factual record on this issue, the Court of Appeals rejected petitioner's argument that the law was motivated by a discriminatory intent on the ground that the recitation of several potentially legitimate purposes in the legislation's preamble rendered any claim that it had been enacted for an invidious purpose "pure speculation." *Crawford* v. *Board of Education* (1980) *(Crawford II)*.

In *Arlington Heights* v. *Metropolitan Housing Development Corporation* (1977), we declared that "[d]etermining whether invidious discriminatory purpose was a motivating factor demands a sensitive inquiry into such circumstantial and direct evidence of intent as may be available." Petitioners assert that the disproportionate impact of Proposition I, combined with the circumstances surrounding its adoption and the history of opposition to integration cited above, clearly indicate the presence of discriminatory intent. Yet despite the fact that *no inquiry* has been conducted into these allegations by either the trial or the appellate court, this Court, in its haste to uphold the banner of "neighborhood schools," affirms a factual determination that was never made. Such blind allegiance to the conclusory statements of a lower court is plainly forbidden by our prior decisions.

IV

Proposition I is in some sense "better" than the Washington initiative struck down in *Seattle*. In their generosity, California voters have allowed those seeking racial balance to petition the very school officials who have steadfastly maintained the color line at the schoolhouse door to comply voluntarily with their continuing state constitutional duty to desegregate. At the same time, the voters have deprived minorities of the only method of redress that has proved effective — the full remedial powers of the state judiciary. In the name of the State's "ability to experiment," the Court today allows this placement of yet another burden in the path of those seeking to counter the effects of nearly three centuries of racial prejudice.

651

Because this decision is neither justified by our prior decisions nor consistent with our duty to guarantee all citizens the equal protection of the laws, I must dissent.

JULY

COURT ON NAACP BOYCOTT
July 2, 1982

In an 8-0 ruling, the Supreme Court held July 2 that the National Association for the Advancement of Colored People (NAACP) could not be held liable for financial damages arising from a 1966 civil rights boycott conducted in Claiborne County, Miss.

The case, NAACP v. Claiborne Hardware Co., had begun in 1969 when a group of white merchants sued the national civil rights organization and 91 individuals for the losses they incurred during the economic boycott of their stores. The boycott had been led by Charles Evers, then the NAACP field secretary in Mississippi.

No Violent Conspiracy

The Mississippi Supreme Court had found the boycott to be a "conspiracy" carried out through illegal force and violence. But Justice John Paul Stevens, writing for the U.S. Supreme Court, declared that the state court had failed to show that the merchants' losses had been caused by specific acts of violence.

"A massive and prolonged effort to change the social, political and economic structure of a local environment cannot be characterized as a violent conspiracy simply by reference to the ephemeral consequences of a relatively few violent acts," he wrote.

Most of the reported violence involved efforts by boycott supporters to prohibit unsympathetic blacks from patronizing the white merchants.

"Unquestionably, these individuals may be held responsible for the injuries that they caused," Stevens wrote. But, he noted, it had not been proven that such violence had "colored the entire collective effort."

Free Speech Boundaries

Referring to speeches delivered by Charles Evers, Stevens noted that the civil rights leader had used "emotionally charged rhetoric." But he concluded that such rhetoric "did not transcend the bounds of protected speech."

"Strong and effective extemporaneous rhetoric cannot be nicely channeled in purely dulcet phrases," Stevens wrote. "An advocate must be free to stimulate his audience with spontaneous and emotional appeals for unity and action in a common cause."

The Mississippi Supreme Court had found that Evers had used threats of violence to enforce the boycott. Evers was quoted: "If we catch any of you going in any one of them racist stores, we're going to break your damn neck."

Marshall Abstention

Joining in the Stevens opinion were Chief Justice Warren E. Burger and Justices William J. Brennan Jr., Byron R. White, Harry A. Blackmun, Lewis F. Powell Jr. and Sandra Day O'Connor. Justice William H. Rehnquist also joined in the judgment but did not sign the opinion. Justice Thurgood Marshall, a former director of the NAACP Legal Defense and Education Fund, did not participate in the case.

Following are excerpts from the Supreme Court's July 2, 1982, decision in National Association for the Advancement of Colored People *v.* Claiborne Hardware Company, *in which the court decided that the civil rights group could not be held liable for damages caused by a boycott:*

No. 81-202

National Association for the
Advancement of Colored People,
et al., Petitioners

v.

Claiborne Hardware Company
et al.

On writ of Certiorari to the Supreme
Court of Mississippi

[July 2, 1982]

JUSTICE STEVENS delivered the opinion of the Court.

The term "concerted action" encompases unlawful conspiracies and constitutionally protected assemblies. The "looseness and pliability" of legal doctrine applicable to concerted action led Justice Jackson to note that certain joint activities have a "chameleon-like" character. The boycott of white merchants in Claiborne County, Mississippi, that gave rise to this litigation had such a character; it included elements of criminality and elements of majesty. Evidence that fear of reprisals caused some black citizens to withhold their patronage from respondents' businesses convinced the Supreme Court of Mississippi that the entire boycott was unlawful and that each of the 92 petitioners was liable for all of its economic consequences. Evidence that persuasive rhetoric, determination to remedy past injustices, and a host of voluntary decisions by free citizens were the critical factors in the boycott's success presents us with the question whether the State Court's judgment is consistent with the Constitution of the United States.

I

In March 1966, black citizens of Port Gibson, Mississippi and other areas of Claiborne County presented white elected officials with a list of particularized demands for racial equality and integration. The complainants did not receive a satisfactory response and, at a local NAACP meeting at the First Baptist Church, several hundred black persons voted to place a boycott on white merchants in the area. On October 31, 1969, several of the merchants filed suit in state court to recover losses caused by the boycott and to enjoin future boycott activity. We recount first the course of that litigation and then consider in more detail the events that gave rise to the merchants' claim for damages.

A

The complaint was filed in the Chancery Court of Hinds County by 17 white merchants. The merchants named two corporations and 146 individuals as defendants: the National Association for the Advancement of Colored People (NAACP), a New York membership corporation; Mississippi Action for Progress (MAP), a Mississippi corporation that implemented the federal "Head Start" program; Aaron Henry, the President of the Mississippi Branch of the NAACP; Charles Evers, the Field Secretary of the NAACP in Mississippi; and 144 other individuals who had participated in the boycott. The complaint sought injunctive relief and an attachment of property, as well as damages. Although it alleged that the plaintiffs were suffering irreparable injury from an ongoing conspiracy, no preliminary relief was sought.

Trial began before a chancellor in equity on June 11, 1973. The court heard the testimony of 144 witnesses during an eight-month trial. In August 1976, the chancellor issued an opinion and decree finding that "an overwhelming preponderance of the evidence" established the joint and several liability of 130 of the defendants on three separate conspiracy theories. First, the court held that the defendants were liable for the tort of malicious interference with the plaintiffs' businesses, which did not necessarily require the presence of a conspiracy. Second, the chancellor found a violation of a state statutory prohibition against secondary boycotts, on the theory that the defendants' primary dispute was with the governing authorities of Port Gibson and Claiborne County and not with the white merchants at whom the boycott was directed. Third, the court found a violation of Mississippi's antitrust statute, on the ground that the boycott had diverted black patronage from the white merchants to black merchants and to other merchants located out of Claiborne County and thus had unreasonably limited competition between black and white merchants that had traditionally existed. The chancellor specifically rejected the defendants' claim that their conduct was protected by the First Amendment.

Five of the merchants offered no evidence of business losses. The chancellor found that the remaining 12 had suffered lost business earnings and lost good will during a seven-year period from 1966 to 1972 amounting to $944,699. That amount, plus statutory antitrust penalties of $6,000 and a $300,000 award of attorney's fees, produced a final judgment of $1,250,699, plus interest from the date of judgment and costs. As noted, the chancellor found all but 18 of the original 148 defendants jointly and severally liable for the entire judgment. The court justified imposing full liability on the national organization of the NAACP on the ground that it had failed to "repudiate" the actions of Charles Evers, its Field Secretary in Mississippi.

In addition to imposing damage liability, the chancellor entered a broad permanent injunction. He permanently enjoined petitioners from stationing "store watchers" at the respondents' business premises; from "persuading" any person to withhold his patronage from respondents; from "using demeaning and obscene language to or about any person" because that person continued to patronize the respondents; from "picketing or patroling" the premises of any of the respondents; and from using violence against any person or inflicting damage to any real or personal property.

In December 1980, the Mississippi Supreme Court reversed significant portions of the trial court's judgment. It held that the secondary boycott statute was inapplicable because it had not been enacted until "the boycott had been in operation for upward of two years." The court declined to rely on the restraint of trade statute, noting that the "United States Supreme Court has seen fit to hold boycotts to achieve political ends are not a violation of the Sherman Act, after which our statute is patterned." Thus, the court rejected two theories of liability that were consistent with a totally voluntary and nonviolent withholding of patronage from the white merchants.

The Mississippi Supreme Court upheld the imposition of liability, however, on the basis of the chancellor's common law tort theory. After reviewing the chancellor's recitation of the facts, the court quoted the following finding made by the trial court:

> "In carrying out the agreement and design, certain of the defendants, acting for all others, engaged in acts of physical force and violence against the persons and property of certain customers and prospective customers. Intimidation, threats, social ostracism, vilification, and traduction were some of the devices used by the defendants to achieve the desired results. Most effective, also, was the stationing of guards ('enforcers,' 'deacons,' or 'black hats') in the vicinity of white-owned businesses. Unquestionably, the evidence shows that the volition of many black persons was overcome out of sheer fear, and they were forced and compelled against their personal wills to withhold their trade and business intercourse from the complainants."

On the basis of this finding, the court concluded that the entire boycott was unlawful. "If any of these factors — force, violence, or threats — is present, then the boycott is illegal regardless of whether it is primary, secondary, economical, political, social or other." In a brief passage, the court rejected petitioners' reliance on the First Amendment:

> "The agreed use of illegal force, violence, and threats against the peace to achieve a goal makes the present state of facts a conspiracy. We know of no instance, and our attention has been drawn to no decision, wherein it has been adjudicated that free speech guaranteed by the First Amendment includes in its protection the right to commit crime."

The theory of the Mississippi Supreme Court, then, was that petitioners had *agreed* to use force, violence, and "threats" to effectuate the boycott. To the trial court, such a finding had not been necessary.

Although the Mississippi Supreme Court affirmed the chancellor's basic finding of liability, the court held that respondents "did not establish their case" with respect to 38 of the defendants. The court found that MAP was a victim, rather than a willing participant, in the conspiracy and dismissed — without further explanation — 37 individual defendants for lack of proof. Finally, the court ruled that certain damages had been improperly awarded and that other damages had been inadequately proved. The court remanded for further proceedings on the computation of damages.

We granted a petition for certiorary. At oral argument, a question arose concerning the factual basis for the judgment of the Mississippi Supreme Court. As noted, that court affirmed petitioners' liability for damages on the ground that each of the petitioners had agreed to effectuate the boycott through force, violence, and threats. Such a finding was not necessary to the trial court's imposition of liability and neither state court had identified the evidence actually linking the petitioners to such an agreement. In response to a request from this Court, respondents filed a supplemental brief "specifying the acts committed by each of the petitioners giving rise to liability for damages." That brief helpfully places the petitioners in different categories; we accept respondents' framework for analysis and identify these classes as a preface to our review of the relevant incidents that occurred during the seven-year period for which damages were assessed.

First, respondents contend that liability is justified by evidence of participation in the "management" of the boycott. Respondents identify two groups of persons who may be found liable as "managers": 79 individuals who regularly attended Tuesday night meetings of the NAACP at the First Baptist Church; and 11 persons who took "leadership roles" at those meetings.

Second, respondents contend that liability is justified by evidence that an individual acted as a boycott "enforcer." In this category, respondents identify 22 persons as members of the "Black Hats" — a special group organized during the boycott — and 19 individuals who were simply "store watchers."

Third, respondents argue that those petitioners "who themselves engaged in violent acts or who threatened violence have provided the best possible evidence that they wanted the boycott to succeed by coercion whenever it could not succeed by persuasion." They identify 16 individuals for whom there is direct evidence of participation in what respondents characterize as violent acts or threats of violence.

Fourth, respondents contend that Charles Evers may be held liable because he "threatened violence on a number of occasions against boycott breakers." Like the chancellor, respondents would impose liability on the national NAACP because Evers "was acting in his capacity as Field Secretary of the NAACP when he committed these tortious and constitutionally unprotected acts."

Finally, respondents state that they are "unable to determine on what record evidence the state courts relied in finding liability on the part of seven of the petitioners." With these allegations of wrongdoing in mind, we turn to consider the factual events that gave rise to this controversy.

B

The chancellor held petitioners liable for all of respondents' lost earnings during a seven-year period from 1966 to December 31, 1972. We first review chronologically the principal events that occurred during that period, describe some features of the boycott that are not in dispute, and then identify the most significant evidence of violent activity.

In late 1965 or early 1966, Charles Evers, the Field Secretary of the NAACP, helped organize the Claiborne County Branch of the NAACP. The pastor of the First Baptist Church, James Dorsey, was elected president of the Branch; regular meetings were conducted each Tuesday evening at the Church. At about the same time, a group of black citizens formed a Human Relations Committee and presented a petition for redress of grievances to civic and business leaders of the white community.

In response, a biracial committee — including five of the petitioners and several of the respondents — was organized and held a series of unproductive meetings.

The black members of the committee then prepared a further petition entitled "Demands for Racial Justice." This petition was presented for approval at the local NAACP meeting conducted on the first Tuesday evening in March. As described by the chancellor, "the approximately 500 people present voted their approval unanimously." On March 14, 1966, the petition was presented to public officials of Port Gibson and Claiborne County.

The petition included 19 specific demands. It called for the desegregation of all public schools and public facilities, the hiring of black policemen, public improvements in black residential areas, selection of blacks for jury duty, integration of bus stations so that blacks could use all facilities, and an end to verbal abuse by law enforcement officers. It stated that "Negroes are not to be addressed by terms as 'boy,' 'girl,' 'shine,' 'uncle,' or any other offensive term, but as 'Mr.,' 'Mrs.,' or 'Miss,' as is the case with other citizens. As described by the chancellor, the purpose of the demands "was to gain equal rights and opportunities for Negro citizens." The petition further provided that black leaders hoped it would not be necessary to resort to the "selective buying campaigns' that had been used in other communities. On March 23, two demands that had been omitted from the original petition were added, one of which provided: "All stores must employ Negro clerks and cashiers." This supplemental petition stated that a response was expected by April 1.

A favorable response was not received. On April 1, 1966, the Claiborne County NAACP conducted another meeting at the First Baptist Church. As described by the chancellor:

> "Several hundred black people attended the meeting, and the purpose was to decide what action should be taken relative to the twenty-one demands. Speeches were made by Evers and others, and a vote was taken. It was the unanimous vote of those present, without dissent, to place a boycott on the white merchants of Port Gibson and Claiborne County."

The boycott was underway.

In September 1966, Mississippi Action for Progress, Inc. (MAP) was organized to develop community action programs in 20 counties of Mississippi. One of MAP's programs — known as Head Start — involved the use of federal funds to provide food for young children. Originally, food purchases in Claiborne County were made alternately from white-owned and black-owned stores, but in February 1967 the directors of MAP authorized their Claiborne County representatives to purchase food only from black-owned stores. Since MAP bought substantial quantities of food, the consequences of this decision were significant. A large portion of the trial was devoted to the question whether MAP participated in the boycott voluntarily and — under the chancellor's theories of liability — could be held liable for the resulting damages. The chancellor found MAP a willing participant, noting that "during the course of the trial, the only Head Start cooks called to the witness stand testified that they refused to go into white-owned stores to purchase groceries for the children in the program *for the reason that they were in favor of the boycott and wanted to honor it.*"

Several events occurred during the boycott that had a strong effect on boycott activity. On February 1, 1967, Port Gibson employed its first black policeman. During that month, the boycott was lifted on a number of merchants. On April 4, 1968, Dr. Martin Luther King, Jr. was assassinated in Memphis. The chancellor found that this tragic event had a depressing effect on the black community and, as a result, the boycott "tightened."

One event that occurred during the boycott is of particular significance. On April 18, 1969, a young black man named Roosevelt Jackson was shot and killed during an encounter with two Port Gibson police officers. Large crowds immediately gathered, first at the hospital and later at the church. Tension in the community neared a breaking point. The local police requested reinforcements from the State Highway Patrol and sporadic acts of violence ensued. The Mayor and Board of Aldermen placed a dawn to dusk curfew into effect.

On April 19, Charles Evers spoke to a group assembled at the First Baptist Church and led a march to the courthouse where he demanded the discharge of the entire Port Gibson Police Force. When this demand was refused, the boycott was reimposed on all white merchants. One of Evers' speeches on this date was recorded by the police. In that speech ... Evers stated that boycott violators would be "disciplined". by their own people and warned that the sheriff could not sleep with boycott violators at night.

On April 20, Aaron Henry came to Port Gibson, spoke to a large gathering, urged moderation, and joined local leaders in a protest march and a telegram sent to the Attorney General of the United States. On April 21, Evers gave another speech to several hundred people, in which he again called for a discharge of the police force and for a total boycott of all white-owned businesses in Claiborne County. Although this speech was not recorded, the chancellor found that Evers stated: "If we catch any of you going in any of them racist stores, we're gonna break your damn neck."

As noted, this lawsuit was filed in October 1969. No significant events concerning the boycott occurred after that time. The chancellor identified no incident of violence that occurred after the suit was brought. He did testify, however, several significant incidents of boycott-related violence that occurred some years earlier.

Before describing that evidence, it is appropriate to note that certain practices generally used to encourage support for the boycott were uniformly peaceful and orderly. The few marches associated with the boycott were carefully controlled by black leaders. Pickets used to advertise the boycott were often small children. The police made no arrests — and no complaints are recorded — in connection with the picketing and occasional demonstrations supporting the boycott. Such activity was fairly irregular, occurred primarily on weekends, and apparently was largely discontinued around the time the lawsuit was filed.

One form of "discipline" of black persons who violated the boycott appears to have been employed with some regularity. Individuals stood outside of boycotted stores and identified those who traded with the merchants. Some of these "store watchers" were members of a group known as the "Black Hats" or the "Deacons." The names of persons who violated the boycott were read at meetings of the Claiborne County NAACP and published in a mimeographed paper entitled the "Black Times." As stated by the chancellor, those persons "were branded as traitors to the black cause, called demeaning names, and socially ostracized for merely trading with whites.

The chancellor also concluded that a quite different form of discipline had been used against certain violators of the boycott. He specifically identified ten incidents that "strikingly" revealed the "atmosphere of fear that prevailed among blacks from 1966 until 1970." The testimony concerning four incidents convincingly demonstrates that they occurred because the victims were ignoring the boycott. In two cases, shots were fired at a house; in a third, a brick was thrown through a windshield; in the fourth, a flower garden was damaged. None of these four victims, however, ceased trading with white merchants....

II

This Court's jurisdiction to review the judgment of the Mississippi Supreme Court is, of course, limited to the federal questions necessarily decided by that court. We consider first whether petitioners' activities are protected in any respect by the Federal Constitution and, if they are, what effect such protection has on a lawsuit of this nature.

A

The boycott of white merchants at issue in this case took many forms. The boycott was launched at a meeting of a local branch of the NAACP attended by several hundred persons. Its acknowledged purpose was to secure compliance by both civic and business leaders with a lengthy list of demands for equality and racial justice. The boycott was supported by speeches and nonviolent picketing. Participants repeatedly encouraged others to join in its cause.

Each of these elements of the boycott is a form of speech or conduct that is ordinarily entitled to protection under the First and Fourteenth Amendments. The black citizens named as defendants in this action banded together and collectively expressed their dissatisfaction with a social structure that had denied them rights to equal treatment and respect. As we so recently acknowledged in *Citizens Against Rent Control* v. *Berkeley* [1981], "the practice of persons sharing common views banding together to achieve a common end is deeply embedded in the American political process." We recognized that "by collective effort individuals can make their views known, when, individually, their voices would be faint or lost." . . . THE CHIEF JUSTICE stated for the Court in *Citizens Against Rent Control*: "There are, of course, some activities, legal if engaged in by one, yet illegal if performed in concert with others, but political expression is not one of them."

The right to associate does not lose all constitutional protection merely because some members of the group may have participated in conduct or advocated doctrine that itself is not protected. In *De Jonge* v. *Oregon* [1937], the Court unanimously held that an individual could not be penalized simply for assisting in the conduct of an otherwise lawful meeting held under the auspices of the Communist Party, an organization that advocated "criminal syndicalism." After reviewing the rights of citizens "to meet peaceably for consultation in respect to public affairs and to petition for a redress of grievances," Chief Justice Hughes, writing for the Court, stated:

> "It follows from these considerations that, consistently with the Federal Constitution, peaceable assembly for lawful discussion cannot be made a crime. The holding of meetings for peaceable political action cannot be proscribed. Those who assist in the conduct of such meetings cannot be branded as criminals on that score. The question, if the rights of free speech and peaceable assembly are to be preserved, is not as to the auspices under which the meeting is held but as to its purpose; not as to the relations of the speakers, but whether their utterances transcend the bounds of the freedom of speech which the Constitution protects." . . .

Of course, the petitioners in this case did more than assemble peaceably and discuss among themselves their grievances against governmental and business policy. Other elements of the boycott, however, also involved activities ordinarily safeguarded by the First Amendment. In *Thornhill* v. *Alabama* [1940], the Court held that peaceful picketing was entitled to constitutional protection, even though, in that case, the purpose of the picketing "was concededly to advise customers and prospective customers of the relationship existing between the employer and its employees and thereby to induce such customers not to patronize the employer." . . . In *Edwards* v. *South Carolina* [1963], we held that a peaceful march and demonstration was protected by the rights of free speech, free assembly, and freedom to petition for a redress of grievances.

Speech itself also was used to further the aims of the boycott. Nonparticipants repeatedly were urged to join the common cause, both through public address and through personal solicitation. These elements of the boycott involve speech in its most direct form. In addition, names of boycott violators were read aloud at meetings at the First Baptist Church and published in a local black newspaper. Petitioners admittedly sought to persuade others to join the boycott through social pressure and the "threat" of social ostracism. Speech does not lose its protected character, however, simply because it may embarrass others or coerce them into action. As Justice Rutledge, in describing the protection afforded by the First Amendment, explained:

> "It extends to more than abstract discussion, unrelated to action. The First Amendment is a charter for government, not for an institution of learning. 'Free trade in ideas' means free trade in the opportunity to persuade to action, not merely to describe facts." *Thomas* v. *Collins* [1945].

In *Organization for a Better Austin* v. *Keefe* [1971], the Court considered the validity of a prior restraint on speech that invaded the "privacy" of the respondent. Petitioner, a racially integrated community organization, charged that respondent, a real estate broker, had engaged in tactics known as "blockbusting" or "panic peddling." Petitioner asked respondent to sign an agreement that he would not solicit property in their community. When he refused, petitioner distributed leaflets near respondent's home that were critical of his business practices. A state court enjoined petitioner from distributing the leaflets; an appellate court affirmed on the ground that the alleged activities were coercive and intimidating, rather than informative, and therefore not entitled to First Amendment protection. This Court reversed. THE CHIEF JUSTICE explained:

> "This Court has often recognized that the activity of peaceful pamphleteering is a form of communication protected by the First Amendment.... In sustaining the injunction, however, the Appellate Court was apparently of the view that petitioners' purpose in distributing their literature was not to inform the public, but to 'force' respondent to sign a no-solicitation agreement. The claim that the expressions were intended to exercise a coercive impact on respondent does not remove them from the reach of the First Amendment. Petitioners plainly intended to influence respondent's conduct by their activities; this is not fundamentally different from the function of a newspaper."...

In dissolving the prior restraint, the Court recognized that "offensive" and "coercive" speech was nevertheless protected by the First Amendment.

In sum, the boycott clearly involved constitutionally protected activity. The established elements of speech, assembly, association and petition, "though not identical, are inseparable." *Thomas* v. *Collins*. Through exercise of these First Amendment rights, petitioners sought to bring about political, social, and economic change. Through speech, assembly, and petition — rather than through riot or revolution — petitioners sought to change a social order that had consistently treated them as second-class citizens.

The presence of protected activity, however, does not end the relevant constitutional inquiry. Governmental regulation that has an incidental effect on First Amendment freedoms may be justified in certain narrowly defined instances. See *United States* v. *O'Brien* [1968]. A nonviolent and totally voluntary boycott may have a disruptive effect on local economic conditions. This Court has recognized the strong governmental interest in certain forms of economic regulation, even though such regulation may have an incidental effect on rights of speech and association. See *Giboney*

v. *Empire Storage* [1949]. . . . The right of business entities to "associate" to suppress competition may be curtailed. *National Soc. of Professional Engineers* v. *United States* [1978]. Unfair trade practices may be restricted. Secondary boycotts and picketing by labor unions may be prohibited, as part of "Congress' striking of the delicate balance between union freedom of expression and the ability of neutral employers, employees, and consumers to remain free from coerced participation in industrial strife." *NLRB* v. *Retail Store Employees Union* [1980] (BLACKMUN, J., concurring. See *International Longshoremen's Assoc.* v. *Allied International.*

While States have broad power to regulate economic activity, we do not find a comparable right to prohibit peaceful political activity such as that found in the boycott in this case. This Court has recognized that expression on public issues "has always rested on the highest rung of the hierarchy of First Amendment values." *Carey* v. *Brown* [1980]. "[S]peech concerning public affairs is more than self-expression; it is the essence of self-government." *Garrison* v. *Louisiana* [1964]. There is a "profound national commitment" to the principle that "debate on public issues should be uninhibited, robust, and wide-open." *New York Times* v. *Sullivan* [1964].

In *Eastern Railroad Presidents Conference* v. *Noerr Motor Freight* [1961], the Court considered whether the Sherman Act prohibited a publicity campaign waged by railroads against the trucking industry that was designed to foster the adoption of laws destructive of the trucking business, to create an atmosphere of distaste for truckers among the general public, and to impair the relationships existing between truckers and their customers. Noting that the "right of petition is one of the freedoms protected by the Bill of Rights, and we cannot, of course, lightly impute to Congress an intent to invade these freedoms," the Court held that the Sherman Act did not proscribe the publicity campaign. The court stated that it could not see how an intent to influence legislation to destroy the truckers as competitors "could transform conduct otherwise lawful into a violation of the Sherman Act." . . .

It is not disputed that a major purpose of the boycott in this case was to influence governmental action. Like the railroads in *Noerr*, the petitioners certainly foresaw — and directly intended — that the merchants would sustain economic injury as a result of their campaign. Unlike the railroads in that case, however, the purpose of petitioners' campaign was not to destroy legitimate competition. Petitioners sought to vindicate rights of equality and of freedom that lie at the heart of the Fourteenth Amendment itself. The right of the States to regulate economic activity could not justify a complete prohibition against a nonviolent, politically-motivated boycott designed to force governmental and economic change and to effectuate rights guaranteed by the Constitution itself. . . .

. . . We hold that the nonviolent elements of petitioners' activities are entitled to the protection of the First Amendment.

B

The Mississippi Supreme Court did not sustain the chancellor's imposition of liability on a theory that state law prohibited a nonviolent, politically-motivated boycott. The fact that such activity is constitutionally protected, however, imposes a special obligation on this Court to examine critically the basis on which liability was imposed. In particular, we consider here the effect of our holding that much of petitioners' conduct was constitutionally protected on the ability of the State to impose liability for elements of the boycott that were not so protected.

The First Amendment does not protect violence. "Certainly violence has no sanctuary in the First Amendment, and the use of weapons, gunpowder, and gasoline may not constitutionally masquerade under the guise of 'advocacy.'" *Samuels* v. *Mackell* [1971] (Douglas, J., concurring). Although the extent and significance of the violence in this case is vigorously disputed by the parties, there is no question that acts of violence occurred. No federal rule of law restricts a State from imposing tort liability for business losses that are caused by violence and by threats of violence. When such conduct occurs in the context of constitutionally protected activity, however, "precision of regulation" is demanded. *NAACP* v. *Button* [1963]. Specifically, the presence of activity protected by the First Amendment imposes restraints on the grounds that may give rise to damage liability and on the persons who may be held accountable for those damages.

In *United Mine Workers* v. *Gibbs* [1966], the Court considered a case in many respects similar to the one before us. The case grew out of the rivalry between the United Mine Workers (UMW) and the Southern Labor Union (SLU) over representation of workers in the southern Appalachian coal fields. A coal company laid off 100 miners of UMW's Local 5881 when it closed one of its mines. That same year, a subsidiary of the coal company hired Gibbs as mine superintendent to attempt to open a new mine on nearby property through use of members of the SLU. Gibbs also received a contract to haul the mine's coal to the nearest railroad loading point. When he attempted to open the mine, however, he was met by armed members of Local 5881 who threatened Gibbs and beat an SLU organizer. These incidents occurred on August 15 and 16. Thereafter, there was no further violence at the mine site and UMW members maintained a peaceful picket line for nine months. No attempts to open the mine were made during that period.

Gibbs lost his job as superintendent and never began performance of the haulage contract. Claiming to have suffered losses as a result of the union's concerted plan against him, Gibbs filed suit in federal court against the international UMW. He alleged an unlawful secondary boycott under the federal labor laws and, as a pendant state law claim, "an unlawful conspiracy and an unlawful boycott aimed at him ... to maliciously, wantonly and willfully interfere with his contract of employment and with his contract of haulage." The federal claim was dismissed on the ground that the dispute was "primary" and therefore not cognizable under the federal prohibition of secondary labor boycotts. Damages were awarded against the UMW, however, on the state claim of interference with an employment relationship.

This Court reversed. The Court found that the pleadings, arguments of counsel, and jury instructions had not adequately defined the compass within which damages could be awarded under state law. The Court noted that it had "consistently recognized the right of States to deal with violence and threats of violence appearing in labor disputes" and had sustained "a variety of measures against the contention that state law was pre-empted by the passage of federal labor legislation." To accommodate federal labor policy, however, the Court in *Gibbs* held: "the permissible scope of state remedies in this area is strictly confined to the direct consequences of such [violent] conduct, and does not include consequences resulting from associated peaceful picketing or other union activity." . . .

The careful limitation on damage liability imposed in *Gibbs* resulted from the need to accommodate state law with federal labor policy. That limitation is no less applicable, however, to the important First Amendment interests at issue in this case. Petitioners withheld their patronage from the white establishment of Claiborne County to challenge a political and economic system that had denied them the basic rights of dignity and equality that this country had fought a civil war to secure. While the State legitimately may impose damages for the consequences of violent conduct, it may not award compensation for the consequences of nonviolent, protected activity. Only those losses proximately caused by unlawful conduct may be recovered.

The First Amendment similarly restricts the ability of the State to impose liability on an individual solely because of his association with another. In *Scales* v. *United States* [1961], the Court noted that a "blanket prohibition of association with a group having both legal and illegal aims" would present "a real danger that legitimate political expression or association would be impaired." The Court suggested that to punish association with such a group, there must be "clear proof that a defendant 'specifically intend[s] to accomplish [the aims of the organization] by resort to violence." ([Q]uoting *Noto* v. *United States* [1961]). Moreover, in *Noto* v. *United States* the Court emphasized that this intent must be judged "according to the strictest law," for "otherwise there is a danger that one in sympathy with the legitimate aims of such an organization, but not specifically intending to accomplish them by resort to violence, might be punished for his adherence to lawful and constitutionally protected purposes, because of other and unprotected purposes which he does not necessarily share."

In *Healy* v. *James* [1972], the Court applied these principles in a non-criminal context. In that case the Court held that a student group could not be denied recognition at a state-supported college merely because of its affiliation with a national organization associated with disruptive and violent campus activity. It noted that "the Court has consistently disapproved governmental action imposing criminal sanctions or denying rights and privileges solely because of a citizen's association with an unpopular organization." The Court stated that "it has been established that 'guilt by association alone, without [establishing] that an individual's association poses the threat feared by the Govenment,' is an impermissible basis upon which to deny First Amendment rights." ([Q]uoting *United States* v. *Robel* [1967]). "The government has the burden of establishing a knowing affiliation with an organization possessing unlawful aims and goals, and a specific intent to further those illegal aims."

The principles announced in *Scales, Noto,* and *Healy* are relevant to this case. Civil liability may not be imposed merely because an individual belonged to a group, some members of which committed acts of violence. For liability to be imposed by reason of association alone, it is necessary to establish that the group itself possessed unlawful goals and that the individual held a specific intent to further those illegal aims. "In this sensitive field, the State may not employ 'means that broadly stifle fundamental personal liberties when the end can be more narrowly achieved.' *Shelton* v. *Tucker* (1960)." *Carroll* v. *Princess Anne* [1968].

III

The chancellor awarded respondents damages for all business losses that were sustained during a seven year period beginning in 1966 and ending December 31, 1972. With the exception of Aaron Henry, all defendants were held jointly and severally liable for these losses. The chancellor's findings were consistent with his view that voluntary participation in the boycott was a sufficient basis on which to impose liability. The Mississippi Supreme Court properly rejected that theory; it nevertheless held that petitioners were liable for all damages "resulting from the boycott." In light of the principles set forth above, it is evident that such a damage award may not be sustained in this case.

The opinion of the Mississippi Supreme Court itself demonstrates that all business losses were not proximately caused by the violence and threats of violence found to be present. The court stated that "coercion, intimidation, and threats" formed "*part* of the boycott activity" and "*contributed* to its almost complete success." The court broadly asserted — without differentiation — that "intimidation, threats, social ostracism, vilification, and traduction" were devices used by the defendants to effectuate the boycott. The court repeated the chancellor's finding that "the volition of *many* black persons was overcome out of sheer fear." These findings are inconsistent with the court's imposition of all damages "resulting from the boycott." To the extent that the court's judgment rests on the ground that "many" black citizens were "intimidated" by "threats" of "social ostracism, vilification, and traduction," it is flatly inconsistent with the First

Amendment. The ambiguous findings of the Mississippi Supreme Court are inadequate to assure the "precision of regulation" demanded by that constitutional provision.

The record in this case demonstrates that all of respondents' losses were not proximately caused by violence or threats of violence. As respondents themselves stated at page 12 of their brief in the Mississippi Supreme Court:

> "Most of the witnesses testified that they voluntarily went along with the NAACP and their fellow black citizens in honoring and observing the boycott because they wanted the boycott."

This assessment is amply supported by the record. It is indeed inconceivable that a boycott launched by the unanimous vote of several hundred persons succeeded solely through fear and intimidation....

Respondents' supplemental brief also demonstrates that on the present record no judgment may be sustained against most of the petitioners. Regular attendance and participation at the Tuesday meetings of the Claiborne County Branch of the NAACP is an insufficient predicate on which to impose liability. The chancellor's findings do not suggest that any illegal conduct was authorized, ratified, or even discussed at any of the meetings. The sheriff testified that he was kept informed of what transpired at the meetings; he made no reference to any discussion of unlawful activity. To impose liability for presence at weekly meetings of the NAACP would — ironically — not even constitute "guilt by association," since there is no evidence that the association possessed unlawful aims. Rather, liability could only be imposed on a "guilt *for* association" theory. Neither is permissible under the First Amendment.

Respondents also argue that liability may be imposed on individuals who were either "store watchers" or members of the "Black Hats." There is nothing unlawful in standing outside of a store and recording names. Similarly, there is nothing unlawful in wearing black hats, although such apparel may cause apprehension in others. As established above, mere association with either group — absent a specific intent to further an unlawful aim embraced by that group — is an insufficient predicate for liability. At the same time, the evidence does support the conclusion that some members of each of these groups engaged in violence or threats of violence. Unquestionably, these individuals may be held responsible for the injuries that they caused; a judgment tailored to the consequences of their unlawful conduct may be sustained.

Respondents have sought separately to justify the judgment entered against Charles Evers and the national NAACP. As set forth by the chancellor, Evers was specially connected with the boycott in four respects. First, Evers signed the March 23 supplemental demand letter and unquestionably played the primary leadership role in the organization of the boycott. Second, Evers participated in negotiation with MAP and successfully convinced MAP to abandon its practice of purchasing food alternately from white-owned and black-owned stores. Third, he apparently presided at the April 1, 1966 meeting at which the vote to begin the boycott was taken; he delivered a speech to the large audience that was gathered on that occasion. Fourth, Evers delivered the speeches on April 19 and 21, 1969, which we have discussed previously.

For the reasons set forth above, liability may not be imposed on Evers for his presence at NAACP meetings or his active participation in the boycott itself. To the extent that Evers caused respondents to suffer business losses through his organization of the boycott, his emotional and persuasive appeals for unity in the joint effort, or his "threats" of vilification or social ostracism, Evers' conduct is constitutionally protected and beyond the reach of a damage award. Respondents point to Evers' speeches, however, as justification for the chancellor's damage award. Since respondents would impose liability on the basis of a public address — which predominantly contained highly charged political rhetoric lying at the core of the First Amendment — we approach this suggested basis of liability with extreme care.

There are three separate theories that might justify holding Evers liable for the unlawful conduct of others. First, a finding that he authorized, directed or ratified specific tortious activity would justify holding him responsible for the consequences of that activity. Second, a finding that his public speeches were likely to incite lawless action could justify holding him liable for unlawful conduct that in fact followed within a reasonable period. Third, the speeches might be taken as evidence that Evers gave other specific instructions to carry out violent acts or threats.

While many of the comments in Evers' speeches might have contemplated "discipline" in the permissible form of social ostracism, it cannot be denied that references to the possibility that necks would be broken and to the fact that the chief of police could not sleep with boycott violators at night implicitly conveyed a sterner message. In the passionate atmosphere in which the speeches were delivered, they might have been understood as inviting an unlawful form of discipline or, at least, as intending to create a fear of violence whether or not improper discipline was specifically intended.

It is clear that "fighting words" — those that provoke immediate violence — are not protected by the First Amendment. *Chaplinsky* v. *New Hampshire* [1942]. Similarly, words that create an immediate panic are not entitled to constitutional protection. *Schenck* v. *United States* [1919]. This Court has made clear, however, that mere *advocacy* of the use of force or violence does not remove speech from the protection of the First Amendment. In *Brandenburg* v. *Ohio* [1969] we reversed the conviction of a Ku Klux Klan leader for threatening "revengeance" if the "suppression" of the white race continued; we relied on "the principle that the constitutional guarantees of free speech and free press do not permit a State to forbid or proscribe advocacy of the use of force or of law violation except where such advocacy is directed to inciting or producing imminent lawless action and is likely to incite or produce such action." ...

The emotionally charged rhetoric of Charles Evers' speeches did not transcend the bounds of protected speech set forth in *Brandenburg*. The lengthy addresses generally contained an impassioned plea for black citizens to unify, to support and respect each other, and to realize the political and economic power available to them. In the course of those pleas, strong language was used. If that language had been followed by acts of violence, a substantial question would be presented whether Evers could be held liable for the consequences of that unlawful conduct. In this case, however — with the possible exception of the Cox incident — the acts of violence identified in 1966 occurred weeks or months after the April 1, 1966 speech; the chancellor made no finding of any violence after the challenged 1969 speech. Strong and effective extemporaneous rhetoric cannot be nicely channeled in purely dulcet phrases. An advocate must be free to stimulate his audience with spontaneous and emotional appeals for unity and action in a common cause. When such appeals do not incite lawless action, they must be regarded as protected speech. . . .

For these reasons, we conclude that Evers' addresses did not exceed the bounds of protected speech. If there were other evidence of his authorization of wrongful conduct, the references to discipline in the speeches could be used to corroborate that evidence. But any such theory fails for the simple reason that there is no evidence — apart from the speeches themselves — that Evers authorized, ratified, or directly threatened acts of violence. . . .

The liability of the NAACP derived solely from the liability of Charles Evers. The chancellor found:

> "The national NAACP was well-advised of Evers' actions, and it had the option of repudiating his acts or ratifying them. It never repudiated those acts, and therefore, it is deemed by this Court to have affirmed them."

Of course, to the extent that Charles Evers' acts are insufficient to impose liability upon him, they may not be used to impose liability on his principal. On the present record, however, the judgment against the NAACP could not stand in any event. . . .

The chancellor made no finding that Charles Evers or any other NAACP member had either actual or apparent authority to commit acts of violence or to threaten violent conduct. The evidence in the record suggests the contrary. Aaron Henry, president of the Mississippi State Branch of the NAACP and a member of the Board of Directors of the national organization, testified that the statements attributed to Evers were directly contrary to NAACP policy. Similarly, there is no evidence that the NAACP ratified — or even had specific knowledge of — any of the acts of violence or threats of discipline associated with the boycott. Henry testified that the NAACP never authorized, and never considered taking, any official action with respect to the boycott. The NAACP supplied no financial aid to the boycott. The chancellor made no finding that the national organization was involved in any way in the boycott.

To impose liability without a finding that the NAACP authorized —

either actually or apparently — or ratified unlawful conduct would impermissibly burden the rights of political association that are protected by the First Amendment. As Justice Douglas noted in *NAACP* v. *Overstreet* [1966], dissenting from a dismissal of a writ of certiorari found to have been improvidently granted;

> "To equate the liability of the national organization with that of the Branch in the absence of any proof that the national authorized or ratified the misconduct in question could ultimately destroy it. The rights of political association are fragile enough without adding the additional threat of destruction by lawsuit. . . .

The chancellor's findings are not adequate to support the judgment against the NAACP.

IV

In litigation of this kind the stakes are high. Concerted action is a powerful weapon. History teaches that special dangers are associated with conspiratorial activity. And yet one of the foundations of our society is the right of individuals to combine with other persons in pursuit of a common goal by lawful means.

At times the difference between lawful and unlawful collective action may be identified easily by reference to its purpose. In this case, however, petitioners' ultimate objectives were unquestionably legitimate. The charge of illegality — like the claim of constitutional protection — derives from the means employed by the participants to achieve those goals. The use of speeches, marches, and threats of social ostracism cannot provide the basis for a damage award. But violent conduct is beyond the pale of constitutional protection.

The taint of violence colored the conduct of some of the petitioners. They, of course, may be held liable for the consequences of their violent deeds. The burden of demonstrating that it colored the entire collective effort, however, is not satisfied by evidence that violence occurred or even that violence contributed to the success of the boycott. A massive and prolonged effort to change the social, political, and economic structure of a local environment cannot be characterized as a violent conspiracy simply by reference to the ephemeral consequences of relatively few violent acts. Such a characterization must be supported by findings that adequately disclose the evidentiary basis for concluding that specific parties agreed to use unlawful means, that carefully identify the impact of such unlawful conduct, and that recognize the importance of avoiding the imposition of punishment for constitutionally protected activity. The burden of demonstrating that fear rather than protected conduct was the dominant force in the movement is heavy. A court must be wary of a claim that the true color of a forest is better revealed by reptiles hidden in the weeds than by the foliage of countless free-standing trees. The findings of the chancellor, framed largely in the light of two legal theories rejected by the Mississippi

Supreme Court, are constitutionally insufficient to support the judgment that all petitioners are liable for losses resulting from the boycott.

The judgment is reversed. The case is remanded for further proceedings not inconsistent with this opinion.

It is so ordered.

COURT ON CHILD PORNOGRAPHY
July 2, 1982

In its first consideration of such legislation, the Supreme Court July 2 unanimously upheld a New York law barring child pornography, saying that the law did not violate rights guaranteed by the First Amendment. The ruling reversed a New York Court of Appeals decision stating that such material must attain the legal standard for obscenity before it may be regulated. The case, New York v. Ferber, *concerned a Manhattan bookstore owner, Paul Ira Ferber, who was convicted of selling two films to an undercover police agent. The films depicted children engaged in sexual activity.*

Background

The obscenity standard established in Miller v. California *(1973) allowed traffic in pornographic material on the basis of its cultural or social validity. In* Miller, *the Supreme Court had defined as obscene materials "which, taken as a whole, appeal to the prurient interest in sex, which portray sexual conduct in a patently offensive way, and which, taken as a whole, do not have serious literary, artistic, political or scientific value."*

In the Ferber *case, a New York court upheld its criminal statute that prohibited material portraying sexual conduct by children under the age of 16, whether or not that material was obscene. Ferber contested the New York law, calling it constitutionally over broad, and his appeal was upheld by the New York Court of Appeals, on the ground that the state could not stop promotion of traditionally protected materials.*

Arguments before the Supreme Court, held April 27, 1982, were highly emotional. Herald Price Fahringer, Ferber's lawyer, was subjected to stern questioning by the bench. Justice Sandra Day O'Connor lectured the lawyer on the state's interest in protecting children from sexual exploitation. Fahringer cited the chilling effect that a restriction on child pornography would have on potentially valuable social and cultural contributions, such as art work or medical studies. The justices were not persuaded.

White's Opinion

Ferber *determined that child pornography not only failed to fall under the Miller standard because it involved children, but also that it was not entitled to protection by the First Amendment. It was legislative judgment that using children as subjects of pornographic material harmed their physiological, mental and emotional health. "That judgment, we think, easily passes muster under the First Amendment," said Justice Byron R. White in the court's opinion.*

Constitutionally, the result of the ruling was that child pornography was placed in the category of speech not deserving protection by the First Amendment, along with libel and language that incites violence. The decision also upheld laws in 19 other states prohibiting such material even if it was not considered legally obscene, allowing states increased discretion to regulate pornographic material involving minors.

In his opinion, joined by Chief Justice Warren E. Burger and Justices Lewis F. Powell Jr. and William H. Rehnquist, White rejected Ferber's argument that the New York statute was unconstitutionally too broad. He stated, "... we consider this the paradigmatic case of a state statute whose legitimate reach dwarfs its arguably impermissible applications."

He also asserted that quite often the fear of censorship in the United States was so great that, even in completely justifiable situations, other laws to circumvent the barring are used. "...[I]t is not rare that a content-based classification of speech has been accepted because it may be appropriately generalized that within the confines of the given classification, the evil to be restricted so overwhelmingly outweighs the expressive interests, if any, at stake, that no process of case-by-case adjudication is required."

Differences Among Justices

Although there were no dissenters to the decision, the concurring opinions revealed some differences among the justices. O'Connor joined White's opinion but, in a separate concurring opinion, said the court's decision did not mean that material with serious literary or scientific value is beyond the reach of the New York statute. Justices William J.

Brennan Jr. and Thurgood Marshall concurred only in the judgment and claimed that application of the statute to material that has legitimate scientific or social value would violate the First Amendment.

Justice John Paul Stevens, concurring in the judgment, saw no reason either to give Ferber the benefit of a full-fledged analysis or, as the majority did, to assume that the statute would have even a few impermissible applications. Justice Harry A. Blackmun concurred in the result without opinion.

Following are excerpts from the Supreme Court's opinion in New York v. Ferber *that child pornography is not entitled to First Amendment protection, decided July 2, 1982:*

No. 81-55

New York, Petitioner
v.
Paul Ira Ferber

} On writ of Certiorari to the Court of Appeals of New York

[July 2, 1982]

JUSTICE WHITE delivered the opinion of the Court.

At issue in this case is the constitutionality of a New York criminal statute which prohibits persons from knowingly promoting sexual performances by children under the age of 16 by distributing material which depicts such performances.

I

In recent years, the exploitive use of children in the production of pornography has become a serious national problem. The federal government and forty-seven States have sought to combat the problem with statutes specifically directed at the production of child pornography. At least half of such statutes do not require that the materials produced be legally obscene. Thirty-five States and the United States Congress have also passed legislation prohibiting the distribution of such materials; twenty States prohibit the distribution of material depicting children engaged in sexual conduct without requiring that the material be legally obscene.

New York is one of the twenty. In 1977, the New York legislature enacted Article 263 of its Penal Law. Section 263.05 criminalizes as a class C felony the use of a child in a sexual performance.

"A person is guilty of the use of a child in a sexual performance if knowing the character and content thereof he employs, authorizes or induces a child less than sixteen years of age to engage in a sexual performance or being a parent, legal guardian or custodian of such child, he consents to the participation by such child in a sexual performance."

A "sexual performance is defined as 'any performance or part thereof which includes sexual conduct by a child less than sixteen years of age,' " § 263.1. "Sexual conduct" is in turn defined in § 263.3:

> " 'Sexual conduct' means actual or simulated sexual intercourse, deviate sexual intercourse, sexual bestiality, masturbation, sado-masochistic abuse, or lewd exhibition of the genitals."

A performance is defined as "any play, motion picture, photograph or dance" or "any other visual presentation exhibited before an audience." § 263.4.

At issue in this case is § 263.15, defining a class D felony:

> "A person is guilty of promoting a sexual performance by a child when, knowing the character and content thereof, he produces, directs or promotes any performance which indicates sexual conduct by a child less than sixteen years of age."

To "promote" is also defined:

> " 'Promote' means to procure, manufacture, issue, sell, give, provide, lend, mail, deliver, transfer, transmute, publish, distribute, circulate, disseminate, present, exhibit or advertise, or to offer or agree to do the same."

A companion provision bans only the knowing dissemination of obscene material. §263.10.

This case arose when Paul Ferber, the proprietor of a Manhattan bookstore specializing in sexually oriented products, sold two films to an undercover police officer. The films are devoted almost exclusively to depicting young boys masturbating. Ferber was indicted on two counts of § 263.10 and two counts of § 263.15, the two New York laws controlling dissemination of child pornography. After a jury trial, Ferber was acquitted of the two counts of promoting an obscene sexual performance, but found guilty of the two counts under § 263.15, which did not require proof that the films were obscene. Ferber's convictions were affirmed without opinion by the Appellate Division of the New York State Supreme Court.

The New York Court of Appeals reversed, holding that § 263.15 violated the First Amendment. (1981). The court began by noting that in light of § 263.10's explicit inclusion of an obscenity standard, § 263.15 could not be construed to include such a standard. Therefore, "the statute would ... prohibit the promotion of materials which are traditionally entitled to constitutional protection from government interference under the First Amendment." Although the court recognized the State's "legitimate interest in protecting the welfare of minors" and noted that this "interest may transcend First Amendment concerns," it nevertheless found two fatal defects in the New York statute. Section 263.15 was underinclusive because it discriminated against visual portrayals of children engaged in sexual activity by not also prohibiting the distribution of films of other dangerous activity. It was also overbroad because it prohibited the distribution of materials produced outside the State, as well as materials, such as medical books and educational sources, which "deal with adolescent sex in a realistic but nonobscene manner." Two judges dissented. We granted the State's petition for certiorari, (1981), presenting the single question:

> "To prevent the abuse of children who are made to engage in sexual conduct for commercial purposes, could the New York State Legislature, consistent with the First Amendment, prohibit the dissemination of material which shows children engaged in sexual conduct, regardless of whether such material is obscene?"

II

The Court of Appeals proceeded on the assumption that the standard of obscenity incorporated in § 263.10, which follows the guidelines enunciated in *Miller* v. *California* (1973), constitutes the appropriate line dividing protected from unprotected expression by which to measure a regulation directed at child pornography. It was on the premise that "nonobscene adolescent sex" could not be singled out for special treatment that the court found § 263.15 "strikingly underinclusive." Moreover, the assumption that the constitutionally permissible regulation of pornography could not be more extensive with respect to the distribution of material depicting children may also have led the court to conclude that a narrowing construction of § 263.15 was unavailable.

The Court of Appeals' assumption was not unreasonable in light of our decisions. This case, however, constitutes our first examination of a statute directed at and limited to depictions of sexual activity involving children. We believe our inquiry should begin with the question of whether a State has somewhat more freedom in proscribing works which portray sexual acts or lewd exhibitions of genitalia by children.

A

In *Chaplinsky* v. *New Hampshire* (1942), the Court laid the foundation for the excision of obscenity from the realm of constitutionally protected expression:

> "There are certain well-defined and narrowly limited classes of speech, the prevention and punishment of which have never been thought to raise any Constitutional problem. These include the lewd and obscene. . . . It has been well observed that such utterances are no essential part of any exposition of ideas and are of such slight social value as a step to truth that any benefit that may be derived from them is clearly outweighed by the social interest and morality. . . ."

Embracing this judgment, the Court squarely held in *Roth* v. *United States* (1957) that "obscenity is not within the area of constitutionally protected speech or press." The Court recognized that "rejection of obscenity as utterly without redeeming social importance" was implicit in the history of the First Amendment: The original states provided for the prosecution of libel, blasphemy and profanity and the "universal judgment that obscenity should be restrained [is] reflected in the international agreement of over 50 nations, in the obscenity laws of all of the 48 states, and in the 20 obscenity laws enacted by Congress from 1842 to 1956."

Roth was followed by fifteen years during which this Court struggled with "the intractable obscenity problem." *Interstate Circuit, Inc.* v. *Dallas* (1968) (Harlan, J.). See, *e.g., Redrup* v. *New York* (1967). Despite considerable vacillation over the proper definition of obscenity, a majority of the members of the Court remained firm in the position that "the States have a legitimate interest in prohibiting dissemination or exhibition of obscene material when the mode of dissemination carries with it a significant danger of offending the sensibilities of unwilling recipients or of exposure to juveniles." *Miller* v. *California; Stanley* v. *Georgia* (1969); *Ginsberg* v. *New York* (1968); *Interstate Circuit, Inc.* v. *Dallas; Redrup* v. *New York; Jacobellis* v. *Ohio* (1964).

Throughout this period, we recognized "the inherent dangers of undertaking to regulate any form of expression." *Miller* v. *California.* Consequently, our difficulty was not only to assure that statutes designed to regulate obscene materials sufficiently defined what was prohibited, but to devise substantive limits on what fell within the permissible scope of regulation. In *Miller* v. *California* a majority of the Court agreed that "a state offense must also be limited to works which, taken as a whole, appeal to the prurient interest in sex, which portray sexual conduct in a patently offensive way, and which, taken as a whole, do not have serious literary, artistic, political, or scientific value." Over the past decade, we have adhered to the guidelines expressed in *Miller*, which subsequently has been followed in the regulatory schemes of most states.

B

The *Miller* standard, like its predecessors, was an accommodation between the state's interests in protecting the "sensibilities of unwilling recipients" from exposure to pornographic material and the dangers of censorship inherent in unabashedly content-based laws. Like obscenity statutes, laws directed at the dissemination of child pornography run the risk of suppressing protected expression by allowing the hand of the censor to become unduly heavy. For the following reasons, however, we are persuaded that the States are entitled to greater leeway in the regulation of pornographic depictions of children.

First. It is evident beyond the need for elaboration that a state's interest in "safeguarding the physical and psychological well being of a minor" is "compelling." *Globe Newspapers* v. *Superior Court* (1982). "A democratic society rests, for its continuance, upon the healthy well-rounded growth of young people into full maturity as citizens." *Prince* v. *Massachusetts* (1944). Accordingly, we have sustained legislation aimed at protecting the physical and emotional well-being of youth even when the laws have operated in the sensitive area of constitutionally protected rights. In *Prince* v. *Massachusetts* the Court held that a statute prohibiting use of a child to distribute literature on the street was valid notwithstanding the statute's effect on a First Amendment activity. In *Ginsberg* v. *New York* (1968) we sustained a New York law protecting children from exposure to nonobscene literature. More recently, we held that the government's interest in the "well-being of its youth" justified special treatment of indecent broadcasting received by adults as well as children. *FCC* v. *Pacifica Foundation* (1978).

The prevention of sexual exploitation and abuse of children constitutes a government objective of surpassing importance. The legislative findings accompanying passage of the New York laws reflect this concern:

> "There has been a proliferation of children as subjects in sexual performances. The care of children is a sacred trust and should not be abused by those who seek to profit through a commercial network based on the exploitation of children. The public policy of the state demands the protection of children from exploitation through sexual performances."

We shall not second-guess this legislative judgment. Respondent has not intimated that we do so. Suffice it to say that virtually all of the States and the United States have passed legislation proscribing the production of or otherwise combating "child pornography." The legislative judgment, as well as the judgment found in the relevant literature, is that the use of children as subjects of pornographic materials is harmful to the physiological, emotional, and mental health of the child. That judgment, we think, easily passes muster under the First Amendment.

Second. The distribution of photographs and films depicting sexual activity by juveniles is intrinsically related to the sexual abuse of children in at least two ways. First, the materials produced are a permanent record of the children's participation and the harm to the child is exacerbated by their circulation. Second, the distribution network for child pornography must be closed if the production of material which requires the sexual exploitation of children is to be effectively controlled. Indeed, there is no serious contention that the legislature was unjustified in believing that it is difficult, if not impossible, to halt the exploitation of children by pursuing only those who produce the photographs and movies. While the production of pornographic materials is a low-profile, clandestine industry, the need to market the resulting products requires a visible apparatus of distribution. The most expeditious if not the only practical method of law enforcement may be to dry up the market for this material by imposing severe criminal penalties on persons selling, advertising, or otherwise promoting the product. Thirty-five States and Congress have concluded that restraints on the distribution of pornographic materials are required in order to effectively combat the problem, and there is a body of literature and testimony to support these legislative conclusions. Cf. *United States* v. *Darby* (1941) (upholding federal restrictions on sale of goods manufactured in violation of Fair Labor Standards Act).

Respondent does not contend that the State is unjustified in pursuing those who distribute child pornography. Rather, he argues that it is enough for the State to prohibit the distribution of materials that are legally obscene under the *Miller* test. While some States may find that this approach properly accommodates its interests, it does not follow that the First Amendment prohibits a state from going further. The *Miller* standard, like all general definitions of what may be banned as obscene, does not reflect the State's particular and more compelling interest in prosecuting those who promote the sexual exploitation of children. Thus, the question under the *Miller* test of whether a work, taken as a whole, appeals to the prurient interest of the average person bears no connection to the issue of whether a child has been physically or psychologically harmed in the production of the work. Similarly, a sexually explicit depiction need not be "patently offensive" in order to have required the sexual exploitation of a child for its production. In addition, a work which, taken on the whole, contains serious literary, artistic, political, or scientific value may nevertheless embody the hardest core of child pornography. "It is irrelevant to the child [who has been abused] whether or not the material ... has a literary, artistic, political, or social value." We therefore cannot conclude that the *Miller* standard is a satisfactory solution to the child pornography problem.

Third. The advertising and selling of child pornography provides an economic motive for and is thus an integral part of the production of such materials, an activity illegal throughout the nation. "It rarely has been suggested that the constitutional freedom for speech and press extends its immunity to speech or writing used as an integral part of conduct in violation of a valid criminal statute." *Giboney* v. *Empire Storage & Ice Co.* (1949). We note that were the statutes outlawing the employment of children in these films and photographs fully effective, and the constitutionality of these laws have not been questioned, the First Amendment implications would be no greater than that presented by laws against distribution: enforceable production laws would leave no child pornography to be marketed.

Fourth. The value of permitting live performances and photographic reproductions of children engaged in lewd sexual conduct is exceedingly modest, if not *de minimis*. We consider it unlikely that visual depictions of children performing sexual acts or lewdly exhibiting their genitals would often constitute an important and necessary part of a literary performance or scientific or educational work. As the trial court in this case observed, if it were necessary for literary or artistic value, a person over the statutory age who perhaps looked younger could be utilized. Simulation outside of the prohibition of the statute could provide another alternative. Nor is there any question here of censoring a particular literary theme or portrayal of sexual activity. The First Amendment interest is limited to that of rendering the portrayal somewhat more "realistic" by utilizing or photographing children.

Fifth. Recognizing and classifying child pornography as a category of material outside the protection of the First Amendment is not incompatible with our earlier decisions. "The question whether speech is, or is not protected by the First Amendment often depends on the content of the speech." *Young* v. *American Mini Theatres* [1976].... See also *FCC* v. *Pacifica Foundation* (1978).... "It is the content of an utterance that determines whether it is a protected epithet or an unprotected 'fighting comment.'" *Young* v. *American Mini Theatres*. See *Chaplinsky* v. *New Hampshire* (1942). Leaving aside the special considerations when public officials are the target, *New York Times* v. *Sullivan* (1964), a libelous publication is not protected by the Constitution. *Beauharnais* v. *Illinois* (1952). Thus, it is not rare that a content-based classification of speech has been accepted because it may be appropriately generalized that within the confines of the given classification, the evil to be restricted so overwhelmingly outweighs the expressive interests, if any, at stake, that no process of case-by-case adjudication is required. When a definable class of material, such as that covered by § 263.15, bears so heavily and pervasively on the welfare of children engaged in its production, we think the balance of competing interests is clearly struck and that it is permissible to consider these materials as without the protection of the First Amendment.

C

There are, of course, limits on the category of child pornography which, like obscenity, is unprotected by the First Amendment. As with all legislation in this sensitive area, the conduct to be prohibited must be adequately defined by the applicable state law, as written or authoritatively construed. Here the nature of the harm to be combatted requires that the state offense be limited to works that *visually* depict sexual conduct by children below a specified age. The category of "sexual conduct" proscribed must also be suitably limited and described.

The test for child pornography is separate from the obscenity standard enunciated in *Miller*, but may be compared to it for purposes of clarity. The *Miller* formulation is adjusted in the following respects: A trier of fact need not find that the material appeals to the prurient interest of the average person; it is not required that sexual conduct portrayed be done so in a patently offensive manner; and the material at issue need not be considered as a whole. We note that the distribution of descriptions or other depictions of sexual conduct, not otherwise obscene, which do not involve live performance or photographic or other visual reproduction of live performances, retains First Amendment protection. As with obscenity laws, criminal responsibility may not be imposed without some element of scienter on the part of the defendant. *Smith* v. *California* (1959); *Hamling* v. *United States* (1974).

D

Section 263.15's prohibition incorporates a definition of sexual conduct that comports with the above-stated principles. The forbidden acts to be depicted are listed with sufficient precision and represent the kind of conduct that, if it were the theme of a work, could render it legally obscene: "actual or simulated sexual intercourse, deviate sexual intercourse, sexual bestiality, masturbation, sado-masochistic abuse, or lewd exhibition of the genitals." The term "lewd exhibition of the genitals" is not unknown in this area and, indeed, was given in *Miller* as an example of a permissible regulation. A performance is defined only to include live or visual depictions: "any play, motion picture, photograph or dance . . . or other visual representation before an audience." Section 263.15 expressly includes a scienter agreement.

We hold that § 263.15 sufficiently describes a category of material the production and distribution of which is not entitled to First Amendment protection. It is therefore clear that there is nothing unconstitutionally "underinclusive" about a statute that singles out this category of material for proscription. It also follows that the State is not barred by the First Amendment from prohibiting the distribution of unprotected materials produced outside the State.

III

It remains to address the claim that the New York statute is unconstitutionally overbroad because it would forbid the distribution of material with serious literary, scientific or educational value or material which does not threaten the harms sought to be combatted by the State. Respondent prevailed on that ground below, and it is to that issue that we now turn.

The New York Court of Appeals recognized that overbreadth scrutiny has been limited with respect to conduct-related regulation, *Broadrick* v. *Oklahoma* (1973), but it did not apply the test enunciated in *Broadrick* because the challenged statute, in its view, was directed as "pure speech." The court went on to find that § 263.15 was fatally overbroad: "[T]he statute would prohibit the showing of any play or movie in which a child portrays a defined sexual act, real or simulated, in a nonobscene manner. It would also prohibit the sale, showing, or distributing of medical or educational materials containing photographs of such acts. Indeed, by its terms, the statute would prohibit those who oppose such portrayals from providing illustrations of what they oppose."

While the construction that a state court gives a state statute is not a matter subject to our review, *Wainright* v. *Stone* (1973); *Gooding* v. *Wilson* (1972), this Court is the final arbiter of whether the federal constitution necessitated the invalidation of a state law. It is only through this process of review that we may correct erroneous applications of the Constitution that err on the side of an overly broad reading of our doctrines and precedents, as well as state court decisions giving the Constitution too little shrift. A state court is not free to avoid a proper facial attack on federal constitutional grounds. *Bigelow* v. *Virginia* (1975).

By the same token, it should not be compelled to entertain an overbreadth attack when not required to do so by the Constitution.

A

The traditional rule is that a person to whom a statute may constitutionally be applied may not challenge that statute on the ground that it may conceivably be applied unconstitutionally to others in situations not before the Court. *Broadrick* v. *Oklahoma*; *United States* v. *Raines* (1960); *Carmichael* v. *Southern Coal & Coke Co.* (1937); *Yazoo & M.V.R. Co.* v. *Jackson Vinegar Co.* (1912). In *Broadrick*, we recognized that this rule reflects two cardinal principles of our constitutional order: the personal nature of constitutional rights, *McGowan* v. *Maryland* (1961), and prudential limitations on constitutional adjudication. In *United States* v. *Raines* we noted the "incontrovertible proposition" that it "would indeed be undesirable for this Court to consider every conceivable situation which might possibly arise in the application of complex and comprehensive legislation," (quoting *Barrows* v. *Jackson* (1953)). By focusing on the factual situation before us, and similar cases necessary for development of a constitutional rule, we face "flesh-and-blood" legal problems with data "relevant and adequate to an informed judgment." This practice also fulfills a valuable institutional purpose: it allows state courts the opportunity to construe a law to avoid constitutional infirmities.

What has come to be known as the First Amendment overbreadth doctrine is one of the few exceptions to this principle and must be justified by "weighty countervailing policies." *United States* v. *Raines*. The doctrine is predicated on the sensitive nature of protected expression: "persons whose expression is constitutionally protected may well refrain from exercising their rights for fear of criminal sanctions by a statute susceptible of application to protected expression." *Village of Schaumburg* v. *Citizens for a Better Environment* (1980); *Gooding* v. *Wilson* (1972). It is for this reason that we have allowed persons to attack overly broad statutes even though the conduct of the person making the attack is clearly unprotected and could be proscribed by a law drawn with the requisite specificity. *Dombrowski* v. *Pfister* (1965); *Thornhill* v. *Alabama* (1940); *United States* v. *Raines*; *Gooding* v. *Wilson*.

The scope of the First Amendment overbreadth doctrine, like most exceptions to established principles, must be carefully tied to the circumstances in which facial invalidation of a statute is truly warranted. Because of the wide-reaching effects of striking a statute down on its face at the request of one whose own conduct may be punished despite the First Amendment, we have recognized that the overbreadth doctrine is "strong medicine" and have employed it with hesitation, and then "only as a last resort." *Broadrick*. We have, in consequence, insisted that the overbreadth involved be "substantial" before the statute involved will be invalidated on its face.

In *Broadrick*, we explained the basis for this requirement:

[T]he plain import of our case is, at the very least, that facial overbreadth adjudication is the exception to our traditional rules of practice and that its function, a limited one at the outset, attenuates as the otherwise protected behavior that it forbids the State to sanction moves from "pure speech" toward conduct and that conduct — even if expressive — falls within the scope of otherwise valid criminal laws that reflect legitimate state interests in maintaining comprehensive controls over harmful, constitutionally unprotected conduct. Although such laws, if too broadly worded, may deter protected speech to some unknown extent, there comes a point where that effect — at best a prediction — cannot, with confidence, justify invalidating a statute on its face and so prohibiting a State from enforcing the statute against conduct that is admittedly within its power to proscribe. Cf. *Alderman* v. *United States* (1969)."

We accordingly held that "particularly where conduct and not merely speech is involved, we believe that the overbreadth of a statute must not only be real, but substantial as well, judged in relation to the statute's plainly legitimate sweep."

Broadrick was a regulation involving restrictions on political campaign activity, an area not considered "pure speech," and thus it was unnecessary to consider the proper overbreadth test when a law arguably reaches traditional forms of expression such as books and films. As we intimated in *Broadrick*, the requirement of substantial overbreadth extended "at the very least" to cases involving conduct plus speech. This case, which poses the question squarely, convinces us that the rationale of *Broadrick* is sound and should be applied in the present context involving the harmful employment of children to make sexually explicit materials for distribution.

The premise that a law should not be invalidated for overbreadth unless it reaches a substantial number of impermissible applications is hardly novel. On most occasions involving facial invalidation, the Court has stressed the embracing sweep of the statute over protected expression. Indeed, JUSTICE BRENNAN observed in his dissenting opinion in *Broadrick*:

"We have never held that a statute should be held invalid on its face merely because it is possible to conceive of a single impermissible application, and in that sense a requirement of substantial overbreadth is already implicit in the doctrine."

The requirement of substantial overbreadth is directly derived from the purpose and nature of the doctrine. While a sweeping statute, or one incapable of limitation, has the potential to repeatedly chill the exercise of expressive activity by many individuals, the extent of deterrence of protected speech can be expected to decrease with the declining reach of the regulation. This observation appears equally applicable to the publication of books and films as it is to activities, such as picketing or participation in election campaigns, which have previously been categorized as involving conduct plus speech. We see no appreciable difference between the position of a publisher or bookseller in doubt as to the reach of New York's child pornography law and the situation faced by the

Oklahoma state employees with respect to that state's restriction on partisan political activity. Indeed, it could reasonably be argued that the bookseller, with an economic incentive to sell materials that may fall within the statute's scope, may be less likely to be deterred than the employee who wishes to engage in political campaign activity. Cf. *Bates* v. *State Bar of Arizona* (1977) (overbreadth analysis inapplicable to commercial speech).

This requirement of substantial overbreadth may justifiably be applied to statutory challenges which arise in defense of a criminal prosecution as well as civil enforcement or actions seeking a declaratory judgment. Cf. *Parker* v. *Levy* (1974). Indeed, the Court's practice when confronted with ordinary criminal laws that are sought to be applied against protected conduct is not to invalidate the law *in toto*, but rather to reverse the particular conviction. *Cantwell* v. *Connecticut* (1940); *Edwards* v. *South Carolina* (1973). We recognize, however, that the penalty to be imposed is relevant in determining whether demonstrable overbreadth is substantial. We simply hold that the fact that a criminal prohibition is involved does not obviate the need for the inquiry or *a priori* warrant a finding of substantial overbreadth.

B

Applying these principles, § 263.15 is not substantially overbroad. We consider this the paradigmatic case of a state statute whose legitimate reach dwarfs its arguably impermissible applications. New York, as we have held, may constitutionally prohibit dissemination of material specified in § 263.15. While the reach of the statute is directed at the hard core of child pornography, the Court of Appeals was understandably concerned that some protected expression, ranging from medical textbooks to pictorials in National Geographic, would fall prey to the statute. How often, if ever, it may be necessary to employ children to engage in conduct clearly within the reach of the § 263.15 in order to produce educational, medical or artistic works cannot be known with certainty. Yet we seriously doubt, and it has not been suggested, that these arguably impermissible applications of the statute amount to more than a tiny fraction of the materials within the statute's reach. Nor will we assume that the New York courts will widen the possibly invalid reach of the statute by giving an expansive construction to the proscription on "lewd exhibitions[s] of the genitals." Under these circumstances, § 263.15 is "not substantially overbroad and whatever overbreadth exists should be cured through case-by-case analysis of the fact situations to which its sanctions, assertedly, may not be applied." *Broadrick* v. *Oklahoma*.

IV

Because § 263.15 is not substantially overbroad, it is unnecessary to consider its application to material that does not depict sexual conduct of a type that New York may restrict consistent with the First Amendment. As applied to Paul Ferber and to others who distribute similar material, the statute does not violate the First Amendment as applied to the States through the Fourteenth. The decision of the New York Court of Appeals is reversed and the case is remanded to that Court for further proceedings not inconsistent with this opinion.

So ordered.

COURT ON WATER RIGHTS
July 2, 1982

In a decision affecting water rights laws in several western states, the Supreme Court July 2 struck down a portion of a Nebraska law forbidding transportation of ground water to states that would not allow their water to be transported to Nebraska.

In defining "water" as an article of commerce, Justice John Paul Stevens, writing for the 7-2 majority, argued that the reciprocity provision of the Nebraska law violated the Commerce Clause of the Constitution by imposing an "impermissible burden" on interstate commerce.

Stevens was joined in the decision by Chief Justice Warren E. Burger and Justices William J. Brennan Jr., Byron R. White, Thurgood Marshall, Harry A. Blackmun and Lewis F. Powell Jr. Justice William H. Rehnquist, joined by Justice Sandra Day O'Connor, filed a dissent.

Background

The case, Sporhase v. Nebraska, *centered on 640 acres of farmland, straddling the border between Nebraska and Colorado. One hundred and forty acres lay in Colorado and 500 in Nebraska. When the farm owners, Joy Sporhase and his son-in-law, Delmer Moss, began irrigating the Colorado land with water from a well located on the Nebraska side of the property, they found themselves in violation of Nebraska law. The law forbade the export of underground water to any state that did not allow water to be exported to Nebraska, as Colorado did not.*

The state of Nebraska filed suit against Sporhase and Moss when the two farmers defied official warnings and continued to pump water onto the Colorado land. In 1981 the Nebraska Supreme Court ruled against the farmers, forcing them to cease operation of the well.

Water as an Article of Commerce

In overturning the state court decision, Stevens said that if Nebraska ground water were not defined as an article of commerce, it would not be subject to scrutiny by Congress, thus curtailing "the affirmative power of Congress to implement its own policies concerning such regulations."

"If Congress chooses to legislate in this area under its commerce power," Stevens wrote, "its regulation need not be more limited in Nebraska than in Texas and states with similar property laws. Ground water overdraft is a national problem and Congress has the power to deal with it on that scale."

Stevens did not rule out the state's right to regulate water exports in order to ensure conservation. A state, he wrote, could prohibit the export of water to another state if the prohibition was "narrowly tailored to the conservation and preservation rationale."

The Dissent

Rehnquist disagreed with the court's finding that water should be considered an item of interstate commerce. He said, "It is difficult, if not impossible, to conclude that 'commerce' exists in an item that cannot be reduced to possession under state law. . . . 'Commerce' cannot exist in a natural resource that cannot be sold, rented, traded, or transferred, but only used."

The Sporhase case was carefully followed by officials in Western states, where water is distributed according to a complex network of rules and regulations. Some feared the decision could allow large energy companies to transport water from one state to another, reducing the amount available to farmers. Others worried that numerous lawsuits could result if states began using the "conservation and preservation" argument to deny water exports.

Following are excerpts from the July 2, 1982, decision by the Supreme Court in Sporhase v. Nebraska, *in which the court ruled that water is subject to the Commerce Clause of the Constitution; and excerpts from the dissent by Justice Rehnquist:*

No. 81-613

Joy Sporhase and Delmer Moss, etc., appellants *v.* Nebraska, ex rel. Paul L. Douglas, attorney general	Appeal from the Supreme Court of Nebraska

[July 2, 1982]

JUSTICE STEVENS delivered the opinion of the Court.

Appellants challenge the constitutionality of a Nebraska statutory restriction on the withdrawal of ground water from any well within Nebraska intended for use in an adjoining State. The challenge presents three questions under the Commerce Clause: (1) whether ground water is an article of commerce and therefore subject to Congressional regulation; (2) whether the Nebraska restriction on the interstate transfer of ground water imposes an impermissible burden on commerce; and (3) whether Congress has granted the States permission to engage in ground water regulation that otherwise would be impermissible.

Appellants jointly own contiguous tracts of land in Chase County, Nebraska, and Phillips County, Colorado. A well physically located on the Nebraska tract pumps ground water for irrigation of both the Nebraska tract and the Colorado tract. Previous owners of the land registered the well with the State of Nebraska in 1971, but neither they nor the present owners applied for the permit required by § 46-613.01 of the Nebraska Revised Statutes. That section provides:

> "Any person, firm, city, village, municipal corporation or any other entity intending to withdraw ground water from any well or pit located in the State of Nebraska and transport it for use in an adjoining state shall apply to the Department of Water Resources for a permit to do so. If the Director of Water Resources finds that the withdrawal of the ground water requested is reasonable, is not contrary to the conservation and use of ground water, and is not otherwise detrimental to the public welfare, he shall grant the permit if the state in which the water is to be used grants reciprocal rights to withdraw and transport ground water from that state for use in the State of Nebraska."

Appellee brought this action to enjoin appellants from transferring the water across the border without a permit. The trial court rejected the defense that the statute imposed an undue burden on interstate commerce and granted the injunction. The Nebraska Supreme Court affirmed. (1981). It held that, under Nebraska law, ground water is not "a marketable item freely transferable for value among private parties, and therefore [is] not an article of commerce." The Chief Justice, while agreeing that the statutory criteria governing the transfer of water to an adjoining State did not violate the Commerce Clause, dissented on the narrow ground that appellee violated both the Federal and Nebraska Constitutions by attempting "to absolutely prohibit the transfer of water, without regard to its need or availability, based solely upon the acts of another state over which citizens of this state have no control."

I

In holding that ground water is not an article of commerce, the Nebraska Supreme Court and appellee cite as controlling precedent *Hudson County Water Co.* v. *McCarter* (1908). In that case a New Jersey statute prohibited the interstate transfer of any surface water located within the State. The Hudson County Water Company nevertheless contracted with New York City to supply one of its boroughs with water from the Passaic River in New Jersey. The state attorney general sought from the New Jersey courts an injunction against fulfillment of the contract. Over the water company's objections that the statute impaired the obligation of contract, took property without just compensation, interfered with interstate commerce, denied New York citizens the privileges afforded New Jersey citizens, and denied New York citizens the equal protection of the laws, the injunction was granted. This Court, in an opinion by Justice Holmes, affirmed.

Most of the Court's opinion addresses the just compensation claim. Justice Holmes refused to ground the Court's holding, as did the New Jersey state courts, on "the more or less attenuated residuum of title that the State may be said to possess." For the statute was justified as a regulatory measure that, on balance, did not amount to a taking of property that required just compensation. Putting aside the "problems of irrigation," the State's interest in preserving its waters was well within its police power. That interest was not dependent on any demonstration that the State's water resources were inadequate for present or future use. The State "finds itself in possession of what all admit to be a great public good, and what it has it may keep and give no one a reason for its will."

Having disposed of the just compensation claim, Justice Holmes turned very briefly to the other constitutional challenges. In one paragraph, he rejected the Contract Clause claim. In the remaining paragraph of the opinion, he rejected all the other defenses. His treatment of the Commerce Clause challenge consists of three sentences: "A man cannot acquire a right to property by his desire to use it in commerce among the States. Neither can he enlarge his otherwise limited and qualified right to the same end. The case is covered in this respect by *Geer* v. *Connecticut* ... [(1896)]."

While appellee relies upon *Hudson County*, appellants rest on our summary affirmance of a three-judge district court judgment in *City of Altus* v. *Carr* (1966). The City of Altus is located near the southern border of Oklahoma. Large population increases rendered inadequate its source of municipal water. It consequently obtained from the owners of land in an adjoining Texas county the contractual right to pump the ground water underlying that land and to transport it across the border. The Texas legislature thereafter enacted a statute that forbade the interstate exportation of ground water without the approval of that body. The City filed suit in federal district court, claiming that the statute violated the Commerce Clause.

The City relied upon *West* v. *Kansas Natural Gas Co.* (1910), which invalidated an Oklahoma statute that prevented the interstate transfer of natural gas produced within the State, and *Pennsylvania* v. *West Virginia* (1923), which invalidated a West Virginia statute that accorded a preference to the citizens of that State in the purchase of natural gas produced therein. The Texas attorney general defended the statute on two grounds. First, he asserted that its purpose was to conserve and protect the State's water resources by regulating the withdrawal of ground water. The district court rejected that defense because similar conservation claims had met defeat in *West* v. *Kansas Natural Gas Co.* and *Pennsylvania* v. *West Virginia*. Second, the State argued that the statute regulated ground water and that ground water is not an article of commerce, citing *Geer* v. *Connecticut* and *Hudson County*. The court rejected this argument since the statute directly regulated the interstate transportation of water that had been pumped from the ground, and under Texas law such water was an article of commerce. The court then had little difficulty in concluding that the statute imposed an impermissible burden on interstate commerce.

In summarily affirming the district court in *City of Altus*, we did not necessarily adopt the court's reasoning. Our affirmance indicates only our agreement with the result reached by the district court. *Metromedia, Inc.* v. *City of San Diego* (1981). That result is not necessarily inconsistent with the Nebraska Supreme Court's holding in this case. For Texas law differs significantly from Nebraska law regarding the rights of a surface owner to ground water that he has withdrawn. According to the district court in *City of Altus*, the "rule in Texas was that an owner of land could use all of the percolating water he could capture from the wells on his land for whatever beneficial purposes he needed it, on or off the land, and could likewise sell it to others for use on or off the land and outside the basin where produced, just as he could sell any other species of property." Since ground water, once withdrawn, may be freely bought and sold in States that follow this rule, in those States ground water is appropriately regarded as an article of commerce. In Nebraska the surface owner has no comparable interest in ground water. As explained by the Nebraska Supreme Court, " 'the owner of land is entitled to appropriate subterranean waters found under his land, but he cannot extract and appropriate them in excess of a reasonable and beneficial use upon the land which he owns, especially if such use is injurious to others who have substantial rights to the waters, and if the natural underground supply is insufficient for all owners, each is entitled to a reasonable proportion of the whole.' " ([Q]uoting *Olson* v. *City of Wahoo* (1933)).

City of Altus, however, is inconsistent with *Hudson County*. For in the latter case the Court found *Geer* v. *Connecticut* to be controlling on the

Commerce Clause issue. *Geer*, which sustained a Connecticut ban on the interstate transportation of game birds captured in that State, was premised on the theory that the State owned its wild animals and therefore was free to qualify any ownership interest it might recognize in the persons who capture them. One such restriction is a prohibition against interstate transfer of the captured animals. This theory of public ownership was advanced as a defense in *City of Altus*. The State argued that it owned all subterranean water and therefore could recognize ownership in the surface owner who withdraws the water, but restrict that ownership to use of the water within the State. That theory, upon which the Commerce Clause issue in *Hudson County* was decided, was rejected by the district court in *City of Altus*. In expressly overruling *Geer* three years ago, this Court traced the demise of the public ownership theory and definitively recast it as " 'but a fiction expressive in legal shorthand of the importance to its people that a State have power to preserve and regulate the exploitation of an important resource.' " *Hughes* v. *Oklahoma* (1979) (quoting *Toomer* v. *Witsell* (1948)). See also *Baldwin* v. *Montana Fish and Game Comm'n* (1978); *Douglas* v. *Seacoast Products, Inc.* (1977). In *Hughes* the Court found the State's interests insufficient to sustain a ban on the interstate transfer of natural minnows seined from waters within the State.

Appellee insists, however, that Nebraska water is distinguishable from other natural resurces. The surface owner who withdraws Nebraska ground water enjoys a lesser ownership interest in the water than the captor of game birds in Connecticut or minnows in Oklahoma or ground water in Texas, for in *Geer*, *Hughes*, and *City of Altus* the States permitted intrastate trade in the natural resources once they were captured. Although appellee's greater ownership interest may not be relevant to Commerce Clause analysis, it does not absolutely remove Nebraska ground water from such scrutiny. For appellee's argument is still based on the legal fiction of state ownership. The fiction is illustrated by municipal water supply arrangements pursuant to which ground water is withdrawn from rural areas and transferred to urban areas. Such arrangements are permitted in Nebraska, see *Metropolitan Utilities District* v. *Merritt Beach Co.* (1966), but the Nebraska Supreme Court distinguished them on the ground that the transferror was only permitted to charge as a price for the water his costs of distribution and not the value of the water itself. Unless demand is greater than supply, however, this reasoning does not distinguish minnows, the price of which presumably is derived from the costs of seining and of transporting the catch to market. Even in cases of shortage, in which the seller of the natural resource can demand a price that exceeds his costs, the State's rate structure that requires the price to be cost-justified is economically comparable to price regulation. A State's power to regulate prices or rates has never been thought to depend on public ownership of the controlled commodity. It would be anomalous if federal power to regulate economic transactions in natural resources depended on the characterization of the payment as compensation for distribution services, on the one hand, or as the price of goods, on the other. Cf. *In re Rahrer* (1891).

The second asserted distinction is that water, unlike other natural resources, is essential for human survival. Appellee, and the *amici curiae* that are vitally interested in conserving and preserving scarce water resources in the arid Western States, have convincingly demonstrated the desirability of state and local management of ground water. But the States' interests clearly have an interstate dimension. Although water is indeed essential for human survival, studies indicate that over 80% of our water supplies is used for agricultural purposes. The agricultural markets supplied by irrigated farms are worldwide. They provide the archtypical example of commerce among the several States for which the Framers of our Constitution intended to authorize federal regulation. The multistate character of the Ogallala aquifer — underlying appellants' tracts of land in Colorado and Nebraska, as well as parts of Texas, New Mexico, Oklahoma, and Kansas — confirms the view that there is a significant federal interest in conservation as well as in fair allocation of this diminishing resource. Cf. *Arizona* v. *California* (1963).

The Western States' interests, and their asserted superior competence, in conserving and preserving scarce water resources are not irrelevant in the Commerce Clause inquiry. Nor is appellee's claim to public ownership without significance. Like Congress' deference to state water law, these factors inform the determination whether the burdens on commerce imposed by state ground water regulation are reasonable or unreasonable. But appellee's claim that Nebraska ground water is not an article of commerce goes too far: it would not only exempt Nebraska ground water regulation from burden-on-commerce analysis, it also would curtail the affirmative power of Congress to implement its own policies concerning such regulation. See *Philadelphia* v. *New Jersey* (1978). If Congress chooses to legislate in this area under its commerce power, its regulation need not be more limited in Nebraska than in Texas and States with similar property laws. Ground water overdraft is a national problem and Congress has the power to deal with it on that scale.

II

Our conclusion that water is an article of commerce raises, but does not answer, the question whether the Nebraska statute is unconstitutional. For the existence of unexercised federal regulatory power does not foreclose state regulation of its water resources, of the uses of water within the State, or indeed, of interstate commerce in water. *Southern Pacific Co.* v. *Arizona* (1945); *United States* v. *South-Eastern Underwriters Assn.* (1944); *Cooley* v. *Board of Wardens* (1851). Determining the validity of state statutes affecting interstate commerce requires a more careful inquiry:

"Where the statute regulates evenhandedly to effectuate a legitimate local public interest, and its effects on interstate commerce are only incidental, it will be upheld unless the burden imposed on such commerce is clearly excessive in relation to the putative local benefits. If a legitimate local purpose is found, then the question becomes one of degree. And the extent of the burden that will be tolerated will of course depend on the nature of the local interest involved, and on whether it could be promoted as well with a lesser impact on interstate activities." *Pike* v. *Bruce Church Inc.* (1970).

The only purpose that appellee advances for § 46-613.01 is to conserve and preserve diminishing sources of ground water. The purpose is unquestionably legitimate and highly important, and the other aspects of Nebraska's ground water regulation demonstrate that it is genuine. Appellants' land in Nebraska is located within the boundaries of the Upper Republican Ground Water Control Area, which was designated as such by the Director of the Nebraska Department of Water Resources based upon a determination "that there is an inadequate ground water supply to meet present or reasonably foreseeable needs for beneficial use of such water supply." Pursuant to § 46-666(1), the Upper Republican Natural Resources District has promulgated special rules and regulations governing ground water withdrawal and use. The rules and regulations define as "critical" those townships in the control area in which the annual decline of the ground water table exceeds a fixed percentage; appellants' Nebraska tract is located within a critical township. The rules and regulations require the installation of flow meters on every well within the control area, specify the amount of water per acre that may be used for irrigation, and set the spacing that is required between wells. They also strictly limit the intrastate transfer of ground water: transfers are only permitted between lands controlled by the same groundwater user, and all transfers must be approved by the district board of directors.

The State's interest in conservation and preservation of ground water is advanced by the first three conditions in § 46-613.01 for the withdrawal of water for an interstate transfer. Those requirements are "that the withdrawal of the ground water requested is reasonable, is not contrary to the conservation and use of ground water, and is not otherwise detrimental to the public welfare." Although Commerce Clause concerns are implicated by the fact that § 46-613.01 applies to interstate transfers but not to intrastate transfers, there are legitimate reasons for the special treatment accorded requests to transport ground water across state lines. Obviously, a State that imposes severe withdrawal and use restrictions on its own citizens is not discriminating against interstate commerce when it seeks to prevent the uncontrolled transfer of water out of the State. An exemption for interstate transfers would be inconsistent with the ideal of evenhandedness in regulation. At least in the area in which appellants' Nebraska tract is located, the first three standards of § 46-613.01 may well be no more strict in application than the limitations upon intrastate transfers imposed by the Upper Republican Natural Resources District.

Moreover, in the absence of a contrary view expressed by Congress, we are reluctant to condemn as unreasonable measures taken by a State to conserve and preserve for its own citizens this vital resource in times of severe shortage. Our reluctance stems from the "confluence of [several] realities." *Hicklin* v. *Orbeck* (1978). First, a State's power to regulate the use of water in times and places of shortage for the purpose of protecting the health of its citizens — and not simply the health of its economy — is at the core of its police power. For Commerce Clause purposes, we have long recognized a difference between economic protectionism, on the one hand, and health and safety regulation, on the other. See *H. P. Hood & Sons* v. *Du Mond* (1949). Second, the legal expectation that under certain circumstances each State may restrict water within its borders had been fostered over the years not only by our equitable apportionment decrees, see, *e.g.*, *Wyoming* v. *Colorado* (1957), but also by the negotiation and enforcement of interstate compacts. Our law therefore has recognized the relevance of state boundaries in the allocation of scarce water resources. Third, although appellee's claim to public ownership of Nebraska ground water cannot justify a total denial of federal regulatory power, it may support a limited preference for its own citizens in the utilization of the resource. See *Hicklin* v. *Orbeck*. In this regard, it is relevant that appellee's claim is logically more substantial than claims to public ownership of other natural resources. Finally, given appellee's conservation efforts, the continuing availability of ground water in Nebraska is not simply happenstance; the natural resource has some indicia of a good publicly produced and owned in which a State may favor its own citizens in time of shortage. See *Reeves, Inc.* v. *Stake* (1980); cf. *Philadelphia* v. *New Jersey*; *Baldwin* v. *Fish and Game Comm'n*. A facial examination of the first three conditions set forth in § 46-613.01 does not, therefore, indicate that they impermissibly burden interstate commerce. Appellants, indeed, seem to concede their reasonableness.

Appellants, however, do challenge the requirement that "the state in which the water is to be used grants reciprocal rights to withdraw and transport ground water from that state for use in the State of Nebraska" — the reciprocity provision that troubled the Chief Justice of the Nebraska Supreme Court. Because Colorado forbids the exportation of its ground water, the reciprocity provision operates as an explicit barrier to commerce between the two States. The State therefore bears the initial burden of demonstrating a close fit between the reciprocity requirement and its asserted local purpose. *Hughes* v. *Oklahoma*; *Dean Milk Co.* v. *City of Madison* (1951).

The reciprocity requirement fails to clear this initial hurdle. For there is no evidence that this restriction is narrowly tailored to the conservation and preservation rationale. Even though the supply of water in a particular well may be abundant, or perhaps even excessive, and even though the most beneficial use of that water might be in another State, such water may not be shipped into a neighboring State that does not permit its water to be used in Nebraska. If it could be shown that the State as a whole suffers a water shortage, that the intrastate transportation of water from areas of abundance to areas of shortage is feasible regardless of distance, and that the importation of water from adjoining States would roughly compensate for any exportation to those States, then the conservation and preservation purpose might be credibly advanced for the reciprocity provision. A demonstrably arid state conceivably might be able to marshal evidence to establish a close mean-end relationship between even a total ban on the exportation of water and a purpose to conserve and preserve water. Appellee, however, does not claim that such evidence exits. We therefore are not persuaded that the reciprocity requirement — when superimposed on the first three restrictions in the statute — significantly advances the State's legitimate conservation and preservation interest; it surely is not narrowly tailored to serve that purpose. The reciprocity requirement does not survive the "strictest scrutiny" reserved for facially discriminatory legislation. *Hughes* v. *Oklahoma*.

III

Appellee's suggestion that Congress has authorized the States to impose otherwise impermissible burdens on interstate commerce in ground water is not well-founded. The suggestion is based on 37 statutes in which Congress has deferred to state water law, and on a number of interstate compacts dealing with water that have been approved by Congress.

Abstracts of the relevant sections of the 37 statutes relied upon by appellee were submitted in connection with the Hearings on S. 1275 before the Senate Subcommittee on Irrigation and Reclamation, 88th Cong., 2d Sess. (1964). Appellee refers the Court to that submission but only discusses § 8 of the Reclamation Act of 1902. That section, it turns out, is typical of the other 36 statutes. It contains two parts. The first provides that "nothing in this Act shall be construed as affecting or intended to affect or to in any way interfere with the laws of any State or Territory relating to the control, appropriation, use, or distribution of water used in irrigation." Such language defines the extent of the federal legislation's preemptive effect on state law. *New England Power Co.* v. *New Hampshire* (1982); *Lewis* v. *BT Investment Managers, Inc.* (1980). The second part provides that "the Secretary of Interior, in carrying out the provisions of this Act, shall proceed in conformity with such laws." Such language mandates that questions of water rights that arise in relation to a federal project are to be determined in accordance with state law. See *California* v. *United States* (1978).

The interstate compacts to which appellee refers are agreements among States regarding rights to surface water.... Appellee emphasizes a compact between Nebraska and Colorado involving water rights to the South Platte River and a compact among Nebraska, Colorado, and Kansas involving water rights to the Republican River.

Although the 37 statutes and the interstate compacts demonstrate

Congress' deference to state water law, they do not indicate that Congress wished to remove federal constitutional constraints on such state laws. The negative implications of the Commerce Clause, like the mandates of the Fourteenth Amendment, are ingredients of the *valid* state law to which Congress has deferred. Neither the fact that Congress has chosen not to create a federal water law to govern water rights involved in federal projects, nor the fact that Congress has been willing to let the States settle their differences over water rights through mutual agreement, constitutes persuasive evidence that Congress consented to the unilateral imposition of unreasonable burdens on commerce. In the instances in which we have found such consent, Congress' " 'intent and policy' to sustain state legislation from attack under the Commerce Clause" was " 'expressly stated' " *New England Power Co.* v. *New Hampshire* (quoting *Prudential Ins. Co.* v. *Benjamin* (1946)). Cf. *Merrion* v. *Jicarilla Apache Tribe* (1982).

The reciprocity requirement of Neb. Rev. Stat. § 46-613.01 violates the Commerce Clause. We leave to the state courts the question whether the invalid portion is severable. The judgment of the Nebraska Supreme Court is reversed and the case is remanded for proceedings not inconsistent with this opinion.

It is so ordered.

JUSTICE REHNQUIST, with whom JUSTICE O'CONNOR joins, dissenting.

The issue presented by this case, and the only issue, is whether the existence of the Commerce Clause of the United States Constitution by itself, in the absence of any action by Congress, invalidates some or all of § 46-613.01 of the Nebraska Revised Statutes, which relates to groundwater. But instead of confining its opinion to this question, the Court first quite gratuitously undertakes to answer the question of whether the authority of Congress to regulate interstate commerce, conferred by the same provision of the Constitution, would enable it to legislate with respect to groundwater overdraft in some or all of the States.

That these two questions are quite distinct leaves no room for doubt. Congress may regulate not only the stream of commerce itself, but activities which affect interstate commerce, including wholly intrastate activities. See, *e.g.*, *Kirschbaum Co.* v. *Walling* (1942); *United States* v. *Darby* (1941); *Houston & Texas Ry.* v. *United States* (1914). The activity upon which the regulatory effect of the congressional statute falls in many of these cases does not directly involve articles of commerce at all. For example, in *Kirschbaum*, the employees were engaged in the operation and maintenance of a loft building in which large quantities of goods for interstate commerce were produced; no one contended that these employees themselves, or the work which they actually performed, dealt with articles of commerce. Nonetheless, the provisions of the Fair Labor Standards Act were applied to them because Congress extended the terms of the Act not only to those who were "engaged in commerce" but to those who were engaged "in the production of goods for commerce."

Thus, the authority of Congress under the power to regulate interstate commerce may reach a good deal further than the mere negative impact of the Commerce Clause in the absence of any action by Congress. Upon a showing that groundwater overdraft has a substantial economic effect on interstate commerce, for example, Congress arguably could regulate groundwater overdraft, even if groundwater is not an "article of commerce" itself. See, *e.g.*, *Hodel* v. *Virginia Surface Mining & Recl. Assn.* (1981); (REHNQUIST, J., concurring in judgment); *Wickard* v. *Filburn* (1942). It is therefore wholly unnecessary to decide whether Congress could regulate groundwater overdraft in order to decide this case; since Congress has not undertaken such a regulation, I would leave the determination of its validity until such time as it is necessary to decide that question.

The question actually involved in this case is whether Neb. Rev. Stat. § 46-613.01 runs afoul of the unexercised authority of Congress to regulate interstate commerce. While the Court apparently agrees that our equitable apportionment decrees in cases such as *Wyoming* v. *Colorado* (1957), and the execution and approval of interstate compacts apportioning water have given rise to "the legal expectation that under certain circumstances each State may restrict water within its borders," it insists on an elaborate balancing process in which the State's "interest" is weighed under traditional Commerce Clause analysis.

I think that in more than one of our cases in which a State has invoked our original jurisdiction, the unsoundness of the Court's approach is manifest. For example, in *Georgia* v. *Tennessee Copper Co.* (1907), the Court said:

> "This is a suit by a State for an injury to it in its capacity of *quasi*-sovereign. In that capacity the State has an interest independent of and behind the titles of its citizens, in all the earth and air within its domain. It has the last word as to whether its mountains shall be stripped of their forests and its inhabitants shall breathe pure air."

Five years earlier, in *Kansas* v. *Colorado* (1902), the Court had made clear that a State's quasi-sovereign interest in the flow of surface and subterranean water within its borders was of the same magnitude as its interest in pure air or healthy forests.

In my view, these cases appropriately recognize the traditional authority of a State over resources within its boundaries which are essential not only to the well-being, but often to the very lives of its citizens. In the exercise of this authority, a State may so regulate a natural resource so as to preclude that resource from attaining the status of an "article of commerce" for the purposes of the negative impact of the Commerce Clause. It is difficult, if not impossible, to conclude that "commerce" exists in an item that cannot be reduced to possession under state law and in which the State recognizes only a usufructuary right. "Commerce" cannot exist in a natural resource that cannot be sold, rented, traded, or transferred, but only *used*.

Of course, a State may not discriminate against interstate commerce when it regulates even such a resource. If the State allows indiscriminate intrastate commercial dealings in a particular resource, it may have a difficult task proving that an outright prohibition on interstate commercial dealings is not such a discrimination. I had thought that this was the basis for this Court's decisions in *Hughes* v. *Oklahoma* (1979), *Pennsylvania* v. *West Virginia* (1923), and *West* v. *Kansas Nat. Gas Co.* (1911). In each case, the State permitted a natural resource to be reduced to private possession, permitted an *intrastate* market to exist in that resource, and either barred *interstate* commerce entirely or granted its residents a commercial preference.

By contrast, Nebraska so regulates groundwater that it cannot be said that the State permits any "commerce," intrastate or interstate, to exist in this natural resource. As with almost all of the Western States, Nebraska does not recognize an absolute ownership interest in groundwater, but grants landowners only a right to *use groundwater on the land from which it has been extracted.* Moreover, the landowner's right to use groundwater is limited. Nebraska landowners may not extract groundwater "in excess of a reasonable and beneficial use upon the land which he owns, especially if such use is injurious to others who have substantial rights to the waters, and if the natural underground supply is insufficient for all owners, each is entitled to a reasonable proportion of the whole." *Olson* v. *City of Wahoo* (1933). With the exception of municipal water systems, Nebraska forbids any transportation of groundwater off the land owned or controlled by the person who has appropriated the water from its subterranean source. . . .

Nebraska places additional restrictions on groundwater users within certain areas, such as the portion of appellant's land situated in Nebraska, where the shortage of groundwater is determined to be critical. Water users in appellants' district are permitted only to irrigate the acreage irrigated in 1977, or the average number of acres irrigated between 1972 and 1976, whichever is greater, and must obtain permission from the water district's board before any additional acreage may be placed under irrigation. The amount of groundwater that may be extracted is strictly limited on an acre-inch-per-irrigated acre basis. . . .

Since Nebraska requires only a limited right to use groundwater on land owned by the appropriator, it cannot be said that "commerce" in groundwater exists as far as Nebraska is concerned. Therefore, it cannot be said that Neb. Rev. Stat. § 46-613.01 either discriminates against, or "burdens," interstate commerce. Section 46-613.01 is simply a regulation of the landowner's *right to use* groundwater extracted from lands he owns within Nebraska. Unlike the Court, I cannot agree that Nebraska's limitation upon a landowner's right to extract water from his land situated in Nebraska *for his own use* on land he owns in an adjoining State runs afoul of Congress' unexercised authority to regulate interstate commerce.

AUGUST

JUSTICES ON WORKLOAD OF SUPREME COURT

August 6-November 18, 1982

In speeches during the summer and fall, seven of the nine Supreme Court justices, including the chief justice, complained of the court's overloaded docket and proposed a number of solutions. The open airing of the court's internal troubles was unusual, and the number of justices speaking out indicated the seriousness of their concerns.

In an address to the American Judicature Society August 6, Justice John Paul Stevens warned that "the heavy flow of litigation is having a more serious impact on the administration of justice than is generally recognized." Stevens disclosed that because of the flood of paperwork, his law clerks screen most of the petitions he receives for Supreme Court review. "As a result, I do not even look at the papers in over 80 percent of the cases that are filed," he said.

Stevens suggested several solutions to the caseload problem. First he urged the court to exercise greater judicial restraint and avoid unnecessary lawmaking. He proposed the formation of a new court to review cases and decide which ones the Supreme Court should hear, thus relieving the justices of the time-consuming screening process. (This proposal was similar to the one advanced in 1972 by a special study committee.) Stevens also suggested creation of a standing congressional committee "to identify conflicts that need resolution and to draft bills to resolve them."

Powell, White and Brennan

Justice Lewis F. Powell Jr., addressing the American Bar Association

(ABA) August 9, discussed the growing volume of cases confronting the Supreme Court and the U.S. judicial system generally. He proposed that Congress make "fundamental changes" in the laws to reduce the number of cases entering federal courts. Otherwise, he feared, the judicial branch may become a third enormous bureaucracy, ever adding personnel to keep up with the workload.

Also speaking to ABA members, Justice Byron R. White pointed out August 10 that the Supreme Court docket was filling up so quickly that the court would not be current in its work. "[C]ases will be ready for argument and we shall not be ready for them. This is something new and disturbing for us," he said.

White proposed the creation of two supreme courts, one to handle civil cases and one criminal; or one for constitutional issues, the other for statutory matters. Alternatively, he proposed formation of new appeals courts to hear appeals in certain types of cases from district courts nationwide. Finally, White suggested requiring "a court of appeals to go en banc [with full judicial authority] before differing with another court of appeals and to make the first en banc decision the nationwide rule."

White's last two suggestions intrigued Justice William J. Brennan Jr., the most senior member of the court, who recommended their "immediate study" in a speech to the Third U.S. Judicial Conference September 9. Brennan agreed that the court is overworked, and he urged greater care in case selection. He sharply criticized Stevens' proposal for creation of a new court to decide which cases the Supreme Court should hear. The screening process, Brennan maintained, is "inextricably linked to the fulfillment of the court's essential duties and is vital to the effective performance of the court's unique mission...." To turn that function over to another panel would be "dangerously" wrong, he contended. And, in an apparent criticism of Stevens, Brennan noted that he screens almost every case himself.

Marshall, Rehnquist and Burger

One consequence of the court's mounting caseload is the increased use of summary dispositions — decisions made without full briefing or oral arguments and issued in unsigned opinions. In an address September 9 to the Second U.S. Circuit Judicial Conference, Justice Thurgood Marshall criticized the court's "all-too-often cavalier treatment of the rights and interests of the parties involved in such cases." He recommended notifying parties that summary disposition was under consideration to allow them time to file briefs on the merits.

Addressing a University of Kentucky audience September 23, Justice William H. Rehnquist, like Powell, warned of the growing number of cases throughout the federal judicial system and resulting bureaucracy.

Federal judges, Rehnquist feared, may soon become mere managers, attended by numerous clerks and attorneys who will "actually do the work of judging."

Chief Justice Warren E. Burger, speaking in New York November 18, said that the increasing caseload of the Supreme Court would make it impossible to "maintain standards of quality the country has a right to expect from its highest court." He suggested considering the division of the court system into criminal and civil tribunals — a system used in some European countries. Burger also supported passage of legislation creating a 14-member bipartisan commission, selected from the three branches of government, to study the problems of the judicial systems and to develop "a long-range plan for the future."

Following are excerpts from speeches by Justice John Paul Stevens, August 6; by Justice Lewis F. Powell Jr., August 9; by Justice Byron R. White, as prepared for delivery August 10; by Justice William J. Brennan Jr., September 9; by Justice Thurgood Marshall, September 9; by Justice William H. Rehnquist, September 23, and by Chief Justice Warren E. Burger, November 18. (Boldface headings in brackets have been added by Congressional Quarterly to highlight the organization of the texts.):

STEVENS' SPEECH

... The Supreme Court is now processing more litigation than ever before. The Court is granting more petitions for certiorari; litigants whose petitions are granted next fall may have to wait a full year before their cases are argued. The Court is issuing more pages of written material; opinions for the Court are longer and more numerous and separate opinions are becoming the norm instead of the exception. The Court is deciding more cases on the merits without the benefit of full briefing and argument, using the currently fashionable technique of explaining its reasons in a "Per Curiam" opinion — a document generally written for the Court by an anonymous member of its ever increasing administrative staff. More and more frequently, after a case has been fully argued, the Court finds it appropriate to dismiss the writ of certiorari without making any decision on the merits because it belatedly learns that certiorari was improvidently granted. As is true in so many courts throughout the country, the heavy flow of litigation is having a more serious impact on the administration of justice than is generally recognized.

Some of the consequences of this increased flow are predictable and have already begun to manifest themselves. The problem of delay — which is not yet serious — in a few years will be a matter of national concern. Of even greater importance, however, is what may happen within the Court itself. For when a court is overworked, the judges inevitably will concentrate their principal attention on the most important business at hand. Matters of secondary importance tend to be put to one side for further study or to be delegated to staff assistants for special consideration. Two examples illustrate this point.

At the beginning of our last Term, after the Court had processed the list of certiorari petitions that had been filed during the summer recess — if my memory serves me correctly there were about a thousand cases on that list — we agreed that it was essential that we confront the question whether the Court should either support legislation that would increase the appellate capacity of the federal judicial system or try to develop new internal procedures that would ameliorate the impact of the case volume on our own work. As the Term developed, however, and we became more and more deeply involved in the merits of a series of difficult cases, our initial recognition of the overriding importance of evaluating our own workload problems — and the desirability of scheduling conferences devoted exclusively to that subject matter — gradually dissipated and no such conference was ever held. We were too busy to decide whether there was anything we could do about the problem of being too busy.

Reviewing approximately 100 certiorari petitions each week and deciding which to grant and which to deny is important work. But it is less important work than studying and actually deciding the merits of cases that have already been accepted for review and writing opinions explaining those decisions. Because there simply is not enough time available to do the more important work with the care it requires and also to read all the certiorari petitions that are filed, I have found it necessary to delegate a great deal of responsibility in the review of certiorari petitions to my law clerks. They examine them all and select a small minority that they believe I should read myself. As a result, I do not even look at the papers in over 80 percent of the cases that are filed. I cannot describe the practice of any of my colleagues, but when I compare the quality of their collective efforts at managing the certiorari docket with the high quality of their work on argued cases, I readily conclude that they also must be treating the processing of certiorari petitions as a form of second-class work. My observation of that process during the past seven Terms has convinced me that the Court does a poor job of exercising its discretionary power over certiorari petitions. Because we are too busy to give the certiorari docket the attention it deserves, we grant many more cases than we should, thereby making our management problem even more unmanageable.

[National Court of Appeals]

At this point I should make clear that I am expressing only my own opinion — an opinion that perhaps none of my colleagues share. Indeed, some of them believe we should be taking many more cases and that our overflow should be decided by a newly created National Court of Appeals.

Under that view, the aggregate lawmaking capacity of the federal judiciary would be enlarged. There would be a significant increase in the number of federal adjudications binding on courts throughout the nation. Moreover, under that view, the management functions performed by the Supreme Court would require a relatively greater portion of the justices' total time. For the Justices would not only decide what cases are important enough to justify decision on the merits at a national level, but they would also decide which of the two courts with nationwide jurisdiction should hear those cases. In other words, they would be managing the docket of two courts instead of just one. The increased national capacity would also make it more difficult for us to resist the temptation to review every case in which we believe the court below has committed an error. Like a new four-lane highway that temporarily relieves traffic congestion, a new national court would also attract greater and greater traffic volumes and create unforeseen traffic problems. In my opinion it would be unfortunate if the function of the Supreme Court of the United States should become one of primarily — or even largely — correcting errors committed by other courts. It is far better to allow the state supreme courts and federal courts of appeals to have the final say on almost all litigation than to embark on the hopeless task of attempting to correct every judicial error that can be found.

[Judicial Restraint]

In my opinion, the Court and the nation would be better served by reexamining the doctrine of judicial restraint and by applying its teachings to the problems that confront us. The doctrine of judicial restraint is often misunderstood. It is not a doctrine that relates to the merits of judicial decisions; it is a doctrine that focuses on the process of making judicial decisions. It is a doctrine that teaches judges to ask themselves whether, and if so when, they should decide the merits of questions that litigants press upon them. It is not a doctrine that denies the judiciary any lawmaking power — our common law heritage and the repeated need to add new stitches in the open fabric of our statutory and constitutional law forecloses the suggestion that judges never make law — but the doctrine of judicial restraint, as explained for example in Justice Brandeis' separate opinion in *Ashwander* v. *Tennessee Valley Authority*, teaches judges to avoid *unnecessary* lawmaking. When it is necessary to announce a new proposition of law in order to decide an actual case or controversy between adversary litigants, a court has a duty to exercise its lawmaking power. But when no such necessity is present, in my opinion there is an equally strong duty to avoid unnecessary lawmaking.

The fact that the Court is granting a larger number of certiorari petitions than ever before raises the question whether it is engaging in unnecessary lawmking. The answer to that question is suggested by a few examples of the way the Court has exercised its discretionary jurisdiction in recent years. For both in deciding when to review novel questions and in deciding what questions need review, the Court often exhibits an unfortunate lack of judicial restraint. Thus, the various opinions in our recent case involving a school library plainly disclose that the Court granted certiorari at an interlocutory stage of a case in which further proceedings in the trial court would either have clarified the constitutional issue or perhaps have mooted the entire case. Similar considerations in the case involving a court clerk's claim of immunity prompted the Court to dismiss the writ as improvidently granted. The Court's *timing* in these cases demonstrates that patience is both a virtue and a characteristic of judgment that judges sometimes forget.

In other cases the Court has displayed a surprising unwillingness to allow other courts to make the final decision in cases that are binding in only a limited geographical area and in which no conflict exists. Thus, in *Watt* v. *Alaska*, apart from the possibility that error had been committed, there was no reason for our Court to involve itself in a dispute between the State of Alaska and one of its counties over the division of mineral leasing revenues that could only arise in the Ninth Circuit. In *Oregon* v. *Kennedy*, the Court elected to review a misapplication of double jeopardy doctrine by the Oregon Court of Appeals even though the particular facts of the case may never be duplicated in other litigation. The fact that the new double jeopardy doctrine pronounced in the opinion of five of my colleagues was totally unnecessary to decide that case adds emphasis to the lack of necessity for granting certiorari at all. Moreover, despite that pronouncement, the Oregon court remained free to reinstate its prior judgment by unambiguously relying on Oregon, rather than federal, law to support its holding. In *South Dakota* v. *Opperman*, the State Supreme Court followed that precise course, thereby proving that our Court had unnecessarily taken jurisdiction of a case in which deference to the state court's judgment would have been appropriate in the first instance.... A willingness to allow the decision of other courts to stand until it is *necessary* to review them is not a characteristic of this Court when it believes that error may have been committed.

The Court's lack of judicial restraint is perhaps best illustrated by the procedure it followed in the *Snepp* case. A former CIA agent filed a petition for certiorari seeking review of a Fourth Circuit decision holding that his publication of a book about Viet Nam violated his secrecy agreement with the CIA; he contended that his contract was unenforceable because it abridged his right to free speech. The Government opposed his petition and also filed a conditional cross-petition, praying that *if* the Court should grant Snepp's petition, it should also consider whether the remedy ordered by the lower court was adequate. The Court denied Snepp's petition, but nevertheless granted the cross-petition and, without hearing argument on the merits, issued a Per Curiam opinion ordering a constructive trust to be imposed on all of the book's earnings even though there was neither a statutory nor contractual basis for that novel remedy.

Since the Government had not even asked the Court to review the remedy issue unless it granted Snepp's petition, it is undeniable that the Court's exercise of lawmaking power in that case was totally unnecessary. . . .

You may think I have wandered away from a discussion of the problems created by the mounting tide of litigation that is threatening to engulf our Court. My purpose in discussing the doctrine of judicial restraint, however, is relevant for two quite different reasons. First, it lends support to a possible solution to the problem that I favor; second, it explains why judges who do not share my respect for the doctrine will surely oppose that solution.

[Need for New Court]

Instead of creating a new court to decide more cases on the merits, thereby increasing the aggregate judicial power that the Supreme Court may exercise, I favor the creation of a new court to which the Supreme Court would surrender some of its present power — specifically, the power to decide what cases the Supreme Court should decide on the merits. In essence, this is the proposal that was made by the committee headed by Professor Paul Freund several years ago with one critical difference. I would allow that court to *decide* — not merely to recommend — that a certiorari petition should be granted or denied. Let me just briefly explain why I believe the creation of a new court with that power would significantly improve the administration of justice.

First, and of greatest importance, I believe an independent tribunal that did not have responsibility for deciding the merits of any case would do a far better job of selecting those relatively few cases that should be decided by the Supreme Court of the United States. As I have already suggested, I think the present Court does a poor job of performing that task. It grants too many cases and far too often we are guilty of voting to grant simply because we believe error has been committed rather than because the question presented is both sufficiently important for decision on a national level and also ripe for decision when action is taken on the certiorari petition. I recognize that a different court might make similar mistakes, but reflection has persuaded me that such a court would be more likely to develop a jurisprudence of its own that properly focused on the factors — other than possible error — that should determine whether or not a certiorari petition should be granted.

Second, if I am correct in my belief that such a court would grant fewer petitions, this Court would be required to decide fewer cases on the merits. Even if that assumption is not correct, if the vast flood of paper and the small army of administrative personnel associated with the processing of our certiorari docket could be entirely removed from the Supreme Court, the time available to the justices for doing their most important work would be dramatically increased. The threat to the quality of that work that is now posed by the flood of certiorari petitions would be entirely removed.

Finally, if the new court were granted the power to control our docket, I believe capable judges would regard membership on that court as worthy of their talent. When the original Freund Committee proposal was made, my initial reaction to it was the same as that of other circuit judges with whom I was serving — it seemed to offer us the opportunity to become law clerks instead of judges. But an important reason for that reaction was the fact that the proposed court was not expected to exercise any real power — it would have done no more than perform a preliminary screening function for the Supreme Court without the actual power of decision. If the Supreme Court surrendered that power to the new court, the status of that court would indeed be significant. I am firmly convinced that a proper performance of the function of selecting the cases for the Supreme Court's docket would be rewarding judicial work, requiring a scholarly understanding of new developments in the law and of our democratic institutions that only our ablest judges possess....

POWELL'S REMARKS

... This audience, better than most, understands that the root cause of the bureaucracy problem is not that judges work less, or are less conscientious. Quite simply, the cause is the escalating extent to which citizens turn to the courts and to administrative tribunals for the resolution of claims and controversies of all kinds. The resort to litigation has accelerated at a rate many times population growth.

Professor [A. E. Dick] Howard of Virginia, recently wrote about our "litigious society." He stated that "the cost of legal services accounts for two percent of America's gross national product, more than the entire steel industry." He documented his thesis with caseload statistics.... Although he relied on federal court statistics, Professor Howard stated that state courts are experiencing a similar surge in litigation.

Judge Robert H. Bork in 1977, then Solicitor General, chaired a Justice Department study that identified the central problem confronting our system of justice as one of "overload." His report described the problem as "so serious that it threatens the capacity of the federal system to function as it should." The Study concluded that this is not a crisis for the courts alone, it is one for "litigants who seek justice, for claims of human rights, for the rule of law, and it is therefore a crisis for the nation."...

If one assumes that the judging function is threatened with being bureaucratized (an assumption I view with considerable skepticism), the proper question is what can be done about the underlying problem. An array of proposals has been made, addressed primarily to the overload at each level of the federal courts. I will identify briefly only a few of the proposals. They fall into several categories. For the Supreme Court, we would like to see our appellate jurisdiction — already limited — replaced entirely by discretionary review on certiorari. Similarly, Courts of Appeals would obtain substantial relief if their review in certain categories of cases were made discretionary. I think it was Judge Friendly who, some years ago, proposed discretionary review of administrative agency action, particularly in cases presenting factual controversies: e.g. social security claims. Since the Pound Conference in 1976, the Justice Department and the organized Bar have considered various alternative means of dispute resolution. Proposals, in addition to neighborhood justice centers, have included expansion of administrative processes like workmen's compensation to deal with a wide variety of subjects.

In the federal system, the fundamental need is to reduce the rate of flow of cases into the district courts. The most familiar proposal is to eliminate diversity jurisdiction, though even this is opposed by much of the organized Bar. Other major reforms also would require congressional action. I will mention two of these without the elaboration they deserve.

[Causes for Case Overload]

The most explosive source of federal jurisdiction is § 1983 (42 U.S.C.). Enacted in 1871, it lay relatively dormant until the 1961 decision in *Monroe* v. *Pape*. The historic purpose of § 1983 was to provide a federal remedy for racial discrimination. This purpose has become irrelevant, as this vaguely drawn statute is now a "font" of constitutional tort claims. Civil rights filings in federal district courts have increased from about 270 in 1961 to some 30 thousand in fiscal year 1981. Many of these were proper and legitimate civil rights complaints. About half of all civil rights suits — actually 15,629 in 1981 — were filed by state prisoners under § 1983. These constituted nearly 9 percent of the civil filings in federal district courts. Many § 1983 claims — and particularly prisoner suits — could be resolved if prior exhaustion of administrative remedies were required where these are adequate. Congress made a half-hearted attempt to curtail this flow by a statute enacted in 1978. But it is a hedged and limited requirement for prior exhaustion, and to date has been wholly ineffectual.

Another cause of overload of the federal system is § 2254, confering federal habeas corpus jurisdiction to review state court criminal convictions. There is no statute of limitations, and no finality of federal review of state convictions. Thus, repetitive recourse is commonplace. I know of no other system of justice structured in a way that assures no end to the litigation of a criminal conviction. Our practice in this respect is viewed with disbelief by lawyers and judges in other countries. Nor does the Constitution require this sort of redundancy. . . .

We have tolerated a system under § 2254 so easily abused because of the rare case — a *Gideon* — in which an unconstitutional and unjust conviction is not identified until years later. One would think that we are wise enough to provide for the exceptional case without continuing a system that otherwise seems indefensible.

There are, of course, responsible organizations and people who oppose any change in § 2254. I would not favor its *repeal*, certainly not without careful study by Congress and the organized Bar. But I agree with Judge [Carl] McGowan in thinking that the time has come for considering means of *limiting* collateral review by federal courts of state convictions to cases of manifest injustice — where the issue is guilt or innocence. . . .

To be sure, as is true of § 1983 suits, most of the § 2254 cases are not burdensome and can be disposed of on order. But every case filed initiates a process, requires staff work, and ultimately a judicial decision. Nor is the problem simply one of overload. As often has been noted — by distinguished judges and commentators — the present dual review system denigrates state courts. Also, as Justice Harlan emphasized, a system that never ends the criminal review process tends to frustrate rehabilitation within the penal system.

Although resort to federal habeas corpus has leveled off in recent years, some 7,700 cases were filed in fiscal 1981. Thus, the total number of state prisoner suits that year, filed under §§ 1983 and 2254, was about 23,000 cases — or some 12 percent of the federal district court civil caseload. Diversity jurisdiction added another 45,000 cases, with the result that these three sources of federal court jurisdiction constituted nearly 40 percent of the total district court civil filings. . . .

. . .At the Supreme Court, the sheer volume of cert petitions and appeals — up nearly 500 this year over two years ago — may prevent the same degree of judicial care, in selecting cases for full review, that probably existed a decade or more ago. Each of us still makes a personal judgment with respect to each petition. In doing so — and I speak for myself — I rely initially on memoranda prepared by law clerks to help me identify petitions that need plenary consideration in our regular Friday conferences.

Of course, when a case is granted, it then receives the most careful judicial review.

At the Court of Appeals level — burdened by appeals of right in every case — it has been necessary to increase staff and personal law clerks more than one would wish. And, to the discomfort of the Bar and litigants, many cases necessarily are decided by order or without published opinion. The full brunt of the litigation explosion falls, of course, on the district courts.

[Need for Change]

No one considers the present situation desirable. The need for fundamental changes — requiring congressional action — is self evident if we are to preserve our federal system of courts, as contemplated by the Constitution. We should maintain a more traditional balance between state and federal courts, and within the federal system reforms — perhaps some of those identified above — seem long overdue. If we continue to encourage a litigious society, in which an ever widening spectrum of claims are asserted only in courts and particularly federal courts — judging itself necessarily may become bureaucratized.

The principal victims of bureaucratizing the federal judicial system

would not be the judges or staffs. Rather, as the study chaired by then Solicitor General Bork concluded, those most likely to suffer would be the
"litigants (with substantial claims) who seek justice." Indeed, the rule of
law — reduced to wholesale justice by the crush of cases — could be the ultimate victim.

My years at the Bar, and my decade of experience as a judge, convince
me that the bench of our country — and I include all components of the judicial system represented in this Division of the ABA [American Bar
Association] — has not yet been bureaucratized. Judges take their oath of
office with the utmost seriousness, and judging remains an individual
function.

This certainly is true at the Supreme Court. I recently heard one of our
Justices say that during May and June his work schedule ran twelve to fifteen hours a day, six days in the week. As Justice Douglas said, after
decades of experience at the Court, Supreme Court Justices — unlike some
high officials in the other branches of government — do their own work.
And although the assistance of able law clerks is essential, the decisions
and opinions are those of the Justices. I have no reason to doubt that this
also generally is true in other tribunals.

At the recent Fourth Circuit Judicial Conference, memorial tributes
were paid to Professor Bernard J. Ward of the Texas Law School, who died
in the spring. Professor Ward had been a regular panelist at the Circuit's
annual conferences. We recalled Bernie Ward's profound respect for the
institution of the judiciary. He often reminded us, however, that the
ultimate strength of a judicial system rests in the courage, conscience and
impartiality of individual judges. He also was convinced that judges,
possessing these qualities, have formed the "thin black line" that has stood
resolutely between human liberty and the awesome power of government. I
agree with Professor Ward. And may it ever be so.

WHITE'S REMARKS

... [I]t is plain, and always has been, that there is a finite limit on the
number of cases that the Court can hear and decide with opinion in any
one term. For more than 20 years prior to 1970, the Court averaged about
100 opinions per term plus a few per curiams in argued cases. That number
crept up during the 1970s. But it has become apparent that it can creep no
more in that direction. As a rule of thumb, the Court should not be
expected to produce, more than 150 opinions per term in argued cases,
including per curiam opinions in such cases. That is about where we were
this past term. Many people are of the view that because of the complexity
of many of the cases that the Court is reviewing in this modern day, the
150 number is too high.

The pressure that drove the argument docket from 100 to 150 was, as
you would suspect, the increased number of filings. That number went up
through the '60s and '70s at the rate of about 5 percent per year, doubling

in 20 years. After leveling off in the late 1970s, it is escalating again. Although the number of cases granted review increased, there were rumblings that many cases deserving review were being denied. The complaint was not that the Court was not hearing all the cases that it had the capacity to hear but that it did not have the capacity to review all those cases that the system contemplated would be reviewed at the Supreme Court level.

Two separate committees gave careful attention to this very issue and arrived at similar conclusions, namely that the Supreme Court did not have the capacity to perform the appellate function that the federal law required. The Freund Committee, an unofficial body chaired by Paul Freund of the Harvard Law School, in 1975 concluded as follows:

> "The statistics of the Court's current workload, both in absolute terms and in the mounting trend, are impressive evidence that the conditions essential for the performance of the Court's mission do not exist. For an ordinary appellate court the burgeoning volume of cases would be a staggering burden; for the Supreme Court the pressures of the docket are incompatible with the appropriate fulfillment of its historic and essential function."

Later, Congress created the Commission on Federal Appellate Court Revision. That Commission was made up of four senators, four representatives, three federal judges, a former chairman of the House Judiciary Committee and two educators, one of whom was Herbert Wechsler, who, if not the most knowledgeable scholar about the federal court system, is certainly one of a select group with such unusual experience and insight. The Commission concluded that the present appellate arrangements leave unresolved too many conflicting decisions and too many unsettled questions of federal law — "that at some point the percentage of cases accorded review will have dipped below the minimum necessary for effective monitoring of the nation's courts on issues of federal statutory and constitutional law" and that this point had then been reached. It recommended that more appellate capacity be provided by creating another court with nationwide appellate jurisdiction. . . .

. . .This last term, however, for the first time since I have been on the Court and for longer ago than that, the Court granted review in more cases than it could hear in a single term. As a general rule, 150 opinions will dispose of approximately 175 cases. During last term, however, we granted review in 210 cases, which is 26 more than the term before and 56 more than two terms ago. Apparently there were just too many petitions for certiorari that we could not conscientiously deny. Our docket is now full through February of next term and will be completely full by the end of November if grants next term proceed at the same rate as they did last term. Of course, what this means is that we shall not be current in our work; cases will be ready for argument and we shall not be ready for them. This is something new and disturbing for us, and it should be [for] those who use the courts as much as you do.

As I have indicated to you, the situation concerning the Court's docket has been on many people's minds for several years. As yet there has been no consensus on the scope of the problem, if there is one, and what to do about it if there is really a problem. For myself, I have thought for some time that there is one and that it will very likely progressively worsen. There were 4,400 new filings during this past term, and there is no indication that this flood will abate. There have always been hard cases on the Court's docket, but it should be no surprise that as filings increase, so do the number of hard cases that must be reviewed. It would be much better if the problem disappeared, but I doubt that it will. For this reason, it is time that the bench, the bar and others interested in the performance of the federal court system seriously consider what should be done and when.

The essence of the National Court of Appeals proposal was this: all certioraris and appeals would come to the Court as they do now. The Court would select cases for its own docket as it does now, but if there were other cases deserving of review that it could not hear, it would have the authority to refer those cases to a so-called national court of appeals that would be created for this purpose. That court's decisions would be subject to certiorari review, but it was thought that only rarely would certiorari be granted in such cases. This is because the cases that would be referred would most often involve statutory issues on which the lower courts are in conflict or which otherwise were deserving of review. This approach to the problem would not disturb the jurisdiction of the Courts of Appeals; nor would it delay decision substantially beyond that which would be involved if the Court itself decided the case. Of course, there would be another 150 to 200 cases in which the decisions of the Courts of Appeals would not be final and the same number of additional decisions and opinions with which the lower courts would have to follow. But that is no more than what would be necessary to ensure that the federal law is not being enforced in substantially different ways in different parts of the country. I should add that a national court of appeals bill is now pending in Congress, but I see no great flurry of activity around it.

There are surely other obvious alternatives, particularly if more fundamental structural changes are thought necessary to remedy the problem. Rather than one Supreme Court, there might be two, one for statutory issues and one for constitutional cases; or one for criminal and one for civil cases. If the resolution of conflicting decisions is at the root of the problem, there is also the option of creating new courts of appeal that would hear appeals from district courts countrywide in certain kinds of cases. For example, the Court of Appeals for the Federal Circuit, created by the merger of the Court of Customs and Patent Appeals and the Court of Claims, will hear all appeals from district courts in cases arising under the patent laws. Another court that hears all appeals from cases arising under specified statutes is the Emergency Court of Appeals. Courts like these of course bypass the regular Courts of Appeals, but they eliminate the possibility of conflicts that normally would have to be heard in the Supreme Court.

Another interesting suggestion to minimize the occurrence of conflicting decisions among the courts of appeals. That is to require a court of appeals to go en banc before differing with another court of appeals and to make the first en banc decision the nationwide rule. I have even heard it argued that this would not require legislation and could be done by rule. . . .

BRENNAN'S REMARKS

You doubtless have read of the concern expressed at the ABA [American Bar Association] meeting in San Francisco by Justices White and Stevens that the Supreme Court confronts a calendar crisis so severe as to threaten the Court's ability effectively to discharge its vital responsibility. Justice Powell also addressed the problem but in the broader context of proposals designed to lessen the burdens of the entire federal court system. I should like in these brief remarks to address the problems of the Supreme Court calendar. . . .

I suppose the solution to the question whether the number of grants can be kept under control and the calendar made manageable without rejection of cases that should be heard and decided depends (a) on what the Court can do for itself to avoid granting cases that should not be granted and (b) on what the Congress and the Courts of Appeal can do to minimize the necessity for granting review of some cases.

What can we do for ourselves? I must admit frankly that we too often take cases that present no necessity for announcement of a new proposition of law but where we believe only that the court below has committed error. But ever since the Congress enacted the Judges Bill of 1925 the Supreme Court of the United States has not been expected to take on the function of primarily — or even largely — correcting errors committed by other courts. . . .

And, too, we have made mistakes in granting certiorari at an interlocutory stage of a case when allowing the case to proceed to its final disposition below might produce a result that makes it unnecessary to address an important and difficult constitutional question. Last Term's school library case is a paradigm example. It presented the question whether school boards were in any wise restrained by the First Amendment in the removal of books from a school library. The District judge held not and granted the school board summary judgment. The Second Circuit reversed on the ground that the case presented a genuine issue of fact as to the school board's motivation and therefore the case should be tried. Obviously further proceedings in the trial court would either have clarified the constitutional issue or perhaps have mooted the entire case. Yet the Court took the case at the interlocutory stage, disposed of it by an affirmance of the remand for trial, and filed eight separate opinions without producing one that commanded the votes of a majority. Surely we should discipline ourselves to be more faithful to the *Ashwander* principle not to address constitutional issues if there is a way properly to avoid doing so.

Congress could afford the Court substantial assistance by repealing to the maximum extent possible the Court's mandatory appellate jurisdiction and shifting those cases to the discretionary certiorari docket. A bill to this end is pending in the Congress and every member of the Court devoutly hopes it will be adopted. Cases on appeal consume a disproportionate amount of the limited time available for oral argument. That's because time and again a Justice who would conscientiously deny review of an issue presented on certiorari cannot conscientiously say that when presented on appeal the issue is insubstantial, the test on appeal. Policy considerations that gave rise to the distinction between review by appeal and review by writ of certiorari have long since lost their force and abandonment of our appellate jurisdiction, (leaving a writ of certiorari as the only means of obtaining Supreme Court review) is simply recognition of reality.

Can we perhaps decide more cases on the merits by denying ourselves the benefit of full briefing and oral argument? There is sentiment among some of my colleagues to do so. Because I wholeheartedly agree with Justice Stevens that "oral argument is a vital component of the appellate process," and have too often witnessed colleagues who favored summary affirmance at the cert stage, change their minds after oral argument — and because I think further that the Court's favorable image in the eyes of both Bar and public rests so heavily on oral audience before us, I have continuously protested against summary dispositions. . . .

[Justice Stevens' Proposal]

. . . Justice Stevens, in his words, "favors the creation of a new court to which the Supreme Court would surrender some of its present power — specifically, the power to decide what cases the Supreme Court should decide on the merits. [Unlike the Freund Committee proposal] I would allow that court to decide — not merely to recommend — that a certiorari petition should be granted or denied" — and that court's decision to deny would not be reviewable.

I completely disagree with my respected and distinguished colleague. I dissented from the form in which the Freund Committee made the proposal and feel even more strongly that adoption of Justice Stevens' proposal would destroy the role of the Supreme Court as the Framers envisaged it.

Justice Stevens believes that the screening function "is less important work than studying and actually deciding the merits of cases that have already been accepted for review and writing opinions explaining those decisions." Apart from the fact that the plan would clearly violate the constitutional provision establishing "one Supreme Court," and therefore require a constitutional amendment, I reject Justice Stevens' fundamental premise that consideration given to the cases actually decided on the merits is compromised by the pressures of processing the inflated docket of petitions and appeals. . . . [M]y view that the screening function is second to none in importance is reflected in my practice of performing the screening function myself. I make an exception only during the summer recess when their initial screening of petitions is invaluable training for next Term's new law clerks. For my own part, I find that I don't need a great deal of time to perform the screening function — certainly not an amount of time that compromises my ability to attend to decisions of argued cases. I should emphasize that the longer one works at the screening function, the less onerous and time-consuming it becomes. Unquestionably the equalizer is experience, and for experience there can be no substitute — not even a second court.

If the screening function were to be farmed out to another Court, some enormous values of the Supreme Court decisional process would be lost. Under the present system, a single Justice may set a case for discussion at conference, and, in many instances that Justice succeeds in persuading three or more of his colleagues that the case is worthy of plenary review. Thus the existing procedure provides a forum in which the particular interests or sensitivities of individual Justices may be expressed, and therefore has a flexibility that is essential to the effective functioning not only of the screening process but also of the decisional process which is an inseparable part.

Similarly, the artificial construction of the Supreme Court's docket by others than the members of the court would seriously undermine the important impact dissents from denials of review frequently have had upon the development of the law. Such dissents often herald the appearance on the horizon of possible re-examination of what may seem to the judges of another court doing the screening work to be an established and unimpeachable principle. Indeed, a series of dissents from denials of review played a crucial role in the Court's reevaluation of the reapportionment question, and the question of the applicability of the Fourth Amendment to electronic searches. The history of the role of such dissents on the right to counsel in criminal cases and the application of the Bill of Rights to the States surely is too fresh in mind to ignore.

Moreover, the assumption that the judges of a national court of appeals could accurately select the "most reviewworthy" cases wholly ignores the inherently subjective nature of the screening process. The thousands upon thousands of cases docketed each Term simply cannot be placed in a computer that will instantaneously identify those that I or any one of my colleagues would agree are "most reviewworthy.". . .

[Importance of Screening Function]

I repeat that a fundamental premise of Justice Stevens' proposal is that the screening function plays only a minor and separable part in the exercise of the Court's fundamental responsibilities. I think that premise is clearly — indeed dangerously — wrong. In my experience over more than a quarter century, the screening process has been, and is today, inextricably linked to the fulfillment of the Court's essential duties and is vital to the effective performance of the Court's unique mission "to define the rights guaranteed by the Constitution, to assure the uniformity of federal law, and to maintain the constitutional distribution of powers in our federal union."

For the choice of issues for decision largely determines the image that the American people have of their Supreme Court. The Court's calendar mirrors the everchanging concerns of this society with ever more powerful and smothering government. The calendar is therefore the indispensable source for keeping the Court abreast of these concerns. Our Constitution is a living document and the Court often becomes aware of the necessity for reconsideration of its interpretation only because filed cases reveal the need for new and previously unanticipated applications of constitutional principles. To adopt Justice Stevens' proposal to limit the Court's consideration to a mere handful of the cases selected by others would obviously result in isolating the Court from many nuances and trends of legal change throughout the land. The point is that the evolution of constitutional doctrine is not merely a matter of hearing arguments and writing opinions in cases granted review. The screening function is an inseparable part of the whole responsibility; to turn over that task to a national court of appeals is to rent a seamless web. And how traumatic and difficult must be the screening task of the judges of a court of appeals required to do major Supreme Court work without being afforded even the slightest glimpse of the whole picture of a Justice's function. It is not only that constitutional principles evolve over long periods and that one must know the history of each before he feels competent to grapple with their application in new contexts never envisioned by the Framers. It is also that he must acquire an understanding of the extraordinarily complex factors that enter into the distribution of judicial power between state and federal courts and other problems of "Our Federalism." The screening function is an indispensable and inseparable part of the entire process and it cannot be withdrawn from the Court without grave risk of impairing the very core of the Court's unique and extraordinary functions.

You may rightly ask me then — what would you do to bring about the shrinking of the size of the calendar to manageable numbers? First, I would urge greater care by the Court in the selection of cases for review. Second, I would urge repeal by Congress of virtually all the Court's mandatory appeal jurisdiction. Third, I would urge an immediate study of the feasibility of Justice White's suggestion of creating new courts of appeals that would hear appeals from district courts countrywide in certain kinds of cases, thus obviating conflicts. Fourth, I would urge an immediate study of Justice White's other suggestion for minimizing conflicts — to require a court of appeals to go *en banc* before differing with another court of appeals and to make the first *en banc* decision the nationwide rule.

But I would most emphatically reject all proposals for the creation of a national court of appeals, or any other court, to which would be assigned the task of doing the Court's work, whether decisional or screening work. Adoption of that proposal would sow the seeds of destruction of the Court's standing as we know it. For remember Justice Brandeis ascribed the great prestige of the Court with the American public to a single thing, "Because we do our own work."

MARSHALL'S REMARKS

Traditionally, I have begun my remarks at these gatherings with a report on how the Second Circuit has fared in the Supreme Court. During the last Term, this Circuit's won-lost record was better than average. Of the 15 cases from the Second Circuit decided on the merits, the Circuit was affirmed in 8 cases and reversed in 7. An 8-and-7 record is pretty good when you consider that, as in past years, the Supreme Court reversed in more than 60% of the cases argued and decided during the 1981 Term....

One case where the Second Circuit did not fare so well involved the *Central Trust Company*. In that case, the Supreme Court summarily reversed the court of appeals in a per curiam opinion. I found the result lamentable, and I therefore joined Justice Stevens' dissent. But equally disturbing was the way in which the Court reached the result. The case exemplifies a growing and inexplicable readiness on the part of the current Court to dispose of cases summarily. When the Court issues a per curiam opinion deciding a case summarily, it does so without full briefing and any oral argument. Instead, the Court has before it only the petitions and responses on the limited issue of certiorari, in which parties are not supposed to debate the merits. Our rules specifically prohibit discussion of the merits....

These summary dispositions pose very real problems. First, significant issues can receive cursory treatment, creating a potential for error and confusion....

The Court has not only used summary dispositions to give short shrift to important issues. It has also used the device to decide cases that do not meet the traditional criteria for Supreme Court review. The nadir was reached at the end of the Term in *Board of Education* v. *McCluskey*, where the Court exercised its mighty power in order to enforce a school board's suspension of a 10th grade student who consumed too much alcohol on a fall day.

In addition, the Court appears to be using summary dispositions in a result-oriented fashion. In a disproportionate number of cases, the Court has employed the device to aid prosecutors, wardens, and school board officials. Last Term, for example, the Court issued 16 per curiam opinions summarily reversing lower courts. Of these 13 involved prosecutors, wardens, or school board officials. In all but one of these cases, the state prevailed. In *McCluskey*, Justice Stevens was forced to wonder whether, if the student had been unjustly suspended, the Court would still have considered the matter of such national importance to require summary reversal.

I am disturbed by the all-too-often cavalier treatment of the rights and interests of the parties involved in such cases. Instead of giving them a full opportunity to be heard on the merits, the Court's rules restrict the parties to a skeletal presentation of the issues. . . .

If these summary dispositions are to continue at all, the Court should undertake one major change in its procedures. Whenever the Court concludes that summary reversal or affirmance may be appropriate, it should notify the parties that summary disposition is under consideration and allow them time to file briefs on the merits. This would give the litigants an opportunity to be heard before their cases are decided, and give the Court the benefit of an adversarial presentation of the issues. An opportunity to brief the merits is the least we should demand before a decision is rendered by the court of last resort.

REHNQUIST'S SPEECH

. . . I have tried to suggest to you this evening that the rapidly escalating case loads of the federal court system, and I am sure of most state court systems, do not bode well in the long run for traditional notions of judging. Escalating case loads of necessity cause a multiplication in the number of judges, with the possibility down the road that indefinite multiplication of judicial positions may well detract from the "prestige" of the job, an important element which has enabled the federal judiciary to command the respect which it has today. But because Congress seems to inevitably lag behind in the creation of judgeships within the federal system, even though these judgeships have multiplied, they have not multiplied enough to keep up with the case load. The federal courts have responded in the only way conceivable; they have attempted to stretch out a smaller number of judge hours per case to cover a great many more cases than formerly. While there was obviously some room for tightening up of the use of judges' time and the separation of strictly judicial functions from managerial functions which could be performed by others, in the end there is a limit to how much these changes can accomplish. To stretch judges more thinly than this limit would suggest is to invite a bureaucratization of the courts, with the judges seen as managers and the numerous types of clerks and attorneys seen as subordinates who actually do the work of judging.

If I am right in these assumptions, those who determine the amount of business which will be transacted in the federal courts face some fairly stark choices in the not too far distant future. Since Congress is the principal determinant of federal court work loads, the choice will be largely one for that body. New claims for relief, new causes of action, however much sense they make in other contexts, can only be created in the future if Congress is willing to either withdraw other categories of jurisdiction already granted, or to willingly face the prospect of a vastly different federal judiciary than anyone would have thought conceivable . . . 45 years ago. . . .

BURGER'S REMARKS

. . . The Supreme Court, at the pinnacle of our judicial system, has long been feeling the brunt of the pressures that begin in both the federal and state trial courts. In recent months there has been a growing awareness about this problem among judges and lawyers who have spoken out. That has refocused attention on the reports of two very important studies — the Freund and Hruska reports, which have too long gathered dust. The Supreme Court's workload is an even more acute problem today than when the Freund Committee was appointed in 1971.

These recent commentaries have presented a variety of possible solutions and I am happy to see that there is recognition that the problem will not solve itself nor can it any longer be brushed under a rug. The suggestions recently advanced serve to revive interest in the problem, and whether we agree or not, this in itself is useful. It serves to stir some horses which have been too long asleep. I am delighted that the Freund and Hruska reports are now coming into their own.

Two bald figures on the Supreme Court's work are striking: In the first year that my distinguished predecessor Chief Justice Warren served, the Court had 1,312 filings and the Court issued 65 signed opinions plus 19 per curiam opinions. Last term, we had 4,422 new filings added to 889 filings carried over or 5,311 in all. We issued 141 signed opinions and 10 per curiam opinions. Ponder on those figures, if you will, as I remind you that a quarter of a century ago when the Supreme Court was averaging 117 opinions a year, Professor Henry Hart of Harvard wrote in his annual survey:

> "The conclusion emerges inexorably that the number of cases which the Supreme Court tries to decide by full opinion, far from being increased, ought to be materially decreased."

"Decreased" from 117 opinions, is what Hart was saying.

Apart from bare numbers, qualified court observers, including practitioners and scholars, have commented on the extraordinary change in the content of the Court's calendar. They point to the novelty of the questions for which, in many instances, there are virtually no precedents. Some observers have said that even if we had only 100 fully argued cases a year, the novelty and complexity of a large proportion of those 100 cases would strain the Court's capacity to the limit.

Computer aids, word processing machines, and increased staffing in the past dozen years have helped some, but if every case in the Supreme Court is to continue receiving close individual attention of Justices, as has been the tradition, the caseload cannot continue at the present rate. It is not just a matter of maintaining the present caseload. That load must be reduced. I emphatically agree with Professor Hart and others who have said the Court cannot continue to turn out more than 100 full scale opinions each year if the quality and depth of treatment is to be maintained at a proper level. If some drastic changes are not made, we will not be able to maintain standards of quality the country has a right to expect from its highest court.

The Freund report made three major points; all related to the growth of filings and the growth of cases calling for plenary treatment. It recommended that the three-judge district court with direct mandatory appeal to the Supreme Court be abolished. Happily, except for reapportionment cases, Congress has abolished that jurisdiction. That gave the Supreme Court only modest relief, however. Second, it recommended that all mandatory statutory rights of appeal be abolished and that all cases be placed under the Court's certiorari, discretionary jurisdiction. This has no opposition from anyone and it has passed each House once. Yet it still languishes in the Congress. That, too, will give only modest relief. The major recommendation of both the Freund and Hruska reports was that an intermediate appellate court be created with power to deal with cases referred to it by the Supreme Court itself.

In approaching any discussions of the Supreme Court's caseload problems, the experience of the highest courts of other highly developed societies is surely relevant. On the continent of Europe we find widespread use of specialized courts, not only at the trial level, but even at the highest level. It is a common pattern to have separation of the jurisdiction of the courts of last resort into two and even three tribunals. For example, criminal appeals in one tribunal, civil and administrative appeals in another and sometimes constitutional cases in a third.

At least two of our own states, Texas and Oklahoma, divide appeals to the state's highest court between civil and criminal reviewing courts. And in intermediate courts of appeal a number of states follow this pattern of separation. It is clear therefore that the concept of separate appellate jurisdiction is not per se an alien or subversive idea.

Here again the English experience especially merits inquiry, for we share with England the common law tradition. The Lord Chief Justice of England presides over the court for criminal appeals; the Master of the Rolls presides over another court for all other appeals. In practice these two specialized appellate courts are, except for about 60 to 70 cases, the courts of last resort in England.

It is significant that the true tribunal of last resort in England, the High Court of Parliament, acts through the Law Lords who sit in two panels of five Justices each. They reserve the calendar for only the most momentous issues. Each panel currently has barely 30 to 35 cases each year. The United States Supreme Court normally hears 24 cases in a two week oral argument session every month until the docket is cleared. That the Law Lords, who have the last word in England, also have other duties, such as sitting as members of the Privy Council, does not significantly alter this enormous disparity between the workload of the Law Lords of last resort in England and the Justices of last resort in this country.

Can it be that England, the "Fountainhead" of our legal concepts — after many more centuries of experience than ours — is wrong, and that our traditional hostility to specialized courts is the correct view? I am not in any sense suggesting that we slavishly copy these models — European or the states of Texas and Oklahoma — that have separated civil and criminal appeals.

What I do suggest is that when the filings of the Supreme Court have almost trebled in my time as a federal judge, and the workings of many courts are falling into disrepair in spite of many improvements, we must reexamine the mind-set that brought us where we are today. We have reached the point where our systems of justice — both state and federal — may literally break down before the end of this century, notwithstanding the great increase in the number of judges and the large infusion of court administrators.

In the face of these constantly rising hydraulic pressures on the courts, the time has come to take a fresh, hard look. We must keep in mind John Locke's admonition that,

> "New opinions are always suspected, and usually opposed, without any other reason but because they are not already common."

As we approach the bicentennial of the Constitution, it is time to embark on a comprehensive study of the judicial process, picking up the work of the Williamsburg and Pound conferences and the Freund and Hruska reports.

I know there are risks even in suggesting that such crucial subjects should be reviewed, and that we should reexamine established patterns. The risk is that it will be said that the speaker is advocating a particular solution. I have never taken a position on the creation of an intermediate court of appeals proposed by the Freund Committee and confirmed by the Hruska Commission. I have, however, emphatically stated, and I repeat now with even more emphasis, that if some changes are not made the work of the Court will fall more and more behind and the quality will suffer.

The basis for one such study is already "in the wings" in Senate Bill S.675. That bill, which passed the Senate on October 1 of this year, would establish a three-branch, bipartisan commission consisting of fourteen members to study the federal and state court systems and recommend improvements. In addition to evaluating current problems facing the courts, that study should also develop a long-range plan for the future of our judicial systems. The long-range plan should include assessments involving alternative methods of dispute resolution, the actual structure and administration of the federal court system, the manner in which courts handle cases, and new methods of resolution of conflicts among circuits.

Enactment of this pending legislation would be one step in the right direction. Many key leaders of Congress have given strong support to proposed changes and some important improvements have been made — the recent addition of federal court administrators among others.

What is important in all these problems is not the differences in view of those who have spoken in the past 10 years, but the harmony of purposes and objectives. A common underlying objective is to assure that the great concept of separation of powers and the checks and balances of our three-branch system are preserved. It can never be perfect, but it is the best so far devised by human minds. That cannot be done if the Supreme Court must carry a load as heavy as it has carried for a quarter of a century.

The danger does not lie in attacks on the Court. Attacks on the Court have been going on for at least 180 years! The real risk is that the institution will be submerged gradually, by placing on it burdens that cannot adequately be carried. . . .

The Constitution must always have pre-eminence and the best guarantee of that is found in our history. But we must face up to the reality that when the demands on the Supreme Court exceed the finite capacity of any nine human beings who could be assembled, they cannot perform the task in keeping with the standards the people of this country have a right to expect. Those standards cannot be maintained with 4,000 to 5,000 filings a year, and 140 or more cases requiring full scale opinions.

For all other courts, a rising caseload can be alleviated by creating more judgeships, but that relief is not available with respect to the Supreme Court. More Justices would hamper rather than aid our work. . . .

But let me close on an optimistic and cheerful note to brighten this otherwise doleful picture. Remember Arthur Vanderbilt's admonition that the solution of these problems is not for the short-winded. Remember too, that John Jay first suggested the creation of what are now the United States Courts of Appeals for the Circuits in 1791, and that Congress responded in 1891.

I leave it to you to decide how long we can wait.

▼▼▼

REPORTS ON SEXUAL ABUSE
OF CAPITOL HILL PAGES
August 16, December 14, 1982

In June and July two former House of Representatives pages made allegations of homosexual activities between members of Congress and pages. These charges, accompanied by stories of illegal drug use on Capitol Hill, led to a review of the House page system and retention of a special counsel by the House Committee on Standards of Official Conduct (ethics committee) to investigate the charges. Although the initial charges were found to be false, the investigation continued into 1983.

Pages are the boys and girls who run errands for members of Congress. They carry documents between the Capitol and members' offices, answer telephones and make sure that necessary papers are in the House and Senate chambers. During the academic year the House employs 71 pages, between the ages of 16 and 18; the Senate hires 30 pages, aged 14-18. Both houses hire additional pages during the summer.

Page salaries are about $9,000 a year and must cover transportation costs to Washington, living expenses and uniforms. Until early 1983, pages had to find their own housing. But in the aftermath of the 1982 scandal, Congress provided a dormitory for them. During the school year the pages attend early morning classes at the Capitol Page School located in the Library of Congress.

Charges

In June, Jeffrey Opp, a 16-year-old page, told staff members in the office of Rep. Patricia Schroeder, D-Colo., that members of Congress were soliciting sex from pages. Schroeder's office arranged for the page to speak with Justice Department investigators. Stories of illegal drug use on Capitol Hill also were circulating at this time, and the Justice Department began investigations into allegations involving cocaine use and sodomy on the part of pages and members of Congress.

On June 30 and July 1, CBS Evening News broadcast separate interviews, which had been recorded a few weeks earlier, with Opp and another former page, 18-year-old Leroy Williams. The former pages stated that they were victims of sexual misconduct by members of Congress and that they knew of other pages who had similar experiences. Williams, who had left the page service in January, said he committed homosexual acts with three representatives and provided male prostitutes for House staffers.

On July 9 Williams failed a FBI lie detector test but insisted on the truth of his story. On August 27 Williams told investigators that he had lied. He claimed to have made up the charges to draw attention to the lack of supervision for pages. A few days later the Justice Department dropped its investigation of the sexual misconduct charges for lack of evidence. Opp later testified that his television interview "was a 16 year old kid satisfying his ego." He said that he did not feel he had acted responsibly in making the charges.

Speaker's Commission on Pages

The charges spotlighted the inadequate supervision and other problems of the page system. On July 14 House Speaker Thomas P. O'Neill Jr., D-Mass., established the Speaker's Commission on Pages to "review the Page system in all its aspects including whether it should be continued, the need for supervised housing or improved education."

On August 16 the panel issued its report. It termed the page system "essential to the efficient functioning of Congress," but recommended several changes. The panel suggested in part that: all pages be juniors in high school and at least 16 years old; pages be housed in a single, supervised dormitory; dining and recreational facilities be provided; and the page school program be improved. Early in 1983, the pages began occupying two floors of a hotel near the Capitol. The dormitory was to be supervised by four resident counselors.

House Ethics Committee Report

On July 27 the House ethics committee retained Joseph A. Califano Jr., former secretary of health, education and welfare, as special counsel to investigate allegations of sexual misconduct and illegal use or distribution of drugs by House members or employees.

Califano issued an interim report on December 14 regarding the work his staff had completed since the end of July. He reported that the specific charges made by Opp and Williams were false but that other allegations of sexual misconduct were still under investigation. Califano's probe into charges of illegal drug use and distribution continued, in coordination with Justice Department and Drug Enforcement Administration efforts. In one case of alleged sexual misconduct by a House employee and in one instance of suspected drug use and distribution by a House employee, Califano found sufficient evidence to recommend the committee begin preliminary inquiries.

Following are excerpts from the report prepared by the Speaker's Commission on Pages, released August 16, 1982; and excerpts from the Interim Report of the Special Counsel to the House Committee on Standards of Official Conduct, released December 14. (Boldface headings in brackets have been added by Congressional Quarterly to highlight the organization of the text.):

PAGE COMMISSION REPORT

Letter of Transmittal

Dear Mr. Speaker: The Speaker's Commission on Pages, established on July 14, 1982, submits the enclosed volume as its report.

The volume contains the recommendations of the Commission regarding the continuation of the Page program, the age and term of service of Pages, the management of the Page program, the supervised housing and education of the Pages, the eating and recreational facilities for Pages, the health care of the Pages, and standardization of the Page-selection process.

The report is intended to give the Leadership a comprehensive review of certain basic issues which the Commission deems most pressing, together with recommendations related thereto.

It should be emphasized that the Commission did not attempt to address any of the matters which are currently the subject of inquiry by the Committee on Standards of Official Conduct.

The Commission recognizes that there are many details yet to be resolved in implementing its recommendations. The Commission urges close coordination with the Senate in this regard. Steps should be taken immediately to begin the process of providing a much improved Page system for the Congress, the Pages, and our Nation.

Sincerely,

Bill Alexander, *Chairman.*
Washington, D.C.
August 11, 1982.

The Work of the Commission

ORGANIZATION OF THE COMMISSION

The Speaker of the House, together with the Minority Leader, established this Commission on July 14, 1982, "to study the Page system of the U.S. House of Representatives with instructions to report recommendations as soon as possible."

The purpose of the Commission was to review the Page system, in all its aspects including whether it should be continued, the need for supervised housing or improved education.

Those appointed to serve as Commissioners were: Bill Alexander (D-Ark), Chairman; John T. Myers (R-Ind); James T. Molloy, Doorkeeper; Joel Jankowsky, Esq. (Former Assistant to Speaker Carl Albert); and Charles E. Wiggins, Esq. (Former Member of Congress from California).

The Commission gave serious consideration to alternative means of providing those services presently provided to the Congress by the Pages and to the modifications which would be required should a form of the Page system be retained.

The Commission's work in no way duplicated the present inquiry of the Committee on Standards of Official Conduct.

In its deliberations, the Commission weighed and balanced the services performed to the Congress and any value that was received by the individuals who performed those services. Further, attention was given to the contribution to the nation which could be derived from certain of the various proposed alternatives.

The Commission recognized that several of the alternatives presented had significant supporting arguments, particularly the proposal to use college-age Pages. However, the recommendations adopted those proposals which had the broadest support within the Commission. . . .

[The Commission's Recommendations]

THE PAGE SYSTEM

The Commission agrees that a Page service is essential to the efficient functioning of Congress, and that service as a Page is a uniquely valuable experience to those selected.

The Commission finds that the Pages have performed this service admirably, but under conditions which need improvement. It therefore recommends that an in-house program with high school students be continued which incorporates the modifications contained in this report.

AGE AND TERM OF PAGE SERVICE

The Commission recommends that the Pages be in their junior year of high school and be at least sixteen (16) years of age. A Page would serve for a maximum of one (1) term.

Further, the Commission recommends that the Page program be divided into three (3) terms with these approximate durations: a Fall Term from August 15 until January 15; a Spring Term from January 16 until June 15; and a Summer Program from June 1 until August 31.

The junior-year requirement should not be applicable to the Summer Program. However, candidates for the Summer Program must be high-school students.

MANAGEMENT OF THE PAGE PROGRAM

The Commission recommends that responsibility for the administration of the Page program be centralized in a Page Board, established by statute, and consisting of the Speaker, the Majority Leader, and the Minority Leader.

It is recommended further that the Page Board: (1) delegate the operational authority for the Page program to the Doorkeeper of the House, or to any other such Official of the House or Committee of the House as is appropriate; (2) appoint an Advisory Committee to assist the Board in the exercise of its responsibilities; and (3) develop a comprehensive "Code of Conduct" for all Pages.

SUPERVISED HOUSING OF THE PAGES

The Commission recommends that housing for the Pages be centralized in existing facilities owned by the Congress and that a reasonable rental fee be charged for the use of such facilities.

Except pursuant to specific regulations promulgated by the Page Board, Pages shall live in the housing facility provided by Congress, and such housing facility shall be for their exclusive use.

Because of its proximity to the Capitol and its immediate availability, the Commission recommends a portion of the House Office Building Annex No. 1 be utilized for this purpose.

For both safety and fiscal reasons, the Commission further recommends that the second and third floors of the House Office Building Annex No. 1 be renovated and made immediately available for residential use by the Pages. Although the Commission understands that House Office Building Annex No. 1 can be available in September, 1982, the Page Board, in conjunction with the House Office Building Commission, should develop a contingency plan should the House Office Building Annex No. 1 not be ready as anticipated. The Commission also recommends that adequate "common" space be made available for Page use on the first floor of the House Office Building Annex No. 1.

The Commission recommends that supervision should be provided by resident counsellors and security provided by the U.S. Capitol Police.

The recommended housing proposal solves the problem of centralized, supervised housing for the foreseeable future. However, should the housing of the Pages at the recommended site become no longer feasible, the Commission recommends that the Page Board ensure that a centralized housing facility be continually maintained. Two of the options which could be utilized in the future are either the inclusion of housing facilities for the Pages in any new House Office Building or the construction of a facility, through either private or public funding, on the property owned by the House which is bounded by Second, Third, "D", and "E" Streets, S.E.

EDUCATION OF THE PAGES

The Commission recommends that the Page Board upgrade the Page School program.

The goal of the educational program for Pages should be to provide an innovative, alternative curriculum in American Studies for junior-year students closely coordinated with the Page's sending school. Such program should incorporate the Page's work experience and the unique resources available in the Capital area. The Commission urges that this program be operational by the Spring Term, 1983.

The Commission further recommends that the contract with the District of Columbia School Board which expires on August 31, 1982, be temporarily renewed on a short-term basis and that legislation be introduced to delete the requirement of existing law that the Page School admit all other minor-age employees of Congress.

[EATING AND RECREATIONAL FACILITIES]

The Commission recommends to the Committee on House Administration that it give special attention to the needs of Pages for cafeteria facilities on week nights and during recesses of the House. The Commission further recommends that limited eating facilities be made available to the Pages in the "common" space of their residence building.

The Commission further recommends that, in addition to the recreational opportunities provided by a "common" space, the Page Board should study means of providing minimal recreational facilities for the Pages.

HEALTH CARE OF THE PAGES

The Commission recommends that the Page Board address the adequacy of the health care of the Pages. This should include health insurance coverage, proper maintenance of health records, and prompt access to outside emergency care.

[PAGE-SELECTION PROCEDURE]

The Commission does not recommend that the general selection procedure presently used by the Personnel Committees be changed. However, the Commission recommends that the selection criteria be reasonbly standardized, with specific attention given to required grade-average, personal recommendations, and certified health condition.

The Commission also recommends that the Page Board should take steps to prohibit employees of Members and Committees from serving in the Page system.

CALIFANO REPORT

On July 13, 1982, the House agreed to House Resolution 518. That resolution authorized and directed this Committee to conduct a full and complete inquiry and investigation of —

(1) alleged improper or illegal sexual conduct by Members, officers, or employees of the House;

(2) illicit use or distribution of drugs by Members, officers, or employees of the House; and

(3) the offering of preferential treatment by Members, officers, or employees of the House to employees of the House, including congressional pages, in exchange for any item referred to in subclause (1) or (2).

On July 27, 1982, this Committee retained Joseph A. Califano, Jr., as Special Counsel to conduct the investigation. The Committee's Special Counsel thereafter assembled a staff and has carried out an extensive investigation.

The Special Counsel has filed an interim report with this Committee, which the Committee has approved, on the investigative work completed during the 97th Congress. The Special Counsel's interim report is attached as an Appendix to this Report. . . .

[Interim Report of the Special Counsel]

I. INTRODUCTION AND SUMMARY

On June 30 and July 1, 1982, tens of millions of Americans watched two teenagers, both former pages of the House of Representatives, with their faces shielded, declare on the CBS Evening News that they had been victims of sexual misconduct by Members of the House of Representatives. One page told of "homosexual advances" by Congressmen and Congressional staff. CBS said the page had been "homosexually harassed."

The experiences described by the other page shocked the nation. He said that he had engaged in sexual relationships with three Members of the

House of Representatives and that he had procured male prostitutes for House staffers. He told his interviewer that homosexual relationships were part of the system of what a page had to do to get ahead in the House. In June and July of 1982, these two former pages repeated those assertions — although with some inconsistencies — to newspapers and other television reporters, to the Federal Bureau of Investigation, and to investigators for the Committee on Standards of Official Conduct....

... At the time of Mr. Califano's appointment as Special Counsel, Committee Chairman Louis Stokes stated that "his charge is clear and straightforward — to conduct the investigation that in his judgment is required and to advise the Committee of his findings and recommendations."

The Speaker, the Majority Leader, and Minority Leader of the House joined Chairman Stokes and the Committee's Ranking Minority Member Floyd Spence in assuring the Special Counsel that he would have the independence and resources to conduct a full and impartial investigation — "whatever investigation is necessary to ascertain the truth about the allegations that have been made."

This interim report details the results of that investigation in the 97th Congress. The report responds to the Chairman's charge that the Special Counsel report to the Committee on his findings and recommendations. This report of the Special Counsel sets out (1) the investigative work completed so far with respect to allegations involving sexual misconduct, (2) his findings and conclusions regarding this work, and (3) his recommendations on the work remaining to be done and on actions the Committee should take at this time.

IMPROPER OR ILLEGAL SEXUAL CONDUCT

The investigation conducted by the Special Counsel has extended beyond the original charges of sexual misconduct made by the two former pages. Pursuant to H. Res 518, the Special Counsel has sought to determine whether there is any responsible evidence of improper or illegal sexual conduct by Members, officers, or employees of the House of Representatives involving congressional pages. The focus of the investigation has been on the period from July, 1981, through June, 1982. To assure completeness, however, the Special Counsel sought to contact every page employed by the House of Representatives during the past three years. The Special Counsel has also investigated allegations that he has received of sexual misconduct involving preferential treatment but not involving pages.

The Special Counsel has found no merit whatsoever in any of the original allegations of sexual misconduct made by the two former pages. One of these pages testified under oath that he lied about having sexual relations with Members of the House and about procuring prostitutes for anyone. The other page, who had referred to homosexual approaches by

Congressmen, testified under oath about three isolated instances of conversations in public places that lasted less than two minutes and involved no improper actions. This page testified that he himself no longer believed, in at least two of these instances, that there were any sexual overtones. The Special Counsel also independently investigated these allegations and has determined that the evidence conclusively indicates that all charges of sexual misconduct made by these two pages were false.

In the course of the investigation, the Special Counsel has received allegations of sexual misconduct from a variety of sources, wholly independent of the two former pages. The Special Counsel has completed investigation of most of these allegations. In most of these cases, the Special Counsel found no evidence to support the allegations.

In one instance, however, the Special Counsel has found reasonable indications that improper or illegal sexual conduct by an employee of the House may have occurred and, therefore, recommends that the Committee open a Preliminary Inquiry.

Under the Committee's rules, a Preliminary Inquiry is convened when evidence has been presented to the Committee that reasonably indicates that a violation may have been committed and the Committee determines that the evidence presented merits further inquiry. The individual named in a Preliminary Inquiry has the opportunity to present to the Committee, orally or in writing, a statement concerning the allegations that have been made. At the conclusion of the Preliminary Inquiry, if the Committee determines that the evidence establishes that there is reason to believe that a violation occurred, the Committee may direct that a Statement of Alleged Violation be issued to the individual involved. Full hearings must be held by the Committee on a Statement of Alleged Violation to determine whether to report a recommendation for disciplinary action to the full House. In this case, the Special Counsel recommends that the name of the individual who is the subject of the Preliminary Inquiry not be released publicly unless and until the Committee votes to issue a Statement of Alleged Violation.

The Special Counsel believes the evidence developed in this case requires the Committee, under its rules, to initiate a Preliminary Inquiry now, even though the full course of the proceedings cannot be completed in this Congress. The Special Counsel recommends that the Committee commence this Preliminary Inquiry, transmit all materials relevant to this matter to the next Congress, and recommend to the House leadership that the Committee on Standards of Official Conduct be constituted immediately upon the convening of the next Congress so that prompt action on this matter can be concluded expeditiously.

A small number of other instances of possible sexual misconduct involving pages or involving preferential treatment remain under investigation, and the Special Counsel recommends that the Committee transmit these matters to the next Congress with its recommendation that investigation of them be completed as early as possible next year.

The Special Counsel has found some evidence of other isolated instances of both heterosexual and homosexual advances to pages by individuals no longer associated with the House. Since these cases are beyond the jurisdiction of the Committee, investigation of these matters has not been pursued.

ILLICIT USE OR DISTRIBUTION OF DRUGS

In coordination with the Department of Justice and its Drug Enforcement Administration, the Special Counsel has been investigating allegations of illicit use and distribution of drugs involving Members, officers, or employees of the House. Both the Department of Justice and the Special Counsel have a number of matters under active investigation.

In one instance the Special Counsel has already found reasonable indications that illicit use and distribution of drugs by an employee of the House may have occurred and, therefore, recommends that the Committee open a Preliminary Inquiry now, under the same conditions described above with respect to the Preliminary Inquiry of sexual misconduct involving pages.

The rest of the Special Counsel's investigation of alleged illicit use or distribution of drugs by Members, officers or employees of the House is not yet at a stage where a report can be made in writing to the Committee. The Special Counsel, therefore, recommends that the Committee transmit the evidence developed in this part of the investigation to the next Congress with the recommendation that the investigation be carried forward expeditiously....

A. Scope

Pursuant to House Resolution 518, the Committee through its Special Counsel undertook an investigation to determine whether any Member, officer, or employee of the House of Representatives had engaged in any way in improper or illegal sexual conduct involving congressional pages.

The investigation focused on the period from July, 1981, to June 1982, and on the allegations of two former pages that received national press attention beginning on June 30, 1982. But to ensure a thorough inquiry into all matters within the scope of H. Res. 518, the Special Counsel sought out information about earlier periods and about any kind of sexual advance, harassment, or relationship involving a congressional page and a Member, officer, or employee of the House. In this connection, the Special Counsel has tried to contact every page employed by the House of Representatives during the past three years. In addition, the Special Counsel investigated all information he received about alleged sexual misconduct by House Members, officers or employees involving preferential treatment even where that information did not involve congressional pages....

D. Origin of allegations

The Special Counsel has found no support whatsoever for the sensational allegations and charges of homosexuality that launched this investigation. To the contrary, the evidence developed contradicts every one of the original highly publicized allegations made by the two former pages. Those allegations resulted either from out-and-out fabrication, overactive teenage imagination stimulated by conversations with a journalist, or teenage gossip which has in virtually every case proved to be utterly inaccurate.

In view of this conclusion, another important set of questions emerged in the course of the investigation: How and why did these charges come to be made? What was the source of the rumors of a "page scandal"?

It is clear that during the 1981-82 academic year, some pages behaved irresponsibly after working hours. There is abundant and convincing evidence, in the case of some pages, of excessive use of alcohol, all-night parties, some drug use, and a variety of other activities that no responsible parent would tolerate.

Leroy Williams, at that time a 17-year-old page in the House, left the page program abruptly at the end of January, 1982, when financial and other troubles became too much for him to handle. Events surrounding Williams' departure triggered an investigation by the Capitol Police of page drinking habits and parties, and of Williams' homosexuality. Two pages, unconnected to Williams, were terminated partly as a result of information developed by the Capitol Police investigation. This investigation, Williams' departure and the termination of the other two pages spawned rumors of a "page scandal." Though unreported in the press, these rumors came to the attention of many reporters.

In June, 1982, a CBS news reporter interviewed a 16-year-old page named Jeffrey Opp in Washington, D.C. and Williams in Little Rock, Arkansas. The Special Counsel requested that the reporter speak to investigators in the Special Counsel's office and offered him the opportunity to do so. The reporter declined that invitation. Thus, the only information available about these interviews comes from the sworn testimony of Williams and Opp themselves. According to Opp, the reporter discussed with him lurid tales of sexual misconduct and homosexual prostitution in the Congress. The reporter asked whether Opp could confirm those stories or provide additional information. According to Williams, the reporter said Williams was being identified in Washington as a drug trafficker and "bad apple" who had been the source of the problems with the page system. The reporter told Williams he was offering him a chance to tell his side of the story.

Following these conversations, and on the basis of assurances that their identities would be kept secret, both teenagers agreed to give on-camera interviews with their faces shielded, to the CBS reporter. Those interviews yielded lies from Williams. In response to the reporter's questions, Opp twisted minor, at best ambiguous conversations with three Congressmen and one lobbyist and characterized them as "homosexual approaches."

Perhaps the most ironic twist of events was the role played by the CBS news reporter in bringing these charges to life. It appears to have been the reporter's discussion with Opp that inspired Opp to repeat these stories, with his own embellishments, to two of his Congressional sponsor's staffers. These staffers were initially suspicious of the sensational nature of Opp's charges. But, then this same news reporter told the staffers that Opp's charges had substance. It was these staffers who decided Opp should tell his story to the Justice Department. The department decided to investigate, at least in part because the staff of a Member of Congress considered the allegations to be serious. That Justice Department investigation itself became the "news" to which CBS pegged its June 30 and July 1 Evening News reports, including the shielded interviews of Williams and Opp. . . . .

PLO DEPARTURE
FROM LEBANON
August 20, 1982

The final act in a summer-long drama in Lebanon was played out September 1 as the last of the trapped Palestine Liberation Organization (PLO) guerrillas departed Beirut for other Arab countries. The evacuation of PLO fighters, trapped since July in west Beirut following an invasion June 6 and the rapid advance into Lebanon by Israeli forces, came as the result of the August 20 agreement among the PLO, Lebanon and Israel negotiated by U.S. Ambassador Philip C. Habib. The settlement called for Israel to lift its siege of west Beirut and allow the PLO safe passage out of Lebanon protected by troops from the United States, France and Italy. Left unsettled was how foreign troops would be withdrawn from Lebanon, the future of the Palestinian people and of relations between Lebanon and Israel.

How It Started

The drama began on the night of June 3 when the Israeli ambassador to Britain, Shlomo Argov, was shot on a London street and critically wounded. Israel blamed the attack on the PLO and launched air strikes on Palestinian positions in southern Lebanon on June 4. The PLO responded with heavy shelling of northern Israel. The air attacks and shelling across the border continued throughout the next day until, on June 6, the Israeli Defense Forces crossed the border into southern Lebanon. Israeli forces moved quickly through Lebanon, taking PLO outposts along the coast and forcing the guerrillas to retreat toward Beirut. By June 9 Israeli forces had advanced to within a few miles of the Lebanese capital.

On June 7 Syrian ground troops occupying the Bekaa Valley in central Lebanon engaged Israeli forces outside the town of Jezzin. At the start of its offensive into Lebanon, Israel had warned Syrian forces, stationed in Lebanon as a peacekeeping force since the 1976 civil war in that country, to stay out of its battle with the PLO. The fighting between Syrian and Israeli troops escalated over the next few days until Israel June 9 launched a massive air strike on Syrian positions in the Bekaa Valley that completely destroyed Syria's Soviet-supplied antiaircraft missile batteries. Two days later, Israel announced a unilateral cease-fire with Syrian forces.

Following a day of heavy fighting around Beirut on June 10, including bombardment of the city and its suburbs, Israel extended the cease-fire June 12 to include Palestinian forces in Beirut. The cease-fire was shattered at dawn the next day. In the subsequent fighting, Israeli forces pushed northeast of Beirut and by June 14 had completely encircled the city. Under a tense truce following the June 21 bombardment of Palestinian positions, Israeli forces began digging in around Beirut, preparing for a final assault on the PLO.

Israel next moved to secure the strategic Beirut-Damascus Highway connecting the capital cities of Lebanon and Syria. Israeli and Syrian forces clashed in a series of fierce battles from June 22 to June 25, when Israeli troops finally broke through the Syrian lines to capture a major portion of the highway, thus cutting off the last possible exit from west Beirut for the trapped PLO guerrillas. Israel further tightened the noose around the PLO on July 3 when Israeli forces began the blockade of west Beirut by taking up positions along the so-called "green line," which had divided Moslem west Beirut from Christian east Beirut since the 1976 civil war. From this point the war evolved into one of nerves, negotiation and political maneuvering, periodically punctuated by Israeli shelling of PLO leadership positions in west Beirut or Palestinian refugee camps on the southwestern outskirts of the city.

Reaction to the Invasion

As Israeli troops dug in for the long siege of west Beirut, world opinion turned against the government of Israeli Prime Minister Menachem Begin. Media reports blamed the Israeli blockade of food and medical supplies and the continued Israeli shelling of Palestinian positions in and around west Beirut for the large numbers of civilians killed and wounded. The United Nations Security Council voted several times on resolutions demanding immediate Israeli withdrawal of its forces. In the United States opinion on the Israeli invasion was divided sharply, as many Americans expressed sympathy for the Palestinian and Lebanese civilians caught in the conflict and urged the Reagan administration to take a harder line toward Israel.

The Negotiations

Serious attempts to negotiate the withdrawal of Israeli and Palestinian forces from Lebanon began on June 26. The basic principles for the final settlement actually were agreed upon early in the negotiation process. On June 27 the PLO agreed to disarm and leave Lebanon. Two days later Israel agreed to allow the Palestinians to carry light weapons with them when they left. Following this basic agreement, however, the negotiations stalled for almost two months.

The main problem centered around where the PLO guerrillas would go when they left Beirut. Israel said it would reject any plan that called for the guerrillas to be relocated elsewhere in Lebanon, insisting that the PLO must leave the country entirely. The PLO in turn refused to be relocated in any country it termed too far from the Palestinian state it hoped to establish in Israel and the occupied territories on the West Bank and Gaza Strip. As world opinion turned against Israel, the PLO also pressed for political concessions in return for its retreat from Beirut, calling on the United States and United Nations to endorse Palestinian self-determination in the Israeli-occupied territories and recognize the Palestinians' right to a state.

After the Damascus government rejected in early July a U.S. proposal for evacuation of the PLO to Syria, Habib and Secretary of State George P. Shultz began a series of missions to individual Arab countries in an effort to find a temporary home for the trapped guerrillas. Their efforts met with little success until the end of July, when Arab leaders offered their own plan for ending the conflict.

The Arab plan called for evacuation of the PLO fighters from Beirut in exchange for lifting of the Israeli siege, coupled with guarantees of safe passage for the PLO and of future security for the 650,000 Palestinian refugees remaining in Lebanon. The PLO meanwhile dropped its demands for political concessions from the United States and United Nations on Palestinian self-determination.

Heavy Fighting Renewed

On July 30 Israeli forces renewed their heavy bombardment of Palestinian positions. After three days of shelling, Israeli troops crossed the green line into west Beirut and began advancing on Palestinian positions. Israeli forces also stepped up bombardment of refugee camps on the outskirts of the city and new Syrian missile emplacements in the Bekaa Valley.

The advance into west Beirut brought the peace talks to an immediate halt and further strained U.S.-Israeli relations. U.S. President Ronald Reagan condemned the invasion of west Beirut and threatened sanctions *against the Begin government, questioning whether Israel really had used its U.S.-supplied weapons in self-defense. Reports of heavy civilian casualties renewed public condemnation of Israel and sympathy for Palestinian and Lebanese civilians caught in the cross-fire. Israel claimed that reports of casualties were grossly exaggerated. As the bombardment continued, civic, religious and political leaders in the United States and other Western nations demanded that the Reagan administration exert pressure on Israel to stop the shelling and withdraw its forces from Lebanon. A cease-fire finally went into effect on August 12, following the heaviest bombardment of the invasion.*

The Settlement

In spite of Israel's renewed shelling of Palestinian positions, or perhaps because of it, the peace talks sputtered toward conclusion in August, halting and starting with each round of Israeli bombardment. On August 6 the United States and the PLO announced agreement on a timetable for the evacuation, as Jordan and Iraq became the first Arab states agreeing to accept PLO guerrillas. Syria, Egypt, Tunisia, Sudan, and North and South Yemen followed suit the next day, announcing their willingness to take in Palestinian fighters. (The PLO subsequently rejected Sudan and North and South Yemen as too far from where they hoped to establish a Palestinian state).

Negotiations on the details of the evacuation continued sporadically over the next two weeks. On August 18 the PLO and the Lebanese government approved an evacuation plan, and Israel accepted it the following day.

The settlement called for evacuation of the PLO guerrillas to begin within two or three days of the final agreement and be completed within 15 days. The Palestinians would be permitted to carry light arms, but all heavy weapons would be turned over to the Lebanese army. Most of the guerrillas would be evacuated overland by bus to Syria, but an initial contingent of wounded Palestinians would be taken by ship to Cyprus where they would board planes for other Arab countries. French paratroopers, the advance party of a multinational peacekeeping force consisting of troops from the United States, France and Italy, would arrive in Lebanon just before the first group of PLO fighters embarked for Cyprus. The multinational force would help the Lebanese army to protect the departing PLO guerrillas and ensure the safety of the Palestinian refugees remaining in Lebanon. (The guarantee of protection for Palestinian refugees, however, failed to prevent a massacre in two refugee camps September 16-18 by Lebanese militiamen of the Christian Phalangist Party. More than 300 people were believed dead and more than 900 were reported missing.) Finally, the Syrian-backed Palestine Liberation Army would return directly to Syria, while the Syrian army

itself would redeploy in the Bekaa Valley region of eastern Lebanon.
(Massacre in Palestinian camps, p. 781)

The first group of Palestinian guerrillas departed Lebanon for Cyprus August 21. Evacuation of the remaining PLO fighters proceeded ahead of schedule, although both the Israelis and Palestinians alleged the other side had violated parts of the agreement. The last contingent of PLO guerrillas left Beirut for Syria September 1.

Following is the text of the evacuation plan agreed to August 20 by the Israeli and Lebanese governments and the PLO, as published by The New York Times:

1

BASIC CONCEPT. All the P.L.O. leadership, offices and combatants in Beirut will leave Lebanon peacefully for prearranged destinations in other countries, in accord with the departure schedules and arrangements set out in this plan. The basic concept in this plan is consistent with the objective of the Government of Lebanon that all foreign military forces withdraw from Lebanon.

2

CEASE-FIRE. A cease-fire in place will be scrupulously observed by all in Lebanon.

3

U.N. OBSERVERS. The U.N. Observer Group stationed in the Beirut area will continue its functioning in that area.

4

SAFEGUARDS. Military forces present in Lebanon — whether Lebanese, Israeli, Syrian, Palestinian, or any other — will in no way interfere with the safe, secure, and timely departure of the P.L.O. leadership, offices and combatants. Law-abiding Palestinian noncombatants left behind in Beirut, including the families of those who have departed, will be subject to Lebanese laws and regulations. The Governments of Lebanon (G.O.L.) and the United States (U.S.) will provide appropriate guarantees of safety in the following ways:

The Lebanese Government will provide its guarantees on the basis of having secured assurances from armed groups with which it has been in touch.

The United States will provide its guarantees on the basis of assurances received from the Government of Israel (G.O.I.) and from the leadership of certain Lebanese groups with which it has been in touch.

5

"Departure-Day" is defined as the day on which advance elements of the Multinational Force (M.N.F.) deploy in the Beirut area, in accordance with arrangements worked out in advance among all concerned, and on which the initial group or groups of P.L.O. personnel commence departure from Beirut in accord with the planned schedule (attached).

6

THE MULTINATIONAL FORCE (M.N.F.). A temporary Multinational Force (M.N.F.), composed of units from France, Italy and the United States, will have been formed — at the request of the G.O.L. — to assist the Lebanese Armed Forces (L.A.F.) in carrying out their responsibilities in this operation. The L.A.F. will assure the departure from Lebanon of the P.L.O. leadership, offices and combatants, from whatever organization in Beirut, in a manner which will:
  (A) Assure the safety of such departing P.L.O. personnel;
  (B) Assure the safety of other persons in the Beirut area; and
  (C) Further the restoration of the sovereignty and authority of the G.O.L. over the Beirut area.

7

SCHEDULE OF DEPARTURES AND OTHER ARRANGEMENTS. The attached schedule of departures is subject to revision as may be necessary because of logistical requirements and because of any necessary shift in the setting of Departure-Day. Details concerning the schedule will be forwarded to the Israeli Defense Forces (I.D.F.) through the Liaison and Coordination Committee. Places of assembly for the departing personnel will be identified by agreement between the G.O.L. and the P.L.O. The P.L.O. will be in touch with governments receiving personnel to coordinate arrival and other arrangements there. If assistance is required, the P.L.O. should notify the Government of Lebanon.

8

M.N.F. MANDATE. In the event that the departure from Lebanon of the P.L.O. personnel referred to above does not take place in accord with the agreed and predetermined schedule, the mandate of the M.N.F. will terminate immediately and all M.N.F. personnel will leave Lebanon forthwith.

9

DURATION OF M.N.F. It will be mutually agreed between the G.O.L. and the governments contributing forces to the M.N.F. that the forces of the M.N.F. will depart Lebanon not later than 30 days after arrival, or sooner at the request of the Government of Lebanon or at the direction of the individual government concerned, or in accord with the termination of the mandate of the M.N.F. provided for above.

10

The P.L.O. leadership will be responsible for the organization and management of the assembly and the final departure of P.L.O. personnel, from beginning to end, at which time the leaders also will all be gone. Departure arrangements will be coordinated so that departures from Beirut take place at a steady pace, day-by-day.

11

L.A.F. CONTRIBUTION. The Lebanese Army will contribute between seven and eight army battalions to the operation, consisting of between 2,500-3,500 men. In addition, the internal security force (I.S.F.) will contribute men and assistance as needed.

12

I.C.R.C. The International Committee of the Red Cross (I.C.R.C.) will be able to assist the G.O.L. and L.A.F. in various ways, including in the organization and management of the evacuation of wounded and ill Palestinian and Syrian personnel to appropriate destinations, and in assisting in the chartering and movement of commercial vessels for use in departure by sea to other countries. The Liaison and Coordination Committee will ensure that there will be proper coordination with any I.C.R.C. activities in this respect.

13

DEPARTURE BY AIR. While present plans call for departure by sea and land, departures by air are not foreclosed.

14

LIAISON AND COORDINATION. The L.A.F. will be the primary point of contact for liaison with the P.L.O. as well as with other armed groups, and will provide necessary information.

The L.A.F. and M.N.F. will have formed prior to Departure-Day a Liaison and Coordination Committee, composed of representatives of the M.N.F. participating governments and the L.A.F. The committee will carry out close and effective liaison with, and provide continuous and detailed information to, the Israeli Defense Forces (I.D.F.). On behalf of the committee, the L.A.F. will continue to carry out close and effective liaison with the P.L.O., and other armed groups in the Beirut area. For convenience, the Liaison and Coordination Committee will have two essential components:

(A) Supervisory liaison; and

(B) Military and technical liaison and coordination.

The Liaison and Coordination Committee will act collectively; however, it may designate one or more of its members for primary liaison contact who would of course act on behalf of all.

Liaison arrangements and consultations will be conducted in such a way as to minimize misunderstandings and to forestall difficulties. Appropriate means of communications between the committee and other groups will be developed for this purpose.

The Liaison and Coordination Committee will continually monitor and keep all concerned currently informed regarding the implementation of the plan, including any revisions to the departure schedule as may be necessary because of logistical requirements.

15

DURATION OF DEPARTURE. The departure period shall be as short as possible and, in any event, no longer than two weeks.

16

TRANSIT THROUGH LEBANON. As part of any departure arrangement, all movements of convoys carrying P.L.O. personnel must be conducted in daylight hours. When moving overland from Beirut to Syria, the convoys should cross the border into Syria with no stops en route. In those instances when convoys of departing-P.L.O. personnel pass through I.D.F. positions, whether in the Beirut area or elsewhere in Lebanon, the I.D.F. will clear the route for the temporary period in which the convoy is running. Similar steps will be taken by other armed groups located in the area of the route the convoy will take.

17

ARMS CARRIED BY P.L.O. PERSONNEL. On their departure, P.L.O. personnel will be allowed to carry with them one individual side weapon (pistol, rifle or submachine gun) and ammunition.

18

HEAVY AND SPARE WEAPONRY, AND MUNITIONS. The P.L.O. will turn over to the L.A.F. as gifts all remaining weaponry in their possession, including heavy, crew-served, and spare weaponry and equipment, along with all munitions left behind in the Beirut area. The L.A.F. may seek the assistance of elements of the M.N.F. in securing and disposing of the military equipment. The P.L.O. will assist the L.A.F. by providing, prior to their departure, full and detailed information as to the location of this military equipment.

19

MINES AND BOOBY TRAPS. The P.L.O. and the Arab Deterrent Force (A.D.F.) will provide to the L.A.F. and M.N.F. (through the L.A.F.) full and detailed information on the location of mines and booby traps.

20

MOVEMENT OF P.L.O. LEADERSHIP. Arrangements will be made so that departing P.L.O. personnel will be accompanied by a proportionate share of the military and political leadership throughout all stages of the departure operation.

21

TURNOVER OF PRISONERS AND REMAINS. The P.L.O. will, through the I.C.R.C., turn over to the I.D.F. all Israeli nationals whom they have taken in custody, and the remains, or full and detailed information about the location of the remains, of all Israeli soldiers who have fallen. The P.L.O. will also turn over to the L.A.F. all other prisoners whom they have taken in custody and the remains, or full and detailed information about the location of the remains, of all other soldiers who have fallen. All arrangements for such turnovers shall be worked out with the I.C.R.C. as required prior to Departure-Day.

22

SYRIAN MILITARY FORCES. It is noted that arrangements have been made between the Governments of Lebanon and Syria for the deployment of all military personnel of the Arab Deterrent Force (A.D.F.) from Beirut during the departure period. These forces will be allowed to take their equipment with them, except for that — under mutual agreement between the two Governments — which is turned over to the L.A.F. All elements of the Palestinian Liberation Army (P.L.A.), whether or not they now or in the past have been attached to the A.D.F., will withdraw from Lebanon.

SEPTEMBER

REAGAN PEACE PLAN
FOR THE MIDDLE EAST
September 1, 1982

Following the withdrawal of the Palestine Liberation Organization (PLO) from Lebanon, President Ronald Reagan, in a televised speech September 1, proposed a new peace plan for the Middle East. The PLO had agreed to leave Lebanon after three months of war between its guerrilla forces and Israeli troops. Calling for a "fresh start," Reagan urged a freeze on Jewish settlement in the Israeli-occupied West Bank and Gaza strip. The Israeli government quickly rejected Reagan's plan, saying that it violated the Camp David accords. (Camp David accords, Historic Documents of 1978, p. 605; war in Lebanon, p. 741)

Reagan suggested that after the five-year transition period of "autonomy" envisioned by the Camp David agreement the territories should have an association with Jordan and should not be subject to Israeli sovereignty. United Nations Resolution 242, approved by the Security Council in 1967, and the 1978 Camp David accords grant Israel recognition and security in exchange for withdrawal from the occupied territory.

Israel regarded the West Bank and the Gaza Strip, captured in the 1967 Middle East war, as integral parts of Israel. When Reagan announced his plan, Israel occupied 30 percent of the land in the territory with 99 settlements in which 30,000 Jews lived among 1.3 million Arabs.

In a special session September 2, the Israeli cabinet rejected Reagan's plan as being "anti-Israel." Anyone in Israel who supported it would be a traitor, Prime Minister Menachem Begin and his cabinet agreed. The government said Reagan's plan would lead to the establishment of a Palestinian state threatening Israel's security.

Shamir's Speech to Knesset

In a September 8 speech before the Knesset, the Israeli parliament, Foreign Minister Yitzhak Shamir denounced the Reagan plan as "negative and harmful. . . . The right of Jews to settle in the Land of Israel is fundamental and beyond question. . . . What this package really means is Israel's return to the partition lines of 1967." Shamir added, "The Camp David agreements are being emptied of their content; everything that was proposed . . . by the Arab side and rejected by Israel reappears in the form of a 'presidential position' . . . to subdue Israel and bend its will."

Four days after Reagan's call for a freeze on Jewish settlements, Israel allocated $18.5 million to build three new settlements in the occupied West Bank and announced approval to build seven others. The United States immediately condemned Israel's settlement plan as "most unwelcome."

Fez Plan

Meanwhile, the Arab countries at the conclusion of a four-day, closed-door Arab League ministers' conference in Fez, Morocco, unanimously approved a Middle East peace plan that appeared to give implicit recognition to Israel.

The 20 Arab League members represented at the conference (only Libya and Egypt were absent) declared that all nations in the region, including an independent Palestinian state, had a right to a peaceful existence. The first of eight points dealing with Arab-Israeli relations called for the return of Israel to its pre-1967 borders and the removal of all Israeli settlements in the occupied territories.

Israel promptly dismissed the Arab League's plan. The Foreign Ministry said "Israel cannot consider seriously the Fez plan. It does not contain any substantial new elements that differ from traditional Arab positions." The ministry also said the call for a Palestinian state "constitutes a threat to Israel's existence."

The peace efforts hit a serious snag April 11, 1983, when Jordan's King Hussein declared an end to attempts to reach accord with the PLO on negotiating positions for the talks. Jordan, said the king, would not act for anybody in peace talks.

> *Following are the texts of President Reagan's speech, nationally televised September 1, 1982; of Israeli Foreign Minister Yitzhak Shamir's speech to the Knesset, September 8; and of the Fez Plan, announced at the conclusion of the 12th Arab Summit, September 9. (Boldface headings in brackets have been added by Congressional Quarterly to highlight the organization of the texts.):*

REAGAN PEACE PROPOSAL

My fellow Americans:

Today has been a day that should make us proud. It marked the end of the successful evacuation of [the] PLO from Beirut, Lebanon. This peaceful step could never have been taken without the good offices of the United States and especially the truly heroic work of a great American diplomat, Ambassador Philip Habib.

Thanks to his efforts, I'm happy to announce that the U.S. Marine contingent helping to supervise the evacuation has accomplished its mission. Our young men should be out of Lebanon within 2 weeks. They, too, have served the cause of peace with distinction, and we can all be very proud of them.

But the situation in Lebanon is only part of the overall problem of conflict in the Middle East. So, over the past 2 weeks, while events in Beirut dominated the front page, America was engaged in a quiet, behind-the-scenes effort to lay the groundwork for a broader peace in the region. For once there were no premature leaks as U.S. diplomatic missions traveled to Mideast capitals, and I met here at home with a wide range of experts to map out an American peace initiative for the long-suffering peoples of the Middle East — Arab and Israeli alike.

It seemed to me that with the agreement in Lebanon we had an opportunity for a more far-reaching peace effort in the region, and I was determined to seize that moment. In the words of the scripture, the time had come to "follow after the things which make for peace." Tonight I want to report to you the steps we've taken and the prospects they can open up for a just and lasting peace in the Middle East.

America has long been committed to bringing peace to this troubled region. For more than a generation, successive United States administrations have endeavored to develop a fair and workable process that could lead to a true and lasting Arab-Israeli peace.

Our involvement in the search for Mideast peace is not a matter of preference; it's a moral imperative. The strategic importance of the region to the United States is well known, but our policy is motivated by more than strategic interests. We also have an irreversible commitment to the survival and territorial integrity of friendly states. Nor can we ignore the fact that the well-being of much of the world's economy is tied to stability in the strife-torn Middle East. Finally, our traditional humanitarian concerns dictated a continuing effort to peacefully resolve conflicts.

[U. S. Middle East Policy]

When our administration assumed office in January of 1981, I decided that the general framework for our Middle East policy should follow the broad guidelines laid down by my predecessors. There were two basic issues we had to address. First, there was a strategic threat to the region posed by the Soviet Union and its surrogates, best demonstrated by the brutal war in Afghanistan, and, second, the peace process between Israel and its Arab neighbors.

With regard to the Soviet threat, we have strengthened our efforts to develop with our friends and allies a joint policy to deter the Soviets and their surrogates from further expansion in the region and, if necessary, to defend against it.

With respect to the Arab-Israeli conflict, we've embraced the Camp David framework as the only way to proceed. We have also recognized, however, solving the Arab-Israeli conflict in and of itself cannot assure peace throughout a region as vast and troubled as the Middle East.

Our first objective under the Camp David process was to ensure the successful fulfillment of the Egyptian-Israeli peace treaty. This was achieved with the peaceful return of the Sinai to Egypt in April 1982. To accomplish this, we worked hard with our Egyptian and Israeli friends and, eventually, with other friendly countries to create the multinational force which now operates in the Sinai. Throughout this period of difficult and time-consuming negotiations, we never lost sight of the next step of Camp David — autonomy talks to pave the way for permitting the Palestinian people to exercise their legitimate rights. However, owing to the tragic assassination of President Sadat and other crises in the area, it was not until January 1982 that we were able to make a major effort to renew these talks.

Secretary of State Haig and Ambassador Fairbanks made three visits to Israel and Egypt early this year to pursue the autonomy talks. Considerable progress was made in developing the basic outline of an American approach which was to be presented to Egypt and Israel after April.

The successful completion of Israel's withdrawal from Sinai and the courage shown on this occasion by Prime Minister Begin and President Mubarak in living up to their agreements convinced me the time had come for a new American policy to try to bridge the remaining differences between Egypt and Israel on the autonomy process. So, in May, I called for specific measures and a timetable for consultations with the Governments of Egypt and Israel on the next step in the peace process. However, before this effort could be launched, the conflict in Lebanon preempted our effort.

The autonomy talks were basically put on hold while we sought to untangle the parties in Lebanon and still the guns of war. The Lebanon war, tragic as it was, has left us with a new opportunity for Middle East peace. We must seize it now and bring peace to this troubled area so vital to world stability while there is still time. It was with this strong conviction that over a month ago, before the present negotiations in Beirut had been completed, I directed Secretary of State Shultz to again review our policy and to consult a wide range of outstanding Americans on the best ways to strengthen chances for peace in the Middle East.

We have consulted with many of the officials who were historically involved in the process, with members of the Congress, and with individuals from the private sector. And I have held extensive consultations with my own advisers on the principles that I will outline to you tonight.

The evacuation of the PLO from Beirut is now complete, and we can now help the Lebanese to rebuild their war-torn country. We owe it to ourselves and to posterity to move quickly to build upon this achievement. A stable and revived Lebanon is essential to all our hopes for peace in the region. The people of Lebanon deserve the best efforts of the international community to turn the nightmares of the past several years into a new dawn of hope. But the opportunities for peace in the Middle East do not begin and end in Lebanon. As we help Lebanon rebuild, we must also move to resolve the root causes of conflict between Arabs and Israelis.

The war in Lebanon has demonstrated many things, but two consequences are key to the peace process. First, the military losses of the PLO have not diminished the yearning of the Palestinian people for a just solution of their claims; and, second, while Israel's military successes in Lebanon have demonstrated that its armed forces are second to none in the region, they alone cannot bring just and lasting peace to Israel and her neighbors.

The question now is how to reconcile Israel's legitimate security concerns with the legitimate rights of the Palestinians. And that answer can only come at the negotiating table. Each party must recognize that the outcome must be acceptable to all and that true peace will require compromises by all.

[Need for a Fresh Start]

So, tonight I'm calling for a fresh start. This is the moment for all those directly concerned to get involved — or lend their support — to a workable basis for peace. The Camp David agreement remains the foundation of our policy. Its language provides all parties with the leeway they need for successful negotiations.

I call on Israel to make clear that the security for which she yearns can only be achieved through genuine peace, a peace requiring magnanimity, vision, and courage.

I call on the Palestinian people to recognize that their own political aspirations are inextricably bound to recognition of Israel's right to a secure future.

And I call on the Arab States to accept the reality of Israel — and the reality that peace and justice are to be gained only through hard, fair, direct negotiation.

In making these calls upon others, I recognize that the United States has a special responsibility. No other nation is in the position to deal with the key parties to the conflict on the basis of trust and reliability.

The time has come for a new realism on the part of all the peoples of the Middle East. The State of Israel is an accomplished fact; it deserves unchallenged legitimacy within the community of nations. But Israel's legitimacy has thus far been recognized by too few countries and has been denied by every Arab State except Egypt. Israel exists; it has a right to exist in peace behind secure and defensible borders; and it has a right to demand of its neighbors that they recognize those facts.

I have personally followed and supported Israel's heroic struggle for survival, ever since the founding of the State of Israel 34 years ago. In the pre-1967 borders Israel was barely 10 miles wide at its narrowest point. The bulk of Israel's population lived within artillery range of hostile Arab armies. I am not about to ask Israel to live that way again.

The war in Lebanon has demonstrated another reality in the region. The departure of the Palestinians from Beirut dramatizes more than ever the homelessness of the Palestinian people. Palestinians feel strongly that their cause is more than a question of refugees. I agree. The Camp David agreements recognized that fact when it spoke of the legitimate rights of the Palestinian people and their just requirements.

For peace to endure it must involve all those who have been most deeply affected by the conflict. Only through broader participation in the peace process, most immediately by Jordan and by the Palestinians, will Israel be able to rest confident in the knowledge that its security and integrity will be respected by its neighbors. Only through the process of negotiation can all the nations of the Middle East achieve a secure peace.

[New American Positions]

These, then, are our general goals. What are the specific new American positions and why are we taking them? In the Camp David talks thus far, both Israel and Egypt have felt free to express openly their views as to what the outcome should be. Understandably their views have differed on many points. The United States has thus far sought to play the role of mediator. We have avoided public comment on the key issues. We have always recognized and continue to recognize that only the voluntary agreement of those parties most directly involved in the conflict can provide an enduring solution. But it's become evident to me that some clearer sense of America's position on the key issues is necessary to encourage wider support for the peace process.

First, as outlined in the Camp David accords, there must be a period of time during which the Palestinian inhabitants of the West Bank and Gaza will have full autonomy over their own affairs. Due consideration must be given to the principle of self-government by the inhabitants of the territory and the legitimate security concerns of the parties involved. The purpose of the 5-year period of transition which would begin after free elections for a self-governing Palestinian authority is to prove to the Palestinians that they can run their own affairs and that such Palestinian autonomy poses no threat to Israel's security.

The United States will not support the use of any additional land for the purpose of settlement during the transitional period. Indeed, the immediate adoption of a settlement freeze by Israel, more than any other action, could create the confidence needed for wider participation in these talks. Further settlement activity is in no way necessary for the security of Israel and only diminishes the confidence of the Arabs that a final outcome can be freely and fairly negotiated.

I want to make the American position well understood. The purpose of this transitional period is the peaceful and orderly transfer of authority from Israel to the Palestinian inhabitants of the West Bank and Gaza. At the same time, such a transfer must not interfere with Israel's security requirements.

Beyond the transition period, as we look to the future of the West Bank and Gaza, it is clear to me that peace cannot be achieved by the formation of an independent Palestinian state in those territories, nor is it achievable on the basis of Israeli sovereignty or permanent control over the West Bank and Gaza. So the United States will not support the establishment of an independent Palestinian state in the West Bank and Gaza. And we will not support annexation or permanent control by Israel.

[Peace for Territory]

There is, however, another way to peace. The final status of these lands must, of course, be reached through the give and take of negotiations. But it is the firm view of the United States that self-government by the Palestinians of the West Bank and Gaza in association with Jordan offers the best chance for a durable, just, and lasting peace. We base our approach squarely on the principle that the Arab-Israeli conflict should be resolved through negotiations involving an exchange of territory for peace.

This exchange is enshrined in United Nations Security Council Resolution 242, which is, in turn, incorporated in all its parts in the Camp David agreements. U.N. Resolution 242 remains wholly valid as the foundation stone of America's Middle East peace effort. It is the United States position that, in return for peace, the withdrawal provision of Resolution 242 applies to all fronts, including the West Bank and Gaza. When the border is negotiated between Jordan and Israel, our view on the extent to which Israel should be asked to give up territory will be heavily affected by the extent of true peace and normalization, and the security arrangements offered in return.

Finally, we remain convinced that Jerusalem must remain undivided. But its final status should be decided through negotiation.

In the course of the negotiations to come, the United States will support positions that seem to us fair and reasonable compromises and likely to promote a sound agreement. We will also put forward our own detailed proposals when we believe they can be helpful. And, make no mistake, the United States will oppose any proposal from any party and at any point in the negotiating process that threatens the security of Israel. America's commitment to the security of Israel is ironclad, and I might add, so is mine.

During the past few days, our Ambassadors in Israel, Egypt, Jordan, and Saudi Arabia have presented to their host governments the proposals, in full detail, that I have outlined here today. Now I'm convinced that these proposals can bring justice, bring security, and bring durability to an Arab-Israeli peace. The United States will stand by these principles with total dedication. They are fully consistent with Israel's security requirements and the aspirations of the Palestinians.

We will work hard to broaden participation at the peace table as envisaged by the Camp David accords. And I fervently hope that the Palestinians and Jordan, with the support of their Arab colleagues, will accept this opportunity.

Tragic turmoil in the Middle East runs back to the dawn of history. In our modern day, conflict after conflict has taken its brutal toll there. In an age of nuclear challenge and economic interdependence, such conflicts are a threat to all the people of the world, not just the Middle East itself. It's time for us all — in the Middle East and around the world — to call a halt to conflict, hatred, and prejudice. It's time for us all to launch a common effort for reconstruction, peace, and progress.

It has often been said — and, regrettably, too often been true — that the story of the search for peace and justice in the Middle East is a tragedy of opportunities missed. In the aftermath of the settlement in Lebanon, we now face an opportunity for a broader peace. This time we must not let it slip from our grasp. We must look beyond the difficulties and obstacles of the present and move with a fairness and resolve toward a brighter future. We owe it to ourselves — and to posterity — to do no less. For if we miss this chance to make a fresh start, we may look back on this moment from some later vantage point and realize how much that failure cost us all.

These, then, are the principles upon which American policy toward the Arab-Israeli conflict will be based. I have made a personal commitment to see that they endure and, God willing, that they will come to be seen by all reasonable, compassionate people as fair, achievable, and in the interests of all who wish to see peace in the Middle East.

Tonight, on the eve of what can be a dawning of new hope for the people of the troubled Middle East — and for all the world's people who dream of a just and peaceful future — I ask you, my fellow Americans, for your support and your prayers in this great undertaking.

Thank you and God bless you.

SHAMIR SPEECH TO KNESSET

Mister Speaker, Members of the Knesset,

When the first stage of Operation Peace for Galilee was completed, and the stronghold of the murder organizations in the Lebanese capital was eliminated, thereby opening up new possibilities for peace in our region, we were prepared to launch a peace offensive, to mobilize all the resources of goodwill in our own country and among our neighbours, in order to complete the process we began five years ago, the Camp David process.

We believed, and we still believe, that the uprooting of the terrorist plague has helped people understand that the path of violence will not lead to Israel's capitulation; there is but one way to solve the problems of the peoples and countries in the region and alleviate their distress, and that is direct negotiations for a comprehensive and honourable peace.

There was no need to rediscover this path or lay it down once again: the road is already paved. Israel, Egypt and the United States invested a great deal of throught and hard work, of mental and spiritual effort in bringing forth the peace treaty between Egypt and Israel and the Camp David Agreements. This past April — only a few months ago — Israel proved its total fidelity to the obligations it had assumed under these agreements. With profound misgivings and mental anguish, witnessed by the entire world, it completed the withdrawal from Sinai, pulling up, for the first time in its history, magnificent settlements built with the blood and sweat of its children.

We were ready to get on with completing the negotiations on autonomy for the Palestinian Arabs, in order to put into effect the remaining section of the Camp David accords and create the conditions for peaceful and honourable coexistence with the Arab residents of Judea, Samaria and Gaza. There is no doubt that, in these negotiations, it was first and foremost Egypt and the United States, partners in the negotiations from the very start, that were to have taken part. Only recently we held talks with representatives of the United States on the next stages in the peace process. We learned that they were busy studying the various issues of Camp David in order to formulate proposals and positions.

The Reagan Programme

Then, last Wednesday, 1 September 1982, the President of the United States delivered a speech to the American people in which he presented the US position on the various issues involved in a political arrangement for the areas of Judea, Samaria and the Gaza district. The main points in the American position were conveyed to the Prime Minister the day before by the US ambassador in Israel. The Cabinet met in special session on Thursday, 2 September 1982, and solemnly deliberated on the American proposals, as presented to the Prime Minister. It decided to reject the proposals, and to refrain from entering into any negotiations with any party whatsoever on the basis of these positions. This decision has now been placed before the Knesset.

The United States Government did not see fit to consult with us on this new programme, which concerns our borders, our security and our positions. This is something that is simply not done. It contradicts an explicit obligation which the US Government undertook on three separate occasions in the past. The Memorandum of Understanding of 20 December 1973, and President Ford's letter of 1 September 1975, which was reaffirmed in the Memorandum of Understanding of 26 March 1979, stated that the United States would confer with Israel fully, step by step, and would make every effort to coordinate its proposals with Israel. On the other hand, the American administration saw fit to confer with Arab countries that have repeatedly ·expressed their opposition to the Camp David Agreements. This is in itself a very serious matter; but the actual contents of the new American ideas are even more serious. We cannot accept them as a basis for the negotiation of peace agreements in the region.

The Camp David Accords

The Camp David Agreements were reached after difficult and penetrating debates. Every word in those agreements was the result of intense discussion. Any matter that was not included had been deliberately omitted. The United States participated in the talks, influenced the positions of the parties and mediated between them. The then-President of the United States signed the Agreements as a witness.

Since that time, and during the entire negotiating process up to 1 September 1982, the United States abstained from taking any explicit public stand on the substantive issues under negotiation. The reason was obvious. Both partners to the agreement well knew that such a stand by the United States would impair the negotiations and the chances of reaching an agreement between the two parties.

The Camp David Agreement constituted a package, whose component parts were interrelated in a logical, political way, although there was no operational connection between them. Israel agreed to make far-reaching concessions in the Sinai in exchange for peace with Egypt, with the understanding that this would be the extent of its security and territorial risk, since, in the eastern sector, autonomy was agreed upon in Judea, Samaria and Gaza for a five-year transition period. During the negotiations, Egypt did indeed call for Arab sovereignty over the territories of Judea, Samaria and Gaza and a freeze on Jewish settlement. But its demand was not accepted, and Egypt agreed to autonomy for five years. This entire structure has now been undermined by the United States move, which ignores the interrelation between the various positions and concessions and revives demands and positions that were considered and rejected during the Camp David negotiating process. Thus the damage wrought by the American move lies not only in its contradiction of the explicit wording of the agreement, but even more in its attack on the whole conception and internal political structure of the Camp David accords. In reading the new US proposals, I can say that if at the time of Camp David the Americans had insisted on the positions they are now putting forth, we would not have signed the agreements.

Contradictions in the US Position

President Ronald Reagan, in his speech to the American people, declared that Israel has the right to exist behind secure and defensible borders, and the right to demand that its neighbours recognize this fact. He even pointed out that under the pre-1967 lines, Israel was less than ten miles wide at certain points, and that a large portion of its population lived within artillery range of hostile Arab armies. He announced that he had no intention of proposing that Israel return to those conditions. President Reagan also said that the peoples of the Middle East could achieve a secure peace only through the negotiating process. He declared that Jerusalem had to remain undivided, although its final status would have to be fixed by negotiations. Finally, he reiterated his earlier declarations concerning the absolute commitment of the United States to Israel's security.

These are important, positive statements, and we believe that they reflect a sincere, profound feeling of friendship toward Israel and of commitment to its future security. We must note with great regret, however, that the operative provisions that accompanied these declarations by the President contradict them; they constitute a danger to Israel's security, to the principle of a negotiated agreement, and to the chances for peace between Israel and its remaining Arab neighbours.

[Erosion of Camp David: Autonomy]

The position paper we received from the US administration stated that full autonomy means that the inhabitants have "full authority" to govern themselves, the land and its water sources. In the Camp David Agreements the language used was the "granting of full autonomy to the inhabitants;" Israel made it clear in the negotiations that this referred to the inhabitants and not the territory.

The operational significance of this point was a subject of negotiations with Egypt. The United States has now taken a definite position of its own that deviates from the agreement and does great harm to the negotiating process. It turns upside down everything that was achieved in this regard by Israel's representatives through difficult, lengthy negotiations. It represents a change in the essence of the Camp David Agreements. We did not accept this position then, and we will not accept it today.

The United States also states that it will support economic, trade, social and cultural ties between Jordan and Judea, Samaria and the Gaza district. The Camp David Agreements refer to the connection between autonomy, Jordan and Israel in careful, thoughtful language. The United States has deemed fit, in its new paper, to emphasize specifically the ties with Jordan and to ignore the ties that in any case already exist with Israel. In so doing, it invites pressure for severing ties with Israel in the future. Open borders and free movement are the fundamental principles which

Israel has always advocated; until now, they were acceptable as well, as far as we know, to the United States. How much more so is this the case when we are speaking of an area that is part and parcel of Eretz Israel (the Land of Israel), from which we will never be separated, not now and not ever.

Jerusalem was not mentioned in the body of the Camp David accords, since Israel did not agree to anything that would impair the status of Israel's united capital. Egypt does indeed differ with Israel's stand on this subject, and the positions of the parties may be found in letters that accompany the agreement. Now the United States has taken a stand completely contradictory to that of Israel. The participation of Jerusalem Arabs in the elections for the autonomy authority can have only one real result: the redivision of Jerusalem. To that we will never agree.

Jewish Settlements

The American call for a freeze on Jewish settlement in Judea, Samaria and Gaza during the transition period is negative and harmful. It is not by chance that there is no mention of this in the Camp David Agreements. No self-respecting Israeli Government could agree that the right of Jews to settle in all parts of Eretz Israel should be an issue for discussion or even for mention in any political document. The right of Jews to settle in the Land of Israel is fundamental and beyond question; it does not require anyone's approval. Even to raise the issue is an insult. Even worse, it will encourage Arab elements to believe that they can continue to strive to cut off segments of Eretz Israel and transfer them — "Judenrein" — to foreign ownership. It is impossible to understand how this position can be reconciled with the President's letter of 31 August to the Prime Minister; I quote: "This position does not contravene his deep recognition of the continued right of the Jews to live in peace in Judea, Samaria and Gaza."

The subject of security was extensively discussed at Camp David. It is divided into two parts: the overall security of Israel from outside attack, and the security of its inhabitants from terror and sabotage attacks from among the Arab population of Judea, Samaria and Gaza. The key sentence in this matter in the Camp David framework states that all steps and measures will be taken to guarantee the security of Israel and its neighbours during the transition period and afterwards. In order to help achieve this security, a strong police force is to be established by the autonomy authority. This means that Israel would remain in charge of its security against both external attacks and terrorist acts during the transition period and beyond.

No Israeli representative to the negotiations conceived that the prevention of terror and the war against terror could possibly be turned over to a foreign element in Judea, Samaria and Gaza. The new American position seeks to give the Arab inhabitants responsibility for internal security, that is, beyond the defined area of police jurisdiction. The new definition differs significantly from that adopted at Camp David. It means turning over all responsibility for internal security to the autonomous authority. In practical terms, responsibility for fighting terror would not be under our jurisdiction. No sensible Israeli would support this position.

UN Security Council Resolution 242

In the preamble to each of the Camp David documents, and later, to the peace agreement between Israel and Egypt, Security Council Resolution 242 is prominently cited.

The participants at Camp David understood that the negotiations were designed, among other things, to fulfil the provisions of the resolution by means of peace treaties between Israel and its neighbours. In this manner, the parties gave the resolution a specific interpretation and agreed to implement it in practice. Now the US comes along and reopens the subject as though there were no Camp David, and as though there were no connections between 242 and the Camp David Agreements. Autonomy implements Resolution 242. But the new American interpretation does not stop there. It demands that Israel specifically withdraw from this area too.

When you put together all the American positions with all their facets — that is, the principle of withdrawal from Judea, Samaria and Gaza, the principle of territories in exchange for peace, the connection between the depth of the withdrawal and the degree of peace, the freezing of settlement, the opposition to Israeli sovereignty over the territories of Judea, Samaria and Gaza, and the granting of voting rights to East Jerusalem Arabs for the autonomy authority — what this package really means is Israel's return to the partition lines of 1967. When we add to this the rejection of Israeli sovereignty as a possible future option, and the equivocal language concerning the possibility of establishing a Palestinian state, the scenario that would result if these positions were realized is very clear and very grim.

The Camp David Agreements are being emptied of their content; everything that was proposed in Camp David by the Arab side and rejected by Israel reappears in the form of a 'presidential position' emanating from above, to subdue Israel and bend its will.

U.S.-Israel Relations

The Government of Israel could not but reject these positions, even though they came to us from our friend, the president of our greatest friend and ally, the United States. Our relations with the United States are of a special character. Between our two nations there is a deep friendship, based on common values and identical interests. At the same time, differences between our two countries crop up occasionally, chiefly on the subject of our borders and how to defend our security. These differences of opinion are natural; they stem from changing conditions, and they express our independence and our separate needs. A true alliance can exist only between independent nations, each one knowing what is unique to it and what they have in common. Israel is a difficult ally, but a faithful and reliable one. We are certain that what we have in common with the United States is permanent and deep, while our disagreements are ephemeral. The permanent will overcome the ephemeral.

Conclusion

The Israeli people have seen changes and fluctuations, ups and downs in their relations with the US. They know and have known that on the fundamental life-and-death issues — such as security, Jerusalem, the 1967 borders, the danger of a Palestinian state — we have no choice but to stand by our position firmly, strongly and clearly — even against our great friend the United States. No different viewpoint, school of thought, or political party can justify taking any position that differs from the one which the Government of Israel has taken. The Israeli people will stand together and overcome.

FEZ PLAN

Given the dangerous and delicate circumstances the Arab nation is going through and the historical feeling of responsibility, their Majesties, their Highnesses and their Excellencies the Arab Kings, Presidents and Emirs of Arab states have examined important issues submitted to the Summit and have made the following decisions:

The Arab-Israeli Conflict

The Summit paid hommage to the resistance of the forces of the Palestinian revolution, of the Lebanese and Palestinian peoples, of the Arab Syrian Armed Forces and reaffirms its support to the Palestinian people in its struggle for the recovering of its inalienable national rights.

The Summit, convinced of the strength of the Arab nation for the achievement of its legitimate objectives and for putting an end to the aggression, on the basis of fundamental principles laid down by Arab Summits and out of Arab countries' concern to carry on the action by all means for the achievement of a just peace in the Middle East, taking into account the plan of His Excellency President Habib Bourguiba who considers the international legality as a basis for settling the Palestinian issue and the plan of His Majesty King Fahd Ibn Abdelaziz, related to peace in the Middle East, and in the light of discussions and remarks made by their Majesties, their Excellencies, and their Highnesses, the Kings, Presidents and Emirs, the Summit has agreed upon the following principles:

1. The withdrawal of Israel from all Arab territories occupied in 1967, including the Arab Al Qods (Jerusalem).

2. The dismantling of settlements established by Israel on the Arab territories after 1967.

3. The guarantee of freedom of worship and practice of religious rites for all religious in the holy shrines.

4. The reaffirmation of the Palestinian people's right to self-determination and the exercise of its imprescriptible and inalienable national rights under the leadership of the Palestine Liberation Organization (PLO), its sole and legitimate representative and the indemnification of all those who do not desire to return.

5. Placing the West Bank and Gaza Strip under the control of the United Nations for a transitory period not exceeding a few months.

6. The establishment of an independent Palestinian state with Al Qods as its capital.

7. The Security Council guarantees peace among all states of the region including the independent Palestinian state.

8. The Security Council guarantees the respect of these principles.

The Israeli Aggression Against Lebanon

1. The Summit strongly condemns the Israeli aggression against Lebanon and the Palestinian and Lebanese peoples, and draws the attention of the international public opinion to the seriousness and the consequences of this aggression on the stability and security of the region.

2. The Summit decides to support Lebanon in everything allowing the implementation of the Security Council resolutions and particularly resolutions 508 and 509 concerning the withdrawal of Israel from the Lebanese territory back to the internationally recognized frontiers.

3. The Summit reaffirms the solidarity of Arab countries with Lebanon in its tragedy and its readiness to grant all assistance that it would demand to solve its problems.

The Summit was informed of the Lebanese Government's decision to put an end to the mission of the Arab deterrent forces in Lebanon. To this effect, the Lebanese and Syrian Governments will start negotiations on measures to be taken in the light of the Israeli withdrawal from Lebanon. . . .

The Summit has decided to set up a committee entrusted with undertaking contact with the permanent members of the United Nations Security Council to follow up the Summit's resolutions on the Arab-Israeli conflict and to get informed on these countries' stance and to get informed concerning the position that the United States of America has made public during the past few days concerning the Arab-Israeli conflict. This committee will report regularly on the results of its contacts and endeavors with the Kings and Heads of State.

SECRETARY-GENERAL ON U. N. ACTIVITIES
September 7, 1982

Secretary-General Javier Pérez de Cuéllar issued his first annual report on the United Nations September 7. Unlike previous U.N. leaders, Pérez de Cuéllar did not survey the organization's accomplishments; rather he addressed the United Nations' increasing inability "to keep the peace and to serve as a forum for negotiations," and he recommended measures to strengthen the organization.

Examples of U.N. ineffectiveness were numerous in 1982, most notably the wars in the Falkland Islands and Lebanon. Despite intense peace efforts by Pérez de Cuéllar, who negotiated with the full backing of the Security Council, Britain and Argentina went to war over the sovereignty of the Falklands. The U.N. Security Council made repeated and unanimous calls for Israeli withdrawal and for a cease-fire in Lebanon, but these demands were defied. (Falkland Islands, p. 283; Lebanon, p. 741)

Pérez de Cuéllar listed other examples of the United Nations' inability to stave off conflicts. The Soviet Union refused to withdraw its troops from Afghanistan, Vietnamese forces remained in Kampuchea (Cambodia), Iraq and Iran waged war and turbulence continued in various Central American countries.

The erosion of U.N. authority must be reversed, Pérez de Cuéllar warned, "before once again we bring upon ourselves a global catastrophe and find ourselves without institutions effective enough to prevent it." He contended that the United Nations' most urgent goal was "to reconstruct the Charter concept of collective action for peace and security." Otherwise, the growing sense of global insecurity would lead governments to continue their arms buildup and would increase the likelihood of conflicts.

Many of Pérez de Cuéllar's recommendations for strengthening the United Nations dealt with the working relations between permanent members of the Security Council, the primary U.N. organ concerned with maintaining international peace and security. Existing differences between countries, which often stymied the council's efforts in recent years, must be left out of council discussions and decisions, Pérez de Cuéllar admonished. He stated that the Security Council must act before crises erupt and not wait for formal complaints to be brought. In this regard, Pérez de Cuéllar intended to use his office for systematic fact finding in areas of potential conflict. The council must act more swiftly and decisively than often has been the case, the secretary-general stated. Once a resolution has been passed, he continued, member nations must be prepared to "follow it up with appropriate support and action."

Pérez de Cuéllar's report was termed "true and accurate" by Jeane J. Kirkpatrick, the U.S. ambassador to the United Nations. The secretary-general himself stated on December 31 that the report was his greatest achievement of his first year in his post.

Pérez de Cuéllar, a Peruvian lawyer and career diplomat, began his five-year term as secretary-general on January 1, 1982, succeeding Kurt Waldheim. After joining the Peruvian diplomatic service in the 1940s, Pérez de Cuéllar served as Peru's ambassador to Venezuela, the Soviet Union, Poland and Switzerland. In his long career at the United Nations, he served as a member of the Peruvian delegation to the first session of the General Assembly in 1946. In 1971 he was appointed Peru's permanent U.N. representative and most recently had served as under secretary-general for special political affairs and special representative on the Afghan situation.

> *Following are excerpts from Javier Pérez de Cuéllar's first annual report on the work of the United Nations, issued September 7, 1982. (Boldface headings in brackets have been added by Congressional Quarterly to highlight the organization of the text.):*

The past year has seen an alarming succession of international crises as well as stalemates on a number of fundamental international issues. The United Nations itself has been unable to play as effective and decisive a role as the Charter certainly envisaged for it. Therefore, in this, my first annual report to the General Assembly, I shall depart from the usual practice of surveying the broad range of the work of the United Nations; instead I shall focus on the central problem of the Organization's capacity to keep the peace and to serve as a forum for negotiations. I shall try to analyse its evident difficulties in doing so, difficulties related to conflicts between national aims and Charter goals and to the current tendency to resort to confrontation, violence and even war in pursuit of what are perceived as vital interests, claims or aspirations. The general international divisions and disorder which have characterized the past year have unquestionably made it even more difficult than usual for the Organization to be, as it was intended to be, a centre for harmonizing the actions of nations in the attainment of common ends.

The problems faced by the United Nations in fulfilling its mission derive in large measure from the difficulties which Governments appear to have in coming to terms, both within and outside the Organization, with the harsh realities of the time in which we live. This question is, of course, highly relevant to the use, misuse or non-use of the United Nations as an instrument for peace and rational change.

I am of the view that we now have potentially better means to solve many of the major problems facing humanity than ever before. For this reason I retain, in the last analysis, a sense of optimism. This basic optimism, however, is tempered by our apparent inability to make adequate use of these means. Instead we sometimes appear still to be in the grip of the dead hand of a less fortunate past. As a result we often lack the vision to differentiate between short-term advantage and long-term progress, between politically expedient positions and the indispensable objective of creating a civilized and peaceful world order. While such attitudes do not affect the validity of the ideas of the Charter, they seriously impair the proper utilization of the machinery of the United Nations for the purposes for which it was set up.

We live today in the presence of a chilling and unprecedented phenomenon. At the peak of world power there exist enough nuclear weapons to destroy life on our planet. It seems evident that nothing worthwhile would survive such a holocaust, and this fact, above all else, contains the nuclear confrontation — for the time being at least.

In the middle level of world power there exist vast quantities of sophisticated, so-called conventional weapons. Indeed we have seen some of them in devastating action this very year. These weapons are, by comparison with those of former times, immensely destructive, and they are actually being used. They are also the objects of a highly profitable international trade.

At yet another level we have the poverty of a vast proportion of the world's population — a deprivation inexplicable in terms either of available resources or of the money and ingenuity spent on armaments and war. We have unsolved but soluble problems of economic relations, trade, distribution of resources and technology. We have many ideas and plans as to how to meet the growing needs of the large mass of humanity, but somehow such human considerations seem to take second place to the technology and funding of violence and war in the name of national security.

It is for these reasons that our peoples, especially the young, take to the streets in their hundreds of thousands in many parts of the world to proclaim their peaceful protest against the existing situation and their deep fear of the consequences of the arms race and nuclear catastrophe. Who can say that these gentle protesters are wrong or misguided? On the contrary, they recall us to the standards and the duties which we set ourselves in the Charter of the United Nations. The States Members of this Organization should not ignore the significance of what they are trying to say.

[Role of the United Nations]

What in reality is the role and the capacity of the United Nations in such a world? Our Charter was born of six years of global agony and destruction. I sometimes feel that we now take the Charter far less seriously than did its authors, living as they did in the wake of a world tragedy. I believe therefore that an important first step would be a conscious recommitment by Governments to the Charter.

Certainly we have strayed far from the Charter in recent years. Governments that believe they can win an international objective by force are often quite ready to do so, and domestic opinion not infrequently applauds such a course. The Security Council, the primary organ of the United Nations for the maintenance of international peace and security, all too often finds itself unable to take decisive action to resolve international conflicts and its resolutions are increasingly defied or ignored by those that feel themselves strong enough to do so. Too frequently the Council seems powerless to generate the support and influence to ensure that its decisions are respected, even when these are taken unanimously. Thus the process of peaceful settlement of disputes prescribed in the Charter is often brushed aside. Sterner measures for world peace were envisaged in Chapter VII of the Charter, which was conceived as a key element of the United Nations system of collective security, but the prospect of realizing such measures is now deemed almost impossible in our divided international community. We are perilously near to a new international anarchy.

I believe that we are at present embarked on an exceedingly dangerous course, one symptom of which is the crisis in the multilateral approach in international affairs and the concomitant erosion of the authority and status of world and regional intergovernmental institutions. Above all, this trend has adversely affected the United Nations, the instrument that was created specifically to prevent such a self-destructive course. Such a trend must be reversed before once again we bring upon ourselves a global catastrophe and find ourselves without institutions effective enough to prevent it.

[Failure to Prevent Wars]

While I do not propose here to review in detail specific situations and developments, it is, of course, my deep concern about them which leads me to examine the underlying deficiencies of our present system. The tragedy of Lebanon and the imperative need to resolve the problem of the Middle East in all its aspects, including the legitimate rights of the Palestinians and the security of all States in the region; the war between Iran and Iraq; the political situation relating to Afghanistan; the prevailing convulsion of Central America; questions relating to Kampuchea; painful efforts to reach a settlement in Cyprus; the situation in Western Sahara and in the Horn of Africa — these and other potential conflict situations, although often differing widely in their nature, should all be responsive to a respected international system for the peaceful settlement of disputes. Even in the sudden crisis over the Falkland/Malvinas Islands, despite the intensive negotiations which I conducted with the full support and encouragement of the Security Council and which endeavoured to narrow the differences between the parties, it nevertheless proved impossible in the end to stave off the major conflict.

Yet in all of these cases, all of the parties would have gained immeasurably in the long run from the effectiveness of a system for the peaceful settlement of disputes. In the case of Namibia we now see some signs of the possibility of a solution after many setbacks. Let us hope that this will prove a welcome exception to the general rule. But the lesson is clear — something must be done, and urgently, to strengthen our international institutions and to adopt new and imaginative approaches to the prevention and resolution of conflicts. Failure to do so will exacerbate precisely that sense of insecurity which, recently, cast its shadow over the second special session of the General Assembly devoted to disarmament. Despite present difficulties, it is imperative for the United Nations to dispel that sense of insecurity through joint and agreed action in the field of disarmament, especially nuclear disarmament....

[Need for Collective Security]

It seems to me that our most urgent goal is to reconstruct the Charter concept of collective action for peace and security so as to render the United Nations more capable of carrying out its primary function. It was the lack of an effective system of collective security through the League of Nations that, among other factors, led to the Second World War. Although we now face a vastly changed world situation, Governments in fact need more than ever a workable system of collective security in which they can have real confidence. Without such a system, Governments will feel it necessary to arm themselves beyond their means for their own security, thereby increasing the general insecurity. Without such a system, the world community will remain powerless to deal with military adventures which threaten the very fabric of international peace, and the danger of the widening and escalation of local conflicts will be correspondingly greater. Without such a system there will be no reliable defence or shelter for the small and weak. And without such a system all of our efforts on the economic and social side, which also need their own collective impetus, may well falter.

There are many ways in which Governments could actively assist in strengthening the system prescribed in the Charter. More systematic, less last-minute use of the Security Council would be one means. If the Council were to keep an active watch on dangerous situations and, if necessary, initiate discussions with the parties before they reach the point of crisis, it might often be possible to defuse them at an early stage before they degenerate into violence.

Unfortunately there has been a tendency to avoid bringing critical problems to the Security Council, or to do so too late for the Council to have any serious influence on their development. It is essential to reverse this trend if the Council is to play its role as the primary world authority for international peace and security. I do not believe that it is necessarily wise or responsible of the Council to leave such matters to the judgement of the conflicting parties to the point where the Council's irrelevance to some ongoing wars becomes a matter of comment by world public opinion.

In recent years the Security Council has resorted increasingly to the valuable process of informal consultations. However there is sometimes a risk that this process may become a substitute for action by the Security Council or even an excuse for inaction. Along the same line of thought, it may be useful for the Council to give renewed consideration to reviewing and streamlining its practices and procedures with a view to acting swiftly and decisively in crises.

Adequate working relations between the permanent members of the Security Council are a *sine qua non* of the Council's effectiveness. What ever their relations may be outside the United Nations, within the Council the permanent members, which have special rights and special responsibilities under the Charter, share a sacred trust that should not go by default owing to their bilateral difficulties. When this happens, the Council and therefore the United Nations are the losers, since the system of collective security envisaged by the Charter pre-supposes, at the minimum, a working relationship among the permanent members. I appeal to the members of the Council, especially its permanent members, to reassess their obligations in that regard and to fulfil them at the high level of responsibility indicated in the Charter....

[Support for U.N. Resolutions]

There is a tendency in the United Nations for Governments to act as though the passage of a resolution absolved them from further responsibility for the subject in question. Nothing could be further from the intention of the Charter. In fact resolutions, particularly those unanimously adopted by the Security Council, should serve as a springboard for governmental support and determination and should motivate their policies outside the United Nations. This indeed is the essence of the treaty obligation which the Charter imposes on Member States. In other words the best resolution in the world will have little practical effect unless Governments of Member States follow it up with the appropriate support and action.

Very often the Secretary-General is allotted the function of following up on the implementation of a resolution. Without the continuing diplomatic and other support of Member States, the Secretary-General's efforts often have less chance of bearing fruit. Concerted diplomatic action is an essential complement to the implementation of resolutions. I believe that in reviewing one of the greatest problems of the United Nations — lack of respect for its decisions by those to whom they are addressed — new ways should be considered of bringing to bear the collective influence of the membership on the problem at hand.

The same consideration applies to good offices and negotiations of various kinds undertaken at the behest of the Security Council. Very often a Member State or group of Member States with a special relationship to those involved in such negotiations could play an extremely important reinforcing role in promoting understanding and a positive attitude.

In order to avoid the Security Council becoming involved too late in critical situations, it may well be that the Secretary-General should play a more forthright role in bringing potentially dangerous situations to the attention of the Council within the general framework of Article 99 of the Charter. My predecessors have done this on a number of occasions, but I wonder if the time has not come for a more systematic approach. Most potential conflict areas are well known. The Secretary-General has traditionally, if informally, tried to keep watch for problems likely to result in conflict and to do what he can to pre-empt them by quiet diplomacy. The Secretary-General's diplomatic means are, however, in themselves quite limited. In order to carry out effectively the preventive role foreseen for the Secretary-General under Article 99, I intend to develop a wider and more systematic capacity for fact-finding in potential conflict areas. Such efforts would naturally be undertaken in close co-ordination with the Council. Moreover, the Council itself could devise more swift and responsive procedures for sending good offices missions, military or civilian observers or a United Nations presence to areas of potential conflict. Such measures could inhibit the deterioration of conflict situations and might also be of real assistance to the parties in resolving incipient disputes by peaceful means.

[Support for Peace-keeping Operations]

Peace-keeping operations have generally been considered to be one of the most successful innovations of the United Nations, and certainly their record over the years is one of which to be proud. They have proved to be a most useful instrument of de-escalation and conflict control and have extended the influence of the Security Council into the field in a unique way. I may add that United Nations peace-keeping operations have traditionally shown an admirable degree of courage, objectivity and impartiality. This record, which is a great credit to the Organization, is sometimes overlooked in the heat of partisanship.

The limitations of peace-keeping operations are less well understood. Thus when, as happened recently, a peace-keeping operation is overrun or brushed aside, the credibility both of the United Nations and of peace-keeping operations as such is severely shaken.

It is not always realized that peace-keeping operations are the visible part of a complex framework of political and diplomatic efforts and of countervailing pressures designed to keep the peace-keeping efforts and related peace-making efforts effective. It is assumed that the Security Council itself and those Member States in a position to bring influence to bear will be able to act decisively to ensure respect for decisions of the Council. If this framework breaks down, as it did for example in Lebanon last June, there is little that a United Nations peace-keeping force can by itself do to rectify the situation. Indeed in such circumstances it tends to become the scapegoat for the developments that follow.

Peace-keeping operations can function properly only with the co-operation of the parties and on a clearly defined mandate from the Security Council. They are based on the assumption that the parties, in accepting a United Nations peace-keeping operation, commit themselves to co-operating with it. This commitment is also required by the Charter, under which all concerned have a clear obligation to abide by the decisions of the Council. United Nations peacekeeping operations are not equipped, authorized, or indeed made available, to take part in military activities other than peace-keeping. Their main strength is the will of the international community which they symbolize. Their weakness comes to light when the political assumptions on which they are based are ignored or overridden.

I recommend that Member States, especially the members of the Security Council, should again study urgently the means by which our peace-keeping operations could be strengthened. An increase in their military capacity or authority is only one possibility — a possibility which may well give rise in some circumstances to serious political and other objections. Another possibility is to underpin the authority of peace-keeping operations by guarantees, including explicit guarantees for collective or individual supportive action.

In recent months, two multinational forces were set up outside the framework of the United Nations to perform peace-keeping tasks, because of opposition to United Nations involvement either within or outside the Security Council. While understanding the circumstances which led to the establishment of these forces, I find such a trend disturbing because it demonstrates the difficulties the Security Council encounters in fulfilling its responsibilities as the primary organ for the maintenance of international peace and security in the prevailing political conditions.

[U.N. as a Negotiating Forum]

We should examine with the utmost frankness the reasons for the reluctance of parties to some conflicts to resort to the Security Council or to use the machinery of the United Nations. The fact is that the Council too often finds itself on the sidelines at a time when, according to the Charter, its possibilities should be used to the maximum. Allegations of partisanship, indecisiveness or incapacity arising from divisions among Member States are sometimes invoked to justify this side-tracking of the Council. We should take such matters with the utmost seriousness and ask ourselves what justifications, if any, there are for them and what can be done to restore the Council to the position of influence it was given in the Charter.

This last problem also applies to other organs of the United Nations and brings me to the question of the validity and utility of the United Nations as a negotiating forum. We have seen, in the case of the law of the sea for example, what remarkable results can be achieved in well-organized negotiations within the United Nations framework, even on the most complex of issues and even though there was no unanimous agreement. On the peace and security side, the Security Council has shown and continues to show that it is often capable of negotiating important basic resolutions on difficult problems. The General Assembly also has to its credit historic documents negotiated in that organ and in its subsidiary organs, not only on the political but also on the economic and social side.

But in spite of all this I am concerned that the possibilities of the United Nations, especially of the Security Council, as a negotiating forum for urgent international problems are not being sufficiently realized or used. Let us consider what is perhaps our most formidable international problem — the Middle East. It is absolutely essential that serious negotiations on the various aspects of that problem involve all the parties concerned at the earliest possible time. Far too much time has already elapsed, far too many lives and far too many opportunities have been lost, and too many *faits accomplis* have been created.

I feel that the Security Council, the only place in the world where all of the parties concerned can sit at the same table, could become a most useful forum for this absolutely essential effort. But if this is to be done, careful consideration will have to be given to what procedures, new if necessary, should be used and what rules should govern the negotiations. I do not believe that a public debate, which could well become rhetorical and confrontational, will be enough. Other means will have to be used as well if negotiations on such a complex and deeply rooted problem are to have any useful outcome. The devising of such means is certainly well within the ingenuity and capacity of concerned Member States.

A related question to which we should give more consideration concerns what are productive and what are counter-productive approaches to the different aspects of our work. Obviously, a parliamentary debate may generate rhetoric, and sometimes even a touch of acrimony. But negotiations and the resolution of urgent problems require a different approach. Debate without effective action erodes the credibility of the Organization. I feel that in the United Nations, if we wish to achieve results, we must make a more careful study of the psychological and political aspects of problems and address ourselves to our work accordingly. It is insufficient to indulge in a course of action that merely tends to strengthen extreme positions.

[Fulfilling the Charter]

The United Nations is now 37 years old. It has survived a period of unprecedented change in almost all aspects of human life. The world of 1982 is vastly different from that of 1945, and that difference is reflected in the United Nations. In other words, the Organization has had to adapt to new circumstances to a quite unexpected extent. But it is not enough for the United Nations merely to reflect change or conflict. The Organization was intended to present to the world the highest common denominator of international behaviour and, in doing so, to develop a binding sense of international community. It was to that end that Governments drafted and ratified the Charter. Amid the various perils that now threaten the orderly progress of humanity, I hope that we can rally once again to the standards of the Charter, beginning with the peaceful settlement of disputes and steadily branching out towards the other objectives of that prophetic document.

Finally let me appeal to all Governments to make a serious effort to reinforce the protective and pre-emptive ring of collective security which should be our common shelter and the most important task of the United Nations. The will to use the machinery of the Charter needs to be consciously strengthened, and all Governments must try to look beyond short-term national interests to the great possibilities of a more stable system of collective international security, as well as to the very great perils of failing to develop such a system. For these reasons I would suggest that consideration be given to the usefulness of holding a meeting of the Security Council at the highest possible level, one object of which might be to discuss in depth some of the problems I have mentioned.

Member States will, I hope, understand if I end this report on a personal note. Last year I was appointed Secretary-General of this Organization, which embodies the noblest hopes and aspirations of the peoples of the world and whose functions and aims under the Charter are certainly the highest and most important ever entrusted to an international institution. This year, time after time we have seen the Organization set aside or rebuffed, for this reason or for that, in situations in which it should, and could, have played an important and constructive role. I think this tendency is dangerous for the world community and dangerous for the future. As one who has to play a highly public role in the Organization, I cannot disguise my deep anxiety at present trends, for I am absolutely convinced that the United Nations is indispensable in a world fraught with tension and peril. Institutions such as this are not built in a day. They require constant constructive work and fidelity to the principles on which they are based.

We take the United Nations seriously when we desperately need it. I would urge that we also seriously consider the practical ways in which it should develop its capacity and be used as an essential institution in a stormy and uncertain world.

MASSACRE IN PALESTINIAN CAMPS
September 16-18, 1982

On September 16, Lebanese militiamen belonging to the Christian Phalangist Party stormed through two Palestinian refugee camps in west Beirut, beginning a massacre of hundreds of men, women and children that continued through September 18. The inhabitants of the camps had been left without protection following the withdrawal of Palestine Liberation Organization (PLO) troops from Beirut at the close of the summer-long war in Lebanon. (PLO surrender, p. 741)

International outrage followed the massacre, and public attention focused on Israel's role. Israeli troops had surrounded the camps, and the Israeli government had given the militiamen permission to enter the areas. In the face of growing international and domestic pressure, the government of Prime Minister Menachem Begin requested an investigation into Israel's role. On October 11 an independent commission began its inquiry.

Background

On September 14 President-elect Bashir Gemayel of Lebanon was killed when a bomb hit the headquarters of his Christian Phalangist Party in east Beirut. No one claimed responsibility for the bombing, which many feared would trigger a new outbreak of violence between Gemayel's forces and Moslem militiamen. Gemayel had been elected president on August 23 amid controversy. Israel supported his election, but opponents (including Moslems and some Christian groups) de-

nounced him as a ruthless, ambitious militia commander and criticized his alliance with the Israelis.

Gemayel's assassination and the subsequent fears of new civil strife prompted Israeli forces to move into west Beirut on September 15. The United States and others called for the Israeli troops to withdraw. But Israel, fearing the reorganization of the PLO and leftist Moslem militias, refused to withdraw until the Lebanese army was strong enough to take control.

Massacre

On September 15 Israeli armor surrounded the Palestinian camps of Sabra and Shatila in west Beirut. Palestinian guerrillas who had escaped evacuation were thought to be hiding in the camps. Israeli troops permitted the Phalangist militiamen to enter the camps September 16 to root out the terrorists. Inside the camps, however, the Phalangists began mass killings of civilians. By the time the massacre had ended two days later, more than 300 people were believed dead, and 900 were reported missing.

Reporters first entered the camps September 18, and their descriptions shocked the world. "Houses had been dynamited and bulldozed into rubble, often with their inhabitants still inside. Groups of bodies lay like mannequins dropped from the sky before bullet-pocked walls where they appeared to have been executed. Others were draped in alleys and streets, apparently shot as they tried to escape," wrote a Washington Post *reporter.*

Israeli Inquiry

As details of the massacre emerged, attention focused on Israel's role in the attack. Israel had suffered a loss of domestic and international esteem after its invasion of Lebanon earlier in the year. Questions regarding Israel's involvement in the massacre brought strained U.S.-Israeli relations to a new low. Demands for an investigation came from American groups, international organizations and the Israeli public.

Begin initially rejected any inquiry because it would be seen as an admission of guilt. Israel, he maintained, was blameless, and allegations of Israeli involvement were a "blood libel." On September 22 Defense Minister Ariel Sharon made a speech to the Knesset, Israel's parliament, defending the army's moves in Beirut.

But Israeli citizens, shocked and shaken by the massacre, September 25 staged the largest rally in Israel's history. Hundreds of thousands of Israelis gathered in Tel Aviv to protest Begin's refusal to hold an inquiry. The prime minister bowed to the mounting pressure and on September 29 formally requested an independent investigation.

On October 11 a three-member commission began its inquiry. Yitzhak Kahan, the chief justice of Israel's Supreme Court, headed the panel. The other two members were Maj. Gen. Yona Efrat, a retired career officer, and Aharon Barak, a Supreme Court justice and former attorney general who had participated in the 1978 Camp David peace agreements. The commission had full subpoena power to investigate all aspects of the massacre, but no judicial authority.

Testimony of Sharon and Begin

Sharon and Begin testified on October 25 and November 8, respectively. Sharon admitted expecting some civilian casualties after the Phalangists entered the camps, but he stated, "[N]one of us foresaw the atrocities that occurred. . . . We were surprised, shocked and disgusted by the massacre." Like Sharon, Begin had foreseen no such horrors. "It did not even occur to me . . . to think that the Phalangists, if they were to enter the camps to fight the terrorists, would commit such atrocities or massacre," he testified. Other officers questioned by the commission, however, admitted they had thought a massacre possible, given the history of Palestinian-Phalangist enmity and the likelihood of retribution for Gemayel's death.

On November 24 the commission warned Begin, Sharon and seven other Israeli leaders that they might "be harmed" by its finding. Through negligence "tantamount to nonfulfillment of a duty," the commission stated, Israel might have abetted the Phalangists. Sharon resigned as defense minister February 11, 1983, but remained in the Cabinet as minister without portfolio.

The investigation continued through 1982, and the commission issued a final report February 8, 1983.

> *Following are the text of a statement by President Ronald Reagan on the massacre of Palestinian residents of refugee camps, delivered September 18, 1982; excerpts from an address by Defense Minister Ariel Sharon to the Knesset, September 22, as translated by* The New York Times; *the text of the announcement of the establishment of the Judicial Commission of Inquiry, released September 29; excerpts from Sharon's October 25 testimony before the commission, as translated by the* Times; *and excerpts from Prime Minister Menachem Begin's testimony November 8, as translated by the* Times. *(Boldface headings in brackets have been added by Congressional Quarterly to highlight the organization of the texts.):*

REAGAN STATEMENT

I was horrified to learn this morning of the killing of Palestinians which has taken place in Beirut. All people of decency must share our outrage and revulsion over the murders, which included women and children. I express my deepest regrets and condolences to the families of the victims and the broader Palestinian community.

During the negotiations leading to the PLO [Palestinian Liberation Organization] withdrawal from Beirut, we were assured that Israeli forces would not enter West Beirut. We also understood that following withdrawal, Lebanese Army units would establish control over the city. They were thwarted in this effort by the Israeli occupation that took place beginning on Wednesday. We strongly opposed Israel's move into West Beirut following the assassination of President-elect Gemayel, both because we believed it wrong in principle and for fear that it would provoke further fighting. Israel, by yesterday in military control of Beirut, claimed that its moves would prevent the kind of tragedy which has now occurred.

We have today summoned the Israeli Ambassador to demand that the Israeli Government immediately withdraw its forces from West Beirut to the positions occupied on September 14. We also expect Israel thereafter to commence serious negotiations which will, first, lead to the earliest possible disengagement of Israeli forces from Beirut and, second, to an agreed framework for the early withdrawal of all foreign forces from Lebanon.

Despite and because of the additional bloody trauma which adds to Lebanon's agonies, we urge the Lebanese to unite quickly in support of their government and their constitutional processes and to work for the future they so richly deserve. We will be with them.

This terrible tragedy underscores the desperate need for a true peace in the Middle East, one which takes full account of the needs of the Palestinian people. The initiative I announced on September 1 will be pursued vigorously in order to achieve that goal.

SHARON ADDRESS TO KNESSET

This is a dark day for all of us. Innocent people, old men, women and children were murdered for no crime in Beirut. In the cruelest possible way. . . .

The human mind cannot accept that such would be the fate of innocent people. How is it possible to explain something for which there can be no explanation, no forgiving and no pardon? I did not come to explain this terrible tragedy, because it is part of a nether world, not ours, but of those who perpetrated this slaughter. I hope they get their just punishment, although this is not under our control.

I came here to report on the matters for which we are responsible, and only on these will I speak. They have no connection whatsoever, in any shape or form, with the criminal acts of murder. For we are not at war with the Palestinian people.

We have declared a war of destruction on Palestinian terror. And if there are those indirectly responsible for these acts of murder — those directly responsible are Lebanese — then those indirectly responsible belong to the P.L.O. terror organization. Therefore, I can say clearly and immediately that no soldier and no commander in the Israel Defense Forces participated in this terrible act. The hands of the I.D.F. are clean. The purity of arms was preserved even there, just as it was throughout the war.

When we agreed to the entry of the Phalangists to the refugee camps, senior commanders distinctly told them, and I quote, that a military force would be allowed into the Shatila camp to seek out and destroy terrorists. In the coordinating meetings, it was stressed that the action was to be against terrorists and not to harm the civilian population, and especially women, children and the elderly, endquote.

[Interrogation of Commanders]

The moment a question arose as to what was happening in the camps, which we recognized as centers of terrorism in West Beirut, the chief of the northern command took immediate steps to halt the action of the Phalangists in Shatila by immediately contacting a liaison officer of the Phalangists who was at our regional headquarters. We have to remember that the Phalangists are not the I.D.F. Their units and their men are not under our command.

And they do not have to report to us. In this sad affair, our senior officer at the scene stubbornly asked the Phalangists for details and asked once again and again for reports from the Phalangist officers: "What did your men say? What did your men do?" We spared no effort. The northern commander, the Chief of Staff and I myself went up there in order to interrogate their commanders, in order to understand and to know that, when and why this tragedy occurred. But these people refuse to this very day to talk. They are not even willing to admit to the act. We ourselves were forced to try — and are still checking and trying to find out — why they did this in violation of their commitment given to us, in violation of our demand....

[Reaction to Acts of Terror]

We are ready to be investigated on everything. There is no problem, but all this is an injustice to the Israel Defense Forces, which are in our charge....

... Our Government, like all our people, is sensitive to acts of terror, more so than any other government or any other people in the world.

The I.D.F., its soldiers and commanders, have been performing for three months a wonderful operation in Lebanon, which has brought and will bring great security gains. Every movement of our soldiers was known to us and was reported immediately. That is the tragedy of the camps. We did not know exactly what was taking place. . . .

There were rumors, partial reports. And when the picture became clear, when we saw the enormity of the tragedy, it was too late, too late to do anything, although we intervened at the rise of the first suspicions. . . .

I am going to read to you from an official document of ours, and I want to stress that as soon as I learned of the outrage, I asked for the preparation of official reports on what occurred. And to the extent that it was possible to obtain testimony as to what took place. Therefore I want to report to you what happened from our standpoint, according to an official military report. I will read the portions that touch on our discussion.

First, the Phalangists entered the refugee camp of Shatila on the night of the 16th of September 1982, and their activities were halted by the I.D.F. on the 17th in the afternoon, after rumors reach us as to what was occurring in the camp. The area was completely evacuated by Saturday the 18th of September in the hours before noon.

Secondly, in the wake of the murder of Bashir Gemayel, a decision was taken that the I.D.F. should gain control of key areas in West Beirut.

The decision was that the northern command should get control of key areas in the western part of the city. This decision was taken on the 15th of September at 12:30 A.M.

Thirdly, this operation was carried out from the 15th of September 1982 beginning with the afternoon hours, starting at 5:00 P.M., and ended on Thursday in the afternoon, with the emphasis being on not hurting civilian residents and their property. And indeed, there were almost no civilian casualties or damage to their property.

Fourth, in a decision reached by the command, it was forbidden absolutely to go into the refugee camps. Search and destroy missions will be carried out by the Phalangists or the Army of Lebanon.

Fifth, on the 15th of September, after the murder of Bashir Gemayel, at 3:30 P.M., a meeting was carried out with the Phalangist command in which the Chief of Staff and northern commander participated, and during which we discussed the operations of the Phalangists and the entry of the I.D.F. into the western part of the city.

And we spoke in principle of their dealing with the camps.

Sixth, on Wednesday the 15th, in the afternoon hours, we received an absolutely negative response from the army of Lebanon in response to our request that the army of Lebanon enter the camps.

Seventh, on Wednesday the 15th in the evening hours, the northern commander met with the commander of the Phalangists and with Col. Michel On, the head of the Lebanese Army units in Beirut, in which the northern commander pressed the Lebanese colonel to persuade the political echelons in the Lebanese Government to approve the entry of the army of Lebanon into the camps.

Eight. After checking, the Lebanese officer claimed that it was impossible and that in a meeting [with] the Prime Minister of Lebanon he was told that he was under orders to open fire on Israeli soldiers entering west Beirut, and he was threatened with a court martial.

[Entry of Phalangists]

Nine. Once again on Thursday the 16th of September, the army of Lebanon passed a negative response to the possibility that the army of Lebanon would go into the camps.

Ten. On the 16th of September in the afternoon, a meeting was held between the northern commander and the commander of the Phalangists with regard to several matters, and on the same day in the afternoon a meeting was held between the division commander in the area and the representative of the Phalangists to coordinate the entry of the Phalangists into the camp of Shatila.

Eleven. The agreement was that the Phalangists would enter the camp from the south and the west to search out terrorist nests. In the coordinating meeting it was stressed that the operation was against terrorists, and that it was forbidden to harm the civilian population, especially women, children and the elderly.

Twelve. On the night of the 16th of September, a force of the Phalangists entered Shatila camp. As per their request they got at a certain time flares fired from 81 millimeter mortars and flares from planes. On the 17th of September 1982, the Phalangists concentrated a force of infantry, artillery and medical personnel in order to continue the mopping-up in the camps.

[No Section Thirteen included.]

Fourteen. The I.D.F. prevented the entry of this force as part of the operation in the camps.

Fifteen. On Friday the 17th around noon — actually around 11 A.M. — the division commander met with the northern commander. The division commander raised suspicions concerning the method of operation of the Phalangists. Even then it was not known what was going on in Shatila camp. The northern commander ordered the immediate halt of the Phalangists activities, by means of the Phalangist liaison officer at the headquarters.

Sixteen. On Friday the 17th at 4:30 P.M., a meeting was held with the Phalangist staff and the Chief of Staff and the northern commander, in which it was agreed that all the Phalangists would leave the refugee camps on Saturday morning, the 18th of September. It was also agreed that no further forces would enter the camps. At this meeting as well, the events in Shatila camp were still not known.

Seventeen. On Friday the 17th of September in the evening, an official announcement was received from the army of Lebanon after a meeting of the Lebanese Government that the army of Lebanon would not go into the camps.

Eighteen. On the 18th of September in the morning, the Phalangist forces left the areas of the refugee camps. And then news began to arrive about the events in the Shatila camp. As a result of this, the northern commander ordered that the I.D.F. enter the camp of Fakhani.

[What the I.D.F. Knew]

And on Sunday the 19th in the morning, into the Sabra camp as well, in order to protect the population and put them at ease, the population which greeted the I.D.F. warmly. Likewise, the northern commander ordered not to go into Shatila camp so that the I.D.F. would not be linked to the events that occurred there. Then, we still did not know who would link the I.D.F. to these events. We never thought that you [the Labor opposition] would be the ones doing the linking.

This sounds to you, and rightfully, like a laconic and dry report, but this is what the I.D.F. knew and did.

I do not come here today to claim that some person or another did not see more, did not hear more than is written in this report. But this was the picture that crystallized in the headquarters of the northern command and in the general staff headquarters. We should always remember that it was not we who entered Shatila camp, but the Phalangists.

In the neighborhoods of Shatila, Sabra and Fakhani, neighborhoods which we call camps, one has to remember that we are talking about urban neighborhoods which contain thousands of buildings. We are talking about thousands of buildings in these neighborhoods, from one story up to 12 stories. It is a built-up, crowded area. It is not a camp in the usual sense of your being able to look in from the outside and see what's going on inside. It is a crowded and built-up area. One has to understand that the operation I described was executed against the background of broad operations carried out by us in West Beirut. After the murder of Gemayel, there was talk of increased preparedness on the part of the the terrorists who suspected an Israeli response in the wake of the murder. I quote here from an authorized [P.L.O.] report from the 15th of September, 12 noon.

In this report, the terrorists speak of the advance of our forces and the fighting along the main arteries of West Beirut. In this context it was reported that not only the terrorists were fighting against the I.D.F., but that at that point the leftist forces were refraining from participating in the fighting. From another I.D.F. report on Sept. 16 at five in the afternoon, that that very day the surrounding of West Beirut was completed, and that the I.D.F. controlled the key areas within it. With the completion of the encirclement, the report continues, the warfare centered in pockets of resistance in parts of the city that were not yet cleaned out: Fakhani, Sabra, Shatila and Hamra.

On Friday the 17th at 11 A.M. — and again I quote from an authorized report — the cleaning out of terrorist nests was continuing in West Beirut. According to reports, the fighting centered in Corniche Mazraa, Talaat al-

Hiraat, the sport stadium and Fakhani. I have been quoting until now from reports that show that in these areas there were still terrorists. And the question is raised why didn't we send in I.D.F. forces? We didn't send I.D.F. forces there because we wanted to save lives. And this objective of saving lives is something every one of us should remember. Therefore, we did not send in I.D.F. soliders when somebody else could carry out this operation.

[Why Decision Was Made]

I now quote from another report from Saturday the 18th, the first day of Rosh ha-Shanah, in which it is stated, "In line with the control of our forces over the northern parts of the city, the Phalangists carried out yesterday" — in other words, the 17th — "search and destroy missions in the neighborhoods of Sabra and Shatila. There it was reported that there were 120 dead." We can see from this that our allowing the Phalangists to enter Shatila came against the background of a presence of many terrorists in the neighborhoods of West Beirut, including Shatila, who fought our soldiers. This decision was made in order to prevent losses among our soldiers.

And didn't you cry out on this point all the time? These neighborhoods — Shatila, Sabra, Fakhani — into which the Phalangists were prepared to enter — were considered strongholds of the terrorists during all the months of the siege of Beirut.

We did not imagine in our worst dreams that the Phalangists would act thus, as they entered the battle at this time of the war. They looked like a regular army in all respects. They promised to fight only against the terrorists. We had a good experience with them in the past, when during the siege of Beirut, they conquered, the Faculty of Sciences, the neighborhood of Reihan, and Jamhour. In addition, they were active in policing the road blocks between the two parts of the city. And they carried out their operations with efficiency. We passed along to them responsibility over various areas which we conquered, and they generally performed — and I emphasize generally, because there were a few mishaps — in good fashion, except for a few small exceptions.

We consented to the entry of the Phalangists in order to save the lives of our soliders, although we never imagined in our worst dreams that these same Phalangists would do the worst thing possible, it is possible that you will come and say that this was an error in judgment in estimating the situation. But I do not say that....

ESTABLISHMENT OF COMMISSION

On Sept. 21, 1982, the Cabinet decided that it would hold a discussion on the manner whereby to conduct an appropriate examination into the facts concerning the atrocities perpetrated by a unit of the Lebanese forces in

Beirut and that it would announce its decision. The Minister of Justice announced in the Knesset, on behalf of the Government, that a decision would be taken in the very near future. On Friday, Sept. 24, 1982, the Cabinet unanimously decided to ask the Chief Justice of the Supreme Court to examine the facts relating to that atrocity.

The Government is convinced that in applying this authority, it was adopting the appropriate means for an absolutely objective investigation to be conducted as speedily as possible of the tragic episode.

The Chief Justice, however, explained to the Minister of Justice that he was not able to consider the Government's request since before the Supreme Court, sitting as the High Court of Justice, were two petitions on this matter awaiting decision, and the issue might be considered *sub judice*. The judicial procedures regarding these positions would take several weeks at least.

To put an end to the baseless libel, alleging that the Government of Israel has something to hide or that it seems to evade a full investigation, the Cabinet decided today on the establishment of an inquiry commission in accordance with the Inquiries Commissions Act of 1969.

The matter to be the subject of the inquiry is all the facts and factors relating to the atrocity perpetrated by a unit of the Lebanese forces against the civilian population in the Shatila and Sabra camps.

The Prime Minister will tomorrow inform the Chief Justice of the establishment of the commission.

SHARON TESTIMONY

. . . **Sharon:** Our aim was one: to root out the remainder of the terrorists and their bases before the situation was reversed. Once again, we did on every level everything humanly possible to refrain from harming civilians. I.D.F. soldiers and commanders, who fought beginning on Sept. 15 in West Beirut and paid for this in blood, behaved according to the strictest ethics of warfare. None of them, just like none of us, ever imagined in his worst dream the disgusting dramas that were revealed to us in Sabra and Shatila.

I want to say in my name and in the name of the entire defense establishment that none of us foresaw the atrocities that occurred in the neighborhoods of Sabra and Shatila, nor could we have foreseen them. Not only are they opposed to the values that we teach and were taught, but they also are opposed to the interests of the state of Israel in every sphere: educational, social, military, national and political. We were surprised, shocked and disgusted by the massacre that occurred in those neighborhoods of Beirut. Foreign elements are the ones that committed this act, which doesn't have a place in the world of cultured people.

I saw the reserve contingent of the Lebanese forces on the 15th of September in the morning, when I visited Beirut. They mobilized the contingent that same day. And I must say to this committee that they appeared to be units that were organized and disciplined. . . .

Barak: In the framework of your evaluations, beforehand you spoke of the possibility that the terrorists would pick up their arms again and would fortify their military forces. Were there any additional considerations beyond the military considerations for the fortifications of the terrorists. Was there a consideration of harm to civilian population by Christians?

Sharon: The Christians of Lebanon, the Lebanese forces, are not a gang of hotheads. Presently, it's a very balanced establishment. . . . It is not an establishment that acts according to emotion. It is a standing establishment which has central control, including, and I stress this, a very blatant patriarchal establishment. And the head of this pyramid stands Pierre Gemayel, an interesting personality in himself.

[Issue of Revenge]

Barak: Is that to say that revenge as a result of Bashir's death was not a relevant consideration?

Sharon: I would like to say a word with the permission of the members of the committee on the subject of revenge, as I know it among the Arabs. Revenge as acceptable among Arabs does not include children, women and the elderly. There are certainly Arabists who are more expert than myself, yes, I say this even in light of my experience. Revenge exists, without any doubt. . . . Amin [Gemayel] himself, to the best of my memory, at the funeral on Sept. 15, used the word revenge. The word revenge also appeared, I would say, in discussions that we had. The word revenge also appeared there. . . .

Kahan: Well, what is meant, of course, is not killing civilians in the course of battle, but rather their intentional killing.

Sharon: Yes, and I would like to add, I don't think that anyone thought that the Lebanese forces would act as we would. . . . The I.D.F. has its own ethics of warfare. Between this and the massacres and atrocities there is a great distance. Concerning the massacres and atrocities such as the ones that were revealed to our eyes later, we never conceived of this, and none of the participants in the various discussions ever conceived of this. Nobody spoke, nobody warned. And I begin with myself, yes. I did not imagine that this is what would happen. It never entered my mind. None of those present on that day, the 15th of the month, during our discussion at the command post of the brigade, where the Chief of Staff reported to me his summary on the matter of the Lebanese forces, and I approved this because this was an acceptable thing, it was a clear thing, it was something that we had strived for all along. During the discussion that I had with the commanders of the Lebanese forces that morning, which was in the presence of all those concerned — I will detail later on exactly what took place in the discussion the 16th of the month. . . .

[News of the Massacre]

Kahan: When did you first hear that something had happened, something unusual had happened in Beirut in the Sabra and Shatila camps?

Sharon: On the eve of Rosh ha-Shanah.

Kahan: That means on the 17th of the month.

Sharon: On the 17th of the month, on the eve of Rosh ha-Shanah, I would say between 8:30 and 9, close to 9, I estimate close to 9.

Barak: In the morning, or in the evening?

Sharon: In the evening. The Chief of Staff called me. It was close to 9 in the evening.

Kahan: And you were where?

Sharon: I was in my home.... The Chief of Staff called me from his home and told me that he had returned from Beirut. He had just returned from Beirut, and he told me that in the course of the operation of the Phalangists in the camps, the Christians had harmed the civilian population beyond what was expected.

I remember that the Chief of Staff used the expression, "They exaggerated" — the Lebanese forces, the forces exaggerated. And he added that during the afternoon the operation was halted by the head of northern command. He added that he flew to Beirut and met with the head of northern command, with army commanders, the commanders of Lebanese forces, and in his words there were three focal points. One, we halted all action. Two, we prevented the entry of additional forces.

Three, we ordered the Phalangists to take out their forces from the terrorists' neighborhoods, the Phalangists organized for the exit. They would complete their exit by 5 in the morning. From the words of the Chief of Staff, then, it was completely clear to me, and this too was mentioned, that civilians had been killed....

Kahan: And what afterward? Did you not telephone, did you not notify the Prime Minister of what the Chief of Staff had informed you that evening?

Sharon: No....

[TV Reporter's Phone Call]

Kahan: That same evening, a television reporter also called you — Ron Ben-Yishai. Yes?

Sharon: Yes.

Kahan: At what time was that, about? After these discussions?

Sharon: Yes, after these discussions. At 11:30 at night, Ron Ben-Yishai called me. It was a short conversation that continued only a few minutes. He told me that he had heard from commanders who had heard from soldiers that they saw Phalangist soldiers murdering, killing civilians in Shatila. I asked him for additional details. What I learned from these things was that he heard it at 4 in the afternoon and that he heard it, if I am not mistaken, at 8 in the evening, or something like that. I definitely asked him, and I also received a clear answer on this, I asked him, did the people who said this see this with their own eyes? He said no, the people did not see it with their own eyes, they heard it. This was repetition in my eyes. It only reinforced what I knew beforehand. It contained nothing new. . . .

Barak: . . . Was there no place, at least at this stage, at 8 in the evening, the Chief of Staff, at 11 in the evening, Ron Ben-Yishai, to take action so they couldn't remain there for the night, so that they would not do that night what they had done beforehand?

Sharon: Honored members of the commission, we are speaking of a crowded built-up area in which combat is taking place. For we did not for one moment believe that in these camps there were only civilians. There would have been no reason to send in Phalangists. It was clear that there was combat going on there. In retrospect, we also know that there were casualties among the Phalangists.

The area is an underground city of tunnels and caches and headquarters, an area which is all dangerous, an area which has minefields. I know what it would take for our forces, let us say, if we were to receive an order in the evening, to evacuate a certain area. . . . You have to gather equipment, you have to gather the wounded and then you have to take precautions at the same time, for you are in an area where combat is taking place — yes, an area where combat is taking place — yes, for that is what we saw all the time before our eyes, fighting. . . .

BEGIN TESTIMONY

. . . **Begin:** I would only like to say that back in a Cabinet meeting on the 15th of June, there was a special discussion concerning the participation of the Lebanese Army and the Lebanese Forces — the Lebanese Forces being the Phalangists — that they would occupy southwestern Beirut. We told them that the I.D.F. was fighting, was sacrificing many lives, we have an interest in liquidating the terrorists, to bring peace to the Galilee, for once and for all to solve the problem of the shellings and disruptions on the inhabitants of the Galilee, and so forth, and to destroy as well the military infrastructure of the terrorist organizations. But the Lebanese Army and the Lebanese Forces as well must do their share, especially while their capital is divided. And they must take part in the fighting in order to bring about the unification of their capital. And this was the decision of the Government, that we must appeal to the Lebanese Army and the Lebanese Forces, so that they would participate in the combat against the terrorists. . . .

Barak: Did the assassination of Bashir Gemayel not bring you to think that maybe at this stage the Phalangists should not be called into action?

Begin: It did not even occur to me, Honored Judge, to think that the Phalangists, if they were to enter the camps to fight the terrorists, would commit such atrocities or massacre. Since that same meeting of the 15th of June, they, the Phalangists conducted certain military operations, with our consent. And they gave no reasons for complaint. We saw them as disciplined, military units. And the whole intention was for them to fight the terrorists. And it did not even occur to me that there was any kind of possibility that they would deal in massacring the civilian population. Therefore the question did not even arise. . . .

Barak: But when you say "bloodshed," who would spill whose blood?

Begin: What I meant by bloodshed was acts of vengeance by Christians against Moslems. Christians in general, not only Phalangists —

Barak: But also Phalangists.

Begin: Of course. Their leader, the President-elect, was assassinated and we saw all the grieving that broke out with his assassination, and therefore I presumed there were liable to be acts of vengeance by everyone.

Barak: On the presumption that there were likely to be acts of vengeance also by the Phalangists. Their leader was assassinated. Under such circumstances, was there no room to ask whether . . . to permit the Phalangists to enter the camps?

Begin: Honored Judge, I can only repeat my previous statement, that in those days, it did not occur to any of us that the Phalangists that were brought into these two camps would not fight the terrorists. They entered in order to fight the terrorists and the terrorists only.

Efrat: Was the problem not discussed, were there no doubts raised, concerning their intentions of solving the Palestinian problem in the area of Beirut, in a certain way, of their heavy feelings toward this group, and the attempt to get rid of them?

Begin: No sir. It did not even occur to us. . . .

Efrat: When did you first learn that something not right had occurred?

Begin: I, toward evening on Saturday, I listened to the BBC.

Efrat: On Saturday, that means after the Sabbath.

Begin: It was the second day of Rosh ha-Shanah, excuse me, the first day of Rosh ha-Shanah, I heard that grave things were happening, I don't remember exactly how the wording went on Radio London, that inside the camps, and then afterward there was a sentence: and Israeli tanks were seen surrounding. Then I called the Chief of Staff and the Defense Minister and I asked what this meant. There is a malicious tendency in saying that Israeli tanks are surrounding, and inside the camps horrible things are happening. Then I was told what happened and I was also told that these things were halted and that the Phalangists were already taken out of the camps. . . .

Barak: At any stage did the intelligence community, whether it be the Mossad or army intelligence, bring to you any material from which it could have been learned that in any case, we needed to be cautious with the Phalangists, that they were likely to be dangerous? That they were likely to harm women and children?

Begin: No, sir. Such a thing was not reported to me, from either of the intelligence establishments. . . .

Efrat: . . . Was there no new basis to consider what the role of the Christians was in light of the events and the danger of vengeance, of sentiments that would be aroused as a result, and so forth? Because we are basing ourselves on a decision that was taken in a different context, it seems to me.

Begin: The decision was in connection with West Beirut, when we decided not to enter West Beirut at all. Afterward, when we decided, following the assassination of Bashir, to enter West Beirut, to capture the traffic points in order to prevent terrible things — atrocities, etc. — then at the same time there still remained in these two camps and also in Fakhani, close to 2,000, some 2,000 armed terrorists. We had to disarm them, of course, or silence them, the danger that they posed. We did not want this to be done by our soldiers. Because as far as we knew they had sacrificed enough in this fighting.

Therefore we said the Christian military units will do this, and they were asked to carry out this operation. This was the entire intention. The tragic development was something else, that's true. But it did not occur to anyone that it would happen, while our whole intention was only to fight the terrorists. . . .

▼▼▼

DETAINEES' PARENTS REPORT ON TORTURE IN SOUTH AFRICA
September 30, 1982

A lobby organization called the Detainees' Parents Support Committee (DPSC), basing its information on first-hand accounts by political prisoners, published September 30 a report that disclosed in graphic detail the extent of human rights violations in the South African security police system.

The event leading to the document's release was the apparent suicide in prison of Dr. Neil Aggett on February 5, 1982. A young white physician, Aggett had worked for the African Food and Canning Workers Union, a primarily black independent labor organization. He had been held at Johannesburg security police headquarters for two months and allegedly had been subjected to intensive interrogation. His death touched off a rampage of protests among workers and students in the Johannesburg area against the treatment of South Africa's political detainees. Protesters demanded a formal inquest.

Security police officials insisted that Aggett committed suicide, but his union countered that "no inquiry by the police or their police minister will convince our union" that he had killed himself. The inquest consisted of 10 weeks of hearings spread over more than eight months and marked by numerous delays and interruptions. On December 21, the verdict completely exonerated the police from any charges. In a statement that took six and a half hours to read, Magistrate Petrus Kotze found that the "balance of probabilities" supported police contention that Aggett had consented to the long interrogation sessions. Kotze added that it was the "moral responsibility" of Aggett's prison mates, such as Auret van Heerden who had testified at the inquest, to alert authorities of Aggett's deteriorating condition.

On September 30, about midway through the hearings, the Detainees' Parents Support Committee issued its report. Several government ministries, bar associations and international organizations received copies for distribution.

Formed in Johannesburg in September 1981, the DPSC was a group of families and friends of primarily white political prisoners interested in abolishing detention laws they thought "uncivilised." Amnesty International reported that the DPSC "quickly developed into an important pressure group campaigning for the release of individual detainees and highlighting the wider problem of detention without trial."

The document sought to increase public awareness of the mental and physical abuse inflicted on detainees, including sleep deprivation, enforced standing, humiliation, beating, electric shock torture, attacks on the genitals and suspension from poles in mid-air. Based on statements made by 70 ex-detainees, the report constituted the first real effort to collect conclusive evidence on the extent of torture practices in prison.

Security Police Practices

South Africa's legal system provided little protection for detainees. Section 22 of the General Law Amendment Act of 1966 gave the security police power to take individuals into custody without a warrant and to hold them without charges for 14 days. This period could then be extended by the police on application to a supreme court judge.

A common practice was for the security police to change the legal basis for detention after passage of the initial 14 days to Section 6 of the Terrorism Act of 1967. This provision empowered officers of the rank of lieutenant colonel or above to authorize continued detention for interrogation without charge or trial for an unlimited period. It also stipulated that detainees were to be held incommunicado.

As a result of several publicized instances of police torture, primarily that of black consciousness leader Stephen Biko in September 1977, Minister of Justice James Kruger in early 1978 appointed prison inspectors as "watchdogs" to examine detainees' conditions, question them about their treatment and prevent further abuse. In practice, this measure was considered ineffective because prison authorities often refused to make detainees available for questioning. Even when they were made available, detainees claimed, inspectors showed only little interest while listening to their complaints.

A revised internal security measure was enacted in 1982 to bring the many legal provisions pertaining to national security under one law. Section 10 of the new act retained many provisions of its predecessors, including indefinite incommunicado detention without trial. According to the DPSC, the act failed to institute certain essential safeguards, such as notification of detainees' names, access to legal counsel and visits from relatives, to prevent further cases of torture.

Human Rights in South Africa

Although its government contended that legal reforms were relaxing the system of apartheid, South Africa remained a battleground for human rights advocates throughout 1982. Blacks, who made up more than 70 percent of the population, still lacked representation in government. The U.S. State Department's annual report on human rights stated that South Africa extended "little or no cooperation" to various United Nations human rights organizations. (Human rights report, p. 107)

The State Department's report also mentioned increased restrictions that prevented journalists from reporting on many police matters. A prevailing fear among members of the news media was that possible restrictions on identifying detainees would cripple any possible monitoring of police actions. Media coverage of arrests had been considered one of the political detainees' few safeguards against virtually unlimited police power.

Following are excerpts from the Detainees' Parents Support Committee's Memorandum on Security Police Abuses of Political Detainees, *released September 30, 1982. (Boldface headings in brackets have been added by Congressional Quarterly to highlight the organization of the text.):*

Background

On 27th April 1982, a delegation representing the Detainees' Parents Support Committees [DPSC] of Johannesburg, Durban and Cape Town met the Ministers of Law and Order and of Justice and presented to them a memorandum in which it was stated that the DPSC was concerned that widespread and systematic use was being made by Security Police of assault and torture during interrogation of detainees. It went on to enumerate many of these abuses, and requested a clear statement from the Ministers as to the official constraints on interrogation procedures. The DPSC called for a Code of Conduct for interrogators and an independent system of monitoring their behaviour.

In reply the Ministers rejected the allegations and said they would deal with them in due course. A few days later, the Commissioner of Police, General Geldenhuys, issued a statement ordering an extensive investigation into the allegations, saying that those making them would be approached for statements, and be afforded an opportunity to substantiate their claims.

A week later members of the DPSC delegation were approached by a high-ranking officer of the CID [Criminal Investigation Department] who had been appointed to investigate the allegations. He also raised the possibility of a prosecution against the persons in terms of Section 27 of the Police Act if the allegations against the police could not be proved. The DPSC was requested to furnish statements to the CID so as to substantiate their claims. The DPSC was further requested to confine their allegations of improper treatment of detainees to the preceding 6 months.

The DPSC rejected the submission that any investigation should confine itself to the period from mid 1981. Firstly, many of the officers alleged to have participated in earlier incidents are still serving in the Security Police. Secondly, the DPSC can see no logical reason in drawing a distinction between alleged practices of torture in 1980 and 1981. Indeed the research and allegations reveal no marked difference between the pattern of abuses alleged to have been committed prior to July 1981 and abuse alleged to have been committed after this period. Finally, the DPSC made it clear that they would draw on all available channels of research to substantiate their claim including court judgements, inquest records and civil actions, and not merely the statements of detainees who were held during that period. The DPSC sought an assurance that the object of the investigation was the practice of torture itself and that the DPSC or individual deponents would themselves not be harrassed.

The DPSC has now submitted to the CID over 70 sets of allegations concerning abuses in one form or another by Police Officers.

It must be stated that the statements so far submitted do not represent the totality of evidence on the systematic use of torture or improper treatment of detainees. For different reasons some statements that were obtained were not relied upon. No thorough attempt was made to collect statements from convicted prisoners who have allegedly been tortured. Some former detainees for reasons ranging from fear to scepticism about the genuineness of the investigation declined to provide statements for remission to the CID. The DPSC has experienced difficulties in tracing informants to obtain permission for the use of their statements. But the research so far should be viewed only as an incomplete sample of the widespread allegations of torture perpetrated on detainees. Copies of the statements have been submitted to the Ministers of Law and Order and of Justice. It is anticipated that further statements will be submitted in due course.

Sources of Statements

The allegations have been drawn from statements by former detainees, admissions by the State itself, court proceedings and actual court judgements. The majority of the allegations deal with the recent period 1981-1982 while some date back to 1978. We have not sought to refer to the much publicised inquests and earlier trials wherein substantial evidence of assault and maltreatment emerged, e.g. the Biko inquest, the Mdludli inquest, the trial of S. v. Ndou and others.

Extent of Malpractices

The statements so far submitted confirm the concern felt by the DPSC regarding the incidence and extent of malpractices in the treatment and interrogation of detainees. While the DPSC is alive to the possibility of an inaccuracy in a particular statement submitted in good faith, the DPSC believes the statements submitted so far reveal a clear picture which as a whole cannot be ignored.

The practices, more fully categorised below, range from mere bullying or neglect to third degree brutal torture.

Furthermore, the allegations of malpractices are not confined to any particular centre. Places at which they are reported to have occurred include police stations at all the major centres in South Africa. The places most commonly cited in the most serious allegations are Protea (Soweto), Sanlam Building (Port Elizabeth), and John Vorster Square (Johannesburg). Included in the scores of Security Police named as being involved in these malpractices are at least 20 commissioned officers up to the rank of major. Some members were categorised as experts in, for example, electric shock torture.

Nine of the statements submitted so far deal with women detainees.

Only a small minority of the persons allegedly assaulted or abused were eventually convicted of any offence. The vast majority were not even charged. Of course even where persons have been convicted the use of cruel or improper treatment can never be condoned.

The DPSC has sought to exclude those statements that deal with torture perpetrated on detainees in the former homelands. However, in this memorandum it must be pointed out that this is not to be interpreted as either an indication that such practices do not occur there *or* that such practices are irrelevant. In the first place allegations of maltreatment of detainees in these territories have become increasingly common. Associated with these allegations have been further allegations of a close working relationship between the security apparatus of these territories and South African security officials. The most recent allegations concern the treatment of Reverends Phosiwe, Phaswana and Farisane in the Republic of Venda. These three priests were so badly assaulted, suffocated, and electrically shocked that they falsely "confessed" to crimes they had not committed. During the course of the investigation one Isaac Muofhe died during interrogation. The inquest magistrate found that two members of the Venda Security Police were responsible for his death as a result of an unlawful assault. The attorney-general of Venda dropped all charges against the priests despite having signed "confessions" from them. Reverend Phosiwe alleges that a white officer from South Africa had been seconded to assist in the investigation.

Nature of Alleged Malpractices

The DPSC believes that the statements submitted to date corroborate the basic pattern of maltreatment alleged by them in their first memorandum to the Minister. In this memorandum the DPSC restates its concern over possible treatment of detainees. The statements submitted to the Ministers reveal a repetition of certain types of malpractice over a wide area. The DPSC summarises the main areas of misconduct revealed in the statements hereunder and specifically draws attention to the seeming pattern of conduct.

PHYSICAL ABUSE

The statements contain numerous complaints of prolonged and intensive interrogation, sometimes by successive teams of interrogators and sometimes for a continuous period of several days. Coupled with this intensive interrogation are alleged practices designed to reduce the detainee to a state of exhaustion and compliance with the interrogators' suggestions. These include the following:

1. Deprivation of sleep in at least 20 cases, some for periods of many days and nights. In one case involving lengthy sleep deprivation the police made payment of substantial damages arising out of their treatment of the detainee culminating in her being found in a comatose condition by the district surgeon. Prolonged sleep deprivation can have serious affects on a person's mental state.

2. Deprivation of food and drink whilst being interrogated.

3. Deprivation of toilet facilities in 8 cases which in some cases led to involuntary urination and the humiliation of cleaning the interrogation room thereafter. In one instance a detainee alleges he was obliged to drag a large chain to which he had been handcuffed when going to the toilet which made access impossible.

4. Enforced standing and arduous physical exercises in over 28 cases for long periods, sometimes days and nights. The exercises included holding heavy objects above the head, standing barefoot on bricks, press-ups, running on the spot.

5. Exposure to cold in 25 cases by being kept naked for long periods sometimes several days and nights. In some cases discomfort was increased by being doused with water, made to stand in front of a fan or open window.

6. Enforced suspension is reported in 11 cases. Most of these involve a method referred to by some Security Policy as the "Helicopter", in which the detainee is handcuffed at the wrists and at the ankles, and while in a

crouching position, a pole is inserted through legs and arms. He is then suspended on the pole between a table and a chair, sometimes for hours on end, while being subjected to a barrage of questions and sometimes blows. Other cases include suspension by the arms while handcuffed. This suspension causes acute and excruciating pain.

7. In 54 cases, including 6 women, hitting with fists, slapping, kicking, beating with sticks, batons, hosepipe, gun butts and other objects, crushing of toes with chairs or bricks, dragging by hair, banging head on wall or table and throwing or pushing against a wall, are the more common forms of assault. Some of the injuries which have resulted are perforated eardrums, broken teeth, loss of sight in an eye, damaged kidneys, and bladder and permanent scarring. One Linda Mogale was found by the court to have had his teeth broken allegedly by pliers.

8. Suffocation is reported in 25 cases, mostly by hooding with a bag made of canvas or plastic. Hooding appears to have several purposes, firstly to induce near suffocation when the bag is pulled tightly around the neck, secondly to heighten the terror of the situation and thirdly to hide the identity of the interrogators or the nature of the equipment when electric shock is being applied. Other forms of suffocation include the use of a wet towel, or choking by hand or cord. In many cases the detainees are alleged to have lost consciousness.

9. Electric shock is alleged in 22 instances. Invariably the detainee is hooded or blindfolded so that he never sees the equipment used or the operator. In one case a detainee alleges he was wrapped tightly in a canvas straightjacket before being shocked. In several cases shocking took place at remote spots away from a police station. Shock torture was allegedly applied for protracted periods in several instances, sometimes resulting in loss of consciousness. In one extreme case, the victim started to experience fits as a result of damage to his nervous system. He continued to have fits for three months after his release from detention and approached the DPSC to assist him to find suitable medical attention. In one case two non Security policemen were actually charged with hooding and administering electric shocks to a man in their custody. They pleaded guilty to common assault and were fined R50. The significance of these allegations, which were obviously accepted by the State, has not received the attention they deserve. What enquiries have been made as to the source of the electrical equipment and the hoods, who trained the policemen in the use of the equipment?

Electric shocks appear to be administered by means of an apparatus which can draw power from a wall plug or a running motor car. The apparatus allows the interrogator to switch the current on and off causing the victim to scream and jerk involuntarily. Electric shocks have allegedly been administered in most of the major centres.

10. Attacks on genitals are reported in 14 cases. These include hitting, kicking and squeezing of testicles, attaching pliers to the penis and the application of electric shock to the genitals.

Psychological Abuse

Reports of psychological abuse contained in the statements fall into several categories, from the more subtle forms such as isolation, humiliation, and concern about loved ones, to the more obvious forms of intimidation and threats to life and limb.

1. *Isolation*: All detainees report being isolated in solitary confinement, as provided for by detention clauses of Security Legislation. The short term and long term effects of solitary confinement have been described by several authorities as more damaging to health than even many extreme forms of physical abuse. Detainees refer to the psychological impact of being transferred from the limited period detention of Section 22 to the indefinite detention provided by Section 6 (a situation which the SP did not fail to exploit). One detainee reports being held for 45 days before interrogation commenced; this constitutes a refined form of torture apart from being a gross violation of the purpose of detention as stated in Security Legislation.

2. *Humiliation and degradation*: Many detainees complain of actions apparently designed to humiliate, degrade and "break" them. The denial of toilet facilities, apart from physical discomfort, has a humiliating effect, especially when the detainee is no longer able to contain himself, and is then compelled to clean up the room. Verbal abuse and ridicule was reported in several cases, sometimes combined with enforced self-abuse, and generally of a personal or racial nature. The statements also include reports of denial of washing facilities and being forced to scrub the floors of the interrogation room.

3. *Intimidation*: The frequent use of highly intimidatory and aggressive situations as a prelude to direct threats or actual violence, is referred to in the statements. The most common of these is being compelled to strip naked or near naked (reported in 25 cases) as in the case of Stephen Biko, which serves to accentuate the vulnerability of the detainee, who may be held in this condition for days.

4. *Hooding*: Another commonly reported practice (19 cases) is hooding, which apart from other purposes, produces disorientation and fear of the unknown. Detainees complained in several instances of being removed from the police cells and driven to isolated spots in the bush which also created a similar condition of disorientation and extreme fear.

5. *Threat to life and limb*: Allegations of death threats to 11 detainees are contained in the statements. Apart from verbal threats, a firearm has been drawn in some cases, in one instance inserted and cocked in the detainee's mouth and in another fired next to the detainee's feet in an isolated area. One detainee alleges that an open knife was held to his throat. Threats to drop from a high building are also reported, or the simulation of being held or thrown out of a window.

In 13 statements, threats of torture and assault are reported. These include being threatened with the use of an undefined apparatus with the appearance of headphones, being burned with a lighted cigarette and being taken to the "waarkamer" (truth room).

6. *Threat to loved ones*: Threats relating to children, parents and wives and close friends are alleged in 6 statements. These include threats to kill or detain such relatives. One woman alleges she was assaulted in the presence of her baby, whilst another had her 2-1/2 year old child taken into custody with her, then forcibly removed a day later. In one case the detainee was told that her young child would be removed from her custody unless she made a statement. The use of untrue reports about the welfare of loved ones is also claimed in some instances.

7. *Indefinite detention*: Many detainees allege that their interrogators have exploited their vulnerability by emphasising that the detainee will not be released until the interrogator is satisfied with the answers. This power to detain people indefinitely is capable of gross abuse and there are cases where persons are held in isolation under security legislation for lengthy periods sometimes in excess of a year for no apparent purpose. The particular abuses which have come to the attention of the DPSC are those where

7.1. a person is questioned at the beginning of his period of detention and may then remain in detention for several months without further questioning. This is an abuse of the law.

7.2. a person is detained and not questioned at all for a lengthy period after his initial detention. This is also an abuse of the law.

7.3. prior to the 1982 Internal Security Act people were detained under Section 22 of the General Law Amendment Act when it was well known to the Security Police that there was no intention to release the detainee within the 14 days provided and that the detention would continue in terms of Section 6 of the Terrorism Act. This was done to facilitate the admission of a confession obtained during the period of 14 days. The Detainee was left with the impression that he might be released after 14 days and this created false expectations which were cruelly unfulfilled and harmful to the morale of the detainee. This was a further abuse of the law.

Health Consequences

In addition to the physical injuries brought about by assaults many detainees complain about the longer term psychiatric effects. The general health of 3 of the detainees concerned deteriorated to the point where the authorities found it necessary to hospitalize them during the course of interrogation. Five detainees had to be hospitalized on release from detention, or required medical attention. One of the detainees, Dr. Neil Aggett, died whilst in detention.

An Examination of Safeguards
CODE OF CONDUCT FOR INTERROGATORS

It is very difficult to establish whether an official code of conduct for interrogators actually exists. No response has been forthcoming from the Minister of Law and Order to this question which was posed by the DPSC in its memorandum, other than to reject allegations of assault and torture. During a Parliamentary debate in February 1982, in response to a question by Mrs Suzman, Mr Le Grange gave a "categorical assurance that inhuman and degrading methods of interrogation of detainees under Section 6 are not used by the Security Police." Later, during the debate on the Internal Security Bill, he announced an investigation into the conditions under which detainees were held and interrogated, to be conducted in consultation with the Commissioner of Police and the Director of Security Legislation, and that broad guidelines would be announced at a later stage.

The "Citizen" newspaper of 11th August 1982 reports that Mr Le Grange, during an interview with foreign reporters, had said that a small number of men had been charged with violating the standards on the treatment of prisoners (detainees), but did not say what these standards were.

The Rand Daily Mail of the same date reported that Mr Le Grange had said he was considering drawing up a voluntary (?) code of conduct for policemen involved in detentions. A week later he referred to the investigation announced in Parliament and went on to say that "what is envisaged is not a statutory code but a set of rules or directions which will be binding on all concerned and will augment the instructions already issued by the Commission of Police in regard to conditions of detention."

It is not known what standing orders or constraints regarding conduct by interrogators are in force. Prima facie the widespread malpractices alleged would indicate that if such code is in existence it is not taken seriously. Indeed such alleged instruments as hoods and electrical apparatuses seem to be conveniently available. Any 'code' that does exist does not appear to have a monitoring or enforcement procedure. A 'voluntary' code for interrogators can only be described as absurd.

"Visits"
[VISITS BY OFFICIALS]

The 1982 Internal Security Act makes provision for compulsory fortnightly visits by a magistrate, District Surgeon and the Inspector of Detainees. The allegations submitted by us indicate that procedure as it existed under previous legislation has provided an appearance of a safeguard against improper treatment of detainees, whilst failing in many instances to be an effective check. The main complaints advanced for this failure have been:

1. the identification by the detainee of the magistrate with the interrogators. This occurs particularly where the magistrate questions the detainee in the presence of the Security Police. On other occasions this is the result of the confusion in the mind of the detainee as to the difference between the branches of the state's judicial and law-enforcement agencies, or simply where the detainee does not accept that the magistrate is the person he purports to be.

2. some detainees complained that they are warned by their alleged assailants not to report any improper treatment to the magistrate on pain of further assaults or removal of privileges etc. The magistrate has no power to restrain the detainee's assailants from having unsupervised access to the detainee. Detainees have reported that they can see little benefit and substantial risk in reporting incidents of maltreatment to the magistrate.

3. some of those detainees who have reported assaults to the magistrate allege that they have indeed been subjected to intimidation and duress which has led them to retract their statements.

4. detainees have alleged that the Security Police are in a position to prevent the magistrate from visiting the detainee by informing him that the detainee concerned is away, or by physically removing him from the cells for the day.

The very same allegations concerning the visiting magistrate pertain to the Inspector of Detainees. . . .

In particular detainees who are alleged to have reported assaults to either of the officials on the condition that such complaint is not relayed to the Security Police who assaulted them have later been confronted by their alleged assailants. In the 1982 Act the Inspector is specifically required to report irregularities to the person in charge of the place where the detainee is being kept.

The District Surgeon and Health Care

There are various allegations that concern the ability of the District Surgeon to protect the detainee from maltreatment and ill health. These are:

1. allegations of cursory examination, e.g. where details of injuries are not recorded or causes inquired into.

2. allegations of detainees being visited or seen by District Surgeons irregularly or not at all. The most serious allegations concern the denial of access to further medical treatment by the police until the detainee has satisfied the police. As detainees' access to medical inspection is vetted by the Security Police they are also able to refuse a request.

3. allegations concerning the administration of medicine by the police themselves or neglect in carrying out the instructions of the District Surgeon. The capacity in law and practice for police officers to overrule the

decision of the District Surgeon on the medical treatment of a detainee is absolutely unacceptable.

4. allegations that examinations and inquiries by the District Surgeon are carried out in the presence of the Security Police.

5. allegations that detainees are warned not to reveal maltreatment to the District Surgeon, or that they are compelled to reveal to the police what transpired in the course of the examination or to retract what they had told the District Surgeon.

6. allegations that a District Surgeon has reported to the police the information he has obtained from his patient.

7. allegations that the District Surgeon attempted to assist the police rather than the detainee. For example where a District Surgeon failed to dress or disinfect 3 bullet wounds in a detainee or to hospitalise him as she felt it was better that he assist the police; or where the District Surgeon asked the police questions about the detainee's health and not the detainee, or where a District Surgeon appears to have falsely reported to the Attorney-General concerning the injuries suffered by persons assaulted.

8. it appears that the District Surgeon in some cases is the doctor who cares for the police personnel in the area and may have a professional or personal relationship with the individual interrogators or Security Policemen.

Laying Charges

There are theoretically several ways in which detainees can or have laid charges against their assailants. They may have complained to the magistrate, the Inspector of Detainees, the District Surgeon or the Station Commander of the police station in which they are being held. In those cases where the complaints have been taken up, the procedure is for the CID of the S A Police to interview the complainant. Where the victim wishes to go ahead with the complaint the CID conduct an investigation, and thereafter the docket is referred to the Attorney-General. There are extremely few cases where Security Policemen have been actually charged, and the DPSC knows of none where any have been convicted. This is revealing, given

1. the many court findings in inquests and trials in which maltreatment was found to have occurred;

2. the assumption of civil liability by the State for alleged assaults or maltreatment;

3. the sheer volume of complaints and allegations of assault on detainees.

The allegations suggested several reasons why the successful prosecution of these assaults is infrequent.

1. *The investigation of the allegations by the CID*: The investigation by the CID is hampered by many of the factors mentioned above, viz the CID

cannot protect the complainant from further assaults; the CID cannot prevent duress being applied on the complainant to withdraw the charge; the CID is associated with the Security Police in the eyes of the complainant. Allegations concerning each one of these factors has been cited in the affidavits.

The impression may be gained that there may be collusion between the CID and their Security Police colleagues, especially where they are based in the very same Police Station. In the Makhoba case the investigating officer was one of the alleged assailants on behalf of whom the State later admitted liability for assaulting the detainee. Where there is an investigation the CID are faced with the difficult task of compiling a docket on the exclusive evidence of the complainant.

2. *Absence of protection:* Because the detainee is in a vulnerable position in relation to his interrogators who may call on him or remove him at will, many of the detainees stated that they felt open to further assaults of the very kind that they wished to complain about and there are allegations that complaints have led to further assaults. Consequently the complainants have alleged that it seemed better to leave things be, rather than complain as the complaint could only worsen their position or delay their release. The only reason for pursuing a charge would be an abstract sense of personal justice. Even this reason counts for little if the complainant believes that it is extremely unlikely that the prosecution would succeed.

3. In addition to the problems faced in laying a charge the detainee faces formidable problems in adducing proof in support of his claim. He has no witnesses. His assailants may lead many witnesses to say how well he was treated, how co-operative he was, how happy he was. If he can actually produce evidence of physical injury the assailants may allege a variety of reasons as to how he acquired these, viz falling down steps, hitting his/her head against a wall.

However the preponderance of cases deal with maltreatment that would leave no physical mark, (see above — deprivation of sleep, exercises, humiliation, exhaustion, electric shocks, suffocation, deprivation of toilet or food, psychological attacks, threats of violence or death, slapping with an open hand, exposure to cold or heat, promises of release, etc.). Even where more violent assaults have allegedly been perpetrated e.g. where bruising is extensive, there is no guarantee that the victim will see a District Surgeon while such bruising is evident. And even where the District Surgeon does record such injuries, the detainee will still have to prove the cause thereof. The accused (i.e. the police) will be entitled to the benefit of the doubt where such injuries may possibly have arisen from another cause.

It is alleged that members of the Security Police openly informed detainees that they can evade conviction for assault while simultaneously bragging about the detainees they have allegedly assaulted. In many cases the detainees do not know the names of their interrogators, or when they have been hooded, who was present and what instruments were used.

In one case where a detainee's complaint led to the alleged assailants actually being charged, the policemen were acquitted, although the District Surgeon stated that she could not have obtained her injuries by inflicting them on herself. The Court effectively accepted this to be the case. Persons following this trial may interpret this case (possibly erroneously) as indicating the futility of laying charges against the Security Police. Some detainees suspect that if charges are successfully laid there may be a lack of rigour or enthusiasm in the investigation of the case.

The Minister's Response

For the above reasons we feel that the Minister's response to allegations of torture (that there has been minimal success in the reporting of assaults, and the prosecution thereof and that accordingly such maltreatment does not occur) is not sufficient to allay the concern of the DPSC that such treatment occurs.

The Minister has also alluded to the disparity between all the allegations and the number of successful civil claims. Here we refer to many of the reasons mentioned above, viz fear of further recrimination by the police felt by many detainees, the problems of adducing proof, the feeling that the Courts will not readily accept the sole evidence of a former detainee against the word of numerous police officers, absence of permanent physical scars. There are however two further reasons specifically relevant. The first is that an action against the police effectively prescribes after five months. Persons held under security legislation are incarcerated without access to their lawyers for periods frequently in excess of this period. Secondly, if they have been too frightened to complain or press charges at the time of the assault this may count against them in the civil proceedings.

Indeed the so called safe-guards against torture appear to be worse than ineffective if regard is to be had to the statements and other evidence. Magistrates' reports that a detainee did not complain of assault when visited have been used against a detainee in subsequent criminal and civil trials. However where persons did complain and their Counsel attempted to subpoena these officials to testify the officials successfully claimed privilege and refused to produce their reports. The very procedure which was supposed to protect detainees appears to operate more effectively to stifle claims of assault than it has done to prevent assaults taking place.

Conclusion and Recommendations

The DPSC has not been convinced by the Minister's denial that cruel or humiliating practices are perpetrated on detainees. Indeed the evidence reveals a clear picture of widespread systemic malpractices. The DPSC believes that it has a duty as parents and as South Africans to draw attention to these allegations of prevalent abuse of detainees.

It is of some concern that the Minister has not answered the legitimate request by the DPSC to explain what official constraints are placed on interrogators. Instead of examining the framework which places unchecked power in the hands of interrogators, instead of recognizing a problem, the Minister has chosen to foreclose any possibility of such an approach by denying outright the existence of such practices and by threatening the DPSC.

The DPSC makes it clear that it is not its primary objective to seek merely the prosecution of individuals but rather a re-examination of the whole system of unchecked power in interrogation of detainees.

The DPSC does not purport to offer elaborate or detailed recommendations. The Association of Law Societies, the Bar Council and other professional bodies have already done so. There is considerable expert evidence of protection available to detainees in other countries.

The DPSC re-iterates its opposition to the current security legislation and in particular the provisions enabling indefinite incommunicado detention without access to the courts. However so long as such legislation is in existence then the DPSC believes the following minimum rights should be accorded to a detainee:

1. access to a lawyer,
2. access to relatives,
3. access to a doctor of choice,
4. access to reading material of choice.

Furthermore there should be

1. an enforceable code setting out standards of interrogation;
2. an effective and independent machinery for enforcing and policing the treatment of detainees;
3. clinical and personal independence of the District Surgeon from the Security Police.

REPORT ON LEAKS
OF SCIENCE DATA
September 30, 1982

In a report issued September 30, a National Academy of Sciences panel concluded there had been "substantial and serious" leakage of U.S. scientific and technological data to the Soviet Union. Soviet espionage efforts accounted for most of the leaks, the panel reported; open scientific exchanges and university research had played only a small part.

Earlier in the year worries over leakage of U.S. scientific and technological information to the Soviet Union had caused a growing conflict between the scientific community and national security officials. The two groups disagreed over the need for tighter controls on scientific communications for national security reasons.

The conflict reached a peak in late August when the Defense Department blocked presentation of about 100 scientific papers at an international symposium sponsored by the Society of Photo-Optical Instrumentation Engineers. The move disrupted the conference by suddenly removing almost one of every six papers on the schedule.

Defense officials believed that information in the banned papers, including such topics as infrared optics, laser communications and reconnaissance sensors, might have been of military use to the Soviets; Soviet scientists were attending the conference.

When the scientific community protested, President Ronald Reagan's science adviser, George A. Keyworth II, explained that defense officials in fact had enforced a rule that had been on the books for some time: every paper written with Defense Department support had to clear for-

mally. But Keyworth admitted the incident had been "both unfortunate and ill-timed."

In April the National Academy of Sciences appointed a 19-member panel to study the problem and the possible need for tighter controls on scientific exchanges. Dale R. Corson, president emeritus of Cornell University, headed the group of experts. The panel had access to top-secret U.S. intelligence reports and heard a variety of viewpoints. After six months of study, the group issued its report.

The panel concluded that transfer of U.S. technology to the USSR existed and "a significant portion" of the leaked information was "damaging to national security." However, open scientific communication was responsible for only a small part of the problem. The panel advocated a policy of open scientific communication in most cases, but recommended that classification be considered for government-supported research that could lead to military application "in a short time."

Following are excerpts from the executive summary of Scientific Communication and National Security, *a report released by the National Academy of Sciences, September 30, 1982:*

Executive Summary

The economic and military strength of the United States is based to a substantial degree on its superior achievements in science and technology and on its capacity to translate those achievements into products and processes that contribute to economic prosperity and national defense. There are concerns, however, that the Soviet Union has gained militarily from access to the results of U.S. scientific and technological efforts. Accordingly, there have been recent suggestions that tighter controls should be established on the transfer of information through open channels to the Soviets. Such controls would, however, also inhibit the free communication of scientific and technical information essential to our achievements. The Panel on Scientific Communication and National Security was asked to examine the various aspects of the application of controls to scientific communication and to suggest how to balance competing national objectives so as to best serve the general welfare. This task has involved a careful assessment of the sources of leakage, the nature of universities and scientific communication, the current systems of information control, and the several costs and benefits of controls. These assessments underlie the Panel's recommendations.

UNWANTED TRANSFER OF U.S. TECHNOLOGY

There has been a substantial transfer of U.S. technology — much of it directly relevant to military systems — to the Soviet Union from diverse sources. The Soviet science and technology intelligence effort has increased in recent years, including that directed at U.S. universities and scientific research. The Soviet Union is exploiting U.S.-U.S.S.R. exchange programs by giving intelligence assignments to some of its participating nationals. This has led to reports of abuses in which the activities of some Soviet bloc exchange visitors have clearly extended beyond their agreed fields of study and have included activities that are inappropriate for visiting scholars.

There is a strong consensus, however, that universities and open scientific communication have been the source of very little of this technology transfer problem. Although there is a net flow of scientific information from the United States to the Soviet Union, consistent with the generally more advanced status of U.S. science, there is serious doubt as to whether the Soviets can reap significant direct military benefits from this flow in the near term. Moreover, U.S. openness gives this nation access to Soviet science in many key areas, and scientific contacts yield useful insights into Soviet institutions and society.

UNIVERSITIES AND SCIENTIFIC COMMUNICATION

The principal mission of universities is education; in many American universities research has also become a major activity, but this research is intertwined with teaching and with the training of advanced research scientists and engineers. Participation in research teaches students to solve difficult, novel problems, often under the guidance of first-rate scientists. Federal policies in support of science have reinforced universities' dual functions.

The system as it has recently evolved has been remarkably successful; American research universities attract some of the best minds from around the world and are the principal source of our scientific preeminence. The effectiveness of this research is now seriously threatened, however, by a number of economic and social forces.

Scientific communication is traditionally open and international in character. Scientific advance depends on worldwide access to all the prior findings in a field — and, often, in seemingly unrelated fields — and on systematic critical review of findings by the world scientific community. In addition to open international publication, there are many informal types of essential scientific communication, including circulation of prepublication drafts, discussions at scientific meetings, special seminars, and personal communications.

THE CURRENT CONTROL SYSTEM

The government can restrict scientific communication in various ways. First, information bearing a particularly close relationship to national security may be subject to classification. This is the most stringent of the control systems because it serves to bar all unauthorized access.

Second, communications with foreign nationals may be restricted by export controls, such as those established by the Export Administration Act (EAA) and its associated Export Administration Regulations (EAR) and by the Arms Export Control Act and its associated International Traffic in Arms Regulations (ITAR). Unless an exemption (or "general license") applies, both systems require prior governmental approval for transfer of technical data — either in written or oral communication — to foreign nationals. Neither EAR nor ITAR is aimed at general scientific communication, and the Constitution limits the government's ability to restrain such communication. Nonetheless, some of the current discussion has focused on the application of export controls to scientific communication. This has proved particularly troubling to the research community in that the current control system appears to be vague in its reach, potentially disruptive, and hard to understand.

Third, the government can include controls on communications in the legal instrument defining the obligations of a recipient of government research funds. A proposal currently under consideration by the Department of Defense would require a DOD funding recipient to allow the government the opportunity for prepublication review of manuscripts dealing with certain research areas of national security concern.

Fourth, the government could attempt to influence conduct by seeking a voluntary agreement with researchers to limit the flow of technical information. Such an agreement is in place to enable the National Security Agency to review manuscripts dealing with cryptography and to negotiate alterations before publication.

Finally, communication with foreign nationals might be inhibited indirectly by limiting their access to the United States. The government can deny a visa request or impose restrictions on activities in this country. In addition, the government can directly regulate the admission of Soviet and East European visitors under particular scientific exchange agreements.

COSTS AND BENEFITS OF CONTROLS

Controls on scientific communications can be considered in the light of several national objectives. Controls can be seen to strengthen national security by preventing the use of American results to advance Soviet military strength. But they can also be seen to *weaken* both military and economic capacities by restricting the mutually beneficial interaction of scientific investigators, inhibiting the flow of research results into military and civilian technology, and lessening the capacity of universities to train advanced researchers. Finally, the imposition of such controls may well erode important educational and cultural values.

With respect to controls and Soviet military gains, the Panel notes that while overall a serious technology transfer problem exists, leakage from the research community has not represented a material danger relative to that from other sources. However, some university scientists will continue to expand their research beyond basic scientific investigations into the application of science to technologies with military relevance. This raises the possibility that the university campus will come to be viewed as a place providing much better opportunities for the illegal acquisition of technology. Information that is of special concern is the "know-how" that is gained by extended participation in U.S. research projects.

With respect to U.S. military and economic progress, controls may slow the rate of scientific advance and thus reduce the rate of technological innovation. Controls also impose economic costs for U.S. high-technology firms, which affect both their prices and their market share in international commerce. Controls may also limit university research and teaching in important areas of technology. The projected shortage of science and engineering talent can become the pacing factor in U.S. technological advance, so maintaining the flow of talented young people to military and commercial technology development efforts is particularly important. A national policy of security by accomplishment has much to recommend it over a policy of security by secrecy.

Apart from these considerations, the U.S. political system and culture are based on the principle of openness. Democracy demands an informed public, and this includes information on science and technology.

In addition, there are some inherent limits on the feasibility and effectiveness of controls. For example, controls cannot be expected to ensure long-term protection of sensitive information, given Soviet determination to procure data and the many parallel leakage channels, some of which are beyond U.S. jurisdiction. Finally, universities and most civilian research organizations lack the logistical capability to monitor the movement of information or personnel.

After weighing these benefits, costs, and feasibility assessments, the Panel arrived at a series of findings and recommendations.

PRINCIPAL FINDINGS AND RECOMMENDATIONS

Control of University Research Activities

The Panel found it possible to define three categories of university research. The first, and by far the largest share, are those activities in which the benefits of total openness overshadow their possible near-term military benefits to the Soviet Union. There are also those areas of research for which classification is clearly indicated. Between the two lies a small "gray area" of research activities for which limited restrictions short of classification are appropriate.

The Panel's critieria leave narrow gray areas for which, in a few instances, limited restrictions short of classification are appropriate. An example of such a gray area may be a situation, anticipated in large-scale integrated circuit work, in which on-campus research merges directly into process technology with possible military application. In its recommendations the Panel has formulated provisions that might be applicable to such a situation.

817

All parties have an interest in having research work done by the most qualified individuals and institutions and in educating a new generation of capable scientists and engineers. These objectives must fit, however, within a system that enables the government to classify work under its sponsorship in accordance with the law and that enables the university to select only work compatible with its principal mission.

Unrestricted Areas of Research

The Panel recommends that no restriction of any kind limiting access or communication should be applied, unless it involves a technology meeting *all* the following criteria:

- The technology is developing rapidly, and the time from basic science to application is short;
- The technology has identifiable direct military applications; or it is dual-use and involves process or production-related techniques;
- Transfer of the technology would give the U.S.S.R. a significant near-term military benefit; and
- The U.S. is the only source of information about the technology, or other friendly nations that could also be the source have control systems as secure as ours.

Classification

The Panel recommends that if government-supported research demonstrably will lead to military products in a short time, classification should be considered. It should be noted that most universities will not undertake classified work, and some will undertake it only in off-campus facilities.

Gray Areas

The Panel recommends that in the limited number of instances in which all of the above four criteria are met but classification is unwarranted, the values of open science can be preserved and the needs of government can [be] met by written agreements no more restrictive than the following:

—a. Prohibition of direct participation in government-supported research projects by nationals of designated foreign countries, with no attempt made to limit physical access to university space or facilities or enrollment in any classroom course of study. Where such prohibition has been imposed by visa or contractually agreed upon, it is not inappropriate for government-university contracts to permit the government to ask a university to report those instances coming to the university's attention in which the stipulated foreign nationals seek participation in any such activities, however supported. It is recognized that some universities will regard such reporting requests as objectionable. Such requests, however, should not require surveillance or monitoring of foreign nationals by the universities.

—b. Submission of stipulated manuscripts simultaneously to the publisher and to the federal agency contract officer, with the federal agency then having 60 days to seek modifications in the manuscript. The review period is not intended to give the government the power to order changes: The right and freedom to publish remain with the university, as they do with all unclassified research. This does not, of course, detract from the government's ultimate power to classify in accordance with law any research it has supported.

The Panel recommends that in cases where the government places such restrictions on scientific communication through contracts or other written agreements, it should be obligated to record and tabulate the instances of those restrictions on a regular basis.

The provisions of EAR and ITAR should not be invoked to deal with gray areas in government-funded unversity research. . . .

Technology Transfer to the Third World

The Panel has concentrated on the U.S.-U.S.S.R. relationship. However, there are clear problems in scientific communication and national security involving Third World countries. These problems in time might overshadow the Soviet dimension. This entire range of issues is both complex and important, and further intensive study is clearly indicated.

The Panel takes note of the current U.S. policy to help the People's Republic of China (PRC) advance its industrial technology. It is generally recognized that the capacity of the PRC to transfer such technologies to the military sector is limited. This technical assistance policy is not reflected, however, in restrictions the government is imposing on cooperative research and activities of PRC students at U.S. universities.

The Panel notes that its deliberations did not extend to the complex issues raised by military-related technology transfer from advanced industrial nations to Third World nations in regionally unstable areas or to those that may be potentially hostile to the United States and its allies. The Panel recommends that this subject receive further attention by the National Academy of Sciences or other qualified study groups under federal sponsorship.

OCTOBER

REPORT ON SOVIET AGRICULTURE
October 2, 1982

In 1982 President Ronald Reagan and private researchers with the Washington-based Worldwatch Institute separately addressed the relationship between U.S. and Soviet farming and the role agricultural trade plays in foreign policy.

Worldwatch Institute, an independent research organization that studies and reports on global resource trends and problems, published a report entitled "U.S. and Soviet Agriculture: The Shifting Balance of Power." The report described the growing Soviet dependence on foreign, particularly American, sources of grain. The U.S.-Soviet food connection, wrote the institute's president, Lester R. Brown, "may represent the most important change in relations between the two countries since the Cold War began a generation ago." Brown suggested that the Soviets' reliance on U.S. agricultural products might even be a deterrent to nuclear attack.

Brown compared American and Soviet farm practices and production. He stated that Soviet agriculture, without major changes, would never be able to meet the needs of its people. The Soviet collective farming system and Five-Year Plans were not flexible enough to cope with unpredictable agricultural problems, such as weather or changing fertilizer needs. Faulty farm equipment, an inadequate transportation system and low morale among farm workers were additional factors contributing to the low level of Soviet agricultural productivity. Despite its own agricultural problems, such as soil erosion and a possible future shortage of fresh water, the United States will continue to increase farm exports, Brown predicted. U.S. farmers, who needed the Soviet market, were, Brown *noted, "the most outspoken advocates of trade with the Soviet Union."*

In several speeches to agricultural groups during 1982, Reagan touched on the issue of U.S.-Soviet trade. Ending the 1980 Soviet grain embargo to resume a more normal trading relationship with Russia was one campaign promise he was "most proud to have kept," Reagan told the National Corn Growers Association in August.

"The bottom line is the Soviet embargo was bad for our farmers, bad for our economy, but not that bad for the aggressors we were supposedly going to punish," the president said in a speech March 22 to representatives of agricultural publications and organizations.

The Carter administration in January 1980 imposed the grain embargo against the Soviets in response to their invasion of Afghanistan. (Soviet invasion of Afghanistan, Historic Documents of 1979, p. 965) However, the Soviets were able to purchase grain elsewhere, primarily from Argentina, and were not severely affected by the embargo.

The Reagan administration resumed grain sales to the Soviets, a move popular with U.S. farmers hard-hit by continuing high interest rates and the depressed economy. In a national radio broadcast October 15, Reagan said the United States would offer the Soviets 23 million metric tons of grain for purchase from October 1982 to September 1983. Denying that the sale aided the Soviets, Reagan said, "We're not providing them with any subsidies or pumping any Western currencies into Soviet pockets."

Following are excerpts from U.S. and Soviet Agriculture: The Shifting Balance of Power, *published by Worldwatch Institute October 2, 1982, and excerpts from statements by President Reagan on March 22, 1982; August 2, 1982; and October 15, 1982:*

WORLDWATCH REPORT

Introduction

Analysts of the U.S.-Soviet balance of power usually focus on relative military strength — the number of tanks, planes, nuclear warheads and other items in the so-called strategic balance. But many other factors determine a country's overall power and influence. Among the most basic is a country's capacity to feed its people. By this measure the Soviet Union appears to be in deep trouble.

Massive spending has increased Soviet military strength in recent years, but the country has become weaker agriculturally. While the two super-powers now appear roughly equal in military strength, the advantage in agriculture has shifted dramatically toward the United States. The U.S.

exportable food surplus is climbing, while Soviet dependence on food imports is growing.

This year the Soviet Union will try to import 46 million tons of grain, more than any country in history. Nearly one-fourth of all Soviet grain, feeding both people and livestock, will come from outside sources. Over one-half of this imported grain will come from the North American breadbasket, most of it from the United States.

The Soviet economy is a planned economy, but these grain imports were not planned. They will fill part of the 68 million ton gap between the 1982 target of 238 million tons of grain and an actual harvest of some 170 million tons. In the past the Soviets blamed bad weather for their shortfalls, but this explanation is beginning to wear thin. Recently the Soviet leadership has acknowledged failures within the agricultural system itself.

Evidence now indicates that the Soviet Union has moved beyond the good year/bad year oscillations of the late sixties and early seventies, when it imported grain only after poor harvests, and must now import massive quantities of grain continuously. The fourth consecutive massive crop shortfall in 1982 signals a broad-based deterioration of Soviet agriculture that will create food shortages well into the future.

In contrast to poor harvests in Third World countries, which can lead to starvation, poor Soviet harvests largely threaten the supply of livestock products. The Soviet food problem is a shortage of meat, not bread. The issue, therefore, is not starvation but worker morale, a question of whether the system can provide the quality of diet that Soviet leaders and planners since Krushchev have promised, and that Soviet citizens have come to expect.

The dramatic shift in the agricultural balance of power between the United States and Soviet Union has been decades in the making. But contrasting food surpluses and deficits have been highly visible only in the last decade or so. As recently as 1970 both countries were exporting grain — the United States 38 million tons and the Soviet Union eight million tons. By 1981, however, U.S. grain exports had jumped to a staggering 115 million tons and the Soviets were importing 43 million tons.

Not surprisingly, these huge food deficits trouble the Soviet leadership. In the Eleventh Five-Year Plan (1981-85), released a year late at the November 1981 meeting of the Central Committee of the Soviet Communist Party, General Secretary Leonid Brezhnev said food was "the central problem of the whole Five-Year Plan." His discussion of Soviet agricultural goals and prospects was extraordinarily dispirited, a far cry from Krushchev's taunting "we will bury you" economic rhetoric of a quarter-century ago.

As the deterioration of Soviet agriculture continues, the need to import food will become even greater. Already the flow of grain from the United States to the Soviet Union is on the verge of being the largest ever between two countries, about to eclipse the current U.S. flow to Japan. The long line of ships that now connects American farms with the dining tables of the Soviet Union constitutes a new economic tie between the two countries, one that could eventually transform their political relations as well. . . .

The Deterioration of Soviet Agriculture

. . . The deterioration of agricultural production in the Soviet Union is too pervasive to blame on the weather. . . . [T]he shortcomings . . . involve nearly every phase of agricultural management. . . .

. . . In the fifties, Krushchev began to elevate agriculture on the Soviet list of priorities. Brezhnev put it front and center following his accession to power in 1964. During the past three Five-Year Plans (1966-1980), as well as the current Plan (1981-1985), investments have been heavy by almost any measure. Since 1966 Soviet investment in agriculture has dwarfed that of the United States. As a share of total Soviet investment, agriculture has claimed a whopping 27 percent in recent years. Few countries, industrial or developing, have been able to commit such a large share of total investment to agriculture.

Since investment in agriculture has been heavy, several questions arise about Soviet agricultural shortcomings: Why is agriculture deteriorating on so many fronts? Why have production trends actually been reversed? And why is this deterioration occurring now?

Discussions of Soviet agriculture, whether by Soviet officials, the Soviet press or Western commentators, tend to focus on specific shortages and shortcomings, but these are commonly symptoms of a more fundamental problem — the nature of the system itself. Evidence now points to a basic conflict between a centrally planned and controlled agriculture and the evolution of a modern, highly productive agriculture. Centralized agriculture and Soviet Plan goals are incompatible. The more the Soviets try to modernize their agriculture, the more obvious the inherent contradiction will become.

Because traditional agriculture is largely self-contained, supplying its own draft power, seed and fertilizer, usually in the form of livestock manure, it is not much affected by central planning. But as agriculture modernizes it becomes even more complex, requiring a range of off-farm physical inputs and support services and the authority to make on-the-spot decisions. Providing the appropriate inputs in the proper amounts and at the right time in response to continually changing conditions on the farm is virtually impossible with a centralized system. . . .

Traditional agriculture, with low but relatively stable productivity, has little need for agricultural research. But as agriculture modernizes and yields rise, research support must become more sophisticated simply to maintain new production levels. In the United States, for example, typical commercial wheat varieties last four years before they are overtaken by evolving strains of wheat rust or other pests, or replaced by newer, more productive varieties. Without research support, high-yield agriculture will gradually deteriorate, with yields eventually returning to traditional levels.

Contrasting approaches to agricultural management in the Soviet Union and the United States are obvious when their respective agricultural structures are compared. In the Soviet Union, 500 million acres of cropland are divided in roughly equal amounts between 20,800 state farms and 26,000 collective farms. Each state farm averages just over 13,000 acres and each collective farm about 9,000.

In the United States, where 2.4 million farmers cultivate some 350 million acres, each farm averages 144 acres of cropland. Including grazing and forest land, the typical farm has close to 400 acres. As is often the case, however, these averages conceal a wide range of farm sizes. The 1974 census reported 225,000 farms with less than 50 acres of land. At the other end of the spectrum, there were 150,000 farms with a thousand acres or more. The vast majority of U.S. farmers — some two million — were in the 50 to 1,000 acre category.

The Soviet Union employs a farm labor force of 26.1 million. Of this group 46,800 are the managers of the state and collective farms. Even allowing for numerous assistant farm managers and other supervisory personnel, the bulk of the 26 million farm labor force are farm workers directed by the 46,800 farm managers, who in turn are directed from Moscow. By contrast, the U.S. farm labor force totals 3.7 million, only a small fraction of that in the Soviet Union. Of this total, 2.4 million are managers of family farms, mostly owner-operators, and fewer than 1.3 million are hired workers.

In the highly competitive U.S. market economy these farm managers must excell to survive. The market is heartless in weeding out poor managers. While the floor price for major commodities may be determined in Washington by the level of price supports, the farmer is largely on his own. For decision making he draws heavily from his own experience and that of his neighbors. For technical and market information, he relies on land grant colleges, state agricultural experiment stations, the U.S. Department of Agriculture, agribusiness firms and a wide range of agricultural magazines, journals, newsletters and radio services. The agricultural media are especially useful for market and weather information. Watching the weather, the U.S. farmer may not decide which crop to plant until the actual day of planting. As far as his equipment and experience permit he can shift from one crop to another to maximize yield and profits by responding to changes in the world market. He is not bound by a long-term production plan.

Individual farmers making day-to-day decisions in response to market signals, changing weather and the conditions of their crops have a collective intelligence far exceeding that of a centralized bureaucracy, however well designed and competently staffed. Consider the simple example of fertilizer use. In the United States a farmer routinely tests the soil in each field and develops a fertilizer application plan according to the soil nutrient content and the crop to be grown there. He may decide to broadcast his fertilizer before plowing or after plowing, depending on the soil type and crop. He may decide to broadcast some of it and sidedress the remainder during the growing season. In some caes he may even resort to foliar application. But even this rather specific plan is revised as the season progresses. For example, a cold wet spring may reduce the amount of phosphorous available to vegetable crops, requiring supplemental application. If the season is dryer than usual in corn growing regions, farmers may apply extra nitrogen in midsummer to help the crop withstand the late summer effects of drought.

A centralized agricultural system relying on Five-Year Plans cannot begin to match the flexibility and sophistication of a system built around the individual farmer. The Soviets already know how much nitrogen fertilizer they are going to use in 1984 because it is spelled out in the 1981-85 Five-Year plan. An American farmer will not know how much nitrogen fertilizer he will use in 1984 until he tests his soil in the spring of that year and decides which crops to plant, and even then he may make adjustments as the season progresses. The fertilizer manufacturer will be expected to meet the farmer's demand. Indeed, the fertilizer firm's success depends on its ability to do so. But it is the farmer who determines how much of what kind of fertilizer is used, not the fertilizer manufacturer or a planning office in Washington. . . .

The U.S.-Soviet Food Connection

Each day two 20,000-ton freighters loaded with grain leave the United States for the Soviet Union. The flow of grain between these two major adversaries, something neither government had planned on, is influenced by economic considerations such as the size of the Soviet grain deficit, the U.S. capacity to supply and the Soviet ability to pay. Political considerations include the risk to both trading partners associated with being heavily dependent on each other, whether as a supplier or a market. . . .

Because of the massive scale of Soviet food imports the United States necessarily figures prominently as a source of food. Indeed, no country has ever dominated world grain trade as the United States does today. Its 55 percent share of world grain exports in 1981 easily overshadows Saudi Arabia's 32 percent share of world oil exports. And while the amount of oil traded internationally has been falling since 1979, grain shipments are continuing to grow. . . .

The U.S. embargo distorted normal grain trade patterns as the Soviet Union turned to other suppliers, all quite small compared with the United States. Tying up the lion's share of exportable supplies from countries such as Argentina, the Soviet Union forced Japan and other major importers to rely even more heavily than usual on the United States. As a result, U.S. restrictions on grain shipments to the Soviet Union effectively altered not only Soviet sources of supply but the entire world pattern of grain trade. The partial embargo did not measurably reduce the amount of grain imported by the Soviets, but it did make grain imports more difficult and somewhat more costly. It also let the Soviets know that food would be used as an instrument of foreign policy.

The current flow of grain from the United States to the Soviet Union takes place within the framework of the U.S.-Soviet Grains Agreement signed in October 1975. Initially a five-year pact that ran from October 1976 to September 1981, it was extended for one year in August of 1981. The United States delayed negotiations, scheduled to begin in early 1982, on a new long-term grain agreement in response to the Soviet Union's role in Poland. In late July 1982, the United States offered another one-year extension of the agreement rather than a new agreement, expressing its displeasure over martial law in Poland. After pondering the proposed one-year extension for a few weeks, the Soviets decided to accept it even though they would have preferred the security of a multi-year agreement.

The Grains Agreement requires that the Soviet Union annually purchase a minimum of six million tons of corn and wheat in roughly equal quantities. It also allows the Soviets to purchase up to eight million tons if needed, but purchases over eight million tons require consultations between the two countries and special permission by the U.S. government. In any year that the U.S. Department of Agriculture estimates the combination of U.S. production and carryover stocks to be less than 225 million tons, the United States may reduce the amount available to the Soviets below the minimum called for.

The original agreement was made when the Soviets were far more hopeful about their long-term food prospects than they are today. As a result, purchases have invariably greatly exceeded the eight million ton maximum automatically permitted in the agreement, requiring numerous consultations from 1976 on. Nonetheless, the agreement has helped stabilize the world grain market. . . .

In the new commercial food relationship between the two superpowers dependence is mutual, but it is not symmetrical. Soviet dependence on U.S. supplies, directly or indirectly, is greater than U.S. dependence on Soviet markets. Whether or not the Soviets import directly from the United States, U.S. export capacity makes Soviet imports possible. For the United States, an embargo on grain exports to the Soviet Union would eliminate direct shipments but would not likely have much effect on total U.S. exports. If Canada and Australia were to join the embargo, as they might in an emergency, then Soviet imports would be reduced, as would overall U.S. grain shipments. In this event, the United States government could idle cropland by supporting farm prices. This technique has been widely used since World War II and was reintroduced on a limited scale in 1982.

The Effect on U.S.-Soviet Relationships

The new food connection between the United States and the Soviet Union may represent the most important change in relations between the two countries since the Cold War began a generation ago. It demonstrates in clear economic terms that the United States and the Soviet Union need each other. This is particularly true at a time when the productive capacity of U.S. farms continues to climb while growth in grain markets outside the Soviet Union has slowed because of a sluggish economy worldwide. The record grain deficits of the early eighties in the Soviet Union show more than ever its dependence on U.S. agriculture. . . .

Although American farmers are the most outspoken advocates of trade with the Soviet Union, the higher level of farm exports that Soviet imports make possible benefits the entire U.S. economy. As the U.S. oil import bill soared after the 1973 price increases, the enormous growth in farm exports paid much of the bill. Traditional export industries, such as automobiles, have sagged in international competition. Even high technology exports, such as commercial jet aircraft, are suffering. In a stagnant economy the productivity and ingenuity of American farmers have helped the United States balance its international payments.

Great as the benefits of this expanded farm trade are for the United States, the Soviet Union has even more to gain. One can only imagine how long the lines would be at Soviet meat counters had it not been for U.S. grain. The Soviet Union is in deep trouble economically because it must import so much food, but it would be in even deeper trouble politically if the food were not available.

Both superpowers at times feel uneasy with their new trade dependency because it complicates a traditional adversarial relationship. The food connection does not ensure peaceful relations between the two countries, but it will make massive arms spending more difficult to justify. The American people and Congress may increasingly doubt that a country depending on the United States for so much of its food could be as dangerous as commonly portrayed. Hard-liners in the Soviet Union may be unable to convince Kremlin colleagues that the country which is feeding them is indeed a mortal enemy. . . .

The advantages of massive U.S. food shipments to the Soviet Union are not limited to economic benefits alone. These shipments are an important commercial transaction for the United States, but they also provide a form of insurance against a Soviet nuclear attack. Although the prospect of destroying its principle source of imported food will not necessarily prevent a Soviet nuclear attack, it is certainly a deterrent. Unlike a U.S. grain export embargo that would simply rearrange trade patterns, a nuclear attack that destroyed U.S. export capacity would decimate the world's exportable grain supplies, particularly since Canada's export capacity might also be destroyed. This would leave over a hundred grain importing countries, including the Soviet Union, scrambling for the exports of Australia and Argentina, plus a few other small exporters. . . .

The food connection between the two superpowers will not automatically usher in a new period of East-West cooperation and peace. But if wisely used, it could become the cornerstone on which to build a better relationship. The food connection between the two superpowers promises other changes in the long run. Frequent consultations under the grain agreement could lead to consultations in other areas as well. Just as the two countries now find it in their mutual interest to engage in massive food trade, they may also find it advantageous to cooperate in nonagricultural trade, scientific research and even space exploration.

The importance of the dramatic shift in the agricultural balance of power lies less in the potential it provides for using food as a political lever than in the psychological effect the new commercial ties will have on political relations between the two countries. The long line of grain-laden ships linking U.S. farmers to Soviet consumers represents a major new economic tie between the two countries, one that could transform long-term political relationships as well.

REAGAN'S MARCH 22 STATEMENT

. . . I believe the first bodyblow to agriculture fell in January 1980, when contracts for the sale of our farm products to the Soviet Union were blocked in retaliation for its invasion of Afghanistan. The impact was immediate and severe. Farm prices declined, and our entire agricultural marketing system — elevators, barge lines, railways, millers, exporters — was disrupted.

According to both private and government estimates, billions of dollars in output and services were lost. Thousands of jobs were lost. And taxpayers immediately had to shell out more than $2 billion to help soften the blow. Other countries didn't hesitate to increase their production and displace U.S. sales. No one knows for sure what the ultimate impact of that ill-advised embargo will be, because such actions effect trade patterns for years.

Now, it's also worth noting that the Soviets are still in Afghanistan suppressing an innocent people, who yearn to be free. And while the Soviets experienced some economic problems, that predicted cutback in their meat production never materialized as a result of our action. By increasing grain imports from other sources, by seeking out meat imports from other countries, and by expanding the use of substitute feeds, the Soviets were able to maintain their meat inventories.

Now, don't get me wrong. There may come a day when our national security is threatened and the issue of an embargo is raised again. In that case, I would not hesitate to declare such an embargo . . . but only if it were part of a complete boycott and if we could have the cooperation of other nations so that we wouldn't end up hurting ourselves, with no harm done to those we were trying to influence. . . .

The bottom line is the Soviet embargo was bad for our farmers, bad for our economy, but not that bad for the aggressors we were supposedly going to punish.

On top of the Soviet embargo, farmers were hard hit by the policies of the late seventies that led to sharing [soaring] inflation and interest rates. Inflation went from 4.8 percent in 1976 to 12.4 percent in 1980. And during that period, interest rates shot all the way up from 6.5 percent to 21.5 percent. The farmer, like any other small businessman lives or dies on his ability to sustain an adequate cash flow. And when that cash flow is reduced to a trickle by high inflation and interest rates, the farmer sometimes has no option but to shut down his operation. And [add] to all this, the recent bumper crops, we understand why the cost-price squeeze is so bad and threatens to strangle the vitality of American agriculture.

Prices received by farmers have gone up 5 percent since 1979. Prices paid by farmers have gone up by 25 percent — or 20 percent, I should say — 4 times as much in this period.

One other problem I didn't mention is that excellent weather overseas has created a large, worldwide surplus. The one exception, of course, is the Soviet Union. You know, I can hardly remember a year when Soviet harvests were not victimized by bad weather. And I've seen a lot of harvest seasons, as I'm constantly being reminded. . . .

We know that the Federal Government also has an important role to play as partner to the farm community. I think the gist of that role is to help the farmer do what he can't do on his own — promote basic research, seek out new markets, counter any unfair trade practices of our trading partners, provide a measure of protection from erratic weather and natural disasters, and create the proper environment so the forces of supply and demand can more efficiently allocate resources. We're fully committed to do this.

We have increased the fiscal year '83 budget for agricultural research by nearly 3 percent above the inflation rate. We've expanded the Federal crop insurance program. We proposed a $4 million increase in the Department of Agriculture's market development program and recommended that the level of agricultural export credit guarantees be maintained at the highest level in history — $2.5 billion. We ended the previous administration's Soviet embargo and withstood pressures to impose agricultural trade sanctions during the Polish crisis. . . .

REAGAN'S AUGUST 2 STATEMENT

. . . [T]he commitment I'm most proud to have kept . . . was a more normal grain trading relationship with the Soviet Union, lifting the last administration's grain embargo.

The lingering effects of that grain embargo are still hanging over the markets, and our Nation's farmers are still suffering from those low prices. We have 70 percent of the Soviet market when the embargo was imposed. That fell to 25 percent during the embargo. At the same time, our competitors took advantage of this market that the last administration threw away. Well, we've restored to the American farmer a fair opportunity to export grain to the U.S.S.R. on a cash basis. We have already begun that difficult road.

After lifting the embargo, we offered the Soviets an additional 15 million metric tons of grain beyond the original 8 million metric tons. Our efforts on behalf of the farmers suffered a setback, however, with the iron repression of the proud people of Poland. When martial law was declared in that country, U.S. officials were developing a negotiating position on a new long-term grain agreement with the U.S.S.R. After the Soviet Union ignored our calls to aid restoration of basic human rights in Poland, we had no choice but to impose a number of sanctions against both countries, including postponement of negotiations on a long-term trade agreement with the Soviet Union.

There is still no cause to celebrate in Poland. I am, however, somewhat encouraged by indications martial law may be relaxing. We'll continue to watch developments there in the hope that life will improve for the Poles and sanctions can be removed. In the meantime we will explore a 1-year extension of the current long-term grain agreement with the Soviet Union. I have also authorized the Secretary of Agriculture to consult with the Soviets on the subject of additional grain sales beyond the minimum purchase requirements of the current agreement.

The extension would have the sanctity of a contract, ensuring U.S. farmers access to the Soviet market. . . . We must restore confidence in U.S. reliability as a supplier. An agreement would, also, protect Americans from possible Soviet disruption of our domestic market.

Indications are that we'll sell a record volume of grain to the Soviet Union this year. With the extension that we're now exploring, we'll be able to sell large quantities during the next year. In other words, the granary door is open, and the exchange will be cash on the barrelhead.

Last March, I outlined this administration's agricultural trade doctrine. . . . There will be no restrictions on farm products proposed because of rising farm prices. Farm exports will not be singled out as an instrument of foreign policy and can be used only as a part of a trade embargo if it is broad and supported by other nations across the board in a situation that would be so serious as to cause this action.

We believe world markets must be freed of trade barriers and unfair trade practices. At home and abroad, we're committed to assuring the American farmer a market that will reward his investment and work, and not punish him for his incomparable success. . . .

REAGAN'S OCTOBER 15 STATEMENT

. . . I'd like to discuss with you for a few moments the plans our administration has to meet important agricultural challenges we face together. I'm talking about increasing American farm exports, restoring our reputation as reliable suppliers, and regaining our world market share. . . .

. . . U.S. agriculture is in the grip of a prolonged economic recession that began in 1980. The record inflation and interest rates of the late seventies and that mistaken Soviet grain embargo laid the seeds for a very different, bitter kind of harvest — a vicious cost-price squeeze and lost markets. Together, they eroded confidence and destroyed too many dreams for prosperity....

As you know, our administration moved early on to end that grain embargo which had hurt farmers so badly. Before the Soviet embargo, American farmers were supplying about 70 percent of Soviet needs. After the embargo, our market share dropped to less than 25 percent. Other nations had quickly moved in to fill the gap left by the embargo, so that our farmers and our farmers almost alone bore the brunt of the embargo. This year, we've fought our way back to 35 percent of the Soviet market. We're on our way back up. We can and we will do better there and around the world.

Nothing is more crucial to the long-term health of agriculture than restoring this Nation's reputation as a reliable supplier of agricultural products around the world. During the past 20 months, we've pursued an agricultural export policy making three things plain: No restrictions will be imposed on farm exports because of rising domestic prices; no farm exports will be singled out as an instrument of foreign policy, except in extreme situations, and then, only as part of a broad embargo supported by our trading partners; and world markets must be freed of trade barriers and unfair trade practices.

On that last point, we've mounted a united front by the Departments of Agriculture, State, Treasury, Commerce, and the U.S. Trade Representative, to speak out and act against the unfair trade practices of our competitors abroad. We're committed to more open agricultural markets in all countries, and we're challenging others in negotiations, particularly our friends in Europe and Japan, to fully match this commitment....

Today, I am directing Secretary of Agriculture Block to take two additional steps. Two weeks from now, U.S. representatives will meet with the Soviets in Vienna for talks concerning additional grain purchases beyond the 8 million metric tons stipulated in article 1 of the existing U.S.-U.S.S.R. grain agreement. I am instructing the Secretary to make available a total of 23 million metric tons for purchase during the October 1, 1982-September 30, 1983 time period.

Second, the Secretary of Agriculture will extend to the additional purchases the same assurances of reliable delivery that the 8 million metric tons are afforded under article 2 of the agreement, if the U.S.S.R. will contract for the additional tonnage during the month of November, and provided that it is shipped within 180 days from the date of the contract.

These same assurances, of course, also apply to soybean and other agricultural exports. We have a large crop. We need commitments to move that crop and strengthen markets. Now, of course, we can't guarantee the Soviets will make these purchases, but we know they're shopping, and they still have large needs.

We want to demonstrate that actions speak louder than words, and we're taking tangible actions to restore this market. Year-in, year-out, there is no better, more reliable producer of food anywhere than the United States of America.

Now, some will say that by offering to sell the Soviets more grain we're sending a weak signal. That's wrong. We're asking the Soviets to give us cash on the line for the food they buy. We're not providing them with any subsidies or pumping any Western currencies into Soviet pockets.

It's always seemed ironic to me that many people who are so quick to sacrifice the interest of farmers in an effort to seem tough are unwilling to do the real things we need to send a signal of national will and strength.

During the last decade, we had two grain embargoes. But during those same years we were also reducing our commitment to a strong national defense, while the Soviets were undertaking the most massive military buildup in history. We're not making that mistake in 1982; we have our priorities straight.

I wish I could tell you today that we've turned everything around for American farmers. I can't. I can only say that we're doing everything we can, as rapidly as we can, to make things right. . . .

POPE'S TRIP TO SPAIN
October 31 - November 9, 1982

During his travels in Spain, Pope John Paul II stressed the need for the country to restore a high standard of morality. About 18 million people, one-half Spain's population, greeted him in 16 cities on his 10-day trip beginning October 31. The journey was the pope's 16th outside Italy and the first of any pope to Spain, one of the world's predominantly Roman Catholic nations. Earlier in 1982, the pope visited Great Britain. (Pope's trip to Britain, p. 409)

Since Francisco Franco, who had ruled as Spain's dictator for 36 years, died in 1975, the power of the Catholic Church in Spain had waned. Spanish bishops issued a report on the eve of the pope's visit complaining of falling church attendance, inadequate numbers of clergy and declining moral standards. Just three days before the pope arrived Spain elected its first Socialist government in 40 years. The Socialists advocated liberalized abortion laws, increased access to contraceptives and a reduction in federal subsidies for parochial schools.

Family Life and Values

At an outdoor mass in Madrid October 31 the pope said "my journey is beyond any political or partisan purpose." Within hours of meeting Prime Minister-elect Felipe González, the pope used one of his first major public addresses to condemn abortion, birth control and divorce. "Matrimony is an indissoluble communion of love," the pope said. In 1981 Spain had liberalized divorce laws.

Turning to the issue of birth control, the pope quoted his predecessor, Paul VI, who said, "Every conjugal act must remain open to the transmission of life." It was on abortion that the pope issued his strongest condemnation. "I speak on the absolute respect for human life, which no person or institution, private or public, can ignore. . . . Nothing can legitimize the death of an innocent," the pope declared.

The pope also spoke strongly on the "inalienable" duty and right of parents to see that their children receive "an education in accordance with their moral and religious convictions."

Pope's Speeches

On his first full day in Spain, the pope journeyed into the heartland of Spanish monasticism in Salamanca. He spoke to theology professors, exploring the relationship of theology to faith, to philosophy and to science.

Speaking to a gathering of scientists on the fourth day of his pastoral tour, the pope said the concentration of scientific effort on development of arms of war was "a scandal of our times. . . . Your responsibility and your power to influence public opinion are immense. Make them serve the cause of peace and real progress of man."

He praised the work of scientists and cited the growing number of contacts between the church and scientists. "The church supports freedom of research, which is one of man's noblest attributes. . . . [T]he church is convinced that there cannot be any real contradiction between science and faith, since all reality proceeds in the ultimate instance from God the creator. . . . [O]ur epoch has need of a science of man, for original reflection and research."

The pope traveled to the troubled Basque region of Spain November 6, just after the assassination of a general there. The killing was thought to be the work of Basque nationalists. The pope appealed to young Basques to reject violence, remembering his own experience with terrorism, the May 1981 attempt on his life by a Turkish gunman. In the city of Saint Ignatius Loyola, who founded the Society of Jesus in the 16th century, Pope John Paul said violence . . . offends God, those who suffer it and those who practice it." (Attempted assassination of pope, Historic Documents of 1981, p. 427)

The pope announced his "gospel of work" in Barcelona November 7. Speaking in a region that has suffered a 10 percent unemployment rate, he discussed the relationship of capital and labor and the problem of unemployment. Ways to a just solution demand a "revision of the economic order as a whole," he said. He referred to unemployment as "this distressing problem — which has become epidemic throughout the world." He described work as a "primordial blessing from the creator, an activity permitting the individual to realize himself and to offer a service to society." (Encyclical on work, Historic Documents of 1981, p. 695)

In an address at the pilgrimage site of Santiago de Compostela November 9, the pope lamented the materialism and hedonism of the modern world, the decline in the values of the large united family and the secularized ideologies that negate God and limit religious liberty.

> *Following are excerpts from the speech of Pope John Paul II at the Pontifical University of Salamanca, November 1, 1982; from remarks at the royal palace in Madrid, November 2; from a speech at the University of Madrid, November 3; from an address in Toledo, November 4; from remarks in Loyola, November 6; and from a speech in Barcelona, November 7:*

SPEECH AT SALAMANCA

1. ... I chose this celebrated and beautiful city of Salamanca for the meeting with you. With its ancient university, it was the center and symbol of the golden period of theology in Spain. Its light shone from here to the Council of Trent, and so made a powerful contribution to the renewal of all Catholic theology. . . .

2. The essential and specific function of the theological task has not changed, nor can it change. St. Anselm of Canterbury formulated this already in the 11th century in a phrase which is admirable for exactitude and substance: *fides quaerens intellectum* — faith seeking understanding.

So, faith is not solely the indispensable presupposition and the fundamental disposition of theology: the connection between the two is much more intimate and profound.

Faith is the vital and permanent root of theology which flows precisely from praying and seeking which are intrinsic to faith itself; that is to say, from its impulse to comprehend itself, both in its radically free option of personal adherence to Christ and in its assent to the content of Christian revelation. Doing theology is, then, a task exclusively proper to the believer as believer; it is a task vitally aroused and sustained at every moment by faith, and so, it is unlimited prayer and seeking.

Theology always maintains itself within the mental process, which ranges from "create" to "comprehend." It is scientific reflection, inasmuch as it is conducted critically, that is to say, with consciousness of its presuppositions and its exigency to be universally valid; methodically, that is, in conformity with the norms imposed by its object and by its end; systematically, that is, by being oriented toward coherent understanding of the revealed truths in their relation with the center of the faith, Christ, and in their salvific significance for man.

The theologian may not limit himself to guarding the doctrinal treasure inherited from the past, but he must seek understanding and expression of the faith that may make reception of it possible in today's way of thinking and speaking. The criterion that ought to guide theological reflection is the search for renewed understanding of the Christian message in the dialectic of renewal in continuity, and vice versa (cf. Discourse to Bishops of Belgium, Sept. 10, 1982).

3. The situation of contemporary culture is dominated by the methods and the form of thought proper to the natural sciences. It is strongly influenced by philosophical currents which proclaim the exclusive validity of the principle of empirical verification. This situation tends to leave the transcendental dimension of man in silence, and thus, logically, to omit or deny the question of God and Christian revelation.

Faced with this situation, theology is called to concentrate its attention on its radical and decisive themes: the mystery of God, the trinitarian God who has revealed himself in Jesus as the God-love; the mystery of Christ, the Son of God made man who, with his life and message, his death and resurrection, definitively illuminated the most profound aspects of human existence; the mystery of man who, in the tension between his finiteness and his unlimited aspiration, bears within himself the irrenounceable question about the last end of his life.

It is theology itself which poses the question of man, so as to be able to understand him as the object of grace and Christ's revelation.

If theology has always had need of the aid of philosophy, today this philosophy will have to be anthropological; that is to say, it will have to search into the essential structures of human existence for the transcendental dimensions which constitute the capacity, radical in man, to be the object of the Christian message, so as to understand it as salvific; that is to say, as the response of gratuitous plenitude to the fundamental questions of human life. This was the process of theological reflection followed by the Second Vatican Council in the constitution *Gaudium et Spes*: the correlation between the deep and decisive problems of man and the new light that the person and the message of Christ shed upon them (cf. 9-21).

We see from this that theology in our time needs the aid not only of philosophy, but also of the sciences, the human sciences above all, as the indispensable basis for replying to the question, "What is man?" Therefore, faculties of theology cannot do without interdisciplinary courses and seminars. . . .

5. The essential connection between theology and faith, founded and centered on Christ, lights up with total clarity the bond between theology and church and the magisterium. One cannot believe in Christ without believing in the church, "the body of Christ"; one cannot believe with Catholic faith within the church without believing in her irrenounceable magisterium.

So, fidelity to Christ implies fidelity to the church; and fidelity to the church entails fidelity to the magisterium in its turn. It is consequently necessary to bear in mind that it is with the same radical freedom of faith with which the Catholic theologian adheres to Christ that he adheres to the church and the magisterium as well.

Therefore, the ecclesial magisterium is not an application alien to theology, but it is intrinsic and essential to it. If the theologian is above all and radically a believer, and if his Christian faith is faith in the church of Christ and in the magisterium, his theological labor can do no less than remain faithfully bound to his ecclesial faith, the authentic and binding interpreter of which is the magisterium.

So be faithful to your faith, without falling into the dangerous illusion of separating Christ from his church, or the church from her magisterium....

SPEECH AT ROYAL PALACE

1. ... Even though my trip to Spain is of an eminently religious nature, through this courtesy visit I would like to pay my respects to the legitimate representatives of the Spanish people. The people have elected them as bearers of their mandate to rule the destinies of the nation. In this way, I would like to remove any doubts — if there were any — about my respect for the country's freely elected leaders.

2. ... It is logical at the same time that, faithful to its duty and yet respecting the autonomy of the temporal order (cf. *Gaudium et Spes*, 16) the church asks the same consideration toward its mission, when it is a question of things having to do with God or the conscience of his sons and daughters in the various manifestations of their personal and social, private and public lives.

3. I am conscious that I come to a nation with a grand Catholic tradition, that many of her children contributed intensely to the humanization and evangelization of other peoples. There are pages of history which speak very highly of your past.

Today, you are involved in a new direction in your public framework which respects the diversity of opinion in the country. Without claiming to give concrete judgments on aspects which do not enter into my competence, I pray God to give you certitude in the solutions to be adopted, for the sake of preserving the harmonious coexistence, the solidarity, the mutual respect and the good of all.

Such equilibrium in Spain will have positive repercussions in the geographical area of which you form a part and into which you legitimately wish to integrate yourselves more fully. A Spain prosperous and at peace, engaged in promoting fraternal relations among her peoples, and not forgetful of her human, spiritual and moral essences, will be able to make a valuable contribution to a future of justice and peace in Europe and in the concert of nations, above all those with which she has special historical links.

4. I know that, in order to attain these objectives, you are making efforts to create civil coexistence in liberty, participation and respect for human rights, within a plurality of legitimate options, and with due respect for them, such as is felt in Spanish society.

I wish for you that a solid and responsible liberty may ever be safeguarded — for it is a precious gift of the human person and a fruit of his dignity — and that your system of liberty may be based at every moment on observance of the moral values of the human person. Thus will liberty be able to be realized truly, individually and collectively....

SPEECH AT UNIVERSITY OF MADRID

... 4. In Spain, as in other countries of Europe, entire generations of researchers, teachers and authors have been very fruitful thanks to freedom of research. This ensured university communities of self-rule, and the king or the church frequently made themselves guarantors of such communities.

Those university centers brought together masters who specialized in various disciplines. They constituted a propitious means for creativity, emulation and constant dialogue with theology. The university appeared above all to be an affair of university members themselves, and conditions favorable to discovery, teaching and diffusion of knowledge were formed in collaboration between masters and disciples.

The masters knew that in the theological field research implies fidelity to the word revealed in Jesus Christ and entrusted to the church. The dialogue between theology and magisterium also proved to be very fruitful. Bishops and theologians were able to meet, with common benefit for pastors and professors.

If moments like that of the Inquisition produced tensions, errors and excesses — facts which the church today evaluates in the objective light of history — it is necessary to recognize that the entirety of the intellectual elements of Spain have known how to reconcile admirably the demands of full freedom of investigation with a profound sense of church. This is attested to by the innumerable creations of classical writings which the masters, sages, scientists and authors of Spain contributed to the church's cultural treasure.

5. We also note an opening to the universal in the intellectual tradition of your nation which has given reputation and fame to your masters.

Your scientists and researchers kept their eyes open to classical and biblical history, to the other countries of Europe, to the ancient and to the new world. Your authors were pioneers of genius in the science of international relations and the law of nations.

Universities of high prestige, modeled on that of Salamanca, were rapidly established. Nearly 30 were implanted in the nascent Americas. That is a further proof of the universalism which characterized your culture over a long time, and that culture was enriched by very many discoveries and discoverers and the profound influence exercised by so many missionaries upon the entire world.

The role of the church which your country acknowledged gave your culture a special dimension. The church was present at all stages of the gestation and progress of Spanish civilization.

Your nation was the crucible where very rich traditions melted together into a unique cultural synthesis. The characteristic features of the Hispanic communities have been enriched by historical contributions from the Arab world — your harmonious language, art and place names give proof of that. They fused into a Christian civilization broadly open to the universal. Both within and outside her frontiers, Spain made herself by receiving the universality of the Gospel and the grand cultural currents of Europe and the world.

6. Your masters and thinkers also had the sense of serving the whole man, integral man, of meeting his psychological, intellectual, moral and spiritual needs. So a science of man arose, and physicians, philosophers, theologians, moralists and jurists all shared in it.

Your great spiritual masters have a place apart. Their work spread so that they rapidly crossed your frontiers and reached the entire church. We have only to think of St. Teresa of Jesus and St. John of the Cross, doctors of the church, St. Dominic, Friar Luis of Granada, St. Ignatius of Loyola, giant figures in the field of spirituality.

They also did great service to the culture of man. They continued a great tradition where eminent precursors stand out, such as St. Isidore of Seville, one of the first Catholic encyclopedists, and St. Raymond of Penafort, author of one of the earliest summaries of law in your country.

All those men and women were masters in the full meaning of the word. With exceptional and prophetic intelligence, they were able to serve man in his highest aspirations. Who can measure their influence and the lasting effect of their teachings, writings and creations? They are marvelous witnesses to a culture which knew man as created in God's likeness, as capable of dominating the world, but called above all to spiritual progress, the perfect model of which is Jesus Christ.

7. These lessons from the story of Spain deserve to be recalled, first of all, in order to do homage to the outstanding contribution made by your masters, sages and scientists, researchers and your saints to the whole of mankind, which would not be what it is without the Hispanic heritage.

There is another reason which invites us today, in a very different historical context, to reflect upon the conditions which can favor promotion of culture and science in our day and stimulate research on man, for which there is so much need in our age. It is greatly beneficial for men and women of culture to meditate on the presuppositions of intellectual and spiritual creation. Today, as yesterday, this calls for a climate of liberty and cooperation among researchers, with an attitude of openness to the universal and with an integral vision of man.

8. The prime condition is that liberty of spirit be assured. It is necessary in research to have freedom to seek and to publish the results. The church supports freedom of research, which is one of man's noblest attributes.

Through searching, man arrives at the truth, one of the most beautiful names that God has given to himself. For the church is convinced that there cannot be any real contradiction between science and faith, since all reality proceeds in the ultimate instance from God the creator. That is what the Second Vatican Council affirmed (cf. *Gaudium et Spes*, 36). I too have recalled this on various occasions to men and women of science.

It is certain that science and faith represent two distinct orders of knowledge which are autonomous in procedures but are finally convergent in discovery of the integral reality which has its origin in God (cf. Discourse in the Cathedral of Cologne, Nov. 15, 1980).

A broad agreement is tending to be established on this point, on the part of the church and on the part of the best modern scientists. Contacts between the world of the sciences and the Holy See have become more and more frequent and have been marked by mutual understanding.

Mainly from the times of my predecessors Pius XII and then Paul VI, popes have entered into increasingly frequent dialogue with numerous groups of scientists, specialists, researchers. These have found the church to be an interlocutor who desires to understand them, to encourage them in their research and to show them at the same time her profound gratitude for the indispensable service that science renders to mankind.

Serious discords and misunderstandings occurred in the past between representatives of science and the church. But those difficulties have now been practically overcome, thanks to the acknowledgement of errors of interpretations which had managed to disfigure relations between faith and science, thanks above all to better understanding of their respective fields of knowledge. Science sets problems at another level in our day. Science and the technology deriving from it have provoked profound changes in society, in institutions and in the behavior of mankind as well. Traditional cultures have been torn apart by new forms of social communication, production, experimentation, exploitation of nature and structuring of society.

Faced with this, science has to feel a much greater responsibility, first of all. The future of humanity depends on it.

Men and women who represent science and culture, your moral power is enormous. Can you succeed in getting the scientific sector to serve the culture of man above all and see that it is never perverted and used for destruction? It is a scandal of our times that many researchers are dedicated to perfecting new arms for war which one day could prove fatal. Consciences must be awakened.

Your responsibility and your power to influence public opinion are immense. Make them serve the cause of peace and man's true progress. How many marvels our world might achieve if the best talents and the best researchers joined hands to explore ways for the development of all mankind and all regions of the earth.

Therefore our epoch has need of a science of man, for original reflection and research. Besides the physical and biological sciences, specialists in the human sciences must make their contribution. Service to man is at stake and man has to be defended in his identity, dignity and moral grandeur, for he is a *res sacra*, as Seneca well said.

9. The size of the concerns mentioned might dishearten isolated researchers or thinkers. So, more than ever, research must be carried through in common.

The specialization of disciplines is such today that researchers should work in common for the sake of effective research, but even more for the sake of serving man: not only because of methodological exigencies, but also so as to avoid dispersion and give an adequate response to the complex problems that they have to face. . . .

The church and Catholics desire to participate actively in dialogue with scientists and researchers. Numerous Catholics already play an eminent part in various sectors of the university world and research. Their faith and culture give them strong reasons for going on with their scientific, humanistic or literary tasks. They are an eloquent testimony to the validity of the Catholic faith and to the church's interest in everything to do with science and culture.

The church follows the life of the university world with particular interest because she is conscious that in it are being formed the generations which will occupy key posts in the society of tomorrow. She, too, desires to be able to accomplish her task in the university field, and so encourages establishment and development of Catholic universities.

It is desirable in a dialogue between church authorities and public powers that practical accords be reached, permitting Catholic universities to give national communities their own original service. By recognizing this contribution, the public powers ultimately serve the cause of the manifold and diverse cultural identities in the pluralistic society of today.

10. A particularly important requirement today for cultural renewal is openness to the universal. We frequently notice that pedagogy is reduced to preparing students for a profession but not for life because, more or less consciously, education has sometimes been dissociated from instruction.

And yet the university must perform its indispensable function of education. This presupposes that teachers will be able to transmit not only science but also knowledge of man himself; that is to say, of his proper dignity, of his history, of his moral and civil responsibilities, of his spiritual destiny, of his ties with all mankind.

This demands that the pedagogy of education be based on a coherent image of man, on a concept of the universal that shall not set out from aprioristic conceptions, yet will also know how to receive the transcendental. For Catholics, man was created in God's image and is called to transcend the universe.

Cultures which have their roots and vitality in Christianity also acknowledge the importance of universal brotherhood among mankind. The new humanism, of which our time has so much need, has to add strength to the solidarity among all human beings. Without that, the great problems, such as establishment of peace, peaceful interchange of natural resources, ecology, the search for employment for all, establishment of social justice, cannot be solved. In the family, in the school and in the university, new generations will learn the requirements of international understanding, mutual respect, and effective cooperation in the tasks of developing the world.

International peace is now a very deep aspiration of mankind. It will be the fruit of universal understanding that is able to do away with prejudices, rancors and conflicts. Yes, the roots of peace are in the cultural and moral order. Yes, peace is a spiritual conquest of man.

11. The progress of culture is united in the end with moral and spiritual growth in man, because it is through his spirit that man realizes himself as such. Therefore he must have a vision of the integral, entire man.

The church therefore feels the responsibility of defending man against theoretical or practical ideologies which reduce him to an object of production or consumption, against fatalistic currents of ideas that paralyze minds, against moral permissiveness which abandons man to the emptiness of hedonism, against agnostic ideologies which tend to remove God from culture. . . .

SPEECH AT TOLEDO

3. . . . It is the apostle of the gentiles himself who speaks to us to teach us what is meant by apostles of Christ; he addresses us in order to show what participation in the church's mission calls for.

Paul teaches with special vigor that we are witnesses of God in Jesus Christ, and him "crucified" (1 Cor. 2, 1-3). Whoever acknowledges and confesses him as Lord stands under the manifestation of the power of the Spirit (cf. 1 Cor. 2,4).

All Christians are called to renew their profession of faith constantly, with the world and with life, as a full adherence to Jesus Christ, the son of God made man, crucified for our salvation and raised up again through the power of God. Such is "God's wisdom, a mysterious, hidden purpose, planned by God before all ages for our glory" (1 Cor. 2,7). This is the fundamental core of the Gospel which Christ entrusted to his church and which she transmits in the living tradition and teaches in the magisterium of the apostolic succession, so enriching the patrimony of the people of God which possesses the "sense of the faith" under the solicitous assistance of the Holy Spirit.

The announcement and testimony of Christian faith is rooted here. Therefore, the prime attitude of a witness to the faith is that of professing the same faith that he preaches, letting himself be gently converted by the Spirit of God and conforming his life to the divine wisdom. . . .

5. The pope exhorts all laity to take up their responsibility with dignity and responsibility. The pope trusts in the Spanish laity, and expects big things from all of them for God's glory and for the service of man. Yes, as I already recalled, the Christian vocation is essentially apostolic: Only in this service to the Gospel will the Christian find the fullness of his dignity and responsibility.

In fact, the laity, "made one body with Christ through baptism, and established among the people of God, are in their own way made sharers in the priestly, prophetic and kingly function of Christ" (*Lumen Gentium*, 31). They are called to sanctity and are sent out to announce and accomplish the reign of Christ until he comes.

If you would be true to this dignity, it is not enough to accept passively the wealth of faith that your tradition and culture have transmitted to you. A treasure is entrusted to you. Talents are granted which have to be taken up with responsibility for them to bear fruit in abundance....

The Second Vatican Council rightly emphasized that the primary task of the Catholic laity is to impregnate and transform the whole fabric of human social living with the values of the Gospel (cf. *LG*, 36), with the announcement of a Christian anthropology deriving from these values.

In his apostolic exhortation *Evangelii Nuntiandi*, (70), Paul VI defines the fields of the lay apostolate in these words: "Their own field of evangelizing activity is the vast and complicated world of politics, of the social field, of economics, but also of culture, of the sciences and of the arts, of international life, of the mass media and of other realities open to evangelization such as love, the family, the education of children and adolescents, professional work, suffering...." There is no human activity foreign to the responsible evangelizing task of the laity.

7. I would now bring out some of the more important of the otherwise pressing commitments of the apostolate of the laity. I am thinking concretely of the witness of life and the evangelizing effort called for by the Christian family.

Christian couples should live the sacrament of matrimony as participation in the fruitful and indissoluble union between Christ and his church. Let them be founders and animators of the domestic church, the family, with commitment to the integral ethical and religious upbringing of the children. Let them open to their youngsters the horizons of the various Christian vocations as a plentiful challenge to the alternatives of hedonist consumerism and atheist materialism....

... The Christian knows from the church's luminous teachings, without any need to follow a onesided or partisan political formula, that he ought to contribute to forming a more worthy society, one more respectful of the rights of man, based on the principles of justice and peace.

I am thinking, finally, of the world of culture. Catholic laity in their tasks as intellectuals, scientists, educations, artists, are called to create a new and authentic culture of truth and goodness, beauty and progress, from the immense cultural wealth of the peoples of Spain. This culture which they are called upon to create can contribute to fruitful dialogue between science and faith, Christian culture and universal civilization....

Before ending my words, I would ask you to raise your prayers for the latest victim and for all victims of terrorism in Spain: That the nation will not feel wounded in its deep aspiration for peace and concord and will obtain the grace from the Lord to free itself from the painful phenomenon of terrorism.

Let us understand that, in addition to always being anti-Christian, violence is not the way to solve human problems.

HOMILY AT LOYOLA

5. . . . The religious world lives immersed in societies and environments, the human and religious values of which it ought to appreciate and promote, because man and his dignity are the church's path, and because the Gospel has to penetrate every people and culture, but without confusing levels and values.

As today's liturgy teaches us, the consecrated know that their activities are not centered on temporal reality nor on what is the field of the laity and ought to be left to them. The consecrated must feel themselves above all to be at the service of God and his cause: "I will bless the Lord at all times, his praise shall ever be in my mouth" (Ps. 33, 2).

The ways of the religious world do not follow the calculations of man. They do not take the worship of power, of riches or of pleasure as their measure. On the contrary, they know that their strength is the grace of the divine acceptance of their oblation: "The poor afflicted man called out, and Yahweh heard" (Ps. 33, 7). This very poetry thus becomes an opening to the divine. Liberty of spirit, readiness without frontiers.

Religious are signposts on the roads of the world: They show the way to God. So there is a strong necessity for imploring prayer: "(The just) cried out and Yahweh heard them" (Ps. 33, 18).

In a world where the aspiration to transcendence is in peril, there is need of those who will halt to pray; of those who will give welcome to those who pray, who will give a supplement of spirit to this world, who time themselves at every moment by God's time.

Above all that, the world of the religious has to keep up its persevering aspiration toward perfection, with conversion renewed every day, for being confirmed in resolve.

What an elevating and humanizing capacity is found in the words of the responsorial Psalm: "Cease from doing evil and do good, seek peace and follow it" (Ps 33, 15). It is a program for every Christian; it is much more so for those who make profession of commitment to the good, to God, the God of love, of peace and concord.

You, dear men and women superiors, dear men and women religious, are called to live this splendid reality. This is the great lesson to be learned from Ignatius of Loyola. It is for his own sons, for each institute and for each man and woman religious.

It is a lesson of absolute fidelity to God, to an ideal without frontiers, to man without distinction, without reneging one's own land, but loving it and its genuine values dearly, with full respect for those not of it.

6. I cannot conclude this homily without addressing a particular word to the church's sons and daughters in the Basque country, in addition to what

I say at these meetings with all the faithful people of Spain.

You are a people rich in Christian, human and cultural values: with your millenniums-old language, your traditions and institutions, the tenacity and quiet character of your people, the noble and gentle sentiments given shape in your songs, the human and Christian dimension of the family among you, the exemplary dynamism of so many missionaries, the profound faith of your people.

I know that you are living a difficult time in the social and religious fields. I know of the efforts of your local churches, your bishops, priests, souls of special consecration and laity, to give a Christian orientation to your life through evangelization and catechesis. I encourage you from my own heart in this effort and in what you achieve for reconciliation of minds.

That is an essential dimension of Christian living, of Christ's prime commandment, which is one of love — a love that unites, that makes brothers and sisters, that therefore does not admit barriers or distinctions, because, as the one people of God (cf. *Lumen Gentium*, 9), the church is and must ever be the sign and sacrament of reconciliation in Christ. "There does not exist among you Jew or Greek, slave or freeman, male or female. All are one in Christ Jesus" (Gal. 3:28).

I cannot but think especially of your young people. So many of them have lived grand ideals and achieved marvelous works in the past and in the present. They are the great majority. I wish to praise them and render them this homage in the face of possible unjust generalizations or accusations. But unfortunately, there are also those who let themselves be tempted by materialistic and violent ideologies.

I would say to them with affection and firmness — and my voice is that of one who has personally suffered from violence — that they should reflect on the path they have taken, that they should not let themselves, their generosity or altruism, be manipulated. Violence is no way to build up. It offends God, those who suffer it and those who practice it.

Once again I repeat that Christianity understands and recognizes the noble and proper fight for justice at all levels but prohibits seeking solutions in paths of hate and death (cf. Homily at Drogheda, Sept. 29, 1979)....

SPEECH AT BARCELONA

1. ... I come to announce the gospel of work to you, dearest men and women workers, present and absent, those born on this land, and those coming from other areas, and those of all Spain.

2. The church believes it has an unavoidable duty in the social field to help "fortify the human community according to the divine law" (*Gaudium et Spes*, 42) by recalling the dignity and rights of workers, by stigmatizing situations where such rights are violated and by favoring

exchanges leading to authentic progress for man and society.

Work corresponds to God's design and will. The first pages of Genesis present creation to us as the work of God, God's labor. So, God calls on many to work, so as to be like him. Hence, work is not something off on the side. Even less is it a curse from heaven. On the contrary, it is a primordial blessing from the creator, an activity permitting the individual to realize himself and to offer a service to society. In addition, he will have a higher reward, for "your toil is not vain when it is done in the Lord" (I Cor. 15:58).

But it was Jesus who delivered the most thorough gospel of work, he who was the son of God made man and a man of manual work, subject to hard effort. He gave the most part of his earthly life to work as a craftsman and incorporated that same work into his task of salvation.

3. For my part, during these four years of my pontificate I have unceasingly proclaimed the centrality of man in my encyclicals and catechesis, insisting on his primacy over things and on the importance of the subjective dimension in work, based on the dignity of the human person.

In fact, inasmuch as he is a person man is the center of creation, for he alone has been created in God's image and likeness. He has been called to "subdue" the earth (Gen. 1:28), with the perspicacity of his intelligence and the activity of his hands. He turns himself into an artificer in work — both manual and intellectual — and communicates his own dignity to his work.

Friends and brother workers, the Christian concept of work sees it as a call to collaborate with God's power and love, maintaining man's life and making it more in accord with his design. When understood in this way, work is not a biological necessity for the sake of subsistence, but a moral duty. It is an act of love and it turns into joy, the deep joy of giving oneself through work to one's own family and to others, the intimate joyousness of offering oneself to God and of serving one's brothers, even though such giving entails sacrifices. Thus Christian work has a paschal meaning.

The logical consequence is that we all have the duty to do our work well. If we wish to realize ourselves properly, we may not avoid our duty or perform our work in a mediocre way, without interest, just to get it over with.

4. Your tenacious hard work and your feeling of responsibility make us understand, dear brothers and sisters, how far from the Christian concept of work — and from a correct vision of the social order — are certain attitudes of lack of interest, of waste of time and resources. These attitudes are spreading in our day, both in the public and in the private sector. . . .

5. . . . The lack of work goes against "the right to work," understood — in the universal context of the rest of the fundamental rights — as a primary necessity, and not a privilege, to satisfy the vital needs of human existence through labor activity. . . .

Prolonged unemployment gives rise to insecurity, lack of initiative, frustration, irresponsibility and lack of trust in society and in oneself. Capacities for personal development are atrophied, enthusiasm and love for the good are lost, family crises and desperate personal situations break out, and so there is an easy fall — especially on the part of the young — into drugs, alcoholism and crime.

It would be false and deceptive to consider this distressing problem — which has become epidemic throughout the world — as the product of passing circumstances or as a purely economic and socio-political problem. It is really an ethical problem, a spiritual problem, because it is a symptom of a moral disorder existing in society when the hierarchy of values is broken.

6. Through its social magisterium the church recalls that the ways to a just solution of this grave problem demand a revision of the economic order as a whole. Comprehensive planning of economic production, not simply planning by sectors, is needed. The correct and rational organization of work is necessary, not only on the national level, but also on the international level. The solidarity of all working men is needed for this.

The state must not resign itself to having to tolerate chronic high unemployment. The creation of new jobs must constitute for it a priority as much economic as political. But businessmen and workers together have to help in overcoming the lack of jobs. The former have to keep up the production rate of their factories, the latter should attend to their work with due efficiency and be disposed through solidarity to give up "double" jobs and recourse to systematic use of overtime, which reduces the possibility of providing work to others.

An economy that is at the service of man must be created by all possible means. To overcome clashes between private and collective interests, to overcome egoisms in the struggle for subsistence, a real change of attitude is demanded of all, a change in lifestyle, minds and wills, a conversion of man to the truth about man.

I have dwelt particularly on this matter because it is so topical. I know that you are preoccupied by many other problems concerning wages, health conditions at work, protection against accidents at work, the role of labor unions, management and profit sharing, and proper protection of workers coming from other places.

These are complex problems and they are vital for you. But I would repeat once again: Do not forget that the primary characteristic of labor is that of uniting humanity. . . .

7. Allow me now, dear men and women workers of Spain, to address my words to another class of workers in Spain: businessmen, industrialists, top administrators, qualified experts in socio-economic life and backers of industrial complexes.

I greet and pay honor to you, the creators of jobs, employment, services and job training. . . . To you, too, I proclaim the gospel of work.

And, as I invite you to reflect upon the Christian concept of enterprise, I would remind you above all that there is a deeper problem, above and beyond technical and economic aspects in which you are masters. I mean the moral dimension. Economics and technology really have no meaning unless they have reference to man, whom they must serve.

Work is actually for man, not man for work. Consequently, enterprise is for man and not man for enterprise.

An indispensable requirement for a society seeking to be a just society is that it overcome the unnatural and illogical antinomy between capital and labor, which has often been artificially sharpened by programed class struggle. This requirement is based on the primacy of man over things. Only man — entrepreneur and worker — is subject to work and is a person. Capital is nothing but "a conjunction of things" (*LE*, 12).

8. You well know that the economic world has been suffering a great crisis for some time. The social question has turned from a class problem into a world problem. Development of energy sources and the effect of strong political interests in this field have created fresh problems. These have led to doubts about certain economic structures until recently considered indispensable and untouchable, making the running of them ever harder.

In the face of such difficulties, do not waver, do not doubt your mission. Do not fall into the temptation to give up business, to shut down, to devote yourselves egoistically to calmer and less demanding professional activities. Overcome such temptations to escape, and keep on bravely at your posts, trying to give a more humane face every day to your enterprise and keeping in mind the great contribution you make to the common good when you open up fresh work possibilities. . . .

9. Because of its intrinsic dynamism, enterprise is called to perform a social function, under your drive, and this social function is profoundly ethical. It is that of contributing to the perfecting of man, of every man without any discrimination by creating conditions making work possible and enabling it to be, at the same time, work in which personal capacities can be developed. In this way effective and reasonable production of goods and services can be attained, and the worker should thus be able to feel that he is really working at something of his own.

So, an enterprise is not just an organism, a production structure. It should also transform itself into a life community, a place where a man lives with and relates with his peers, where personal development is not only allowed but encouraged as well. Is not the main enemy of the Christian sense of enterprise perhaps a certain functionalism that makes efficiency the one and only and the immediate requirement for production and work?

Work relations are first of all relations among human beings. They cannot be measured by the sole rule of efficiency. . . .

When times are difficult for all — as times of economic crisis are — workers cannot be left to their fate, especially those who, like the poor and the immigrants, have nothing but their hands to support themselves. It is proper always to remember an important principle of Catholic social teaching: "The hierarchy of values and the deep meaning of work itself demand that capital be a function of work and not work a function of capital." (*LE*, 23). . . .

10. . . . Work has a power in itself that can give life to a community, to

solidarity: the solidarity of work, which spontaneously develops among those sharing the same kind of work or profession, so as to embrace, through the interests of all individuals and groups, the common good of all society; solidarity with work, that is to say, with each man who works, which by overcoming all class egoisms and one-sided political interests makes its own the drama of the unemployed and those in hard working conditions; finally, solidarity in work, a solidarity without boundaries because it is based on the naturalness of human work, that is to say, on the priority of the human person over things.

Such solidarity, open, dynamic and universal by nature, will never be negative. It will be a "solidarity against," but a positive and constructive one, a "solidarity for," for work, for justice, for peace, for well-being and for truth in social life. . . .

NOVEMBER

PRELIMINARY REPORT
ON SOVIET LABOR CAMPS
November 4, 1982

In late September Congress directed the secretary of state to investigate the reported use of forced labor and violations of human rights in connection with the construction of the Soviet Union's Yamal natural gas pipeline. On November 4 the State Department sent to Capitol Hill a "Preliminary Report to the Congress on Forced Labor in the USSR," the first published U.S. government study on Soviet labor camps. (A final report was submitted to Congress in February 1983.)

The preliminary report consisted of six parts:
* *A letter of transmittal to Sen. William L. Armstrong, R-Colo., from Powell A. Moore, assistant secretary for congressional relations in the State Department.*
* *A Reagan administration press statement of September 22, expressing concern over reports of forced labor in the U.S.S.R., particularly on the pipeline construction.*
* *A Labor Department summary of efforts by the United Nations' International Labor Organization "to bring Soviet law and practice into line with international treaties on forced labor."*
* *A Central Intelligence Agency (CIA) study of the Soviet forced labor system, the heart of the State Department report.*
* *Documents and testimony gathered by the Frankfurt-based International Society for Human Rights, including eyewitness accounts from former prison and labor camp inmates.*
* *A brief summary of actions by European governments and international labor groups seeking investigations of the forced labor charges.*

Pipeline Labor

Reports that forced labor was being used to construct the 3,000-mile Soviet pipeline that would supply Siberian natural gas to Western Europe came to public attention during the summer. These reports added to the controversy already surrounding the project. Upon its completion, scheduled for early 1984, the pipeline would deliver some 40,000 million cubic meters of gas annually to West Europe, in exchange for hard currency. West European nations were contributing technological and financial support to the pipeline project.

Opponents of the pipeline deal, including the Reagan administration, argued that the $8 billion-$10 billion the Russians would receive annually would finance a Soviet technological buildup and that the gas supply would be a powerful lever for the Kremlin to have over Europe. In moves that irritated American allies supporting the pipeline, President Ronald Reagan barred export of U.S. goods for use in pipeline construction and later extended this ban to prohibit sales of equipment produced by foreign subsidiaries of U.S. companies. (Pipeline sanctions, p. 879)

The reports of forced labor, including the alleged use of political dissidents, religious prisoners and Vietnamese laborers, gave pipeline opponents a moral argument. Senate Resolution 449, submitted by Armstrong on August 17, expressed the Senate's concern: "... [I]f allegations of forced labor prove to be true, the participation of the West in furnishing either technology or financing to make construction of the pipeline possible is tantamount to unwitting collaboration by the West in one of the most massive abuses of human rights in history."

The State Department came up with no hard proof of forced labor use on the pipeline, and Moscow vehemently denied any such charges. However, the CIA study contained in the State Department report stated: "In view of the past use of unconfined forced laborers and the current shortage of labor, it seems that some forced labor would be used along the export pipeline route for compressor stations and auxiliary construction unless the Soviets depart from their usual practice because of the exposure in the Western media." Reinforcing this conjecture were the repeated Soviet refusals to allow Western press or diplomats to visit the pipeline construction sites, the location of many labor camps close to the pipeline route and eyewitness reports of compulsory labor on the pipeline gathered by international human rights groups.

Soviet Forced Labor System

Forced labor long has been a part of the Soviet penal system, allowing the state to benefit economically from an individual's "rehabilitation." Forced labor reportedly played a part in construction of the trans-

Siberian railroad, the White Sea Canal, the Moscow subway system and other major construction projects in the Soviet Union.

The CIA estimated that in 1982 approximately 4 million Soviet citizens were serving sentences of forced labor. Half of these were confined, either in labor camps or in prisons; the others were either on probation or parole, forced to work but not strictly confined.

The labor camps, which the CIA estimated numbered more than 1,000, engaged in a variety of activities including construction work, manufacturing, mining, logging and agriculture. On large construction projects, such as the gas pipeline, forced laborers would be used to clear land, dig trenches, lay cables and do other heavy work that required no special skills.

Accounts from former prisoners and others described poor conditions at the camps, including overcrowding, malnutrition, inadequate health care and unsafe working conditions.

Following are excerpts from the preliminary report to Congress on forced labor within the Soviet Union, submitted to Sen. William Armstrong November 4, 1982:

LETTER OF TRANSMITTAL

Dear Senator Armstrong:

Conference Report No. 97-891 dated September 29 accompanying H.R. 6956 directed the Secretary to undertake an investigation into allegations that forced labor is being employed, and human rights violated, by the Soviet authorities in the construction of the Trans-Siberian gas pipeline.

There is clear evidence that the Soviet Union is using forced labor on a massive scale. This includes the use of political prisoners. We have information from a variety of sources which confirms that the Soviets routinely employ a portion of their 4 million forced laborers, the world's largest forced labor population, as unskilled workers on domestic pipeline construction. It cannot yet be conclusively established whether such labor is being used specifically on the export pipeline project, but a number of reports suggest that forced labor has been used in some of the site preparation and other preliminary work on the export pipeline including clearing the forests, leveling the right of way, building roads, and constructing living quarters.

There is, in fact, a long history to the use of forced labor in the Soviet Union. This has included the use of forced labor — including thousands of political prisoners — on numerous large-scale development projects. The Baikal-Amur rail line, the Bielomorsk and Volga-Don canals, the Moscow subway, and the Kama River truck plant are a few of the better known Soviet projects built with forced labor. Among the groups that Soviet authorities traditionally press into forced labor are political prisoners and prisoners of conscience convicted for "anti-Soviet agitation" or under broadly-worded "hooliganism" and "parasitism" laws. For nearly thirty years, complaints have been registered in the International Labor Organization [ILO], and in other international bodies, against the use of such laws to punish and exploit political and religious dissidents in the Soviet Union.

The Soviet authorities not only have failed to provide responses satisfactory to the ILO on any of these complaints, but also have attacked the ILO supervisory machinery itself. Their continuing refusal to cooperate with the ILO authorities puts the burden of proof on the Soviet Union with regard to the numerous and grave charges of forced labor lodged against them. We strongly believe that the Soviet authorities should open all of their labor camps and large-scale labor brigades to independent international investigation.

We welcome Congressional interest in this question. Forced labor in the USSR is a human rights issue of deep concern to the Administration, as expressed most recently in our official statement of September 22. Decency compels us to express our distress at the Soviet Union's exploitation of forced labor. For those who believe in the promotion of world peace through law, it is crucial that the international community investigate and demand remedial action when confronted with serious charges of violations of international agreements. Obviously, the closed nature of Soviet society renders difficult the discovery of facts on this issue, as well as the production of convincing evidence. But be assured that we will continue diligently to conduct this investigation. We also are pursuing this issue vigorously through the ILO. . . .

Sincerely,

Powell A. Moore
Assistant Secretary for
Congressional Relations

PRELIMINARY REPORT

Preface

To enable observers of the Soviet Union to better assess the reports of use of forced labor in the USSR, especially reports of its use on the gas export pipeline to Western Europe, this study has been prepared on the overall system of forced labor in the Soviet Union. Various aspects of the system as outlined in Soviet official documents, such as The Russian Soviet Federated Socialist Republic (RSFSR) Criminal Code, are examined in the light [of] the accounts by former prisoners and other emigres that have been published in Western news media about the realities of the system. The report has been prepared from a broad array of documents, scholarly studies, and other source materials relating to the subject of the Soviet penal system in general and forced labor in particular.

The Soviet Forced Labor System

The Soviet Penal system is remarkable for its huge size and its systematic employment of labor. The labor camps so vividly described by Solzhenitsyn are only one element of a system that also includes prisons as well as a growing cadre of forced labor without confinement. The Soviets have an ideological commitment to the rehabilitative role of labor in the social adjustment of the individual, and accordingly refer to the forced labor camps as "correctional" labor colonies.*

Correctional labor colonies were first established in 1919 on the Solovetskiy Islands in the White Sea, but until Stalin assumed power the system grew rather slowly. Stalin's forced labor system reached a peak of perhaps 15 million persons in 1947. After Stalin's death liberal reforms reduced the camp population, and in 1957 P. I. Kudryavtsev, Deputy Procurator General of the Soviet Union, asserted that the number had been reduced to about 800,000 to 900,000, and that 1 to 2 percent were "politicals." Toward the end of the Khrushchev era, criminal penalties were toughened, the crime rate increased, and the camp system began to expand again. Criminal charges were used increasingly to control political dissidents. Although many of the old camps in Siberia and the Far East were abandoned, others were built closer to population centers.

In addition, an extensive system of forced labor without confinement had its inception in the early 1960s and has grown rapidly in scope since then; the number of non-confined forced laborers now more than equals the number of those confined, and it is continuing to rise. Given the worsening labor shortage in parts of the Soviet Union, this relatively efficient, flexible method of deriving some economic benefit from an increasing crime rate is likely to continue to grow.

In the Soviet Union nine out of every 10 persons convicted of crimes more serious than misdemeanors receive sentences that include forced labor. About half of these sentences also include confinement. Although approximately half of those sentenced to confinement are paroled from confinement, they continue in the forced labor system until they finish their terms.

---

* The term *forced labor camps* is used in this report as a general appellation for *correctional labor colonies*, *educational labor colonies*, and *correctional labor colony settlements*; the specific terms will be used when particular types of facilities are being discussed.

HOW MANY FORCED LABORERS?

We currently estimate that some 4 million Soviet citizens — about 1.5 percent of the population — are now serving sentences of forced labor.

— About 2 million of these are confined, 85 percent in forced labor camps — of which there are over 1,100 — and the remainder in prisons.

— Approximately 1.5 million, convicted of crimes for which they could have received sentences of confinement, have been sentenced instead to probation with "compulsory involvement in labor." Most of them are working at construction jobs far from their homes.

— About 500,000 have been paroled from confinement but remain obligated to perform forced labor for the remainder of their terms. Many of them also are working at construction sites.

— In addition an undetermined number are sentenced to "correctional tasks" without confinement; they are working at their own jobs for reduced pay or in more menial jobs for low pay while continuing to live at home.

Among these forced laborers are dissidents (political prisoners) whose numbers may reach as high as 10,000, the figure claimed by [Andrei D.] Sakharov and Amnesty International. A former Soviet official reports that Ministry of Internal Affairs (MVD) records listed 10,358 political prisoners at the beginning of 1977. Aleksandr Ginsburg, a prominent political dissident, estimated that there were 5,000 political prisoners in 1979. Dissidents in the Soviet Union fall into at least six categories: refuseniks (those refused permission to leave the USSR), religious nonconformists, human and civil rights activists, minority nationalists, discontented workers, and Russian nationalists. The higher estimates above probably include some who, in addition to being dissidents, are accused of crimes of "hooliganism" and "parasitism."

FORCED LABOR WITH CONFINEMENT

The Correctional Labor Code of the RSFSR establishes four basic types of confinement facilities: correctional labor colonies, education labor colonies (for juveniles), colony settlements, and prisons. Each type of facility is differentiated by the amount of freedom and privileges granted to the prisoners; the degree of supervision, regimentation, and restraint to which they are subjected; the difficulty of their labor; and the conditions under which they must live and work. The regimes in effect at prisons are the most harsh; the ones in effect at correctional labor colonies and educational labor colonies somewhat less harsh; and the regime at colony settlements is the mildest in the system.

The gravity of the offender's crime and whether or not he is a recidivist determines in which of the following facilities incarceration will occur.

• Correctional labor colonies constitute the bulk of the traditional Soviet confinement system where convicts are closely guarded, supervised, and regimented. Labor colonies are enclosed by as many as six or seven fences and walls with towers on each corner manned by armed guards. A typical one-story wooden barracks houses a detachment of 140 to 160 prisoners divided into two sections. The legal minimum living area per prisoner (2.0 square meters in prisons; 2.5 square meters in camps) is not much larger than an American-style twin bed.

• Educational labor colonies are correctional institutions for juvenile criminals aged 14 through 17. Inmates of educational labor colonies are usually transferred to correctional labor colonies when they reach age 18. Those who have less than two years of a sentence remaining and who seem well on the way to rehabilitation, however, may be allowed to remain at the education labor colony.

• Correctional labor colony settlements are milder forms of confinement that were introduced in 1977. Often referred to by prisoners as the "fifth regime," these colony settlements are located in areas where new industries are being built and at other construction sites. Many regular camps — especially in Kazakhstan, Siberia, the Far East, and the Far North — have associated colony settlements. Colony settlements are the least onerous facilities in the penal system and the only ones in which the sexes are not segregated. For instance, prisoners must observe a curfew and perform the labor designated for them, but they may wear ordinary clothing, and few restrictions are placed on their private behavior or their privileges.

• Soviet prisons are urban facilities, most of which have been expanded and reconstructed since Czarist times, and present the harshest confinement in the system. All major cities have at least one large prison. Major prisons number about 300 and house some 300,000 inmates at any one time. Prisons are differentiated by primary function; four types may be distinguished: penitentiaries, transit prisons, investigatory prisons and psychiatric prisons.

PAYMENT OF PRISONERS

Soviet law stipulates that inmates in prisons and labor colonies are to be paid at least the minimum wage for their work. Since inmates are not permitted to keep money in their possession (a rule constantly abused), wages are credited to the prisoners' accounts. Theoretically, after deductions for their upkeep have been made, the balance is credited to their accounts and paid to them when they depart; however, many prisoners reportedly have no money when they are released.

Prisoners are allowed as much as 5 rubles monthly in credit at the prison or colony commissary on what are termed "food items and basic necessities." Soap, tooth powder, envelopes, postage stamps, tobacco, cigarettes, black bread, margarine, candy, jam and canned fish are typical commissary items, but reportedly many of these are frequently unavailable. There are no restrictions placed on the amount of money a prisoner may spend on books, educational supplies, and stationery. The number of letters prisoners may send and receive and the number of packages and parcels they may receive are closely regulated; such privileges are commonly used as a means of enforcing prison discipline.

INCENTIVES AND PENALTIES

The Correctional Labor Code specifies incentives that "may be employed to encourage convicts' good behavior and honest attitude toward work and training." These incentives include the granting of additional privileges — perhaps permission to spend an extra couple of rubles in the commissary. More significant measures entail transfer of prison inmates to labor colonies, or transfer of inmates of labor colonies of other than special regime to colony settlements. Such transfers may not take place until at least half the sentence has been served.

The Correctional Labor Code also specifies penalties that "may be applied to convicts for violating the requirement of the regime." Not surprisingly, most of the penalties are mirror images of the incentives: a warning or reprimand, withdrawal of privileges, and transfer to harsher confinement conditions. For major infractions, inmates of both labor camps and prisons may be put in "punitive isolation." First offenders are sentenced for as long as 15 days to a punishment isolation cell, better known as the *shizo*, or cooler.

WORKING CONDITIONS

The RSFSR Correctional Labor Code provides guidelines on the general work conditions of prisoners, while specific conditions are established by the prison and colony administrators. Work is compulsory, and those who do not work receive a reduced food ration and no pay. Inmates are required to work eight hours per day, six days a week. Prisoners who must travel to work sites, such as those in logging or construction areas, "donate" this extra time to the state. Most camps work two shifts, from 0800 to 1700 and from 1700 to 0100.

According to many former prisoners from many different camps, violations of good safety and health practices are common throughout the system, even though the Correctional Labor Code stipulates that "convicts' work is organized so as to observe labor protection rules and industrial safety measures as established by labor law." At a sawmilling camp in Riga, for example, serious accidents were reported to occur frequently. Prisoners in this camp work without helmets, gloves, or safety goggles.

FORCED LABOR WITHOUT CONFINEMENT

Persons sentenced to forced labor without confinement fall in [sic] two categories: those assigned to correctional *tasks* without confinement, an administrative penalty that amounts to little more than a fine, and those sentenced to correctional *labor* without confinement. The latter comprises two sub-categories: parolees (also known as khimiki*) and probationers with compulsory labor.

The penalty of correctional tasks without confinement is meted out to offenders whose crimes are deemed not serious enough to justify sentences of confinement. The compulsory tasks may be performed either at the offender's regular workplace or at some other nearby place so that he may continue to live at home. The offender's pay is docked as much as 20 percent, and the time spent performing correctional tasks (maximum sentence: one year) may not count towards his job seniority. The number of Soviet citizens who receive such sentences annually is difficult to estimate but could number about a half million, judging from fragmentary information.

In 1964 the Supreme Soviet of the USSR decreed that certain prisoners then under confinement could be released — in effect, paroled — from penal institutions and sent to construction sites to work out the balance of their sentences without confinement. Article 44 of the Criminal Code was amended to establish eligibility requirements for this program. Those not eligible include prisoners undergoing compulsory treatment for alcoholism, drug addiction, or venereal disease; foreign prisoners, and prisoners "who systematically or maliciously" violate the terms of their confinement. All others were eligible — those confined for the most serious offenses (intentional homicide, crimes against the state) after serving three-quarters of their time, and those serving for lesser offenses after lesser amounts of time.

The MVD serves as a clearing house — a kind of employment agency — keeping track on the one hand of requests from other ministries for forced laborers, and on the other of eligible prisoners who might be paroled to fulfill these requirements. Periodically (perhaps two or three times a year), groups of eligible prisoners are freed from confinement in what are called "amnesties" and sent in guarded batches to the forced labor sites. Until recently, prisoners convicted of especially dangerous crimes against the state had little chance of being granted parole. However, demands for forced laborers have become so insistent that even some political prisoners have been paroled. Overall, roughly one-half of all persons under confinement are now being paroled before the end of their terms and are serving an average of two years at compulsory labor without confinement. Approximately 500,000 parolees are currently performing forced labor under this system.

In 1970, another decree of the Supreme Soviet authorized courts to issue sentences of "probation with compulsory labor" as an alternative to

---

* When the parole program started, most parolees were sent to construction sites of the chemical industry, which was then undergoing a major expansion. The prisoners therefore referred to the program as *khimiya* — chemistry — and to the parolees (and, later, also to the probationers) as *khimiki* — chemists. The term *khimiya* remains in use to this day.

"confinement with compulsory involvement in labor." In such sentences, the confinement portion is suspended but the labor portion remains. The new decree greatly widened the scope of the program of forced labor without confinement, for now the entire sentence could be so served. The stated intent of the decree was to allow courts more latitude in determining the sentence when they decided that an offender could be reformed without confinement. Perhaps not coincidentally, however, treating offenders in this way permits the state to extract maximum economic benefit from their labor at minimum cost.

Estimating the number of persons serving sentences of probation with compulsory involvement in labor is difficult. In 1973 the Chief Justice of the Lithuania Supreme Court commented that nearly 20 percent of the court sentences issued in Lithuania fell into this category and that this percentage was rising. A Ukrainian court lawyer until 1979 estimated at least 30 percent of all criminal court cases received sentences to compulsory labor. Recent information suggests that this has risen to about half of current sentences. Assuming this is correct, and that the average sentence is 3 to 4 years, there are now 1.4 million to 1.8 million persons on probation with compulsory involvement in labor.

Persons sentenced to correctional *tasks* without confinement never leave home and suffer minimal disruption in their lives, but the parolees and probationers sentenced to correctional *labor* without confinement may be sent to large construction sites far from their homes. When assigned to work outside their immediate home areas, parolees are usually transported to their assigned work sites in guarded groups on trains, and if they travel long distances, they spend several periods in transit prisons en route. Probationers are usually permitted to make their own travel arrangements and travel to their assigned work sites unescorted.

At the work sites the forced laborers live in barracks similar to those in correctional labor colonies. The facilities are not guarded, but the convicts must observe a daily curfew, normally at 2200 hours. As a rule a laborer's special skills will be utilized as much as possible at the work site, but there are reports that some laborers are required to perform heavy manual labor regardless of their skills. They are paid the Soviet minimum wage for such labor and after paying for room and board (no more than 50 percent) are allowed to keep or spend the rest of their money as they wish. They are permitted to eat wherever they wish. It is not unusual for such convicts, especially probationers, to be granted permission to leave the work site to visit relatives, conduct personal business, or even to take vacations.

The time spent at forced labor without confinement counts toward fulfillment of the confinement sentence at the rate of one day for one day. But if the parolee or probationer violates the terms of his sentence or commits a new crime at his work site, he is sent back to the penal institution from whence he came (or would have gone, in the case of a probationer) and forfeits all of the time spent outside confinement. Authorities apparently try to avoid applying this drastic punishment to convicts nearing the ends of their sentences.

ROLE OF FORCED LABOR IN THE ECONOMY

Forced laborers engage in nearly all forms of economic activity. They constitute about 3 percent of the total Soviet labor force, which now is estimated at 147 million. In the 1980s, labor force growth will be less than half of what it was in the 1970s. Forced labor is thus likely to become a more important means of relieving serious manpower shortages, particularly in inhospitable areas, and there is likely to be much greater use of forced laborers who are not confined. Unconfined forced labor provides a flexible and inexpensive source of labor for hazardous or unhealthy duty or for work in remote locations.

Most inmates of prisons, correctional labor colonies, and colony settlements work full time in a broad variety of economic activities, including manufacturing, construction, logging and wood processing, mining, producing building materials, and agriculture.

Construction. Under Stalin, forced labor was used heavily in the development of remote areas of the Far North, Siberia, and the Far East. Cities such as Noril'sk, Vorkuta, Magnitogorsk, and Magadan were built largely by forced labor. Major construction projects such as the Baltic-White Sea and Volga-Don Canals, as well as parts of the Trans-Siberian and Kotlas-Vorkuta Railroads, relied heavily upon forced labor.

In recent years, more than 100 camps, or approximately 10 percent of the total, have been associated with construction activities. Construction camps are scattered throughout the USSR, most of them in or near cities. The heaviest concentrations are in Kazakhstan and Central Asia. The inmates usually work at sites throughout the cities in which the camps are located; hence they are more visible to the general populace than those in other kinds of camps. One source reported watching 40 trucks, each loaded with 40 prisoners, drive off daily from the labor colony at Nizhnekamsk to nearby sites where a petrochemical complex, a large automotive repair facility, and a concrete products plant were under construction. In many large cities apartment houses, hotels, hospitals, government office buildings, and the like have been built by convict labor.

The practice of using forced labor for the clearing and construction work for entire new towns continues. Examples include Shevchenko, a showplace city on the Caspian Sea containing a nuclear-powered desalination plant, and Navoi, a petrochemical city in Central Asia near a large deposit of natural gas. Both cities still contain major concentrations of forced labor.

Forced laborers on probation or parole from confinement are being employed at a multitude of major construction projects throughout the country. Especially large concentrations of them, numbering in the thousands, have been used in construction of the huge Kama River truck plant (the world's largest) and the Baykal-Amur Mainline (BAM) railroad. Parolees and probationers are also employed in industrial production and other economic activities, including pipeline construction.

Pipeline Construction. Forced labor has been used as an integral part of pipeline construction work crews in the Ukraine, Kazakhstan, and the central RSFSR. The forced laborers in pipeline construction have come largely from parolees and probationers, and have been used in unskilled jobs such as clearing forests, draining swamps, and preparing roads. Forced labor crews are usually removed before skilled workers arrive, minimizing contact between the groups. In some areas, however, unconfined forced laborers have worked directly with free workers doing low-skilled jobs. Parolees are usually released to a specific work site, for example, a construction site for a compressor station, where they must remain until completion of their assignment. They often live in trailers or barracks similar to those of other workers. If local labor is not available, construction authorities may appeal to the oblast executive committee and the local organs of the MVD to assign paroled prisoners to a work site. Paroled prisoners and probationers are not generally employed in laying pipe, which requires mobile crews. They reportedly are used in the construction and repair of gas compressor stations, service roads, and workers' housing. Many of these unconfined forced laborers are young people who have been convicted of petty crimes and are serving relatively light sentences.

SIBERIAN GAS EXPORT PIPELINE

In view of the past use of unconfined forced laborers and the current shortage of labor, it seems that some forced labor would be used along the export pipeline route for compressor station and auxiliary construction unless the Soviets depart from their usual practice because of the exposure in the Western media. There are about 100 heavily secured forced labor camps close to the proposed route, all of which existed before the start of construction of the export pipeline. Prisoners in the camps are engaged in a variety of activities, but they could be tapped for pipeline construction work if needed. However, it is more likely that forced laborers will come from the ranks of parolees and probationers.

Manufacturing. Well over half of the USSR's forced labor camps and numerous large prisons contain some type of manufacturing facility. These institutions associated with manufacturing are most heavily concentrated in the western USSR, especially in the Ukraine. Industrial camps tend to be larger and more complex than the other types, and there is a great diversity of manufacturing activities, for example:

— 17 camps in the Mordovskaya ASSR Complex produce a variety of manufactures including metal products, clothing, clocks, automotive parts, furniture, and souvenirs;

— 12 Latvian camps produce metal goods, wooden furniture and souvenirs, clothing, footwear, and electrical equipment;

— eight camps in Lithuania produce electrical sockets and plugs, home appliances, clothing, plastic and rubber products, and furniture;

— in a Siberian camp near Ulan-Ude, 1,500 prisoners produce furniture, glass, and clothing.

Typically, the prisoner work force at a manufacturing camp is supplemented by free laborers, some of them former prisoners, who may account for as much as 15 percent of the total. Most of this latter group serve as foremen, technicians, engineers, and quality control experts.

Logging and Other Activities. About 350 camps are engaged in logging, sawmilling, and related activities. These operations are concentrated in the Urals, the Northwest, the Volga-Vyatka, and the Siberian economic regions. Most logging camps are by nature temporary and crude in construction; they are abandoned as surrounding areas are depleted of trees. In the past, abandoned logging camps were usually replaced by new ones elsewhere. Now, however, the use of forced labor in logging and wood processing seems to be declining, and relatively few new camps of this type are being constructed.

Approximately 50 camps are associated with mineral extraction, far fewer than in former years when forced labor was extensively used in mining, especially in the Kolyma Basin, where gold mining and some lead and coal mining were carried on by prisoners. Coal mining was also pursued in Kazakhstan and in the Russian North at Vorkuta and on Novaya Zemlya. Today coal is still mined by forced laborers at Vorkuta and Karaganda as is uranium at Zheltyye Vody in the Ukraine, gold at Zarafshan in Central Asia, iron ore at Rudnyy, and bauxite at Arkalyk — the last two in Kazakhstan. At Vasalemma, Estonia, prisoners work a large linestone deposit.

Camps producing construction materials have in recent years increased slightly, to about 60, and are scattered throughout the USSR. Camps in this category engage primarily in producing bricks and blocks used in the construction industry.

Agricultural camps number about 20 and play a small and decreasing role in the Soviet forced labor system. Conditions in agricultural camps are less severe than in other camps: the work is less strenuous, and agricultural camps are located in more hospitable regions of the USSR, such as the North Caucasus.

▼▼▼

DEATH OF BREZHNEV
November 10, 1982

Long-time Soviet leader Leonid I. Brezhnev died November 10, touching off widespread speculation about a successor. Within days after Brezhnev's death, 68-year-old Yuri V. Andropov succeeded Brezhnev as the most powerful political figure in the Soviet Union. For 15 years, from 1967 to 1982, he had headed the country's intelligence and internal security agency, the Committee for State Security, known as the KGB. The speed and smoothness of the transition, without an apparent power struggle, surprised many Western analysts.

Brezhnev's death marked the end of a long period of stability in Soviet internal affairs, following the turbulent years of Nikita Khrushchev's leadership. Brezhnev held the post of general secretary of the Communist Party's Central Committee for 18 years, a term exceeded only by Joseph Stalin's tyrannical 29 years. Brezhnev simultaneously held the top government post of Presidium chairman for six years.

He considered détente and disarmament his greatest accomplishments. One of his last speeches, to 500 generals and defense ministry officials, however, marked a turn from an emphasis on negotiation to a blunter approach. He referred to "Washington's aggressive policy which is threatening to push the world into the flames of nuclear war" and the "adventurism, rudeness and undisguised egoism of this policy."

A super apparatchik (high-level bureaucrat) with strong army ties (he was a major general), Brezhnev promoted détente while presiding over almost two decades of Soviet military expansion. His tenure bracketed the flowering and collapse of the human rights and emigration move-

ments. Emigration, primarily of Jews, began under Brezhnev in the late 1960s and reached its height in the mid-1970s.

Domestically the Brezhnev era saw a sharp rise in the Soviet standard of living despite periodic setbacks in the agricultural and industrial sectors. Brezhnev modernized and built up the nation's conventional and nuclear defense systems, centralized the economy and tightened the party hold on the KGB.

Brezhnev was born in 1906 in the Ukraine. In 1931 he became a member of the Communist Party. Six years later he was promoted to a party secretaryship in the Ukraine under Khrushchev, the Ukrainian Communist Party leader. Brezhnev became Khrushchev's protégé in a close association lasting until Khrushchev's ouster from party leadership in October 1964.

In 1960 Brezhnev became chairman of the Presidium of the Supreme Soviet (parliament), a post equivalent to president. He relinquished the presidency the following year to serve as Khrushchev's deputy on the Central Committee Secretariat. He helped bring about his mentor's downfall in 1964 and subsequently replaced Khrushchev. He was elected president in 1977, replacing the ousted Nikolai Podgorny. The three living former U.S. presidents who negotiated with Brezhnev — Richard Nixon, Gerald R. Ford and Jimmy Carter — each recalled the Soviet leader as a formidable adversary.

In poor health for several years, Brezhnev was 75 when he died of a heart attack. He was buried in front of the Kremlin Wall in a spot behind the Lenin mausoleum that is symbolically the most distinguished burial place of any modern Soviet leader.

Brezhnev's successor, Andropov, one of the few members of the Soviet hierarchy to speak English, reportedly was fascinated with Western culture, especially that of the United States.

American leaders regarded Andropov as a tougher, smarter and shrewder competitor than Brezhnev. As KGB chief, he presided over the systematic suppression of the dissident movement and was a key member of the leadership group that ordered the invasion of Czechoslovakia in 1968. He pressured the Communist Polish regime to crush the Solidarity labor union and impose martial law in December 1981. (End of martial law, p. 947; martial law in Poland, Historic Documents of 1981, p. 881.)

Andropov was the first secret police chief to rise to any of the top political positions in the Soviet Union. As the Soviet ambassador to Hungary from 1954 to 1957, he played a major role in quelling the 1956 Hungarian uprising. In 1962 he was promoted to Communist Party Central Committee secretary. In 1982 he was named to the party's secretariat. Two days after Brezhnev's death, on November 12, he replaced Brezhnev as Communist Party Central Committee general secretary. On November 23 he was elected to the 38-member Presidium of the Supreme Soviet.

Following is the text of the announcement of the death of Soviet leader Leonid I. Brezhnev and a statement to the Soviet people by the CPSU Central Committee, both November 11, 1982; and the text of the eulogy by Yuri V. Andropov given at Brezhnev's funeral, November 15:

ANNOUNCEMENT OF DEATH

The Central Committee of the Communist Party of the Soviet Union, the Presidium of the USSR Supreme Soviet and the Council of Ministers of the USSR hereby inform with deep sorrow the party and the entire Soviet people that Leonid Ilyich Brezhnev, General Secretary of the Central Committee of the Communist Party of the Soviet Union and President of the Presidium of the USSR Supreme Soviet, died a sudden death at 8:30 A.M. on November 10, 1982.

The name Leonid Ilyich Brezhnev, a true continuer of Lenin's great cause and an ardent champion of peace and communism, will live forever in the hearts of the Soviet people and all progressive people throughout the world.

CENTRAL COMMITTEE STATEMENT

Dear comrades,

The Communist Party of the Soviet Union, the entire Soviet people have suffered a grave loss. The true follower of the great cause of Lenin, fiery patriot, outstanding revolutionary and fighter for peace and communism, the most prominent politician and statesman of our times, Leonid Ilyich Brezhnev, has passed away.

All of the diverse activities and the life of L. I. Brezhnev are inseparable from the most important stages in the history of the Land of the Soviets. Collectivization and industrialization, the Great Patriotic War and the postwar rebirth, the opening up of the virgin lands and the organization of space exploration — these are also landmarks in the biography of the glorious son of the working class, Leonid Ilyich Brezhnev. Wherever the party sent him, Leonid Ilyich selflessly, with the energy, persistence, daring and principledness typical of him, struggled for its great ideas.

The Soviet people and our friends all over the world by right associate the consistent assertion of the Leninist norms in party and state life and the perfection of socialist democracy with the name of Comrade Brezhnev and with his tireless work in the posts of General Secretary of the Central Committee of the Communist Party of the Soviet Union and President of the Presidium of the USSR Supreme Soviet. He wisely steered the activities of the Leninist headquarters of the party — its Central Committee, the Politburo of the Central Committee — setting an example of the masterful organization of concerted collective work. He played an outstanding role in drafting and implementing the economic and sociopolitical strategy of the party at the stage of developed socialism, in laying down and pursuing the course of improving the well-being of the people and in the further strengthening of the economic and defense might of our country.

Leonid Brezhnev made an everlasting contribution to the formulation and implementation of the policy of our party on the international scene, a policy of peace, peaceful cooperation, detente, disarmament, giving a strong rebuff to the aggressive intrigues of imperialism and preventing nuclear catastrophe. Great was his contribution to the consolidation of the world socialist community and the development of the international communist movement.

While Leonid Brezhnev's heart was beating, his thoughts and deeds were entirely dedicated to the interests of the working people. He was always linked vitally and inseparably with the masses of working people. He was and remains an embodiment of Leninist ideological devotion, consistent internationalism, revolutionary optimism and humanism in the minds of Communists and hundreds of millions of people in all continents.

Grave is our loss, profound is our grief. At this hour of mourning the Communists and all the working people of the Soviet Union rally still closer behind the Leninist CPSU Central Committee, its steering nucleus, that was established under the beneficial influence of Leonid Ilyich Brezhnev. The people have faith in the party, its mighty collective reason and will. They wholeheartedly support its domestic and foreign policy. The Soviet people know well that the banner of Lenin, the banner of the October Revolution, under which historic victories of world significance were attained, is in reliable hands.

The party and the people have the grandiose program of communist construction worked out by the 23rd — 26th CPSU Congresses. That program is being steadily implemented. The party will continue doing its utmost to raise the well-being of the people through intensifying production, enhancing its efficiency and quality of work and fulfilling the food program of the USSR.

The party will continue showing great concern for consolidating the alliance of the working class, collective farmers and the intelligentsia, for strengthening the sociopolitical and ideological unity of Soviet society, the fraternal friendship of the peoples of the USSR and for ideologically steeling the working people in the spirit of Marxism-Leninism and proletarian, socialist internationalism.

Invariable is the Soviet people's will for peace. The lodestar leading to tomorrow is not preparations for war, which doom the people to a senseless squandering of their material and spiritual wealth, but consolidation of peace. This noble idea permeates the Peace Program for the 1980s and all the foreign policy activities of the party and the Soviet state.

We see the entire complexity of the international situation, the attempts by the aggressive circles of imperialism to undermine peaceful coexistence, to push the people to the path of enmity and military confrontation. But this cannot shake our resolve to uphold peace. We will do everything necessary for those who are fond of military ventures not to catch the Land of the Soviets unawares, for the potential aggressor to know: A crushing retaliatory strike ineluctably awaits him.

Relying on its might, displaying the greatest vigilance and self-control and retaining invariable loyalty to the peace-loving principles and aims of its foreign policy, the Soviet Union will perseveringly struggle to ward off from humankind the threat of nuclear war and to ensure detente and disarmament.

Together with us in this struggle are the fraternal countries of socialism, the fighters for national and social liberation, the peace-loving countries of all continents, all the upstanding people of the Earth. The policy of peace expresses the fundamental vital interests of humanity, and therefore the future is with this policy.

The Soviet people view the party as their tried and tested collective guide, wise leader and organizer. Serving the working class, the working people — this is the highest goal and meaning of the party's activity. The unshakable unity of the party and the people was and remains a source of the unconquerable strength of Soviet society.

The CPSU cherishes as sacred the trust of the working people and is constantly strengthening its links with the masses. The people have learned in practice that, faced with any turn of developments and any trials, the party is a match for its historical mission. The domestic and foreign policy of the CPSU formulated under the leadership of Leonid Brezhnev will continue to be pursued consistently and purposefully.

The life and work of Leonid Brezhnev will always be an inspiring example of dedicated service to the Communist Party and the Soviet people.

The Central Committee of the Communist Party of the Soviet Union, the Presidium of the USSR Supreme Soviet and the Council of Ministers of the USSR express the confidence that the Communists and all the Soviet people will show a high sense of awareness and organization and ensure by their selfless and creative work under the leadership of the Leninist party the implementation of the plans of communist construction and the further flourishing of our socialist homeland.

ANDROPOV'S SPEECH AT FUNERAL

Comrades, our party, our people and all progressive people on Earth have suffered a heavy loss. Today we are paying our last respects to Leonid Ilyich Brezhnev, a glorious son of our homeland, a fiery Marxist-Leninist, an outstanding leader of the Communist Party and the Soviet state, a prominent leader of the international communist and working class movement, a tireless fighter for peace and friendship of the peoples.

Let me first of all express profound condolences to Leonid Brezhnev's family and relatives.

Leonid Ilyich belonged to the group of political leaders who grew up and were tempered during the years of the Soviet people's selfless struggle for consolidating the gains of the Great October Revolution, for the fulfillment of Lenin's behests, for building socialism in our country and for its freedom and independence.

A worker and soldier, an outstanding organizer and a wise political leader, Leonid Ilyich Brezhnev was flesh of the flesh and bone of the bone of the people and was linked with them by unbreakable bonds. All his life and activities were subordinated to serving the interests of the working people. He devoted all his great talent, all his tremendous energies to the cause of building a society of developed socialism, a society of freedom and social justice, of brotherhood of the working people.

An extremely important period in the history of our party and country was associated with the activities of Leonid Ilyich Brezhnev in the highest positions of authority in the party and the state. It was under his leadership that the party's policy, permeated with constant concern for the working man, for raising the people's welfare, was worked out and consistently translated into life and the Leninist standards for party and state life and a fruitful atmosphere of joint work was firmly established.

Leonid Ilyich Brezhnev will be always remembered by the world as an outstanding fighter for a lasting peace and peaceful cooperation between peoples. He consistently fought, with all the ardor of his soul, for the relaxation of international tension, for delivering humankind from the threat of nuclear war, for strengthening the cohesion of the socialist community and the unity of the international communist movement.

Comrades, at this hour of grief, paying our last homage to Leonid Ilyich Brezhnev, all our party and its Central Committee declare their determination to pursue firmly and consistently the strategic line in domestic and foreign policy, which was worked out under the beneficial influence of Leonid Ilyich Brezhnev.

Rallying still closer round the party, its Leninist Central Committee and its collective leadership, the Soviet people voice their support for the policy of the party and their boundless trust in it. The party will continue to do everything necessary for further raising the living standards of the people, for developing the democratic mainstays of Soviet society, for strengthening the economic and defensive might of the country, for strengthening the friendship of the fraternal peoples of the USSR. The CPSU Central Committee will undeviatingly translate into life the decisions of the 26th Congress of the party and the will of the Soviet people.

We shall do everything possible for further increasing the cohesion of the great community of socialist states and unity in the ranks of Communists throughout the whole world in the struggle for common aims and ideals. We shall guard and develop our solidarity and our cooperation with the countries that have gained freedom from colonial oppression, with the struggle of the peoples for national independence and social progress. We shall always be loyal to the cause of the struggle for peace, for the relaxation of international tension.

In the complicated international situation, as the forces of imperialism are trying to push the peoples onto the road of hostility and military confrontation, the party and the state will firmly uphold the vital interests of our homeland and maintain great vigilance and readiness to give a crushing rebuff to any attempt at aggression. They will redouble their efforts in the struggle for the security of the people and strengthen cooperation with all the peace forces of the world. We are always ready for honest, equal and mutually beneficial cooperation with any state that is willing to cooperate.

In these days of sorrow we are keenly aware of the support and solidarity of the working people of the socialist countries, of the fraternal parties and all fighters for social progress with our party and the Soviet people. We are grateful to the governments and peoples of numerous countries in all continents who paid homage these days to the memory of Leonid Ilyich Brezhnev.

Comrades, the Communist Party of the Soviet Union firmly declares that the cause of the working class, the working people, the cause of communism and peace, to which Leonid Ilyich Brezhnev devoted all his life, will continue to be the supreme aim and meaning behind all its activities.

Farewell, dear Leonid Ilyich. The memory of you will never dim in our hearts. Your cause will be continued in the deeds of our party and people!

I declare the funeral meeting devoted to the memory of Leonid Ilyich Brezhnev open.

REAGAN ON PIPELINE SANCTIONS
November 13, 1982

Bowing to the wishes of West European allies and of U.S. businesses, President Ronald Reagan on November 13 lifted embargoes directed against companies involved in the construction of the Soviet natural gas pipeline. The sanctions were designed to thwart construction of the 3,700-mile gas pipeline from Siberia to Western Europe. Economic sanctions first had been imposed against Poland and the Soviet Union December 29, 1981, in a move to counteract the imposition of marital law in Poland. (Martial law in Poland, p. 947; Historic Documents of 1981, p. 881)

The pipeline, long opposed by the Reagan administration, would supply gas to nearly all the countries of Western Europe. The administration feared that the pipeline not only would make those countries increasingly dependent upon the Soviet Union but also would provide the Soviets with much needed foreign currency to boost their sagging economy.

Reagan on June 18 extended sanctions on the selling of U.S. oil and natural gas equipment by West European nations to Russia. The original sanctions had banned the sale of such equipment to the Soviet Union. The June sanctions, issued after Reagan failed to win allied cooperation at the Versailles economic summit meeting with Western leaders, ordered foreign subsidiaries of U.S. companies and independent companies under license to U.S. companies to stop supplying materials to the Soviets for the construction of the pipeline. The new sanctions included prohibiting foreign companies using American technology from delivering their *products to the Soviets.* (Economic summit in Versailles, p. 469)

Allies' Failure to Comply

European leaders immediately voiced their disagreement with the administration's demands and on August 12 issued a formal protest charging that the ban was "an unacceptable interference" in European economic affairs. Contracts among West European countries for supplying equipment for the pipeline involved millions of dollars — dollars that an already economically depressed Europe desperately needed. In addition, European leaders saw the embargo as evidence of their belief that the United States was going its own way in fiscal and trade matters without consulting its European allies.

In defiance of the ban, France August 24 ordered Dresser (France) S.A., a wholly owned subsidiary of Dresser Industries, Inc. of Dallas, to ship three 60-ton compressors to the Soviets. The compressors had been manufactured under contract to a French engineering company, Creusot-Loire, for use in the Soviet pipeline. The same day Dresser France resumed production on 18 additional compressors.

In response the United States imposed trade sanctions against the two French companies. The companies were placed on a "temporary denial list" that prohibited them from buying U.S. goods and services for 30 days. Several days later John Brown P.L.C., a Glasgow-based engineering firm, shipped six giant turbines to the Soviets. British Prime Minister Margaret Thatcher had ordered that the shipment be made on schedule. "The question is whether one very powerful nation can prevent existing contracts being fulfilled," said Thatcher. "I think it is wrong to do that."

West Germany and Italy joined France and Britain in refusing to comply with the bans and in ordering companies to fulfill their contractual obligations with the Soviets. West German Chancellor Helmut Schmidt said on July 22, "The U.S. embargo is a serious matter. By claiming the right to extend American law to other territories, it is affecting not only the interests of the European trading nations, but also their sovereignty." Two days later, French Foreign Minister Claude Cheysson warned that a "progressive divorce" was developing between the United States and Europe because "we no longer speak the same language" on trade and East-West relations.

Although displeased with the defiance of the ban by U.S. allies, Reagan also reportedly was reluctant to pull back his sanctions because of a letter he had sent to Soviet leader Leonid Brezhnev in December 1981. Reagan had said in the letter that, if the repression in Poland continued, the United States would have to take specific political and economic steps affecting relations between the countries. The United States also protested the alleged use of forced labor by the Soviet Union at pipeline construction sites. (Report on forced labor, p. 857)

Easing of Sanctions

After an attempt to repeal the sanctions narrowly failed in the U.S. House of Representatives, the administration began to question its own actions. Popular European opinion was strongly against the embargo and major American corporations such as Caterpillar Tractor Co. and General Electric, which had hoped to sell more than $2 billion worth of equipment for the pipeline, argued that the sanctions were hurting U.S. businesses.

On October 16, the United States presented France, West Germany, Britain and Italy with an alternative draft proposal for establishing trade relations with the Soviets. France and Britain refused to accept these new proposals.

Finally, on November 13, Reagan lifted all the sanctions, saying that the United States and its allies had reached "substantial agreement" on an overall economic strategy toward the Soviet Union. Reagan said he had lifted the sanctions because an accord had been reached among West European nations that would restrict Soviet trade and commerce more efficiently than had the sanctions on pipeline equipment.

The accord included agreements that East-West trade would not "contribute to the military or strategic advantage of the U.S.S.R.," that no new natural gas contracts would be signed pending a study of alternative Western sources of energy and that procedures for monitoring financial relations with the Soviet Union would be established. The agreement was seen by many Europeans as a "face-saving" gesture for the administration. France promptly refused to acknowledge the new strategy, causing confusion about European acceptance of the deal.

Martin S. Feldstein, chairman of the president's Council of Economic Advisers, said the sanctions had "worked temporarily. . . . I think we have inflicted some pain, "but we were also creating some side effects for our allies and ourselves so it was an inefficient way to penalize the Russians. We were hurting the allies and ourselves."

Following is the text of President Ronald Reagan's radio address to the nation November 13, 1982, announcing the end of sanctions against West European companies supplying equipment for the Soviet natural gas pipeline. (Boldface headings in brackets have been added by Congressional Quarterly to highlight the organization of the text.):

My fellow Americans:
During the campaign 2 years ago, I spoke of the need for the United States to restore the balance in our relationship with the Soviet Union. For too many years we had stood still while the Soviets increased their military strength and expanded their influence from Afghanistan to Ethiopia and

beyond. I expressed a belief, which you seemed to share, that it was time for the United States to chart a new course. Since then, we've embarked upon a buildup of our defense forces in order to strengthen our security and, in turn, to strengthen the prospects for peace. We still have a long way to go. But the fact that we've started on a new course has enabled us to propose the most comprehensive set of proposals for arms reduction and control in more than a quarter of a century. It's always been my belief that if the Soviets knew we were serious about maintaining our security, they might be more willing to negotiate seriously at the bargaining table.

In the near future, I will be speaking to you in more detail about this matter of arms control and, more importantly, arms reductions. But right now I have something in the nature of news I'd like to bring you.

[Soviet Economic Problems]

The balance between the United States and the Soviet Union cannot be measured in weapons and bombers alone. To a large degree, the strength of each nation is also based on economic strength. Unfortunately, the West's economic relations with the U.S.S.R. have not always served the national security goals of the Alliance.

The Soviet Union faces serious economic problems. But we — and I mean all of the nations of the free world — have helped the Soviets avoid some hard economic choices by providing preferential terms of trade, by allowing them to acquire militarily relevant technology, and by providing them a market for their energy resources, even though this creates an excessive dependence on them. By giving such preferential treatment, we've added to our own problems — creating a situation where we have to spend more money on our defense to keep up with Soviet capabilities which we helped create.

Since taking office, I have emphasized to our allies the importance of our economic as well as our political relationship with the Soviet Union. In July of 1981 at the economic summit meeting in Ottawa, Canada, I expressed to the heads of state of the other major Western countries and Japan my belief that we could not continue conducting business as we had. I suggested that we forge a new set of rules for economic relations with the Soviet Union which would put our security concerns foremost. I wasn't successful at that time in getting agreement on a common policy.

Then in December of 1981 the Polish Government, at Soviet instigation, imposed martial law on the Polish people and outlawed the Solidarity union. This action showed graphically that our hopes for moderation in Soviet behavior were not likely to be fulfilled.

In response to that action, I imposed an embargo on selected oil and gas equipment to demonstrate our strong opposition to such actions and to penalize this sector of the Soviet economy which relies heavily on high technology, much of it from the United States. In June of this year I extended our embargo to include not only U.S. companies and their products but subsidiaries of U.S. companies abroad and on foreign licensees of U.S. companies.

[New Agreement with Allies]

Well, it's no secret that our allies didn't agree with this action. We stepped up our consultations with them in an effort to forge an enduring, realistic, and security-minded economic policy toward the Soviet Union. These consultations have gone on over a period of months.

Well, I'm pleased today to announce that the industrialized democracies have this morning reached substantial agreement on a plan of action. The understanding we've reached demonstrates that the Western Alliance tends to give consideration to strategic issues when making decisions on trade with the U.S.S.R.

As a result, we have agreed not to engage in trade arrangements which contribute to the military or strategic advantage of the U.S.S.R. or serve to preferentially aid the heavily militarized Soviet economy. In putting these principles into practice, we will give priority attention to trade in high technology products, including those used in oil and gas production. We will also undertake an urgent study of Western energy alternatives, as well as the question of dependence on energy imports from the Soviet Union.

In addition, we've agreed on the following immediate actions. First, each partner has affirmed that no new contracts for the purchase of Soviet natural gas will be signed or approved during the course of our study of alternative Western sources of energy. Second, we and our partners will strengthen existing controls on the transfer of strategic items to the Soviet Union. Third, we will establish without delay procedures for monitoring financial relations with the Soviet Union and will work to harmonize our export credit policies.

The understanding we and our partners have reached and the actions we are taking reflect our mutual determination to overcome differences and strengthen our cohesion. I believe this new agreement is a victory for all the Allies. It puts in place a much needed policy in the economic area to complement our policies in the security area.

As I mentioned a moment ago, the United States imposed sanctions against the Soviet Union in order to demonstrate that their policies of oppression would entail substantial costs. Well, now that we've achieved an agreement with our allies which provides for stronger and more effective measures, there is no further need for these sanctions, and I am lifting them today.

The process of restoring a proper balance in relations with the Soviet Union is not ended. It will take time to make up for the losses incurred in past years. But acting together, we and our allies are making major progress. And I'm happy to say the prospects for peace are higher.

I have just returned to the White House from the Soviet Embassy, where I signed the book of condolence for President Brezhnev. New leaders are

883

coming to power in the Soviet Union. If they act in a responsible fashion, they will meet a ready and positive response in the West.

Till next Saturday at this time, goodby, and God bless you.

PASTORAL LETTER
ON NUCLEAR WAR
November 15-18, 1982

The passage of nuclear freeze resolutions on Election Day in November by eight states and the District of Columbia, plus 27 cities and counties, highlighted a year in which the nuclear freeze movement gained in strength and organization. More than 200 city councils and 400 New England town meetings approved freeze resolutions starting in the early months of 1982.

The town of Buckland, Mass., for example, passed the following resolution April 10:

> *RESOLUTION VOTED: Because it is impossible to defend against nuclear war, and because there can be no winner of a nuclear war, we*
>
> *Call upon the President of the U.S. to propose to the U.S.S.R. that together, both countries negotiate an immediate halt to the nuclear arms race. Specifically, we call upon each country to adopt an immediate mutual freeze on all further testing, production and deployment of all nuclear warheads, missiles and delivery systems.*

One of the more striking examples of the seriousness with which the problem of nuclear arms was regarded was a proposed pastoral letter by U.S. bishops of the Roman Catholic Church. The second draft of the letter was discussed at the bishops' meeting in Washington, D.C., November 15-18, and plans were made at that time for revising the letter a third time.

Other evidence of the movement's growing momentum included the following events:

● *On February 21 an anti-nuclear concert performed by 200 musicians at Boston's Symphony Hall grossed approximately $77,000.*

● *On June 12 more than 500,000 persons marched in Manhattan against nuclear arms. The demonstration was planned to coincide with the United Nations Second Special Session on Disarmament.*

● *On June 14 more than 1,600 persons were arrested in Manhattan for blocking the entrances of five United Nations mission offices of countries that have nuclear weapons.*

● *On June 21 more than 1,300 protesters were arrested in Livermore, Calif., during a demonstration at the Lawrence Livermore Laboratories, where nuclear weapons are designed.*

Emphasizing the grass-roots spirit, the 1982 nuclear freeze movement was loosely centralized, composed primarily of local and state freeze campaigns. Its members included citizen activists and volunteers, many of whom were medical, scientific, legal, religious and business professionals. In New York City, the movement spawned such professional organizations as Dancers for Disarmament, Architects for Social Responsibility, Nurses for a Non-Nuclear Future and Performing Artists for Nuclear Disarmament.

Bishops' Pastoral Letter

Work on the pastoral letter was begun by the National Conference of Catholic Bishops in July 1981. Archbishop Joseph Bernadin of Chicago chaired the committee of five responsible for the draft. In releasing the second draft of the letter, the U.S. Catholic Conference said it "addresses the relationship of the church to the world on one of the most urgent issues of our day." The letter condemned any first use of nuclear weapons, declared nuclear war immoral and called for a bilateral verifiable freeze on nuclear weapons by the United States and Soviet Union. But, the letter emphasized, the bishops were not condoning the use of conventional weapons: the letter was to serve as "an invitation to continue the new appraisal of war and peace. . . ."

In November 1982 the Reagan administration took steps to influence the content of the pastoral letter. In a letter to the bishops dated November 16, President Reagan's assistant for national security affairs, William P. Clark, defended the administration's nuclear policy. "It is important for the bishops' conference to know our decisions on nuclear armaments and our defense posture are guided by moral considerations as compelling as any which have faced mankind," he wrote.

Clark said that the Reagan administration "welcomed the involvement of the Catholic bishops in the effort to secure effective arms control and to reduce the risks of war." But, he added: "We therefore regret all the more that the committee's latest draft continues to reflect fundamental misreadings of American policy and continues to ignore the far-reaching administration proposals that are currently being negotiated with the Soviet Union. . . ."

The national security adviser defended the policy of deterrence, an issue that provoked some disagreement among the bishops. Some believed deterrence should be condemned as morally indefensible because it involves threatening to use force. Others argued it was morally justifiable to use the threat of force to prevent the greater evil of war.

"The nature of the deterrent in the nuclear age has raised the most severe moral questions for Catholic teaching on warfare," the bishops' draft letter stated. It argued, among other things, that the strategy might be considered impermissible if it were based on the "addition of weapons which are likely to invite attack and therefore give credence to the concept that the United States seeks a first strike, 'hard-target kill' capability. . . ."

The final draft of the pastoral letter, addressed to all American Catholics, was released in April 1983. According to reports, this version was somewhat more moderate in its tone and expectations.

Reagan Opposition

The Reagan administration opposed an immediate halt to the production of Soviet and American weapons, arguing that a freeze would put the United States at a serious military disadvantage. The administration's position was that the Russians would abandon their superiority in large missiles only if they were faced with the alternative of a nuclear buildup by the United States.

During 1982 the administration moved on several fronts to challenge freeze proposals. In August, for example, it spearheaded an intense lobbying effort in the House of Representatives against a nuclear freeze proposal sponsored by Rep. Clement J. Zablocki, D-Wis. The Zablocki resolution, which called for a "mutual and verifiable" freeze, was narrowly defeated August 5 by an administration-supported substitute, which called for a freeze at "equal and substantially reduced levels." The administration prevailed by only two votes, however, and the narrow margin of victory was interpreted as a lack of confidence on the part of House members in the president's commitment to arms control negotiations.

Freeze proponents renewed the debate during the first session of the 98th Congress.

Issue of Soviet Involvement

Several times during 1982 the president suggested that the Soviet Union was manipulating proponents of the nuclear freeze in the United

States and Western Europe. At a fund-raiser in Columbus, Ohio, October 4, Reagan said the movement was inspired by people who "want the weakening of America." At a news conference November 11 Reagan stated that there was "plenty of evidence" that the nuclear freeze movement had been infiltrated by foreign agents. He emphasized, however, that he felt the overwhelming majority of people involved in the movement were "sincere and well-intentioned." A report issued by the House Select Committee on Intelligence December 9 indicated that the Soviet Union had attempted to capitalize on the nuclear freeze movement, but had had little success in manipulating events in the United States. The major emphasis of the report was not on the freeze movement, but on the Soviet Union's use of "disinformation" as a propaganda tool. Responding to the House report, Reagan reiterated his claim December 10, stating that freeze supporters unintentionally were aiding the Soviet Union.

Following are excerpts from the second draft of the pastoral letter, entitled "The Challenge of Peace: God's Promise and Our Response," released during the annual meeting of the U.S. Conference of Bishops, November 15-18, 1982; and excerpts from a letter to Archbishop Joseph Bernadin from William P. Clark, presidential assistant for national security affairs, dated November 16. (Boldface headings in brackets have been added by Congressional Quarterly to highlight the organization of the texts.):

DRAFT OF PASTORAL LETTER

II. War and Peace in the Modern World: Problems and Principles

. . . In the nuclear arsenals of the United States or the Soviet Union alone, there exists a capacity to do something no other age could imagine. We can threaten the created order. For people of faith this means we read the Book of Genesis with a new awareness; the moral issue at stake in nuclear war involves the meaning of sin in its most graphic dimensions. Every sinful act is a confrontation of the creature and the Creator. Today the destructive potential of the nuclear powers threatens the sovereignty of God over the world he has brought into being. We could destroy his work.

We live today, therefore, in the midst of a cosmic drama; we possess a power which should never be used, but which might be used if we do not reverse our direction. We live with nuclear weapons on the basis of an assumption we would not tolerate in any other area of life: We know we cannot afford one mistake. This fact dramatizes the precariousness of our position, politically, morally and spiritually.

A prominent "sign of the times" today is a sharply increased awareness of the danger of the nuclear arms race. Such awareness has produced a public discussion about nuclear policy here and in other countries which is unprecedented in its scope and depth. What has been accepted for years with almost no question is now being subjected to the sharpest criticism. What had been previously defined as a safe and stable system of deterrence is today viewed with political and moral skepticism. There are many forces at work in this new evaluation and we believe one of the crucial elements is the gospel vision of peace which guides our work in this pastoral letter. The nuclear age has been the theater of our existence for almost four decades; today it is being evaluated with a new perspective; the leaven of the Gospel and the light of the Holy Spirit create for many the decisive dimension of this new perspective. . . .

A. THE NEW MOMENT

. . . Papal teaching has consistently addressed the folly and danger of the arms race; but the new perception in the general public about it is due in large measure to the work of scientists and physicians who have described for citizens the concrete human consequences of a nuclear war.

In a striking demonstration of his personal and pastoral concern for preventing nuclear war, Pope John Paul II commissioned a study by the Pontifical Academy of Sciences which reinforced the findings of other scientific bodies. The Holy Father had the study transmitted by personal representatives to the leaders of the United States, the Soviet Union, the United Kingdom, France and the president of the General Assembly of the United Nations. One of the conclusions of the study is especially pertinent to the public debate in the United States:

"Recent talk about winning or even surviving a nuclear war must reflect a failure to appreciate a medical reality: Any nuclear war would inevitably cause death, disease and suffering of pandemonic proportions and without the possibility of effective medical intervention. That reality leads to the same conclusion physicians have reached for life-threatening epidemics throughout history: Prevention is essential for control."

This medical conclusion has a moral corollary. Traditionally the church's moral teaching sought first to prevent war and then to limit its consequences if it occurred. Today the possibilities for placing political and moral limits on nuclear war are so infinitesimal that the moral task, like the medical, is prevention: As a people we must refuse to legitimate the idea of nuclear war. Such a refusal will require not only new ideas and new vision, but what the Gospel calls conversion of the heart. . . .

We see with clarity the political folly of a system which threatens mutual suicide; the psychological damage this does to ordinary people, especially the young; the economic distortion of priorities — billions readily spent for destructive instruments and pitched battles being waged daily in our legislatures about a fraction of this amount for the homeless, the hungry and the helpless here and abroad. We see with much less clarity how we translate a "no" to nuclear war into the personal and public choices which can move us in a new direction, toward a national policy and an international system which more adequately reflect the values and vision of the kingdom of God....

Precisely because of the destructive nature of nuclear weapons, strategies have been developed which previous generations would have found unintelligible. Today military preparations are undertaken on a vast and sophisticated scale, but the declared purpose is not to use the weapons produced. Threats are made which would be suicidal to implement. The key to security is no longer only military secrets, but in many instances it requires informing one's adversary publicly what weapons one has and what plans exist for their use. The presumption of the nation-state system, that sovereignty implied an ability to protect a nation's territory and population, is precisely the presumption denied by the nuclear capacities of both superpowers. In a sense each is at the mercy of the other's perception of what strategy is "rational," what kind of damage is "unacceptable," how "convincing" one side's threat is to the other.

The political paradox of deterrence has also strained our moral conception. May a nation threaten what it may never do? May it possess what it may never use? Who is involved in the threat each superpower makes: government officials? or military personnel? or the citizenry in whose "defense" the threat is made?

In brief, the danger of the situation is clear: The dilemma of how to prevent the use of nuclear weapons, how to assess deterrence and how to delineate moral responsibility in the nuclear age is less clearly seen or stated. Reflecting the complexity of the nuclear problem, our arguments in this pastoral must be detailed and nuanced; but our "no" to nuclear war must, in the end, be definitive and decisive....

B. RELIGIOUS LEADERSHIP IN THE PUBLIC DEBATE

... The "new moment" which exists in the public debate about nuclear weapons provides a creative opportunity and a moral imperative to examine the relationship between public opinion and public policy. We believe it is necessary, for the sake of prevention, to build a barrier against the concept of nuclear war as a viable strategy for defense. There should be a clear public resistance to the rhetoric of "winnable" nuclear wars, "surviving" nuclear exchanges and strategies of "protracted nuclear war."

We seek to encourage a public attitude which sets stringent limits on the kind of actions our government will take on nuclear policy in our name. We believe religious leaders have a task in concert with public officials, analysts, private organizations and the media to set the limits beyond which our military policy should not move in word or action. Charting a moral course in a complex public policy debate involves several steps. We will address four questions, offering our reflections on them as an invitation to a public moral dialogue: 1) the use of nuclear weapons; 2) the policy of deterrence in principle and in practice; 3) specific steps to reduce the danger of war; 4) long-term measures of policy and diplomacy.

C. THE USE OF NUCLEAR WEAPONS

... For the tradition which acknowledges some legitimate use of force, contemporary nuclear strategies push the moral limits beyond the permissible. A justifiable use of force must be both discriminatory and proportionate. Certain aspects of both U.S. and Soviet strategies fail both tests. The technical literature and the personal testimony of public officials who have been closely associated with U.S. nuclear strategy have both convinced us of the overwhelming probability that a nuclear exchange would have no limits.

On the more complicated issue of "limited" nuclear war, we are aware of the extensive literature and discussion this topic has generated. As a general statement it does seem to us that public officials have been unable to refute the following conclusion of the study made by the Papal Academy of Science:

"Even a nuclear attack directed only at military facilities would be devastating to the country as a whole. This is because military facilities are widespread rather than concentrated at only a few points. Thus, many nuclear weapons would be exploded.

"Furthermore, the spread of radiation due to the natural winds and atmospheric mixing would kill vast numbers of people and contaminate large areas. The medical facilities of any nation would be inadequate to care for the survivors. An objective examination of the medical situation that would follow a nuclear war leads to but one conclusion: Prevention is our only recourse."

In light of these perspectives we address three questions more explicitly: 1) counterpopulation warfare; 2) initiation of nuclear war; and 3) limited nuclear war.

1. Counterpopulation Warfare: *Under no circumstances may nuclear weapons or other instruments of mass slaughter be used for the purpose of destroying population centers or other predominantly civilian targets.* Popes have repeatedly condemned such use. For example, as early as 1954 Pope Pius XII condemned nuclear warfare "when it entirely escapes the control of man" and results in "the pure and simple annihilation of all human life within the radius of action." The condemnation was repeated by the Second Vatican Council: "Any act of war aimed indiscriminately at the destruction of entire cities or of extensive areas along with their population is a crime against God and man himself. It merits unequivocal and unhesitating condemnation."

The council's condemnation referred to "direct" attacks on civilian populations; these clearly violate the traditional principle of non-combatant immunity. An equally troublesome problem, which the nature of modern warfare makes all too likely, is an attack on military targets or militarily significant industrial targets which would involve "indirect" (i.e., unintended) but massive civilian casualties. The problem is aggravated when one side deliberately positions military targets in the midst of a civilian population. These pose a different question than the one addressed by Vatican II, and moralists are divided in their response to this question.

Aware of the controverted nature of the issue, we nonetheless feel obliged as a matter of practical moral guidance to register our opposition to a policy of attacking targets which lie so close to concentrations of population that destruction of the target would devastate the nearby population centers. The relevant moral principle in this case is the disproportionate damage which would be done to human life. We are moved to specify this practical moral conclusion because recent policy proposals seek to justify attacks on militarily related industries situated in populated areas.

Retaliatory action which would take many wholly innocent lives, lives of people who are in no way responsible for reckless actions of their government, must also be condemned. Our condemnation applies especially to the retaliatory use of weapons striking enemy cities after our own have already been struck. Retaliation in such circumstances would serve no rational or moral purpose and might be considered to be only an act of vengeance. No Christian can rightfully carry out orders or policies deliberately aimed at killing non-combatants.

2. Initiation of Nuclear War: *We do not perceive any situation in which the deliberate initiation of nuclear warfare, on however restricted a scale, can be morally justified. Non-nuclear attacks by another state must be resisted by other than nuclear means.*

There is a serious debate on this issue under way. It is cast in political terms, but it has a significant moral dimension. Some have argued that at the very beginning of a war nuclear weapons might be used only against military targets, perhaps in limited numbers. Indeed, it has long been American and NATO policy that nuclear weapons, especially so-called tactical nuclear weapons, would likely be used if NATO forces in Europe seemed in danger of losing a conflict that until then had been restricted to conventional weapons. Large numbers of tactical nuclear weapons are now deployed in Europe by the NATO forces and about as many by the Soviet Union. Some are substantially smaller than the bomb used on Hiroshima, some are larger. Very many such weapons, if employed, would totally devastate the densely populated countries of Western and Central Europe.

Whether under conditions of war in Europe, parts of Asia or the Middle East, or the exchange of strategic weapons directly between the United States and the Soviet Union, the difficulties of limiting the use of nuclear weapons are immense. Expert witnesses advise us that commanders operating under conditions of battle would not be able to exercise strict control: The number of weapons used would rapidly increase, the targets would be expanded beyond the military and the level of civilian casualties would rise enormously. No one can be certain that this escalation would not occur even in the face of political efforts to keep such an exchange "limited.". . .

D. DETERRENCE IN PRINCIPLE AND PRACTICE

2. The Moral Issues

. . . It is generally agreed by moralists, by religious and secular analysts, by citizens and public officials alike that one of the worst political and moral evils which could be perpetrated would be the actual initiation of nuclear war with its enormous potential for destruction.

The purpose of deterrence is to prevent this eventuality, but the moral problem of nuclear deterrence relates to the method by which prevention is accomplished. An extract from the U.S. Military Posture Statement for FY 1983 describes certain elements of the method of deterrence:

"The prime objective of U.S. strategic forces and supporting C³ [command, control, and communication] is deterrence of Soviet nuclear attack on the United States and its allies. Deterrence depends upon the assured capability and manifest will to inflict damage on the Soviet Union disproportionate to any goals that rational Soviet leaders might hope to achieve."

The concept of "disproportionate" or "unacceptable" damage implies (more strongly in some variants of deterrence than in others) the willingness to strike targets of "value" in the adversary's country. "Targets of value" either explicitly include the civilian population or include industrial targets which inevitably would involve killing large numbers of civilians.

The moral questions about deterrence focus on five issues: 1) the *possession* of weapons of mass destruction; 2) the accompanying *threat* and or *intention* to use them; 3) the declared, or at least not repudiated, willingness *to use such weapons on civilians*; 4) the moral significance of *the prevention of use* of nuclear weapons through a strategy which could not morally be implemented; and 5) *the continued escalation of the nuclear arms race* with its diversion of resources from other needs. . . .

The moral and political paradox posed by deterrence was concisely stated by Vatican II:

"Undoubtedly, armaments are not amassed merely for use in wartime. Since the defensive strength of any nation is thought to depend on its capacity for immediate retaliation, the stockpiling of arms which grows from year to year serves, in a way hitherto unthought of, as a deterrent to potential attackers. Many people look upon this as the most effective way known at the present time for maintaining some sort of peace among nations.

"Whatever one may think of this form of deterrent, people are convinced that the arms race, which quite a few countries have entered, is no infallible way of maintaining real peace and that the resulting so-called balance of power is no sure and genuine path to achieving it. Rather than eliminate the causes or [sic] war, the arms race serves only to aggravate the position. As long as extravagant sums of money are poured into the development of new weapons, it is impossible to devote adequate aid in tackling the misery which prevails at the present day in the world. Instead of eradicating international conflict once and for all, the contagion is spreading to other parts of the world. . . .

The Holy Father's delicate assessment of deterrence reflects the complexity of the concept. He emphasizes these two necessary elements in any discussion on deterrence: 1) that deterrence, even if based on balance, cannot be accepted as an end in itself; and 2) deterrence must be a step on the way toward progressive disarmament. The emphasis on these two elements helps form the basis for our judgment on deterrence in this pastoral letter. . . .

This strictly conditioned judgment yields criteria for morally assessing the elements of deterrence strategy. Clearly these criteria demonstrate that we cannot approve of every weapons system, strategic doctrine or policy initiative advanced in the name of strengthening deterrence.

On the contrary, these criteria require continual public scrutiny of what our government proposes to do with the deterrent:

1) If deterrence exists only to prevent the *use* of nuclear weapons by others, then proposals to go beyond this objective to encourage war-fighting capabilities must be resisted. We must continually say "no" to the idea of nuclear war.

2) If deterrence is our goal, "sufficiency" to deter is an adequate strategy; the quest for superiority must be resisted.

3) If deterrence is to be used as "a step on the way toward progressive disarmament," then each proposed addition to our strategic system or change in strategic doctrine must be assessed precisely in light of whether it will render steps toward arms control and disarmament more or less likely.

Moreover, these criteria provide us with the means to make some recommendations and judgments about the present direction of U.S. strategic policy. Progress toward a world free of the threat of deterrence must be carefully carried out. But it must not be delayed. There is an urgent moral and political responsibility to use the "peace of a sort" we have as a framework to move toward authentic peace through nuclear arms control, reductions and disarmament. Of primary importance in this process is the need to prevent the development and deployment of destabilizing weapons systems on either side; a second requirement is to ensure that the more sophisticated command and control systems are no less open to human intervention; a third is the need to prevent the proliferation of nuclear weapons in the international system.

In light of these general principles we oppose some specific goals for our present deterrence posture:

1) The addition of weapons which are likely to invite attack and therefore give credence to the concept that the United States seeks a first strike, "hard-target kill" capability; the MX missile might fit into this category;

2) The willingness to foster strategic planning which seeks a nuclear-war fighting capability;

3) Proposals which have the effect of lowering the nuclear threshold and blurring the difference between nuclear and conventional weapons.

In support of the concept of "sufficiency" as an adequate deterrent and in light of the present size and composition of both the U.S. and Soviet strategic arsenals, *we recommend:*

1) Support for immediate, bilateral verifiable agreements to halt the testing, production and deployment of new strategic systems;

2) Support for negotiated bilateral deep cuts in the arsenals of both superpowers, particularly of those weapons systems which have destabilizing characteristics;

3) Support for a comprehensive test ban treaty;

4) Removal by all parties of nuclear weapons from border areas and the strengthening of command and control over tactical nuclear weapons to prevent inadvertent and unauthorized use.

These judgments are meant to exemplify how a lack of unequivocal condemnation of deterrence is meant only to be an attempt to acknowledge the role attributed to deterrence, but not to support its extension beyond the prevention of use of nuclear weapons. . . .

III. The Promotion of Peace:
Proposals and Policies

. . . At the beginning of this letter we affirmed the need for a more fully developed theology of peace. The basis of such a theology is found in the papal teaching of this century. . . .

A. SPECIFIC STEPS TO REDUCE THE DANGER OF WAR

. . . While we do not advocate a policy of unilateral disarmament, we believe the urgent need for control of the arms race requires a willingness for each side to take some first steps; the United States should be prepared, in our view, to take some independent initiatives, beyond those already taken, to reduce some of the gravest dangers and to encourage a constructive Soviet response. By independent initiatives we mean carefully chosen limited steps which the United States could take for a defined period of time, seeking to elicit a comparable step from the Soviet Union. If an appropriate response is not forthcoming, the United States would no longer be bound by the steps taken. . . .

As with nuclear proliferation, we seem to be witnessing a relaxation of earlier concerns to restrain the international commerce in conventional arms. Sales of increasingly sophisticated military aircraft, missiles, tanks, anti-tank weapons, anti-personnel bombs and other systems by the major supplying countries (especially the Soviet Union, the United States, France and Great Britain) have reached unprecedented levels. . . .

U.S. arms sales policies have in the last decade become more expansive. Precisely the opposite course is needed. The United States should renew earlier efforts to develop multilateral controls on arms exports, and should in this case also be willing to take carefully chosen independent initiatives to restrain the arms trade....

... The arts of diplomacy, negotiation and compromise must be developed and fully exercised. Non-violent means of resistance to evil should be carefully weighed. For example, there have been instances when people have successfully resisted oppressors without taking up arms. Non-violent resistance requires the united will of a people and may demand patience and suffering from those who practice it. It may not always succeed. But before the possibility is dismissed as impractical or unrealistic we urge that it be measured against the almost certain effects of a major war....

We do not in any way want to contribute to a notion of "making the world safe for conventional war," which introduces its own horrors. It may well be, however, that some strengthening of conventional defense would be a proportionate price to pay, if indeed this will reduce the possibility of nuclear war. We must re-emphasize with all our being, nonetheless, that it is not only nuclear war that must be prevented, but war itself, the scourge of humanity. History has demonstrated that an upward spiral even in conventional arms and a continuing unbridled increase in armed forces, rather than securing true peace, are provocative of war....

CLARK LETTER TO ARCHBISHOP

I would like to take this opportunity to respond, on behalf of President Reagan, Secretary Shultz, Secretary Weinberger, Director Rostow and other administration officials, to the request for our views on the second draft of the pastoral letter recently prepared by the ad hoc committee on war and peace for review by the National Conference of Catholic Bishops. Let me assure you that we have read these drafts with great interest and care.

As officials, citizens and laymen, we share a profound interest in your answer to the question posed in the draft letter of "whether and how our religious-moral tradition can assess, direct, contain and hopefully help eliminate the threat posed to the human family by the nuclear arsenals of the world." We note that in your attempt to answer this question, you are drawing upon "a broad spectrum of advisers of varying persuasions" to examine the nature of weapons systems, military doctrines and consequences. We recognize both the seriousness and the difficulty of the task you have set for yourself "in concert with public officials" to try "charting a moral course in a complex public policy debate." All must surely work together conscientiously if we are "to persevere in the long-term effort needed to move the world toward a stable and secure peace."

It is because of such objectives expressed by your committee that at the time when the first draft of the pastoral letter was circulated earlier this year, we provided extensive commentaries in response to your request. I am enclosing copies of our prior correspondence for consideration by your committee. We understood then that our comments would be fully considered by the committee as it continued its important work. We commented in some detail because we recognized fully that while the issues are complex and involve serious moral dilemmas, "the possibility of peace must be continually protected and preserved in the face of obstacles and attacks upon it."

I believe we can agree that the purpose of any moral theory of defense is "not, in the first place, to legitimize war, but to prevent it," and this, of course, is what American deterrence policy is designed to achieve. I believe we can also agree that any proposed change in strategic systems or doctrines, as well as any recommendation, whether proposed by the U.S. government or by your committee, should be judged "in light of whether it will render steps toward arms control and disarmament more or less likely." We believe that our weapons systems (which are not designed to be "first-strike" systems), our deterrence posture (which is defensive) and our arms control initiatives (which call for deep and verifiable reductions) do conform to these objectives.

['Fundamental Misreadings' of Policy]

Because we share an enormous sense of responsibility for the protection of our people and our values, we have welcomed the involvement of the Catholic bishops in the effort to secure effective arms control and to reduce the risks of war. We, therefore, regret all the more that the committee's latest draft continues to reflect fundamental misreadings of American policies and continues essentially to ignore the far-reaching American proposals that are currently being negotiated with the Soviet Union on achieving steep reductions in nuclear arsenals, on reducing conventional forces and, through a variety of verification and confidence-building measures, on further reducing the risks of war. Thus, while the committee's draft calls for alternative approaches to current nuclear arsenals and strategies, it does so without presenting the citizen who is concerned with issues of peace and war with any information whatsoever about the initiatives undertaken by the United States to bring the world closer to arms reductions, peace and reconciliation.

Previous administration comments that were forwarded to you ... summarized a number of these arms control initiatives and sought to correct the prior draft's mistaken depictions of U.S. nuclear strategy. We find the virtual omission of these perspectives puzzling, in view of the stated purpose expressed in the pastoral letter that "our arguments in this pastoral must be detailed and nuanced," and that "this pastoral letter in its complexities be used as a framework in forming consciences," so as to "learn together how to make correct and responsible moral judgments."

As with the committee's first draft, I am especially troubled in reading the second draft of the pastoral letter to find none of the serious U.S. arms control efforts, including major initiatives and ongoing U.S.-Soviet negotiations, described or even noted in the text. Ours are not proposals for freezes on current high ceilings. Such freezes would remove incentives for achieving reductions and would, in any case, require extensive prior negotiations to reach agreement on what numbers and systems to freeze and on how such freezes might be effectively verified. Ours are initiatives for reduction, or even elimination, of the most destabilizing systems. They involve new verification and confidence-building measures designed both to build trust and to assure compliance.

Because these important initiatives and negotiations have again been ignored in the draft pastoral letter, although they so clearly conform to the hopes of all concerned with reducing the arsenals and the risks of war and promoting the path of peace, I would like to summarize them for you again. I do so with a renewed hope that the comments your committee receives from U.S. government officials in response to the committee's requests will be carefully considered, just as your committee asks that its draft letter "receive a respectful consideration" from others.

[Administration's Initiatives]

This administration's arms control efforts include the following major initiatives:

— In the U.S.-Soviet negotiations on strategic arms (START), which began on June 30, 1982, we are proposing to begin with a one-third reduction in the number of warheads on the land- and sea-based ballistic missiles and a reduction in the most destabilizing systems of all, the land-based ballistic missiles, to about one-half of the current U.S. levels. In a second phase we propose to reduce the destructive potential of the remaining missiles to equal levels, lower than we now have, and we could include other strategic systems as well.

— In the U.S.-Soviet negotiations on intermediate-range nuclear forces (INF), which began Nov. 30, 1981, we have proposed to begin with the total elimination of the forces considered the most destablilizing and threatening by both sides, the land-based missile systems. We and our NATO allies have offered to cancel plans for the deployment of U.S. Pershing and ground-launched cruise missiles in exchange for the corresponding destruction of Soviet SS-20, SS-4 and SS-5 missiles. Other elements of the balance could be limited subsequently.

— In the multilateral negotiations on mutual and balanced force reductions (MBFR), the United States and its NATO allies are proposing to the Warsaw Pact nations major initial reductions in military personnel to common ceilings and a wide range of new verification measures.

— In the areas of limiting nuclear testing and chemical and biological weapons, the United States is actively participating in discussions in the Committee on Disarmament in Geneva to develop the verification and compliance procedures that would make such limitations truly effective. We are, of course, particularly distressed by the extensive and inhuman use by the Soviet Union and its allies of toxins and chemicals against the defenseless populations of Afghanistan, Laos and Cambodia.

In all of our ongoing arms control negotiations and discussions we are emphasizing the importance of substantial early reductions and of effective verification and confidence-building measures. Your committee will surely recognize that the administration's nuclear-reductions proposals clearly conform to the pastoral letter's recommendations for cuts in nuclear arsenals, and that the other multilateral efforts in which we are currently engaged conform closely with the letter's call for efforts "aimed at reducing and limiting conventional forces and at building confidence between possible adversaries, especially in regions of major military confrontation, as well as those addressed to outlawing effectively the use of chemical and biological weapons."

I continue to believe that as the bishops' conference reviews new drafts of the pastoral letter, a clear presentation of these initiatives should lead to the bishops' conference strong support for them. As I noted in my comments on the first draft, such support would prove enormously helpful in making clear to the world America's seriousness in our efforts and would, in particular, add to Soviet incentives to agree to the reductions and verifiable limitations that we are seeking.

In urging you to assure that the commission's future drafts include a description, and I hope support for, the important American arms control initiatives currently being negotiated, it also appears particularly significant to note that the deterrent posture upon which our nation's armed forces and our nuclear strategy are based is judged in the pastoral letter as being morally defensible. It is quite clear that the judgments cited in the letter as reflecting the views of Pope John Paul II and of the bishops' conference support the continued requirement and morality of maintaining effective nuclear deterrent forces. This pastoral judgment is supported because, while nuclear deterrence is considered "unsatisfactory," unilateral disarmament is rejected, and we are urged instead to seek truly effective arms limitations agreements of the kind we are, in fact, currently seeking. I believe this is a fact of critical importance for conscientious clergy, laymen and citizens to understand.

Let me explain further what I mean by the above. According to the pastoral letter, the bishops state that "we do not advocate a policy of unilateral disarmament," and the letter, in fact, argues that if, in the face of independent U.S. initiatives for arms control, "an appropriate response is not forthcoming, the United States would no longer be bound to steps taken." Pope John Paul II is cited in his message of Dec. 13, 1981, as stating that we must move, as we have, to the "reduction of nuclear armaments, while waiting for their future complete elimination, carried out simultaneously by all parties, by means of explicit agreements and with the commitment of accepting effective controls."

Pope John Paul II is further cited, in his address to the United Nations' June 1982 Special Session on Disarmament, as stating that "deterrence based on balance, certainly not as an end in itself but as a step on the way toward progressive disarmament, may still be judged morally acceptable." Cardinal Krol is cited as stating for the bishops' conference that "it is of the utmost importance that negotiations proceed to meaningful and continuing reductions" and that "as long as there is hope of this occurring, Catholic moral teaching is willing, while negotiations proceed, to tolerate possession of nuclear weapons for deterrence as the lesser of the two evils."

In recognition that our deterrent forces have the critical positive role of preventing war, the draft pastoral letter reflects the bishops' conclusion that "as clearly unsatisfactory as the deterrent posture of the United States is from a moral point of view, use of nuclear weapons by any of the nuclear powers would be an even greater evil." In sum, as the letter says, "we have held that possession of nuclear weapons may be tolerated as deterrents, while meaningful efforts are under way to achieve multilateral disarmament."

As we negotiate seriously to achieve the steep reductions and the effective limitations we all want in the arsenals of war, it must be clearly understood that our military forces are armed and organized to deter attack and coercion and to prevent war. It is our policy and that of our allies not to use any force, whether nuclear or non-nuclear, except to deter and defend against aggression. We must, therefore, assure that, in view of the unprecedented Soviet military buildup of the last decade and longer, our deterrent forces remain sufficiently strong and credible to assure effective deterrence.

[Earlier Initiatives Ignored]

The draft pastoral letter does not describe either the facts or the impact of the Soviet buildup which we face and which goes far beyond defensive needs. Neither does the letter describe any of the many past unilateral initiatives taken for arms limitation in the last decade by the United States, including reduction in our defense budgets, in real terms, and the eliminating or delay of important U.S. military modernization programs. These are important factors the commission will need to take into account in its future assessments.

The draft pastoral letter reminds the reader that the bishops' 1980 pastoral letter on Marxism described significant differences between Christian teaching and Marxism. The letter also notes that the "fact of a Soviet threat, as well as the existence of a Soviet imperial drive for hegemony, at least in regions of major strategic interest, cannot be denied." The letter recalls memories of repressive Soviet policies in Eastern Europe and recently in Afghanistan and Poland. It might have added Southeast Asia, Africa and Central America as areas where the military power of the Soviet Union and its allies has increasingly expanded by force of arms. In this connection the draft letter importantly urges its readers to reject "romantic idealism about Soviet intentions and capabilities," and declares that "Americans need have no illusions about the Soviet system of repression or about the lack of respect in that system for human rights."

It is important for the bishops' conference to know our decisions on nuclear armaments and our defense posture are guided by moral considerations as compelling as any which have faced mankind. The strategy of deterrence on which our policies are based is not an end in itself but a means to prevent war and preserve the values we cherish — individual liberty, freedom of worship, freedom of conscience and expression, respect for the sanctity of human life and the rule of law through representative institutions. As Americans, we are among the fortunate few in the world who enjoy these blessings.

These traditions and values are not shared by the Soviet Union, which subordinates all individual rights to the needs of a totalitarian state. Individual voices, including those who seek to worship freely and who raise concern about the preservation of peace, are uncompromisingly suppressed, both within the Soviet Union and in those countries to which it has extended its sway. While oppression is common to much of the world, in the case of the Soviet Union it has been wedded to military arsenals and a militant dogma that threaten peace and freedom everywhere.

We are confident that as the bishops continue to study the problem of reducing arms, preventing war and fostering genuine peace, you will also take note of the importance to this effort of building support for international standards of rights and law, such as those proclaimed in the U.N. Charter and in the Helsinki agreement. As we work to reduce the risks and the causes of war, we have more than just an interest in preserving the traditions of freedom; we have a moral responsibility to future generations. As heirs to the tradition of freedom, we must carry the burden of its preservation and growth.

We believe that by sustaining effective deterrence and working for effective arms control we will preserve the peace while protecting the fundamental values of Western civilization which you share. We would value opportunities to discuss these vital issues with you and your colleagues, and we ask that you consider and circulate our comments. As we continue our earnest efforts toward genuine peace, we believe that to turn our backs on a course that has kept the peace for over three decades of the nuclear age would increase the risks of war and endanger the cause of freedom throughout the world.

REAGAN ON MX MISSILE
November 22, 1982

The pursuit of equitable and viable arms control agreements while continuing to build up America's defenses in the face of a Soviet challenge were the two central themes of a November 22 nationally televised address by President Ronald Reagan. Armed with an array of charts denoting the Soviet buildup in "a great deal of red," in contrast to the American standstill depicted by "a much lesser amount of U.S. blue," the president declared, "You often hear that the United States and the Soviet Union are in an arms race. Well, the truth is that while the Soviet Union has raced, we have not." To rectify what he considered a dangerous situation, Reagan restated his commitment to pursue arms reduction agreements and at the same time to continue production of the controversial new land-based intercontinental ballistic missile (ICBM), the MX (missile experimental), scheduled for deployment in 1986.

Reagan's emphasis on the need to strengthen national defense was in keeping with his longstanding views on nuclear arms. During his campaign for the presidency, Reagan had emphasized the need to strengthen U.S. defenses to counter the growing Soviet military threat. His administration's policy would aim to deter nuclear war through readiness to fight one if challenged, and to deny Moscow the diplomatic leverage it might gain from a perception of Soviet nuclear superiority.

Reagan's position struck a responsive chord in a Congress and a public disillusioned with the meager successes of the U.S.-Soviet détente so eagerly sought by Republican and Democratic administrations alike since the 1960s. A rapid Soviet defense buildup, undertaken while the United

903

States initially slowed down its defense spending and then continued to lag behind the Soviet Union throughout the 1970s, fed apprehension that Moscow would be emboldened to take political and military advantage of America's loss of superiority.

At the same time, the growing momentum for a "freeze" on nuclear weapons deployment symbolized a widespread desire on the part of Congress and the public to reduce defense spending and to initiate serious arms control efforts. Faced with those anxieties about the risks of nuclear war, Reagan May 9, 1982, offered his proposals on strategic arms reduction talks (START) with Moscow. The president and his defense advisers argued that the talks would be grounded in a more "realistic" approach than were the strategic arms limitation talks (SALT) under President Jimmy Carter. Reagan emphasized that any agreement would preserve an "equitable" balance between the superpowers. The goal would be not simply to freeze but actually to reduce levels and capabilities of nuclear destruction without endangering U.S. security, he said. (Freeze movement, p. 885; START proposal, p. 385)

Nonetheless, the administration continued to maintain that a strong national defense was the only way to deter an attack and prod the enemy to the negotiating table. The elements of that defense included the means not only to retaliate massively against Soviet aggression, but to respond "selectively" and "appropriately" to different kinds of threats wherever they might occur.

Reagan's Strategic Policy

Reagan's November 22 speech embodied two fundamental premises of his defense policy:

● Peace depends on a nearly symmetrical balance of U.S. and Soviet forces, especially land-based ICBMs.

● The Soviets would agree to reduce their nuclear arsenals only if confronted with clear indications that the United States would match Soviet forces in the absence of an arms control agreement.

"What we are saying to them is this," Reagan summed up. "We will modernize our military in order to keep the balance for peace, but wouldn't it be better if we simply reduced our arsenals to a much lower level."

"The Soviet military buildup must not be ignored," the president warned. "We must replace and modernize our forces. . . . [T]he MX is the right missile at the right time."

In shaping a nuclear force to meet its general doctrine, the Reagan administration shared these principles with its Democratic and Republican predecessors of the 1970s:

● *Diversity and Endurance. The administration maintained the long-standing dependence on a diversified "triad" of nuclear launchers (ICBMs, submarine-launched ballistic missiles and long-range bombers), assuming that no two of those forces would be wiped out by a Soviet attack. To ensure that invulnerability, administration officials argued that the three legs of the triad should be not only retained but reinforced. However, the U.S. land-based arsenal of Minuteman ICBMs had become vulnerable to destruction by extremely powerful and highly accurate Soviet MIRV (multiple, independently targetable re-entry vehicle) warheads. Deployment of the MX was essential to remedy that nuclear weapons imbalance, Reagan concluded.*

● *Flexibility. The U.S. arsenal must be flexible; that is, it must contain weapons that could be used to cover the gamut of possible Soviet targets under various scenarios of "limited" nuclear war. MX missiles, each armed with an average of 10 powerful and accurate MIRVed warheads, could selectively destroy even the most heavily armored Soviet military targets.*

If the United States were able to respond to a limited act of aggression, Reagan and his defense advisers reasoned, it was more likely that an all-out holocaust could be avoided. This was one of the arguments the administration marshaled in its campaign to deploy the MX, as well as intermediate-range Pershing IIs and ground-launched cruise missiles (small, pilotless drone jets carrying nuclear warheads) in Western Europe. By 1982 those weapons — and their Soviet counterparts — had become both symbols and concrete evidence of the evolving U.S.-Soviet strategic balance and a major subject of arms control negotiations. They were part of the larger debate over what type of and how much capability U.S. strategic forces should have. (Soviet offer on intermediate-range nuclear weapons in Europe, p. 225)

Issues in MX Debate

MX was the centerpiece of the Reagan team's strategic defense structure. It was viewed by its supporters as a counterweight to existing Soviet missiles, as a replacement for the aging U.S. ICBMs and as an incentive to prod Moscow to the negotiating table. It was the last attribute that prompted the administration to confer on MX the title "Peacekeeper," a somewhat inappropriate accolade in the view of the missile's critics. They argued that the theoretical ability of the MX to destroy Soviet missiles in their armored underground silos would only elicit from Moscow some new escalation in the nuclear arms race. Reagan countered that view in his November 22 address. "Unless we demonstrate the will to rebuild our strength and restore the military balance, the Soviets, since they are so far ahead, have little incentive to negotiate with us," he said.

From the beginning, one of the key issues in the MX debate was the design of a basing method to protect the large missiles from destruction by Soviet nuclear warheads. Most of the MX basing modes that had been proposed were designed to bar a successful Soviet attack by hiding the missiles among thousands of possible launch sites. To be sure of killing each missile, Moscow would have to destroy all of the sites, the numbers of which could be expanded more cheaply than the attacking missiles. The theory was that Moscow might not have enough accurate warheads to demolish the MX fleet or — at worst — that it would have to use up most of its ICBMs to wipe out the U.S. missiles.

This theory was embodied in the so-called "race track," or multiple protected structure (MPS), basing plan adopted by Carter in September 1979. Carter's design would have linked 23 launch sites on an oval-shaped track. Each of 200 missiles would be moved at random among sites scattered across 10,000 square miles in Utah and Nevada, for a total of 4,600 sites. The goal of the MPS system was to ensure that 100 missiles (with 1,000 warheads) would survive any possible Soviet attack.

Many groups were unhappy with the race-track plan. Traditional arms control advocates disliked the threat to future arms limits posed by mobile missiles. Residents of Utah and Nevada feared the adverse impact of the system on local water supplies as well as the economic and social strains brought by the tens of thousands of workers who would move into sparsely populated regions to build the system. To non-specialists in strategic weaponry, the sheer complexity of playing a shell game with 100-ton nuclear missiles had more than a little bit of Alice-in-Wonderland improbability to it. And to many observers the plan simply was too expensive.

Although both the House and Senate rejected efforts to eliminate or cut Carter's requests for MX development funds, doubts persisted in Congress about the best system for basing and protecting MX.

'Dense-Pack' Basing Plan

Reagan scrapped the mobile basing plan October 2, 1981, announcing that the first few dozen missiles would be put in 20-40 existing silos that would be "superhardened" with additional concrete armor. He said the administration would select by 1984 one of three long-term basing methods: large airplanes that could cruise for days and launch an MX in midair; silos thousands of feet underground, too deep to be destroyed by attacking missiles; or silos defended by anti-ballistic missile defenses.

The administration's technical argument against MPS was that an untrammeled expansion of the Soviet missile force could simply overwhelm the system. With enough warheads, Moscow could fire at all 4,600 planned launch sites, thus ensuring the destruction of all 200 MXs.

"There is no way the United States can build [launch] shelters faster than the Soviet Union can build missiles," Secretary of Defense Caspar W. Weinberger testified during congressional hearings October 5, 1981.

Reagan disclosed the administration's plan for basing the missile in his November 22 address a year later. The plan envisioned clustering the missiles in a "dense pack," more formally known as a Closely Spaced Basing mode. The plan called for building 100 MX launch sites 1,800 feet apart in a column 14 miles long at Warren Air Force Base near Cheyenne, Wyo. In contrast to the mobile basing design, the dense pack presented Moscow with only a small number of concentrated targets, but relied on the literally self-defeating effects of Soviet weapons to protect the U.S. missiles. In theory, the MX missiles would be close enough to each other that the first few attacking missiles to explode would destroy or disable all the other incoming Soviet missiles (this lethal effect of an exploding nuclear warhead on nearby warheads is called "fratricide"). At the same time, the MXs would be far enough apart that any Soviet warhead could destroy only one MX.

Under dense pack, the MX missiles would be placed in very hard silos — resistant to 5,000 pounds of pressure per square inch from a warhead exploded next to it in the ground, and up to 20 times that much pressure from a warhead exploding overhead. Proponents of this basing mode argued that if an array of 100 such silos were attacked simultaneously by Soviet warheads, each with an explosive force equal to one million tons of TNT (one megaton), most of the U.S. missiles would survive and would be usable for a counterattack against the Soviet Union. The Soviet warheads aimed at the surviving MXs would be neutralized by the first Soviet warheads to explode. Either they would malfunction because of the intense radiation, or they would be blown off course by the blast from the explosions.

Skepticism in Congress

Despite high-powered lobbying by the administration, the dense-pack scheme failed to sway congressional critics, whose principal objections were the program's cost, its impact on the arms race and, finally, uncertainty about whether it would work as planned. On December 7, 1982, by a decisive vote of 245-176, the House deleted from the fiscal 1983 defense budget $988 million to procure the first five MXs.

In striking out the funds, the House rejected repeated administration warnings that a vote against MX would undermine the U.S. bargaining position in arms reduction talks with the Soviet Union; unless deployment of MX was likely, Moscow would have no incentive to agree to reductions in its ICBM force. "We must move forward with the MX to have any hope of achieving meaningful progress at the arms negotiations in Geneva," Reagan said in a December 6 letter to House members.

However, during floor debate on the measure, some MX opponents denounced this logic. "The history of the arms race shows that weapons which are intended to force the other side to the negotiating table simply add more momentum to the arms race," said Rep. Mike Lowry, D-Wash. (After Reagan announced the dense-pack plan, the Soviets responded that deployment of MX would lead to production of a "not inferior" weapon on their part.)

Critics of the MX procurement funding also stressed the novel and untested character of the dense-pack system. It was attacked by some members for violating the common-sense rule against putting all one's eggs in a single basket. Les AuCoin, D-Ore., likened it to the decision by military chiefs in Hawaii before the Japanese attack on Pearl Harbor, that "the one way to make sure the planes would be safe is to cluster them on the runway. . . ."

Ten days after the House rejected MX procurement funds, the Senate December 17 voted to restore the funds, but with the proviso that the money not be spent until Congress approved an MX basing method by concurrent resolution. In other words, either house could reject a basing method by majority vote. The refusal to go along with dense pack symbolized a weakening of previous consensus on strategic defense policy by a Congress that historically had been reluctant to deny presidents major strategic weapons they deemed essential.

Congress also required the administration to establish an advisory commission to study alternative basing modes. The MX controversy was renewed by the panel's April 1983 report, which recommended a return to Reagan's interim basing plan to deploy 100 MX missiles in existing silos. At the same time the report urged a crash program to develop smaller, mobile (and less vulnerable) ICBMs.

> *Following are the texts of President Ronald Reagan's nationally televised address on nuclear arms control and production and deployment of the MX missile and of his statement sent to Congress on the basing mode for the missile, both November 22, 1982. (Boldface headings in brackets have been added by Congressional Quarterly to highlight the organization of the text.):*

REAGAN'S TELEVISED SPEECH

Good evening.

The week before last was an especially moving one here in Washington. The Vietnam veterans finally came home once and for all to America's heart. They were welcomed with tears, with pride, and with a monument to their great sacrifice. Many of their names, like those of our Republic's greatest citizens, are now engraved in stone in this city that belongs to all of us. On behalf of the Nation, let me again thank the Vietnam veterans from the bottom of my heart for their courageous service to America.

Seeing those moving scenes, I know mothers of a new generation must have worried about their children and about peace. And that's what I'd like to talk to you about tonight — the future of our children in a world where peace is made uneasy by the presence of nuclear weapons.

A year ago, I said the time was right to move forward on arms control. I outlined several proposals and said nothing would have a higher priority in this administration. Now, a year later, I want to report on those proposals and on other efforts we're making to ensure the safety of our children's future.

The prevention of conflict and the reduction of weapons are the most important public issues of our time. Yet, on no other issue are there more misconceptions and misunderstandings. You, the American people, deserve an explanation from your Government on what our policy is on these issues. Too often, the experts have been content to discuss grandiose strategies among themselves, and cloud the public debate in technicalities no one can understand. The result is that many Americans have become frightened and, let me say, fear of the unknown is entirely understandable. Unfortunately, much of the information emerging in this debate bears little semblance to the facts.

To begin, let's go back to what the world was like at the end of World War II. The United States was the only undamaged industrial power in the world. Our military power was at its peak, and we alone had the atomic weapon. But we didn't use this wealth and this power to bully; we used it to rebuild. We raised up the war-ravaged economies, including the economies of those who had fought against us. At first, the peace of the world was unthreatened, because we alone were left with any real power, and we were using it for the good of our fellow man. Any potential enemy was deterred from aggression because the cost would have far outweighted the gain.

As the Soviets' power grew, we still managed to maintain the peace. The United States had established a system of alliances, with NATO [North Atlantic Treaty Organization] as the centerpiece. In addition, we grew even more respected as a world leader with a strong economy and deeply held moral values.

With our commitment to help shape a better world, the United States also pursued, and always pursued, every diplomatic channel for peace. And for at least 30 years after World War II, the United States still continued to possess a large military advantage over the Soviet Union. Our strength deterred, that is, prevented, aggression against us.

This nation's military objective has always been to maintain peace by preventing war. This is neither a Democratic nor a Republican policy. It's supported by our allies. And most important of all, it's worked for nearly 40 years.

What do we mean when we speak of "nuclear deterrents"? Certainly, we don't want such weapons for their own sake. We don't desire excessive forces or what some people have called "overkill." Basically, it's a matter of others knowing that starting a conflict would be more costly to them than anything they might hope to gain. And, yes, it is sadly ironic that in these modern times, it still takes weapons to prevent war. I wish it did not.

We desire peace. But peace is a goal, not a policy. Lasting peace is what we hope for at the end of our journey; it doesn't describe the steps we must take nor the paths we should follow to reach that goal.

[Paths to Peace]

I intend to search for peace along two parallel paths: deterrents and arms reductions. I believe these are the only paths that offer any real hope for an enduring peace.

And let me say I believe that if we follow prudent policies, the risk of nuclear conflict will be reduced. Certainly, the United States will never use its forces except in response to attack. Through the years, Soviet leaders have also expressed a sober view of nuclear war. And if we maintain a strong deterrent, they are exceedingly unlikely to launch an attack.

Now, while the policy of deterrence has stood the test of time, the things we must do in order to maintain deterrence have changed. You often hear that the United States and the Soviet Union are in an arms race. Well, the truth is that while the Soviet Union has raced, we have not. As you can see from this blue U.S. line,[1] in constant dollars, our defense spending in the 1960s went up because of Vietnam. And then it went downward through much of the 1970s. And now follow the red line, which is Soviet spending. It's gone up and up and up. In spite of a stagnating Soviet economy, Soviet leaders invest 12 to 14 percent of their country's gross national product in military spending — two to three times the level we invest.

I might add that the defense share of our United States Federal budget has gone way down, too. Watch the blue line again. In 1962, when John Kennedy was President, 46 percent, almost half of the Federal budget, went to our national defense. In recent years, about one quarter of our budget has gone to defense, while the share for social programs has nearly doubled. And most of our defense budget is spent on people, not weapons.

[Soviet Military Advantage]

The combination of the Soviets spending more and the United States spending proportionately less changed the military balance, and weakened our deterrent. Today, in virtually every measure of military power, the Soviet Union enjoys a decided advantage.

---

[1] *At this point and during later portions of this address, the President referred to charts which could be seen by the television audience.*

This chart shows the changes in the total number of intercontinental missiles and bombers. You will see that in 1962 and in 1972, the United States' forces remained about the same — even dropping some by 1982. But take a look now at the Soviet side. In 1962, at the time of the Cuban missile crisis, the Soviets could not compare with us in terms of strength. In 1972, when we signed the SALT I treaty, we were nearly equal. But in 1982 — well, that red Soviet bar stretching above the blue American bar tells the story.

I could show you chart after chart where there is a great deal of red and a much lesser amount of U.S. blue. For example, the Soviet Union has deployed a third more land-based intercontinental ballistic missiles than we have. Believe it or not, we froze our number in 1965 and have deployed no additional missiles since then.

The Soviet Union put to sea 60 new ballistic missile submarines in the last 15 years. Until last year, we hadn't commissioned one in that same period.

The Soviet Union has built over 200 modern backfire bombers and is building 30 more a year. For 20 years, the United States has deployed no new strategic bombers. Many of our B-52 bombers are now older than the pilots who fly them.

The Soviet Union now has 600 of the missiles considered most threatening by both sides — the intermediate-range missiles based on land. We have none. The United States withdrew its intermediate-range land-based missiles from Europe almost 20 years ago.

The world has also witnessed unprecedented growth in the area of Soviet conventional forces. The Soviets far exceed us in the number of tanks, artillery pieces, aircraft, and ships they produce every year. What is more, when I arrived in this office, I learned that in our own forces we had planes that couldn't fly and ships that couldn't leave port mainly for lack of spare parts and crew members.

The Soviet military buildup must not be ignored. We have recognized the problem and, together with our allies, we've begun to correct the imbalance. Look at this chart of projected real defense spending for the next several years. Here is the Soviet line. Let us assume the Soviets [*sic*] rate of spending remains at the level they have followed since the 1960's. The blue line is the United States. If my defense proposals are passed, it will still take five years before we come close to the Soviet level. Yet, the modernization of our strategic and conventional forces will assure that deterrence works and peace prevails.

[MX Missile]

Our deployed nuclear forces were built before the age of microcircuits. It is not right to ask our young men and women in uniform to maintain and operate such antiques. Many have already given their lives in missile explosions and aircraft accidents caused by the old age of their equipment.

We must replace and modernize our forces, and that's why I decided to proceed with the production and deployment of the new ICBM known as the MX.

Three earlier Presidents worked to develop this missile. Based on the best advice that I could get, I concluded that the MX is the right missile at the right time. On the other hand, when I arrived in office I felt the proposal on where and how to base the missile simply cost too much in terms of money and the impact on our citizens' lives. I've concluded, however, it's absolutely essential that we proceed to produce this missile and that we base it in a series of closely based silos at Warren Air Force Base, near Cheyenne, Wyoming.

This plan requires only half as many missiles as the earlier plan and will fit in an area of only 20 square miles. It is the product of around-the-clock research that has been underway since I directed a search for a better, cheaper way. I urge the Members of Congress who must pass this plan to listen and examine the facts before they come to their own conclusion.

Some may question what modernizing our military has to do with peace. Well, as I explained earlier, a secure force keeps others from threatening us, and that keeps the peace. And just as important, it also increases the prospects of reaching significant arms reductions with the Soviets, and that's what we really want.

The United States wants deep cuts in the world's arsenal of weapons, but unless we demonstrate the will to rebuild our strength and restore the military balance, the Soviets, since they are so far ahead, have little incentive to negotiate with us. Let me repeat that point because it goes to the heart of our policies. Unless we demonstrate the will to rebuild our strength, the Soviets have little incentive to negotiate. If we hadn't begun to modernize, the Soviet negotiators would know we had nothing to bargain with except talk. They would know that we were bluffing without a good hand, because they know what cards we hold just as we know what is in their hand.

You may recall that in 1969 the Soviets did not want to negotiate a treaty banning anti-ballistic missiles. It was only after our Senate narrowly voted to fund an anti-ballistic missile program that the Soviets agreed to negotiate. We then reached an agreement. We also know that one-sided arms control doesn't work. We've tried time and time again to set an example by cutting our own forces in the hope that the Soviets would do likewise. The result has always been that they keep building.

I believe that our strategy for peace will succeed. Never before has the United States proposed such a comprehensive program of nuclear arms control. Never in our history have we engaged in so many negotiations with the Soviets to reduce nuclear arms and to find a stable peace. What we are saying to them is this: We will modernize our military in order to keep the balance for peace, but wouldn't it be better if we both simply reduced our arsenals to a much lower level?

Let me begin with the negotiations on the intermediate-range nuclear forces that are currently underway in Geneva. As I said earlier, the most threatening of these forces are the land-based missiles which the Soviet Union now has aimed at Europe, the Middle East, and Asia.

This chart shows the number of warheads on these Soviet missiles. In 1972 there were 600. The United States was at zero. In 1977 there were 600. The United States was still at zero. Then the Soviets began deploying powerful new missiles with three warheads and a reach of thousands of miles — the SS-20. Since then, the bar has gone through the roof — the Soviets have added a missile with three warheads every week. Still, you see no United States blue on the chart. Although the Soviet leaders earlier this year declared they'd frozen deployment of this dangerous missile, they have in fact continued deployment.

[Peace Initiatives]

Last year, on November 18th, I proposed the total, global elimination of all these missiles. I proposed that the United States would deploy no comparable missiles which are scheduled for late 1983, if the Soviet Union would dismantle theirs. We would follow agreement on the land-based missiles with limits on other intermediate-range systems.

The European governments strongly support our initiative. The Soviet Union has thus far shown little inclination to take this major step to zero levels. Yet I believe, and I'm hoping, that as the talks proceed and as we approach the scheduled placement of our new systems in Europe, the Soviet leaders will see the benefits of such a far-reaching agreement.

This summer we also began negotiations on strategic arms reductions, the proposal we call START. Here we're talking about intercontinental missiles, the weapons with a longer range than the intermediate-range ones I was just discussing. We're negotiating on the basis of deep reductions. I proposed in May that we cut the number of warheads on these missiles to an equal number, roughly one-third below current levels. I also proposed that we cut the number of missiles themselves to an equal number, about half the current U.S. level. Our proposals would eliminate some 4,700 warheads and 2,250 missiles. I think that would be quite a service to mankind.

This chart shows the current level of United States ballistic missiles, both land- and sea-based. This is the Soviet level. We intend to convince the Soviets it would be in their own best interest to reduce these missiles. Look at the reduced numbers both sides would have under our proposal — quite a dramatic change. We also seek to reduce the total destructive power of these missiles and other elements of United States and Soviet strategic forces.

In 1977, when the last administration proposed more limited reductions, the Soviet Union refused even to discuss them. This time their reaction has been quite different. Their opening position is a serious one, and even though it doesn't meet our objective of deep reductions, there's no question we're heading in the right direction. One reason for this change is clear. The Soviet Union knows that we are now serious about our own strategic programs and that they must be prepared to negotiate in earnest.

We also have other important arms control efforts underway. In the talks in Vienna on mutual and balanced force reductions, we've proposed cuts in military personnel to a far lower and equal level. And in the 40-nation Committee on Disarmament in Geneva, we're working to develop effective limitations on nuclear testing and chemical weapons. The whole world remains outraged by the Soviets and their allies [sic] use of biological and chemical weapons against defenseless people in Afghanistan, Cambodia, and Laos. This experience makes ironclad verification all the more essential for arms control.

There is, of course, much more that needs to be done. In an age when intercontinental missiles can span half the globe in less than half an hour, it's crucial that Soviet and American leaders have a clear understanding of each other's capabilities and intentions.

Last June in Berlin, and again at the United Nations Special Session on Disarmament, I vowed that the United States would make every effort to reduce the risks of accident and misunderstanding and thus to strengthen mutual confidence between the United States and the Soviet Union. Since then, we've been actively studying detailed measures to implement this Berlin initiative.

[Reagan Proposals]

Today I would like to announce some of the measures which I've proposed in a special letter just sent to the Soviet leadership and which I've instructed our Ambassadors in Geneva to discuss with their Soviet counterparts. They include but also go beyond some of the suggestions I made in Berlin.

The first of these measures involves advance notification of all United States and Soviet test launches of intercontinental ballistic missiles. We will also seek Soviet agreement on notification of all sea-launched ballistic missiles as well as intermediate-range land-based ballistic missiles of the type we're currently negotiating. This would remove surprise and uncertainty at the sudden appearance of such missiles on the warning screens of the two countries.

In another area of potential misunderstanding, we propose to the Soviets that we provide each other with advance notification of our major military exercises. Here again, our objective is to reduce the surprise and uncertainty surrounding otherwise sudden moves by either side.

These sorts of measures are designed to deal with the immediate issues of miscalculation in time of crisis. But there are deeper, longer-term problems as well. In order to clear away some of the mutual ignorance and suspicion between our two countries, I will propose that we both engage in a broad-ranging exchange of basic data about our nuclear forces. I am instructing our ambassadors at the negotiations on both strategic and intermediate forces to seek Soviet agreement on an expanded exchange of information. The more one side knows about what the other side is doing, the less room there is for surprise and miscalculation.

Probably everyone has heard of the so-called Hotline, which enables me to communicate directly with the Soviet leadership in the event of a crisis. The existing Hotline is dependable and rapid, with both ground and satellite links. But because it's so important, I've also directed that we carefully examine any possible improvements to the existing Hotline system.

Now, although we've begun negotiations on these many proposals, this doesn't mean we've exhausted all the initiatives that could help to reduce the risk of accidental conflict. We'll leave no opportunity unexplored, and we'll consult closely with Senators Nunn, Jackson, and Warner, and other Members of the Congress who have made important suggestions in this field.

We're also making strenuous efforts to prevent the spread of nuclear weapons to additional countries. It would be tragic if we succeeded in reducing existing arsenals only to have new threats emerge in other areas of the world.

Earlier, I spoke of America's contributions to peace following World War II, of all we did to promote peace and prosperity for our fellow man. Well, we're still those same people. We still seek peace above all else.

I want to remind our own citizens and those around the world of this tradition of American good will, because I am concerned about the effects the nuclear fear is having on our people. The most upsetting letters I receive are from schoolchildren who write to me as a class assignment. It's evident they've discussed the most nightmarish aspects of a nuclear holocaust in their classrooms. Their letters are often full of terror. Well, this should not be so.

The philosopher, Spinoza, said, "Peace is a virtue, a state of mind, a disposition for benevolence, confidence, justice." Well, those are the qualities we want our children to inherit, not fear. They must grow up confident if they're to meet the challenges of tomorrow as we will meet the challenges of today.

I began these remarks speaking of our children. I want to close on the same theme. Our children should not grow up frightened. They should not fear the future. We're working to make it peaceful and free. I believe their future can be the brightest, most exciting of any generation. We must reassure them and let them know that their parents and the leaders of this world are seeking, above all else, to keep them safe and at peace. I consider this to be a sacred trust.

My fellow Americans, on this Thanksgiving, when we have so much to be grateful for, let us give special thanks for our peace, our freedom, and our good people.

I've always believed that this land was set aside in an uncommon way, that a divine plan placed this great continent between the oceans to be found by a people from every corner of the earth who had a special love of faith, freedom, and peace.

Let us reaffirm America's destiny of goodness and good will. Let us work for peace and, as we do, let us remember the lines of the famous old hymn "O God of Love, O King of Peace, make wars throughout the world to cease."

STATEMENT ON MX MISSILE

For nearly 2 years my administration has examined the matter of the MX missile, the development of which has been supported by my three immediate predecessors. Presidents Carter, Ford, and Nixon. We all have strongly agreed that strengthening our land-based missile system is absolutely essential to maintain America's deterrent capability to deter war and to protect our nation.

I have sought the counsel of my predecessors, the opinion of Members of Congress, and the advice of the best technical and scientific minds in the field. My administration, as well as the ones before it, has examined a wide variety of options, including smaller or bigger missiles, the development of one missile for common use on land or at sea, and the possibility of greater mobility. And, like the preceding administrations, we have concluded that MX is the right missile and that now is the time.

Deciding how to deploy the missile has not been that easy. A variety of basing modes has been studied by previous administrations and by ours. The concept of deceptive basing, as employed in previous planning, was a fundamentally sound one for assuring the stability of land-based ICBM forces in times of crisis. It complied with our strategic arms control objectives. Other sensible growth options were studied as well. As these plans progressed through the two previous administrations, however, they grew enormously in cost. Not only was the financial cost high — $40-$50 billion — but the cost of our western citizens in terms of water, land, social disruption, and environmental damage seemed unreasonable.

For these reasons, we considered other approaches while proceeding with the development of the MX missile itself. The missile work is now nearly complete. The first test flight is scheduled for early next year. While test flights are just that — tests — I have no doubts about the technical success, in fact excellence, of this missile.

In reexamining how to base the missiles, we concluded that by pulling the launch sites much closer together and making them a great deal harder, we could make significant savings. We would need fewer silos, much less land, and in fact fewer missiles. We would achieve a system that could survive against the current and projected Soviet rocket inventory. Deployment of such a system would require the Soviets to make costly new technical developments if they wish to even contemplate a surprise attack. Most of the Soviet countermeasures proposed are really no more than technical dreams on which no Soviet planner or politician would bet the fate of his country. Thus, Closely Spaced Basing is a reasonable way to deter attack — which is our objective.

[Plan for ICBM Force]

Now let me outline our overall plan for our ICBM force.

First, we recognize that the best survivability, and thus the best deterrence, lies in the modernization of all three legs of the Triad: submarines, bombers, and land-based ballistic missiles. Each gains security as all are rendered less susceptible to technological or operational surprise.

Second, we are closing down our force of huge Titan missiles at the rate of one missile every month or two. Their immense warheads and antiquated fuels have no place in our current inventory.

Third, we will maintain an appropriate Minuteman force, but many of these could be removed if we reach agreement with the Soviets on strategic arms reductions.

And fourth, we plan to produce the MX missile, now named "Peacekeeper," and deploy it in superhard silos at Francis E. Warren Air Force Base, near Cheyenne, Wyoming.

That seems to be the most cost-effective location, but I appreciate the enthusiastic offers by the citizens of Nevada to base the missile in their State.

We will emplace 100 of these missiles (versus the 200 in some of the earlier plans) in launch canisters which can be moved, if necessary, between closely spaced superhard silos. We plan to build only 100 such silos, but we will design the system so that we can add more silos later, again within the confines of a small land area, if the Soviets will not agree to strategic arms reductions, or if they persist in the development and production of more powerful and deadly weapons. We would prefer that the Soviets dismantle SS-18's, rather than we build more holes. But we can accommodate either and maintain stability.

As far as an active defense is concerned, we do not wish to embark on any course of action that could endanger the current ABM treaty so long as it is observed by the Soviet Union. Likewise, we do not wish to build even the minimal ABM system allowed us by the treaty, even though the Soviets have done so.

We plan to continue research on ballistic missile defense technology — the kind of smart, highly accurate, hopefully non-nuclear, weapons that utilize the microelectronic and other advanced technologies in which we excel. The objective of this program is stability for our ICBM forces in the nineties, a hedge against Soviet breakout of the ABM treaty, and the technical competence to evaluate Soviet ABM developments. We currently have no plan to deploy any ballistic missile defense system.

[Cost of Program]

The entire missile and basing program will cost about $26 billion in 1982 dollars, commencing with this fiscal year. That's a reduction by half, both in cost and in numbers of missiles deployed, from the other plans on the drawingboards when I entered office. The ongoing ballistic missile defense research and development will cost about $2.5 billion. Both of these programs are already reflected in the FY 83 budget projections, but the specific decisions announced today allow us to proceed with the reductions from my February budget request for this year of a billion dollars, which we have so carefully worked out with the Congress.

Continuity of effort in national security affairs is essential. Turbulence is wasteful beyond words. These programs to increase the stability and security of our strategic nuclear forces are urgently needed. The planning by my predecessors made them possible, but it is for my successor that I make these decisions. With every effort, the Peacekeeper missile still will not be fully deployed until the late 1980s, when yet another President shoulders these burdens.

I urge the Congress, and all Americans, to support this program, developed under several Presidents: those in the past who conceived and urged the deployment of MX and the current President, who has made these difficult decisions. It is only by such steadfastness of purpose that we can maintain the peace which every nation needs to work out the hopes and dreams of its own people.

REPORT ON EMPLOYMENT
OF MINORITIES AND WOMEN
November 23, 1982

The United States Commission on Civil Rights issued a 98-page report November 23 stating that employment disparities were so pervasive they were present everywhere in the United States. The study found that unemployment and underemployment of minorities and women existed at all educational, age, skill and training levels and in all geographic regions. Commission Chairman Clarence M. Pendleton Jr. said at a press conference the day the study was released, "We must strongly suspect that discrimination continues to be a factor."

"The presence of discrimination cannot be measured in a statistical study," the commission stated in its report Unemployment and Underemployment Among Blacks, Hispanics, and Women. *It further asserted, "The suspicion remains that discrimination continues to have a major effect on blacks, Hispanics and women in their struggle to find jobs commensurate with their qualifications and experience."*

When the commission issued the report, the United States was in its eighth recession since World War II. The frequency of recessions hurt minorities most because they were concentrated in industries with high cyclical unemployment. They have "insufficient time to recover from the employment hardships of one recession before being subjected to another," the study said.

One of the reasons cited for minority unemployment was lack of education. The less educated were more often employed in marginal jobs (those requiring three months or less of vocational training or experi-

ence). Among workers of the same educational level, majority males had the lowest rates of underemployment (defined as having less than full-time or adequate employment). Increased education produced lower rates of unemployment and underemployment for all groups, but especially for majority males. Blacks and Hispanics had more difficulty securing jobs that matched their educational levels than did majority males.

Employers' preference for experienced workers affected blacks and Hispanics because they had a higher proportion of younger people than the majority population. "Many of the jobs young people have are unstable and have low pay.... Younger workers are more likely than older workers to switch jobs, also resulting in higher unemployment rates (and higher rates of intermittent employment as well)," the commission reported. People with intermittent employment were defined as those unemployed at least 15 weeks or having at least three separate spells of unemployment during the year studied.

High rates of unemployment and underemployment for blacks and Hispanics were due also to jobs being located in areas where few of them lived. Since 1960 there had been a redistribution of employment from the central cities to the suburbs and to the Sun Belt region. This decline affected blacks and Hispanics because most lived in the declining central cities and in the older northern industrial regions of the country.

Lack of training was another reason why minorities and women were disproportionately unemployed or underemployed. Majority males were the most likely to receive vocational training. Minorities and women, when they were able to find jobs, usually found marginal ones that required little skill, and they found they had substantially more education than their jobs required. They received wages far below those paid to majority males with similar qualifications. They were most often the "working poor."

Following are excerpts from Unemployment and Underemployment Among Blacks, Hispanics, and Women, *issued November 23, 1982, by the United States Commission on Civil Rights:*

Introduction

The lack of adequate employment for many of this Nation's citizens has become a problem of considerable national concern. For minorities and women, who have traditionally been discriminated against in the labor market, employment problems have become critical. A 1980 survey of the National Urban League found that unemployment is "unequivocally" the number one problem in the black community. In 1982, with one out of every eight Hispanics, and nearly one out of every five blacks, officially counted as "unemployed," problems of employment have become greater than ever.

Although much has been written about employment problems during the 1981-82 recession, the crucial role of employment in securing equal benefits of citizenship has long been recognized. In 1968 the Kerner Commission studied the causes of racial disturbances in American cities and concluded that lack of adequate employment was of "critical significance." The report stressed the role of employment:

> The capacity to obtain and hold a "good job" is the traditional test of participation in American society. Steady employment with adequate compensation provides both purchasing power and social status. It develops the capabilities, confidence, and self-esteem an individual needs to be a responsible citizen and provides a basis for a stable family life.

Civil rights organizations have also emphasized the key role of jobs. In the words of Vernon Jordan, former president of the National Urban League:

> It is too often forgotten that the 1963 March on Washington was for more than just abstract rights. It was for jobs and freedom. To a large extent, we won the freedoms, but we still do not have the jobs. There are today half a million more black people unemployed than at the time of the March on Washington. . . .
>
> Despite some gains in employment and education, the masses of black people did not witness significant changes in their lives because of the rights they won in the 1960s. We were poor then, we're poor today; we were disadvantaged then, we remain so today. . . .

Social scientists also have noted that adequate employment is critical for minorities. In *The Chicano Worker*, Vernon M. Briggs, Jr., Walter Fogel, and Fred H. Schmidt discuss the link between adequate employment and full participation in other aspects of American society:

> . . . Chicanos are becoming increasingly aware of the problems they face in their efforts to obtain an equitable share of the benefits of American society — problems of schooling, housing, health, employment, social status, and cultural identity. . . .

The struggle for employment equality affects women as well as minorities; it is central to the battle against sex discrimination. Economist and former Secretary of Commerce Juanita Kreps has noted that "the most glaring complaints have to do with . . . employment. . . ." Janet Norwood, Commissioner of the Bureau of Labor Statistics, has noted that women have higher unemployment rates than men "in good times as well as bad."

Federal legislation has played a crucial role in the progress of minorities and women toward equality in employment. Title VII of the Civil Rights Act of 1964 prohibits discrimination based on race, color, religion, sex, or national origin in all employment practices, including hiring, firing, promotion, compensation, and provision of benefits. The Equal Pay Act prohibits employers from maintaining different pay scales for men and women who perform "equal work." These laws have challenged longstanding practices of limiting employment opportunities for minorities and women. Discrimination on the basis of race, sex, and national origin in virtually all phases of employment is now illegal.

Despite these laws, however, there is ample evidence that minorities and women continue to lag well behind majority [white, not of Hispanic origin] males in their employment status. In 1978 the U.S. Commission on Civil Rights documented widespread inequalities in the labor force. Minorities and women were more often unemployed than majority males. Employed minorities and women were more often in less remunerative occupations than were majority males. Similarly, minorities and women more frequently had higher levels of formal education than their jobs required compared with majority males. Recent statistics from the U.S. Department of Labor make clear that women, blacks, and Hispanics remain disadvantaged in the labor market. Comparable data from the Department of Labor for other minority groups are not available.

The purpose of this report is to examine the status of minorities and women compared with majority males in terms of unemployment and several forms of underemployment in the labor market. Unemployment is a serious burden for individuals and families. In addition to the obvious problem of no earnings, unemployment has been found to be associated with a range of personal, emotional, and even physiological problems. According to Johns Hopkins University sociologist Harvey Brenner, a 1.4 percent increase in the unemployment rate has been associated with a 5.7 percent increase in the suicide rate, a 4.7 percent increase in admissions to State mental hospitals, and an 8.0 percent increase in homicides.

Unemploymnent is a highly visible problem. Less visible is the problem of underemployment. People who are underemployed have jobs, but their jobs fail to use or to compensate adequately their abilities, education, or willingness to work. This report develops and examines several indicators of underemployment — intermittent employment, involuntary part-time employment, overeducation, marginal jobs, workers in poverty households, and inequitable compensation. In all cases, the proportions of Hispanic and black males and females and majority females who are unemployed and underemployed are contrasted with the proportions of majority males in similar situations, to assess the extent of disparity in the labor force.

Historically, employment disparities have resulted from discrimination in the labor market. Although discrimination in employment is illegal, the long history of discrimination has not been readily put aside. The Commission has previously stated that discrimination should be viewed as an interlocking process of attitudes and actions, some seemingly neutral, that continue to disadvantage minorities and women. For example, hiring officials, who have traditionally been majority males, may rely on "word-of-mouth" recruiting, with the result that few minorities or women are considered for vacancies. Guidance counselors may steer minorities and women into nonacademic curricula. Organizations may discriminate through the use of well-established rules, policies, and practices that are neutral on their face but discriminatory in effect. Seniority rules, for instance, are often applied to jobs historically held by majority males and make minorities and females more subject to layoff and less eligible for advancement. Restrictive leave policies often make full-time employment difficult for heads of single-parent families, who are usually women. Minorities and women may also be the victims of structural discrimination, in which discrimination in one area leads to unequal opportunity in other areas. For example, discrimination in education may deny minorities and women the career-oriented credentials to get well-paying jobs; lack of good jobs denies minorities the economic resources needed to move to areas with better schools.

This report examines the nature and extent of employment disparities; it also examines statistically several factors other than discrimination that could have caused those disparities. This report cannot make a determination that discrimination is a contributing factor, because the statistical analysis presented here is based only on quantitative labor market information. Quantitative evidence alone cannot be used to determine the role of discrimination in producing disparities; such a determination requires a qualitative analysis of the behaviors, motivations, and patterns that caused the statistical disparities. Because nationwide data on behaviors, motivations, and patterns are not available, the exact role of discrimination cannot be measured here. Instead, statistical analysis is presented to determine the extent of the disparities. Pervasive employment disparities may indicate that discrimination is continuing.

Data are available to analyze statistically two possible causes of disparities other than discrimination. One possible cause is poor economic conditions. According to this line of reasoning, the best way to eliminate employment disparities is to improve the overall health of the economy. . . .

Second, differences in the employment status of minorities and women may be due to their demographic characteristics, which differ in key respects from those of majority males. Blacks, Hispanics, and women often have less vocational training, for example, and blacks and Hispanics have lower levels of education than majority males. Blacks and Hispanics are also younger, on the average, than the majority population. Geographic location, too, affects employment, and blacks and Hispanics tend to live in central cities in the older, industrial regions at a time when the greatest growth is said to be in the "Sunbelt" regions. . . .

As noted above, the role of discrimination, if any, cannot be statistically ascertained. If, however, disparities are persistent, and the other possible causes described above are shown to be inadequate explanations, this would serve as a basis for hypothesizing that discrimination continues.

The Extent of Disparities
In Unemployment and Underemployment

This chapter examines levels of disparities in the labor force by presenting several statistical indicators of unemployment and underemployment for majority males, minorities, and women.... Some of these indicators are standard statistical measures frequently reported by the Department of Labor's Bureau of Labor Statistics (BLS); others have been developed specifically for this report. The Current Population Survey (CPS), conducted monthly by the Bureau of the Census, is the data set used for these statistics. The CPS data are used by the BLS to provide the monthly employment and unemployment statistics, and are widely used by analysts as a barometer of the state of the economy. The CPS is the only current data set large enough to develop measures of underemployment for minority groups.

UNEMPLOYMENT

With the amount of publicity given to unemployment and the importance of the problem for individuals and the economy, it might be presumed that very precise information is available on the extent of unemployment for the Nation and in all major segments of the economy. In fact, however, unemployment is not simple to define or measure. Any calculation of the rate of unemployment in the labor force will be influenced greatly by the way unemployment is defined and by the research procedures used to estimate or count the persons fitting the definition. The official U.S. unemployment rates are published by the Bureau of Labor Statistics and are based on the following statistical definition:

> People are classified as unemployed, regardless of their eligibility for unem-
> ployment benefits or public assistance, if they meet all of the following criteria:
> They had no employment during the survey week; they were available for work
> at that time; and they made specific efforts to find employment sometime
> during the prior 4 weeks. Also included among the unemployed are persons not
> looking for work because they were laid off and waiting to be recalled and
> those expecting to report to a job within 30 days.

This definition of the unemployed does not include all jobless persons, however. Many people, including a disproportionate number of minorities and women, are not working yet are not counted as unemployed because they are "not in the labor force." People not in the labor force may want or need employment, but may not be actively seeking work because of disability, illness, school attendance, home responsibilities, or the belief that there is no work to be found....

The official unemployment rate is used in this report as a *relative* index of the level of unemployment, rather than as an absolute measure of the full extent of joblessness, because it is the group differences in rates of unemployment and underemployment that are the central issues here. This rate has the advantage of being consistent with that used in other studies. The unemployment rate is created by dividing the number of persons who are jobless and looking for work by the number of persons in the labor force. The labor force is defined as the sum of persons who are working plus those who are not working but are looking for work. An 8 percent unemployment rate, for example, refers to the part of the population either working or looking for work; it does not indicate anything about those who are neither working nor looking for work. . . .

The data . . . show that unemployment does not affect all groups equally. In March 1980, 6.0 percent of majority males were unemployed, about 1 out of 16. By contrast, the percentage of black males out of work was more than double, 13.0 percent, or about 1 out of 8. The percentage of Hispanic males unemployed, 8.1 percent, was considerably above the percentage of majority males. Black and Hispanic women, too, suffered unemployment more frequently than majority men. Black females were unemployed as often as black males (13.0 percent), and 10.4 percent of Hispanic females were out of work, or more than 1 out of 10.

Only majority females had a lower unemployment rate than majority males, for two reasons. First, majority females continue to be concentrated in three occupations — secretaries, nurses, and teachers. In two of these occupations, secretaries and nurses, the demand for workers has continued to exceed the supply, due to low wages and poor working conditions. Second, majority women are more likely than members of other groups to stop actively looking for work when it becomes unavailable. As a result, majority females are more often classified as "not in the labor force" and are, therefore, not counted as unemployed.

UNDEREMPLOYMENT

The concept of underemployment has received considerable attention by the Federal Government, as well as in scholarly and popular publications, even though no official government definition of underemployment exists. The dictionary definition of "having less than full time or adequate employment" reflects a lay consensus that exists on the essential components of underemployment.

Some implications of the nature and extent of underemployment were recognized by the Kerner Commission:

> Even more important perhaps than unemployment is the related problem of the undesirable nature of many jobs open to Negroes. Negro workers are concentrated in the lowest-skilled and lowest-paying occupations. These jobs often involve substandard wages, great instability and uncertainty of tenure, extremely low status in the eyes of both the employer and employee, little or no chance for meaningful advancement, and unpleasant or exhausting duties. . . . The concentration of male Negroes at the lowest end of the occupational scale is . . . the single most important source of poverty among Negroes. It is even more important than unemployment, . . .

One aspect of underemployment that increases the effect on workers and their families is its duration. Whereas unemployment is often temporary, lasting less than a few months for most individuals, underemployment can be permanent. A person can be underemployed for an entire worklife by being intermittently employed, employed part time involuntarily, marginally employed, working for poverty wages, being overeducated for a job, or by being paid inequitably.

In the discussion that follows, several forms of underemployment are examined, each relating to a different aspect of work. Statistics are presented to establish degrees of disparity among blacks, Hispanics, and majority females compared to majority males. The primary objective is to identify the underemployed and to see how employment problems are distributed among groups. . . .

Intermittent Employment

Intermittent workers are individuals who experienced a significant amount of underemployment during the previous year and, therefore, do not have a stable work history. Specifically, persons are defined as intermittently employed if they were unemployed at least 15 weeks or had at least three separate spells of unemployment during the past year.

Persons intermittently employed may experience several hardships. First, they have little opportunity to obtain seniority, and their earnings suffer as a result. Second, an unstable work history is often associated with difficulty in obtaining or keeping employment in the future. Traditionally, minorities have experienced higher levels of intermittent employment than majority males, in part because minorities are employed in industries more subject to frequent layoffs and in part because, regardless of industry or occupation, they are more likely than majority males to be laid off.

. . . [M]ajority males and females work intermittently much less frequently than Hispanics and blacks. The percentage of Hispanic males who were intermittent workers in March 1980, for example, (9.0 percent) is almost double the percentage of majority males (5.3 percent). Black males worked intermittently at an even higher rate (11.5 percent). Black females and Hispanic females, too, experienced higher levels of intermittent employment than majority males (8.1 percent and 7.4 percent, respectively). Only majority females had a lower rate of intermittent employment than majority males. . . .

Involuntary Part-Time Employment

Some workers are partly unemployed. These "involuntary part-time workers" have jobs and are, therefore, not counted among the unemployed, but they work less than a full workweek due to economic factors beyond their control. Unlike workers who are intermittently employed, involuntary part-time workers experience some unemployment each week. Workers in the Current Population Survey who reported working less than 35 hours were asked why they worked less than full time. Those who gave economic reasons, such as material shortages, slack work, partial layoffs, or an inability to find full-time work, are considered involuntary part-time workers. Involuntary part-time work can leave workers doubly disadvantaged: they are not eligible for unemployment benefits because they are employed, but because they do not work full time their earnings may not be adequate for their needs.

Involuntary part-time workers are most often found in clerical jobs, retail sales, and services. Traditionally, minorities and women have been disproportionately represented in these occupations, and they have been overrepresented among involuntary part-time workers.

... [M]inorities and women are more likely to be employed part-time involuntarily than majority males. In March 1980 involuntary part-time work affected 2.7 percent of majority males and 3.6 percent of majority females. The percentage of Hispanics and blacks who were involuntarily working part time was roughly double that of majority males: 5.0 percent of black males, 5.7 percent of Hispanic males, 6.1 percent of black females, and 5.5 percent of Hispanic females.

Marginal Jobs

People employed in marginal jobs represent a different form of underemployment, in that they may work full time all year, yet their jobs offer little chance for advancement or economic incentive. The concept of marginal jobs is used to refer to jobs in the "secondary" labor market. These jobs were described by economists Peter Doeringer and Michael Piore as jobs that "tend to have low wages and fringe benefits, poor working conditions, high labor turnover, little chance of advancement, and often arbitrary and capricious supervision."

Historically, jobs in the secondary labor market have been filled by minorities and women. Because of occupational segregation, potential skills of minorities and women were ignored, and they were relegated to the least desirable jobs. A study of labor supply for the least desirable jobs in the economy noted that in "1910, about 90 percent of the Negro workers were still in the South and nearly three-fourths were confined to the two traditional black occupations of farming and menial service activities." A 1919 study of laundry workers in El Paso, Texas, reported that non-Hispanic workers were given the desirable jobs and Hispanic workers were relegated to the jobs non-Hispanics rejected. This situation was repeated throughout the Southwest. The historical pattern of occupational concentration of women in marginal jobs is also clear and striking. In 1870, for example, 60 percent of all working women were servants or had taken up similar employment; and in 1910, 60 percent were employed in just five occupations.

Discrimination that concentrated minorities and women in marginal jobs was legally sanctioned prior to 1964. For example, a 1963 study of Birmingham, Alabama, listed the following reasons given by managers for limiting *all* blacks to unskilled, low-paid positions:

> [lack of] education and training; the inability to use Negroes where they must meet the public; fear of the reaction of white workers. . . ; belief that Negroes lack a sense of responsibility; separate rest rooms would have to be installed; Negro workers are "well suited" to the type of work they are performing and

are more productive than whites in jobs requiring a lot of strength, or which are repetitive or require intense heat.

Although the importance of marginal jobs as a form of underemployment has long been recognized, no consensus has been reached on which jobs are "marginal." Marginal jobs are often discussed in abstract terms, such as jobs with low "worker satisfaction" or jobs that are "out of the economic mainstream." Jobs that require little training, however, are commonly included in descriptions of marginal jobs, and this characteristic appears to be crucial. That is, marginal jobs require little, if any, job-specific skills. The analysis in this section defines marginal jobs as those that require 3 months or less of specific vocational training or experience.

The fact that a job requires little or no vocational training or has few or no job skill requirements is especially important, as it has been shown that specific on-the-job training and experience are key determinants both to present earnings and to increasing an employee's value to an employer. Occupations that require fewer than 3 months' training are likely to offer little in the way of present or future earnings potential, are unlikely to have much promotion possibility, and as a result are likely to have high turnover. These jobs were described by economist Harold Wool as the "jobs of last resort," positions people take, for the most part, not because they want them or because they are lacking in ability, but because they are denied access to better jobs that provide training and opportunities for career advancement....

... [I]n March 1980, more than 1 out of 10 black and Hispanic males were in marginal jobs (11.9 percent and 11.2 percent, respectively), more than double the proportion of majority males (5.3 percent). Among women, the percentages are even higher. About one out of five black and Hispanic women (21.6 percent and 18.5 percent) were in marginal jobs, as were about one out of eight majority women (13.9 percent).

Workers in Poverty Households

The number of workers in poverty households shows a different aspect of underemployment in the form of the "working poor." Some individuals work steadily all year, but have household incomes below the poverty level.

Historically, workers in poverty households were more likely to be blacks or Hispanics than majority males for two reasons. First, majority males were usually paid more than those in other groups for doing identical or similar work. Second, as discussed above, blacks and Hispanics were subject to legally sanctioned discrimination, which restricted their moving into high-paying occupations. Recent studies have found that male and female Hispanics and blacks continue to be more often in low-paid occupations than majority males. These two factors have resulted in a higher proportion of blacks and Hispanics who work but remain in poverty compared with majority males.

The measure used here defines workers in poverty households as persons who remained below the Federal poverty level even though they worked at least 9 of the preceding 12 months. Unlike the other measures of underemployment used in this report, this measure uses a characteristic of families, not individuals, because "poverty" is a family characteristic. The Federal poverty level is based on total family income, family size, and farm-nonfarm residence. Therefore, not every worker with low wages is included. Most families now have two or more wage earners, so it is necessary to consider the family income to determine who is in poverty. People who had low salaries but had high family incomes (for example, a low-paid worker whose spouse earned a high salary) would not be considered working poor because they do not meet the federally established standard of poverty.

. . . [I]n 1980 only 2.1 percent of majority males in the labor force worked but remained in poverty. By contrast, the proportion of blacks and Hispanics in poverty households shows that they suffered this form of underemployment far more often; 4.5 percent of black males, 5.4 percent of Hispanic males, 6.7 percent of black females, and 3.6 percent of Hispanic females had earnings that failed to raise their families out of poverty. Majority females, often married to majority males, were consequently in poverty households less often.

These findings do not reflect the high concentration of women in poverty, because only full-year workers (that is, the "working poor") are included in the definition. Among female-headed households, the proportion in poverty is far higher. A Commission report found that in 1975, one out of five female-headed families with income were below the poverty level. Women also represented three-quarters of all persons receiving public assistance, and more than half were living in poverty. Moreover, the financial distress caused by unemployment is felt most keenly in families headed by women. Women who head families are more likely than others to be unemployed and, when unemployed, are less likely to have other sources of income.

Overeducation

Overeducation is a form of underemployment in which the individual's formal education and skills are not adequately used. Overeducation, in contrast to the forms of underemployment described above, refers only to formal education, while the emphasis in "marginal jobs" is on vocational skills and on-the-job training. Traditionally, the link between formal education and employment in American society has been direct:

> Education is valued by Americans because of the outcomes associated with it, not the least of these being the provision of a suitably skilled labor force. From the perspective of the individual, education is a means of acquiring those skills that provide the transition to employment.

To distinguish those who are overeducated from those who are not, some approximate educational requirement for categories of occupations must be used. The *Dictionary of Occupational Titles* contains an approximation of educational requirements for detailed occupational categories, and the actual years of schooling for each person are available in the Current Population Survey. Given these two essential items, it is possible to identify persons with college degrees who are in occupations typically not requiring a college degree, persons with some college in occupations typically requiring no more than a high school education, and persons with a high school education in occupations requiring an elementary school education.

The data ... show that overeducation affects all groups, but it especially affects minority males. In 1980 fewer than one-quarter of majority males (23.4 percent) were counted as overeducated for their jobs. By contrast, almost one-third of Hispanic males (31.2 percent) and over one-third of black males (37.0 percent) were in jobs requiring substantially less education than they had attained. These data show that minority males are less likely to see their education translated into better jobs than majority males.

The situation for females was somewhat different. Black females (26.2 percent) were more often overeducated for their jobs than majority males; Hispanic females (23.2 percent) were overeducated for their jobs about as often as majority males. Majority females, however, had this form of underemployment less often (20.3 percent), a result that is related to the fact that many majority women continue to be concentrated in a small number of jobs — nurses, teachers, secretaries — that, although low-paid, have relatively high educational requirements. As a result, overeducation is less of a problem for majority women.

Inequitable Pay

Inequitable pay refers to earnings that are not commensurate with a person's qualifications. Traditionally, majority males have experienced inequitable pay far less often than blacks, Hispanics, or women, who have had more difficulty translating their qualifications into jobs that pay well. Several recent studies have examined earnings and found that majority males continue to have the highest earnings of any group. A recent study by the National Academy of Sciences, for example, found that in the period 1975 to 1978, minority males employed full time all year earned 75.3 percent of the salary [of] similarly employed majority males; majority females, 58.6 percent; and minority females, 55.8 percent.

Similarly, economist Ronald Oaxaca, using a 1967 national sample of workers, found that majority males earned, on the average, $2.95 per hour. By contrast, majority females earned $1.92 per hour, black males earned $2.16 per hour, and black females earned $1.45 per hour.

Earnings discrepancies such as these have been attributed to a number of factors, including differences in the levels of education, job experience, age, and region of the country. Two sets of factors have been cited to account for these differences. First, some of these factors refer to the worker's qualifications or characteristics. The amount of education people have, for example, makes them more valuable to an employer, so they are expected to have relatively high salaries. Majority males, who have higher levels of education than other groups, could expect to receive higher earnings as a result. Similarly, since younger workers on the average earn less than older workers, the average age of workers would affect their average earnings. Second, employment factors need to be considered. People who work longer hours or in areas with higher pay rates would be expected to have higher average earnings.

To determine whether the earnings of minorities and women were disproportionately low when compared with similar majority males, both sets of factors were taken into account. Multiple regression, a common method of statistical analysis, was used to determine and control for the effects on earnings of various individual characteristics (education, age, general educational development, and specific vocational training) that are important in determining earnings, as well as employment characteristics (local pay rate, number of weeks worked, and average number of hours worked). If the actual earnings for an individual were under half of the earnings expected on the basis of individual and employment characteristics, the person was considered to be "inequitably paid." ...

... About one in seven majority males (13.8 percent) was inequitably paid; that is, their earnings in 1980 were under half of their expected earnings given their individual and employment characteristics. By contrast, nearly one in five black males and Hispanic males was inequitably paid (19.0 percent and 18.9 percent, respectively).

Females received inequitable pay far more often than majority males, and the percentage of females with this form of underemployment was larger than with any other form. Majority females, for instance, who had relatively low rates of unemployment, had rates of inequitable pay double those of majority males. Black and Hispanic women had rates of inequitable pay that were also substantially higher than those of majority males. Receiving a rate of pay incommensurate with their qualifications is therefore a particular problem for female workers. ...

Cyclical Trends In Unemployment And Underemployment

Workers in Poverty Households

Households in poverty are predominantly headed by women, and minority women have a particularly high incidence of poverty. According to the data ... 53.1 percent of households headed by Hispanic women and 50.6 percent of households headed by black women were below the poverty level, compared with 23.5 percent of households headed by majority women in 1978. In contrast, only 4.7 percent of households headed by majority men were below the poverty level in 1978. The percentage of households headed by black men in poverty was 11.8 percent, and for Hispanic men the rate was 12.4 percent.

Marital condition is an important factor when considering the economic status of a household. Researcher Marta Tienda notes:

> Female family heads include women not currently living with a spouse or another adult relative who is the household head, while male family heads may be living with their spouses and/or children. Obviously, these two forms of family headship imply different economic circumstances and needs, including eligibility for public assistance.

The high incidence of poverty among female-headed households can be attributed in part to the fact that women heading families often find full-year, full-time work impractical given their family responsibilities; in part to the fact that only one wage earner is contributing to household income; and in part to the fact that women receive lower earnings than men with similar educational backgrounds. The latter point was addressed by the National Commission for Employment Policy in a recent report:

> Women's earnings remain far below those of men, regardless of race, educational attainment, or age, though the difference is smaller among minorities. The average woman who works full-time, year-round earns about 60 percent of the wages of the average male worker. This gap has hardly changed over the past two decades. Women — black, Hispanic, and white — earn much less than men [with similar education] within every age group. In the youngest category (ages 18-24) their earnings are about 75 percent of those of men. But men's earnings increase more than women's earnings, so that by ages 40-44 women's earnings are only 50 percent of those of men. . . .

Overeducation

The white-collar job market is expanding, but the number of persons trying to enter the market is growing at a faster rate. At the same time, some workers who have white-collar jobs are exchanging them for blue-collar occupations that are less stressful, offer adequate pay and advancement, and are more conducive to personal leisure. By March 1981 approximately 40 percent of all workers between the ages of 25 and 64 had completed a year or more of college, compared with 23 percent in 1970. Some analysts maintain that as many as half of all college graduates are in jobs that do not fully use their education. As the educational level of the labor force increases, employers' preference for employees with higher educational attainment also increases, although it may not be necessary for the job. . . .

A higher incidence of mismatch between education and occupation is found among blacks and Hispanics than among majority males. Hispanic and black men consistently experienced the highest levels of overeducation during the 10-year period, and the largest disparities were between their rates and those of majority men. Majority women had the lowest rates of overeducation, but like most of the other groups, their rates also show a continuing upward trend. Hispanic women are the only group with rates that, during the latter part of the decade, appear to be moving downward. Indeed, the persistent upward trend in rates of overeducation for the other groups suggests that this form of underemployment will continue as the educational attainment level of the labor force rises.

Recent research suggests that the low overeducation rates for women in general, and majority women in particular, may be due to occupational segregation. Indeed, patterns of occupational segregation are so prevalent that some analysts suggest "the existence of a separate female labor market characterized by low paying jobs, fluid entry and exit patterns, and limited prospects for upward mobility." Economist Ralph Smith goes farther:

> The majority of women in the labor force are engaged in activities that could be characterized as "women's work." Most are clerical workers, nurses, elementary school teachers, salesclerks, and waitresses — not managers, physicians, college and university professors or skilled craft workers.

One possible explanation for the overrepresentation of women in clerical and service occupations is offered by economist Nancy Barrett:

> To the extent that women discount their probable labor market participation, they will invest in less education and training, but because of externally imposed barriers to their upward mobility, women also get less payoff for education and training than do men. Thus women have less incentive to undertake costly education and training than men do, not only because they expect to spend less time in the labor market, but also because education and training do not pay off in higher earnings for women to the same degree that they do for men.

The data ... show that overeducation is a continuing condition for all groups in the labor market. It is also clear that the trends indicated are not just simple ramifications of short-term economic trends; as mentioned previously, as the educational levels of workers continue to increase, this particular form of underemployment will probably also continue to increase.

Summary

This chapter has examined the disparities between the employment status of women and minorities and that of majority males to determine whether they persist through upswings and downturns of the business cycle. The consistency in the continuing disparity between the unemployment rates of blacks, Hispanics, and women and that of majority males suggests a pervasive and entrenched pattern.

Measures of underemployment were examined to determine if the pattern established for unemployment rates also prevailed in those areas of employment. The rates for minorities and women for some measures were, indeed, more affected by cyclical fluctuations than the rates for majority men.

● In terms of intermittent employment, majority and minority males exhibited the sharpest increases in their rates during the 1973-75 recession and the sharpest decreases during the subsequent recovery. The situation of Hispanic males improved relative to that of majority males by the end of the 10-year period, but for black males and females, the gap between their rates and that of majority males increased markedly. Only majority women fared better over the 10-year period than majority males. The gap in rates for Hispanic women and majority men was relatively stable.

• Involuntary part-time employment over the study period is disproportionately concentrated among minorities, particularly Hispanic and black women. The rates for majority males were relatively stable over the 1971-80 period, but the rates for blacks, Hispanics, and women appeared more responsive to cyclical pressures in the economy. The smallest disparity in rates relative to majority males was that of majority women. The largest disparities occurred for black and Hispanic women. Following the 1973-75 recession, the rates for black and Hispanic women improved slightly relative to majority males, while the rate for majority women was slightly worse. The disparities for black and Hispanic males relative to majority males were relatively consistent toward the recovery years, but each experienced sharp increases toward the end of the decade.

• Marginal employment was a significant problem for all minorities and women compared to majority males; however, Hispanics and blacks consistently experienced the highest rates of marginal employment over the 10-year period. Although the rates for majority males and females showed relatively little change over the period, the rates for minorities appeared responsive to cyclical variations. The dissimilarity in the group patterns, however, suggests that the effects of cyclical changes on marginal employment are more adverse for minorities than for majority males.

• Those workers who were fully employed but whose household income was below the poverty level were disproportionately minorities. Furthermore, the rates for members of the majority for 1971-80 did not appear as cyclically responsive as those for blacks and Hispanics, indicating that blacks and Hispanics are more likely to experience household income below the poverty level during recessionary periods than are members of the majority.

• Overeducation is a problem that affects all groups; however, the highest rates during the 1971-80 period were for black and Hispanic males. . . .

Short-run cyclical unemployment and underemployment problems are caused by a declining gross national product and the resultant decline in aggregate demand for goods and services. The analysis of measures of unemployment and underemployment in this chapter demonstrates that the employment hardships of economic downtuns disproportionately affect blacks and Hispanics. Nevertheless, as the economy recovers, and employment opportunities increase, the group disparities persist. Although a healthy economy certainly improves employment opportunities for blacks, Hispanics, and majority women, it is not sufficient to diminish the disparities in the employment status of minorities and women compared to majority men. The next two chapters examine other factors that could account for these disparities.

Variations by Location and Industry

The previous chapter demonstrated that blacks, Hispanics, and women generally had higher levels of unemployment and underemployment than majority males from 1971 to 1980, regardless of the state of the overall economy. These disparities may be due, not to discrimination, but to regional or industrial factors. This chapter examines whether those disparities may arise from higher levels of unemployment or underemployment in the areas of industries in which blacks, Hispanics, and women tend to live or work.

Over the past two decades, two major changes in regional development have occurred that have affected the economic status of blacks and Hispanics. Since 1960 there has been a "substantial redistribution of employment" from central cities to suburbs, according to sociologist Franklin D. Wilson.

During this time most new employment has occurred in the suburbs, and the result has been a trend toward "metropolitan decline" in the older cities.

Those most affected by this decline are blacks and Hispanics, who disproportionately live in central cities. Over one-half of all blacks, and nearly one-half of all Hispanics in the Nation, live in central cities. By contrast, about 30 percent of the total U.S. population resides in central cities.

The fact that many blacks and Hispanics live in declining central cities is called by some economists a "market imperfection." Lack of jobs for blacks and Hispanics, according to this line of reasoning, is due not to discrimination, but to the fact that the jobs are located in areas in which relatively few blacks and Hispanics live or in parts of the metropolitan area to which commuting is time consuming or expensive.

A second and equally important trend has been the rapid growth of industry in the "Sunbelt" regions of the Nation, the Southern and Western States. Many industries have relocated from the Northeastern and Central States to areas with warmer climates and lower labor costs. For example, the number of manufacturing jobs in the United States declined by 393,000 between 1970 and 1976, but the number of such jobs increased in the Sunbelt. The growth of industry in the South and West might make geographical variations an important factor in economic disparities. . . .

Variations by Individual Characteristics

Previous chapters have shown that the disparities between groups remained despite economic fluctuations, location, or industry. Although discrimination is certainly a possible cause of employment disparities, other factors could also account for the differences such as in the characteristics of individuals. This chapter goes beyond general conditions to look at more specific comparisons that take into account individual factors such as age and education that are relevant to employment.

Economist Thomas Sowell has discussed how factors other than discrimination could account for disparities. . . . For example, since black males in the labor force are on the average younger and have less education than majority males, the higher average rates of unemployment and underemployment, Sowell argues, could simply be a reflection of these differences in age and education and not a result of anything else. . . .

The characteristics of individuals undoubtedly play an important part in employers' decisions on whom to hire or promote. Frequently, researchers suggest thinking of the labor supply as a long "queue," with the most desirable potential employees at the beginning and the least desirable at the end. People with the same characteristics, such as educational background or age, should be at the same position in the queue, regardless of their race or sex, according to this theory. When an employer has a vacancy, he fills it from the front of the queue, that is, with the worker perceived as most desirable.

The groups in this report differ in their composition in terms of their demographic, educational, and employment characteristics. This is partly a manifestation of historical conditions and past patterns of legally-sanctioned discrimination experienced by blacks, Hispanics, and women. It is possible, therefore, that the disparities observed . . . reflect these differences in the composition of groups. That is, the disparities could simply reflect the results of hiring from the labor pool to obtain the best worker for each job without regard to race, national origin, or sex.

Critics of this view, however, charge that it cannot fully explain differences in unemployment between majority males and other groups. Economist William Darity, Jr., has claimed that "black workers who share the same 'productivity characteristics' with whites typically earn less and are more frequently jobless." This chapter examines characteristics of individuals that are said to affect their desirability to employers to determine whether disparities in unemployment or underemployment remain when these characteristics are held constant. Comparisons of unemployment and underemployment rates for workers with equivalent qualifications — people who should have the same position in the labor queue — are made to determine whether differences in qualifications between majority males, Hispanics, blacks, and women can account for the differences in unemployment and underemployment.

EDUCATION

Previous Studies

Education is a key characteristic that employers look for in potential or current employees. Those with more education are usually regarded as more desirable employees, and increased levels of education are related to decreased levels of unemployment and underemployment. People with more education, in short, more often have better jobs.

All groups do not have equivalent levels of education, however. Minorities, who have long been discriminated against in the educational process, continue to have lower levels of educational attainment than majority males.

Most studies of the effect of education on employment disparities have looked at earnings, a factor in two of the underemployment measures used in this report (workers in poverty households and inequitable pay). In one such study, economists Farrell F. Bloch and Sharon P. Smith examined a number of human capital characteristics using data from the 1973 Current Population Survey (CPS). They found that more years of education were associated with higher earnings for both whites and blacks. They also reported, however, that more education increased the earnings of whites to a greater extent than it did for blacks.

Sociologists Donald Treiman and Kermit Terrell examined the relationship between education and earnings for black and white men and women. They found that higher levels of education increased the earnings of white men more than white women. They also reported that on the average black women appeared to earn "substantially less than white women with comparable characteristics."

In a study of Hispanic workers in the Southwest, economists Briggs, Fogel, and Schmidt reported that increased education was associated with increased earnings for Hispanics, but the increase was less than for non-Hispanics. In California during the 1960s, for example, they found that relative educational levels of Hispanics rose compared to those of non-Hispanics, but that Hispanic relative income did not increase accordingly. Future increases in education, they concluded, would not lead to income equality for Hispanics.

Sociologists David Featherman and Robert Hauser compared 1962 and 1973 samples of married men and women. They controlled for family background factors (father's occupation, farm origins, and number of siblings), occupation, and experience. They found that women's "returns to" education (that is, the average increase in earnings associated with an additional year of education) in 1973 were just under 40 percent of those for men. This represented an improvement over the situation in 1962 when the returns to education for women were 25 percent of the male rate of return. They also found that increased years of education for blacks in 1973 increased their earnings 63 percent as much as it did for whites.

1980 Data on Education

The above-noted studies indicate that differences in education alone do not account for differences in earnings, which suggests that education cannot fully explain disparities, but these studies did not examine education as it affects the specific forms of underemployment in this report.

This section examines unemployment and underemployment rates of persons with comparable amounts of schooling to determine how much of the inequalities can be attributed to different levels of education attained by majority males, blacks, Hispanics, and females.

Data from the March 1980 CPS reveal a clear and unambiguous relationship between education and unemployment for each group: the more schooling, the less unemployment. Persons with less than a high school education experienced unemployment rates of more than 10 percent. By contrast, fewer than 6 percent of college graduates were unemployed. . . .

More striking than the overall differences due to education are the disparities between groups at the same educational level. At every level of education, large differences exist in unemployment rates between majority males and blacks, Hispanics, and women. Among high school graduates, for example, blacks were unemployed more than twice as often as majority males, and Hispanics were also unemployed more often than majority males. Black males who had attended college were unemployed as frequently (10.9 percent) as majority males who had not graduated from high school (10.8 percent). The only exceptions to this pattern were majority females with less than a college degree and Hispanic males who had not finished high school. These groups had unemployment rates slightly below those of comparably educated majority males.

On the measures of underemployment, too, majority males generally fared best at each educational level. The proportion of involuntary part-time workers, for example, decreased with higher levels of education. As with unemployment, however, involuntary part-time work affects majority males less often than any other group. Among high school graduates, for example, 3.3 percent of majority males were involuntary part-time workers. Among other workers with the same level of education, involuntary part-time work affected 4.7 percent of black males, 6.0 percent of black females, and 3.8 percent of majority females. Majority males who never graduated from high school had lower rates of involuntary part-time work than blacks and Hispanics who were high school graduates.

The proportion of workers in marginal jobs also clearly demonstrates the relationship between education and the ability to get a "good job." For each group, the more education, the smaller the percentage who had marginal jobs. At each level of education, however, the smallest percentage of those who worked in marginal jobs were majority males. Among majority males who graduated from high school, for example, 3.8 percent held marginal jobs. Among majority females who graduated from high school, however, 12.7 percent held marginal jobs, more than triple the proportion of majority males.

GENERAL EDUCATIONAL DEVELOPMENT

A somewhat different way of looking at education has been developed by the U.S. Department of Labor in its general educational development

(GED) scale. This scale measures the amount of reasoning development, mathematical development, and language development required of an average worker in each job listed in the *Dictionary of Occupational Titles*. Each job has a GED score ranging from 1 to 7.

The GED score for each job is a measure of how much education is needed actually to carry out the responsibilities of the job, not how much education is needed for a worker to be hired for the job. The GED score, therefore, measures the amount of education workers use in performing their work. It measures both how educated and, in a general sense, how skilled the employees are. GED scores are useful because they avoid the problem of the "quality" of the worker's education. Everyone who works in an occupation with an average GED of 4-5, for example, is performing work that requires knowledge gained through an average high school education.

. . . Majority males continue to fare better than women, Hispanics, and blacks when using this measure. Among majority males in occupations that use the education acquired in high school, 3.7 percent had intermittent employment. Among black males in jobs using a high school education, 7.2 percent had that form of underemployment, nearly twice the proportion of majority males. Other groups, except majority females, had rates lower than black males, but higher than majority males. Only majority females continued to have a lower rate of intermittent employment than majority males when using this method of analysis. . . .

On the measure of inequitable pay, the disparities continue to display the same pattern. Inequitable pay is primarily a problem for females, with their rates being twice as high as the rate for majority males. Among workers using the education acquired in high school, nearly one out of three women were inequitably paid, making inequitable pay for women the largest underemployment problem experienced by any group. Black and Hispanic males had rates higher than majority males, but lower than females.

TRAINING

Previous Studies

Training can be obtained either through vocational education or on the job. The amount of training required for a job is, along with education, one of the key "human capital" characteristics of workers. People in jobs that require a longer period of training are more valuable to employers because they cannot be quickly or inexpensively replaced by other workers.

Despite the importance of training, few empirical studies have specifically examined its importance as a factor in unemployment or underemployment. The disproportionate distribution of training, however, has been noted by several studies; majority males are more likely to receive vocational training than minorities and women. Economists Greg J. Duncan and Saul Hoffman, working at the Institute for Social Research at the University of Michigan, examined the extent of on-the-job and specific vocational training experienced by whites and blacks, males and females.

They found that the amount of on-the-job training was considerably higher for white males than for blacks and women. Duncan and Hoffman concluded that "minority workers are placed on different promotion ladders from white men, or are relegated to secondary sector jobs with a high degree of turnover." In a later analysis of these data, Hoffman found that the average training period for white males was 2.25 years, and for women and minorities it was under 1 year. These differences persisted within age and educational levels. . . .

Differences in on-the-job training acquired by men and women were studied by economist Ronald Oaxaca. He found differences either in the amount of on-the-job training received by men and women or the increase in earnings for that training. Economist Barbara R. Bergmann, in a discussion of these findings, noted that women do not necessarily choose to receive less training. Employers often exclude women from the opportunity to receive training. Women and minorities, she concluded, "very frequently are barred from accumulating as much human capital as they would like."

1980 Data on Training

Does the fact that majority males have more training than other groups help explain differences in rates of unemployment and underemployment? This section controls for these differences by examining unemployment and underemployment rates for majority males, blacks, Hispanics, and women who have similar training requirements for their occupations. Data on training requirements for different occupations are available from the *Dictionary of Occupational Titles* published by the U.S. Department of Labor. Training requirements are referred to in the *Dictionary of Occupational Titles* as "specific vocational preparation.". . .

. . . [T]he amount of training required for a job is, in fact, related to the level of unemployment. Of those people whose last jobs required up to 3 months' training, unemployment rates were as high as 22.4 percent (the rate experienced by black famales). Of those in jobs requiring over 1 year of training, unemployment rates were no higher than 6.7 percent (the rate experienced by black males).

Although the rate of unemployment declines for jobs that require more training, at all levels blacks and Hispanics, both males and females, experienced higher levels of unemployment than majority males. Among workers in jobs that require more than 1 year of training, for example, black males were unemployed nearly twice as often as majority males (6.7 percent and 3.7 percent, respectively). . . .

The same general pattern holds when examining underemployment: majority males continued to have lower rates than other groups, with the exception of majority females who were intermittently employed or in poverty households, as discussed previously. For example, blacks and

Hispanics were overrepresented among involuntary part-time workers, at each level of training. . . .

Finally, on the measure of inequitable pay, majority males were consistently the group least often underemployed. For example, fewer than 1 in 10 majority males in jobs requiring less than 3 months' training received inequitable pay (9.3 percent). By contrast, more than one in five black females (22.9 percent) and Hispanic females (22.8 percent) received inequitable pay. The proportion of majority females who received inequitable pay was only slightly smaller (17.1 percent), still nearly double the proportion of majority males. Black and Hispanic males in occupations requiring less than 3 months' training also received inequitable pay more often than majority males.

AGE

Previous Studies

Age is known to have a bearing on employment. Workers who have been in the labor force several years have more experience, and for this reason many employers may view them as more desirable than younger workers. The relatively high unemployment rate for teenagers, compared with adults, confirms this view that young people are considered to be less desirable as employees. Age, in this sense, may serve as a proxy for experience, and employers frequently prefer experienced to inexperienced workers.

The preference for experienced workers disproportionately affects blacks and Hispanics because of the demographic fact that the black and Hispanic populations in the United States have a higher proportion of younger people than the majority population. Total group differences in unemployment and underemployment may, therefore, be misleading, unless these age differences are taken into consideration. . . .

In addition to having less experience, younger workers also have less commitment to specific jobs, according to sociologist Teresa A. Sullivan, who studied underutilization of workers using 1960 and 1970 data from the Current Population Survey. Further, they are more likely to be terminated during layoffs. Finally, Sullivan notes that many of the jobs young people typically have are unstable and have low pay. For these reasons, she concludes, "We would expect underutilization to be higher among young persons. . . ."

These differences based on youth are not necessarily undesirable, Edward Banfield has argued. Young people are more likely to work out of choice rather than necessity and are, therefore, more likely to be unemployed. Younger workers are more likely than older workers to switch jobs, also resulting in higher unemployment rates (and higher rates of intermittent employment as well). Higher unemployment and underemployment rates among minorities, therefore, could be explained by the fact that minority populations are younger than the majority population, and

941

younger workers, regardless of race or ethnic group, are more likely to be unemployed.

1980 Data on Age

To determine the degree to which disparities in unemployment and underemployment are related to different age structures of the majority, black, and Hispanic populations, it is necessary to control for age by looking at each age group separately.... The data show that unemployment is highest for younger workers. Among teenagers in the labor force, unemployment was as high as 38.7 percent (the rate experienced by black females). Among older workers, a smaller proportion of each age group was unemployed. Therefore, as the literature suggests, age is related to the percentage unemployed. The fact that minority populations have a larger proportion of teenagers could, in this manner, help explain the higher total minority unemployment rates.

Differences in unemployment by age, however, cannot explain why minority teenagers are disproportionately unemployed compared to majority teenagers. Among majority males ages 14 to 19, 14.6 percent were out of work. Among black males and females, more than twice that percentage was unemployed, and the proportion of Hispanic females unemployed was one-third higher than majority males. Majority female and Hispanic male teenagers had unemployment rates about equal to majority males. Majority females, however, were more often employed in marginal jobs, and Hispanic males had high rates of intermittent employment and involuntary part-time work....

Similar patterns are evident in the underemployment rates. For example, marginal jobs are sometimes seen as disproportiontely affecting younger workers because these jobs require the least amount of training and the least experience. The data ... show that younger workers, especially teenage workers, were more often in marginal jobs than older workers.... Among workers in the next age bracket, ages 20 to 24, the situation changed markedly. Majority males in marginal jobs dropped from over one-quarter of teenagers (28.6 percent) to fewer than 1 in 10 workers ages 20 to 24 (9.1 percent). Among blacks, Hispanics, and women, by contrast, the decline was much smaller — about one worker in seven remained in marginal jobs. Thus, although teenage majority males may have been in marginal jobs about as often as other groups, they moved out of these jobs as they got older much more quickly than blacks, Hispanics, or women.

Inequitable pay, too, affected majority male teenagers (4.2 percent) more often than black male teenagers (2.1 percent) or black female teenagers (2.7 percent). Among older workers, however, majority males received inequitable pay less often than any other groups, and the older the workers, the greater the disparities. Majority male teenagers may have no more success than other groups in obtaining good jobs, but after the teenage years they do progressively better while blacks, Hispanics, and women do not. . . .

Further Observations
By the Commissioners

We believe this report does an excellent job of exploding the myth that the younger age of black and Hispanic populations, the lack of adequate education and skills, or the changes in economic cycles are the principal causes of minority underemployment and unemployment. By controlling for those factors in given cases, the report suggests the need not only for greater efforts to provide equality of opportunity for effective education and training, but also reminds us that effective implementation of our national policy against racial and ethnic discrimination in employment is a goal that has not yet been achieved. Even when minority youths and white youths of the same age and educational attainment are competing for jobs, black and Hispanic youths are less likely to receive them. Even when blacks of the same age and with more education compete with whites, blacks are likely either to be unemployed or underemployed.

Not only are the age of populations and lack of education not the principal causes of minority unemployment and underemployment, but cultural factors that are usually advanced as reasons appear to have little validity. Empirical evidence suggests that these cultural explanations of why European immigrants have advanced economically more than blacks are very suspect. Consider education, for example. Blacks have been as strongly oriented toward education as any of the European immigrants of the late 19th and early 20th centuries. In fact, many of the new European immigrants were so eager for their children to leave school for work that compulsory school attendance laws were passed in many States. Blacks wanted a quality education, but history indicates that poverty and discrimination prevented their acquiring it. Furthermore, historically, even when levels of education among European immigrants were lower than among blacks, the European immigrants were preferred over blacks for jobs that required little or no skill. All immigrants — Chinese, Japanese, and southern Europeans — have been discriminated against. But an exceptionally unfavorable disposition towards blacks because of the legacy of the slave period has perpetuated the discrimination against them.

When we consider the relative success of some Asian groups compared to blacks, we are reminded that discriminatory immigration laws cut off Asian immigration while their numbers were quite small. For example, even in the 1970 census there were 22,580,000 blacks, compared with 591,000 Japanese and 435,000 Chinese. An indirect result was that Asians were regarded as less of an actual threat to whites than blacks. In the relatively small number of occupations in which Asians were allowed to participate, they were able to attain a moderate level of economic success.

Blacks from the West Indies have often achieved more mobility in the United States than American-born blacks. Slavery in the West Indies, however, differed in key respects from slavery in the United States. In the West Indies, slavery ended well before it did here. Moreover, slaves in the West Indies were permitted to obtain an education and often had their own land, which enabled them to become more self-sufficient. In addition, families were not separated as they were here. This different heritage has made it easier for West Indians to overcome obstacles to success.

This report makes clear that we should not blame historically disadvantaged groups for lacking a strong work ethic or for having a different outlook on education. We also cannot blame economic cycles or the age of the population in a particular group. Instead, we must try to end discrimination directly by enforcing the law. The groups involved must not be shortchanged by finding the paths to employment opportunities blocked even when they have acquired education and skills.

DECEMBER

EASING OF MARTIAL LAW IN POLAND

December 12, 1982

On December 12 Gen. Wojciech Jaruzelski, Communist Party leader and premier of Poland, announced that the basic restrictions of martial law would be suspended by the end of the year. Jaruzelski emphasized, however, that this move was merely the first step toward the complete lifting of martial law and that certain restrictions would remain in effect.

The Polish government had imposed martial law on December 13, 1981, in response to growing civil unrest and challenges to the government's authority. The establishment of the independent trade union Solidarity in 1980 and its increasing popularity and power were central to the government's growing uneasiness and its eventual crackdown. (Polish workers' demands, Historic Documents of 1980, p. 793; Martial law in Poland, Historic Documents of 1981, p. 881)

A Difficult Year

One year after imposition of martial law, Jaruzelski declared in his address, an improving economy and easing of social turmoil merited the suspension of some restrictions. But that year had been a most difficult one for Poland. Thousands of people were arrested and interned, including many Solidarity supporters. Authorities held in isolation for most of the year Solidarity leader Lech Walesa, arrested in December 1981. Communications within Poland and with other countries were limited; independent-minded journalists were rounded up and detained. Mail was censored and telephone calls were monitored. A nationwide curfew kept people off the streets at night. All public gatherings were banned, except church services. As a result, religious events often became shows of support for Solidarity and all it represented. In October, for example, the funeral of a 20-year-old Solidarity supporter who was shot by police erupted into a pro-Solidarity rally of 10,000 people.

Demonstrations and protests against the government's restrictions occurred throughout 1982. Underground Solidarity members organized most of these activities. The first serious disturbance of the year took place January 30 when 200 protesters were arrested during a demonstration in Gdansk. A 48-hour police crackdown followed, and an estimated 140,000 persons were either warned, fined, given court summonses or detained.

Despite government crackdowns and reports of brutal treatment of political prisoners, underground Solidarity leaders continued to urge resistance. In April Radio Solidarity made two pirate broadcasts. In August underground union members called for mass demonstrations to take place on August 31, the second anniversary of the union's formation. Five persons were killed and more than 4,000 arrested that day. Disruptions continued in the fall. On October 8 the Polish parliament passed a law banning all existing labor organizations, including the suspended Solidarity. Thousands of workers participated in strikes October 11 and 12 to protest the action.

The government's pressure tactics, however, began to take effect. In November Solidarity's calls for a nationwide demonstration and strike were largely ignored. The government waged a well-organized campaign against the strike call, intimidating factory workers and engaging in great displays of police power. But the most effective move authorities made was to imply that the Roman Catholic Church had joined the government in opposing the strike.

For most of the year the church was openly sympathetic to the cause of Solidarity. On several occasions the Roman Catholic primate, Archbishop Jozef Glemp, spoke out against government restrictions and appealed for the release of Walesa and other political detainees. In October Polish-born Pope John Paul II sharply condemned the government for its ban of Solidarity, terming the action "a violation of the fundamental rights of man."

On November 8, however, Glemp met with Jaruzelski in a widely publicized meeting. An announcement followed that the pope would visit Poland in June 1983. This news elated the overwhelmingly Catholic country and suggested some degree of reconciliation between the church and government.

The government's campaign against the strike call proved effective. In tape recordings later made public by authorities, underground leaders were heard admitting defeat and expressing their frustration over the waning of public support. On November 14 Walesa was released; he had spent 11 months in confinement. Walesa remained under close watch, however, and in mid-December authorities picked him up before his scheduled appearance at a rally in Gdansk. In a bizarre episode, his captors drove Walesa round and round the ring highway linking the Baltic cities of Gdansk and Gdynia for eight hours, finally returning him to his home.

U.S. Reactions to Events in Poland

After the announcement of martial law, the United States in December 1981 imposed economic sanctions against Poland and the Soviet Union. Early in 1982 the Reagan administration began to pressure reluctant European allies to join the United States in its sanctions against the Soviets. Relations between the United States and West European nations became strained when the latter refused to support the American ban on export of equipment for the Soviet natural gas pipeline. (Pipeline sanctions, p. 879)

Throughout the year the Reagan administration condemned the Polish government for its repressive regime. In October, when Polish authorities banned Solidarity, the United States responded by suspending Poland's "most-favored-nation" trading status, thereby increasing tariffs on imported Polish goods. The move was primarily a symbolic gesture that had little impact on the Polish economy, given the declining volume of trade between the two countries.

In November and December reports reached the United States that Polish officials were considering suspension of some martial law restrictions. In a speech December 10 Reagan stated, "[I]f the Polish Government introduces meaningful liberalizing measures, we will take equally significant and concrete actions of our own. However, it will require the end of martial law, the release of political prisoners, and the beginning of dialogue with truly representative forces of the Polish nation, such as the church and the freely formed trade unions to make it possible for us to lift all the sanctions."

Jaruzelski's Speech

The lack of public support for Solidarity's strike call in November buoyed Polish authorities and, perhaps more than any other factor, led to the lifting of some restrictions. In his December 12 address Jaruzelski said, "November . . . saw further clear progress. The patriotism of the society, wisdom, the attitude of the working class, made it that the enemy's calls went unheeded."

Jaruzelski did not specify which restrictions would be eased, but on

December 13 the Polish parliament received three bills dealing with the modification of martial law. Parliament passed the government-approved legislation five days later. The major provisions of martial law to be lifted effective December 31 included the routine monitoring of every phone call and examination of mail, domestic travel restrictions and internment of political prisoners. Yet the government had the power to reimpose restrictions at any time, and the new legislation appeared to strengthen many of the sweeping powers authorities had adopted during their year of military rule.

Looking ahead to the new period of suspension of martial law, Jaruzelski asserted that the time was coming for the "birth and development of the independent, self-governed trade unions." Most observers believed, however, that these would be little more than Communist Party extensions.

Elsewhere in his speech, Jaruzelski praised the Soviet Union for its friendship and support during 1982 and denounced the United States for its sanctions and criticisms. "We have survived the boycott, restrictions and the barrage of an instigatory propaganda. The Government of the United States and some of its customers could see for themselves the evidence of bankruptcy of the attempts to interefere in the Polish internal affairs," he stated.

The United States and its allies responded coolly to Jaruzelski's announcement, and the Reagan administration did not lift any sanctions. A State Department spokesman said the easing of martial law was "in name only and certainly does not meet our conditions for the lifting of sanctions."

> *Following are excerpts from Gen. Wojciech Jaruzelski's speech to the Polish nation December 12, 1982, as released by the Polish Embassy in Washington.* (Boldface headings in brackets have been added by Congressional Quarterly to highlight the organization of the text.):

Exactly one year ago, the martial law was introduced. Some call it "war". Yes. That really was and is a war for preserving and continuity of the socialist statehood, for salvaging the dying-out economy, for the irreversibility of the line of reforms and renewal.

We have got the worst behind us, but the road ahead of Poland is not an easy one. It is not possible to come out of so deep a crisis right away. However, we behold a clearer horizon. With this thought we are coming to the New Year.

We counted that the martial law could be ended earlier. Social calm was the primary condition. Unfortunately, it came to notorious disturbances many a time. Despite that the situation in this country was steadily improving. November, the recent period, saw further clear progress. The patriotism of the society, wisdom, the attitude of the working class, made it that the enemy's calls went unheeded. An advantageous tendency took hold in economy. Observance of law and order is getting ever stronger. That allows to positively answer the appeal of the Patriotic Movement for National Rebirth, as well as the other social initiatives aiming at similar direction. The Martial Council of National Redemption is of the opinion that conditions have arisen for suspending the martial law. I would like to state this just today — on the eve of the anniversary of its introduction.

[First Step]

The suspension of the martial law means that its basic rigours will cease to function before the end of this year. Only such regulations should be binding either in full or limited dimension, which directly protect the basic interest of the state, create the shield for economy and strengthen the personal security of citizens.

This will be a weighty step towards complete lifting of the martial law. We would like to realize this intention in the feasibly near perspective, as it is simply impossible to jump into a full normalization. One should move towards it step by step, consistently, by a common effort.

The enemy's actions have not stopped. Hopes are still lingering for "another stage" of the fight against the socialist state.

So we cannot afford yet to renounce all the extraordinary measures. We did not reach for the martial law to squander today what we have managed to achieve by such an effort, by the effort of millions of Poles, during that year.

I do not make any promises, but I do promise one thing — anarchy will not be allowed into Poland. Let nobody, in Poland or outside, cherish any illusions that present decisions will allow another round. I do not say this admonition flippantly....

We are living at a time of heightened tensions and dangers provoked by imperialism. Our Polish affairs are not taking place on an empty arena. The sooner we regain balance, the greater will be our contribution to the edifice of peace in Europe. Poland has ceased to be the potential hotbed of a conflict. Now the important thing for her is to become again a durable factor of international cooperation and stability.

We have survived the boycott, restrictions and the barrage of an instigatory propaganda. The Government of the United States and some of its customers could see for themselves the evidence of bankruptcy of the attempts to interfere in the Polish internal affairs. The Polish destinies are being decided not there and not in their way. They are being decided only here, on the Vistula and Odra rivers.

The Sejm has not taken the decision on martial law yet, but the foreign, uninvited reviewer has already spoken up. He seems to know the best what Poland needs. We have supplied enough proofs that we shall not swerve from the road we have chosen. We shall act according to only one guidepost — this is the well-being of the nation, of the socialist Polish statehood. We will answer with appropriate decisions to those who are hitting out so venomously at this well-being.

The past years have once again strengthened the rank of our alliances, the importance of the assistance which we experience from our Soviet friends. Thus the importance of the principle "one for all and all for one" has been borne out. In the mutual interdependence of the national interest of each socialist country with the interest of the socialist community resides the strength and resistance of all of its members. A new period is beginning in the life of Poland, a period of suspension of martial law. We want to use it effectively.

[Future of Poland]

What is waiting for us in this period?

Waiting for us is first of all "a great collective duty": strengthening of the socialist state. Saved from disintegration, regaining strength, it can and should creatively absorb and actively use the various broadly developing forms of socialist democracy and self-management.

We also expect that this will be the time of birth and development of the independent, self-governed trade unions. The gaining by them of the high position which they deserve. The Party, the people's authority, will show them understanding and will wish them best.

Awaiting is the great task of rebuilding the confidence and strengthening the bond of the people's authority with the society, especially the working class. We do not forget about social agreements. We all should learn with perserverance the difficult art of a frank, constructive dialogue, mutual contact and consultation. We must create such an atmosphere, such conditions as to ensure that every conscious, honestly-working citizen feels to be the real co-manager of his establishment and his own country.

Some time is necessary to gradually untangle our Polish matters, improve the living conditions. Strained work is necessary. Mutual confidence is necessary. The road to this goal is charted by the Party, its 9th Congress. There is not and will not be a U-turn from this road.

The time has come for construction of institutional foundations of agreement. We need not talk all with one voice on every separate matter. A new democratic forum — The Patriotic Movement for National Rebirth — is formed. Its National Council will soon begin to act. Next year the first Congress of this Movement can be held. It can be expected that an original programme, in keeping with the social expectations, will be worked out.

Only he who wants to be an enemy is one. We shall be impatient with evil but patient with human doubts. I say this to those who did not find a place for themselves throughout the past year. I also speak to those who are still wandering in the blind corner of the underground. The suspension of martial law gives a successive chance.

Internment will cease to be applied. Pardons on a socially-purposeful scale are envisaged. The people's authority is stern when necessary, tolerant when possible. Perhaps sensational statements were expected. I think, however, that it is better when we solve the Polish matters realistically, with prudence, when we discuss them calmly, normally.

COURT ON CHURCH AND STATE
December 13, 1982

By a vote of 8-1, the Supreme Court December 13 struck down as unconstitutional a Massachusetts law allowing churches and schools to veto the issuance of liquor licenses to nearby establishments. The majority opinion, written by Chief Justice Warren E. Burger, held that the law violated the Establishment Clause of the First Amendment, which requires separation between church and state.

The case of Larkin v. Grendel's Den *began in 1977 when Grendel's Den restaurant applied for a license to sell alcoholic beverages. The restaurant is located in the Harvard Square area of Cambridge, Mass., 10 feet from the Holy Cross Armenian Catholic Church.*

In accordance with Massachusetts law, which gave schools and churches the power to prevent the issuance of liquor licenses to premises located within a 500-foot radius, the church chose to object to the restaurant's application. On that basis, the application was denied.

Church-State Conflict

In ruling for the restaurant, Burger wrote that the Massachusetts law gave churches "unilateral and absolute power" over governmental decision making and thus "enmeshes churches in the process of government." He stated, "The Framers did not set up a system of government in which important, discretionary governmental powers would be delegated to or shared with religious institutions."

The Burger opinion hinted that a zoning law barring liquor licenses to establishments located near churches or schools would be constitutionally acceptable, because the decision-making power would be vested in governmental agencies and not delegated to private, non-governmental entities. ". . . [T]here can be little doubt about the power of a state to regulate the environment in the vicinity of schools, churches, hospitals and the like by exercise of reasonable zoning laws," the chief justice wrote.

Burger was joined in the opinion by Justices William J. Brennan Jr., Byron R. White, Thurgood Marshall, Harry A. Blackmun, Lewis F. Powell Jr., John Paul Stevens and Sandra Day O'Connor.

Rehnquist Dissent

Only Justice William H. Rehnquist dissented, describing the Massachusetts law as "sensible and unobjectionable." He said, "The state can constitutionally protect churches from liquor for the same reasons it can protect them from fire, noise and other harm."

Following are excerpts from the Supreme Court's December 13, 1982, decision in Larkin v. Grendel's Den, *in which Massachusetts' law giving churches the power to veto liquor licenses was declared an unconstitutional intrusion by religion into governmental affairs, and the dissent by Justice Rehnquist:*

No. 81-878

John P. Larkin et al., Appellants *v.* Grendel's Den, Inc.	On appeal from the United States Court of Appeals for the First Circuit

[December 13, 1982]

CHIEF JUSTICE BURGER delivered the opinion of the Court.

The question presented by this appeal is whether a Massachusetts statute, which vests in the governing bodies of churches and schools the power effectively to veto applications for liquor licenses within a five hundred foot radius of the church or school, violates the Establishment Clause of the First Amendment or the Due Process Clause of the Fourteenth Amendment.

I

A

Appellee operates a restaurant located in the Harvard Square area of Cambridge, Massachusetts. The Holy Cross Armenian Catholic Parish is located adjacent to the restaurant; the back walls of the two buildings are ten feet apart. In 1977, appellee applied to the Cambridge License Commission for approval of an alcoholic beverages license for the restaurant.

Section 16C of Chapter 138 of the Massachusetts General Laws provides: "Premises ... located within a radius of five hundred feet of a church or school shall not be licensed for the sale of alcoholic beverages if the governing body of such church or school files written objection thereto."

Holy Cross Church objected to the appellee's application, expressing concern over "having so many licenses *so* near" (emphasis in original). The License Commission voted to deny the application, citing only the objection of Holy Cross Church and noting that the church "is within 10 feet of the proposed location."

On appeal, the Massachusetts Alcoholic Beverages Control Commission upheld the License Commission's action. The Beverages Control Commission found that "the church's objection under Section 16C was the only basis on which the [license] was denied."

Appellee then sued the License Commission and the Beverages Control Commission in United States District Court. Relief was sought on the grounds that § 16C, on its face and as applied, violated the Equal Protection and Due Process Clauses of the Fourteenth Amendment, the Establishment Clause of the First Amendment, and the Sherman Act.

The suit was voluntarily continued pending the decision of the Massachusetts Supreme Judicial Court in a similar challenge to § 16C, *Arno* v. *Alcoholic Beverages Control Commission* (1979). In *Arno*, the Massachusetts court characterized § 16C as delegating a "veto power" to the specified institutions but upheld the statute against Due Process and Establishment Clause challenges. Thereafter, the District Court denied appellants' motion to dismiss.

On the parties' cross-motions for summary judgment, the District Court declined to follow the Massachusetts Supreme Judicial Court's decision in *Arno*. The District Court held that § 16C violated the Due Process Clause and the Establishment Clause and held § 16C void on its face. The District Court rejected appellee's equal protection arguments, but held that the state's actions were not immune from antitrust review under the doctrine of *Parker* v. *Brown* (1942). It certified the judgment to the First Circuit Court of Appeals pursuant to 28 U.S.C. § 1292, and the Court of Appeals accepted certification.

A panel of the First Circuit, in a divided opinion, reversed the District Court on the Due Process and Establishment Clause arguments, but affirmed its antitrust analysis.

Appellee's motion for rehearing *en banc* was granted and the *en banc* court, in a divided opinion, affirmed the District Court's judgment on Establishment Clause grounds without reaching the due process or antitrust claims.

B

The Court of Appeals noted that appellee does not contend that § 16C lacks a secular purpose, and turned to the question of "whether the law 'has the *direct* and *immediate* effect of advancing religion' as contrasted with 'only a *remote* and *incidental* effect advantageous to religious institutions'" (emphasis in original), quoting *Committee for Public Education* v. *Nyquist* (1973). The court concluded that § 16C confers a direct and substantial benefit upon religions by "the grant of a veto power over liquor sales in roughly one million square feet ... of what may be a city's most commercially valuable sites."

The court acknowledged that § 16C "extends its benefit beyond churches to schools," but concluded that the inclusion of schools "does not dilute [the statute's] forbidden religious classification," since § 16C does not "encompass all who are otherwise similarly situated to churches in all respects except dedication to 'divine worship.'" In the view of the Court of Appeals, this "explicit religious discrimination" provided an additional basis for its holding that § 16C violates the Establishment Clause.

The court found nothing in the Twenty-First Amendment to alter its conclusion, and affirmed the District Court's holding that § 16C is facially unconstitutional under the Establishment Clause of the First Amendment.

We noted probable jurisdiction (1982), and we affirm.

II

A

Appellants contend that the State may, without impinging on the Establishment Clause of the First Amendment, enforce what it describes as a "zoning" law in order to shield schools and places of divine worship from the presence nearby of liquor dispensing establishments. It is also contended that a zone of protection around churches and schools is essential to protect diverse centers of spiritual, educational and cultural enrichment. It is to that end that the State has vested in the governing bodies of all schools, public or private, and all churches, the power to prevent the issuance of liquor licenses for any premises within 500 feet of their institutions.

Plainly schools and churches have a valid interest in being insulated from certain kinds of commercial establishments, including those dispensing liquor. Zoning laws have long been employed to this end, and there can be little doubt about the power of a state to regulate the environment in the vicinity of schools, churches, hospitals and the like by exercise of reasonable zoning laws.

We have upheld reasonable zoning ordinances regulating the location of so-called "adult" theaters, see *Young* v. *American Mini Theatres, Inc.* (1976); and in *Grayned* v. *City of Rockford* (1972), we recognized the legitimate governmental interest in protecting the environment around certain institutions when we sustained an ordinance prohibiting willfully making, on grounds adjacent to a school, noises which are disturbing to the good order of the school sessions.

The zoning function is traditionally a governmental task requiring the "balancing [of] numerous competing considerations," and courts should properly "refrain from reviewing the merits of [such] decisions, absent a showing of arbitrariness or irrationality." *Village of Arlington Heights* v. *Metropolitan Housing Development Corp.* (1977). See also, *e.g., Village of Belle Terre* v. *Boraas* (1974). Given the broad powers of states under the Twenty-First Amendment, judicial deference to the legislative exercise of zoning powers by a city council or other legislative zoning body is especially appropriate in the area of liquor regulation. See, *e.g., California* v. *Larue* (1972); *California Retail Liquor Dealers Association* v. *Midcal Aluminum, Inc.* (1980).

However, § 16C is not simply a legislative exercise of zoning power. As the Massachusetts Supreme Judicial Court concluded, § 16C delegates to private, nongovernmental entities power to veto certain liquor license applications, *Arno* v. *Alcoholic Beverages Control Commission*. This is a power ordinarily vested in agencies of government. See, *e.g., California* v. *Larue*, commenting that a "state agency . . . is itself the repository of the State's power under the Twenty-First Amendment." We need not decide whether, or upon what conditions, such power may ever be delegated to nongovernmental entities; here, of two classes of institutions to which the legislature has delegated this important decisionmaking power, one is secular, but one is religious. Under these circumstances, the deference normally due a legislative zoning judgment is not merited.

B

The purposes of the First Amendment guarantees relating to religion were twofold: to foreclose state interference with the practice of religious faiths, and to foreclose the establishment of a state religion familiar in other Eighteenth Century systems. Religion and government, each insulated from the other, could then coexist. Jefferson's idea of a "wall," see *Reynolds* v. *United States* (1878), *quoting* Reply from Thomas Jefferson to an address by a committee of the Danbury Baptist Association (January 1, 1802), was a useful figurative illustration to emphasize the concept of separateness. Some limited and incidental entanglement between church and state authority is inevitable in a complex modern society, see, *e.g., Lemon* v. *Kurtzman* (1971); *Walz* v. *Tax Commission* (1970), but the concept of a "wall" of separation is a useful signpost. Here that "wall" is substantially breached by vesting discretionary governmental powers in religious bodies.

This Court has consistently held that a statute must satisfy three criteria to pass muster under the Establishment Clause:

> First, the statute must have a secular legislative purpose; second, its principal or primary effect must be one that neither advances nor inhibits religion ... ; finally, the statute must not foster "an excessive government entanglement with religion."

Lemon v. *Kurtzman, quoting Walz* v. *Tax Commission.* See also *Widmar* v. *Vincent* (1981); *Wolman* v. *Walter* (1977). Independent of the first of those criteria, the statute, by delegating a governmental power to religious institutions, inescapably implicates the Establishment Clause.

The purpose of § 16C, as described by the District Court, is to "protec[t] spiritual, cultural, and educational centers from the 'hurly-burly' associated with liquor outlets." There can be little doubt that this embraces valid secular legislative purposes. However, these valid secular objectives can be readily accomplished by other means — either through an absolute legislative ban on liquor outlets within reasonable prescribed distances from churches, schools, hospitals and like institutions, or by ensuring a hearing for the views of affected institutions at licensing proceedings where, without question, such views would be entitled to substantial weight.

Appellants argue that § 16C has only a remote and incidental effect on the advancement of religion. The highest court in Massachusetts, however, has construed the statute as conferring upon churches a veto power over governmental licensing authority. Section 16C gives churches the right to determine whether a particular applicant will be granted a liquor license, or even which one of several competing applicants will receive a license.

The churches' power under the statute is standardless, calling for no reasons, findings, or reasoned conclusions. That power may therefore be used by churches to promote goals beyond insulating the church from undesirable neighbors; it could be employed for explicitly religious goals, for example, favoring liquor licenses for members of that congregation or adherents of that faith. We can assume that churches would act in good faith in their exercise of the statutory power, see *Lemon* v. *Kurtzman*, yet § 16C does not by its terms require that churches' power be used in a religiously neutral way. "[T]he potential for conflict inheres in the situation," *Levitt* v. *Committee for Public Education* (1973); and appellants have not suggested any "effective means of guaranteeing" that the delegated power "will be used exclusively for secular, neutral, and nonideological purposes." *Committee for Public Education* v. *Nyquist.* In addition, the mere appearance of a joint exercise of legislative authority by Church and State provides a significant symbolic benefit to religion in the minds of some by reason of the power conferred. It does not strain our prior holdings to say that the statute can be seen as having a "primary" and "principal" effect of advancing religion.

Turning to the third phase of the inquiry called for by *Lemon* v. *Kurtzman*, we see that we have not previously had occasion to consider the entanglement implications of a statute vesting significant governmental authority in churches. This statute enmeshes churches in the exercise of substantial governmental powers contrary to our consistent interpretation of the Establishment Clause; "[t]he objective is to prevent, as far as possible, the intrusion of either [Church or State] into the precincts of the other." *Lemon* v. *Kurtzman*. We went on in that case to state:

> Under our system the choice has been made that government is to be entirely excluded from the area of religious instruction *and churches excluded from the affairs of government*. The Constitution decrees that religion must be a private matter for the individual, the family, and the institutions of private choice, and that while some involvement and entanglement are inevitable, lines must be drawn.

([E]mphasis added).

Our contemporary views do no more than reflect views approved by the Court more than a century ago:

> "The structure of our government has, for the preservation of civil liberty, rescued the temporal institutions from religious interference. On the other hand, it has secured religious liberty from the invasion of the civil authority."

Watson v. *Jones* (1871), quoting *Harmon* v. *Dreher* (S.C. Ct. App. 1843).

As these and other cases make clear, the core rationale underlying the Establishment Clause is preventing "a fusion of governmental and religious functions," *School District of Abington Township* v. *Schempp* (1963). See, *e.g.*, *Walz* v. *Tax Commission*; *Everson* v. *Board of Education* (1947). The Framers did not set up a system of government in which important, discretionary governmental powers would be delegated to or shared with religious institutions.

Section 16C substitutes the unilateral and absolute power of a church for the reasoned decisionmaking of a public legislative body acting on evidence and guided by standards, on issues with significant economic and political implications. The challenged statute thus enmeshes churches in the processes of government and creates the danger of "[p]olitical fragmentation and divisiveness along religious lines," *Lemon* v. *Kurtzman*. Ordinary human experience and a long line of cases teach that few entanglements could be more offensive to the spirit of the Constitution.

The judgment of the Court of Appeals is affirmed.

So ordered.

JUSTICE REHNQUIST, dissenting.

Dissenting opinions in previous cases have commented that "great" cases, like "hard" cases, make bad law. *Northern Securities Co.* v. *United States* (1904) (Holmes, J., dissenting); *Nixon* v. *Administrator of General Services Administration* (1977) (BURGER, C. J., dissenting). Today's opinion suggests that a third class of cases — silly cases — also make bad law. The Court wrenches from the decision of the Massachusetts Supreme Judicial Court the word "veto," and rests its conclusion on this single term. The aim of this effort is to prove that a quite sensible Massachusetts liquor zoning law is apparently some sort of sinister religious attack on secular government reminiscent of St. Bartholomew's Night. Being unpersuaded, I dissent.

In its original form, § 16C imposed a flat ban on the grant of an alcoholic beverage license to any establishment located within 500 feet of a church or a school. This statute represented a legislative determination that worship and liquor sales are generally not compatible uses of land. The majority concedes, as I believe it must, that "an absolute legislative ban on liquor outlets within reasonable prescribed distances from churches, schools, hospitals, and like institutions" would be valid. See *California* v. *LaRue* (1972) (Stewart, J., concurring).

Over time, the legislature found that it could meet its goal of protecting people engaged in religious activities from liquor-related disruption with a less absolute prohibition. Rather than set out elaborate formulae or require an administrative agency to make findings of fact, the legislature settled on the simple expedient of asking churches to object if a proposed liquor outlet would disturb them. Thus, under the present version of § 16C, a liquor outlet within 500 feet of a church or school can be licensed unless the affected institution objects. The flat ban, which the majority concedes is valid, is more protective of churches and more restrictive of liquor sales than the present § 16C.

The evolving treatment of the grant of liquor licenses to outlets located within 500 feet of a church or a school seems to me to be the sort of legislative refinement that we should encourage, not forbid in the name of the First Amendment. If a particular church or a particular school located within the 500 foot radius chooses not to object, the state has quite sensibly concluded that there is no reason to prohibit the issuance of the license. Nothing in the Court's opinion persuades me why the more rigid prohibition would be constitutional, but the more flexible not.

The Court rings in the metaphor of the "wall between church and state," and the "three part test" developed in *Walz* v. *Tax Commission* (1970) to justify its result. However, by its frequent reference to the statutory provision as a "veto," the Court indicates a belief that § 16C effectively constitutes churches as third houses of the Massachusetts legislature. Surely we do not need a three part test to decide whether the grant of actual legislative power to churches is within the proscription of the Establishment Clause of the First and Fourteenth Amendments. The question in this case is not whether such a statute would be unconstitutional, but whether § 16C is such a statute. The court in effect answers this question in the first sentence of its opinion without any discussion or statement of reasons. I do not think the question is so trivial that it may be answered by simply affixing a label to the statutory provision.

Section 16C does not sponsor or subsidize any religious group or activity.

It does not encourage, much less compel, anyone to participate in religious activities or to support religious institutions. To say that it "advances" religion is to strain at the meaning of that word.

The Court states that § 16C "advances" religion because there is no guarantee that objections will be made "in a religiously neutral way." It is difficult to understand what the Court means by this. The concededly legitimate purpose of the statute is to protect citizens engaging in religious and educational activities from the incompatible activities of liquor outlets and their patrons. The only way to decide whether these activities are incompatible with one another in the case of a church is to ask whether the activities of liquor outlets and their patrons may interfere with religious activity; this question cannot, in any meaningful sense, be "religiously neutral." In this sense, the flat ban of the original § 16C is no different from the present version. Whether the ban is unconditional or may be invoked only at the behest of a particular church, it is not "religiously neutral" so long as it enables a church to defeat the issuance of a liquor license when a similarly situated bank could not do the same. The state does not, in my opinion, "advance" religion by making provision for those who wish to engage in religious activities, as well as those who wish to engage in educational activities, to be unmolested by activities at a neighboring bar or tavern that have historically been thought incompatible.

The Court is apparently concerned for fear that churches might object to the issuance of a license for "explicitly religious" reasons, such as "favoring liquor licenses for members of that congregation or adherents of that faith." If a church were to seek to advance the interests of its members in this way, there would be an occasion to determine whether it had violated any right of an unsuccessful applicant for a liquor license. But our ability to discern a risk of such abuse does not render § 16C violative of the Establishment Clause. The state can constitutionally protect churches from liquor for the same reasons it can protect them from fire, see *Walz* (1970), noise, see *Grayned* v. *City of Rockford* (1972), and other harm.

The heavy First Amendment artillery that the Court fires at this sensible and unobjectionable Massachusetts statute is both unnecessary and unavailing. I would reverse the judgment of the Court of Appeals.

GORSUCH CONTEMPT CITATION

December 16, 1982

The House of Representatives December 16 by a vote of 259-105 held Anne M. Gorsuch, administrator of the Environmental Protection Agency (EPA), in contempt of Congress. It was the first time a Cabinet-level official had been held in contempt. Gorsuch was cited for refusing, at the direction of President Ronald Reagan, to comply in full with a November 16 House subpoena for documents pertaining to EPA's enforcement of the $1.6 billion "superfund" law. The law required the cleanup of 160 abandoned toxic waste dump sites. EPA withheld 74 of the documents demanded, less than 1 percent of those subpoenaed.

The president, advised by Attorney General William French Smith, instructed Gorsuch November 30 not to provide the 74 documents because, according to the administration, they contained vital information pertaining to ongoing investigations that could jeopardize enforcement of the superfund law.

Congress created the superfund in 1980 to pay for the cleanup of hazardous waste dumps, such as the one at Love Canal in New York. It was meant to pay for immediate cleanup, avoiding the delay of lawsuits. It contained liability provisions under which the government could recover cleanup costs and collect damages from polluters. Some 86 percent of the revenue for the fund was provided by a tax on the chemical and oil industries, and the rest from congressional appropriations. Congress was obliged to appropriate the money to EPA after it was deposited into the fund. Gorsuch refused to release documents on three superfund sites. (Chromosome report on Love Canal residents, Historic

965

Documents of 1980, p. 445)

With its vote, the Democrat-controlled House asked the United States attorney for the District of Columbia to present a criminal contempt case against Gorsuch to a grand jury. The misdemeanor charge carried a penalty of up to a year in jail and a fine from $100 to $1,000.

Promptly afterward the Justice Department, representing Gorsuch, filed a civil lawsuit against the House seeking to have its subpoena declared unconstitutional. The department's suit charged that the House subpoena was illegal and improper because the documents demanded were protected by executive privilege, because the subpoena was too broad and because the subcommittee of the Public Works and Transportation Committee that was seeking the documents failed to demonstrate specific need for those that Gorsuch withheld. With its lawsuit the Justice Department put the confrontation between the legislative and executive branches squarely before the judicial branch to settle. This challenge was dismissed February 3, 1983, by U.S. District Judge John Lewis Smith Jr. Smith, refusing to rule on the matter of executive privilege, urged both sides to settle their differences without further judicial involvement.

Lavelle Investigation

Far from settling down, the EPA investigation became more dramatic when Rita Lavelle, the assistant administrator in charge of the superfund, was fired February 7. It had been alleged that Lavelle had "politicized" the superfund by delaying payments for cleanups in certain areas. Her relationship with officials of major chemical companies was also under investigation. After failing to honor a subpoena to appear at House hearings, Lavelle February 23 testifed before the Senate Environment Committee that she had not given favorable treatment to any company. She denied having participated in decisions involving the waste dump of her former employer, Aerojet General Corp. When she appeared before the the House Public Works and Transportation Subcommittee on Investigation and Oversight (the committee that had issued the original subpoena) the next day, Chairman Elliott H. Levitas, D-Ga., said that Lavelle's attitude seemed to be to settle toxic waste cleanup issues to the satisfaction of the polluters, not the public.

The subcommittee took the position that it was inappropriate for the administration to decide unilaterally what Congress could or could not review. Levitas said the inquiry indicated that "major chemical companies are not being held liable for the full costs of cleaning up their portion of the wastes in the country." Without more information, he said, the subcommittee could neither confirm nor deny the findings.

The contempt citation itself may have become a moot point when

Gorsuch (who changed her name to Anne McGill Burford February 20, 1983, when she married Robert Burford, director of the Bureau of Land Management) resigned her post at EPA March 9. Levitas, whose sub-committee originated the citation, said the matter was under discussion. And at EPA major personnel changes continued with further resignations and dismissals, at least one related to the discovery of a "hit list" that contained the names of agency employees considered too liberal for the administration's policies. On March 21, 1983, Reagan asked William D. Ruckelshaus, the agency's first administrator during the Nixon administration, to take the head position again.

Executive Privilege

The clash between Congress and Gorsuch posed the first major test of executive privilege since President Richard Nixon tried in 1974 to withhold White House tapes from Watergate prosecutors. Nixon was unsuccessful. A unanimous Supreme Court ruled that his claim of executive privilege had to yield to the criminal prosecution of Watergate defendants. The court ruled then that presidents are entitled to claim executive privilege in certain circumstances but did not specify when such claims were valid. Presidents have relied on executive privilege 64 times since 1792. The outcome of the Gorsuch case involved the same sort of legal issue that existed in the Nixon case — defining the limits of executive privilege when that doctrine collided with the interests of another branch of government.

A difference between the two cases was that Gorsuch's did not involve personal, presidential communications but rather an agency within the executive branch that tried to keep certain documents from the legislative branch.

The broad issues at stake in the Gorsuch case were: How much power did Congress have in overseeing government operations? And should the documents be protected by executive privilege?

Following are excerpts from H Rept 97-968, as read into the Congressional Record, and the text of the citation finding Anne Gorsuch in contempt of Congress, both December 16, 1982:

REPORT

What the subcommittee is trying to assess

The Subcommittee's hearings and field investigations have raised a number of concerns about the adequacy of the Superfund law, and the extent to which the EPA's efforts to carry it out are both satisfactory and in keeping with the intent of the law. Further, public disclosure of alleged illegal hazardous waste disposal activities by a Waterbury, Connecticut chemical handling firm, activities that may also be in violation of the Federal Clean Water Act, suggest that current efforts to prevent improper and illegal disposal of hazardous wastes are inadequate.

Testimony and additional evidence available to the Subcommittee also suggests that many identified hazardous waste sites are not being fully, nor expeditiously cleaned up, and that many of the companies responsible for the wastes are not being held fully liable for their share of the cleanup costs, as the Superfund law intended.

There is also evidence suggesting that resources devoted to the EPA for pursuing leads about responsible parties are inadequate; that documents that would help to establish the responsibility of parties for some of these sites have not been expeditiously obtained; that contracts for cleaning up hazardous waste sites may be going to the very companies that had a hand in creating them; that wastes from some sites being cleaned up at public expense may appear to have been improperly disposed of, creating new cleanup problems; and, that EPA's efforts to impose administrative penalties on violators of hazardous chemical and waste laws over the past several years, have been oriented toward seeking minimum penalties, which are often further reduced during negotiations with responsible parties.

As a result, the Subcommittee's inquiry continued following the July 9, 1982, hearing and, with respect to the Superfund statute, focused heavily on the following areas:

Whether there are statutory requirements and/or administrative policies, practices and procedures that affect the government's (EPA's) ability to function effectively and achieve the objectives of the law, or whether amendments to the statute are needed;

Whether the Superfund law's enforcement provisions are being fully and effectively carried out;

Whether adequate efforts have been, or are being made to obtain and/or recover the full costs of cleaning up hazardous waste sites from responsible parties;

Whether the Fund, and the existing sources and amounts of revenue for it, particularly the tax on oil and chemicals, is adequate to address both known and potential hazardous waste sites and chemical spills; and

What information is being considered, or not being considered by the EPA, in its administration and management of the Fund, and its execution of responsibilities under the Superfund law.

Answers to these concerns will, in turn, assist the subcommittee in identifying weaknesses and/or deficiencies in the framework of Federal laws and the ways they are being carried out that may be inhibiting or precluding regulation and enforcement of hazardous waste disposal activities; in assessing the adequacy of existing statutory penalties for deterring the continuance of illegal or improper disposal of hazardous wastes; and in demonstrating how the several Federal statutes and their implementing regulations may be combining to create incentives and methods for generators of hazardous wastes to dispose of toxins illegally.

In pursuit of information that would help the subcommittee make these assessments, efforts were undertaken by the Subcommittee's investigators to interview EPA Officials and others, and to review the agency's enforcement files. Among the questions needing answers:

Why aren't responsible parties being held liable for their full share of the costs of cleaning up a hazardous waste site?

Why is the EPA agreeing to limit the liability of some responsible parties, and not others; and what is the effect of this on the program and the Fund's resources?

What is the basis for the agency deciding whether it will assess civil penalties, and how much those penalties should be?

What is the EPA's basis for deciding whether it will refer a case to the Justice Department for prosecution of either civil or criminal concerns?

What does the agency do when it finds that one or more of the responsible parties may be judgment proof?

Why are some cases being settled or handled administratively, and others going to litigation?

Is the agency capable of making substantive financial analyses of the responsible parties, and how does this affect their decisions on obtaining or recovering cleanup costs from responsible parties, or on pursuing penalties through litigation?

To what extent does the ability to identify responsible parties affect agency enforcement decisions about who should pay how much of the cleanup costs and whether efforts should be made to litigate, or settle out of court?

Is the agency able to move rapidly enough to ensure that valuable and critical evidence, particularly potentially criminal evidence, is not lost, or destroyed?

Is any consideration given to whether a responsible party is involved in more than one site?

Are cleanup and other efforts to negotiate settlements or proceed with litigation hindered in any way, or being stalled, and if so, why?

Are there weaknesses or deficiencies in the statute that affect EPA's ability to enforce?

The Attorney General and Administrator Gorsuch have repeatedly asserted that congressional inquiry into these matters wrest from the Executive its ability to "take Care That the Laws be faithfully executed," U.S. Const. art. II, Sec. 3.

As the opinion of the General Counsel to the Clerk in response to the Attorney General's opinion states: "Congress does not forgo inquiry simply because it may produce information on the government's strategies and weaknesses; the only way to correct either bad law or bad administration is to examine these matters.". . .

The position of the EPA would mean that Congress would, in effect, destroy or diminish its own oversight power in passing laws, for once passed, administration of the law would fall exclusively within the "take care" clause power to the exclusion of oversight, sealing off from Congress an effective means for determining the sufficiency of existing law. This argument falls of its own weight. The power conferred by the Constitution under Article II, Sec. 3 is primarily to empower the President simply to carry out the laws enacted by Congress. It neither expressly nor impliedly authorizes the President, or any agency, to withhold documents essential to evaluating the administration of the laws passed by Congress which the President is to "faithfully" execute.

This kind of slipshod constitutional construction and the unsupported equivalency drawn between oversight and interference in execution of the law cannot withstand scrutiny and is rejected by your Committee....

H RES 632

Resolved, That the Speaker of the House of Representatives certify the report of the Committee on Public Works and Transportation as to the contumacious conduct of Anne M. Gorsuch, as Administrator, United States Environmental Protection Agency, in failing and refusing to furnish certain documents in compliance with a subpena duces tecum of a duly constituted subcommittee of said committee served upon Anne M. Gorsuch, as Administrator, United States Environmental Protection Agency, and as ordered by the subcommittee, together with all of the facts in connection therewith, under seal of the House of Representatives, to the United States attorney for the District of Columbia, to the end that Anne M. Gorsuch, as Administrator, United States Environmental Protection Agency, may be proceeded against in the manner and form provided by law.

OECD REPORT
ON THIRD WORLD DEBT
December 16, 1982

Debt and the inability of many Third World countries to make payments on their debts became a major subject of discussion among international government leaders and financial analysts in the early 1980s. Dramatic fluctuations in world oil prices, soaring interest rates and low prices for Third World exports shook the international financial system to its core, as nation after nation found it necessary to reschedule its debt payments. In December 1982, after a financial crisis twice forced Mexico to devalue its peso, the Organization for Economic Cooperation and Development (OECD) issued a survey examining the external debt problem in developing nations.

The report concluded that a handful of heavily indebted developing countries would require substantial international financial help to endure the crisis and would have to undergo significant economic adjustment. Most other Third World nations, however, seemed to be weathering the world economic recession well and remained financially sound enough to be considered creditworthy by Western banks and international aid organizations.

The 1982 debt problems of Third World countries stemmed from the two oil shocks of the previous decade. Oil producers belonging to the Organization of Petroleum Exporting Countries (OPEC) quadrupled oil prices in 1973-74 and tripled them again in 1979-81. Flush with funds from consuming nations, many oil-producing nations flooded international banks with their riches. Banks in turn lent the money to nonproducing nations that needed to borrow to pay for their oil imports. This system of "recycling" oil money worked well after the first round of OPEC price hikes, when most Third World countries enjoyed rapid economic growth rates at home and high prices for their commodity exports abroad to help service their growing debts. High inflation rates, which meant greater availability of money, also eased the burden of debt service for these countries.

The second round of oil price increases, however, came at a time when the world economic situation was much worse. The U.S. Federal Reserve tightened monetary policy in 1981, pushing up interest rates and reducing inflation. Throughout the inflationary 1970s, many Third World countries had borrowed at low real interest rates from banks anxious to lend. These loans, however, tended to be at floating rather than fixed interest rates. As the money supply shrank and interest rates soared, Third World nations saw the interest payments on their external debt skyrocket, raising the entire cost of the outstanding debt. At the same time, commodity prices for Third World exports dropped, cutting severely the export incomes of the most heavily indebted nations such as Brazil, Mexico, Argentina and Venezuela. In addition the phenomenal 5 to 6 percent growth rate these nations had experienced in the 1970s dropped off to around 2 percent or less, further inhibiting the ability of Third World countries to pay the interest on their debts.

Reaction of International Banks

By the end of 1982, the total external debt of Third World nations had grown to $500 billion from $100 billion in 1973, with most of the debts concentrated in a handful of countries. The Mexican financial crisis focused world attention on the international banking system and the suddenly real possiblity of its collapse under the weight of billions of dollars in loans to developing countries. As these nations ran out of funds to service their outstanding external debt, the specter of default arose. Default by a country on a loan of such magnitude would force banks to call in their loans to other developing nations. The international banking system, based on the confidence of banks in the ability of a sovereign government to repay loans, would collapse. Banks, standing to lose billions of dollars, had no choice but to extend further loans to Third World nations and reschedule debt payments.

The OECD survey noted that, in retrospect, some developing nations borrowed unwisely during the 1970s, funneling the loans into unsound projects rather than using the funds to strengthen and diversify their productive capabilities.

International banks were at fault as well because their overeagerness to lend induced some Third World governments to delay making needed internal adjustments to their economic systems and encouraged them to continue borrowing.

Relief for Debtor Nations

The financial crisis arising in late 1982 involved only a handful of the advanced developing nations heavily indebted to Western banks. Many financial analysts believed the problem was not so much a long-term, fundamental crisis as a short-term liquidity problem — the heavily indebted countries were economically capable of meeting their debt obligations over time, but simply did not have the cash to service their debts immediately, given the existing world economic situation. The OECD survey essentially agreed with this evaluation, citing improved world economic conditions, including lower interest rates, higher prices for commodity exports and a resurgence of economic activity and foreign trade, as the only true solution to the crisis.

In the short run, however, Western governments, international financial institutions and private banks were forced to put together individual "survival packages" for Mexico and other Third World governments about to default on loans. Western governments, particularly the United States, drew upon reserve funds to advance developing nations cash to meet short-term debt obligations. The International Monetary Fund (IMF) offered new funds to troubled countries and pressured private banks to keep lending. Private banks rescheduled the debt service payments of debtor governments and, in some instances, agreed to postpone interest payments for a few months.

Critics of this ad hoc system pointed out several obstacles to long-term economic recovery. First, this approach did not guarantee that new loans would enable the countries to achieve an increased rate of economic growth. Without real growth, new loans would only allow debtor governments to service existing debts, without sufficient funds for economic recovery.

In addition, to qualify for IMF aid, Third World governments had to accept austerity measures designed to increase exports and reduce imports. Aside from the political risks inherent in requiring volatile developing nations to adopt such measures in the midst of a world recession, critics again noted that, without continuing capital flow, growth in Third World economies was impossible.

Long-Range Reform

Many financial experts believed that only significant reform of the international banking structure would prevent the Third World debt crisis from happening again. Most reform proposals centered around the lending practices of private banks, specifically requiring banks to stretch out loan payments over a longer period of time at reduced interest rates. Rep. Charles E. Schumer, D-N.Y., proposed such legislation at the start of the 98th Congress and included a provision requiring banks to *establish large loan loss reserves for their Third World debtors if they refused to comply. Other proposals suggested creation of a new international financial agency to buy up outstanding loans to developing nations and structure lenient payment plans for them. At the end of 1982, however, serious discussions on revision of the international banking system had not yet begun, and attention remained focused on ad hoc assistance to individual troubled Third World nations.*

Following are excerpts from the introductory chapter of External Debt of Developing Countries, *released December 16, 1982, by the Organization for Economic Cooperation and Development.* (Boldface headings in brackets have been added by Congressional Quarterly to highlight the organization of the text.):

Introduction and Overview

This Report presents the latest statistics on external debt, including preliminary data for 1981 and estimates up to the end of 1982, for all developing countries and territories combined, for the group of non-OPEC developing countries, for major sub-categories of developing countries, and for the individual 20 largest debtor countries. The data concern mainly medium- and long-term debt (i.e. with original maturities of more than one year), but estimates of short-term assets and liabilities are also presented so that a more complete assessment of the total net debt position of developing countries can be derived. . . .

The stock of debt and the volume of current debt-service obligations are a measure of a long-term cumulative process of loan inflows to developing countries. In principle, this is the natural situation for countries at a stage of economic evolution where the demand for resources for investment runs ahead of domestic savings capacity. (There are, of course, some capital-surplus developing countries just as there are a number of capital-importing developed countries.) In this light, it is normal to expect the debt stock and debt service to increase continuously over time, at both the aggregate and individual country level — with no net repayment of debt. The additional net financial resources made available by foreign borrowing year by year are therefore equivalent to the increase in the total stock of debt outstanding.

Over the post-World War II period as a whole, the long-run processes of international capital transfer have materially helped to foster prosperity and development progress. However, the viability and success of capital-transfer processes cannot be assessed in isolation from the general economic environment in which they occur. The fundamental point is whether, over the medium and longer term, economic policies and conditions are such that foreign borrowing can make a net contribution to economic growth in the capital-importing countries.

The data aggregates presented in this Survey largely reflect the performance of major developing countries over the last decade in the context of the evolution of the world economy. The most evident features of this period have been the pervasive presence of inflation, but with an abrupt onset of a period of disinflation in the last two years; major episodes of payments imbalances, including the two oil-price shocks; and significant structural changes in the pattern of capital flows and in the institutional basis of international financial intermediation.

The current world economic environment is characterized by what are generally recognized to be the most serious economic difficulties experienced since the 1930's. Both developed and developing countries are affected by this situation. Financial stresses are increasingly evident in all countries and at all levels in both the public and private sectors. The overall debt situation of developing countries, with the recent emergence of an increasing number of problems and a few very acute cases, must be seen in this broad context.

The present Survey cannot and does not amount to a comprehensive assessment of the total financial position of developing countries and its implications for the global financial situation. A much wider range of information and analysis would be required for such a study. It is important, therefore, that the limitations of what may be concluded on the basis of the data presented are clearly borne in mind. Moreover, statistics on debt are difficult to handle, involving a range of different financial instruments, terms and conditions. Debt aggregates and averages are therefore not easy to interpret, and such parameters as outstanding debt and debt-service ratios can often be misleading for inter-country comparisons and policy assessments.

[PRESENT SITUATION]

Bearing this need for caution in mind, there are a number of main points that emerge from the analysis and data.

— The sharp change in world economic conditions at the beginning of the 1980's — with the advent of rising real interest rates, low trade growth and falling commodity prices — has fundamentally affected the relative positions of creditors and debtors as compared with the previous decade. Whereas for most of the 1970's the real burden of debt and debt service was being eroded by inflation, it is now being radically increased in a context of economic stagnation.

— It appears in retrospect that certain developing countries have borrowed unwisely (as indeed have some other borrowers), using some of the resources to finance consumption and investments of dubious value, rather than to strengthen their productive potential; overeagerness by banks to lend has sometimes allowed borrowing governments to delay necessary adjustments.

— The emergence of debt problems is concentrated on two very different kinds of developing countries: (i) a small number of poorer commodity-dependent countries with mainly official debt (Official Development Assistance and officially extended or guaranteed export credits) and amounts which are minor in world terms and (ii) a few advanced developing countries which have massively increased their borrowing from commercial sources at high floating interest rates and now suffer from depressed export markets.

— For most other developing countries, external debt cannot be isolated as a major constraint and their debt structures are such that they are not much affected, at least directly, by major fluctuations in floating interest rates. The overall deterioration of the world economic and financial environment, especially with its consequences for trade and commodity prices, is however a real concern for these countries.

— On the basis of outstanding stocks, the overall lending of the private banking community to the developing world represents about one-third of their total international lending but only about 6 percent of their total domestic and international lending combined. These shares include significant amounts of bank credits which are guaranteed by OECD [Organization for Economic Cooperation and Development] governments.

— There is an extreme concentration of private bank exposure in a few countries — Argentina, Brazil, South Korea and Mexico (which, however, present highly differentiated cases in terms of both their debt profiles and their economic structures and policies). Between end-1978 and end-1982, there have been major increases in net floating-interest debt (including short-term) for Argentina (from $0.8 billion to $20.5 billion), Brazil (from $18.5 billion to $45.5 billion), South Korea (from $1.2 billion to $15.5 billion) and Mexico (from $19.9 billion to $59.3 billion). The exposure of banks in these four countries alone is thus estimated to have increased by about $100 billion (from $40 billion to $140 billion) between end-1978 and end-1982. About one-half of this increase is accounted for by short-term lending (maturities of less than one year) and about one-half by medium- and long-term lending. Significant increases in the floating-interest debt of some other countries (e.g. Chile) have also occurred.

— The increase in the volume of floating-interest debt, together with the sharp rise in its cost, largely explains the major increase in interest payments of developing countries in recent years. A decrease in floating interest rates (such as has been occurring since mid-1982) will thus bring significant reductions in interest payments of those developing countries holding large volumes of floating-interest debt. The much lower interest payments of other developing countries will not be much affected.

— While much of the banking systems' exposure is to the governments of developing countries (whether directly or through guarantees), significant amounts are owed by private sector enterprises. In some countries, individual entities (in both public and private sectors) have come to rely heavily on external financing. In such cases, changes in international interest rates — and also, where revenues are entirely or mainly in local currency, changes in the exchange rate — have major effects on the financial balances of such entities. Thus, problems associated with reliance on external financing may arise not only at the macro-economic level but also at the enterprise level, often compounding the difficulty of retaining or restoring overall economic stability and growth.

These various elements suggest that two essential factors need to be kept in the foreground in discussions of the debt problems of developing countries.

World Economic Environment. A basic component of the debt picture is the sharp change in the world economic environment occurring from 1979. . . . Recycling after the first oil shock was accomplished with the balance-sheet positions of developing countries suffering a relatively small deterioration, partly because of the effects of inflation on debt and generally permissive monetary conditions accompanied by relatively low interest rates. But in addition, developing countries for the most part succeeded in raising their investment and domestic savings ratios (as a percent of GNP) and maintaining relatively high rates of economic growth. They also managed to restore foreign exchange reserves. In contrast, the smaller OECD countries suffered a major deterioration in their balance sheets because their borrowing from capital markets was accompanied by falling investment and savings ratios, relatively low growth and a fall in foreign exchange reserves.

The recycling experience after the second oil shock, however, has taken place in quite different circumstances. Interest rates are a quite dramatic illustration of this. But equally dramatic has been the trend in the export revenues of non-OPEC developing countries (including Mexico), especially on the side of prices, but in the current period also on the side of volumes. The abrupt break in the trend of export receipts which occurred between 1980 and 1981 is evident. . . . The deterioration in the net external-asset position vis-a-vis GNP has been, in these circumstances, much more serious and of about the same magnitude as in the case of the smaller OECD countries.

The data . . . reflect the importance of the relationships between the level and structure of capital flows, world trade volumes and prices and economic growth rates. While the evidence is that the much increased degree of external indebtedness of developing countries has a "real" counterpart in increased productive capacity, this can only be turned to positive account in the context of renewed growth in world trade and economic activity. The financial structures created over the last decade are hardly tenable in a context of prolonged stagnation in world trade and economic activity.

Concentration of Private Bank Exposure. For the international financial system, the essential problem may be seen to be the concentration of private bank exposure in a few very large developing countries. Just four advanced developing countries — Mexico, Brazil, Argentina and South Korea — account for more than half of the total outstanding loans of private banks to non-OPEC developing countries, for some 85 percent of the net floating-interest debt and almost all of total net private bank "exposure" (excluding guaranteed export credits) to non-OPEC developing countries.

Essentially, there is no "developing country debt problem" in any general sense. Debt problems are country specific. Broader financial problems currently affecting developing countries are related to conditions in the world economy. Advanced and middle-income countries should remain fundamentally creditworthy and have good growth potential. New bank lending to developing countries is in the process of being adjusted to more realistic levels, but this adjustment is concentrated largely on lending to Brazil, Mexico and Argentina. The level of bank lending to most other developing countries and regions is likely to be maintained or even increased. Reduced lending to the three countries mentioned may, in fact, help to maintain or increase flows to those developing countries which presently retain a capacity to productively use a higher level of external financing. Low-income countries have, in the past, received about 80 percent of their external financing in the form of low-cost aid loans or grants. Bank lending to such countries is largely in the form of officially guaranteed export credits. "Debt problems" among these countries usually reflect broader underlying development problems and/or depressed commodity prices.

[ECONOMIC RECOVERY]

In principle, the main features of financial and economic stress at the present time are reversible. A return to more moderate rates of interest should already ease the situation significantly in 1983. A recovery of commodity prices in the context of an improving world economy would also do much to restore and underpin the positive role of private capital transfers to developing countries. However, for those countries which have borrowed heavily while not implementing the kind of economic policies which enable these capital flows to be adequately productive, a major period of adjustment lies ahead, in which the financial community will need to play a constructive role. Effective economic adjustment must rest on retaining or achieving adequate social consensus and political cohesion. This underlines the need for parallel and co-operative action. . . .

Clearly, the combination of increased debt and current world economic conditions is reason for concern. It is important that the competent international organizations, including the OECD, follow closely the debt situation of developing countries. Particular attention has to be paid to the questions of how far the external deficits of problem countries can realistically be expected to be brought down by appropriate adjustment policies; the scope and nature of the remaining financing requirements; and the potential further difficulties if real interest rates were to continue at high levels, commodity prices to remain low and world trade to remain depressed.

OPEC EFFORT
TO LIMIT PRODUCTION
December 19-20, 1982

In 1982 the 13-member oil cartel, the Organization of Petroleum Exporting Countries (OPEC), faced its greatest problems since its creation 23 years earlier. The group's principal challenge was to agree on production limits for each member country that would not result in an increase in the overall ceiling so large that the OPEC price structure of $34 a barrel (42 gallons each) would be threatened. At the close of a two-day, ministerial-level meeting December 19-20 at its Vienna headquarters, OPEC agreed that "Every effort should be made by each member country to preserve the price structure and to stabilize the market conditions." The failure to set individual ceilings raised questions among analysts about OPEC's ability to remain an effective bargaining force.

The group also decided in Vienna that total OPEC production for 1983 should not exceed 18.5 million barrels a day. But OPEC countries already were estimated to be producing 19.5 million barrels a day. In 1979 OPEC members produced 31 million barrels of oil a day.

Oil Glut

The disagreements within OPEC resulted from a worldwide oversupply of oil. The surplus, caused principally by the international recession and energy conservation, reduced the demand for oil exports and cut into OPEC's share of the world market. An increase in oil production by non-OPEC countries also contributed to the surplus. For the first time in two decades, non-communist nations outside OPEC pumped in 1982 more crude oil than the members. The non-OPEC countries charged prices below OPEC's. In 1979 OPEC countries produced 64.0 percent of the non-communist world's total oil.

In an effort to bolster their sagging economies and defend their share of the world market, several OPEC members in 1982 lowered prices and increased production in contravention of joint decisions made by the group earlier in the year. Iran, for example, produced three million barrels a day, instead of its OPEC quota of 1.2 million barrels a day.

Iran, leader of a group of nations (Algeria, Nigeria, Venezuela and Libya) forming one of the two factions in OPEC, wanted to increase production at the expense of Saudi Arabia, leader of the other faction, the Persian Gulf states. Saudi Arabia, OPEC's largest oil producer with one-fourth the world's known oil, needed money to finance foreign trade, while Iran needed increased revenues to finance its two-year-old war with Iraq.

The Saudis called for a sharper price differential for the higher quality African crude oil that Nigeria, Libya and Algeria produced. The existing price of the African oil was $35.50 a barrel, only $1.50 above the benchmark price of Saudi Arabia's $34.00. The Saudis claimed the low price differential hurt their market by encouraging customers to buy the African oil.

Effect on Third World Debt

The international banking system, some analysts feared, could be jeopardized by a sharp drop in OPEC prices. In Mexico, for example, a large reduction in prices could lead to defaults on its huge international debts. (Third World debt, p. 971)

The oil market moved into excess supply, about three million barrels a day in 1981, a phenomenon that American consumers noticed when gasoline prices reversed course and headed down. This slide in world oil prices, however, could have negative effects, resulting in a tightening of international lending, especially to the more impoverished countries of the Third World. Africa's most populous country with nearly 100 million inhabitants, Nigeria early in 1982 froze virtually all imports because of the decline in its oil revenues.

> *Following is the text of the communiqué issued at the end of the meeting of the Organization of Petroleum Exporting Countries, as it appeared in* The New York Times, *December 20, 1982:*

The 66th meeting of the conference of the Organization of Petroleum Exporting Countries [OPEC] was held in Vienna, Austria, on 19th and 20th December, 1982. Yahaya Dikko, presidential adviser on petroleum and energy affairs of Nigeria, an alternate president of the 65th (extraordinary) meeting of the conference, addressed and formally opened the conference.

The conference unanimously elected as its president Yahaya Dikko, presidential adviser on petroleum and energy affairs of Nigeria and head of its delegation. Gustavo Galindo Velasco, minister of natural and energy resources of Ecuador and head of its delegation, was unanimously elected alternate president.

The conference examined the market situation and decided to take the necessary measure to stabilize the market and to defend the OPEC price structure. For this purpose the conference decided that total OPEC production for the year 1983 should not exceed 18.5 million barrels a day. However, an agreement on establishing national quotas for the distribution of that total amount would require further consultations among the respective governments.

The conference, therefore, decided to keep its deliberations open and to meet at a later stage in the light of those consultations. Meanwhile, the conference decided that every effort should be made by each member country to preserve the price structure and to stabilize the market conditions.

The conference approved the budget of the organization for the year 1983.

The conference appointed Mr. Ir. Wijarso, governor for Indonesia, to be chairman of the board of governors for the year 1983, and Dr. Abbas Honardoost, governor for the Islamic Republic of Iran, to be alternate chairman for 1983.

The conference expressed its sincere gratitude to the Government of the Federal Republic of Austria and the authorities of the city of Vienna for their warm hospitality and the excellent arrangements made for the meeting.

The conference passed resolutions which will be published on January 20, 1983, after ratification by member countries.

The next ordinary meeting of the conference will be convened on 18th July, 1983.

ANDROPOV ON ARMS CONTROL
December 21, 1982

In his first major address on arms-control measures, Soviet party leader Yuri V. Andropov proposed December 21 that the Soviet Union would reduce its medium-range missiles in Europe from more than 600 to 162 if the United States and its allies abandoned plans in 1983 to deploy there 572 new medium-range missiles. The United States, France, Britain and West Germany rejected Andropov's idea, believing it created a Soviet advantage in modern nuclear missiles in Europe. Andropov's 80-minute speech, delivered several weeks after he succeeded the late Leonid Brezhnev, emphasized that Brezhnev's policies, stated earlier in negotiations in Geneva, were to be maintained under Andropov's new leadership. (Brezhnev on nuclear arms, p. 225)

"We are prepared, among other things," Andropov said, "to agree that the Soviet Union should retain in Europe only as many missiles as are kept there by Britain and France — and not a single one more. This means that the Soviet Union would reduce hundreds of missiles, including tens of the latest missiles known in the West as SS-20." Each SS-20 missile carries three warheads and has a range of 3,000 miles. The Soviets earlier counted 162 medium-range missiles in Britain and France's arsenals.

Andropov's proposal would leave the United States without any missiles in Europe, the Reagan administration pointed out. The State Department said, "The Soviet proposal contained in Mr. Andropov's speech today is unacceptable because it would leave the Soviets with several hundred warheads on SS-20's while denying us the means to deter that threat. We cannot accept that the United States should agree to allow the Soviets superiority over us because the British and French maintain their own national deterrent forces."

Andropov also told the Reagan administration that any attempt to use new weapons systems as bargaining chips in arms negotiations would fail. "We will be compelled to counter the challenge of the American side," he said, "by deploying corresponding weapons systems of our own — an analogous missile to counter the MX missile, and our own long-range cruise missile, which we are already testing, to counter the U.S. long-range cruise missiles."

He said the threat of war would be heightened if the administration used bargaining chips as it did earlier when it debated the MX question. "... [I]f the people in Washington really believe that new weapons systems will be a 'trump' for the Americans at negotiations, we want them to know that these 'trumps' are false," Andropov said.

Along with scaling down missiles in Europe, Andropov proposed an "accord on reducing to equal levels on both sides the number of medium-range nuclear-delivery aircraft" both sides have stationed in Europe. Andropov suggested that the United States and the Soviet Union reach overall agreement soon. "Given the swift action and power of modern weapons, the atmosphere of mutual suspicion is especially dangerous," he warned. "Even a mere accident, miscalculation or technical failure can have tragic consequences. It is therefore important to take the finger off the trigger, and put a reliable safety catch on all weapons."

> *Following are excerpts from a speech outlining arms control proposals by Yuri V. Andropov, delivered December 21, 1982. (Boldface headings in brackets have been added by Congressional Quarterly to highlight the organization of the text.):*

... The war preparations of the United States and the NATO bloc which it leads have grown to an unheard-of, record scale. Official spokesmen in Washington are heard to discourse on the possibility of "limited", "sustained" and other varieties of nuclear war. This is intended to reassure people, to accustom them to the thought that such war is acceptable. Veritably, one has to be blind to the realities of our time not to see that wherever and however a nuclear whirlwind arises, it will inevitably go out of control and cause a worldwide catastrophe.

Our position on this issue is clear: a nuclear war — whether big or small, whether limited or total — must not be allowed to break out. No task is more important today than to stop the instigators of another war. This is required by the vital interests of all nations. That is why the unilateral commitment of the Soviet Union not to use nuclear weapons first was received with approval and hope all over the world. If our example is followed by the other nuclear powers, this will be a truly momentous contribution to the efforts of preventing nuclear war.

It is said that the West cannot take such a commitment because, allegedly, the Warsaw Treaty has an advantage in conventional armaments. To begin with, this is untrue, and the facts and figures bear witness to it. Furthermore, as everybody knows, we are in favour of limiting such armaments as well, and of searching for sensible, mutually acceptable solutions to this end. We are also prepared to agree that the sides should renounce first use of conventional, as well as nuclear arms.

Of course, one of the main avenues leading to a real scaling down of the threat of nuclear war is that of reaching a Soviet-American agreement on limitation and reduction of strategic nuclear arms. We approach negotiations on the matter with the utmost responsibility, and seek an honest agreement that will do no damage to either side and will, at the same time, lead to a reduction of their nuclear arsenals.

So far, unfortunately, we see a different approach by the American side. While calling for "radical reductions" in word, what it really has in mind is essentially a reduction of the Soviet strategic potential. For itself, the United States would like to leave a free hand in building up strategic armaments. It is absurd even to think that we can agree to this. It would, of course, suit the Pentagon, but can on no account be acceptable to the Soviet Union and, for that matter, to all those who have a stake in preserving and consolidating peace.

[Soviet Proposals]

Compare to this the proposals of the USSR. They are based on the principle of preserving parity. We are prepared to reduce our strategic arms by more than 25 per cent. US arms, too, must be reduced accordingly, so that the two states have the same number of strategic delivery vehicles. We also propose that the number of nuclear warheads should be substantially lowered and that improvement of nuclear weapons should be maximally restricted.

Our proposals refer to all types of strategic weapons without exception, and envisage reduction of their stockpiles by many hundreds of units. They close all possible channels for any further arms race in this field. And that is only a start: the pertinent agreement would be the point of departure for a still larger mutual reduction of such weapons, which the sides could agree upon, with due account of the general strategic situation in the world.

And while the negotiations are under way, we offer what is suggested by common sense: to freeze the strategic arsenals of the two sides. The US government does not want this, and now everyone can understand why: it has embarked on a new, considerable build-up of nuclear armaments.

Washington's attempts to justify this build-up are obviously irrelevant. The allegation of a "lag" behind the USSR which the Americans must close, is a deliberate untruth. This has been said more than once. And the talk that new weapons systems, such as the MX missile, are meant "to facilitate disarmament negotiations" is altogether absurd.

No programmes of a further arms build-up will ever force the Soviet Union to make unilateral concessions. We will be compelled to counter the challenge of the American side by deploying corresponding weapons systems of our own — an analogous missile to counter the MX missile, and our own long-range cruise missile, which we are now testing, to counter the US long-range cruise missile.

Those are not threats at all. We are wholly averse to any such course of events, and are doing everything to avoid it. But it is essential that those who shape US policy, as well as the public at large, should be perfectly clear on the real state of affairs. Hence, if the people in Washington really believe that new weapons systems will be a "trump" for the Americans at negotiations, we want them to know that these "trumps" are false. Any policy directed to securing military superiority over the Soviet Union has no future and can only heighten the threat of war.

[Confidence-building Measures]

Now a few words about what are known as confidence-building measures. We are serious about them.

Given the swift action and power of modern weapons, the atmosphere of mutual suspicion is especially dangerous. Even a mere accident, miscalculation, or technical failure can have tragic consequences. It is therefore important to take the finger off the trigger, and put a reliable safety catch on all weapons. A few things have already been accomplished to this effect, particularly in the framework of the Helsinki accords. As everybody knows, the Soviet Union is also offering measures of a more far-reaching nature and of broader scope. Our proposals on this score have been tabled at the Soviet-American negotiations in Geneva on limitation and reduction of nuclear armaments.

We are also prepared to consider pertinent proposals made by others, including the recent ones by the US President. But the measures he referred to are not enough to dispel the atmosphere of mutual suspicion, and to restore confidence. Something more is needed: to normalise the situation, and to renounce incitement of hostility and hatred, and propaganda of nuclear war. And, surely, the road to confidence, to preventing any and all wars, including an accidental one, is that of stopping the arms race and going back to calm, respectful relations between states, back to detente.

We consider this important for all regions of the world, and especially for Europe, where a flare-up of any kind may trigger a worldwide explosion.

At present, that continent is beset by a new danger — the prospect of several hundred US missiles being deployed in Western Europe. I must say bluntly: this would make peace still more fragile.

As we see it, the peril threatening the European nations, and, for that matter, the nations of the whole world, can be averted. It is definitely possible to save and strengthen peace in Europe — and this without damage to anyone's security. It is, indeed, for this purpose that we have been negotiating with the United States in Geneva for already more than a year on how to limit and reduce nuclear weapons in the European zone.

[Reduction of Weapons in Europe]

The Soviet Union is prepared to go very far. As everybody knows, we have suggested an agreement renouncing all types of nuclear weapons — both of medium range and tactical — designed to strike targets in Europe. But this proposal has come up against a solid wall of silence. Evidently, they do not want to accept it, but are afraid to reject it openly. I want to reaffirm again that we have not withdrawn this proposal.

We have also suggested another variant: that the USSR and the NATO countries reduce their medium-range weaponry by more than two-thirds. So far, the United States will not have it. For its part, it has submitted a proposal which, as if in mockery, is called a "zero option". It envisages elimination of all Soviet medium-range missiles not only in the European, but also in the Asian part of the Soviet Union, while NATO's nuclear-missile arsenal in Europe is to remain intact and may even be increased. Does anyone really think that the Soviet Union can agree to this? It appears that Washington is out to block an agreement and, citing the collapse of the talks, to station, in one way or another, its missiles on European soil.

The future will show if this is so. We, for our part, will continue to work for an agreement on a basis that is fair to both sides. We are prepared, among other things, to agree that the Soviet Union should retain in Europe only as many missiles as are kept there by Britain and France — and not a single one more. This means that the Soviet Union would reduce hundreds of missiles, including tens of the latest missiles known in the West as SS-20. In the case of the USSR and the USA this would be a really honest "zero" option as regards medium-range missiles. And if, later, the number of British and French missiles were scaled down, the number of Soviet ones would be additionally reduced by as many.

Along with this there must also be an accord on reducing to equal levels on both sides the number of medium-range nuclear-delivery aircraft stationed in this region by the USSR and the NATO countries.

We call on the other side to accept these clear and fair terms, to take this opportunity while it still exists. But let no one delude himself: we will never let our security or the security of our allies be jeopardised. It would also be a good thing if thought were given to the grave consequences that the stationing of new US medium-range weapons in Europe would entail for all further efforts to limit nuclear armaments in general. In short, the ball is now in the court of the USA.

In conclusion, let me say the following. We are for broad, fruitful cooperation among all nations of the world to their mutual advantage and the good of all mankind, free from diktat and interference in the affairs of other countries. The Soviet Union will do everything it can to secure a tranquil, peaceful future for the present and coming generations. That is the aim of our policy, and we shall not depart from it. . . .

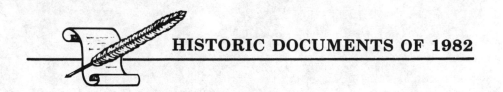

CUMULATIVE INDEX, 1978-82

CUMULATIVE INDEX, 1978-82

A

J

O